CURRENT LAW
STATUTES
ANNOTATED
1990

VOLUME TWO

CURRENT LAW EDITORIAL TEAM
SARAH ANDREWS
CAROLINE EADIE
BARBARA GRANDAGE
PHILIPPA JOHNSON
ROSANNA ROTHERY
ALAN THOMPSON
CLARE TURNER

LONDON
SWEET & MAXWELL

EDINBURGH
W. GREEN & SON

1991

Published by
SWEET & MAXWELL LIMITED
of South Quay Plaza, 183 Marsh Wall, London,
and W. GREEN & SON LIMITED
of St. Giles Street, Edinburgh,
and printed in Great Britain
by The Bath Press,
Bath, Avon.

ISBN This Volume only : 0 421 44230 1
As a set   : 0 421 44250 6

CONTENTS

CHRONOLOGICAL TABLE

STATUTES 1990

VOLUME TWO

INDEX OF SHORT TITLES 1990

(References are to chapter numbers of 1990)

PLANNING (LISTED BUILDINGS AND CONSERVATION AREAS) ACT 1990*

(1990 c. 9)

A Table showing the derivation of the provisions of this consolidation Act will be found at the end of the Act. The Table has no official status.

ARRANGEMENT OF SECTIONS

PART I

LISTED BUILDINGS

CHAPTER 1

LISTING OF SPECIAL BUILDINGS

CHAPTER II

AUTHORISATION OF WORKS AFFECTING LISTED BUILDINGS

Control of works in respect of listed buildings

Applications for listed building consent

Grant of consent subject to conditions

Appeals

Revocation and modification of consent

---

* Annotations by Professor Malcolm Grant, LL.D., Faculty of Laws, University College, London.

CHAPTER III

RIGHTS OF OWNERS ETC.

Compensation

Listed building purchase notices

CHAPTER IV

ENFORCEMENT

CHAPTER V

PREVENTION OF DETERIORATION AND DAMAGE

Compulsory acquisition of listed building in need of repair

Acquisition by agreement

Management of acquired buildings

Urgent preservation

Town schemes

PART III

GENERAL

Authorities exercising functions under Act

Special cases

Miscellaneous provisions

PART IV

SUPPLEMENTAL

An Act to consolidate certain enactments relating to special controls in
respect of buildings and areas of special architectural or historic interest
with amendments to give effect to recommendations of the Law
Commission.   [24th May 1990]

PARLIAMENTARY DEBATES
  Hansard, H.L. Vol. 515, col. 1093; Vol. 516, col. 21; Vol. 517, col. 977; Vol. 518, col.
437; H.C. Vol. 173, col. 251.
  The Bill was examined by the Joint Committee on Consolidation Bills on February 28,
March 7 and 14, 1990.

INTRODUCTION

Outline
  This Act is one of the four 1990 Acts consolidating the legislation on town and country
planning. It consolidates the provisions in the Town and Country Planning Act 1971 relating
to listed buildings and conservation areas, together with other related legislation. It now
provides a self-contained code for the protection of the architectural heritage. It ties in
closely with the principal Act, the Town and Country Planning Act 1990 (T.C.P.A. 1990),
but instead of incorporating references to listed buildings and conservation areas into that

Act, several of its provisions as they apply to listed buildings—such as the validity of enforcement notices, action taken by the Secretary of State and Crown land—are specially replicated in this Act. The rules relating to scheduled monuments remain in entirely separate legislation (the Ancient Monuments and Archaeological Areas Act 1979), and although a building which has been listed under this Act may also be a scheduled monument under that Act, the provisions of that Act prevail.

Pt. I of this Act deals with listed buildings, and assembles the various provisions that formerly were dispersed throughout the 1971 Act relating to the process of listing buildings, obtaining listed building consent, the rights of owners to compensation and to serve purchase notices, enforcement of listed building control and the prevention of deterioration and damage to listed buildings. Once a building has been listed as a building of special architectural or historic interest, it becomes a criminal offence to execute works affecting its character as a building of special interest except in accordance with listed building consent. Enforcement action may also be taken where those controls are breached, requiring the building to be restored. Although the Act stops short of imposing positive duties on owners of listed buildings to keep them in good repair, it does allow local planning authorities to commence proceedings for the compulsory purchase of any building in disrepair, and allows for reduced compensation in a case where the building has been deliberately allowed to fall into disrepair with a view to redevelopment of the site. There are also wide-ranging powers for the local planning authority itself to undertake works urgently needed to preserve unoccupied listed buildings, and to charge the cost to the owners.

Pt. II relates to conservation areas, including their designation and effect, and control of demolition and development within the areas. A conservation area is an area which it is special architectural or historic interest, the character or appearance of which it is desirable to preserve or enhance. The consolidation legislation, like the 1971 Act, then proceeds to apply to conservation areas, by complex process of cross-reference, many of the controls in Pt. I relating to listed buildings. The provisions are modified as necessary for this quite different role by the Town and Country Planning (Listed Buildings and Conservation Areas) Regulations 1990.

Pt. III contains supplementary provisions.

Who does what

Functions under the Act are conferred on
   (1)   the Secretary of State, who has the usual powers of call-in, determining appeals and several reserve powers;
   (2)   local planning authorities, who are the London boroughs and the metropolitan district planning authorities. In the shire counties the districts have most of the functions exclusively, but some of the powers are exercisable concurrently by the counties. In the Norfolk and Suffolk Broads the Broads Authority are the sole district planning authority for many purposes of the Act. In the National Parks the powers are exercisable by the two special planning boards in the Lake District and Peak National Parks, and elsewhere by the county planning authority. These authorities may be supplanted in any area for which urban development corporation or housing action trust has been established, and where the powers have been transferred to the corporation or the trust. Not all powers under the Act are so transferrable.
   (3)   the Historic Buildings and Monuments Commission: the Commission was established by the National Heritage Act 1983, with the general duties of, so far as practicable, securing the preservation of ancient monuments and historic buildings situated in England, promoting the preservation and enhancement of the character and appearance of conservation areas in England and promoting the public's enjoyment of, and advancing their knowledge of, ancient monuments and historic buildings and their preservation. It immediately adopted the name of "English Heritage", and is best known by that title. In order to avoid confusion, however, it is referred to in the Notes to the Act (as in the Act itself) as "the Commission". Although responsibility for the listing of buildings remains with the Secretary of State, the Commission compiles lists of buildings for inclusion in the statutory list, and the Secretary of State is required to consult with the Commission before compiling, approving or amending any list. The Commission has special responsibilities in London, as successor to some of the statutory functions previously exercised by the Greater London Council. Advice on the role of the Commission is contained in D.O.E. Circular 8/87. The Commission's functions extend only to England. Different arrangements exist in Wales, and are outlined in W.O. Circular 61/81.

Parliamentary proceedings

The consolidation was undertaken by the Law Commission, which consulted widely on its proposals and reported to the House in February 1990 (*Report on the Consolidation of Certain Enactments Relating to Town and Country Planning*) with 65 recommendations for amendments necessary to produce a satisfactory consolidation. The Bills were introduced in the Lords in February 1990, and were referred to the Joint Committee on Consolidation Bills which met on February 28, March 7 and March 14, 1990. The Committee reported (*Third Report, Session 1989–90*; H.L. Paper 38–II, p. vi) that they were satisfied that, apart from those parts which were the subject of Law Commission recommendations, the Bills as amended by the Committee were pure consolidation and represented the existing law. The Committee were also satisfied that the Law Commission's recommended amendments were necessary for the purpose of producing a satisfactory consolidation of the law. The Committee did, however, draw attention to two of the Law Commission's recommendations: Recommendation 18, intended to resolve an ambiguity in relation to offences in respect of applications for established use certificates; and Recommendation 46, relating to the exercise of functions relating to listed buildings.

The Bill had its Second Reading in the Commons on May 15, 1990 (*Hansard*, H.C., Vol. 172, cols. 714–716), and further minor amendments were made during the Commons Committee stage (*Hansard*, H.C. Vol. 173, cols. 245–254; May 22, 1990). The Bill had a formal third reading on the same day, and received Royal Assent on May 24.

Commencement

This Act came into force on August 24, 1990, three months after Royal Assent (s.94(2)).

ABBREVIATIONS

the Commission : The Historic Buildings and Monuments Commission.
T.C.P.A. 1990 : Town and Country Planning Act 1990.

PART I

LISTED BUILDINGS

CHAPTER 1

LISTING OF SPECIAL BUILDINGS

Listing of buildings of special architectural or historic interest

1.—(1) For the purposes of this Act and with a view to the guidance of local planning authorities in the performance of their functions under this Act and the principal Act in relation to buildings of special architectural or historic interest, the Secretary of State shall compile lists of such buildings, or approve, with or without modifications, such lists compiled by the Historic Buildings and Monuments Commission for England (in this Act referred to as "the Commission") or by other persons or bodies of persons, and may amend any list so compiled or approved.

(2) The Secretary of State shall not approve any list compiled by the Commission if the list contains any building situated outside England.

(3) In considering whether to include a building in a list compiled or approved under this section, the Secretary of State may take into account not only the building itself but also—

(a) any respect in which its exterior contributes to the architectural or historic interest of any group of buildings of which it forms part; and

(b) the desirability of preserving, on the ground of its architectural or historic interest, any feature of the building consisting of a man-made object or structure fixed to the building or forming part of the land and comprised within the curtilage of the building.

(4) Before compiling, approving (with or without modifications) or amending any list under this section the Secretary of State shall consult—

(a) in relation to buildings which are situated in England, with the Commission; and

(b) with such other persons or bodies of persons as appear to him appropriate as having special knowledge of, or interest in, buildings of architectural or historic interest.

(5) In this Act "listed building" means a building which is for the time being included in a list compiled or approved by the Secretary of State under this section; and for the purposes of this Act—

(a) any object or structure fixed to the building;

(b) any object or structure within the curtilage of the building which, although not fixed to the building, forms part of the land and has done so since before 1st July 1948,

shall be treated as part of the building.

(6) Schedule 1 shall have effect for the purpose of making provision as to the treatment as listed buildings of certain buildings formerly subject to building preservation orders.

DEFINITIONS

"building": s.91.
"functions": s.91(2).
"land": s.91(2).
"listed building": s.1(5).
"the commission": s.1(1).
"the Principal Act": s.91(1).

GENERAL NOTE

Introduction

Protection for buildings of special architectural or historic interest is provided by this and the succeeding sections. It is a system of selective protection, in that buildings are individually identified as being of special interest and then "listed" under this section. The consequence of listing is that it becomes an offence to carry out any works for the demolition of the building or for its alteration without consent ("listed building consent") granted under s.10. Those provisions are supplemented by a procedure which enables the local planning authority to secure interim protection of an unlisted building, by serving a building preservation notice under s.3, to preserve the status quo whilst consideration is given to whether the building should be listed.

Control over the unauthorised demolition of buildings of buildings is also extended to unlisted buildings in conservation areas by Part II, though subject to certain exceptions prescribed by way of Direction issued by the Secretary of State in DOE Circular 8/87, para. 97. Ancient monuments are protected under an entirely separate system of controls, now contained in the Ancient Monuments and Archaeological Areas Act 1979.

Background: the development of listing

There are currently around 450,000 listed buildings in England and Wales. The process effectively began as a reaction to the losses of the Second World War, and in the first national listing survey, carried out between 1947 and 1969, some 120,000 buildings were listed. However, during the 1960s "public tastes reflected a growing awareness of the value of Victorian and early twentieth century buildings, and an appreciation of the contribution which individual buildings might make when sited attractively together" (Memorandum submitted by the Department of the Environment to the House of Commons Environment Committee (Historic Buildings and Ancient Monuments; H.C. 146–II, p.13; Session 1986–87)). A national resurvey was then launched in 1970, but made slow progress until it was accelerated following the demolition of the Firestone Factory in 1980 when its listing was being considered. The systematic national resurvey was initially conducted by the Department's Inspectorate of Ancient Monuments and Historic Buildings, now part of the Commission. They also supervised fieldwork by 22 local authorities and 11 firms of private consultants.

For many years the Secretary of State was unwilling to list post-war buildings, except in quite exceptional circumstances. But in 1988 he announced the introduction in England of a rolling 30-year rule, and a competition was held to identify the best 50 candidates for listing from the period 1939–1958 (*Observations on the First Report of the Environment Committee in Session 1986–87* H.C. 268 (1987–88) para. 1.)

The listing procedure

General survey. The procedure by which buildings are added to the list is informal. In order to avoid anticipatory demolition, there is no formal requirement of preliminary notification to owners; and as between a vendor and purchaser of a building, listing after the exchange of contracts is an inherent and not unforeseeable risk accepted by the purchaser (*Amalgamated Investment and Property Co.* v. *Walker (John) & Sons* [1977] 1 W.L.R. 164 (C.A.)). However, it is now Commission policy that, except in cases of threatened demolition, fieldworkers should make themselves known to owners and occupiers of the buildings they are surveying. In 1987 the Government rejected a recommendation by the House of Commons Environment Committee that there should be a statutory requirement always to notify owners of an intended inspection, because of the risk of pre-emptive demolition (*Observations on the First Report of the Environment Committee in Session 1986–87* H.C. 268 (1987–88) para. 2). A right of entry is conferred on authorised persons by s.88.

For England the Secretary of State is required under this section either to compile lists himself, or to approve (with or without modifications) lists approved by the Historic Buildings and Monuments Commission or by other bodies or persons. He must in any event consult with the Commission (subs. (4)(a)) and the normal course is for lists to be compiled by the Commission and submitted to the Secretary of State for approval. Each recommendation by a Commission fieldworker is checked by a supervising inspector, who looks at the buildings on the ground with the fieldworker; and each list, which covers a group of parishes or a whole town or city, is then examined by a Principal Inspector before it is submitted to the Secretary of State. The Principal Inspector also visits some of the buildings and settles the difficult cases. The draft lists are submitted by the Commission to the Department, where they are checked and edited into volumes and signed on behalf of the Secretary of State. The Secretary of State takes the final decision, but usually follows the recommendation of the Commission, though marginal cases are sometimes referred back for detailed opinion.

"Spot" listing. Listing is ideally undertaken on a programmed basis, but when in the 1980s revision of the lists fell behind schedule, resort was had increasingly to the practice of "spot-listing" buildings under threat. Spot-listing is also carried out in resurveyed areas where a building has been overlooked, or new evidence about it (such as its internal features) has since been made available. This has often meant that the ban on unauthorised demolition has been imposed at a comparatively late stage in the formulation of proposals for redevelopment, and s.6 was therefore enacted to enable developers to obtain an advance ruling on whether a building is to be listed or not. A decision under that section to include a building in the list is effectively a spot-listing.

Additionally, a local planning authority may serve a building preservation notice under s.3, which has the effect of temporarily listing the building.

What is a building?

Only a "building" may be listed, although that expression is widely defined by s.336(1) of the principal Act so as to include "any structure or erection, and any part of a building as so defined, but does not include plant or machinery comprised in a building". A fixture attached to a building, or in its curtilage—such as a statue—cannot therefore be listed in its own right, but the Secretary of State is entitled under subs. (3)(b) to take into account the desirability of preserving such a feature when deciding whether to list the building. The listing is then effective to protect the feature (except in the case of free standing buildings erected in the curtilage after July 1, 1948).

A building does not cease to be a listed building if it is demolished without authorisation, and is no longer a building: in *R.* v. *Leominster District Council,* ex p. *Antique Country Buildings* (1988) 56 P. & C.R. 240 and *Leominster District Council* v. *British Historic Buildings and S.P.S. Shipping* [1987] J.P.L. 350 the courts held that it was possible to serve a listed building enforcement notice requiring the restoration of such a building where sufficient of its components remained extant: see further the notes to s.38.

Listing is not, however, an appropriate method of protection generally for the remains of historic buildings. Instead, there is the possibility of scheduling as an ancient monument under the Ancient Monuments and Archaeological Areas Act 1979. The two codes operate alongside one another, and it is possible for a building to be both listed under this Act and scheduled as an ancient monument. In such a case, however, the scheduled monument controls take precedence over the prohibition against unauthorised demolition contained in this Act (s.61).

Criteria for listing

Two main classifications are employed in listing buildings. Grade I buildings are those of exceptional interest, and only around two per cent. of all listed buildings appear on this list. Grade II buildings are those of special interest, and some particularly important buildings in this category are distinguished as Grade II*.

The current criteria for listing, contained in Appendix I to DOE Circular 8/87, provide for the inclusion of:

(1) all buildings built before 1700 which survive in anything like their original condition;
(2) most buildings built between 1700 and 1840, although selection is necessary;
(3) buildings of definite quality built between 1840–1914, where the selection is designed to include the principal works of the principal architects;
(4) selected buildings of high quality built between 1914–1939, and a few outstanding buildings after 1939. Since 1981 (details now in Appendix I to DOE Circular 8/87) the range of buildings in this category qualifying for listing has been widened very substantially so as to represent three main building styles (modern, classical and vernacular) and nine categories of building types:
    (a) churches, chapels and other places of public worship;
    (b) cinemas, theatres, hotels and other places of public entertainment;
    (c) commercial and industrial premises including shops and offices;
    (d) schools, colleges and educational buildings;
    (e) flats;
    (f) houses and housing estates;
    (g) municipal and other public buildings;
    (h) railway stations, airport terminals and other places associated with public transport;
    (i) miscellaneous.

In addition, selection is to include the work of the principal architects of the period. In 1987 the Secretary of State announced the introduction of a "rolling 30-year rule", under which all buildings over 30 years old would be regarded as eligible for listing, and, in exceptional cases, some buildings only 10 years or more.

In choosing buildings, particular attention is paid to:

"Special value within certain types, either for architectural or planning reasons or as illustrating social and economic history (for instance, industrial buildings, railway stations, schools, hospitals, theatres, town halls, markets, exchanges, almshouses, prisons, lock-ups, mills).

Technological innovation or virtuosity (for instance, cast iron, prefabrication or the early use of concrete).

Association with well-known characters or events.

Group value, especially as examples of town planning (for instance, squares, terraces or model villages)" (DOE Circular 8/87, Appendix 1.)

In general, the age or the architecture of the building is of greater importance than its condition. As the Department of the Environment explained in 1986 (Memorandum of Evidence to House of Commons Environment Committee, H.C. 146–II Session 1986–87; p.15), the historic core of a building is often concealed under a later skin or a tin roof. Some buildings are derelict or decaying. Provided, however, that the special architectural or historic interest survives, the Secretary of State sees it as his statutory duty to list such structures.

Group value

The Secretary of State is not confined to considering the merits of a building in isolation. He may have regard to the building's contribution to a group of buildings, and to any man-made structures or objects fixed to the building or part of the land within the curtilage (although only those dating from before 1948 will automatically fall within the scope of the listing: see further below) (subs. (3)(b); confirming *Corthorn Land and Timber Co.* v. *Minister of Housing and Local Government* (1965) 63 L.G.R. 490).

Deemed listing: pre-1969 preservation orders

Any building which was immediately before January 1, 1969 subject to a building preservation order under the Town and Country Planning Act 1962 but was not then included in a list, is deemed to be a listed building by virtue of Sched. 1, para. 1 to this Act, unless the Secretary of State otherwise directs under para. 2 of that Schedule.

The extent of the listing

Objects and structure fixed to the building. The listing of a building confers protection not only on the building, but also on any object or structure fixed to the building (subs. 3). The case law suggests that an ordinary common law construction should be given to the word fixed.

In *Corthorn Land and Timber Co.* v. *Minister of Housing and Local Government* (1965) L.G.R. 490 a building preservation order had been made under the Town and Country Planning Act 1962 in respect of a mansion, requiring that not only should the building itself not be demolished, altered or extended without consent, but also that the following items should not be altered or removed: (1) 27 portrait panels in the King's Room, being nineteenth century copies of Tudor and Stuart kings and queens; (2) carved oak panels in the wall of the Oak Room dating from the fifteenth to mid-seventeenth centuries; (3) a large wood carving in the Great Hall; (4) large wooden mediaeval figures on the main landing; (5) a pair of painted wooden panels depicting the hall in the ornate mantlepiece in one of the drawing rooms. The court rejected an application by the owner to quash the order, holding that all the items were fixtures as that phrase was commonly applied by law. In *Debenhams* v. *Westminster City Council* [1987] A.C. 396 Lord Mackay of Clashfern followed that analysis and observed that

". . . it appears to me that the word 'fixed' is intended in [s.1(3)] to have the same connotation as in the law of fixtures and that what is achieved by the latter part of [s.1(3)] is that the ordinary rule of common law is applied so that any object or structure fixed to a building should be treated as part of it."

Objects or structures within the curtilage. Any object or structure within the curtilage of the building which, although not fixed to it, forms part of the land and has done so since before July 1, 1948 is also protected by the listing (subs. (5)). The courts originally construed this concept broadly. In *Attorney-General*, ex rel. *Sutcliffe, Rouse and Hughes* v. *Calderdale Borough Council* [1983] 46 P. & C.R. 399 the Court of Appeal held that three factors had to be taken into account in deciding whether a structure or object was within the curtilage of a listed building: (1) the physical layout of the building and the structure; (2) their ownership, past and present, and (3) their use of function, past and present. Applying these criteria, the Court held that a terrace of cottages which had been constructed as mill-workers' dwellings adjacent to, and linked by a bridge to, a mill which was now a listed building, was within the curtilage of the mill and thus included in the listing by virtue of subs. (5).

However, in *Debenhams* v. *Westminster City Council* [1987] A.C. 396 the House of Lords (Lord Ackner dissenting) held that a "structure fixed to a building" within subs. (5) meant only a structure which was ancillary and subordinate to the listed building itself and which was either fixed to the main building or within its curtilage, such as the stable block of a listed mansion house or the steading of a listed farmhouse. If there were no concept of subordination, then the listing of a single building in a terrace would have the effect of listing the whole terrace, which could not have been the intention of Parliament. The fact that one building was subordinated to another for the commercial purposes of the occupier, or that a completely distinct building was connected to a listed building, did not make it a "structure fixed to a [listed] building". Thus where a building on the other side of a street was connected to a listed building by an underground tunnel and by a footbridge at second floor level, it did not thereby fall within the scope of the listing. The House of Lords did not, however, overrule the *Calderdale* case on its facts, since it was possible there, given the history of the properties, to regard the mill and the terrace as a single unit.

The potential for confusion has been recognised by the Commission and their practice in preparing the revised lists has been to:

"consider individually all the structures and buildings on a site which can be construed as separate buildings and to list those, and only those, which qualify. The new lists will therefore leave little room for doubt whether a building is listed or not" (*Hansard*, H.L. Vol. 480, col. 625; October 13, 1986).

Although listed building consent is not normally required for the erection of a free-standing building in the curtilage of a listed building, once erected the building would formerly have been subject to listed building control. That rule was modified by the Housing and Planning Act 1986, and the scope of the listing is now restricted to any object or structure in the curtilage which has, since before July 1, 1948, formed part of the land. Transitional provisions in the 1986 Act (Sched. 9, para. 1) provide that:

"(2) Where by virtue of this paragraph an object or structure ceases to be treated as part of a listed building—

(a) liabilities incurred before the commencement of this paragraph by reason of the object or structure being so treated cease to have effect, and

(b) a condition attached to a listed building consent ceases to have effect if, or to the extent that, it could not have been attached if this paragraph had been in force;

except for the purposes of criminal proceedings begun before the commencement of this paragraph."

Applications to de-list buildings

Although there is no right of appeal against the listing of a building, the Secretary of State is empowered (subs. (1)) to amend any list, and (for England) the Department of the Environment is willing to entertain a request, which may be made at any time, for the listing to be reviewed. The arrangements are entirely non-statutory, and they are outlined in DOE Circular 8/87, para. 40. A guidance note issued by the Department of the Environment in 1986 observed:

"We cannot take a building off the list just because an owner feels aggrieved. We have to be convinced that a mistake has been made in adding the building to the list in the first place; or that a building has become so altered or mutilated over the years it is no longer worthy of listing."

The Note goes on to explain the procedure which will be followed by the Department. The request will be forwarded to the Historic Buildings and Monuments Commission for England, and examined by a different expert from the one who conducted the initial survey. The inspector will, if requested, make an appointment to see the applicant when reviewing the case. He will then make a recommendation which will go through his principal inspector. The final decision will be taken by the Head of the Department's Listing Branch, but in some exceptional cases it will be taken by the Minister or the Secretary of State personally. The Department indicates that it will be sympathetic to requests for urgency, and that its aim throughout "is to be as open as possible about the listing or delisting of your property."

The effect of listing

Listing of a building brings into play all the protective provisions of this Act. It becomes an offence to carry out unauthorised works to a building (ss.7–9), and if the building is allowed to fall into disrepair there is power for it to be acquired compulsorily by the local planning authority or the Secretary of State. Moreover, there is some diminution of permitted development rights under the Town and Country Planning General Development Order 1988. There is no right under Pt. 1 of Sched. 2 to the Order to erect (or to improve or alter) any building exceeding 10 cubic metres in the curtilage of a listed building (Part 1, Class A.1(g)) and Class E.1(f)).

The controls under this Act have immediate effect upon the inclusion of a building in the list, and the Secretary of State is required by s.2(3) as soon as possible thereafter to notify the council, and they are similarly required to notify all owners and occupiers. The offence of carrying out unauthorised works to a listed building is an offence of strict liability (see the notes to s.9) and therefore does not require proof that the defendant knew the building was listed (although it would be unreasonable to bring proceedings in a case where it was clear that an owner had not at that stage been notified that the building had been listed).

Publication of lists

2.—(1) As soon as possible after any list has been compiled or approved under section 1 or any amendments of such a list have been made, a copy of so much of the list as relates to any district or London borough or, as the case may be, of so much of the amendments as so relates, certified by or on behalf of the Secretary of State to be a true copy, shall be deposited—

(a) in the case of a London borough, with the council of the borough and with the chief officer of the Commission; and

(b) in the case of a district—

(i) with the district council;

(ii) with the county planning authority whose area or any part of whose area includes the district, or any part of it; and

(iii) where the district council are not the district planning authority, with that authority.

(2) Any copy deposited under subsection (1) shall be a local land charge, and the council with whom a copy is deposited shall be treated for the purposes of the Local Land Charges Act 1975 as the originating authority as respects the charge constituted by the deposit.

(3) As soon as possible after the inclusion of any building in a list under section 1 (whether it is included when the list is compiled, approved or amended) or as soon as possible after any such list has been amended by the exclusion of any building from it—

(a) the Secretary of State shall inform the council of the district or London borough in whose area the building is situated of the inclusion or exclusion; and

(b) the council shall serve a notice in the prescribed form on every owner and occupier of the building, stating that the building has been included in or excluded from the list.

(4) The Secretary of State shall keep available for public inspection free of charge at reasonable hours and at a convenient place, copies of all lists and amendments of lists, compiled, approved or made by him under section 1.

(5) Every authority with whom copies of any list or amendments are deposited under this section shall similarly keep available copies of so much of any such list or amendment as relates to buildings within their area.

(6) For the purposes of subsection (5) the Commission shall be taken to be an authority whose area is Greater London.

DEFINITIONS
  "authority": s.2(6).
  "building": s.91.
  "land": s.91(2).
  "London borough": s.91(2).
  "owner": s.91(2).
  "prescribed": s.91(1).
  "the Commission": s.91(1).

ALLOCATION OF FUNCTIONS
  The authority with whom copies of the list are required to be deposited, and kept available by, is:
Greater London: the borough council and the Commission (subss. (1)(a) and (6));
Elsewhere: the district council, and, where applicable, the county council (subs. (1)).
  The authority that is required to notify owners and occupiers is the district council or London borough council in whose area the building is situated (subs. (3)).

GENERAL NOTE

Introduction
  This section prescribes the procedures consequent upon a decision to list a building, or to amend a list. As a matter of practice the Department notifies the owner of a building informally upon the approval of the list, but is also formally required under subs. (1) to notify the local authorities for the area. The district council (or London borough) is required to notify every owner and occupier (subs. (3)(b)) in the prescribed form (prescribed by the Town and Country Planning (Listed Buildings and Conservation Areas) Regulations 1990). For Wales, a form in the Welsh language is prescribed by the Town and Country Planning (Listed Buildings in Wales and Buildings in Conservation Areas in Wales) (Welsh Forms) Regulations 1990 (No. 1147), reg. 4 and Sched. 4, which may be used instead of the English form.

Listing as land charge
  The copy of the deposited list is a local land charge by virtue of subs. (2), and the listing is required to be registered accordingly against the land affected. Registration gives notice of the building's listed status to prospective purchasers and others dealing with the land. But failure to register does not affect the enforceability of the charge, although it may confer entitlement to compensation (Local Land Charges Act 1975, s.10(1)). In the case of

registered land, such charges are overriding interests under the Land Registration Act 1925, s.70(1)(i) unless and until registered and protected.

However, none of the provisions relating to registration affects liability for the purposes of listed building control. Criminal liability under s.9 is not dependent upon proof by the prosecution that the defendant had been notified or otherwise knew of the listing. Thus it is no defence to prosecution for carrying out unauthorised works, for example, that the listing had not been registered, or had not taken effect as an overriding interest. The view expressed in *Abbey National Building Society* v. *Cann* [1990] 2 W.L.R. 833 by Lord Oliver and Lord Jauncey that a listing might bind a purchaser only through land law principles is difficult to square with the provisions of this Act.

Service of notice: ecclesiastical property

Where the land concerned is ecclesiastical property, notice is required to be served not only on any owner under this section, but also on the Church Commissioners (s.86(1)).

Copies of the list

Copies of the lists are distributed to the county and district councils, to the main amenity societies and some other bodies. They are available for inspection at the offices of the local planning authority, the Commission (in respect of Greater London) and at the National Monuments Record, thus satisfying the obligation on the Secretary of State under subs. (4).

Temporary listing: building preservation notices

3.—(1) If it appears to a local planning authority, other than a county planning authority, that a building in their area which is not a listed building—

(a) is of special architectural or historic interest; and

(b) is in danger of demolition or of alteration in such a way as to affect its character as a building of such interest,

they may serve on the owner and occupier of the building a notice (in this Act referred to as a "building preservation notice").

(2) A building preservation notice served by a local planning authority shall—

(a) state that the building appears to them to be of special architectural or historic interest and that they have requested the Secretary of State to consider including it in a list compiled or approved under section 1; and

(b) explain the effect of subsections (3) to (5) and Schedule 2.

(3) A building preservation notice—

(a) shall come into force as soon as it has been served on both the owner and occupier of the building to which it relates; and

(b) subject to subsection (4), shall remain in force for six months from the date when it is served or, as the case may be, last served.

(4) A building preservation notice shall cease to be in force if the Secretary of State—

(a) includes the building in a list compiled or approved under section 1, or

(b) notifies the local planning authority in writing that he does not intend to do so.

(5) While a building preservation notice is in force with respect to a building, the provisions of this Act (other than section 59) and the principal Act shall have effect in relation to the building as if it were a listed building.

(6) If, following the service of a building preservation notice, the Secretary of State notifies the local planning authority that he does not propose to include the building in a list compiled or approved under section 1, the authority shall immediately give notice of that decision to the owner and occupier of the building.

(7) Following such a notification by the Secretary of State no further building preservation notice in respect of the building shall be served by the local planning authority within the period of 12 months beginning with the date of the notification.

(8) The Commission shall, as respects any London borough, have concurrently with the council of that borough the functions of a local planning authority under this section; and references to the local planning authority shall be construed accordingly.

DEFINITIONS
"building": s.91.
"building preservation notice": ss.3(3); 91(1).
"functions": s.91(2).
"listed building": ss.1(5); 91(1).
"local planning authority": s.81, and see below.
"London borough": s.91(2).
"owner": s.91(2).
"the Commission": s.91(1).
"the Principal Act": s.91(1).

ALLOCATION OF FUNCTIONS
The functions of a local planning authority under this section are exercisable solely by:—
London boroughs: the council of the borough (T.C.P.A. 1990, s.1(2)) which has the functions concurrently with the Commission (subs. (8)).
Metropolitan areas: the metropolitan district council (T.C.P.A. 1990, s.1(2)).
Non-metropolitan areas: the district planning authority. Although the county planning authority would normally have concurrent powers (T.C.P.A. 1990, s.1(1)), county jurisdiction is excluded by subs. (1).
National Parks (outside a metropolitan county): the county planning authority (T.C.P.A. 1990, s.4) or joint planning board in areas where one has been established as county planning authority (T.C.P.A. 1990, s.2).
Norfolk and Suffolk Broads: the Broads Authority (Sched. 4, para. 5).
Urban development areas: the urban development corporation where an order has been made under the Local Government, Planning and Land Act 1980, s.149(1), transferring the function to the corporation (T.C.P.A. 1990, s.7(1)): for a list of current orders see the General Note to s.81.
Housing action trust areas: the housing action trust has the functions under this section to the exclusion of any other authority (other than the Secretary of State) where an order has been made under the Housing Act 1988, s.67(3) transferring the function (as a function within s.67(3A), as substituted by the Planning (Consequential Provisions) Act 1990, Sched. 2, para. 79(3)) to the trust (T.C.P.A. 1990, s.8(2)).
Enterprise zones: the enterprise zone authority, where so provided by order under the Local Government, Planning and Land Act 1980, Sched. 32, para. 5.

GENERAL NOTE

Introduction
This section supplements listed building control by enabling an authority to extend that control on an interim basis to an unlisted building. The purpose is to forestall a threatened demolition or alteration whilst consideration is given to whether the building should be formally listed, and the power is only exercisable where in their opinion the building is in danger of demolition, or of alteration in such a way as to affect its character as a building of special architectural or historic interest.
By serving a building preservation notice on both the owner and occupier, the authority are able to give immediate protection to the building. The notice remains in force for six months. During that period the Secretary of State may:
(1) list the building, in which event it will become subject to the usual controls and the notice lapses (subs. (4)); or
(2) notify the authority that he proposes not to list it, in which case the interim protection lapses (subs. (4)) and no further notice may be served for a further 12 months from the date of the notification (subs. (7)); or
(3) fail to notify the local planning authority of any such decision within the six month period, in which case the notice lapses (subs. (3)).

Exceptions
A building preservation notice may not be served in respect of:
(1) any ecclesiastical building which is for the time being used for ecclesiastical purposes (s.60);
(2) a scheduled monument (s.61);
(3) Crown land, except to the extent of any interest in the land which is for the time being held otherwise than by or on behalf of the Crown (s.83(1)(b));
(4) a building in respect of which a certificate has been granted under s.6 that the building is not intended to be listed, for a period of five years from the date the certificate was issued (s.6(2)(b)).

Effect of a building preservation notice
During the period that it remains in force, a building preservation notice confers on the building a status akin to listing. All the provisions of this Act except s.59 (acts causing damage to listed buildings) have effect in relation to the building as if it were listed (subs. (5)).
Hence, it becomes an offence to execute (or cause to be executed) any works for its demolition or extension in any manner which would affect its character as a building of special architectural or historic interest, except in accordance with the terms of a listed building consent (ss.7, 9(1)). Any infringement of the notice whilst it is in force is not excused by virtue of it lapsing subsequently (Sched. 2, para. 2); but any proceedings on an application for listed building consent and any listed building enforcement notice based on the building preservation notice will lapse upon notification by the Secretary of State that the building is not to be listed, or the expiry of the six month period without it being listed (Sched. 2, paras. 3 and 4).

Service of the notice
A building preservation notice may be served in the normal way prescribed by s.329 of the T.C.P.A. 1990. Alternatively, the authority may use the urgent procedure provided by s.4 below, which allows service to be effected by affixing the notice conspicuously to some object on the building.

Liability to compensate where building not subsequently listed
If the Secretary of State does not list the building within the six month period, any person owning an interest in it is entitled under s.29 to compensation in respect of any loss or damage directly attributable to the effect of the notice.

Arrangements for specialist advice
The Secretary of State may from time to time direct a district planning authority, under Sched. 4, para. 7, to submit for approval by him the arrangements they propose to make to obtain specialist advice in connection with their functions under this section, and, if not satisfied about the arrangements, may direct them to enter into an agreement with another local planning authority.

Temporary listing in urgent cases

4.—(1) If it appears to the local planning authority to be urgent that a building preservation notice should come into force, they may, instead of serving the notice on the owner and occupier of the building, affix the notice conspicuously to some object on the building.

(2) The affixing of a notice under subsection (1) shall be treated for all the purposes of section 3, this section, sections 5 and 10 to 26 and Schedule 2 as service of the notice.

(3) A notice which is so affixed must explain that by virtue of being so affixed it is treated as being served for those purposes.

(4) The Commission shall, as respects any London borough, have concurrently with the council of that borough the functions of a local planning authority under this section; and references to the local planning authority shall be construed accordingly.

DEFINITIONS
"building": s.91.
"building preservation notice": ss.3(3); (91)(1).

"functions": s.91(2).
"listed building": ss.1(5); 91(1).
"local planning authority": s.81, and see below.
"London borough": s.91(2).
"owner": s. 91(2).
"the Commission": s.91(1).

ALLOCATION OF FUNCTIONS
See the notes to s.3. The Commission also has concurrent powers in Greater London for the purposes of this section, by virtue of subs. (4).

GENERAL NOTE

Introduction
This section allows a building preservation notice to be served urgently by affixing it conspicuously to some object on the building, rather than having to rely upon the normal provisions of s.329 of the T.C.P.A. 1990. The urgency provisions were introduced following the ruling in *Maltglade* v. *St. Albans Rural District Council* [1972] 1 W.L.R. 1230 that, because the effectiveness of the notice depended upon it being received before the work of demolition began, it was open to the appellant to assert that it had not been served in time under the normal rules of service (s.329).
    A building preservation notice posted under this section has immediate effect, and it must therefore contain an explanation (subs. (3)) that by virtue of being affixed conspicuously to some object on the building, it is to be treated as having been served.

Provisions applicable on lapse of building preservation notice

5. Schedule 2 to this Act shall have effect as respects the lapse of building preservation notices.

DEFINITIONS
"building": s.91
"building preservation notice": s.91(1).

GENERAL NOTE

    Sched. 2 ensures that the lapse of a building preservation notice does not affect the liability of a person for an offence under ss.9 (unauthorised works to listed building) or 43 (penalties for non-compliance with listed building enforcement notice) committed before the notice ceased to have effect; but provides that any proceedings on listed building consent or enforcement should lapse.

Issue of certificate that building not intended to be listed

    6.—(1) Where—
        (a) application has been made for planning permission for any development involving the alteration, extension or demolition of a building; or
        (b) any such planning permission has been granted;
the Secretary of State may, on the application of any person, issue a certificate stating that he does not intend to list the building.
    (2) The issue of such a certificate in respect of a building shall—
        (a) preclude the Secretary of State for a period of 5 years from the date of issue from exercising in relation to that building any of the powers conferred on him by section 1; and
        (b) preclude the local planning authority for that period from serving a building preservation notice in relation to it.
    (3) Notice of an application under subsection (1) shall be given to the local planning authority within whose area the building is situated at the same time as the application is submitted to the Secretary of State.
    (4) In this section "local planning authority", in relation to a building in Greater London, includes the Commission.

DEFINITIONS
    "building": s.91.
    "building preservation notice": s.91(1).
    "development": s.91(2).
    "functions": s.91(2).
    "local planning authority": s.81, and see below.
    "London borough": s.91(2).
    "owner": s.91(2).
    "planning permission": s.91(2).
    "the Commission": s.91(1).

ALLOCATION OF FUNCTIONS
    The local planning authority for the purposes of this section, and to which notice of an application must be given at the same time the application is submitted to the Secretary of State, is:—
    Greater London: the London borough council (T.C.P.A. 1990, s.1(2)) and the Commission (subs. (4)).
    Metropolitan areas: the metropolitan district council (T.C.P.A. 1990, s.1(2)).
    Non-metropolitan areas: the district planning authority and the county planning authority have concurrent powers (T.C.P.A. 1990, s.1(1)), and notification should therefore be given to both.
    National Parks (outside a metropolitan county): the county planning authority (T.C.P.A. 1990, s.4) or joint planning board in areas where one has been established as county planning authority (T.C.P.A. 1990, s.2)
    Norfolk and Suffolk Broads: "local planning authority" includes the Broads Authority, but that authority does not have exclusive jurisdiction (Sched. 4, para.5(b)), and notification should therefore also be given to the district planning authority.
    Urban development areas: the urban development corporation where an order has been made under the Local Government, Planning and Land Act 1980, s.149(1), transferring the function to the corporation (T.C.P.A. 1990, s.7(1)): for a list of current orders see the General Note to s.81.
    Housing action trust areas: the housing action trust has the functions under this section to the exclusion of any other authority (other than the Secretary of State) where an order has been made under the Housing Act 1988, s.67(3) transferring the function (as a function within s.67(3A), as substituted by the Planning (Consequential Provisions) Act 1990, Sched. 2, para. 79(3)) to the trust (T.C.P.A. 1990, s.8(2)).
    Enterprise zones: the enterprise zone authority, where so provided by order under the Local Government, Planning and Land Act 1980, Sched. 32, para. 5.

GENERAL NOTE

Introduction
    This section enables a prospective developer (or any other person) to obtain either an immediate decision listing a building or a guarantee against listing for the ensuing five years. The Secretary of State has undertaken that a certificate will be refused only if he proposes to list the building immediately, because·it will have been found to possess some special architectural or historic interest. Application for a certificate under this section may be made only where an application (whether pending or granted) has been made for planning permission for development which involves the alteration, extension or demolition of the building, although the applicant for that permission and the applicant under this section need not be the same person.

Procedure
    DOE Circular 8/87, para. 42 advises that applications in England for a certificate of immunity under this section should be made to the Department of the Environment, and that a plan showing the position of the building or buildings involved and black and white photographs of each elevation of the building and any notable interior features should be supplied, together with details of the approximate date of its construction, the architect (if known) and any available information about the architectural or historical interest of the building.

Special cases
    The procedure under this section extends to all listed ecclesiastical buildings, whether or not for the time being used for ecclesiastical purposes (s.60(1)); and also to buildings which

are also scheduled monuments under the Ancient Monuments and Archaeological Areas Act 1979 (s.61).

The procedure applies to Crown land to the extent of any interest held in it otherwise than by the s.83(1)(b), but the Crown is not empowered by s.84 to seek such a certificate in anticipation of disposal of Crown land.

Effect of certificate

A certificate that the Secretary of State does not intend to list the building also precludes the local planning authority from serving a building preservation notice under s.3 (subs. (2)(b)). A certificate does not, however, affect a local planning authority's power to designate conservation areas, and thus does not obviate the need for conservation area consent to demolition if the building is within a conservation area, whenever designated.

CHAPTER II

AUTHORISATION OF WORKS AFFECTING LISTED BUILDINGS

Control of works in respect of listed buildings

Restriction on works affecting listed buildings

7. Subject to the following provisions of this Act, no person shall execute or cause to be executed any works for the demolition of a listed building or for its alteration or extension in any manner which would affect its character as a building of special architectural or historic interest, unless the works are authorised.

DEFINITIONS
"authorised": s.(8).
"building": s.91.
"listed building": ss.1(5); 91(1).

GENERAL NOTE

Introduction

This section establishes the legal basis of listed building control. It contains a straight prohibition of unauthorised works to listed buildings, breach of which is then translated by s.9 into an offence. By virtue of s.8, works are authorised only if consent ("listed building consent") has been granted for them and they are carried out in accordance with that consent, and (for demolition) if requirements relating to notification and provision of access to the Royal Commission are satisfied.

Extension of the prohibition

The prohibition is extended also to:

(1) unauthorised demolition of certain buildings in conservation areas, by virtue of s.74(3) and the Town and Country Planning (Listed Buildings and Conservation Areas) Regulations 1990;
(2) buildings which are subject to building preservation notices, which are treated as if they were listed buildings for the purposes of the section (s.3(5)).

Exceptions

(1) an ecclesiastical building which is for the time being used for ecclesiastical purposes is exempt from the prohibition contained in this section, by virtue of s.60(1);
(2) the demolition of all or part of a redundant church building in pursuance of a pastoral or redundancy scheme (under the Pastoral Measure 1983) is excluded by s.60(7);
(3) the section does not, by virtue of s.61, apply to any building which is a scheduled monument under the Ancient Monuments and Archaeological Areas Act 1979 s.1;
(4) although buildings owned by the Crown may be listed under s.1, the Crown is exempt from the prohibition contained in this section. However, the Crown has undertaken to consult local planning authorities before undertaking works which would otherwise require listed building consent, and a set of shadow procedures is established by DOE Circular 18/84, Memorandum, Pt. IV, paras. 31 and 32: see further the notes to s.10. The legal requirement to obtain listed building consent does apply to Crown land to

the extent of any interest in it for the time being held otherwise than by or on behalf of the Crown (s.83(1)(b)).

Obtaining authorisation

Works are authorised for the purposes of this section if listed building consent has been granted for them, and they are carried out in accordance with the terms and conditions of that consent. There is a further requirement, in cases involving demolition, that the Royal Commission should have been notified, and provided with the requisite opportunity to enter the land for the purposes of making a record. See further the notes to ss.8 and 9.

Relationship to planning control

The prohibition under this section is independent of the requirement in s.57 of the T.C.P.A. 1990 that planning permission be obtained for works constituting development. Works of demolition, alteration or extension of a listed building will also frequently constitute development requiring permission under that Act, for which application must be made separately. This may be the case even in respect of relatively minor works. In *Windsor and Maidenhead Borough Council* v. *Secretary of State for the Environment* (1988) 86 L.G.R. 402 the High Court (Mann J.) held that the repainting of a listed building was capable of constituting both a building operation within the definition of development, and an alteration for the purposes of this section, and hence required listed building consent where it affected the character of the building as a building of special architectural or historic interest.

Up until 1980, application for planning permission and listed building consent could be made on the same form, unless demolition of all or part of the building was involved. But this practice proved confusing, and was abolished by the Local Government, Planning and Land Act 1980. Today the two systems are separately administered. Although application for listed building consent and for planning permission for the same works will normally be made to the same planning authority, there are different publicity, notification and consultation requirements for each. The fact that planning permission has been granted for works does not constitute an authorisation for the purposes of liability under this Act (except in respect of the offence under s.59 of causing intentional damage to a listed building).

Works may, however, require consent under these provisions, notwithstanding that they do not constitute "development" (such as works of maintenance or repair, or internal alterations) or that they constitute permitted development under the Town and Country Planning General Development Order 1988 (such as extensions to dwelling-houses or industrial buildings, or agricultural operational development). In such cases there may be entitlement to compensation under s.27 for the additional restrictions imposed by listing building control.

Authorisation of works: listed building consent

8.—(1) Works for the alteration or extension of a listed building are authorised if—

(a) written consent for their execution has been granted by the local planning authority or the Secretary of State; and

(b) they are executed in accordance with the terms of the consent and of any conditions attached to it.

(2) Works for the demolition of a listed building are authorised if—

(a) such consent has been granted for their execution;

(b) notice of the proposal to execute the works has been given to the Royal Commission;

(c) after such notice has been given either—

    (i) for a period of at least one month following the grant of such consent, and before the commencement of the works, reasonable access to the building has been made available to members or officers of the Royal Commission for the purpose of recording it; or

    (ii) the Secretary of the Royal Commission, or another officer of theirs with authority to act on their behalf for the purposes of this section, has stated in writing that they have completed their recording of the building or that they do not wish to record it; and

  (d) the works are executed in accordance with the terms of the consent and of any conditions attached to it.

(3) Where—
  (a) works for the demolition of a listed building or for its alteration or extension are executed without such consent; and
  (b) written consent is granted by the local planning authority or the Secretary of State for the retention of the works,
the works are authorised from the grant of that consent.

(4) In this section "the Royal Commission" means—
  (a) in relation to England, the Royal Commission on the Historical Monuments of England; and
  (b) in relation to Wales, the Royal Commission on Ancient and Historical Monuments in Wales.

(5) The Secretary of State may by order provide that subsection (2) shall have effect with the substitution for the references to the Royal Commission of references to such other body as may be so specified.

(6) Such an order—
  (a) shall apply in the case of works executed or to be executed on or after such date as may be specified in the order; and
  (b) may apply in relation to either England or Wales, or both.

(7) Consent under subsection (1), (2) or (3) is referred to in this Act as "listed building consent".

DEFINITIONS
  "building": s.91.
  "land": s.91(2).
  "listed building": ss.1(5); 91(1).
  "listed building consent": subs. (7).
  "local planning authority": s.81.
  "the Royal Commission": subs. (4).

ALLOCATION OF FUNCTIONS
  As to the local planning authority with the function of granting listed building consent for the purposes of authorisation under this section, see the notes to s.10.

GENERAL NOTE

Introduction
  It is an offence under ss.7 and 9 for works of demolition, alteration or extension to be executed to a listed building unless they are authorised. This section establishes the preconditions to that authorisation. Works are authorised only if they have listed building consent, and are executed in accordance with the terms and conditions of that consent. An additional requirement in cases of demolition is that notice of the proposal has been given to the Royal Commission, and an opportunity provided for the Royal Commission to have access to the building for the purpose of recording it.
  Although listed building consent can be granted for works which have already been executed, it does not confer retrospective immunity from prosecution under s.9 (subs. (3)).

Extension of the section
  The authorisation requirements of this section are extended also to:
  (1) the demolition of certain buildings in conservation areas, by virtue of s.74(3) but subject to modifications made by the Town and Country Planning (Listed Buildings and Conservation Areas) Regulations 1990, reg.12 and Sched. 3. Demolition is authorised only if it has "conservation area consent": see further the notes to s.74.
  (2) buildings which are subject to building preservation notices: these are treated as if they were listed buildings for the purposes of the section (s.3(5)).

Exceptions
  (1) an ecclesiastical building which is for the time being used for ecclesiastical purposes is exempt from listed building requirements, by virtue of s.60(1);
  (2) the demolition of all or part of a redundant church building in pursuance of a pastoral or redundancy scheme (under the Pastoral Measure 1983) (s.60(7));

(3) the section does not, by virtue of s.61, apply to any building which is a scheduled monument under the Ancient Monuments and Archaeological Areas Act 1979, s.1;

(4) although buildings owned by the Crown may be listed under s.1, the Crown is exempt from listed building control. However, the Crown has undertaken to consult local planning authorities before undertaking works which would otherwise require listed building consent, and a set of shadow procedures is established by DOE Circular 18/84, Memorandum, Pt.IV, paras. 31 and 32: see further the notes to s.10. The legal requirement to obtain listed building consent applies to Crown land to the extent of any interest in it for the time being held otherwise than by or on behalf of the Crown (s.83(1)(b)).

Deemed consent: Private Bill procedure

Where works are authorised by a Private Act of Parliament, it is common for a provision to be inserted in the Act granting any necessary listed building consent and conservation area consent. This procedure overrides the normal planning and consultation processes, and although the statutory agencies may seek to petition against such a Bill in either House of Parliament, there may be difficulty in establishing *locus* if the matter is challenged by the Bill's promoters. The Court of Referees rejected in 1989 a petition lodged by English Heritage against the King's Cross Bill, although the Select Committee subsequently rejected the clause which would have allowed the Bills promoters to demolish listed buildings without further consent.

The Select Committee on Private Bill Procedure in its report published in 1987 (*Report of the Joint Committee on Private Bill Procedure*; H.L. Paper 97, Session 1987–88) recognised this anomaly, together with the risk that promoters might choose deliberately to pursue Private Bill authorisation rather than face normal planning and listed building procedures. The Committee's recommendations for reforms of Private Bill procedure were largely accepted by the Government, which announced in 1990 (*Private Bills and News Procedures – A Consultation Document*, Cm. 1110) that it proposed to seek legislative powers to deal with the approval of railway, light rapid transit and harbour works by ministerial order rather than Private Bill. Any other consents which were required, such as listed building consent or conservation area consent, would be obtained either separately by the promoter of the order, or by including the application for the consent as part of the order. In the latter case a single public inquiry would be held to examine all issues, and the Secretary of State for the Environment would be jointly responsible with the Secretary of State for Transport for deciding whether the order should be confirmed (para. 19).

Listed building consent procedure

The procedures governing the making and determination of applications for listed building consent are prescribed by ss.10–16, and by the Town and Country Planning (Listed Buildings and Conservation Areas) Regulations 1990, and are discussed in detail in the notes to each section.

Notification to the Royal Commission

The demolition of a listed building is authorised only if, in addition to obtaining listed building consent and complying with it, the requirements of subs. (2) as to notification to, and provision of access for, the Royal Commission on the Historical Monuments of England (or, in Wales, the Royal Commission on Ancient and Historical Monuments in Wales) are met.

There are two notification requirements. First, any application for consent to demolish any listed building has to be notified as a matter of course to the Royal Commission and the national amenity societies, followed by notification of the decision taken (Direction by the Secretary of State, DOE Circular 8/87, para. 81: see further the notes to s.13). The second requirement arises under this section. The section does not specify when notice must be given, other than it must be after listed building consent has actually been granted. But no works may commence under the consent unless notice has been given of the proposal to execute the works, and for a period of at least one month reasonable access has been made available to the Royal Commission for the purpose of recording the building (unless they complete their recording earlier or do not wish to record the building).

The English Royal Commission was established by Royal Warrant in 1908 "to make an inventory of the Ancient and Historical Monuments and Constructions connected with or illustrative of the contemporary culture, civilisation and conditions of life of the people of England . . . and to specify those which seem most worthy of preservation". In 1985 the Royal Commission received 5,000 notifications of listed building consent. Of those where consent was granted, 650 buildings were surveyed photographically, and 150 of those merited written reports on the basis of the resources that were available (Memorandum submitted by the Royal Commission of Historical Monuments of England, *Historic Buildings and Ancient Monuments*, 1st Report from the Environment Committee, Session 1986–87; H.C. 146–III, p.415).

Listed buildings in despair

The Act imposes no positive duties on owners of listed buildings to maintain them in good repair, but it confers powers on local planning authorities:

(1)   to carry out works urgently necessary for the preservation of an unoccupied listed building upon giving not less than seven days' prior notification of their intention to the owner (s.54); and

(2)   to acquire compulsorily any listed building in need of repair (s.47), subject, in the case of a building which has deliberately been allowed to fall into disrepair for the purpose of justifying its demolition and the redevelopment of the site, to the payment of minimum compensation calculated on the assumption that neither planning permission nor listed building consent would be forthcoming except for maintaining the building in a proper state of repair (s.50).

Compensation for refusal of listed building consent

Compensation is payable under s.27 in respect of the refusal of listed building consent for the alteration or extension of a listed building (but not for its demolition, and the provisions are therefore inapplicable to unlisted buildings in conservation areas) where:—

(1)   the Secretary of State has refused consent for the alteration or extension, or granted it subject to conditions; and

(2)   the works do not constitute development, or if they do, permission is granted by a development order; and

(3)   the value of the relevant interest in the land is less than it would have been if listed building consent had been granted unconditionally.

Liability to value added tax on alterations to listed buildings

By virtue of the Value Added Tax Act 1983, s.16 and Sched. 5, Group 8, the supply of works, services and materials in the construction, alteration and demolition of buildings was formerly zero-rated for VAT purposes. Works of alteration lost that exemption in 1984 when the 1983 Act was amended by the Finance Act 1984, s.10 and Sched. 6, Pt. II. But the Act retained zero-rating for the supply of any service (other than the services of an architect, surveyor or any person acting as consultant or in a supervisory capacity) made in connection with an approved alteration (not including purely repair or maintenance) of a "protected building", which included any listed building or scheduled monument. An alteration is "approved" only if it has the necessary scheduled monument consent or listed building consent, or is exempt from it (Value Added Tax Act 1983, s.16 and Sched. 5, Group 8A (as inserted by Finance Act 1984, s.10 and Sched. 16)).

That category was subsequently narrowed by the Finance Act 1989, Sched. 3, para. 2, following the ruling by the European Court in *EC Commission* v. *U.K.* [1988] 3 C.M.L.R. 437 that the former zero-rating provisions did not satisfy EC requirements, particularly in connection with the construction of new commercial buildings. Amendments made by the 1989 Act retained zero-rating for protected buildings only to the extent that they are non-commercial buildings. "Protected building" is now defined as:

"a building which is designed to remain as or become a dwelling or number of dwellings or is intended for use solely for a residential purpose or a relevant charitable purpose after the reconstruction or alteration and which, in either case, is [a listed building or a scheduled monument]".

The definition of "use for a relevant residential purpose" includes a variety of non-commercial residential uses; and "use for a relevant charitable purpose" means use by a charity otherwise than in the course or furtherance of a business, or as a village hall or similarly in providing social or recreational facilities for a local community.

Arrangements for specialist advice

The Secretary of State may from time to time direct a district planning authority, under Sched. 4, para. 7, to submit for approval by him the arrangements they propose to make to obtain specialist advice in connection with their functions under this section, and, if not satisfied about the arrangements, may direct them to enter into an agreement with another local planning authority.

Offences

9.—(1) If a person contravenes section 7 he shall be guilty of an offence.

(2) Without prejudice to subsection (1), if a person executing or causing to be executed any works in relation to a listed building under a listed building consent fails to comply with any condition attached to the consent, he shall be guilty of an offence.

(3) In proceedings for an offence under this section it shall be a defence to prove the following matters—

(a) that works to the building were urgently necessary in the interests of safety or health or for the preservation of the building;

(b) that it was not practicable to secure safety or health or, as the case may be, the preservation of the building by works of repair or works for affording temporary support or shelter,

(c) that the works carried out were limited to the minimum measures immediately necessary; and

(d) that notice in writing justifying in detail the carrying out of the works was given to the local planning authority as soon as reasonably practicable.

(4) A person who is guilty of an offence under this section shall be liable—

(a) on summary conviction to imprisonment for a term not exceeding three months or a fine not exceeding the statutory maximum, or both; or

(b) on conviction on indictment to imprisonment for a term not exceeding twelve months or a fine, or both.

(5) In determining the amount of any fine to be imposed on a person convicted on indictment of an offence under this section, the court shall in particular have regard to any financial benefit which has accrued or appears likely to accrue to him in consequence of the offence.

DEFINITIONS
"building": s.91.
"listed building": ss.1(5); 91(1).
"listed building consent": ss.8(7); 91(1).
"local planning authority": s.81.

ALLOCATION OF FUNCTIONS
The local planning authority to which notice must be given under subs. (3)(d) is:—
Greater London: the London borough council (T.C.P.A. 1990, s.1(2).
Metropolitan areas: the metropolitan district council (T.C.P.A. 1990, s.1(2)).
Non-metropolitan areas: the district planning authority (Sched. 4, para. 2).
National Parks (outside a metropolitan county): the county planning authority (T.C.P.A. 1990, s.4) or joint planning board in areas where one has been established as county planning authority (T.C.P.A. 1990, s.2).
Norfolk and Suffolk Broads: the Broads Authority (Sched. 4, para. 5).
Urban development areas: the urban development corporation where an order has been made under the Local Government, Planning and Land Act 1980, s.149(1), transferring the function to the corporation (T.C.P.A. 1990, s.7(1)): for a list of current orders see the General Note to s.81.
Housing action trust areas: the housing action trust has the functions under this section to the exclusion of any other authority (other than the Secretary of State) where an order has been made under the Housing Act 1988, s.67(3) transferring the function (as a function within s.67(3A), as substituted by the Planning (Consequential Provisions) Act 1990, Sched. 2, para. 79(3)) to the trust (T.C.P.A. 1990, s.8(2)): see the General Note to s.81.
Enterprise zones: the enterprise zone authority, where so provided by order under the Local Government, Planning and Land Act 1980, Sched. 32, para. 5.

GENERAL NOTE

Introduction
This section creates two offences. It is an offence to contravene s.7 (unauthorised execution of works for demolition of a listed building, or its alteration or extension in any

manner which would affect its character as a building of special architectural or historic interest). What constitutes authorisation for the purposes of that offence is defined by s.8. It is a further offence (subs. (2)) to fail to comply with any condition attached to a listed building consent. Subs. (3) of this section creates a specific statutory defence to prosecution for both offences.

Extension of the section

The offences under this section are extended also to:
(1) the demolition of certain buildings in conservation areas, by virtue of s.74(3) but subject to modifications made by the Town and Country Planning (Listed Buildings and Conservation Areas) Regulations 1990, reg. 12 and Sched. 3. Demolition is authorised only if it has "conservation area consent" (see further the notes to s.74);
(2) buildings which are subject to building preservation notices: these are treated as if they were listed buildings for the purposes of the section (s.3(5)).

Exceptions

It is not an offence under this section to carry out unauthorised works in relation to listed buildings in the following cases:
(1) an ecclesiastical building which is for the time being used for ecclesiastical purposes is exempt from listed building requirements, by virtue of s.60(1);
(2) the demolition of all or part of a redundant church building in pursuance of a pastoral or redundancy scheme (under the Pastoral Measure 1983): s.60(7);
(3) works to any building which is a scheduled monument under the Ancient Monuments and Archaeological Areas Act 1979, s.1 (s.61);
(4) works to listed buildings owned by the Crown, because of the Crown's immunity from listed building control. That immunity extends not only to Crown land but also to any liability of the Crown in relation to any listed building (*Lord Advocate* v. *Dumbarton District Council* [1990] 3 W.L.R. 1346. Although the Crown has undertaken to consult local planning authorities before undertaking works which would otherwise require listed building consent, and a set of shadow procedures is established by DOE Circular 18/84, Memorandum, Pt. IV, paras. 31 and 32 (see further the notes to s.10) the arrangements are wholly non-statutory and non-compliance with them does not create liability under this section. The legal requirement to obtain listed building consent does however apply to Crown land to the extent of any interest in it for the time being held otherwise than by or on behalf of the Crown (s.83(1)(b)).

Unauthorised works: the nature of the offence

The offence of executing unauthorised works for the demolition or alteration of a listed building is an offence of strict liability; the prosecution is not required to prove that the defendant was aware that the building was listed. In *R.* v. *Wells Street Metropolitan Stipendiary Magistrates*, ex p. *Westminster City Council* [1986] 1 W.L.R. 1046 the court rejected the submissions that the provisions of subs. (5) relating to punishment were a strong indication that proof of intent should be required, and that it was wrong for third parties to be fixed with strict liability. These fears were capable of being allayed by the discretion as to whether to prosecute, and in the power to refrain from punishment by either fine or imprisonment in appropriate cases, and there was therefore no injustice in holding that the offence was absolute. The court accepted the submission for the local planning authority that the circumstances of that case (where the defendant had been discovered stripping the fixtures and fittings from a listed building) clearly gave rise to an issue of social concern, and that the creation of strict liability would be effective to promote the objectives of the statute by encouraging greater vigilance to prevent breaches, and by creating a deterrent to those tempted to breach it. This approach to liability is in line with that taken by the courts in relation to breaches of tree preservation orders: see, *e.g.* *Maidstone Borough Council* v. *Mortimer* [1980] 3 All E.R. 552.

Liability attaches only to somebody who executes works, or causes works to be executed, and this requires some positive act. It is not an offence merely to permit works to be executed; nor does the offence include damage to a building which is caused by accident (see, *e.g.* the ministerial decision reported at [1981] J.P.L. 443). Moreover, "works" implies some deliberate alteration to the building, and it is doubtful how far the term covers action that is purely vandalistic. There is therefore a separate offence under s.59 of deliberately causing damage to a listed building: see further the notes to s.59.

Liability commences as soon as a building becomes listed: there is no provision that renders liability dependent upon notification to owners and occupiers of the fact of listing. But it is unlikely that a prosecution could ever reasonably be brought in a case where, for want of notification, the alleged offender could not have known that the building had become listed.

Non-compliance with condition

This offence (subs. (2)) overlaps substantially with that created by subs. (1), because works of demolition, alteration and extension are authorised only if listed building consent has been granted for them, and they are executed in accordance with its terms "and of any conditions attached to it" (s.8(2)(d)). Thus, non-compliance with a condition is already within subs. (1), and it is not clear at first glance how far this separate offence adds anything to that offence. Its purpose seems to be to avoid the difficulty which might arise if works have been carried out in accordance with listed building consent but some additional requirement imposed by a condition, such as making good any damage to the building, or carrying out reconstruction works (see s.17(1)) has not been carried through. Prosecution for the more specific offence of failure to comply with a condition is then perhaps more straightforward for the local planning authority than having to prove that the works that have actually been carried out, though fully in accordance with the consent so far as they go, had nonetheless to be regarded as unauthorised because separate works required by a condition had not been completed.

Prior notice of demolition to local authority

A separate requirement is imposed by the Building Act 1984, s.80, of notification to the local authority prior to the demolition of any building, with a view to their ensuring that proper steps are taken for the protection of adjacent buildings, the removal of materials and rubbish, and the sealing up of drains and pipes.

The statutory defence

There is a statutory defence to prosecution under this section, the burden of proof of which lies with the defendant (see also *R.* v. *Brightman* [1990] L.S. Gaz. April 11, 42, C.A. in relation to tree preservation orders). Subs. (3) (as originally substituted by the Housing and Planning Act 1986) provides that it shall be a defence to any proceedings for an offence under the section to prove that the works were urgently necessary (and no more than the minimum required) in the interests of safety or health or for the preservation of the building, which it was not practicable to secure by temporary or repair works, and that notice had been given to the local planning authority. In *R.* v. *Stroud District Council*, ex p. *Goodenough Usborne and Tomlin* [1982] J.P.L. 246, the Divisional Court accepted that although the subsection as previously worded (s.55(6) of the 1971 Act, which required the defence to prove only that "the works were urgently necessary in the interests of safety or health, or for the preservation of the building, and that notice in writing of the need for the works was given to the local planning authority as soon as reasonably practicable") did not in terms render demolition lawful in such a case, the intent of the legislation was that in appropriate cases the owner should be able to demolish notwithstanding that he had not obtained listed building consent.

The defence under subs. (3) is now tightly limited. Not only must the works have been urgently necessary (to the extent that repair or temporary support or shelter would have been insufficient), but they must have been confined to the minimum immediately necessary and written notice must have been given to the local planning authority as soon as reasonably practicable. If that notice were to be given to the authority before the works were carried out, it might beg the question of how urgently necessary they were; but it would also allow the authority to consider whether to use its powers under ss.47 and 48 of this Act (compulsory acquisition of a listed building in need of repair) or 54 (urgent works to preserve unoccupied listed buildings).

A similarly worded provision, but excluding the requirement of notice to the local planning authority, is provided under s.39(1)(d) as a ground of appeal against a listed building enforcement notice.

Liability where demolition required under another enactment

The potential conflict between liability under this section, and a requirement to repair or demolish an unsafe building imposed under other legislation, was highlighted in the *Stroud* case, where the local authority had taken the view that there was no further action they could take when an owner proposed to demolish a listed building in reliance on the statutory defence (as it then stood) following the making of an order under s.58 of the Public Health Act 1936 (now the Building Act 1984, s.77) requiring the execution of works necessary to make the buildings safe or their demolition. The court held that this was wrong: the authority should have given consideration to whether action should be taken under ss.54 or 47 and 48 (carrying out urgent repairs themselves or issuing a repairs notice prior to commencing compulsory purchase proceedings). Subsequently, amendments made by the 1986 Act, now to be found in s.56 of this Act, imposed a duty on a local planning authority to consider using their powers under this Act before making an order or serving a notice under the Building Act 1984 or the London Building Acts (Amendment) Act 1939; and amendments made by the 1986 Act to those two Acts also require a local authority to consider using their powers under ss.47, 48 and 54 of this Act before making a dangerous structures order in respect of a listed building (or an unlisted building in a conservation area). Moreover, the provisions of this Act now take priority: demolition of a listed building by virtue of an order made under those powers is authorised only if listed building consent has been granted (and the requirements of notification and access to the Royal Commission have been complied with). Only in the limited circumstances defined in subs. (3) will unauthorised demolition not attract criminal liability.

Residential properties unfit for human habitation

There is no power to make a demolition order under the Housing Act 1985 in respect of a listed building or a building which is subject to a building preservation notice, and the authority are instead limited to making a closing order (Housing Act 1985, s.304). If a building is listed after being included in a slum clearance area then:

(1) if it has been purchased by the local authority by agreement, they may apply within three months to the Secretary of State for his consent to demolition. If the application is refused or none is made within the prescribed period, the authority cease to be subject to the duty under s.291 of the Housing Act 1985 to demolish the building. If it is a house, it is thereupon appropriated to the purposes of Pt. II of the 1985 Act; otherwise, it is appropriated to the purposes of Pt. IX of the T.C.P.A. 1990 (Housing Act 1985, s.306);

(2) if the authority have not acquired the building but have made a compulsory purchase order in respect of it, they may within three months of the listing apply to the Secretary of State for listed building consent. If the application is refused, or none is made within the period, and the building has not been vested in the authority and no notice to treat has been served, the compulsory purchase order ceases to have effect in relation to the building, and the building ceases, where applicable, to be comprised in the clearance area. Otherwise, unless listed building consent is granted, the authority cease to be subject to the duty under s.291 of the 1985 Act to demolish the building, and the compulsory purchase order has effect as if (in the case of a house) it had been made and confirmed under Pt. II of the 1985 Act, or (in any other case) as if it had been made and confirmed under Pt. IX of the T.C.P.A. 1990 (Housing Act 1985, s.305).

The level of penalties

The special provisions of subs. (5) are intended to counteract the temptation that an offender might have to accept a modest court fine as, in effect, a licence fee for unauthorised demolition, given the very substantial financial return, such as an enhancement in development value of the land, that may ensue. Two instances of fines being imposed under these provisions are reported at [1990] J.P.L. 397.

Listed building enforcement procedures

In addition to the offences created by this section and s.59, specific enforcement powers are conferred by ss.38–46 which allow the local planning authority, where it appears to them that works have been or are being executed to a listed building which are such as to involve a contravention of subss. (1) or (2) of this section, to issue a listed building enforcement notice specifying the alleged contravention and requiring steps to be taken for its remedy.

Applications for listed building consent

Making of applications for listed building consent

10.—(1) Except as provided in sections 12 to 15, an application for listed building consent shall be made to and dealt with by the local planning authority.

(2) Such an application shall be made in such form as the authority may require and shall contain—

(a) sufficient particulars to identify the building to which it relates, including a plan;

(b) such other plans and drawings as are necessary to describe the works which are the subject of the application; and

(c) such other particulars as may be required by the authority.

(3) Provision may be made by regulations under this Act with respect to—

(a) the manner in which such applications are to be made;

(b) the manner in which they are to be advertised; and

(c) the time within which they are to be dealt with by local planning authorities or, as the case may be, by the Secretary of State.

DEFINITIONS
"building": s.91.
"listed building": ss.1(5); 91(1).
"listed building consent": ss.8(7); 91(1).
"local planning authority": s.81.

ALLOCATION OF FUNCTIONS
The local planning authority to whom application must be made under this section for listed building consent (or conservation area consent) is:—

Greater London: the London borough council (T.C.P.A. 1990, s.1(2).

Metropolitan areas: the metropolitan district council (T.C.P.A. 1990, s.1(2)).

Non-metropolitan areas: the district authority (Sched. 4, para. 2).

National Parks (outside a metropolitan county): the district planning authority, who shall, unless it falls to be determined by them, send it on to the county planning authority (Sched. 4, para. 3(1)). An application as respects a building situated in an area of a National Park within a metropolitan county must be made to the joint planning board (Town and Country Planning (Listed Buildings and Conservation Areas) Regulations 1990

Norfolk and Suffolk Broads: the Broads Authority (Sched. 4, para. 5).

Urban development areas: the urban development corporation where an order has been made under the Local Government, Planning and Land Act 1980, s.149(1), transferring the function to the corporation (T.C.P.A. 1990, s.7(1)): for a list of current orders see the notes to s.81.

Housing action trust areas: the housing action trust has the functions under this section to the exclusion of any other authority (other than the Secretary of State) where an order has been made under the Housing Act 1988, s.67(3) transferring the function (as a function within s.67(3A), as substituted by the Planning (Consequential Provisions) Act 1990, Sched. 2, para. 79(3)) to the trust (T.C.P.A. 1990, s.8(2)): see the notes to s.81.

Enterprise zones: the enterprise zone authority, where so provided by order under the Local Government, Planning and Land Act 1980, Sched. 32, para. 5.

As to the local planning authority with the function of *determining* applications made under this section, see the note to s.16.

GENERAL NOTE

Introduction
This section prescribes the form and content of applications for listed building consent. It extends also to:

(1) buildings subject to building preservation notices under s.3, which are treated as listed buildings (s.3(5));

(2) applications for conservation area consent, with the substitution of the words "conservation area consent" for "listed building consent" (s.74 and Town and Country Planning (Listed Buildings and Conservation Areas) Regulations 1990, reg. 12 and Sched. 3);

(3) applications for the modification or discharge of conditions attached to listed building consent (s.19(3)) or to conservation area consent (s.74 and Town and Country Planning (Listed Buildings and Conservation Areas) Regulations 1990, reg. 12 and Sched. 3).

Form of application
The procedures for making and determining applications for listed building consent are prescribed by the Town and Country Planning (Listed Buildings and Conservation Areas) Regulations 1990. Applications are required to be made on a form issued by the relevant local planning authority (see under Allocation of Functions above), and to be lodged with that authority accompanied by two further copies of the form, plans and drawings. The

authority may entertain the application only if it is accompanied by an ownership certificate (see below).

No fee is payable in respect of applications under this section.

Content of application

The application must contain (subs. (2)) (1) sufficient particulars to identify the building to which it relates, including a plan; (2) such other plans and drawings as are necessary to describe the works which are the subject of the application; and (3) such other particulars as may be required by the authority.

The degree of detail that is required is thus a matter primarily for the local planning authority. An application that fails to provide the details required by the section, or required by the authority exercising their powers under para. (c), may be refused for lack of sufficient information, or simply not determined within the prescribed eight week period (subject in each case to the right of appeal to the Secretary of State); or treated by them as invalid (in which case they are required to notify the applicant accordingly, "as soon as may be"; reg. 3(4)). Such a determination could presumably also be challenged by an appeal to the Secretary of State for failure to determine the application within the prescribed eight week period, and the issue of validity considered in the course of those proceedings.

Ownership certificates

The application must be accompanied by the appropriate certificate in the form prescribed by Sched. 2 to the 1990 Regulations (pursuant to the powers in s.11(1)), to the effect either that (1) the applicant was, 20 days before the date of the application, the sole owner of the building to which the application relates (Certificate A); (2) that the requisite notice has been given to all owners (Certificate B); or (3) that the requisite notice has been given to such owners as were ascertainable (Certificate C); or (4) that no other owners were ascertainable (Certificate D).

In the latter two cases the certificate must also describe the steps taken to ascertain the owners, and be accompanied by a copy of notice of the application (in the form prescribed by Pt. II of Sched. 2 to the 1990 Regulations) published in a newspaper circulating in the locality. Alternative forms of certificate in the Welsh language for use at the option of Welsh authorities, are prescribed by the Town and Country Planning (Listed Buildings in Wales and Buildings in Conservation Areas in Wales) (Welsh Forms) Regulations 1990 (No. 1147), reg. 3(1) and Sched. 2. Where the applicant has given notice to some or all of the owners, the certificate must also set out their names and addresses, and the date of service on them (s.11(2)).

An application for consent under this section may not be entertained by the local planning authority unless it is accompanied by a certificate; and the eight week period allowed for determining the application under the Town and Country Planning (Listed Buildings and Conservation Areas) Regulations 1990, reg. 3(4), does not begin to run until the certificate has been lodged with them. The fact that the incorrect certificate, or a false certificate, has been submitted does not necessarily invalidate any consent which is subsequently granted (see further the notes to the T.C.P.A., s.66).

Duty to take owners' representations into account

Where an application is accompanied by a certificate other than Certificate A, the local planning authority are required, in determining the application, to take into account any representations made by any person who satisfies them that he is an owner of the building, and to give notice of their decision to any such person (Town and Country Planning (Listed Buildings and Conservation Areas) Regulations 1990, reg. 6(3)(b)).

Handling applications

The local planning authority are required to acknowledge receipt of an application in the terms prescribed by the Town and Country Planning (Listed Buildings and Buildings in Conservation Areas) Regulations 1987 (No. 349), Sched. 1, Pt. I; and, if they form the view that the application is invalid, to notify the applicant accordingly (reg. 3(2)).

Advertisement of applications

The local planning authority are required to publish notice of all applications, except those relating only to works affecting the interior of Grade II (unstarred) buildings. The notice must be published in a local newspaper circulating in the locality in which the building is situated, and must indicate the nature of the works proposed, and name a place where the application and the plans and documents submitted with it will be open to public inspection (1990 Regulations, reg. 5(1)). In addition, the local planning authority must ensure that a site notice, containing the same information, is displayed on or near the building for not less than seven days. The authority have no power to proceed to determine the application until after 21 days from the date of publication of the notice or the display off the site notice (whichever is later), and they must take into account any representations relating to the application received by them within that period.

Applications by local planning authorities

The normal provisions of the Town and Country Planning General Regulations 1976 (No. 1419) under which local planning authorities may authorise their own development proposals do not extend to applications for development which consists of or includes works for the alteration or extension of a listed building (reg. 7), nor to applications for listed building consent (Town and Country Planning (Listed Buildings and Conservation Areas) Regulations 1990, reg. 13). Instead, the authorities are required to apply to the Secretary of State when they require listed building consent. In the case of a county council, the application is required to be made to the district council, who must then "forthwith" send it on to the Secretary of State (reg. 13(8)). For other authorities the application is made direct to the Secretary of State, though in the form of an application to themselves, which is then deemed to have been referred to the Secretary of State (reg. 13(3)). The regulations do not, however, apply to applications made by third parties in relation to land owned by the local planning authority, even where the local planning authority proposes to dispose of that land to the applicant for development (*R.* v. *Merton London Borough Council*, ex p. *Burnett* [1990] 1 P.L.R. 72).

Crown land

Although the Crown is immune from listed building requirements, it becomes involved in the system in four ways:

(1) where an interest is held in a listed building which is Crown land other than by the Crown: in this case the owner of the interest is required to obtain authorisation in the usual way, and to certify under s.11 that the Crown had been notified of the application as an owner of the land;

(2) where the Crown proposes itself to carry out works to a listed building: although not requiring consent, the Crown has undertaken to observe a set of non-statutory shadow procedures, contained in DOE Circular 18/84, Memorandum, Pt. IV, paras. 31–33. Departments will consult about any proposal to demolish a listed building, or to alter or extend it in such a way as to affect its character as a building of special architectural or historic interest. The local planning authority are asked to advertise such proposals and to notify national and local amenity societies in the same way as if a formal application had been made to them. Objections made by third parties are conveyed by the local planning authority to the developing department who will consider whether to proceed in light of the objections, or whether to refer the matter to the Secretary of State for the Environment. If there is an unresolved objection from the local planning authority, the matter must be referred to the Secretary of State, to be dealt with in accordance with a procedure model on the statutory appeals procedure. Similar shadow arrangements apply (paras. 34 and 35) to proposals for the demolition of buildings in conservation areas;

(3) where the Crown proposes to dispose of land, and seeks listed building consent (or conservation area consent) in anticipation of disposal. The purpose of these provisions is to allow the Crown to enhance the value of the land on disposal by establishing in advance the necessary planning backing for any appropriate development or redevelopment. Application for consent may be made by virtue of s.84, and this section is modified by the Town and Country Planning (Crown Land Applications) Regulations 1984 (No. 1015) by the insertion of a further subsection:

(AA) Where an application in respect of Crown land is made (otherwise than as part of an application for planning permission) under this section by virtue of the provisions of [section 84] and it is made by a person authorised in writing by the appropriate authority, the application shall be accompanied by a copy of the relevant authorisation.

Moreover, such applications, where there is no private interest in the land, are required to be accompanied by a statement to that effect: Town and Country Planning (Listed Buildings and Conservation Areas) Regulations 1990, reg. 6, as modified by reg. 15(1)(c).

Any consent granted on such an application applies only to works carried out after the land has ceased to be Crown land; and, so long as it continues to be Crown land, to works carried out by virtue of a private interest in the land (s.84(3)). The appropriate Crown authority is required to give written notification to the local planning authority after disposing of, or of any interest in, the land (Town and Country Planning (Crown Land Applications) Regulations 1984 (No. 1015), reg. 4);

(4) where the Crown disposes of land its immunity continues to protect its successors in title in relation to works carried by or on behalf of the Crown during its ownership: s.83(3).

Notification of applications

The Act prescribes a complex system of relationships between local planning authorities (to which all applications are made in the first instance), the Commission and the Secretary of State. Local planning authorities outside London are required by s.13 to notify the Secretary of State of all applications for listed building consent and conservation area consent, but a direction made under s.15 has relaxed that requirement in relation to certain categories of application: see further the notes to s.13. Any application that is not required to be notified may be determined by the local planning authority in any manner they think fit (s.15(2)), although there is a residential power for the Secretary of State to reintroduce the notification requirement for any particular application or description of applications (s.15(4)).

The notification requirement provides a trigger for the exercise of the Secretary of State's powers to call-in an application for his own determination, and there is a 28 day moratorium period following notification during which the authority may not proceed to determine the application unless notified by the Secretary of State that he does not propose to call it in.

For London boroughs, the requirement is (under s.14) to notify the HBMC of any application which they do not propose to refuse. The Commission then, depending on its view on the application, may be required to notify it to the Secretary of State.

Consultation

Where an application relating to land in a National Park falls to be determined by a county planning authority, they are required before determining it to consult with the district planning authority for the area where the land is located (Sched. 4, para. 3(2)).

Arrangements for specialist advice

The Secretary of State may from time to time direct as district planning authority, under Sched. 4, para. 7, to submit for approval by him the arrangements they propose to make to obtain specialist advice in connection with their functions under this section through to s.26, and, if not satisfied about the arrangements, may direct them to enter into an agreement with another local planning authority.

Certificates as to applicant's status etc.

11.—(1) Regulations under this Act may provide that an application for listed building consent shall not be entertained unless it is accompanied by one of the following certificates in the prescribed form and signed by or on behalf of the applicant—

(a) a certificate stating that, at the beginning of the period of 21 days ending with the date of the application, no person (other than the applicant) was the owner of any of the building to which the application relates;

(b) a certificate stating that the applicant has given the requisite notice of the application to all the persons (other than himself) who at the beginning of that period were owners of any of the building to which the application relates;

(c) a certificate stating—

(i) that the applicant is unable to issue a certificate in accordance with paragraph (a) or (b);

(ii) that he has given the requisite notice of the application to such one or more of the persons mentioned in paragraph (b) as are specified in the certificate; and

(iii) that he has taken such steps as are reasonably open to him (specifying them) to ascertain the names and addresses of the remainder of those persons but has been unable to do so;

(d) a certificate stating—

(i) the applicant is unable to issue a certificate in accordance with paragraph (a); and

(ii) that he has taken such steps as are reasonably open to him (specifying them) to ascertain the names and addresses of the persons mentioned in paragraph (b) but has been unable to do so.

(2) Where such provision is made any such certificate as is mentioned in subsection (1)(b) or (c) must set out—

(a) the names of the persons to whom the applicant has given the requisite notice of the application;

(b) the addresses at which notice was given to them; and

(c) the date of service of each such notice.

(3) Such regulations may require that any such certificate as is mentioned in subsection (1)(c) or (d) shall also contain a statement that the requisite notice of the application, as set out in the certificate, has on a date specified in the certificate (which must not be earlier than the beginning of the period mentioned in subsection (1)(a)) been published in a local newspaper circulating in the locality in which the building is situated.

(4) Such regulations may also require that where an application is accompanied by such a certificate as is mentioned in subsection (1)(b), (c) or (d), the local planning authority—

(a) shall not determine the application before the end of the period of 21 days beginning with the date appearing from the certificate to be the latest of the dates of service of notices as mentioned in the certificate, or, if later, the date of publication of a notice as so mentioned;

(b) shall in determining the application take into account any representations relating to it which are made to them before the end of that period by any person who satisfies them that he is an owner of any of the building to which the application relates; and

(c) shall give notice of their decision to every person who has made representations which they were required to take into account in accordance with paragraph (b).

(5) Such regulations may also make provision as to who, in the case of any building, is to be treated as the owner for the purposes of any provision made by virtue of this section.

(6) If any person—

(a) issues a certificate which purports to comply with the requirements of regulations made by virtue of this section and contains a statement which he knows to be false or misleading in a material particular; or

(b) recklessly issues a certificate which purports to comply with those requirements and contains a statement which is false or misleading in a material particular,

he shall be guilty of an offence and liable on summary conviction to a fine not exceeding level 3 on the standard scale.

(7) Subject to subsection (5), in this section "owner" means a person who is for the time being the estate owner in respect of the fee simple or is entitled to a tenancy granted or extended for a term of years certain of which not less than seven years remain unexpired.

DEFINITIONS
  "building": s.91.
  "listed building": ss.1(5); 91(1).
  "listed building consent": ss.8(7); 91(1).
  "local planning authority": see notes to s.16.
  "owner": subs. (5).
  "prescribed": s.91(1).

ALLOCATION OF FUNCTIONS
As to the local planning authority with the function of determining applications (subs. (4)), see the note to s.16.

GENERAL NOTE

Introduction
An application for listed building consent may be made by any person, whether or not the owner of the building. This section makes provision for requiring the notification of applications for listed building consent to owners of the building concerned. Effect is given to these provisions by the Town and Country Planning (Listed Buildings and Conservation Areas) Regulations 1990, reg. 6 and Sched. 2.

Extension of the requirement
The requirement extends also to
(1) applications in relation to a building which is not listed, but is the subject of a building preservation notice under s.3, and is therefore to be treated for the purposes of this Act as if it were listed (s.3(5));
(2) applications for conservation area consent, with the substitution of the words "conservation area consent" for "listed building consent" (s.74 and Town and Country Planning (Listed Buildings and Conservation Areas) Regulations 1990, reg.12 and Sched. 3);
(3) applications for the modification or discharge of conditions attached to listed building consent (s.19(3)) or to conservation area consent (s.74 and Town and Country Planning (Listed Buildings and Conservation Areas) Regulations 1990, reg. 12 and Sched. 3). Such an application may, however, be made only by a person "interested" in the building (s.19(1));
(4) appeals to the Secretary of State against refusal of consent, the imposition of conditions or refusal to vary or discharge a condition. By virtue of s.21(5) and the 1990 Regulations, reg. 6(6), such an appeal may not be entertained unless it is accompanied by a fresh certificate in the prescribed form corresponding to one of those described in subs. (1) of this section. A person so notified, who makes representations within the prescribed time to the Secretary of State, is entitled under the Town and Country Planning (Inquiries Procedure) Rules 1988 to appear at any public local inquiry held for the purposes of the appeal.

What owners are entitled to be notified
The definition of "owner" in subs. (7) includes not only fee simple owners, but also tenants, provided that not less than seven years of the term of the lease remain. It does not therefore include short-term periodic tenants (*e.g.* from month to month, or from year to year), nor tenants in occupation by virtue of statutory tenancies. The requirement which exists in the corresponding provisions relating to planning applications (s.66 of the T.C.P.A. 1990) to notify certain agricultural tenants, is not carried across to listed building consent applications.

Alternative forms of certificate in Wales
It is open to an applicant in Wales to submit a certificate in the Welsh language, in the form prescribed by the Town and Country Planning (Listed Buildings in Wales and Buildings in Conservation Areas in Wales) (Welsh Forms) Regulations 1990 (No. 1147), reg. 3(1) and Sched. 2.

Duty to take owners' representations into account
Where an application is accompanied by a certificate other than Certificate A, the local planning authority are required, in determining the application, to take into account any representations made by any person who satisfies them that he is an owner of the building, and to give notice of their decision to any such person (Town and Country Planning (Listed Buildings and Buildings in Conservation Areas) Regulations 1990 reg. 6(4)).

The offence of providing false or misleading information
The offence under subs. (6) is triable only summarily and not on indictment, and thus is subject to the time limitation of the Magistrates' Court Act 1980, s.127, which requires that the information be laid within six months from the time when the offence was committed.

Reference of certain applications to Secretary of State

12.—(1) The Secretary of State may give directions requiring applications for listed building consent to be referred to him instead of being dealt with by the local planning authority.

(2) A direction under this section may relate either to a particular application, or to applications in respect of such buildings as may be specified in the direction.

(3) An application in respect of which a direction under this section has effect shall be referred to the Secretary of State accordingly.

(4) Before determining an application referred to him under this section, the Secretary of State shall, if either the applicant or the authority so wish, give each of them an opportunity of appearing before, and being heard by, a person appointed by the Secretary of State.

(5) The decision of the Secretary of State on any application referred to him under this section shall be final.

DEFINITIONS
  "building": s.91.
  "listed building": s.1(5); 91(1).
  "listed building consent": ss.8(7); 91(1).
  "local planning authority": s.81.

ALLOCATION OF FUNCTIONS
  As to the local planning authority with the function of determining listed building consent applications up until the point of call-in, and who is thus entitled under subs. (4) to be heard, see the note to s.16.

GENERAL NOTE

Introduction
  The section provides the Secretary of State with the power, modelled on s.77 of the T.C.P.A. 1990, to "call-in" an application for listed building consent for determination by himself. This power plays a central part in the planning process. It allows the Secretary of State to exercise highly selective control over local planning authorities' decision-making and is operated to some extent as a balance to the lack of third-party rights of appeal where local planning authorities propose to grant consent. Where consent is refused, the applicant has a right of appeal, the Secretary of State has an opportunity to review the issues and third parties have a right to make representations. But if consent is to be granted, such opportunities arise only if the application is called-in.

Extension of the power
  The call-in power under this section extends also to:
  (1) applications in relation to a building which is not listed, but is the subject of a building preservation notice under s.3, and is therefore to be treated for the purposes of this Act as if it were listed (s.3(5));
  (2) applications for conservation area consent, with the substitution of the words "conservation area consent" for "listed building consent" (s.74 and Town and Country Planning (Listed Buildings and Conservation Areas) Regulations 1990, reg. 12 and Sched. 3)
  (3) applications for the modification or discharge of conditions attached to listed building consent (s.19(3)) or to conservation area consent (s.74 and Town and Country Planning (Listed Buildings and Conservation Areas) Regulations 1990, reg. 12 and Sched. 3).

Directions relating to pending applications
  There are two modes of exercise of the power: in relation to pending applications, and in relation to specified buildings.
  The power may be used in respect of any particular application that has been made to the local planning authority, and the trigger for its exercise in this way will normally be the notification requirements of ss.13 and 14. Under s.13, a local planning authority (outside London) is required to notify the Secretary of State of all applications for listed building consent (except those excepted by the Secretary of State: see the notes to that section), and

9–33

to proceed no further in determining the application over the following 28 days unless notified by him that he does not propose to call-in the application under this section. The 28 day period may be extended if the Secretary of State needs further time to consider whether to call-in the application, and a call-in direction may be issued, even after the expiry of that period, at any time before the local planning authority determines the application.

On the face of this section, the power of call-in is exercisable also in relation to applications which are excepted from the notification requirements under ss.13 or 14. But that inter-pretation would conflict with the guarantee in s.15(2) that excepted applications may be dealt with by the local planning authority in any manner they think fit without notification to the Secretary of State or the Commission. The means of reconciliation of the two provisions would seem to be the power to make a further direction under s.15(4) requiring either a particular application, or specified descriptions of application, to be notified to the Secretary of State, and thereby bringing into play the suspensive provisions of those sections. Such a direction is only effective if made prior to the local planning authority's determination of the application.

The Secretary of State has advised that:

"It is open to the Commission or national or local amenity societies to alert the authority to any application which they consider falls into a category requiring reference to the Department. They may also ask the Department to withdraw the direction in an individual case if they consider that the proposals raise issues which ought to be considered by the Secretary of State." (DOE Circular 8/87, para. 84).

Directions relating to specified buildings

This power allows the Secretary of State to make pre-emptive call-in directions in relation to specified buildings, in advance of any application for listed building consent. Such a direction must be building-specific: there is no power to make a general direction in relation to specified descriptions of buildings, or in relation to specified types of authority.

Discretion to call-in applications

The Secretary of State's discretion is couched in broad terms, and there are no procedural preconditions to its exercise. In the context of the similar power to call-in planning applications and local plans for ministerial determination, the courts have been reluctant to intervene. They have held, for example, that there is no duty to consult the local planning authority before exercising a call-in power (for a local plan). This section does not impose an obligation to consult, and such an obligation would not arise under the rules of natural justice because a decision to call-in is not a decision on the merits of the application (*R.* v. *Secretary of State for the Environment*, ex p. *Southwark London Borough Council* (1987) 54 P. & C.R. 226).

Although a decision by the Secretary of State to call-in, or not to call-in, an application for listed building consent is challengeable in the courts by application for judicial review, the courts have laid particular emphasis on the breadth of the Secretary of State's discretion under this section, and have been unwilling to uphold applications for judicial review of his decision whether or not to call-in an application.

In what appears to have been the first case in which exercise of a call-in power under planning legislation was challenged, *R.* v. *Secretary of State for the Environment*, ex p. *Newprop* [1983] J.P.L. 386, Forbes J. expressed the view that the section did not require the Secretary of State to entertain any request that he should call-in any application, and his refusal to exercise his discretion under the section could be challenged in the courts only if it were "wildly perverse". He was under no obligation to give reasons for such refusal, although if reasons were given which were clearly wrong the court might interfere. But in *Williams* v. *Secretary of State for Wales (Sir Brandon Meredith Rhys) and the Welsh Water Authority and Taff Ely Borough Council* [1985] J.P.L. 29 the Court of Appeal preferred the straight application of the *Wednesbury* principles, and were prepared to examine the question whether, in all the circumstances of the case, the only reasonable course must have been for the Minister to call-in the particular application. In *R.* v. *Secretary of State for the Environment*, ex p. *Middlesbrough Borough Council* [1988] 3 P.L.R. 52 the High Court refused to quash a decision by the Secretary of State not to call-in an application. Although there was no reference in his decision to his policy on call-in, it could not be concluded that he had ignored it. The court concluded that, given the wide area of discretion allowed to the Secretary of State, he had arrived at his conclusion in a perfectly reasonable way.

The Scots Court of Session in *Lakin* v. *Secretary of State for Scotland* 1988 S.L.T. 780 was prepared to quash the Secretary of State's exercise of his discretion (in that case, under the parallel provisions of the Town and Country Planning (Scotland) Act 1972, s.32), where his refusal to call-in an application was found effectively to have prejudiced the outcome of an application made by the applicants, and to have defeated their legitimate expectation of a hearing being held into the alternative sites.

Locus standi to challenge refusal to call-in
It is open to any member of the public to request the Secretary of State to exercise his call-in powers under this section. He is not obliged to entertain such a request, and not obliged to give reasons; but as a matter of good practice he will normally do so. Where the reasons disclose an error of law, the decision is prima facie challengeable by an applicant with sufficient standing. But the High Court has suggested (in a passage which is purely *obiter*) in *R.* v. *Secretary of State for the Environment*, ex p. *Rose Theatre Trust Co.* [1990] Q.B. 504 (request to Secretary of State to schedule a monument) that such a decision was:
"one of those governmental decisions in respect of which the ordinary citizen does not have a sufficient interest to entitle him to obtain leave to move for judicial review. Clearly a person cannot obtain a sufficient interest by writing a letter to the Secretary of State. I approach with reluctance the submission that because the Secretary of State sent a considered reply, that gives the recipient an interest which he would not have had if no reply had been sent beyond a formal acknowledgement. If the court were to sanction such an arrangement it might cause the decision-makers to be less helpful to the general public. Further, what about the man who appears in the decision-maker's office, the man who telephones the decision-maker and so on?"
This dictum does not, however, exclude all challenges: a neighbour whose property is affected by the proposal may be found to have sufficient standing, for example; and perhaps also in an appropriate case one of the national amenity societies, who are given a special rôle in relation to listed building controls (see further the notes to s.16).

Deemed call-in: applications by local planning authorities
An application for listed building consent by a local planning authority is required to be made in the form of an application to the authority in the usual way, but is then deemed to be referred to the Secretary of State under this section for determination by him (Town and Country Planning (Listed Buildings and Conservation Areas) Regulations 1990, reg. 13. Before sending it to the Secretary of State the authority are required (unless the application relates to works affecting only the interior of a Grade II (unstarred) building) to publish notice of the application in a newspaper circulating in the locality, and to post a site notice. These requirements are modelled on those applicable to applications made to the authority by others: see the notes to s.10. Their application to the Secretary of State must be accompanied by a copy of all representations duly made in relation to it (reg. 13(4), (5) and (6)).

Effect of a direction
The effect of a direction under this section is to deprive the local planning authority of any further jurisdiction to determine the application. The matter becomes one solely for the Secretary of State, and the procedure followed by him resembles that for an appeal under s.20.

Notification of call-in
The local planning authority are required to notify the applicant in writing of a direction by the Secretary of State under this section (Town and Country Planning (Listed Buildings and Conservation Areas) Regulations 1990, reg. 3(5)).

Determining called-in applications
The Secretary of State is required by subs. (4) to offer the parties an opportunity to be heard (in practice, a public local inquiry). The procedure is governed by the Town and Country Planning (Inquiries Procedure) Rules 1988 (No. 944). Jurisdiction to determine called-in cases has not been transferred to planning inspectors. The procedure to be followed corresponds with that for planning appeals: see further the notes to s.20.

Reasons for the Secretary of State's decision
The Secretary of State is required to notify in writing his decision on a called in application, and his reasons for it, to all perons entitled to appear at the inquiry and who did appear (r.17(1)). The extent of the duty to give reasons was examined by the Court of Appeal in *Save Britain's Heritage* v. *Secretary of State for the Environment, The Times*, April 4, 1990. The Secretary of State's decision letter had repeated the conclusions reached by his inspector, but had failed to address the central questions raised by the inspector. The Court reasoned that where a decision involved a departure from a formal policy statement, then as part of

the obligation of the Secretary of State to deal with all substantial points in his decision letter he should make it clear that this was the case and give reasons for the departure. The principal issue in that case had been whether the benefits of the proposals for redevelopment were sufficient to override the undoubted presumption in favour of the preservation of the existing listed buildings on the site. The Secretary of State's decision letter had failed to express any view about the merits of those buildings. To grant listed building consent for the demolition of existing buildings that were capable of being used economically after refurbishment was without precedent and a total departure from previous policy, and without an assessment by the Secretary of State of the merits of the existing buildings it was impossible to tell whether the decision was unlawful or not.

Power to remove building from the list
The section does not, as does s.20 in the case of appeals, confer power on the Secretary of State to remove the building from the list. But a general power to amend the list at any time (following consultation with the Commission) is conferred by s.1, and that power would prima facie be exercisable in the course of proceedings on a called-in application; although in the interests of natural justice it would be subject to consultation with all the parties, particularly if a local public inquiry had already been opened into the referred application.

Secretary of State's decision to be final
The finality conferred by subs. (5) is qualified by s.63, which allows any person aggrieved by a decision under this section (s.63(1)), or the local planning authority which referred the matter to him (s.63(2) and (7)(b)) to apply to the High Court on a point of law to quash the decision.

Duty to notify Secretary of State of applications

13.—(1) If a local planning authority, (other than a London borough council), to whom application is made for listed building consent, or a London borough council to whom such an application is made by the Commission intend to grant listed building consent they shall first notify the Secretary of State of the application giving particulars of the works for which the consent is required.

(2) The Secretary of State may within the period of 28 days beginning with the date of such a notification—

(a) direct the reference of the application to him under section 12; or
(b) give notice to the authority that he requires further time in which to consider whether to require such a reference.

(3) The local planning authority shall not grant listed building consent until—

(a) the period mentioned in subsection (2) has expired without the Secretary of State directing the reference of the application to him or giving them notice under paragraph (b) of that subsection; or
(b) the Secretary of State has notified them that he does not intend to require the reference of the application.

DEFINITIONS
   "building": s.91.
   "listed building": ss.1(5); 91(1).
   "listed building consent": ss.8(7); 91(1).
   "local planning authority": s.81.
   "London borough": s.91(2).
   "the Commission": s.91(1).

ALLOCATION OF FUNCTIONS
   As to the local planning authority to whom application for listed building consent must be made (subs. (1)), see the notes to s.10; and as to the authority by whom it falls to be determined (subs. (3)), see the notes to s.16.

GENERAL NOTE
Introduction
   This section imposes a duty on local planning authorities outside London to notify the Secretary of State of applications for listed building consent. It applies also to applications

in respect of buildings subject to preservation notices, and applications for the modification or discharge of conditions subject to which listed building consent has been granted (s.19(3)). But it does not apply to applications for conservation area consent (as to which, see further below).

The notification requirement is in addition to a requirement, applicable to all English local planning authorities, that applications be notified to the Commission. There is a further duty on all authorities to notify certain other bodies, including national amenity societies of certain applications.

Different criteria apply to each requirements, and it is therefore convenient to deal with all three notification duties in the notes to this section.

Notification to amenity bodies and others

Local planning authorities are required (by direction of the Secretary of State; DOE Circular 8/87, para. 81) to notify all applications for the demolition of any listed building, and the decisions thereon, to the following societies: The Ancient Monuments Society; The Council for British Archaeology; The Georgian Group, The Society for the Protection of Ancient Buildings, The Victorian Society; The Royal Commission on the Historical Monuments of England.

Notification is required to the Royal Commission simply because of the possible need for them to record the site in the event that consent is granted, but further notification to them by the applicant, offering an opportunity of access to the site for the purpose of recording the building, is required as a pre-condition of authorising the demolition (s.8(2)). For the other bodies, the Secretary of State has suggested (DOE Circular 8/87, para. 81) that they should be notified immediately upon receipt of an application, and that it would be helpful for a quick response if they could receive appropriate supporting information at the time of notification. Where the application is retrospective, this should be indicated.

Notification is the first step in a process of consultation. There is no formal requirement upon local planning authorities to take into account representations received following the notification, but these would clearly be relevant to an authority's decision and should in accordance with ordinary public law principles be taken into account. That proposition is underpinned by the fact that the consultees specified in the Direction are all parties to the National Development Control Forum's *Code of Practice* (reproduced in the notes to s.62 of the T.C.P.A. 1990), and in accordance with the Code local planning authorities will give them 28 days' notice intimating that the application will not be determined within the 28 day period (or such extended time as may be requested by the consultee), and the local planning authority will take into account any representation received. The local planning authorities have agreed to provide copies of the appropriate application form, and such supporting information as is deemed appropriate (Code, para. 3).

Notification to the Commission

The Secretary of State has directed, under s.15(5), that local planning authorities in England (outside London) must notify the Commission of all applications for listed building consent to alter, extend or demolish any Grade I or Grade II* building (DOE Circular 8/87, para. 82), and to notify the Commission in due course of their decision on the application. Works to Grade II (unstarred) buildings are outside those requirements. The aim of the procedure "is to allow the Commission to comment helpfully on applications at the earliest possible stage and before the local planning authorities have reached their own conclusions upon them." (DOE Circular 8/87, para. 82). If they hear nothing from the Commission within 28 days, they may assume that the Commission has no comment. Authorities are asked to submit appropriate supporting information, including plans, photographs and other relevant documentation accompanying the application.

In relation to applications to local planning authorities outside London, the Commission does not have the power (which it has in relation to London) to direct authorities as to how the application should be determined; but it may make representations to the Secretary of State if of the opinion that an application should be called in for determination by him.

Notification to the Secretary of State

The authority have no power to proceed to grant listed building consent without first having notified the application to the Secretary of State (in London, to the Commission under s.14), and 28 days have elapsed without the Secretary of State having either called-in the application under s.12 for determination, or having notified the authority that he does not propose to issue such a direction. This is a separate notification requirement from notification to the Commission.

The Secretary of State has power under s.15 to relax the notification requirement, and has directed that it should not apply to applications for listed building consent for the carrying out of works for the demolition, alteration or extension of a Grade II (unstarred) listed building with the exception of applications of any one of the following descriptions:—

(a) for the total demolition of a principal building;

(b) for the total demolition of a curtilage building where such a building is recorded in the list description, (unless it is expressly stated that it is not of special interest);

(c) (i) subject to (ii) below, for the demolition of any part of a principal building where the cubic content of that part (as ascertained by external measurement), taken with any other part demolished since the building was listed, exceeds ten per cent. of the cubic content of the building when listed;

(ii) sub-paragraph (i) above does not apply to applications for the demolition of any part of a principal building which:

—was primarily erected before January 1, 1914 provided that the part to be demolished was erected since that date, or

—was primarily erected between January 1, 1914 and December 31, 1939 provided that the part to be demolished was erected after July 1, 1948;

(d) for the total demolition of an elevation of a principal building;

(e) for the demolition of substantially all of the interior of a principal building;

(f) for the demolition (in whole or in part) of any object or structure fixed to a principal or curtilage building where that object or structure is recorded in the list description (unless it is expressly stated that it is not of special interest);

(g) for the demolition (in whole or in part) of a principal or curtilage building where within five years of the application a previous application for demolition involving that building was determined by the Secretary of State under para. 4 or para. 8 of Sched. 11 to the 1971 Act (ss.12, 21 and 22 of the 1990 Act).

The full text of the Direction appears in DOE Circular 8/87, para. 86.

Unlike the requirement to notify certain planning applications to the Secretary of State under the various Development Plan Directions (see the notes to s.70 of the T.C.P.A. 1990) this requirement is statutory. The Secretary of State has in the past applied to the High Court for judicial review where an authority has failed to comply, and "he will not hesitate to take similar action in appropriate cases should an authority fail to refer a case to him" (DOE Circular 8/87, para. 87.)

Policy advice on the direction

The Secretary of State has advised local planning authorities (DOE Circular 8/87, para. 85) that the wording of the Direction reflects the criteria for listing, but that:

"Authorities should not spend too much time establishing the precise date of erection where this is relevant to a decision whether to refer [notify] the application to the Department; if there is any doubt, the application should be referred. The directions include references to the list description. List descriptions are not, of course, statutory and the amount of information given in them varies. Absence of a reference to a feature in the list description does not indicate that it can be removed without consent, but if it is mentioned there is a presumption that the feature is of importance."

Applications by the Commission

This section extends only to local planning authorities outside London, except in relation to applications made by the Commission. It would clearly be inappropriate for those applications to be dealt with under the London provisions in s.14 below, which require notification to the Commission itself, and so they are routed instead through this section. Crown immunity extends to land owned by the Commission, and proposals in respect of the Commission's own listed buildings are therefore handled through the non-statutory consultation procedures of DOE Circular 18/84. This section therefore extends only to applications in respect of listed buildings owned by others.

Applications to the London Docklands Development Corporation

Applications relating to listed buildings in the area of the LDDC are made to, and dealt with by, the Corporation as local planning authority. They are processed under this section rather than under s.14 below, which relates to applications made to London borough councils.

The Secretary of State has directed that the Corporation should notify the Commission of all applications for listed building consent, that they should not determine such application until 21 days following such notification, and that they should take into account any representations made by the Commission and notify the Commission of their decision.

Applications for conservation area consent
This section does not apply to conservation area consent (Town and Country Planning (Listed Buildings and Conservation Areas) Regulations 1990).

Duty of London borough councils to notify Commission

14.—(1) Where application for listed building consent is made to a local planning authority which is a London borough council—
  (a) unless the authority have determined to refuse it, they shall notify the Commission of the application, giving particulars of the works for which the consent is required; and
  (b) the authority shall not grant the consent unless they are authorised or directed to do so under subsection (2)(a).
(2) On receipt of such a notification the Commission may—
  (a) subject to subsection (6), give the local planning authority directions as to the granting of the application or authorise them to determine the application as they think fit; or
  (b) direct them to refuse the application.
(3) If the Commission intend to exercise either of their powers under subsection (2)(a), they shall notify the Secretary of State of the application giving particulars of the works for which the consent is required.
(4) Where the Commission direct the local planning authority under subsection (2)(b) to refuse listed building consent, the authority may, within 28 days from the date of the direction, notify the Secretary of State of the application giving particulars of the works for which the consent is required.
(5) The Secretary of State may within the period of 28 days beginning with the date of a notification under subsection (3) or (4)—
  (a) direct the reference of the application to him; or
  (b) give notice to the authority who notified him or, as the case may be, the Commission that he requires further time in which to consider whether to require such a reference.
(6) The Commission shall not direct the local planning authority under subsection (2)(a) to grant the application or authorise them to determine it as they think fit unless—
  (a) the period mentioned in subsection (5) has expired without the Secretary of State directing the reference of the application to him or giving them notice under paragraph (b) of that subsection; or
  (b) he has notified them that he does not intend to require the reference of the application.
(7) Where the local planning authority notify the Secretary of State as mentioned in subsection (4), they shall not refuse the application unless—
  (a) a period of 28 days beginning with the date of the notification has expired without the Secretary of State directing the reference of the application to him or giving them notice under subsection (5)(b); or
  (b) he has notified the authority that he does not intend to require the reference of the application.
(8) Where, after receiving notification under subsection (4), the Secretary of State directs the reference of the application to him, before determining the application he shall, if either the applicant or the authority or, as the case may be, the Commission so desire, give each of them an opportunity of appearing before, and being heard by, a person appointed by the Secretary of State.
(9) Subsection (1) shall not apply where the application for listed building consent is made by the Commission.

DEFINITIONS
    "building": s.91.
    "listed building": ss.1(5); 91(1).
    "listed building consent": ss.8(7); 91(1).
    "local planning authority": s.81.
    "London borough": s.91(2).
    "the Commission: s.91(1).

ALLOCATION OF FUNCTIONS
    This section applies only to London borough councils.

GENERAL NOTE

Introduction
    This section applies only to applications for listed building consent in London (except for
London Docklands, and for applications by the Commission: see the notes to s.13), where
the arrangements for supervision of the boroughs' exercise of listed building control differ
from the rest of the country. Until its abolition in 1986, the Greater London Council had to
be notified of all applications that the boroughs intended to grant and could direct how they
should be dealt with. That function was then transferred, with some modifications, to the
Commission, which also inherited the Historic Buildings Bureau of the GLC.
    The section does not apply to applications for conservation area consent (as to which see
further below), but it does apply to applications in respect of buildings subject to building
preservation notices (s.3(9)), and applications for the modification or discharge of conditions
attached to listed building consent (s.19(3)).
    There are thus three notification duties on the London boroughs: notification to amenity
societies, to the Commission and to the Secretary of State.

Notification to amenity bodies and others
    The London boroughs are required (by direction of the Secretary of State; DOE Circular
8/87, para. 81) to notify all applications for the demolition of any listed building, and the
decisions thereon, to the amenity societies listed in the notes to s.13 above.

Notification to the Commission
    No notification duty arises under this section if a London borough council decides to
refuse an application for listed building consent. However, a direction made by the Secretary
of State under s.15(5) and (6) requires the notification to the Commission of all applications
in London to alter, extend or demolish any grade of listed building (DOE Circular 8/87,
para. 82). Notification of an application under this section must give particulars of the works
for which consent is required (subs. (1)).
    The Commission may then do any of the following:
    (1) direct the local planning authority to grant the application: this option is not
        available (subs. (6)) unless they have first notified the Secretary of State of the
        application under subs. (3), giving particulars of the works for which the consent
        is required, and he has not within 28 days (or such longer period as he requires)
        called-in the application, or he has notified the Commission that he does not
        intend to call it in.
            Not all applications need to be so notified. The Secretary of State has made
        a direction under s.15 excluding applications for listed building consent for the
        carrying out of works for:—
            "(a) the alteration or extension of any listed building;
            (b) the demolition of a Grade II (unstarred) listed building with the
            exception of applications of any one of the following descriptions:—
                (i) for the total demolition of a principal building;
                (ii) for the total demolition of a curtilage building where such a
            building is recorded in the list description (unless it is expressly stated
            that it is not of special interest);
                (iii) subject to the exceptions mentioned in this sub-paragraph, for
            the demolition of any part of a principal building where the cubic
            content of that part (as ascertained by external measurement), taken
            with any other part demolished since the building was listed, exceeds
            ten per cent. of the cubic content of the building when listed. This
            sub-paragraph does not apply to applications for the demolition of any
            part of a principal building which

— was primarily erected before January 1, 1914 provided that the part to be demolished was erected on or after that date; or

— was primarily erected between January 1, 1914 and December 31, 1939 provided that the part to be demolished was erected after July 1, 1948;

(iv) for the total demolition of an elevation of a principal building;

(v) for the demolition of substantially all of the interior of a principal building;

(vi) for the demolition of any object or structure fixed to a principal or curtilage building where that object or structure is recorded in the list description (unless it is expressly stated that it is not of special interest); or

(vii) for the demolition (in whole or in part) of a principal or curtilage building where within five years of the application a previous application involving that demolition was determined by the Secretary of State under para. 4. or para. 8 of Sched. 11 of the 1971 Act [ss.12, 21 and 22 of the 1990 Act]".

(2) authorise the London borough to determine the application as they think fit: this option requires the same procedure to be followed as (1) above;

(3) direct the London borough to refuse the application: in this case the authority have the option of notifying the Secretary of State of the application within 28 days of the Commission's direction. If they do so, their power to refuse consent is suspended until the Secretary of State notifies them that he does not propose to call-in the application, or 28 days pass without him calling it in (subs. (5)). In the event of an appeal against the decision, the Commission is entitled to appear at any public local inquiry, and will be required to provide for a representative to be made available at the inquiry: see further the notes to s.20;

(4) fail to make any direction or authorisation: until directed or authorised by the Commission, a London borough has no power to grant listed building consent, but only to refuse it. If, however, no decision is issued by the borough to the applicant within eight weeks of the application (or such longer period as may have been agreed upon in writing), the applicant may appeal to the Secretary of State under s.20(2) as if the authority had decided to refuse the application.

Notification to the Secretary of State

Notification to the Secretary of State by the Commission is required only where they propose to direct a London borough to grant an application, or to authorise them to determine the application as they wish. It is at the option of the borough to notify the Secretary of State where refusal has been directed by the Commission. In such a case, the Secretary of State has asked (DOE Circular 8/87, para. 88) that the notification not only give the particulars of the works for which the consent is required, as the Act requires, but also:

(1) a copy of the completed application form and relevant certificate of ownership with any accompanying plans, drawings or schedules of work;

(2) copies of any representations received by the local planning authority as a result of any advertisement, consultation or notification;

(3) recent photographs of the building concerned (if they are not available this should be made clear);

(4) a statement giving the local planning authority's reasons for wishing to grant consent and for notifying the Secretary of State of the application. A copy of the Commission's formal direction should also be given;

(5) if demolition is proposed it should be made clear whether this is in respect of the entire building or parts of the building and there should also be confirmation that the national amenity societies have been notified in accordance with the direction set out above.

The Secretary of State expects the Commission and local planning authority to have made every attempt to reconcile differences of opinion in order to reach a solution before any application is notified to him under these arrangements.

Applications in London Docklands

Within the urban development area of the London Docklands Development Corporation the Corporation is the local planning authority for all purposes of this section. This section applies only to London boroughs, and applications to the Corporation for listed building consent are instead processed under s.13 above. The Commission therefore has the rights under that section to be consulted, but no power to direct how the Corporation should determine an application.

Conservation area consent

This section does not apply to conservation area consent, and the following section is substituted instead by the Town and Country Planning (Listed Buildings and Conservation Areas) Regulations 1990, s.12 and Sched. 3:

"Where application for listed building consent is made as respects a building situated in Greater London, the local planning authority shall notify the Historic Buildings and Monuments Commission for England of that application, shall not determine such application until the expiry of a period of 28 days from such notification, shall take into account any representations made by the Commission within such period in respect of that application, and shall notify the Commission of their decision on that application."

Referral of planning applications to the Commission

A separate power is conferred on the Secretary of State by s.68 to require by regulations that planning applications in London involving the demolition or material alteration of a listed building should be referred to the Commission before being dealt with by the local planning authority: see further the notes to that section.

Directions concerning notification of applications etc.

15.—(1) The Secretary of State may direct that, in the case of such descriptions of applications for listed building consent as he may specify, sections 13 and 14 shall not apply.

(2) Where a direction is in force under subsection (1) in respect of any description of application, local planning authorities may determine applications of that description in any manner they think fit, without notifying the Secretary of State or, as the case may be, the Commission.

(3) Before giving a direction under subsection (1) in respect of any description of application for consent to the demolition of a building in England, the Secretary of State shall consult the Commission.

(4) Where a direction is in force under subsection (1), the Secretary of State may direct a local planning authority that section 13 or, as the case may be, section 14 shall nevertheless apply—

(a) to a particular application for listed building consent; or

(b) to such descriptions of application for listed building consent as are specified in the direction;

and such a direction has effect in relation to any such application which has not been disposed of by the authority by their granting or refusing consent.

(5) Without prejudice to sections 10 to 14, the Secretary of State may give directions to local planning authorities requiring them, in such cases or classes of case as may be specified in the directions, to notify him and such other persons as may be so specified—

(a) of any applications made to the authorities for listed building consent; and

(b) of the decisions taken by the authorities on those applications.

(6) Directions under subsection (1) or (5) may be given to authorities generally or to particular authorities or descriptions of authority.

DEFINITIONS
"building": s.91.
"land": s.91(2).
"listed building": ss.1(5); 91(1).
"listed building consent": ss.8(7); 91(1).
"local planning authority": s.81.
"the Commission": s.91(1).

ALLOCATION OF FUNCTIONS
As to the local planning authority with the function of determining applications for listed building consent, see the notes to s.16.

Introduction

This section gives the Secretary of State power to supplement the procedures prescribed by the Act, by making directions. This is an informal type of quasi-legislation, which requires no Parliamentary supervision. There are two powers. The first (subs. (1)) is a power to relax the notification requirements of ss.13 and 14. The second power (subs. (5)) allows the Secretary of State to direct local planning authorities to notify him or such other persons as may be specified of any applications for listed building consent, and of the decisions taken thereon. This power has been exercised so as to require notification to national amenity societies and the Royal Commission on the Historical Monuments of England: see further the notes to s.13.

Decision on application

16.—(1) Subject to the previous provisions of this Part, the local planning authority or, as the case may be, the Secretary of State may grant or refuse an application for listed building consent and, if they grant consent, may grant it subject to conditions.

(2) In considering whether to grant listed building consent for any works the local planning authority or the Secretary of State shall have special regard to the desirability of preserving the building or its setting or any features of special architectural or historic interest which it possesses.

(3) Any listed building consent shall (except in so far as it otherwise provides) enure for the benefit of the building and of all persons for the time being interested in it.

DEFINITIONS
  "building": s.91.
  "listed building": ss.1(5); 91(1).
  "listed building consent": ss.8(7); 91(1).
  "local planning authority": s.81.

ALLOCATION OF FUNCTIONS
  The functions of a local planning authority for determining applications for listed building consent are exercisable solely by:—
  Greater London: the London borough council (T.C.P.A. 1990, s.1(2).
  Metropolitan areas: the metropolitan district council (T.C.P.A. 1990, s.1(2)).
  Non-metropolitan areas: the district planning authority (Sched. 4, para. 2).
  National Parks (outside a metropolitan county): the county planning authority (T.C.P.A. 1990, s.4) or joint planning board in areas where one has been established as county planning authority (T.C.P.A. 1990, s.2).
  Norfolk and Suffolk Broads: the Broads Authority (Sched. 4, para. 5).
  Urban development areas: the urban development corporation where an order has been made under the Local Government, Planning and Land Act 1980, s.149(1), transferring the function to the corporation (T.C.P.A. 1990, s.7(1)): for a list of current orders see the notes to s.81.
  Housing action areas: the housing action trust has the functions under this section to the exclusion of any other authority (other than the Secretary of State) where an order has been made under the Housing Act 1988, s.67(3) transferring the function to the trust (T.C.P.A. 1990, s.8(2)): see the notes to s.81.
  Enterprise zones: the enterprise zone authority, where so provided by order under the Local Government, Planning and Land Act 1980, Sched. 32, para. 5.

GENERAL NOTE

Introduction

This section establishes the powers of the local planning authority or the Secretary of State to grant or refuse consent, and to impose conditions. It is subject to the previous provisions of the Act, which implies that the power arises only when the requirements as to notification to the Commission and/or the Secretary of State have been met, and the 28 day suspension period observed where applicable.

Which authority?
The local planning authority which is responsible for determining an application for listed building consent, save where it is referred to the Secretary of State, is set out under Allocation of Functions above. The validity of a consent may not be called in question in any legal proceedings, or in any proceedings under this Act which are not legal proceedings, on the ground that the consent should have been granted by some other local planning authority (Sched. 4, para. 6).

Time limit for decisions
Local planning authorities are required to give notice of their decisions within eight weeks of the date when the form of application and the ownership certificate were lodged with them, or such longer period as may be agreed in writing with the applicant (Town and Country Planning (Listed Building and Conservation Areas) Regulations 1990, reg. 3(4)). Agreement on an extension may be reached at any time before the applicant has given notice of appeal to the Secretary of State. Failure to notify a decision within the time prescribed or agreed entitles the applicant to appeal to the Secretary of State under s.20(2), as if the authority had decided to refuse consent. The authority's duty to determine the application is not lifted by the expiry of the period, however, and an application for mandamus may lie to compel them to notify a decision: see further the notes to s.74 of the T.C.P.A. 1990.

The criteria for the decision
Statutory duty. The local planning authority (or Secretary of State) is required to have "special regard to the desirability of preserving the building or its setting or any features of special architectural or historic interest which it possesses" (subs. (2)). The duty to pay "special" regard makes this a positive duty, not merely one to take this matter into account (see, *e.g.* the extensive litigation on the parallel duty in conservation areas to have regard to the desirability of character or appearance of the area, discussed in the notes to s.72). Moreover, the "desirability" of preserving the building will normally be something which must be taken for granted under this section, as flowing from the decision to list the building. The local planning authority have no power to question the listing, although it is open to the Secretary of State to amend the list.
This section is not extended to cover applications made under s.19 for the variation or discharge of conditions, and the statutory duty does not therefore apply in such cases.
Policy advice. The Secretary of State's guidance on the criteria which authorities should apply in determining applications is set out in DOE Circular 8/87, para. 90:
(a) the importance of the building, both intrinsically and relatively, bearing in mind the number of other buildings of special architectural or historic interest in the neighbourhood. In some cases a building may be important because there are only a few of its type in the neighbourhood or because it has a fine interior, while in other cases its importance may be enhanced because it forms part of a group or series. Attention should also be paid to the contribution to the local scene made by a building, particularly if it is in a conservation area, but the absence of such a contribution is not a reason for demolition or alteration;
(b) in assessing the importance of the building, attention should be paid to both its architectural merit and to its historical interest. This includes not only historical associations but also the way the design, plan, materials or location of the building illustrates the character of a past age; or the development of a particular skill, style or technology;
(c) the condition of the building, the cost of repairing and maintaining it in relation to its importance, and whether it has already received or been promised grants from public funds. In estimating cost, however, due regard should be paid to the economic value of the building when repaired and to any saving through not having to provide alternative accommodation in a new building. Old buildings generally suffer from some defects, but the effects of these can easily be exaggerated;
(d) the importance of any alternative use for the site and, in particular, whether the use of the site for some public purpose would make it possible to enhance the environment and especially other listed buildings in the area; or whether, in a rundown area, a limited redevelopment might bring new life and make the other listed buildings more economically viable.
The circular also suggests (para. 91) that there should be a presumption in favour of preservation, and that presumption is given additional force by the advice contained in para. 89 of the Circular to the effect that the Secretary of State

". . . will not be prepared to grant listed building consent for the demolition of a listed building unless he is satisfied that every possible effort has been made to continue the present use or to find a suitable alternative use for the building. He would normally expect to see evidence that the freehold of the building had been offered for sale on the open market. There would need to be exceptional circumstances to justify the offer of a lease or the imposition of restrictive covenants which would unreasonably limit the chances of finding a new use for the building."

Relevance of redevelopment proposals

The Secretary of State originally took the view that the quality of the proposed redevelopment was not a material consideration in determining whether to allow demolition of a listed building, but the question was specifically left open by Phillips J. in *Kent Messenger* v. *Secretary of State for the Environment* [1976] J.P.L. 372. However, in *Save Britain's Heritage* v. *Secretary of State for the Environment, The Times*, April 4, 1990, the Secretary of State decisively departed from that principle, and accepted his inspector's recommendation that listed building consent should be granted for the demolition of a group of buildings (on a site adjoining Mansion House in the City of London), notwithstanding that they were capable of being economically refurbished and retained. He took the view that the design and quality of the proposed redevelopment scheme would contribute more to the environment and architectural heritage than the retention of the existing buildings. They were only of relative importance, whereas the redevelopment was a considered mature work of a British architect of international status, and deserved to be built. In the special circumstances of the case the presumption in favour of retention should be overridden. That principle was not challenged in the court, although the Court of Appeal quashed the Secretary of State's decision letter for failure to set out his views on the merits of the existing buildings, which made it impossible to decide whether he had failed to have special regard to the desirability of preserving them, as required by subs. (2).

Duty to take owner's representations into account

Where an application is accompanied by a certificate other than Certificate A, the local planning authority are required, in determining the application, to take into account any representations made by any person who satisfies them that he is an owner of the building, and to give notice of their decision to any such person (Town and Country Planning (Listed Buildings and Conservation Areas) Regulations 1990, reg. 6(3)(b)).

Power to impose conditions

Consent may be granted subject to conditions, and this power is expanded upon by s.17 which specifies some particular tyes of condition which may be imposed, though without prejudice to the general power under this section. In addition, s.18 requires the imposition of a condition limiting the life of any unimplemented consent. The criteria for validity of conditions are discussed in the notes to s.17; see also the analysis of validity of planning conditions in the notes to s.70 of the T.C.P.A. 1990.

It is particularly important that conditions attached to listed building consent should impose clearly specified obligations, because (unlike planning conditions) they create direct criminal liability: it is an offence, under ss.7 and 9, to execute any works to a listed building otherwise than in accordance with the terms and conditions of listed building consent, or to breach any condition (s.9(2)).

Application may be made under s.19 to vary or discharge any condition attached to listed building consent.

Consent to enure for benefit of building

Listed building consent runs with the land, unless it otherwise so provides (subs. (3)). Thus the section envisages the possibility of a personal consent.

Form of decision

The local planning authority's decision is required to be in writing, and to state the reasons for refusing consent, or for imposing conditions (Town and Country Planning (Listed Buildings and Conservation Areas) Regulations 1990, regs. 3(4) and (5)). There must also be a notification to the applicant, in a prescribed form, of his rights of appeal and his right to claim compensation (*ibid.*, Sched. 1, Pt. II: for an optional Welsh version, see the Town and Country Planning (Listed Buildings in Wales and Buildings in Conservation Areas in Wales) (Welsh Forms) Regulations 1990 (No. 1147), reg. 2(2) and Sched. 1). The duty to give reasons is not as tightly drawn as that for planning applications under art. 25 of the Town and Country Planning General Development Order 1988, where the authority are required to "state clearly and precisely their full reasons for the refusal or for any condition imposed".

Notification of decision

The local planning authority are required to notify their decision on an application for listed building consent to the amenity societies listed in the notes to s.13. Decisions on conservation area consent applications in London must be notified to the Commission (1990 Regs., Sched. 3). Where representations have been made by any person who satisfied the local planning authority that he was an owner of the building, they must also give notice of their decision to that person (Town and Country Planning (Listed Buildings and Conservation Areas) Regulations 1990, reg. 6(4)).

Revocation and modification of listed building consent

The local planning authority may by order revoke or modify a consent under s.23, subject to confirmation of any opposed order by the Secretary of State (s.24), and subject to the right of any person interested in the building to claim compensation under s.28 for abortive expenditure and any other loss or damage sustained by him which is directly attributable to the revocation or modification. The Secretary of State also has a reserve power to revoke or modify a consent (s.26), with similar procedural safeguards and with compensation liability falling on the local planning authority.

Compensation: consent refused, or granted subject to conditions

Compensation is not normally payable for the refusal of listed building consent, or the imposition of conditions. But there are two cases in which entitlement arises:

(1)   where the application is for consent to works of alteration or extension which either do not constitute development requiring planning permission under the T.C.P.A. 1990, or for which such permission is granted by development order (*e.g.* the rights to alter and extend dwelling-houses and industrial buildings under the Town and Country Planning General Development Order 1988, Sched. 2, Pts. 1 and 8 respectively). In this case, the purpose of the compensation provisions (under s.27) appears to be to compensate the applicant for any loss in land values as a result of listed building control, going beyond that attributable to planning control for which there is, in general, no entitlement to compensation. It is a necessary precondition, however, that the decision has been taken by the Secretary of State (whether on call-in or appeal): decisions by local planning authorities do not qualify for compensation under this head;

(2)   where listed building consent has been refused, or granted subject to conditions, and where the owner of the building claims that the building and land have become incapable of reasonably beneficial use in their existing state, and cannot be rendered capable of such use by carrying out works in accordance with the conditions imposed, or carrying out any other works for which listed building consent has been granted or for which the Secretary of State or the local planning authority has undertaken to grant consent (ss.32–37). In such a case, the claimant may serve a listed building purchase notice which, if accepted, by the local planning authority or confirmed by the Secretary of State, will compel them to acquire the claimant's interest and to pay compensation accordingly.

Grant of consent subject to conditions

Power to impose conditions on grant of listed building consent

17.—(1) Without prejudice to the generality of section 16(1), the conditions subject to which listed building consent may be granted may include conditions with respect to—

(a)   the preservation of particular features of the building, either as part of it or after severance from it;

(b)   the making good, after the works are completed, of any damage caused to the building by the works;

(c)   the reconstruction of the building or any part of it following the execution of any works, with the use of original materials so far as practicable and with such alterations of the interior of the building as may be specified in the conditions.

(2) A condition may also be imposed requiring specified details of the works (whether or not set out in the application) to be approved subsequently by the local planning authority or, in the case of consent granted by the Secretary of State, specifying whether such details·are to be approved by the local planning authority or by him.

(3) Listed building consent for the demolition of a listed building may be granted subject to a condition that the building shall not be demolished before—

(a) a contract for the carrying out of works of redevelopment of the site has been made; and

(b) planning permission has been granted for the redevelopment for which the contract provides.

DEFINITIONS
  "building": s.91.
  "development": s.91(2).
  "listed building": ss.1(5); 91(1).
  "listed building consent": ss.8(7); 91(1).
  "local planning authority": s.81.
  "planning permission": s.91(2).
  "use": s.91(2).

ALLOCATION OF FUNCTIONS
  See the notes to s.16.

GENERAL NOTE

Introduction
  This section specifies certain types of condition which may be attached to listed building consent. They are without prejudice to the general discretionary power conferred by s.16, although that power needs to be interpreted in light of the approach by the courts to the validity of planning conditions. The specific conditions are

(1) requiring preservation, making good or reconstruction;

(2) requiring subsequent approval of details: the Secretary of State has stressed (DOE Circular 8/87, para. 112) that this is not intended to provide a procedure akin to outline planning permissions. Proposed works must still be described in sufficient detail in the application for listed building consent for their effect to be fully assessed before consent is granted. But the power under this section may be useful where more information needs to be given before particular parts of the works are carried out, if the remaining details can safely be left to later approval;

(3) requiring that the building not be demolished until redevelopment is imminent. The Secretary of State (DOE Circular 8/87, para. 111) has urged local planning authorities to impose such a condition in all cases where it is appropriate, and advises that its purpose is to ensure that premature demolition does not take place and leave an empty gap long before planning permission is sought and rebuilding starts:
  "The condition will be particularly useful in cases where the demolition of listed buildings is essential if a particular scheme of redevelopment or road widening is to be carried out but the preparation and execution of detailed plans will take a long time, or if the implementation of the project is dependent upon some other factors, *e.g.* a place in a financial programme. Consent should not, however, be granted subject to this condition in the hope that it will never be exercised. If the case for demolition has not been fully established, consent should be refused."
  (DOE Circular 8/87, para. 111.)
  A model condition has been proposed by the Secretary of State (*ibid.*, Appendix VIII):
  "The demolition hereby permitted shall not be undertaken before a contract for the carrying out of the works of redevelopment of the site has been made and planning permission has been granted for the redevelopment for which the contract provides."

(4) personal consents: s.16(3) provides that a listed building consent runs with the land, unless limited by a condition to an individual.

Appeal against conditions
The applicant for listed consent is entitled to appeal under s.20 against any conditions subject to which the consent has been granted. Such an appeal is a precondition to compensation entitlement under s.27 (see further below), although it puts the whole consent at risk because it is possible for the Secretary of State to treat the matter as if it were an application to him in the first instance and to determine it accordingly.

Compensation for conditions
Compensation is payable under s.27 in respect of conditional grant of listed building consent by the Secretary of State on an application solely for works of alteration or extension of a listed building which do not require planning permission, if it can be shown that the conditions have resulted in a diminution in the value of a claimant's interest in the land.
A listed building purchase notice may be served under s.32 where the building and land are incapable of reasonably beneficial use and cannot be rendered capable of such use by carrying out the works in accordance with the conditions attached to listed building consent, having regard to any other works for which consent has been granted or promised.

Limit of duration of listed building consent

18.—(1) Subject to the provisions of this section, every listed building consent shall be granted subject to the condition that the works to which it relates must be begun not later than the expiration of—

(a) five years beginning with the date on which the consent is granted; or

(b) such other period (whether longer or shorter) beginning with that date as the authority granting the consent may direct, being a period which the authority considers appropriate having regard to any material considerations.

(2) If listed building consent is granted without the condition required by subsection (1), it shall be deemed to have been granted subject to the condition that the works to which it relates must be begun not later than the expiration of five years beginning with the date of the grant.

(3) Nothing in this section applies to any consent to the retention of works granted under section 8(3).

DEFINITIONS
"building": s.91.
"listed building": ss.1(5); 91(1).
"listed building consent": ss.8(7); 91(1).

ALLOCATION OF FUNCTIONS
The local planning authority with the functions under this section is the authority with the function of granting the relevant listed building consent: see further the notes to s.16.

GENERAL NOTE

Introduction
This section imposes time limits on the implementation of listed building consent comparable to those limiting the life of planning permissions under s.91 of the T.C.P.A. 1990. The authority are required to impose an express condition, specifying the period within which the works are to begin; otherwise a time limit of five years is imposed automatically under subs. (2). Advice on the use of this power is contained in DOE Circular 8/87, para. 113.

Failure to commence works within period allowed
The requirements of subss. (1) and (2) are not clearly expressed. The clear intention of the provisions is not to impose an absolute requirement that authorised works should be commenced by the specified date, but that the right to carry them out should lapse if they are not commenced by that date, and that it should be an offence to begin them later than the time allowed. The provisions on which this section is modelled (ss.91–94 of the T.C.P.A. 1990, relating to planning permission) make this clear by providing (s.91(3)) that development carried out after the date by which the time-limiting condition requires it to be carried out is to be treated as not authorised by the permission. That in turn is not a well drafted

provision, because the time-limiting condition will require only that the development be begun by the specified date, not that it be carried out by that date; and development may be begun by the carrying out of preliminary works not in themselves constituting development. But there is not even that underpinning to the condition imposed under or by this section, and no express sanction for breach is provided for in the section. Breach of the condition would not normally be an appropriate case for listed building enforcement proceedings under s.37, except to require the restoration of the building where any works that had been undertaken were unauthorised because they were not begun in time.

However, to carry out works without having complied with the commencement requirement would be to commit an offence under s.9 by failing to comply with any condition attached to the consent. As originally enacted, that provision did not extend to a condition attached under this section, which was inserted in the Act in 1980, and confusion persisted even after an attempt had been made to put the matter straight in the Housing and Planning Act 1986. The opportunity was taken in the consolidation legislation to clarify the point (*Law Commission Report*, para. 36).

What constitutes the "beginning" of works
The Act offers no guidance on this point, unlike the corresponding provisions of the T.C.P.A. 1990 dealing with planning permission. It may, therefore, require something more than purely token commencement (which is all the T.C.P.A. 1990 requires for planning permission), but to require any substantial implementation of the consent would go beyond the requirements of the section.

Conservation area consent
This section is extended so as to apply also to applications for conservation area consent, by the Town and Country Planning (Listed Buildings and Conservation Areas) Regulations 1990, reg. 12 and Sched. 3, with the substitution of the words "conservation area consent" for "listed building consent".

Application for variation or discharge of conditions

19.—(1) Any person interested in a listed building with respect to which listed building consent has been granted subject to conditions may apply to the local planning authority for the variation or discharge of the conditions.

(2) The application shall indicate what variation or discharge of conditions is applied for.

(3) Sections 10 to 15 apply to such an application as they apply to an application for listed building consent.

(4) On such an application the local planning authority or, as the case may be, the Secretary of State may vary or discharge the conditions attached to the consent, and may add new conditions consequential upon the variation or discharge, as they or he thinks fit.

DEFINITIONS
   "building": s.91.
   "listed building": ss.1(5); 91(1).
   "listed building consent": ss.8(7); 91(1).
   "local planning authority": s.81.

ALLOCATION OF FUNCTIONS
   The functions of a local planning authority under this section are exercisable solely by:—
   Greater London: the London borough council (T.C.P.A. 1990, s.1(2).
   Metropolitan areas: the metropolitan district council (T.C.P.A. 1990, s.1(2)).
   Non-metropolitan areas: the district planning authority (Sched. 4, para. 2).
   National Parks (outside a metropolitan county): the county planning authority (T.C.P.A. 1990, s.4) or joint planning board in areas where one has been established as county planning authority (T.C.P.A. 1990, s.2).
   Norfolk and Suffolk Broads: the Broads Authority (Sched. 4, para. 5).
   Urban development areas: the urban development is not the local planning authority for the purposes of this section, the function not being one listed in Sched. 29 to the Local Government, Planning and Land Act 1980 as capable of being transferred to a corporation.

Housing action trust areas: the housing action trust has the functions under this section to the exclusion of any other authority (other than the Secretary of State) where an order has been made under the Housing Act 1988, s.67(3) transferring the function (as a function within s.67(3A), as substituted by the Planning (Consequential Provisions) Act 1990, Sched. 2, para. 79(3)) to the trust (T.C.P.A. 1990, s.8(2)): see the notes to s.81.

Enterprise zones: the enterprise zone authority, where so provided by order under the Local Government, Planning and Land Act 1980, Sched. 32, para. 5.

GENERAL NOTE

Introduction

This section, inserted originally into the 1971 Act by the Housing and Planning Act 1986, introduced a new procedure allowing application to be made to vary or discharge any condition attached to a grant of listed building consent. A parallel procedure, though quite differently drafted, was also introduced by that Act (Sched. 11, para. 4) in respect of conditions on planning permissions. To seek variation of a condition in the past, it was necessary either to pursue an appeal or to apply for fresh consent.

Who may apply for variation or discharge

An application for listed building consent may be made by any person, and not merely the landowner or lessee, although an applicant is required to notify any owners of interests in the land concerned. But under this section, the power to apply is limited to persons "interested" in the building concerned. This distinction is significant. The wording implies that once a variation or discharge has been made, the pre-existing consent is supplanted by the new, unlike the position if an entirely fresh consent were granted which would not, unless it specifically so provided, override the previous consent, and the owner or occupier would be entitled to implement either. The intention of the section is to restrict the power to make applications, in cases where the existing consent is liable to be amended, to applicants who at least have some property interest in the land. There is some justification for this. Unlike planning conditions, conditions on a listed building consent create direct criminal liability: it is an offence under s.7 for works to be executed other than in accordance with listed building consent and any conditions attached to it. If third parties were able to seek variation or discharge of a condition, their action could affect the liability of the building's owners; if a fresh condition were imposed, it would create wholly new liability.

But it is unfortunate that resort has been had to the ambiguous phrase "any person interested". In the context of planning agreements under s.52 of the Act of 1971, the word "interested" has been held to mean holding a proprietary interest in the land (*Jones* v. *Secretary of State for Wales* (1974) 28 P. & C.R. 280), though a wider view was mooted by Eveleigh L.J. in *Pennine Raceway* v. *Kirklees Metropolitan Council* [1983] Q.B. 382. If the narrow view is the correct one under this section, then it must preclude any application being made by a potential purchaser of the property except through the present owner; yet since there is no such restriction on applications for listed building consent itself, he could seek the same end through the alternative route of applying for a fresh consent.

Non-metropolitan areas: county jurisdiction

When the provision was introduced by the Housing and Planning Act 1986, responsibility was assigned to the "local planning authority" without specifically assigning it to either tier of local government in the non-metropolitan areas. Hence counties were left with concurrent powers under the section. The Joint Committee on Consolidation Bills (*Report*, H.L. Paper 38–II, pp. 22–25; March 7, 1990) was unhappy with the draftsman's proposal to assign the function for the future exclusively to the districts who had exclusive jurisdiction over all other listed building consent matters. Members of the Committee were unwilling to regard the 1986 Act's allocation as a mistake, without evidence that counties were not actually exercising the function, and the Committee determined not to reject the recommendation, but nonetheless to draw it to the attention of the House. The Law Commission's recommendation was subsequently accepted by the House.

Form of application

An application under this section is required to be made on a form issued by the local planning authority and obtainable from that authority, and to be lodged with the relevant authority (see under Allocation of Functions above) together with two further copies of the form, plans and drawings (Town and Country Planning (Listed Buildings and Conservation Areas) Regulations 1987, reg. 4(1)).

Handling the application

The local planning authority are required to acknowledge the application; to notify the applicant if they form the opinion that the application is invalid; to determine the application within eight weeks of receipt (or such longer period as may be agreed in writing) and to give notice of their decision with reasons if they refuse to vary or modify the conditions, or impose fresh conditions (Town and Country Planning (Listed Buildings and Conservation Areas) Regulations 1990, reg. 3, as applied by reg. 4(2)).

Power of local planning authority to impose further conditions

The applicant is required to indicate what variation or discharge is applied for, but the section does not expressly limit the local planning authority to granting or refusing the application. The power for them under subs. (4) to "vary or discharge the conditions attached to the consent" suggests that they may be empowered to vary or discharge conditions other than those to which the application relates. But it is unlikely that this power would be regarded as extending beyond changes purely incidental to the main purpose of the application, particularly in view of the direct criminal liability imposed by s.7, and if the effect of the section is to give immediate effect to the consent as varied (see above); nor as providing an opportunity for the local planning authority to impose additional requirements beyond those sanctioned in subs. (4) as being "conditions consequential upon the variation or discharge". If the local planning authority take the view that consent should not be granted except on a wholly different basis, then the proper course would be to refuse the application and invite an application for fresh consent under s.10.

Right of appeal

Where a local planning authority refuse an application under this section, or grant it and add new conditions, the applicant may appeal to the Secretary of State under s.20. There is also a right of appeal (s.20(2)) if the local planning authority fail to give notice of their decision on the application within eight weeks of the application (or such longer period as may have been agreed with the applicant in writing), or to notify the applicant that the application has been called-in by the Secretary of State under s.12.

Extension to conservation area consent

This section is extended to applications for conservation area consent, by the Town and Country Planning (Listed Buildings and Conservation Areas) Regulations 1990, reg. 12 and Sched. 3, with the substitution of the words "conservation area consent" for "listed building consent".

Appeals

Right to appeal against decision or failure to take decision

20.—(1) Where a local planning authority—
  (a) refuse an application for listed building consent or grant it subject to conditions;
  (b) refuse an application for the variation or discharge of conditions subject to which such consent has been granted or grant it and add new conditions; or
  (c) refuse an application for approval required by a condition imposed on the granting of listed building consent with respect to details of works or grant it subject to conditions,
the applicant, if aggrieved by the decision, may appeal to the Secretary of State.

(2) A person who has made such an application may also appeal to the Secretary of State if the local planning authority have neither—
  (a) given notice to the applicant of their decision on the application; nor
  (b) in the case of such an application as is mentioned in paragraph (a) or (b) of subsection (1), given notice to the applicant that the application has been referred to the Secretary of State in accordance with directions given under section 12,

within the relevant period from the date of the receipt of the application, or within such extended period as may at any time be agreed upon in writing between the applicant and the authority.

(3) In this section "the relevant period" means—

    (a) in the case of such an application as is mentioned in paragraph (a) or (b) of subsection (1), such period as may be prescribed; and

    (b) in the case of such an application for approval as is mentioned in paragraph (c) of subsection (1), the period of eight weeks from the date of the receipt of the application.

(4) For the purposes of the application of sections 22(1) and 63(7)(b) in relation to an appeal under subsection (2) it shall be assumed that the authority decided to refuse the application in question.

DEFINITIONS
"building": s.91.
"listed building": ss.1(5); 91(1).
"listed building consent": ss.8(7); 91(1).
"local planning authority": s.81.
"prescribed": s.91(1).

ALLOCATION OF FUNCTIONS
The local planning authority for the purposes of this section is the local planning authority with the function under s.16 of determining the application: see the notes to s.16.

GENERAL NOTE

Introduction
This section establishes the right to appeal to the Secretary of State against the determination by a local planning authority of an application to it under this Part of the Act. It is supplemented by s.21, which deals with procedural matters relating to listed building consent appeals, and s.22, which prescribes the Secretary of State's powers in determining appeals.

What decisions are appealable
An appeal may be made against
(1) the refusal of listed building consent (subs. (1)(a));
(2) any condition imposed on a grant of consent (subs. (1)(a)), although here there is the alternative option of applying to the local planning authority under s.19 for the variation or discharge of the condition, and then appealing against a refusal on that application. On such an appeal, only the condition is at stake, whereas on an appeal against a conditional consent the Secretary of State is empowered to review the grant of consent itself (s.22(1));
(3) refusal of an application for the variation or discharge of a condition attached to listed building consent, or the imposition of new conditions (subs. (1)(b));
(4) refusal or conditional grant of an application for approval required by a condition attached to listed building consent which requires such approval to details of works (subs. (1)(c));
(5) the refusal or conditional grant of conservation area consent: this section is extended to cover such appeals by s.74(3), but with modifications made by the Town and Country Planning (Listed Buildings and Conservation Areas) Regulations 1990;
(6) the refusal of an application to vary or discharge conditions attached to conservation area consent, or the imposition of new conditions on such an application (s.19, as applied by s.74(3);
(7) failure by the local planning authority to determine the application for listed building consent or conservation area consent within the prescribed (by the 1990 Regulations) period of eight weeks (or such longer period as may have been agreed) (subs. (2)). The same period is specified by subs. (3) in respect of applications for approval under conditions (under heading (4) above).

Relationship to planning appeals
In cases where planning permission is also required for the works, and is refused by the local planning authority, a separate appeal will be necessary under s.78 of the T.C.P.A. 1990, although the two may then be processed and considered together.

Who may appeal

The only person who may appeal is an applicant who is aggrieved by the decision, although a subsequent owner may continue an appeal lodged by the applicant, and may apply to the High Court under s.63 as a "person aggrieved" (*Times Investment* v. *Secretary of State for the Environment and London Borough of Tower Hamlets, The Times*, June 21, 1990).

Making an appeal

The appellant is required to give notice of appeal, on a form obtained from the Secretary of State, within six months (1990 Regulations, reg. 8(1)) of the notice of decision or the expiry of the prescribed or agreed period, or such longer time as the Secretary of State may allow, and is obliged to furnish to the Secretary of State a copy of each of the following documents:

(1) the application;
(2) all relevant plans, drawings, particulars and documents submitted with the application, including a copy of a further ownership/notification certificate;
(3) the notice of the decision, if any;
(4) all other relevant correspondence with the local planning authority (Town and Country Planning (Listed Buildings and Conservation Areas) Regulations 1990, reg. 8(2)).

Grounds of appeal

The notice of appeal may include as a ground of appeal a claim that the building is not of special architectural or historic interest and ought to be removed from the list (s.21(3)); or, in the case of a building for which there is a building preservation notice in force, a claim that the building should not be included in the list (s.21(4)).

Ownership certificates

The appellant is required under s.21(5) to submit a fresh certificate as to the notification of the appeal to owners of the land concerned, as prescribed by the Town and Country Planning (Listed Buildings and Conservation Areas) Regulations 1990. As to the alternative notices, see the notes to s.11. It is an offence under s.21(7) knowingly or recklessly to issue a false or misleading certificate.

Transferred jurisdiction

Jurisdiction is now transferred to inspectors, by the Town and Country Planning (Determination of Appeals by Appointed Persons) (Prescribed Classes) Regulations 1981 (No. 804), as amended by S.I. 1986 No. 623 and S.I. 1989 No. 1087, to determine listed building consent appeals, conservation area consent appeals and listed building enforcement appeals, except

(1) appeals relating to Grade I and Grade II* buildings;
(2) appeals relating to buildings for which grants have been made under ss.3A or 4 of the Historic Buildings and Ancient Monuments Act 1953; and
(3) appeals relating to buildings in Wales.

Appeals procedure

Procedure on appeals under this section corresponds to that for planning appeals under s.78 of the T.C.P.A. 1990 except that, although appeals may be determined either on the basis of a local public inquiry or written representations, the Town and Country Planning (Appeals) (Written Representations) Regulations 1987 (No. 701) do not apply.

Appeals: inquiry procedure

The Secretary of State is required to offer the parties an opportunity to be heard (s.22(2)), and in practice this is normally undertaken through the holding of a public local inquiry. Inquiry procedure is governed by the Town and Country Planning (Inquiries Procedure) Rules 1988 (No. 944) and the Town and Country Planning Appeals (Determination by Appointed Persons) (Inquiries Procedure) Rules 1988 (No. 945). The effect of these provisions is analysed in the notes to s.79 of the T.C.P.A. 1990. Where the Commission have given a direction in respect of the application, the local planning authority may request from them a written statement of their reasons which must then be included in the authority's own statement. The applicant or local planning authority may also require, by application to the Secretary of State, the attendance at the inquiry of a representative of the Commission to give evidence as a witness called by the local planning authority.

Reasons for the decision

The Secretary of State (or his inspector) is required to give written reasons for his decision on an appeal under this section: as to the scope of that requirement, see the notes to s.14 of this Act, and s.79 of the T.C.P.A. 1990.

Application to the High Court

The Secretary of State's decision on an appeal is final (s.22(3)), subject to the right of any person aggrieved (or the local authority from whose decision the appeal was made) to apply to the High Court under s.63(1) on the grounds that the decision is not within the powers of this Act, or that any of the relevant requirements have not been complied with in relation to it. The validity of the Secretary of State's decision may not otherwise be questioned in any legal proceedings whatever (s.62(1)). Application to the High Court must be made within six weeks of the date the decision is taken (s.62(3)).

Appeals: supplementary provisions

21.—(1) An appeal under section 20 must be made by notice served in the prescribed manner within such period as may be prescribed.

(2) The period which may be prescribed under subsection (1) must not be less than—

(a) in the case of an appeal under subsection (1) of section 20, 28 days from the receipt by the applicant of notification of the decision; or

(b) in the case of an appeal under subsection (2) of that section, 28 days from the end of the relevant period (within the meaning of that section) or, as the case may be, the extended period there mentioned.

(3) The notice of appeal may include as the ground or one of the grounds of the appeal a claim that the building is not of special architectural or historic interest and ought to be removed from any list compiled or approved by the Secretary of State under section 1.

(4) In the case of a building with respect to which a listed building preservation notice is in force, the notice may include a claim that the building should not be included in such a list.

(5) Regulations under this Act may provide that an appeal in respect of an application for listed building consent or for the variation or discharge of conditions subject to which such consent has been granted shall not be entertained unless it is accompanied by a certificate in the prescribed form and corresponding to one of those described in subsection (1) of section 11.

(6) Any such regulations may also include provisions corresponding to those which may be included in the regulations which may be made by virtue of section 11.

(7) If any person—

(a) issues a certificate which purports to comply with the requirements of regulations made by virtue of subsection (5) or (6) and contains a statement which he knows to be false or misleading in a material particular; or

(b) recklessly issues a certificate which purports to comply with those requirements and contains a statement which is false or misleading in a material particular,

he shall be guilty of an offence and liable on summary conviction to a fine not exceeding level 3 on the standard scale.

DEFINITIONS

"building": s.91.

"building preservation notice": s.91(1).

"listed building": ss.1(5); 91(1).

"listed building consent": ss.8(7); 91(1).

"prescribed": s.91(1).

Determination of appeals

22.—(1) The Secretary of State may allow or dismiss an appeal under section 20 or may reverse or vary any part of the authority's decision (whether or not the appeal relates to that part), and—

   (a) may deal with the application as if it had been made to him in the first instance; and

   (b) may exercise his power under section 1 to amend any list compiled or approved under that section by removing from it the building to which the appeal relates.

(2) Before determining the appeal, the Secretary of State shall, if either the applicant or the local planning authority so wish, give each of them an opportunity of appearing before, and being heard by, a person appointed by the Secretary of State for the purpose.

(3) The decision of the Secretary of State on the appeal shall be final.

(4) Schedule 3 applies to appeals under section 20.

DEFINITIONS
  "building": s.91.
  "local planning authority": s.81.

ALLOCATION OF FUNCTIONS
  As to the local planning authority under this section, see the notes to s.16.

GENERAL NOTE
  See the General Note to s.20.

Revocation and modification of consent

Revocation and modification of listed building consent by local planning authority

23.—(1) If it appears to the local planning authority that it is expedient to revoke or modify any listed building consent granted on an application under this Act, the authority may by order revoke or modify the consent to such extent as they consider expedient.

(2) In performing their functions under subsection (1) the local planning authority shall have regard to the development plan and to any other material considerations.

(3) The power conferred by this section to revoke or modify listed building consent in respect of any works may be exercised at any time before those works have been completed, but the revocation or modification shall not affect so much of those works as has been previously carried out.

DEFINITIONS
  "building": s.91.
  "development": s.91(2).
  "development plan": s.91(2).
  "functions": s.91(2).
  "listed building": ss.1(5); 91(1).
  "listed building consent": ss.8(7); 91(1).
  "local planning authority": s.81.

ALLOCATION OF FUNCTIONS
  The functions of a local planning authority under this section are exercisable solely by:—
  Greater London: the council of the borough (T.C.P.A. 1990, s.1(2)).

Metropolitan areas: the metropolitan district council (T.C.P.A. 1990, s.1(2)).

Non-metropolitan areas: the district planning authority (Sched. 4, para. 2).

National Parks (outside a metropolitan county): the county planning authority (T.C.P.A. 1990, s.4) or joint planning board in areas where one has been established as county planning authority (T.C.P.A. 1990, s.2).

Norfolk and Suffolk Broads: the Broads authority (Sched. 4, para. 5).

Urban development areas: the urban development corporation where an order has been made under the Local Government, Planning and Land Act 1980, s.149(1), transferring the function to the corporation (T.C.P.A. 1990, s.7(1)): for a list of current orders see the notes to s.81.

Housing action trust areas: the housing action trust has the functions under this section to the exclusion of any other authority (other than the Secretary of State) where an order has been made under the Housing Act 1988, s.67(3) transferring the function (as a function within s.67(3A), as substituted by the Planning (Consequential Provisions) Act 1990, Sched. 2, para. 79(3)) to the trust (T.C.P.A. 1990, s.8(2)): see the notes to s.81.

Enterprise zones: the enterprise zone authority, where so provided by order under the Local Government, Planning and Land Act 1980, Sched. 32, para. 5.

GENERAL NOTE

Introduction

The section allows for a change of mind by a local planning authority. They may revoke or modify a consent, but subject to the procedural safeguards provided by this and the two following sections, and subject to liability to pay compensation.

Scope of the power

The power to revoke or modify is exercisable at any time before the works have been completed, and it is ineffective against any of the works that have already been carried out. Thus there is no power to act at all if the works have already been completed. If works have not been begun, and the time allowed under a condition imposed pursuant to s.18 has expired, the consent is dead and there is no need to resort to the power under this section.

But the effectiveness of the procedure is greatly reduced by the fact that an order made by the local planning authority has no effect until confirmed by the Secretary of State (or settled as an unopposed order under s.25). Although the relevant time is the time the order is made by the authority, and not the date of its confirmation (*Caledonian Terminal Investments* v. *Edinburgh Corporation* 1970 S.C. 271, decided in relation to the corresponding Scottish provisions relating to revocation or modification of planning permission), the owner may nonetheless lawfully continue to carry on the authorised works in the meantime, making it impossible to undo the damage caused.

Reform of the procedure was heralded in a consultation paper published by the Department of the Environment in 1989, *Listed Buildings and Conservation Areas*, in which the Department accepted that the present procedure was unduly cumbersome, and proposed to provide that once a revocation order had been served in respect of a listed building consent, no further work could be carried out under the consent until the order had been either confirmed or rejected.

Extension of the power

The power under this section is extended also to conservation area consents, by virtue of s.74(3). It does not, however, extend to a consent granted under s.19 (application for variation or discharge of conditions).

The discretion to revoke or modify a consent

As with a decision to issue a planning enforcement notice or listed building enforcement notice, the authority may act only where they consider it "expedient" to do so, and they may only seek to revoke or modify the consent to the extent that they think expedient. The authority are required also to have regard to the provisions of the development plan and any other material considerations. That obligation is imported from the corresponding provisions of the T.C.P.A. 1990 relating to determination of planning applications, and the revocation or modification of planning permissions, but it does not govern the determination of listed building consent applications under s.16.

The Secretary of State's reserve power

The Secretary of State may himself make an order under s.26, having first consulted the local planning authority. Such an order has the same effect as if made by the local planning authority, and that authority bears the compensation liability (s.28); and he has a further reserve power under the Town and Country Planning (Listed Buildings and Conservation Areas) Regulations 1990, reg. 13(8) in respect of any building owned by a local planning authority.

Procedure

Opposed cases. The local planning authority are required to serve notice of the making of the order on the owner and any occupier of the building concerned, and on any other person who in their opinion will be affected by the order (s.24). The order has effect only once it is confirmed by the Secretary of State, and any person on whom it is served has the right to require an opportunity to be heard before the order is confirmed (s.24(3)). The Secretary of State may confirm the order with or without modifications, or reject it.

Unopposed cases. In a case where the owner and occupier of the land, and all persons who in the authority's opinion will be affected by the order, have notified the authority in writing that they do not object to the order, there is no need for it to be referred to the Secretary of State for confirmation. Instead, the authority are required to advertise the fact of the making of the order under s.25(2) in a local newspaper circulating in the area in which the building is situated (Town and Country Planning (Listed Buildings and Conservation Areas) Regulations 1990, reg. 10), to serve notice on those affected and to forward a copy of the advertisement to the Secretary of State. There is no right to compensation under s.28 when an order is unopposed.

This is a cumbersome procedure, and, where there is agreement between the local planning authority and those interested in the land, it may be more convenient for an application to be made under s.19 for the variation of a condition and the imposition of a new condition, where that would satisfy the authority's objectives; or to explore the possibility of an agreement under s.106 of the T.C.P.A. 1990.

Compensation

Except in the case of an unopposed order, there is entitlement to compensation under s.28 for any loss or damage, including expenditure carried out on abortive works, resulting from the order.

Listed building purchase notice

Where, following the making of a revocation or modification order under this section, the owner claims that the land has become incapable of reasonably beneficial use in its existing state, he may be entitled to serve a listed building purchase notice under s.32, requiring the local planning authority to acquire his interest in it.

Procedure for s.23 orders: opposed cases

24.—(1) Except as provided in section 25, an order made by a local planning authority under section 23 shall not take effect unless it is confirmed by the Secretary of State.

(2) Where a local planning authority submit such an order to the Secretary of State for confirmation they shall serve notice on—

(a) the owner of the building affected;

(b) the occupier of that building; and

(c) any other person who in their opinion will be affected by the order.

(3) The notice shall specify the period (which must not be less than 28 days after its service) within which any person on whom it is served may require an opportunity of appearing before and being heard by a person appointed by the Secretary of State for the purpose.

(4) If within that period a person on whom the notice is served so requires, the Secretary of State shall give such an opportunity both to that person and to the local planning authority before he confirms the order.

(5) The Secretary of State may confirm an order submitted to him under this section either without modification or subject to such modifications as he considers expedient.

DEFINITIONS

"building": s.91.

"local planning authority": s.81.

"owner": s.91(2).

Procedure for s.23 orders: unopposed cases

25.—(1) This section shall have effect where—
 (a) the local planning authority have made an order under section 23 revoking or modifying a listed building consent granted by them; and
 (b) the owner and occupier of the land and all persons who in the authority's opinion will be affected by the order have notified the authority in writing that they do not object to the order.
 (2) Where this section applies, instead of submitting the order to the Secretary of State for confirmation the authority shall—
 (a) advertise in the prescribed manner the fact that the order has been made, specifying in the advertisement—
   (i) the period within which persons affected by the order may give notice to the Secretary of State that they wish for an opportunity of appearing before and being heard by a person appointed by him for the purpose; and
   (ii) the period at the end of which, if no such notice is given to the Secretary of State, the order may take effect by virtue of this section without being confirmed by him;
 (b) serve notice to the same effect on the persons mentioned in subsection (1)(b);
 (c) send a copy of any such advertisement to the Secretary of State not more than three days after its publication.
 (3) If—
 (a) no person claiming to be affected by the order has given notice to the Secretary of State as mentioned in subsection (2)(a)(i) within the period referred to in that subsection; and
 (b) the Secretary of State has not directed within that period that the order be submitted to him for confirmation,
the order shall take effect at the end of the period referred to in subsection (2)(a)(ii) without being confirmed by the Secretary of State as required by section 24(1).
 (4) The period referred to in subsection (2)(a)(i) must not be less than 28 days from the date on which the advertisement first appears.
 (5) The period referred to in subsection (2)(a)(ii) must not be less than 14 days from the end of the period referred to in subsection (2)(a)(i).

DEFINITIONS
 "building": s.91.
 "land": s.91(2).
 "listed building": ss.1(5); 91(1).
 "listed building consent": ss.8(7); 91(1).
 "local planning authority": s.81.
 "owner": s.91(2).
 "prescribed": s.91(1).

GENERAL NOTE
See the General Note to s.23.

Revocation and modification of listed building consent by the Secretary of State

26.—(1) If it appears to the Secretary of State that it is expedient that an order should be made under section 23 revoking or modifying any listed building consent granted on an application under this Act he may himself make such an order revoking or modifying the consent to such extent as he considers expedient.

(2) In performing his functions under subsection (1) the Secretary of State shall have regard to the development plan and to any other material considerations.

(3) The Secretary of State shall not make an order under that subsection without consulting the local planning authority.

(4) Where the Secretary of State proposes to make such an order he shall serve notice on—

(a) the owner of the building affected;

(b) the occupier of that building; and

(c) any other person who in his opinion will be affected by the order.

(5) The notice shall specify the period (which must not be less than 28 days after its service) within which any person on whom it is served may require an opportunity of appearing before and being heard by a person appointed by the Secretary of State for the purpose.

(6) If within that period a person on whom it is served so requires, before the Secretary of State makes the order he shall give such an opportunity both to him and to the local planning authority.

(7) The power conferred by this section to revoke or modify listed building consent in respect of any works may be exercised at any time before those works have been completed, but the revocation or modification shall not affect so much of those works as has been previously carried out.

(8) An order under this section shall have the same effect as if it had bccn made by the local planning authority under section 23 and confirmed by the Secretary of State under section 24.

DEFINITIONS
  "building": s.91.
  "development": s.91(2).
  "development plan": s.91(2).
  "functions": s.91(2).
  "listed building": ss.1(5); 91(1).
  "listed building consent": ss.8(7); 91(1).
  "local planning authority": s.81.
  "owner": s.91(2).

ALLOCATION OF FUNCTIONS
  The local planning authority which must be consulted by the Secretary of State under subs. (3) is:—
  Greater London: the London borough council (T.C.P.A. 1990, s.1(2).
  Metropolitan areas: the metropolitan district council (T.C.P.A. 1990, s.1(2)).
  Non-metropolitan areas: the district planning authority (Sched. 4, para. 2).
  National Parks (outside a metropolitan county): the county planning authority (T.C.P.A. 1990, s.4) or joint planning board in areas where one has been established as county planning authority (T.C.P.A. 1990, s.2).
  Norfolk and Suffolk Broads: the Broads Authority (Sched. 4, para. 5).
  Urban development areas: the urban development corporation where an order has been made under the Local Government, Planning and Land Act 1980, s.149(1), transferring the function to the corporation (T.C.P.A. 1990, s.7(1)): for a list of current orders see the note to s.81.
  Housing action trust areas: the housing action trust has the functions under this section to the exclusion of any other authority (other than the Secretary of State) where an order has been made under the Housing Act 1988, s.67(3) transferring the function (as a function within s.67(3A), as substituted by the Planning (Consequential Provisions) Act 1990, Sched. 2, para. 79(3)) to the trust (T.C.P.A. 1990, s.8(2)): see the note to s.81.
  Enterprise zones: the enterprise zone authority, where so provided by order under the Local Government, Planning and Land Act 1980, Sched. 32, para. 5.

GENERAL NOTE
  See the General Note to s.23.

RIGHTS OF OWNERS ETC.

Compensation

Compensation for refusal of consent to alteration, etc. of listed building

27.—(1) This section shall have effect where—

    (a) an application is made for listed building consent for the alteration or extension of a listed building;

    (b) the works do not constitute development or they do so but the development is such that planning permission for it is granted by a development order; and

    (c) the Secretary of State, either on appeal or on the reference of the application to him, refuses such consent or grants it subject to conditions.

(2) If, on a claim made to the local planning authority within the prescribed time and in the prescribed manner, it is shown that the value of the interest of any person in the land is less than it would have been if listed building consent had been granted or, as the case may be, had been granted unconditionally, the local planning authority shall pay that person compensation of an amount equal to the difference.

(3) In determining for the purposes of subsection (2) whether or to what extent the value of an interest in land is less than it would have been if listed building consent had been granted, or had been granted unconditionally—

    (a) it shall be assumed that any subsequent application for listed building consent for the alteration or extension in question would be determined in the same way; but

    (b) in the case of a refusal of listed building consent, regard shall be had to any undertaking given by the Secretary of State on that refusal to grant such consent for some other works to the building if an application were made for it.

(4) No compensation shall be payable under this section in respect of an interest in land in respect of which a notice is served under section 32 of this Act or under section 137 of the principal Act (circumstances in which purchase notices may be served) by virtue of subsection (1)(a) or (b) of that section, being a notice which takes effect.

(5) The local planning authority need not pay compensation under this section in respect of a building in respect of which a building preservation notice is in force unless and until the building is included in a list compiled or approved by the Secretary of State under section 1, but a claim for such compensation may be made before the building is so included.

DEFINITIONS

    "building": s.91.
    "building preservation notice": s.91(1).
    "development": s.91(2).
    "development order": s.91(2).
    "land": s.91(2).
    "listed building": ss.1(5); 91(1).
    "listed building consent": ss.8(7); 91(1).
    "local planning authority": s.81.
    "owner": s.91(2).
    "planning permission": s.91(2).
    "prescribed": s.91(1).
    "the Principal Act": s.91(1).

ALLOCATION OF FUNCTIONS

    Claims for compensation under this section are to be made to and paid by:
    Greater London: the London borough council as local planning authority (T.C.P.A. 1990, s.1)

Elsewhere: the local planning authority to whom the application for listed building consent was made (s.30(1)(a)).

GENERAL NOTE

Purpose of the section
This section establishes a limited right to compensation for loss or damage arising from listed building control. It arises only where consent is refused for the alteration or extension to a listed building, and there is no entitlement where consent is refused for demolition (or conservation area consent is refused). There may be, however, entitlement under s.32 to serve a listed building purchase notice in cases where the owner claims that the building (or associated land) has become incapable of reasonably beneficial use.

Where consent is refused to works of alteration or extension
Although there is an entitlement to compensation for cases involving the proposed alteration (which may include partial demolition) or extension of a listed building, it is tied in closely to planning control. There is normally no entitlement to compensation for the refusal, or conditional grant, of planning permission, and hence there is no compensation under this Act where listed building consent is refused to the extent that planning permission would also be required for the proposed works. A claim may be made only where the works involved do not constitute development under the T.C.P.A. 1990 (s.55), or where they are covered by a planning permission under the Town and Country Planning General Development Order 1988, or a special development order. For example, under s.55 of the T.C.P.A. 1990, works of alteration affecting only the interior of the building, or not affecting its external appearance, do not constitute development at all; and under the 1988 Order there is a general grant of planning permission for certain alterations and extensions to dwelling-houses (Sched. 2, Pt. 1), and industrial buildings (Sched. 2, Pt. 8). There may be some difficulty in applying the section in cases where some of the proposed works require express planning permission and some do not, but it would appear to be the intention of the section that compensation should be limited to those which do not.

Requirement of Secretary of State's decision
There is no entitlement to claim compensation in respect of a decision by the local planning authority, although it is they who must pay any compensation. The right arises only where the Secretary of State has, on an appeal or call-in, refused consent or granted it subject to conditions (subs. (1)(c)). He may, however, undertake to grant consent for other works to the building if application were made for it, and such an undertaking is then relevant to the assessment of compensation (subs. (3)(b)) and to the ability of an owner to serve a listed building purchase notice (s.32(2)(c)).

Claims procedure
A claim for compensation under this section must be made in writing to the local planning authority within six months from the date of the decision in respect of which it is made (or such longer period as the Secretary of State may allow in any particular case) (Town and Country Planning (Listed Buildings and Conservation Areas) Regulations 1990, reg. 9).

Assessment of compensation
Compensation is payable to the extent that the claimant can show that the value of his interest in the land is less than it would have been if consent had been granted, or granted unconditionally. The possibility that consent might be granted for other works to the building must be ignored, unless the Secretary of State has undertaken on a refusal, to grant such an alternative consent if application were made (subs. (3)). A claim under this section is effectively a claim relating to depreciation in the value of the land, and the rules of the Land Compensation Act 1961, s.5, are applicable (by virtue of s.31).

Relationship to purchase notice procedure
In a case where the building and its associated land has no reasonably beneficial use, a purchase notice may be served under s.32, (or an ordinary purchase notice served under s.137 of the T.C.P.A. 1990) but the two remedies are exclusive and where such a notice takes effect no compensation is payable under this section (subs. (5)).

Building preservation notice cases
This section applies to buildings subject to building preservation notices as if they were listed buildings (s.3), but entitlement to compensation arises only once the building is listed (subs. (5)), although a claim may be made in advance. Where the building does not become

9–61

listed, a claim may be made under s.29 for any loss or damage directly attributable to the effect of the notice.

Compensation where listed building consent revoked or modified

28.—(1) This section shall have effect where listed building consent is revoked or modified by an order under section 23 (other than an order which takes effect by virtue of section 25).

(2) If on a claim made to the local planning authority within the prescribed time and in the prescribed manner, it is shown that a person interested in the building—

(a) has incurred expenditure in carrying out works which are rendered abortive by the revocation or modification; or

(b) has otherwise sustained loss or damage which is directly attributable to the revocation or modification,

the authority shall pay that person compensation in respect of that expenditure, loss or damage.

(3) Subject to subsection (4), no compensation shall be paid under this section in respect of—

(a) any works carried out before the grant of the listed building consent which is revoked or modified; or

(b) any other loss or damage (not being loss or damage consisting of depreciation of the value of an interest in land) arising out of anything done or omitted to be done before the grant of that consent.

(4) For the purposes of this section, expenditure incurred in the preparation of plans for the purposes of any works, or upon other similar matters preparatory to any works, shall be taken to be included in the expenditure incurred in carrying out those works.

DEFINITIONS
    "building": s.91.
    "land": s.91(2).
    "listed building": ss.1(5); 91(1).
    "listed building consent": ss.8(7); 91(1).
    "local planning authority": s.81.
    "prescribed": s.91(1).

ALLOCATION OF FUNCTIONS
    Claims under this section are to be made to and paid by:
    Greater London: the London borough council as local planning authority (T.C.P.A. 1990, s.1).
    Elsewhere: the local planning authority who made the order in question or, where it was made by the Secretary of State under s.26, the local planning authority who are treated as having made it under that section: s.30(1)(b).

GENERAL NOTE

Introduction
    This section creates compensation entitlement in respect of the revocation or modification of listed building consent, otherwise than in an unopposed case under s.25.

Claims procedure
    A claim for compensation under this section must be made in writing to the local planning authority within six months from the date of the decision in respect of which it is made (or such longer period as the Secretary of State may allow in any particular case) (Town and Country Planning (Listed Buildings and Conservation Areas) Regulations 1990, reg. 9).

Assessment of compensation
    Compensation does not extend to works carried out before the grant of consent, or any other loss or damage, nor (except for depreciation in value) to any other loss or damage arising from events before the grant of consent. The applicability of these rules to the

revocation or modification of retrospective grants for the retention of works, under s.8(3), is therefore somewhat uncertain: whilst no compensation is payable in respect of expenditure incurred in carrying out those works, nor perhaps for being subsequently required to remedy them, there may nonetheless be compensatable loss or damage in terms of depreciation in the value of the building. Entitlement to compensation exists also in respect of preparatory expenditure, even where no works have been carried out (subs. (4)).

To the extent that a claim under this section includes a claim relating to depreciation in the value of the land, the rules of the Land Compensation Act 1961, s.5, are applicable (by virtue of s.31).

Compensation for loss or damage caused by service of building preservation notice

29.—(1) This section applies where a building preservation notice ceases to have effect without the building having been included in a list compiled or approved by the Secretary of State under section 1.

(2) Any person who at the time when the notice was served had an interest in the building shall, on making a claim to the authority within the prescribed time and in the prescribed manner, be entitled to be paid compensation by the local planning authority in respect of any loss or damage directly attributable to the effect of the notice.

(3) The loss or damage in respect of which compensation is payable under subsection (2) shall include a sum payable in respect of any breach of contract caused by the necessity of discontinuing or countermanding any works to the building on account of the building preservation notice being in force with respect to it.

DEFINITIONS
"building": s.91.
"building preservation notice": s.91(1).
"local planning authority": s.81.
"prescribed": s.91(1).

ALLOCATION OF FUNCTIONS
Claims under this section are to be made to and paid by the local planning authority who served the building preservation notice: s.30(1)(c).

GENERAL NOTE

Introduction
This section confers an entitlement to compensation for loss or damage caused by the service under s.3 of a building preservation notice. The right arises only if the building is not listed within the period allowed under that section. If it is so listed, compensation liability is limited to that for a listed building under s.27 (compensation for refusal of consent to alteration or extension) or s.32 (listed building purchase notice).

Claims procedure
A claim for compensation under this section must be made in writing to the local planning authority within six months from the date of the decision in respect of which it is made (or such longer period as the Secretary of State may allow in any particular case) (Town and Country Planning (Listed Buildings and Conservation Areas) Regulations 1990, reg. 9).

Assessment of compensation
Any loss or damage directly applicable to the effect of the notice is compensatable (subs. (2)), and to the extent that it relates to depreciation in the value of the interest in the land, the rules of the Land Compensation Act 1961, ss.2–5, are applicable by virtue of s.31.

Local planning authorities for compensation purposes

30.—(1) Subject to subsection (2)—
    (a) claims under section 27 shall be made to and paid by the local planning authority to whom the application for listed building consent was made;

    (b) claims under section 28 shall be made to and paid by the local planning authority who made the order in question or, where it was made by the Secretary of State under section 26, the local planning authority who are treated as having made it under that section;

    (c) claims under section 29 shall be made to and paid by the local planning authority who served the building preservation notice,

and references in those sections to a local planning authority shall be construed accordingly.

(2) The Secretary of State may after consultation with all the authorities concerned direct that where a local planning authority is liable to pay compensation under section 27, 28 or 29 in any particular case or class of case they shall be entitled to be reimbursed the whole of the compensation or such proportion of it as he may direct from one or more authorities specified in the direction.

(3) This section does not apply in Greater London.

DEFINITIONS
    "building": s.91.
    "building preservation notice": s.91(1).
    "listed building": ss.1(5); 91(1).
    "listed building consent": ss.8(7); 91(1).
    "local planning authority": s.81.

GENERAL NOTE
    This section allocates responsibility, outside Greater London, for paying compensation under the preceding sections.

General provisions as to compensation for depreciation under this Part

    31.—(1) For the purpose of assessing any compensation to which this section applies, the rules set out in section 5 of the Land Compensation Act 1961 shall, so far as applicable and subject to any necessary modifications, have effect as they have effect for the purpose of assessing compensation for the compulsory acquisition of an interest in land.

(2) This section applies to any compensation which is payable under sections 27 to 29 in respect of depreciation of the value of an interest in land.

(3) Where an interest in land is subject to a mortgage—

    (a) any compensation to which this section applies, which is payable in respect of depreciation of the value of that interest, shall be assessed as if the interest were not subject to the mortgage;

    (b) a claim for any such compensation may be made by any mortgagee of the interest, but without prejudice to the making of a claim by the person entitled to the interest;

    (c) no compensation to which this section applies shall be payable in respect of the interest of the mortgagee (as distinct from the interest which is subject to the mortgage); and

    (d) any compensation to which this section applies which is payable in respect of the interest which is subject to the mortgage shall be paid to the mortgagee, or, if there is more than one mortgagee, to the first mortgagee, and shall in either case be applied by him as if it were proceeds of sale.

(4) Except in so far as may be otherwise provided by any regulations made under this Act, any question of disputed compensation under sections 27 to 29 shall be referred to and determined by the Lands Tribunal.

(5) In relation to the determination of any such question, the provisions of sections 2 and 4 of the Land Compensation Act 1961 shall apply subject

to any necessary modifications and to the provisions of any regulations made under this Act.

DEFINITIONS
   "building": s.91.
   "compulsory acquisition": s.91(2).
   "land": s.91(2).
   "listed building": ss.1(5); 91(1).
   "listed building purchase notice": ss.32(1); 91(1).

GENERAL NOTE

Introduction
   This section establishes the compensation rules for claims made under the preceding sections, so far as they relate to the depreciation of the value of an interest in land. It applies the ordinary rules for compulsory acquisition of interests in land, under the Land Compensation Act 1961, so far as applicable and with any necessary modifications. Disputed compensation claims must be referred to, and determined by, the Lands Tribunal (subs. (4)).

Assessment of compensation
   The rules set out in s.5 of the Land Compensation Act 1961 are as follows:
   (1) No allowance shall be made on account of the acquisition being compulsory;
   (2) The value of land shall, subject as hereinafter provided, be taken to be the amount which the land if sold in the open market by a willing seller might be expected to realise;
   (3) The special suitability or adaptability of the land for any purpose shall not be taken into account if that purpose is a purpose to which it could be applied only in pursuance of statutory powers, or for which there is no market apart from the special needs of a particular purchaser or the requirements of any authority possessing compulsory purchase powers;
   (4) Where the value of the land is increased by reason of the use thereof or of any premises thereon in a manner which could be restrained by any court, or is contrary to law, or is detrimental to the health of the occupants of the premises or to the public health, the amount of that increase shall not be taken into account;
   (5) Where land is, and but for the compulsory acquisition would continue to be, devoted to a purpose of such a nature that there is no general demand or market for land for that purpose, the compensation may, if the Lands Tribunal is satisfied that reinstatement in some other place is bona fide intended, be assessed on the basis of the reasonable cost of equivalent reinstatement;
   (6) The provisions of rule (2) shall not affect the assessment of compensation for disturbance or any other matter not directly based on the value of land.

Mortgagees
   Where the interest is subject to a mortgage, subs. (3) requires that compensaton be paid to the mortgagee as if it were the proceeds of sale of the property; and the mortgagee himself may make the claim (without prejudice to the rights of the mortgagor). The fact that the interest is mortgaged is not to affect its valuation, and there is no special allowance to be made in respect of the existence of the mortgage.

Listed building purchase notices

Purchase notice on refusal or conditional grant of listed building consent

   32.—(1) Where—
      (a) listed building consent in respect of a building is refused, or granted subject to conditions, or is revoked or modified by an order under section 23 or 26; and
      (b) any owner of the building claims—
               (i) that the conditions mentioned in subsection (2) are satisfied with respect to it and any land comprising the building, or contiguous or adjacent to it, and owned with it; and

(ii) that the conditions mentioned in subsection (3) are
satisfied with respect to that land,
he may, within the prescribed time and in the prescribed manner, serve
on the council of the district or London borough in which the building
and land are situated a notice (in this Act referred to as a "listed building
purchase notice") requiring that council to purchase his interest in the
building and land in accordance with sections 33 to 37.

(2) The conditions mentioned in subsection (1)(b)(i) are—

(a) that the building and land in respect of which the notice is
served have become incapable of reasonably beneficial use in
their existing state;

(b) in a case where listed building consent has been granted subject
to conditions with respect to the execution of the works or has
been modified by the imposition of such conditions, that the
land cannot be rendered capable of such use by the carrying
out of the works in accordance with those conditions; and

(c) in any case, that the land cannot be rendered capable of such
use by the carrying out of any other works for which listed
building consent has been granted or for which the local
planning authority or the Secretary of State has undertaken to
grant such consent.

(3) The conditions mentioned in subsection (1)(b)(ii) are that the use
of the land is substantially inseparable from that of the building and that
it ought to be treated, together with the building, as a single holding.

(4) In determining for the purpose of subsection (2) what is or would
in any particular circumstances be a reasonably beneficial use of land, no
account shall be taken of any prospective use which would involve the
carrying out of new development or any works requiring listed building
consent which might be executed to the building, other than works for
which the local planning authority or the Secretary of State have undertaken to grant such consent.

(5) References in sections 33 to 37 to the land are to the building and
the land in respect of which the notice under subsection (1) is served.

DEFINITIONS
"building": s.91.
"development": s.91(2).
"land": s.91(2).
"listed building": ss.1(5); 91(1).
"listed building consent": ss.8(7); 91(1).
"listed building purchase notice": subs. (1).
"local planning authority": s.81.
"London borough": s.91(2).
"new development": s.91(2).
"owner": s.91(2).
"prescribed": s.91(1).
"use": s.91(2).

ALLOCATION OF FUNCTIONS
A listed building purchase notice must be served, in Greater London, on the London
borough council, and elsewhere on the district council. The Secretary of State, if he confirms
the notice, may under s.35(6) substitute another local authority or statutory undertaker for
the council on whom the notice was served. In this section, and ss.34–36, "local authority"
in relation to a building or land in the Broads, includes the Broads Authority (s.91(6)).

GENERAL NOTE

Introduction
A purchase notice is a form of inverse compulsory purchase. It is a special machinery
which allows a landowner to require a local authority to acquire his interest in the land. It
is limited to cases where his inability to obtain a consent has left the land without any

reasonably beneficial use. A general power to serve a purchase notice is conferred by the T.C.P.A. 1990, s.137, where there has been a refusal or conditional grant of planning permission; this section adapts that general model to the specific case of refusal or conditional grant of listed building consent or conservation area consent.

A listed building purchase notice is served on the relevant council, and may be accepted by them, or by another council or statutory undertaker. If they serve a counter-notice rejecting the notice, it is referred to the Secretary of State, who may confirm the purchase notice. Once a notice has been accepted or confirmed, the parties are locked into ordinary compulsory purchase procedures: the notice has effect as if a compulsory purchase order were in effect, and a notice to treat had been served on the owner.

The particular value of the provisions to a landowner lies in the assumptions which are used for the assessment of compensation, which may provide a higher sum than the land would obtain if sold on the open market.

Policy advice

Advice on the use of listed building purchase notices is contained in DOE Circular 13/83, *Purchase Notices*, and DOE Circular 8/87, *Historic Buildings and Conservation Areas— Policy and Procedures*, para. 120.

Relationship with planning purchase notice

A purchase notice and a listed building purchase notice may both be served in respect of the same building, and this may be the appropriate course where both planning permission and listed building consent have been refused, or conditionally granted, for the works, since both planning control and listed building control will normally be involved. The Secretary of State has power, instead of confirming a listed building purchase notice, to direct that not only listed building consent but also planning permission should be granted for any works or development, upon an application being made to the local planning authority (s.35(5)).

Where a repairs notice has been served

If the local planning authority have served a repairs notice under s.40, as a preliminary to the compulsory acquisition of a listed building which is not being properly preserved, the person on whom the notice was served is not entitled to serve a listed building purchase notice for the ensuing three months or, if during that period compulsory acquisition proceedings are commenced, unless and until the compulsory acquisition is discontinued (s.48(5)). The advantage to an authority of being able to pursue an acquisition under those provisions, rather than accepting a purchase notice under this section, lies in the different compensation rules, and particularly the possibility of obtaining an order for minimum compensation under s.50 in the case of a building which has been deliberately allowed to fall into disrepair for the purpose of justifying its demolition and redevelopment.

Acquisition by agreement

Purchase notice procedure imposes an obligation to acquire on the local authority. A local authority may in any event under s.52 acquire by agreement any building which appears to them to be of special architectural or historic interest (whether or not it is listed), together with any contiguous or adjacent land required for preserving the building or its amenities, for affording access to it, or for its proper control or management.

Conditions of service of a notice

The following conditions must be satisfied:

(1) that listed building consent (or conservation area consent: s.74(3)) has been refused, or conditionally granted, or revoked or modified (subs. (1)(a)); and

(2) that any owner of the building claims (and the notice need be accepted or confirmed only if the claim is made out) that the building and land are incapable of reasonably beneficial use in their existing state and cannot be rendered capable of such use by carrying out works in accordance with conditions attached to the consent, or with a consent that the local planning authority or Secretary of State have undertaken to grant.

Crown land

No listed building purchase notice may be served in relation to any interest in Crown land unless there has been a prior offer of that interest to the appropriate Crown authority: see further s.82(4).

The area covered by the notice

The notice need not be confined to the listed building itself. It may include any land comprising the building, or contiguous or adjacent to it, and owned with it (subs. (1)(b)). This land need not itself be incapable of reasonably beneficial use, though it and the listed building taken together must so qualify (subs. (1)(b)(i)); and its use must be substantially inseparable from that of the building such that it ought to be treated, together with the building, as a single holding. The importance of this requirement lies in the fact that the Secretary of State is not permitted to confirm the notice unless he is satisfied that such contiguous or adjacent land is comprised in the notice for preserving the building or its amenities, or for affording access to it, or for its proper control or management (s.35(3)). The area covered by the notice may therefore be greater than that covered by the relevant application for listed building consent.

Reasonably beneficial use

The purchase notice procedure is designed to provide a compensatory remedy where the value of a building is effectively wiped-out by listed building control. To the extent that listed building control imposes requirements over and above those of planning control, there is a right to seek compensation under s.27, even though the building remains capable of reasonably beneficial use. Where, however, there is no longer any reasonably beneficial use to which it may be put, a notice may be served under this section. In litigation under corresponding provisions which are now incorporated under the T.C.P.A. 1990, the courts have held that it is not incumbent on the claimant to show that it is the refusal of planning permission that has caused the land to become incapable of reasonably beneficial use ([1958] J.P.L. 897). It may be no more than the owner's past neglect (see, *e.g.* [1967] J.P.L. 491 and *Leominster Borough Council* v. *Minister of Housing and Local Government* (1971) 218 E.G. 1419), or his failure to plan his building scheme properly (see, *e.g.* [1967] J.P.L. 299, upheld in *West Bromwich County Borough Council* v. *Minister of Housing and Local Government* (1968) R.V.R. 349). But the test is not satisfied if the condition of the land is due to unlawful activity, such as the carrying out of unauthorised development (*Purbeck District Council* v. *Secretary of State for the Environment* (1983) 46 P. & C.R. 1); providing that the breach of planning control concerned could still be the subject of an enforcement notice requiring the owner to restore the land to its previous condition in which it would then be capable of resonably beneficial use (*Balco Transport Services* v. *Secretary of State for the Environment* (*No. 2*) [1986] 1 W.L.R. 88). Those principles appear to be equally applicable to listed building purchase notices, particularly in light of the power under s.39 (which has no time-limit) to serve a listed building enforcement notice in relation to unauthorised works.

The Secretary of State has advised that:

"In considering what capacity for use the land has, relevant factors are the physical state of the land, its size, shape and surroundings and the general pattern of land-uses in the area; a use of relatively low value may be regarded as reasonably beneficial if such a use is common for similar land in the vicinity. It may sometimes be possible for an area of land to be rendered capable of reasonably beneficial use by being used in conjunction with neighbouring or adjoining land, provided that a sufficient interest in that land is held by the server of the notice, or by a prospective owner of the purchase notice land. Use by a prospective owner cannot be taken into account unless there is a reasonably firm indication that there is in fact a prospective owner of the purchase notice site. (In this paragraph the word 'owner' is used to include a person who has a tenancy of the land or some other interest which is sufficient to enable him to use the land.) Profit may be a useful comparison in certain circumstances, but the absence of profit (however calculated) is not necessarily material: the concept of reasonably beneficial use is not synonymous with profit." (DOE Circular 13/83, para. 13).

In determining what might be a reasonably beneficial use, subs. (4) requires that no account is to be taken of:

(1) any prospective use which would involve the carrying out of new development: "new development" is a term of art meaning any development which is not comprised in the limited existing use concept (formerly Eighth Schedule rights) which are now defined by s.55(6) and Sched. 3 to the T.C.P.A. 1990. It is, however, permissible to have regard to any prospective use for which planning permission has been granted (*Gavaghan* v. *Secretary of State for the Environment* [1989] 1 P.L.R. 88; reversed on other grounds: [1990] J.P.L. 273).

(2) any prospective use which would involve the carrying out of any works requiring listed building consent, except where the local planning authority or Secretary of State have undertaken to grant such a consent. There is great practical difficulty in applying this provision. The Secretary of State, advising on the corresponding

provisions relating to planning purchase notices, has insisted that it is insufficient for the local planning authority simply to promise "to give favourable consideration" to an application (DOE Circular 13/83, para. 15). Yet for an authority to give a binding undertaking may be impossible, in the light of their duty to consult on any application and to take representations into account, and also in the light of the powers of the Secretary of State and, in London, the Commission to issue directions under ss.12–15. The Secretary of State is expressly empowered, however, instead of confirming a notice, to direct that listed building consent or planning permission be granted in the event of an application being made, if this would in his opinion render the land capable of reasonably beneficial use within a reasonable time (s.35(4)).

Service of the notice
A listed building purchase notice is required to be served within 12 months of the decision of the local planning authority or the Secretary of State (Town and Country Planning General Regulations 1976 (No. 1419), reg. 14). The Regulations confer power on the Secretary of State to extend that period and he has indicated that he is normally prepared to grant an extension where service is delayed for good reasons, such as awaiting a decision on a related planning appeal to the Secretary of State, or negotiations with the local planning authority (DOE Circular 13/83, Memorandum, para. 4).

Purchase notice procedure: notice and counter-notice
When a listed building purchase notice has been served on a borough or district council, the council must notify the claimant within three months
(1) that they (or some other local authority or statutory undertakers) are prepared to accept the notice and purchase the building (s.33(1)(a) and (b)) in which event the authority (or the other authority named) is empowered to purchase it and deemed to have served a notice to treat (s.33(2)). Under the 1971 Act, that notice was not capable of being withdrawn (Act of 1971, s.208), but that restriction has been lost, presumably by oversight, in the 1990 consolidation, although it remains in place for purchase notices and blight notices under the T.P.C.A. 1990, s.167;
(2) that neither they nor any such other authority are prepared to purchase the building. They are required to give reasons, and authorities have been advised by the Secretary of State that fair reasons for their refusal to comply with the purchase notice should be given, and that it would be helpful if their statement of reasons were sufficiently explicit to serve as a statement of their case for any hearing that may subsequently be required (DOE Circular 13/83, Memorandum, para. 26). Before serving such a counter-notice, the authority are required to have sent a copy of it to the Secretary of State, together with a copy of the listed building purchase notice (s.33(4)).

Action by the Secretary of State
The Secretary of State is required to come to a preliminary view on the notice, and then to give notice of his proposed action to the parties specified in s.34(2), giving them an opportunity to be heard. If he is satisfied that the requirements in subs. (2) of this section are fulfilled he must
(1) confirm the notice, but:
   (a) if he is satisfied that the conditions are fulfilled only in respect of part of the land, he may confirm it only in respect of that part (s.35(2));
   (b) if there is insufficient land contiguous or adjacent to the building as is in his opinion required to preserve it or its amenities, for access or for its proper management or control, he must not confirm the notice (s.35(3));
   (c) he may confirm it on a different local authority or statutory undertaker from that on which the notice was served (s.35(6)). He will do this only where it is shown that the building is to be used in the reasonably near future for purposes related to the exercise of the functions of that other body (DOE Circular 13/83, para. 33). (See below for the definition of "local authority" and "statutory undertaker" for the purposes of these provisions);
(2) grant the listed building consent which was applied for (or, where appropriate, cancel the revocation order; substitute new conditions on the modification order; or, in the case of a claim based on a conditional consent, revoke or amend those conditions) if the land is then capable of reasonably beneficial use (s.35(4)); or
(3) direct that listed building consent or planning permission should be granted for any other works or development which the Secretary of State considers could render the land or part of it capable of reasonably beneficial use within a reasonable time (s.35(4)).

If he is not satisfied that the requirements are fulfilled, he is obliged to reject the notice.

Deemed confirmation
If the Secretary of State does not take any of the above action within six months from the time the notice was transmitted to him (or within nine months of service of the notice, if the end of that period is earlier) and has not by that time notified the owner by whom the notice was served that he does not propose to confirm the notice, he is then deemed to have confirmed the notice (s.36(2)). That time limit is lifted, however, if there is a contemporaneous appeal under other provisions of this Act (s.36(6)).

Confirmation on another local authority or statutory undertaker
A listed building purchase notice may be confirmed on another local authority which is not a planning authority: see the definition in s.336(1) of the T.C.P.A. 1990, which is extended to this Act by s.91(2). In relation to land in the area of the Broads, it also includes the Broads Authority (s.91(6)).
"Statutory undertaker" includes (T.C.P.A. 1990, s.262, as applied by s.91(3)) "persons authorised by any enactment to carry on any railway, light railway, tramway, road transport, water transport, canal, inland navigation, dock, harbour, pier or lighthouse undertaking, or any undertaking for the supply of hydraulic power and a relevant airport operator (within the meaning of Part V of the Airports Act 1986)."
In addition, for the purposes of these sections (ss.33–36), the expression includes (s.91(3)):
(1) a public telecommunications operator;
(2) the Post Office;
(3) the Civil Aviation Authority;
(4) a public gas supplier;
(5) a holder of a licence under section 6 of the Electricity Act 1989;
(6) the National Rivers Authority;
(7) every water or sewerage undertaker.

Acquisition and compensation
Where a purchase notice is accepted by an authority, they are deemed to be authorised to acquire the owner's interest under s.47 and to have served a notice to treat in respect of it on the date of service of the notice (s.33(3)); and likewise where a notice is confirmed by the Secretary of State, except that it is for him to direct the date upon which the notice to treat is to be deemed to have served (s.36(1)). Compensation is then assessable under s.49, but without the power to seek a reduction to minimum compensation under s.50 in a case where the building has been deliberately left derelict. If compensation has already become payable (following the revocation or modification of listed building consent) for expenditure incurred in carrying out works to a building, s.37 requires that it be off-set against compensation payable upon the acquisition of the building under this section.

Applications to the High Court
Any person aggrieved by a decision of the Secretary of State to confirm a purchase notice or not to confirm a listed building enforcement notice, including a decision to confirm only in part, or to grant any consent or give any direction in lieu of confirming the notice wholly or in part, may question the validity of the decision by application to the High Court under s.63. Except by such an application such action cannot be challenged (s.62(2)). If the Secretary of State's decision should be quashed by the High Court, the original purchase notice is deemed to be cancelled, but it is open to the person who served it to start over again (s.36(7)).

Action by council on whom listed building purchase notice served

33.—(1) The council on whom a listed building purchase notice is served by an owner shall serve on him a notice stating either—
(b) that another local authority or statutory undertakers specified in the notice under this subsection have agreed to comply with it in their place; or
(c) that for reasons so specified the council are not willing to comply with the purchase notice and have not found any other local authority or statutory undertakers who will agree to comply with it in their place and that they have transmitted to the Secretary of

State a copy of the purchase notice and of the notice under this
subsection.

(2) A notice under subsection (1) must be served before the end of the
period of three months beginning with the date of service of the listed
building purchase notice.

(3) Where such a notice as is mentioned in paragraph (a) or (b) of
subsection (1) has been duly served, the council or, as the case may be,
the other local authority or statutory undertakers specified in the notice
shall be deemed—

(a) to be authorised to acquire the interest of the owner compulsorily
in accordance with the provisions of section 47; and

(b) to have served a notice to treat in respect of it on the date of
service of the notice under that subsection.

(4) Where the council propose to serve such a notice as is mentioned in
subsection (1)(c), they shall first send to the Secretary of State a copy
of—

(a) the proposed notice; and

(b) the listed building purchase notice which was served on them.

DEFINITIONS
"building": s.91.
"listed building": ss.1(5); 91(1).
"listed building purchase notice": ss.32(1); 91(1).
"local authority": s.91(2).
"owner": s.91(2).
"statutory undertaker": s.91(3).

GENERAL NOTE
See the General Note to s.32.

Procedure on reference of listed building purchase notice to Secretary of State

34.—(1) Where a copy of a listed building purchase notice is sent to the
Secretary of State under section 33(4), he shall consider whether to
confirm the notice or to take other action under section 35 in respect of
it.

(2) Before confirming such a notice or taking such other action, the
Secretary of State shall give notice of his proposed action—

(a) to the person who served the notice;

(b) to the council on whom it was served;

(c) outside Greater London—

(i) to the county planning authority and also, where that
authority is a joint planning board, to the county council; and

(ii) if the district council on whom the purchase notice in
question was served is a constituent member of a joint planning
board, to that board; and

(d) if the Secretary of State proposes to substitute any other local
authority or statutory undertakers for the council on whom the
notice was served, to them.

(3) A notice under subsection (2) shall specify the period (which must
not be less than 28 days from its service) within which any of the persons
on whom it is served may require the Secretary of State to give him an
opportunity of appearing before and being heard by a person appointed
by him for the purpose.

(4) If any of those persons so require, before the Secretary of State
confirms the listed building purchase notice or takes any other action
under section 35 in respect of it, he shall give such an opportunity to each
of them.

(5) If after any of those persons have appeared before and been heard by the appointed person, it appears to the Secretary of State to be expedient to take action under section 35 otherwise than in accordance with the notice given by him, the Secretary of State may take that action accordingly.

DEFINITIONS
"building": s.91.
"joint planning board": s.91(2).
"listed building": ss.1(5); 91(1).
"listed building purchase notice": ss.32(1); 91(1).
"local authority": s.91(2).
"statutory undertaker": s.91(3).

GENERAL NOTE
See the General Note to s.32.

Action by Secretary of State in relation to listed building purchase notice

35.—(1) Subject to the following provisions of this section, if the Secretary of State is satisfied that the conditions specified in section 32(2)(a) to (c) are satisfied in the case of any listed building purchase notice, he shall confirm the notice.

(2) If the Secretary of State is satisfied that those conditions are fulfilled only in respect of part of the land, he shall confirm the notice only in respect of that part and the notice shall have effect accordingly.

(3) The Secretary of State shall not confirm the notice unless he is satisfied that the land comprises such land contiguous or adjacent to the building as is in his opinion required—

(a) for preserving the building or its amenities, or
(b) for affording access to it, or
(c) for its proper control or management.

(4) If it appears to the Secretary of State to be expedient to do so he may, instead of confirming the notice—

(a) in the case of a notice served on account of the refusal of listed building consent for any works, grant such consent for those works;
(b) in the case of a notice served on account of such consent being granted subject to conditions, revoke or amend those conditions so far as it appears to him to be required in order to enable the land to be rendered capable of reasonably beneficial use by the carrying out of those works;
(c) in the case of a notice served on account of such consent being revoked by an order under section 23 or 26, cancel the order revoking the consent; or
(d) in the case of a notice served on account of such consent being modified by such an order by the imposition of conditions, revoke or amend those conditions so far as appears to him to be required in order to enable the land to be rendered capable of reasonably beneficial use by the carrying out of the works in respect of which the consent was granted.

(5) If it appears to the Secretary of State that the land (or any part of it) could be rendered capable of reasonably beneficial use within a reasonable time by the carrying out—

(a) of any other works for which listed building consent ought to be granted, or
(b) of any development for which planning permission ought to be granted,

he may, instead of confirming the listed building purchase notice (or confirming it so far as it relates to that part), direct that if an application is made for such consent for those works or, as the case may be, for planning permission for that development, it shall be granted.

(6) If it appears to the Secretary of State, having regard to the probable ultimate use of the building or its site, that it is expedient to do so, he may, if he confirms the notice, modify it either in relation to the whole or any part of the land, by substituting another local authority or statutory undertakers for the council on whom the notice was served.

(7) Any reference in section 34 to the taking of action by the Secretary of State under this section includes a reference to the taking by him of a decision not to confirm the notice on the grounds that any of the conditions referred to in subsection (1) are not satisfied.

DEFINITIONS
  "building": s.91.
  "development": s.91(2).
  "land": s.32(5).
  "listed building": ss.1(5); 91(1).
  "listed building consent": ss.8(7); 91(1).
  "listed building purchase notice": ss.32(1); 91(1).
  "local authority": s.91(2).
  "planning permission": s.91(2).
  "statutory undertaker": s.91(3).
  "use": s.91(2).

GENERAL NOTE
  See the General Note to s.32.

Effect of Secretary of State's action in relation to listed building purchase notice

36.—(1) Where the Secretary of State confirms a listed building purchase notice, the council on whom the notice was served shall be deemed—
  (a) to be authorised to acquire the owner's interest in the land compulsorily in accordance with the provisions of section 47; and
  (b) to have served a notice to treat in respect of it on such date as the Secretary of State may direct.

(2) If before the end of the relevant period the Secretary of State has neither—
  (a) confirmed the listed building purchase notice; nor
  (b) notified the owner by whom it was served that he does not propose to confirm it; nor
  (c) taken any such action in respect of it as is mentioned in subsection (4) or (5) of section 35,
the notice shall be deemed to be confirmed at the end of that period and the council on whom it was served shall be deemed to have been authorised as mentioned in subsection (1)(a) and to have served a notice to treat in respect of the owner's interest at the end of that period.

(3) Where a listed building purchase notice is confirmed in respect of only part of the land, references in this section to the owner's interest in the land are references to the owner's interest in that part.

(4) Where a listed building purchase notice is modified under section 35(6) by the substitution of another local authority or statutory undertakers for the council on whom the notice was served, the reference in subsection (1) to that council is to that other local authority or those statutory undertakers.

(5) In this section "the relevant period" means, subject to subsection (6) below—
  (a) the period of nine months beginning with the date of the service of the listed building purchase notice; or

(b) if it ends earlier, the period of six months beginning with the date on which a copy of the notice was sent to the Secretary of State.

(6) The relevant period does not run if the Secretary of State has before him at the same time both—

(a) a copy of the listed building purchase notice sent to him under section 33(4); and

(b) a notice of appeal under section 20 or section 39 relating to any of the land to which the listed building purchase notice relates.

(7) Where any decision by the Secretary of State to confirm or not to confirm a listed building purchase notice (including any decision to confirm the notice only in respect of part of the land, or to give any direction as to the granting of listed building consent or planning permission) is quashed under section 63, the notice shall be treated as cancelled but the owner may serve a further notice in its place.

(8) For the purposes of determining whether such a further notice has been served within the period prescribed for the service of listed building purchase notices, the decision concerning listed building consent on account of which the notice has been served shall be treated as having been made on the date on which the Secretary of State's decision was quashed.

DEFINITIONS
   "building": s.91.
   "land": s.32(5).
   "listed building": ss.1(5); 91(1).
   "listed building consent": ss.8(7); 91(1).
   "listed building purchase notice": ss.32(1); 91(1).
   "local authority": s.91(2).
   "owner": s.91(2).
   "planning permission": s.91(2).
   "prescribed": s.91(1).
   "statutory undertaker": s.91(3).

GENERAL NOTE
   See the General Note to s.32.

Reduction of compensation on acquisition where s.28 compensation payable

37. Where compensation is payable under section 28 in respect of expenditure incurred in carrying out any works to a building any compensation which then becomes payable in respect of the acquisition of an interest in the land in pursuance of a listed building purchase notice shall be reduced by an amount equal to the value of those works.

DEFINITIONS
   "building": s.91.
   "land": s.32(5).
   "listed building": ss.1(5); 91(1).
   "listed building purchase notice": ss.32(1); 91(1).

GENERAL NOTE
   This provision prevents compensation being paid twice: under the provisions for compensation for revocation or modification of listed building consent (s.28), and again in consequence of a listed building purchase notice under s.32.

CHAPTER IV

ENFORCEMENT

Power to issue listed building enforcement notice

38.—(1) Where it appears to the local planning authority—
  (a) that any works have been or are being executed to a listed building in their area; and
  (b) that the works are such as to involve a contravention of section 9(1) or (2),
they may, if they consider it expedient to do so having regard to the effect of the works on the character of the building as one of special architectural or historic interest, issue a notice under this section (in this Act referred to as a "listed building enforcement notice").

(2) A listed building enforcement notice shall specify the alleged contravention and require such steps as may be specified in the notice to be taken within such period as may be so specified—
  (a) for restoring the building to its former state; or
  (b) if the authority consider that such restoration would not be reasonably practicable or would be undesirable, for executing such further works specified in the notice as they consider necessary to alleviate the effect of the works which were carried out without listed building consent; or
  (c) for bringing the building to the state in which it would have been if the terms and conditions of any listed building consent which has been granted for the works had been complied with.

(3) A listed building enforcement notice shall specify the date on which it is to take effect (in this section referred to as "the specified date").

(4) A copy of a listed building enforcement notice shall be served, not later than 28 days after the date of its issue and not later than 28 days before the specified date—
  (a) on the owner and on the occupier of the building to which it relates; and
  (b) on any other person having an interest in that building which in the opinion of the authority is materially affected by the notice.

(5) The local planning authority may withdraw a listed building enforcement notice (without prejudice to their power to issue another) at any time before it takes effect.

(6) If they do so, they shall immediately give notice of the withdrawal to every person who was served with a copy of the notice.

(7) Where a listed building enforcement notice imposes any such requirement as is mentioned in subsection (2)(b), listed building consent shall be deemed to be granted for any works of demolition, alteration or extension of the building executed as a result of compliance with the notice.

DEFINITIONS
  "building": s.91.
  "listed building": ss.1(5); 91(1).
  "listed building consent": ss.8(7); 91(1).
  "listed building enforcement notice": ss.38(1); 91(1).
  "local planning authority": s.81.
  "owner": s.91(2).

ALLOCATION OF FUNCTIONS
  The functions of a local planning authority of issuing a listed building enforcement notice under this section are exercisable solely by:—
  Greater London: the London borough council (T.C.P.A. 1990, s.1(2) and the Commission, concurrently (s.45)).

Metropolitan areas: the metropolitan district council (T.C.P.A. 1990, s.1(2)).

Non-metropolitan areas: the district planning authority (Sched. 4, para. 2).

National Parks (outside a metropolitan county): the county planning authority (T.C.P.A. 1990, s.4) or joint planning board in areas where one has been established as county planning authority (T.C.P.A. 1990, s.2).

Norfolk and Suffolk Broads: the Broads Authority (Sched. 4, para. 5).

Urban development areas: the urban development corporation where an order has been made under the Local Government, Planning and Land Act 1980, s.149(1), transferring the function to the corporation (T.C.P.A. 1990, s.7(1)): for a list of current orders see the notes to s.81.

Housing action trust areas: the housing trust has the functions under this section to the exclusion of any other authority (other than the Secretary of State) where an order has been made under the Housing Act 1988, s.67(3) transferring the function (as a function within s.67(3A), as substituted by the Planning (Consequential Provisions) Act 1990, Sched. 2 para.79(3)) to the trust (T.C.P.A. 1990, s.8(2)): see the notes to s.81.

Enterprise zones: the enterprise zone authority, where so provided by order under the Local Government, Planning and Land Act 1980, Sched. 32, para. 5.

The Secretary of State: the Secretary of State has power under s.46(1) to issue a listed building enforcement notice in respect of any land.

GENERAL NOTE

Introduction

The enforcement procedure for listed buildings is similar to that for breaches of planning control, but with the important difference that criminal liability arises under s.9 independently of enforcement action under these provisions (for which a separate criminal liability is created by s.43). Because of this immediate criminal liability there is no provision for stop notices where the unauthorised works continue despite the issuing of a listed building enforcement notice under this section. Failure to comply with the requirements of an enforcement notice under this section within the period allowed by the notice is itself an offence, under s.43; and the local planning authority has power itself under s.42 to enter the land and to carry out the required works at the owner's expense.

The original listed building enforcement provisions were recast by the Local Government and Planning (Amendment) Act 1981 so as to confer more flexible powers upon the local planning authority, enabling them to require works to be carried out to alleviate the effect of the contravening works where they consider that restoration to the building's former state would not be reasonably practicable or would be undesirable.

Pre-conditions to exercise of enforcement powers

An authority may issue a listed building enforcement notice where it "appears" to them that certain unauthorised works have been or are being executed to a listed building in their area (subs. (1)). The works that may give rise to enforcement action are (subs. (1)(b), applying ss.7 and 9(1) and (2)): (1) unauthorised works for the demolition of a listed building; or (2) unauthorised works for the alteration or extension of a listed building in any manner which would affect its character as a building of special architectural or historic interest; or (3) any works executed in relation to a listed building under a listed building consent which fail to comply with any condition attached to the consent.

Failure simply to keep a listed building in repair is not a matter for enforcement under these provisions. Instead, local planning authorities have extensive powers under Chapter V of this Part of the Act (powers for prevention of deterioration and damage). The distinction is significant. Action under the present section is directed to acts of commission, not omission, and it places on the owner the financial burden of remedying that which has been done. Lord Bridge in *Robbins* v. *Secretary of State for the Environment* [1989] 1 All E.R. 878 observed that:

> "An enforcement notice under [this section] is both penal and coercive: it compels the owner to restore the building or to bear the cost of restoration. A repairs notice [under s.48] is in no way either penal or coercive: it is a procedural preliminary to compulsory acquisition designed to give the owner the opportunity, if he chooses, to undertake the works reasonably necessary for the proper preservation of the building as an alternative to selling it at its market value to the acquiring authority."

Limitation period for enforcement action

There is no limitation period on the issuing of a listed building enforcement notice. Thus the present owner of a listed building may be liable to enforcement action in respect of breaches by his predecessors in title, whenever committed. Once a listed building enforcement notice has been issued, however, liability under s.43 (penalties for non-compliance) remains with the person who was the owner at the time the notice was issued, unless he can show that he ceased to be owner before the end of the compliance period and the failure to take the required steps was attributable to the default of the subsequent owner (s.43(2) and (3)).

Exceptions and immunities
No listed building enforcement notice may be issued in respect of works executed
(1) by or on behalf of the Crown, in respect of a building which was Crown land at the time the works were executed (s.83(3)). However, the enforcement power applies in relation to Crown land to the extent of any interest held in it other than by the Crown (s.83(1)(b)), except that no notice may be issued or served under this section without the consent of the appropriate Crown authority (s.83(2)(a));
(2) to any ecclesiastical building which is for the time being used for ecclesiastical purposes: although these provisions are not expressly excluded by the ecclesiastical exemption contained in s.60, such works would not, by virtue of s.60(2), constitute a contravention of s.9 and are therefore outside subs. (1) of this section;
(3) to scheduled monuments, which similarly are exempt from the requirements of s.9 (s.61(2)), but subject to a different regime under the Ancient Monuments and Archaeological Areas Act 1979.

Discretion to take enforcement action
Enforcement action is discretionary. Although the local planning authority must exercise their discretion according to law, they cannot be required to issue an enforcement notice (*Perry* v. *Stanborough (Development)* [1978] J.P.L. 36). They may issue a notice "if they consider it expedient to do so having regard to the effect of the works on the character of the building as one of special architectural or historic interest". In the case of unauthorised works of extension or alteration, their power to enforce in any event only arises if the works have affected the building's character (see above). The implication is that insignificant infringements should not attract action under these provisions.

Obtaining information
A right of entry on to the land for the purpose of surveying it with a view to issuing a notice under this section is conferred by s.88(2)(a). The power under the T.C.P.A. 1990, s.330, to require information to be supplied as to interests in the land, is extended to this Act by s.89(1).

Matters to be specified in the enforcement notice
(1) The alleged contravention: the requirement to "specify" the alleged contravention (subs. (2)) implies that the notice will be a nullity if it fails to indicate clearly the substance of the authority's complaint. The distinction between the different heads may not always be clear, particularly as between works which have no authorisation and works undertaken in purported reliance on a grant of listed building consent. The fact that the authority may have chosen the wrong ground of complaint, or that there has been in fact no contravention at all, does not affect the performance of the duty under this subsection. The authority may take action where it appears to them that a contravention has occurred, and are required only to specify their allegation. Any informality, defect or error in the notice can be corrected by the Secretary of State on appeal, under s.41(2). But there must be some specification of the matters alleged to constitute the contravention in order to allow the appellant's exercise of the ground of appeal in s.39(1)(b); moreover, the choice of steps required to be taken under subs. (2) depends on the type of contravention specified (as between unauthorised works and breach of consent).
(2) The specified date: the notice is required (subs. (3)) to specify the date on which it is to take effect. It must be a date at least 28 days following the date of service of the notice, and its importance lies not only in determining when the notice will become effective but also in defining the period within which an appeal may be made to the Secretary of State under s.39.
(3) The steps to be taken: the section offers the local planning authority three alternatives: (a) to seek restoration of the building to its former state; (b) to have works carried out to alleviate the effect of the contravention; or (c) to secure compliance with the terms of listed building consent. The section does not indicate whether all of the steps specified in a notice must be directed to only one of these alternatives, or whether different steps may pursue different objectives. In the case of a single specified

contravention, the alternatives would appear to be exclusive. Alternative (b), for example, can be pursued only if option (a) is considered impracticable or undesirable; option (c) is applicable only where the contravention complained of relates to non-compliance with the terms of listed building consent. But where more than one contravention is complained of, the authority may serve a separate notice in respect of each; each notice may then pursue the appropriate option. If the authority instead consider it more convenient or appropriate to issue a single notice for multiple contraventions, there would seem to be no barrier to it pursuing the appropriate option in respect of each contravention, particularly in light of the Secretary of State's power under s.41(2) on appeal to vary the terms of the notice. The court in *Bath City Council* v. *Secretary of State for the Environment and Grosvenor Hotel (Bath)* (1984) 47 P. & C.R. 663 appeared to accept that there was power to vary a notice so as to ensure that it was based on the correct option.

(a) Restoring the building to its former state: in cases where restoration of the building would not be reasonably practicable, or would be undesirable, the authority may instead require alleviating works to be carried out. But it is clear that even a listed building that has been totally dismantled or demolished may still be a "building" for the purposes of requiring steps for its restoration under this option. In *Leominster District Council* v. *British Historic Buildings and S.P.S. Shipping* [1987] J.P.L. 350 the court ruled, in *inter partes* proceedings for an injunction, that to hold otherwise would be to draw a silly semantic distinction which would encourage people to demolish listed buildings as quickly and thoroughly as possible before the local planning authority could take action under this section. That view was supported in an appeal in subsequent proceedings on two listed building enforcement notices served in relation to the same building, *R.* v. *Leominster District Council*, ex p. *Antique Country Buildings* [1988] J.P.L. 554, although Mann J. stressed the problems of applying it in a case of total demolition where only rubbish or ash was left. In those circumstances the power to require "restoration" could not require the construction of a replica. Nonetheless, it was not a pre-requisite to requiring restoration of a building that all the original components still had to be extant. Thus, the authority were entitled to issue an enforcement notice requiring restoration on the facts of that case, because 70 to 80 per cent. of the structural timbers were extant. Moreover, the applicants, being the owners of the disassembled parts, were the "owners" of the building for the purpose of serving a listed building enforcement notice under this section. See also the appeal decision reported at [1990] J.P.L. 444, where the inspector took the view that a requirement that British Telecom should replace a K6 telephone kiosk that had been demolished in a motor accident, with another identical K6 kiosk, would not amount to the construction of a "replica".

It is a ground of appeal in relation to this option (though not in relation to options (b) and (c)) that the requirements of the notice exceed what is necessary for restoring the building to its condition before the works were carried out, and the Secretary of State may vary the notice accordingly. Difficulties in determining precisely what steps would be required to restore the building need not therefore deter authorities from selecting this option, and in *Bath City Council* v. *Secretary of State for the Environment and Grosvenor Hotel (Bath)* (1984) 47 P. & C.R. 663 the court accepted that

"the person carrying out the works should be in the best position to know what steps were needed to rectify the breach of the listed building provisions which he had committed and if he did not know he could not complain if this meant, for example, he must retile the whole roof, although otherwise he would only be required to retile part. He could not . . . refuse to comply because his own default had made it more difficult for him to do so."

The restoration option is appropriate to an alleged contravention of carrying out unauthorised works, but not to a failure to comply with the terms and conditions of a listed building consent where the objective is to bring the building, not to its former state, but to its "future" state (*i.e.* its state if the terms and conditions of the consent had been complied with).

(b) Requiring works to alleviate the effect of unauthorised works: this option is available to the authority when they consider that restoration of the building to its former state would not be reasonably practicable or desirable. In *Bath City Council* v. *Secretary of State for the Environment and Grosvenor Hotel (Bath)* 47 P. & C.R. 663, Woolf J. insisted that the approach of the courts to this provision should not be a narrow one, and that it was important that the powers of the enforcement authority should not be too restrictively construed. However, the option could not be used to secure an improvement to the listed building compared with its state prior to the carrying out of the unauthorised works. The object of the new provisions was not to provide a punishment in the form of a requirement to carry out work over and above that required to remedy the unauthorised works.

"Alleviation" presumably falls to be considered against listed building criteria, rather than planning criteria. From a planning point of view, it may be sufficient alleviation to provide adequate landscaping to soften the visual effect of unauthorised works; but for listed building purposes the whole point of the controls is the preservation of the character of the building as a building of special historic or architectural interest.

Where requirements are imposed under this option, listed building consent is deemed by subs. (7) to be granted for the necessary works. But there is no deemed grant of planning permission, which may be necessary where the required works of demolition, alteration or extension go beyond those permitted by the T.C.P.A. 1990 or the General Development Order 1988.

(c) securing compliance with terms of consent: this option allows the authority to require that the building be brought to the state in which it would have been if the terms and conditions of any listed building consent *which had been granted for the works* had been complied with. Thus it is available only where the contravention complained of is a failure to comply with any condition attached to a listed building consent when carrying out works authorised by the consent. Since its purpose is to remedy that breach of condition, it does not confer a general power to require the execution of all works authorised by the consent.

(4) The specified period for compliance: the notice must also specify the period within which the required steps must be taken. It is a ground of appeal to the Secretary of State under s.39(2)(h) that the period falls short of what should reasonably be allowed. The section does not expressly provide, as does s.172 of the T.C.P.A. 1990 in relation to enforcement of planning control, that different periods may be specified in relation to different steps. That may, however, be inherent in the section, and the existence of such a power is implied by s.39(1)(h), which refers to "the period within which any step required by the notice".

The validity of a listed building enforcement notice

The validity of a notice may not, except by appeal to the Secretary of State, be questioned in any proceedings whatsoever on any of the grounds on which such an appeal may be brought (s.64). Failure to specify anything required by this section is not such a ground, and a notice which so fails may be challenged as a nullity. But mis-specification, or the inclusion of unreasonable or excessive requirements, are matters within the scope of the grounds of appeal in s.39: see further the notes to that section.

Service of the notice

A copy of the enforcement notice must be served on the owner and the occupier of the building to which it relates, and on any other person having an interest in the building which in the opinion of the planning authority is materially affected by the notice. In the case of a dismantled building, "owner" should be taken to include the owners of the disassembled parts, even where they have now been removed from the site where the building formerly stood (*R.* v. *Leominster District Council*, ex p. *Antique Country Buildings* (1988) 56 P. & C.R. 240).

The machinery of service is prescribed by the T.C.P.A. 1990, s.329 (applied to this Act by s.89(1)).

Failure to serve the notice properly is not a matter affecting its validity, because improper service constitutes a ground of appeal to the Secretary of State under s.39(1)(f), and he is empowered by s.41(5) to disregard the fact that a person who should have been served was not, if neither the appellant nor that person has been substantially prejudiced by the failure to serve him. Moreover, if any person has appealed to the Secretary of State, no person may in any other proceedings instituted thereafter claim that the notice was not duly served on the appellant (s.39(6)).

In *R.* v. *Greenwich London Borough Council*, ex p. *Patel* [1985] 129 S.J. 654 the Court of Appeal rejected a landowner's application for judicial review of a planning enforcement notice which had never been served on him. The court held that it was bound by the preclusive provisions of the legislation (see now s.64 of this Act), and was satisfied that sufficient protection was provided for landowners by what is now s.287(1) of the T.C.P.A. 1990, which lifts the privative provisions of that Act so as not to prevent challenge to the validity of an enforcement notice by an owner on whom the notice was never served, by way of defence to prosecution for non-compliance. That provision does not apply to listed building enforcement notices, but broader protection is instead conferred by s.43 of this Act. Under that section, criminal liability is expressly limited to the person who was the owner of the building at the time the notice was served, and upon whom it was served.

Listed building enforcement notice as local land charge
A notice issued under this section must be registered as a local land charge (Local Land Charges Act 1975, s.1(1)(c)).

Withdrawal of an enforcement notice
A listed building enforcement notice may be withdrawn by the authority at any time before it takes effect and without prejudice to their power to serve another (subs. (5)). They must immediately notify all those who were served (subs. (6)). The power to withdraw a notice is not limited to the local planning authority which served it and it may therefore be possible for a notice to be withdrawn by another authority possessing concurrent powers (as in Greater London), although it may be difficult to conceive of circumstances in which this would be an appropriate course of action.

Deemed grant of listed building consent
Where an enforcement notice requires alleviating works to be carried out, listed building consent is deemed by subs. (7) to be granted for any necessary works of demolition, alteration or extension of the building. That does not carry with it, however, any grant of planning permission. Moreover, the Secretary of State, on appeal, may grant listed building consent for all or part of the works to which the notice relates, or discharge any condition or limitation on the consent alleged to have been conravened (s.41(6)).

Right of appeal
There is a right of appeal to the Secretary of State, under s.39, against a listed building enforcement notice. An appeal must be made before the date specified in the notice as that on which it is to take effect, and the making of an appeal has effect to suspend the requirements of the notice pending the final determination or withdrawal of the appeal (s.39(3)), though without prejudice to any criminal liability under s.9.

Use of injunctions in support of enforcement powers
A local planning authority may enlist the aid of the courts to supplement their enforcement powers under this Act, relying upon their power under the Local Government Act 1972, s.222 (power to institute civil proceedings in their own name where they consider it expedient for the promotion or protection of the interests of the inhabitants of their area). But relief will not be automatically granted, and the authority needs to show some special reason why the court's inherent powers should be used to reinforce the statutory system of remedies. The general principles are analysed in the notes to s.172 of the T.C.P.A. 1990.
In *Runnymede Borough Council* v. *Ball* [1986] 1 W.L.R. 353 the Court of Appeal laid great stress on the duty of the local authorities under planning law as being not merely to enforce penalties for past offences but also to do all within their power to ensure through properly observed planning control the natural amenities of their area. The court endorsed the rule that it was unnecessary for the authority first to have exhausted criminal proceedings where prosecution would have been futile and too slow; Purchas L.J. observed that the right to act under s.222 should not therefore be restricted to any particular class or classes of infringement, but should depend on the facts of the individual case:
   "Obvious instances where s.222 applies are those cases where the conduct past and intended of the offender shows that process in the magistrates' court will be inadequate to afford protection to the interests of the local inhabitants ('the deliberate and flagrant flouting cases'). Other circumstances may well arise, *e.g.* the failure to avoid fire hazards or the execution of development on land which may well in practice prove irreversible."
That approach was endorsed in the Court of Appeal in *City of London Corp.* v. *Bovis Construction* (1988) 84 L.G.R. 660, where Bingham L.J. observed that the guiding principles were:
   (1) that the jurisiction was to be invoked and exercised exceptionally and with great caution;
   (2) that there had certainly to be something more than mere infringement of the criminal law before the assistance of civil proceedings could be invoked and accorded for the

protection or promotion of the interests of the inhabitants of the area: see the Stoke-on-Trent case, and *Wychavon District Council* v. *Midland Enterprises (Special Events)* (1988) 86 L.G.R. 83;

(3) that the essential foundation for the exercise of the court's discretion to grant an injunction was not that the offender was deliberately and flagrantly flouting the law but the need to draw the inference that the defendant's unlawful operations would continue unless and until effectively restrained by law and that nothing short of an injunction would be effective to restrain them: see *Wychavon* at p.89.

In *Runnymede Borough Council* v. *Smith* (1987) 53 P. & C.R. 132 the court distinguished the *Ball* case and refused an injunction. There had been no breach of the criminal law, because by virtue of s.90(2)(b) of the 1971 Act the stop notices which had been served were ineffective against the occupants of caravans on the site; but even if they had been effective, there had been no deliberate or flagrant breach of the criminal law, nor any permanent development of the site which would warrant the grant of an injunction.

In *Leominster District Council* v. *British Historic Buildings and S.P.S. Shipping* [1987] J.P.L. 350 the local planning authority successfully sought an injunction to prevent the defendants from removing from the country the timbers of two old barns which had been dismantled without listed building consent, and in respect of which notices under this section had been served requiring their re-erection. The defendants had appealed to the Secretary of State, and the notices were currently suspended under s.39(3)). The court accepted that the local planning authority had an arguable case and that the balance of convenience plainly favoured the retention of the timbers in the jurisdiction until the matter was resolved.

Effect of subsequent grant of listed building consent

A grant of listed building consent after a listed building enforcement notice has been issued overrides the notice to the extent that it permits the retention of any work to which the notice relates, or discharges a condition on which the notice was based (s.44) but without affecting liability up until that time (ss.44(2); 8(3)).

Demolition of unlisted buildings in conservation areas

This section is extended to breach of conservation area consent requirements, by the Town and Country Planning (Listed Buildings and Conservation Areas) Regulations 1990, reg. 12 and Sched. 3, with the substitution of the words "conservation area consent" for "listed building consent", and "conservation area enforcement notice" for "listed building enforcement notice"; and with the following modifications: in subs. (1), for the words "the character of the building as one of special architectural or historic interest", substitute the words "the character or appearance of the conservation area in which the building is situated".

Arrangements for specialist advice

The Secretary of State may from time to time direct a district planning authority, under Sched. 4, para. 7, to submit for approval by him the arrangements they propose to make to obtain specialist advice in connection with their functions under this section, and, if not satisfied with the arrangements, may direct them to enter into an agreement with another local planning authority.

Appeal against listed building enforcement notice

39.—(1) A person having an interest in the building to which a listed building enforcement notice relates or a relevant occupier may appeal to the Secretary of State against the notice on any of the following grounds—

(a) that the building is not of special architectural or historic interest;
(b) that the matters alleged to constitute a contravention of section 9(1) or (2) do not involve such a contravention;
(c) that the contravention of that section alleged in the notice has not taken place;
(d) that works to the building were urgently necessary in the interests of safety or health or for the preservation of the building, that it was not practicable to secure safety or health or, as the case may be, the preservation of the building by works of repair or works for affording temporary support or shelter, and that the works carried out were limited to the minimum measures immediately necessary;

(e) that listed building consent ought to be granted for the works, or that any relevant condition of such consent which has been granted ought to be discharged, or different conditions substituted;
(f) that copies of the notice were not served as required by section 38(4);
(g) except in relation to such a requirement as is mentioned in section 38(2)(b) or (c), that the requirements of the notice exceed what is necessary for restoring the building to its condition before the works were carried out;
(h) that the period specified in the notice as the period within which any step required by the notice is to be taken falls short of what should reasonably be allowed;
(i) that the steps required by the notice for the purpose of restoring the character of the building to its former state would not serve that purpose;
(j) that steps required to be taken by virtue of section 38(2)(b) exceed what is necessary to alleviate the effect of the works executed to the building;
(k) that steps required to be taken by virtue of section 38(2)(c) exceed what is necessary to bring the building to the state in which it would have been if the terms and conditions of the listed building consent had been complied with.

(2) An appeal under this section must be made by notice in writing to the Secretary of State before the day specified in the listed building enforcement notice as that on which it is to take effect.

(3) Where such an appeal is brought the listed building enforcement notice shall be of no effect pending the final determination or the withdrawal of the appeal.

(4) A person who gives notice of appeal under this section shall submit to the Secretary of State, either when giving the notice or within such time as may be prescribed, a statement in writing—
(a) specifying the grounds on which he is appealing against the listed building enforcement notice; and
(b) giving such further information as may be prescribed.

(5) If, where more than one ground is specified in the statement, the appellant does not give information required under subsection (4)(b) in relation to each of those grounds within the prescribed time, the Secretary of State may determine the appeal without considering any ground as to which the appellant has failed to give such information within that time.

(6) Where any person has appealed to the Secretary of State under this section against a notice, no person shall be entitled, in any other proceedings instituted after the making of the appeal, to claim that the notice was not duly served on the person who appealed.

(7) In this section "relevant occupier" means a person who—
(a) on the date on which the listed building enforcement notice is issued occupies the building to which the notice relates by virtue of a licence in writing; and
(b) continues so to occupy the building when the appeal is brought.

DEFINITIONS
"building": s.91.
"listed building": ss.1(5); 91(1).
"listed building consent": ss.8(7); 91(1).
"listed building enforcement notice": ss.38(1); 91(1).
"prescribed": s.91(1).
"relevant occupier": subs. (7).

GENERAL NOTE

Introduction

This section creates a right of appeal against a listed building enforcement notice issued under the preceding section. In 1988–89 there were 337 appeals under these provisions in England, of which 82 were subsequently withdrawn or turned away, 130 were determined by inspectors and 182 determined by the Secretary of State (*Chief Planning Inspector's Report April 1988 to March 1989*; HMSO 1989; Table A2.3).

The right to appeal

An appeal may be made by any person having an interest in the building (*i.e.* an ownership interest), or a person who was in occupation under a written licence at the time the notice was issued, and who is still in occupation when the appeal is made (subss. (1) and (7)). This is a narrower class than the class of those required to be served with copies of the notice, which includes all occupiers whether or not their occupation is authorised. The inclusion of occupiers authorised in writing came about as a result of concern that, in the case of planning enforcement notices, such occupiers might be criminally liable for non-compliance with the notice, yet be without a right of appeal against it (see further the notes to s.174 of the T.C.P.A. 1990). That situation does not arise with listed building enforcement notices, where criminal liability under s.43 is limited to the owner of the building, but an occupier's rights could nonetheless be adversely affected by the carrying out of remedial works required by a notice, and by any exercise by the local planning authority of its powers to enter the land and carry out the works themselves under s.42.

The grounds of appeal

The grounds of appeal set out in subs. (1) provide a comprehensive code. No challenge may be brought to the validity of an enforcement notice on any of these grounds except by way of an appeal under this section (s.43). There may be other public law challenges which are outside this list, such as where the authority's officers had been bribed to issue the notice, or it had been served without the authority of the local planning authority, where challenge by application for judicial review is not precluded (*Davy* v. *Spelthorne Borough Council* [1984] A.C. 262 at 272, *per* Lord Fraser).

(a) building not of special interest:

This ground effectively constitutes an application to the Secretary of State to remove the building from the statutory list, which he is empowered to do by s.41(6)(c). It is also a ground of appeal against refusal or conditional grant of listed building consent, under s.21(3). The time at which the question falls to be considered must be the time before the alleged works were carried out rather than the date of the issuing of the notice, because otherwise the enforcement procedure would be totally ineffective where the works had destroyed the special interest of the building.

(b) and (c) no contravention:

The allegations on which a listed building enforcement notice must be based are analysed in the notes to s.38 above. These grounds of appeal allow it to be argued that the matters alleged do not constitute a contravention, or that they have not taken place. There must have been some "works" for the demolition, alteration or extension of the building, and that suggests that there has been some premeditated or planned action: the view has been taken by the Secretary of State (see decisions reported at [1981] J.P.L. 443, and [1990] J.P.L. 444) that where a building has been damaged by something outside the owner's control, such as by being hit by a motor vehicle, there is no contravention of listed building control; and that it is beyond the power of the enforcement procedures to require the reinstatement of property damaged or destroyed by accident.

(d) works urgently necessary:

This ground of appeal constitutes a restatement of the defence to prosecution under s.9 for carrying out unauthorised works, or breaching the terms of a consent, save that there is an additional requirement in that section that notice should have been given in writing to the local planning authority as soon as reasonably practicable, justifying in detail the carrying out of the works. In an appeal reported at [1989] 4 P.A.D. 355 (*Wellingborough Borough Council* v. *Shah*) the inspector took the view that the unauthorised replacement of sliding sash windows by aluminium windows was not justifiable under this head, because no evidence had been given that temporary repairs would have been inadequate, and the works carried out far exceeded what might have been necessary in the interests of health and safety. But in a appeal reported at [1990] J.P.L. 444 the Secretary of State accepted an inspector's recommendation that an appeal be upheld on this ground where a K6 telephone kiosk had been destroyed in a motor accident: the remains of the kiosk were a danger to the general public, the provision of props and temporary fencing to support and enclose the damaged remains of a mass-produced structure which was incapable of satisfactory repair would have been totally inappropriate, the works carried out were the minimum required and the appellants had informed the local planning authority of their intention before carrying out the works.

(e) consent should be granted:
The Secretary of State has broad jurisdiction on appeal, comparable to that on appeals against refusal of listed building consent. He has power under s.41(6), irrespective of whether this ground has been pleaded, to grant listed building consent for all or part of the works to which the notice relates, or to discharge any condition or limitation and to substitute any other condition (whether more or less onerous).

(f) defective service:
As to the consequences of defective service, see the notes to s.38 above.

(g)–(k) excessive requirements:
A successful appeal on any of these grounds would not normally be a ground for quashing the notice, but merely for the exercise by the Secretary of State of his powers of variation under s.41(2) so as to extend time for compliance or to alter the steps required by the notice to be taken. There may, however be cases—particularly under ground (i), that the steps required would not serve the purpose of restoring the character of the building—where the difficulties of devising an alternative formula may force the Secretary of State to quash the notice.

Appeal procedure: making an appeal
Procedure on an appeal under this section is regulated in part by the section itself, in part by Sched. 3 and in part by the Town and Country Planning (Enforcement Notices and Appeals) Regulations 1981 (No. 1742).
An appeal is required to be made by notice in writing to the Secretary of State before the date specified in the notice as that on which it is to take effect (subs. (2)). That time is absolute. The notice of appeal must actually be received by the Secretary of State by that date (*Lenlyn* v. *Secretary of State for the Environment* (1984) 50 P. & C.R. 129, and he has no power to extend the period (*Howard* v. *Secretary of State for the Environment* [1975] Q.B. 235): see further the discussion in the context of planning enforcement appeals in the notes to s.174 of the T.C.P.A. 1990.

Statement of grounds of appeal
A written statement specifying the grounds of appeal must be submitted either at the time of giving notice of appeal, or within 28 days of being required by the Secretary of State to submit such a statement: subs. (4), and reg. 5 of the Town and Country Planning (Enforcement Notices and Appeals) Regulations 1981 (No. 1742). The Secretary of State may dismiss the appeal if the requirement is not met within the period allowed (s.41(3)(a)).

Suspended effect of notice pending determination of appeal
If an appeal is made before the date specified for the notice to take effect, it does not take effect until the withdrawal or final determination of the appeal (subs. (3)). An appeal is not finally determined until the Secretary of State has given his decision, and the time for appealing to the High Court, or from there to the Court of Appeal or House of Lords, has expired. An appeal cannot be regarded as having been finally determined until there is no longer a possibility of it being remitted by a court under s.65 for redetermination by the Secretary of State (*R.* v. *Kuxhaus* [1988] Q.B. 631).

Local planning authority's response
The local planning authority may be required by the Secretary of State to send him, within 14 days of being notified by him that an appeal has been made, a copy of the enforcement notice and a list of the names and addresses of the persons on whom a copy of it was served (Town and Country Planning (Enforcement Notices and Appeals) Regulations 1981 (No. 1742), reg. 8).
The local planning authority are also required to serve a statement on the Secretary of State and the appellant, indicating the submissions they propose to put forward on the appeal and including the following matters:

(1) a summary of the authority's response to each ground of appeal pleaded by the appellant;

(2) a statement as to whether the authority would be prepared to grant listed building consent for the works to which the listed building enforcement notice relates, and if so, any conditions which they would wish to attach to such consent (reg. 6 of the Town and Country Planning (Enforcement Notices and Appeals) Regulations 1981 (No. 1742)). The notice must be served not later than 28 days before the date fixed for the inquiry, if there is to be one (or such later date as may be agreed in writing between the parties and the Secretary of State); or otherwise 28 days from the date the Secretary of State sends a notice to the authority requiring such a statement.

Failure by the local planning authority to comply with these requirements entitles the Secretary of State summarily to allow the appeal and quash the notice under s.41(4).

Transferred jurisdiction

Jurisdiction to determine appeals under this section may be transferred from the Secretary of State to planning inspectors by virtue of powers conferred by Sched. 3, para. 1. That power has been exercised so as to transfer to inspectors all appeals concerning Grade II listed buildings, by the Town and Country Planning (Determination of Appeals by Appointed Persons) (Prescribed Classes) Regulations 1981 (No. 804). The Regulations were amended in 1989 to extend inspectors' jurisdiction to include appeals involving demolition as well as extension and alteration; but jurisdiction in all appeals involving Grade I and Grade II* buildings remains with the Secretary of State. Power for the Secretary of State to recover jurisdiction in any particular case is conferred by Sched. 3, para. 3. Where an appeal is determined by an inspector, his decision is to be treated as that of the Secretary of State (Sched. 3, para. 2(5)).

Inquiries procedure: preliminary statements

The Secretary of State is required, if either the appellant or the local planning authority so wish, to give each of them an opportunity of appearing before and being heard by an inspector (s.40(2) (Secretary of State cases); Sched 3, para. 2(2) (inspectors' cases)). This normally takes the form of a public local inquiry, although in appropriate cases the Secretary of State may offer the parties instead an informal hearing: see further the notes to s.79 of the T.C.P.A. 1990. Procedure at an inquiry is governed by the Town and Country Planning (Enforcement) (Inquiry Procedure) Rules 1981 (No. 1743).

The statement submitted by the local planning authority summarising its responses to the grounds of appeal (see above) is required in inquiry cases to be supplemented by a further statement under r. 6 of the Town and Country Planning (Enforcement) (Inquiries Procedure) Rules 1981 (No. 1743), which requires the local planning authority to serve on the appellant, not later than 28 days before the inquiry:

(1) a statement of any expression of view or opinion expressed by a government department or local authority on which the local planning authority propose to rely at the inquiry; and

(2) a list of any documents (including maps and plans) they propose to refer to, or put in evidence at the inquiry.

By virtue of r. 11(5) the local planning authority may be permitted by the inspector to alter or add to the submissions contained in their statement under r. 6, or in the statement under the Town and Country Planning (Enforcement Notices and Appeals) Regulations 1981 (No. 1742), so far as may be necessary for the purpose of determining the questions in controversy between the parties, and subject to allowing the appellant an adequate opportunity of considering any fresh submission or document.

If the local planning authority fail to comply with the requirement to serve the first statement (their response to each ground of appeal, and statement as to whether they are prepared to grant conditional permission), the Secretary of State is authorised to quash the listed building enforcement notice. The Secretary of State takes the view that this will be an exceptional step, and has undertaken that authorities will be sent an urgent warning letter within one week of the commencement of the 28 day period if no statement has been issued (DOE Circular 38/81, para. 39).

Appellant's statement

A statement by the appellant may also be required by the Secretary of State, under r. 6(5) of the Town and Country Planning (Enforcement) (Inquiries Procedure) Rules 1981 (No. 1743). When the regulations were made in 1981, the Secretary of State announced that he proposed to make greater use of this power (DOE Circular 38/81, para. 36), but non-compliance with a request by him under r. 6(5) does not give him the right to dismiss the appeal summarily.

Procedure at the inquiry
Inquiry procedure is regulated by the Town and Country Planning (Enforcement) (Inquiry Procedure) Rules 1981 No. 1743, analysed in the notes to s.79 of the T.C.P.A 1990.

Written representations procedure
Where neither party insists upon an inquiry or hearing, the appeal may be determined by written representations. The local planning authority are required to give notification of the appeal to occupiers of properties in the locality of the site, and to any other persons who in their opinion are affected by the contravention of listed building control alleged in the notice (Town and Country Planning (Enforcement Notices and Appeals) Regulations 1981 (No. 1742), reg. 7). The notification must describe the alleged breach, the grounds of appeal, and a statement that interested persons may submit written comments to the authority within a specified time. The Town and Country Planning (Appeals) (Written Representations Procedure) Regulations 1987 do not apply to appeals under this section.

Powers exercisable on appeal
The Secretary of State under s.41:
(1) may quash or vary the listed building enforcement notice, or correct any informality, defect or error in it;
(2) may grant listed building consent for all or part of the works to which it relates;
(3) may discharge any condition or limitation subject to which listed building consent was granted and substitute another; or
(4) may remove the building from the statutory list.

Costs
The Secretary of State or inspector has power to make an order for costs against a party to the appeal (whether or not an inquiry is held), by virtue of Sched. 3, para. 6(4) and (8). Government policy on the award of costs is contained in DOE Circular 2/87.

Appeal to the High Court
There is a right of appeal on a point of law to the High Court against a decision of the Secretary of State under this section (s.65). The court has power only to remit the appeal for redetermination by the Secretary of State.

Appeals: supplementary provisions

40.—(1) The Secretary of State may by regulations prescribe the procedure which is to be followed on appeals under section 39, and in particular, but without prejudice to the generality of this subsection may—
(a) require the local planning authority to submit, within such time as may be prescribed, a statement indicating the submissions which they propose to put forward on the appeal;
(b) specify the matters to be included in such a statement;
(c) require the authority or the appellant to give such notice of such an appeal as may be prescribed, being notice which in the opinion of the Secretary of State is likely to bring the appeal to the attention of persons in the locality in which the building in question is situated;
(d) require the authority to send to the Secretary of State, within such period from the date of the bringing of the appeal as may be prescribed, a copy of the enforcement notice and a list of the persons served with copies of it.

(2) Subject to section 41(4), the Secretary of State shall, if either the appellant or the local planning authority so wish, give each of them an opportunity of appearing before and being heard by a person appointed by the Secretary of State for the purpose.

(3) Schedule 3 applies to appeals under section 39.

Definitions
"building": s.91.
"local planning authority": s.81.
"prescribed": s.91(1).

Allocation of Functions
See the note to s.38 above.

General Note
The regulations made under this section are the Town and Country Planning (Enforcement Notices and Appeals) Regulations 1981 No. 1742. Their effect in relation to listed building enforcement appeals is summarised in the notes to s.39 above.

Determination of appeals under s.39

41.—(1) On the determination of an appeal under section 39, the Secretary of State shall give directions for giving effect to the determination, including where appropriate directions for quashing the listed building enforcement notice or for varying its terms.

(2) On such an appeal if the Secretary of State is satisfied that to do so will not cause injustice to the appellant or to the local planning authority, he may—

(a) correct any informality, defect or error in the listed building enforcement notice, or

(b) give directions for varying its terms.

(3) The Secretary of State—

(a) may dismiss such an appeal if the appellant fails to comply with section 39(4) within the prescribed time; and

(b) may allow such an appeal and quash the listed building enforcement notice if the local planning authority fail to comply within the prescribed period with any requirement imposed by regulations made by virtue of section 40(1)(a), (b) or (d).

(4) If the Secretary of State proposes to dismiss an appeal under paragraph (a) of subsection (3) or to allow an appeal and quash the listed building enforcement notice under paragraph (b) of that subsection he need not comply with section 40(2).

(5) Where it would otherwise be a ground for determining an appeal in favour of the appellant that a person required to be served with a copy of the listed building enforcement notice was not served, the Secretary of State may disregard that fact if neither the appellant nor that person has been substantially prejudiced by the failure to serve him.

(6) On the determination of an appeal the Secretary of State may—

(a) grant listed building consent for the works to which the listed building enforcement notice relates or for part only of those works;

(b) discharge any condition or limitation subject to which listed building consent was granted and substitute any other condition, whether more or less onerous;

(c) if he thinks fit, exercise his power under section 1 to amend any list compiled or approved under that section by removing from it the building to which the appeal relates.

(7) Any listed building consent granted by the Secretary of State under subsection (6) shall be treated as granted on an application for the same consent under section 10 and the Secretary of State's decision in relation to the grant shall be final.

Definitions
"building": s.91.
"listed building": ss.1(5); 91(1).
"listed building consent": ss.8(7); 91(1).

"listed building enforcement notice": ss.38(1); 91(1).
"local planning authority": s.81.
"prescribed": s.91(1).

GENERAL NOTE

Introduction
   The Secretary of State is not limited merely to upholding or dismissing an appeal, but is given a range of powers to enable him to address legal objections to the enforcement notice, and the merits of the notice as an instrument for the restoration or preservation of a building of special architectural or historic interest.

Variation of the notice
   This power was conferred originally in relation to planning enforcement notices so as to overcome technical legal objections to the validity of notices (see further the notes to s.176 of the T.C.P.A. 1990). In *Bath City Council* v. *Secretary of State for the Environment and Grosvenor Hotel (Bath)* (1984) 47 P. & C.R. 663 the court took the view that, even where the matter had not been argued before the inspector, the Secretary of State should have considered the question of amending a listed building enforcement notice, and, in addition, if he decided not to amend it he should have given reasons so that the planning authority would know why he had come to that conclusion.

Power to grant consent, or discharge conditions
   The Secretary of State is empowered to treat the appeal as, in effect, an application for listed building consent or for the discharge of conditions or limitations attached to an existing consent. This allows him to take a broad view of the merits of seeking to restore the building, or carrying through the terms of the consent.

Power to remove building from statutory list
   The Secretary of State's power under subs. (6) to remove the building to which the appeal relates from the statutory list is exercisable only in accordance with s.1, which requires that he must first consult with the Commission (where the building is in England) and with such other bodies or persons as appear to him appropriate as having special knowledge of, or interest in, buildings of architectural or historic interest.

Execution of works required by listed building enforcement notice

   42.—(1) If any of the steps specified in the listed building enforcement notice have not been taken within the compliance period, the authority may—
   (a) enter the land and take those steps, and
   (b) recover from the person who is then the owner of the land any expenses reasonably incurred by them in doing so.
   (2) Where a listed building enforcement notice has been served in respect of a building—
   (a) any expenses incurred by the owner or occupier of the building for the purpose of complying with it, and
   (b) any sums paid by the owner of the building under subsection (1) in respect of expenses incurred by the local planning authority in taking steps required by it,
shall be deemed to be incurred or paid for the use and at the request of the person who carried out the works to which the notice relates.
   (3) Regulations under this Act may provide that all or any of the following sections of the Public Health Act 1936, namely—
   (a) section 276 (power of local authorities to sell materials removed in executing works under that Act subject to accounting for the proceeds of sale);
   (b) section 289 (power to require the occupier of any premises to permit works to be executed by the owner of the premises);
   (c) section 294 (limit on liabilities of persons holding premises as agents or trustees in respect of the expenses recoverable under that Act),

shall apply, subject to such adaptations and modifications as may be specified in the regulations, in relation to any steps required to be taken by a listed building enforcement notice.

(4) Regulations under subsection (3) applying all or any of section 289 of that Act may include adaptations and modifications for the purpose of giving the owner of land to which such a notice relates the right, as against all other persons interested in the land, to comply with the requirements of the notice.

(5) Regulations under subsection (3) may also provide for the charging on the land on which the building stands of any expenses recoverable by a local planning authority under subsection (1).

(6) Where any expenses are recoverable by a local planning authority by virtue of this section, those expenses shall be recoverable as a simple contract debt in any court of competent jurisdiction.

(7) In this section and in section 43 references to "the compliance period", in relation to a listed building enforcement notice, are references to the period specified in the notice as that within which the steps specified in it are to be taken, or such extended period as the local planning authority may allow for the taking of those steps.

DEFINITIONS
   "building": s.91.
   "compliance period": subs. (7).
   "land": s.91(2).
   "listed building": ss.1(5); 91(1).
   "listed building enforcement notice": ss.38(1); 91(1).
   "local planning authority": s.81.
   "owner": s.91(2).
   "use": s.91(2).

ALLOCATION OF FUNCTIONS
   The functions of a local planning authority under this section are exercisable solely by:—
   Greater London: the London Borough Council (T.C.P.A. 1990, s.1(2) and the Commission concurrently (s.45).
   Metropolitan areas: the metropolitan district council (T.C.P.A. 1990, s.1(2))
   Non-metropolitan areas: the district planning authority (Sched. 4, para. 2).
   National Parks (outside a metropolitan county): the county planning authority (T.C.P.A. 1990, s.4) or joint planning board in areas where one has been established as county planning authority (T.C.P.A. 1990, s.2).
   Norfolk and Suffolk Broads: the Broads Authority (Sched. 4, para. 5).
   Urban development areas: the urban development corporation where an order has been made under the Local Government, Planning and Land Act 1980, s.149(1), transferring the function to the corporation (T.C.P.A. 1990, s.7(1)): for a list of current orders see the notes to s.81.
   Housing action trust areas: the housing action trust has the functions under this section to the exclusion of any other authority (other than the Secretary of State) where order has been made under the Housing Act 1988, s.67(3) transferring the function (as a function within s.67(3A), as substituted by the Planning (Consequential Provisions) Act 1990, Sched. 2, para. 79(3)) to the trust (T.C.P.A. 1990, s.8(2)): see the notes to s.81.
   Enterprise zones: the enterprise zone authority, where so provided by order under the Local Government, Planning and Land Act 1980, Sched. 32, para. 5.

GENERAL NOTE
Judicial review of authority's decision to take action
   The Court of Appeal in *R.* v. *Greenwich London Borough Council,* ex p. *Patel* (1985) 129 S.J. 654 accepted that a local planning authority ought to be willing, before taking action under this section, to look at evidence put before it by an owner who had not been served with a copy of the notice, and who had not appealed, if it tended to show, for example, that there had been no breach. Although the court could not review the validity of the enforcement notice, it could in an appropriate case intervene to review on *Wednesbury* principles a decision to take action under these provisions.

Adaptation of Public Health Act 1936

The provisions of the 1936 Act specified in subs. (3), as adapted by the Town and Country Planning General Regulations 1976 (No. 1419), reg. 16, are printed below with the modifications required by the regulations indicated by square brackets.

276.—(1) A [local planning authority] may sell any materials which have been removed by them from any premises, including any street, when [taking steps required to be taken by an enforcement notice] and which are not before the expiration of three days from the date of their removal claimed by the owner and taken away by him.

(2) Where a [local planning authority] sell any materials under this section, they shall pay the proceeds to the person to whom the materials belonged after deducting the amount of any expenses recoverable by them from him.

(3) This section does not apply to refuse removed by a [local planning authority].

289. If on a complaint made by the owner of any premises, it appears to a court of summary jurisdiction that [a person having an interest in the premises other than the owner] of those premises prevents the owner from [taking steps required to be taken by an enforcement notice] the court may order the [person] to permit the [taking of such steps].

294. Where a [local planning authority] claim to recover any [expenses incurred in the taking of such steps as aforesaid] from a person as being the owner of the premises in respect of which the expenses were incurred and that person proves that he—

  (a) is receiving the rent of those premises merely as agent or trustee for some other person; and

  (b) has not, and since the date of the service on him of a demand for payment has not had, in his hands on behalf of that other person sufficient money to discharge the whole demand of that authority.

his liability shall be limited to the total amount of the money which he has or has had in his hands as aforesaid but a [local planning authority] who are, or would be debarred by the foregoing provisions from recovering the whole of any such expenses from an agent or trustee may recover the whole of any unpaid balance thereof from the person on whose behalf the agent or trustee receives the rent.

Although the modified provisions do not in terms apply to listed building enforcement notices as opposed to planning enforcement notices, the corresponding provision of the T.C.P.A. 1990 is simply extended to listed building enforcement by reference to the powers of entry and execution applicable to planning enforcement, and thus the powers under these provisions remain applicable unless and until new regulations are made. The possibilities provided for by subss. (4) and (5) have not yet been carried through to the regulations.

Recovery of establishment expenses

In addition to the sums they are entitled to recover under this section, a local planning authority may recover, "together with and in like manner as" those expenses, such sums as appears to them to be reasonable in respect of their establishment charges (Local Government Act 1974, s.36). This power extends to any local authority, but not to the Commission or the Secretary of State.

Arrangements for specialist advice

The Secretary of State may from time to time direct a district planning authority, under Sched. 4, para. 7, to submit for approval by him the arrangements they propose to make to obtain specialist advice in connection with their functions under this section, and, if not satisfied with the arrangements, may direct them to enter into an agreement with another local planning authority.

Penalties for non-compliance with listed building enforcement notice

43.—(1) Where a listed building enforcement notice has been served on the person who at the time when the notice was served was the owner of the building to which it relates, and any steps required by the notice have not been taken within the compliance period, then subject to the provisions of this section, that person shall be guilty of an offence and liable—

  (a) on summary conviction, to a fine not exceeding the statutory maximum, or

(b) on conviction on indictment, to a fine.

(2) Where proceedings have been brought under subsection (1) against a person ("the original owner") who ceased to be the owner of the building before the end of the compliance period, if he—

(a) duly lays information to that effect; and

(b) gives the prosecution not less than three clear days' notice of his intention,

he shall be entitled to have the person who then became the owner of the building ("the subsequent owner") brought before the court in the proceedings.

(3) Where in such proceedings—

(a) it is proved that any steps required by the notice have not been taken within the compliance period; and

(b) the original owner proves that the failure to take those steps was attributable, in whole or in part, to the default of the subsequent owner,

then—

(i) the subsequent owner may be convicted of the offence; and

(ii) if the original owner also proves that he took all reasonable steps to secure compliance with the notice, he shall be acquitted of the offence.

(4) If, after a person has been convicted under the previous provisions of this section, he does not as soon as practicable do everything in his power to secure compliance with the notice, he shall be guilty of a further offence and liable—

(a) on summary conviction, to a fine not exceeding £200 for each day following his first conviction on which any of the requirements of the notice remains unfulfilled; or

(b) on conviction on indictment, to a fine.

DEFINITIONS

"building": s.91.
"compliance period": s.42(7).
"listed building": ss.1(5); 91(1).
"listed building enforcement notice": ss.38(1); 91(1).
"owner": s.91(2).

GENERAL NOTE

Introduction

This section gives legal effect to listed building enforcement procedures by making it an offence to fail to comply with the requirements of a notice (subs. (1)), and upon conviction, a further continuing offence of failure to do everything practicable to secure compliance with the notice (subs. (5)).

Bringing prosecution under this section

The right to bring a prosecution under this section is not restricted to the local planning authority (although it is they who will normally have the necessary evidence in their possession), and private prosecution may therefore be brought. Both of the offences are triable either way, and are therefore not subject to the six-month time limit under the Magistrates' Court Act 1980, s.127.

The date a listed building enforcement notice takes effect

The offence under subs. (1) is committed only where the required steps have not been taken within the "compliance period". Subject to s.39 (appeals) a listed building enforcement notice takes effect on the date specified in it (s.38(3)), and the "compliance period" is the period specified in the notice, "or such extended period as the local planning authority may allow for compliance with it" (s.42(7)). The compliance period begins when the notice takes effect. If, however, an appeal is lodged to the Secretary of State under s.39 before the notice takes effect, the notice is of no effect pending the final determination or the withdrawal of the appeal: see further the notes to the T.C.P.A. 1990, ss.174 and 179, where there is a detailed analysis of the case law on the directly corresponding provisions relating to planning enforcement notices.

Failure to comply with a notice

Liability under this section is restricted to owners upon whom a copy of the notice was served. Thus, to succeed in a prosecution, it is incumbent upon the local planning authority to prove that the defendant was the owner of the land and that a copy of the notice was served upon him. In *R.* v. *Ruttle*, ex p. *Marshall* (1988) 57 P. & C.R. 299 the information laid against the defendant did not allege, nor prove, that he was the owner of the land when a planning enforcement notice was served. The Divisional Court held that the fact that he had appealed against the notice did not absolve the authority from proving ownership, notwithstanding the provisions of s.175(5). That subsection was concerned with proof of service, but not with proof of ownership, and a statement reported in the inspector's decision letter on the enforcement appeal as having been made by the defendant, to the effect that he had admitted buying the relevant property, was hearsay and inadmissible. It would have been admissible only if somebody present at the inquiry had produced the inspector's decision letter and then stated that the relevant passage was an accurate account of the evidence given by the defendant at the inquiry.

Where, however, there is evidence that the accused was the owner of the land at a date before the notice was issued, there is, in the absence of anything to the contrary, a presumption of continuing ownership by him thereafter (*Whitfield* v. *Gowling* (1974) 118 S.J. 716).

Shifting of liability to new owner

If the original owner parted with ownership of the land before the end of the compliance period, he may attempt to have liability apportioned between himself and the new owner. The new owner will have acquired the land with notice of the enforcement notice, as a consequence of it being registered as a local land charge. The original owner is entitled under subs. (2) to lay information to the effect that he has ceased to be the owner of the land, and to have the subsequent owner brought before the court by giving the prosecution three clear days' notice. The prosecution must still prove that any steps required by the notice to be taken have not been taken within the compliance period, but the original owner may then prove that failure to take the steps was attributable in whole or in part to the default of the subsequent owner. The subsequent owner may then be convicted of the offence. If the original owner is also able to prove that he took all reasonable steps to secure compliance with the notice, he must be acquitted.

Single offences and continuing offences

See the notes to s.179 of the T.C.P.A. 1990.

Effect of listed building consent on listed building enforcement notice

44.—(1) If, after the issue of a listed building enforcement notice, consent is granted under section 8(3)—

(a) for the retention of any work to which the notice relates; or

(b) permitting the retention of works without compliance with some condition subject to which a previous listed building consent was granted,

the notice shall cease to have effect in so far as it requires steps to be taken involving the works not being retained or, as the case may be, for complying with that condition.

(2) The fact that such a notice has wholly or partly ceased to have effect under subsection (1) shall not affect the liability of any person for an offence in respect of a previous failure to comply with that notice.

DEFINITIONS

"building": s.91.
"listed building": ss.1(5); 91(1).
"listed building consent": ss.8(7); 91(1).
"listed building enforcement notice": ss.38(1); 91(1).

GENERAL NOTE

A listed building enforcement notice remains effective until its requirements have been met, or are overridden by the grant of listed building consent permitting the retention of works (or retention without compliance with some previous condition). There is no separate offence under this Act of reinstating works, akin to that of s.181 of the T.C.P.A. 1990 in relation to planning enforcement notices, because such reinstatement would itself normally constitute unauthorised works to the listed building and thus be an offence under s.9.

Moreover, there is no power for the local planning authority to enter the land and themselves carry out the steps required by the enforcement notice (*cf.* T.C.P.A. 1990, s.178). But there is a general power under s.54 for an authority to carry out any works which appear to them to be urgently necessary for the preservation of any unoccupied listed building in their area.

Commission to have concurrent enforcement functions in London

45. The Commission shall, as respects any London borough, have concurrently with the council of that borough the functions of a local planning authority under sections 38 to 43; and references to the local planning authority in those provisions shall be construed accordingly.

DEFINITIONS
  "functions": s.91(2).
  "local planning authority": s.81.
  "London borough": s.91(2).
  "the Commission": s.91(1).

GENERAL NOTE
  Under this section the Historic Buildings and Monuments Commission (English Heritage) has concurrent enforcement powers in Greater London. The Commission also has concurrent powers under ss.3 and 4 (building preservation notices), 47 (compulsory acquisition of listed buildings in need of repair), 54 (works for urgent preservation of unoccupied listed buildings) and 69 (designation of conservation areas).

Enforcement by the Secretary of State

46.—(1) If it appears to the Secretary of State to be expedient that a listed building enforcement notice should be issued in respect of any land he may issue such a notice.

(2) Before the Secretary of State serves a notice under subsection (1) he shall consult—

  (a) the local planning authority; and
  (b) if the land is situated in England, the Commission.

(3) A listed building enforcement notice issued by the Secretary of State shall have the same effect as a notice issued by the local planning authority.

(4) In relation to a listed building enforcement notice issued by the Secretary of State, sections 42 and 43 shall apply as if for any reference in those sections to the local planning authority there were substituted a reference to the Secretary of State.

(5) References in this section to the local planning authority shall in the case of an authority for an area outside Greater London be construed as references to the district planning authority.

DEFINITIONS
  "building": s.91.
  "land": s.91(2).
  "listed building": ss.1(5); 91(1).
  "listed building enforcement notice": ss.38(1); 91(1).
  "local planning authority": s.81.
  "the Commission": s.91(1).

ALLOCATION OF FUNCTIONS
  The local planning authority with whom the Secretary of State must consult is, in Greater London, the London borough council (T.C.P.A. 1990, s.1) and elsewhere, the district planning authority (subs. (5)).

GENERAL NOTE

This section confers on the Secretary of State a reserve power to issue a listed building enforcement notice, with the same effect as a notice issued by a local planning authority. He must first consult the local planning authority.

The procedure would not allow effective enforcement action to be taken against a local planning authority itself, because a notice issued by the Secretary of State would have the same effect as one issued by the authority, and thus could be withdrawn by the authority. However, a separate enforcement power is conferred on the Secretary of State by the Town and Country Planning (Listed Buildings and Conservation Areas) Regulations 1990, reg. 13(8) which enables the Secretary of State to serve, in relation to a building owned by a local planning authority, any notice authorised to be served by a local planning authority in relation to a listed building.

CHAPTER V

PREVENTION OF DETERIORATION AND DAMAGE

Compulsory acquisition of listed building in need of repair

Compulsory acquisition of listed building in need of repair

47.—(1) If it appears to the Secretary of State that reasonable steps are not being taken for property preserving a listed building he—

(a) may authorise the appropriate authority to acquire compulsorily under this section the building and any relevant land; or

(b) may himself compulsorily acquire them under this section.

(2) The Acquisition of Land Act 1981 shall apply to compulsory acquisition under this section.

(3) The Secretary of State shall not make or confirm a compulsory purchase order for the acquisition of any building by virtue of this section unless—

(a) in the case of the acquisition of a building situated in England otherwise than by the Commission, he has consulted with the Commission; and

(b) in any case, he is satisfied that it is expedient to make provision for the preservation of the building and to authorise its compulsory acquisition for that purpose.

(4) Any person having an interest in a building which it is proposed to acquire compulsorily under this section may, within 28 days after the service of the notice required by section 12 of that Act of 1981 or, as the case may be, paragraph 3(1) of Schedule 1 to that Act, apply to a magistrates' court acting for the petty sessions area within which the building is situated for an order staying further proceedings on the compulsory purchase order.

(5) If on an application under subsection (4) the court is satisfied that reasonable steps have been taken for property preserving the building, the court shall make an order accordingly.

(6) Any person aggrieved by the decision of a magistrates' court on an application under subsection (4) may appeal against the decision to the Crown Court.

(7) In this section—

"the appropriate authority" means—

(a) the council of the county or district in which the building is situated, or

(b) in the case of a building situated in Greater London, the Commission or the council of the London borough in which the building is situated, or

(c) in the case of a building situated outside Greater London, the joint planning board for the area in which the building is situated; or

(d) in the case of a building situated within the Broads, the Broads Authority;

"relevant land", in relation to any building, means the land comprising or contiguous or adjacent to it which appears to the Secretary of State to be required for preserving the building or its amenities, or for affording access to it, or for its proper control or management.

DEFINITIONS
"appropriate authority": subs. (7).
"building": s.91.
"compulsory acquisition": s.91(2).
"joint planning board": s.91(2).
"land": s.91(2).
"listed building": ss.1(5); 91(1).
"London borough": s.91(2).
"relevant land": subs. (7).
"the Broads": s.91(2).
"the Commission": s.91(1).

ALLOCATION OF FUNCTIONS
The appropriate authority who may be authorised by the Secretary of State to acquire a listed building compulsorily under this section is (subs. (7)):
Greater London: the London borough council, and the Commission.
Metropolitan and non-metropolitan areas: the district council, or, where applicable, the joint planning board, and the Broads Authority.

GENERAL NOTE

Introduction
This section enables an authority or the Secretary of State to acquire compulsorily a listed building in need of repair. The other coercive powers under the Act fall short of requiring the owners of listed buildings to keep them in good repair, whilst attempting to control positive acts of destruction by making it an offence to damage a building or carry out unauthorised works of demolition, alteration or extension to it; and short-term "shoring-up" repairs can be undertaken under the emergency powers of s.54 if the building is unoccupied. Compulsory acquisition is therefore a reserve power, designed to secure longer term preservation, and the procedures are designed accordingly. They are unique amongst compulsory acquisition powers, in that they confer jurisdiction on the magistrates' court to make orders. The magistrates may stay the proceedings in certain cases, and they may agree to waive the normal compensation rules and instead order that only minimum compensation should be paid where a building has been deliberately left derelict.
The first step is the service of a repairs notice under s.48, which must be served at least two months before the compulsory purchase is started (s.48(1)). Its purpose is to offer the owner of the building a prior opportunity himself to carry out all necessary repairs, so that compulsory acquisition under this section becomes the sanction for failure to comply with the notice. It may be appropriate for the authority to combine it with an offer of financial assistance under s.57. The repairs notice specifies the repairs that the local planning authority (or the Secretary of State) consider "reasonably necessary for the proper preservation of the building". Then, if after the expiry of the two month period it appears to the authority or Secretary of State that reasonable steps are not being taken for properly preserving the building, they may serve notice of a compulsory purchase order on every owner, lessee and occupier. Any person having an interest in the building may then within 28 days apply to the magistrates' court for an order staying the compulsory purchase on the grounds that reasonable steps have been taken for preserving the building properly (subs. (6)). Compensation is payable on the usual basis for compulsory acquisition under this section, but special rules apply where the building has been deliberately allowed to fall into despair.

Listed buildings in dangerous or ruinous state
Before taking any steps with a view to making orders or serving notices under the Building Act 1984, ss.77 and 79 or the London Building Acts (Amendment) Act 1939, ss.69(1) and

(2), a local planning authority are required by s.56 to consider whether they should instead exercise their powers under this section, s.48 (repairs notices) or s.54 (urgently necessary works for preservation of listed building).

Acquisition with a view to disposal

By virtue of s.53 an authority may acquire a building under this section with a view to its immediate disposal for the purposes of its preservation (*Rolf* v. *North Shropshire District Council* (1988) 55 P. & C.R. 242).

Acquisition of additional land

An order under this section may extend not only to the building, but also to any land comprising or contiguous or adjacent to it which appears to be required for preserving it or its amenities, or for affording access to it, or for its proper control or management (subs. (7)). Such land need not necessarily be in the same ownership as the building, but the power could work harshly in such a case. Someone who owned only the contiguous land would lack altogether the ability to resist the order by putting in hand steps for the proper preservation of the building, and could be wrongly penalised by a direction for minimum compensation.

Acquisition by agreement

There is a broad power under s.52 for any council or joint planning board to acquire by agreement any building of special architectural or historic interest together with adjacent land, whether listed or not and whether or not located in their area.

Urgent works

A special power for an authority to undertake urgently needed repair work on unoccupied listed buildings is conferred by s.54

Exceptions

The compulsory purchase power does not extend to
(1) Crown land, except that it may be exercised in relation to any interest in Crown land which is for the time being held otherwise than by or on behalf of the Crown (s.83(1)(c)), provided that the acquisition has the consent of the appropriate Crown authority (s.83(2)(b));
(2) an ecclesiastical building which is for the time being used for ecclesiastical purposes (s.60(1));
(3) scheduled monuments (s.61). Alternative powers of compulsory acquisition and guardianship are conferred by the Ancient Monuments and Archaeological Areas Act 1979.

Function of the Secretary of State

The Secretary of State may either initiate compulsory acquisition proceedings himself, or authorise a council to acquire the building compulsorily. In either case, he may proceed only upon consulting the Commission (where the building is in England), and only where satisfied that it is expedient to make provision for the preservation of the building and to authorise compulsory acquisition for the purpose.

Serving a repairs notice

A repairs notice must be served under s.48 as a preliminary step, and the power of compulsory acquisition under this section does not arise until two months from the date of service. The purpose is to allow the owner an opportunity to take reasonable steps for properly preserving the building, and that objective is reinforced by the right (under subs. (4)) of any person with an interest in the building, within 28 days of service of the draft compulsory purchase order, to apply to the magistrates' court for an order staying further proceedings on the compulsory order, on the ground that reasonable steps have been taken for properly preserving the building. Similarly, the Secretary of State may confirm an order only if it appears to him that reasonable steps are not being taken for properly preserving the building (subs. (1)).

The relevant date for determining "preservation"

The works that may be required by a notice under this section to be carried out include not only works necessary to prevent the building deteriorating further or falling into further disrepair, but also works of repair, and any works reasonably necessary for the proper preservation of the building as a building of special architectural or historic importance. In

Robbins v. *Secretary of State for the Environment* [1989] 1 W.L.R. 201, the House of Lords rejected the submission that a repairs notice under [this section] could include only those works that were necessary for the proper preservation of a listed building as it subsisted at the date the notice was served, and could not specify further works of restoration. The House held that the relevant date for determining what works were required for the "preservation" of a building was not the date of the notice, but the date the building was listed. It could not be earlier than that, because ". . . the legislature cannot have intended that immediately following the listing of a building it should be liable to compulsory purchase on the ground that steps were not being taken for properly preserving it because the owner was unwilling to restore features of the building that had ceased to exist before listing" (*per* Lord Bridge at p.884). The House took the view that the line between repair and restoration may not be an easy one to draw with precision, but that in practice there should be little difficulty in determining whether any works fell on one side of the line or the other (*idem*).

Effect of excessive requirements on validity of repairs notice
    The House of Lords in *Robbins* v. *Secretary of State for the Environment* held that even if a notice went further than the Act allowed, and required works to be carried out to restore features which were missing at the date a building was listed, it was not necessarily invalid. On the face of the language of this section a notice listing a number of valid items was a notice "specifying the works which they consider reasonably necessary for the proper preservation of the building" notwithstanding that it also included invalid items. Provided, therefore, that the list of valid items was sufficiently substantial to support a conclusion by the Secretary of State that, in the event that the specified works were not carried out, reasonable steps were not being taken for properly preserving the building, it was difficult to see why the invalid items should not simply be disregarded, particularly given the further protection available to the owner through application to the magistrates' court under subs. (4) (application to magistrates' court to stay further proceedings). An owner who disputed items contained in the repairs notice could undertake the other items, and on receipt of notice under s.12 of the Acquisition of Land Act 1981 initiating the compulsory purchase notice proceedings he could apply under subs. (4) to the magistrates' court for a stay, to which he would be entitled if he satisfied the court that the works already put in hand constituted reasonable steps for preserving the building, and the remainder were excessive. Lord Ackner agreed with that approach, provided that preservation requirements were not inextricably mingled in the repairs notice with the repairs requirements (p.218).
    In *Rolf* v. *North Shropshire District Council* (1988) 55 P. & C.R. 242 the Court of Appeal held that this section does not require a council to take into account the means of an owner of a listed building, when specifying the works which it considers reasonably necessary for the preservation of the building.

Withdrawal of repairs notice
    A repairs notice may be withdrawn at any time, but notice of the withdrawal must be given immediately to any person on whom the notice was served (s.48(3)).

Making of order by local authority
    Where the procedure is initiated by the local authority, the requirement in subs. (1), that the Secretary of State authorise the appropriate authority, extends only to his confirmation of the order, and not also to their making a draft order: *Robbins* v. *Secretary of State for the Environment* [1989] 1 W.L.R. 201 (this point does not appear to have been taken in the subsequent appeal to the House of Lords, reported at [1989] 1 W.L.R. 201). Notice of the order must be published in one or more local newspapers, and copies served on every owner, lessee and occupier (except tenants for a month or lesser period) of any land comprised in the order, stating the effect of the order, that it is about to be submitted for confirmation and specifying the time (not less than 21 days) within which objections to the order can be made (Acquisition of Land Act 1981, ss.11 and 12(1)). Within 28 days of service of that notice, any person interested may apply to the magistrates' court for an order staying further proceedings (subs. (4)). If the proceedings are not stayed by the magistrates, the Secretary of State may proceed to confirm the order, but if any duly made objection to it has not been withdrawn, he is obliged first to offer the objector an opportunity to be heard (Acquisition of Land Act 1981, s.13). Procedure at an inquiry is governed by the Compulsory Purchase by Non-Ministerial Acquiring Authorities (Inquiries Procedure) Rules 1990 (No. 512).

Making of draft order by Secretary of State

Similar requirements are imposed where acquisition is by the Secretary of State, except that the order is first issued in draft form for publicity, objection and consultation prior to it being made by him (Sched. 1 to the Acquisition of Land Act 1981).

Application to magistrates' court to stay further proceedings

In *Robbins* v. *Secretary of State for the Environment* [1989] 1 W.L.R. 201 Lord Bridge remarked that this unusual provision empowers the magistrates' court to override the opinion of the acquiring authority and to pre-empt the decision of the Secretary of State in determining what works are reasonably necessary for the proper preservation of the listed building. The magistrates could assess what works were reasonably necessary for the preservation of the building, and whether the owner had taken reasonable steps for properly preserving the building by the works he had already put in hand. If there are disputed items, and the magistrates rule that they should be carried out, then the owner will be able to put them in hand, and it would be inconceivable that the authority would then wish to proceed with the acquisition. His Lordship suggested that, if they did, the owner would be able to make a fresh application to the magistrates' court under subs. (4), but it must be noted that this course would be possible only if the magistrates made an order staying the compulsory purchase proceedings. This they could do, even where all the works validly required by the notice had not been carried out, because their power is exercisable where they are satisfied only that "reasonable steps have been taken for properly preserving the building". Indeed, Lord Ackner recorded that:

"Both counsel for the appellant and counsel for the respondents accepted that before the magistrates or at the inquiry it was not essential for the owner to actually have carried out any work, so long as he could establish that he had taken reasonable steps with a view to carrying out such work. For example, he may have instructed surveyors to advise him as to which of the items in the repairs notice could fairly be said to be reasonably necessary for the proper preservation of the building and, having received their report and found that only certain items fell within that category, instructed them to carry out such work after the proceedings before the magistrates or the inquiry had terminated."

If the magistrates refuse an order and the proceedings continue, it remains open to the owner to persuade the Secretary of State that he is, by then, taking reasonable steps for the preservation of the building. The Secretary of State may only confirm the order if it appears to him that reasonable steps are not being taken (subs. (1)).

Compensation

The starting point for compensation is the market value of the land with the protected building on it. The valuer may assume that consent would be forthcoming for any works of alteration or extension of the building, but not for its demolition (except for the limited assumption of permission to rebuild a building of the same size plus 10 per cent., under Sched. 3 of the T.C.P.A. 1990).

Direction for minimum compensation

If an authority proposing to acquire a building under this section are satisfied that it has been deliberately allowed to fall into disrepair for the purpose of justifying its demolition and the redevelopment of the site, they may include in the compulsory purchase order a direction for minimum compensation. In such a case, as with an application under subs. (4) to stay proceedings, application may be made to the magistrates' court by any person having an interest in the building within 28 days of the service of notice of the order, for an order that the direction should not be included in the compulsory purchase order (s.50).

Financial assistance for acquisition

Power is conferred by the Historic Buildings and Ancient Monuments Act 1953, ss.5B and 6, on the Commission (or, in Wales, the Secretary of State) to make grants for the purpose of defraying all or part of a local authority's expenses in acquiring any property under this section.

Repairs notice as preliminary to acquisition under s.47

48.—(1) The compulsory purchase of a building under section 47 shall not be started by the appropriate authority or by the Secretary of State unless at least two months previously the authority or, as the case may be, the Secretary of State has served on the owner of the building a notice under this section (in this section referred to as a "repairs notice")—

(a) specifying the works which the appropriate authority or, as the case may be, the Secretary of State considers reasonably necessary for the proper preservation of the building; and
(b) explaining the effect of sections 47 to 50,
and the repairs notice has not been withdrawn.
(2) Where—
  (a) a building is demolished after a repairs notice has been served in respect of it by an appropriate authority or the Secretary of State, but
  (b) the Secretary of State is satisfied that he would have confirmed or, as the case may be, would have made a compulsory purchase order in respect of the building had it not been demolished,
the demolition of the building shall not prevent the authority or the Secretary of State from being authorised under section 47 to acquire compulsorily the site of the building.
(3) An appropriate authority or the Secretary of State may at any time withdraw a repairs notice served by them on any person; and if they do so, they shall immediately give him notice of the withdrawal.
(4) The Secretary of State shall consult with the Commission before he serves or withdraws a repairs notice in relation to a building situated in England.
(5) Where a repairs notice has been served on a person in respect of a building, he shall not be entitled to serve a listed building purchase notice in respect of it—
  (a) until the expiration of three months beginning with the date of the service of the repairs notice; or
  (b) if during that period the compulsory acquisition of the building is begun under section 47, unless and until the compulsory acquisition is discontinued.
(6) For the purposes of this section a compulsory acquisition—
  (a) is started when the notice required by section 12 of the Acquisition of Land Act 1981 or, as the case may be, paragraph 3(1) of Schedule 1 to that Act is served; and
  (b) is discontinued—
    (i) in the case of acquisition by the Secretary of State, when he decides not to make the compulsory purchase order; and
    (ii) in any other case when the order is withdrawn or the Secretary of State decides not to confirm it.
(7) In this section "appropriate authority" has the same meaning as in section 47.

DEFINITIONS
  "appropriate authority": subs. (7); s.47(7).
  "building": s.91.
  "compulsory acquisition": s.91(2).
  "land": s.91(2).
  "listed building": ss.1(5); 91(1).
  "listed building purchase notice": ss.32(1); 91(1).
  "owner": s.91(2).
  "repairs notice": subs. (1).
  "the Commission": s.91(1).

ALLOCATION OF FUNCTIONS
  By virtue of subs.(7), the appropriate authority under this section is as for s.47: see further the notes to that section.

GENERAL NOTE
  See the notes to s.47.

Compensation on compulsory acquisition of listed building

49. Subject to section 50, for the purpose of assessing compensation in respect of any compulsory acquisition of land including a building which immediately before the date of the compulsory purchase order was listed, it shall be assumed that listed building consent would be granted for any works—

(a) for the alteration or extension of the building; or

(b) for the demolition of the building for the purpose of development of any class specified in Schedule 3 to the principal Act (development not constituting new development),

other than works in respect of which such consent has been applied for before the date of the order and refused by the Secretary of State, or granted by him subject to conditions, the circumstances having been such that on that refusal or grant compensation became payable under section 27.

DEFINITIONS

"building": s.91.

"compulsory acquisition": s.91(2).

"development": s.91(2).

"land": s.91(2).

"listed building": ss.1(5); 91(1).

"listed building consent": ss.8(7); 91(1).

"new development": s.91(2).

"the principal Act": s.91(1).

GENERAL NOTE

Basis for compensation

The primary purpose of the compulsory acquisition procedures is to secure the preservation of the building, not to penalise its owner. Its effect is to transfer the burden of future maintenance from private owner to public funds. This section therefore secures compensation for the owner on an "extended market value" basis. As a general rule the owner is entitled to have the actual market value of the building, under the compensation regime established by the Land Compensation Act 1961, but enhanced by a valuation assumption that listed building consent would be forthcoming for any works of alteration or extension (but not demolition) to the building. Valuation therefore proceeds on the assumption that there is no special control over alterations and extensions (although planning control has still to be taken into account). There is thus a compromise: the fact of listing is not ignored altogether, and although it is to be assumed that owners would be entitled to undertake limited works, the assumption is that the building stays where it is and the local planning authority should not be required to pay full redevelopment values on the basis of a cleared site. There is also a complex interaction between these assumptions and those applicable to planning control.

But in exceptional cases, where the building has been deliberately left derelict and a direction for minimum compensation is made under s.50, the only assumption that can be made is that listed building consent would be forthcoming for works necessary for restoring the building and maintaining it in a proper state of repair (s.50(4)).

Compensation falls to be assessed by the Lands Tribunal (Land Compensation Act 1961, s.1) in default of agreement between the claimant and the authority (or, as the case may be, the Commission acting on behalf of the Secretary of State).

The valuation assumptions

(1) it is to be assumed that listed building consent would be granted for any works for the alteration or extension of the building: the purpose appears to be to allow listed building control over alterations and extensions to be ignored entirely, and thus to assume that any necessary consent would be granted unconditionally. But the assumption does not carry with it an assumption that planning permission would be granted for the works, to the extent that it is required. However:

  (a) works for the maintenance, improvement or other alteration of a building which do not materially affect its external appearance do not generally constitute development requiring planning permission (T.C.P.A. 1990, s.55(2)(a));

  (b) for certain dwelling-houses and industrial buildings there are permitted development rights for specified works of alteration and extension under the Town and Country Planning General Development Order 1988; and

  (c) planning permission may be assumed (Land Compensation Act 1961, s.15(3)) for development within Sched. 3 of the T.C.P.A. 1990 (see further below).

  Moreover, the assumption is only that consent would be forthcoming, not that such works had been carried out; so it allows only for an enhancement in development value to be taken into account;

(2) there is no assumption that listed building consent would be granted for the demolition of the building, save for the purposes of Sched. 3 development. Demolition does not normally require planning permission (see further the notes to s.55 of the T.C.P.A. 1990), and so this exclusion of listed building consent means that the owner is required to bear the direct cost of listed building control on the same basis as if the sale were by private treaty. The incorporation of Sched. 3 rights is not easy to reconcile with the assumption as to demolition, because many of those rights are to do with changes in use or other works not requiring demolition, but the Schedule does include a right to rebuild existing buildings so long as the cubic content of the original building is not substantially exceeded (by more than one-tenth, or if a dwelling-house, up to 1,750 cubic feet if that is the greater) (T.C.P.A. 1990, Sched. 3, paras. 1 and 10(2));

(3) where compensation has already been paid under s.27 for the refusal or conditional grant of listed building consent, the works to which it relates are to be left out of the assumption under the two preceding headings;

(4) where a direction for minimum compensation has been made, the above assumptions are inapplicable, and instead it is to be assumed that no planning permission or listed building consent would be forthcoming at all, save for the restoration and maintenance of the building in a proper state of repair (s.51(4)).

Minimum compensation in case of listed building deliberately left derelict

50.—(1) Where the appropriate authority within the meaning of section 47—

  (a) propose to acquire a building compulsorily under that section; and

  (b) are satisfied that the building has been deliberately allowed to fall into disrepair for the purpose of justifying its demolition and the development or redevelopment of the site or any adjoining site,

they may include in the compulsory purchase order as submitted to the Secretary of State for confirmation a direction for minimum compensation.

(2) Subject to the provisions of this section, where the Secretary of State acquires a building compulsorily under section 47, he may, if he is satisfied as mentioned in subsection (1)(b), include a direction for minimum compensation in the compulsory purchase order.

(3) Without prejudice to so much of section 12 of the Acquisition of Land Act 1981 or, as the case may be, paragraph 3(1) of Schedule 1 to that Act (notices stating effect of compulsory purchase order or, as the case may be, draft order) as requires the notice to state the effect of the order, the notice required to be served in accordance with that provision shall—

  (a) include a statement that a direction for minimum compensation has been included in the order or, as the case may be, in the draft order prepared by the Secretary of State in accordance with Schedule 1 to that Act; and

(b) explain the meaning of the expression "direction for minimum compensation".

(4) A direction for minimum compensation, in relation to a building compulsorily acquired, is a direction that for the purpose of assessing compensation it is to be assumed, notwithstanding anything to the contrary in the Land Compensation Act 1961, the principal Act, or this Act—

(a) that planning permission would not be granted for any development or redevelopment of the site of the building; and

(b) that listed building consent would not be granted for any works for the demolition, alteration or extension of the building other than development or works necessary for restoring it to and maintaining it in a proper state of repair.

(5) If a compulsory purchase order is confirmed or made with the inclusion of a direction for minimum compensation, the compensation in respect of the compulsory acquisition shall be assessed in accordance with the direction.

(6) Where such a direction is included in a compulsory purchase order or, as the case may be, in a draft order prepared by the Secretary of State, any person having an interest in the building may, within 28 days after the service of the notice mentioned in subsection (3), apply to a magistrates' court acting for the petty sessions area in which the building is situated for an order that no such direction be included in the compulsory purchase order as confirmed or made by the Secretary of State.

(7) If the court to which an application is made under subsection (6) is satisfied that the building in respect of which the application is made has not been deliberately allowed to fall into disrepair for the purpose mentioned in subsection (1)(b) the court shall make the order applied for.

(8) A person aggrieved by the decision of a magistrates' court on an application under subsection (6) may appeal against the decision to the Crown Court.

(9) The rights conferred by subsections (6) and (8) shall not prejudice those conferred by section 47(4) and (6).

DEFINITIONS
"appropriate authority": s.47(7).
"building": s.91.
"compulsory acquisition": s.91(2).
"development": s.91(2).
"direction for minimum compensation": subs. (4).
"land": s.91(2).
"listed building": ss.1(5); 91(1).
"listed building consent": ss.8(7); 91(1).
"planning permission": s.91(2).
"the principal Act": s.91(1).

ALLOCATION OF FUNCTIONS
The "appropriate authority" under this section is the same as for s.47 (subs. (1)): see the notes to that section.

GENERAL NOTE
Purpose of a direction
A direction for minimum compensation under this section is intended to have the punitive effect of reducing compensation entitlement where a building has been deliberately allowed to fall into disrepair for the purpose of justifying its demolition to allow redevelopment to occur. It falls to the acquiring authority to make the direction in the first instance, by including it in the compulsory purchase order. They must first be satisfied that there has been deliberate neglect, which requires something more than merely the fact of dereliction. The section does not require that it should be the present owner who has deliberately allowed the building to fall into disrepair. However, any person interested in the building

may then apply to the magistrates' court for an order that no such direction should be
included in the order. At that point the burden of proof appears to shift: the magistrates
may make such an order only if satisfied that the building has not been deliberately allowed
to fall into disrepair for the purpose of justifying its demolition and redevelopment of the
site (subs. (6)). If the applicant fails to satisfy them of that, there is a right of appeal under
subs. (9) to the Crown Court. Moreover, it remains open to an unsuccessful owner still to
avoid compulsory purchase by setting in hand steps for the proper preservation of the
building.

Form of direction
   DOE Circular 6/85, Appendix J, suggests that a direction under this section might be in
the following terms (editorially amended to take account of the consolidation legislation):
   "Under the provisions of [section 50 of the Planning (Listed Buildings and Conservation
   Areas) Act 1990] it is hereby directed that for the purpose of assessing compensation it is
   to be assumed, notwithstanding anything to the contrary in the Land Compensation Act
   1961 or the [Town and Country Planning Act 1990], that planning permission would not
   be granted for any development or redevelopment of the site of the listed building
   described in the Schedule to this Order and that listed building consent would not be
   granted for any works for the demolition, alteration or extension of that building other
   than development or works necessary for restoring it to, and maintaining it in, a proper
   state of repair".

Right of appeal
   A "person aggrieved" may (subs. (8)) appeal to the Crown Court against the magistrates'
decision, and this expression includes not only the applicant but also the local planning
authority (*Cook* v. *Southend Borough Council* [1990] 2 W.L.R. 61).

Effect of direction
   The effect of a direction under this section is that compensation for the building is
restricted to its market value as it stands, without any prospect of development value. The
value of the site for redevelopment is especially excluded, although that is limited in any
event by the general rule (s.49) that listed building consent could not be assumed for
demolition except for Third Schedule redevelopment.

Ending of rights over land compulsorily acquired

   51.—(1) Subject to the provisions of this section, upon the completion
of a compulsory acquisition of land under section 47—
   (a) all private rights of way and rights of laying down, erecting,
       continuing or maintaining any apparatus on, under or over the land
       shall be extinguished, and
   (b) any such apparatus shall vest in the acquiring authority.
   (2) Subsection (1) shall not apply—
   (a) to any right vested in, or apparatus belonging to, statutory
       undertakers for the purpose of the carrying on of their under-
       taking, or
   (b) to any right conferred by or in accordance with the telecom-
       munications code on the operator of a telecommunications
       code system, or
   (c) to any telecommunication apparatus kept installed for the
       purposes of any such system.
   (3) In respect of any right or apparatus not falling within subsection
(2), subsection (1) shall have effect subject—
   (a) to any direction given by the acquiring authority before the com-
       pletion of the acquisition that subsection (1) shall not apply to any
       right or apparatus specified in the direction; and
   (b) to any agreement which may be made (whether before or after the
       completion of the acquisition) between the acquiring authority and
       the person in or to whom the right or apparatus in question is
       vested or belongs.

(4) Any person who suffers loss by the extinguishment of a right or the vesting of any apparatus under this section shall be entitled to compensation from the acquiring authority.

(5) Any compensation payable under this section shall be determined in accordance with the Land Compensation Act 1961.

DEFINITIONS
"acquiring authority": s.91.
"compulsory acquisition": s.91(2).
"land": s.91(2).
"statutory undertaker": s.91(3) and see below.

GENERAL NOTE

Introduction
The general rule is that compulsory purchase of a listed building under s.47 extinguishes all private rights of way, together with all rights to have apparatus on the land, and the apparatus vests in the acquiring authority (subs. (1)). The rights of the owners are translated into a right to claim compensation (subs. (5)).

Exceptions
The following cases are excepted from the general rule:
(1) where the parties so agree (subs. (3)(b));
(2) where the acquiring authority have directed, before the completion of the acquisition, that the general rule should not apply to any specified right or apparatus (subs. (3)(a));
(3) rights and apparatus of statutory undertakers (as defined below). Special rules are prescribed by s.271 of the T.C.P.A. 1990 in relation to their rights and equipment;
(4) telecommunications code rights (under the Telecommunications Act 1984, Sched. 2) and apparatus kept installed for the purpose of such a system. A special regime is created by s.272 of the T.C.P.A. 1990 for telecommunications rights and apparatus upon compulsory purchase.

Statutory undertakers
"Statutory undertaker" includes (T.C.P.A. 1990, s.262, as applied by s.91(3)):
"persons authorised by any enactment to carry on any railway, light railway, tramway, road transport, water transport, canal, inland navigation, dock, harbour, pier or lighthouse undertaking, or any undertaking for the supply of hydraulic power and a relevant airport operator (within the meaning of Part V of the Airports Act 1986)."
In addition, for the purposes of these sections (ss.33–36), the expression includes (s.91(3)):
(1) every water or sewerage undertaker;
(2) the Post Office;
(3) the Civil Aviation Authority;
(4) a public gas supplier;
(5) a holder of a licence under s.6 of the Electricity Act 1989;
(6) the National Rivers Authority.

Acquisition by agreement

Acquisition of land by agreement

52.—(1) The council of any county, district or London borough or a joint planning board for an area outside Greater London may acquire by agreement—
(a) any building appearing to them to be of special architectural or historic interest; and
(b) any land comprising or contiguous or adjacent to such a building which appears to the Secretary of State to be required—
(i) for preserving the building or its amenities, or
(ii) for affording access to it, or
(iii) for its proper control or management.
(2) The provisions of Part I of the Compulsory Purchase Act 1965 (so far as applicable), other than sections 4 to 8, 10 and 31, shall apply in

relation to the acquisition of land under subsection (1), but references in that Part to the execution of the works shall be construed as including references to—

(a) any erection, construction or carrying out of buildings or works authorised by section 237 of the principal Act; and

(b) any erection, construction or carrying out of buildings or works on behalf of a Minister or statutory undertakers on land acquired by that Minister or those undertakers, where the buildings or works are erected, constructed or carried out for the purposes for which the land was acquired.

DEFINITIONS

"building": s.91.
"joint planning board" s.91(2).
"land": s.91(2).
"London borough": s.91(2).
"Minister": s.91(2).
"statutory undertaker": s.91(3).
"the principal Act": s.91(1).

ALLOCATION OF FUNCTIONS

The power to acquire buildings and land under this section is exercisable by any county or district council, London borough council or joint planning board (subs. (1)).

GENERAL NOTE

Introduction

A local planning authority may under this section acquire by agreement any building appearing to them to be of special architectural or historic interest. It need not be a listed building, and it need not be in a state of disrepair; nor need it be within the council's area. They may make such arrangements as to its management, use or disposal as they consider appropriate for the purposes of its preservation (s.53(1)).

Contiguous or adjacent land

The requirement of subs. (2), that the authority should only acquire land comprising or adjacent to such a building where it appears to the Secretary of State to be required, appears anomalous. Originally, the Secretary of State's consent was required to all acquisitions under the section (s.119 of the 1971 Act) except where the land was immediately required by the council, or was within the council's area. But that requirement was repealed by the Local Government, Planning and Land Act 1980, Sched. 23, para. 8. Given that the Act provides no statutory mechanism for obtaining the view of the Secretary of State that the land needs to be acquired for the purposes specified in subs. (1)(b), and given also that the acquisition is by agreement and involves no coercion, it seems likely that the retention of this requirement has been by error.

Alternative powers

There are two principal alternative authorisations for land acquisition by agreement. Under s.227 of the T.C.P.A. 1990 a local authority may acquire by agreement any land which is "suitable for and required in order to secure the carrying out of development, re-development or improvement", or is "required for a purpose which it is necessary to achieve in the interests of the proper planning of an area in which the land is situated" (s.226(1), as applied by s.227). A broader power is conferred by s.120 of the Local Government Act 1972 on principal councils (*i.e.* county councils, district councils and London borough councils). That section authorises acquisition by agreement by a council for the purpose of—

(a) any of their functions under that or any other enactment, or

(b) the benefit, improvement or development of their area.

There is further under that section an authorisation to acquire land for any purposes for which it is not immediately required, and that authorisation extends to acquisition under any other enactment, including this section. By virtue of s.122(2), any land so acquired may be used for the purpose of any of the Council's functions until it is required for the purpose for which it was acquired.

Acquisition of land for purposes of exchange
Under the 1971 Act, s.119, from which this section derives, the power to acquire land included power to acquire land required for giving in exchange
(a) for land appropriated under that Act; or
(b) for Green Belt land, within the meaning of the Green Belt (London and Home Counties) Act 1938, appropriated in accordance with that Act for any purpose specified in a development plan.
That power, which was in any event anomalous in relation to acquisition of buildings of special architectural or historic interest, was lost in the 1990 Consolidation, and now exists solely in supplementation of s.226 of the T.C.P.A. 1990.

Management of acquired buildings
Special management powers are conferred by s.53.

Financial assistance for acquisition
Power is conferred by the Historic Buildings and Ancient Monuments Act 1953, ss.5B and 6, on the Commission (or, in Wales, the Secretary of State) to make grants for the purpose of defraying all or part of a local authority's expenses in acquiring any property under this section.

Management of acquired buildings

Management of listed buildings acquired under this Act

53.—(1) Where—
(a) a local authority or joint planning board acquire any building or other land under section 47(1) or 52(1)(a) or (b); or
(b) the Commission acquire any building or other land under section 47(1),
they may make such arrangements as to its management, use or disposal as they consider appropriate for the purpose of its preservation.
(2) Where the Secretary of State acquires any building or other land under section 47(1), he may—
(a) make such arrangements as he thinks fit as to the management, custody or use of the building or land; and
(b) dispose of or otherwise deal with any such building or land as he may from time to time determine.
(3) The Commission may be a party to such arrangements as are mentioned in subsection (2) if they relate to property situated in England.

DEFINITIONS
"building": s.91.
"disposal": s.91(2).
"joint planning board": s.91(2).
"land": s.91(2).
"listed building": ss.1(5); 91(1).
"local authority":s.91(2).
"the Commission": s.91(1).
"use": s.91(2).

ALLOCATION OF FUNCTIONS
In relation to land or buildings in the Broads, "local authority" in subs. (1) includes the Broads Authority (s.91(6)).

GENERAL NOTE
Where a listed building is acquired by the Secretary of State, he has broad power under subs. (2) to secure the management, custody or use of it, or to dispose of it, and the Commission may be party to such arrangements. Moreover, under the National Heritage Act 1983, s.34, any functions of management exercisable by the Secretary of State in relation to any historic building in England may be exercised by the Commission as directed by the Secretary of State on his behalf.

For buildings acquired by local authorities or by the Commission, there are also powers to make arrangements as to the building's management, use or disposal, but the arrangements must be such as the authority consider appropriate for the purposes of its preservation. In *Rolf* v. *North Shropshire District Council* (1988) 55 P. & C.R. 242 the Court of Appeal held that a council has power to make a compulsory purchase order under s.47 on the basis of a proposed immediate disposal under this section to another body, since the section contemplates the acquisition of land with a view to its subsequent disposal.

Urgent preservation

Urgent works to preserve unoccupied listed buildings

54.—(1) A local authority may execute any works which appear to them to be urgently necessary for the preservation of a listed building in their area.

(2) If it appears to the Secretary of State that any works are urgently necessary for the preservation of a listed building—

  (a) if the building is in England, he shall authorise the Commission to execute any works specified in the authorisation which appear to him to be urgently necessary for its preservation; or

  (b) if the building is in Wales, he may himself execute any works which appear to him to be urgently necessary for its preservation.

(3) The works which may be executed under this section may consist of or include works for affording temporary support or shelter for the building.

(4) If the building is occupied works may be carried out only to those parts which are not in use.

(5) The owner of the building must be given not less than seven days notice in writing of the intention to carry out the works and, in the case of works authorised under subsection (2)(a), the Commission shall give that notice.

(6) A notice under subsection (5) shall describe the works proposed to be carried out.

(7) As respects buildings in Greater London, the functions of a local authority under this section are exercisable concurrently by the Commission and the relevant London borough council.

DEFINITIONS
  "building": s.91.
  "functions": s.91(2).
  "land": s.91(2).
  "listed building": ss.1(5); 91(1).
  "local authority": s.91(2).
  "London Borough": s.91(2).
  "owner": s.91(2).
  "the Commission": s.91(1).

ALLOCATION OF FUNCTIONS
  The power to execute works under this section is exercisable by any local authority (subs. (1)), by the Secretary of State (subs. (2)), though, in England, only through the Commission; and, in Greater London, by the Commission (subs. (7)). In relation to a building or land in the Broads, "local authority" also includes the Broads Authority (s.91(6)).

GENERAL NOTE

Introduction
  Under this section a local authority may carry out any works urgently necessary for the preservation of an unoccupied listed building, after given seven days' notice to the owner, and may under s.55 require him to pay their expenses of so doing, subject to the owner's right of appeal to the Secretary of State against such a requirement.

Exercise of power by Secretary of State
The power may be exercised by the Secretary of State in Wales, but in England his power is to authorise the Commission to exercise any works specified in the authorisation which appear to him to be urgently necessary for the preservation of the building (subs. (2)). Prior notice must still be given to the owner under subs. (5). Such works as are carried out by the Commission are carried out on behalf of the Secretary of State, who has the power under s.55 to recover the expenses from the owner. In Greater London the Commission also has concurrent power with the relevant London borough council themselves to carry out works (subs. (7)).

Listed buildings in dangerous or ruinous state
Before taking any steps with a view to making orders or serving notices under the Building Act 1984, ss.77 and 79 or the London Building Acts (Amendment) Act 1939, ss.69(1) and (2), a local planning authority are required by s.56 to consider whether they should instead exercise their powers under this section, s.47 (compulsory acquisition) or s.48 (repairs notices).

Exceptions
The power under this section may not be used in relation to:
(1) an ecclesiastical building which is for the time being used for ecclesiastical purposes: s.60(1);
(2) any building which is a scheduled monument under the Ancient Monuments and Archaeological Areas Act 1979, s.1. (s.61);
(3) Crown land, except that the power does extend to Crown land to the extent of any interest in it for the time being held otherwise than by or on behalf of the Crown (s.83(1)(b)), including the rights of a person entitled to occupy the land by virtue of a written licence (s.84(6));
(4) any listed building which is occupied, although where the building is occupied in part the powers may be used in relation to those parts that are not in use (subs. (4)).

Extension
The Secretary of State may direct under s.76 that this section shall apply to an unlisted building in a conservation area, where it appears to him that its preservation is important for maintaining the character or appearance of that area.

Written notice describing proposed works
In *R.* v. *Secretary of State for the Environment*, ex p. *Hampshire County Council* (1982) 44 P. & C.R. 343 the Divisional Court upheld a ruling by the Secretary of State under an earlier version of this section that a notice under subs. (5) should specify in detail the works believed to be urgently necessary. The purpose of the seven days' notice was to enable the owner to discuss the matter with the local authority and perhaps to volunteer to do the works himself. The power subsequently to make representations to the Secretary of State under s.55 could not therefore be relied upon to take care of inadequacies in the notice itself. That decision was followed in *R.* v. *Camden London Borough Council*, ex p. *Comyn Ching & Co. (London)* (1984) 47 P. & C.R. 417, where a notice under this section requiring the taking of "all such steps as may be necessary to preserve the structure of the building" was held to be invalid for failing to give sufficient particularity. Subs. (6) now expressly requires that the notice should describe the works proposed.

Works of temporary support or shelter
The Court in *R.* v. *Secretary of State for the Environment*, ex p. *Hampshire County Council* (above) had also declined to hold that the old section could apply to works which could involve the owner in continuing liability, such as the maintenance of scaffolding erected to give structural support to a building. In *R.* v. *Camden London Borough Council*, ex p. *Comyn Ching & Co. (London)* (above), however, Woolf J. expressed reservations as to that ruling; and subs. (3) (originally substituted by the Housing and Planning Act 1986, Sched. 9, para. 7) now makes it clear that the works may include works for affording temporary support or shelter for the building. Continuing expenditure incurred in undertaking such works may be recovered from the owner under s.55 by notices given from time to time (s.55(3)).

Recovery of expenses
Under s.55 the local authority, the Secretary of State and the Commission may recover from the owner of a building their expenses of carrying out works under this section. They

are required to give notice to the owner of the building requiring him to pay the expenses, and the owner has 28 days in which to challenge the requirements, by making representations to the Secretary of State.

Recovery of expenses of works under s.54

55.—(1) This section has effect for enabling the expenses of works executed under section 54 to be recovered by the authority who carried out the works, that is to say the local authority, the Commission or the Secretary of State or, in the case of works carried out by the Commission on behalf of the Secretary of State, the Secretary of State.

(2) That authority may give notice to the owner of the building requiring him to pay the expenses of the works.

(3) Where the works consist of or include works for affording temporary support or shelter for the building—

(a) the expenses which may be recovered include any continuing expenses involved in making available the apparatus or materials used; and

(b) notices under subsection (2) in respect of any such continuing expenses may be given from time to time.

(4) The owner may within 28 days of the service of the notice represent to the Secretary of State—

(a) that some or all of the works were unnecessary for the preservation of the building; or

(b) in the case of works for affording temporary support or shelter, that the temporary arrangements have continued for an unreasonable length of time; or

(c) that the amount specified in the notice is unreasonable; or

(d) that the recovery of that amount would cause him hardship,

and the Secretary of State shall determine to what extent the representations are justified.

(5) The Secretary of State shall give notice of his determination, the reasons for it and the amount recoverable—

(a) to the owner of the building; and

(b) if the authority who gave notice under subsection (2) is a local authority or the Commission, to them.

(6) Any expenses recoverable by virtue of this section shall be recoverable as a simple contract debt in any court of competent jurisdiction.

DEFINITIONS
  "building": s.91.
  "local authority": s.91(2).
  "owner": s.91(2).
  "the Commission": s.91(1).

GENERAL NOTE

Introduction
  The local authority (or the Secretary of State or the Commission) who incur expenditure under s.54 in carrying out urgently necessary works for the preservation of a listed building are entitled under this section to seek to recover their expenses from the owner of the building.

Notice to the owner
  The authority which carried out the works must first give notice to the owner requiring him to pay the expenses. He is then entitled to make representations to the Secretary of State. In *Bolton Metropolitan Borough Council* v. *Jolley* [1989] 1 P.L.R. 97, the Court of Appeal held that the giving of "notice" for the purpose of the corresponding provision of the previous legislation (before it was amended by the Housing and Planning Act 1986), required something more than the issuing of a bare account by the authority to the owner.

Bingham L.J., whilst accepting that the statute did not prescribe any form for the notice, stated (at 101):
"But the statute does unquestionably require notice to be given, and the council never gave the defendant anything which, in my view, could reasonably be regarded as a notice requiring him to pay the expenses of the works executed. An advance warning, although proper and valuable, is not a notice such as the Act requires. Parliament must, in my judgment, have intended, in the interests of good administration, that the citizen should be plainly told in language, however untechnical, that the council was seeking to exercise a statutory power to seek reimbursement; otherwise the citizen might reasonably conclude that he was not obliged to pay for work he had never asked to be done. In the absence of such notice, he would not be prompted to seek advice on his rights, if any, under the statute. Parliament must also, in my judgment, have intended that the notice should not be misleading, and the council's account calling for immediate payments was, no doubt unintentionally, misleading, given the provision of subsections (7), (8) and (9) of section 101 [see now s.55]."
Parker L.J. accepted that the notice was inaccurate and inadequate, and suggested, without expressing a concluded view, that to be valid, a notice might also have to contain sufficient detail to enable representations to be made to the Secretary of State upon which he would be able to form some conclusion as to its validity or otherwise (at 100):
"The bill, which was presented, would not enable, as I see it, anybody to say that there has been, for example windows boarded up which were unnecessary, or that some of the repairs to the brickwork and gutters were unnecessary, because there was no detail whatever given of the works which had been carried out."

Recovery of overheads
A local authority are entitled under the Local Government Act 1974, s.36 to recover in addition to the expenses recoverable under this section, "such sum as appears to them to be reasonable in respect of their establishment charges".

Dangerous structure orders in respect of listed buildings

56. Before taking any steps with a view to—
  (a) the making of an order in respect of a listed building under section 77(1)(a) of the Building Act 1984 or section 65 or 69(1) of the London Building Acts (Amendment) Act 1939; or
  (b) the service of a notice under section 79(1) of that Act of 1984 or section 62(2) of that Act of 1939,
a local planning authority shall consider whether they should instead exercise their powers under sections 47 and 48 or section 54.

DEFINITIONS
  "building": s.91.
  "listed building": ss.1(5); 91(1).
  "local planning authority": s.81.

ALLOCATION OF FUNCTIONS
The functions of a local planning authority under this section are exercisable solely by:—
  Greater London: the London borough council (T.C.P.A. 1990, s.1(2)).
  Metropolitan areas: the metropolitan district council (T.C.P.A. 1990, s.1(2)).
  Non-metropolitan areas: the district planning authority and the county planning authority have the functions concurrently (T.C.P.A. 1990, s.1(3)).
  National Parks (outside a metropolitan county): the county planning authority (T.C.P.A. 1990, s.4) or joint planning board in areas where one has been established as county planning authority (T.C.P.A. 1990, s.2).
  Norfolk and Suffolk Broads: the Broads Authority (Sched. 4, para. 5).
  Urban development areas: the urban development corporation where an order has been made under the Local Government, Planning and Land Act 1980, s.149(1), transferring the function to the corporation (T.C.P.A. 1990, s.7(1)): for a list of current see the notes to s.81.
  Housing action trust areas: the housing action trust has the functions under this section to the exclusion of any other authority (other than the Secretary of State) where an order has been made under the Housing Act 1988, s.67(3) transferring the function (as a function

within s.67(3A), as substituted by the Planning (Consequential Provisions) Act 1990, Sched. 2, para. 79(3)) to the trust (T.C.P.A. 1990, s.8(2)): see the notes to s.81.

Enterprise zones: the enterprise zone authority, where so provided by order under the Local Government, Planning and Land Act 1980, Sched. 32, para. 5.

GENERAL NOTE

Purpose of the section

This section requires a local planning authority to consider using their powers under this Act in ss. 47 and 48 (compulsory purchase of listed buildings and preliminary repairs notices) and s.55 (power to carry out urgently necessary repairs for preservation of a listed building) before serving certain orders under the Building Act 1984 and the London Building Acts (Amendment) Act 1939. The section therefore gives statutory backing to the decision in *R. v. Stroud District Council*, ex p. *Goodenough Usborne and Tomlin* [1982] J.P.L. 246.

In addition, amendments made by the Housing and Planning Act 1986, Sched. 9, para. 6(2) to the relevant provisions of the 1984 and 1939 Acts provide that they are to have effect subject to the provisions of this Act relating to listed buildings, buildings subject to building preservation notices and buildings in conservation areas. Thus, such a building may be demolished in pursuance of an order under those provisions only if the requisite consent has been obtained under this Act, although it is open to a defendant in a prosecution under s.9 for unauthorised demolition to rely upon the limited defence in that section (subs. (3)) that the works were urgently necessary in the interests of safety or health.

Dangerous and ruinous buildings: orders under the Building Act 1984

The Building Act 1984, s.77 authorises a local authority, where it appears to them that a building or structure is in such a condition, or is used to carry such loads, as to be dangerous, to apply to a magistrates' court for an order requiring works to be carried out to obviate the danger, or, if the owner so elects, to demolish the building or structure or any dangerous part of it.

An order under s.79 of the Building Act 1984 may be made by the local authority itself, where it appears that a building or structure is "by reason of its ruinous or dilapidated condition seriously detrimental to the amenities of the neighbourhood", requiring the owner to execute works of repair or restoration, or if he so elects, to demolish it or any part of it.

Orders under the London Building Acts (Amendment) Act 1939

Under s.62 of this Act the local authority are entitled to shore up or otherwise secure the structure of a building in a dangerous state, and are required to serve notice on the owner or occupier requiring him forthwith to take down, repair or otherwise secure the structure, as the case requires. By way of enforcement, under s.65 the authority may complain to the court, which may make any order it thinks fit for remedying the dangerous state of the building, or taking it down, repairing it or otherwise securing it.

Grants for repair and maintenance

Power of local authority to contribute to preservation of listed buildings etc.

57.—(1) A local authority may contribute towards the expenses incurred or to be incurred in the repair or maintenance—

(a) of a listed building which is situate in or in the vicinity of their area; or

(b) of a building in their area which is not listed but appears to them to be of architectural or historic interest.

(2) At the time of making such a contribution the local authority may also contribute towards the expenses incurred, or to be incurred, in the upkeep of any garden occupied with the building and contiguous or adjacent to it.

(3) A contribution under this section may be made by grant or loan.

(4) A contribution by way of loan may be made upon such terms and conditions as the local authority may determine including (but without prejudice to the foregoing) a term that the loan shall be free of interest.

(5) A local authority—

(a) may renounce their right to repayment of such a loan or any interest for the time being outstanding, and

(b) by agreement with the borrower may otherwise vary any of the terms and conditions on which such a loan is made.

(6) A local authority may require as a condition of the making by them of a contribution under this section by way of grant towards the expenses of the repair or maintenance or upkeep of any property that the person to whom the grant is made shall enter into an agreement with them for the purpose of enabling the public to have access to the property or part of it during such period and at such times as the agreement may provide.

(7) In this section and in section 58 "local authority" means—

(a) the council of a county, borough or district,

(b) a joint planning board constituted under section 2 of the principal Act, and

(c) in relation to a building or land in the Broads, the Broads Authority.

DEFINITIONS
"building": s.91 (but see below).
"joint planning board": s.91(2).
"land": s.91(2).
"listed building": ss.1(5); 91(1).
"local authority": s.91(2).
"the Broads": s.91(2).
"the Principal Act": s.91(1).

GENERAL NOTE

Introduction
This section establishes a power for local authorities to contribute to the upkeep of listed buildings (and other non-listed buildings of special interest) and any garden occupied with them. The authority may provide an outright grant, or a loan (which may be interest free), and they may renounce their right to repayment.

Other powers
Other powers for providing financial assistance for the upkeep of listed buildings are provided by

(1) Historic Buildings and Ancient Monuments Act 1953, ss.3A and 4: these sections confer power on the Commission within England (in Wales, the Secretary of State) to make grants or loans for the upkeep of buildings of "outstanding historic or architectural interest" and their gardens;

(2) Historic Buildings and Ancient Monuments Act 1953, ss.5B and 6: power is conferred on the Commission (or, in Wales, the Secretary of State) to make grants to local authorities to defray their costs in acquiring listed buildings under ss.47 and 54, and also to the National Trust;

(3) Local Government Act 1985, Sched. 2, para. 3(i): power for the Commission to make grants for the repair of any building, within Greater London, which appears to be of historic or architectural interest;

(4) National Heritage Act 1980: the Trustees of the National Heritage Memorial Fund are enabled to make grants or loans towards the acquisition, maintenance or preservation of any land, building, structure, object or group of objects which in their opinion is of outstanding scenic, historic, aesthetic, architectural or scientific interest;

(5) Housing Act 1985: housing improvement grants under this Act may be used for repairs and improvements to historic buildings.

Further powers are conferred in relation to buildings in conservation areas, by ss.77–80 and by the Town and Country Planning (Amendment) Act 1972: see further the notes to s.77. There is a full analysis of sources of financial assistance in Roger Suddards, *Listed Buildings* (2nd ed., 1987), Ch. 10.

Policy advice
Appendix VI of DOE Circular 8/87 offers further advice to authorities on their powers under this section regarding the nature of contributions, buildings outside the area of the contributing authority, gardens, the consent of the Secretary of State and rights of access.

Definition of "building"

For the purposes of subss. (1)(b), and (2) as it applies for the purposes of that subsection, the definition of "building" in the T.C.P.A. 1990 applies with the omission of the words "but does not include any plant or machinery comprised in a building" (s.91(7)).

Gardens

There is no statutory protection for historic gardens, but the Commission is empowered by the Historic Buildings and Monuments Act 1953, ss.8B and 8C (inserted by the National Heritage Act 1983, Sched. 4, para. 10), to accept endowments for the upkeep of gardens, and to compile and maintain a register of gardens appearing to them to be of special historic interest. After including any entry in the register they are required to notify the owner and occupier of the garden, the local planning authorities and the Secretary of State. The Commission has undertaken such a compilation, and has observed (*Historic Buildings and Ancient Monuments*, First Report from the Environment Committee, Session 1986–87; H.C. 146–II, p.208) that

> "The register is being produced to draw attention to important gardens and parks as an essential part of the nation's heritage. Whilst their existence is not widely enough known they are too easily overlooked or undervalued for example in plans for redevelopment or motorway building. The Commission believes that the Register will be helpful to planners, developers, statutory bodies and all those concerned to protect the heritage."

Recovery of grants under s.57

58.—(1) If, during the period of three years beginning with the day on which a grant is made under section 57 towards the repair or maintenance or upkeep of any property ("the grant property"), the grantee disposes of the interest held by him in the property on that day or any part of that interest, by way of sale or exchange or lease for a term of not less than 21 years, the local authority may recover the amount of the grant, or such part of it as they think fit, from the grantee in any court of competent jurisdiction.

(2) If the grantee gives the whole of that interest to any person (whether directly or indirectly, but otherwise than by will) subsection (1) shall have effect as if the donee were the grantee.

(3) If the grantee gives part of that interest to any person (whether directly or indirectly, but otherwise than by will) subsection (1) shall have effect as if any disposal or part disposal of that interest by the donee were a disposal by the grantee.

(4) If any condition imposed on the making of a grant to which this section applies is contravened or not complied with, the grantor may recover the amount of the grant, or such part of it as he thinks fit, from the grantee.

(5) Nothing in this section entitles a grantor to recover amounts in the aggregate exceeding the amount of the grant (for example by virtue of a breach of more than one condition or disposals of several parts of an interest in the grant property).

DEFINITIONS
   "building": s.91.
   "disposal": s.91(2).
   "lease": s.91(2).
   "listed building": ss.1(5); 91(1).
   "local authority": s.91(2).

GENERAL NOTE

Introduction

This section enables local authorities to recover all or part of a grant made under s.57 if the grantee's interest is disposed of by way of sale, exchange or lease, within three years of the grant. In the case of grants made under s.4 of the Historic Buildings and Ancient

Monuments Act 1953 or s.10 of the Town and Country Planning (Amendment) Act 1972, the period during which recovery may be sought is, by comparison, up to ten years.

Liability to repay under this section is personal and enforceable only against the original grantee, except where the grantee's interest is transferred by way of *inter vivos* gift, in which case the donee becomes liable under this section. Gifts by will are not treated as disposals for the purpose of liability to repay. "Disposal" for these purposes is limited to disposal by the grantee by way of sale, exchange or lease (for not less than 21 years). It does not therefore include a mortgage or charge, and disposal by the mortgagee exercising a power of sale conferred by the mortgage does not attract the repayment liability imposed by this section (*Canterbury City Council* v. *Quine* (1988) 55 P. & C.R. 1).

Policy advice

The Secretary of State's advice to authorities acting under this section is contained in para. 11 of Appendix VI to DOE Circular 8/87.

Damage to listed buildings

Acts causing or likely to result in damage to listed buildings

59.—(1) If, with the intention of causing damage to a listed building, any relevant person does or permits the doing of any act which causes or is likely to result in damage to the building, he shall be guilty of an offence and liable on summary conviction to a fine not exceeding level 3 on the standard scale.

(2) A person is a relevant person for the purpose of subsection (1) if apart from that subsection he would be entitled to do or permit the act in question.

(3) Subsection (1) does not apply to an act for the execution—

    (a) of works authorised by planning permission granted or deemed to be granted in pursuance of an application under the principal Act; or

    (b) of works for which listed building consent has been given under this Act.

(4) If a person convicted of an offence under this section fails to take such reasonable steps as may be necessary to prevent any damage or further damage resulting from the offence, he shall be guilty of a further offence and liable on summary conviction to a fine not exceeding £40 for each day on which the failure continues.

DEFINITIONS

    "building": s.91.
    "listed building": ss.1(5); 91(1).
    "listed building consent": ss.8(7); 91(1).
    "planning permission": s.91(2).
    "the Principal Act": s.91(1).
    "relevant person": subs. (2).

GENERAL NOTE

Intentional damage to a listed building

This section creates a separate offence from that of carrying out unauthorised works, under s.9. It extends to intentional "damage", rather than "works", so that it covers any harm that is deliberately caused. The damage need not be such as would affect the character of the building as a building of special architectural or historic interest. Where a building is deliberately damaged by somebody who has no right to damage it, there is criminal liability under s.1(1) of the Criminal Damage Act 1971, which provides:

"(1) A person who without lawful excuse destroys or damages any property belonging to another intending to destroy or damage any such property or being reckless as to whether any such property would be destroyed or damaged shall be guilty of an offence."

But that does not apply where the person involved is the owner of the property and hence is entitled to do, or to permit, the act in question. Therefore the offence created by this section is designed to extend to such a person, signifying the public interest in protecting listed buildings from being damaged even by their owners.

Exceptions

The offence created by this section does not apply to
(1) any acts carried out by or on behalf of the Crown, which is immune from listed building control. However, the section does apply to Crown land to the extent of any interest in it for the time being held otherwise than by or on behalf of the Crown (s.83(1)(b));
(2) any ecclesiastical building which is for the time being used for ecclesiastical purposes (s.60(1));
(3) any building which is a scheduled monument under the Ancient Monuments and Archaeological Areas Act 1979, s.1 (s.61);
(4) unlisted buildings in conservation areas: the section is not extended by s.74(3);
(5) any works authorised by planning permission (though only if granted on an application, thus excluding permitted development rights under the Town and Country Planning General Development Order 1988) or listed building consent (subs. (3)).This exception is broader than that under s.9, which treats works as authorised only if they have listed building consent, are executed in accordance with the consent and if, in the case of demolition, prior notice and a right of access have been given to the Royal Commission.

The further offence

Conviction under subs. (1) carries with it an obligation to take any necessary reasonable steps to prevent any damage or further damage resulting from the offence, and failure to do so is a further offence under subs. (4), which carries a daily penalty.

CHAPTER VI

MISCELLANEOUS AND SUPPLEMENTAL

Exceptions for church buildings and ancient monuments

Exceptions for ecclesiastical buildings and redundant churches

60.—(1) The provisions mentioned in subsection (2) shall not apply to any ecclesiastical building which is for the time being used for ecclesiastical purposes.

(2) Those provisions are sections 3, 4, 7 to 9, 47, 54 and 59.

(3) For the purposes of subsection (1), a building used or available for use by a minister of religion wholly or mainly as a residence from which to perform the duties of his office shall be treated as not being an ecclesiastical building.

(4) For the purposes of sections 7 to 9 a building shall be taken to be used for the time being for ecclesiastical purposes if it would be so used but for the works in question.

(5) The Secretary of State may by order provide for restricting or excluding the operation of subsections (1) to (3) in such cases as may be specified in the order.

(6) An order under this section may—
   (a) make provision for buildings generally, for descriptions of building or for particular buildings;
   (b) make different provision for buildings in different areas, for buildings of different religious faiths or denominations or according to the use made of the building;
   (c) make such provision in relation to a part of a building (including, in particular, an object or structure falling to be treated as part of the building by virtue of section 1(5)) as may be made in relation to a building and make different provision for different parts of the same building;
   (d) make different provision with respect to works of different descriptions or according to the extent of the works;

(e) make such consequential adaptations or modifications of the operation of any other provision of this Act or the principal Act, or of any instrument made under either of those Acts, as appear to the Secretary of State to be appropriate.

(7) Sections 7 to 9 shall not apply to the execution of works for the demolition, in pursuance of a pastoral or redundancy scheme (within the meaning of the Pastoral Measure 1983), of a redundant building (within the meaning of that Measure) or a part of such a building.

DEFINITIONS
"building": s.91.
"the Principal Act": s.91(1).
"use": s.91(2).

GENERAL NOTE

Introduction
The exemption of ecclesiastical buildings from listed building control dates back to the Ancient Monuments Consolidation and Amendment Act 1913, s.22, which defined a "monument" as including "any structure or erection, other than an ecclesiastical building which is for the time being used for ecclesiastical purposes". The formula remains the same today, notwithstanding the great growth since 1913 in the scope of listed building control powers, the difficulties in applying the formula to buildings other than those of the Church of England, and the perennial controversy as to whether the churches should be entitled to such special exemption.

The exemption operates at two levels: first, although any ecclesiastical building may be listed, it is not subject to any of the controls under this Act so long as it remains in ecclesiastical use. It is not, however, exempt from the requirement under the T.C.P.A. 1990 to obtain planning permission for works constituting development. Second, under subs. (7) (previously the Redundant Churches and Other Religious Buildings Act 1969, s.2), listed building control does not extend to the execution of works for the demolition of a redundant building of the Church of England in pursuance of a pastoral or redundancy scheme under the Pastoral Measure 1983.

These exemptions extend also to conservation area control, but are conferred separately for those purposes by s.75(1)(b) and (7).

Further reference
For detailed analysis of the history and scope of the ecclesiastical exemption, and the current debate, see
Peter Boydell Q.C., "Special situations: ecclesiastical buildings and ancient monuments", in *A future for old Buildings?* JPEL Occasional Paper, 1977.
Charles Mynors, *Listed Buildings and Conservation Areas* (Longman, 1988) Ch. 13; and "'Render unto Caesar . . .' The ecclesiastical exemption from listed building control" [1985] J.P.L.
J.D.C. Harte, "Church *v.* State—The faculty jurisdiction; a case for conservation" [1985] J.P.L. 611 (Pt. I); 690 (Pt. II).
Roger Suddards, *Listed Buildings* (2nd ed., 1988), paras. 5.28–5.32.

Exclusion of rectories and vicarages
A building used or available for use by a minister of religion wholly or mainly as a residence from which to perform the duties of his office is not to be treated as an ecclesiastical building (s.60(3)). This proviso was first introduced by the Civic Amenities Act 1967, s.9, in order to reverse the ruling in *Phillips* v. *Minister of Housing and Local Government* [1965] 1 Q.B. 156 that a rectory was an ecclesiastical building.

"Used for the time being for ecclesiastical purposes"
The building is to be taken to be used for the time being for ecclesiastical purposes if it would so be used but for the works in question (s.60(4)), but the exemption is nonetheless effectively limited to works falling short of total demolition, because the relevant time for the purposes of the formula "for the time being used" is the time of the commission of the offence under s.9 and a building is not being used for ecclesiastical purposes when it is being demolished (*Att.-Gen., ex rel. Bedfordshire County Council* v. *Howard United Reform Church Trustees, Bedford* [1976] A.C. 363). Thus listed building consent is necessary for the

total demolition of an ecclesiastical building, except when it is undertaken in pursuance of a pastoral or redundancy scheme (subs. (7), and see further below).

Churches other than the established church

The exception is not limited to the Church of England, but how far it extends to non-Christian sects remains an open question: see, *e.g. Phillips* v. *Minister of Housing and Local Government* [1965] 1 Q.B. 156, at 162 *per* Roskill J. In *Att.-Gen., ex rel. Bedfordshire County Council* v. *Howard United Reform Church Trustees, Bedford* [1976] A.C. 363 the House of Lords ruled that it extended to a Congregational church, but Lord Cross at 376 observed:

"The argument as to what buildings could and what buildings could not properly be described as 'ecclesiastical buildings' ranged over a wide field and raised many questions to which, as I see it, it is unnecessary and would be unwise for us to give answers. For example, is the expression confined to Christian religious buildings or does it extend to synagogues and mosques? To what extent is the ownership of the building a relevant consideration? Does it make any difference whether the building was built as a church or not? Must one exclude all considerations of user in deciding whether or not the building is an ecclesiastical building?"

In the Court of Appeal, Lord Denning M.R. had thought it sufficient that "the building must be owned by the ecclesiastical authorities—as freehold or leasehold—and it must have some other ecclesiastical attribute marking it out as ecclesiastical" [1974] 3 All E.R. 273 at 276. Stephenson L.J. at 278 said:

"In my judgment an ecclesiastical building is a building owned by a Christian church and built or used mainly for religious worship or for what is necessarily ancillary to it. The legal ownership may be in any recognised authority of the church, the beneficial ownership must be in its members or congregation. The word 'ecclesia', whether written in Greek or Latin letters, has for centuries meant either a Christian congregation or a place where a Christian congregation assembles. 'Ecclesiastical' means belonging to the one or the other. Since the Reformation it applies to the Church of England and to the different Christian churches which have come into existence in this country".

Note, however, the narrow definition of "ecclesiastical property" adopted for other purposes in s.86(4), which effectively confines it to the Anglican church, as land belonging to an ecclesiastical benefice or a church "subject to the jurisdiction of a bishop of any diocese".

Reform: the 1986 agreement

The scope of the exemption from listed building controls of ecclesiastical buildings has provoked much controversy, particularly in light of the increasing number of redundant churches which are listed buildings. After some years of negotiations, agreement was reached in 1986 between the Government and representatives of the Church of England and other religious organisations, through the Churches Main Committee, to extend listed building control to include the partial demolition of non-Anglican buildings. Listed building consent is required already to total demolition, since the building can no longer at that stage be regarded as still being in ecclesiastical use; and demolition of churches of the Church of England is governed by the special requirements of the Pastoral Measure 1983. The terms of the agreement were announced in the House of Lords in 1986 during the Committee stage of the Housing and Planning Bill (*Hansard*, H.L. Vol. 480, cols. 608–611; October 13, 1986) and provisions (now subss. (5) and (6)) were inserted into the Bill at the Report stage to give statutory effect where necessary to the agreement.

Subss. (5) and (6) allow the Secretary of State by order to restrict the scope of the ecclesiastical exemption, and to discriminate in doing so between different types of building and between different areas and the buildings of different denominations. The intention is that consent should be required for the partial demolition of a church if it would materially affect the architectural or historic interest of the building, such as the removal of a spire, tower or cupola, or if the works were otherwise to affect the interest of the building to such an extent that its value as a listed building, or the contribution an unlisted church makes to a conservation area, is brought into question. There is to be consultation as to how the necessary order will need to be drafted to achieve these ends (*Hansard*, H.L. Vol. 481, col. 187; October 22, 1986).

Treatment of redundant churches under the Pastoral Measure

The Minister also announced in the course of his statement at the Committee stage in the Lords that the Church of England had further agreed to accept greater consultation with the Department of the Environment in relation to historic churches. In particular, when it is proposed to demolish a listed church (or a church in a conservation area), wholly or partly, under the Pastoral Measure 1983, the Church Commissioners have agreed always to ask the Secretary of State for the Environment whether he wishes to hold a non-statutory local public inquiry into the proposal if there are reasoned objections to it from the Commission, the Advisory Board for Redundant Churches, the local planning authority or a national amenity society. The Church Commissioners have undertaken to accept a recommendation from the Secretary of State, following such an inquiry, that the church is of sufficient importance to be vested in the Redundant Churches Fund, or, in cases where the recommendation was not that the building should go to the Fund, to make further efforts to find an alternative use and to engage in further consultation with the Secretary of State before using the Pastoral Measure powers to demolish.

Under s.28 of the Pastoral Measure 1983 a pastoral scheme may make a declaration of redundancy in respect of a church (or part of a church) which is no longer required as a parish church or chapel of ease or will cease to be so required as a result of any provision of the scheme. Provision may then be made, either in the pastoral scheme itself or in a redundancy scheme made under Pt. III of the Measure, for "the use, the care and maintenance, the vesting in the diocesan board of finance or the demolition of the church or part of a church to which the declaration relates" (s.28(1)). A redundancy scheme may provide for appropriation of the building to any other use, for its vesting in the Redundant Churches Fund for preservation, for remaining vested in the diocesan board of finance for other purposes, or demolition. The arrangements are reviewed in *The Care of Redundant Churches*, Report by Richard Wilding C.B. (HMSO 1990).

Faculty jurisdiction of the Church of England
One justification for the retention of the ecclesiastical exemption for churches of the Church of England lies in the existence of a separate authorisation procedure through ecclesiastical law for works and other changes affecting a church. The ecclesiastical courts have come to insist that the power to grant a faculty should be exercised, in relation to listed churches, on similar principles to those applicable in listed building control. In *St. Mary's, Banbury, Re* [1986] Fam. 24 the Chancellor (Mr P. Boydell, Q.C.) observed:
    "This is a Grade A [Grade I] listed building; and any proposal to alter the structure of such a building must be approached with the same care and be subject to the same detailed consideration as would be necessary if churches were to lose their ecclesiastical immunity and if, therefore, this were an application for listed building consent pursuant to the provisions of the [Planning (Listed Buildings and Conservation Areas) Act 1990]."
On appeal, that statement was endorsed, although the Consistory Court then went so far as to insist that a faculty should only be granted where there was a clearly proved necessity for it ([1987] 1 All E.R. 247). Subsequently, that dictum has been overridden. In *St. Stephen's Walbrook, Re* [1987] 2 All E.R. 578 the Court of Ecclesiastical Causes Reserved ruled that the fact that an ecclesiastical building is listed is a relevant consideration in considering whether to grant a faculty permitting alterations to it, but there is no rule that a faculty can only be granted in cases of clearly proved necessity. The Chancellor must have:
    "full regard to all the circumstances including the interest of the community as a whole in the special architectural or historic attributes of the building and to the desirability of preserving the building and any features of special architectural or historic interest which it possesses" (*per* Sir Ralph Gibson at 585–600).
Sir Anthony Lloyd similarly remarked (at 604) that:
    "Listed building consent is given every day in ordinary cases which fall far short of 'clearly proved necessity'. I see no reason why a different standard should prevail in the case of ecclesiastical buildings."
For a detailed discussion of faculty jurisdiction see G.H. Newsom, *Faculty Jurisdiction of the Church of England* (Sweet and Maxwell, 1988).
New powers were introduced by the Care of Cathedrals Measure 1990 to ensure that no works which would materially affect a cathedral church should be carried out without prior approval by the Cathedrals Fabric Commission.

Exceptions for ancient monuments etc

61.—(1) The provisions mentioned in subsection (2) shall not apply to any building for the time being included in the schedule of monuments compiled and maintained under section 1 of the Ancient Monuments and Archaeological Areas Act 1979.
    (2) Those provisions are sections 3, 4, 7 to 9, 47, 54 and 59.

DEFINITIONS
    "building": s.91.

GENERAL NOTE

Scheduled monuments
    A building may be both a listed building under this Act, and a scheduled monument under the Ancient Monuments and Archaeological Areas Act 1979. In such a case, the provisions of the 1979 Act take precedence. Under s.2 of that Act, it is an offence, except in accordance with a grant of scheduled monument consent, to carry out:
    (a) any works resulting in the demolition or destruction of or any damage to a scheduled monument;
    (b) any works for the purpose of removing or repairing a scheduled monument or any part of it or of making any alterations or additions thereto; and
    (c) any flooding or tipping operations on land in, on or under which there is a scheduled monument.
    The section provides, however, that it is a defence for the accused to prove that he took all reasonable precautions and exercised all due diligence to avoid or prevent damage to the monument; and that (except under (b) above) it is a defence for the accused to prove that he did not know and had no reason to believe that the monument was within the area affected by the works or (as the case may be) that it was a scheduled monument.

Distinction between listing and scheduling
    There are no absolute distinctions between a scheduled monument and a listed building, but certain characteristics were noted in the Department of the Environment's evidence in 1986 to the House of Commons Environment Committee (*Historic Buildings and Ancient Monuments*; Session 1985–86, H.C. 146–II, p.57):
    "Scheduled monuments are few in number (about 13,000) and tend to be older. Their importance usually lies in their historical or archaeological value. As ruins or remains of the past they are not typically lived in. Their variety is wide, from ancient burial mounds and Saxon field systems to relatively modern industrial archaeology. Any works to a scheduled monument require consent from the Secretary of State.
    "Listed buildings are more numerous (over 450,000), are between 50 and 500 years old and are most likely to consist of a dwelling-house, shop, factory or public building in use. Their importance nearly always derives from their architecture, any alteration to which requires a consent from the local planning authority (though the Secretary of State can become involved in particularly controversial development proposals)."

Validity of instruments, decisions and proceedings

Validity of certain orders and decisions

    62.—(1) Except as provided by section 63, the validity of—
    (a) any order under section 23 or 26 (whether before or after it has been confirmed); or
    (b) any such decision by the Secretary of State as is mentioned in subsection (2),
shall not be questioned in any legal proceedings whatsoever.
    (2) Those decisions are—
    (a) any decision on an application referred to the Secretary of State under section 12 or on an appeal under section 20;
    (b) any decision to confirm or not to confirm a listed building purchase notice including—
        (i) any decision not to confirm such a notice in respect of part of the land to which it relates, and
        (ii) any decision to grant any consent, or give any direction, in lieu of confirming such a notice, either wholly or in part;
    (c) any decision to grant listed building consent under paragraph (a) of section 41(6) or to discharge a condition or limitation under paragraph (b) of that section.
    (3) Nothing in this section shall affect the exercise of any jurisdiction of any court in respect of any refusal or failure on the part of the Secretary of State to take any such decision as is mentioned in subsection (2).

DEFINITIONS
"building": s.91.
"land": s.91(2).
"listed building": ss.1(5); 91(1).
"listed building consent": ss.8(7); 91(1).
"listed building purchase notice": ss.32(1); 91(1).

GENERAL NOTE

Introduction
This section and the following section establish a system of protection for certain categories of decisions taken under this Act. Their validity can be challenged only by application to the High Court by a person aggrieved within six weeks from the decision (s.63), and may otherwise not be questioned in any legal proceedings whatsoever (subs. (1)). Similar provision is made by ss.64 and 65 for listed building enforcement notices, although there the right is to appeal to the High Court within 28 days of the Secretary of State's decision on the notice. All four sections are directly parallel to ss.284, 285, 287–289 of the T.C.P.A. 1990. Prior to the 1990 consolidation the one set of provisions governed all relevant decisions.

Decisions and actions within this section
This section is extended with modifications to conservation area consent, by s.74(3). The following decisions and actions are therefore protected from legal challenge (subject to s.63) by this section:
   (1) revocation orders and modification orders of listed building consent (or conservation area consent), whether made by the local planning authority (s.23) or the Secretary of State (s.26), and whether before or after confirmation;
   (2) any decision by the Secretary of State on an application for listed building consent (or conservation area consent) referred to him under s.12, or taken by him on appeal under s.20. The protection of decisions taken on referred applications and appeals appears not to cover interlocutory decisions, for which judicial review may lie instead: see, *e.g. Co-operative Retail Services* v. *Secretary of State for the Environment and City of Wakefield Metropolitan District Council and William Morrison Supermarkets* [1980] 1 W.L.R. 271; *Solihull Metropolitan Borough Council* v. *Secretary of State for the Environment and Tesco Stores* [1987] J.P.L. 208;
   (3) any decision by the Secretary of State on a listed building (or conservation area) enforcement notice, including a decision to confirm (in whole or part) or not to confirm (including a decision to grant any consent or give any direction in lieu of confirmation);
   (4) a decision to grant listed building consent or conservation area consent or discharge a condition or limitation under s.41(6) (listed building enforcement notice appeals and conservation area consent enforcement appeals). The validity of the enforcement notice itself is protected by ss.64 and 65.

Decisions and actions not protected by this section
   (1) the section only protects decisions and actions taken by the Secretary of State, and does not extend to the final actions of a local planning authority (as opposed to orders made by them and confirmed by the Secretary of State). Such actions, including decisions on applications for listed building consent and conservation area consent, may be challenged in the ordinary way by application for judicial review (see, *e.g. R.* v. *North Hertfordshire District Council*, ex p. *Sullivan* [1981] J.P.L. 752);
   (2) listed building enforcement notices, whose validity is protected by ss.64 and 65;
   (3) subs. (3) preserves the jurisdiction of the High Court to grant mandamus against the Secretary of State for refusal or failure to take any decision;
   (4) decisions by the Secretary of State under s.55 (expenses recoverable from owner in respect of urgent works carried out on an unoccupied listed building), for which judicial review will therefore lie instead (see, *e.g. R.* v. *Secretary of State for the Environment*, ex p. *Hampshire County Council* (1982) 44 P. & C.R. 343);
   (5) compulsory purchase orders under s.47: the validity of these orders is protected instead by the Acquisition of Land Act 1981, ss.23–25.

Effect of ouster clause
The effect of the ouster provision is that s.63 provides the only opportunity for challenge to a decision defined in this section, and its validity is otherwise unchallengeable, even if it would have been a nullity had it been challenged in the appropriate manner (*R.* v. *Secretary of State for the Environment*, ex p. *Ostler* [1977] Q.B. 122) and even although the challenging

party did not know, and could not reasonably have known, of the decision in time to challenge it under s.63 (*R.* v. *Secretary of State for the Environment*, ex p. *Kent* [1988] 3 P.L.R. 17; [1990] 1 P.L.R. 17).

Other ouster clauses
By virtue of Sched. 4, para. 6, the validity of any consent or determination given by a local planning authority on an application for listed building consent (or conservation area consent) may not be called into question in any proceedings on the ground that it should have been given by some other local planning authority.

Proceedings for questioning validity of other decisions and directions

63.—(1) If any person is aggrieved by any such order or decision as is mentioned in section 62(1) and wishes to question its validity on the grounds—
  (a) that it is not within the powers of this Act, or
  (b) that any of the relevant requirements have not been complied within relation to it,
he may make an application to the High Court under this section.

(2) Without prejudice to subsection (1), if the authority directly concerned with any such order or decision wish to question its validity on any of those grounds, the authority may make an application to the High Court under this section.

(3) An application under this section must be made within six weeks from the date on which the order is confirmed (or, in the case of an order under section 23 which takes effect under section 25 without confirmation, the date on which it takes effect) or, as the case may be, the date on which the action is taken.

(4) On any application under this section the High Court—
  (a) may by interim order suspend the operation of the order or decision, the validity of which is questioned by the application, until the final determination of the proceedings; and
  (b) if satisfied—
      (i) that the order or decision is not within the powers of this Act, or
      (ii) that the interests of the applicant have been substantially prejudiced by a failure to comply with any of the relevant requirements in relation to it,
may quash that order or decision.

(5) References in this section to the confirmation of an order include the confirmation of an order subject to modifications.

(6) In this section "the relevant requirements", in relation to any order or decision, means any requirements of this Act or of the Tribunals and Inquiries Act 1971 or of any order, regulations or rules made under either of those Acts which are applicable to that order or decision.

(7) For the purposes of subsection (2) the authority directly concerned with an order or decision is—
  (a) in relation to any such decision as is mentioned in section 62(2)(b)—
      (i) the council on whom the listed building purchase notice was served, and
      (ii) in a case where the Secretary of State has modified the notice wholly or in part by substituting another local authority or statutory undertakers for that council, also that authority or those statutory undertakers; and
  (b) otherwise, the authority who—
      (i) made the order or decision to which the proceedings in question relate, or
      (ii) referred the matter to the Secretary of State, or

(iii) if the order was made by him, are the authority named in it.

DEFINITIONS
"building": s.91.
"listed building": ss.1(5); 91(1).
"listed building purchase notice": ss.32(1); 91(1).
"local authority": s.91(2).
"relevant requirements": subs. (6).
"statutory undertaker": s.91(3).

GENERAL NOTE

Introduction
This section creates a right to challenge the validity of certain decisions of the Secretary of State. By virtue of s.62, it is the only way in which their validity may be challenged. For an analysis of the grounds of application, the scope of the court's jurisiction, and proceedings by application for judicial review, see the notes to the parallel provision of the T.C.P.A. 1990, s.288.

Standing
An application may be made by any "person aggrieved" (as to which see the notes to s.287 of the T.C.P.A. 1990), and by the authority directly concerned with the order or decision (subs. (2)), who would now in any event be normally regarded as a person aggrieved for these purposes (*Cook* v. *Southend Borough Council* [1990] 2 W.L.R. 61).

Procedure
An application to the High Court under this section must be by originating motion in the Queen's Bench Division (Rules of the Supreme Court 1965, Ord. 94). The notice of motion must state the grounds of the application, and the notice of motion must be served on the authority directly concerned with the decision, order or action (or, if the authority is the applicant, on every person who would, if he were aggrieved by the decision, be entitled to apply to the High Court under this section (Ord. 94, r. 2(2)). Jurisdiction is exercisable by a single judge of the Queen's Bench Division (Ord. 94, r. 1(1)).

Validity of listed building enforcement notices

64. The validity of a listed building enforcement notice shall not, except by way of an appeal under section 39, be questioned in any proceedings whatsoever on any of the grounds on which such an appeal may be brought.

DEFINITIONS
"building": s.91.
"listed building": ss.1(5); 91(1).
"listed building enforcement notice": ss.38(1); 91(1).

GENERAL NOTE

Introduction
This section protects listed building enforcement notices from legal challenge, conferring upon them a status of deemed validity. The only route through which a challenge may be made is by appeal to the Secretary of State under s.39. However, the protection conferred by this section extends only to challenge on any of the grounds on which such an appeal may be made; there is a separate right of appeal to the High Court on a point of law under s.65 against any determination by the Secretary of State on a listed building enforcement appeal.
    Although the section runs parallel with s.285 of the T.C.P.A. 1990 (and prior to the 1990 consolidation the two were combined in one section) it does not contain the protection given by s.285(2) to a person who held an interest in the land before an enforcement notice was served, but did not have a copy served on him, and who did not and could not reasonably have known that the notice had been issued. Where such a person can satisfy the court that his interests have been substantially prejudiced, the prohibition against challenge does not apply. The reason is no doubt that under s.43 of this Act, criminal liability attaches only to someone on whom a copy of the notice was served.

The grounds on which an appeal may be made

An appeal may be made to the Secretary of State under s.39 on any of the following grounds:

(a) that the building is not of special architectural or historic interest;

(b) that the matters alleged to constitute a contravention of s.9(1) or (2) do not involve such a contravention;

(c) that the contravention of that section alleged in the notice has not taken place;

(d) that works to the building were urgently necessary in the interests of safety or health or for the preservation of the building, that it was not practicable to secure safety or health or, as the case may be, the preservation of the building by works of repair or works for affording temporary support or shelter, and that the works carried out were limited to the minimum measures immediately necessary;

(e) that listed building consent ought to be granted for the works, or that any relevant condition of such consent which has been granted ought to be discharged, or different conditions substituted;

(f) that copies of the notice were not served as required by s.38(4);

(g) except in relation to such a requirement as is mentioned in s.38(2)(b) or (c), that the requirements of the notice exceed what is necessary for restoring the building to its condition before the works were carried out;

(h) that the period specified in the notice as the period within which any step required by the notice is to be taken falls short of what should reasonably be allowed;

(i) that the steps required by the notice for the purpose of restoring the character of the building to its former state would not serve that purpose;

(j) that the steps required to be taken by virtue of s.38(2)(b) exceed what is necessary to alleviate the effect of the works executed to the building;

(k) that the steps required to be taken by virtue of section 38(2)(c) exceed what is necessary to bring the building to the state in which it would have been if the terms and conditions of the listed building consent had been complied with.

Those grounds are not exhaustive of possible grounds of legal challenge to the validity of a notice. It may be asserted, for example, that the authority had no power to issue the notice, or that it was not properly authorised by them, or that it was improperly issued, or that the notice is a nullity. In such cases a challenge by application for judicial review is not precluded by this section (see, *e.g. Davy* v. *Spelthorne Borough Council* [1984] A.C. 262 at 272, *per* Lord Fraser).

Moreover, the section does not prevent an application being made for judicial review (for example, for a declaration as to the lawfulness of works that have been carried out, or as to the interpretation of a listed building consent or the validity of its conditions), provided it is done before an enforcement notice is issued; it may be appropriate to stay proceedings on that application if a notice is subsequently issued (see, *e.g. Square Meals Frozen Foods* v. *Dunstable Corporation* [1974] 1 W.L.R. 59).

Appeals to High Court relating to listed building enforcement notices

65.—(1) Where the Secretary of State gives a decision in proceedings on an appeal under section 39 against a listed building enforcement notice, the appellant or the local planning authority or any other person having an interest in the land to which the notice relates may, according as rules of court may provide, either appeal to the High Court against the decision on a point of law or require the Secretary of State to state and sign a case for the opinion of the High Court.

(2) At any stage of the proceedings on any such appeal, the Secretary of State may state any question of law arising in the course of the proceedings in the form of a special case for the decision of the High Court.

(3) A decision of the High Court on a case stated by virtue of subsection (2) shall be deemed to be a judgment of the court within the meaning of section 16 of the Supreme Court Act 1981 (jurisdiction of the Court of Appeal to hear and determine appeals from any judgment of the High Court).

(4) In relation to any proceedings in the High Court or the Court of Appeal brought by virtue of this section the power to make rules of court shall include power to make rules—

    (a) prescribing the powers of the High Court or the Court of Appeal with respect to the remitting of the matter with the opinion or direction of the court for re-hearing and determination by the Secretary of State; and

    (b) providing for the Secretary of State, either generally or in such circumstances as may be prescribed by the rules, to be treated as a party to any such proceedings and to be entitled to appear and to be heard accordingly.

    (5) No appeal to the Court of Appeal shall be brought by virtue of this section except with the leave of the High Court or the Court of Appeal.

    (6) In this section "decision" includes a direction or order, and references to the giving of a decision shall be construed accordingly.

    (7) In the case of a listed building enforcement notice issued by the Commission subsection (1) shall apply as if the reference to the local planning authority were a reference to the Commission.

DEFINITIONS
    "building": s.91.
    "decision": subs. (6).
    "functions": s.91(2).
    "land": s.91(2).
    "listed building": ss.1(5); 91(1).
    "listed building enforcement notice": ss.38(1); 91(1).
    "local planning authority": s.81.
    "prescribed": s.91(1).
    "the Commission": s.91(1).

GENERAL NOTE

Introduction
    This section provides a right of appeal to the High Court against a decision of the Secretary of State on a listed building enforcement appeal. The validity of a notice can be questioned only by appeal to the Secretary of State, and hence be reviewed in the High Court only by means of further appeal under this section, on any of the grounds of appeal in s.39.

Appeals procedure
    Appeal to the High Court is by way of originating motion, under the Rules of the Supreme Court, Ord. 94, r. 12. Notice of the motion must be served, and the appeal entered, within 28 days after the date of the decision against which it is brought. Although Ord. 55, r. 4(4) requires that period to be calculated from the time that notice of the decision was given to the appellant, the Divisional Court in *Ringroad Investments and Courtburn* v. *Secretary of State for the Environment* (1979) 40 P. & C.R. 99 felt obliged by earlier authority to hold that the relevant date was the date on which the decision letter was posted, not when it was received. The Court of Appeal in *Griffiths* v. *Secretary of State for the Environment* [1983] 2 A.C. 51, expressed the view *obiter* that the latter date more obviously satisfied the requirements of r. 4(4). There is, in any event, power for the court under Ord. 3, r. 5, to extend the time for appeal but in *Smith* v. *Secretary of State for the Environment, The Times*, July 6, 1987, the Court of Appeal insisted that it is not a sufficient explanation of delay when seeking an extension of time in relation to an appeal under these provisions merely to set out the chronology of events which had resulted in delay without giving any reasons which would tend to excuse it. The time limits must normally be complied with, and Ord. 3, r. 5 did not provide an easy escape route for practitioners who did not conduct their clients' cases with reasonable expedition.
    Jurisdiction is now vested in a single judge unless the court otherwise directs (Ord. 94, r. 12(2A)); and further appeal to the Court of Appeal requires the leave of either the Divisional Court or the Court of Appeal (subs. (4)).

Appeal by case stated
    Although subs. (1) allows a party to require the Secretary of State to state and sign a case for the opinion of the High Court, it is subject to rules of the High Court. No rules have ever been made, and the procedure is therefore not available (*Hoser* v. *Minister of Housing and Local Government* [1963] Ch. 428).

Evidence
Although power is conferred by Ord. 55, r.7(2) for the court to receive further evidence on questions of fact, it does not allow the court to conduct a rehearing of the primary facts since the appeal is limited to a point of law (*Green* v. *Minister of Housing and Local Government* [1967] 2 Q.B. 606). In *Forkhurst* v. *Secretary of State for the Environment and Brentwood District Council* (1982) 46 P. & C.R. 89 the court held that where an appeal under this section was directed to persuading the court that it ought to quash the inspector's decision on the ground that no reasonable inspector could have so decided the appeal, and there was foundation for the claim in the appellant's affidavits, the court should look at the uncontroverted evidence as to the material that had actually been before the inspector. Moreover, Ord. 55, r. 7(4) is applicable to appeals under this section, but Hodgson J. suggested that a sensible construction to place upon it was that the duty to apply to the inspector for a signed copy of any note made by him of the evidence only applied where the appellant wished to place before the court all the material that had been before the inspector, either (a) because the decision letter did not itself contain a record of the evidence or (b) because a ground of appeal was that the inspector's record was so inaccurate that the appellant was entitled to supplement his record. A similar approach was taken by Woolf J. in *Weitz (J.R.), F.D.S. (Market Research)* v. *Secretary of State for the Environment and Camden London Borough Council* (1983) 43 P. & C.R. 150, when he ruled that the ordinary principle should continue to be that it was inappropriate to apply Ord. 55, r. 7(4) in an ordinary case, and that it was not necessary for the inspector's note to be made available to the appellant. There might be exceptional cases, but he did not propose to deal with them in the present judgment.

Powers of the court
The power of the court where an appeal is made out is limited to remitting the matter to the Secretary of State with the opinion of the court, for rehearing and redetermination by him (Ord. 94, r. 12(5)). The general power under Ord. 55, r. 7(5) for the court to give any decision which ought to have been given by the Secretary of State is expressly excluded by Ord. 94, r. 12(6). There is thus no power to quash a decision or to set aside an enforcement notice, and the intention is that the Secretary of State should be able to correct any error provided the enforcement notice itself is not invalid. There is no burden upon the appellant to establish that he has been substantially prejudiced, and the view has been expressed that the matter should be remitted to the Secretary of State if there was any possibility that he was influenced by an error, however slight (*LTSS Print and Supply Services* v. *Hackney London Borough Council* [1978] Q.B. 663, 681–2, C.A.).

But the right of appeal under this section is an appeal against a decision of the Secretary of State, and the court ought not therefore to use the procedure as a vehicle for testing the validity of reasoning of the inspector or Secretary of State when the points in issue did not affect their decision (see, *e.g. Miah* v. *Secretary of State for the Environment and Hillingdon Borough Council* [1986] J.P.L. 756, where, however, the court was prepared to indicate its view of the proper interpretation of a planning condition which the inspector had upheld).

Given the limited powers of the court, there is no power to make any finding of facts, and therefore allegations which were neither put to nor determined by the Secretary of State or his inspector cannot be raised on an appeal under this section (*London Parachuting* v. *Secretary of State for the Environment* [1986] J.P.L. 428).

Special considerations affecting planning functions

General duty as respects listed buildings in exercise of planning functions

66.—(1) In considering whether to grant planning permission for development which affects a listed building or its setting, the local planning authority or, as the case may be, the Secretary of State shall have special regard to the desirability of preserving the building or its setting or any features of special architectural or historic interest which it possesses.

(2) Without prejudice to section 72, in the exercise of the powers of appropriation, disposal and development (including redevelopment) conferred by the provisions of sections 232, 233 and 235(1) of the principal Act, a local authority shall have regard to the desirability of preserving features of special architectural or historic interest, and in particular, listed buildings.

(3) The reference in subsection (2) to a local authority includes a reference to a joint planning board and a board reconstituted in pursuance of Schedule 17 to the Local Government Act 1972.

DEFINITIONS
"building": s.91.
"development": s.91(2).
"disposal": s.91(2).
"functions": s.91(2).
"joint planning board": s.91(2).
"listed building": ss.1(5); 91(1).
"local authority": s.91(2); subs. (3).
"local planning authority": s.81.
"planning permission": s.91(2).

ALLOCATION OF FUNCTIONS
The functions of a local planning authority under subs. (1) are exercisable solely by:—
Greater London: the London borough council (T.C.P.A. 1990, s.1(2).
Metropolitan areas: the metropolitan district council (T.C.P.A. 1990, s.1(2)).
Non-metropolitan areas: the district planning authority and the county planning authority have the functions concurrently (T.C.P.A. 1990, s.1(3)).
National Parks (outside a metropolitan county): the county planning authority (T.C.P.A. 1990, s.4) or joint planning board in areas where one has been established as county planning authority (T.C.P.A. 1990, s.2).
Norfolk and Suffolk Broads: the Broads Authority (Sched. 4, para. 5).
Urban development areas: the urban development corporation where an order has been made under the Local Government, Planning and Land Act 1980, s.149(1), transferring the function to the corporation (T.C.P.A. 1990, s.7(1)): for a list of current orders see the notes to s.81.
Housing action trust areas: the housing action trust has the functions under this section to the exclusion of any other authority (other than the Secretary of State) where an order has been made under the Housing Act 1988, s.67(3) transferring the function (as a function within s.67(3A), as substituted by the Planning (Consequential Provisions) Act 1990, Sched. 2, para. 79(3)) to the trust (T.C.P.A. 1990, s.8(2)): see the notes to s.81.
Enterprise zones: the enterprise zone authority, where so provided by order under the Local Government, Planning and Land Act 1980, Sched. 32, para. 5.
The reference to a local authority under subs. (2) includes a joint planning board (subs. (3)).

GENERAL NOTE

Introduction
Listed building control cannot properly operate in isolation, and the purpose of this section is to integrate these controls with general planning control under the T.C.P.A. 1990. The section requires local planning authorities, when determining planning applications, to have special regard to the desirability of preserving
  (1) the building itself: listed building consent will also normally be required for works which would affect the character of the building, but the present duty applies even where those works would be immune from listed building control;
  (2) the building's setting: this component of the duty is reinforced by s.67, which requires the authority to give publicity to any planning application which would, in their opinion, affect the setting of a listed building;
  (3) any special features it possesses: most features of special interest will also be protected by listed building control (see further the notes to s.1).
Subs. (2) also requires authorities to "have regard" (not "special" regard) to the desirability of preserving features of special architectural or historic interest, and in particular listed buildings, when appropriating, disposing of or developing land under ss.232, 233 and 235 of the T.C.P.A. 1990.

Parallel duty in determining applications for listed building consent
Local planning authorities are under an identical duty by virtue of s.16(2), when determining applications for listed building consent.

Special cases

The duty under subs. (1)

(1) does not extend to conservation areas: although nominally extendable by virtue of s.74(3), it is excluded by the Town and Country Planning (Listed Buildings and Conservation Areas) Regulations 1990, Sched. 3. There is, however, a separate duty under s.72, when exercising any powers under the Planning Acts with respect to any buildings or land in a conservation area, to pay special attention to the desirability of preserving or enhancing the character or appearance of the area;

(2) does apply where the listed building in question is an ecclesiastical building, or a scheduled monument: it is not excluded by s.60 and 61 respectively;

(3) does apply to Crown land, at least to the extent of any interest held in it for the time being otherwise than by the Crown (s.83(1)(b)). Where the duty is relevant to the determination of a planning application relating to development affecting the setting of a listed building owned by the Crown, then whether there is a private interest in that building must be irrelevant to the performance of the duty.

The nature of the duty

The duty to have "special regard" is not simply a meaningless formality, and where it can be shown that an authority have failed to pay any attention at all to the desirability of preservation their decision may be set aside by the court. The corresponding duty in relation to conservation areas, under s.72, has generated a volume of recent litigation: see further the notes to that section.

"Enabling development"

The courts have indicated that it may be a material consideration in determining an application for planning permission that, even although there are policy objections to it, to allow the development to proceed will help to achieve some other planning objective, such as the preservation of a listed building. For a practical application of this doctrine (which derives from cases such as *R.* v. *Westminster City Council*, ex p. *Monahan* [1989] 3 W.L.R. 408 and *Northumberland County Council* v. *Secretary of State for the Environment* [1989] J.P.L. 700, analysed in the notes to s.70 of the T.C.P.A.), see the ministerial decisions reported at [1990] J.P.L. 453 (*Broadlands House*) and [1990] 5 P.A.D. 116 (*Malvern Hills District Council* v. *Period & County Homes*).

Operations of telecommunications operators

Telecommunications operators have permitted development rights under the Town and Country Planning General Development Order 1988, Sched. 2, Pt. 24, but under a condition imposed by Sched. 4 of the Licence (HMSO 1984) granted by the Secretary of State for Trade and Industry to British Telecommunications under s.7 of the Telecommunications Act 1984, British Telecommunications are required to give written notice to the local planning authority (except in the case of emergency works) before installing lines, poles or other telecommunication apparatus in proximity to any Grade I listed building. Where the installation would detrimentally affect the character and appearance of the building and the planning authority indicates within 28 days of the giving of the notice that the installation should not take place, British Telecommunication may instal the apparatus only if the Secretary of State so directs in writing, or with the agreement of the planning authority.

Similar conditions have been imposed in the licences granted to other telecommunications operators, though with some variations according to the nature of the undertaking involved, and the outcome of pre-licensing consultations with local planning and highway authorities. Licence conditions relating to planning and environmental issues are included when the licence concerned applies to the licensee the powers of the telecommunication code (contained in Sched. 2 to the Telecommunications Act 1984). These powers have to date been applied to British Telecom, Mercury Communications, Kingston upon Hull City Council, the water authorities and 10 local broadband operators. They have also been applied to the cellular radiophone operators, Telecom Securicor Cellular Radio and Racal Vodaphone, with certain exceptions.

Arrangements for specialist advice

The Secretary of State may from time to time direct a district planning authority, under Sched. 4, para. 7, to submit for approval by him the arrangements they propose to make to obtain specialist advice in connection with their functions under subs. (1), and, if not satisfied with the arrangements, may direct them to enter into an agreement with another local planning authority.

Publicity for applications affecting setting of listed buildings

67.—(1) This section applies where an application for planning permission for any development of land is made to a local planning authority and the development would, in the opinion of the authority affect the setting of a listed building.

(2) The local planning authority shall—

(a) publish in a local newspaper circulating in the locality in which the land is situated; and

(b) for not less than seven days display on or near the land,

a notice indicating the nature of the development in question and naming a place within the locality where a copy of the application, and of all plans and other documents submitted with it, will be open to inspection by the public at all reasonable hours during the period of 21 days beginning with the date of publication of the notice under paragraph (a).

(3) In a case where the land is situated in England, the local planning authority shall send a copy of the notice to the Commission.

(4) Where the Secretary of State, after consulting with the Commission, notifies a local planning authority in writing that subsection (3) shall not affect the authority as regards any notice relating to any kind of application specified in the notification, then that subsection shall not affect the authority as regards any such notice.

(5) The Secretary of State shall send the Commission a copy of any notification made under subsection (4).

(6) The application shall not be determined by the local planning authority before—

(a) the expiry of the period of 21 days referred to in subsection (2); or

(b) if later, the expiry of the period of 21 days beginning with the date on which the notice required by that subsection to be displayed was first displayed.

(7) In determining any application for planning permission to which this section applies, the local planning authority shall take into account any representations relating to the application which are received by them before the periods mentioned in subsection (6) have elapsed.

(8) Subsection (3) of section 63 of the principal Act (references to applications for planning permission to include applications for permission to retain existing works and uses) does not apply to the construction of this section.

DEFINITIONS
  "building": s.91.
  "development": s.91(2).
  "land": s.91(2).
  "listed building": ss.1(5); 91(1).
  "local planning authority": s.81.
  "planning permission": s.91(2).
  "the Commission": s.91(1).
  "the Principal Act": s.91(1).

ALLOCATION OF FUNCTIONS
  The functions of a local planning authority under subss. (2) and (3) are exercisable solely by:—
  Greater London: the London borough council as local planning authority under the T.C.P.A. 1990, s.1(2): Sched. 4, para. 4(1).
  Metropolitan areas: the metropolitan district council as local planning authority under the T.C.P.A. 1990, s.1(2): Sched. 4, para. 4(1).
  Non-metropolitan areas: the district planning authority (Sched. 4, para. 4(1)(c)), but they are required, where the application is to be determined by the county, to notify the county of the steps that they have taken under this section and the date on which they took them (Local Government Act 1972, Sched. 16, para. 21(2)).

National Parks (outside a metropolitan county): the county planning authority (T.C.P.A. 1990, s.4) or joint planning board in areas where one has been established as county planning authority: Sched. 4, para. 4(1)(b).

Norfolk and Suffolk Broads: the Broads Authority (Sched. 4, para. 5).

Urban development areas: the urban development corporation, where an order has been made under the Local Government, Planning and Land Act 1980, s.149(1), transferring the function to the corporation (T.C.P.A. 1990, s.7(1)): for a list of current orders see the notes to s.81.

Housing action trust areas; the housing action trust has the functions under this section to the exclusion of any other authority (other than the Secretary of State) where an order has been made under the Housing Act 1988, s.67(3) transferring the function (as a function within s.67(3A), as substituted by the Planning (Consequential Provisions) Act 1990, Sched. 2, para. 79(3)) to the trust (T.C.P.A. 1990, s.8(2)): see the notes to s.81.

Enterprise zones: the enterprise zone authority, where so provided by order under the Local Government, Planning and Land Act 1980, Sched. 32, para. 5.

GENERAL NOTE

Introduction
This section reinforces the substantive duty in the preceding section, to have regard to the desirability of preserving a listed building or its setting when determining planning applications, by requiring all applications for development which would affect the setting of a listed building to be advertised. In some cases such development will involve works to the building itself which will require listed building consent, and the application for that consent will require to be advertised under the Town and Country Planning (Listed Buildings and Conservation Areas) Regulations 1990, reg. 5: see further the notes to s.10.

Newspaper advertisement and site notice
This section requires the local planning authority (not the applicant) to give publicity by way of newspaper advertisement and site notice to any application for development which would, in their opinion, affect the setting of a listed building. The requirements also apply, by virtue of s.73(2), to planning applications for any development of land which would in the authority's opinion affect the character or appearance of a conservation area.

Policy advice
The Secretary of State has advised authorities (DOE Circular 8/87, para. 25) that:
"The setting of a building of special architectural or historic interest is often an essential feature of its character, especially if a garden or grounds have been laid out as an integral part of the design and layout of a listed house. It is important to consider the effect that proposed development may have on such buildings. In addition, many attractive streets or villages owe their character not so much to buildings of great individual merit but to the harmony produced by a whole range or complex of buildings. Such areas require the same careful consideration when proposals for redevelopment are under consideration, even if the redevelopment only replaces a building that is neither of great merit in itself nor is immediately adjacent to a listed building."
The advice (DOE Circular 8/87, para. 27) also reminds authorities that the "setting" of a building may be limited to its immediate surroundings, but often may include land some distance from it:
"For example, where a listed building forms an important visual element in a street, it would probably be right to regard any development in the street as being within the setting of the building. A proposed high or bulky building might also affect the setting of a listed building some distance away. The character and appearance of a conservation area could be affected by proposed development outside the designated area but visible from it. This provision should therefore not be interpreted too narrowly, and, if there is doubt, it is better to advertise."
In *R.* v. *South Hereford District Council*, ex p. *Felton* [1989] 3 P.L.R. 81 the High Court quashed a planning permission which had been granted without having been properly advertised or notified to the Commission. The court emphasised that although the wording of the section made it a matter for the opinion of the local planning authority, it did not require that the proposed development would "substantially" affect the setting of a listed building: it was amazing, on the facts before the court, that anybody could have thought that the proposed building would not affect the setting of the listed buldings: such a decision had been unreasonable verging on an absurdity (at p.87). The decision was upheld in the Court of Appeal ([1990] E.G.C.S. 34).

Notification to the Historic Buildings and Monuments Commission
Subs. (3) imposes an additional duty on English local planning authorities to send a copy
of the notice required under subs. (2) to the Commission. Subs. (4) makes provision for
exceptions from this requirement to be prescribed by the Secretary of State, and authorities
were formally notified in DOE Circular 8/87, para. 29 that they are not required to send to
the Commission any notice relating to applications for planning permission for development
which affects the setting of a Grade II (unstarred) listed building situated outside Greater
London; or is for the development of land in Greater London which in the opinion of the
local planning authority, involves the demolition, in whole or in part, or the material
alteration of a listed building, which falls to be notified to the Commission pursuant to the
provisions of the current General Development Order (at present the Town and Country
Planning General Development Order 1988 (No. 1813), art. 18(1)(m)). For listed buildings
in London the Commission has powers under s.68 to give directions to the local planning
authority as to how the application is to be dealt with.

Determination of the application
The application may not be determined within the ensuing 21 days (subs. (5)), and the
authority are required, in determining it, to take into account any representations relating
to it and received within that period (subs. (7), and T.C.P.A. 1990, s.70(3)).

Development affecting the character or appearance of a conservation area
Subss. (2) to (7) of this section apply (by virtue of s.73(1)), to planning applications for
development which would, in the opinion of the local planning authority, affect the character
or appearance of a conservation area. However, the requirement to notify the Commission
under subs. (3) is modified by a direction under subs. (4), so as to exclude a proposal which
"affects the character or appearance of a conservation area and which is for the
development of any land by—
    (i) the erection of a new building or the alteration or extension of an existing
        building where the new building, the part of the building being altered, or the
        extension, is of a cubic content (ascertained by external measurement) not
        exceeding 3,000 cubic metres or where the area of ground to be developed does
        not exceed 1,000 square metres; or
   (ii) the material change of use of any building having a cubic content (ascertained
        by external measurement) not exceeding 3,000 cubic metres or where the area
        of ground to be developed does not exceed 1,000 square metres."

Development proposals of local planning authorities
This section does not extend to the development proposals of local planning authorities,
by virtue of s.82, but a comparable duty is imposed by the Town and Country Planning
General Regulations 1976 (No. 1419), reg. 4(2)(c) in these terms:
    "where the development consists of or includes development within any of the
    descriptions set out in [section 67(1) of the Planning (Listed Buildings and Conservation
    Areas) Act 1990], publish in a local newspaper circulating in the locality in which the
    land is situated, and display (for not less than 7 days) on or near the land, notices
    describing the development; and . . . such notice shall state that any objection to the
    proposal should be made to the authority in writing within such period (not being less
    than 21 days) as may be specified in the notice."
The obligation extends not only to development which is proposed to be carried out by
the local planning authority and in respect of which permission is sought under reg. 4 of the
Regulations, but also where the authority seek deemed permission for development of land
vested in them which they do not themselves propose to carry out, by virtue of reg. 5(2).
In *R.* v. *Lambeth London Borough Council,* ex p. *Sharp* (1988) 55 P. & C.R. 232 the
Court of Appeal held that the requirements of the Regulations were mandatory, and strict
compliance was required. The Court quashed a deemed grant of planning permission which
had been preceded by a notice under the Regulations (though dealing with an application
affecting a conservation area, now dealt with under s.73 which applies this section) which
referred to representations instead of objections, and failed to specify the period within
which objections should be made and to indicate that they should be in writing.
Since the section does not apply to local authorities' own development proposals, there is
no legal requirement that they should be notified to the Commission under subs. (3).
Although DOE Circular 23/84, para. 2, formerly asserted that the effect of the Secretary of
State's notification contained therein was that local authorities should inform the Commission
of all applications within the specified categories, "including their own proposals to seek

such permission," there was no statutory backing for that requirement and it does not now appear in DOE Circular 8/87.

Reference to Commission of planning applications involving listed buildings in Greater London

68.—(1) Without prejudice to his powers by virtue of section 74(1) of the principal Act, the Secretary of State may by regulations provide for any application for planning permission to which this section applies to be referred to the Commission before it is dealt with by the local planning authority.

(2) This section applies to an application for planning permission for any development in Greater London which would, in the opinion of the local planning authority to which the application is made, involve the demolition, in whole or in part, or a material alteration, of a listed building.

(3) Regulations under this section may—
  (a) provide for the Commission to give the referring authority directions as to the manner in which an application is to be dealt with; and
  (b) provide that an application which satisfies such conditions as may be specified in the regulations need not be referred to the Commission.

DEFINITIONS
  "building": s.91.
  "development": s.91(2).
  "listed building": ss.1(5); 91(1).
  "local planning authority": s.81.
  "planning permission": s.91(2).
  "the Commission": s.91(1).
  "the Principal Act": s.91(1).

ALLOCATION OF FUNCTIONS
  The section applies only to Greater London, where the local planning authority is the London borough council, except where the function has been transferred to an urban development corporation or housing action trust.

GENERAL NOTE
  This section allows power to be conferred on the Commission to direct a London borough how to deal with a planning application for development involving the demolition of a listed building. It is dependent upon regulations being made for the purpose, and none have yet been made.
  To the extent that the objective of the section is to establish a supervisory rôle for the Commission over authorisation of demolition of listed buildings in Greater London, it is met already by two other provisions:
  (1) s.14, under which all applications for listed building consent for such demolition must be referred to the Commission, and which confers on them extensive powers to direct the local planning authority as to how the application should be determined;
  (2) Town and Country Planning General Development Order 1988, art. 18(1)(m), which requires the local planning authority to consult the Commission on any planning application for the development of land in Greater London involving the demolition, in whole or in part, or the material alteration of a listed building.

PART II

CONSERVATION AREAS

Designation

Designation of conservation areas
  69.—(1) Every local planning authority—
    (a) shall from time to time determine which parts of their area are

areas of special architectural or historic interest the character or appearance of which it is desirable to preserve or enhance, and

(b) shall designate those areas as conservation areas.

(2) It shall be the duty of a local planning authority from time to time to review the past exercise of functions under this section and to determine whether any parts or any further parts of this area should be designated as conservation areas; and, if they so determine, they shall designate those parts accordingly.

(3) The Secretary of State may from time to time determine that any part of a local planning authority's area which is not for the time being designated as a conservation area is an area of special architectural or historic interest the character or appearance of which it is desirable to preserve or enhance; and, if he so determines, he may designate that part as a conservation area.

(4) The designation of any area as a conservation area shall be a local land charge.

DEFINITIONS
"conservation area": s.91(1).
"functions": s.91(2).
"land": s.91(2).
"local planning authority": s.81.

ALLOCATION OF FUNCTIONS
The functions of a local planning authority under this section are exercisable solely by:—

Greater London: the London borough council as local planning authority under the T.C.P.A. 1990, s.1(2) (Sched. 4, para. 4(1)). The functions are also exercisable in Greater London by the Commission (s.70(1)).

Metropolitan areas: the metropolitan district council as local planning authority under the T.C.P.A. 1990, s.1(2) (Sched. 4, para. 4(1)).

Non-metropolitan areas: the district planning authority (Sched. 4, para. 4(1)(c)). The county planning authority, outside a National Park, also has power to make determinations and designations under this section, but before making any determination is required to consult with the council of each district of which any part is included in the area to which the proposed determination relates (Sched. 4, para. 4(1) and (2)).

National Parks (outside a metropolitan county): the county planning authority (T.C.P.A. 1990, s.4) or joint planning board in areas where one has been established as county planning authority (Sched. 4, para. 4(1)(b)).

Norfolk and Suffolk Broads: the Broads Authority (Sched. 4, para. 5).

Urban development areas: the urban development corporation where an order has been made under the Local Government, Planning and Land Act 1980, s.149(1), transferring the function to the corporation (T.C.P.A. 1990, s.7(1)): for a list of current orders see the notes to s.81.

Housing action trust areas: the housing action trust has the functions under this section to the exclusion of any other authority (other than the Secretary of State) where an order has been made under the Housing Act 1988, s.67(3) transferring the function (as a function within s.67(3A), as substituted by the Planning (Consequential Provisions) Act 1990, Sched. 2, para. 79(3)) to the trust (T.C.P.A. 1990, s.8(2)): see the notes to s.81.

Enterprise zones: the enterprise zone authority, where so provided by order under the Local Government, Planning and Land Act 1980, Sched. 32, para. 5.

The Secretary of State has power under subs. (3) to designate any area as a conservation area.

GENERAL NOTE

History and purpose of conservation areas
The concept of conservation areas was introduced by the Civic Amenities Act 1967, in recognition of the need to look beyond listing of individual buildings, and to secure protection for groupings of buildings.

A conservation area is an area of special architectural or historic interest, the character or appearance of which it is desirable to preserve or enhance. Although the formula "special architectural or historic interest" is borrowed from the criteria for listing buildings (s.1), the purpose of conservation areas is to provide a broader form of protection than listed building control. It recognises that historic buildings and architecturally interesting buildings do not exist in a vacuum, but in a particular urban or rural context which provides a setting for the building and may itself have a special character or appearance which it is desirable to preserve. Moreover, conservation areas are by no means tied to listed buildings: they may be designated anywhere if the local planning authority so determine under subs. (1), including a rural area that has no architectural interest but special historic interest, the character or appearance of which it is desirable to preserve or enhance.

The duty under subss. (1) and (2) is a continuing duty, requiring the authority from to time to determine which parts of their area should be designated, and from time to time to review the past exercise of the power and to determine whether any further parts should be designated.

Designation criteria: policy advice

The Secretary of State has advised local planning authorities (DOE Circular 8/87, para. 54) that:

"Clearly there can be no standard specification for conservation areas. The statutory definition is 'areas of special architectural or historic interest, the character or appearance of which it is desirable to preserve or enhance'. These areas will naturally be of many different kinds. They may be large or small, from whole town centres to squares, terraces and smaller groups of buildings. They will often be centred on listed buildings, but not always. Pleasant groups of other buildings, open spaces, trees, an historic street pattern, a village green or features of historic or archaeological interest may also contribute to the special character of an area. Areas appropriate for designation as conservation areas will be found in almost every town and many villages. It is the character of areas, rather than the individual buildings, that [section 69 of the Planning (Listed Buildings and Conservation Areas) Act 1990] seeks to preserve or enhance."

Designation procedure

There is no formal designation procedure. In the non-metropolitan areas, the district planning authority is not required to consult the county authority (although, since they have concurrent powers, prior consultation is obviously desirable); but the county is required to consult before making any designation (Sched. 4, para. 4(1) and (2)). Moreover, the Commission's concurrent power to designate conservation areas in Greater London is exercisable only upon consultation with the London borough, and only with the prior approval of the Secretary of State (s.70(2) and (4)).

Designation of an area takes effect from the date of the appropriate resolution of the authority, and must then be notified. There is no requirement to notify it individually to owners and occupiers of premises in the area, although their criminal liability under s.9 (as extended by s.74(3) to conservation area) commences from the date of designation.

Designation operates entirely outside the local plan preparation process, although the local plan is commonly the vehicle for policies of conservation and protection applicable within an authority's conservation areas. The Government announced proposals, in a Consultation Paper in 1990, to tie the two systems together more closely, through amending legislation which will allow conservation areas to be designated, varied or cancelled only in the context of a district-wide development plan.

Notification of designation

Notice of designation, with particulars of its effect, is required to be published in the London Gazette and in at least one newspaper circulating in the area of the local planning authority (s.70(8)). The local planning authority must also notify the designation to the Secretary of State and (if in England) to the Commission (s.70(5)), giving sufficient particulars to identify the area affected (s.70(7)).

Cancellation or variation of designation

Although subs. (1) confers no power to cancel or vary a designation, such a power is assumed by s.70 to exist and requires any variation or cancellation to be notified in the same way as a designation. It follows that a designation by one authority may be liable to be cancelled or varied by another authority exercising concurrent powers, or by the Secretary of State under subs. (3).

Consequences of designation
Designation of an area as a conservation area has several formal consequences:
(1) the demolition of certain buildings is brought within conservation area control, under s.74, and may only be demolished with the consent of the appropriate authority ("conservation area consent"): for the scope of these controls, see the notes to s.74.
(2) it becomes an offence to cut down, top, lop, uproot, wilfully damage or wilfully destroy any tree in the area except with the consent of the local planning authority, although it is a defence to prosecution to prove that prior notice of intention was served on the local planning authority and the act was done either with their consent, or after the expiry of six weeks from the date of the notice and before the expiry of two years from that date (T.C.P.A., ss.211–214)). Exceptions to this control are provided for by the Town and Country Planning (Tree Preservation Order) (Amendment) and (Trees in Conservation Areas) (Exempted Cases) Regulations 1975 (No. 148): see further the notes to s.211 of the T.C.P.A. 1990;
(3) the authority come under a duty under s.71 to formulate and publish proposals for the preservation and enhancement of the area;
(4) the authority come under a duty to pay special attention to the desirability of preserving or enhancing the character or appearance of the area in the exercise of their powers under the planning Acts and Pt. I of the Historic Buildings and Ancient Monuments Act 1953 (s.72);
(5) planning applications for development which would, in the opinion of the local planning authority, affect the character or appearance of the conservation area must be given publicity under s.67 (as applied by s.73), and representations received in consequence taken into account in determining the application (s.67(7));
(6) permitted development rights under the General Development Order 1988 are more restricted than in other areas: see further below;
(7) specific statutory duties are imposed on telecommunications operators (by virtue of licences granted under the Telecommunications Code 1984: see further below);
(8) the right to display certain types of illuminated advertisement without express consent under the Town and Country Planning (Control of Advertisements) Regulations 1989 (No. 670) Sched. 3, Class 4A and 4B is excluded;
(9) grants and loans become payable under ss.77–80: see further below.

Permitted development rights in conservation areas
    Under the Town and Country Planning General Development Order 1988, a conservation area designated by a local planning authority (but not, remarkably, one designated by the Commission or by the Secretary of State) falls within the definition of "article 1(5) land", together with national parks and areas of outstanding natural beauty (Sched. 1). More restrictive development tolerances apply under Sched. 2 on art. 1(5) land than elsewhere, as follows:
Part 1 (householder development):
(1) the right to enlarge, improve or otherwise alter a dwelling-house is restricted to increases in cubic capacity not exceeding 50 cubic metres or 10 per cent., and any building erected within the curtilage with a cubic capacity exceeding 10 cubic metres is treated as an enlargement of the dwelling-house for these purposes (Class A.1(a) and A.3).
(2) permitted development rights do not extend to cladding any part of the exterior with stone, artificial stone, timber, plastic or tiles (Class A.2).
(3) the right to carry out roof alterations under Class B is excluded.
(4) no building incidental to the enjoyment of the dwelling-house may be provided, altered or improved if its cubic capacity would exceed 10 cubic metres (Class E.1(f)).
Part 8 (industrial development):
    the extension or alteration of an industrial building or warehouse is permitted only up to an increase of 10 per cent. over the cubic content of the original building, as opposed to 25 per cent. elsewhere.
Part 17 (statutory undertakers): Class G (electricity):
    the extension or alteration of buildings by electricity operators on operational land is permitted only up to 10 per cent. or 500 square metres (instead of 25 per cent. or 1,000 square metres).
Part 24 (telecommunications):
(1) the installation, alteration or replacement of a microwave antenna or of its support apparatus is excluded from permitted development rights (Class A.1(g)).
(2) there is a requirement that the operator give eight weeks' prior notice to the local planning authority of his intention to carry out any permitted development (or give

written notice as soon as possible where works have been begun in an emergency): Class A.2(3).
Part 25 (other telecommunications development): Class A.1(g)
the installation, alteration or replacement of a terrestrial microwave antenna is not permitted development (Class A.1(g)).
At one time, the more restrictive regime applied only to conservation areas that had been designated before the relevant development order was made, but that limitation was lifted with the 1988 General Development Order. The regime now applies automatically upon the designation of an area as a conservation area, and there is no entitlement to compensation for it.

Article 4 direction withdrawing permitted development rights
Other permitted development rights under the 1988 Order may be withdrawn by the local planning authority by means of an article 4 direction. The Secretary of State's policy on Directions in conservation areas is set out in DOE Circular 8/87, para. 64:
". . . unless there are obvious and immediate reasons for it, a direction should not be made until it is clear that there will not be adequate public co-operation in the improvement of the area. Although the Secretary of State will generally be in favour of approving directions relating to these areas, a special need for them must be clearly shown (such as a known or potential threat to the character of the area), because the fact that they are conservation areas is not itself a justification for a direction. However, where there is no threat, known or potential, the question of need may be satisfied if the authority can show how a direction would assist a positive policy which they had adopted for enhancing the character or appearance of the conservation area. For example, it would be justifiable to make a direction to bring under control permitted development which would be unsympathetic to a programme or scheme of conservation work. It is important in this respect that permitted development in neighbouring buildings should not be allowed to detract from the appearance of works or buildings which have been or are being, grant aided for conservation reasons."
Earlier advice by the Secretary of State is also reproduced in Appendix II to that circular:
"Although, in general, the Secretary of State will be favourably disposed towards approving an Article 4 Direction relating to land included in a conservation area, it must be emphasised that the existence of a designated conservation area is not, in itself, automatic justification for a direction. A special need for it must be shown. This may be done by reference either to known threats to the character of the area from 'permitted development' or to pressures which would create such threats in the future. Where there is no threat known or potential, the question of need may be satisfied if the authority can show how a direction would assist a positive policy which they had adopted for improving the environment of the designated area including the improvement by the appropriate authority of street furniture."
The circular goes on to advise that the extent of control, and the boundaries of the direction, should be drawn as tightly as possible; and it gives advice on proposals to control external painting.

Compensation for loss of permitted development rights
The withdrawal of permitted development rights by an art. 4 Direction may give rise to liability to compensate for abortive expenditure, or other loss or damage directly attributable to the withdrawal of the permitted development rights (T.C.P.A. 1990, s.107, applied by s.108). But the Act requires that a planning application should first have been made, and permission refused or granted only subject to conditions other than those previously by the development order (s.108(1)).

Areas of special control for advertisements
Provision is made by the Town and Country Planning (Control of Advertisements) Regulations 1989, Pt. IV, (made in accordance with s.221 of the T.C.P.A. 1990) for the designation of area of special control of advertisements. Their principal use is in rural areas, and the Secretary of State has been more cautious in allowing designations in urban areas because of the possible effect on the commercial life of the town. In DOE Circular 15/89, however, local planning authorities are invited to submit for the Secretary of State's approval an order designating the whole, or any part, of a conservation area as an area of special control of advertisements. They must be able to show that there are compelling and relevant planning considerations to justify their view (para. 26), and (para. 25):
"An important consideration in justifying the view that 'special protection' is required is to be able to show the Secretary of State that the proposed area requires a stricter

degree of advertisement control than the LPA are able to exercise by alternative means already available in the Regulations, such as the discontinuance powers in regulation 8. It is never enough to say that the area has already been defined as a conservation area, under [section 69 of the Planning (Listed Buildings and Conservation Areas) Act 1990]; or that the discontinuance powers in regulation 8 are inadequate, or too cumbersome in their operation, to remove, or prevent, the display of visually harmful advertisements."

Financial assistance
A special regime of financial assistance is established by ss.77–80, which allows the Commission (in Wales the Secretary of State) to make grants and loans towards expenditure incurred in the preservation or enhancement of the character or appearance of any conservation area, and to establish with one or more local authorities a funding agreement (a town scheme) setting aside a specified sum for a specified period of years for the purpose of making grants for the repair of buildings in conservation areas.

Special rôle of the Commission
In addition to its function under this Act, the Commission is under a duty imposed by the National Heritage Act 1983, s.33, so far as practicable to promote the preservation and enhancement of the character and appearance of conservation areas situated in England, and to provide educational facilities and services, instruction and information to the public in relation to such conservation areas.

Arrangements for specialist advice
The Secretary of State may from time to time direct a district planning authority, under Sched. 4, para. 7, to submit for approval by him the arrangements they propose to make to obtain specialist advice in connection with their functions under this section, and, if not satisfied about the arrangements, may direct them to enter into an agreement with another local planning authority.

Designation of conservation areas: supplementary provisions

70.—(1) The functions of a local planning authority under section 69 and this section shall also be exercisable in Greater London by the Commission.

(2) Before making a determination under section 69 the Commission shall consult the council of each London borough of which any part isincluded in the area to which the proposed determination relates.

(3) Before making a determination under section 69(3) the Secretary of State shall consult the local planning authority.

(4) Before designating any area in Greater London as a conservation area the Commission shall obtain the consent of the Secretary of State.

(5) A local planning authority shall give notice of the designation of any part of their area as a conservation area under section 69(1) or (2) and of any variation or cancellation of any such designation—
   (a) to the Secretary of State; and
   (b) if it affects an area in England and the designation or, as the case may be the variation or cancellation was not made by the Commission, to the Commission.

(6) The Secretary of State shall give notice of the designation of any part of the area of a local planning authority as a conservation area under section 69(3) and of any variation or cancellation of any such designation—
   (a) to the authority; and
   (b) if it affects an area in England, to the Commission.

(7) A notice under subsection (5) or (6) shall contain sufficient particulars to identify the area affected.

(8) Notice of any such designation, variation or cancellation as is mentioned in subsection (5) or (6), with particulars of its effect, shall be published in the London Gazette and in at least one newspaper circulating

in the area of the local planning authority, by that authority or, as the case may be, the Secretary of State.

DEFINITIONS
  "conservation area": s.91(1).
  "functions": s.91(2).
  "land": s.91(2).
  "local planning authority": s.81.
  "London borough": s.91(2).
  "the Commission": s.91(1).

GENERAL NOTE
  See the notes to s.69.

General duties of planning authorities

Formulation and publication of proposals for preservation and enhancement of conservation areas

71.—(1) It shall be the duty of a local planning authority from time to time to formulate and publish proposals for the preservation and enhancement of any parts of their area which are conservation areas.

(2) Proposals under this section shall be submitted for consideration to a public meeting in the area to which they relate.

(3) The local planning authority shall have regard to any views concerning the proposals expressed by persons attending the meeting.

DEFINITIONS
  "conservation area": s.91(1).
  "local planning authority": s.81.

GENERAL NOTE
  The duty of a local planning authority under this section is loosely prescribed. The formulation and publication of proposals for conservation areas is not governed by any procedural regime comparable to that regulating the development process. There is no public local inquiry into objections, only a public meeting for consideration of the proposals; and there is no legal requirement to consult other statutory agencies or amenity societies. However, it is a common practice for local planning authorities to incorporate conservation area designations and enhancement proposals into the local planning process, and the Government has proposed that the two should be formally integrated by legislation (see the notes to s.69).

General duty as respects conservation areas in exercise of planning functions

72.—(1) In the exercise, with respect to any buildings or other land in a conservation area, of any powers under any of the provisions mentioned in subsection (2), special attention shall be paid to the desirability of preserving or enhancing the character or appearance of that area.

(2) The provisions referred to in subsection (1) are the planning Acts and Part I of the Historic Buildings and Ancient Monuments Act 1953.

DEFINITIONS
  "building": s.91.
  "conservation area": s.91(1).
  "functions": s.91(2).
  "land": s.91(2).
  "the planning Acts": s.91(2).

GENERAL NOTE

Introduction

This section imposes a wide-ranging duty on all persons exercising any statutory powers under the 1990 Planning Acts, and the Historic Buildings and Ancient Monuments Act 1953, with respect to any buildings or other land in a conservation area, to pay special attention to the desirability of preserving or enhancing the special character or appearance of the area.

Functions under the 1953 Act

The functions under Pt. I of the Historic Buildings and Ancient Monuments Act 1953, to which this duty applies, are principally those of making grants available for the preservation of historic buildings, their contents and adjoining land, and the acquisition of historic buildings by the Secretary of State.

The Steinberg doctrine

Determining the true scope of this duty has generated some difficulties in recent years. The courts have been unwilling to insist that mention of it should be expressly made wherever it is relevant in decision-making in order to prove that the duty to pay "special attention" has actually been performed, yet have wanted to ensure that it has nonetheless been given effect and not simply overlooked. The leading case is *Steinberg* v. *Secretary of State for the Environment* [1989] 2 P.L.R. 9, where the High Court (Mr Lionel Read, Q.C., sitting as Deputy Judge) quashed a decision of the Secretary of State to grant planning permission for development in a conservation area, on the ground that the inspector had failed to comply with the duty to pay "special attention". The court accepted that it was not necessary that the inspector's report should say that he was discharging or was conscious of the duty. What mattered was that he should discharge the duty, and if he made no reference to it, then it must be apparent from his decision that he had discharged it or otherwise there would be an error of law. Mr Read observed ([1989] 2 P.L.R. 9 at 12):

"There is, in my judgment, a world of difference between the issue which the inspector defined for himself—whether the proposed development would 'harm' the character of the conservation area—and the need to pay special attention to the desirability of preserving or enhancing the character or appearance of the conservation area. In short, harm is one thing; preservation or enhancement is another. No doubt the inspector has demonstrated his concern that the character of the conservation area should not be harmed. That, in my judgment, is not the same as paying special attention to the desirability of preserving or enhancing that character as well as its appearance. The concept of avoiding harm is essentially negative. The underlying purpose of [section 72(1)] seems to me to be essentially positive."

That decision was followed in *Harrow London Borough Council* v. *Secretary of State for the Environment, The Times*, December 15, 1989, where, however, the court found that there had been no breach of the duty.

The *Steinberg* decision was also endorsed by the Court of Appeal in *Ward on behalf of Torlangton Villagers* v. *Secretary of State for the Environment, Harborough District Council, and Mosley* [1990] 1 P.L.R. 85, where an inspector's decision letter stated the principal issue "in an unfortunate way in so far as it concentrates on whether the development would cause an unacceptable degree of harm and fails to make reference to the approach required by [section 72(1)] of preserving or enhancing" (*per* Woolf L.J. at 89). The court found, however, that the rest of the decision letter made it quite clear that the inspector was very familiar with the approach required by the section, but proceeded nonetheless to quash his decision on the ground that he had misconstrued the reference in DOE Circular 8/87 to the contribution made by open spaces to the character and appearance of conservation areas. The Court held that a pattern of private gardens would be capable of being a feature of a conservation area which would have to be taken into account by an inspector in complying with the duty under this section. Having regard to the inspector's misconstruction of this point, he had failed to perform a most important task because he had misapplied the circular and had failed to apply his mind to the question of whether what was there at present would be less beneficial or more beneficial to the area than what was proposed.

Further, in *Bath Society* v. *Secretary of State for the Environment*, March 30, 1990 (Hutchison J.) no mention of the duty was made in the inspector's report, but it was common ground that in evidence and argument at the inquiry much was made of the fact that the site was in a conservation area and of the the duty under this section. The court held that it was clear also from the inspector's report and the decision letter that both the inspector and the Secretary of State had in mind and gave full effect to the duty. The court stressed that nothing in the section required that planning permission should be refused unless the development would preserve or enhance the character or appearance of the area.

See also *South Hams District Council* v. *Secretary of State for the Environment* [1988] 3 P.L.R. 57 and *Westminster City Council* v. *Secretary of State for the Environment* [1988] 3 P.L.R. 104, where the High Court reviewed decisions by the Secretary of State in advertisement appeals on the ground (*inter alia*) of failure to have proper regard to the duty under this subsection.

The duty also extends to the giving of notice by an officer of the authority, under the Town and Country Planning General Regulations 1976 (S.I. 1976 No. 1419) reg. 6, of intention to seek planning permission for development by the authority or on land owned by the authority: *R.* v. *Lambeth London Borough Council,* ex p. *Sharp* [1986] J.P.L. 201 (although this point was not taken in the subsequent appeal to the Court of Appeal, reported at (1988) 55 P. & C.R. 232).

Publicity for applications affecting conservation areas

73.—(1) Where an application for planning permission for any development of land is made to a local planning authority and the development would, in the opinion of the authority, affect the character or appearance of a conservation area, subsections (2) to (7) of section 67 shall apply as they apply in the circumstances mentioned in subsection (1) of that section.

(2) Subsection (3) of section 63 of the principal Act (references to applications for planning permission to include applications for permission to retain existing works and uses) does not apply to the construction of this section.

DEFINITIONS
"conservation area": s.91(1).
"development": s.91(2).
"land": s.91(2).
"local planning authority": s.81.
"planning permission": s.91(2).
"the Principal Act": s.91(1).

GENERAL NOTE
This section extends the requirements of s.67 (publicity for planning applications affecting the setting of listed buildings) to planning applications for development affecting the character or appearance of a conservation area. See further the notes to s.67.

Control of demolition

Control of demolition in conservation areas

74.—(1) A building in a conservation area shall not be demolished without the consent of the appropriate authority (in this Act referred to as "conservation area consent").

(2) The appropriate authority for the purposes of this section is—
    (a) in relation to applications for consent made by local planning authorities, the Secretary of State; and
    (b) in relation to other applications for consent, the local planning authority or the Secretary of State.

(3) Sections 7 to 26, 28, 32 to 46, 56, 62 to 65, 66(1), 82(2) to (4), 83(1)(b), (3) and (4) and 90(2) to (4) have effect in relation to buildings in conservation areas as they have effect in relation to listed buildings subject to such exceptions and modifications as may be prescribed by regulations.

(4) Any such regulations may make different provision—
    (a) in relation to applications made by local planning authorities, and
    (b) in relation to other applications.

DEFINITIONS
  "building": s.91.
  "conservation area": s.91(1).
  "conservation area consent": subs. (1).
  "listed building": ss.1(5); 91(1).
  "local planning authority": s.81.
  "prescribed": s.91(1).

ALLOCATION OF FUNCTIONS
  The references to a local planning authority are references solely to:—
  Greater London: the London borough council as local planning authority under the
T.C.P.A. 1990, s.1(2): Sched. 4, para. 4(1).
  Metropolitan areas: the metropolitan district council as local planning authority under
T.C.P.A. 1990, s.1(2): Sched. 4, para. 4(1).
  Non-metropolitan areas: the district planning authority (Sched. 4, para. 4(1)(c)).
  National Parks (outside a metropolitan county): the county planning authority (T.C.P.A.
1990, s.4) or joint planning board in areas where one has been established as county
planning authority: Sched. 4, para. 4(1)(b).
  Norfolk and Suffolk Broads: the Broads Authority (Sched. 4, para. 5).
  Urban development areas: the urban development corporation where an order has been
made under the Local Government, Planning and Land Act 1980, s.149(1), transferring the
function to the corporation (T.C.P.A. 1990, s.7(1)): for a list of current orders see the notes
to s.81.
  Housing action trust areas: the housing action trust has the functions under this section to
the exclusion of any other authority (other than the Secretary of State) where an order has
been made under the Housing Act 1988, s.67(3) transferring the function (as a function
within s.67(3A), as substituted by the Planning (Consequential Provisions) Act 1990, Sched.
2, para. 79(3)) to the trust (T.C.P.A. 1990, s.8(2)): see the notes to s.81.
  Enterprise zones: the enterprise zone authority, where so provided by order under the
Local Government, Planning and Land Act 1980, Sched. 32, para. 5.

GENERAL NOTE

Introduction
  This section establishes a system of controls over the demolition of buildings situated in
conservation areas. Not all buildings are within the control: some are excluded by s.70, and
others are excluded by a direction made by the Secretary of State (see further below). A
building to which the control applies may be demolished only with the consent of the local
planning authority, known as conservation area consent. The control is more limited than
listed building control. It does not, for example, control works of extension or alteration to
such a building (although partial demolition in the course of carrying out alterations may be
sufficient to constitute demolition for these purposes).
  Effect is given to conservation area control in a remarkably complicated and awkward
manner, by extending all of the sections specified in subs. (3), which relate to listed building
control, to conservation area control, with modifications made by the Secretary of State by
regulations. Each section is modified by the Town and Country Planning (Listed Buildings
and Conservation Areas) Regulations 1990, reg. 12, so as to substitute "conservation area
consent" for any reference to "listed building consent"; the substitution of "conservation
area enforcement notice" for "listed building enforcement notice" and of "conservation area
purchase notice" for "listed building purchase notice". Sched. 3 to the Regulations then
makes further modifications to the individual sections.
  The effect of these arrangements is that all of the provisions of the Act applicable to listed
buildings apply equally to the demolition of buildings in conservation areas with the following
principal exceptions:
  Pt. I, Chap. I: listing of buildings.
  s.27:   compensation for refusal of consent to alteration of listed building.
  s.29–31:   compensation provisions.
  ss.47–53:   acquisition of listed buildings.
  ss.54–55:   urgent works to unoccupied listed buildings (but note the power of
                   the Secretary of State under s.76 to extend this section to specified
                   buildings in conservation areas).
  ss.57–58:   grants for preservation of listed buildings (a separate grants regime
                   is established for conservation areas by ss.77–80).
  s.59:   acts likely to cause damage to listed buildings.

ss.60–61:   ecclesiastical exemption and scheduled monuments (these are
                         excepted separately by s.75).
s.66(2) and (3):   general duties in exercising planning functions (separate duty
                         imposed by s.72).
s.67:   publicity for applications (separate duty imposed by s.73).
s.68:   reference of London applications to the Commission.

Exceptions from conservation area control
Control over demolition of buildings in conservation areas does not extend to:
(1) listed buildings (s.75(1)), because these are subject to listed building control, which
    is more extensive than conservation area control;
(2) ecclesiastical buildings which are for the time being used for ecclesiastical purposes
    (s.75(1); and see the notes to s.60);
(3) buildings for the time being included in the schedule of monuments compiled and
    maintained under s.1 of the Ancient Monuments and Archaeological Areas Act 1979
    (s.75(1), and see the notes to s.61);
(4) buildings in relation to which a direction under subs. (2) is for the time being in
    force. The Secretary of State has directed (DOE Circular 8/87, para. 97) that the
    control should not apply to the following descriptions of buildings:—
    (a) any building with a total cubic content not exceeding 115 cubic metres or any
        part of such building, and in this sub-paragraph "building" does not include part
        of a building;
    (b) any gate, wall, fence or railing which is less than one metre high where abutting
        on a highway (including a public footpath or bridleway) or public open space,
        or two metres high in any other case;
    (c) any building erected since January 1, 1914 and used, or last used, for the
        purposes of agriculture or forestry;
    (d) any part of a building used, or last used, for an industrial process, provided that
        such part (taken with any other part which may have been demolished) does not
        exceed ten per cent. of the cubic content of the original building (as ascertained
        by external measurement) or 500 square metres of floor space, whichever is the
        greater;
    (e) any building required to be demolished by virtue of an order made under section
        [102] of the Act;
    (f) any building required to be demolished by virtue of any provision of an
        agreement made under [section 106] of the Act;
    (g) any building in respect of which the provisions of an enforcement notice served
        under section [172 or section 182] of the Act [or section 38 of the Planning
        (Listed Buildings and Conservation Areas) Act 1990] require its demolition, in
        whole or in part, however expressed;
    (h) any building required to be demolished by virtue of a condition of planning
        permission granted under section [70] of the Act, other than a permission
        deemed to be granted to a local planning authority by virtue of regulation 4(5)
        or regulation 5(4) of the Town and Country Planning General Regulations 1976
        (S.I. 1976, No. 1419);
    (i) any building to which a demolition order made under Part IX of the Housing
        Act 1985 applies;
    (j) any building included in a compulsory purchase order made under the provisions
        of Part IX of the Housing Act 1985 and confirmed by the Secretary of State;
    (k) a redundant building (within the meaning of the Pastoral Measure 1983) or part
        of such a building where demolition is in pursuance of a pastoral or redundancy
        scheme (within the meaning of that measure).
        [(2) In this direction:—
        "the Act" means the [Town and Country Planning Act 1990];
        "forestry" means the growing of a utilisable crop of timber; and
        "industrial process" means any process for or incidental to any of the following
        purposes, namely:—
        (a) the making of any article or part of an article, or
        (b) the altering, repairing, ornamenting, finishing, cleaning, washing, packing
            or canning, or adapting for sale, or breaking up, or demolition, of any
            article, or
        (c) without prejudice to the foregoing paragraphs, the getting, dressing or
            treatment of minerals,

being a process carried out in the course of trade or business, and for the purposes of this definition the expression "article" means an article of any description, including a ship or vessel.]

Arrangements for specialist advice
The Secretary of State may from time to time direct a district planning authority, under Sched. 4, para. 7, to submit for approval by him the arrangements they propose to make to obtain specialist advice in connection with their functions under this section, and, if not satisfied about the arrangements, may direct them to enter into an agreement with another local planning authority.

Cases in which s.74 does not apply

75.—(1) Section 74 does not apply to—
  (a) listed buildings;
  (b) ecclesiastical buildings which are for the time being used for ecclesiastical purposes;
  (c) buildings for the time being included in the schedule of monuments compiled and maintained under section 1 of the Ancient Monuments and Archaeological Areas Act 1979; or
  (d) buildings in relation to which a direction under subsection (2) is for the time being in force.
  (2) The Secretary of State may direct that section 74 shall not apply to any description of buildings specified in the direction.
  (3) A direction under subsection (2) may be given either to an individual local planning authority exercising functions under that section or to local planning authorities generally.
  (4) The Secretary of State may vary or revoke a direction under subsection (2) by a further direction under that subsection.
  (5) For the purposes of subsection (1)(b), a building used or available for use by a minister of religion wholly or mainly as a residence from which to perform the duties of his office shall be treated as not being an ecclesiastical building.
  (6) For the purposes of sections 7 to 9 as they apply by virtue of section 74(3) a building shall be taken to be used for the time being for ecclesiastical purposes if it would be so used but for the works in question.
  (7) The Secretary of State may by order provide for restricting or excluding the operation of subsection (1)(b) in such cases as may be specified in the order.
  (8) An order under subsection (7) may—
  (a) make provision for buildings generally, for descriptions of building or for particular buildings;
  (b) make different provision for buildings in different areas, for buildings of different religious faiths or denominations or according to the use made of the building;
  (c) make such provision in relation to a part of a building (including, in particular, an object or structure falling to be treated as part of the building by virtue of section 1(5)) as may be made in relation to a building and make different provision for different parts of the same building;
  (d) make different provision with respect to works of different descriptions or according to the extent of the works;
  (e) make such consequential adaptations or modifications of the operation of any other provision of this Act or the principal Act, or of any instrument made under either of those Acts, as appear to the Secretary of State to be appropriate.
  (9) Regulations under this Act may provide that subsections (5) to (8) shall have effect subject to such exceptions and modifications as may be prescribed, and any such regulations may make different provision—

(a) in relation to applications made by local planning authorities, and
(b) in relation to other applications.

(10) Any proceedings on or arising out of an application for conservation area consent made which section 74 applies to a building shall lapse if it ceases to apply to it, and any such consent granted with respect to the building shall also lapse.

(11) The fact that that section has ceased to apply to a building shall not affect the liability of any person to be prosecuted and punished for an offence under section 9 or 43 committed with respect to the building while that section did apply to it.

DEFINITIONS
"building": s.91.
"conservation area": 91(1).
"conservation area consent": 91(1).
"functions": s.91(2)
"listed buildings": ss.1(5); 91(1).
"local planning authority": s.81.
"prescribed": s.91(1).
"the principal Act": s.91(1).
"use": s.91(2).

GENERAL NOTE
The section prescribes the exceptions from conservation area controls established under the preceding section.
The provisions relating to ecclesiastical buildings (subss. (1)(b) and (5) to (8)) mirror exactly those under s.60 in respect of listed building control. The power under subs. (7) to restrict or exclude the ecclesiastical exemption under subs. (1)(b) is exercisable by order subject to negative resolution procedure, and the order may contain such supplementary and incidental provision as may appear to the Secretary of State to be appropriate (s.93(4)).

Urgent works to preserve unoccupied buildings in conservation areas

76.—(1) If it appears to the Secretary of State that the preservation of a building in a conservation area is important for maintaining the character or appearance of that area, he may direct that section 54 shall apply to it as it applies to listed buildings.

(2) The Secretary of State shall consult the Commission before giving a direction under subsection (1) in respect of a building in England.

DEFINITIONS
"building": s.91.
"conservation area": s.91(1).
"land": s.91(2).
"listed building": ss.1(5); 91(1).
"the Commission": s.91(1)

GENERAL NOTE
The section extends the applicability of s.54, which allows a local planning authority to carry out urgently necessary works for the preservation of an unoccupied listed building. It empowers the Secretary of State to direct that the section should apply also to a specific unlisted building in a conservation area. The test is not, as it would be with listing, the special architectural or historic interest of the building itself, but its importance in maintaining the character or appearance of the conservation area. It is unlikely to be a widely used power, because it will be rare that a building of such importance will not qualify also for listing.

Grants

Grants and loans for preservation or enhancement of conservation areas

77.—(1) If in the opinion of the Commission any relevant expenditure has made or will make a significant contribution towards the preservation or enhancement of the character or appearance of any conservation area situated in England or any part of such an area they may make grants or loans for the purposes of defraying the whole or part of that expenditure.

(2) If in the opinion of the Secretary of State any relevant expenditure has made or will make a significant contribution towards the preservation or enhancement of the character or appearance of any conservation area situated in Wales or any part of such an area, he may make grants or loans for the purposes of defraying the whole or part of that expenditure.

(3) Expenditure is relevant for the purposes of subsection (1) or (2) if it has been or is to be incurred in or in connection with, or with a view to the promotion of, such preservation or enhancement as is mentioned in that subsection.

(4) A grant or loan under this section may be made subject to such conditions as the Commission or; as the case may be, the Secretary of State may think fit to impose.

(5) Any loan under subsection (1) shall be made on such terms as to repayment, payment of interest and otherwise as the Commission may determine.

(6) Any loan under subsection (2) shall be made on such terms as to repayment, payment of interest and otherwise as the Secretary of State may with the approval of the Treasury determine.

(7) Unless the making of a grant or loan under this section appears to the Secretary of State to be a matter of immediate urgency, before making the grant or loan, the Secretary of State shall consult the Historic Buildings Council for Wales as to its making and the conditions subject to which it should be made.

(8) The Secretary of State may pay such remuneration and allowances as he may with the approval of the Treasury determine to any member of the Historic Buildings Council for Wales by whom services are rendered in connection with any question as to the exercise of his powers under this section.

(9) If any such member is also a member of the House of Commons, those payments shall extend only to allowances in respect of travelling and subsistence expenses, and any other expenses necessarily incurred by him in connection with those services.

DEFINITIONS
   "building": s.91.
   "conservation area": s.91(1).
   "land": s.91(2).
   "the Commission": s.91(1)
   "relevant expenditure": subs. (3).

GENERAL NOTE
   The function of making grants under this section was formerly conferred on the Secretary of State, but for England was transferred to the Commission by the National Heritage Act 1983. Details of the grants available are therefore no longer specified in Government circulars, but may be obtained from the Commission. Further financial powers are conferred by ss.79 and 80, which allow the Commission (or in Wales, the Secretary of State) to enter into a town scheme agreement with one or more local authorities for the purpose of committing expenditure to the repair of buildings.
   Grants made under this section may be recoverable under s.78 in certain circumstances.

Recovery of grants under s.77

   78.—(1) This section applies to any grant under section 77 made on terms that it shall be recoverable under this section.

   (2) A grant shall only be regarded as made on those terms if before or on making the grant the grantor gives the grantee notice in writing—
   (a) summarising the effect of this section; and

(b) if the grant is made for the purpose of defraying the whole or part of expenditure in relation to any particular property ("the grant property"), specifying the recovery period.

(3) In this section "the recovery period" means the period, beginning with the day on which the grant is made and ending not more than ten years after that day, during which the grant is to be recoverable in accordance with subsection (4).

(4) If during the recovery period the grantee disposes of the interest which was held by him in the grant property on the day on which the grant was made or any part of that interest, by way of sale or exchange or lease for a term of not less than 21 years, the grantor may recover the amount of the grant, or such part of it as the grantor thinks fit, from the grantee.

(5) If the grantee gives the whole of that interest to any person (whether direction or indirectly, but otherwise than by will) subsection (4) shall have effect as if the donee were the grantee.

(6) If the grantee gives part of that interest to any person (whether directly or indirectly, but otherwise than by will) subsection (4) shall have effect as if any disposal or part disposal of that interest by the donee were a disposal by the grantee.

(7) If any condition imposed on the making of a grant to which this section applies is contravened or not complied with, the grantor may recover the amount of the grant, or such part of it as he thinks fit, from the grantee.

(8) Nothing in this section entitles a grantor to recover amounts in the aggregate exceeding the amount of the grant (for example by virtue of a breach of more than one condition or disposals of several parts of an interest in the grant property).

DEFINITIONS
   "disposal": s.91(2).
   "grant property": subs. (2)(b).
   "lease": s.91(2).
   "the recovery period": subs. (3).

GENERAL NOTE

Recovery of grant
   This section enables the Commission (or in Wales, the Secretary of State) to recover all or part of a grant made under s.77 if the grantee's interest is disposed of by way of sale, exchange or lease, within three years of the grant. Similar provision is made by s.58 in relation to grants made by local planning authorities under s.57 (though with a recovery period of only three years), and for grants made under s.4 of the Historic Buildings and Ancient Monuments Act 1953.
   Liability to repay under this section is personal and enforceable only against the original grantee, except where the grantee's interest is transferred by way of *inter vivos* gift, in which case the donee becomes liable under this section. Gifts by will are not treated as disposals for the purpose of liability to repay. "Disposal" for these purposes is limited to disposal by the grantee by way of sale, exchange or lease for not less than 21 years (subs. (4)). It does not therefore include a mortgage or charge, and disposal by the mortgagee exercising a power of sale conferred by the mortgage does not attract the repayment liability imposed by this section (*Canterbury City Council* v. *Quine* (1988) 55 P. & C.R. 1 (decided on the corresponding provisions of s.1 of the Local Authorities (Historic Buildings) Act 1962, now s.58 of this Act)).

Town schemes

Town scheme agreements

79.—(1) The Commission and one or more local authorities in England, or the Secretary of State and one or more local authorities in Wales, may enter an agreement (in this Act referred to as a "town scheme agreement") that a specified sum of money shall be set aside for a specified period of years for the purpose of making grants for the repair of buildings which are—

(a) included in a list compiled for the purposes of such an agreement by the parties to the agreement, or by them and other such authorities, or

(b) shown on a map prepared for those purposes by the parties, or by them and such other authorities.

(2) Before such a list is compiled or such a map is prepared by the Secretary of State and any local authorities as respects any buildings in Wales they shall consult the Historic Buildings Council for Wales.

(3) In this section "local authority" means—

(a) a county council;

(b) a district council;

(c) in relation to any building situated within the Broads, the Broads Authority;

(d) a London borough council or the Common Council of the City of London;

(e) the Council of the Isles of Scilly.

DEFINITIONS
"building": s.91.
"land": s.91(2).
"local authority": subs. (3).
"London borough": s.91(2)
"the Broads": s.91(2).
"the Commission": s.91(1).   .
"town scheme agreement": subs. (1); s.91(1).

GENERAL NOTE

Town scheme agreements
   This section authorises the Commission (in Wales, the Secretary of State) to enter into town scheme agreements with one or more local authorities. The purpose is to establish a programme of grant-aid, to which the Commission contributes but which is delegated to local authorities for administration under s.80(5)(b). Current policy on town schemes was explained by the Commission in its evidence to the House of Commons Environment Committee in 1986 (*Historic Buildings and Ancient Monuments*, Session 1986–87, H.C. 146; Vol. II, p. 230), as follows:
   "Town schemes are agreements by which the Commission and local authorities jointly set aside funds for grants to historic buildings within a defined area. Whereas other grant schemes concentrate mainly on buildings, conservation grants attempt to preserve a very much wider range of vernacular buildings, as well as actually to improve the environment of historic areas. They cover not only the centres of the classic historic cities, such as Bath, but also hundreds of small towns, and range from small domestic terraces to large warehouses. Increasingly, additional demands are coming from the run-down inner city areas, where grants at a comparatively low level can give a significant stimulus to urban regeneration and improve the quality of life for those living or working there. The effects of conservation grants probably bring public benefit to more people than any other single activity of the Commission."

Grants for town scheme agreements
   Under s.80 the Commission (in Wales, the Secretary of State) may provide grants to defray all or part of the repair cost for any building within a town scheme agreement, if it is situated in a conservation area and appears to be of architectural or historic interst. Grants are recoverable in certain circumstances, under s.78 as applied by s.80(7).

Grants for repairing of buildings in town schemes

   80.—(1) The Commission may make grants for the purpose of defraying the whole or part of any expenditure incurred or to be incurred in the repair of any building which—

(a) is the subject of a town scheme agreement;
(b) is situated in a conservation area in England; and
(c) appears to the Commission to be of architectural or historic interest.

(2) The Secretary of State may make grants for the purpose of defraying the whole or part of any expenditure incurred or to be incurred in the repair of any building which—
(a) is the subject of a town scheme agreement;
(b) is situated in a conservation area in Wales; and
(c) appears to him to be of architectural or historic interest.

(3) A grant under this section may be made subject to conditions imposed by the Commission or, as the case may be, the Secretary of State for such purposes as the Commission or, as the case may be, the Secretary of State thinks fit.

(4) Unless the making of a grant under this section appears to the Secretary of State to be a matter of immediate urgency, before he makes such a grant he may consult with the Historic Buildings Council for Wales as to the making of the grant and as to the conditions subject to which it should be made.

(5) The Commission or the Secretary of State may—
(a) pay any grant under this section to any authority which is a party to a town scheme agreement; and
(b) make arrangements with any such authority for the way in which the agreement is to be carried out.

(6) Those arrangements may include such arrangements for the offer and payment of grants under this section as the parties may agree.

(7) Section 78(4) to (8) shall apply to a grant under this section as it applies to a grant under that section, but taking the recovery period to be three years beginning with the day on which the grant is made.

DEFINITIONS
  "building": s.91.
  "conservation area": s.91(1).
  "land": s.91(2).
  "the Commission: s.91(1).
  "town scheme agreement": ss.79; 91(1).

GENERAL NOTE
  See the notes to s.79.

PART III

GENERAL

Authorities exercising functions under Act

Authorities exercising functions under Act

81. In this Act "local planning authority" shall be construed in accordance with Part I of the principal Act and Schedule 4 to this Act (which makes further provision as to the exercise of functions under this Act).

DEFINITIONS
  "functions": s.91(2).
  "local planning authority": s.81.
  "the principal Act": s.91(1).

GENERAL NOTE

Allocation of functions

Ascertaining which authorities have the function of local planning authority for each provision of this Act is a particularly complex task, because the allocation of responsibilities varies for each section. The notes to the Act therefore include, where relevant, a statement of how the function of local planning authority has been allocated for that section.

The validity of anything done in purported reliance on powers conferred by this Act depends upon it being done by the authority to whom the necessary power has been allocated under these provisions, but there is a special saving under Sched. 4, para. 6 in respect of any consent or determination made or granted in respect of an application for listed building consent or conservation area consent: such a consent or determination may not be questioned in any legal proceedings on the ground that it should have been granted or made by some other local planning authority.

The general rule

The basic allocation, established by s.1 of the T.C.P.A. 1990, is that
(1) within Greater London the London borough council (including the Common Council of the City of London) is the local planning authority for its area;
(2) for metropolitan areas outside London (*i.e.* the former metropolitan counties of West Midlands, Greater Manchester, Merseyside, Tyne and Wear, South Yorkshire and West Yorkshire) the metropolitan district council is the local planning authority; and
(3) for non-metropolitan areas (the "shire counties") the function is shared by the district council (as district planning authority) and the county council (as county planning authority).

However, special arrangements exist in the National Parks, the Norfolk and Suffolk Broads, urban development areas, in Greater London respecting the rôle of the Commission enterprise zones and, in housing action trust areas, and these are set out below. Moreover, the majority of planning functions in the shire counties are allocated under Sched. 4 specifically to the districts, with the counties enjoying concurrent powers only in a few cases.

Housing action trust areas

Housing action trust areas are designated under the Housing Act 1988, s.60. Their purpose is to improve conditions in the most run-down council housing estates. The objectives of a trust are (Housing Act 1988, s.63(1)):
(a) to secure the repair or improvement of housing accommodation for the time being held by the trust;
(b) to secure the proper and effective management and use of that housing accommodation;
(c) to encourage diversity in the interests by virtue of which housing accommodation in the area is occupied and, in the case of accommodation which is occupied under tenancies, diversity in the identity of the landlords; and
(d) generally to secure or facilitate the improvement of living conditions in the area and the social conditions and general environment of the area.

Under s.67 of the 1988 Act the Secretary of State may provide by order for a housing action trust to be the local planning authority for the whole or such part as may be specified of its area in place of any authority which would otherwise be the local planning authority, and may also confer on the trust exclusively other functions under the planning Acts that are conferred on any authority.

To date, no designation orders have been made under the 1988 Act, and thus no planning functions have been transferred to any housing action trust.

Urban development areas

By orders made under the Local Government, Planning and Land Act 1980, s.149(1), the urban development corporations have all (except for Cardiff Bay) been created by the local planning authority for specified functions under the T.C.P.A. 1990 (including development control under Pt. III of that Act), and for the following functions under this Act in place of any other authority which would otherwise have had the function. The list is as substituted in Sched. 28 to the 1980 Act by Sched. 2, para. 44(12) of the Town and Country Planning (Consequential Provisions) Act 1990:

Sections 3 and 4 (previously s.58 of the 1971 Act): building preservation notice in respect of building not listed.
Section 8 (previously s.55 of the 1971 Act): control of works of demolition, alteration or extension of listed buildings.

Sections 10, 11, 13 to 16, 20, 23 to 25 (previously Sched. 11 to the 1971 Act): control of works for demolition, alteration or extension of listed buildings.

Section 38 (previously s.96 of the 1971 Act): power to serve listed building enforcement notice.

Section 42 (previously s.99 of the 1971 Act): execution and cost of works required by listed building enforcement notice.

Section 47 (previously s.114 of the 1971 Act): compulsory acquisition of listed building in need of repair.

Section 48 (previously s.115 of the 1971 Act): repairs notice as preliminary to compulsory acquisition under s.47).

Section 50 (previously s.117 of the 1971 Act): minimum compensation in case of listed building deliberately left derelict.

Section 53 (previously s.126 of the 1971 Act): management, etc. of listed buildings acquired by local authority or Secretary of State.

Section 54 (previously s.101 of the 1971 Act): urgent works for preservation of certain unoccupied buildings.

Sections 69 to 72 (previously ss.277, 277B of the 1971 Act): designation of conservation area.

Sections 74 and 75 (previously s.277A of the 1971 Act): control of demolition in conservation areas.

Section 82 (previously s.271 of the 1971 Act): application to local planning authorities of provisions as to listed buildings.

The following orders have been made under s.149 transferring all the above powers to the specified urban development corporations:

Merseyside Development Corporation (Planning Functions) Order 1981 (S.I. 1981 No. 561)

London Dockland Development Corporation (Planning Functions) Order 1981 (S.I. 1981 No. 1081)

Black Country Development Corporation (Planning Functions) Order 1987 (S.I. 1987 No. 1340)

Teesside Development Corporation (Planning Functions) Order 1987 (S.I. 1987 No. 1341)

Tyne and Wear Development Corporation (Planning Functions) Order 1987 (S.I. 1987 No. 1342)

Black Country Development Corporation (Planning Functions) (Wolverhampton) Order 1988 No. 1399.

Leeds Development Corporation (Planning Functions) Order 1988 No. 1551

Central Manchester Development Corporation (Planning Functions) Order 1988 No. 1552

Sheffield Development Corporation (Planning Functions) Order 1988 No. 1553

Merseyside Development Corporation (Planning Functions) (Liverpool and Wirral) Order 1988 No. 1968

Bristol Development Corporation (Planning Functions) Order 1989 No. 93.

National Parks

All functions under this Act are exercisable by the two special planning boards in their areas (Lake District and Peak Park) and elsewhere by the county planning authority, except that an application under s.10 for listed building consent or conservation area consent is to be made to the district planning authority who must, if it is not to be determined by them, forward it to the county (Sched. 4, para. 3(1)), and the county must consult the district before determining such an application.

The Commission

The Historic Buildings and Monuments Commission for England is neither a local authority nor a local planning authority for any of the purposes of the Act, but it has certain special powers in Greater London (as successor in some respects to the Greater London Council), and concurrent power to designate conservation areas in Greater London.

Enterprise zones

An order designating an enterprise zone under the Local Government, Planning and Land Act 1980, Sched. 32, para. 5, may provide that the enterprise zone authority shall be the local planning authority for the zone for the purposes of the planning Acts, and in relation to such kinds of development, as may be prescribed in the order (para. 5(7)). The enterprise zone authorities for the zones designated to date in England and Wales have already been the local planning authorities, and further designations have therefore not been undertaken under these powers.

Special cases

Application of Act to land and works of local planning authorities

82.—(1) In relation to land of a local planning authority, section 1(1), (2) and 4) and sections 2, 39(6), 42(6) and 55(6) shall have effect subject to such exceptions and modifications as may be prescribed.

(2) The provisions mentioned in subsection (3) shall have effect for the purpose of applications by local planning authorities relating to the execution of works for the demolition, alteration or extension of listed buildings, subject to such exceptions and modifications as may be prescribed.

(3) Those provisions are sections 1(3), (5) and (6), 3 to 5, 7 to 29, 32 to 50 (except sections 39(6) and 42(6)), 60(1) to (4) (as it applies as respects the provisions mentioned in this subsection), 62 to 65, 67(2)(b), (6) and (7), 73(1), Schedules 1 and 2, paragraph 2 of Schedule 4 (as it applies to Schedule 1) and paragraph 4(1) of Schedule 4 (as it applies as respects the provisions mentioned in this subsection).

(4) Regulations under this section may in particular provide—

    (a) for the making of applications for listed building consent to the Secretary of State; and

    (b) for the issue or service by him of notices under section 2(3) and the provisions mentioned in subsection (3).

DEFINITIONS
    "building": s.91.
    "land": s.91(2).
    "listed building": ss.1(5); 91(1).
    "listed building consent": ss.8(7); 91(1).
    "local planning authority": s.81.
    "prescribed": s.91(1).

GENERAL NOTE
This Act applies to the land of, and development by, local authorities to the same extent as it applies to any other land and development. However, this section confers power on the Secretary of State to modify, and to make exceptions from, certain provisions of the Act in their applicability to local planning authorities. Subss. (2)–(4) are extended by s.74(3) to buildings in conservation areas.

The Town and Country Planning (Listed Buildings and Conservation Areas) Regulations 1990, reg. 13, modify the procedural requirements of this Act by prescribing that where a local planning authority require listed building consent or conservation area consent for the demolition of a building in their area, they must apply to the Secretary of State for that consent. As to the scope of this requirement, see further the notes to s.10.

Exercise of powers in relation to Crown land

83.—(1) Notwithstanding any interest of the Crown in Crown land, but subject to the following provisions of this section—

    (a) a building which for the time being is Crown land may be included in a list compiled or approved by the Secretary of State under section 1;

    (b) any restrictions imposed or powers conferred by sections 1 to 26, 32 to 46, 54 to 56, 59 to 61, 66(1), 67, 68, 73 or 76 or Schedule 1, 2 or 3 shall apply and be exercisable in relation to Crown land, to the extent of any interest in it for the time being held otherwise than by or on behalf of the Crown;

    (c) any power to acquire land compulsorily under section 47 may be exercised in relation to any interest in the land which is for the time being held otherwise than by or on behalf of the Crown.

(2) Except with the consent of the appropriate authority—

    (a) no notice shall be issued or served under section 38 in relation to land which for the time being is Crown land;

    (b) no interest in land which for the time being is Crown land shall be acquired compulsorily under section 47.

(3) No listed building enforcement notice shall be issued in respect of works executed by or on behalf of the Crown in respect of a building which was Crown land at the time when the works were executed.

(4) No listed building purchase notice shall be served in relation to any interest in Crown land unless—

    (a) an offer has been previously made by the owner of that interest to dispose of it to the appropriate authority on terms that the price payable for it—

        (i) shall be equal to the compensation which would be payable in respect of it if it were acquired in pursuance of such a notice, or

        (ii) in default of agreement, shall be determined in a similar manner to that in which that compensation would be determined; and

    (b) that offer has been refused by the appropriate authority.

(5) In this section—

    "Crown land" means land in which there is a Crown interest or a Duchy interest;

    "Crown interest" means an interest belonging to Her Majesty in right of the Crown, or belonging to a government department, or held in trust for Her Majesty for the purposes of a government department;

    "Duchy interest" means an interest belonging to Her Majesty in right of the Duchy of Lancaster, or belonging to the Duchy of Cornwall.

(6) A person who is entitled to occupy Crown land by virtue of a licence in writing shall be treated as having an interest in land for the purposes of subsection (1)(b) so far as applicable to sections 1 to 26, 38 to 46, 54 to 56, 59 to 61, 66(1), 67, 68, 73 and 76 and Schedule 1, 2 or 3.

(7) For the purposes of this section "the appropriate authority", in relation to any land—

    (a) in relation to land belonging to Her Majesty in right of the Crown and forming part of the Crown Estate, means the Crown Estate Commissioners;

    (b) in relation to any other land belonging to Her Majesty in right of the Crown, means the government department having the management of that land;

    (c) in relation to land belonging to Her Majesty in right of the Duchy of Lancaster, means the Chancellor of the Duchy;

    (d) in relation to land belonging to the Duchy of Cornwall, means such person as the Duke of Cornwall or the possessor for the time being of the Duchy of Cornwall appoints;

    (e) in the case of land belonging to a government department or held in trust for Her Majesty for the purposes of a government department, means that department.

(8) If any question arises as to what authority is the appropriate authority in relation to any land, that question shall be referred to the Treasury, whose decision shall be final.

DEFINITIONS
"the appropriate authority": subs. (7).
"building": s.91.
"Crown interest": subs. (5).
"Crown land": subs. (5).
"Duchy interest": subs. (5)
"government department": s.91(2).
"land": s.91(2).
"listed building": ss.1(5); 91(1).
"listed building enforcement notice": ss.38(1); 91(1).
"listed building purchase notice": ss.32(1); 91(1).
"owner": s.9(2).

GENERAL NOTE
Crown immunity: the general rule
   The Crown is immune from the coercive components of listed building control and
conservation area control, as it is from general planning control (*Lord Advocate* v.
Dumbarton District Council [1990] 3 W.L.R. 1346). But this section carves out several
exceptions from that immunity, and the following section confers special power on the
Crown to seek listed building consent and conservation area consent in advance of disposing
of any interest in Crown land.

What is Crown land
   The definition of Crown land in subs. (5) is broad, and encompasses not merely the private
estate of the monarch but also any land belonging to a government department. DOE
Circular 18/84, *Memorandum*, Pt. IV, para. 1, indicates that the Crown claims this immunity
also in respect of health authorities and the Metropolitan Police.

Where a private interest is held in Crown land
   Where an interest in a listed building which is Crown land is held other than by the
Crown, all of the provisions specified in subs. (2)(b) apply to the land to the extent of that
interest. The owner of the interest is able (and required) to obtain authorisations to works
in the usual way, but must certify under s.11 that the Crown had been notified of the
application as an owner of the land.
   An interest held otherwise than by the Crown would normally need to be a property
interest, but subs. (6) widens the category so as to include the rights of a person occupying
Crown land under a written licence, except for ss.32–37 (listed building purchase notices).

Works carried out by the Crown
   Despite the immunity from controls, the Crown has undertaken to observe a set of non-
statutory shadow procedures, contained in DOE Circular 18/84, *Memorandum*, Pt. IV,
paras. 31–33, before carrying out works which would otherwise have required consent.
Government departments (together with the Crown Estate Commissioners and the Duchies
of Cornwall and Lancaster) will consult about any proposal to demolish a listed building, or
to alter or extend it in such a way as to affect its character as a building of special
arrchitectural or historic interest. The local planning authority are asked to advertise such
proposals and to notify national and local amenity societies in the same way as if a formal
application had been made to them. Objections made by third parties are conveyed by the
local planning authority to the developing department who will consider whether to proceed
in light of the objections, or whether to refer the matter to the Secretary of State for the
Environment. If there is an unresolved objection from the local planning authority, the
matter must be referred to the Secretary of State, to be dealt with in accordance with a
procedure modelled on the statutory appeals procedure. Similar shadow arrangements apply
(paras. 34 and 35) to proposals for the demolition of buildings in conservation areas.

Obtaining consent in advance of land disposal
   Where the Crown proposes to dispose of land, and seeks listed building consent (or
conservation area consent) in anticipation of disposal, application for consent may be made
by virtue of s.84. Any consent granted on such an application applies only to works carried
out after the land has ceased to be Crown land; and, so long as it continues to be Crown
land, to works carried out by virtue of a private interest in the land (s.84(3)). The
appropriate Crown authority is required to give written notification to the local planning
authority after disposing of, or of any interest in, the land (Town and Country Planning
(Crown Land Applications) Regulations 1984 (No. 1015), reg. 4).

Similar procedures are established under the T.C.P.A. 1990 for obtaining planning permission (s.299) and tree preservation order consent (s.300) prior to disposal of any interest in the land.

Applicability to conservation areas
Subss. (1)(b) and (3) and (4) are extended by s.74(3) to conservation areas. All the provisions of this Act that are applied to conservation areas are set out, as modified by the Regulations, in the *Conservation Area Code*.

Application for listed building or conservation area consent in anticipation of disposal of Crown land

84.—(1) This section has effect for the purpose of enabling Crown land, or an interest in Crown land, to be disposed of with the benefit of listed building consent or conservation area consent.

(2) Notwithstanding the interest of the Crown in the land in question, an application for any such consent may be made—
(a) by the appropriate authority; or
(b) by any person authorised by that authority in writing;
and, subject to subsections (3) and (4), all the statutory provisions relating to the making and determination of any such application shall accordingly apply as if the land were not Crown land.

(3) Any listed building consent or conservation area consent granted by virtue of this section shall apply only—
(a) to works carried out after the land in question has ceased to be Crown land; and
(b) so long as that land continues to be Crown land, to works carried out by virtue of a private interest in the land.

(4) The Secretary of State may by regulations—
(a) modify or exclude any of the statutory provisions referred to in subsection (2) in their application by virtue of that subsection and any other statutory provisions in their application to consents granted or made by virtue of this section;
(b) make provision for requiring a local planning authority to be notified of any disposal of, or of an interest in, any Crown land in respect of which an application has been made by virtue of this section; and
(c) make such other provision in relation to the making and determination of applications by virtue of this section as he thinks necessary or expedient.

(5) This section shall not be construed as affecting any right to apply for any listed building consent or conservation area consent in respect of Crown land in a case in which such an application can be made by virtue of a private interest in the land.

(6) In this section—
"statutory provisions" means provisions contained in or having effect under any enactment;
"private interest" means an interest which is neither a Crown interest nor a Duchy interest;
and references to the disposal of an interest in Crown land include references to the grant of an interest in such land.

(7) Subsections (5), (7) and (8) of section 83 apply for the purposes of this section as they apply for the purposes of that section.

(8) A person who is entitled to occupy Crown land by virtue of a licence in writing shall be treated for the purposes of this section as having an interest in land and references to the disposal or grant of an interest in Crown land and to a private interest in such land shall be construed accordingly.

DEFINITIONS
   "building": s.91.
   "conservation area": s.91(1).
   "conservation area consent": s.91(1).
   "disposal": s.91(2).
   "enactment": s.91(2).
   "land": s.91(2).
   "listed building": ss.1(5); 91(1).
   "listed building consent": ss.8(7); 91(1).
   "local planning authority": s.81.

GENERAL NOTE

Introduction
   This section, introduced originally by the Town and Country Planning Act 1984, allows
the Crown to obtain listed building consent and conservation area consent in advance of
disposal by it of an interest in the land, thereby resolving a constitutional uncertainty as to
whether the Crown's general immunity from planning control deprived it of the right to take
advantage of planning legislation when it chose to do so. Corresponding provision is made
in the T.C.P.A. 1990 for obtaining planning permission (s.299) and tree preservation order
consent (s.300) prior to disposal of any interest in the land. The section does not affect the
right of the owner of any other interest in Crown land to seek consent in the usual manner
(subs. (5)).

Procedure
   An application for consent may be made to the local planning authority in the usual way,
but it is required to be accompanied by (1) where there is no private interest held in the
land, a statement to that effect; and (2) a copy of the consent of the appropriate authority
(Town and Country Planning (Listed Buildings and Conservation Areas) Regulations 1990,
reg. 6(1A), inserted by way of modification under reg. 15(1)(c)).

Effect of consent
   Any consent granted on such an application applies only to works carried out after the
land has ceased to be Crown land; and, so long as it continues to be Crown land, to works
carried out by virtue of a private interest in the land (subs. (3)). Any refusal of consent, or
conditions, may be appealed against to the Secretary of State, and the usual remedies of
listed building (or conservation area) purchase notice, and compensation entitlement, are
available to the Crown.

Notification of disposal
   The appropriate Crown authority is required to give written notification to the local
planing authority after disposing of, or of any interest in, the land (Town and Country
Planning (Crown Land Applications) Regulations 1984 (No. 1015), reg. 4).

Effect of Crown immunity following disposal
   Where the Crown had disposed of an interest in land, the immunity under this Act in
respect of the carrying out by the Crown of any unauthorised works transfers to subsequent
owners; and by virtue of subs. (3) no listed building enforcement notice may be issued in
respect of it.

British Coal

   85.—(1) The Secretary of State for the Environment and the Secretary
of State for Energy with the consent of the Treasury may by regulations
direct that any of the provisions of sections 1(1) to (5), 2(1) to (3), 51, 52,
83, 88 (except subsection (3)) and 90(1) to (6) relating to statutory
undertakers and land of such undertakers and any of the other provisions
of this Act as they have effect for the purposes of any of those provisions
shall apply to the British Coal Corporation as if it were a statutory
undertaker.

   (2) Such regulations may apply those provisions subject to such adaptations, modifications and exceptions as may be specified in the
regulations.

GENERAL NOTE
    British Coal (formerly the National Coal Corporation) is not a statutory undertaker for the purposes of this Act under s.91, but this section allows the two Secretaries of State by regulations to direct that the provisions specified in subs. (1) should apply to the Board as if it were a statutory undertaker.
    The Town and Country Planning (National Coal Board) Regulations 1972 (No. 1006) do apply some of the provisions of the T.C.P.A. 1990 (under the parallel power conferred by s.317 of that Act) but do not apply to any of the provisions specified in this section.

Ecclesiastical property

86.—(1) Without prejudice to the provisions of the Acquisition of Land Act 1981 with respect to notices served under that Act, where under any of the provisions of this Act a notice or copy of a notice is required to be served on an owner of land, and the land is ecclesiastical property, a similar notice or copy of a notice shall be served on the Church Commissioners.

(2) Where the fee simple of any ecclesiastical property is in abeyance—

(a) if the property is situated in England, then for the purposes of section 11, this subsection (other than paragraph (b)) and sections 62, 63 and 83(1) and any other provisions of this Act so far as they apply or have effect for the purposes of any of those provisions, the fee simple shall be treated as being vested in the Church Commissioners;

(b) in any case, the fee simple shall, for the purposes of a compulsory acquisition of the property under section 47, be treated as being vested in the Church Commissioners, and any notice to treat shall be served, or be deemed to have been served, accordingly.

(3) Any compensation payable under section 29 in respect of land which is ecclesiastical property—

(a) shall be paid to the Church Commissioners, and

(b) shall be applied by them for the purposes for which the proceeds of a sale by agreement of the land would be applicable under any enactment or Measure authorising or disposing of the proceeds of such a sale.

(4) In this section "ecclesiastical property" means land belonging to an ecclesiastical benefice, or being or forming part of a church subject to the jurisdiction of a bishop of any diocese or the site of such a church, or being or forming part of a burial ground subject to such jurisdiction.

Settled land

87. The classes of works specified in Part II of Schedule 3 to the Settled Land Act 1925 (which specifies improvements which may be paid for out of capital money, subject to provisions under which repayment out of income may be required to be made) shall include works specified by the Secretary of State as being required for property maintaining a listed building which is settled land within the meaning of that Act.

DEFINITIONS
  "building": s.91.
  "land": s.91(2).
  "listed building": ss.1(5); 91(1).

Miscellaneous provisions

Rights of entry

88.—(1) Any person duly authorised in writing by the Secretary of State
may at any reasonable time enter any land for the purpose of surveying
any building on it in connection with a proposal to include the building in,
or exclude it from, a list compiled or approved under section 1.

(2) Any person duly authorised in writing by the Secretary of State, a
local planning authority or, where the authorisation relates to a building
situated in Greater London, the Commission may at any reasonable time
enter any land for any of the following purposes—

  (a) surveying it in connection with any proposal by the authority or
       the Secretary of State to make, issue or serve any order or notice
       under any of the provisions of sections 1 to 26, 38, 40, 46, 54, 55,
       60, 68, 75 or 76 or under any order or regulations made under any
       of them, or any notice under section 48;

  (b) ascertaining whether any such order or notice has been complied
       with;

  (c) ascertaining whether an offence has been, or is being, committed
       with respect to any building on the land, under section 9, 11 or 43;

  (d) ascertaining whether any such building is being maintained in a
       proper state of repair.

(3) Any person duly authorised in writing by the Secretary of State, a
local authority or, where the authorisation relates to a building situated
in Greater London, the Commission may at any reasonable time enter
any land for any of the following purposes—

  (a) ascertaining whether an offence has been or is being committed
       under section 59;

  (b) ascertaining whether any of the functions conferred by section 54
       should or may be exercised in connection with the land; or

  (c) exercising any of those functions in connection with the land.

(4) Any person who is an officer of the Valuation Office or is duly
authorised in writing by a local planning authority may at any reasonable
time enter any land for the purpose of surveying it, or estimating its value,
in connection with a claim for compensation payable by the authority
under section 27, 28 or 29 in respect of any land.

(5) Any person who is an officer of the Valuation Office or is duly
authorised in writing by a local authority having power to acquire land
under sections 47 to 52 may at any reasonable time enter any land for the
purpose of surveying it, or estimating its value, in connection with any
proposal to acquire that land or any other land, or in connection with any
claim for compensation in respect of any such acquisition.

(6) Subject to subsection (7), any power conferred by this section to
survey land shall be construed as including power to search and bore for
the purpose of ascertaining the nature of the subsoil or the presence of
minerals in it.

(7) Section 325 of the principal Act (supplementary provisions as to
rights of entry) applies in relation to this section as it applies in relation
to section 324 of that Act taking the reference in section 325(8) to section
324(8) as a reference to subsection (6) of this section.

DEFINITIONS
  "building": s.91.
  "functions": s.91(2).

"land": s.91(2).
"local authority": s.91(2).
"local planning authority": s.81.
"minerals": s.91(2).
"the Commission": s.91(1).
"the Principal Act": s. 91(1).
"Valuation Office": s.91(2).

ALLOCATION OF FUNCTIONS
The functions of a local planning authority under subss.(2) and (3) are exercisable solely by:—
Greater London: the London borough council as local planning authority under the T.C.P.A. 1990, s.1(2): Sched. 4, para. 4(1).
Metropolitan areas: the metropolitan district council as local planning authority under the T.C.P.A. 1990, s.1(2): (Sched. 4, para. 4(1).
Non-metropolitan areas: the district planning authority (Sched. 4, para. 4(1)(c)).
National Parks (outside a metropolitan county): the county planning authority (T.C.P.A. 1990, s.4) or joint planning board in areas where one has been established as county planning authority: Sched. 4, para. 4(1)(b).
Norfolk and Suffolk Broads: for the purposes of subs. (2)(a) and (b) "local planning authority" includes the Broads Authority (Sched. 4, para. 5(b)) and for the purposes of subs. (3), "local authority" includes the Broads Authority (s.91(6)).
Urban development areas: the urban development corporation where an order has been made under the Local Government, Planning and Land Act 1980, s.149(1), transferring the function to the corporation (T.C.P.A. 1990, s.7(1)): for a list of current orders see the notes to s.81.
Housing action trust areas: the housing action trust has the functions under this section to the exclusion of any other authority (other than the Secretary of State) where an order has been made under the Housing Act 1988, s.67(3), transferring the function (as a function within s.67(3A), as substituted by the Planning (Consequential Provisions) Act 1990, Sched. 2, para. 79(3)) to the trust (T.C.P.A. 1990, s.8(2)): see the notes to s.81.
Enterprise zones: the enterprise zone authority, where so provided by order under the Local Government, Planning and Land Act 1980, Sched. 32, para. 5.

Application of certain general provisions of principal Act

89.—(1) Subject to subsection (2), the following provisions of the principal Act shall apply for the purposes of this Act as they apply for the purposes of that Act, namely—
    section 320 (local inquiries),
    section 322 (orders as to costs of parties where no inquiry held),
    section 323 (procedure on certain appeals and applications),
    section 329 (service of notices),
    section 330 (power to require information as to interests in land),
    section 331 (offences by corporations).
  (2) Section 331 of that Act shall not apply to offences under section 59 of this Act.

DEFINITIONS
"land": s.91(2).
"the Principal Act": s.91(1).

Financial provisions

90.—(1) Where—
    (a) compensation is payable by a local authority under this Act in consequence of any decision or order given or made under Chapters I, II or IV of Part I or sections 32 to 37, 60 or Schedule 3; and
    (b) the decision or order in consequence of which it is payable was given or made wholly or partly in the interest of a service

which is provided by a government department and the cost of
which is defrayed out of money provided by Parliament,
the Minister responsible for the administration of that service may pay
that authority a contribution of such amount as he may with the consent
of the Treasury determine.

(2) Any local authority and any statutory undertakers may contribute
towards any expenses incurred by a local planning authority in or in
connection with the performance of any of their functions under the
provisions of Chapters I to V of Part I (other than sections 27 to 31, 53,
54, 55, 57, 58) and sections 66 and 68 and Schedule 1.

(3) Where any expenses are incurred by a local authority in the payment
of compensation payable in consequence of anything done under Chapters
I, II or IV of Part I or sections 32 to 37, 56, 59, 60, 66(1), 67, 68 or 73 the
Secretary of State may, if it appears to him to be expedient to do so,
require any other local authority to contribute towards those expenses
such sum as appears to him to be reasonable, having regard to any benefit
accruing to that authority by reason of the proceeding giving rise to the
compensation.

(4) For the purposes of subsections (2) and (3), contributions made by
a local planning authority towards the expenditure of a joint advisory
committee shall be deemed to be expenses incurred by that authority for
the purposes for which that expenditure is incurred by the committee.

(5) The council of a county may direct that any expenses incurred by
them under the provisions specified in subsection (6) shall be treated as
special expenses of a county council chargeable upon such part of the
county as may be specified in the directions.

(6) Those provisions are—

(a) sections 1(1) to (5), 2(1) to (3), 51, 52, 64, 65, 66(2), 82(1) and
    (4)(b), 83, 86 (except subsection (2)(a)) 87, 88 (except subsec-
    tion (3)) and subsections (1) to (4) of this section and any other
    provisions of the planning Acts in so far as they apply, or have
    effect for the purposes of, any of those provisions; and

(b) sections 1(6), 3, 4, 5, 7 to 29, 32 to 50 (except 39(6) and 42(6)),
    60(1) to (4), 61, 66(1), 67(2)(b),(6) and (7), 73(1) (so far as it
    applies to section 67(2)(b), (6) and (7)), 82(2), (3) and (4)(a)
    and Schedules 1, 2 and 3.

(7) There shall be paid out of money provided by Parliament—

(a) any sums necessary to enable the Secretary of State to make
    any payments becoming payable by him under sections 27 to
    29;

(b) any expenses incurred by any government department (includ-
    ing the Secretary of State) in the acquisition of land under
    sections 47 to 52 or in the payment of compensation under
    section 51(4) or 88(7) or under subsection (1);

(8) Any sums received by the Secretary of State under this Act shall be
paid into the Consolidated Fund.

DEFINITIONS
  "functions": s.91(2).
  "government department": s.91(2).
  "land": s.91(2).
  "local authority": s.91(2).
  "local planning authority": s.81.
  "Minister": s.91(2).
  "statutory undertaker": s.91(3).
  "the planning Acts": s.91(2).

Definition of statutory undertakers
"Statutory undertaker" includes (s.262, as applied by s.91(3)):
> "persons authorised by an enactment to carry on any railway, light railway, tramway, road transport, water transport, canal, inland navigation, dock, harbour, pier or lighthouse undertaking, or any undertaking for the supply of hydraulic power and a relevant airport operator (within the meaning of Part V of the Airports Act 1986)."

In addition, for the purposes of subs. (2) of this section, the expression includes (s.91(3)):
(1) every water or sewerage undertaker;
(2) the Post Office;
(3) the Civil Aviation Authority;
(4) a public gas supplier;
(5) a holder of a licence under section 6 of the Electricity Act 1989;
(6) the National Rivers Authority.

PART IV

SUPPLEMENTAL

Interpretation

91.—(1) In this Act, except in so far as the context otherwise requires—
> "building preservation notice" has the meaning given in section 3(1);
> "the Commission" means the Historic Buildings and Monuments Commission for England;
> "conservation area" means an area for the time being designated under section 69;
> "conservation area consent" has the meaning given in section 74(1);
> "listed building" has the meaning given in section 1(5);
> "listed building consent" has the meaning given in section 8(7);
> "listed building enforcement notice" has the meaning given in section 38(1);
> "listed building purchase notice" has the meaning given in section 32(1);
> "local planning authority" shall be construed in accordance with section 81;
> "prescribed", except in relation to matters expressly required or authorised by this Act to be prescribed in some other way, means prescribed by regulations under this Act;
> "the principal Act" means the Town and Country Planning Act 1990;
> "town scheme agreement" has the meaning given in section 79.

(2) Subject to subsections (6) and (7) and except in so far as the context otherwise requires, the following expressions have the same meaning as in the principal Act—
> "the 1962 Act"
> "acquiring authority"
> "the Broads"
> "building"
> "compulsory acquisition"
> "development"
> "development order"
> "development plan"
> "disposal"
> "enactment"
> "functions"
> "government department"

"joint planning board"
"land"
"lease"
"local authority"
"London borough"
"minerals"
"Minister"
"new development"
"owner"
"the planning Acts"
"planning permission"
"public gas supplier"
"use"
"Valuation Office",
but this subsection does not affect the meaning of "owner" in section 11.

(3) In this Act "statutory undertakers" has the same meaning as in the principal Act except that—

   (a) in sections 33 to 36 it shall be deemed to include references to a public telecommunications operator;

   (b) in sections 33 to 36, 51(2)(a) and 90(2) it shall be deemed to include the Post Office, the Civil Aviation Authority, a public gas supplier, a holder of a licence under section 6 of the Electricity Act 1989, the National Rivers Authority and every water or sewerage undertaker.

(4) References in the planning Acts to any of the provisions mentioned in section 82 include, except where the context otherwise requires, references to those provisions as modified under that section.

(5) Words in this Act importing a reference to service of a notice to treat shall be construed as including a reference to the constructive service of such a notice which, by virtue of any enactment, is to be deemed to be served.

(6) In sections 33 to 36, 53(1) 54, 55 and 88(3) "local authority", in relation to a building or land in the Broads, includes the Broads Authority.

(7) For the purposes of subsection (1)(b) of section 57 and subsection (2) of that section as it applies for the purposes of that subsection the definition of "building" in the principal Act shall apply with the omission of the words "but does not include any plant or machinery comprised in a building".

Application of Act to Isles of Scilly

92.—(1) The Secretary of State shall, after consultation with the Council of the Isles of Scilly, by order provide for the application to those Isles of the provisions of this Act specified in subsection (2) as if those Isles were a separate county.

(2) The provisions referred to in subsection (1) are—

   (a) sections 1(1) to (5), 2(1) to (3), 51, 52, 64, 65, 66(2), 82(1) and (4)(b), 83, 84, 86 (except subsection (2)(a)) 87, 88 (except subsection (3)), 90(1) to (4) and any other provisions of the planning Acts in so far as they apply, or have effect for the purposes of, any of those provisions; and

   (b) sections 1(6), 3, 4, 5, 7 to 29, 32 to 50 (except 39(6) and 42(6)), 60(1) to (4), 61, 66(1), 67(2)(b),(6) and (7), 73(1) (so far as it applies to section 67(2)(b), (6) and (7)), 75(1), (5) and (6), 30082(2), (3) and (4)(a) and Schedules 1, 2 and 3.

(3) The Secretary of State, may, after consultation with the Council of the Isles of Scilly, by order provide for the application to those Isles of sections 2(4) and (5), 53 to 55, 59, 67(1) to (6), 69 to 72, 73(1), 74 to 76

and 88(3) and paragraph 4 of Schedule 4 as if those Isles were a separate county or district.

(4) Any order under this section may provide for the application of provisions to the Isles subject to such modifications as may be specified in the order.

DEFINITIONS
"the planning Acts": s.91(2).

GENERAL NOTE
Various provisions of the Town and Country Planning Act 1971 were extended to the Isles of Scilly by the Town and Country Planning (Isles of Scilly) Order 1973 (No. 1285).

Regulations and orders

93.—(1) The Secretary of State may make regulations under this Act—
  (a) for prescribing the form of any notice, order or other document authorised or required by any of the provisions of this Act to be served, made or issued by any local authority;
  (b) for any purpose for which regulations are authorised or required to be made under this Act.

(2) Any power conferred by this Act to make regulations shall be exercisable by statutory instrument.

(3) Any statutory instrument containing regulations made under this Act shall be subject to annulment in pursuance of a resolution of either House of Parliament.

(4) The power to make orders under sections 8(5), 60, 75(7) and 92 shall be exercisable by statutory instrument.

(5) Any statutory instrument which contains an order under section 60 or 75(7) shall be subject to annulment in pursuance of a resolution of either House of Parliament.

(6) Any order under section 60 or 75(7) may contain such supplementary and incidental provisions as may appear to the Secretary of State appropriate.

(7) Without prejudice to section 14 of the Interpretation Act 1978, any power conferred by this Act to make an order shall include power to vary or revoke any such order by a subsequent order.

DEFINITIONS
"local authority": s.91(2).

Short title, commencement and extent

94.—(1) This Act may be cited as the Planning (Listed Buildings and Conservation Areas) Act 1990.

(2) Except as provided in Schedule 4 to the Planning (Consequential Provisions) Act 1990, this Act shall come into force at the end of the period of three months beginning with the day on which it is passed.

(3) This Act extends to England and Wales only.

DEFINITIONS
"building": s.91.
"conservation area": s.91(1).
"land": s.91(2).
"listed building": ss.1(5); 91(1).

GENERAL NOTE
This Act received Royal Assent on May 24, 1990, and accordingly (subs. (3)) came into force on August 24, 1990.

SCHEDULES

Section 1(6)   SCHEDULE 1

BUILDINGS FORMERLY SUBJECT TO BUILDING PRESERVATION ORDERS

1. Subject to paragraph 2, every building which immediately before January 1, 1969 was subject to a building preservation order under Part III of the 1962 Act, but was not then included in a list compiled or approved under section 32 of that Act, shall be deemed to be a listed building.

2.—(1) The Secretary of State may at any time direct, in the case of any building, that paragraph 1 shall no longer apply to it.

(2) The local planning authority in whose area a building in respect of which such a direction is given is situated shall, on being notified of the direction, give notice of it to the owner and occupier of the building.

(3) Before giving such a direction in relation to a building situated in England, the Secretary of State shall consult with the Commission who shall in turn consult with the local planning authority and the owner and the occupier of the building.

(4) Before giving such a direction in relation to a building not situated in England the Secretary of State shall consult with the local planning authority and the owner and occupier of the building.

3. In the case of a building to which paragraph 1 applies—

(a) a notice of appeal under section 20 may include a claim that the Secretary of State should give a direction under paragraph 2 with respect to the building and on such an appeal the Secretary of State may give such a direction; and

(b) such a direction may also be given on an appeal under section 39.

DEFINITIONS
"building": s.91.
"land": s.91(2).
"listed building": ss.1(5); 91(1).
"local planning authority": s.81.
"owner": s.91(2).
"the Commission": s.91(1).

GENERAL NOTE
The Schedule makes provision for transition from the old system of building preservation orders that existed prior to 1969, to the contemporary listing system. It deems a building formerly subject to an order to be now a listed building, unless the Secretary of State otherwise directs (para. 2(1)).

Section 5   SCHEDULE 2

LAPSE OF BUILDING PRESERVATION NOTICES

1. This Schedule applies where a building preservation notice ceases to be in force by virtue of—

(a) the expiry of the six month period mentioned in subsection (3)(b) of section 3; or

(b) the service of a notification by the Secretary of State under subsection (4)(b) of that section.

2. The fact that the notice has ceased to be in force shall not affect the liability of any person to be prosecuted and punished for an offence under section 9 or 43 committed with respect to the building while it was in force.

3. Any proceedings on or arising out of an application for listed building consent with respect to the building made while the notice was in force and any such consent granted while it was in force shall lapse.

4.—(1) Any listed building enforcement notice served by the local planning authority while the building preservation notice was in force shall cease to have effect.

(2) Any proceedings on it under sections 38 to 40 shall lapse.

(3) Notwithstanding sub-paragraph (1), section 42(1) and (2) shall continue to have effect as respects any expenses incurred by the local authority, owner or occupier as mentioned in that section and with respect to any sums paid on account of such expenses.

Definitions
  "building": s.91.
  "building preservation notice": s.91(1).
  "listed building": ss.1(5); 91(1).
  "listed building consent": ss.8(7); 91(1).
  "listed building enforcement notice": ss.38(1); 91(1).
  "local authority": s.91(2).
  "local planning authority": s.81.
  "owner": s.91(2).

General Note
A building preservation notice lapses when the Secretary of State has failed within six months to list the building, or has notified the local planning authority that he does not propose to do so. This Schedule preserves the criminal liability of parties for the period the notice remained in force, but overrides any listed building enforcement notice that had already been served.

Sections 22 and 40   SCHEDULE 3

Determination of Certain Appeals by Person Appointed by Secretary of State

Determination of appeals by appointed person

1.—(1) The Secretary of State may by regulations prescribe the classes of appeals under sections 20 and 39 which are to be determined by a person appointed by the Secretary of State for the purpose instead of by the Secretary of State.
(2) Appeals of a prescribed class shall be so determined except in such classes of case as may for the time being be prescribed or as may be specified in directions given by the Secretary of State.
(3) Regulations made for the purpose of this paragraph may provide for the giving of publicity to any directions given by the Secretary of State under this paragraph.
(4) This paragraph shall not affect any provision in this Act or any instrument made under it that an appeal shall lie to, or a notice of appeal shall be served on, the Secretary of State.
(5) A person appointed under this paragraph is referred to in this Schedule as "an appointed person".

Powers and duties of appointed person

2.—(1) An appointed person shall have the same powers and duties—
  (a) in relation to an appeal under section 20, as the Secretary of State has under subsection (1) of section 22 and paragraph 2 of Schedule 1; and
  (b) in relation to an appeal under section 39, as he has under section 41(1), (2), (5) or (6) and paragraph 2 of Schedule 1.
(2) Sections 22(2) and 40(2) shall not apply to an appeal which falls to be determined by an appointed person, but before it is determined the Secretary of State shall ask the appellant and the local planning authority whether they wish to appear before and be heard by the appointed person.
(3) If both the parties express a wish not to appear and be heard the appeal may be determined without their being heard.
(4) If either of the parties expresses a wish to appear and be heard, the appointed person shall give them both an opportunity of doing so.
(5) Where an appeal has been determined by an appointed person, his decision shall be treated as that of the Secretary of State.
(6) Except as provided by sections 62 to 65, the validity of that decision shall not be questioned in any proceedings whatsoever.
(7) It shall not be a ground of application to the High Court under section 63, or of appeal to the High Court under section 65, that an appeal ought to have been determined by the Secretary of State and not by an appointed person, unless the appellant or the local planning authority challenge the appointed person's power to determine the appeal before his decision on the appeal is given.
(8) Where in any enactment (including this Act) there is a reference to the Secretary of State in a context relating or capable of relating—
  (a) to an appeal under section 20 or 39, or

(b) to anything done or authorised or required to be done by, to or before the Secretary of State on or in connection with any such appeal,

then so far as the context permits it shall be construed, in relation to an appeal determined or falling to be determined by an appointed person, as a reference to him.

Determination of appeals by Secretary of State

3.—(1) The Secretary of State may, if he thinks fit, direct that an appeal which would otherwise fall to be determined by an appointed person shall instead be determined by the Secretary of State.

(2) Such a direction shall state the reasons for which it is given and shall be served on the appellant, the local planning authority, any person who made representations relating to the subject matter of the appeal which the authority were required to take into account by regulations made under section 11(4) and, if any person has been appointed under paragraph 1, on him.

(3) Where in consequence of such a direction an appeal under section 20 or 39 falls to be determined by the Secretary of State himself, the provisions of this Act which are relevant to the appeal shall, subject to the following provisions of this paragraph, apply to the appeal as if this Schedule had never applied to it.

(4) The Secretary of State shall give the appellant, the local planning authority and any person who has made such representations as are referred to in sub-paragraph (2) an opportunity of appearing before and being heard by a person appointed by the Secretary of State for that purpose if—

   (a) the reasons for the direction raise matters with respect to which any of those persons have not made representations; or

   (b) in the case of the appellant and the local planning authority, either of them was not asked in pursuance of paragraph 2(2) whether they wished to appear before and be heard by the appointed person, or expressed no wish in answer to that question, or expressed a wish to appear and be heard but was not given an opportunity of doing so.

(5) Except as provided by sub-paragraph (4), the Secretary of State need not give any person an opportunity of appearing before and being heard by a person appointed for the purpose, or of making fresh representations or making or withdrawing any representations already made.

(6) In determining the appeal the Secretary of State may take into account any report made to him by any person previously appointed to determine it.

4.—(1) The Secretary of State may by a further direction revoke a direction under paragraph 3 at any time before the determination of the appeal.

(2) Such a further direction shall state the reasons for which it is given and shall be served on the person, if any, previously appointed to determine the appeal, the appellant, the local planning authority and any person who made representations relating to the subject matter of the appeal which the authority were required to take into account by regulations made under section 11(4).

(3) Where such a further direction has been given the provisions of this Schedule relevant to the appeal shall apply, subject to sub-paragraph (4), as if no direction under paragraph 3 had been given.

(4) Anything done by or on behalf of the Secretary of State in connection with the appeal which might have been done by the appointed person (including any arrangements made for the holding of a hearing or local inquiry) shall unless that person directs otherwise, be treated as having been done by him.

Appointment of another person to determine appeal

5.—(1) At any time before the appointed person has determined the appeal the Secretary of State may—

   (a) revoke his appointment; and

   (b) appoint another person under paragraph 1 to determine the appeal instead.

(2) Where such a new appointment is made the consideration of the appeal or any inquiry or other hearing in connection with it shall be begun afresh.

(3) Nothing in sub-paragraph (2) shall require—

   (a) the question referred to in paragraph 2(2) to be asked again with reference to the new appointed person if before his appointment it was asked with reference to the previous appointed person (any answers being treated as given with reference to the new appointed person); or

  (b) any person to be given an opportunity of making fresh representations or modifying or withdrawing any representations already made.

Local inquiries and hearings

6.—(1) Whether or not the parties to an appeal have asked for an opportunity to appear and be heard, an appointed person—

  (a) may hold a local inquiry in connection with the appeal; and

  (b) shall do so if the Secretary of State so directs.

(2) Where an appointed person—

    (a) holds a hearing by virtue of paragraph 2(4); or

    (b) holds an inquiry by virtue of this paragraph,

an assessor may be appointed by the Secretary of State to sit with the appointed person at the hearing or inquiry to advise him on any matters arising, notwithstanding that the appointed person is to determine the appeal.

(3) Subject to sub-paragraph (4), the costs of any such hearing or inquiry shall be paid by the Secretary of State.

(4) Section 250(2) to (5) of the Local Government Act 1972 (local inquiries: evidence and costs) applies to an inquiry held by virtue of this paragraph with the following adaptations—

  (a) for the references in subsection (4) (recovery of costs of holding the inquiry) to the Minister causing the inquiry to be held, there shall be substituted references to the Secretary of State; and

  (b) for the reference in subsection (5) (orders as to the costs of the parties) to the Minister causing the inquiry to be held, there shall be substituted a reference to the appointed person or the Secretary of State.

(5) Subject to sub-paragraph (6), at any such inquiry oral evidence shall be heard in public and documentary evidence shall be open to public inspection.

(6) If the Secretary of State is satisfied in the case of any such inquiry—

  (a) that giving evidence of a particular description or, as the case may be, making it available for inspection would be likely to result in the disclosure of information as to any of the matters mentioned in sub-paragraph (7); and

  (b) that the public disclosure of that information would be contrary to the national interest,

he may direct that evidence of the description indicated in the direction shall only be heard or, as the case may be, open to inspection at that inquiry by such persons or persons of such descriptions as he may specify in that direction.

(7) The matters referred to in sub-paragraph (6)(a) are—

  (a) national security; and

  (b) the measures taken or to be taken to ensure the security of any premises or property.

(8) The appointed person or the Secretary of State has the same power to make orders under section 250(5) of the Local Government Act 1972 (orders with respect to costs of the parties) in relation to proceedings under this Schedule which do not give rise to an inquiry as he has in relation to such an inquiry.

Supplementary provisions

7.—(1) The Tribunals and Inquiries Act 1971 shall apply to a local inquiry or other hearing held in pursuance of this Schedule as it applies to a statutory inquiry held by the Secretary of State, but as if in section 12(1) of that Act (statement of reasons for decisions) the reference to any decision taken by the Secretary of State were a reference to a decision taken by an appointed person.

(2) Where an appointed person is an officer of the Department of the Environment or the Welsh Office the functions of determining an appeal and doing anything in connection with it conferred on him by this Schedule shall be treated for the purposes of the Parliamentary Commissioner Act 1967—

  (a) if he was appointed by the Secretary of State for the time being having general responsibility in planning matters in relation to England, as functions of that Department; and

  (b) if he was appointed by the Secretary of State for the time being having general responsibility in planning matters in relation to Wales, as functions of the Welsh Office.

DEFINITIONS
"enactment": s.91(2).
"functions": s.91(2).
"land": s.91(2).
"local planning authority": s.81.
"Minister": s.91(2).
"prescribed": s.91(1).

GENERAL NOTE
The Schedule regulates appeal procedure where an appeal is to be determined by an inspector. See further the notes to s.20.

Section 81   SCHEDULE 4

FURTHER PROVISIONS AS TO EXERCISE OF FUNCTIONS BY DIFFERENT AUTHORITIES

1. Subsection (3) of section 1 of the principal Act (which provides that outside London, the metropolitan counties and the Isles of Scilly planning functions are exercisable by both county and district planning authorities) shall have effect subject to paragraphs 2, 4 and 5, and that section and section 2 of the principal Act (joint planning boards) shall have effect subject to paragraph 3.

2. Subject to sections 4, 6, 7 and 8 of the principal Act (which make provision as to the exercise of planning functions in National Parks, enterprise zones, urban development areas and housing action areas) and to the following provisions, outside Greater London the functions of a local planning authority under sections 7 to 26, 38, 42, paragraph 2(2) of Schedule 1 and Schedule 2 shall be exercised by the district planning authority.

3.—(1) Any application for listed building consent under section 10 shall, if relating to land in a National Park, be made to the district planning authority who shall, unless it falls to be determined by them, send it on to the county planning authority.

(2) Where any such application relating to land in a National Park falls to be determined by a county planning authority, that authority shall before determining it consult with the district planning authority for the area in which the land to which the application relates is situated.

4.—(1) Subject to sections 4(3) and (4), 6, 7 and 8 of the principal Act, the functions of a local planning authority under sections 67(2) and (3), 69, 70 and 74 and paragraph 2(3) and (4) of Schedule 1 shall be exercisable—

(a) in Greater London or a metropolitan county, by the local planning authority;
(b) in any part of a National Park outside a metropolitan county, by the county planning authority; and
(c) elsewhere, by the district planning authority;

but outside a National Park a county planning authority shall also have power to make determinations and designations under section 69.

(2) Before making a determination under section 69 a county planning authority shall consult the council of each district of which any part is included in the area to which the proposed determination relates.

(3) Where it is the duty of the district planning authority to take the steps required by section 67(2) in relation to an application which falls to be determined by the county planning authority, the district planning authority shall as soon as possible after taking those steps notify the county planning authority of the steps which they have taken and the date on which they took them.

5. For the purposes of sections 3 and 4, 7 to 26, 38, 42, 56, 66(1), 67, 69 to 75, 82, 84 and 88(2)(c) and (d) and the provisions of this Schedule so far as they relate to those provisions, the Broads Authority shall be the sole district planning authority in respect of the Broads, and in relation to a building or land within the Broads—

(a) the references to the district planning authority in section 2(1)(b)(iii) and in paragraph 4(1)(c) of this Schedule, so far as that paragraph relates to paragraph 2(3) and (4) of Schedule 1, include that Authority; and
(b) for the purposes of sections 6 and 88(2)(a) and (b) "local planning authority" includes that Authority.

6. The validity of any consent or determination granted or made or purported to be granted or made by a local planning authority in respect of an application for listed building consent or conservation area consent shall not be called in question in any legal proceedings, or in any proceedings under this Act which are not legal proceedings, on the ground that the

consent or determination should have been granted or made by some other local planning
authority.

7.—(1) The Secretary of State may from time to time direct a district planning authority
to submit to him for his approval within a period specified in the direction the arrangements
which the authority propose to make to obtain specialist advice in connection with their
functions under sections 3, 4, 8, 10 to 26, 38, 42, 66(1), 69 to 72, 74 and 75.

(2) If the Secretary of State is not satisfied about any such arrangements he may direct the
district planning authority and another local planning authority specified in the direction—

   (a) to enter into an agreement under section 113 of the Local Government Act 1972 for
       the placing at the disposal of the district planning authority, for the purpose of giving
       them any such specialist advice, of the services of officers employed by that other
       authority who are qualified to give such advice; or

   (b) to enter into arrangements, containing terms specified in the direction or terms on
       lines laid down by him, for the discharge by that other authority of any of those
       functions.

(3) Before giving a direction under sub-paragraph (2) the Secretary of State shall consult
with the district planning authority and the other authority concerned.

DEFINITIONS
   "building": s.91.
   "conservation area": s.91(1).
   "conservation area consent": s.91(1).
   "disposal": s.91(2).
   "enactment": s.91(2).
   "functions": s.91(2).
   "joint planning board": s.91(2).
   "land": s.91(2).
   "listed building": ss.1(5); 91(1).
   "listed building consent": ss.8(7); 91(1).
   "local planning authority": s.81.
   "the Broads": s.91(2).
   "the Principal Act": s.91(1).

GENERAL NOTE
   The general allocation of responsibilities betwen local planning authorities is undertaken
by Pt. I of the T.C.P.A. 1990. This schedule makes further provision for the purposes of
this Act: see further the notes to s.81.

TABLE OF DERIVATIONS

Notes:

1. The following abbreviations are used in this Table:—

1953 c.49 = The Historic Buildings and Ancient Monuments Act 1953
1962 c.36 = The Local Authorities (Historic Buildings) Act 1962
1962 c.22 = The Redundant Churches and Other Religious Buildings Act 1969
1969 c.48 = The Post Office Act 1969
1971 c.78 = The Town and Country Planning Act 1971
1972 c.42 = The Town and Country Planning (Amendment) Act 1972
1972 c.70 = The Local Government Act 1972
1974 c.7 = The Local Government Act 1974
1974 c.32 = The Town and Country Amenities Act 1974
1975 c.10 = The Statute Law (Repeals) Act 1975
1975 c.76 = The Local Land Charges Act 1975
1977 c.38 = The Administration of Justice Act 1977
1978 c.30 = The Interpretation Act 1978
1979 c.46 = The Ancient Monuments and Archaeological Areas Act 1979
1980 c.43 = The Magistrates' Courts Act 1980
1980 c.65 = The Local Government, Planning and Land Act 1980
1981 c.41 = The Local Government and Planning (Amendment) Act 1981
1981 c.54 = The Supreme Court Act 1981
1981 c.67 = The Acquisition of Land Act 1981
1982 c.16 = The Civil Aviation Act 1982
1982 c.21 = The Planning Inquiries (Attendance of Public) Act 1982
1982 c.30 = The Local Government (Miscellaneous Provisions) Act 1982
1982 c.48 = The Criminal Justice Act 1982
1983 c.47 = The National Heritage Act 1983
1984 c.10 = The Town and Country Planning Act 1984
1984 c.12 = The Telecommunications Act 1984
1985 c.51 = The Local Government Act 1985
1986 c.44 = The Gas Act 1986
1986 c.63 = The Housing and Planning Act 1986
1987 c.3 = The Coal Industry Act 1987
1988 c.4 = The Norfolk and Suffolk Broads Act 1988
1989 c.15 = The Water Act 1989
1989 c.29 = The Electricity Act 1989

2. The Table does not show the effect of Transfer of Function orders.

3. The letter R followed by a number indicates that the provision gives effect to the Recommendation bearing that number in the Law Commission's Report on the Consolidation of Certain Enactments relating to Town and Country Planning (Cmnd. 958).

4. The entry "drafting" indicates a provision of a mechanical or editorial nature only affecting the arrangement of the consolidation.

Provision	Derivation
1(1)	1971 c.78 s.54(1); 1983 c.47 Sch. 4 para. 16(2).
(2)	1971 c.78 s.54(1)(part); 1983 c.47 Sch. 4 para. 16(2).
(3)	1971 c.78 s.54(2).
(4)	1971 c.78 s.54(3); 1983 c.47 Sch. 4 para. 16(3).
(5)	1971 c.78 s.54(9); 1986 c.63 Sch. 9 para 1(1).
(6)	Drafting.
2(1)	1971 c.78 s.54(4),(5); 1972 c.70 s.179(3), Sch. 16 para. 28, Sch. 30; 1985 c.51 Sch. 2 para. 1(3); R 34.
(2)	1971 c.78 s.54(6); 1972 c.70 Sch. 30; 1975 c.76 Sch. 1.
(3)	1971 c.78 s.54(7); 1972 c.70 s.179(3), Sch. 30.
(4)	1971 c.78 s.54(8).
(5)	1971 c.78 s.54(8); 1985 c.51 Sch. 2 para. 1(3); R 34.
(6)	1971 c.78 s.54(8); 1985 c.51 Sch. 15 para. 1(3).
3(1)	1971 c.78 s.58(1); 1980 c.65 Sch. 15 para. 12; 1985 c.51 Sch. 2 para. 1(5).
(2)	1971 c.78 s.58(1); 1980 c.65 Sch. 15 para. 12; 1985 c.51 Sch. 2 para. 1(5).

Provision	Derivation
3(3)	1971 c.78 s.58(3); 1980 c.65 Sch. 15 para. 12; 1985 c.51 Sch. 2 para. 1(5).
(4)	1971 c.78 s.58(3); 1980 c.65 Sch. 15 para. 12; 1985 c.51 Sch. 2 para. 1(5).
(5)	1971 c.78 s.58(4)(part).
(6)	1971 c.78 s.58(5)(a); 1980 c.65 Sch. 15 para. 12; 1985 Sch. 2 para. 1(5).
(7)	1971 c.78 s.58(5)(b); 1980 c.65 Sch. 15 para. 12; 1985 c.51 Sch. 2 para. 1(5).
(8)	1971 c.78 s.58(7); 1985 c.51 Sch. 2 para. 1(5)(c).
4(1) to (3)	1971 c.78 s.58(6); 1972 c.42 s.7(1); 1985 c.51 Sch. 2 para. 1(5).
(4)	1971 c.78 s.58(7); 1985 c.51 Sch. 2 para. 1(5)(c).
5	Drafting.
6(1)	1971 c.78 s.45A(1); 1980 c.65 Sch. 15 para. 5.
(2)	1971 c.78 s.54A(2); 1980 c.65 Sch. 15 para. 5; R 35.
(3)	1971 c.78 s.54A(3); 1980 c.65 Sch. 15 para. 5.
(4)	1971 c.78 s.54A(4); 1980 c.65 Sch. 15 para. 5; 1985 c.51 Sch. 2 para. 1(4).
7	1971 c.78 s.55(1)(part); 1980 c.65 Sch. 15 para. 6(1).
8(1), (2)	1971 c.78 s.55(2); 1980 c.65 Sch. 34, Pt X; R 36.
(3)	1971 c.78 s.55(2A); 1980 c.65 Sch. 15 para. 6(2).
(4) to (6)	1971 c.78 s.55(3).
(7)	1971 c.78 s.55(3A); 1980 c.65 Sch. 15 para. 6(3).
9(1)	1971 c.78 s.55(1)(part).
(2)	1971 c.78 s.55(4); 1986 c.63 Sch. 11 para. 19.
(3)	1971 c.78 s.55(6); 1986 c.63 Sch. 9 para. 2(1).
(4), (5)	1971 c.78 s.55(5); 1980 c.43 s.32(2); 1982 c.48 s.74(1).
10(1)	1971 c.78 s.56(6) (part), Sch. 11 para. 1(1A) (part); 1986 c.63 Sch. 9 para. 9.
(2)	1971 c.78 Sch. 11 para. 1(1); 1986 c.63 Sch. 9 para. 9.
(3)	1971 c.78 Sch. 11 para. 1(1A); 1986 c.63 Sch. 9 para. 9.
11(1) to (5)	1971 c.78 ss.27(1) (except (cc)), (2), (4), 29(3), Sch. 11 para. 2(1).
(6)	1971 c.78 Sch. 11 para. 2(2); 1982 c.48 ss.38, 46.
(7)	1971 c.78 s.27(7), Sch. 11 para. 2(1).
12(1)	1971 c.78 Sch. 11 para. 4(1).
(2)	1971 c.78 Sch. 11 para. 4(2).
(3)	1971 c.78 Sch. 11 para. 4(3).
(4)	1971 c.78 Sch. 11 para. 4(4).
(5)	1971 c.78 Sch. 11 para. 4(5).
13(1)	1971 c.78 Sch. 11 para. 5(1), (3); 1985 c.51 Sch. 2 para. 1(17).
(2)	1971 c.78 Sch. 11 para. 5(1).
(3)	1971 c.78 Sch. 11 para. 5(2); 1986 c.63 Sch. 9 para. 10(1).
14(1)	1971 c.78 Sch. 11 para. 6(1); 1985 c.51 Sch. 2 para. 1(17)(b).
(2)	1971 c.78 Sch. 11 para. 6(2); 1985 c.51 Sch. 2 para. 1(17)(b).
(3)	1971 c.78 Sch. 11 para. 6(3); 1985 c.51 Sch. 2 para. 1(17)(b).
(4)	1971 c.78 Sch. 11 para. 6(5); 1985 c.51 Sch. 2 para. 1(17)(b).
(5)	1971 c.78 Sch. 11 para. 6(4), (6); 1985 c.51 Sch. 2 para. 1(17)(b); 1986 c.63 Sch. 9 para. 10.
(6)	1971 c.78 Sch. 11 para. 6(3), (4); 1985 c.51 Sch. 2 para. 1(17)(b); 1986 c.63 Sch. 9 para. 10.
(7)	1971 c.78 Sch. 11 para. 6(5); 1985 c.51 Sch. 2 para. 1(17)(b).
(8)	1971 c.78 Sch. 11 para. 6(7); 1985 c.51 Sch. 2 para. 1(17)(b).
(9)	1971 c.78 Sch. 11 para. 6(8); 1985 c.51 Sch. 2 para. 1(17)(b).
15(1)	1971 c.78 Sch. 11 para. 7(1); 1986 c.63 Sch. 9 para. 11(2).
(2)	1971 c.78 Sch. 11 para. 7(1); 1985 c.51 Sch. 2 para. 1(17)(c).
(3)	1971 c.78 Sch. 11 para. 7(1A); 1986 c.63 Sch. 9 para. 11(2).
(4)	1971 c.78 Sch. 11 para. 7(1B); 1986 c.63 Sch. 9 para. 11(3).
(5)	1971 c.78 Sch. 11 para. 7(2).
(6)	1971 c.78 Sch. 11 para. 7(3); 1986 c.63 Sch. 9 para. 11(4).
16(1)	1971 c.78 s.56(3)(part), (4); 1980 c.65 Sch. 15 para. 9.

Provision	Derivation
16(2)	1971 c.78 s.56(3)(part); 1980 c.65 Sch. 15 para. 8.
(3)	1971 c.78 Sch. 11 para. 1(2).
17(1)	1971 c.78 s.56(4A); 1980 c.65 Sch. 15 para. 9.
(2)	1971 c.78 s.56(4B); 1986 c.63, Sch. 9 para. 3(1).
(3)	1971 c.78 s.56(5); 1980 c.65, Sch. 15 para. 10.
18(1)	1971 c.78 s.56A(1); 1980 c.65 Sch. 15 para. 11.
(2)	1971 c.78 s.56A(2); 1980 c.65 Sch. 15 para. 11.
(3)	1971 c.78 s.56A(5); 1980 c.65 Sch. 15 para. 11.
19(1)	1971 c.78 s.56B(1); 1986 c.63 Sch. 9 para. 4.
(2)	1971 c.78 s.56B(2); 1986 c.63 Sch. 9 para. 4.
(3)	1971 c.78 s.56B(2); 1986 c.63 Sch. 9 para. 4.
(4)	1971 c.78 s.56B(3); 1986 c.63 Sch. 9 para. 4.
20(1)	1971 c.78 s.56B(2)(part), Sch. 11 para. 8(1); 1986 c.63 Sch. 9 para. 3(2), para. 4.
(2), (3)	1971 c.78 Sch. 11 para. 9; 1986 c.63 Sch. 9 para. 3(3).
(4)	1971 c.78 Sch. 11 para. 9(1) (part); 1986 c.63 Sch. 9 para. 3(3); R 8(a).
21(1)	1971 c.78 Sch. 11 para. 8(1), 9; 1986 c.63 Sch. 9 para. 3(2), (3).
(2)	1971 c.78 Sch. 11 para. 8(1), 9; 1986 c.63 Sch. 9 para. 3(2), (3).
(3), (4)	1971 c.78 Sch. 11 para. 8(2) (part).
(5), (6)	1971 c.78 s.56B(2)(part), Sch. 11 para. 2 (part); 1986 c.63 Sch. 9 para. 4.
(7)	1971 c.78 Sch. 11 para. 2(2); 1982 c.48, ss.38, 46.
22(1)	1971 c.78 Sch. 11 para. 8(3).
(2)	1971 c.78 Sch. 11 para. 8(4).
(3)	1971 c.78 Sch. 11 para. 8(5).
(4)	1971 c.78 Sch. 11 para. 8(6).
23(1), (2)	1971 c.78 Sch. 11 para. 10(1).
(3)	1971 c.78 Sch. 11 para. 10(4).
24(1)	1971 c.78 Sch. 11 para. 10(2) (part).
(2) to (4)	1971 c.78 Sch. 11 para. 10(3).
(5)	1971 c.78 Sch. 11 para. 10(2) (part).
25(1)	1971 c.78 Sch. 11 para. 12(1), (6); 1980 c.65 Sch. 15 para. 25.
(2)	1971 c.78 Sch. 11 para. 12(2), (3), (4); 1980 c.65 Sch. 34 Pt. X.
(3)	1971 c.78 Sch. 11 para. 12(5).
(4)	1971 c.78 Sch. 11 para. 12(2)(a).
(5)	1971 c.78 Sch. 11 para. 12(2)(b).
26	1971 c.78 Sch. 11 para. 11; 1974 c.7 Sch. 6 para. 25(14).
27(1)	1971 c.78 s.171(1).
(2)	1971 c.78 s.171(2).
(3)	1971 c.78 s.171(3).
(4)	1971 c.78 s.171(4).
(5)	1971 c.78 s.173(1) (part), (2).
28(1), (2)	1971 c.78 s.172(1).
(3)	1971 c.78 s.172(3).
(4)	1971 c.78 s.172(2).
29(1)	1971 c.78 s.173(1), (3).
(2)	1971 c.78 s.173(3).
(3)	1971 c.78 s.173(4).
30(1)	1972 c.70 Sch. 16 para. 34(1), (2); R 37.
(2)	1972 c.70 Sch. 16 para. 34(3).
(3)	1972 c.70 Sch. 16 para. 52.
31(1)	1971 c.78 s.178(1).
(2)	1971 c.78 s.178(2).
(3)	1971 c.78 s.178(3).
(4)	1971 c.78 s.179(1).
(5)	1971 c.78 s.179(2).
32(1)	1971 c.78 s.190(1), (3), (5); 1972 c.70 s.179(3); 1975 c.10 Sch. Pt. XII.
(2)	1971 c.78 s.190(1); 1975 c.10 Sch. Pt. XII.

Provision	Derivation
32(3)	1971 c.78 s.190(3).
(4)	1971 c.78 s.190(2).
(5)	1971 c.78 s.190(3), drafting.
33(1), (2)	1971 c.78 Sch. 19 para. 1(1); 1986 c.63 Sch. 11 para. 5(2)(a).
(3)	1971 c.78 Sch. 19 para. 1(2).
(4)	1971 c.78 Sch. 19 para. 1(3); 1986 c.63 Sch. 11 para. 5(2)(b).
34(1)	1971 c.78 s. 182(1), Sch. 19 para. 1(3).
(2)	1971 c.78 s. 182(2), Sch. 19 para. 1(3); 1972 c.70 Sch. 16 paras. 37, 52.
(3), (4)	1971 c.78 s. 182(3), Sch. 19 para. 1(3).
(5)	1971 c.78 s.182(4), Sch. 19 para. 1(3).
35(1), (2)	1971 c.78 Sch. 19 para. 2(1).
(3)	1971 c.78 Sch. 19 para. 2(2).
(4)	1971 c.78 Sch. 19 para. 2(3), (4).
(5)	1971 c.78 Sch. 19 para. 2(5), (6).
(6)	1971 c.78 Sch. 19 para. 2(7).
(7)	1971 c.78 Sch. 19 para. 2(8).
36(1)	1971 c.78 Sch. 19 para. 3(1).
(2)	1971 c.78 Sch. 19 para. 3(2).
(3)	1971 c.78 Sch. 19 para. 3(3)(a).
(4)	1971 c.78 Sch. 19 para. 3(1).
(5)	1971 c.78 Sch. 19 para. 3(3)(b); 1986 c.63 Sch. 11 para. 7(2).
(6)	1971 c.78 Sch. 19 para. 3(3A); 1986 c.63 Sch. 11 para. 7(2).
(7)	1971 c.78 Sch. 19 para. 3(4); R 38.
(8)	1971 c.78 Sch. 19 para. 3(5); R 39.
37	1971 c.78 Sch. 19 para. 4.
38(1)	1971 c.78 s.96(1), (2); 1981 c.41 Sch. para. 9.
(2)	1971 c.78 s.96(1); 1981 c.41 Sch. para. 9.
(3)	1971 c.78 s.96(3), (4); 1981 c.41 Sch. para. 9.
(4)	1971 c.78 s.96(3); 1981 c.41 Sch. para. 9.
(5) to (7)	1971 c.78 s.96(5) to (7); 1981 c.41 Sch. para. 9.
39(1)	1971 c.78 s.97(1); 1981 c.41 Sch. para. 9; 1984 c.10 s.4(2); 1986 c.63 Sch. 9 para. 2(2).
(2)	1971 c.78 s.97(1), (2): 1981 c.41 Sch. para. 9.
(3)	1971 c.78 s.97(9); 1981 c.41 Sch. para. 9.
(4)	1971 c.78 s.97(3); 1981 c.41 Sch. para. 9.
(5)	1971 c.78 s.97(8): 1981 c.41 Sch. para. 9.
(6)	1971 c.78 s.110(2)(part).
(7)	1984 c.10 s.4(2).
40(1)	1971 c.78 ss.88(5), 97(4); 1981 c.41 Sch. paras. 1, 9.
(2)	1971 c.78 s.97(6); 1981 c.41 Sch. para. 9.
(3)	1971 c.78 s.97(10); 1981 c.41 Sch. para. 9.
41(1)	1971 c.78 s.97A(1); 1981 c.41 Sch. para. 9.
(2)	1971 c.78 s.97A(2); 1981 c.41 Sch. para. 9.
(3)	1971 c.78 s.97(5); 1981 c.41 Sch. para. 9.
(4)	1971 c.78 s.97(7); 1981 c.41 Sch. para. 9.
(5)	1971 c.78 s.97A(3); 1981 c.41 Sch. para. 9.
(6)	1971 c.78 s.97A(4); 1981 c.41 Sch. para. 9.
(7)	1971 c.78 s.97A(5); 1981 c.41 Sch. para. 9.
42(1)	1971 c.78 s.99(1).
(2)	1971 c.78 s.99(2).
(3)	1971 c.78 ss.91(3), (4), 99(3); 1974 c.7 Sch. 8.
(4)	1971 c.78 ss.91(3), 99(3).
(5)	1971 c.78 s.99(3).
(6)	1971 c.78 s.111.
(7)	1971 c.78 s.99(1).
43(1)	1971 c.78 s.98(1); 1980 c.43 s.32(2), (9); 1982 c.48 s.74(1).
(2)	1971 c.78 s.98(2).
(3)	1971 c.78 s.98(3).

Provision	Derivation
43(4)	1971 c.78 s.98(4); 1980 c.43 s.32(2), (9); 1981 c.41 Sch. para. 10; 1986 c.63 Sch. 11 para. 13.
44(1)	1971 c.78 s.99A(1), (2); 1980 c.65 Sch. 15 para. 17.
(2)	1971 c.78 s.99A(3); 1980 c.65 Sch. 15 para. 17.
45	1971 c.78 s.99B; 1985 c.51 Sch. 2 para. 1(7).
46(1)	1971 c.78 ss.100(1), 276(5A); 1981 c.41 Sch. paras. 11, 24; 1985 c.51 Sch. 17.
(2)	1971 c.78 ss.100(1), 276(5A); 1981 c.41 Sch. paras. 11, 24; 1983 c.47 Sch. 4 para. 17; 1985 c.51 Sch. 17.
(3)	1971 c.78 ss.100(1), 276(5A); 1981 c.41 Sch. para. 11; 1983 c.47 Sch. 4 para. 17; 1985 c.51 Sch. 17.
(4)	1971 c.78 ss.100(2), 276(5B); 1981 c.41 Sch. paras. 11, 24; R 40.
(5)	1972 c.70 Sch. 16 paras. 47(2), 52.
47(1)	1971 c.78 s.114(1) to (3); 1972 c.70 Sch. 30; 1985 c.51 Sch. 2 para. 1(9); 1988 c.4 Sch. 3 para. 15.
(2)	1971 c.78 s.114(5); 1981 c.67 Sch. 4 para. 1, Sch. 6 Pt. I.
(3)	1971 c.78 s.114(3A), (4); 1983 c.47 Sch. 4 para. 19; 1985 c.51 Sch. 2 para. 1(9).
(4)	1971 c.78 s.114(6); 1981 c.67 Sch. 4 para. 21(1), (2); R 41.
(5)	1971 c.78 s.114(6); 1981 c.67 Sch. 4 para. 21(1), (2).
(6)	1971 c.78 s.114(7).
(7)	1971 c.78 s.114(1), (1A); 1972 c.70 s.179(3), Sch. 16 paras. 31, 52; 1988 c.4 Sch. 3 para. 16.
48(1)	1971 c.78 s.115(1); 1985 c.51 Sch. 2 para. 1(10)(a).
(2)	1971 c.78 s.115(2); 1985 c.51 Sch. 2 para. 1(10)(b).
(3)	1971 c.78 s.115(3); 1985 c.51 Sch. 2 para. 1(10)(b).
(4)	1971 c.78 s.115(3A); 1983 c.47 Sch. 4 para. 20; 1985 c.51 Sch. 2 para. 1(10)(c).
(5)	1971 c.78 ss.180(5), 190(4); R 12.
(6)	1971 c.78 ss.115(4), 180(6), 190(4); 1981 c.67 Sch. 4 para. 21(3); 1985 c.51 Sch. 2 para. 1(10)(d); R 12, R 41.
(7)	1971 c.78 ss.114(1), 115(5); 1972 c.70 s.179(3), Sch. 16 paras. 31, 52; 1988 c.4 Sch. 3 para. 16.
49	1971 c.78 s.116; 1974 c.32 s.6.
50(1)	1971 c.78 s.117(1), (8); 1974 c.7 Sch. 6 para. 25(8); 1985 c.51 Sch. 2 para. 1(11)(a); 1988 c.4 Sch. 3 para. 17; R 42.
(2)	1971 c.78 s.117(2).
(3)	1971 c.78 s.117(3); 1974 c.7 Sch. 6 para. 25(8); 1981 c.67 Sch. 4 para. 21(4)(b); R 41.
(4)	1971 c.78 s.117(4).
(5)	1971 c.78 s.117(4).
(6)	1971 c.78 s.117(5); 1974 c.7 Sch. 6 para. 25(8), Sch. 8; 1981 c.67 Sch. 4 para. 21(5)(b); 1985 c.51 Sch. 2 para. 1(11)(b).
(7)	1971 c.78 s.117(5).
(8)	1971 c.78 s.117(6).
(9)	1971 c.78 s.117(7).
51(1)	1971 c.78 s.118(1).
(2)	1971 c.78 s.118(2); 1984 c.12 Sch. 4 para. 53(3).
(3) to (5)	1971 c.78 s.118(3) to (5).
52(1)	1971 c.78 s.119(1); 1972 c.70 s.179(3), Sch. 16 paras. 31, 52, Sch. 30.
(2)	1971 c.78 s.119(3), 132(4)(a), (c).
53(1)	1971 c.78 s.126(1); 1972 c.70 Sch. 16 paras. 31, 52; 1985 c.51 Sch. 2 para. 1(12); R 43.
(2)	1953 c.49 s.5(3); 1971 c.78 s.126(2).
(3)	1953 c.49 s.5(3A); 1983 c.47 Sch. 4 para. 6(2).
54(1)	1971 c.78 s.101(1); 1986 c.63 Sch. 9 para. 7.
(2)	1971 c.78 s.101(1), (5)(c); 1986 c.63 Sch. 9 para. 7.
(3)	1971 c.78 s.101(1); 1986 c.63 Sch. 9 para. 7.
(4)	1971 c.78 s.101(3); 1986 c.63 Sch. 9 para. 7.
(5), (6)	1971 c.78 s.101(4); 1986 c.63 Sch. 9 para. 7.

Provision	Derivation
54(7)	1971 c.78 s.101(5)(a); 1986 c.63, Sch. 9 para. 7.
55(1) to (5)	1971 c.78 s.101A(1) to (5); 1986 c.63 Sch. 9 para. 7.
(6)	1971 c.78 s.111; R 40.
56	1971 c.78 s.56C(1); 1986 c.63, Sch. 9 para. 6(1).
57(1) to (3)	1962 c.36 s.1(1).
(4), (5)	1962 c.36 s.1(2).
(6)	1962 c.36 s.1(3).
(7)	1962 c.36 s.1(4), (5); 1988 c.4 Sch. 3 para. 4.
58(1)	1962 c.36 s.2(1).
(2), (3)	1962 c.36 s.2(2).
(4)	1962 c.36 s.2(2); R 44.
(5)	1962 c.36 s.2(3); R 45.
59(1)	1971 c.78 s.57(1)(part): 1982 c.48 ss.38, 46.
(2)	1971 c.78 s.57(1)(part).
(3)	1971 c.78 s.57(2).
(4)	1971 c.78 s.57(3); 1982 c.48 ss.38, 46; 1986 c.63 Sch. 11 para. 13.
60(1) to (3)	1971 c.78 ss.56(1), 57(1), 58(2), 101(3), 114(3); 1979 c.46 Sch. 4 para. 11; 1986 c.63 Sch. 9 para. 7.
(4)	1971 c.78 s.56(1)(a).
(5)	1971 c.78 s.58AA(1); 1986 c.63 Sch. 9 para. 5(1).
(6)	1971 c.78 s.58AA(2); 1986 c.63 Sch. 9 para. 5(1).
(7)	1969 c.22 s.2; 1971 c.78 Sch. 23 Pt. II; 1978 c.30 ss.17(2)(a), 22(3).
61	1971 c.78 ss.56(1)(part), 57(1), 58(2), 101(3), 114(3); 1979 c.46 Sch. 4 para. 11; 1986 c.63 Sch. 9 para. 7.
62(1)	1971 c.78 ss.242(1)(d)(e), (2)(e).
(2)	1971 c.78 s.242(3)(h) to (k); 1982 c.30 Sch. 6 para. 7(b).
(3)	1971 c.78 s.242(4).
63(1)	1971 c.78 s.245(1).
(2)	1971 c.78 s.245(2).
(3)	1971 c.78 s.245(1), (2); R 25(b).
(4)	1971 c.78 s.245(4).
(5)	1971 c.78 s.245(6).
(6)	1971 c.78 s.245(7); 1972 c.70 Sch. 16 para. 46.
(7)	1971 c.78 s.245(3), (7); 1972 c.70 Sch. 16 para. 46; R 26.
64	1971 c.78 s.243(1)(b); 1981 c.41 Sch. para. 18(1).
65(1)	1971 c.78 s.246(1); 1981 c.41 Sch. para. 19.
(2), (3)	1971 c.78 s.246(2); 1981 c.54 Sch. 5.
(4)	1971 c.78 s.246(3).
(5)	1971 c.78 s.246(4); 1977 c.38 Sch. 5 Pt. IV.
(6)	1971 c.78 s.246(5).
(7)	1971 c.78 s.246(6); 1985 c.51 Sch. 2 para. 1(13).
66(1)	1971 c.78 s.56(3); 1980 c.65 Sch. 15 para. 8.
(2)	1971 c.78 ss.125(1), (3), (4); 1974 c.7 Sch. 6 para. 25(10).
(3)	1980 c.65 s.119(3).
67(1)	1971 c.78 s.28(1); 1974 c.7 Sch. 6 para. 25(1); 1974 c.32 s.4(1).
(2)	1971 c.78 s.28(2); 1972 c.70 Sch. 16 para. 21(1); 1985 c.51 Sch. 2 para. 1(2).
(3)	1971 c.78 s.28(2A); 1983 c.47 Sch. 4 para. 15(2).
(4)	1971 c.78 s.28(2B); 1983 c.47 Sch. 4 para. 15(2).
(5)	1971 c.78 s.28(2C); 1983 c.47 Sch. 4 para. 15(2).
(6)	1971 c.78 s.28(3); 1983 c.47 Sch. 4 para. 15(3).
(7)	1971 c.78 s.29(4).
(8)	1971 c.78 s.32(2) proviso.
68(1)	1971 c.78 s.58A(1); 1985 c.51 Sch. 2 para. 1(6).
(2)	1971 c.78 s.58A(2); 1985 c.51 Sch. 2 para. 1(6).
(3)	1971 c.78 s.58A(3); 1985 c.51 Sch. 2 para. 1(6).
69(1)	1971 c.78 s.277(1); 1974 c.32 s.1(1).
(2)	1971 c.78 s.277(2); 1974 c.32 s.1(1); 1980 c.65 Sch. 15 para. 26(1).
(3)	1971 c.78 s.277(4); 1974 c.32 s.1(1).
(4)	1971 c.78 s.277(9); 1974 c.32 s.1(1); 1975 c.76 Sch. 1.

Provision	Derivation
70(1)	1971 c.78 s.277(10)(a); 1974 c.32 s.1(1); 1985 c.51 Sch. 2 para. 1(14)(b).
(2)	1971 c.78 s.277(5); 1974 c.32 s.1(1); 1985 c.51 Sch. 2 para 1(14)(a).
(3)	1971 c.78 s.277(4)(part); 1974 c.32 s.1(1).
(4)	1971 c.78 s.277(5); 1974 c.32 s.1(1); 1985 c.51 Sch. 2 para. 1(14)(a).
(5)	1971 c.78 s.277(6), (6A); 1974 c.32, s.1(1); 1983 c.47 Sch. 4 para. 21.
(6)	1971 c.78 s.277(6), (6A); 1974 c.32 s.1(1); 1983 c.47 Sch. 4 para. 21.
(7)	1971 c.78 s.277(6); 1974 c.32 s.1(1).
(8)	1971 c.78 s.277(7); 1974 c.32 s.1(1).
71(1)	1971 c.78 s.277B(1); 1974 c.32 s.1(1); 1980 c.65 Sch. 15 para. 26(3).
(2), (3)	1971 c.78 s.277B(2); 1974 c.32, s.1(1).
72	1971 c.78 s.277(8); 1974 c.32 s.1(1).
73(1)	1971 c.78 ss.28(1) to (3), 29(4); 1972 c.70 Sch. 16 para. 21; 1974 c.7 Sch. 6 para. 25(1); 1974 c.32, s.4(1); 1983 c.47 Sch. 4 para. 15(2), (3); 1985 c.51 Sch. 2 para. 1(2).
(2)	1971 c.78 s.32(2) proviso.
74(1)	1971 c.78 s.277A(1), (2); 1974 c.32 s.1(1).
(2)	1971 c.78 s.277A(7); 1974 c.32, s.1(1).
(3)	1971 c.78 s.277A(8); 1974 c.32, s.1(1); 1984 c.10, s.4(3); 1986 c.63, Sch. 9 para. 8(2).
(4)	1971 c.78 s.277A(9); 1974 c.32 s.1(1).
75(1)	1971 c.78 ss.58(2), 277A(1); 1974 c.32 s.1(1); 1979 c.46 Sch. 4, para. 11.
(2)	1971 c.78 s.277A(4); 1974 c.32 s.1(1); 1980 c.65 Sch. 15 para. 26(2)(b).
(3)	1971 c.78 s.277A(5); 1974 c.32 s.1(1).
(4)	1971 c.78 s.277A(6); 1974 c.32 s.1(1).
(5)	1971 c.78 ss.58(2), 277A(1); 1974 c.32 s.1(1).
(6)	1971 c.78 s.56(1).
(7)	1971 c.78 s.58AA(1); 1986 c.63 Sch. 9 para. 5(1).
(8)	1971 c.78 s.58AA(2); 1986 c.63 Sch. 9 para. 5(1).
(9)	1971 c.78 s.277A(8), (9); 1974 c.32 s.1(1); 1986 c.63 Sch. 9 para. 8(2).
(10), (11)	1971 c.78 s.277A(10); 1974 c.32 s.1(1).
76(1)	1971 c.78 s.101(1)(b), (2); 1986 c.63 Sch. 9 para. 7.
(2)	1971 c.78 s.101(5)(b); 1986 c.63 Sch. 9 para. 7.
77(1)	1972 c.42 s.10(1AA); 1983 c.47 Sch. 4 para. 22.
(2)	1972 c.42 s.10(1); 1980 c.65 Sch. 15 para. 27; 1983 c.47 Sch. 4 para. 22.
(3)	1972 c.42 s.10(1), (1AA); 1980 c.65 Sch. 15 para. 27; 1983 c.47 Sch. 4 para. 22.
(4)	1972 c.42 s.10(2); 1983 c.47 Sch. 4 para. 22.
(5)	1972 c.42 s.10(3A); 1983 c.47 Sch. 4 para. 22.
(6)	1972 c.42 s.10(3); 1983 c.47 Sch. 4 para. 22.
(7)	1972 c.42 s.10(4); 1983 c.47 Sch. 6.
(8)	1972 c.42 s.10(5).
(9)	1972 c.42 s.10(5).
78(1)	1972 c.42 s.10A(1); 1979 c.46 s.48(1); 1983 c.47 Sch. 4 para. 23(2).
(2)	1972 c.42 s.10A(1), (4); 1979 c.46 s.48(1); 1983 c.47 Sch. 4 para. 23(2).
(3)	1972 c.42 s.10A(2); 1979 c.46 s.48(1).
(4)	1972 c.42 s.10A(5); 1979 c.46 s.48(1); 1983 c.47 Sch. 4 para. 23(2), (3).
(5)	1972 c.42 s.10A(7); 1979 c.46 s.48(1).
(6)	1972 c.42 s.10A(6); 1979 c.46 s.48(1).
(7)	1972 c.42 s.10A(3); 1979 c.46 s.48(1); 1983 c.47 Sch. 4 para. 23(2), (3).
(8)	1972 c.42 s.10A(8); 1979 c.46 s.48(1); 1983 c.47 Sch. 4 para. 23(2); R 45.

Provision	Derivation
79(1)	1972 c.42 s.10B(3), (4); 1980 c.65 Sch. 15 para. 28; 1983 c.47 Sch. 4 para. 24(4), (5).
(2)	1972 c.42 s.10B(3); 1980 c.65 Sch. 15 para. 28; 1983 c.47 Sch. 4 para. 24(4).
(3)	1972 c.42 s.10B(11); 1980 c.65 Sch. 15 para. 28; 1983 c.47 Sch. 4 para. 24(11); 1988 c.4 Sch. 3 para. 27.
80(1)	1972 c.42 s.10B(1A), (2); 1980 c.65 Sch. 15 para. 28; 1983 c.47 Sch. 4 para. 24(3).
(2)	1972 c.42 s.10B(1), (2); 1980 c.65 Sch. 15 para. 28; 1983 c.47 Sch. 4 para. 24(2).
(3)	1972 c.42 s.10B(5); 1980 c.65 Sch. 15 para. 28; 1983 c.47 Sch. 4 para. 24(6).
(4)	1972 c.42 s.10B(6), (7); 1980 c.65 Sch. 15 para. 28; 1983 c.47 Sch. 4 para. 24(7).
(5)	1972 c.42 s.10B(8); 1980 c.65 Sch. 15 para. 28; 1983 c.47 Sch. 4 para. 24(8).
(6)	1972 c.42 s.10B(9); 1980 c.65 Sch. 15 para. 28; 1983 c.47 Sch. 4 para. 24(9).
(7)	1972 c.42 s.10B(10)(part); 1980 c.65 Sch. 15 para. 28; 1983 c.47 Sch. 4 para. 24(10); R 44.
81	Drafting.
82(1)	1971 c.78 s.270(1), Sch. 21 Pt. V.
(2)	1971 c.78 s.271; 1974 c.32 s.7(1).
(3)	1971 c.78 s.271, Sch. 21 Pt. VI; 1974 c.32 s.7(1); 1986 c.63 Sch. 9 para. 12; R47, R 48.
(4)	1971 c.78 ss.270(2)(b), 271; 1974 c.32 s.7(1); 1981 c.41 Sch. paras. 21, 22.
83(1)	1971 c.78 s.266(1)(part).
(2)	1971 c.78 s.266(2)(part); 1981 c.41 Sch. para. 20.
(3)	1971 c.78 s.266(4); 1981 c.41 Sch. para. 20.
(4)	1971 c.78 s.266(5).
(5)	1971 c.78 s.266(7).
(6)	1984 c.10 s.4(1).
(7), (8)	1971 c.78 s.266(7).
84(1)	1984 c.10 s.1(1)(a).
(2)	1984 c.10 s.1(2).
(3)	1984 c.10 s.1(3).
(4)	1984 c.10 s.1(5).
(5)	1984 c.10 s.1(7).
(6)	1984 c.10 ss.1(6), 6(1).
(7)	1984 c.10 s.6(1).
(8)	1984 c.10 s.4(1).
85	1971 c.78 s.273; 1987 c.3 Sch. 1 para. 19; R 48.
86(1)	1971 c.78 s.274(1); 1981 c.41 Sch. para. 23; 1981 c.67 Sch. 4 para. 1.
(2)	1971 c.78 s.274(2).
(3)	1971 c.78 s.274(3).
(4)	1971 c.78 s.274(5).
87	1971 c.78 s.275(2).
88(1)	1971 c.78 s.280(2).
(2)	1971 c.78 s.280(1)(c), (3), (8), (10); 1981 c.41 Sch. para. 25; 1985 c.51 Sch. 2 para. 1(16).
(3)	1971 c.78 s.280(4), (10); 1985 c.51 Sch. 2 para. 1(16); R 49.
(4)	1971 c.78 s.280(6).
(5)	1971 c.78 s.280(7).
(6)	1971 c.78 s.280(9).
(7)	1971 c.78 s.281.
89(1)	1971 c.78 ss.282, 282A, 282B, 283, 284, 285; 1986 c.63, Sch. 11 paras. 9, 10.
(2)	1971 c.78 s.285(1).

Provision	Derivation
90(1)	1971 c.78 s.254; R 50.
(2)	1971 c.78 s.255(2).
(3)	1971 c.78 s.255(3).
(4)	1971 c.78 s.255(5).
(5)	1971 c.78 s.263(1); 1972 c.70 Sch. 29 Pt. I para. 3(b).
(6)	1971 c.78 s.263(1); R 47, R 48.
(7)	1971 c.78 s.260(1)(b)(f), (2).
(8)	1971 c.78 s.262.
91(1)	1971 c.78 s.290(1).
(2)	1971 c.78 s.290(1); 1972 c.70 Sch. 30; 1985 c.51 Sch. 17; 1986 c.63 Sch. 12 Pt. III; 1988 c.4 Sch. 3 para. 25.
(3)	1969 c.48 Sch. 4 para. 93(1)(xxxiii); 1971 c.78 s.191A; 1982 c.16, Sch. 2 para. 4; 1984 c.12 Sch. 4 para. 53(5); 1986 c.44 Sch. 7 para. 2; 1989 c.15 Sch. 25 para. 1(1), (2); 1989 c.29 Sch. 16 para. 1(1)(xxii).
(4)	1971 c.78 s.290(8).
(5)	1971 c.78 s.290(3).
(6)	1971 c.78 ss.101(6), 126(3), 280(10), Sch. 19 para. 1(4); 1988 c.4 Sch. 3 paras. 14, 18, 23, 26.
(7)	1962 c.36 s.1.
92(1)	1971 c.78 s.269(1).
(2)	1971 c.78 s.269(1); 1984 c.10 s.6(3); R 47, R 48.
(3)	1971 c.78 s.269(3); 1972 c.70 s.179(3).
(4)	1971 c.78 s.269(4).
93(1)	1971 c.78 s.287(1).
(2), (3)	1971 c.78 s.287(2).
(4)	1971 c.78 s.287(4); 1986 c.63 Sch. 9 para. 5(2).
(5)	1971 c.78 s.287(5)(b); 1986 c.63 Sch. 9 para. 5(2).
(6)	1971 c.78 s.287(9); 1986 c.63 Sch. 9 para. 5(2); R 51.
(7)	1971 c.78 s.287(3).
94	Drafting.
Sch. 1	
para. 1	1971 c.78 s.54(10).
para. 2(1)	1971 c.78 ss.54(10).
(2)	1971 c.78 s.54(10); 1972 c.70 s.179(3), Sch. 30.
(3)	1971 c.78 s.54(12); 1983 c.47 Sch. 4 para. 16(5).
(4)	1971 c.78 s.54(11); 1972 c.70 Sch. 16 para. 28(2); 1983 c.47 Sch. 4 para. 16(4); 1985 c.51 Sch. 2 para. 1(3).
para. 3	1971 c.78 s.97A(4)(c)(ii), Sch. 11 paras. 8(2)(a), (3)(b); 1981 c.41, Sch. para. 9.
Sch. 2	
para. 1	1971 c.78 Sch. 11 para. 13.
para. 2	1971 c.78 Sch. 11 para. 14.
para. 3	1971 c.78 Sch. 11 para. 15.
para. 4	1971 c.78 Sch. 11 para. 16.
Sch. 3	
para. 1(1), (2)	1971 c.78 Sch. 9 para. 1(1).
(3)	1971 c.78 Sch. 9 para. 1(2).
(4)	1971 c.78 Sch. 9 para. 1(3).
(5)	Drafting.
para. 2(1)	1971 c.78 Sch. 9 para. 2(1)(d), (f); 1981 c.41 Sch. para. 27.
(2)	1971 c.78 Sch. 9 para. 2(2); 1981 c.41 Sch. para. 27.
(3)	1971 c.78 Sch. 9 para. 2(2)(a); 1981 c.41 Sch. para. 27.
(4)	1971 c.78 Sch. 9 para. 2(2)(b); 1981 c.41 Sch. para. 27.
(5)	1971 c.78 Sch. 9 para. 2(3).
(6)	1971 c.78 Sch. 9 para. 2(3)(a).
(7)	1971 c.78 Sch. 9 para. 2(3)(b).
(8)	1971 c.78 Sch. 9 para. 2(4).
para. 3(1)	1971 c.78 Sch. 9 para. 3(1).
(2)	1971 c.78 Sch. 9 para. 3(2); R 52.

Provision	Derivation
para. 3(3)	1971 c.78 Sch. 9 para. 3(3).
(4)	1971 c.78 Sch. 9 para. 3(4); R 52.
(5), (6)	1971 c.78 Sch. 9 para. 3(5).
para. 4(1)	1971 c.78 Sch. 9 para. 3A(1); 1986 c.63 Sch. 11 para. 11.
(2)	1971 c.78 Sch. 9 para. 3A(2); 1986 c.63 Sch. 11 para. 11; R 52.
(3)	1971 c.78 Sch. 9 para. 3A(3); 1986 c.63 Sch. 11 para. 11.
(4)	1971 c.78 Sch. 9 para. 3A(4); 1986 c.63 Sch. 11 para. 11.
para. 5(1)	1971 c.78 Sch. 9 para. 4(1).
(2)	1971 c.78 Sch. 9 para. 4(2)(a).
(3)	1971 c.78 Sch. 9 para. 4(2).
para. 6(1)	1971 c.78 Sch. 9 para. 5(1).
(2)	1971 c.78 Sch. 9 para. 5(1A); 1986 c.63 Sch. 11 para. 12.
(3)	1971 c.78 Sch. 9 para. 5(2).
(4)	1971 c.78 Sch. 9 para. 5(3); 1986 c.63 Sch. 11 para. 8(2).
(5)	1982 c.21 s.1(1).
(6)	1982 c.21 s.1(2), (3).
(7)	1982 c.21 s.1(4).
(8)	1971 c.78 Sch. 9 para. 5(4); 1986 c.63 Sch. 11 para. 9(2).
para. 7(1)	1971 c.78 Sch. 9 para. 7(1).
(2)	1971 c.78 Sch. 9 para. 7(2).
Sch. 4	
para. 1	Drafting.
para. 2	1971 c.78 s.54(10); 1972 c.70 s.179(3), Sch. 16 paras. 25(1), 52; R 46.
para. 3(1)	1972 c.70 Sch. 16 paras. 16(1), 52.
(2)	1972 c.70 Sch. 16 paras 16(2), 52.
para. 4(1)	1971 c.78 ss.28(2), (2A), 54(11), (12), 277(10), 277A(11); 1972 c.70 Sch. 16 paras. 21(1), 28; 1974 c.32 s.1(1); 1983 c.47 Sch. 4 para. 15; 1985 c.51 Sch. 2 para. 1(2), (3), (14), (15); 1986 c.63 Sch. 9 para. 8(3).
(2)	1971 c.78 s.277(5); 1974 c.32 s.1(1); 1985 c.51 Sch. 2 para. 1(14).
(3)	1972 c.70 Sch. 16 para. 21(2).
para. 5	1971 c.78 ss.54(13), 54A(4), 273A, 280(10); 1984 c.10 s.6(5), (6); 1985 c.51 Sch. 2 para. 1(16); 1988 c.4 Sch. 3 paras. 7, 8, 12, 13, 23, 32.
para. 6	1972 c.70 Sch. 16 para. 51(1); R 53.
para. 7(1)	1972 c.70 Sch. 16 para. 58.
(2)	1972 c.70 Sch. 16 para. 59; 1978 c.30 s.17(2)(a).
(3)	1972 c.70 Sch. 16 para. 59(part).

TABLE OF DESTINATIONS

HISTORIC BUILDINGS AND ANCIENT MONUMENTS ACT 1953
c.49

1953	1990
s.5(3)	s.53(2)
(3A)	(3)

LOCAL AUTHORITIES (HISTORIC BUILDINGS) ACT 1962
c.36

1962	1990
s.1	91(7)
(1)	57(1)–(3)
(2)	(4), (5)
(3)	(6)
(4), (5)	(7)
2(1)	58(1)
(2)	(2), (3), (4)
(3)	(5)

REDUNDANT CHURCHES AND OTHER RELIGIOUS BUILDINGS ACT 1969
c.22

1969	1990
s.2	s.60(7)

POST OFFICE ACT 1969
c.48

1969	1990
Sched. 4, para. 93(1)(xxiii)	s.91(3)

TOWN AND COUNTRY PLANNING ACT 1971
c.78

1971	1990	1971	1990	1971	1990
s.27(1) (except cc), (2), (4)	s.11(1)–(5)	s.54(12)	Sched. 1, para. 2(3), Sched. 4, para. 4(1)	s.56B(1)	s.19(1)
(7)	(7)	(13)	Sched. 4, para. 5	(2)	(2), (3)
28(1)	67(1), 73(1)	54A(1)	s.6(1)	(2)	
(2)	(2), 73(1), Sched. 4, para. 4(1)	(2)	(2)	(part)	20(1), 21(5), (6)
(2A)	(3), 73(1), Sched. 4, para. 4(1)	(3)	(3)	(3)	19(4)
		(4)	(4), Sched. 4, para. 5	56C(1)	56
(2B)	(4)	55(1)(part) .	(7), 9(1)	57(1)	61
(2C)	(5)	(2)	8(1), (2)	(1) (part)	59(1), (2),60(1)–(3)
(3)	(6)	(2A)	(3)	(2)	59(3)
29(3)	11(1)–(5)	(3)	(4)–(6)	(3)	(4)
(4)	67(7), 73(1)	(3A)	(7)	58(1)	3(1), (2)
32(2)		(4)	9(2)	(2)	60(1)–(3), 61, 75(1), (5)
proviso	(8), 73(2)	(5)	(4), (5)	(3)	3(3), (4)
54(1)	1(1)	(6)	(3)	(4) (part)	(5)
(1) (part)	(2)	56(1)	60(1)–(3), 75(6)	(5)(a)	(6)
(2)	(3)			(5)(b)	(7)
(3)	(4)	(1)(a)	(4)	(6)	4(1)–(3)
(4), (5) ...	2(1)	(1) (part)	61	(7)	3(8), 4(4)
(6)	(2)	(3)	66(1)	58A(1)	68(1)
(7)	(3)	(3) (part)	16(1), (2)	(2)	(2)
(8)	(4)–(6)	(4)	(1)	(3)	(3)
(9)	1(5)	(4A)	17(1)	58AA(1) ...	60(5), 75(7)
(10)	Sched. 1, para. 1, 2(1), 2(2), Sched. 4, para. 2	(4B)	(2)	(2) ...	(6)
		(5)	(3)	88(5)	40(1)
		(6) (part)	10(1)	91(3)	42(3), (4)
		56A(1)	18(1)	(4)	(3)
(11)	Sched. 1, para. 2(4), Sched. 4, para. 4(1)	(2)	(2)	96(1)	38(1)
		(5)	(3)	(2)	(2)
				(3)	(3), (4)
				(4)	(3)
				(5)–(7) ...	(5)–(7)

TABLE OF DESTINATIONS

1971	1990
s.97(1)	s.39(1)
(2)	(2)
(3)	(4)
(4)	40(1)
(5)	41(3)
(6)	40(2)
(7)	41(4)
(8)	39(5)
(9)	(3)
(10)	40(3)
97A(1)	41(1)
(2)	(2)
(3)	(5)
(4)	(6)
(4) (c)	
(ii)	Sched. 1, para. 3
(5)	(7)
98(1)	43(1)
(2)	(2)
(3)	(3)
(4)	(4)
99(1)	42(1), (7)
(2)	(2)
(3)	(2), (4), (5)
99A(1), (2)	44(1)
(3)	(2)
99B	45
101(1)	54(1)–(3)
(1)(b)	76(1)
(2)	(1)
(3)	54(4), 60(1)–(3), 61
(4)	(5), (6)
(5)(a)	(7)
(b)	76(2)
(c)	54(2)
(6)	91(6)
A(1)–(5)	55(1)–(5)
110(2)	
(part)	39(6)
111	42(6), 55(6)
114(1)	47(1), (7), 48(7)
(1A)	(7)
(2)	(1)
(3)	(1), 60(1) to (3), 61
(3A)	(3)
114(4)	(3)
(5)	(2)
(6)	(4),(5)
(7)	(6)
115(1)	48(1)
(2)	(2)
(3)	(3)
(3A)	(4)
(4)	(6)
(5)	(7)
116	49
117(1)	50(1)
(2)	(2)
(3)	(3)
(4)	(4), (5)
(5)	(6), (7)
(6)	(8)
(7)	(9)
(8)	(1)

1971	1990
s.118(1)	s.51(1)
(2)	(2)
(3)	(3)
(4)	(4)
(5)	(5)
119(1)	52(1)
(3)	(2)
125(1)	66(2)
(3)	(2)
(4)	(2)
126(1)	53(1)
(2)	(2)
(3)	91(6)
132(4)(a),	
(c)	52(1)
171(1)	27(1)
(2)	(2)
(3)	(3)
(4)	(4)
172(1)	28(1), (2)
(2)	(4)
(3)	(3)
173(1)	
(part)	(5), 29(1)
(2)	(5)
(3)	29(1), (2)
(4)	(3)
178(1)	31(1)
(2)	(2)
(3)	(3)
179(1)	(4)
(2)	(5)
180(5)	48(5)
(6)	(6)
182(1)	34(1)
(2)	(2)
(3)	(3), (4)
(4)	(5)
190(1)	82(1), (2)
(2)	(4)
(3)	(1), (3), (5)
(4)	48(5), (6)
(5)	32(1)
242(1)(d),	
(e)	62(1)
(2)(e)	(1)
(3)(h)–	
(k)	(2)
(4)	(3)
243(1)(b)	64
245(1)	63(1), (3)
(2)	(2)
(3)	(7)
(4)	(4)
(6)	(5)
(7)	(6), (7)
246(1)	65(1)
(2)	(2), (3)
(3)	(4)
(4)	(5)
(5)	(6)
(6)	(7)
254	90(1)
255(2)	(2)
(3)	(3)
(5)	(4)
260(1)(b)(f)	(7)
(2)	(7)

1971	1990
s.262	s.90(8)
263(1)	(5), (6)
266(1)	
(part)	83(1)
(2)	
(part)	(2)
(4)	(3)
(5)	(4)
(7)	(5), (7), (8)
269(1)	92(1), (2)
(3)	(3)
(4)	(4)
270(1)	82(1)
(2)(b)	(4)
271	(2)–(4)
273	85
273A	Sched. 4, para. 5
274(1)	86(1)
(2)	(2)
(3)	(3)
(5)	(3)
275(2)	87
276(5A)	46(1)–(4)
277(1)	69(1)
(2)	(2)
(4)	(3)
(4)	
(part)	70(3)
(5)	(2), (4), Sched. 4, para. 4(2)
(6)	(5) to (7)
(6A)	(6)
(7)	(8)
(8)	72
(9)	69(4)
(10)	Sched. 4, para. 4(1)
(10)(a)	70(1)
277A(1)	74(1), 75(1), (5)
(2)	(1), 75(8)
(4)	75(2)
(5)	(3)
(6)	(4)
(7)	74(2)
(8)	(3), 75(9)
(9)	(4), 75(9)
(10)	75(10), (11)
(11)	Sched. 4, para. 4(1)
277B(1)	71(1)
(2)	(2), (3)
280(1)(c)	88(2)
(2)	(1)
(3)	(2)
(4)	(3)
(6)	(4)
(7)	(5)
(8)	(2)
(9)	(6)
(10)	(2), (3), 91(6), Sched. 4, para. 5
281	(7)
282	89(1)
282A	(1)

1971	1990
s.282B	s.89(1)
283	(1)
284	(1)
285	(1)
285(1)	(2)
287(1)	93(1)
(2)	(2), (3)
(3)	(7)
(4)	(4)
(5)(b) ...	(5)
(9)	(6)
290(1)	91(1), (2)
(3)	(5)
(8)	(4)
Sched. 9, ...Sched. 3,	
para. 1(1) .. para. 1(1),	
	(2)
(2) ..	(3)
(3) ..	(4)
2(1)	
(d),	
(f) ...	2(1)
(2) ..	(2)
(2)(a)	(3)
(b)	(4)
(3) ..	(5)
(3)(a)	(6)
(b)	(7)
(4) ..	(8)
3(1) ..	3(1)
(2) ..	(2)
(3) ..	(3)
(4) ..	(4)
(5) ..	(5),
	(6)
3A(1)	(1)
(2)	(2)
(3)	(3)
(4)	(4)
4(1) ..	5(1)
(2)(a)	(2)
(2) ..	(3)
5(1) ..	6(1)
(1A)	(2)
(2) ..	(3)
(3) ..	(4)
(4) ..	(8)
7(1) ..	7(1)
(2) ..	(2)

1971	1990
Sched. 11,	
para. 1(1) ..	s.10(2)
(1A)	
(part)	(1)
(1A)	(3)
(2) ..	16(3)
2	
(part)	21(5), (6)
2(1) ..	11(1)–(5),
	(7)
2(2) ..	(6), 21(7)
4(1) ..	12(1)
(2) ..	(2)
(3) ..	(3)
(4) ..	(4)
(5) ..	(5)
5(1) ..	13(1), (2)
(2) ..	(3)
(3) ..	(1)
6(1) ..	14(1)
(2) ..	(2)
(3) ..	(3), (6)
(4) ..	(5), (6)
(5) ..	(4), (7)
(6) ..	(5)
(7) ..	(8)
(8) ..	(9)
7(1) ..	15(1), (2)
(1A)	(3)
(1B)	(4)
(2) ..	(5)
(3) ..	(6)
8(1) ..	20(1), 21(1),
	(2)
(2)	
(part)	21(3), (4)
(2)(a) Sched. 1,	
	para. 3
(3) ..	s.22(1)
(3)(b) Sched. 1,	
	para. 3
(4) ..	s.22(2)
(5) ..	(3)
(6) ..	(4)
9	20(2), (3),
	21(1), (2)
(1)	
(part)	(4)

1971	1990
para. 10(1) .	s.23(1), (2)
(2)	
(part)	24(1), (5)
(3) .	(2) to (4)
(4) .	23(3)
11	26
12(1) .	25(1)
(2) .	(2)
(2)	
(a) ...	(4)
(2)	
(b) ...	(5)
(3) .	(2)
(4) .	(2)
(5) .	(3)
(6) .	(1)
13 .....Sched. 2,	
	para. 1
14	2
15	3
16	4
Sched. 19,	
para. 1(1) ..	s.33(1), (2)
(2) ..	(3)
(3) ..	(4),
	34(1)–(5)
(4) ..	91(6)
2(1) ..	35(1), (2)
(2) ..	(3)
(3) ..	(4)
(4) ..	(4)
(5) ..	(5)
(6) ..	(5)
(7) ..	(6)
(8) ..	(7)
3(1) ..	36(1), (4)
(2) ..	(2)
(3)	
(a)	(3)
(b)	(5)
(3A)	(6)
(4) ..	(7)
(5) ..	(8)
4	37
Sched. 21,	
Pt. V	82(1)
Pt. VI	(3)
Pt. II	60(7)
Sched. 30 ......Sched. 1,	
	para. 2(2)

TOWN AND COUNTRY PLANNING (AMENDMENT) ACT 1972
(c.42)

1972	1990
s.7(1)	s.4(1)–(3)
10(1)	77(2), (3)
(1AA) ...	(1), (3)
(2)	(4)
(3)	(6)
(3A)	(5)
(4)	(7)
(5)	(8), (9)
10A(1)	78(1), (2)
(2)	(3)

1972	1990
s.10A(3)	s.78(7)
(4)	(2)
(5)	(4)
(6)	(6)
(7)	(5)
(8)	(8)
10B(1)	80(2)
(1A)	(1)
(2)	(1), (2)

1972	1990
s.10B(3)	s.79(1), (2)
(4)	(1)
(5)	80(3)
(6)	(4)
(7)	(4)
(8)	(5)
(9)	(6)
(10)	
(part)	(7)
(11)	79(3)

LOCAL GOVERNMENT ACT 1972
c.70

1972	1990
s.179(3)	s.2(1), (3), 32(1), 47(7), 48(7), 52(1), 92(3), Sched. 1, para. 2(2), Sched. 4, para. 2
Sched. 16,	.....Sched. 4,
para. 16(1) .	para. 3(1)
(2) .	(2)
21	s.73(1)
(1) .	67(2), Sched. 4, para. 4(1)
(2) .	Sched. 4, para. 4(3)
25(1) .	Sched. 4, para. 2

1972	1990
Sched. 16,	
para. 28	s.2(1), Sched. 4, para. 4(1)
(2) .	Sched. 5, para. 2(4)
31	ss.47(7), 48(7), 52(1), 53(1)
34(1),	
(2) .	s.30(1)
(3) .	(2)
37	34(2)
46	63(6), (7)
47(2) .	46(5)
51(1) .	Sched. 4, para. 6

1972	1990
Sched. 16,	
para. 52	ss.34(2), 46(5), 47(7), 48(7), 52(1), 53(1), Sched. 4, para.2, 3(1), (2)
55	s.30(3)
58	Sched. 4, para. 7(1)
59	(2)
59	
(part)	(3)
Sched. 29, Pt. I,	
para. 3(b)	s.90(5)
Sched. 30	ss.2(1), (2), (3), 47(1), 52(1), 91(2)

LOCAL GOVERNMENT ACT 1974
c.7

1974	1990
Sched. 6,	
para. 25(1) .	ss.67(1), 73(1)
(8) .	50(1), (3), (6)
(10)	s.66(2)
(14)	26
Sched. 8	ss.42(3), 50(6)

TOWN AND COUNTRY AMENITIES ACT 1974
c.32

1974	1990
s.1(1)	ss.69(1), (2), (3), (4), 70(1), (2), (3), (4), (5), (6), (7), (8), 71(1), (2), (3), 72, 74(1), (2), (3), (4), 75(1), (2), (3), (4), (5), (9), (10), (11), Sched. 4, para. 4(1), (2)
4(1)	67(1), 73(1)
6	s.49
7(1)	82(2), (3), (4)

STATUTE LAW (REPEALS) ACT 1975
c.10

1975	1990
Sched.,	
Pt. XII	s.32(1), (2)

LOCAL LAND CHARGES ACT 1975
c.76

1975	1990
Sched. 1	ss.2(2), 69(4)

ADMINISTRATION OF JUSTICE ACT 1977
c.38

1977	1990
Sched. 5,	
Pt. IV	s.65(5)

Table of Destinations

INTERPRETATION ACT 1978
c.30

1978	1990
s.17(2) (a)	s.60(7), Sched. 4, para. 7(2)
22(3)	(7)

ANCIENT MONUMENTS AND ARCHAEOLOGICAL AREAS ACT 1979
c.46

1979	1990
s.48(1)	s.78(1)–(8)
Sched. 4,	
para. 11	60(1)–(3), 61, 75(1)

MAGISTRATES' COURTS ACT 1980
c.43

1980	1990
s.32(2)	ss.9(4), (5), 43(1), (4)
(9)	s.43(1), (4)

LOCAL GOVERNMENT, PLANNING AND LAND ACT 1980
c.65

1980	1990	1980	1990	1980	1990
s.119(3)	s.66(3)	Sched. 15,		Sched. 15,	
Sched. 15,		para. 10	s.17(3)	para. 26(2)	
para. 5	s.6(1)–(4)	11	18(1)–(3)	(b) .	s.75(2)
6(1) ..	6(7)	12	3(1)–(4),	(3) .	71(1)
(2) ..	8(3)		(6), (7)	27	77(2), (3)
(3) ..	(7)	17	44(1), (2)	28	79(1)–(3),
8	16(2), 66(1)	25	25(1)		80(1)–(7)
9	(1), 17(1)	26(1) .	69(2)	34,	
				Pt. X	8(1), (2), 25(2)

LOCAL GOVERNMENT AND PLANNING (AMENDMENT) ACT 1981
c.41

1981	1990	1981	1990	1981	1990
Sched. 1,		Sched. 1,		Sched. 1,	
para. 1	s.40(1)	para. 10	s.43(4)	para. 23	s.86(1)
9	38(1) to (7),	11	46(1)–(4)	24	46(1), (2),
	39(1)–(5),	18(1) .	64		(4)
	40(1) to (3),	19	65(1)	25	88(2)
	41(1)–(7),	20	83(2), (3)	27	Sched. 3,
	Sched. 1, para.	21	82(4)		para.
	3	22	(4)		2(1)–(4)

SUPREME COURT ACT 1981
c.54

1981	1990
Sched. 5	s.65(2), (3)

ACQUISITION OF LAND ACT 1981
c.67

1981	1990
Sched. 4,	
para. 1	s.47(2), 86(1)
21(1),	
(2)	(4), (5)
(3) .	48(6)
(4)	
(b)	50(3)
(5)	
(b)	(6)

TABLE OF DESTINATIONS

LOCAL GOVERNMENT ACT 1985
c.51

1985	1990	1985	1990	1985	1990
Sched. 2,		Sched. 2,		Sched. 2,	
para. 1(2	.......ss.67(2), 73(1),	1(10)		para. (14)	.Sched. 14,
	Sched. 4, para.	(a)	.... s.48(1)		para. 4(1),
	4(1)	(b) .	(2), (3)		(2)
(3)	.. 2(1), (5),	(c) ..	(4)	(a)	. 70(2), (4)
	(6), Sched. 1,	(d) .	(6)	(b)	. (1)
	para. 2(4),	(11)		(15)	.Sched. 4,
	Sched. 4, para.	(a)	.. 50(1)		para. 4(1)
	4(1)	(b)	. (6)	(16)	. 88(2), (3),
(4)	.. 6(4)	(12)	. 53(1)		Sched. 4, para.
(5)	.. 3(1)–(4),	(13)	. 65(7)		5
	(6), (7),			(17)	. 13(1)
	4(1)–(3)			(b)	. 14(1)–(9)
(5)(c)	3(8), 4(4)			(c)	.. 15(2)
(6)	.. 68(1)–(3)				
(7)	.. 45				
(9)	.. 47(1), (3)				

GAS ACT 1986
c.44

1986	1990
Sched. 7,	
para. 2	...... s.91(3)

HOUSING AND PLANNING ACT 1986
c.63

1986	1990	1986	1990	1986	1990
Sched. 9,		Sched. 9,		Sched. 11,	
para. 1(1)	.. s.1(5)	para. 7	...... s.54(1)–(6),	para. 5(2)(a) s.33(1), (2)	
(1)	.. 9(3)		55(1)–(5),	(b)	.... 33(4)
(2)	.. 39(1)		60(1)–(3), 61,	7(2)	.. 36(5), (6)
3(1)	.. 17(2)		75(7), (8),	8(2)	..Sched. 3,
(2)	.. 20(1), 21(1)		76(1), (2)		para. 6(4)
(3)	.. 20(2)–(4),	8(2)	.. 74(3), 75(9)	9(2)	.. (8)
	21(2)	8(3)	..Sched. 4,	10	..... s.89(1)
4	...... 19(1)–(4),		para. 4(1)	11	.....Sched. 3,
	20(1), 21(5),	9	...... 10(1)–(3)		para. 4(1) to
	(6)	10	..... 14(5), (6)		(4)
5(1)	.. 60(5), (6)	(1)	. 13(3)	12	..... 6(2)
(2)	.. 93(4)–(6)	11(2)	. 15(1), (3)	13	..... s.43(4), 59(4)
6(1)	.. 56	(3)	. (4)		
		(4)	. (6)		
		12	..... 82(3)		

COAL INDUSTRY ACT 1987
c.3

1987	1990
Sched. 1,	
para. 19	..... s.85

NORFOLK AND SUFFOLK BROADS ACT 1988
c.4

1988	1990	1989	1990	1988	1990
Sched. 3,		Sched. 3,		Sched. 3,	
para. 4	...... s.57(7)	para. 15	..... s.47(1)	para. 25	..... (2)
7	......Sched. 4,	16	..... (7), 48(7)	26	..... (6)
	para. 5	17	..... 50(1)	27	..... 79(3)
8	 5	18	..... 91(6)	32	.....Sched. 4,
12	 5	23	..... (6),		para. 5
13	 5		Sched. 4,		
14	..... s.91(6)		para. 5		

TABLE OF DESTINATIONS

WATER ACT 1989
c.15

1989	1990
Sched. 25,	
para. 1(1)	.. s.91(3)
(2)	.. (3)

ELECTRICITY ACT 1989
c.29

1989	1990
Sched. 16,	
para.	
1(1)(xxii)	...... s.91(3)

The Law Commission's Report on the Consolidation of Certain Enactments relating to Town and Country Planning (Cmnd. 958)

Rec.	1990	Rec.	1990	Rec.	1990
8(a)	.... s.20(4)	41	.... 47(4), 48(6), 50(3)	48	.... 82(3), 85, 90(6), 92(2)
12	.... 48(5), (6)	42	.... 50(1)	49	.... 88(3)
25(b)	.... 63(3)	43	.... 53(1)	50	.... 90(1)
26	.... 63(7)	44	.... 58(4), 80(7)	51	.... 93(6)
34	.... 2(1), (5)	45	.... 58(5), 78(8)	52	............Sched. 3,
35	.... 6(2)	46	............Sched. 4, para.		para. 3(2),
36	.... 8(1), (2)		2		(4), 4(2)
37	.... 30(1)	47	.... 82(3), 90(6),	53	............Sched. 4, para.
38	.... 36(7)		92(2)		6
39	.... 36(8)				
40	.... 46(4), 55(6)				

INDEX

References are to section numbers

INDEX

PLANNING (HAZARDOUS SUBSTANCES) ACT 1990*

(1990 c. 10)

A table showing the derivation of the provisions of this consolidation Act will be found at the end of the Act. The table has no official status.

ARRANGEMENT OF SECTIONS

---

* Annotations by Professor Malcolm Grant, LL.D., Faculty of Laws, University College, London.

General

Supplemental

An Act to consolidate certain enactments relating to special controls in
respect of hazardous substances with amendments to give effect to
recommendations of the Law Commission.   [24th May 1990]

PARLIAMENTARY DEBATES
   Hansard, H.L. Vol. 515, col. 1094; Vol. 516, col. 21; Vol. 517, col. 978; Vol. 518, col.
437; H.C. Vol. 173, col. 253.
   The Bill was considered in Committee from March 1–14, 1990.

INTRODUCTION
   This Act derives from provisions inserted in the Town and Country Planning Act 1971 by
the Housing and Planning Act 1986, which introduced a new system of control over
hazardous substances. The draftsman of that Act went to considerable pains to integrate the
new regime over hazardous substances with the planning provisions of the 1971 Act, but in
the 1990 consolidation that integration was unstitched and the hazardous substances
provisions divorced from the planning powers and placed in a separate Act. This is a logical
approach, because although there is a close relationship between the two systems, they are
conceptually and functionally different.
   The reason for the introduction of a special regime in 1986 was the increased concern over
the lack of any coherent controls over the storage of hazardous substances on land. The
influence of planning control over the design and siting of new hazardous uses had been
steadily increasing through the 1970s and 1980s, led by local planning authorities and
reinforced by consultation on safety issues with the Health and Safety Executive (HSE). But
the major drawback of the ordinary development control system in this context had been
that it was limited to acts constituting "development" of land, whilst a new hazardous use
could be introduced without any development occurring at all. An established industry might
commence new hazardous operations, or intensify existing operations, without any further
planning consent being required.
   Planning arrangements had, however, been strengthened over the years preceding the
1986 Act. Local planning authorities have since 1972 (DOE Circulars 1/72; 97/74) been
urged to take safety factors into account on applications involving a major hazard, and to
consult with the HSE, particularly in cases involving the storage of large quantities of
hazardous materials. But the comparative informality of these arrangements continued to
cause concern, and the Advisory Committee on Major Hazards, in its *First Report* (HMSO
1976), urged that consultation with the HSE should be mandatory in all cases of applications
involving, affecting or affected by, a notifiable installation. In its *Second Report* (HMSO
1979) the Committee proposed that development control should be extended by bringing
within the statutory definition of "development" the introduction of a notifiable activity, so
that planning permission would always be required. Although there were obvious problems
in implementing this proposal and incorporating it into the overall structure of development
control (should it, for example, be regarded as operational development or material change

of use?), the Committee were firm in their preference for control to be exercised through the planning system rather than by a specialised licensing system administered by the HSE, since only the planning system would in their view give the community the opportunity of deciding whether they were prepared to accept the introduction of the hazard.

In 1983 the Government introduced amendments to the General Development Order and the Use Classes Order. Their effect was to take away the immunity from planning control (under the Use Classes Order) and the deemed planning permission (under the General Development Order) in cases of development involving a notifiable quantity of hazardous substances. But the changes still did not catch those cases where the introduction of hazardous substances did not involve any material change in the use of the land. Moreover, where development rights under the General Development Order were restricted by the amendment, and the local planning authority subsequently refused permission, a claim could be made for compensation under what is now s.107 of the T.C.P.A. 1990. Although the Town and Country Planning (Compensation) Act 1985 limited such claims to those based on applications for planning permission made within twelve months of the amendment to the General Development Order, it did not otherwise restrict the extent of local planning authorities' liability.

The regime established by this Act was foreshadowed in a consultation paper issued by the Department of the Environment in 1984, *Planning Control over Hazardous Development*, in which the Department argued against a straightforward extension of planning control, and suggested the setting up of a separate procedural regime, though still administered by local planning authorities. The procedures would be modelled on planning procedures, with comparable provision for applications, appeals and call-in. This model was adopted by the 1986 Act, although the basic planning regime is substantially modified to accommodate the different problems of hazardous substances.

Commencement

There has been considerable delay in the implementation of these measures. A commencement order is required to bring the Act into force, but no order has yet been made. Detailed regulations will also be required to give effect to its provisions.

Prospective amendment

The Environmental Protection Bill, presently before Parliament, contains amendments to this Act which were introduced by the Government at the Committee stage in the House of Lords. Their principal effect will be to repeal s.2 (special arrangements for statutory undertakers), to clarify the arrangements for deemed consent under ss.11 and 12, and to insert a new s.26A (power to charge fees for consent applications).

Outline of hazardous substances control

Upon the coming into force of this Act, the presence on, over or under land of any hazardous substance in excess of the controlled quantity requires consent from the hazardous substances authority: in Greater London and the metropolitan counties, the London boroughs and the district councils (s.1); in the non-metropolitan counties, the district councils will generally have the function (s.1), but the county councils in relation to National Parks (outside the Peak Park and Lakes District where the function vests in the Planning Board) and in relation to land used for mineral working or waste disposal (s.3). An exception is in the case of operational land of statutory undertakers where the function vests in "the appropriate Minister" (s.2), and urban development corporations and housing action trusts will have the function in their areas if they are the local planning authority in relation to all kinds of development (s.4(4) and (5)). The Secretary of State has power to specify the control figures, and to carve out exceptions from control (s.5).

Applications for consent are made to the hazardous substances authority, who are to be required by regulations to consult with the HSE in prescribed cases (s.7), and are empowered to grant consent either unconditionally or subject to such conditions as they think fit, or to refuse it; and in dealing with the application they are required to "have regard to any material considerations", and in particular to the considerations specified in s.9(2).

There is a right of appeal to the Secretary of State against refusal or conditions imposed on a grant of consent (s.21) and a right of call-in (s.20), power to revoke or modify a grant of consent (ss.14–16) and special provision for emergencies.

Transitional provisions

The new controls are to be phased in, with a transitional period of six months during which consent may be claimed in respect of any hazardous substance which was present on land at any time within the 12 months immediately preceding the commencement date (the "establishment period") for these provisions (s.11).

Application of provisions to hazardous substances authorities
The regime established by these provisions extends also to the grant of consent to hazardous substances authorities themselves, but subject to such exceptions and modifications as may be prescribed by the Secretary of State. The regulations may require that any such application should be made to him, rather than to the hazardous substances authority (s.30).

Redrafting amendments on the consolidation
These provisions were not particularly well designed or drafted in the first place, and several technical difficulties have arisen with them. In particular, the drafting style of the original relied heavily on cross-referenced incorporation of provisions in the Town and Country Planning Act 1971 with suitable modifications, but without full consideration of their consequences. Some of the difficulties have been resolved in the course of consolidation, and the planning provisions that have been translated across to hazardous substances are now instead separately enacted in this Act, although many more are yet to be applied by regulations.
The following further drafting amendments, proposed by the Law Commission in its *Report on the Consolidation of Certain Enactments Relating to Town and Country Planning,* Cm. 958 (1990) have been made:
(1) hazardous substances authorities in special areas: the ambiguity that previously existed has been overcome by specifying clearly that in a National Park the authority will always be the county council or the National Park authority rather than the Broads Authority, an urban development corporation or a housing action trust;
(2) for the purposes of ss.10 and 28 housing action trusts are equated with non-ministerial authorities;
(3) when a non-ministerial authority is determining an application under s.18 they are limited in imposing certain conditions, in the same way as they are limited under s.10, to acting on advice from the HSE, by s.18(6);
(4) the right to appeal to the Secretary of State against a refusal or conditional grant of consent, agreement or approval is extended to a case where that is required by a condition on a hazardous substance consent (ss.21 and 22);
(5) the challenge and ouster provisions of s.22 are now clearly applied to decisions of the Secretary of State on called-in applications, and s.22(2) makes it clear that it is the hazardous substances authority rather than the local planning authority which has a right of application to the High Court;
(6) the registers to be kept by non-Ministerial authorities are now required to contain information in relation to consents deemed to be granted under s.12;
(7) it is to the hazardous substances authority, rather than the local planning authority, that notification of disposal of Crown land may be required by regulations to be made under s.32;
(8) the power of entry to land under s.36 is clarified and adapted to the particular requirements of hazardous substance control;
(9) the power to contribute to the expenses of authorities under s.38 is clarified by a substitution of hazardous substances authorities for local planning authorities.

ABBREVIATIONS
HSE : Health and Safety Executive
T.C.P.A. 1990 : Town and Country Planning Act 1990
the Commission : Health and Safety Commission
the Committee : Advisory Committee on Major Hazards.

Hazardous substances authorities

Hazardous substances authorities: general

1. The council of the district or London borough in which land is situated shall be the hazardous substances authority in relation to the land except in cases where section 2 or 3 applies.

DEFINITIONS
"land": s.39(2).
"London borough": s.39(2).

GENERAL NOTE

Purpose of the section

This and the two following sections designate which authority is to have the functions under this Act of "hazardous substances authority". For the most part it is the authority which would be the local planning authority in respect of the development concerned, but special arrangements are made by s.2 in relation to the operational land of statutory undertakers.

Designation of hazardous substances authority

The hazardous substances authority is:

(1) Greater London: the London borough council (s.1);

(2) metropolitan areas: the metropolitan district council (s.1);

(3) non-metropolitan areas: the district council (s.1), but the function vests in the county council in relation to land used for mineral working or (in England only) waste disposal (s.3(1)(c));

(4) national parks (outside the Peak Park and Lake District where the function vests in the Planning Board): the county council (s.3(1)(a)). The subsequent subsections of s.3 are drafted so as to make it clear that this allocation takes priority over the allocation of the function in those provisions to the Broads Authority, an urban development corporation or a housing action trust;

(5) the Norfolk and Suffolk Broads: the Broads Authority (s.3(3));

(6) urban development areas: the urban development corporation has the function in its area if it is the local planning authority in relation to all kinds of development. This is presently the case in relation to all the urban development corporations except for Cardiff Bay. For a list of current designations, see the notes to s.7 of the T.C.P.A. 1990;

(7) housing action trust areas: the housing action trust under the Housing Act 1988, if it is the local planning authority for all kinds of development (s.3(5)). No housing action trusts have yet been created;

(8) operational land of statutory undertakers (including land held or proposed to be acquired with a view to being used as operational land): the "appropriate Minister" (s.2).

Application of the Act to authorities themselves

Regulations may be made under s.30 dealing with the application of the Act to hazardous substances authorities themselves, with such exceptions and modifications as may be prescribed. In particular (s.30(2)), the regulations may require that any application by such an authority for consent should be made to the Secretary of State and not to the authority itself.

Hazardous substances authorities: statutory undertakers

2.—(1) The appropriate Minister shall be the hazardous substances authority for—

(a) operational land of statutory undertakers; and

(b) land in which statutory undertakers hold or propose to acquire an interest with a view to the land being used as operational land.

(2) For the purposes of this section a wharf or harbour land which is not operational land of statutory undertakers authorised to carry on a harbour shall be treated as if it were such operational land.

(3) Any question whether subsection (2) applies to land shall be determined by the Secretary of State and the Minister who is the appropriate Minister in relation to operational land of statutory undertakers who are authorised to carry on harbour undertakings.

(4) In this section "wharf" and "harbour land" have the same meaning as in the Harbours Act 1964.

DEFINITIONS

"harbour land": subs. (4).

"hazardous substances authority": ss.1, 2, 3, 39(1).

"land": s.39(2).

"Minister": s.39(2).

"operational land": s.39(2) and (8).
"statutory undertakers": s.39(2), (4), (5), (6), (7) and (8).
"the appropriate Minister": s.39(2).
"use": s.39(2).
"wharf": subs. (4).

GENERAL NOTE
The hazardous substances authority in relation to operational land, or prospective operational land, of statutory undertakers is to be the "appropriate Minister", as defined by s.265 of the T.C.P.A. 1990.

Statutory undertakers
"Statutory undertaker" includes T.C.P.A. 1990, s.262, as applied by s.39(2)).
"persons authorised by any enactment to carry on any railway, light railway, tramway, road transport, water transport, canal, inland navigation, dock, harbour, pier or lighthouse undertaking, or any undertaking for the supply of hydraulic power and a relevant airport operator (within the meaning of Part V of the Airports Act 1986)."
In addition, for the purposes of this section, the expression includes (s.39):
(1) a public gas supplier;
(2) the National Rivers Authority; and
(3) every water or sewerage undertaker.
Regulations may be made under s.33 extending this section to British Coal as if it were a statutory undertaker, and to any of its land (including mines) as if it were operational land.

Operational land
The primary definition of operational land is given by ss.263 to 264 of the T.C.P.A. 1990. In addition, all wharves and harbour land are to be treated for the purposes of this section as if they were operational land of statutory undertakers. Any question as to whether land of statutory undertakers is operational land is to be determined by the appropriate Minister in relation to the undertaking concerned (s.39(8)).

Wharves and harbour land
The definitions of "harbour" and "wharf" in the Harbours Act 1964, s.57 are as follows:
"'harbour' . . . means any harbour, whether natural or artificial, and any port, haven, estuary, tidal or other river or inland waterway navigated by ocean-going ships and includes a dock, a wharf . . ."
"'harbour land' means land adjacent to a harbour and occupied wholly or mainly for the purposes of activities there carried on."
"wharf means any wharf, quay, pier, jetty or other place at which sea-going ships can ship or unship goods or embark or disembark passengers."

Prospective repeal
Provisions repealing this section were inserted in the Environmental Protection Bill during the House of Lords Committee stage in July 1990.

Hazardous substances authorities: other special cases

3.—(1) The county council shall be the hazardous substances authority for land which is in a non-metropolitan county and—
(a) is situated in a National Park;
(b) is used for the winning and working of minerals (including their extraction from a mineral-working deposit); or
(c) is situated in England and used for the disposal of refuse or waste materials,
unless subsection (2) applies.
(2) If the land is in a National Park for which a joint planning board or special planning board has been constituted, the board shall be the hazardous substances authority for the land.
(3) The Broads Authority is the hazardous substances authority for the Broads unless subsection (1) or (2) applies.
(4) If the land is in an area for which an urban development corporation is the local planning authority in relation to all kinds of development, the

corporation shall be the hazardous substances authority for the land unless subsection (1) or (2) applies.

(5) If the land is in an area for which a housing action trust established under Part III of the Housing Act 1988 is the local planning authority in relation to all kinds of development, the trust shall be the hazardous substances authority for the land unless subsection (1) or (2) applies.

(6) This section does not apply to land to which section 2 applies.

DEFINITIONS
   "development": s.39(2).
   "hazardous substances authority": ss.1, 2, 3, 39(1).
   "joint planning board": s.39(2).
   "land": s.39(2).
   "local planning authority": s.39(2).
   "minerals": s.39(2).
   "the Broads": s.39(2).
   "urban development corporation": s.39(2).
   "use": s.39(2).

GENERAL NOTE
   For the overall allocation of functions, see the notes to s.1.

Control over presence of hazardous substances

Requirement of hazardous substances consent

4.—(1) Subject to the provisions of this Act, the presence of a hazardous substance on, over or under land requires the consent of the hazardous substances authority (in this Act referred to as "hazardous substances consent").

(2) Subsection (1) does not apply if the aggregate quantity of the substance—
   (a) on, over or under the land;
   (b) on, over or under other land which is within 500 metres of it and controlled by the same person; or
   (c) in or on a structure controlled by the same person any part of which is within 500 metres of it,
is less than the quantity prescribed as the controlled quantity for that substance.

(3) The temporary presence of a hazardous substance while it is being transported from one place to another is not to be taken into account unless it is unloaded.

(4) The Secretary of State may by regulations provide that hazardous substances consent is not required or is only required—
   (a) in relation to land of prescribed descriptions;
   (b) by reason of the presence of hazardous substances in prescribed circumstances.

(5) Regulations under this section may make different provision for different cases or descriptions of cases.

DEFINITIONS
   "hazardous substances authority": ss.1, 2, 3, 39(1).
   "hazardous substances consent": subs. (1).
   "land": s.39(2).
   "prescribed": s.39(2).

ALLOCATION OF FUNCTIONS
   See the Commentary to s.1.

GENERAL NOTE

Purpose of the section
   This section establishes the basis of control over hazardous substances, by requiring that
the presence of a hazardous substance requires consent. Deemed consent is available under
s.11 where there is an established presence of substances on the land for 12 months prior to
the Act coming into force, though it must be claimed within six months of that date; consent
must otherwise be applied for and granted under the following provisions of the Act. There
are special rules relating to grants of consent in the context of an authorisation by a
Government department (s.12), for hazardous substance authorities themselves (s.30) and
for Crown land; but overall the procedures for obtaining consent are closely modelled on
those for obtaining planning permission under T.C.P.A. 1990.

What is a hazardous substance
   The Act does not define "hazardous substance". It is for the Secretary of State under s.5
to make regulations specifying the substances that are hazardous substances, and the quantity
which is to be the controlled quantity of any such substance.

Exceptions from the requirement of consent
   Hazardous substances consent is not required
   (1) for the temporary presence of a hazardous substance while it is being transported
       from one place to another, unless it is unloaded (subs. (3));
   (2) for the presence of a substance in a quantity less than the prescribed controlled
       quantity (subs. (2)). The relevant control zone is "the land" (although the Act
       does not specify what land this is, and whether it is intended to cover the whole
       of a planning unit, or all land owned or occupied as a single unit), together with
       any other land controlled by the same person within a radius of 500 metres. The
       concept of "control" is central to the Act, but not defined: see further the notes
       to s.17;
   (3) for land of descriptions that may be prescribed by the Secretary of State under
       subs. (4)(a);
   (4) in circumstances that may be prescribed by the Secretary of State (subs. (4)(b));
   (5) where a temporary exemption direction has been issued the Secretary of State
       under s.27;
   (6) for Crown land, except to the extent of any interest in it for the time being held
       otherwise than by or on behalf of the Crown (s.31). The Crown may, however,
       seek hazardous substances consent for the purpose of enabling Crown land, or
       an interest in it, to be disposed of with the benefit of consent (s.32);
   (7) during the transitional six-month period following the coming into force of the
       Act, in respect of any presence of hazardous substances which has been
       established for the preceding 12 months (s.29), although a claim for deemed
       consent must be made under s.11 to continue this exemption beyond that period.

Consequences of failure to obtain consent
   It is an offence under s.23 to have hazardous substances in excess of the controlled
quantity without consent, or to exceed the maximum quantity permitted by a consent, or to
fail to comply with a consent condition. In addition, the hazardous substances authority is
empowered to serve, under s.24, a hazardous substances contravention notice specifying the
alleged contravention, and requiring specified steps to be taken to remedy it.

Power to prescribe hazardous substances

   5.—(1) For the purposes of this Act the Secretary of State—
      (a) shall by regulations specify—
               (i) the substances that are hazardous substances; and
               (ii) the quantity which is to be the controlled quantity of
         any such substance; and
      (b) may by regulations provide that, except in such circumstances
         as may be prescribed, all hazardous substances falling within a
         group specified in the regulations are to be treated as a single
         substance.
   (2) Regulations which—
      (a) are made by virtue of subsection (1)(a)(i); or

(b) are made by virtue of subsection (1)(a)(ii) and reduce the
        controlled quantity of a substance,
may make such transitional provision as appears to the Secretary of State
to be appropriate.

(3) The power to make such transitional provision includes, without
prejudice to its generality, power to apply sections 11 and 26 subject to
such modifications as appear to the Secretary of State to be appropriate.

(4) Regulations under this section may make different provision for
different cases or descriptions of cases.

DEFINITION
    "prescribed": s.39(2).

GENERAL NOTE

Power to prescribe
    The extent of control attainable under this Act is dependent on the regulations to be
made by the Secretary of State under this section. Those regulations will determine what is
a hazardous substance, and what the controlled quantity of each substance is.

Power to make more restrictive provision
    The section contemplates that the Secretary of State may in the future wish to make
further regulations that are more restrictive than those initially made under this section.
There is therefore express power in subss. (2) and (3), where regulations reduce the
controlled quantity of a substance, to make transitional provision by applying ss.11 and 26,
which allow for claims to be made for deemed consent in respect of an established presence
of a hazardous substance.

Obtaining hazardous substances consent

Hazardous substances consent: general

6.—(1) Hazardous substances consent—
        (a) may be granted on an application under this Act, or
        (b) may be deemed to have been granted by virtue of section 11
            or 12.

(2) Without prejudice to the provisions of this Act, any hazardous
substances consent shall (except in so far as it otherwise provides) enure
for the benefit of the land to which it relates and of all persons for the
time being interested in the land.

DEFINITIONS
    "hazardous substances consent": ss.4, 39(1).
    "land": s.39(2).

GENERAL NOTE

Hazardous substances consent
    Hazardous substances consent may be either express or deemed. Express consent is
granted on an application, which is to be handled and determined in accordance with the
following sections of this Act and the detailed procedural rules which are to be prescribed
by the Secretary of State. The system is closely modelled on the development control system
under the T.C.P.A. 1990 including a power of call-in and a right of appeal to the Secretary
of State.
    Deemed consent is available in two unconnected cases.

Protection for established uses
    Deemed consent is available as a transitional arrangement in relation to an established
presence of a hazardous substance on, over or under land, which has existed for 12 months
prior to the Act coming into force (s.11). Such a consent must be claimed within six months
of the Act coming into force, but it is not then dependent upon any response by the
hazardous substances authority to the claim (unless within two weeks of receiving it they
notify the claimant that in their opinion the claim is invalid, with their reasons).

Government authorisations

Deemed consent may be directed under s.12 by a government department in a case where its authorisation is required in respect of development to be carried out by a local authority or statutory undertakers, or in connection with the grant of a consent by the Secretary of State for Energy under s.36 of the Electricity Act 1989 (construction of electricity generating stations). This arrangement corresponds to that under s.90 of the T.C.P.A. 1990.

Consent to run with the land

Any consent runs with the land, unless it provides otherwise (subs. (2)). But that principle yields to s.17, which provides that a consent is revoked if there is a change in the person in control of part of the land to which it relates, unless a prior application has been made for the continuation of the consent. The authority has broad powers under s.18 in determining an application for the continuation of a consent.

Applications for hazardous substances consent

7.—(1) Provision may be made by regulations with respect to—
    (a) the form and manner in which applications for hazardous substances consent are to be made;
    (b) the particulars which they are to contain and the evidence by which they are to be verified;
    (c) the manner in which they are to be advertised; and
    (d) the time within which they are to be dealt with.
  (2) Regulations—
    (a) may require an applicant for hazardous substances consent or the hazardous substances authority or both to give publicity to an application for hazardous substances consent in such manner as may be prescribed;
    (b) may require hazardous substances authorities to conduct appropriate consultations before determining applications for hazardous substances consent;
    (c) may provide for the manner in which such a consultation is to be carried out and the time within which—
        (i) such a consultation; or
        (ii) any stage in such a consultation,
    is to be completed;
    (d) may require hazardous substances authorities to determine applications for hazardous substances consent within such time as may be prescribed;
    (e) may require hazardous substances authorities to give prescribed persons or bodies prescribed information about applications for hazardous substances consent, including information as to the manner in which such applications have been dealt with.
  (3) In subsection (2) above "appropriate consultations" means—
    (a) consultations—
        (i) in the case of a hazardous substances authority other than the appropriate Minister, with the Health and Safety Executive; and
        (ii) in the case of the appropriate Minister, with the Health and Safety Commission; and
    (b) consultations with such persons or bodies as may be prescribed.
  (4) Regulations under this section may make different provision for different cases or descriptions of cases.

DEFINITIONS
  "appropriate consultations": subs. (3).
  "the appropriate Minister": s.39(2).
  "hazardous substances authority": ss.1, 2, 3, 39(1).
  "hazardous substances consent": ss.4, 39(1).

"Minister": s.39(2).
"prescribed": s.39(2).

ALLOCATION OF FUNCTIONS
See the Commentary to s.1.

GENERAL NOTE

Purpose of the section
The Act sets only a broad framework for hazardous substance control, and empowers the Secretary of State by regulations under this section to prescribe the detailed procedures. There is no requirement in the Act that an applicant for consent should be the owner or occupier of the land, or the person in control of it. Regulations made under s.8 may, however, require that all owners of the relevant land be notified by the applicant before he lodges the application.

Relationship with planning control
There is no requirement in the Act that the site to which the application relates should already have planning permission, or established use rights, for the use to which the proposed hazardous substance consent will relate. However, the planning status of the land is a material consideration under s.9 in determining applications made under this section.

Register of applications
Every hazardous substance authority is required to maintain a register, in a form to be prescribed under s.28, containing information as to applications made for consent, either to the authority itself or to the appropriate Minister in respect of land for which the authority would otherwise be the hazardous substances authority.

Certificates as to applicant's status etc.

8.—(1) Regulations under this Act may provide that an application for hazardous substances consent or an appeal against the refusal of such an application or against the imposition of a condition on such a consent shall not be entertained unless it is accompanied by one of the following certificates in the prescribed form and signed by or on behalf of the applicant—

(a) a certificate stating that, at the beginning of the period of 21 days ending with the date of the application, no person (other than the applicant) was the owner of any of the land to which the application relates;

(b) a certificate stating that the applicant has given the requisite notice of the application to all the persons (other than himself) who, at the beginning of that period, were owners of any of the land to which the application relates;

(c) a certificate stating that—
(i) the applicant is unable to issue a certificate in accordance with paragraph (a) or (b);
(ii) he has given the requisite notice of the application to such one or more of the persons mentioned in paragraph (b) as are specified in the certificate;
(iii) he has taken such steps as are reasonably open to him (specifying them) to ascertain the names and addresses of the remainder of those persons but has been unable to do so;

(d) a certificate stating that—
(i) the applicant is unable to issue a certificate in accordance with paragraph (a);
(ii) he has taken such steps as are reasonably open to him (specifying them) to ascertain the names and addresses of the persons mentioned in paragraph (b) but has been unable to do so.

(2) Where such provision is made any such certificate as is mentioned in subsection (1)(b) or (c) must set out—

(a) the names of those persons to whom the applicant has given the requisite notice of the application;

(b) the addresses at which notice was given to them;

(c) the date of service of each such notice.

(3) Such regulations may require that any such certificate as is mentioned in subsection (1)(c) or (d) shall also contain a statement that the requisite notice of the application, as set out in the certificate, has on a date specified in the certificate (which must not be earlier than the beginning of the period mentioned in subsection (1)(a)) been published in a local newspaper circulating in the locality in which the land in question is situated.

(4) Such regulations may also require that where an application is accompanied by such a certificate as is mentioned in subsection (1)(b), (c) or (d) the hazardous substances authority—

(a) shall not determine the application before the end of the period of 21 days beginning with the date appearing from the certificate to be the latest of the dates of service of notices as mentioned in the certificate or, if later, the date of publication of a notice as so mentioned;

(b) in determining the application, shall take into account any representations relating to it which are made to them before the end of that period by any person who satisfies them that he is an owner of any land to which the application relates; and

(c) shall give notice of their decision to every person who has made representations which they were required to take into account in accordance with paragraph (b).

(5) Such regulations may also make provision as to who is to be treated as the owner of land for the purposes of any provisions of the regulations.

(6) If any person—

(a) issues a certificate which purports to comply with the requirements of regulations made by virtue of this section and contains a statement which he knows to be false or misleading in a material particular; or

(b) recklessly issues a certificate which purports to comply with those requirements and contains such a statement,

he shall be guilty of an offence and liable on summary conviction to a fine not exceeding level 3 on the standard scale.

(7) Regulations under this section may make different provision for different cases or descriptions of cases.

(8) Subject to subsection (5), in this section "owner," in relation to any land, means a person who is for the time being the estate owner in respect of the fee simple in the land or is entitled to a tenancy of the land granted or extended for a term of years certain of which not less than seven years remain unexpired.

DEFINITIONS

"hazardous substances authority": ss.1, 2, 3, 39(1).

"hazardous substances consent": ss.4, 39(1).

"land": s.39(2).

"owner": subs. (5).

"prescribed": s.39(2).

"tenancy": s.39(2).

ALLOCATION OF FUNCTIONS

See the Commentary to s.1.

GENERAL NOTE

Ownership certificates
This section is modelled on s.66 of the T.C.P.A. 1990 and it carries across to hazardous substances control the requirement (though here to be prescribed by regulations) that an applicant for consent should provide a certificate to the effect that he is the sole owner of the land to which the application relates, or that, if he is not, he has notified or attempted to notify all other owners.

Determination of applications for hazardous substances consent

9.—(1) Subject to the following provisions of this Act, where an application is made to a hazardous substances authority for hazardous substances consent, that authority—
  (a) may grant hazardous substances consent, either unconditionally or subject to such conditions as they think fit; or
  (b) may refuse hazardous substances consent.
  (2) In dealing with such an application the hazardous substances authority shall have regard to any material considerations and, in particular, but without prejudice to the generality of the foregoing—
  (a) to any current or contemplated use of the land to which the application relates;
  (b) to the way in which land in the vicinity is being used or is likely to be used;
  (c) to any planning permission that has been granted for development of land in the vicinity;
  (d) to the provisions of the development plan; and
  (e) to any advice which the Health and Safety Executive or Health and Safety Commission have given following consultations in pursuance of regulations under section 7(2).
  (3) If an application relates to more than one hazardous substance, the authority may make different determinations in relation to each.
  (4) It shall be the duty of a hazardous substances authority, when granting hazardous substances consent, to include in that consent—
  (a) a description of the land to which the consent relates;
  (b) a description of the hazardous substance or substances to which it relates; and
  (c) in respect of each hazardous substance to which it relates, a statement of the maximum quantity allowed by the consent to be present at any one time.

DEFINITIONS
  "development": s.39(2).
  "development plan": s.39(2).
  "hazardous substances authority": ss.1, 2, 3, 39(1).
  "hazardous substances consent": ss.4, 39(1).
  "land": s.39(2).
  "use": s.39(2).

ALLOCATION OF FUNCTIONS
  See the Commentary to s.1.

GENERAL NOTE

Criteria for determining applications
This section lays the basis for decision-making by the hazardous substances authority on applications for consent. Although modelled on s.70 of the T.C.P.A. 1990, especially in its formulation of the requirement to have regard to material considerations and the power to impose conditions, it contains special provisions in subs. (2) which specifically require the authority to have regard to other land uses in the vicinity and any planning permission that may have been granted for other land in the vicinity. This provides hazardous substances control with a planning context. Although it is not a precondition to the grant of consent

that there should be planning permission (or an existing use or established use right) for the land-use to which the consent will relate, the authority are entitled to look at any current or contemplated use of the land. Moreover, they may make any consent conditional upon the commencement or partial or complete execution of development on the land which is authorised by a specified planning permission (s.10(1)). In some cases there will be a parallel application for planning consent, and locational considerations and public safety can be dealt with together on the joint applications. But the introduction of hazardous substances to a site will not always of itself require planning permission, because it may require no physical development (where, for example, it is proposed to use exising storage facilities) nor constitute a material change in the use of the land; and, in such cases, only the controls under this Act are available.

The public safety aspect of hazardous substance control is underpinned by the power for the authority to have regard to the locality as a whole, so as to see what safety margins are available in terms of other uses existing or proposed in the vicinity of the site. Advice from the HSE may, for example, require that there be a minimum safety cordon around the site for certain types of substances.

Relevance of the person in control

Although the person in control of the site is of central importance to the hazardous substances scheme, and consent is automatically revoked if there is a change in relation to part of the site, there are no requirements imposed by the Act as to the qualifications or experience of that person in relation to handling hazardous substances, and that is not made a material consideration in determining an application for consent.

Imposition of conditions

The authority may impose such conditions as they think fit when granting consent. Special conditions which may be imposed are specified in s.10, though a local hazardous substances authority are permitted to impose conditions relating to how a hazardous substance is to be kept or used only on the basis of advice provided by the HSE (s.10(3)). Moreover, if there is any conflict between conditions imposed under these powers and the requirements of the HSE, the latter take precedence (s.29) and to the extent that any consent or notice issued by the hazardous substances authority requires or allows anything to be done in contravention of Pt. 1 of the Health and Safety at Work etc. Act 1974, or of any improvement notice or prohibition notice served under it, it is void.

General conditions may be imposed relating to the site, and specific conditions may be imposed relating to each substance included in the consent; and the authority are required by s.10(3) to provide a statement of all conditions relating to each substance.

Call-in

The Secretary of State may call-in an application, under s.20, although that power does not apply to cases where, under s.2 (operational land of statutory undertakers), the matter is already in the hands of the "appropriate Minister" as hazardous substances authority.

Appeals

Where consent is refused under this section, or the application not determined within the prescribed time, an aggrieved applicant may appeal under s.21 to the Secretary of State. Again, there is no right of appeal in s.2 cases (s.21(7)).

Power to impose conditions on grant of hazardous substances consent

10.—(1) Without prejudice to the generality of section 9(1), a hazardous substances authority may make the grant of hazardous substances consent conditional on the commencement or partial or complete execution of development on the land which is authorised by a specified planning permission or may grant hazardous substances consent subject to conditions with respect to any of the following—

  (a) how and where any hazardous substance to which the consent relates is to be kept or used;

  (b) the times between which any such substance may be present;

  (c) the permanent removal of any such substance—

    (i) on or before a date specified in the consent; or

    (ii) before the end of a period specified in it and commencing on the date on which it is granted.

(2) An authority who are a hazardous substances authority by virtue of section 1 or 3 may only grant consent subject to conditions as to how a hazardous substance is to be kept or used if the conditions are conditions to which the Health and Safety Executive have advised the authority that any consent they might grant should be subject.

(3) It shall be the duty of a hazardous substances authority when granting hazardous substances consent to include in that consent in respect of each hazardous substance to which it relates a statement of all conditions relating to that substance subject to which the consent is granted.

DEFINITIONS
"development": s.39(2).
"hazardous substances authority": ss.1, 2, 3, 39(1).
"hazardous substances consent": ss.4, 39(1).
"land": s.39(2).
"use": s.39(2).

ALLOCATION OF FUNCTIONS
See the Commentary to s.1.

GENERAL NOTE

The power to impose conditions
Section 9 confers a general power to impose conditions when granting consent, and that power is extended by this section to authorise conditions relating to specific matters. To the extent that any conditions relate to how a hazardous substance is to be kept or used, their use must have been advised by the HSE.

Conditions relating to planning permission
Subs. (1) specifically empowers the authority to require by condition that consent should not take effect until development on the land authorised by a specified planning permission has been commenced, or has been partially or completely executed.

Discharge of condition
Application may be made under s.13 for discharge of a condition attached to a consent, and the authority may agree to grant consent without that condition or to refuse the application.

Conditions attached to deemed consents
Where consent is deemed under s.11 (transitional provisions for established presence), it is subject to the conditions (s.11(7)) that
(a) the maximum aggregate quantity of the substance that may be present
  (i) on, over or under the land to which the claim for the consent relates;
  (ii) on, over or under other land which is within 500 metres of it and controlled by the same person; or
  (iii) in or on a structure controlled by the same person any part of which is within 500 metres of it,
  at any one time shall not exceed the established quantity;
(b) the substance shall be kept and used in the place and manner in which information supplied in pursuance of regulations made by virtue of subs. (2) [claim to contain prescribed information as to the presence of the substance during the establishment period and how and where it was kept and used immediately before the relevant date] shows that it was kept and used immediately before the relevant date; and
(c) none of the substance shall be kept or used in a container greater in capacity than the container, or the largest of the containers, in which the substance was kept or used immediately before that date.

Deemed hazardous substances consent: established presence

11.—(1) Where a hazardous substance was present on, over or under any land at any time within the establishment period hazardous substances consent may be claimed in respect of its presence.

(2) A claim shall be made in the prescribed form before the end of the transitional period and shall contain the prescribed information as to the presence of the substance during the establishment period and as to how and where it was kept and used immediately before the relevant date.

(3) Subject to subsections (4) to (6), the hazardous substances authority shall be deemed to have granted any hazardous substances consent which is claimed under subsection (1).

(4) If at the relevant date notification in respect of the substance was required by regulation 3 or 5 of the Notification Regulations, hazardous substances consent is only to be deemed to be granted under this section if notification in respect of the substance was given before that date in accordance with those regulations.

(5) If at the relevant date such notification was not so required, hazardous substances consent is only to be deemed to be granted under this section if an aggregate quantity of the substance not less than the controlled quantity was present at any one time within the establishment period.

(6) If it appears to the hazardous substances authority that a claim for hazardous substances consent does not comply with subsection (2), it shall be their duty, before the end of the period of two weeks from their receipt of the claim—

(a) to notify the claimant that in their opinion the claim is invalid; and
(b) to give their reasons for that opinion.

(7) Hazardous substances consent which is deemed to be granted under this section is subject to the conditions that—

(a) the maximum aggregate quantity of the substance that may be present—
 (i) on, over or under the land to which the claim for the consent relates;
 (ii) on, over or under other land which is within 500 metres of it and controlled by the same person; or
 (iii) in or on a structure controlled by the same person any part of which is within 500 metres of it,
 at any one time shall not exceed the established quantity;
(b) the substance shall be kept and used in the place and manner in which information supplied in pursuance of regulations made by virtue of subsection (2) shows that it was kept and used immediately before the relevant date; and
(c) none of the substance shall be kept or used in a container greater in capacity than the container, or the largest of the containers, in which the substance was kept or used immediately before that date.

(8) In this section—
"establishment period" means the period of 12 months immediately preceding the relevant date;
"established quantity" means, in relation to any land—
 (a) where before the relevant date there was a notification in respect of a substance in accordance with any of the Notification Regulations—
  (i) the quantity notified or last notified before that date; or
  (ii) a quantity equal to twice the quantity which was so notified or last notified before the start of the establishment period,
 whichever is the greater;
 (b) where a notification was not required before that date by any of those regulations, a quantity exceeding by 50 per cent. the maximum quantity which was present on, over or under the land at any one time within that period;

"Notification Regulations" means the Notification of Installations Handling Hazardous Substances Regulations 1982;

"the relevant date" means the date on which Part IV of the Housing and Planning Act 1986 came into force or, if that Part of that Act is not in force immediately· before the date on which this Act comes into force, that date.

"the transitional period" means the period of 6 months beginning with the relevant date.

DEFINITIONS
"established quantity": subs. (8).
"establishment period": subs. (8).
"hazardous substances authority": ss.1, 2, 3, 39(1).
"hazardous substances consent": ss.4, 39(1).
"land": s.39(2).
"Notification Regulations": subs. (8).
"prescribed": s.39(2).
"the relevant date": subs. (8).
"the transitional period": subs. (8).
"use": s.39(2).

ALLOCATION OF FUNCTIONS
See the Commentary to s.1.

GENERAL NOTE

Purpose of the section
The transitional arrangements established by this section are important because the hazardous substances regime does not have a purely prospective effect: the control extends not only to the introduction of hazardous substances on to land in the future, but also to existing sites where hazardous substances are present. Consent must therefore be obtained where necessary for all existing sites.

Entitlement to deemed consent
Although hazardous substances consent is required whether or not land has previously been used for the storage of use of hazardous substances, there is an entitlement to receive consent if a hazardous substance was present at the land at any time within the period of 12 months preceding the commencement date (subs. (3)); and such consent is deemed to have been granted by the hazardous substances authority upon a valid claim being submitted under subs. (3). The authority need not issue a consent as such, since it is deemed to be granted upon the making of the claim. Subs. (8) therefore requires the authority to notify a claimant within two weeks of the claim if they are of the opinion that the claim is invalid, and give their reasons.
The deemed consent is, however, subject to the conditions imposed by subs. (9).

Transitional immunity
The Act allows a six month transitional period following the commencement date of these provisions for consent to be claimed. During the period no offence is committed under s.23, and no contravention notice may be issued under s.24, provided that, if notification was required under the Notification Regulations, it had been given before the commencement date, and the volume of the substance remains at or below the "established quantity" (s.26).

Deemed hazardous substances consent: government authorisation

12.—(1) Where—
(a) the authorisation of a government department is required by virtue of an enactment in respect of development to be carried out by a local authority, or by statutory undertakers who are not a local authority; and
(b) the development would involve the presence of a hazardous substance in circumstances requiring hazardous substances consent,

the department may, on granting that authorisation, also direct that hazardous substances consent shall be deemed to be granted subject to such conditions (if any) as may be specified in the direction.

(2) On granting a consent under section 36 of the Electricity Act 1989 in respect of any operation or change of use that would involve the presence of a hazardous substance in circumstances requiring hazardous substances consent, the Secretary of State may direct that hazardous substances consent shall be deemed to be granted, subject to such conditions (if any) as may be specified in the direction.

(3) The department or, as the case may be, the Secretary of State shall consult the Health and Safety Commission before giving any such direction.

(4) For the purposes of this section development shall be taken to be authorised by a government department if—

(a) any consent, authority or approval to or for the development is granted by the department in pursuance of an enactment;

(b) a compulsory purchase order is confirmed by the department authorising the purchase of land for the purpose of the development;

(c) consent is granted by the department to the appropriation of land for the purpose of the development or the acquisition of land by agreement for that purpose;

(d) authority is given by the department for the borrowing of money for the purpose of the development, or for the application for that purpose of any money not otherwise so applicable; or

(e) any undertaking is given by the department to pay a grant in respect of the development in accordance with an enactment authorising the payment of such grants,

and references in this section to the authorisation of a government department shall be construed accordingly.

(5) The provisions of this Act (except section 22) shall apply in relation to any hazardous substances consent deemed to be granted by virtue of directions under this section as if it had been granted by the Secretary of State on an application referred to him under section 20.

DEFINITIONS
"development": s.39(2).
"enactment": s.39(2).
"government department": s.39(2).
"hazardous substances consent": ss.4, 39(1).
"land": s.39(2).
"local authority": s.39(2).
"statutory undertakers": s.39(2), (4), (5), (6), (7) and (8).
"use": s.39(2).

GENERAL NOTE

Purpose of the section
This section extends s.90 of the Town and Country Planning Act 1990, which allows planning permission to be granted directly by a Government department where the development also requires authorisation under another enactment, to the new controls over hazardous substances. Hazardous substances consent may now also be deemed to be granted upon the issuing of such authorisation where the development is to be carried out by a local authority or statutory undertaker.

The procedure allows all material considerations to be taken into account in the authorisation process, and planning permission can also be deemed to be granted for any necessary associated development under s.90 of the T.C.P.A. 1990.

Definition of statutory undertaker
"Statutory undertaker" includes (T.C.P.A. 1990, s.262, as applied by s.91(3)):
"persons authorised by any enactment to carry on any railway, light railway, tramway, road transport, water transport, canal, inland navigation, dock, harbour, pier or light-house undertaking, or any undertaking for the supply of hydraulic power and a relevant airport operator (within the meaning of Part V of the Airports Act 1986)."
In addition, for the purposes of this section, the expression includes (s.39):
(1) a public gas supplier;
(2) the National Rivers Authority;
(3) every water or sewerage undertaker.

Variation and revocation of consents

Applications for removal of conditions attached to hazardous substances consent

13.—(1) This section applies to an application for hazardous substances consent without a condition subject to which a previous hazardous substances consent was granted.

(2) On such an application the hazardous substances authority shall consider only the question of the conditions subject to which hazardous substances consent should be granted.

(3) If on such an application the hazardous substances authority determine—

(a) that hazardous substances consent should be granted subject to conditions differing from those subject to which the previous consent was granted; or

(b) that it should be granted unconditionally,

they shall grant hazardous substances consent accordingly.

(4) If on such an application the hazardous substances authority determine that hazardous substances consent should be granted subject to the same conditions as those subject to which the previous consent was granted, they shall refuse the application.

(5) Where—

(a) hazardous substances consent has been granted or is deemed to have been granted for the presence on, over or under land of more than one hazardous substance; and

(b) an application under this section does not relate to all the substances,

the hazardous substances authority shall only have regard to any condition relating to a substance to which the application does not relate to the extent that it has implications for a substance to which the application does relate.

(6) Where—

(a) more than one hazardous substances consent has been granted or is deemed to have been granted in respect of the same land; and

(b) an application under this section does not relate to all the consents,

the hazardous substances authority shall only have regard to any consent to which the application does not relate to the extent that it has implications for consent to which the application does relate.

(7) Regulations may make provision in relation to applications under this section corresponding to any provision that may be made by regulations under section 7 or 8 in relation to applications for hazardous substances consent.

DEFINITIONS
"hazardous substances authority": ss.1, 2, 3, 39(1).
"hazardous substances consent": ss.4, 39(1).

"land": s.39(2).
"use": s.39(2).

ALLOCATION OF FUNCTIONS
See the Commentary to s.1.

GENERAL NOTE
Power to seek discharge of conditions
This section confers power on the hazardous substances authority to review the conditions subject to which consent has previously been granted, and corresponds to the powers that were also introduced by the Housing and Planning Act 1986 in relation to planning conditions generally and listed building consents. Unlike the situation with listed building consent, however, (see the Planning (Listed Buildings and Conservation Areas) Act 1990, s.19) the power to apply under this section is not limited to persons interested in land, with the consequence that an owner's criminal liability, if a condition is discharged and a fresh condition imposed, may be affected by the application of an unconnected third party (unless the substitution is effective only upon acceptance by the owner or occupier of the land: see further below). Moreover, only that third party would enjoy a right of appeal to the Secretary of State under s.21.

Discretion of the authority
The authority's discretion is confined to reviewing the conditions attached to the consent, and does not extend to reviewing whether consent should or should not have been granted (but without prejudice to their power under s.14 to make revocation and modification orders). Moreover, where the consent relates to more than one substance, they are required to have regard only to the conditions imposed in respect of the substance to which the condition which is the subject of the application relates. They are permitted to have regard to a condition relating to any other substance to the extent to which it has implications for a substance to which the application relates (subs. (5)).

Power of the authority
The authority may grant the application unconditionally, or they may refuse or grant it subject to different conditions. There is a right of appeal to the Secretary of State against refusal or substituted conditions. It is uncertain, however, whether any substituted condition would have immediate effect, or would require some prior act of implementation or acceptance by the applicant. If it did not, then an unwelcome substituted condition, even one imposed upon an application under this section by an unconnected third party, would affect the criminal liability of operators of the site, even pending the outcome of an appeal to the Secretary of State against the decision.

General power by order to revoke or modify hazardous substances consent

14.—(1) The hazardous substances authority may by order revoke a hazardous substances consent or modify it to such extent as they consider expedient if it appears to them, having regard to any material consideration, that it is expedient to revoke or modify it.

(2) The hazardous substances authority may also by order revoke a hazardous substances consent if it appears to them—

(a) that there has been a material change of use of land to which a hazardous substances consent relates; or

(b) that planning permission has been granted for development the carrying out of which would involve a material change of use of such land and the development to which the permission relates has been commenced; or

(c) in the case of a hazardous substances consent which relates only to one substance, that that substance has not for at least five years been present on, over or under the land to which the consent relates in a quantity equal to or exceeding the controlled quantity; or

(d) in the case of a hazardous substances consent which relates to a number of substances, that none of those substances has for at least five years been so present.

(3) An order made by virtue of subsection (2)(a) or (b) in the case of a consent relating to more than one substance may revoke it entirely or only so far as it relates to a specified substance.

(4) An order under this section shall specify the grounds on which it is made.

DEFINITIONS
"development": s.39(2).
"hazardous substances authority": ss.1, 2, 3, 39(1).
"hazardous substances consent": ss.4, 39(1).
"land": s.39(2).
"use": s.39(2).

ALLOCATION OF FUNCTIONS
See the Commentary to s.1.

GENERAL NOTE
Power to revoke or modify consent
The Act prescribes for several different circumstances in which hazardous substances consent may be revoked or modified, or will cease to have effect, for only some of which is there liability to pay compensation:

(1) the general power: the authority may by order revoke any consent or modify it to such extent as they think expedient (subs. (1)). An order made under these powers takes effect only upon being confirmed by the Secretary of State (s.15), except where it relates to operational land of a statutory undertaker, for which the hazardous substances authority is the "appropriate Minister" under s.2. The authority are liable to pay full compensation for exercise of this general power, under s.16;

(2) material change of use: where there has been an actual material change of use of the land to which a consent relates, or planning permission has been granted for development involving such a change and the development to which it relates has commenced, then the hazardous substances authority may by order revoke the consent either in full, or so far as it relates to a specified substance (subs. (2)(a)). Although such an order also requires confirmation by the Secretary of State under s.15, there is no liability to pay compensation;

(3) less than five years' presence: the authority may also by order revoke a consent where the substance or substances have not been present in a controlled quantity for a period of at least five years (subs. (2)(b)). The order requires confirmation (s.15), but there is no compensation liability;

(4) change of person in control of part of the land: consent is automatically revoked without compensation if there is a change of person in control of any part of the land to which the consent relates, unless an application for continuance of the consent has previously been made to the hazardous substances authority (s.17); and where such an application is made, the authority may modify or revoke the consent (s.18(1)) subject to compensation liability (s.19);

(5) contravention notice under s.24: where there has been a contravention of hazardous substances control, the authority may issue a notice requiring steps to be taken to remedy the contravention, and also include a requirement that the substance be removed altogether from the land and that any consent for it should cease to have effect at the end of a specified period (s.24(6) and (7)). Although there is a right of appeal to the Secretary of State against such a notice, there is no compensation payable if its requirements are upheld;

(6) on an application to discharge a condition, under s.13, there is power for the authority to modify the consent by the substitution of a different condition (s.13(3)).

The purpose of powers (2) and (3) above is apparently to allow the non-compensable revocation of a consent where it has, in effect, been abandoned. The Minister explained in Standing Committee (Standing Committee H, March 25, 1986, col. 437) that the possibility that hazardous substances may be kept on land often restricts the development permitted on neighbouring land, and if the use to which a consent relates has ceased the consent should therefore be revoked as soon as possible.

No order is to take effect without confirmation by the Secretary of State, and owners and other persons on whom notice of the order is served (s.14(3)) have the right to appear before, and be heard by an inspector (s.14(4)) before any order is confirmed.

There is, surprisingly, no right of entry under s.36 in connection with the exercise of powers under this section.

Crown land
An order may be made under this section in respect of Crown land only
  (1) to the extent of any interest in it for the time being held otherwise than by or on behalf of the Crown (s.31(1)); and
  (2) with the consent of the appropriate authority (s.31(2)).

Confirmation by Secretary of State of s.14 orders

15.—(1) An order under section 14 (other than an order relating to land to which section 2 applies) shall not take effect unless it is confirmed by the Secretary of State.

(2) The Secretary of State may confirm any such order submitted to him either without modification or subject to such modification as he considers expedient.

(3) Where a hazardous substances authority submit an order under section 14 to the Secretary of State for his confirmation under this section, the authority shall serve notice of the order—
  (a) on any person who is an owner of the whole or any part of the land to which the order relates;
  (b) on any person other than an owner who appears to them to be in control of the whole or any part of that land;
  (c) on any other person who in their opinion will be affected by the order.

(4) A notice under subsection (3) shall specify the period (which must not be less than 28 days from the service of it) within which any person on whom the notice is served may require an opportunity of appearing before and being heard by a person appointed by the Secretary of State for that purpose.

(5) If such a person so requires, the Secretary of State, before confirming the order, shall give that person and the hazardous substances authority such an opportunity.

(6) Where an order under section 14 has been confirmed by the Secretary of State, the hazardous substances authority shall serve a copy of the order on every person who was entitled to be served with notice under subsection (3).

DEFINITIONS
  "hazardous substances authority": ss.1, 2, 3, 39(1).
  "land": s.39(2).
  "owner": s.39(2).

ALLOCATION OF FUNCTIONS
  See the Commentary to s.1.

GENERAL NOTE
  Any order made under s.14 for the revocation or modification of a consent may take effect only if confirmed by the Secretary of State, even if it is unopposed.

Service of order
Notice of the order must be served by the authority on
  (1) any person who is an owner of the land: as to this expression, see the notes to s.336 of the Town and Country Planning Act 1990;
  (2) any other person appearing to be in control of the land: the operator of the site may have a short lease which puts him outside the definition of "owner" above, or occupy the land by virtue of a licence rather than a proprietary interest;
  (3) any other person who in their opinion will be affected.
  The mode of service is prescribed by the T.C.P.A. 1990, s.329 (as applied by s.37 of this Act).

Confirmation of the order
   The Secretary of State may modify the order when confirming it (subs. (2)).

   16.—(1) This section applies where an order is made under section 14(1) revoking or modifying a hazardous substances consent.
   (2) If, on a claim made to the hazardous substances authority within the prescribed time and in the prescribed manner, it is shown that any person has suffered damage in consequence of the order—
   (a) by depreciation of the value of an interest to which he is entitled in the land or in minerals in, on or under it; or
   (b) by being disturbed in his enjoyment of the land or of minerals in, on or under it,
the authority shall pay him compensation in respect of that damage.
   (3) Without prejudice to subsection (2), any person who carries out any works in compliance with the order shall be entitled, on a claim made as mentioned in that subsection, to recover from the hazardous substances authority compensation in respect of any expenses reasonably incurred by him in that behalf.
   (4) Any compensation payable to a person under this section by virtue of an order shall be reduced by the value to him of any timber, apparatus or other materials removed for the purpose of complying with the order.
   (5) Sections 117 and 118 of the principal Act (which contain general provisions as to the assessment of and the determination of claims for compensation) shall apply as if compensation under this section were compensation under section 115 of that Act.

DEFINITIONS
   "hazardous substances authority": ss.1, 2, 3, 39(1).
   "hazardous substances consent": ss.4, 39(1).
   "land": s.39(2).
   "minerals": s.39(2).
   "prescribed": s.39(2).
   "the principal Act": s.39(1).

ALLOCATION OF FUNCTIONS
   See the Commentary to s.1.

GENERAL NOTE
Entitlement to compensation
   Compensation is payable under this section only in respect of orders made under s.14(1), and a separate entitlement to compensation is conferred by s.19 in respect of revocations under s.18. There is no compensation entitlement for revocation orders made under s.14(2).
   The right to claim compensation is not restricted to owners of any interest in the land, but extends to any person who has suffered damage in consequence of the order (subs. (2)), or who has carried out works in compliance with the order (subs. (3)). As to the general principles involved in calculation of compensation, see the notes to the Town and Country Planning Act 1990, ss.117 and 118 (applied by subs. (5) of this section).

Claims procedure
   The period for making claims, and the manner of making them, are to be prescribed (subs. (1)) by regulations (T.C.P.A. 1990, s.336(1)).

Ecclesiastical property
   Any compensation payable under this section in respect of land which is ecclesiastical property must be paid to the Church Commissioners and be applied by them under s.34(3)(b).

Revocation of hazardous substances consent on change of control of land

   17.—(1) A hazardous substances consent is revoked if there is a change in the person in control of part of the land to which it relates, unless an application for the continuation of the consent has previously been made to the hazardous substances authority.

(2) Regulations may make provision in relation to applications under subsection (1) corresponding to any provision that may be made by regulations under section 7 or 8 in relation to applications for hazardous substances consent.

DEFINITIONS
"hazardous substances authority": ss.1, 2, 3, 39(1).
"hazardous substances consent": ss.4, 39(1).
"land": s.39(2).

ALLOCATION OF FUNCTIONS
See the Commentary to s.1.

GENERAL NOTE

Automatic revocation
Although hazardous substances consent, like a planning permission, enures for the benefit of land unless it is expressly limited to a personal consent, it will be revoked automatically in the event of a change in the person in control of part of the land unless an application for the continuance of the consent has previously been made to the hazardous substances authority. This section applies whether the consent was granted originally on an application, or claimed on the basis of an established presence under the transitional arrangements upon the Act coming into force.

A change of control of the whole of the land does not trigger off the revocation, and the power seems intended to be directed at sub-division of the planning unit. Its purpose is presumably to ensure that all conditions attached to the consent would still be capable of being complied with despite a change in control of part of the land. Therefore any change in control of part of the land will result in revocation of the whole of the relevant consent, unless there has been prior application. Moreover, the authority will have power on such application to modify or revoke the whole of the consent, though subject to payment of compensation to the person in control of the whole of the land before the change (s.19).

The person in control
The Act nowhere defines this concept. It uses the expression as one distinct from ownership or occupation of the land (see, *e.g.* for criminal liability under s.23 and the service of contravention notices under s.24), but it is ambiguous as to whether it is a reference to a particular individual, such as a site manager (in which case there might be frequent changes in the person in control), or to a legal person such as a corporate owner (in which case there might be no change even if the ownership of the company changed). The latter construction is indicated by s.39(3) which extends the definition of "person" for these sections so as to include any two bodies corporate to be treated as being one person if one is a subsidiary of the other, or if both are subsidiaries of one and the same corporate body.

The land to which the consent relates
The consent need not relate to the whole of the land under the control of the same person, and this fact to some extent undermines this provision. In order to mitigate the risk of automatic revocation, an applicant may seek to confine the area covered by an application to the smallest practical unit, such as a particular storage tank. This section would not then inhibit disposal of other parts of the land.

Determination of applications for continuation of hazardous substances consent

18.—(1) When an application is made under section 17 for the continuation of a hazardous substances consent the hazardous substances authority—

(a) may modify the consent in any way they consider appropriate; or
(b) may revoke it.

(2) In dealing with such an application the authority shall have regard to any material consideration and, in particular, but without prejudice to the generality of the foregoing—

(a) to the matters to which a hazardous substances authority are required to have regard by section 9(2)(a) to (d); and

(b) to any advice which the Health and Safety Executive or Health and Safety Commission have given following consultations in pursuance of regulations under section 17(2).

(3) If an application relates to more than one consent, the authority may make different determinations in relation to each.

(4) If a consent relates to more than one hazardous substance, the authority may make different determinations in relation to each.

(5) It shall be the duty of a hazardous substances authority, when continuing hazardous substances consent, to attach to the consent either—

(a) a statement that it is unchanged in relation to the matters included in it by virtue of sections 9(4) and 10(3); or

(b) a statement of any change in respect of those matters.

(6) The modifications which a hazardous substances authority may make by virtue of subsection (1)(a) include, without prejudice to the generality of that subsection, the making of the consent subject to conditions with respect to any of the matters mentioned in subsection (1) of section 10; and subsection (2) of that section shall apply as respects those conditions as it applies to the grant of consent subject to conditions.

(7) Where any application under section 17(1) is made to a hazardous substances authority then, unless within such period as may be prescribed, or within such extended period as may at any time be agreed upon in writing between the applicant and the hazardous substances, authority, the hazardous substances authority either—

(a) give notice to the applicant of their decision on the application; or

(b) give notice to him that the application has been referred to the Secretary of State in accordance with directions given under section 20,

the application shall be deemed to have been granted.

DEFINITIONS
"hazardous substances authority": ss.1, 2, 3, 39(1).
"hazardous substances consent": ss.4, 39(1).
"prescribed": s.39(2).

ALLOCATION OF FUNCTIONS
See the Commentary to s.1.

GENERAL NOTE

Applications for continuation of consent
An application must be made under s.17 prior to any change in the person in control of part of the land to which a consent relates. If such a change takes place without a prior application, the whole of the consent is automatically revoked under s.17, although there is no revocation—and no trigger for the exercise of the powers under this section—if a change in control of the whole of the land occurs.

On an application under this section the authority may revoke the consent or modify it (subject in both cases to liability to pay compensation under s.19), including power to impose further conditions (subs. (6)). Unlike the general powers in s.14, their action under this section does not require confirmation by the Secretary of State. It has immediate effect: it becomes an offence under s.23 to fail to comply with any new condition imposed, or to allow the presence of hazardous substances to continue if consent is revoked. However, there is entitlement to compensation under s.19 for any loss or damage sustained by the person in control of the whole of the land, and there is a right of appeal to the Secretary of State under s.21 against any decision by the authority under this section.

Failure to determine within prescribed time
Subs. (7) reverses the normal rule for planning applications, under which the failure by a planning authority to determine an application within the prescribed or agreed time

constitutes a deemed refusal. On a continuation application such a failure by a hazardous substances authority constitutes a deemed consent.

Compensation on revocation or modification of consent under s.18

19. Where on an application under section 17(1) the hazardous substances authority modify or revoke the hazardous substances consent, they shall pay to the person in control of the whole of the land before the change in control by virtue of which the application was made compensation in respect of any loss or damage sustained by him and directly attributable to the modification or revocation.

DEFINITIONS
"hazardous substances authority": ss.1, 2, 3, 39(1).
"hazardous substances consent": ss.4, 39(1).
"land": s.39(2).

ALLOCATION OF FUNCTIONS
See the Commentary to s.1.

GENERAL NOTE
Entitlement to compensation
Compensation is payable under this section only for modification or revocation of a consent under s.19. A separate entitlement is conferred by s.16 where consent is revoked or modified by an order under s.14(1). Compensation is payable to the person who was in control of the whole of the land prior to the making of the application. But the section fails to specify any of the normal requirements as to compensation, such as a power for the Secretary of State to prescribe the period for and method of claiming compensation.

Compensation where revocation by Secretary of State
The section refers to compensation being payable only where the authority modify or revoke the consent. But a consent may also be revoked or modified by the Secretary of State, whether on call-in under s.20, or appeal by an aggrieved applicant under s.21. In both cases it is clear that the decision is then a decision of the Secretary of State and not of the hazardous substances authority, and thus there is no entitlement to compensation under this section.

Contribution to compensation
The Secretary of State may direct other authorities to contribute towards an authority's compensation liability under this section, having regard to any benefit accruing to those other authorities by reasons of the revocation or modification (s.38(3)).

Secretary of State's powers

Reference of applications to Secretary of State

20.—(1) The Secretary of State may give directions requiring applications for hazardous substances consent or applications under section 17(1) to be referred to him instead of being dealt with by hazardous substances authorities.

(2) A direction under this section—
    (a) may be given either to a particular hazardous substances authority or to hazardous substances authorities generally; and
    (b) may relate either to a particular application or to applications of a class specified in the direction.

(3) Any application in respect of which a direction under this section has effect shall be referred to the Secretary of State accordingly.

(4) Before determining an application referred to him under this section, the Secretary of State shall, if either the applicant or the hazardous substances authority so wish, give to each of them an opportunity of appearing before, and being heard by, a person appointed by the Secretary of State for the purpose.

(5) The decision of the Secretary of State on any application referred to him under this section shall be final.

(6) This section does not have effect in relation to applications for hazardous substances consent relating to land to which section 2 applies or to decisions on such applications.

DEFINITIONS
"hazardous substances authority": ss.1, 2, 3, 39(1).
"hazardous substances consent": ss.4, 39(1).
"land": s.39(2).

ALLOCATION OF FUNCTIONS
See the Commentary to s.1.

GENERAL NOTE

Power of call-in
This section confers a power of call-in on the Secretary of State, corresponding to the general planning call-in power under the T.C.P.A. 1990, s.77. As to the ability of the courts to question the exercise of this discretion by the Secretary of State, see the notes to that section. It does not extend to ministerial authorities under s.2, where the decision is already in the hands of central government (subs. (5)).
A decision given by the Secretary of State on a called-in s.17 application, to revoke or modify a consent, is not a decision by the authority qualifying for compensation under s.19: see further the notes to that section.

Finality of Secretary of State's decision
The finality which attaches under subs. (5) to the decisions of the Secretary of State yields to the right under s.22 to apply to the High Court for review of such decisions on a point of law.

Appeals against decisions or failure to take decisions relating to hazardous substances

21.—(1) Where a hazardous substances authority refuse an application for hazardous substances consent or an application under section 17(1) or an application for any consent, agreement or approval of the authority required by a condition imposed on the grant of such consent, or grant it subject to conditions, the applicant may, if he is aggrieved by their decision, appeal to the Secretary of State.

(2) A person who has made an application for hazardous substances consent may also appeal to the Secretary of State if the hazardous substances authority have neither—

(a) given notice to the applicant of their decision on the application; nor

(b) given notice to him that the application has been referred to the Secretary of State in accordance with directions given under section 20,

within such period as may be prescribed, or within such extended period as may at any time be agreed upon in writing between the applicant and the hazardous substances authority; and for the purposes of this Act in such a case the authority shall be deemed to have decided to refuse the application.

(3) An appeal under this section must be made by notice served in the prescribed manner within such period as may be prescribed.

(4) The Secretary of State may allow or dismiss an appeal under this section or may reverse or vary any part of the decision of the hazardous substances authority (whether or not the appeal relates to that part of it) and may deal with the application as if it had been made to him in the first instance.

(5) Before determining an appeal under this section, the Secretary of State shall, if either the applicant or the hazardous substances authority so wish, give each of them an opportunity of appearing before and being heard by a person appointed by the Secretary of State for the purpose.

(6) The decision of the Secretary of State on any appeal under this section shall be final.

(7) This section does not have effect in relation to applications for hazardous substances consent relating to land to which section 2 applies or to decisions on such applications.

(8) The Schedule to this Act applies to appeals under this section.

DEFINITIONS
"hazardous substances authority": ss.1, 2, 3, 39(1).
"hazardous substances consent": ss.4, 39(1).
"land": s.39(2).
"prescribed": s.39(2).
"use": s.39(2).

ALLOCATION OF FUNCTIONS
See the Commentary to s.1.

GENERAL NOTE

When an appeal may be made
An appeal may be made under this section where
(1) hazardous substances consent has been refused, or conditions have been imposed on the grant of consent (subs. (1)). Alternatively, the applicant may choose to challenge a condition by applying to the authority under s.13 for consent without such a condition, since on that application only the condition is at stake (s.13(2)) and on any subsequent appeal, and not the question of whether consent should be granted at all which will be at issue in an appeal under this section;
(2) the authority have failed to notify the applicant of their decision, or to notify him that the application has been called-in, within the prescribed time (yet to be prescribed by regulations) (subs. (2));
(3) an application under s.17 for the continuation of a consent upon a change in the person in control of the land is refused or granted subject to conditions: the wording of this formula is inappropriate, because the only choice available to an authority under s.18 is to grant the application, or to modify or revoke the consent. Moreover, an unsuccessful appeal may deprive the applicant of any compensation under s.19, to the extent that it results in the Secretary of State rather than the authority modifying or revoking the consent (see further the notes to s.19). There is no appeal in default of a determination under this section, because if the authority fail to notify their decision within the prescribed time the application is deemed to be granted (under s.18(7));
(4) an application for any consent, agreement or approval of the authority required by a condition attached to a consent has been refused, or granted subject to conditions (subs. (1)).
Where the terms of any consent infringe health and safety requirements, they are to that extent void under s.29 without any need to pursue an appeal.

An appeal may not be made in a case falling within s.2 (operational land of statutory undertakers) where the determining authority is already central government, in the form of the "appropriate Minister".

Appeal procedure
The procedure is to be prescribed by regulations made under subs. (3), and the Schedule to the Act prescribes the arrangements for determination of appeals by inspectors rather than by the Secretary of State. No regulations have yet been made transferring jurisdiction to inspectors.

The right of appeal
An appeal may be made under this section only by the original applicant, and not a successor in title.

Further appeal

A right of further appeal by way of application to the High Court is conferred by s.22, but otherwise the validity of any decision taken by the Secretary of State under this section (or on call-in under s.20) may not be called in question in any legal proceedings whatsoever (s.20(5)) and the Secretary of State's decision is "final" (subs. (6)).

Validity of decisions as to applications

22.—(1) If any person is aggrieved by any decision of the Secretary of State under section 20 or 21 and wishes to question the validity of that decision on the grounds—

    (a) that it is not within the powers of this Act; or

    (b) that any of the relevant requirements have not been complied with in relation to that decision,

he may within six weeks from the date on which the decision is taken make an application to the High Court under this section.

(2) Without prejudice to subsection (1), if the hazardous substances authority who made the decision on the application to which the proceedings relate or, as the case may be, referred the application wish to question the validity of any such decision as is mentioned in that subsection on any of the grounds there mentioned, the authority may within six weeks from the date on which the decision is taken make an application to the High Court under this section.

(3) On any application under this section the High Court—

    (a) may by interim order suspend the operation of the decision the validity of which is questioned by the application until the final determination of the proceedings;

    (b) if satisfied that the decision in question is not within the powers of this Act, or that the interests of the applicant have been substantially prejudiced by a failure to comply with any of the relevant requirements in relation to it, may quash that decision.

(4) In this section "the relevant requirements," in relation to any decision, means any requirements of this Act or the 1971 Act or of the Tribunals and Inquiries Act 1971, or of any order, regulations or rules made under this Act or under either of those Acts which are applicable to that decision.

(5) Except as provided by this section, the validity of any such decision as is mentioned in subsection (1) shall not be questioned in any legal proceedings whatsoever.

(6) Nothing in subsection (5) shall affect the exercise of any jurisdiction of any court in respect of any refusal or failure on the part of the Secretary of State to take any such decision as is there mentioned.

DEFINITIONS

    "hazardous substances authority": ss.1, 2, 3, 39(1).

    "the 1971 Act": s.39(2).

    "the relevant requirements": subs. (4).

ALLOCATION OF FUNCTIONS

    See the Commentary to s.1.

GENERAL NOTE

The section creates a right to question the validity of the Secretary of State's decision on an appeal or called-in application, by applying to the High Court within six weeks of the decision. It is the only means by which the validity of such decisions may be tested, and the section therefore excludes applications for judicial review in respect of them. The section is in the familiar form of the ouster provisions of the T.C.P.A. 1990: for a full analysis see the notes to ss.284–292 of that Act.

The section does not apply to directions made under s.12 (deemed consent upon authorisation of government department), although such directions may be similarly protected by ouster provisions contained in the legislation under which the primary authorisation is made.

Contraventions of hazardous substances control

Offences

    23.—(1) Subject to the following provisions of this section, if there is a contravention of hazardous substances control, the appropriate person shall be guilty of an offence.

    (2) There is a contravention of hazardous substances control—

      (a) if a quantity of a hazardous substance equal to or exceeding the controlled quantity is or has been present on, over or under land and either—

        (i) there is no hazardous substances consent for the presence of the substance; or

        (ii) there is hazardous substances consent for its presence but the quantity present exceeds the maximum quantity permitted by the consent;

      (b) if there is or has been a failure to comply with a condition subject to which a hazardous substances consent was granted.

    (3) In subsection (1) "the appropriate person" means—

      (a) in relation to a contravention falling within paragraph (a) of subsection (2)—

        (i) any person knowingly causing the substance to be present on, over or under the land;

        (ii) any person allowing it to be so present; and

      (b) in relation to a contravention falling within paragraph (a) or (b) of that subsection, the person in control of the land.

    (4) A person guilty of an offence under this section shall be liable—

      (a) on summary conviction, to a fine not exceeding the statutory maximum; or

      (b) on conviction on indictment, to a fine,

and if the contravention is continued after the conviction he shall be guilty of a further offence and liable—

    (i) on summary conviction to a fine not exceeding £200 for each day on which it continues, or

    (ii) on conviction on indictment to a fine.

    (5) In any proceedings for an offence under this section it shall be a defence for the accused to prove—

      (a) that he took all reasonable precautions and exercised all due diligence to avoid commission of the offence, or

      (b) that commission of the offence could be avoided only by the taking of action amounting to a breach of a statutory duty.

    (6) In any proceedings for an offence consisting of a contravention falling within subsection (2)(a), it shall be a defence for the accused to prove that at the time of the alleged commission of the offence he did not know, and had no reason to believe—

      (a) if the case falls within paragraph (a)(i)—

        (i) that the substance was present; or

        (ii) that it was present in a quantity equal to or exceeding the controlled quantity;

      (b) if the case falls within paragraph (a)(ii), that the substance was present in a quantity exceeding the maximum quantity permitted by the consent.

    (7) In any proceedings for an offence consisting of a contravention falling within subsection (2)(b), it shall be a defence for the accused to prove that he did not know, and had no reason to believe, that there was

a failure to comply with a condition subject to which hazardous substances consent had been granted.

DEFINITIONS
"contravention of hazardous substances control": subs. (2).
"hazardous substances consent": ss.4, 39(1).
"land": s.39(2).
"the appropriate person": subs. (3).
"use": s.39(2).

ALLOCATION OF FUNCTIONS
See the Commentary to s.1.

GENERAL NOTE

Purpose of the section
This section renders contravention of hazardous substances control a criminal offence. There is a contravention if there has been a quantity of hazardous substance equal to or exceeding the controlled quantity without consent, or in excess of consent, or if there has been any breach of a condition on a hazardous substances consent. In the special circumstances specified in s.27 the Secretary of State is permitted to exclude certain contraventions from liability under this section for up to three months.

Further enforcement powers are contained in s.24, allowing the authority to issue a special enforcement notice (a hazardous substances contravention notice) specifying the contravention and requiring specified steps to be taken to remedy it.

Subs. (2)(a)
Excessive quantity. It is an offence under this provision for the appropriate person knowingly to cause, or to allow, an excessive quantity of a hazardous substance to be present on, over or under land. It is excessive if it is equal to or exceeds the controlled quantity (as prescribed under s.5) and there is no consent for it; or if the quantity exceeds the maximum permitted by the consent (subs. (2)(a).

The offence is committed by the "appropriate person", who is (subs. (3)) any one or more of the following: (1) any person who knowingly causes the substance to be present; (2) any person allowing it to be present; and (3) the person in control of the land. Thus knowledge is an ingredient in the offence in the first two cases, but not in the third. However, in addition to the general defence (see below) it is a specific statutory defence in relation to this offence under subs. (6), for the accused to prove that at the time of the alleged commission of the offence he did not know and had no reason to know that the substance was present, or that its quantity was in excess of the controlled quantity (or the maximum permitted in the consent).

Subs. (2)(b)
Breach of condition. It is an offence under this provision for the person in control of the land to fail to comply with a condition attached to hazardous substances consent. In addition to the general defence (see below) it is a defence (subs. (5)) for the accused to prove that he did not know, and had no reason to believe, that there was such a failure.

The general defence
It is a defence (subs. (5)) for the accused to prove that he took all reasonable precautions and exercised due diligence, or that the commission of the offence could only have been avoided by the taking of action amounting to a breach of a statutory duty.

Further enforcement action
The authority may take action under s.24 where it appears to them that there has been a breach of control under this section, by issuing a contravention notice specifying the alleged breach and requiring steps to be taken to remedy it. The objective of this procedure is remedial rather than penal, and there is a right of appeal to the Secretary of State against any such notice.

Power to issue hazardous substances contravention notice

24.—(1) Where it appears to the hazardous substances authority that there is or has been a contravention of hazardous substances control, they may issue a notice—

(a) specifying an alleged contravention of hazardous substances control; and

(b) requiring such steps as may be specified in the notice to be taken to remedy the contravention,

if they consider it expedient to do so having regard to any material consideration.

(2) Such a notice is referred to in this Act as a "hazardous substances contravention notice."

(3) A hazardous substances authority shall not issue a hazardous substances contravention notice where it appears to them that a contravention of hazardous substances control can be avoided only by the taking of action amounting to a breach of a statutory duty.

(4) A copy of a hazardous substances contravention notice shall be served—

(a) on the owner of the land to which it relates;

(b) on any person other than the owner who appears to the hazardous substances authority to be in control of the land; and

(c) on such other persons as may be prescribed.

(5) A hazardous substances contravention notice shall also specify—

(a) a date not less than 28 days from the date of service of copies of the notice as the date on which it is to take effect;

(b) in respect of each of the steps required to be taken to remedy the contravention of hazardous substances control, the period from the notice taking effect within which the step is to be taken.

(6) Where a hazardous substances authority issue a hazardous substances contravention notice the steps required by the notice may, without prejudice to the generality of subsection (1)(b), if the authority think it expedient, include a requirement that the hazardous substance be removed from the land.

(7) Where a notice includes such a requirement, it may also contain a direction that at the end of such period as may be specified in the notice any hazardous substances consent for the presence of the substance shall cease to have effect or, if it relates to more than one substance, shall cease to have effect so far as it relates to the substances which are required to be removed.

(8) The hazardous substances authority may withdraw a hazardous substances contravention notice (without prejudice to their power to issue another) at any time before it takes effect.

(9) If they do so, they shall immediately give notice of the withdrawal to every person who was served with a copy of the notice.

DEFINITIONS
"contravention of hazardous substances control": ss.23(2); s.39(1).
"hazardous substances authority": ss.1, 2, 3, 39(1).
"hazardous substances consent": ss.4, 39(1).
"hazardous substances contravention notice": subs. (2).
"land": s.39(2).
"owner": s.39(2).
"prescribed": s.39(2).

ALLOCATION OF FUNCTIONS
See the Commentary to s.1.

GENERAL NOTE

Purpose of the section
This section makes provision for enforcement of hazardous substances control, through procedures modelled on those relating to the enforcement of planning control. Liability to contravention action is independent from, and additional to, criminal liability under s.23,

although the pre-conditions to liability are the same. Enforcement action may only be taken under this section in circumstances where there has been a contravention of hazardous substances control. The defences that are available under s.23(5), (6) and (7) are not reproduced in this section, but would presumably need to be incorporated into the grounds of appeal (yet to be prescribed) against a contravention notice under this section (as with the statutory defence to breach of listed building control under the Planning (Listed Buildings and Conservation Areas) Act 1990: see s.38 of that Act).

The contravention procedures in this section are intended to be remedial: the authority are empowered to serve a notice requiring the owner, or person otherwise in control, of the land to take such steps as are specified in the notice, within such time as may be specified, to remedy the contravention. The section does not impose any direct criminal liability for failure to comply with a notice, but the Secretary of State is empowered by s.25 to make regulations for the purpose, *inter alia*, of directing that certain of the enforcement provisions of the T.C.P.A. 1990 shall extend to notices under this section, subject to such modifications as he may specify. Nor is there provision for a stop notice procedure corresponding to that under planning enforcement, because criminal liability exists under s.23 independently of contravention proceedings under this section.

Exemptions from enforcement

A contravention notice may not be issued
(1) where a temporary exemption direction has been issued by the Secretary of State under s.27, for the period of the exemption;
(2) in respect of Crown land, except to the extent of any interest in it for the time being held otherwise than by or on behalf of the Crown, and then only with the prior consent of the appropriate Crown authority (s.31(1) and (2));
(3) during the transitional six-month period following the coming into force of the Act, in respect of any presence of hazardous substances which has been established for the preceding 12 months (s.26(1));
(4) where it appears to the authority that a contravention of hazardous substances control can only be avoided by the taking of action amounting to a breach of statutory duty (subs. (3)).

Exclusion for health and safety requirements

Nothing in a contravention notice may require or allow anything to be done in contravention of any relevant statutory provisions, prohibition notice or improvement notice under the Health and Safety at Work Act 1974, and to the extent that it does so it is void (s.29(1) and (2)). If it appears to the authority that a notice or part of it is rendered void by these provisions, they are required by s.29(3) as soon as is reasonably practicable to consult the HSE (the Commission where the authority is the appropriate Minister), and revoke it or modify it in accordance with their advice.

What a contravention notice must specify

A contravention notice must specify
(1) the alleged contravention of control (subs. (1)(a));
(2) the steps required by the authority to be taken to remedy the contravention (subs. (1)(b)), which may include:
  (a) a requirement that the hazardous substance be removed from the land (subs. (6)); and,
  (b) in such a case, a direction that at the end of a specified period any consent for the presence of the substance shall cease to have effect or, if it relates to more than one substance, shall cease to have effect so far as it relates to the substances which are to be removed;
(3) a date of not less than 28 days from the date of service, as the date on which the notice is to take effect (subs. (5)(a));
(4) the period in which each of the required steps is to be taken (subs. (5)(b));
(5) such other matters as may be prescribed by the Secretary of State (s.25(1)).

Service of the notice

The notice must be served on the owner, the person appearing to be in control of the land and such other persons as may be prescribed (subs. (4)). The mechanism for service is prescribed by the T.C.P.A. 1990, s.329, applied by s.37 of this Act. No-one is entitled to claim that a notice has not been properly served on a person if that person has appealed to the Secretary of State against the notice (s.25(4)).

Appeal against contravention notice
There is to be a right of appeal to the Secretary of State under regulations made under s.25, and the contravention notice has no effect pending the final determination or the withdrawal of the appeal (s.25(2)).

Hazardous substances contravention notices: supplementary provisions

25.—(1) The Secretary of State may by regulations—

(a) specify matters which are to be included in hazardous substances contravention notices, in addition to those which are required to be included in them by section 24;

(b) provide—

(i) for appeals to him against hazardous substances contravention notices;

(ii) for the persons by whom, grounds upon which and time within which such an appeal may be brought;

(iii) for the procedure to be followed on such appeals;

(iv) for the directions that may be given on such an appeal;

(v) for the application to such appeals, subject to such modifications as the regulations may specify, of any of the provisions of sections 174, 175(1) to (4) and (6), 176, 177, 285 and 289 of the principal Act;

(c) direct that any of the provisions of sections 178(1) to (5) and (7), 179 to 181, 183, 184, 187 and 188 of that Act shall have effect in relation to hazardous substances contravention notices subject to such modifications as he may specify in the regulations;

(d) make such other provision as he considers necessary or expedient in relation to hazardous substances contravention notices.

(2) If any person appeals against a hazardous substances contravention notice, the notice shall be of no effect pending the final determination or the withdrawal of the appeal.

(3) Regulations under section 24 or this section may make different provision for different cases or descriptions of cases.

(4) Where any person has appealed to the Secretary of State under this section against a hazardous substances contravention notice, no person shall be entitled, in any other proceedings instituted after the making of the appeal, to claim that the notice was not duly served on the person who appealed.

DEFINITIONS
"hazardous substances contravention notice": ss.24(1), 39(1).
"the principal Act": s.39(1).

ALLOCATION OF FUNCTIONS
See the Commentary to s.1.

GENERAL NOTE
The Secretary of State has power to fill in all the details of contravention notice appeals procedure, by regulations made under this section.

Transitional exemptions

26.—(1) No offence is committed under section 23 and no hazardous substances contravention notice may be issued in relation to a hazardous substance which is on, over or under any land, if—

(a) the substance was present on, over or under the land at any time within the establishment period; and

(b) in a case in which at the relevant date notification in respect of that substance was required by any of the Notification Regulations, both the conditions specified in subsection (2) were satisfied; and

(c) in a case in which at that date such notification was not so required, the condition specified in paragraph (b) of that subsection is satisfied.

(2) The conditions mentioned in subsection (1) are—

(a) that notification required by the Notification Regulations was given before the relevant date; and

(b) that the substance has not been present during the transitional period in a quantity greater in aggregate than the established quantity.

(3) Expressions used in this section and in section 11 have the same meanings as in that section.

DEFINITIONS
"established quantity": s.11(8).
"establishment period": s.11(8).
"hazardous substances contravention notice": ss.24(1), 39(1).
"land": s.39(2).
"Notification Regulations": s.11(8).
"the relevant date": s.11(8).
"the transitional period": s.11(8).

GENERAL NOTE
This section carries through the provisions of s.11, under which deemed consent may be claimed for any established presence of hazardous substances, by conferring an immunity from prosecution and contravention proceedings for the six month claim period following the Act's entry into force.

Miscellaneous provisions

Temporary exemption directions

27.—(1) If it appears to the Secretary of State—

(a) either—

(i) that the community or part of it is being or is likely to be deprived of an essential service or commodity; or

(ii) that there is or is likely to be a shortage of such a service or commodity affecting the community or part of it; and

(b) that the presence of a hazardous substance on, over or under land specified in the direction in circumstances such that hazardous substances consent would be required, is necessary for the effective provision of that service or commodity,

he may direct that, subject to such conditions or exceptions as he thinks fit, the presence of the substance on, over or under the land is not to constitute a contravention of hazardous substances control so long as the direction remains in force.

(2) A direction under this section—

(a) may be withdrawn at any time;

(b) shall in any case cease to have effect at the end of the period of three months beginning with the day on which it was given, but without prejudice to the Secretary of State's power to give a further direction.

(3) The Secretary of State shall send a copy of any such direction to the authority who are the hazardous substances authority for the land.

(4) Where the land is land to which section 2 applies subsection (3) shall not apply but instead the Secretary of State shall send the copy to the authority who would be the hazardous substances authority for the land but for that section.

DEFINITIONS
"contravention of hazardous substances control": s.39(1).
"hazardous substances authority": ss.1, 2, 3, 39(1).
"hazardous substances consent": ss.4, 39(1).
"land": s.39(2).

ALLOCATION OF FUNCTIONS
See the Commentary to s.1.

GENERAL NOTE
This section confers on the Secretary of State a special power to extend exemption from criminal liability under s.23, and from contravention action under s.24, where an essential service or commodity is at stake and the presence of some hazardous substance requiring consent is necessary for the effective provision of the service or commodity. It is a temporary exception, limited to a maximum period of three months, although with power for the Secretary of State to make further orders. If it is intended that the presence of the substance should continue beyond that period, then application for express consent may be made within the exemption period.
The heading to the section as originally enacted (as s.58L of the T.C.P.A. 1971) was "Emergencies", but that did not accurately reflect its content and it has been discarded in the consolidation.

Registers etc.

28.—(1) Every authority who are a hazardous substances authority by virtue of section 1 or 3 shall keep, in such manner as may be prescribed, a register containing such information as may be prescribed with respect—
  (a) to applications for hazardous substances consent—
      (i) made to that authority; or
      (ii) made to the appropriate Minister with respect to land for which, but for section 2, that authority would be the hazardous substances authority;
      and including information as to the manner in which such applications have been dealt with;
  (b) to hazardous substances consent having effect by virtue of section 11 or 12 with respect to land for which that authority is, or but for section 2 would be, the hazardous substances authority;
  (c) to revocations or modifications of hazardous substances consent granted with respect to such land; and
  (d) to directions under section 27 sent to the authority by the Secretary of State.
(2) Where the appropriate Minister exercises any of the functions of a hazardous substances authority with respect to any land he shall send to the authority which but for section 2 would be the hazardous substances authority for the land any such information as appears to him to be required by them for the purposes of maintaining a register under this section.
(3) Every register kept under this section shall be available for inspection by the public at all reasonable hours.

DEFINITIONS
"the appropriate Minister": s.39(2).
"functions": s.39(2).
"hazardous substances authority": ss.1, 2, 3, 39(1).
"hazardous substances consent": ss.4, 39(1).
"land": s.39(2).
"Minister": s.39(2).
"prescribed": s.39(2).

ALLOCATION OF FUNCTIONS
See the Commentary to s.1.

Every local hazardous substances authority is required to keep a public register of applications, consents, revocations, modifications and directions issued under s.27. Where the hazardous substances authority is a Minister under s.2, he is required to forward any such information relating to his exercise of that function to the local hazardous substances authority for the area.

General

Health and safety requirements

29.—(1) Nothing in—
  (a) any hazardous substances consent granted or deemed to be granted or having effect by virtue of this Act; or
  (b) any hazardous substances contravention notice issued under section 24,
shall require or allow anything to be done in contravention of any of the relevant statutory provisions or any prohibition notice or improvement notice served under or by virtue of any of those provisions.

(2) To the extent that such a consent or notice purports to require or allow any such thing to be done, it shall be void.

(3) Where it appears to a hazardous substances authority who have granted, or are deemed to have granted, a hazardous substances consent or who have issued a hazardous substances contravention notice that the consent or notice or part of it is rendered void by subsection (2), the authority shall, as soon as is reasonably practicable, consult the appropriate body with regard to the matter.

(4) If the appropriate body advise the authority that the consent or notice is rendered wholly void, the authority shall revoke it.

(5) If they advise that part of the consent or notice is rendered void, the authority shall so modify it as to render it wholly operative.

(6) In this section—
    "the appropriate body" means—
        (a) in relation to a hazardous substances authority other than the appropriate Minister, the Health and Safety Executive; and
        (b) in relation to the appropriate Minister, the Health and Safety Commission; and
    "relevant statutory provisions," "improvement notice" and "prohibition notice" have the same meanings as in Part I of the Health and Safety at Work etc. Act 1974.

DEFINITIONS
  "the appropriate body": subs. (6).
  "the appropriate Minister": s.39(2).
  "hazardous substances authority": ss.1, 2, 3, 39(1).
  "hazardous substances consent": ss.4, 39(1).
  "hazardous substances contravention notice": ss.24(1), 39(1).
  "improvement notice": subs. (6), and see below.
  "Minister": s.39(2).
  "prohibition notice": subs. (6), and see below.
  "relevant statutory provisions": subs. (6), and see below.

ALLOCATION OF FUNCTIONS
  See the Commentary to s.1.

GENERAL NOTE
  Where there is any conflict between action taken by a hazardous substances authority under these provisions, and any requirement of Pt. I of the Health and Safety at Work etc. Act 1974, or an improvement notice or prohibition notice issued thereunder, then those requirements prevail.

Definitions in the Health and Safety at Work Act

The Health and Safety at Work Act 1974 defines the following terms used in this section: "relevant statutory provisions": this means the powers of Pt. I of that Act, and of any health and safety regulations, and the "existing statutory provisions." (in Sched. 1 to that Act) to the extent that they are still in force.

A "prohibition notice" is a notice served under s.22 of that Act by an inspector in order to prohibit an activity carried on, or about to be carried on, which would involve a risk of serious personal injury.

An improvement notice may be served by an inspector under s.21 where a person is (or has been) contravening one or more of the relevant statutory provisions in circumstances that make it likely that the contravention will continue or will be repeated. The notice may require the person to remedy the contravention (or, as the case may be, the matters occasioning it) within a period specified in the notice.

Application of this Act to certain authorities and persons

30.—(1) The provisions of this Act shall have effect, subject to such exceptions and modifications as may be prescribed in relation to granting hazardous substances consent for authorities who are hazardous substances authorities by virtue of section 1 or 3.

(2) Subject to the provisions of section 12, any such regulations may in particular provide for securing—

(a) that any application by such an authority for hazardous substances consent in respect of the presence of a hazardous substance on, over or under land shall be made to the Secretary of State and not to the hazardous substances authority;

(b) that any order or notice authorised to be made, issued or served under those provisions shall be made, issued or served by the Secretary of State and not by the hazardous substances authority.

DEFINITIONS

"hazardous substances authority": ss.1, 2, 3, 39(1).
"hazardous substances consent": ss.4, 39(1).
"land": s.39(2).
"prescribed": s.39(2).

ALLOCATION OF FUNCTIONS

See the Commentary to s.1.

GENERAL NOTE

This section makes special provision for handling applications for hazardous substances consent in cases where the consent is required for the hazardous substances authority themselves. It extends only to non-ministerial authorities under s.2 who enjoy Crown immunity from the requirement of obtaining consent under the Act. The Secretary of State is to have power to require the authority to make application to him for consent.

Exercise of powers in relation to Crown land

31.—(1) Notwithstanding any interest of the Crown in Crown land, but subject to subsection (2), any restrictions imposed or powers conferred by sections 4 to 29 (except section 22) shall apply and be exercisable in relation to Crown land to the extent of any interest in it for the time being held otherwise than by or on behalf of the Crown.

(2) Except with the consent of the appropriate authority, no order or notice shall be made, issued or served under any of the provisions of section 14, 15 or 24 in relation to land which for the time being is Crown land.

(3) In this section—

"Crown land" means land in which there is a Crown interest or a Duchy interest;

"Crown interest" means an interest belonging to Her Majesty in right of the Crown, or belonging to a government department or held in trust for Her Majesty for the purposes of a government department;

"Duchy interest" means an interest belonging to Her Majesty in right of the Duchy of Lancaster, or belonging to the Duchy of Cornwall.

(4) A person who is entitled to occupy Crown land by virtue of a licence in writing shall be treated for the purposes of subsection (1) as having an interest in land.

(5) For the purposes of this section "the appropriate authority," in relation to any land—

(a) in the case of land belonging to Her Majesty in right of the Crown and forming part of the Crown Estate, means the Crown Estate Commissioners, and, in relation to any other land belonging to Her Majesty in right of the Crown, means the government department having the management of that land;

(b) in relation to land belonging to Her Majesty in right of the Duchy of Lancaster, means the Chancellor of the Duchy;

(c) in relation to land belonging to the Duchy of Cornwall, means such person as the Duke of Cornwall, or the possessor for the time being of the Duchy of Cornwall, appoints;

(d) in the case of land belonging to a government department or held in trust for Her Majesty for the purposes of a government department, means that department.

(6) If any question arises as to what authority is the appropriate authority in relation to any land, that question shall be referred to the Treasury, whose decision shall be final.

DEFINITIONS
"the appropriate authority": subs. (5).
"Crown interest": subs. (3).
"Crown land": subs. (3).
"Duchy interest": subs. (3).
"government department": s.39(2).
"land": s.39(2).

ALLOCATION OF FUNCTIONS
See the Commentary to s.1.

GENERAL NOTE
Purpose of the section
The Crown is immune from the controls introduced by this Act, in respect both of Crown land and of any acts done by or on behalf of the Crown (*Ministry of Agriculture, Fisheries and Food* v. *Jenkins* [1963] 2 Q.B. 317; *Lord Advocate* v. *Dumbarton District Council* [1989] 3 W.L.R. 1346). This section waives that immunity to the extent of any interest in Crown land held otherwise than by the Crown (including the rights of a person entitled to occupy Crown land by virtue of a written licence), but subject to the requirement in subs. (2) that the consent of the appropriate Crown authority is necessary before any order is made under ss.14 or 15 (revocation of consent) or any contravention notice is issued under s.24.

In addition, special power is conferred by s.32 to allow the Crown to seek consent under this Act for the purpose of allowing Crown land to be disposed of with the benefit of consent.

Application for hazardous substances consent in anticipation of disposal of Crown land

32.—(1) Subsections (2) to (4) have effect for the purpose of enabling Crown land, or an interest in Crown land, to be disposed of with the benefit of hazardous substances consent.

(2) Notwithstanding the interest of the Crown in the land in question, an application for such consent may be made by—
(a) the appropriate authority; or
(b) any person authorised by that authority in writing;
and, subject to subsections (3) and (4), all the statutory provisions relating to the making and determination of such an application shall accordingly apply as if the land were not Crown land.

(3) Any hazardous substances consent granted by virtue of this section shall apply only—
(a) to the presence of the substance to which the consent relates after the land in question has ceased to be Crown land; and
(b) so long as that land continues to be Crown land, to the presence of the substance by virtue of a private interest in the land.

(4) The Secretary of State may by regulations—
(a) modify or exclude any of the statutory provisions referred to in subsection (2) in their application by virtue of that subsection and any other statutory provisions in their application to consents granted by virtue of this section;
(b) make provision for requiring a hazardous substances authority to be notified of any disposal of, or of an interest in, any Crown land in respect of which an application has been made by virtue of this section; and
(c) make such other provision in relation to the making and determination of applications by virtue of this section as he thinks necessary or expedient.

(5) This section shall not be construed as affecting any right to apply for hazardous substances consent in respect of Crown land in a case in which such an application can be made by virtue of a private interest in the land.

(6) In this section—
"private interest" means an interest which is neither a Crown interest nor a Duchy interest;
"statutory provisions" means provisions contained in or having effect under any enactment;
and references to the disposal of an interest in Crown land include references to the grant of an interest in such land.

(7) Subsections (3), (5) and (6) of section 31 apply for the purposes of this section as they apply for the purposes of that section.

(8) A person who is entitled to occupy Crown land by virtue of a licence in writing shall be treated for the purposes of this section as having an interest in land and references to the disposal or grant of an interest in Crown land and to a private interest in such land shall be construed accordingly.

DEFINITIONS
"enactment": s.39(2).
"hazardous substances authority": ss.1, 2, 3, 39(1).
"hazardous substances consent": ss.4, 39(1).
"land": s.39(2).
"private interest": subs. (6).
"statutory provisions": subs. (6).

ALLOCATION OF FUNCTIONS
See the Commentary to s.1.

GENERAL NOTE

Under this section the Crown is entitled to apply for hazardous substances consent to enable Crown land to be disposed of with the benefit of consent. Unlike the situation under the corresponding provisions of the Planning (Listed Buildings and Conservation Areas) Act

1990, s.83(3), a purchaser or subsequent owner inherits no express immunity from contra-vention proceedings in respect of a presence of hazardous substances that was established whilst the land was in Crown ownership. Thus it would appear that consent must be sought under this section for the continuation of a presence of a hazardous substance on land, as well as for any prospective use of the land for this purpose upon disposal.

British Coal

33.—(1) The Secretary of State for the Environment and the Secretary of State for Energy with the consent of the Treasury may by regulations direct that any of the provisions specified in subsection (2) relating to statutory undertakers and to land of such undertakers—

(a) shall apply to the British Coal Corporation as if it were a statutory undertaker; and

(b) shall apply to land (including mines) of that Corporation of any such class as may be specified in the regulations as if it were operational land.

(2) Those provisions are sections 1 to 3, 16, 20, 21, 31 (the reference in subsection (1) to sections 4 to 29 not being construed as including a reference to section 8(1) to (3)), 34(1), (3) and (4), 36 and 38(1) to (5), and any other provisions of the planning Acts so far as they apply or have effect for the purposes of any of those provisions.

(3) Such regulations may apply those provisions subject to such adap-tations, modifications and exceptions as may be specified in the regulations.

DEFINITIONS
"land": s.39(2).
"operational land": s.39(2) and (8).
"the planning Acts": s.39(2).
"statutory undertakers": s.39(2), (4), (5), (6), (7) and (8).

ALLOCATION OF FUNCTIONS
See the Commentary to s.1.

GENERAL NOTE

British Coal is not a statutory undertaker for the general purposes of the Planning Acts, but the Secretaries of State may direct that it be so treated, and that certain of its land be treated as operational land, for the provisions of this Act specified in subs. (2). No regulations have yet been made under this section.

Ecclesiastical property

34.—(1) Where under any of the provisions of this Act a notice or copy of a notice is required to be served on an owner of land and the land is ecclesiastical property, a similar notice or copy of a notice shall be served on the Church Commissioners.

(2) Where the fee simple of any ecclesiastical property is in abeyance and the property is situated elsewhere than in Wales, then for the purposes of this section, sections 8 and 22 and section 31(1), so far as it applies to section 8, and any other provisions of the planning Acts so far as they apply, or have effect for the purpose of, any of those provisions, the fee simple shall be treated as being vested in the Church Commissioners.

(3) Any compensation payable under section 16 in respect of land which is ecclesiastical property—

(a) shall be paid to the Church Commissioners, and

(b) shall be applied by them for the purposes for which the proceeds of a sale by agreement of the land would be applicable under any enactment or Measure authorising or disposing of the proceeds of such a sale.

(4) In this section "ecclesiastical property" means land belonging to an ecclesiastical benefice, or being or forming part of a church subject to the jurisdiction of a bishop of any diocese or the site of such a church, or being or forming part of a burial ground subject to such jurisdiction.

DEFINITIONS
"enactment": s.39(2).
"land": s.39(2).
"owner" s.39(2).
"the planning Acts": s.39(2).

GENERAL NOTE
This section requires notices under this Act respecting ecclesiastical property to be served on the Church Commissioners as well as on the owners; and compensation payable under s.16, for the revocation or modification of consent affecting such property, to be paid to the Church Commissioners and applied by them to the purposes specified in subs. (3)(b).

Application of Act to Isles of Scilly

35. In relation to land in the Isles of Scilly the provisions of this Act, and any other provisions of the planning Acts in so far as they apply or have effect for the purposes of those provisions, shall have effect as if those Isles were a district and the Council of the Isles were the council of that district.

DEFINITIONS
"land": s.39(2)
"the planning Acts": s.39(2).

GENERAL NOTE
The Act extends to the Scilly Isles as if its council were a district council and hence a hazardous substances authority under s.1.

Rights of entry

36.—(1) Any person duly authorised in writing by the Secretary of State or by a hazardous substances authority may at any reasonable time enter any land for the purpose of surveying it in connection with—
  (a) any application for hazardous substances consent;
  (b) any proposal to issue a hazardous substances contravention notice.
  (2) Any person duly authorised in writing by the Secretary of State or by a hazardous substances authority may at any reasonable time enter any land for the purpose of ascertaining whether an offence appears to have been committed under section 23.
  (3) Any person who is an officer of the Valuation Office or a person duly authorised in writing by a hazardous substances authority may at any reasonable time enter any land for the purpose of surveying it, or estimating its value, in connection with a claim for compensation in respect of that land or any other land made by virtue of section 16 or 19.
  (4) Any person duly authorised in writing by the Secretary of State or by a hazardous substances authority may at any reasonable time enter any land in respect of which a hazardous substances contravention notice has been issued for the purpose of ascertaining whether the notice has been complied with.
  (5) Subject to subsection (6), any power conferred by this section to survey land shall be construed as including power to search and bore for the purpose of ascertaining the nature of the subsoil or the presence of minerals in it.
  (6) Section 325 of the principal Act (supplementary provisions as to rights of entry) applies in relation to this section as it applies in relation

to section 324 of that Act, but taking the reference in section 325(8) to section 324(8) as a reference to subsection (5).

DEFINITIONS
  "hazardous substances authority": ss.1, 2, 3, 39(1).
  "hazardous substances consent": ss.4, 39(1).
  "hazardous substances contravention notice": ss.24(1), 39(1).
  "land": s.39(2).
  "minerals": s.39(2).
  "the principal Act": s.39(1).
  "Valuation Office": s.39(2).

ALLOCATION OF FUNCTIONS
  See the Commentary to s.1.

GENERAL NOTE
  The right of entry conferred by the T.C.P.A. 1990, s.324, does not apply to the exercise of functions under this Act. Instead, this section confers a restricted right, limited to entry in connection with an application for consent, or a proposal to issue a hazardous substances contravention notice. There is no right of entry in connection with the exercise of other powers under the Act, such as the revocation or modification of consent, deemed consents for an established presence of hazardous substances, or applications for the continuation of consent under s.17.

Application of certain general provisions of principal Act

37.—(1) The provisions of the principal Act specified in subsection (2) shall apply for the purposes of this Act as they apply for the purposes of that Act.

(2) Those provisions are—
  section 320 (local inquiries)
  section 322 (orders as to costs of parties where no inquiry held)
  section 323 (procedure on certain appeals and applications)
  section 329 (service of notices)
  section 330 (power to require information as to interests in land)
  section 331 (offences by corporations).

Financial provisions

38.—(1) Where—
  (a) compensation is payable by a local authority under this Act in consequence of any decision or order given or made under sections 4 to 21 or the Schedule,
  (b) that decision or order was given or made wholly or partly in the interest of a service which is provided by a government department and the cost of which is defrayed out of money provided by Parliament,
the Minister responsible for the administration of that service may pay to that authority a contribution of such amount as he may with the consent of the Treasury determine.

(2) Any local authority and any statutory undertakers may contribute towards any expenses incurred by a hazardous substances authority (being a local planning authority) in or in connection with the performance of any of their functions under sections 4 to 29.

(3) Where any expenses are incurred by a local authority in the payment of compensation payable in consequence of anything done under sections 4 to 21, the Secretary of State may, if it appears to him to be expedient to do so, require any other local authority to contribute towards those expenses such sum as appears to him to be reasonable, having regard to

any benefit accruing to that authority by reason of the proceeding giving rise to the compensation.

(4) For the purposes of subsections (2) and (3), contributions made by an authority towards the expenditure of a joint advisory committee shall be deemed to be expenses incurred by that authority for the purposes for which that expenditure is incurred by the committee.

(5) The council of a county may direct that any expenses incurred by them under sections 1 to 3, 16, 20, 21, 31, 34 and 36, the previous provisions of this section or the Schedule shall be treated as special expenses of a county council chargeable upon such part of the county as may be specified in the directions.

(6) There shall be paid out of money provided by Parliament any expenses of the Secretary of State or any government department under this Act.

(7) Any sums received by the Secretary of State under this Act shall be paid into the Consolidated Fund.

DEFINITIONS
  "functions": s.39(2).
  "government department": s.39(2).
  "hazardous substances authority": ss.1, 2, 3, 39(1).
  "local authority": s.39(2).
  "local planning authority": s.39(2).
  "Minister": s.39(2).
  "statutory undertakers": s.39(2), (4), (5), (6), (7) and (8).

ALLOCATION OF FUNCTIONS
  See the Commentary to s.1.

GENERAL NOTE

Financial provisions
  The section empowers Ministers to contribute towards the compensation costs of a local hazardous substances authority, and empowers the Secretary of State to require local authorities to contribute. It also empowers local authorities and statutory undertakers to contribute towards any of a hazardous substances authority's expenses under the Act.

Definition of statutory undertaker
  For the purposes of subs. (2), "statutory undertaker" includes (T.C.P.A. 1990, s.262, as applied by s.91(3)):
  "persons authorised by any enactment to carry on any railway, light railway, tramway, road transport, water transport, canal, inland navigation, dock, harbour, pier or lighthouse undertaking, or any undertaking for the supply of hydraulic power and a relevant airport operator (within the meaning of Part V of the Airports Act 1986)."
  In addition, for the purposes of this subsection, the expression includes (s.39): (1) the Post Office (s.39(6)); (2) the Civil Aviation Authority (s.39(6)); (3) a public gas supplier (s.39(4)); (4) a holder of a licence under section 6 of the Electricity Act 1989 (s.39(6)); (5) the National Rivers Authority (s.39(5)); (6) every water or sewerage undertaker (s.39(5)).

Supplemental

Interpretation

39.—(1) In this Act—
  "contravention of hazardous substances control" has the meaning given in section 23(2);
  "hazardous substances authority" is to be construed in accordance with sections 1 to 3;
  "hazardous substances consent" means consent required by section 4;
  "hazardous substances contravention notice" means such a notice as is mentioned in section 24(1);

"the principal Act" means the Town and Country Planning Act 1990.

(2) In this Act, except in so far as the context otherwise requires and subject to the following provisions of this section, the following expressions have the same meaning as in the principal Act—

"the 1971 Act";
"the appropriate Minister";
"the Broads";
"development";
"development plan";
"enactment";
"functions";
"government department";
"joint planning board";
"land";
"local authority";
"local planning authority";
"London borough";
"mineral working deposit";
"minerals";
"Minister";
"operational land";
"owner";
"the planning Acts";
"prescribed";
"public gas supplier";
"statutory undertakers";
"tenancy";
"urban development area" and "urban development corporation";
"use";
"Valuation Office";

but this subsection does not affect the meaning of "owner" in section 8.

(3) For the purposes of sections 4 to 21 and 23 to 26 any two bodies corporate are to be treated as being one person if—

(a) one of them is a body corporate of which the other is a subsidiary (within the meaning of section 736 of the Companies Act 1985); or

(b) both of them are subsidiaries (within the meaning of that Act) of one and the same body corporate.

(4) For the purposes of sections 2, 12 and 38(2) a public gas supplier shall be deemed to be a statutory undertaker and his undertaking a statutory undertaking.

(5) For the purposes of sections 2, 12 and 38(2) the National Rivers Authority and every water or sewerage undertaker shall be deemed to be a statutory undertaker and its undertaking a statutory undertaking; and for the purposes of sections 2, 7, 28 and 29 and subsections (7) and (8) of this section, "the appropriate Minister"—

(a) in relation to the National Rivers Authority, means the Secretary of State or the Minister of Agriculture; and

(b) in relation to a water or sewerage undertaker, means the Secretary of State.

(6) For the purposes of section 38(2) the Post Office, the Civil Aviation Authority and any holder of a licence under section 6(1) of the Electricity Act 1989 shall be deemed to be statutory undertakers and their undertakings statutory undertakings.

(7) If, in relation to anything required or authorised to be done under this Act, any question arises as to which Minister is or was the appropriate Minister in relation to any statutory undertakers, that question shall be determined by the Treasury.

(8) If any question so arises whether land of statutory undertakers is operational land, that question shall be determined by the Minister who is the appropriate Minister in relation to those undertakers.

DEFINITIONS
"Minister": s.39(2).
"use": s.39(2).

Regulations

40.—(1) The Secretary of State may make regulations under this Act for any purpose for which regulations are authorised or required to be made under this Act, not being a purpose for which regulations are authorised or required to be made by another Minister.

(2) Any power conferred by this Act to make regulations shall be exercisable by statutory instrument.

(3) Any statutory instrument containing regulations made under this Act shall be subject to annulment in pursuance of a resolution of either House of Parliament.

GENERAL NOTE
No regulations have yet been made under this section.

Short title, commencement and extent

41.—(1) This Act may be cited as the Planning (Hazardous Substances) Act 1990.

(2) If an order has been made under section 57(2) of the Housing and Planning Act 1986 appointing a date during or at the end of the period of three months beginning with the day on which this Act is passed as the date on which all or any of the provisions of that Act relating to control over hazardous substances come into force, then the corresponding provisions of this Act (and, subject to Schedule 4 to the Planning (Consequential Provisions) Act 1990, the remaining provisions of it so far as they relate to them) shall come into force at the end of that period.

(3) Except so far as subsection (2) applies, the provisions of this Act (other than this section) shall come into force on such day as may be appointed by the Secretary of State by order made by statutory instrument and—

(a) different days may be appointed for different provisions or for different purposes; and

(b) an order may make such transitional provision as the Secretary of State thinks appropriate.

(4) This Act extends to England and Wales only.

GENERAL NOTE
This Act has not yet been brought into force.

Section 26   SCHEDULE

DETERMINATION OF APPEALS BY PERSON APPOINTED BY SECRETARY OF STATE

Determination of appeals by appointed person

1.—(1) The Secretary of State may by regulations prescribe the classes of appeals under section 21 which are to be determined by a person appointed by the Secretary of State for the purpose instead of by the Secretary of State.

(2) Appeals of a prescribed class shall be so determined except in such classes of case as may for the time being be prescribed or as may be specified in directions given by the Secretary of State.

(3) Regulations made for the purpose of this paragraph may provide for the giving of publicity to any directions given by the Secretary of State under this paragraph.

(4) This paragraph shall not affect any provision in this Act or any instrument made under it that an appeal shall lie to, or a notice of appeal shall be served on, the Secretary of State.

(5) A person appointed under this paragraph is referred to in this Schedule as "an appointed person."

Powers and duties of appointed person

2.—(1) An appointed person shall have the same powers and duties as the Secretary of State has under subsection (4) of section 21.

(2) Subsection (5) of that section shall not apply to an appeal which falls to be determined by an appointed person, but before it is determined the Secretary of State shall ask the appellant and the hazardous substances authority whether they wish to appear before and be heard by the appointed person.

(3) If both the parties express a wish not to appear and be heard the appeal may be determined without their being heard.

(4) If either of the parties expresses a wish to appear and be heard, the appointed person shall give them both an opportunity of doing so.

(5) Where an appeal has been determined by an appointed person, his decision shall be treated as that of the Secretary of State.

(6) Except as provided by section 22, the validity of that decision shall not be questioned in any proceedings whatsoever.

(7) It shall not be a ground of application to the High Court under that section, that an appeal ought to have been determined by the Secretary of State and not by an appointed person, unless the appellant or the hazardous substances authority challenge the appointed person's power to determine the appeal before his decision on the appeal is given.

(8) Where in any enactment (including this Act) there is a reference to the Secretary of State in a context relating or capable of relating—

(a) to an appeal under section 21, or

(b) to any thing done or authorised or required to be done by, to or before the Secretary of State on or in connection with any such appeal,

then so far as the context permits it shall be construed, in relation to an appeal determined or falling to be determined by an appointed person, as a reference to him.

Determination of appeals by Secretary of State

3.—(1) The Secretary of State may, if he thinks fit, direct that an appeal which would otherwise fall to be determined by an appointed person shall instead be determined by the Secretary of State.

(2) Such a direction shall state the reasons for which it is given and shall be served on the appellant, the hazardous substances authority, any person who made representations relating to the subject matter of the appeal which the authority were required to take into account by regulations made under section 8(4) or, as the case may be, regulations made under section 17(2) making provision corresponding to section 8(4) and, if any person has been appointed under paragraph 1, on him.

(3) Where in consequence of such a direction an appeal under section 21 falls to be determined by the Secretary of State, the provisions of this Act which are relevant to the appeal shall, subject to the following provisions of this paragraph, apply to the appeal as if this Schedule had never applied to it.

(4) The Secretary of State shall give the appellant, the hazardous substances authority and any person who has made such representations as are referred to in sub-paragraph (2) an opportunity of appearing before and being heard by a person appointed by the Secretary of State for that purpose if—

(a) the reasons for the direction raise matters with respect to which any of those persons have not made representations; or

(b) in the case of the appellant or the hazardous substances authority, either of them was not asked in pursuance of paragraph 2(2) whether they wished to appear before and be heard by the appointed person, or expressed no wish in answer to that question, or expressed a wish to appear and be heard but was not given an opportunity of doing so.

(5) Except as provided by sub-paragraph (4), the Secretary of State need not give any person an opportunity of appearing before and being heard by a person appointed for the purpose, or of making fresh representations or making or withdrawing any representations already made.

(6) In determining the appeal the Secretary of State may take into account any report made to him by any person previously appointed to determine it.

4.—(1) The Secretary of State may by a further direction revoke a direction under paragraph 3 at any time before the determination of the appeal.

(2) Such a further direction shall state the reasons for which it is given and shall be served on the person, if any, previously appointed to determine the appeal, the appellant, the hazardous substances authority and any person who made representations relating to the subject matter of the appeal which the authority were required to take into account by regulations made under section 8(4) or, as the case may be, regulations made under section 17(2) making provision corresponding to section 8(4).

(3) Where such a further direction has been given the provisions of this Schedule relevant to the appeal shall apply, subject to sub-paragraph (4), as if no direction under paragraph 3 had been given.

(4) Anything done by or on behalf of the Secretary of State in connection with the appeal which might have been done by the appointed person (including any arrangements made for the holding of a hearing or local inquiry) shall, unless that person directs otherwise, be treated as having been done by him.

Appointment of another person to determine appeal

5.—(1) At any time before the appointed person has determined the appeal the Secretary of State may—

(a) revoke his appointment; and

(b) appoint another person under paragraph 1 to determine the appeal instead.

(2) Where such a new appointment is made the consideration of the appeal or any inquiry or other hearing in connection with it shall be begun afresh.

(3) Nothing in sub-paragraph (2) shall require—

(a) the question referred to in paragraph 2(2) to be asked again with reference to the new appointed person if before his appointment it was asked with reference to the previous appointed person (any answers being treated as given with reference to the new appointed person); or

(b) any person to be given an opportunity of making fresh representations or modifying or withdrawing any representations already made.

Local inquiries and hearings

6.—(1) Whether or not the parties to an appeal have asked for an opportunity to appear and be heard, an appointed person—

(a) may hold a local inquiry in connection with the appeal; and

(b) shall do so if the Secretary of State so directs.

(2) Where an appointed person—

(a) holds a hearing by virtue of paragraph 2(4); or

(b) holds an inquiry by virtue of this paragraph,

an assessor may be appointed by the Secretary of State to sit with the appointed person at the hearing or inquiry to advise him on any matters arising, notwithstanding that the appointed person is to determine the appeal.

(3) Subject to sub-paragraph (4), the costs—

(a) of any hearing held by virtue of paragraph 2(4); and

(b) of any inquiry held under this paragraph,

shall be defrayed by the Secretary of State.

(4) Section 250(2) to (5) of the Local Government Act 1972 (local inquiries: evidence and costs) applies to an inquiry held by virtue of this paragraph with the following adaptations—

(a) for the references in subsection (4) (recovery of costs of holding the inquiry) to the Minister causing the inquiry to be held there shall be substituted references to the Secretary of State; and

(b) for the reference in subsection (5) (orders as to the costs of the parties) to the Minister causing the inquiry to be held there shall be substituted a reference to the appointed person or the Secretary of State.

(5) Subject to sub-paragraph (6), at any such inquiry oral evidence shall be heard in public and documentary evidence shall be open to public inspection.

(6) If the Secretary of State is satisfied in the case of any such inquiry—

    (a) that giving evidence of a particular description or, as the case may be, making it available for inspection would be likely to result in the disclosure of information as to any of the matters mentioned in sub-paragraph (7), and

    (b) that the public disclosure of that information would be contrary to the national interest,

he may direct that evidence of the description indicated in the direction shall only be heard or, as the case may be, open to inspection at that inquiry by such persons or persons of such descriptions as he may specify in that direction.

(7) The matters referred to in sub-paragraph (6)(a) are—

    (a) national security; and

    (b) the measures taken or to be taken to ensure the security of any premises or property.

(8) The appointed person or the Secretary of State has the same power to make orders under section 250(5) of the Local Government Act 1972 (orders with respect to costs of the parties) in relation to proceedings under this Schedule which do not give rise to an inquiry as he has in relation to such an inquiry.

Supplementary provisions

7.—(1) The Tribunals and Inquiries Act 1971 shall apply to a local inquiry or other hearing held in pursuance of this Schedule as it applies to a statutory inquiry, held by the Secretary of State, but as if in section 12(1) of that Act (statement of reasons for decisions) the reference to any decision taken by the Secretary of State were a reference to a decision taken by an appointed person.

(2) Where an appointed person is an officer of the Department of the Environment or the Welsh Office the functions of determining an appeal and doing anything in connection with it conferred on him by this Schedule shall be treated for the purposes of the Parliamentary Commissioner Act 1967—

    (a) if he was appointed by the Secretary of State for the time being having general responsibility in planning matters in relation to England, as functions of that Department; and

    (b) if he was appointed by the Secretary of State for the time being having general responsibility in planning matters in relation to Wales, as functions of the Welsh Office.

DEFINITIONS

    "functions": s.39(2).
    "hazardous substances authority": ss.1, 2, 3, 39(1).
    "land": s.39(2).
    "Minister": s.39(2).
    "prescribed": s.39(2).

GENERAL NOTE

    The Schedule corresponds to Sched. 6 to the T.C.P.A. 1990, and Sched. 3 to the Planning (Listed Buildings and Conservation Areas) Act 1990. See further the notes to s.79 of the T.C.P.A. 1990.

TABLE OF DERIVATIONS

Notes:

1. The following abbreviations are used in this Table:—

1969 c.48	=	The Post Office Act 1969
1971 c.78	=	The Town and Country Planning Act 1971
1973 c.41	=	The Fair Trading Act 1973
1981 c.41	=	The Local Government and Planning (Amendment) Act 1981
1982 c.16	=	The Civil Aviation Act 1982
1982 c.21	=	The Planning Inquiries (Public) Act 1982
1984 c.10	=	The Town and Country Planning Act 1984
1985 c.9	=	The Companies (Consequential Provisions) Act 1985
1986 c.44	=	The Gas Act 1986
1986 c.63	=	The Housing and Planning Act 1986
1988 c.4	=	The Norfolk and Suffolk Broads Act 1988
1988 c.50	=	The Housing Act 1988
1989 c.15	=	The Water Act 1989
1989 c.29	=	The Electricity Act 1989

2. The letter R followed by a number indicates that the provision gives effect to the Recommendation bearing that number in the Law Commission's Report on the Consolidation of Certain Enactments relating to Town and Country Planning (Cmnd. 958).

3. The entry "drafting" indicates a provision of a mechanical or editorial nature only affecting the arrangement of the consolidation.

Provision	Derivation
1	1971 c.78 s.1A(1); 1986 c.63 s.30.
2(1)	1971 c.78 s.1B(1), (2); 1986 c.63 s.30.
(2)	1971 c.78 s.1B(3)(4); 1986 c.63 s.30.
(3)	1971 c.78 s.1B(5); 1986 c.63 s.30.
(4)	1971 c.78 s.1B(4); 1986 c.63 s.30.
3(1)	1971 c.78 s.1A(2); 1986 c.63 s.30.
(2)	1971 c.78 s.1A(3); 1986 c.63 s.30.
(3)	1971 c.78 s.1A(3A); 1988 c.4 Sch. 3 para. 9; R 54.
(4)	1971 c.78 s.1A(4); 1986 c.63 s.30; R 54.
(5)	1988 c.50 s.67(6); R 54.
(6)	1971 c.78 s.1A(1)(part); 1986 c.63 s.30.
4(1), (2)	1971 c.78 s.58B(1); 1986 c.63 s.31.
(3)	1971 c.78 s.58B(2); 1986 c.63 s.31.
(4)	1971 c.78 s.58B(3)(b); 1986 c.63 s.31.
(5)	1971 c.78 s.58B(6); 1986 c.63 s.31.
5(1)	1971 c.78 s.58B(3)(a), (3)(c); 1986 c.63 s.31.
(2)	1971 c.78 s.58B(4); 1986 c.63 s.31.
(3)	1971 c.78 s.58B(5); 1986 c.63 s.31.
(4)	1971 c.78 s.58B(6); 1986 c.63 s.31.
6(1)	1971 c.78 ss.58C, 58F; 1986 c.63 s.34.
(2)	1971 c.78 s.58J(1); 1986 c.63 s.31.
7(1)	1971 c.78 s.58C(1); 1986 c.63 s.31.
(2)	1971 c.78 s.58C(4); 1986 c.63 s.31.
(3)	1971 c.78 s.58C(5); 1986 c.63 s.31.
(4)	1971 c.78 s.58C(6); 1986 c.63 s.31.
8(1) to (5)	1971 c.78 s.58C(2); 1986 c.63 s.31.
(6)	1971 c.78 s.58C(3); 1986 c.63 s.31.
(7)	1971 c.78 s.58C(6); 1986 c.63 s.31.
(8)	1971 c.78 s.27(7).
9(1)	1971 c.78 s.58D(1) (part); 1986 c.63 s.31.
(2)	1971 c.78 s.58D(1)(2); 1986 c.63 s.31.
(3)	1971 c.78 s.58D(3); 1986 c.63 s.31.
(4)	1971 c.78 s.58D(4) (part); 1986 c.63 s.31.
10(1)	1971 c.78 s.58D(5); 1986 c.63 s.31.
(2)	1971 c.78 s.58D(5); 1986 c.63 s.31; R 55.
(3)	1971 c.78 s.58D(4)(c); 1986 c.63 s.31.

Provision	Derivation
11(1)	1986 c.63 s.34(3).
(2)	1986 c.63 s.34(4).
(3)	1986 c.63 s.34(5).
(4)	1986 c.63 s.34(6).
(5)	1986 c.63 s.34(7).
(6)	1986 c.63 s.34(8).
(7)	1986 c.63 s.34(9).
(8)	1986 c.63 s.34(10).
12(1)	1971 c.78 s.58F(1); 1986 c.63 s.31.
(2)	1989 c.29 Sch. 8 para. 7(2).
(3)	1971 c.78 s.58F(2); 1986 c.63 s.31; 1989 c.29 Sch. 8 para. 7(2).
(4)	1971 c.78 s.58F(4); 1986 c.63 s.31.
(5)	1971 c.78 s.58F(3); 1986 c.63 s.31.
13(1)	1971 c.78 s.58G(1); 1986 c.63 s.31.
(2) to (4)	1971 c.78 s.58G(2); 1986 c.63 s.31.
(5) to (7)	1971 c.78 s.58G(3) to (5); 1986 c.63 s.31.
14(1)	1971 c.78 s.58H(3); 1986 c.63 s.31.
(2), (3)	1971 c.78 s.58H(1) (part), (2); 1986 c.63 s.31.
(4)	1971 c.78 s.58H(4); 1986 c.63 s.31.
15(1), (2)	1971 c.78 s.58H(5); 1986 c.63 s.31.
(3) to (5)	1971 c.78 s.58H(6); 1986 c.63 s.31.
(6)	1971 c.78 s.58H(7); 1986 c.63 s.31.
16(1)	1971 c.78 s.58H(8); 1986 c.63 s.31.
(2) to (4)	1971 c.78 s.170(2) to (4).
(5)	Drafting.
17(1)	1971 c.78 s.58J(2); 1986 c.63 s.31.
(2)	1971 c.78 s.58J(3); 1986 c.63 s.31.
18(1)	1971 c.78 s.58J(4) (part); 1986 c.63 s.31.
(2)	1971 c.78 s.58J(4) (part), (5); 1986 c.63 s.31.
(3)	1971 c.78 s.58J(6); 1986 c.63 s.31.
(4)	1971 c.78 s.58J(7); 1986 c.63 s.31.
(5)	1971 c.78 s.58J(8); 1986 c.63 s.31.
(6)	1971 c.78 s.58J(9); 1986 c.63 s.31; R. 56.
(7)	1971 c.78 s.58J(10), (11), (a), (d), s.37; 1986 c.63 s.31.
19	1971 c.78 s.58J(12); 1986 c.63 s.31.
20(1)	1971 c.78 ss.35(1), 58E, 58J(10), (11); 1986 c.63 s.31.
(2)	1971 c.78 ss.35(2), 58E, 58J(10), (11); 1986 c.63 s.31.
(3)	1971 c.78 ss.35(3), 58E, 58J(10), (11); 1986 c.63 s.31.
(4)	1971 c.78 ss.35(5), 58E, 58J(10), (11); 1986 c.63 s.31.
(5)	1971 c.78 ss.35(6), 58E, 58J(10), (11); 1986 c.63 s.31.
(6)	1971 c.78 s.58E(3); 1986 c.63 s.31.
21(1)	1971 c.78 ss.58E, 58J(10), (11), 36(1); 1986 c.63 s.31; R 57.
(2)	1971 c.78 ss.58E, 58J(10), (11), 37; 1986 c.63 s.31; R 8(a).
(3)	1971 c.78 ss.58E, 58J(10), (11), 36(2); 1986 c.63 s.31.
(4)	1971 c.78 ss.58E, 58J(10), (11), 36(3); 1986 c.63 s.31.
(5)	1971 c.78 ss.58E, 58J(10), (11), 36(4); 1986 c.63 s.31.
(6)	1971 c.78 ss.58E, 58J(10), (11), 36(6); 1986 c.63 s.31.
(7)	1971 c.78 s.58E(3); 1986 c.63 s.31.
(8)	1971 c.78 ss.36(8), 58E, 58J(10), (11); 1986 c.63 s.31.
22(1)	1971 c.78 s.245(1); R 57 and R 58.
(2)	1971 c.78 s.245(2) (7); R 57 and R 58.
(3)	1971 c.78 s.245(4).
(4)	1971 c.78 s.245(7) (part); 1972 c.70 Sch. 16 para. 46.
(5)	1971 c.78 s.242(1)(e), (3)(dd); 1986 c.63 Sch. 7 para. 2; R 57.
(6)	1971 c.78 s.242(4).
23	1971 c.78 s.58K; 1986 c.63 s.31.
24(1)	1971 c.78 s.101B(1), (3); 1986 c.63 s.32.
(2)	1971 c.78 s.101B(3) (part); 1986 c.63 s.32.
(3)	1971 c.78 s.101B(2); 1986 c.63 s.32.
(4) to (9)	1971 c.78 s.101B(4) to (9); 1986 c.63 s.32.

Provision	Derivation
25(1) to (3)	1971 c.78 s.101B(10) to (12); 1986 c.63 s.32.
(4)	1971 c.78 s.110(2).
26	1986 c.63 s.34(1), (2), (10).
27	1971 c.78 s.58L; 1986 c.63 s.31.
28	1971 c.78 s.58M; 1986 c.63, s.31; R 55, R 59.
29(1), (2)	1971 c.78 s.58N(1); 1986 c.63 s.31.
(3)	1971 c.78 s.58N(2); 1986 c.63 s.31.
(4)	1971 c.78 s.58N(3); 1986 c.63 s.31.
(5)	1971 c.78 s.58N(4); 1986 c.63 s.31.
(6)	1971 c.78 s.58N(5); 1986 c.63 s.31.
30(1)	1971 c.78 s.271A(1); 1986 c.63 Sch. 7 Part I para. 5.
(2)	1971 c.78 s.271A(2); 1986 c.63 Sch. 7 Part I para. 5.
31(1)	1971 c.78 s.266(1)(b).
(2)	1971 c.78 s.266(2)(a); 1981 c.41 Sch. para. 20; 1986 c.63 Sch. 7 Part I para. 3.
(3)	1971 c.78 s.266(7).
(4)	1984 c.10 s.4(1).
(5)	1971 c.78 s.266(7); 1984 c.10 s.6(1).
(6)	1971 c.78 s.266(7) (part).
32(1)	1984 c.10 s.1(1); 1986 c.10 Sch. 7 Part I para. 8.
(2)	1984 c.10 s.1(2).
(3)	1984 c.10 s.1(3A); 1986 c.10 Sch. 7 para. 8.
(4)	1984 c.10 s.1(5); R 60.
(5)	1984 c.10 s.1(7).
(6)	1984 c.10 ss.1(6), 6(1), (2).
(7)	1984 c.10 s.6(1), (2).
(8)	1984 c.10 s.4(1).
33	1971 c.78 s.273.
34(1) to (3)	1971 c.78 s.274(1) to (3).
(4)	1971 c.78 s.274(5).
35	1971 c.78 s.269(2); 1986 c.63 Sch. 7 Part I para. 4.
36(1)	1971 c.78 s.280(1A); 1986 c.63 Sch. 7 Part I para. 6.
(2)	1971 c.78 s.280(4) (part); 1986 c.63 Sch. 7 Part I para. 6.
(3)	1971 c.78 s.280(6), (6A); 1986 c.63 Sch. 7 Part I para. 6.
(4)	1971 c.78 s.280(8); 1986 c.63 Sch. 7 Part I para. 6; R 61.
(5)	1971 c.78 s.280(9).
(6)	1971 c.78 s.281, drafting.
37	1971 c.28 ss.282, 282A, 282B, 283, 284, 285; 1986 c.63 Sch. 11 paras. 9, 10.
38(1)	1971 c.78 s.254.
(2)	1971 c.78 s.255(2)(b); R 62.
(3)	1971 c.78 s.255(3).
(4)	1971 c.78 s.255(5).
(5)	1971 c.78 s.263(1); 1972 c.70 Sch. 29 Part I para. 3(b).
(6), (7)	1971 c.78 ss.260(1) (part), 262; 1986 c.63 s.56.
39(1), (2)	1971 c.78 s.290(1); 1986 c.44 Sch. 7 para. 2(9)(e); 1986 c.63 Sch. 7 Part I para. 7(a), (b).
(3)	1971 c.78 s.58B(7); 1973 c.41 s.137(5); 1985 c.9 Sch.2; 1986 c.63, s.31.
(4)	1986 c.44 Sch. 7 para. 2(1), (9).
(5)	1989 c.15 Sch. 25 para. 1(1), (2), (10).
(6)	1969 c.49 Sch. 4 para. 93; 1982 c.16 Sch. 2 para. 4; 1989 c.29 Sch. 16 para. 1(1)(xxii).
(7), (8)	1971 c.78 s.290(2).
40(1)	1971 c.78 s.287(1)(b).
(2), (3)	1971 c.78 s.287(2).
41(1)	Drafting.
(2)	Drafting.
(3)	1986 c.63 s.57(2).
(4)	Drafting.

Provision	Derivation
Sch.	
para. 1(1)	1971 c.78 Sch. 9 para. 1(1).
(2)	1971 c.78 Sch. 9 para. 1(1).
(3)	1971 c.78 Sch. 9 para. 1(2).
(4)	1971 c.78 Sch. 9 para. 1(3).
(5)	Drafting.
para. 2(1)	1971 c.78 Sch. 9 para. 2(1).
(2)	1971 c.78 Sch. 9 para. 2(2).
(3)	1971 c.78 Sch. 9 para. 2(2)(a).
(4)	1971 c.78 Sch. 9 para. 2(2)(b).
(5)	1971 c.78 Sch. 9 para. 3.
(6)	1971 c.78 Sch. 9 para. 2(3)(a).
(7)	1971 c.78 Sch. 9 para. 2(3)(b).
(8)	1971 c.78 Sch. 9 para. 2(4).
para. 3(1)	1971 c.78 Sch. 9 para. 3(1).
(2)	1971 c.78 Sch. 9 para. 3(2); R 52.
(3)	1971 c.78 Sch. 9 para. 3(3).
(4)	1971 c.78 Sch. 9 para. 3(4); R 52.
(5)	1971 c.78 Sch. 9 para. 3(5).
(6)	1971 c.78 Sch. 9 para. 3(5).
para. 4(1)	1971 c.78 Sch. 9 para. 3A(1); 1986 c.63 Sch. 11 para. 11.
(2)	1971 c.78 Sch. 9 para. 3A(2); 1986 c.63 Sch. 11 para. 11; R 52.
(3)	1971 c.78 Sch. 9 para. 3A(3); 1986 c.63 Sch. 11 para. 11.
(4)	1971 c.78 Sch. 9 para. 3A(4); 1986 c.63 Sch. 11 para. 11.
para. 5(1)	1971 c.78 Sch. 9 para. 4(1).
(2)	1971 c.78 Sch. 9 para. 4(2)(a).
(3)	1971 c.78 Sch. 9 para. 4(2).
para. 6(1)	1971 c.78 Sch. 9 para. 5(1).
(2)	1971 c.78 Sch. 9 para. 5(1A); 1986 c.63 Sch. 11 para. 12.
(3)	1971 c.78 Sch. 9 para. 5(2).
(4)	1971 c.78 Sch. 9 para. 5(3); 1986 c.63 Sch. 11 para. 8(2).
(5)	1982 c.21 s.1(1).
(6)	1982 c.21 s.1(2),(3).
(7)	1982 c.21, s.1(4).
(8)	1971 c.78 Sch. 9 para. 5(4); 1986 Sch. 11 para. 9(2).
para. 7	1971 c.78 Sch. 9 para. 7.

TABLE OF DESTINATIONS

POST OFFICE ACT 1969
c.48

1969	1990
Sched. 4, para. 93	s.39(6)

TOWN AND COUNTRY PLANNING ACT 1971
c.78

1971	1990	1971	1990	1971	1990
s.1A(1)	s.1	(3)	(1)	266(1)(b) ...	31(1)
(1) (part)	3(6)	(4)	(4)	(2)(a) ...	(2)
(2)	(1)	(5)	15(1), (2)	(7)	(3), (5)
(3)	(2)	(6)	(3)–(5)	(7)	
(3A)	(3)	(7)	(6)	(part)	(6)
(4)	(4)	(8)	16(1)	269(2)	35
1B(1)	2(1)	58J(1)	6(2)	271A(1)	30(1)
(2)	(1)	(2)	17(1)	(2)	(2)
(3)	(2)	(3)	(2)	273	33
(4)	(2), (4)	(4)		274(1)–(3) ..	34(1)–(3)
(5)	(3)	(part)	18(1), (2)	(5)	(4)
27(7)	8(8)	(6)	(3)	280(1A)	36(1)
35(1)	20(1)	(7)	(4)	(4)	
(2)	(2)	(8)	(5)	(part)	(2)
(3)	(3)	(9)	(6)	(6)	(3)
(5)	(4)	(10)	(7),	(6A)	(3)
(6)	(5)		20(1)–(5),	(8)	(4)
36(1)	21(1)		21(1)–(6), (8)	(9)	(5)
(2)	(3)	(11)	20(1), (2),	281	(6)
(3)	(4)		(3), (4), (5),	282	37
(4)	(5)		21(1), (2), (3),	282A, 282B	37
(6)	(6)		(4), (5), (6),	283, 284,	
(8)	(8)		(8)	285	37
37	18(7), 21(2)	(a), (d) .	18(7)	287(1)(b) ...	40(1)
58B(1)	4(1), (2)	(12)	19	(2)	(2), (3)
(2)	(3)	58K 23		290(1)	39(1), (2)
(3)(a) ..	5(1)	58L	27	(2)	(7), (8)
(b) ..	4(4)	58M	28	Sched. 9, ...	Sched.,
(4)	5(2)	58N(1)	29(1), (2)	para. 1(1) ..	para. 1(1),
(5)	(3)	(2)	(3)		(2)
(6)	4(5), 5(4)	(3)	(4)	(2) ..	(3)
(7)	39(3)	(4)	(5)	(3) ..	(4)
58C	6(1)	(5)	(6)	2(1) ..	2(1)
(1)	7(1)	101B(1), (3)	24(1)	(2) ..	(2)
(2)	8(1)–(5)	(2)	(3)	(a)	(3)
(4)	7(2)	(3)		(b)	(4)
(5)	(3)	(part)	(2)	(3)(a)	(6)
(6)	(4), 8(7)	(4)–		(b)	(7)
58D(1)		(9)	(4)–(9)	(4) ..	(8)
(part)	9(1)	(10)–		3	(5)
(1), (2)	(2)	(12) ...	25(1)–(3)	(1) ..	3(1)
(3)	(3)	110(2)	(4)	(2) ..	(2)
(4)		170 (2)–(4) .	16(2)–(4)	(3) ..	(3)
(part)	(4)	242(1)(e) ...	22(5)	(4) ..	(4)
(4)(c) ..	10(3)	(3)(dd) .	(5)	(5) ..	(5),
(5) ......10(1), (2)		(4)	(6)	(6)	
58E	20(1), (2),	245(1)	(1)	3A(1)	4(1)
	(3), (4), (5),	(2)	(2)	(2)	(2)
	21(1)–(6), (8)	(4)	(3)	(3)	(3)
(3)	20(6), 21(7)	(7)	(2)	(4)	(4)
58F	6(1)	(7)		4(1) ..	5(1)
(1)	12(1)	(part)	(4)	(2) ..	(3)
(2)	(3)	254	38(1)	(a)	(2)
(3)	(5)	255(2)(b) ...	(2)	5(1) ..	6(1)
(4)	(4)	(3)	(3)	(1A)	(2)
58G(1)	13(1)	(5)	(4)	(2) ..	(3)
(2)	(2)–(4)	260(1)		(3) ..	(4)
(3)–(5) .	(5)–(7)	(part)	(6)	(4) ..	(8)
58H(1)		262	(7)	7	7
(part)	14(2), (3)	263(1)	(5)		

TABLE OF DESTINATIONS

LOCAL GOVERNMENT ACT 1972
c.70

1972	1990
Sched. 16,	
para. 46	s.22(4)
Sched. 29,	
para. 3(b) ..	38(5)

FAIR TRADING ACT 1973
c.41

1973	1990
s.137(5)	s.39(3)

LOCAL GOVERNMENT AND PLANNING (AMENDMENT) ACT 1981
c.41

1981	1990
Sched.,	
para. 20	s.31(2)

CIVIL AVIATION ACT 1982
c.16

1982	1990
Sched. 2,	
para. 4	s.39(6)

PLANNING INQUIRIES (PUBLIC) ACT 1982
c.21

1982	1990
s.1(1) ....Sched.,	
	para. 6(5)
(2), (3)	(6)
(4)	(7)

COMPANIES (CONSEQUENTIAL PROVISIONS) ACT 1984
c.10

1984	1990	1984	1990	1984	1990
s.1(1)	s.32(1)	(5)	(4)	4(1)	31(4), 32(8)
(2)	(2)	(6)	(6)	6(1)	(5), 32(6)
(3A)	(3)	(7)	(5)	(2)	32(6), 32(7)

COMPANIES (CONSEQUENTIAL PROVISIONS) ACT 1985
c.9

1985	1990
Sched. 2	s.39(3)

GAS ACT 1986
c.44

1986	1990
Sched. 7,	
para. 2(1) ..	s.39(4)
(9)(e)	(1), (2)
(9) ..	(4)

TABLE OF DESTINATIONS

HOUSING AND PLANNING ACT 1986
c.63

1986	1990	1986	1990	1986	1990
s.30	s.1, 2(1), 2(2),	1986	17(2),	57(2)	41(3)
	2(3), 2(4),		18(1)–(7), 19,	Sched. 7,	
	3(1), 3(2),		20(1)–(6),	para. 2	22(5)
	3(4), 3(6)		21(1)–(8), 23,	Pt. I,	
31	4(1), 4(2),		27, 28,	para. 3 ...	31(2)
	4(3), 4(4),		29(1)–(6),	4 ...	35
	4(5), 5(1),		39(3)	5 ...	30(1), (2)
	5(2), 5(3),	32	24(1)–(9),	6 ...	36(1)–(4)
	5(4), 6(2),		25(1)–(3)	7(a),	
	7(1), 7(2),	34	6(1)	(b).	39(1), (2)
	7(3), 7(4),	(1)	26	8 ...	32(1), 32(3)
	8(1)–(5), 8(7),	(2)	26	(2)	6(4)
	9(1), 9(2),	(3)	11(1)	Sched. 11,	
	9(3), 9(4),	(4)	(2)	paras. 9, 10	37
	10(1), 10(2),	(5)	(3)	para. 9(2) ..	6(8)
	10(3), 12(1),	(6)	(4)	11 .....Sched.,	
	12(3)–(5),	(7)	(5)	para.	
	13(1)–(7),	(8)	(6)	4(1)–(4)	
	14(1)–(4),	(9)	(7)	12 .....Sched.,	
	15(1)–(6),	(10)	(8), 26	para. 6(2)	
	16(1), 17(1),	56	38(6), (7)		

NORFOLK AND SUFFOLK BROADS ACT 1988
c.4

1988	1990
Sched. 3,	
para. 9	s.3(3)

HOUSING ACT 1988
c.50

1988	1990
s.67(6)	s.3(5)

WATER ACT 1989
c.15

1989	1990
Sched. 25,	
para. 1(1),	
(2), (10)	s.39(5)

ELECTRICITY ACT 1989
c.29

1989	1990
Sched. 8,	
para. 7(2) ..	12(2), (3)
Sched. 16,	
para.	
1(1)(xxii)	s.39(6)

The Law Commission Report on the Consolidation of certain Enactments relating to Town and Country Planning (Cmnd. 958)

Recommen-dation	1990				
Rec. 8(a)	s.21(2)	55	10(2), 28	59	28
52 ....Sched.,		56	18(6)	60	32(4)
para. 3(2),		57	21(1), 22(1),	61	36(4)
(4), 4(2)			(2), (5)	62	38(2)
54	s.3(3)–(5)	58	22(1), (2)		

INDEX

References are to section numbers

Index

PLANNING (CONSEQUENTIAL PROVISIONS) ACT 1990

(1990 c. 11)

An Act to make provision for repeals, consequential amendments, transitional and transitory matters and savings in connection with the consolidation of enactments in the Town and Country Planning Act 1990, the Planning (Listed Buildings and Conservation Areas) Act 1990 and the Planning (Hazardous Substances) Act 1990 (including provisions to give effect to recommendations of the Law Commission).

[24th May 1990]

PARLIAMENTARY DEBATES
Hansard, H.L. Vol. 515, col. 1094; Vol. 516, col. 21; Vol. 517, cols. 978, 1528; Vol. 518, col. 437; H.C. Vol. 173, col. 254.
The Bill was considered in Committee from March 1–14, 1990.

INTRODUCTION
The Planning (Consequential Provisions) Act complements the major pieces of planning legislation which have been passed this year, namely the Town and Country Planning Act 1990, the Planning (Listed Buildings and Conservation Areas) Act 1990 and the Planning (Hazardous Substances) Act 1990. It provides the relevant repeals, consequential amendments, transitional provisions and savings and transitory modifications in connection with the consolidation of enactments in these three Acts.
The Act also defines certain terms used for and relating to these pieces of legislation and allows for the continuity and construction of references to new and old law.

Meaning of "the consolidating Acts", "the repealed enactments", etc.

1.—(1) In this Act—
"the consolidating Acts" means the principal Act, the Planning (Listed Buildings and Conservation Areas) Act 1990, the Planning (Hazardous Substances) Act 1990 and, so far as it reproduces the effect of the repealed enactments, this Act,
"the principal Act" means the Town and Country Planning Act 1990, and
"the repealed enactments" means the enactments repealed by this Act.
(2) Expressions used in this Act and in any of the other consolidating Acts have the same meaning as in those Acts.

C.L. STATS. (4)—18

Continuity, and construction of references to old and new law

2.—(1) The substitution of the consolidating Acts for the repealed enactments does not affect the continuity of the law.

(2) Anything done or having effect as if done under or for the purposes of a provision of the repealed enactments has effect, if it could have been done under or for the purposes of the corresponding provision of the consolidating Acts, as if done under or for the purposes of that corresponding provision.

(3) Any reference, whether express or implied, in the consolidating Acts or any other enactment, instrument or document to a provision of the consolidating Acts shall, so far as the context permits, be construed as including, in relation to the times, circumstances and purposes in relation to which the corresponding provision of the repealed enactments has effect, a reference to that corresponding provision.

(4) Any reference, whether express or implied, in any enactment, instrument or document to a provision of the repealed enactments shall be construed, so far as is required for continuing its effect, as including a reference to the corresponding provision of the consolidating Acts.

Repeals

3.—(1) The enactments specified in Schedule 1 are repealed to the extent specified in the third column of that Schedule.

(2) Those repeals include the repeal, in accordance with Recommendations of the Law Commission, of section 105(4) and (5) of the 1968 Act and section 21(7A) and (8) of the 1971 Act as no longer of practical utility.

(3) The repeals have effect subject to any relevant savings in Schedule 3.

Consequential amendments

4. Schedule 2 (which makes consequential amendments) shall have effect, subject to any relevant transitional provisions in Schedule 3.

Transitional provisions and savings

5.—(1) Schedule 3 (which makes transitional provision and contains savings in connection with the repeals made by this Act) shall have effect.

(2) Nothing in that Schedule affects the general operation of section 16 of the Interpretation Act 1978 (general savings implied on repeal) or of the previous provisions of this Act.

Transitory modifications

6. Schedule 4 (which makes transitory modifications of the consolidating Acts) shall have effect.

Short title, commencement and extent

7.—(1) This Act may be cited as the Planning (Consequential Provisions) Act 1990.

(2) This Act shall come into force at the end of the period of three months beginning with the day on which it is passed.

(3) This Act does not extend to Scotland or Northern Ireland except (subject to subsection (4)) so far as it affects other enactments so extending.

(4) The repeals in Part II of Schedule 1 extend to England and Wales only and those in Part III of that Schedule to Scotland only.

SCHEDULES

SCHEDULE 1

REPEALS

PART I

GENERAL

Chapter	Short title	Extent of repeal
10 & 11 Geo. 6 c. 51.	The Town and Country Planning Act 1947.	The whole Act.
10 & 11 Eliz. 2 c. 36.	The Local Authorities (Historic Buildings) Act 1962.	The whole Act.
10 & 11 Eliz. 2 c.38.	The Town and Country Planning Act 1962.	The whole Act.
1963 c. 33.	The London Government Act 1963.	In section 85, in subsection (3) the words from "or by" to "1971" and from "(or as" to "paragraph 6)" and in subsection (4) the words from "or of" to "1971".
1967 c. 69.	The Civic Amenities Act 1967.	In section 5, paragraph (a) and in section 30(1), the definition of "the Planning Act".
1968 c. 72.	The Town and Country Planning Act 1968.	The whole Act.
1969 c. 22.	The Redundant Churches and Other Religious Buildings Act 1969.	Section 2.
1969 c. 48.	The Post Office Act 1969.	In Schedule 4, paragraph 89 and in paragraph 93, sub-paragraphs (1)(xxxiii) and (4)(j).
1971 c. 78.	The Town and Country Planning Act 1971.	The whole Act.
1972 c. 5.	The Local Employment Act 1972.	In Schedule 3, the entry relating to the Town and Country Planning Act 1971.
1972 c. 70.	The Local Government Act 1972.	In section 182, subsections (1) and (2), in subsection (3) paragraphs (a) and (c) and subsections (4) to (6). Section 183. In Schedule 16, paragraphs 4 to 54, 58 and 59.
1973 c. 26.	The Land Compensation Act 1973.	In section 53(5) the words from "sections 180" to "or". Sections 68 to 82.
1973 c. 37.	The Water Act 1973.	In Schedule 8, paragraph 94.
1974 c. 7.	The Local Government Act 1974.	In Schedule 6, paragraph 25.
1974 c. 32.	The Town and Country Amenities Act 1974.	Section 1(1). Section 4(1). In section 6, the words from "section 116" to "and in" and the words from "Schedule 8" to "or". Section 7(1). Section 8. Section 10. Section 13(1)(a).
1975 c. 76.	The Local Land Charges Act 1975.	In Schedule 1, the entry relating to the Town and Country Planning Act 1971.
1977 c. 29.	The Town and Country Planning (Amendment) Act 1977.	The whole Act.

Chapter	Short title	Extent of repeal
1979 c. 46.	The Ancient Monuments Act and Archaeological Areas 1979.	In Schedule 4, paragraph 11.
1980 c. 65.	The Local Government, Planning and Land Act 1980.	Section 86(1) to (6). Sections 89 and 90. Section 91(1). Section 119. In section 122, in subsection (1) the words "section 113 of the Town and Country Planning Act 1971" and "and 113", and in subsections (2), (3), (6) and (8) the word "113". In section 147, in subsection (1) the words from the beginning to "and", in subsection (3) the words from "sections 192" to "Act and" and in subsection (5) the words from the beginning to "Scotland". In section 149, in subsection (1) the words from "in place" to "planning authority", in subsection (3)(a) the words from "and in place" to "them" and subsection (5). Section 150. Schedule 14. In Schedule 15, paragraphs 2 to 15, 17 to 20, 22, 23 and 25 to 28. In Schedule 23, paragraphs 8 to 11. In Schedule 32, paragraph 5(7), in paragraph 15(2)(b), sub-paragraph (i), in paragraph 17(7) the words "the 1971 Act or", in the first place where they occur, and "Part III of the 1971 Act or", paragraphs 18, 20(1), 22(2)(a), 23 and 26(1A)(a). In Schedule 33, paragraph 12.
1980 c. 66.	The Highways Act 1980.	In Schedule 24, paragraphs 20 and 22, and in paragraph 23, sub-paragraphs (d) to (h).
1981 c. 36.	The Town and Country Planning (Minerals) Act 1981.	Sections 1 to 18. In section 34, the words from the beginning to "Act, and" and the words "in each case". Schedule 1.
1981 c. 38.	The British Telecommunications Act 1981.	In Schedule 3, paragraph 10(2)(c).
1981 c. 41.	The Local Government and Planning (Amendment) Act 1981.	The whole Act.
1981 c. 43.	The Disabled Persons Act 1981.	Section 3.
1981 c. 54.	The Supreme Court Act 1981.	In Schedule 5, the entry relating to the Town and Country Planning Act 1971.
1981 c. 64.	The New Towns Act 1981.	In Schedule 12, paragraph 11.
1981 c. 67.	The Acquisition of Land Act 1981.	In Schedule 4, in the Table in paragraph 1, the entry relating to the Town and Country Planning Act 1971 and paragraph 21.
1981 c. 69.	The Wildlife and Countryside Act 1981.	In Schedule 16, paragraphs 1 to 4.

Chapter	Short title	Extent of repeal
1982 c. 16.	The Civil Aviation Act 1982.	In Schedule 2, in paragraphs 4 and 5 the entries relating to the Town and Country Planning Act 1971 and paragraph 6. In Schedule 10, in paragraphs 4(c) and 8(c), the words from "either" to "or".
1982 c. 21.	The Planning Inquiries (Attendance of Public) Act 1982.	The whole Act.
1982 c. 30.	The Local Government (Miscellaneous Provisions) Act 1982.	Sections 35 and 36. In Schedule 5, paragraphs 2 and 3. In Schedule 6, paragraph 7.
1982 c. 52.	The Industrial Development Act 1982.	In Part II of Schedule 2, paragraph 7(2).
1983 c. 47.	The National Heritage Act 1983.	In Schedule 4, paragraphs 15 to 17 and 19 to 21, 22(1) to (5) and (7), 23 and 24.
1984 c. 12.	The Telecommunications Act 1984.	In Schedule 4, paragraph 53.
1984 c. 32.	The London Regional Transport Act 1984.	In Schedule 6, paragraph 9.
1985 c. 19.	The Town and Country Planning (Compensation) Act 1985.	Section 1.
1985 c. 51.	The Local Government Act 1985.	In section 3, subsections (1), (3) and (4). Sections 4 and 5. Schedule 1. In Schedule 2, paragraph 1. In Schedule 3, paragraphs 2 and 3(1) and in paragraph 4 the words "54(2) and". In Schedule 4, paragraph 50. In Schedule 14, paragraph 48.
1985 c. 52.	The Town and Country Planning (Amendment) Act 1985.	Section 1.
1985 c. 68.	The Housing Act 1985.	In section 256(4), paragraph (b).
1985 c. 71.	The Housing (Consequential Provisions) Act 1985.	In Schedule 2, paragraphs 22 and 24(8).
1986 c. 31.	The Airports Act 1986.	In Schedule 2, in paragraph 1(1) and (2), the words "the Town and Country Planning Act 1971". In Schedule 4, paragraph 1.
1986 c. 44.	The Gas Act 1986.	In Schedule 7, in paragraph 2, sub-paragraph (1)(xxiv) and (xxvi) and in (xxvii) the words "and 71" and sub-paragraphs (2)(c) and (9)(e) and paragraph 12.
1986 c. 63.	The Housing and Planning Act 1986.	Section 25. Sections 30 to 34. Section 41. Sections 45 and 46. In section 58(1), the words from "in Part II" to "Schedule 6" and the words from "in Part IV" to "Schedule 7". In Schedule 6, Parts I and II. In Schedule 7, Part I. In Schedule 9, paragraphs 1 to 5, 6(1) and 7 to 12. Schedule 10. In Schedule 11, paragraphs 1 to 24, 26 and 27.
1987 c. 3.	The Coal Industry Act 1987.	In Schedule 1, paragraph 19.

11–5

Chapter	Short title	Extent of repeal
1988 c. 4.	The Norfolk and Suffolk Broads Act 1988.	In Schedule 3, paragraphs 4, 7 to 28, 32 and 48.
1988 c. 40.	The Education Reform Act 1988.	In Schedule 12, paragraphs 40 and 70.
1988 c. 50.	The Housing Act 1988.	In section 67, in subsection (1) the words from "in place" onwards and in subsection (3) the words from "and in place" to "them", and subsections (5) and (6). In Schedule 17, paragraph 18.
1989 c. 15.	The Water Act 1989.	In Schedule 25, in paragraph 1, in sub-paragraph (2), paragraphs (xvi) and (xvii) and in paragraph (xviii) the words "and 71", and sub-paragraphs (10)(iv) and (11)(ii), and paragraph 42.
1989 c. 29.	The Electricity Act 1989.	In Schedule 16, in paragraph 1, in sub-paragraph (1), paragraphs (xxii) and (xxiv) and in paragraph (xxv) the words "and 71", paragraphs 2(2)(c), (4)(c) and (5)(b) and 3(1)(d).
1989 c. 42.	The Local Government and Housing Act 1989.	In Schedule 11, paragraphs 19 and 20.

Part II

England and Wales only

Chapter	Short title	Extent of repeal
9 & 10 Geo. 6. c.35.	The Building Restrictions (War-Time Contraventions) Act 1946.	The whole Act.
14 & 15 Geo. 6. c. 60.	The Mineral Workings Act 1951.	Section 32. Section 40(6).
1969 c. 48.	The Post Office Act 1969.	In Schedule 9, paragraph 27(8).
1972 c. 42.	The Town and Country Planning (Amendment) Act 1972.	The whole Act.
1980 c. 65.	The Local Government, Planning and Land Act 1980.	Section 87.
1984 c. 10.	The Town and Country Planning Act 1984.	The whole Act.
1989 c. 29.	The Electricity Act 1989.	In Schedule 8, paragraph 7.

Part III

Scotland only

Chapter	Short title	Extent of repeal
14 & 15 Geo. 6. c. 60.	The Mineral Workings Act 1951.	In section 40(6), the words "section forty-nine of the principal Act or" and "as the case may be".

Chapter	Short title	Extent of repeal
1972 c. 42.	The Town and Country Planning (Amendment) Act 1972.	In section 10, in subsection (1), the words from "Subject" to "this section" and "section 277" to "1971 or", subsection (1AA), in subsection (2) the words from "or" to "Commission", subsections (3A) and (3B), in subsection (4) the words from "the appropriate" to "Monmouthshire)" and the words from "or the" to "Wales". In section 10A, in subsection (1) the words from "or" to "Commission", in subsections (3) and (5) the words "or (as the case may be) the Commission" and "or (as the case may be) they think", in subsection (8) the words "or (as the case may be) the Commission" and subsection (9).
1980 c. 65.	The Local Government, Planning and Land Act 1980.	In section 87, in subsection (1) the words "a local planning authority in England or Wales or", in subsection (2) paragraph (a) and in subsection (8) paragraph (a).
1984 c. 10.	The Town and Country Planning Act 1984.	In section 1, in subsection (1)(b) the words from "section 53" to "or", in subsection (5)(b) the words from "a local" to "Scotland" and in subsection (6) the words from "section 277A" to "1971 or". In section 2, in subsection (1) the words from the beginning to "Scotland" and in subsection (4) the words from "section 60" to "1971 or". In section 3, in subsection (2), the words "a local planning authority or, in Scotland" and subsection (8). In section 4, in subsection (1) the words "a licence in writing or, in Scotland" and the words from "section 266(1)(b)" to "be" and subsections (2) and (3). In section 5, in subsection (1) the words from the beginning to "Scotland", in subsection (2) the words "the Act of 1971 or, as the case may be", in subsection (3) the words "local planning authority or" and subsection (4). In section 6, in subsection (1), the definition of "the Act of 1971" and in the definition of "the appropriate authority" the words from "section 266(7)" to "Scotland" and subsections (2) and (3). Section 7(2)(b).
1989 c. 29.	The Electricity Act 1989.	In Schedule 8, in paragraph 7(4), in the definition of "the Planning Act" the words from "the Town and Country Planning Act 1971" to "Wales and" and in the definition of "the relevant section" the words from "section 35" to "1971 and".

SCHEDULE 2

CONSEQUENTIAL AMENDMENTS

The Finance Act 1931 (c. 28)

1.—(1) In section 28(6) of the Finance Act 1931, for the words "the Town and Country Planning Act 1971" there shall be substituted the words "the Town and Country Planning Act 1990".

(2) In paragraph (viii) of Schedule 2 to that Act, for the words "section 34(1) of the Town and Country Planning Act 1971" there shall be substituted the words "section 69(1) of the Town and Country Planning Act 1990".

The Mineral Workings Act 1951 (c. 60)

2. In section 41(2A) of the Mineral Workings Act 1951 for the words "the Town and Country Planning Act 1971", in both places where they occur, there shall be substituted the words "the Town and Country Planning Act 1990".

The Agricultural Land (Removal of Surface Soil) Act 1953 (c. 10)

3.—(1) In section 1(1)(b) of the Agricultural Land (Removal of Surface Soil) Act 1953 for the words "the Town and Country Planning Act, 1947" there shall be substituted the words "the Town and Country Planning Act 1990".

(2) In section 2(3) of that Act for the words "section seventeen of the Town and Country Planning Act, 1947" there shall be substituted the words "section 64 of the Town and Country Planning Act 1990".

(3) In section 4 of that Act for the words "the Town and Country Planning Act, 1947" and "section seventeen" there shall be substituted respectively the words "the Town and Country Planning Act 1990" and "section 64".

(4) In section 5(2) of that Act for the words "the Town and Country Planning Act, 1947" there shall be substituted the words "the Town and Country Planning Act 1990".

The Historic Buildings and Ancient Monuments Act 1953 (c. 49)

4.—(1) In section 5A(1)(b) of the Historic Buildings and Ancient Monuments Act 1953, for the words "section 277 of the Town and Country Planning Act 1971" there shall be substituted the words "section 69 of the Planning (Listed Buildings and Conservation Areas) Act 1990".

(2) In section 5B(1) of that Act, for the words "section 114 or 119(1)(b) or (c) of the Town and Country Planning Act 1971" there shall be substituted the words "section 47 or 52 of the Planning (Listed Buildings and Conservation Areas) Act 1990".

The Opencast Coal Act 1958 (c. 69)

5. In the Opencast Coal Act 1958—
     (a) in section 13—
               (i) in subsection (1) for the words from "provisions", in the first place where it occurs, to "(which" there shall be substituted the words "provisions of section 271 of the Act of 1990 (which" and in paragraph (d) of that subsection for the words from "subsection (4)" to "shall" there shall be substituted the words "subsection (5) of the said section 271 shall";
               (ii) in subsection (2) for the words from "the said" to "shall" there shall be substituted the words "the said section 271 shall";
               (iii) in subsection (3) for the words from "by virtue" to "(which" in the second place it occurs and the words from "the said" onwards there shall be substituted respectively the words "by virtue of section 271 of the Act of 1990 as applied by either of the preceding subsections, the provisions of sections 275 to 277 of that Act (which relate to the powers, duties and obligations of statutory undertakers) and of sections 278 to 282 of that Act (which" and "the said section 271";
               (iv) in subsection (5) for the words "the said" to "shall" there shall be substituted the words "section 219 of the Town and Country Planning (Scotland) Act 1972 to roads stopped up or diverted by virtue of section 198 of that Act) shall";
               (v) in subsection (6) for the words from "for references" in the first place they occur to " "highway" " there shall be substituted the words "for refer-

ences to section 271, subsection (5) of that section and sections 275 to 282 of the Act of 1990 there shall be substituted respectively references to section 219, subsection (4) of that section, and sections 222 to 229 of the said Act of 1972; "highway" ";
(b) in section 15(6) and (7) for the words "the Act of 1971" in each place where they occur there shall be substituted the words "the Act of 1990";
(c) in section 51(1)—
(i) there shall be inserted at the appropriate place " "the Act of 1990" means the Town and Country Planning Act 1990"; and
(ii) in the definition of "planning permission" for the words "the Act of 1971" there shall be substituted the words "the Act of 1990".

The Town and Country Planning Act 1959 (c. 53)

6. For paragraph (c) of section 26(5) of the Town and Country Planning Act 1959 there shall be substituted—
"(c) to section 233 of the Town and Country Planning Act 1990 (which relates to the disposal of land for planning purposes)".

The Radioactive Substances Act 1960 (c. 34)

7. After paragraph 8A of Schedule 1 to the Radioactive Substances Act 1960, there shall be inserted—
"8AA. The Planning (Hazardous Substances) Act 1990".

The Caravan Sites and Control of Development Act 1960 (c. 62)

8. At the end of section 29(4) of the Caravan Sites and Control of Development Act 1960 there shall be inserted the words "or granted on the designation of an enterprise zone under Schedule 32 to the Local Government, Planning and Land Act 1980".

The Land Compensation Act 1961 (c. 33)

9.—(1) In paragraph 1 of Schedule 2 to the Land Compensation Act 1961—
(a) in sub-paragraph (2)(b) for the words from "under" to "1971" there shall be substituted the words "under Part IX of the Town and Country Planning Act 1990 or sections 47 to 52 of the Planning (Listed Buildings and Conservation Areas) Act 1990";
(b) in sub-paragraph (2)(c) for the words "Part IX of that Act" there shall be substituted the words "Part VI of the Town and Country Planning Act 1990 or sections 32 to 37 of the Planning (Listed Buildings and Conservation Areas) Act 1990".
(2) In paragraph 3(2) of that Schedule—
(a) in paragraph (a) for the words from "section 180" to "1971" there shall be substituted the words "section 137 of the Town and Country Planning Act 1990";
(b) in paragraph (b) for the words "Part IX" there shall be substituted the words "Part VI" and at the end of that paragraph there shall be added the words "or
(c) sections 32 to 37 of the Planning (Listed Buildings and Conservation Areas) Act 1990".

The Public Health Act 1961 (c. 64)

10. In Schedule 4 to the Public Health Act 1961 for the second item in the Table there shall be substituted—

"A building which is included in a list com-   The Secretary of State."
piled or approved under section 1 of the
Planning (Listed Buildings and Conservation
Areas) Act 1990.

The Harbours Act 1964 (c. 40)

11. In section 52(2) of the Harbours Act 1964 for the words "section 266 of the Town and Country Planning Act 1971; and the provisions of subsection (7) of that section" there shall be substituted the words "subsection (2) of section 293 of the Town and Country Planning Act 1990; and the provisions of subsection (3) of that section".

The Gas Act 1965 (c. 36)

12.—(1) In section 4(6) of the Gas Act 1965—
  (a) for the words "the Town and Country Planning Act 1971" there shall be substituted the words "the Town and Country Planning Act 1990";
  (b) for the words "section 40 of that Act" there shall be substituted the words "section 90 of that Act".
(2) In section 28(1) of that Act—
  (a) in the definition of "local planning authority", for the words "section 1 of the Town and Country Planning Act 1971" there shall be substituted the words "section 336(1) of the Town and Country Planning Act 1990";
  (b) in the definition of "planning permission", for the words "Part III of the Town and Country Planning Act 1971" there shall be substituted the words "Part III of the Town and Country Planning Act 1990 (other than sections 88 and 89)".
(3) In Schedule 3 to that Act—
  (a) in paragraph 3, for the words "section 146 of the Town and Country Planning Act 1971" and "Part VII of that Act, together with sections 38 and 39" there shall be substituted respectively the words "section 120 of the Town and Country Planning Act 1990" and "Part V of that Act, together with sections 80 and 81";
  (b) in paragraph 7(2), for the words "the Town and Country Planning Act 1971" there shall be substituted the words "the Town and Country Planning Act 1990";
  (c) in paragraph 9(a) for the words "section 146 of the Town and Country Planning Act 1971", "Part VII of the said Act of 1971" and "sections 38 and 39 of the said Act of 1971" there shall be substituted respectively "section 120 of the Town and Country Planning Act 1990", "Part V of the said Act of 1990" and "sections 80 and 81 of the said Act of 1990".

The Compulsory Purchase Act 1965 (c. 56)

13.—(1) In section 1(4) of the Compulsory Purchase Act 1965—
  (a) for the words "Part VI of the Town and Country Planning Act 1971" there shall be substituted the words "Part IX of the Town and Country Planning Act 1990 or section 52 of the Planning (Listed Buildings and Conservation Areas) Act 1990";
  (b) for the words "section 132(4) of that Act" there shall be substituted the words "section 245(4) of the Town and Country Planning Act 1990 or, as the case may be, section 52(2) of the Planning (Listed Buildings and Conservation Areas) Act 1990".
(2) In section 10(3) of that Act—
  (a) for the words "Part VI of the Town and Country Planning Act 1971" there shall be substituted the words "Part IX of the Town and Country Planning Act 1990";
  (b) for the words "section 132(4)(b) of that Act" there shall be substituted the words "section 245(4)(b) of that Act".

The Forestry Act 1967 (c. 10)

14.—(1) In section 9(4)(d) of the Forestry Act 1967, for the words "the Town and Country Planning Act 1971" there shall be substituted the words "the Town and Country Planning Act 1990".
(2) In the definition of "tree preservation order" in section 35 of that Act, for the words "section 60 of the Town and Country Planning Act 1971" there shall be substituted the words "section 198 of the Town and Country Planning Act 1990".
(3) In Schedule 3 to that Act—
  (a) in paragraph 2—
      (i) in sub-paragraph (a), for the words "section 35 of the Town and Country Planning Act 1971" there shall be substituted the words "section 77 of the Town and Country Planning Act 1990";
      (ii) in sub-paragraph (b), for the words "the said section 35" there shall be substituted the words "the said section 77";
  (b) in paragraph 3, for the words "the Town and Country Planning Act 1971" there shall be substituted the words "the Town and Country Planning Act 1990".

The Agriculture Act 1967 (c. 22)

15.—(1) In section 49(5)(a) of the Agriculture Act 1967—
  (a) for the words "section 246 of the Town and Country Planning Act 1971" there

shall be substituted the words "section 289 of the Town and Country Planning Act 1990";
  (b) for the words "Part V of that Act" there shall be substituted the words "Part VII of that Act".

(2) In section 50(3)(b) of that Act, for the words "section 290(1) of the Town and Country Planning Act 1971" there shall be substituted the words "section 336(1) of the Town and Country Planning Act 1990".

(3) In section 52(2)(g) of that Act, for the words "the Town and Country Planning Act 1971" there shall be substituted the words "the Town and Country Planning Act 1990".

The Civic Amenities Act 1967 (c. 69)

16. In section 5 of the Civic Amenities Act 1967—
  (a) for the words "Sections 1 and 2 of the Local Authorities (Historic Buildings) Act 1962" there shall be substituted the words "Sections 57 and 58 of the Planning (Listed Buildings and Conservation Areas) Act 1990";
  (b) paragraph (a) shall be omitted;
  (c) in paragraph (b)—
    (i) for the words "subsection (4) of section 1" there shall be substituted the words "subsection (7) of section 57";
    (ii) after the definition of "local authority" there shall be inserted—
      " "listed building" means a building for the time being included in a list of buildings of special architectural or historic interest compiled or approved under section 52 of the Scottish Planning Act";
  (d) in paragraph (c) for the words "section 2" there shall be substituted the words "section 58".

The Leasehold Reform Act 1967 (c. 88)

17.—(1) In section 28(6) of the Leasehold Reform Act 1967, for the words from "that authority" to "is situated" there shall be substituted the words "that authority, in order to secure—
  (a) the development or redevelopment of an area defined by a development plan under the Town and Country Planning Act 1990 as an area of comprehensive development; or
  (b) the treatment as a whole, by development, redevelopment or improvement, or partly by one and partly by another method, of any area in which the property is situated".

(2) In paragraph 1(7) of Schedule 4 to that Act, for the words "the Town and Country Planning Act 1971" there shall be substituted the words "the Town and Country Planning Act 1990".

The Public Expenditure and Receipts Act 1968 (c. 14)

18. For paragraph 7(b) of Schedule 3 to the Public Expenditure and Receipts Act 1968 there shall be substituted—
  "(b) The Town and Country Planning Act 1990 (c. 8), paragraph 20(9) of Schedule 12.".

The Agriculture (Miscellaneous Provisions) Act 1968 (c. 34)

19. In section 13(2) of the Agriculture (Miscellaneous Provisions) Act 1968 for the words "section 112 or 120 of the Town and Country Planning Act 1971" there shall be substituted the words "section 226 or 230 of the Town and Country Planning Act 1990".

The Countryside Act 1968 (c. 41)

20. In section 40(1) of the Countryside Act 1968, for the words "section 1 of the Town and Country Planning Act 1971" there shall be substituted the words "section 2 of the Town and Country Planning Act 1990".

The Caravan Sites Act 1968 (c. 52)

21.—(1) In section 8(3) of the Caravan Sites Act 1968, for the words "section 35 of the Town and Country Planning Act 1971" there shall be substituted the words "section 77 of the Town and Country Planning Act 1990".

(2) In the definition of "planning permission" in section 16 of that Act (as it applies in England and Wales), for the words "Part III of the Town and Country Planning Act 1971" there shall be substituted the words "Part III of the Town and Country Planning Act 1990".

The Transport Act 1968 (c. 73)

22.—(1) In paragraph (a) of the definition of "planning authority" in section 63(6) of the Transport Act 1968, for the words "Part III of the Town and Country Planning Act 1971" there shall be substituted the words "Part III of the Town and Country Planning Act 1990".
(2) In section 108 of that Act—
    (a) in subsection (1) for paragraph (b) there shall be substituted—
        "(b) land to which section 215 of the Town and Country Planning Act 1990 applies;";
        and for the words "the said Act of 1971" and "the said section 65" there shall be substituted respectively the words "the said Act of 1990" and "the said section 215"; and
    (b) in subsection (3) for the words from "Part III" to "or" there shall be substituted the words "Part III of the Town and Country Planning Act 1962 or".
(3) In section 112(3)(d) of that Act, for the words "section 65 of the Town and Country Planning Act 1971" there shall be substituted the words "section 215 of the Town and Country Planning Act 1990".
(4) In section 141(2) of that Act, for the words "section 290(1) of the Town and Country Planning Act 1971" there shall be substituted the words "section 336(1) of the Town and Country Planning Act 1990".
(5) In section 142(2) of that Act—
    (a) for the words "the Town and Country Planning Act 1971" there shall be substituted the words "the Town and Country Planning Act 1990 or the Planning (Listed Buildings and Conservation Areas) Act 1990 or the Planning (Hazardous Substances) Act 1990";
    (b) for the words from "Part III" to "notices" there shall be substituted the words "Part III or Part VIII of the Town and Country Planning Act 1990 or the provisions of Part VI of that Act relating to purchase notices or the Planning (Listed Buildings and Conservation Areas) Act 1990 or the Planning (Hazardous Substances) Act 1990".

The Finance Act 1969 (c. 32)

23. In the Table in section 58(4)(c) of the Finance Act 1969, in the entry relating to the Town and Country Planning Act 1971—
    (a) in the first column for the words "the Town and Country Planning Act 1971" there shall be substituted the words "the Town and Country Planning Act 1990"; and
    (b) for the entry in the second column there shall be substituted the words "Part II of the Town and Country Planning Act 1990".

The Post Office Act 1969 (c. 48)

24.—(1) In section 57 of the Post Office Act 1969—
    (a) in subsection (2)—
        (i) for the words "Sections 280(9) and 281(1) to (3) and (6) of the Town and Country Planning Act 1971" there shall be substituted the words "Sections 324(8), 325(1) to (5), (8) and (9) of the Town and Country Planning Act 1990";
        (ii) for the words "section 280(1) to (8) thereof" there shall be substituted the words "section 324(1) to (7) and (9) thereof";
        (iii) for the words "the said section 280" there shall be substituted the words "the said section 324";
        (iv) in paragraph (a) for the words "section 280(9)" and the word "therein", in both places where it occurs, there shall be substituted respectively the words "section 324(8)" and "in it";
        (v) in paragraph (b) for the words "section 281(1)" there shall be substituted the words "section 325(1)";
    (b) in subsection (4)—
        (i) for the words "Section 179 of the Town and Country Planning Act 1971" there shall be substituted the words "Section 118 of the Town and Country Planning Act 1990";

(ii) for the words "Part VIII of that Act" there shall be substituted the words "Part IV of that Act".

(2) In paragraph 93(1) of Schedule 4 to that Act for the words from "Subject" to "1958" there shall be substituted the words "Subject to this exception, namely, that in relation to Scotland it shall not be so deemed for the purposes of section 271 of the Town and Country Planning Act 1990, as applied by section 13 of the Opencast Coal Act 1958".

(3) In Schedule 9 to that Act—

    (a) in paragraph 27—

        (i) in sub-paragraph (7) (as it applies in England and Wales), for the words "Parts VII and XII of the Town and Country Planning Act 1971" there shall be substituted the words "Parts V and XII of the Town and Country Planning Act 1990";

        (ii) in sub-paragraph (9) (as it applies in England and Wales), for the words "section 34 of the Town and Country Planning Act 1971" there shall be substituted the words "section 69 of the Town and Country Planning Act 1990";

        (iii) in sub-paragraph (12)(a), for the words "the Town and Country Planning Act 1971" there shall be substituted the words "the Town and Country Planning Act 1990";

        (iv) in sub-paragraph (14), for the words "Sections 41 and 42 of the Town and Country Planning Act 1971" there shall be substituted the words "Sections 91 and 92 of the Town and Country Planning Act 1990";

        (v) in sub-paragraph (15) (as it applies in England and Wales), for the words "Subsections (5) and (7) of section 43 of the Town and Country Planning Act 1971" there shall be substituted the words "Subsections (2) and (4) of section 93 of the Town and Country Planning Act 1990"; and for the words "sections 41 and 42 of that Act" there shall be substituted the words "sections 91 and 92 of that Act of 1990";

    (b) in paragraph 28—

        (i) in sub-paragraph (1), for the words "section 266 of the Town and Country Planning Act 1971" and "section 27 of the said Act of 1971" there shall be substituted respectively the words "section 296 of the Town and Country Planning Act 1990" and "sections 66 and 67 of the said Act of 1990";

        (ii) in sub-paragraph (2), for the words "the said Act of 1971" there shall be substituted the words "the said Act of 1990";

    (c) in paragraph 29 for the words "paragraph 34 of Schedule 24 to the Town and Country Planning Act 1971" and "section 87 of the said Act of 1971" there shall be substituted respectively the words "paragraph 34 of Schedule 24 to the Town and Country Planning Act 1971 (as it continues in effect by virtue of Schedule 3 to the Planning (Consequential Provisions) Act 1990)" and "section 172 of the Town and Country Planning Act 1990".

The Courts Act 1971 (c. 23)

25. In section 28(2) of the Courts Act 1971 for paragraph (b) there shall be substituted—

"(b) section 228(1) of the Town and Country Planning Act 1990 (power of Secretary of State to acquire compulsorily land necessary for the public service)".

The Town and Country Planning (Amendment) Act 1972 (c. 42)

26. In section 10C(10) of the Town and Country Planning (Amendment) Act 1972, for the words "Section 2 of the Local Authorities (Historic Buildings) Act 1962" there shall be substituted the words "Section 58 of the Planning (Listed Buildings and Conservation Areas) Act 1990".

The Town and Country Planning (Scotland) Act 1972 (c. 52)

27.—(1) In section 47(1) of the Town and Country Planning (Scotland) Act 1972, for the words "section 48 of the Town and Country Planning Act 1971" there shall be substituted the words "section 101 of the Town and Country Planning Act 1990".

(2) In Schedule 9 to that Act—

    (a) in the Table in paragraph 1 for the words "section 225(1) of the Act of 1971" and "section 40 of the Act of 1971" there shall be substituted respectively the words "section 266(1) of the Act of 1990" and "section 90(1) of the Act of 1990";

(b) in paragraph 2, for the words " 'Act of 1971' means the Town and Country Planning Act 1971" there shall be substituted the words " 'Act of 1990' means the Town and Country Planning Act 1990";

(c) in paragraph 7—

    (i) in sub-paragraph (2), for the words "section 35 of the Act of 1971", "section 36 of the Act of 1971" and "section 29(2) or (3) of the Act of 1971" there shall be substituted respectively the words "section 77 of the Act of 1990", "section 78 of the Act of 1990" and "section 71(1) or (2) of the Act of 1990";

    (ii) in sub-paragraph (3), for the words "section 40 of the Act of 1971" there shall be substituted the words "section 90(1) of the Act of 1990";

    (iii) in sub-paragraph (4), for the words "the Act of 1971" there shall be substituted the words "the Act of 1990";

(d) in paragraph 9(b), for the words "section 48(1)(a), (b) or (c) of the Act of 1971" there shall be substituted the words "section 101(2)(a), (b) or (c) of the Act of 1990";

(e) in paragraph 9(c)—

    (i) for the words "the said section 48(1)(a) or (b)" there shall be substituted the words "the said section 101(2)(a) or (b)";

    (ii) for the words "section 29(2) or (3) of the Act of 1971" there shall be substituted the words "section 71(1) or (2) of the Act of 1990";

(f) in paragraph 10—

    (i) for the words "sections 35(5) and 36(4) of the Act of 1971" there shall be substituted the words "sections 77(5) and 79(2) of the Act of 1990";

    (ii) for the words "Schedule 9 to the Act of 1971" there shall be substituted the words "Schedule 6 to the Act of 1990".

The Local Government Act 1972 (c. 70)

28.—(1) In sections 122(2) and 126(4) of the Local Government Act 1972 for the words "section 121 of the Town and Country Planning Act 1971" and "the said section 121" there shall be substituted respectively the words "section 229 of the Town and Country Planning Act 1990" and "the said section 229".

(2) In paragraph (a) of the definition of "local authority" in section 140A(2) of that Act, for the words "section 1 of the Town and Country Planning Act 1971" there shall be substituted the words "section 2 of the Town and Country Planning Act 1990".

(3) In the definition of "open space" in section 270(1) of that Act, for the words "section 290(1) of the Town and Country Planning Act 1971" there shall be substituted the words "section 336(1) of the Town and Country Planning Act 1990".

(4) In the definition of "protected informant" in paragraph 1(1) of Part III of Schedule 12A to that Act, for the words "section 87(3) of the Town and Country Planning Act 1971" there shall be substituted the words "section 172(3) of the Town and Country Planning Act 1990".

(5) In paragraph 55(7) of Schedule 16 to that Act for the words "paragraph 32 of this Schedule" there shall be substituted the words "paragraph 1 of Schedule 1 to the Town and Country Planning Act 1990".

(6) In Schedule 17 to that Act—

(a) in paragraph 1 for the words "Schedule 1 to that Act" there shall be substituted the words "section 2 of the Town and Country Planning Act 1990";

(b) in paragraph 2 for the words "the Town and Country Planning Act 1971" there shall be substituted the words "the Town and Country Planning Act 1990 and the Planning (Listed Buildings and Conservation Areas) Act 1990";

(c) in paragraph 3 for the words "section 1 of the Town and Country Planning Act 1971" there shall be substituted the words "section 2 of the Town and Country Planning Act 1990";

(d) in paragraph 4 for the words "section 1" there shall be substituted the words "section 2";

(e) in paragraph 6 for the words "the Town and Country Planning Act 1971" and the words "Part V" there shall be substituted respectively the words "the Town and Country Planning Act 1990" and "Part VII";

(f) in paragraph 7 for the words "the Town and Country Planning Act 1971" there shall be substituted the words "the Town and Country Planning Act 1990";

(g) in paragraph 15 for the words "section 1 of the Town and Country Planning Act 1971" there shall be substituted the words "section 2 of the Town and Country Planning Act 1990";

(h) in paragraph 20 for the words "and the Town and Country Planning Act 1971" there shall be substituted the words "and the Town and Country Planning Act 1990, the Planning (Listed Buildings and Conservation Areas) Act 1990 and the Planning (Consequential Provisions) Act 1990".

The Land Compensation Act 1973 (c. 26)

29.—(1) In section 2(6) of the Land Compensation Act 1973—
(a) for the words "section 192(4)(a) of the Town and Country Planning Act 1971" there shall be substituted the words "section 149(3)(a) of the Town and Country Planning Act 1990";
(b) for the words "section 207" there shall be substituted the words "section 171";
(c) for the words "section 193" there shall be substituted the words "section 150".
(2) In section 5 of that Act—
(a) in subsection (2), for the words "Schedule 8 to the Town and Country Planning Act 1971" there shall be substituted the words "Schedule 3 to the Town and Country Planning Act 1990";
(b) in subsection (3)—
  (i) in paragraph (a), for the words "Part II of the said Schedule 8" there shall be substituted the words "Part II of the said Schedule 3" and for the words "section 169 of the said Act of 1971" there shall be substituted the words "section 114 of the said Act of 1990";
  (ii) in paragraph (b), for the words "the said section 169" there shall be substituted the words "the said section 114";
  (iii) in paragraph (c), for the words "section 51 of the said Act of 1971" and "section 170" there shall be substituted respectively the words "section 102 of or paragraph 1 of Schedule 9 to the said Act of 1990" and "section 115";
*(c) in subsection (5), for the words "the said Act of 1971" there shall be substituted the words "the said Act of 1990".
(3) In section 26(6) of that Act, for the words "section 290(1) of the Town and Country Planning Act 1971" there shall be substituted the words "section 336(1) of the Town and Country Planning Act 1990".
(4) In section 29(5) of that Act, for the words "section 192 of the Town and Country Planning Act 1971" there shall be substituted the words "section 149 of the Town and Country Planning Act 1990".
(5) In section 34(6) of that Act, for the words "section 192 of the Town and Country Planning Act 1971" there shall be substituted the words "section 149 of the Town and Country Planning Act 1990".
(6) In section 39(2) of that Act, for the words "section 192 of the Town and Country Planning Act 1971" there shall be substituted the words "section 149 of the Town and Country Planning Act 1990".
(7) In section 46(2) of that Act—
(a) for the words "section 192(4)(a) of the Town and Country Planning Act 1971" there shall be substituted the words "section 149(3)(a) of the Town and Country Planning Act 1990";
(b) for the words "section 207" there shall be substituted the words "section 171";
(c) for the words "section 193" there shall be substituted the words "section 150".
(8) In section 51(6)(b) of that Act, for the words "the Town and Country Planning Act 1971" there shall be substituted the words "the Town and Country Planning Act 1990".
(9) In section 53 of that Act—
(a) in subsection (4), after the words "(3) above" there shall be inserted the words "or such a notice is deemed to have been served by virtue of sections 137 to 144 of the Town and Country Planning Act 1990"; and
(b) in subsection (5) the words from "sections 180" to "or" shall be omitted.
(10) In section 58(1) of that Act, for the words "section 202(2) of the Town and Country Planning Act 1971" there shall be substituted the words "section 166(2) of the Town and Country Planning Act 1990".
(11) In the definition of "agricultural unit" in section 87(1) of that Act for the words "section 207(1) of the Town and Country Planning Act 1971" there shall be substituted the words "section 171(1) of the Town and Country Planning Act 1990".

---

* Misprinted in Queen's Printer's copy as 29(2)(e).

The Employment and Training Act 1973 (c. 50)

30. In section 4 of the Employment and Training Act 1973—
   (a) in subsection (3)(e), for the words "the Town and Country Planning Act 1971" there shall be substituted the words "the Town and Country Planning Act 1990";
   and
   (b) in subsection (5)(d), for the words "the said Act of 1971" there shall be substituted the words "the said Act of 1990".

The Control of Pollution Act 1974 (c. 40)

31.—(1) In section 5(2) of the Control of Pollution Act 1974, for the words "the Town and Country Planning Act 1971" there shall be substituted the words "the Town and Country Planning Act 1990".
   (2) In section 105(3) of that Act, for the words "subsection (7) of section 266 of the Town and Country Planning Act 1971" there shall be substituted the words "subsection (1) of section 293 of the Town and Country Planning Act 1990".

The House of Commons Disqualification Act 1975 (c. 24)

32. In Part II of Schedule 1 to the House of Commons Disqualification Act 1975, in the first entry relating to "A Planning Inquiry Commission", for the words "Part III of the Town and Country Planning Act 1971" there shall be substituted the words "Part III of the Town and Country Planning Act 1990".

The Coal Industry Act 1975 (c. 56)

33. In section 2(3) of the Coal Industry Act 1975, for the words "the Town and Country Planning Act 1971" there shall be substituted the words "the Town and Country Planning Act 1990".

The Welsh Development Agency Act 1975 (c. 70)

34.—(1) In section 7(1) of the Welsh Development Agency Act 1975, for the words "section 29 of the Town and Country Planning Act 1971" there shall be substituted the words "section 70 of the Town and Country Planning Act 1990".
   (2) In section 26 of that Act, for the words "section 266(7) of the Town and Country Planning Act 1971" and "that subsection" there shall be substituted respectively the words "section 293(1) and (2) of the Town and Country Planning Act 1990" and "those subsections".
   (3) In section 27(1) of that Act—
   (a) in the definition of "the appropriate Minister", for the words "section 224 of the Town and Country Planning Act 1971" there shall be substituted the words "section 265 of the Town and Country Planning Act 1990";
   (b) in paragraph (b) of the definition of "statutory undertakers", for the words "the Town and Country Planning Act 1971" there shall be substituted the words "the Town and Country Planning Act 1990".

The Local Government (Miscellaneous Provisions) Act 1976 (c. 57)

35.—(1) In section 7(5) of the Local Government (Miscellaneous Provisions) Act 1976—
   (a) in paragraph (a)(i), for the words "the Town and Country Planning Act 1971" there shall be substituted the words "the Town and Country Planning Act 1990";
   (b) in paragraph (a)(iii), for the words "section 87 of that Act" there shall be substituted the words "section 172 of that Act".
   (2) In section 15(9) of that Act, for the words "section 280(7) of the Town and Country Planning Act 1971" there shall be substituted the words "section 324(6) of the Town and Country Planning Act 1990, section 88(5) of the Planning (Listed Buildings and Conservation Areas) Act 1990".
   (3) In section 26(6) of that Act, for the words "section 222 of the Town and Country Planning Act 1971" there shall be substituted the words "section 263 of the Town and Country Planning Act 1990".

The Race Relations Act 1976 (c. 74)

36. In section 19A(3)(a) of the Race Relations Act 1976, for the words "the Town and Country Planning Act 1971" there shall be substituted the words "the Town and Country

Planning Act 1990, the Planning (Listed Buildings and Conservation Areas) Act 1990 and the Planning (Hazardous Substances) Act 1990".

The Development of Rural Wales Act 1976 (c. 75)

37.—(1) In section 30 of the Development of Rural Wales Act 1976, for the words "section 266(7) of the Town and Country Planning Act 1971" and "that subsection" there shall be substituted respectively the words "subsections (1) and (2) of section 293 of the Town and Country Planning Act 1990" and "those subsections".

(2) In Schedule 3 to that Act—
 (a) in paragraph 1—
  (i) in sub-paragraph (2), for the words "section 24 of the Town and Country Planning Act 1971" and "that section" there shall be substituted respectively the words "sections 59 to 61 of the Town and Country Planning Act 1990" and "section 59";
  (ii) in sub-paragraph (3), for the words "section 54(1) of the Town and Country Planning Act 1971" there shall be substituted the words "section 1 of the Planning (Listed Buildings and Conservation Areas) Act 1990";
  (iii) in sub-paragraph (6), for the words "paragraph 32 of Schedule 16 to the Local Government Act 1972" there shall be substituted the words "paragraph 1 of Schedule 1 to the Town and Country Planning Act 1990";
 (b) in the definition of "planning permission" in paragraph 56(1), for the words "Part III of the Town and Country Planning Act 1971" there shall be substituted the words "Part III of the Town and Country Planning Act 1990".

The Rent (Agriculture) Act 1976 (c. 80)

38. In section 33(4) of the Rent (Agriculture) Act 1976, for the words "section 32(1)(b) of the Town and Country Planning Act 1971" there shall be substituted the words "section 63(2)(b) of the Town and Country Planning Act 1990".

The Health Services Act 1976 (c. 83)

39.—(1) In section 12(1)(b) of the Health Services Act 1976, for the words "the Town and Country Planning Act 1971" there shall be substituted the words "the Town and Country Planning Act 1990".

(2) In section 15(5) of that Act—
 (a) in the definition of "local planning authority", for the words "the Town and Country Planning Act 1971" there shall be substituted the words "the Town and Country Planning Act 1990";
 (b) in the definition of "planning permission", for the words "the said Act of 1971" there shall be substituted the words "the said Act of 1990".

The National Health Service Act 1977 (c. 49)

40. For subsection (6) of section 87 of the National Health Service Act 1977 there shall be substituted—

 "(6) Sections 238 and 239 of the Town and Country Planning Act 1990 (use and development of consecrated land and burial grounds) shall apply to consecrated land or, as the case may be, land comprised in a burial ground (within the meaning of section 240 of that Act) which—
 (a) the Secretary of State holds for the purposes of the health service, and
 (b) has not been the subject of a relevant acquisition (within the meaning of that section) by the Secretary of State,
 as if that land had been the subject of such an acquisition by him for those purposes.".

The Refuse Disposal (Amenity) Act 1978 (c. 3)

41. In section 8 of the Refuse Disposal (Amenity) Act 1978—
 (a) in subsection (2)—
  (i) for the words "Section 281(1) to (5) of the Town and Country Planning Act 1971" there shall be substituted the words "Section 325(1) to (7) of the Town and Country Planning Act 1990";
  (ii) for the words "section 280", in both places where they occur, there shall be substituted the words "section 324";
 (b) in subsection (3), for the words from "Sections" to "1971" there shall be

substituted the words "Sections 320, 322, 323, 329 and 330 of the said Act of 1990".

The Estate Agents Act 1979 (c. 38)

42. In section 1(2)(e) of the Estate Agents Act 1979, for the words "the Town and Country Planning Act 1971" there shall be substituted the words "the Town and Country Planning Act 1990, the Planning (Listed Buildings and Conservation Areas) Act 1990, the Planning (Hazardous Substances) Act 1990".

The Ancient Monuments and Archaeological Areas Act 1979 (c. 46)

43.—(1) In section 32(1) of the Ancient Monuments and Archaeological Areas Act 1979—
   (a) for the words "the Town and Country Planning Act 1971" there shall be substituted the words "the Town and Country Planning Act 1990 or the Planning (Listed Buildings and Conservation Areas) Act 1990";
   (b) for the words "the said Act of 1971" there shall be substituted the words "the said Acts of 1990".
(2) In section 61 of that Act, in the definition of "works" in subsection (1) and in subsection (2)(b), for the words "the Town and Country Planning Act 1971" there shall be substituted the words "the Town and Country Planning Act 1990".

The Local Government, Planning and Land Act 1980 (c. 65)

44.—(1) In section 3(5)(c) of the Local Government, Planning and Land Act 1980, for the words "the Town and Country Planning Act 1971" there shall be substituted the words "the Town and Country Planning Act 1990".
(2) In section 99(6)(a) of that Act, for the words "the Town and Country Planning Act 1971" there shall be substituted the words "the Town and Country Planning Act 1990".
(3) In section 108 of that Act, in subsections (1)(b) and (2)(a), for the words "the 1971 Act" there shall be substituted the words "the 1990 Act".
(4) In section 109 of that Act—
   (a) in the definition of "agriculture" for the words "section 290 of the 1971 Act" there shall be substituted the words "section 336 of the 1990 Act";
   (b) in the definition of "development" for the words "section 22 of the 1971 Act" there shall be substituted the words "section 55 of the 1990 Act"; and
   (c) for the definition of "the 1971 Act" there shall be substituted the words " "the 1990 Act" means the Town and Country Planning Act 1990".
(5) In section 148 of that Act—
   (a) in subsection (2), for the words "section 24 of the 1971 Act" there shall be substituted the words "section 59 of the 1990 Act";
   (b) in subsection (3), for the words "section 54(1) of the 1971 Act" there shall be substituted the words "section 1 of the Planning (Listed Buildings and Conservation Areas) Act 1990";
   (c) in subsection (4)—
        (i) in paragraph (a), for the words "paragraph 32 of Schedule 16 to the Local Government Act 1972" there shall be substituted the words "paragraph 1 of Schedule 1 to the 1990 Act";
        (ii) in paragraph (b), for the words "Schedule 3 to the Town and Country Planning Act 1971" there shall be substituted the words "Part I of the 1990 Act".
(6) In section 149 of that Act—
   (a) in subsection (1) for the words "Part III of the 1971 Act" there shall be substituted the words "Part III of the 1990 Act";
   (b) in subsection (3)(a) for the words "the 1971 Act" there shall be substituted the words "the 1990 Act and the Planning (Listed Buildings and Conservation Areas) Act 1990";
   (c) in subsection (3)(b) for the words "the 1971 Act" there shall be substituted the words "those Acts".
(7) In section 170(1)(b) and (3)(a) of that Act for the words "the 1971 Act" there shall be substituted the words "the 1990 Act".
(8) In section 171 of that Act, for the word "1971" in both places where it occurs there shall be substituted the word "1990".
(9) In Schedule 20 to that Act—
   (a) in paragraph 12(6) for the words "Sections 238 and 240 of the 1971 Act" and

"section 237(2) of the 1971 Act" there shall be substituted respectively the words "Sections 280 and 282 of the 1990 Act" and "section 279(2) of the 1990 Act"; and

(b) in paragraph 14(8) for the words "Sections 238 and 240 of the 1971 Act" and "section 237(3) of the 1971 Act" there shall be substituted respectively the words "Sections 280 and 282 of the 1990 Act" and "section 279(4) of the 1990 Act".

(10) In Schedule 21 to that Act, in paragraph 15(2) for the words "section 266(7) of the 1971 Act" there shall be substituted the words "section 293(2) of the 1990 Act".

(11) In Schedule 28 to that Act—

(a) in paragraph 14(6) for the words "Sections 238 and 240 of the 1971 Act" and "section 237(2) of the 1971 Act" there shall be substituted respectively the words "Sections 280 and 282 of the 1990 Act" and "section 279(2) of the 1990 Act";

(b) in paragraph 16(8) for the words "Sections 238 and 240 of the 1971 Act" and "section 237(3) of the 1971 Act" there shall be substituted respectively the words "Sections 280 and 282 of the 1990 Act" and "section 279(4) of the 1990 Act".

(12) In Schedule 29 to that Act for the enactments referred to in Part I there shall be substituted—

"Sections 172, 173, 178, 183, 184, 188, 197, 198, 199, 201, 206, 207, 209, 211, 213 to 215, 219, 220 and 224 of the 1990 Act.

Sections 3, 4, 8, 10, 11, 13 to 16, 20, 23 to 25, 38, 42, 47, 48, 50, 53, 54, 60, 69 to 72, 74, 75 and 82 of the Planning (Listed Buildings and Conservation Areas) Act 1990."

(13) For paragraphs 1 to 9 of Part II of that Schedule there shall be substituted—

"1. Section 139 of the 1990 Act shall have effect as if after the word "undertakers" there were inserted—

(a) in paragraph (b) of subsection (1), the words "or an urban development corporation";

(b) in paragraph (c) of that subsection, the words "or any urban development corporation"; and

(c) in subsection (3), the words "or urban development corporation".

2. Section 140(2)(d) of that Act shall have effect as if after the word "undertakers" there were inserted the words "or an urban development corporation".

3. Section 141(4) of that Act shall have effect as if after the word "undertakers" there were inserted the words "or an urban development corporation".

4. Section 143(1)(b) of that Act shall have effect as if—

(a) after the word "undertakers" in the first place where it occurs, there were inserted the words "or an urban development corporation"; and

(b) after that word, in the second place where it occurs, there were inserted the words "or that corporation".

5. The definition of "relevant provisions" in section 148 of that Act shall have effect as if after the word "undertaking" there were added the words "or, in the case of an urban development corporation, section 142 of the Local Government, Planning and Land Act 1980.".

6. Section 249 of that Act shall have effect as if—

(a) in subsection (1) after the word "applies" there were inserted the words "subject to subsection (1A)"; and

(b) the following subsection were inserted after that subsection—

"(1A) Any reference in this section and in section 250 to a local planning authority is to be construed as including a reference to an urban development corporation."

7. Section 251 of that Act shall have effect as if—

(a) in subsection (1), for the word "Where" there were substituted the words "Subject to subsection (1A), where"; and

(b) the following subsection were inserted after that subsection—

"(1A) Where any land has been acquired by an urban development corporation or has vested in such a corporation and is for the time being held by them for the purpose of regenerating their area, the Secretary of State may by order extinguish any public right of way over the land if he is satisfied that an alternative right of way has been or will be provided or that the provision of an alternative right of way is not required.".

8. Section 258 of that Act shall have effect as if—

(a) in subsection (1), for the word "Where" there were substituted the words "Subject to subsection (1A), where"; and

(b) the following subsection were inserted after that subsection—

"(1A) Where any land has been acquired by an urban development corporation or has vested in such a corporation and is for the time being held by them for the purpose of regenerating their area, then, subject to section 259, the urban development corporation may by order extinguish any public right of way over the land being a footpath or bridleway, if they are satisfied that an alternative right of way has been or will be provided or that the provision of an alternative right of way is not required.".

9. Section 330 of that Act shall have effect as if—

   (a) after the words "local authority" in the first place where they occur in subsection (1), there were inserted the words "or an urban development corporation"; and

   (b) after those words, in the second place where they occur in subsection (1) and in subsection (3), there were inserted the words "or corporation".

10. Section 33 of the Planning (Listed Buildings and Conservation Areas) Act 1990 shall have effect as if—

   (a) in subsection (1)(b) after the word "undertakers" there were inserted the words "or an urban development corporation";

   (b) in subsection (1)(c), after the word "undertakers" there were inserted the words "or an urban development corporation";

   (c) in subsection (3), after the word "undertakers" there were inserted the words "or corporation".

11. Section 34(2)(d) of that Act shall have effect as if after the word "undertakers" there were inserted the words "or an urban development corporation".

12. Section 35(6) of that Act shall have effect as if after the word "undertakers" there were inserted the words "or an urban development corporation".

13. Section 36(4) of that Act shall have effect as if after the word "undertakers" in the first place where it occurs there were inserted the words "or an urban development corporation" and in the second place where it occurs there were inserted the words "or that corporation".

14. Section 91(2) of that Act shall have effect as if the words "urban development corporation" were inserted at the appropriate place."

(14) In Schedule 32 to that Act—

   (a) in paragraph 7(2) for the words "subsection (9) of section 280 and subsections (1) to (6) of section 281 of the 1971 Act" and "to section 280" there shall be substituted respectively the words "subsection (8) of section 324 and section 325 of the 1990 Act" and "to section 324";

   (b) in paragraph 8, for the word "1971", in both places where it occurs, there shall be substituted the word "1990";

   (c) in paragraph 17—

       (i) in sub-paragraph (1) after the word "zone" there shall be inserted the words "in Scotland";

       (ii) in sub-paragraph (2) after the word "scheme" there shall be inserted the words "as respects land in Scotland";

    *(d) in paragraph 26—

       (i) in sub-paragraph (1) for the words "the 1971 Act", in the first place where they occur, there shall be substituted the words "the 1990 Act, the Planning (Listed Buildings and Conservation Areas) Act 1990, the Planning (Hazardous Substances) Act 1990";

       (ii) in that sub-paragraph for the definition of "the 1971 Act" there shall be substituted the words " "the 1990 Act" means the Town and Country Planning Act 1990"; and

       (iii) in sub-paragraph (2)(a) for the word "1971" there shall be substituted the word "1990".

The Highways Act 1980 (c. 66)

45.—(1) In section 21 of the Highways Act 1980—

   (a) in subsection (1)—

       (i) for the words "sections 230 to 232 of the Town and Country Planning Act 1971" there shall be substituted the words "sections 271 to 274 of the Town and Country Planning Act 1990";

       (ii) for the words "Part VI of that Act" there shall be substituted the words "Part IX of that Act";

---

* Misprinted in Queen's Printer's copy as 44(14)(f).

(iii) for the words "sections 237(2) and (3), 238 and 240, which provide for the payment of compensation, and sections 233 to 236, which contain provisions consequential on the extinguishment of any rights under section 230" there shall be substituted the words "sections 279(2) to (4), 280 and 282, which provide for the payment of compensation, and sections 275 to 278 which contain provisions consequential on the extinguishment of any rights under section 271 or 272";

(b) in subsection (3), for the words "the said Act of 1971" there shall be substituted the words "the said Act of 1990";

(c) in subsection (4), for the words "section 230 or 232 of the said Act of 1971" there shall be substituted the words "section 271, 272 or 273 of the said Act of 1990".

(2) In section 25(2)(a) of that Act, for the words "the Town and Country Planning Act 1971" there shall be substituted the words "the Town and Country Planning Act 1990".

(3) In section 36(2)(d) of that Act, for the words "section 209 of the Town and Country Planning Act 1971 or by a competent authority under section 210 of that Act" there shall be substituted the words "section 247 of the Town and Country Planning Act 1990 or by a competent authority under section 257 of that Act".

(4) In section 80(3)(c) of that Act, for the words "the Town and Country Planning Act 1971" there shall be substituted the words "the Town and Country Planning Act 1990".

(5) In section 105A(4)(b) of that Act for the words "the Town and Country Planning Act 1971" there shall be substituted the words "the Planning (Listed Buildings and Conservation Areas) Act 1990".

(6) In the definition of "pedestrian planning order" in section 115A(2) of that Act, for the words "section 212(2) of the Town and Country Planning Act 1971" there shall be substituted the words "section 249(2) of the Town and Country Planning Act 1990".

(7) In sections 115H(1)(b)(ii), 118(7) and 123(2) of that Act, for the words "the Town and Country Planning Act 1971" there shall be substituted the words "the Town and Country Planning Act 1990".

(8) In section 125 of that Act—

(a) in subsections (1) and (2)(a), for the words "section 211 of the Town and Country Planning Act 1971" there shall be substituted the words "section 248 of the Town and Country Planning Act 1990";

(b) in subsection (4) for the words "Section 215 of the Town and Country Planning Act 1971", "section 211 of that Act" and "section 215(2) and (7)" there shall be substituted respectively the words "Section 252 of the Town and Country Planning Act 1990", "section 248 of that Act" and "section 252(2), (3), (10) and (11)".

(9) In section 126(1)(b) of that Act, for the words "section 211 of the Town and Country Planning Act 1971" there shall be substituted the words "section 248 of the Town and Country Planning Act 1990".

(10) In section 166(3) of that Act for the words "section 290(1) of the Town and Country Planning Act 1971" there shall be substituted the words "section 336(1) of the Town and Country Planning Act 1990".

(11) In sections 184(3) and 203(2)(b)(i) of that Act, for the words "the Town and Country Planning Act 1971" there shall be substituted the words "the Town and Country Planning Act 1990".

(12) In section 232 of that Act—

(a) in subsection (8), for the words "the Town and Country Planning Act 1971" there shall be substituted the words "the Town and Country Planning Act 1990";

(b) in subsection (9), in the definition of "development plan", for the words "section 20 of the Town and Country Planning Act 1971" there shall be substituted the words "sections 27 and 54 of the Town and Country Planning Act 1990".

(13) In section 246(2) of that Act—

(a) for the words "section 192(3) to (5) of the Town and Country Planning Act 1971" there shall be substituted the words "subsection (2) of section 149 of the Town and Country Planning Act 1990";

(b) for the word "references", in the first place where it occurs, there shall be substituted the words "the reference in subsection (4) of that section"; and

(c) for the words "section 193 of that Act as references" there shall be substituted the words "section 150 of that Act as a reference".

(14) In section 253(5) of that Act, for the words "section 52 of the Town and Country Planning Act 1971" there shall be substituted the words "section 106 of the Town and Country Planning Act 1990".

(15) In section 262 of that Act—
    (a) in subsection (1)—
        (i) in paragraph (b), for the words "section 180, 188 or 189 of the Town and Country Planning Act 1971" there shall be substituted the words "section 137 of the Town and Country Planning Act 1990";
        (ii) in paragraph (c), for the words "section 193 of that Act or section 78 of the Land Compensation Act 1973" and "section 196 of the said Act of 1971" there shall be substituted respectively the words "section 150 or 161 of that Act" and "section 154 of that Act";
    (b) in subsection (2)—
        (i) in paragraph (b), for the words "section 180, 188 or 189 of the Town and Country Planning Act 1971" there shall be substituted the words "section 137 of the Town and Country Planning Act 1990";
        (ii) in paragraph (c), for the words "section 193 of that Act or section 78 of the Land Compensation Act 1973" there shall be substituted the words "section 150 or 161 of that Act" and for the words "section 196 of the said Act of 1971" there shall be substituted the words "section 154 of that Act";
(16) In section 272(1)(i) of that Act, for the words "section 211 of the Town and Country Planning Act 1971" there shall be substituted the words "section 248 of the Town and Country Planning Act 1990".
(17) In the definition of "local planning authority" in section 329(1) of that Act, for the words "the Town and Country Planning Act 1971" there shall be substituted the words "the Town and Country Planning Act 1990".
(18) In section 337 of that Act, for the words "section 23 of the Town and Country Planning Act 1971" there shall be substituted the words "section 57 of the Town and Country Planning Act 1990".
(19) In Schedule 5 to that Act—
    (a) in the heading of that Schedule for the words "the Town and Country Planning Act 1971" there shall be substituted the words "the Town and Country Planning Act 1990";
    (b) in paragraph 1 of Part I for the words from "sections" to "Act")" there shall be substituted the words "sections 271, 272, 274, 279(2) to (4), 280 and 282 of the Town and Country Planning Act 1990 (referred to in this Schedule as "the 1990 Act")";
    (c) for paragraph 2 of that Part there shall be substituted—
        "2. In subsection (2) of section 271 and of section 272 for the words from "any development" to "appropriated" substitute "any works in pursuance of the scheme or order, or as the case may be, for the purpose of ensuring that the highway can be safely used as a special road". ";
    (d) in paragraph 3 of that Part for the words from "subsection (4)" to "section 231" there shall be substituted the words "subsection (5) of the said section 271 and of the said section 272 and subsections (2) and (3) of the said section 274";
    (e) in paragraph 4 of that Part for the words "section 232(1) of the 1971 Act" there shall be substituted the words "section 273(1) of the 1990 Act";
    (f) in paragraphs 5 and 6 of that Part for the words "section 232" there shall be substituted the words "section 273";
    (g) in paragraph 1 of Part II for the words from "sections" to "1971 Act" there shall be substituted the words "sections 271, 272, 274, 279(2) to (4), 280 and 282 of the 1990 Act";
    (h) for paragraph 2 of that Part there shall be substituted—
        "2. In subsection (2) of section 271 and of section 272 for the words from "is necessary" to "appropriated" substitute "is made necessary by the works in connection with which the stopping up or diversion of the highway is or was authorised". ";
    (i) in paragraph 3 of that Part for the words from "subsection (4)" to "section 231" there shall be substituted the words "subsection (5) of the said section 271 and of the said section 272 and subsections (2) and (3) of the said section 274";
    (j) in paragraph 4 of that Part for the words "section 232 of the 1971 Act" there shall be substituted the words "section 273 of the 1990 Act";
    (k) in paragraph 5 of that Part for the words "the said section 232" there shall be substituted the words "the said section 273".

The Water Act 1981 (c. 12)

46. In section 6(7)(c)(i) of the Water Act 1981, for the words "section 290(1) of the Town and Country Planning Act 1971" there shall be substituted the words "section 336(1) of the Town and Country Planning Act 1990".

The English Industrial Estates Corporation Act 1981 (c. 13)

47. In section 9(3) of the English Industrial Estates Corporation Act 1981, for the words "section 29 of the Town and Country Planning Act 1971" there shall be substituted the words "section 70 of the Town and Country Planning Act 1990".

The Disused Burial Grounds (Amendment) Act 1981 (c. 18)

48. In section 7 of the Disused Burial Grounds (Amendment) Act 1981, for the words "the Town and Country Planning Acts 1971 and 1972" there shall be substituted the words "the planning Acts (within the meaning of the Town and Country Planning Act 1990)".

The Zoo Licensing Act 1981 (c. 37)

49. In section 4(6) of the Zoo Licensing Act 1981, for the words "the Town and Country Planning Act 1971" and "the said Act of 1971" there shall be substituted respectively the words "the Town and Country Planning Act 1990" and "the said Act of 1990".

The Transport Act 1981 (c. 56)

50. In paragraph 9 of Schedule 4 to the Transport Act 1981, for the words "section 290(1) of the Town and Country Planning Act 1971" there shall be substituted the words "section 262(1) of the Town and Country Planning Act 1990".

The New Towns Act 1981 (c. 64)

51.—(1) In section 7 of the New Towns Act 1981—
   (a) in subsection (2) for the words "section 24 of the Town and Country Planning Act 1971" and "section 24 of that Act of 1971" there shall be substituted respectively the words "section 59 of the Town and Country Planning Act 1990" and "sections 59 to 61 of that Act of 1990"; and
   (b) in subsection (3) for the words "paragraph 32 of Schedule 16 to the Local Government Act 1972" there shall be substituted the words "paragraph 1 of Schedule 1 to the Town and Country Planning Act 1990".

(2) In section 8 of that Act, for the words "section 54(1) of the Town and Country Planning Act 1971" there shall be substituted the words "section 1 of the Planning (Listed Buildings and Conservation Areas) Act 1990".

(3) In the definition of "planning permission" in section 80(1) of that Act, for the words "the Town and Country Planning Act 1971" there shall be substituted the words "the Town and Country Planning Act 1990".

(4) In paragraph 3(3)(a) of Schedule 10 to that Act, for the words "section 24 of the Town and Country Planning Act 1971" there shall be substituted the words "section 59 of the Town and Country Planning Act 1990".

The Compulsory Purchase (Vesting Declarations) Act 1981 (c. 66)

52.—(1) In section 2(3) of the Compulsory Purchase (Vesting Declarations) Act 1981, for the words "Section 284 of the Town and Country Planning Act 1971" there shall be substituted the words "Section 330 of the Town and Country Planning Act 1990".

(2) In section 6(2) of that Act, for the words "Section 283 of the Town and Country Planning Act 1971" there shall be substituted the words "Section 329 of the Town and Country Planning Act 1990".

(3) In section 11(6) of that Act, for the words "section 290(1) of the Town and Country Planning Act 1971" there shall be substituted the words "section 336(1) of the Town and Country Planning Act 1990".

The Acquisition of Land Act 1981 (c. 67)

53.—(1) In the definition of "listed building" in section 20(5) of the Acquisition of Land Act 1981, for the words "section 54 of the Town and Country Planning Act 1971" there shall be substituted the words "section 1 of the Planning (Listed Buildings and Conservation Areas) Act 1990".

(2) In section 31 of that Act—
    (a) in subsection (1)(a), for the words "the Town and Country Planning Act 1971" there shall be substituted the words "the Town and Country Planning Act 1990 or the Planning (Listed Buildings and Conservation Areas) Act 1990";
    (b) in subsection (4), for the words "sections 238 to 240 of the Town and Country Planning Act 1971" and "section 238(1)(c)" there shall be substituted respectively the words "sections 280 to 282 of the Town and Country Planning Act 1990" and "section 280(1)(c)".

(3) In section 32(7) of that Act, for the words "section 214 of the Town and Country Planning Act 1971" there shall be substituted the words "section 251 or 258 of the Town and Country Planning Act 1990".

(4) In the definition of "listed building" in paragraph 7(5) of Schedule 3 to that Act, for the words "section 54 of the Town and Country Planning Act 1971" there shall be substituted the words "section 1 of the Planning (Listed Buildings and Conservation Areas) Act 1990".

The Wildlife and Countryside Act 1981 (c. 69)

54.—(1) In sections 28(8)(a), 29(9)(a) and 34(5) of the Wildlife and Countryside Act 1981, for the words "Part III of the Town and Country Planning Act 1971" there shall be substituted the words "Part III of the Town and Country Planning Act 1990".

(2) In section 70A of that Act—
    (a) in subsection (1), for the words "section 283 of the Town and Country Planning Act 1971" there shall be substituted the words "section 329 of the Town and Country Planning Act 1990";
    (b) in subsection (2), for the words "Subsections (2) and (3) of the said section 283" there shall be substituted the words "Subsections (2) and (3) of the said section 329".

The Civil Aviation Act 1982 (c. 16)

55.—(1) In section 48(9) of the Civil Aviation Act 1982, for the words "subsections (1) and (2) of section 220 of the Town and Country Planning Act 1971" and "section 209 of the said Act of 1971" there shall be substituted respectively the words "subsections (1) to (4) of section 256 of the Town and Country Planning Act 1990" and "section 247 of the said Act of 1990".

(2) In section 51 of that Act—
    (a) in subsection (2)(a), for the words "section 238(2), (3), (5) and (6) of the Town and Country Planning Act 1971" there shall be substituted the words "section 280(2) to (5), (7) and (8) of the Town and Country Planning Act 1990";
    (b) in subsection (5)—
        (i) for the words "Subsections (2), (3), (5) and (6) of the said sections 238 and" there shall be substituted the words "Subsections (2) to (5), (7) and (8) of the said section 280 and subsections (2), (3), (5) and (6) of the said section";
        (ii) in paragraph (a), for the words "section 238" and "section 237(2)" there shall be substituted respectively the words "section 280" and "section 279(2) or (3)";
        (iii) in paragraph (c), for the words "subsection (6) of each of the said sections" there shall be substituted the words "subsection (8) of the said section 280 and subsection (6) of the said section 227";
    (c) in subsection (7), for the words "sections 233 to 235 of the Town and Country Planning Act 1971" there shall be substituted the words "sections 275 to 277 of the Town and Country Planning Act 1990".

(3) In section 53 of that Act—
    (a) in subsection (1)—
        (i) in paragraph (a), for the words "section 164, 165, 169, 187(2) or 237(1) of the Town and Country Planning Act 1971" there shall be substituted the words "section 107, 108, 114, 144(2) or 279(1) of the Town and Country Planning Act 1990";
        (ii) in paragraph (b), for the words "the said section 164" and "section 45 of the said Act of 1971" there shall be substituted respectively the words "the said section 107" and "section 97 of the said Act of 1990";
    (b) in subsection (2), for the words "section 168 of the said Act of 1971" there shall be substituted the words "sections 111 and 112 of the said Act of 1990";
    (c) in subsection (3) for the words "section 180 of the said Act of 1971" and "section 181(2) or 186(1) of the said Act of 1971" there shall be substituted respectively

the words "section 137 of the said Act of 1990" and "section 139(3) or 143(1) of the said Act of 1990";

(d) in subsection (5), for the words "the said section 45" there shall be substituted the words "the said section 97";

(e) in subsection (6), for the words "the said Act of 1971" there shall be substituted the words "the said Act of 1990".

(4) In section 54 of that Act—

(a) in subsection (1) for the words "section 128 of the Town and Country Planning Act 1971" and "Part VI of the said Act of 1971" there shall be substituted respectively the words "sections 238 to 240 of the Town and Country Planning Act 1990" and "Part IX of the said Act of 1990";

(b) in subsection (2) for the words "The said sections 128" and "Part VI of the said Act of 1971" there shall be substituted respectively the words "The said sections 238 to 240" and "Part IX of the said Act of 1990".

(5) In Schedule 10 to that Act—

(a) in paragraph 4—

(i) for the words "section 236 of the Town and Country Planning Act 1971" there shall be substituted the words "section 278 of the Town and Country Planning Act 1990";

(ii) in sub-paragraph (a), for the words "the said section 236 to section 233 of the said Act of 1971" there shall be substituted the words "the said section 278 to section 275 or 276 of the said Act of 1990";

(iii) in sub-paragraph (c), the words from "either" to "or" shall be omitted;

(b) in paragraph 8—

(i) for the words "section 236 of the Town and Country Planning Act 1971" there shall be substituted the words "section 278 of the Town and Country Planning Act 1990";

(ii) in sub-paragraph (a), for the words "the said section 236 to section 235 of the said Act of 1971" there shall be substituted the words "the said section 278 to section 277 of the said Act of 1990";

(iii) in sub-paragraph (c), the words from "either" to "or" shall be omitted.

The Local Government (Miscellaneous Provisions) Act 1982 (c. 30)

56.—(1) In section 33(9)(a) of the Local Government (Miscellaneous Provisions) Act 1982, for the words "section 1 of the Town and Country Planning Act 1971" there shall be substituted the words "section 2 of the Town and Country Planning Act 1990".

(2) In section 37(8) of that Act, for the words "Part III of the Town and Country Planning Act 1971" there shall be substituted the words "Part III of the Town and Country Planning Act 1990".

(3) In paragraph (b) of the definition of "local authority" in section 41(13) and in section 45(2)(b) of that Act, for the words "section 1 of the Town and Country Planning Act 1971" there shall be substituted the words "section 2 of the Town and Country Planning Act 1990".

The Industrial Development Act 1982 (c. 52)

57. In section 14(6) of the Industrial Development Act 1982, for the words "subsection (9) of section 280 and subsections (1) to (4) and (6) of section 281 of the Town and Country Planning Act 1971" and "the said section 280" there shall be substituted respectively the words "subsection (8) of section 324 and subsections (1) to (6), (8) and (9) of section 325 of the Town and Country Planning Act 1990" and "the said section 324".

The Conwy Tunnel (Supplementary Powers) Act 1983 (c. 7)

58.—(1) In the definition of "Crown land" in section 22(1) of the Conwy Tunnel (Supplementary Powers) Act 1983, for the words "Part XIV of the Town and Country Planning Act 1971" there shall be substituted the words "Part XIII of the Town and Country Planning Act 1990".

(2) In paragraph 8(1) of Schedule 1 to that Act—

(a) for the words "Sections 230 to 232 of the Town and Country Planning Act 1971" there shall be substituted the words "Sections 271 to 274 of the Town and Country Planning Act 1990";

(b) for the words "section 230(1) of that Act" there shall be substituted the words "section 271(1) or 272(1) of that Act";

(c) for the words "section 230(1) and 232(1)" there shall be substituted the words "sections 271(2), 272(2) and 273(1)";

    (d) for the words "section 232(2)" there shall be substituted the words "section 273(2)";

    (e) for the words "sections 230 to 232 (including sections 237(2) and (3), 238 and 240, which provide for the payment of compensation, and sections 233 to 236, which contain provisions consequential on the extinguishment of any rights under section 230)" there shall be substituted the words "sections 271 to 274 (including sections 279(2) to (4), 280 and 282, which provide for the payment of compensation, and sections 275 to 278 which contain provisions consequential on the extinguishment of any rights under section 271 or 272)".

  (3) In paragraph 1(2) of Schedule 3 to that Act, for the words "section 230(1)(b) of the Town and Country Planning Act 1971" there shall be substituted the words "paragraph (b) of section 271(1) or of section 272(1) of the Town and Country Planning Act 1990".

The Mobile Homes Act 1983 (c. 34)

59. In the definition of "planning permission" in section 5(1) of the Mobile Homes Act 1983, for the words "Part III of the Town and Country Planning Act 1971" there shall be substituted the words "Part III of the Town and Country Planning Act 1990".

The National Heritage Act 1983 (c. 47)

60. In the definition of "conservation area" in section 33(8) of the National Heritage Act 1983, for the words "section 277 of the Town and Country Planning Act 1971" there shall be substituted the words "section 69 of the Planning (Listed Buildings and Conservation Areas) Act 1990".

The Value Added Tax Act 1983 (c. 55)

61. In Group 8A of Schedule 5 to the Value Added Tax Act 1983—

    (a) in Note (1)(a)(i) for the words "the Town and Country Planning Act 1971" there shall be substituted the words "the Planning (Listed Buildings and Conservation Areas) Act 1990";

    (b) in Note (3)(c)(i) for the words "Part IV of the Town and Country Planning Act 1971" there shall be substituted the words "Part I of the Planning (Listed Buildings and Conservation Areas) Act 1990".

The Town and Country Planning Act 1984 (c. 10)

62.—(1) In section 1(4) of the Town and Country Planning Act 1984, for the words "of each of the sections" there shall be substituted the words "of the section".

  (2) In section 6(1) of that Act for the words "the said section 266(7)" there shall be substituted the words "section 293(1) and (2) of the Town and Country Planning Act 1990".

The Telecommunications Act 1984 (c. 12)

63.—(1) In section 34(4) of the Telecommunications Act 1984, for the words "the Town and Country Planning Act 1971", "section 128", "section 129" and "sections 230 to 232" there shall be substituted respectively the words "the Town and Country Planning Act 1990", "sections 238 to 240", "section 241" and "sections 271 to 274".

  (2) In section 37 of that Act—

    (a) in subsection (2) for the words "Sections 280(9) and 281(1) to (3) and (6) of the Town and Country Planning Act 1971", "section 280(1) to (8)", "the said section 280," "section 280(9)" and "section 281(1)" there shall be substituted respectively the words "Sections 324(8), 325(1) to (5), (8) and (9) of the Town and Country Planning Act 1990", "section 324(1) to (7)", "the said section 324", "section 324(8)" and "section 325(1)";

    (b) in subsection (4) for the words "Section 179 of the said Act of 1971" and "Part VIII of that Act" there shall be substituted respectively the words "Section 118 of the said Act of 1990" and "Part IV of that Act".

The Road Traffic Regulation Act 1984 (c. 27)

64.—(1) In section 75(3)(b) of the Road Traffic Regulation Act 1984, for the words "section 54 of the Town and Country Planning Act 1971" there shall be substituted the words "section 1 of the Planning (Listed Buildings and Conservation Areas) Act 1990".

  (2) In Schedule 4 to that Act—

    (a) in paragraph 12(2), for the words "any specified operation within the meaning

of section 43(1) of the Town and Country Planning Act 1971" there shall be substituted the words "any material operation within the meaning of section 56(4) of the Town and Country Planning Act 1990";
  (b) in paragraph 20(a)(ii), for the words "section 290(1) of the Town and Country Planning Act 1971" there shall be substituted the words "section 336(1) of the Town and Country Planning Act 1990";
  (c) in paragraph 22—
      (i) in sub-paragraph (4) for the words "Section 178 of the Town and Country Planning Act 1971" there shall be substituted the words "Section 117 of the Town and Country Planning Act 1990";
      (ii) in sub-paragraph (5) for the words "section 45 or 51 of the said Act of 1971" and "section 164 or, as the case may be, section 170 of that Act" there shall be substituted respectively the words "section 97 or 102 of or paragraph 1 of Schedule 9 to the said Act of 1990" and "section 107 or, as the case may be, section 115 of that Act".

The London Regional Transport Act 1984 (c. 32)

65. In section 7(9) of the London Regional Transport Act 1984, for the words "section 20 of the Town and Country Planning Act 1971" there shall be substituted the words "sections 27 and 54 of the Town and Country Planning Act 1990".

The Cycle Tracks Act 1984 (c. 38)

66. In section 3(10) of the Cycle Tracks Act 1984 for the words "the Town and Country Planning Act 1971" there shall be substituted the words "the Town and Country Planning Act 1990".

The Building Act 1984 (c. 55)

67.—(1) In section 19(1) of the Building Act 1984, for the words "the Town and Country Planning Act 1971" there shall be substituted the words "the Town and Country Planning Act 1990".
  (2) In section 20(1) of that Act, for the words "Part III or IV of the Town and Country Planning Act 1971" there shall be substituted the words "Part III or Part VIII of the Town and Country Planning Act 1990 or under the Planning (Listed Buildings and Conservation Areas) Act 1990 or the Planning (Hazardous Substances) Act 1990".
  (3) In section 77(3) of that Act, for the words "the Town and Country Planning Act 1971" and "orders" there shall be substituted respectively the words "the Planning (Listed Buildings and Conservation Areas) Act 1990" and "notices".
  (4) In section 79 of that Act—
      (a) in subsection (4), for the words "section 290(1) of the Town and Country Planning Act 1971" there shall be substituted the words "section 336(1) of the Town and Country Planning Act 1990";
      (b) in subsection (5), for the words "the Town and Country Planning Act 1971" and "orders" there shall be substituted respectively the words "the Planning (Listed Buildings and Conservation Areas) Act 1990" and "notices".

The Town and Country Planning (Compensation) Act 1985 (c. 19)

68. In section 3 of the Town and Country Planning (Compensation) Act 1985—
      (a) in subsection (2) for the words "Sections 1(1) and 2(1) above have" there shall be substituted the words "Section 2(1) above has"; and
      (b) in subsection (3) for the words "Sections 1(2) and 2(2) above have" there shall be substituted the words "Section 2(2) above has".

The Local Government Act 1985 (c. 51)

69.—(1) In section 3(5) of the Local Government Act 1985 for the words from the beginning to "that Schedule" there shall be substituted the words "In paragraph 55(1) of Schedule 16 to the Local Government Act 1972".
  (2) In Schedule 13 to that Act—
      (a) in paragraph 13(d), for the words "section 215 of the Town and Country Planning Act 1971" there shall be substituted the words "section 252 of the Town and Country Planning Act 1990";
      (b) in paragraph 19, for the words "paragraph 1(3) of Schedule 20 to the Town and

Country Planning Act 1971" there shall be substituted the words "paragraph 1(3) of Schedule 14 to the Town and Country Planning Act 1990".

The Town and Country Planning (Amendment) Act 1985 (c. 52)

70. In section 3(4) of the Town and Country Planning (Amendment) Act 1985 for the words "sections 1 and 2" there shall be substituted the words "section 2".

The Housing Act 1985 (c. 68)

71.—(1) In section 256 of the Housing Act 1985—
  (a) in subsection (1) for the words "section 212 of the Town and Country Planning Act 1971" there shall be substituted the words "sections 249 and 250 of the Town and Country Planning Act 1990";
  (b) in subsection (2) for the words "subsection (2) or (8) of that section" there shall be substituted the words "subsection (2) or (6) of section 249";
  (c) in subsection (4) for the words "subsection (2) of that section" and "subsection (5) of that section" there shall be substituted respectively the words "subsection (2) of section 249" and "subsection (1) of section 250".

(2) In section 303 of that Act, for the words "section 54 of the Town and Country Planning Act 1971" there shall be substituted the words "section 1 of the Planning (Listed Buildings and Conservation Areas) Act 1990".

(3) In section 305 of that Act—
  (a) in subsection (1), for the words "under section 55 of the Town and Country Planning Act 1971 (listed building consent) for his consent" there shall be substituted the words "for his consent under section 8 of the Planning (Listed Buildings and Conservation Areas) Act 1990";
  (b) in subsection (6)(a) and (b), for the words "Part VI of the Town and Country Planning Act 1971" there shall be substituted the words "Part IX of the Town and Country Planning Act 1990";

(4) In section 306 of that Act—
  (a) in subsection (1), for the words "under section 55 of the Town and Country Planning Act 1971 for his consent" there shall be substituted the words "for his consent under section 8 of the Planning (Listed Buildings and Conservation Areas) Act 1990";
  (b) in subsection (2)(b), for the words "Part VI of the Town and Country Planning Act 1971" there shall be substituted the words "Part IX of the Town and Country Planning Act 1990".

(5) In section 610(1)(b) of that Act, for the words "the Town and Country Planning Act 1971" there shall be substituted the words "the Town and Country Planning Act 1990".

(6) In paragraph 3(2) of Schedule 1 to that Act, for the words "section 22 of the Town and Country Planning Act 1971" there shall be substituted the words "section 55 of the Town and Country Planning Act 1990".

The Agricultural Holdings Act 1986 (c. 5)

72. In paragraph 8(2) of Part II of Schedule 3 to the Agricultural Holdings Act 1986, for the words "section 30A(2) of the Town and Country Planning Act 1971" there shall be substituted the words "section 336(1) of the Town and Country Planning Act 1990".

The Airports Act 1986 (c. 31)

73.—(1) In section 59(6) of the Airports Act 1986, for the words "section 128 of the Town and Country Planning Act 1971" and "Part VI of that Act of 1971" there shall be substituted respectively the words "sections 238 to 240 of the Town and Country Planning Act 1990" and "Part IX of that Act of 1990".
  (2) In section 61 of that Act—
    (a) in subsection (1)—
       (i) in paragraph (a), for the words "section 164, 165, 169, 187(2), or 237(1) of the Town and Country Planning Act 1971 ("the 1971 Act")" there shall be substituted the words "section 107, 108, 114, 144(2) or 279(1) of the Town and Country Planning Act 1990 ("the 1990 Act")";
       (ii) in paragraph (b), for the words "section 164 of the 1971 Act" and "section 45 of the 1971 Act" there shall be substituted respectively the words "section 107 of the 1990 Act" and "section 97 of the 1990 Act";

(b) in subsection (2), for the words "section 168 of the 1971 Act" there shall be substituted the words "sections 111 and 112 of the 1990 Act";

(c) in subsection (3) for the words "section 180 of the 1971 Act" and "section 181(2) or 186(1) of the 1971 Act" there shall be substituted respectively the words "section 137 of the 1990 Act" and "section 139(3) or 143(1) of the 1990 Act";

(d) in subsection (5), for the words "section 45 of the 1971 Act" there shall be substituted the words "section 97 of the 1990 Act";

(e) in subsection (6), for the words "the 1971 Act" there shall be substituted the words "the 1990 Act".

The Finance Act 1986 (c. 41)

74. In paragraph (a) of the definition of "the relevant planning enactment" in paragraph 1(1) of Schedule 13 to the Finance Act 1986, for the words "section 290(1) of the Town and Country Planning Act 1971" there shall be substituted the words "section 336(1) of the Town and Country Planning Act 1990".

The Channel Tunnel Act 1987 (c. 53)

75. In Part III of Schedule 2 to the Channel Tunnel Act 1987, in paragraph 27(8) for the words "section 290(1) of the Town and Country Planning Act 1971" there shall be substituted the words "section 336(1) of the Town and Country Planning Act 1990".

The Norfolk and Suffolk Broads Act 1988 (c. 4)

76. In section 25(1) of the Norfolk and Suffolk Broads Act 1988, in paragraph (a) of the definition of "statutory undertaker" for the words "the Town and Country Planning Act 1971" there shall be substituted the words "the Town and Country Planning Act 1990".

The Dartford-Thurrock Crossing Act 1988 (c. 20)

77. In section 30 of the Dartford-Thurrock Crossing Act 1988, for the words "the Town and Country Planning Act 1971" there shall be substituted the words "the Town and Country Planning Act 1990".

The Education Reform Act 1988 (c. 40)

78. In section 90(2) of the Education Reform Act 1988, for the words "the Town and Country Planning Act 1971" there shall be substituted the words "the Town and Country Planning Act 1990".

The Housing Act 1988 (c. 50)

79.—(1) In section 28(6) of the Housing Act 1988, for the words "has the same meaning as in section 43(3) of the Town and Country Planning Act 1971" there shall be substituted the words "has the meaning given in section 56(6) of the Town and Country Planning Act 1990".

(2) In section 66 of that Act—

(a) in subsection (2) for the words "section 24 of the 1971 Act" and "that section" there shall be substituted respectively the words "sections 59 to 61 of the 1990 Act" and "section 59";

(b) in subsection (3) for the words "section 54(1) of the 1971 Act" there shall be substituted the words "section 1 of the Planning (Listed Buildings and Conservation Areas) Act 1990";

(c) in subsection (4)(a) for the words "section 1 of the 1971 Act" there shall be substituted the words "sections 1 and 2 of the 1990 Act";

(d) in subsection (4)(b) for the words "paragraph 32 of Schedule 16 to the Local Government Act 1972" there shall be substituted the words "paragraph 1 of Schedule 1 to the 1990 Act".

(3) In section 67 of that Act—

(a) in subsection (1) for the words from the beginning to "Act" there shall be substituted the words "The Secretary of State may by order provide that, for such purposes of Part III of the 1990 Act and sections 67 and 73 of the Planning (Listed Buildings and Conservation Areas) Act 1990," and the words from "in place" onwards shall be omitted;

(b) in subsection (3)—

(i) in paragraph (a) for the words from "Parts" to "Act" there shall be substituted the words "the provisions mentioned in subsection (3A) below";

(ii) in paragraph (b) for the words from "Part" to "Act" there shall be substituted the words "Part VI and sections 249 to 251 and 258 of the 1990 Act and sections 32 to 37 of the Planning (Listed Buildings and Conservation Areas) Act 1990";

(c) after subsection (3) there shall be inserted—

"(3A) The provisions referred to in subsection (3)(a) above are sections 96, 100, 104, 172 to 185, 187 to 202, 206 to 222, 224, 225, 231 and 320 to 336 of and paragraph 11 of Schedule 9 to the 1990 Act, Chapters I, II and IV of Part I and sections 54 to 56, 59 to 61, 66, 68 to 72, 74 to 76 and 88 of the Planning (Listed Buildings and Conservation Areas) Act 1990 and sections 4 to 15, 17 to 21, 23 to 25 and 36 of the Planning (Hazardous Substances) Act 1990.";

(d) subsections (5) and (6) shall be omitted.

(4) For paragraph (g) of section 92(1) of that Act there shall be substituted—

"(g) "the 1990 Act" means the Town and Country Planning Act 1990".

(5) In Part I of Schedule 9 to that Act—

(a) in paragraph 3(1)(a) for the words "the Town and Country Planning Act 1971" there shall be substituted the words "the Town and Country Planning Act 1990";

(b) in paragraph 4(b) for the words "the Town and Country Planning Act 1971" there shall be substituted the words "the Town and Country Planning Act 1990, the Planning (Listed Buildings and Conservation Areas) Act 1990 or the Planning (Hazardous Substances) Act 1990".

(6) In Part II of Schedule 10 to that Act—

(a) in paragraph 12(6) for the words "Sections 238 and 240 of the Town and Country Planning Act 1971" and "section 237(2)" there shall be substituted respectively the words "Sections 280 and 282 of the Town and Country Planning Act 1990" and "section 279(2)";

(b) in paragraph 14(8) for the words "Sections 238 and 240 of the Town and Country Planning Act 1971" and "section 237(3)" there shall be substituted respectively the words "Sections 280 and 282 of the Town and Country Planning Act 1990" and "section 279(4)".

The National Maritime Museum Act 1989 (c. 8)

80. In section 1(4) of the National Maritime Museum Act 1989, for the words "the Town and Country Planning Act 1971" there shall be substituted the words "the Town and Country Planning Act 1990, the Planning (Listed Buildings and Conservation Areas) Act 1990".

The Water Act 1989 (c. 15)

81.—(1) In section 130(8) of the Water Act 1989 for the words "the Town and Country Planning Act 1971" there shall be substituted the words "the Town and Country Planning Act 1990".

(2) In section 163 of that Act for the words "section 40 of the Town and Country Planning Act 1971" and "the said Act of 1971" there shall be substituted respectively the words "section 90 of the Town and Country Planning Act 1990" and "the said Act of 1990".

(3) In section 192(5) of that Act for the words "section 266 of the Town and Country Planning Act 1971" and "subsection (7) of the said section 266" there shall be substituted respectively the words "section 293 of the Town and Country Planning Act 1990" and "subsection (3) of the said section 293".

The Road Traffic (Driver Licensing and Information Systems) Act 1989 (c. 22)

82. In Schedule 4 to the Road Traffic (Driver Licensing and Information Systems) Act 1989, in paragraph 1 for the words "Sections 230 to 232 of the Town and Country Planning Act 1971" and "the 1971 Act" there shall be substituted respectively the words "Sections 271 to 274 of the Town and Country Planning Act 1990" and "the 1990 Act".

The Electricity Act 1989 (c. 29)

83.—(1) In paragraph 2(5) of Schedule 3, paragraph 12 of Schedule 4 and paragraph 2(6)(a) of Schedule 8 to the Electricity Act 1989, for the words "the Town and Country Planning Act 1971" there shall be substituted the words "the Town and Country Planning Act 1990".

(2) In Part II of Schedule 17 to that Act, in paragraph 37(1)(b) for the words "section 1B of the Town and Country Planning Act 1971" there shall be substituted the words "section 2 of the Planning (Hazardous Substances) Act 1990".

The Local Government and Housing Act 1989 (c. 42)

84. In section 94 of the Local Government and Housing Act 1989—
   (a) in subsection (1) for the words "section 212 of the Town and Country Planning Act 1971" there shall be substituted the words "sections 249 and 250 of the Town and Country Planning Act 1990";
   (b) in subsection (2) for the words "subsection (2) or subsection (8) of that section" there shall be substituted the words "subsection (2) or subsection (6) of section 249";
   (c) in subsection (4) for the words "subsection (2) of that section" and "subsection (5) of that section" there shall be substituted respectively the words "subsection (2) of section 249" and "subsection (1) of section 250".

Sections 3, 4 and 5 SCHEDULE 3

TRANSITIONAL PROVISIONS AND SAVINGS

1. The repeal by this Act of a provision relating to the coming into force of a provision reproduced in the consolidating Acts does not affect the operation of that provision, in so far as it is not specifically reproduced in the consolidating Acts but remains capable of having effect, in relation to the corresponding provision of the consolidating Acts.

2.—(1) The repeal by this Act of an enactment previously repealed subject to savings does not affect the continued operation of those savings.

(2) The repeal by this Act of a saving to which a previous repeal of an enactment is subject does not affect the operation of the saving in so far as it is not specifically reproduced in the consolidating Acts but remains capable of having effect.

3. Without prejudice to the generality of paragraphs 1 and 2, notwithstanding the repeal by this Act of Schedule 24 to the 1971 Act, the provisions of that Schedule shall continue to have effect, in so far as they are not specifically reproduced in this Schedule and remain capable of having effect, with any reference in those provisions to any provision of the repealed enactments which is reproduced in the consolidating Acts being taken, so far as the context permits, as including a reference to the corresponding provision of those Acts.

4. The repeal by this Act of an enactment which has effect as respects any provision of the repealed enactments (being a provision which is not reproduced in the consolidating Acts but continues in effect by virtue of this Schedule or the Interpretation Act 1978) does not affect its operation as respects that provision.

5. Any document made, served or issued after this Act comes into force which contains a reference to any of the repealed enactments shall be construed, except so far as a contrary intention appears, as referring or, as the context may require, including a reference to the corresponding provision of the consolidating Acts.

6. Where any provision of the repealed enactments amends an enactment (not being an enactment reproduced in the consolidating Acts) which is repealed or partly repealed by another enactment which is not in force when this Act comes into force, that provision shall continue to have effect, notwithstanding its repeal by this Act, but subject to section 2(4) of this Act.

7.—(1) In any regulations in force under section 91 of the 1971 Act (execution and cost of works required by enforcement notice) references to an enforcement notice, and an enforcement notice a copy of which has been served in respect of any breach of planning control, include a reference to a notice served under section 103 of that Act or section 207 of the principal Act (enforcement of duties as to replacement of trees).

(2) Section 319(3) of the principal Act shall apply to this paragraph as it applies to the provisions there mentioned.

8.—(1) Where the planning permission referred to in section 257 of the principal Act relates to a transferred matter, as defined in section 86(11) of the Local Government, Planning and Land Act 1980, but was granted by a county planning authority before the transfer date, as so defined, the district planning authority shall be the competent authority for the purposes of that section.

(2) Section 319(1) of the principal Act shall apply to this paragraph as it applies to the provisions there mentioned.

9. The expression "statutory undertakers" in any provision of the consolidating Acts shall, as respects any time when the corresponding provision in the repealed enactments (or any enactment replaced by them) was in force, have the same meaning as that expression had at that time in that provision.

10.—(1) In the case of an enforcement notice served before 27th July 1981, section 285(2) of the principal Act has effect with the following modifications.

(2) In paragraph (a) for the words "issued under that Part" there shall be substituted the words "served under Part V of the 1971 Act".

(3) For paragraph (b) there shall be substituted—

"(b)   did not have the enforcement notice or a copy of it served on him under that Part of that Act".

(4) In paragraph (c)—

(a)   in sub-paragraph (i) for the word "issued" there shall be substituted the word "served"; and

(b)   in sub-paragraph (ii) the words "with a copy of it" shall be omitted.

(5) References in the principal Act to section 285(2) shall, so far as the context permits, be construed as including references to this paragraph.

11.—(1) The repeal by Part II of Schedule 1 to this Act of section 1(8) of the Town and Country Planning Act 1984 (which validates certain permissions granted in respect of Crown land before 12th August 1984) shall not affect any permission to which that section applies immediately before the date on which the principal Act comes into force (and accordingly any such permission has effect and is deemed always to have had effect as provided in section 299(3) of the principal Act).

(2) The repeal by that Part of that Schedule of section 2(7) of that Act of 1984 (which makes similar provision as to orders for the preservation of trees) shall not affect any order to which that section applies immediately before the date on which the principal Act comes into force (and accordingly any such order has effect and is deemed always to have had effect as provided in section 300(3) of the principal Act).

(3) The repeal by that Part of that Schedule of section 1(8) of that Act of 1984 (which makes similar provision as to listed building consents and conservation area consents) shall not affect any order to which that section applies immediately before the date on which the Planning (Listed Buildings and Conservation Areas) Act 1990 comes into force (and accordingly any such consent has effect and is deemed always to have had effect as provided in section 84(3) of the Planning (Listed Buildings and Conservation Areas) Act 1990).

(4) Section 319(1) of the principal Act applies to sub-paragraphs (1) and (2) as it applies to the provisions there mentioned, and section 92(1) of the Planning (Listed Buildings and Conservation Areas) Act 1990 applies to sub-paragraph (3) as it applies to the provisions mentioned in subsection (2)(a) of that section.

12. The repeal by this Act of section 266(1)(a) of the 1971 Act shall not affect the validity of anything contained in the Greater London Development Plan.

13. The expression "local authority" in any provision of the consolidating Acts shall, as respects any time when the corresponding provision in the repealed enactments (or any enactment replaced by them) was in force, have the same meaning as that expression had at that time in that provision.

14. References in the consolidating Acts to the British Coal Corporation have effect as respects any time before 5th March 1987 as references to the National Coal Board.

15.—(1) Where the functions of a Minister under any enactment re-enacted or referred to in this Act have at any time been exercisable by another Minister or other Ministers, references in the relevant provision of this Act shall, as respects any such time, be construed as references to the other Minister or Ministers.

(2) In this paragraph "Minister" includes the Board of Trade and the Treasury.

16. The repeal by this Act of section 56A of the 1971 Act (duration of listed building consents granted before 13th November 1980) shall not affect any consent to which that section applies immediately before this Act comes into force.

17. No sum may be recovered under section 58(4) of the Planning (Listed Buildings and Conservation Areas) Act 1990 or under subsection (7) of section 78 of that Act, as applied by section 80(7) of that Act, in respect of any grant made before that Act comes into force.

Section 6   SCHEDULE 4

TRANSITORY MODIFICATIONS

1.—(1) If—

(a)   no date has been appointed as the date on which a provision mentioned in

column 1 of the following Table is to come into force before the relevant
commencement date for a paragraph of this Schedule mentioned in column 2 of
the Table opposite that provision, or

(b)   a date has been appointed which is later than the relevant commencement date
for that paragraph,

then that paragraph shall have effect until the appointed day.

TABLE

Provision	Paragraph of this Schedule
Section 9(4) of the 1971 Act.	Paragraph 2.
Paragraph 1 of Part I of Schedule 7 to the Housing and Planning Act 1986 (c. 63).	Paragraph 17.
Paragraph 9(1) of Schedule 11 to the Housing and Plannng Act 1986 (c. 63).	Paragraphs 6, 11 and 14.
Paragraph 9(2) of Schedule 11 to the Housing and Planning Act 1986 (c. 63).	Paragraphs 7, 12 and 16.
The repeal of section 110(1) of the 1971 Act in Part III of Schedule 12 to the Housing and Planning Act 1986 (c. 63).	Paragraphs 3, 4, 5, 8, 9. 10, 13 and 15.

(2) If—

(a)   a date has been appointed as the date on which a provision mentioned in column
1 of the Table in sub-paragraph (1) is to come into force for some purposes of
that provision but not for others, and

(b)   that date is on or before the relevant commencement date for a paragraph of
this Schedule mentioned in column 2 of the Table opposite that provision,

then that paragraph shall have effect for those other purposes of that provision (in so far as
it is capable of doing so) until the relevant appointed day.

(3) In this paragraph—

"the relevant commencement date", in relation to a paragraph of this Schedule,
means the date on which the provision of the consolidating Acts referred to in
that paragraph comes into force;

"the appointed day" means—

(a)   in the case mentioned in paragraph (a) of sub-paragraph (1), such day
as may be appointed by the Secretary of State by order made by
statutory instrument; and

(b)   in the case mentioned in paragraph (b) of that sub-paragraph, the day
appointed as the day on which the provision mentioned in column 1 of
the Table is to come into force.

(4) An order under sub-paragraph (3) (other than an order appointing a day until which
paragraph 2 has effect) may—

(a)   appoint different days for different provisions and for different purposes, and

(b)   make such transitional provision as the Secretary of State thinks appropriate;

and in sub-paragraph (2) "the relevant appointed day", in relation to any purpose of a
provision, means the day appointed as the day on which the provision is to come into force
for that purpose.

The principal Act

2. In section 35 of the principal Act subsection (5) shall be omitted.

3. At the end of section 175 of that Act there shall be inserted—

"(7) Subsection (5) of section 250 of the Local Government Act 1972 (which
authorises a Minister holding an inquiry under that section to make orders with
respect to the costs of the parties) shall apply in relation to any proceedings before
the Secretary of State on an appeal under section 174 as if those proceedings were an
inquiry held by the Secretary of State under section 250.".

4. At the end of section 196 of that Act there shall be inserted—

"(8) Subsection (5) of section 250 of the Local Government Act 1972 (which authorises a Minister holding an inquiry under that section to make orders with respect to the costs of the parties) shall apply in relation to any proceedings before the Secretary of State on an appeal under section 195 as if those proceedings were an inquiry held by the Secretary of State under section 250.".

5. At the end of section 208 of that Act there shall be inserted—

"(11) Subsection (5) of section 250 of the Local Government Act 1972 (which authorises a Minister holding an inquiry under that section to make orders with respect to the costs of the parties) shall apply in relation to any proceedings before the Secretary of State on an appeal under this section as if those proceedings were an inquiry held by the Secretary of State under section 250.".

6. Section 322 of that Act shall be omitted.

7. In paragraph 6 of Schedule 6 to that Act sub-paragraph (5) shall be omitted.

8. In Schedule 16 to that Act—

(a) in Part I the words "Section 175(7)", "Section 196(8)" and "Section 208(11)"; and

(b) in Part V the words "Section 208(11)",

shall be inserted at the appropriate places.

The Planning (Listed Buildings and Conservation Areas) Act 1990

9. At the end of section 41 of the Planning (Listed Buildings and Conservation Areas) Act 1990 there shall be inserted—

"(8) Subsection (5) of section 250 of the Local Government Act 1972 (which authorises a Minister holding an inquiry under that section to make orders with respect to the costs of the parties) shall apply in relation to any proceedings before the Secretary of State on an appeal under section 39 as if those proceedings were an inquiry held by the Secretary of State under section 250.".

10. In sections 85(1), 90(6)(a) and 92(2)(a) of that Act after "2(1) to (3)", and in section 82(1) after "39(6)", there shall be inserted "41(8)".

11. In section 89(1) of that Act the words from "section 322" to "held)" shall be omitted.

12. In paragraph 6 of Schedule 3 to that Act sub-paragraph (8) shall be omitted.

The Planning (Hazardous Substances) Act 1990

13. In section 25 of the Planning (Hazardous Substances) Act 1990, at the end there shall be inserted—

"(5) Subsection (5) of section 250 of the Local Government Act 1972 (which authorises a Minister holding an inquiry under that section to make orders with respect to the costs of the parties) shall apply in relation to any proceedings before the Secretary of State on an appeal under this section as if those proceedings were an inquiry held by the Secretary of State under section 250.".

14. In section 37 of that Act the words from "section 322" to "held" shall be omitted.

15. In section 38(5) of that Act, after "21" there shall be inserted "25(5)".

16. In paragraph 6 of the Schedule to that Act sub-paragraph (8) shall be omitted.

This Act

17. The amendment of the Radioactive Substances Act 1960 in Schedule 2 to this Act shall be omitted.

PROPERTY SERVICES AGENCY AND CROWN SUPPLIERS ACT 1990

(1990 c. 12)

ARRANGEMENT OF SECTIONS

An Act to make provision for the transfer of the Crown services known as the Property Services Agency and the Crown Suppliers; and for connected purposes.   [29th June 1990]

PARLIAMENTARY DEBATES
Hansard H.C. Vol. 163, col. 345; Vol. 167, col. 72; Vol. 174, col. 108; H.L. Vol. 515, col. 1282; Vol. 516, col. 986; Vol. 518, col. 359; Vol. 519, cols. 76, 477.
The Bill was considered in Standing Committee D from January 9–23, 1990.

INTRODUCTION

The Act aims to facilitate the sale of the Property Services Agency and The Crown Suppliers; the provisions enacted here will enable such a sale by conferring wide powers on the Secretary of State relating to the transfer of property, rights and liabilities. Not only does this provide the Secretary of State with powers of disposal, it also entitles him to acquire or form in advance a company for the purpose of inheriting an interest in the two entities; this may be manifest in the form of shares or securities being issued to the Secretary of State or the right to be issued them being reserved and loans may be made to any such transferee company even whilst still wholly owned by the Crown.

In addition, The Crown Suppliers' trading fund will be wound up and provision is made to allow for all liabilities of the fund to be extinguished.

The Secretary of State's powers are curtailed somewhat in that the acquisition or formation of a company and the disposal of shares or securities may not be undertaken without the consent of the Treasury.

Any expenditure involved in the acquisition of shares or the making of loans can be rightly incurred by the Secretary of State and in turn any sum received either by way of consideration for sale, dividends or interest is to be paid into either the Consolidated Fund, the National Loans Fund or into both, depending on the direction given by the Treasury.

Lastly, the Act makes provisions concerning the future of existing employees. It is intended there will be no increase in public sector manpower; a proportion of central Government staff will be transferred to the transferee company and any employee whose employment is automatically transferred in this way will not be entitled to redundancy pay.

Transfer of Property Services Agency and Crown Suppliers

1.—(1) The Secretary of State may make a scheme or schemes which provide for the transfer to any person or persons of such property, rights and liabilities as are specified in or determined in accordance with the scheme, being property, rights or liabilities—

(a) to which a Minister of the Crown (or in the case of copyright Her Majesty) is entitled or subject immediately before the day on which the scheme providing for the transfer comes into force; and

(b) which then subsisted for the purposes of or in connection with or are otherwise attributable (wholly or partly) to either of the Crown services known respectively as the Property Services Agency and the Crown Suppliers.

(2) Without prejudice to the generality of paragraph (b) of subsection (1) above any property, rights or liabilities shall be taken to fall within that paragraph so far as relating to the Property Services Agency or, as the case may be, to the Crown Suppliers if the Secretary of State issues a certificate to that effect.

(3) A scheme under this section may confer or impose such rights and liabilities as appear to the Secretary of State to be requisite for the purpose of converting into a contract between a transferee under the scheme and a Minister of the Crown any arrangement existing immediately before the coming into force of the scheme under which goods or services are being, or are to be, provided for that Minister as part of either of the services mentioned in subsection (1)(b) above.

(4) In subsection (3) above references to a Minister of the Crown include references to a Northern Ireland department.

(5) A scheme under this section may apply to property wherever situated and to property, rights and liabilities whether or not capable of being transferred or assigned by a Minister of the Crown or, as the case may be, by Her Majesty.

(6) A scheme under this section shall come into force on such day as may be specified for that purpose in the scheme; and on that day the property, rights and liabilities to which the scheme applies shall be transferred and vest in accordance with the scheme.

(7) A scheme under this section may contain such supplementary, incidental, consequential or transitional provisions as appear to the Secretary of State to be necessary or expedient; and the Schedule to this Act shall have effect in relation to any such scheme.

Transferred staff

2.—(1) No scheme under section 1 above shall provide for the transfer of any rights or liabilities relating to a person's employment.

(2) Where by reason of the operation of the Transfer of Undertakings (Protection of Employment) Regulations 1981 in relation to the transfer of any such property, rights or liabilities as are mentioned in section 1(1) above a person ceases to be employed in the civil service of the State and becomes employed by a transferee—

(a) he shall not, on so ceasing, be treated for the purposes of any scheme under section 1 of the Superannuation Act 1972 as having retired on redundancy; and

(b) his ceasing to be employed in that service shall not be regarded as an occasion of redundancy for the purpose of the agreed redundancy procedures applicable to persons employed in that service.

Transferee companies

3.—(1) The person or persons to whom anything is transferred by a scheme under section 1 above may be or include one or more companies ("transferee companies") formed or acquired by the Secretary of State for that purpose.

(2) Subject to subsections (4) and (5) below, the Secretary of State may—

(a) subscribe for or otherwise acquire shares in or securities of a transferee company, or rights to subscribe for such shares or securities;

(b) from time to time by a direction given to a transferee company require it to issue to him such shares or securities as are specified in the direction;

(c) make loans to a transferee company on such terms and conditions as he may determine.

(3) A direction under subsection (2)(b) above may require any shares to which it relates to be issued as fully or partly paid up.

(4) The Secretary of State shall not subscribe for or otherwise acquire shares in or securities of a transferee company, or rights to subscribe for such shares or securities, unless all the company's issued shares are to be held by or on behalf of the Crown and shall not at any time give a direction or make a loan to a transferee company under subsection (2) above unless all its issued shares are then held as aforesaid.

(5) The Secretary of State shall not exercise any of the powers conferred by the foregoing provisions in this section or dispose of any shares in or securities of a transferee company without the consent of the Treasury.

(6) If the articles of association of a transferee company confer on the Secretary of State powers exercisable with the consent of the Treasury for, or in connection with, restricting the sums of money which may be borrowed or raised by the company during any period, those powers shall be exercisable in the national interest notwithstanding any rule of law and the provisions of any enactment.

(7) For the purposes of subsection (6) above there shall be disregarded any alteration of the articles of association of a transferee company which has the effect of conferring or extending any such power as is mentioned in that subsection and is made at a time when the issued shares in the company are no longer all held by or on behalf of the Crown.

Winding up of Crown Suppliers trading fund

4.—(1) The Secretary of State may with the consent of the Treasury by order—
  (a) extinguish to such extent as may be specified in the order all or any of the liabilities which subsist in respect of—
       (i) the public dividend capital designated in respect of the trading fund of the Crown Suppliers under section 2(2) of the Government Trading Funds Act 1973; or
       (ii) the principal of any loan made, or treated as made, to the fund under section 2(2) or (3) of that Act;
  (b) repeal section 1(3)(e) of that Act (by virtue of which that fund was established).

(2) Where liabilities are extinguished by an order under subsection (1)(a) above the assets of the Consolidated Fund or, as the case may be, of the National Loans Fund shall be reduced by amounts corresponding to the liabilities extinguished.

(3) An order under subsection (1)(b) above may contain such supplementary, incidental, consequential or transitional provisions relating to the winding up of the trading fund as appear to the Secretary of State, after consulting the Treasury, to be necessary or expedient.

(4) The power to make an order under this section shall be exercisable by statutory instrument subject to annulment in pursuance of a resolution of either House of Parliament.

Expenses and receipts

5.—(1) Any sums required by the Secretary of State for making payments or for defraying his administrative expenses under this Act shall be paid out of money provided by Parliament.

(2) Any sums received by the Secretary of State by virtue of this Act shall be paid into the Consolidated Fund or the National Loans Fund, or partly into one and partly into the other, as the Treasury may direct.

Short title and extent

6.—(1) This Act may be cited as the Property Services Agency and Crown Suppliers Act 1990.

(2) This Act extends to Northern Ireland.

Section 1(7)   SCHEDULE

TRANSFER SCHEMES: SUPPLEMENTARY PROVISIONS

Certificate of vesting

1. A certificate by the Secretary of State that anything specified in the certificate has vested in any person by virtue of a scheme under section 1 of this Act shall be conclusive evidence for all purposes of that fact.

Construction of agreements etc.

2.—(1) This paragraph applies to any agreement made, transaction effected or other thing (not contained in an enactment) which—

   (a) has been made, effected or done by, to or in relation to a transferor under a scheme under section 1 of this Act;

   (b) relates to any property, right or liability transferred from the transferor in accordance with the scheme; and

   (c) is in force or effective immediately before the day on which the scheme comes into force.

(2) The agreement, transaction or other thing shall have effect on and after that day as if made, effected or done by, to or in relation to the corresponding transferee under the scheme.

(3) Accordingly, references to the transferor which relate to or affect any property, right or liability of the transferor vesting by virtue of the scheme in the transferee and which are contained—

   (a) in any agreement (whether or not in writing), deed, bond or instrument;

   (b) in any process or other document issued, prepared or employed for the purpose of any proceeding before a court or other tribunal or authority; or

   (c) in any other document whatever (other than an enactment) relating to or affecting any property, right or liability of the transferor which vests by virtue of the scheme in the transferee,

shall be taken on and after that day to refer to the transferee concerned.

(4) In this paragraph "transferee" and "transferor", in relation to a scheme, mean respectively a person to whom, and one from whom, a scheme provides for a transfer.

Stamp duty

3. Stamp duty shall not be chargeable on any instrument which is certified to the Commissioners of Inland Revenue by the Secretary of State as being a scheme under section 1 of this Act (or as having been made or executed in pursuance of such a scheme) and as effecting a transfer of property, rights or liabilities to a company all the issued shares in which are held by or on behalf of the Crown; but no such instrument shall be taken to be duly stamped unless—

   (a) it is stamped with the duty to which it would but for this paragraph be liable; or

   (b) it has, in accordance with section 12 of the Stamp Act 1891, been stamped with a particular stamp denoting that it is not chargeable with any duty or that it is duly stamped.

INDEX

References are to sections

GREENWICH HOSPITAL ACT 1990

(1990 c. 13)

An Act to enable the Royal Hospital School to admit both girls and boys and, in either case, regardless of any seafaring family connection; and for purposes connected therewith.

[29th June 1990]

PARLIAMENTARY DEBATES
Hansard, H.L. Vol. 513, col. 1404; Vol. 517, col. 110; H.C. Vol. 172, col. 502; Vol. 174, col. 897.
The Bill was considered in Second Reading Committee on May 9, 1990 and in Standing Committee H on June 12, 1990.

INTRODUCTION
The terms of the Royal Charter 1694 which founded the Greenwich Hospital provided for the "maintenance and education of the children of certain seafaring families". Although not specifically restrictive it was feared that the terms might be construed in such a way as to deny access to the Royal Hospital School by children from a non-seafaring background. This Act therefore makes provision for the admittance of children of either sex to the school regardless of their family connections, and for funds to be expended accordingly. However, the power to make regulations restricting the entry of certain children under the Greenwich Hospital Act 1865 (c.89) (s.20) is still preserved.
No repercussions in relation to finance or public service manpower are intended.

Power of Royal Hospital School to admit girls and boys regardless of any seafaring family connection

1.—(1) It shall be lawful for any child to be admitted to the Royal Hospital School regardless of sex and of whether the child has any seafaring family connection; and funds of Greenwich Hospital may be expended accordingly.

(2) Subsection (1) above is without prejudice to the power to make regulations under section 20 of the Greenwich Hospital Act 1865 restricting the descriptions of children who may from time to time be admitted to the school.

Short title and citation

2.—(1) This Act may be cited as the Greenwich Hospital Act 1990.

(2) This Act and the Greenwich Hospital Acts 1865 to 1967 may be cited together as the Greenwich Hospital Acts 1865 to 1990.

INDEX

References are to section numbers.

PAKISTAN ACT 1990

(1990 c. 14)

An Act to make provision in connection with the re-admission of Pakistan as a member of the Commonwealth.

[29th June 1990]

PARLIAMENTARY DEBATES
Hansard, H.L. Vol. 513, col. 21; Vol. 514, col. 356; Vol. 515, col. 526; H.C. Vol. 172, col. 694; Vol. 175, col. 285.
The Bill was considered in Standing Committee F on June 7, 1990.

INTRODUCTION
On October 1, 1989 Pakistan was re-admitted as a member of the Commonwealth and the Government have responded by providing in this Act for the modification of certain other enactments in accordance with this change in affairs, namely legislation relating to the Commonwealth Institute, the Imperial War Museum, visiting forces, the services, shipping and to the reciprocal enforcement of judgments. The Pakistan Acts 1973 and 1974 are repealed. The specific changes are set out in the schedule to this Act.

Consequential provisions relating to Pakistan

1. The provisions in the Schedule to this Act shall have effect, being amendments and other provisions consequential on the re-admission of Pakistan as a member of the Commonwealth.

Short title, repeals and commencement

2.—(1) This Act may be cited as the Pakistan Act 1990.
(2) The Pakistan Acts 1973 and 1974 are hereby repealed.
(3) This Act shall be deemed to have come into force on 1st October 1989.

Section 1   SCHEDULE

CONSEQUENTIAL PROVISIONS RELATING TO PAKISTAN

Commonwealth Institute

1. In section 8(2) of the Imperial Institute Act 1925, as amended by the Commonwealth Institute Act 1958 (power to vary the provisions of the said Act of 1925 if an agreement for the purpose is made with the governments of certain territories which for the time being are contributing to the expenses of the Commonwealth Institute) after "India," there shall be inserted "Pakistan,".

Imperial War Museum

2.—(1) In the Schedule to the Imperial War Museum Act 1920 in paragraph (1) for the words "nineteen other members" there shall be substituted the words "twenty other members" and in the first and second columns of the Table in that paragraph after the entries relating to the Government of India there shall be inserted "1" and "the Government of Pakistan" respectively.
(2) The above amendments are without prejudice to the power to vary the said paragraph (1) conferred by section 1 of the Imperial War Museum Act 1955.

The Services

3. In the definition of "Commonwealth force" in section 225(1) of the Army Act 1955 and section 223(1) of the Air Force Act 1955 and in the definition of "Commonwealth country" in section 135(1) of the Naval Discipline Act 1957 after "India," there shall be inserted "Pakistan,".

14–1

Visiting forces

4. In the Visiting Forces (British Commonwealth) Act 1933 section 4 (attachment of personnel and mutual powers of command) shall apply in relation to forces raised in Pakistan as it applies to forces raised in Dominions within the meaning of the Statute of Westminster 1931.

5. In the Visiting Forces Act 1952, in section 1(1)(a) (countries to which the Act applies) after "India," there shall be inserted "Pakistan,"; and any Order in Council under section 8 of that Act for the time being in force (applying to visiting forces the law relating to home forces) shall be deemed to apply to the visiting forces of Pakistan until express provision with respect to that country is made under that section.

6. In section 84(2) of the Offices, Shops and Railway Premises Act 1963 and section 78(2) of the Office and Shop Premises Act (Northern Ireland) 1966 (exclusion of visiting forces from Act) after "India," there shall be inserted "Pakistan,".

Shipping

7. In the Whaling Industry (Regulation) Act 1934 the expression "British ship to which this Act applies" shall not include a British ship registered in Pakistan.

Enforcement of judgments

8. The operation of the Reciprocal Enforcement of Judgments (Pakistan) Order 1958 shall not be affected by any change in the status of Pakistan since the making of that Order; and, for the purposes of any further Order in relation to Pakistan under Part I of the Foreign Judgments (Reciprocal Enforcement) Act 1933, section 7 of that Act and any Order in Council under that section (application of Part I to Her Majesty's dominions outside the United Kingdom) shall have effect as if references to Her Majesty's dominions outside the United Kingdom included references to any Commonwealth country.

INDEX

References are to section numbers of the Act and to paragraph numbers of the Schedule.
Section numbers are in roman type and paragraph numbers are in italic.

AGRICULTURAL HOLDINGS (AMENDMENT) ACT 1990*

(1990 c. 15)

An Act to amend Case B in Part I of Schedule 3 to the Agricultural Holdings Act 1986; and for connected purposes.

[29th June 1990]

PARLIAMENTARY DEBATES

Hansard, H.C. Vol. 167, col. 614; Vol. 171, col. 663; H.L. Vol. 519, col. 376; Vol. 520, col. 1443.

The Bill was considered in Standing Committee C on April 18, 1990.

GENERAL NOTE

This Act received the Royal Assent on June 29, 1990 and came into force one month thereafter.

The purpose of the Act is to correct an anomaly of drafting in the 1986 Act, which is the most recent of a succession of statutes enacted since 1875, conferring on the tenants of agricultural land the security of tenure needed to ensure that farmland remains in good heart through adequate investment and sound husbandry.

The 1986 Act restricts the exercise by agricultural landlords of their common law right to determine such farm tenancies by service of a notice to quit. Normally, if a notice to quit is served on an agricultural tenant, the tenant may serve a counter-notice under s.26(1) of the Act, requiring the landlord to secure the consent of the Agricultural Lands Tribunal. Until the Tribunal gives its consent, the notice to quit is ineffective.

There are, however, some exceptions to this right to serve a counter-notice. In some special circumstances, the landlord can serve an "incontestable" notice to quit, against which no counter-notice can be served and no recourse to the Tribunal can be had.

One of these grounds, set out in Case B of Sched. 3 to the 1986 Act, was intended to govern cases in which the landlord wished to recover possession in order to use the land in question for non-agricultural purposes, a provision not unlike those governing repossession in the course of redevelopment in residential and other lettings. The Act required that the intended use must either have received planning permission or that it was a use "for which, otherwise than by virtue of any provision of [the planning legislation], such permission is not required".

For about forty years, it has been assumed that this latter phrase referred exclusively to development carried on by the Crown, which was exempt from the need to obtain planning consent.

The decision of the Court of Appeal in the recent case of *Bell* v. *McCubbin* [1990] 1 All E.R. 54 showed that this venerable assumption was in fact ill-founded. In that case, an agricultural landlord served a notice to quit on the tenant of a farmhouse which was sublet as a dwelling-house, clearly a non-agricultural purpose. The landlord's reason for serving the notice was that he himself wished to let the house on a residential tenancy. His counsel argued, to the satisfaction of the Court of Appeal, that the landlord did not require planning permission, by virtue of the fact that, there being no material change of use, there was no development requiring such permission to be sought. The Court of Appeal accordingly allowed the notice to quit to operate without reference to the Agricultural Lands Tribunal.

The decision was one which had the potential for far-reaching, and perhaps unforeseen consequences. As a result of the down-turn in many farm incomes, subsequent to the introduction of milk quotas and the reform of the Common Agricultural Policy, etc., many tenant farmers are attempting to diversify the activities being carried out on their land. Amongst other things, unwanted farm buildings are being converted for other uses (including bunk-house barns and farm-shops) and other value-added activities are being encouraged (such as the construction of golf-courses or for educational uses), not all of which might be regarded as "agricultural" for the purposes of the 1986 Act. Quite a number of these activities are actually being grant-aided by the Ministry of Agriculture itself! The possibility therefore existed, at least in principle, that the landlord could thus take the holding back into hand, which also raised the spectre of agricultural tenants being dispossessed on a

---

* Annotations by Malcolm Forster, Director, Centre for Environmental Law, Faculty of Law, University of Southampton.

technicality, with inadequate compensation for the loss of home and livelihood, and with little prospect of finding another farm in the currently very inelastic tenancy market.

The present Act is an attempt to avoid these new threats to tenant farmers' security by tightening up the drafting of Case B.

ABBREVIATIONS
1986 Act : the Agricultural Holdings Act 1986
1990 Act : the Town and Country Planning Act 1990

Agricultural Holdings Act 1986 (Amendment)

1.—(1) Schedule 3 to the Agricultural Holdings Act 1986 shall be amended as follows.

(2) In Part I for Case B there shall be substituted—

"CASE B

The notice to quit is given on the ground that the land is required for a use, other than for agriculture—
  (a) for which permission has been granted on an application made under the enactments relating to town and country planning,
  (b) for which permission under those enactments is granted by a general development order by reason only of the fact that the use is authorised by—
       (i) a private or local Act,
       (ii) an order approved by both Houses of Parliament, or
       (iii) an order made under section 14 or 16 of the Harbours Act 1964,
  (c) for which any provision that—
       (i) is contained in an Act, but
       (ii) does not form part of the enactments relating to town and country planning,
     deems permission under those enactments to have been granted,
  (d) which any such provision deems not to constitute development for the purposes of those enactments, or
  (e) for which permission is not required under the enactments relating to town and country planning by reason only of Crown immunity,
and that fact is stated in the notice."

(3) In Part II after paragraph 8 there shall be inserted—
  "8A.—(1) For the purposes of Case B—
       (a) 'general development order' means an order under section 59 of the Town and Country Planning Act 1990 which is made as a general order, and
       (b) 'the enactments relating to town and country planning' means the planning Acts (as defined in section 336(1) of the Town and Country Planning Act 1990) and any enactment amending or replacing any of those Acts.
     (2) In relation to any time before the commencement of Part III of the Town and Country Planning Act 1990, sub-paragraph (1) above shall have effect as if—
       (a) in paragraph (a), for '59' there were substituted '24' and for '1990' there were substituted '1971', and
       (b) in paragraph (b), for the words from 'planning Acts' onwards there were substituted 'repealed enactments (as defined in section 1(1) of the Planning (Consequential Provisions) Act 1990)'."

DEFINITIONS
"agriculture": s.96(1) of the 1986 Act.
"general development order": s.2(3); s.59 of the 1990 Act.

GENERAL NOTE
The provisions of s.2 of the Act represent a complete replacement of the former Case B in Sched. 3 of the 1986 Act, which is repealed with effect from the date of the coming into force of the Act. (For notices to quit served under the old Case B prior to the commencement date, or subject to proceedings arising out of such a notice, see s.2.)

Thus, a landlord can only now regain possession under Case B if:—

(a) he can show that he needs the land for a non-agricultural use for which he has obtained planning permission in the usual way. This represents no change in the existing law under the 1986 Act;

(b) if permission has been granted under a General Development Order for a non-agricultural use. Note that this does not extend to all "permitted development", but only to development authorised by a private Act of Parliament or certain other statutory means. Ss.14 and 16, Harbours Act 1964, respectively cover "harbour revision orders" and "harbour empowerment orders". These are special procedures for passing subordinate legislation needed by harbour authorities, which were introduced in order to avoid the complex and expensive business of obtaining the passage of private Bills;

(c) any provision in a statute (other than the 1990 Planning Acts) deems permission to have been granted under those Acts for the non-agricultural use in question;

(d) the non-agricultural use in question is deemed not to constitute development for planning purposes by the terms of any statute other than the 1990 Planning Acts; or

(e) where planning permission is not required only on the grounds of Crown immunity.

The effect of these provisions is effectively to exclude recovery of possession for a non-agricultural use which is merely continued by the landlord for his own purposes, while at the same time stating expressly the position relating to Crown land and the various special Parliamentary procedures. It should be noted that Case B can *never* be used to obtain possession of an agricultural holding if the use to which the landlord seeks to put it himself is either the same, or another agricultural use within the meaning of the 1986 Act (as to which, see the definitions contained in s.96(1) and (5) of that Act).

Savings

2.—(1) Nothing in this Act shall apply in relation to—
    (a) a notice to quit an agricultural holding or part of an agricultural holding given before the commencement of this Act, or
    (b) any application, arbitration or other proceedings which relate to, or arise out of, such a notice.

(2) In this section "agricultural holding" has the same meaning as in the Agricultural Holdings Act 1986.

DEFINITION
"agricultural holding": s.2(2); s.1(1) of the 1986 Act.

GENERAL NOTE
This transitional section makes it clear that the old rule in *Bell* v. *McCubbin* [1990] 1 All E.R. 54, will continue to apply to notices to quit given before the Act came into force and to proceedings deriving from such notices.

Citation, commencement and extent

3.—(1) This Act may be cited as the Agricultural Holdings (Amendment) Act 1990.

(2) This Act shall come into force at the end of the period of one month beginning with the day on which it is passed.

(3) This Act extends to England and Wales only.

INDEX

References in roman type are to sections of this Act: references in italic are to Schedule 3 of the Agricultural Holdings Act 1986 (as amended).

FOOD SAFETY ACT 1990*

(1990 c. 16)

---

* Annotations by Dr. Alistair Clark, Senior Lecturer, The Law School, University of Strathclyde.

An Act to make new provision in place of the Food Act 1984 (except Parts III and V), the Food and Drugs (Scotland) Act 1956 and certain other enactments relating to food; to amend Parts III and V of the said Act of 1984 and Part I of the Food and Environment Protection Act 1985; and for connected purposes.

PARLIAMENTARY DEBATES
Hansard, H.L. Vol. 513, cols. 21, 744, 756; Vol. 514, cols. 417, 741; Vol. 515, cols. 1132, 1184, 1209; Vol. 520, col. 1619; H.C. Vol. 168, col. 1023; Vol. 173, col. 812.
The Bill was considered in Standing Committee B from March 20–April 3, 1990.

INTRODUCTION AND GENERAL NOTE
The late 1980s witnessed a spate of food safety scares, involving such things as salmonella, listeria, botulism and bovine spongiform encephalopathy. At the same time there was concern that production processes of foods and the use of additives, ingredients and pesticides had developed beyond the scope of existing legislation. Moreover, there was much debate about the usefulness and desirability of irradiation as a means of reducing the incidence of food contamination. Against this background the Food Safety Act 1990 was passed. These great issues of the day gave rise to debates which took up many of the pages of the Parliamentary debates on the Bill. However, the precise measures to be taken in order to deal with these matters will, in the main, be left to be dealt with in regulations or orders to be made under the new Act. The Act itself is broadly an enabling measure, although the opportunity has been taken to create a more systematic structure of food law and to tighten up the offences, the enforcement powers and the penalties.

Part I of the Act deals with preliminary matters such as the definition of the central concepts used, including *food*, *business*, *food source* and *food premises*. The term *sale* is given an extended meaning (see s.2), and the Act creates presumptions that food is intended for human consumption. The Minister or Ministers having functions under the Act (in particular, the extensive and flexible regulation-making powers given by provisions such as s.16) are specified, and the Act goes on to establish *food authorities* and *enforcement authorities*.

Part II contains the main provisions of the Act, including the major offences of rendering food injurious to health (s.7), selling food which does not comply with food safety requirements (s.8), selling food not of the nature or substance or quality demanded (s.14), and falsely describing or presenting food (s.15). Each of the offences has some basis in the precursor legislation, but all have been amended and s.8 is essentially a new offence. Powers are given to an *authorised officer of a food authority* to inspect, seize and condemn food which does not comply with food safety requirements. A new scheme of notices and orders is introduced, including in particular: *improvement notices* issued by an authorised officer when it is suspected that an offence under the regulations has been committed; *prohibition orders* (covering processes, treatments, premises, equipment, and persons involved) issued by a court following upon a conviction where there is a risk of injury to health; *emergency prohibition notices* issued by an authorised officer of an enforcement authority and *emergency prohibition orders* issued by a court, where there is imminent risk to health; *emergency control orders* issued by the Minister prohibiting commercial operations in relation to food where there is a risk of such food causing imminent injury to health. The Government hopes that control orders will rarely be used and that the existing voluntary compliance of the industry will cope with most contamination incidents.

Section 16 gives to Ministers a wide range of regulation-making powers. The main controversy about these powers concerns irradiation. This was the subject of intense and heated debate during the passage of the legislation and the result is that the Minister now has powers to bring in regulations permitting irradiation.

Under the regulations, consumers are to be given the choice as to whether to purchase irradiated food or non-irradiated food. This will be done by placing an obligation upon those in the food supply industry to label irradiated food clearly. However, if, as some MPs argued, it is not possible to test whether food has been irradiated, there may be some operators who will ignore the labelling requirement and hope that a workable test will not be available to Environmental Health Officers.

As well as permitting irradiation, it is expected that regulations to be issued will deal with the presence of residues on animals and crops, microbiological standards, food processes and treatments, and hygienic conditions and practices. A further provision gives power to deal with such things as novel foods or genetically modified foods.

Section 19 permits the Minister to make regulations which require the registration and licensing of food premises. Unregistered premises are to be prohibited from operating. If the Government deems it necessary, it may require that in the interests of public health or consumer protection certain food businesses will be able to operate only if in addition to being registered they obtain a licence. Regulations will specify the types of businesses which will require licences, and it is expected that licensing will be limited to businesses producing irradiated foods, dairy farms and dairies. It is also expected that licences to carry out

16–3

irradiation will be issued by the government and licences for the others will be issued by local authorities.

This Part of the Act also specifies the defences which are available to offences under Part II. There is the standard "by-pass" provision whereby the authorities can prosecute the real offender rather than, or as well as, the immediate offender. A new defence of having taken all reasonable precautions and exercised all due diligence is introduced and the former "warranty" defence (see s.102 of the Food Act 1984) has been removed. A special defence for advertisers is provided. There is also provision in this part of the Act allowing local authorities to provide training courses for food handlers, giving statutory backing to what are at present informal arrangements.

Part III of the Act deals with administration and enforcement, covering *inter alia* the procuring and analysing of samples, entry by officers to premises, inspection of records, obstruction, time limits for prosecutions, penalties and appeals.

Part IV covers miscellaneous and supplemental matters. Important provisions include amendments to the Food and Environment Protection Act 1985, with retrospective effect, allowing it to be used to deal with incidents likely to create a hazard to human health through human consumption of food, and amendments to the Water Act 1989 and the Water (Scotland) Act 1980, to extend the controls over water used for domestic purposes to water used for food production.

ABBREVIATION
the 1984 Act: the Food Act 1984.

PART I

PRELIMINARY

Meaning of "food" and other basic expressions

1.—(1) In this Act "food" includes—
   (a) drink;
   (b) articles and substances of no nutritional value which are used for human consumption;
   (c) chewing gum and other products of a like nature and use; and
   (d) articles and substances used as ingredients in the preparation of food or anything falling within this subsection.

(2) In this Act "food" does not include—
   (a) live animals or birds, or live fish which are not used for human consumption while they are alive;
   (b) fodder or feeding stuffs for animals, birds or fish;
   (c) controlled drugs within the meaning of the Misuse of Drugs Act 1971; or
   (d) subject to such exceptions as may be specified in an order made by the Ministers—
      (i) medicinal products within the meaning of the Medicines Act 1968 in respect of which product licences within the meaning of that Act are for the time being in force; or
      (ii) other articles or substances in respect of which such licences are for the time being in force in pursuance of orders under section 104 or 105 of that Act (application of Act to other articles and substances).

(3) In this Act, unless the context otherwise requires—
   "business" includes the undertaking of a canteen, club, school, hospital or institution, whether carried on for profit or not, and any undertaking or activity carried on by a public or local authority;
   "commercial operation", in relation to any food or contact material, means any of the following, namely—

(a) selling, possessing for sale and offering, exposing or advertising for sale;

(b) consigning, delivering or serving by way of sale;

(c) preparing for sale or presenting, labelling or wrapping for the purpose of sale;

(d) storing or transporting for the purpose of sale;

(e) importing and exporting;

and, in relation to any food source, means deriving food from it for the purpose of sale or for purposes connected with sale;

"contact material" means any article or substance which is intended to come into contact with food;

"food business" means any business in the course of which commercial operations with respect to food or food sources are carried out;

"food premises" means any premises used for the purposes of a food business;

"food source" means any growing crop or live animal, bird or fish from which food is intended to be derived (whether by harvesting, slaughtering, milking, collecting eggs or otherwise);

"premises" includes any place, any vehicle, stall or moveable structure and, for such purposes as may be specified in an order made by the Ministers, any ship or aircraft of a description so specified.

(4) The reference in subsection (3) above to preparing for sale shall be construed, in relation to any contact material, as a reference to manufacturing or producing for the purpose of sale.

DEFINITIONS

"animal": s.53(1).

"article": s.53(1).

"fish": s.53(1).

"human consumption": s.53(1).

"preparation": s.53(1).

"the Ministers: s.4(1).

"sale and related expressions": s.2.

"ship": s.53(1).

"substance": s.53(1).

GENERAL NOTE

Subss. (1) and (2)

These subsections state the meaning of "food" for the purposes of the Act. "Food," as the short title makes clear, is the central concept in the Act. However, there is no general definition of "food." The definitions in earlier legislation (see, *e.g.* Food and Drugs Act 1938; Food and Drugs Act 1955) were inadequate to cope with the multitude of food products now in existence. *Articles and substances of no nutritional value* would include certain slimming aids. *Other products of a like nature and use* to chewing gum may be thought to include, for example, chewing tobacco, but it could be argued that such a product, while of a like use to chewing gum, is not of a like nature. Water, including tapwater, is included within *drink* and may also be covered by s.1(1)(d). However, by virtue of ss.55 and 56, water up to the point of supply to premises is not dealt with by this Act but by the Water Act 1989 and the Water (Scotland) Act 1980. Live fish used for human consumption while alive would include oysters and elvers. Vitamin and mineral supplements, and such things as herbal tea are covered by the word "food."

Animal feedstuffs are excluded; controls over such feedstuffs exist under the Agriculture Act 1970, the Animal Health Act 1981, and various E.C. regulations.

Subs. (3)

The definition of business is derived from s.132(1) of the Food Act 1984 (s.58(1) of the Food and Drugs (Scotland) Act 1956) and includes a wide range of food suppliers. *Commercial operation* would appear to cover any person, body or organisation which has any involvement in the chain of derivation, production, distribution, and sale of food. *Contact material* could include, *e.g.* packaging, plastic film, containers, water, chemicals, equipment and machinery. *Premises* is wide enough to cover hamburger stalls, mobile sandwich bars and the like.

Subs. (4)

By virtue of subs. (3), various activities not only in relation to food but also in relation to a contact material are included in the meaning of *commercial operation*. Subs. 4 makes it clear that preparation for sale of a contact material shall include manufacturing or producing it. Accordingly, the Ministers' powers under s.16(2) can apply to the making of contact materials.

Extended meaning of "sale" etc.

2.—(1) For the purposes of this Act—
   (a) the supply of food, otherwise than on sale, in the course of a business; and
   (b) any other thing which is done with respect to food and is specified in an order made by the Ministers,
shall be deemed to be a sale of the food, and references to purchasers and purchasing shall be construed accordingly.
   (2) This Act shall apply—
   (a) in relation to any food which is offered as a prize or reward or given away in connection with any entertainment to which the public are admitted, whether on payment of money or not, as if the food were, or had been, exposed for sale by each person concerned in the organisation of the entertainment;
   (b) in relation to any food which, for the purpose of advertisement or in furtherance of any trade or business, is offered as a prize or reward or given away, as if the food were, or had been, exposed for sale by the person offering or giving away the food; and
   (c) in relation to any food which is exposed or deposited in any premises for the purpose of being so offered or given away as mentioned in paragraph (a) or (b) above, as if the food were, or had been, exposed for sale by the occupier of the premises;
and in this subsection "entertainment" includes any social gathering, amusement, exhibition, performance, game, sport or trial of skill.

DEFINITIONS
   "advertisement": s.53(1).
   "business": s.1(3).
   "food: s.1(1), (2) and (4).
   "occupier": s.53(1).
   "premises: s.1(3).
   "the Ministers": s.4(1).

GENERAL NOTE

Many of the Act's provisions concern the sale of food. S.2 revises provisions from earlier legislation to the effect that any supply of food in the course of business (not necessarily from food premises) is deemed to be a sale. For example, charities which give away food to the elderly are caught. Similarly, free condiments supplied in a restaurant will be regarded as being sold. Domestic supply of food is excluded. The Ministers' powers in s.2(1)(b) are extensive and are expected to be used *inter alia* in relation to the implementation of E.C. measures on non-commercial supply of food. S.2(2) identifies the persons who are regarded as having exposed for sale food which is offered as a prize or reward or given away.

Presumptions that food intended for human consumption

3.—(1) The following provisions shall apply for the purposes of this Act.

(2) Any food commonly used for human consumption shall, if sold or offered, exposed or kept for sale, be presumed, until the contrary is proved, to have been sold or, as the case may be, to have been or to be intended for sale for human consumption.

(3) The following, namely—

    (a) any food commonly used for human consumption which is found on premises used for the preparation, storage, or sale of that food; and

    (b) any article or substance commonly used in the manufacture of food for human consumption which is found on premises used for the preparation, storage or sale of that food,

shall be presumed, until the contrary is proved, to be intended for sale, or for manufacturing food for sale, for human consumption.

(4) Any article or substance capable of being used in the composition or preparation of any food commonly used for human consumption which is found on premises on which that food is prepared shall, until the contrary is proved, be presumed to be intended for such use.

DEFINITIONS
"article": s.53(1).
"food": s.1(1), (2) and (4).
"human consumption": s.53(1).
"premises": s.1(3).
"preparation": s.53(1).
"sale and related expressions": s.2.
"substance": s.53(1).

GENERAL NOTE
Presumptions that food is intended for human consumption were an important part of previous food legislation (see s.98 of the Food Act 1984; s.43 of the Food and Drugs (Scotland) Act 1956; see also *Hooper* v. *Petrou* (1973) 71 L.G.R. 347) and the new provisions are largely a repetition of the previous rules. Each of the presumptions is rebuttable by the defendant proving to the contrary. The major provisions of the Act apply only to food which is intended for human consumption. S.3 will make it difficult if not impossible for a butcher, for example, to argue that meat in his premises which is unfit for human consumption (see s.8) was in fact being kept for other purposes, such as the feeding of his pet dog (see *Skinner* v. *McLean* 1979 S.L.T. (Notes) 35).

Ministers having functions under Act

4.—(1) In this Act—

"the Minister" means, subject to subsection (2) below—

    (a) in relation to England and Wales, the Minister of Agriculture, Fisheries and Food or the Secretary of State;

    (b) in relation to Scotland, the Secretary of State;

"the Ministers" means—

    (a) in relation to England and Wales, the following Ministers acting jointly, namely, the Minister of Agriculture, Fisheries and Food and the Secretaries of State respectively concerned with health in England and food and health in Wales;

    (b) in relation to Scotland, the Secretary of State.

(2) In this Act, in its application to emergency control orders, "the Minister" means the Minister of Agriculture, Fisheries and Food or the Secretary of State.

DEFINITION
"emergency control order": s.13(1).

GENERAL NOTE
Later provisions of the Act refer to regulation-making powers of *the Minister* or *the
Ministers*. This section states the meaning of these terms. Under subs. (1) the term *Secretary
of State* in theory means any Secretary of State, but in practice the relevant person will be
the Secretary of State for Health or the Secretary of State for Wales. In Scotland, the
Secretary of State for Scotland is *the Minister*. *The Ministers* in England and Wales means
three Secretaries of State acting jointly, while in Scotland, curiously, *the Ministers* and *the
Minister* each appear to mean the same thing—the Secretary of State for Scotland. Where
the Act gives powers to *the Ministers* (for example, ss.16–19) and these powers are exercised
in respect of the whole of Great Britain the term *the Ministers* means all four Ministers
acting jointly. It will be noticed that where swift action is required (for example an
emergency control order under s.13) the Act gives powers to the Minister rather than
requiring joint action. Some provisions confer regulation-making powers on either *the
Minister* or *the Ministers* (see, for example, s.40 regarding the power to issue codes of
practice). Subs. (2) is in different terms from the meaning ascribed to *the Minister* in subs.
(1). Arguably, on the basis that *Secretary of State* means any Secretary of State, this extends
the power to make emergency control orders (s.13) covering Scotland to a Minister other
than the Secretary of State for Scotland and in theory permits the Secretary of State for
Scotland to make such orders covering England and Wales.

Food authorities and authorised officers

5.—(1) Subject to subsections (3) and (4) below, the food authorities in
England and Wales are—
   (a) as respects each London borough, district or non-metropolitan
       county, the council of that borough, district or county;
   (b) as respects the City of London (including the Temples), the
       Common Council;
   (c) as respects the Inner Temple or the Middle Temple, the appropriate
       Treasurer.
   (2) Subject to subsection (3)(a) below, the food authorities in Scotland
are the islands or district councils.
   (3) Where any functions under this Act are assigned—
       (a) by an order under section 2 or 7 of the Public Health (Control
           of Disease) Act 1984, to a port health authority or, by an order
           under section 172 of the Public Health (Scotland) Act 1897, to
           a port local authority;
       (b) by an order under section 6 of the Public Health Act 1936, to
           a joint board for a united district; or
       (c) by an order under paragraph 15(6) of Schedule 8 to the Local
           Government Act 1985, to a single authority for a metropolitan
           county,
any reference in this Act to a food authority shall be construed, so far as
relating to those functions, as a reference to the authority to whom they
are so assigned.
   (4) The Ministers may by order provide, either generally or in relation
to cases of a particular description, that any functions under this Act
which are exercisable concurrently—
       (a) as respects a non-metropolitan district, by the council of that
           district and the council of the non-metropolitan county;
       (b) as respects the Inner Temple or the Middle Temple, by the
           appropriate Treasurer and the Common Council,
shall be exercisable solely by such one of those authorities as may be
specified in the order.
   (5) In this section—
       "the appropriate Treasurer" means the Sub-Treasurer in relation to
           the Inner Temple and the Under Treasurer in relation to the
           Middle Temple;
       "the Common Council" means the Common Council of the City of
           London;

"port local authority", includes a joint port local authority.

(6) In this Act "authorised officer", in relation to a food authority, means any person (whether or not an officer of the authority) who is authorised by them in writing, either generally or specially, to act in matters arising under this Act; but if regulations made by the Ministers so provide, no person shall be so authorised unless he has such qualifications as may be prescribed by the regulations.

DEFINITIONS
"functions": s.53(1).
"officer": s.53(1).
"the Ministers": s.4(1).

GENERAL NOTE
The intention of this provision is to state which authorities are *food authorities* and to define *authorised officer* of a food authority. This should avoid complications which existed under previous legislation (for example, the distinct terms "authorised officers" and "sampling officers"). An order will be made under s.6(4) laying down the precise distribution of enforcement responsibilities in England and Wales. These are expected to follow the existing pattern. In Scotland, the food authorities are the Island or District councils, enforcement being carried out by their Environmental Health Officers.

Under subs. (3) orders made under other legislation can assign functions to bodies not designated as food authorities under subss. (1) and (2), and in relation to these functions the bodies are regarded as food authorities.

The definition of *authorised officer* in subs. (6) covers persons other than those employed by food authorities, so that, for example, a private veterinary surgeon may be engaged to carry out meat inspection duties in remote areas.

Enforcement of Act

6.—(1) In this Act "the enforcement authority", in relation to any provisions of this Act or any regulations or orders made under it, means the authority by whom they are to be enforced and executed.

(2) Every food authority shall enforce and execute within their area the provisions of this Act with respect to which the duty is not imposed expressly or by necessary implication on some other authority.

(3) The Ministers may direct, in relation to cases of a particular description or a particular case, that any duty imposed on food authorities by subsection (2) above shall be discharged by the Ministers or the Minister and not by those authorities.

(4) Regulations or orders under this Act shall specify which of the following authorities are to enforce and execute them, either generally or in relation to cases of a particular description or a particular area, namely—

(a) the Ministers, the Minister, food authorities and such other authorities as are mentioned in section 5(3) above; and

(b) in the case of regulations, the Commissioners of Customs and Excise;

and any such regulations or orders may provide for the giving of assistance and information, by any authority concerned in the administration of the regulations or orders, or of any provisions of this Act, to any other authority so concerned, for the purposes of their respective duties under them.

(5) An enforcement authority in England and Wales may institute proceedings under any provisions of this Act or any regulations or orders made under it and, in the case of the Ministers or the Minister, may take over the conduct of any such proceedings which have been instituted by some other person.

DEFINITIONS
"food authority": s.5.
"the Minister": s.4(1) and (2).
"the Ministers": s.4(1).

GENERAL NOTE
This section introduces the term enforcement authority. Unless duties are imposed expressly or by necessary implication on some other authority, the enforcement authority will be the food authority within each area. The Ministers or the Minister may have enforcement duties assigned to them, either in a class of cases or one particular case. Subs. (4) largely repeats existing provisions. In England and Wales enforcement authorities can institute proceedings, while in Scotland prosecutions will continue to be instituted by the Procurator Fiscal Service. The Minister or Ministers can take over the conduct of proceedings, and it is expected that this power will be used in important test cases, or where resources greater than those at the disposal of the local authority are required to conduct the proceedings.

PART II

MAIN PROVISIONS

Food safety

Rendering food injurious to health

7.—(1) Any person who renders any food injurious to health by means of any of the following operations, namely—
(a) adding any article or substance to the food;
(b) using any article or substance as an ingredient in the preparation of the food;
(c) abstracting any constituent from the food; and
(d) subjecting the food to any other process or treatment,
with intent that it shall be sold for human consumption, shall be guilty of an offence.

(2) In determining for the purposes of this section and section 8(2) below whether any food is injurious to health, regard shall be had—
(a) not only to the probable effect of that food on the health of a person consuming it; but
(b) also to the probable cumulative effect of food of substantially the same composition on the health of a person consuming it in ordinary quantities.

(3) In this Part "injury", in relation to health, includes any impairment, whether permanent or temporary, and "injurious to health" shall be construed accordingly.

DEFINITIONS
"article": s.53(1).
"food": s.1(1), (2) and (4).
"human consumption: s.53(1).
"preparation": s.53(1).
"substance": s.53(1).
"treatment": s.53(1).

GENERAL NOTE
This provision is principally a restatement of the offence first introduced in the Adulteration of Food and Drink Act 1860, latterly found in s.1 of the Food Act 1984 and s.1 of the Food and Drugs (Scotland) Act 1956. For an offence to be committed a person must *render* food injurious to health, so that the mere sale of food which is so injurious (for example, a species of poisonous mushroom) is not an offence under this provision but may be caught by a later provision, for example, s.8. The rendering of food injurious to health involves a positive act so that a failure to do something (*e.g.* failure properly to pasteurise milk, or

fully to thaw frozen poultry) is not an offence under s.7, but may be an offence under s.8. The provision in previous legislation used the words *with intent that the food be sold for human consumption in that state*. The final three words have been deleted, with the result that any person who renders food injurious either accidentally or by design, intending to sell the food for human consumption, will be caught by the provisions. The offence is capable of applying not only to those in the food industry but also to those who add articles or substances (such as glass) to food, for example on a supermarket shelf, although it is likely that such persons would be charged with crimes carrying greater sentences than are available under the Act. *Abstracting* (subs. (1)(c)) has been discussed in relation to milk in *Penrice* v. *Brander* 1921 J.C. 63 and *Bridges* v. *Griffin* [1925] 2 K.B. 233. Dilution has been held not to amount to abstraction (*Deardon* v. *Whiteley* (1916) 85 L.J.K.B. 1420).

The probable cumulative effect, as well as the effect of any particular consumption of such food, is to be looked at in determining whether food is injurious to health (see *Cullen* v. *McNair* (1908) 99 L.T. 358). For example, a one-off consumption of a meat product which has had excess preservative (*e.g.* E220—sulphur dioxide) added may not be injurious, but the cumulative effect of consumption may well be injurious. A statement, for example on a label, disclosing the presence of the injurious ingredient, has been held not to constitute a defence (*Haigh* v. *Aerated Bread Co.* [1916] 1 K.B. 878). *Injury* and *injurious to health* include any impairment, covering, for example, temporary sickness as well as conditions such as permanent renal disease which become apparent only after the passage of time.

Selling food not complying with food safety requirements

8.—(1) Any person who—
   (a) sells for human consumption, or offers, exposes or advertises for sale for such consumption, or has in his possession for the purpose of such sale or of preparation for such sale; or
   (b) deposits with, or consigns to, any other person for the purpose of such sale or of preparation for such sale,
any food which fails to comply with food safety requirements shall be guilty of an offence.
   (2) For the purposes of this Part food fails to comply with food safety requirements if—
   (a) it has been rendered injurious to health by means of any of the operations mentioned in section 7(1) above;
   (b) it is unfit for human consumption; or
   (c) it is so contaminated (whether by extraneous matter or otherwise) that it would not be reasonable to expect it to be used for human consumption in that state;
and references to such requirements or to food complying with such requirements shall be construed accordingly.
   (3) Where any food which fails to comply with food safety requirements is part of a batch, lot or consignment of food of the same class or description, it shall be presumed for the purposes of this section and section 9 below, until the contrary is proved, that all of the food in that batch, lot or consignment fails to comply with those requirements.
   (4) For the purposes of this Part, any part of, or product derived wholly or partly from, an animal—
   (a) which has been slaughtered in a knacker's yard, or of which the carcase has been brought into a knacker's yard; or
   (b) in Scotland, which has been slaughtered otherwise than in a slaughterhouse,
shall be deemed to be unfit for human consumption.
   (5) In subsection (4) above, in its application to Scotland, "animal" means any description of cattle, sheep, goat, swine, horse, ass or mule; and paragraph (b) of that subsection shall not apply where accident, illness or emergency affecting the animal in question required it to be slaughtered as mentioned in that paragraph.

DEFINITIONS
"advertises": s.53(1).
"animal": s.53(1).
"food": s.1(1), (2) and (4).
"human consumption": s.53(1).
"injurious to health": s.7(3).
"knacker's yard": s.53(1).
"preparation": s.53(1).
"sale and related expressions": s.2.
"slaughterhouse": s.53(1).

GENERAL NOTE
This section introduces a new offence of selling food which does not comply with food safety requirements. Food will fail to comply if it has been rendered injurious to health within the meaning of s.7 or is unfit for human consumption or is so contaminated that it would not be reasonable to expect it to be used for human consumption in that state.

These provisions effectively combine the previous offences in s.1 and s.8 of the Food Act 1984 (ss.1 and 8 of the Food and Drugs (Scotland) Act 1956). However, a wider range of activities relating to the selling of contaminated food or food which has been rendered injurious to health, for example depositing or consigning or preparing the food, is now covered. Food which is contaminated but not unfit or rendered injurious had to have been sold before an offence was committed under the previous rules, but the other activities listed now suffice. On the meaning of *sale*, see s.1(1), (2) and (4); see also *Watson* v. *Coupland* [1945] 1 All E.R. 217 and *Mischeff* v. *Springett* [1942] 2 K.B. 331. As to the meaning of *exposes*, see *e.g. Wheat* v. *Brown* [1892] 1 Q.B. 418 and *Clark* v. *Strachan* 1940 J.C. 29. Food can of course be unfit for human consumption while not actually injurious to health: see, *e.g. David Greig* v. *Goldfinch* (1961) 105 S.J. 367. The presence of a foreign body or substance may not necessarily render the food unfit for human consumption, but may constitute an offence under s.14; see, *e.g. J. Miller* v. *Battersea Borough Council* [1956] 1 Q.B. 43; *Turner & Son* v. *Owen* [1956] 1 Q.B. 48; but see also *Barton* v. *Unigate Dairies* (1987) 151 J.P. 113; *Gateway Foodmarkets* v. *Simmonds* [1988] TLR 26.

The effect of subs. (3) is that the whole of a batch, lot or consignment can be seized under s.9 without having been inspected.

The intended effect of subs. (4) is to deem meat and other products derived from an animal slaughtered otherwise than in a slaughterhouse to be unfit for human consumption, since such meat is not the subject of statutory inspection. The definition of *knacker's yard* in s.53 restricts the meaning of that term to premises used in connection with the business of slaughtering, flaying or cutting up animals, the flesh of which is not intended for human consumption.

Subs. (5) excludes from the application of subs. (4) in Scotland such things as poultry or deer. Accordingly, where such animals have been slaughtered outside a slaughterhouse the resulting food is not deemed to be unfit for human consumption. Subs. (5) is also designed to permit meat and other products from an animal slaughtered outside a slaughterhouse not to be deemed to be unfit in the circumstances mentioned in that subsection.

Inspection and seizure of suspected food

9.—(1) An authorised officer of a food authority may at all reasonable times inspect any food intended for human consumption which—
 (a) has been sold or is offered or exposed for sale; or
 (b) is in the possession of, or has been deposited with or consigned to, any person for the purpose of sale or of preparation for sale;
and subsections (3) to (9) below shall apply where, on such an inspection, it appears to the authorised officer that any food fails to comply with food safety requirements.

(2) The following provisions shall also apply where, otherwise than on such an inspection, it appears to an authorised officer of a food authority that any food is likely to cause food poisoning or any disease communicable to human beings.

(3) The authorised officer may either—
 (a) give notice to the person in charge of the food that, until the notice is withdrawn, the food or any specified portion of it—

(i) is not to be used for human consumption; and

(ii) either is not to be removed or is not to be removed except to some place specified in the notice; or

(b) seize the food and remove it in order to have it dealt with by a justice of the peace;

and any person who knowingly contravenes the requirements of a notice under paragraph (a) above shall be guilty of an offence.

(4) Where the authorised officer exercises the powers conferred by subsection (3)(a) above, he shall, as soon as is reasonably practicable and in any event within 21 days, determine whether or not he is satisfied that the food complies with food safety requirements and—

(a) if he is so satisfied, shall forthwith draw the notice;

(b) if he is not so satisfied, shall seize the food and remove it in order to have it dealt with by a justice of the peace.

(5) Where an authorised officer exercises the powers conferred by subsection (3)(b) or (4)(b) above, he shall inform the person in charge of the food of his intention to have it dealt with by a justice of the peace and—

(a) any person who under section 7 or 8 above might be liable to a prosecution in respect of the food shall, if he attends before the justice of the peace by whom the food falls to be dealt with, be entitled to be heard and to call witnesses; and

(b) that justice of the peace may, but need not, be a member of the court before which any person is charged with an offence under that section in relation to that food.

(6) If it appears to a justice of the peace, on the basis of such evidence as he considers appropriate in the circumstances, that any food falling to be dealt with by him under this section fails to comply with food safety requirements, he shall condemn the food and order—

(a) the food to be destroyed or to be so disposed of as to prevent it from being used for human consumption; and

(b) any expenses reasonably incurred in connection with the destruction or disposal to be defrayed by the owner of the food.

(7) If a notice under subsection (3)(a) above is withdrawn, or the justice of the peace by whom any food falls to be dealt with under this section refuses to condemn it, the food authority shall compensate the owner of the food for any depreciation in its value resulting from the action taken by the authorised officer.

(8) Any disputed question as to the right to or the amount of any compensation payable under subsection (7) above shall be determined by arbitration.

(9) In the application of this section to Scotland—

(a) any reference to a justice of the peace includes a reference to the sheriff and to a magistrate;

(b) paragraph (b) of subsection (5) above shall not apply;

(c) any order made under subsection (6) above shall be sufficient evidence in any proceedings under this Act of the failure of the food in question to comply with food safety requirements; and

(d) the reference in subsection (8) above to determination by arbitration shall be construed as a reference to determine by a single arbiter appointed, failing agreement between the parties, by the sheriff.

DEFINITIONS

"authorised officer of a food authority": s.5(6).

"food": s.1(1), (2) and (4).

"food authority": s.5.

"food safety requirements and related expressions": s.8(2).
"human consumption": s.53(1).
"officer": s.53(1).
"preparation": s.53(1).
"sale and related expressions": s.2.

GENERAL NOTE

This provision brings together and strengthens the powers given in s.9 of the Food Act 1984 (s.9 of the Food and Drugs (Scotland) Act 1956), and ss.28 and 31 of the Food Act 1984. The intention of the new provisions is to provide a flexible system whereby enforcement officers can choose the appropriate course of action in a particular case.

Subs. (1)

Authorised officer of a food authority. The term *food authority* rather than "enforcement authority" (see, *e.g.* ss.10 and 12) is used, so that, for example, Customs and Excise Officers have no powers under this section.

Intended for human consumption. The presumption in s.3 applies.

Subs. (2)

This permits the application of subss. (3)–(9) where without inspecting the food the authorised officer suspects that the food is likely to cause food poisoning or any disease communicable to human beings, for example that a salmonella outbreak can be traced to a particular batch of poultry. *Food poisoning* is not defined.

Subs. (3)

The authorised officer has power either to detain the food or to seize it. The *person in charge of the food* may well be someone other than the proprietor of the food business, for example, an employee. It is likely that managers or supervisors are persons in charge but that those who simply serve food are not.

Subs. (5)

The person who under ss.7 or 8 may be liable to prosecution can appear in person and can call witnesses but may wish to have legal representation. Legal costs would not be recoverable under subs. (7) below.

Subs. (6)

Condemned food may be ordered to be disposed of, for example by being fed to animals, rather than destroyed. The justice must order the costs of destroying or disposing of the food to be met by the owner of the food.

Subs. (7)

The right to compensation arises in the circumstances mentioned in the provision. There is no right of compensation where the authorised officer gives notice that the food is to be detained but then decides that the food does comply with food safety requirements.

Subs. (8)

Disputes as to compensation under subs. (7) must be settled by arbitration.

Subs. (9)

This recognises the different legal procedures in Scotland.

Improvement notices

10.—(1) If an authorised officer of an enforcement authority has reasonable grounds for believing that the proprietor of a food business is failing to comply with any regulations to which this section applies, he may, by a notice served on that proprietor (in this Act referred to as an "improvement notice")—

    (a) state the officer's grounds for believing that the proprietor is failing to comply with the regulations;

    (b) specify the matters which constitute the proprietor's failure so to comply;

(c) specify the measures which, in the officer's opinion, the proprietor must take in order to secure compliance; and

(d) require the proprietor to take those measures, or measures which are at least equivalent to them, within such period (not being less than 14 days) as may be specified in the notice.

(2) Any person who fails to comply with an improvement notice shall be guilty of an offence.

(3) This section and section 11 below apply to any regulations under this Part which make provision—

(a) for requiring, prohibiting or regulating the use of any process or treatment in the preparation of food; or

(b) for securing the observance of hygienic conditions and practices in connection with the carrying out of commercial operations with respect to food or food sources.

DEFINITIONS
"business": s.1(3).
"commercial operation": s.1(3) and (4).
"enforcement authority": s.6(1).
"food": s.1(1), (2) and (4).
"food business": s.1(3).
"food sources": s.1(3).
"officer": s.53(1).
"preparation": s.53(1).
"proprietor": s.53(1).
"treatment": s.53(1).

GENERAL NOTE
If an authorised officer of an enforcement authority has reasonable grounds for believing that a proprietor of a food business is failing to comply with food processing or food hygiene regulations (made under Pt. II of the Act; see in particular ss.16–19 and also ss.25–26) the officer may serve an *improvement notice* on the proprietor, requiring him to take measures to secure compliance with the regulations within a specified period. Failure to comply with an improvement notice is an offence (subs. (2)). These provisions replace the current system of informal notices with statutory improvement notices.

Subs. (1)
   Authorised officer of an enforcement authority. Enforcement authority rather than "food authority" is used; *cf.* s.9.

Subs. (2)
   Ss.37 and 39 allow for appeals against improvement notices.

Subs. (3)
   S.16 will be the major source of regulations made regarding food processing and food hygiene.

Prohibition orders

   11.—(1) If—
   (a) the proprietor of a food business is convicted of an offence under any regulations to which this section applies; and
   (b) the court by or before which he is so convicted is satisfied that the health risk conditions is fulfilled with respect to that business.
the court shall by an order impose the appropriate prohibition.

   (2) The health risk condition is fulfilled with respect to any food business if any of the following involves risk of injury to health, namely—
   (a) the use for the purposes of the business of any process or treatment;

(b) the construction of any premises used for the purposes of the business, or the use for those purposes of any equipment; and

(c) the state or condition of any premises or equipment used for the purposes of the business.

(3) The appropriate prohibition is—

(a) in a case falling within paragraph (a) of subsection (2) above, a prohibition on the use of the process or treatment for the purposes of the business;

(b) in a case falling within paragraph (b) of that subsection, a prohibition on the use of the premises or equipment for the purposes of the business or any other food business of the same class or description;

(c) in a case falling within paragraph (c) of that subsection, a prohibition on the use of the premises or equipment for the purposes of any food business.

(4) If—

(a) the proprietor of a food business is convicted of an offence under any regulations to which this section applies by virtue of section 10(3)(b) above; and

(b) the court by or before which he is so convicted thinks it proper to do so in all the circumstances of the case,

the court may, by an order, impose a prohibition on the proprietor participating in the management of any food business, or any food business of a class or description specified in the order.

(5) As soon as practicable after the making of an order under subsection (1) or (4) above (in this Act referred to as a "prohibition order"), the enforcement authority shall—

(a) serve a copy of the order on the proprietor of the business; and

(b) in the case of an order under subsection (1) above, affix a copy of the order in a conspicuous position on such premises used for the purposes of the business as they consider appropriate;

and any person who knowingly contravenes such an order shall be guilty of an offence.

(6) A prohibition order shall cease to have effect—

(a) in the case of an order under subsection (1) above, on the issue by the enforcement authority of a certificate to the effect that they are satisfied that the proprietor has taken sufficient measures to secure that the health risk condition is no longer fulfilled with respect to the business;

(b) in the case of an order under subsection (4) above, on the giving by the court of a direction to that effect.

(7) The enforcement authority shall issue a certificate under paragraph (a) of subsection (6) above within three days of their being satisfied as mentioned in that paragraph; and on an application by the proprietor for such a certificate, the authority shall—

(a) determine, as soon as is reasonably practicable and in any event within 14 days, whether or not they are so satisfied; and

(b) if they determine that they are not so satisfied, give notice to the proprietor of the reasons for that determination.

(8) The court shall give a direction under subsection (6)(b) above if, on an application by the proprietor, the court thinks it proper to do so having regard to all the circumstances of the case, including in particular the conduct of the proprietor since the making of the order; but no such application shall be entertained if it is made—

(a) within six months after the making of the prohibition order; or

(b) within three months after the making by the proprietor of a previous application for such a direction.

(9) Where a magistrates' court or, in Scotland, the sheriff makes an order under section 12(2) below with respect to any food business, subsection (1) above shall apply as if the proprietor of the business had been convicted by the court or sheriff of an offence under regulations to which this section applies.

(10) Subsection (4) above shall apply in relation to a manager of a food business as it applies in relation to the proprietor of such a business; and any reference in subsection (5) or (8) above to the proprietor of the business, or to the proprietor, shall be construed accordingly.

(11) In subsection (10) above "manager", in relation to a food business, means any person who is entrusted by the proprietor with the day to day running of the business, or any part of the business.

DEFINITIONS
"business": s.1(3).
"enforcement authority": s.6(1).
"equipment": s.53(1).
"food business": s.1(3).
"injury to health and injurious to health": s.7(3).
"premises": s.1(3).
"proprietor": s.53(1).
"treatment": s.53(1).

GENERAL NOTE
This section extends and strengthens current legislation by covering all food businesses, and by being capable of application to particular uses of premises, particular pieces of equipment, particular processes and particular persons.

Where there is a risk of injury to health, a court may make a *prohibition order* which may prohibit the use of a process or treatment for the purposes of a food business, the use of premises (either for particular kinds of food business or entirely) or equipment, and may prohibit a person from carrying on or managing a food business.

Subs. (1)
Regulations to which this section applies. This is as provided in s.10(3).
Health risk condition. See subs. (2).
Appropriate prohibition. See subs. (3).
This subsection does not apply to prohibitions of persons.

Subs. (4)
The court may. The court has discretion as to whether to impose a prohibition on persons, whereas under subs. (1) if its provisions are satisfied the court is required to impose the appropriate prohibition. The offence must be under the regulations mentioned in s.10(3)(b) rather than s.10(3).

Subs. (5)
S.38 gives a right of appeal to the Crown Court to a person who is aggrieved by any decision of a magistrates' court to make a prohibition order. There is no specific reference to such a right of appeal in Scotland and it seems that this matter is being left to be dealt with in regulations.

Subs. (7)
This provision sets out the method of cancellation of a prohibition order made under subs. 6(a).
S.37(1)(b) provides for a right to appeal to a magistrates' court or sheriff by any person who is aggrieved by a decision of an enforcement authority to refuse to issue the certificate mentioned in s.11(6).

Subs. (8)
This provision sets out the the method of cancellation of a prohibition order made under subs. 6(b). Six months must elapse before a proprietor can apply to have the order lifted and if the application is refused the proprietor must wait a further three months before re-applying.

Subs. (9)

The court is permitted to impose the appropriate prohibition under s.11(3) where a proprietor has not been convicted but where an emergency prohibition order under s.12(2) has been made.

Subs. (10)

Under this provision the court has power to prohibit a manager in the same way as a proprietor.

Emergency prohibition notices and orders

12.—(1) If an authorised officer of an enforcement authority is satisfied that the health risk condition is fulfilled with respect to any food business, he may, by a notice served on the proprietor of the business (in this Act referred to as an "emergency prohibition notice"), impose the appropriate prohibition.

(2) If a magistrates' court or, in Scotland, the sheriff is satisfied, on the application of such an officer, that the health risk condition is fulfilled with respect to any food business, the court or sheriff shall, by an order (in this Act referred to as an "emergency prohibition order"), impose the appropriate prohibition.

(3) Such an officer shall not apply for an emergency prohibition order unless, at least one day before the date of the application, he has served notice on the proprietor of the business of his intention to apply for the order.

(4) Subsections (2) and (3) of section 11 above shall apply for the purposes of this section as they apply for the purposes of that section, but as if the reference in subsection (2) to risk of injury to health were a reference to imminent risk of such injury.

(5) As soon as practicable after the service of an emergency prohibition notice, the enforcement authority shall affix a copy of the notice in a conspicuous position on such premises used for the purposes of the business as they consider appropriate; and any person who knowingly contravenes such a notice shall be guilty of an offence.

(6) As soon as practicable after the making of an emergency prohibition order, the enforcement authority shall—

    (a) serve a copy of the order on the proprietor of the business; and

    (b) affix a copy of the order in a conspicuous position on such premises used for the purposes of that business as they consider appropriate;

and any person who knowingly contravenes such an order shall be guilty of an offence.

(7) An emergency prohibition notice shall cease to have effect—

    (a) if no application for an emergency prohibition order is made within the period of three days beginning with the service of the notice, at the end of that period;

    (b) if such an application is so made, on the determination or abandonment of the application.

(8) An emergency prohibition notice or emergency prohibition order shall cease to have effect on the issue by the enforcement authority of a certificate to the effect that they are satisfied that the proprietor has taken sufficient measures to secure that the health risk condition is no longer fulfilled with respect to the business.

(9) The enforcement authority shall issue a certificate under subsection (8) above within three days of their being satisfied as mentioned in that subsection; and on an application by the proprietor for such a certificate, the authority shall—

    (a) determine, as soon as is reasonably practicable and in any event within 14 days, whether or not they are so satisfied; and

   (b) if they determine that they are not so satisfied, give notice to the proprietor of the reasons for that determination.

   (10) Where an emergency prohibition notice is served on the proprietor of a business, the enforcement authority shall compensate him in respect of any loss suffered by reason of his complying with the notice unless—

   (a) an application for an emergency prohibition order is made within the period of three days beginning with the service of the notice; and

   (b) the court declares itself satisfied, on the hearing of the application, that the health risk condition was fulfilled with respect to the business at the time when the notice was served;

and any disputed question as to the right to or the amount of any compensation payable under this subsection shall be determined by arbitration or, in Scotland, by a single arbiter appointed, failing agreement between the parties, by the sheriff.

DEFINITIONS
  "enforcement authority": s.6(1).
  "food business": s.1(3).
  "health risk condition": s.11(2).
  "injury to health and injurious to health": s.7(3).
  "officer": s.53(1).
  "premises": s.1(3).
  "proprietor": s.53(1).

GENERAL NOTE
  The effect of this section is to permit an authorised officer of an enforcement authority, or the court, to issue a prohibition order in the same terms as under s.11 (except that there is no ability to prohibit a person: subs. 12(4)) without the precondition that the proprietor of the food business has been convicted as in s.11. These powers are designed to be used when there is an *imminent* risk to health (s.12(4)).

Subs. (1)
  Service of the notice by the officer (commonly by an environmental health officer) is all that is required in order to impose the prohibition, which will therefore have immediate effect.

Subs. (2)
  Under subs. (7) below, a notice under subs. (1) above shall cease to have effect if no application is made within three days for an order under subs. (2).
  S.38 gives a right of appeal to the Crown Court to a person who is aggrieved by any decision of a magistrates' court to make an emergency prohibition order. There is no specific reference to such a right of appeal in Scotland and it seems that this matter is being left to be dealt with in regulations.

Subs. (3)
  The intention of the provisions of s.12 is that an enforcement officer will apply for an emergency prohibition order within three days of issuing an emergency prohibition notice. However, it is of course possible for the enforcement officers to go directly to the court for an emergency prohibition order under subs. (2). Subs. (3) is designed to give the proprietor notice of the the intention to apply for the order.

Subs (4)
  As noted above, this gives the same powers as in s.11 except the power to prohibit persons.
  Imminent risk of injury. The risk rather than necessarily the actual injury must be imminent; for example, ingestion of a chemical which is known to cause cancers manifest only after some years.

Subs. (8)
  Either before or after the issue of an emergency prohibition order the enforcement authority can certify that the health risk condition is no longer fulfilled, so that a notice or order shall cease to have effect.

Subs. (9)

It is possible for the certificate under subs. (8) above to be issued without application by the proprietor of the food business, *e.g.* following a further visit by the enforcement officers. However, it is likely in practice that proprietors will apply for a prohibition to be lifted and subs. (9) means that the authority must determine whether to lift the prohibition "as soon as is reasonably practicable" and in any event within 14 days.

S.37(1)(b) gives a right to appeal to any person who is aggrieved by a decision of an enforcement authority to refuse to issue a certificate under subs.(8).

Subs. (10)

Compensation is payable to the proprietor of a food business unless an application for an emergency prohibition order is made within three days (see subs. (7)) and the court is satisfied that no *imminent* (see subs. (4)) risk to health was posed when the notice was served.

As in s.9(9)(d), there is separate provision for arbitration in Scotland since the Arbitration Act 1950 does not apply to Scotland.

Emergency control orders

13.—(1) If it appears to the Minister that the carrying out of commercial operations with respect to food, food sources or contact materials of any class or description involves or may involve imminent risk of injury to health, he may, by an order (in this Act referred to as an "emergency control order"), prohibit the carrying out of such operations with respect to food, food sources or contact materials of that class or description.

(2) Any person who knowingly contravenes an emergency control order shall be guilty of an offence.

(3) The Minister may consent, either unconditionally or subject to any condition that he considers appropriate, to the doing in a particular case of anything prohibited by an emergency control order.

(4) It shall be a defence for a person charged with an offence under subsection (2) above to show—

(a) that consent had been given under subsection (3) above to the contravention of the emergency control order; and

(b) that any condition subject to which that consent was given was complied with.

(5) The Minister—

(a) may give such directions as appear to him to be necessary or expedient for the purpose of preventing the carrying out of commercial operations with respect to any food, food sources or contact materials which he believes, on reasonable grounds, to be food, food sources or contact materials to which an emergency control order applies; and

(b) may do anything which appears to him to be necessary or expedient for that purpose.

(6) Any person who fails to comply with a direction under this section shall be guilty of an offence.

(7) If the Minister does anything by virtue of this section in consequence of any person failing to comply with an emergency control order or a direction under this section, the Minister may recover from that person any expenses reasonably incurred by him under this section.

DEFINITIONS

"commercial operation": s.1(3) and (4).
"contact material": s.1(3).
"contravention": s.53(1).
"food": s.1(1), (2) and (4).
"food source": s.1(3).
"injury to health and injurious to health": s.7(3).
"the Minister": s.4(1) and (2).

GENERAL NOTE
This provision introduces new statutory powers to strengthen the current controls which rely upon the voluntary co-operation of the industry. Emergency control orders are likely to be used where there is contamination of food and that contamination cannot be dealt with under voluntary arrangements.

If it appears to the Minister. As in the power given to enforcement officers under s.12(1) there is no need for the imminent risk of injury to health to be established by proof.

Of any class or description. This allows the order to be focused upon, for example, a particular batch or type of food, food source or contact material.

Subs. (3)
The intention of s.13 is to confer flexible powers to respond to contamination incidents. Subs. (3) thus permits the Minister to release activities from the scope of the order.

Subs. (5)
The Minister may direct that food be removed from premises, for example, or that premises where a contamination incident has occurred be closed down.

Consumer protection

Selling food not of the nature or substance or quality demanded

14.—(1) Any person who sells to the purchaser's prejudice any food which is not of the nature or substance or quality demanded by the purchaser shall be guilty of an offence.

(2) In subsection (1) above the reference to sale shall be construed as a reference to sale for human consumption; and in proceedings under that subsection it shall not be a defence that the purchaser was not prejudiced because he bought for analysis or examination.

DEFINITIONS
"analysis": s.53(1).
"examination": s.28(2).
"food": s.1(1), (2) and (4).
"human consumption": s.53(1).
"sale and related expressions": s.2.

GENERAL NOTE
This provision mirrors with some very minor and technical amendments the offence found in s.2 of the Food Act 1984 (s.2 of the Food and Drugs (Scotland) Act 1956) which is based upon the offence set out in the Food and Drugs Act 1875. Many food safety prosecutions are brought under this head. In appropriate cases the prosecuting authorities will be able to bring a case under this provision or under the new offence set out in s.8(2)(c), or under both provisions. However, *sale* (as defined, see also *Watson* v. *Coupland* [1945] 1 All E.R. 217 and *Mischeff* v. *Springett* [1942] 2 K.B. 331) is crucial to the commission of the s.14 offence.

Nature. See *Meah* v. *Roberts* [1977] 1 W.L.R. 1187; *Knight* v. *Bowers* (1885) 14 Q.B. 845.

Substance. The presence of extraneous matter will commonly but not necessarily (see *Edwards* v. *Llaethdy Meirion* (1957) Crim. L.R. 402) give rise to an offence. See, for example, *J. Miller* v. *Battersea Borough Council* [1956] 1 Q.B. 43; *Turner & Son* v. *Owen* [1956] 1 Q.B. 48; *Chibnall's Bakeries* v. *Cope-Brown* [1956] Crim. L.R. 263; *Newton* v. *West Vale Creamery Co.* (1956) 120 J.P. 318; *Southworth* v. *Whitewell Dairies* (1958) 122 J.P. 322; *Smedleys* v. *Breed* [1974] A.C. 839; *Arun District Council* v. *Argyle Stores* (1986) 150 J.P. 552; *Barton* v. *Unigate Dairies* (1987)151 J.P. 113.

Quality. This does not mean simply *description* or *type* of food: *Anness* v. *Grivell* [1915] 3 K.B. 685; *Barber* v. *Co-operative Wholesale Society* [1983] Crim. L.R. 476; but see also *McDonald's Hamburgers* v. *Windle* (1987) 151 J.P. 333.

Purchaser. This means any purchaser, not necessarily the ultimate consumer.

To the purchaser's prejudice. See, for example, *Hoyle* v. *Hitchman* (1879) 4 Q.B.D. 233; *Evans* v. *Jones* [1953] 1 W.L.R. 1056; *Collett* v. *Walker* (1895) 59 J.P. 600; *Williams* v. *Friend* [1912] 2 K.B. 471; *Rodburn* v. *Hudson* [1925] 1 K.B. 225.

The defences formerly provided by s.3 of the Food Act 1984 (s.3 of the Food and Drugs (Scotland) Act 1956) have been removed. In particular, the defence under s.3(2) of the Food Act 1984 that the presence of extraneous matter in food was an unavoidable consequence of the process of collection or preparation, had proved of little worth to defendants: " . . . no one has been able to think of any circumstances in which the defence . . . could be applicable. So local authorities and magistrates can in practice ignore the subsection altogether. This has the merit of simplicity" (*per* Lord Diplock, *Smedleys* v. *Breed* [1974] A.C. 839 at p.859; see also *Greater Manchester Council* v. *Lockwood Foods* [1979] Crim. L.R. 593). Attempts to re-instate the defence during the passage of the legislation failed. However, the defence under s.21 below may well be available and it is strongly arguable that if the circumstances of *Smedleys* v. *Breed* (above) arose again the s.21 defence would preclude conviction.

Falsely describing or presenting food

15.—(1) Any person who gives with any food sold by him, or displays with any food offered or exposed by him for sale or in his possession for the purpose of sale, a label, whether or not attached to or printed on the wrapper or container, which—
 (a) falsely describes the food; or
 (b) is likely to mislead as to the nature or substance or quality of the food,
shall be guilty of an offence.
 (2) Any person who publishes, or is a party to the publication of, an advertisement (not being such a label given or displayed by him as mentioned in subsection (1) above) which—
 (a) falsely describes any food; or
 (b) is likely to mislead as to the nature or substance or quality of any food,
shall be guilty of an offence.
 (3) Any person who sells, or offers or exposes for sale, or has in his possession for the purpose of sale, any food the presentation of which is likely to mislead as to the nature of substance or quality of the food shall be guilty of an offence.
 (4) In proceedings for an offence under subsection (1) or (2) above, the fact that a label or advertisement in respect of which the offence is alleged to have been committed contained accurate statement of the composition of the food shall not preclude the court from finding that the offence was committed.
 (5) In this section references to sale shall be construed as references to sale for human consumption.

DEFINITIONS
 "advertisement": s.53(1).
 "container": s.53(1).
 "food": s.1(1), (2) and (4).
 "human consumption": s.53(1).
 "presentation": s.53(1).
 "sale and related expressions": s.2.

GENERAL NOTE
 This provision amends but re-enacts the substance of s.6 of the Food Act 1984 (s.6 of the Food and Drugs (Scotland) Act 1956). Possession for sale of food which is falsely described or presented is now an offence.

Subs. (1)
 Any food offered or exposed. The words *offered or* are new and would include food which is offered but not exposed.
 Or in his possession for the purpose of sale. These words are also new and are intended to take account of the new approach to enforcement of labelling rules in the factory as brought in by the E.C. Directive on Official Control of Foodstuffs.
 (*a*) *Falsely describes the food; or.* The semi-colon replaces a comma in the previous provision, thus ensuring that the provision is interpreted as creating two distinct offences.

Is likely to mislead. This replaces *is calculated to mislead* by giving an objective rather than a subjective standard.

Subs. (2)
The final two points made above in respect of subs. (1) apply here also.

Subs. (3)
S.6 of the Food Act 1984 did not apply to *presentation* of food, but the matter was dealt with in the Food Labelling Regulations 1984. Subs. (3) in the current Act brings misleading presentation of food within the ambit of the primary legislation, and includes food in possession for the purpose of sale.

Subss. (4) and (5)
These provisions largely reiterate existing provisions: ss.6(5) and 6(6) of the Food Act 1984. Subs. (4) of the new Act refers only to the offences under subss. (1) and (2) above.

Regulations
Food safety and consumer protection
   16.—(1) The Ministers may by regulations make—
   (a) provision for requiring, prohibiting or regulating the presence in food or food sources of any specified class, and generally for regulating the composition of food;
   (b) provision for securing that food is fit for human consumption and meets such microbiological standards (whether going to the fitness of the food or otherwise) as may be specified by or under the regulations;
   (c) provision for requiring, prohibiting or regulating the use of any process of treatment in the preparation of food;
   (d) provision for securing the observance of hygienic conditions and practices in connection with the carrying out of commercial operations with respect to food or food sources;
   (e) provision for imposing requirements or prohibitions as to, or otherwise regulating, the labelling, marking, presenting or advertising of food, and the descriptions which may be applied to food; and
   (f) such other provision with respect to food or food sources, including in particular provision for prohibiting or regulating the carrying out of commercial operations with respect to food or food sources, as appears to them to be necessary or expedient—
      (i) for the purpose of securing that food complies with food safety requirements or in the interests of the public health; or
      (ii) for the purpose of protecting or promoting the interests of consumers.
   (2) The Ministers may also by regulations make provision—
   (a) for securing the observance of hygienic conditions and practices in connection with the carrying out of commercial operations with respect to contact materials which are intended to come into contact with food intended for human consumption;
   (b) for imposing requirements or prohibitions as to, or otherwise regulating, the labelling, marking or advertising of such materials, and the descriptions which may be applied to them; and
   (c) otherwise for prohibiting or regulating the carrying out of commercial operations with respect to such materials.
   (3) Without prejudice to the generality of subsection (1) above, regulations under that subsection may make any such provision as is mentioned in Schedule 1 to this Act.

(4) In making regulations under subsection (1) above, the Ministers shall have regard to the desirability of restricting, so far as practicable, the use of substances of no nutritional value as foods or as ingredients of foods.

(5) In subsection (1) above and Schedule 1 to this Act, unless the context otherwise requires—

(a) references to food shall be construed as references to food intended for sale for human consumption; and

(b) references to food sources shall be construed as references to food sources from which such food is intended to be derived.

DEFINITIONS

"commercial operation": s.1(3) and (4).
"contact material": s.1(3).
"food": s.1(1), (2) and (4).
"food safety requirements and related expressions": s.8(2).
"food source": s.1(3).
"human consumption": s.53(1).
"preparation": s.53(1).
"substance": s.53(1).
"the Ministers": s.4(1).
"treatment": s.53(1).

GENERAL NOTE

This provision introduces sweeping new regulation-making powers in an attempt to establish a framework within which Ministers can react in a swift and flexible way to developments within the food industry. Regulation-making powers did of course exist in precursor legislation but the new provision gives much wider powers. Substantive provisions of earlier legislation (including some of those in Pt. II of the Food Act 1984 relating to Milk, Dairies and Cream Substitutes) will now be dealt with in regulations made under s.16. The powers cover, in addition to food, the new concepts introduced in s.1 *i.e.* "food sources" and "food contact materials," so that for example under s.16(1)(a) maximum levels of antibiotic residue in meat or indeed in live animals can be stipulated. S.16(1)(c) will be used to introduce *inter alia* food irradiation, and there are likely to be detailed rules about type of radiation, dosage, identification of irradiated foods, labelling (which may also be dealt with under s.16(1)(e) below), packaging and record-keeping. S.16(1)(f) gives catch-all powers in respect of food and food sources. It is expected that the powers in s.16(2) which apply to food contact materials will be used to replace and extend the Materials and Articles in Contact with Food Regulations (S.I. 1987 No. 1523). S.16(3) permits regulations under s.16(1) to make such provision as is set out in Sched. 1. S.16(4) is merely hortatory, and reiterates the existing provision (s.4(2) of the Food Act 1984). The Ministers will be aware that some 3,800 substances are used either as colours, flavours, flavour enhancers, sweeteners, texture modifiers, preservatives and processing aids. However, attempts during the passage of the Bill to require Ministers positively to restrict such substances were defeated. S.16(5) confines the meaning of "food" and "food sources" for the purposes of s.16 and Sched. 1 to that which is intended for human consumption.

Enforcement of Community provisions

17.—(1) The Ministers may by regulations make such provision with respect to food, food sources or contact materials, including in particular provision for prohibiting or regulating the carrying out of commercial operations with respect to food, food sources or contact materials, as appears to them to be called for by any Community obligation.

(2) As respects any directly applicable Community provision which relates to food, food sources or contact materials and for which, in their opinion, it is appropriate to provide under this Act, the Ministers may by regulations—

(a) make such provision as they consider necessary or expedient for the purpose of securing that the Community provision is administered, executed and enforced under this Act; and

(b) apply such of the provisions of this Act as may be specified in the regulations in relation to the Community provision with such modifications, if any, as may be so specified.

(3) In subsections (1) and (2) above references to food or food sources shall be construed in accordance with section 16(5) above.

"commercial operation": s.1(3) and (4).
"contact material": s.1(3).
"food": s.1(1), (2) and (4).
"food source": s.1(3).
"the Ministers": s.4(1).

GENERAL NOTE
The intention of this provision is that regulations applying to food, food sources or contact materials in implementation of any Community obligation can all emanate from this Act without need to use the European Communities Act 1972, which had been used *inter alia* for the Materials and Articles in Contact with Food Regulations referred to above. Subs. (1) refers to the fulfilment of *any* Community obligation, including directly applicable obligations (*i.e.* E.C. Regulations). Subs. (2) refers to administration, execution and enforcement of directly applicable obligations, and permits modification of the provisions of the Act in relation to the Community provision. Under s.48(4) Ministers have no obligation to consult with organisations representing consumers or others affected before making regulations under s.17(2).

Special provisions for particular foods etc.

18.—(1) The Ministers may by regulations make provision—
(a) for prohibiting the carrying out of commercial operations with respect to novel foods, or food sources from which such foods are intended to be derived, of any class specified in the regulations;
(b) for prohibiting the carrying out of such operations with respect to genetically modified food sources, or foods derived from such food sources, of any class so specified; or
(c) for prohibiting the importation of any food of a class so specified,
and (in each case) for excluding from the prohibition any food or food source which is of a description specified by or under the regulations and in the case of a prohibition on importation, is imported at an authorised place of entry.

(2) The Ministers may also by regulations—
(a) prescribe, in relation to milk of any description, such a designation (in this subsection referred to as a "special designation") as the Ministers consider appropriate;
(b) provide for the issue by enforcement authorities of licences to producers and sellers of milk authorising the use of a special designation; and
(c) prohibit, without the use of a special designation, all sales of milk for human consumption, other than sales made with the Minister's consent.

(3) In this section—
"authorised place of entry" means any port, aerodrome or other place of entry authorised by or under the regulations and, in relation to food in a particular consignment, includes any place of entry so authorised for the importation of that consignment;
"description", in relation to food, includes any description of its origin or of the manner in which it is packed;
"novel food" means any food which has not previously been used for human consumption in Great Britain, or has been so used only to a very limited extent.

(4) For the purposes of this section a food source is genetically modified if any of the genes or other genetic material in the food source—

(a) has been modified by means of an artificial technique; or

(b) is inherited or otherwise derived, through any number of replications, from genetic material which was so modified;

and in this subsection "artificial technique" does not include any technique which involves no more than, or no more than the assistance of, naturally occurring processes of reproduction (including selective breeding techniques or *in vitro* fertilisation).

DEFINITIONS

"commercial operation": s.1(3) and (4).
"enforcement authority": s.6(1).
"food": s.1(1), (2) and (4).
"food source": s.1(3).
"human consumption": s.53(1).
"importation": s.53(1).
"milk": s.53(1).
"the Minister": s.4(1) and (2).
"the Ministers": s.4(1).

GENERAL NOTE

Developments in food technology have resulted in the creation of novel foods and the existing procedures for the approval of such foods for human consumption have operated on a voluntary basis. Like other provisions of the Act, s.18 *inter alia* introduces statutory control of a previously voluntary system.

Subs. (1)

Paragraph (a)

Food sources. The definition in s.1 restricts this term to crops and animals, so that the invention of a new food source, *e.g.* chemically based, will not be covered, although the novel food itself derived from such a source will be covered.

Paragraph (b)

Genetically modified food sources. This is one particular method of creating novel food, but the separate provision for such food and food sources makes it clear that even if such food is not regarded as novel, it can be the subject of regulation under this paragraph.

Paragraph (c)

This permits prohibition of the importation of novel foods, genetically modified foods, and food sources from which either of these is derived.

The subsection permits exemption from the prohibitions above; food exempted from the prohibition on importation must be imported at an authorised place of entry.

Subs. (2)

Similar regulation-making powers in relation to milk exist in the Food Act 1984 and the Food and Drugs (Scotland) Act 1956, and have been used to introduce the Milk (Special Designations) Regulations 1988 and Milk (Special Designations) (Scotland) Regulations 1988. Special designations of milk include UHT (ultra heat treated), pasteurised, sterilised, and untreated. The Scottish regulations do not permit the retail sale of untreated milk. The regulations give the Minister power to license producers of untreated milk in England and local authorities in England and Scotland power to license distributors and dealers. S.18(2)(b) permits regulations to provide for the enforcement authorities (see s.6) to issue licences. It is likely that similar arrangements to those currently in place will be introduced under this section.

Subs. (4)

Subs. (4) is designed to clarify the scope of s.18. All foods produced as a result of genetic manipulation are brought within the section. The powers set out in s.16(1) (c) can be used to regulate novel processes for the production of food. Genetically modified foods are not wholly new, for example a genetically modified yeast is currently available in Britain, and work continues on the creation of new fruits. Manipulation of the sperm of an animal is covered but simple *in vitro* fertilisation is not an *artificial technique.*

Registration and licensing of food premises

19.—(1) The Ministers may by regulations make provision—

(a) for the registration by enforcement authorities of premises used or proposed to be used for the purposes of a food business, and for prohibiting the use for those purposes of any premises which are not registered in accordance with the regulations; or

(b) subject to subsection (2) below, for the issue by such authorities of licences in respect of the use of premises for the purposes of a food business, and for prohibiting the use for those purposes of any premises except in accordance with a licence issued under the regulations.

(2) The Ministers shall exercise the power conferred by subsection (1)(b) above only where it appears to them to be necessary or expedient to do so—

(a) for the purpose of securing that food complies with food safety requirements or in the interests of the public health; or

(b) for the purpose of protecting or promoting the interests of consumers.

DEFINITIONS
"enforcement authority": s.6(1).
"food business": s.1(3).
"food safety requirements and related expressions": s.8(2).
"premises": s.1(3).
"the Ministers": s.4(1).

GENERAL NOTE

Subs. (1)
The intention is that food businesses will be required to register premises with the enforcement authority and will be prohibited from using the premises on failure to register. Change of use of the premises for use in another type of food business or change of owner are likely to require re-registration. Licensing is to be used only where a particular type of food business gives rise to a risk to health or where licensing is otherwise desirable for consumer protection (subs. (2)). The Government has already made it clear that dairy farms and dairies will require a licence, as will businesses which produce irradiated food under regulations to be brought in under s.16(1)(c) above.

Defences etc.

Offences due to fault of another person

20. Where the commission by any person of an offence under any of the preceding provisions of this Part is due to an act or default of some other person, that other person shall be guilty of the offence; and a person may be charged with and convicted of the offence by virtue of this section whether or not proceedings are taken against the first-mentioned person.

GENERAL NOTE
This is a standard provision in modern food or consumer protection legislation and similar provisions are to be found in the Trade Descriptions Act 1968, the Health and Safety at Work Act 1974, the Food Act 1984, the Weights and Measures Act 1985 and the Consumer Protection Act 1987. S.20 makes a number of changes to the wording of s.100(3) of the Food Act 1984 but the minor amendments do not result in any substantial differences in the applicability or scope of the provision.
Some other person. See, *e.g. Tesco Supermarkets* v. *Nattrass* [1972] A.C. 153.

Defence of due diligence

21.—(1) In any proceedings for an offence under any of the preceding provisions of this Part (in this section referred to as "the relevant provision"), it shall, subject to subsection (5) below, be a defence for the person charged to prove that he took all reasonable precautions and exercised all due diligence to avoid the commission of the offence by himself or by a person under his control.

(2) Without prejudice to the generality of subsection (1) above, a person charged with an offence under section 8, 14 or 15 above who neither—

(a) prepared the food in respect of which the offence is alleged to have been committed; nor

(b) imported it into Great Britain,

shall be taken to have established the defence provided by that subsection if he satisfies the requirements of subsection (3) or (4) below.

(3) A person satisfies the requirements of this subsection if he proves—

(a) that the commission of the offence was due to an act or default of another person who was not under his control, or to reliance on information supplied by such a person;

(b) that he carried out all such checks of the food in question as were reasonable in all the circumstances, or that it was reasonable in all the circumstances for him to rely on checks carried out by the person who supplied the food to him; and

(c) that he did not know and had no reason to suspect at the time of the commission of the alleged offence that his act or omission would amount to an offence under the relevant provision.

(4) A person satisfies the requirements of this subsection if he proves—

(a) that the commission of the offence was due to an act or default of another person who was not under his control, or to reliance on information supplied by such a person;

(b) that the sale or intended sale of which the alleged offence consisted was not a sale or intended sale under his name or mark; and

(c) that he did not know, and could not reasonably have been expected to know, at the time of the commission of the alleged offence that his act or omission would amount to an offence under the relevant provision.

(5) If in any case the defence provided by subsection (1) above involves the allegation that the commission of the offence was due to an act or default of another person, or to reliance on information supplied by another person, the person charged shall not, without leave of the court, be entitled to rely on that defence unless—

(a) at least seven clear days before the hearing; and

(b) where he has previously appeared before a court in connection with the alleged offence, within one month of his first such appearance,

he has served on the prosecutor a notice in writing giving such information identifying or assisting in the identification of that other person as was then in his possession.

(6) In subsection (5) above any reference to appearing before a court shall be construed as including a reference to being brought before a court.

DEFINITIONS
   "food": s.1(1), (2) and (4).
   "sale and related expressions": s.2.

GENERAL NOTE

This is one of the most important provisions in the Act since it introduces a new "due diligence" defence in place of the long established "warranty" defence which had been of particular value to the retailer of food. Under s.102 of the Food Act 1984, and equivalent Scottish legislation, the defendant could plead that he had a written warranty to the effect that the article or substance could be lawfully sold or otherwise dealt with. S.102(5) was of particular value to retailers as it provided that an invoice constituted a written warranty. The "due diligence" defence found in s.21 is similar to that in the Trade Descriptions Act 1968, and in the Weights and Measures Act 1985, and in the Consumer Protection Act 1987, but there are important modifications designed to protect those who take reasonable precautions.

Subs. (1)

In any proceedings for an offence under any of the preceding provisions of this Part. Accordingly, the defence applies in respect of offences under Pt. II, and not for example to offences such as obstruction of officers (see s.33).

Subject to subsection (5) below. If it is argued that another person was responsible then the defendant must identify that person within the time limits set out in subs. (5).

Took all reasonable precautions and exercised all due diligence. Both aspects of the defence must be satisfied. For an example of satisfaction of this test under other legislation, see *Naish* v. *Gore* [1971] 3 All E.R. 737. For examples of failure to satisfy the test see *Sherrat* v. *Gerald's The American Jewellers* (1970) 1 S.J. 147; *Read* v. *West Wales Bakeries* [1962] Crim. L.R. 477; *Richmond upon Thames London Borough Council* v. *Motor Sales (Hounslow)* 115 S.J. 156; *Aitchison* v. *Reith and Anderson (Dingwall and Tain)* 1974 S.L.T. 282; *Taylor* v. *Fraser (Lawrence) (Bristol)* (1977) 121 S.J. 757; *Simmons* v. *Ravenhill* (1984) 148 J.P. 109.

Subs. (2)

The requirement to have taken *all reasonable precautions and exercised all due diligence* may be unduly burdensome, particularly to those who did not prepare the food or who simply imported it into Great Britain. Accordingly, subs. (2) provides this special defence to a person charged under s.8 (selling food not complying with food safety requirements), s.14 (selling food not of the nature or substance or quality demanded) or s.15 (falsely describing or presenting food). Such a person will be taken to have established the defence if he satisfies the requirements of subs. (3) *or* subs. (4). In practice, most retailers will arguably be able to obtain protection similar to and in some cases stronger than that afforded by the old warranty defence by invoking s.21(3)(b) (where the sale or intended sale is under his own name or mark) or s.21(4)(b) (where the sale or intended sale is not under his own name or mark). S.21(3)(b) clearly requires more in the way of checks since it applies to those using their own name or mark (including of course own-branders).

Subs. (6) seems to be intended to avoid any doubt that a person who is brought before the court (for example, following arrest for failure to answer a summons) is treated as a person who appears before a court.

Defence of publication in the course of business

22. In proceedings for an offence under any of the preceding provisions of this Part consisting of the advertisement for sale of any food, it shall be a defence for the person charged to prove—

  (a) that he is a person whose business it is to publish or arrange for the publication of advertisements; and

  (b) that he received the advertisement in the ordinary course of business and did not know and had no reason to suspect that its publication would amount to an offence under that provision.

DEFINITIONS

"advertisement": s.53(1).
"business": s.1(3).
"food": s.1(1), (2) and (4).
"sale and related expressions": s.2.

GENERAL NOTE

This defence is available to publishers of advertisements and it corresponds with the provision in s.25 of the Trade Descriptions Act 1968. The defence is needed because of the difficulty which publishers would otherwise face in seeking to establish the "due diligence" defence in s.21.

Miscellaneous and supplemental

Provision of food hygiene training

23.—(1) A food authority may provide, whether within or outside their area, training courses in food hygiene for persons who are or intend to become involved in food businesses, whether as proprietors or employees or otherwise.

(2) A food authority may contribute towards the expenses incurred under this section by any other such authority, or towards expenses incurred by any other person in providing, such courses as are mentioned in subsection (1) above.

DEFINITIONS

"food authority": s.5.
"food business": s.1(3).
"proprietor": s.53(1).

GENERAL NOTE

Or otherwise. This means, *e.g.* those who volunteer to serve food in a club or charitable organisation.

This is a further example of previously voluntary arrangements being given statutory backing under the Act. The provisions are self-explanatory but the comma after "providing" in subs. (2) seems otiose, and may have been intended to be after "person."

S.45 gives the Ministers power to require or authorise charges to be imposed by enforcement authorities for such courses.

Provision of facilities for cleansing shellfish

24.—(1) A food authority may provide, whether within or outside their area, tanks or other apparatus for cleansing shellfish.

(2) A food authority may contribute towards the expenses incurred under this section by any other such authority, or towards expenses incurred by any other person in providing, and making available to the public, tanks or other apparatus for cleansing shellfish.

(3) Nothing in this section authorises the establishment of any tank or other apparatus, or the execution of any other work, on, over or under tidal lands below high-water mark of ordinary spring tides, except in accordance with such plans and sections, and subject to such restrictions and conditions as may before the work is commenced be approved by the Secretary of State.

(4) In this section "cleansing", in relation to shellfish, includes subjecting them to any germicidal treatment.

DEFINITION

"food authority": s.5.

GENERAL NOTE

Powers to provide facilities for the cleansing of shellfish exist under current legislation (s.30 of the Food Act 1984; s.20 of the Food and Drugs (Scotland) Act 1956). S.24 re-enacts these provisions with minor amendments.

Subs. (1)

The provision in precursor legislation referred to county councils and local authorities. These terms have been replaced with the term "food authority" in line with the scheme of the new Act. The provision that authorities may make charges for use of cleansing facilities is dealt with not in this provision, as in previous legislation, but by regulations made under s.45 below. The provisions of s.30(3) of the Food Act 1984 have been transferred to s.46(2) below.

Orders for facilitating the exercise of functions

25.—(1) For the purpose of facilitating the exercise of their functions under this Part, the Ministers may by order require every person who at the date of the order, or at any subsequent time, carries on a business of a specified class or description (in this section referred to as a "relevant business")—

    (a) to afford to persons specified in the order such facilities for the taking of samples of any food, substance or contact material to which subsection (2) below applies; or

    (b) to furnish to persons so specified such information concerning any such food, substance or contact material,

as (in each case) is specified in the order and is reasonably required by such persons.

    (2) This subsection applies to—

    (a) any food of a class specified in the order which is sold or intended to be sold in the course of a relevant business for human consumption;

    (b) any substance of a class so specified which is sold in the course of such a business for use in the preparation of food for human consumption, or is used for that purpose in the course of such a business; and

    (c) any contact material of a class so specified which is sold in the course of such a business and is intended to come into contact with food intended for human consumption.

    (3) No information relating to any individual business which is obtained by means of an order under subsection (1) above shall, without the previous consent in writing of the person carrying on the business, be disclosed except—

    (a) in accordance with directions of the Minister, so far as may be necessary for the purposes of this Act or of any corresponding enactment in force in Northern Ireland, or for the purpose of complying with any Community obligation; or

    (b) for the purposes of any proceedings for an offence against the order or any report of those proceedings;

and any person who discloses any such information in contravention of this subsection shall be guilty of an offence.

    (4) In subsection (3) above the reference to a disclosure being necessary for the purposes of this Act includes a reference to it being necessary—

    (a) for the purpose of securing that food complies with food safety requirements or in the interests of the public health; or

    (b) for the purpose of protecting or promoting the interests of consumers;

and the reference to a disclosure being necessary for the purposes of any corresponding enactment in force in Northern Ireland shall be construed accordingly.

DEFINITIONS
    "business": s.1(3).
    "contact material": s.1(3).
    "contravention": s.53(1).
    "food": s.1(1), (2) and (4).
    "food safety requirements and related expressions": s.8(2).
    "functions": s.53(1).
    "human consumption": s.53(1).

"preparation": s.53(1).
"substance": s.53(1).
"the Minister": s.4(1) and (2).
"the Ministers": s.4(1).

GENERAL NOTE
This provision is designed to replace and extend the powers currently set out in s.5 of the Food Act 1984 (s.5 Food and Drugs (Scotland) Act 1956) with new powers to make orders to require facilities to be afforded for the taking of samples of, or to furnish information concerning, any food, substance or contact material. Voluntary co-operation of the industry will continue to be the main method of obtaining samples to be analysed; the new rules give statutory backing which can be used if required.

Subs. (2)
This qualifies the definitions of food, contact material and substance referred to above.

Subs. (3)
This provision is designed to ensure that information relating to an individual business is kept confidential, so that, for example, there is no unnecessary disruption of the business following unauthorised disclosure. Disclosure is permitted in the circumstances set out in s.25(3)(a) (on direction by the Minister) and s.25(3)(b). S.35 states the penalties for disclosure in contravention of the subsection.

Subs. (4)
Necessary for the purposes of this Act. These words occur in s.25(3)(a) above, and refer to the power of the Minister to direct disclosure of information. Subs. (4) gives clarification as to when disclosure will be necessary.

Regulations and orders: supplementary provisions

26.—(1) Regulations under this Part may—
(a) make provision for prohibiting or regulating the carrying out of commercial operations with respect to any food, food source or contact material—
(i) which fails to comply with the regulations; or
(ii) in relation to which an offence against the regulations has been committed, or would have been committed if any relevant act or omission had taken place in Great Britain; and
(b) without prejudice to the generality of section 9 above, provide that any food which, in accordance with the regulations, is certified as being such food as is mentioned in paragraph (a) above may be treated for the purposes of that section as failing to comply with food safety requirements.
(2) Regulations under this Part may also—
(a) require persons carrying on any activity to which the regulations apply to keep and produce records and provide returns;
(b) prescribe the particulars to be entered on any register required to be kept in accordance with the regulations;
(c) require any such register to be open to inspection by the public at all reasonable times and, subject to that, authorise it to be kept by means of a computer;
(d) prescribe the periods for which and the conditions subject to which licences may be issued, and provide for the subsequent alteration of conditions and for the cancellation, suspension or revocation of licences;
(e) provide for an appeal to a magistrates' court or, in Scotland, to the sheriff, or to a tribunal constituted in accordance with the regulations, against any decision of an enforcement authority, or of an authorised officer of such an authority; and

    (f) provide, as respects any appeal to such a tribunal, for the procedure in the appeal (including costs) and for any appeal against the tribunal's decision.

(3) Regulations under this Part or an order under section 25 above may—

    (a) provide that an offence under the regulations or order shall be triable in such way as may be there specified; and

    (b) include provisions under which a person guilty of such an offence shall be liable to such penalties (not exceeding those which may be imposed in respect of offences under this Act) as may be specified in the regulations or order.

DEFINITIONS
"commercial operation": s.1(3) and (4).
"contact material": s.1(3).
"enforcement authority": s.6(1).
"food": s.1(1), (2) and (4).
"food safety requirements and related expressions": s.8(2).
"food source": s.1(3).
"officer": s.53(1).

GENERAL NOTE
This provision is a re-enactment and extension of the subordinate legislation-making powers set out in s.118 of the Food Act 1984, and its wording takes account of the terminology introduced by the new Act.

Subs. (1)
Regulations under this Part. This means under ss.16, 17, 18 and 19. For example, suppose that injection of a certain antibiotic drug into cattle were prohibited by regulations in Great Britain, but that meat with residues of the drug were being imported into Great Britain. Ministers would be able to prohibit commercial operations with respect to such food.

Paragraph (b)
This provision replaces s.4(4) of the Food Act 1984 (s.4(4) Food and Drugs (Scotland) Act 1956) and has the effect of permitting (by bringing such food as is mentioned in paragraph (a) within the ambit of s.9 above) the inspection, seizure and destruction of the food.

Subs. (2)
Further matters which may be covered by regulations are listed here. Detailed provisions *inter alia* dealing with issuing, cancelling, altering or revoking licences, and provisions supplementing the rights of appeal granted under ss.37–39 are expected under this subsection.

Subs. (3)
The regulations or orders referred to may specify particular modes of trial and penalties.

PART III

ADMINISTRATION AND ENFORCEMENT

Administration

Appointment of public analysts

27.—(1) Every authority to whom this section applies, that is to say, every food authority in England and Wales and every regional or islands council in Scotland, shall appoint in accordance with this section one or more persons (in this Act referred to as "public analysts") to act as analysts for the purposes of this Act within the authority's area.

(2) No person shall be appointed as a public analyst unless he possesses—

(a) such qualifications as may be prescribed by regulations made by the Ministers; or

(b) such other qualifications as the Ministers may approve,

and no person shall act as a public analyst for any area who is engaged directly or indirectly in any food business which is carried on in that area.

(3) An authority to whom this section applies shall pay to a public analyst such remuneration as may be agreed, which may be expressed to be payable either—

(a) in addition to any fees received by him under this Part; or

(b) on condition that any fees so received by him are paid over by him to the authority.

(4) An authority to whom this section applies who appoint only one public analyst may appoint also a deputy to act during any vacancy in the office of public analyst, or during the absence or incapacity of the holder of the office, and—

(a) the provisions of this section with respect to the qualifications, appointment, removal and remuneration of a public analyst shall apply also in relation to a deputy public analyst; and

(b) any reference in the following provisions of this Act to a public analyst shall be construed as including a reference to a deputy public analyst appointed under this subsection.

(5) In subsection (1) above "food authority" does not include the council of a non-metropolitan district, the Sub-Treasurer of the Inner Temple or the Under Treasurer of the Middle Temple; and in subsection (2) above the reference to being engaged directly or indirectly in a food business includes a reference to having made such arrangements with a food business as may be prescribed by regulations made by the Ministers.

DEFINITIONS
"food authority": s.5.
"food business": s.1(3).
"public analyst": s.27(1).
"the Ministers": s.4(1).

GENERAL NOTE
This section re-enacts with minor amendments the provisions contained in s.76 of the Food Act 1984 and s.27 of the Food and Drugs (Scotland) Act 1956. Public analysts must be appointed by every food authority to whom the section applies, and must possess the prescribed or approved qualifications. Food authorities must pay the analyst. A deputy analyst may be appointed and references in the Act to a public analyst include a deputy.

Subs. (2)
Who is engaged directly or indirectly in any food business which is carried out on that area.
Subs. (5) permits the Ministers to prescribe in regulations *arrangements with a food business* which will be included within the meaning of *engaged directly or indirectly in any food business.*

Provision of facilities for examinations

28.—(1) A food authority, or a regional council in Scotland, may provide facilities for examinations for the purposes of this Act.

(2) In this Act "examination" means a microbiological examination and "examine" shall be construed accordingly.

DEFINITION
"food authority": s.5.

GENERAL NOTE
This provision re-enacts the substance of s.77 of the Food Act 1984 (s.27 of the Food and Drugs (Scotland) Act 1956). However, for the purpose of clarification, *bacteriological and*

other examinations in the 1984 Act is replaced with *examinations* which mean *microbiological examination* in the new Act. *Microbiological* is the wider term and would more clearly include, for example, examinations for contamination by a viral agent.

Sampling and analysis etc.

Procurement of samples

29. An authorised officer of an enforcement authority may—

(a) purchase a sample of any food, or any substance capable of being used in the preparation of food;

(b) take a sample of any food, or any such substance, which—

(i) appears to him to be intended for sale, or to have been sold, for human consumption; or

(ii) is found by him on or in any premises which he is authorised to enter by or under section 32 below;

(c) take a sample from any food source, or a sample of any contact material, which is found by him on or in any such premises;

(d) take a sample of any article or substance which is found by him on or in any such premises and which he has reason to believe may be required as evidence in proceedings under any of the provisions of this Act or of regulations or orders made under it.

DEFINITIONS
"article": s.53(1).
"contact material": s.1(3).
"enforcement authority": s.6(1).
"food": s.1(1), (2) and (4).
"food source": s.1(3).
"human consumption": s.53(1).
"officer": s.53(1).
"premises": s.1(3).
"preparation": s.53(1).
"sale and related expressions": s.2.
"substance": s.53(1).

GENERAL NOTE
This is substantially a re-enactment of s.78 of the Food Act 1984 (s.28 of the Food and Drugs (Scotland) Act 1956). However, specific sampling powers set out in the precursor legislation have been replaced with general sampling powers and the regulation-making powers under s.31 will be used to introduce specific sampling powers. Procurement of samples applies to articles or substances (*e.g.* dirt) found on premises which the officer is entitled to enter in terms of s.32 as well as to food, food sources, and contact materials. Sampling of food sources will allow sampling of, for example, live poultry.

An authorised officer of an enforcement authority. This states "of an enforcement authority" (see s.6 above) rather than of a food authority, so that persons other than officers of food authorities (*e.g.* persons employed by the state veterinary service) have sampling powers.

Analysis etc. of samples

30.—(1) An authorised officer of an enforcement authority who has procured a sample under section 29 above shall—

(a) if he considers that the sample should be analysed, submit it to be analysed either—

(i) by the public analyst for the area in which the sample was procured; or

(ii) by the public analyst for the area which consists of or includes the area of the authority;

(b) if he considers that the sample should be examined, submit it to be examined by a food examiner.

(2) A person, other than such an officer, who has purchased any food, or any substance capable of being used in the preparation of food, may submit a sample of it—

(a) to be analysed by the public analyst for the area in which the purchase was made; or

(b) to be examined by a food examiner.

(3) If, in any case where a sample is proposed to be submitted for analysis under this section, the office of public analyst for the area in question is vacant, the sample shall be submitted to the public analyst for some other area.

(4) If, in any case where a sample is proposed to be or is submitted for analysis or examination under this section, the food analyst or examiner determines that he is for any reason unable to perform the analysis or examination, the sample shall be submitted or, as the case may be, sent by him to such other food analyst or examiner as he may determine.

(5) A food analyst or examiner shall analyse or examine as soon as practicable any sample submitted or sent to him under this section, but may, except where—

(a) he is the public analyst for the area in question; and

(b) the sample is submitted to him for analysis by an authorised officer of an enforcement authority,

demand in advance the payment of such reasonable fee as he may require.

(6) A food analyst or examiner who has analysed or examined a sample shall give to the person by whom it was submitted a certificate specifying the result of the analysis or examination.

(7) Any certificate given by a food analyst or examiner under subsection (6) above shall be signed by him, but the analysis or examination may be made by any person acting under his direction.

(8) In any proceedings under this Act, the production by one of the parties—

(a) of a document purporting to be a certificate given by a food analyst or examiner under subsection (6) above; or

(b) of a document supplied to him by the other party as being a copy of such a certificate,

shall be sufficient evidence of the facts stated in it unless, in a case falling within paragraph (a) above, the other party requires that the food analyst or examiner shall be called as a witness.

(9) In this section—

"food analyst" means a public analyst or any other person who possesses the requisite qualifications to carry out analyses for the purposes of this Act;

"food examiner" means any person who possesses the requisite qualifications to carry out examinations for the purposes of this Act;

"the requisite qualifications" means such qualifications as may be prescribed by regulations made by the Ministers, or such other qualifications as the Ministers may approve;

"sample", in relation to an authorised officer of an enforcement authority, includes any part of a sample retained by him in pursuance of regulations under section 31 below.

and where two or more public analysts are appointed for any area, any reference in this section to the public analyst for that area shall be construed as a reference to either or any of them.

DEFINITIONS
"analysis": s.53(1).
"enforcement authority": s.6(1).
"examination and examine": s.28(2).

"food": s.1(1), (2) and (4).
"officer": s.53(1).
"preparation": s.53(1).
"substance": s.53(1).
"the Ministers": s.4(1).

GENERAL NOTE
This provision restates and extends s.79 of the Food Act 1984 (s.29 of the Food and Drugs (Scotland) Act 1956). Officers of enforcement authorities may have the sample *analysed* (by sending it to the public analyst) or *examined* (by sending it to a food examiner—defined in subs. (9)). The definition of *analysis* in s.53 is to be contrasted to that of *examine* in s.28(2). Under subs. (5) a fee may be charged where the sample is submitted other than by an authorised officer to the public analyst for the area in question. *Food analyst* is defined in subs. (9). The food analyst or examiner provides a certificate showing the results which can then (subs. (8)) be used in court proceedings.

Regulation of sampling and analysis etc.

31.—(1) The Ministers may by regulations make provision for supplementing or modifying the provisions of sections 29 and 30 above.

(2) Without prejudice to the generality of subsection (1) above, regulations under that subsection may make provision with respect to—

(a) the matters to be taken into account in determining whether, and at what times, samples should be procured;

(b) the manner of procuring samples, including the steps to be taken in order to ensure that any samples procured are fair samples;

(c) the method of dealing with samples, including (where appropriate) their division into parts;

(d) the persons to whom parts of samples are to be given and the persons by whom such parts are to be retained;

(e) the notices which are to be given to, and the information which is to be furnished by, the persons in charge of any food, substance, contact material or food source of or from which samples are procured;

(f) the methods which are to be used in analysing or examining samples, or parts of samples, or in classifying the results of analyses or examinations;

(g) the circumstances in which a food analyst or examiner is to be precluded, by reason of a conflict of interest, from analysing or examining a particular sample or part of a sample; and

(h) the circumstances in which samples, or parts of samples, are to be or may be submitted for analysis or examination—

(i) to the Government Chemist, or to such other food analyst or examiner as he may direct; or

(ii) to a person determined by or under the regulations.

(3) In this section "food analyst" and "food examiner" have the same meanings as in section 30 above.

DEFINITIONS
"analysis": s.53(1).
"contact material": s.1(3).
"examination and examine": s.28(2).
"food": s.1(1), (2) and (4).
"food source": s.1(3).
"substance": s.53(1).
"the Ministers": s.4(1).

GENERAL NOTE
Sections 80, 81, 84, 99 and Sched. 7 of the Food Act 1984 (ss. 29–31, 33 and 44 of the Food and Drugs (Scotland) Act 1956) state in detail the treatment of samples taken for analysis, including sampling of milk, samples from unopened containers, movement of

imported food, and analysis by the Government Chemist. These provisions are replaced by the simpler and more flexible provision in this section to permit the Ministers to supplement or modify the sampling and analysis, etc., provisions of s.29 and s.30.

Powers of entry and obstruction etc.

Powers of entry

32.—(1) An authorised officer of an enforcement authority shall, on producing, if so required, some duly authenticated document showing his authority, have a right at all reasonable hours—

(a) to enter any premises within the authority's area for the purpose of ascertaining whether there is or has been on the premises any contravention of the provisions of this Act, or of regulations or orders made under it; and

(b) to enter any business premises, whether within or outside the authority's area, for the purpose of ascertaining whether there is on the premises any evidence of any contravention within that area of any of such provisions; and

(c) in the case of an authorised officer of a food authority, to enter any premises for the purpose of the performance by the authority of their functions under this Act;

but admission to any premises used only as a private dwelling-house shall not be demanded as of right unless 24 hours' notice of the intended entry has been given to the occupier.

(2) If a justice of the peace, on sworn information in writing, is satisfied that there is reasonable ground for entry into any premises for any such purpose as is mentioned in subsection (1) above and either—

(a) that admission to the premises has been refused, or a refusal is apprehended, and that notice of the intention to apply for a warrant has been given to the occupier; or

(b) that an application for admission, or the giving of such a notice, would defeat the object of the entry, or that the case is one of urgency, or that the premises are unoccupied or the occupier temporarily absent,

the justice may by warrant signed by him authorise the authorised officer to enter the premises, if need be by reasonable force.

(3) Every warrant granted under this section shall continue in force for a period of one month.

(4) An authorised officer entering any premises by virtue of this section, or of a warrant issued under it, may take with him such other persons as he considers necessary, and on leaving any unoccupied premises which he has entered by virtue of such a warrant shall leave them as effectively secured against unauthorised entry as he found them.

(5) An authorised officer entering premises by virtue of this section, or of a warrant issued under it, may inspect any records (in whatever form they are held) relating to a food business and, where any such records are kept by means of a computer—

(a) may have access to, and inspect and check the operation of, any computer and any associated apparatus or material which is or has been in use in connection with the records; and

(b) may require any person having charge of, or otherwise concerned with the operation of, the computer, apparatus or material to afford him such assistance as he may reasonably require.

(6) Any officer exercising any power conferred by subsection (5) above may—

(a) seize and detain any records which he has reason to believe may be required as evidence in proceedings under any of the provisions of this Act or of regulations or orders made under it; and

(b) where the reords are kept by means of a computer, may require the records to be produced in a form in which they may be taken away.

(7) If any person who enters any premises by virtue of this section, or of a warrant issued under it, discloses to any person any information obtained by him in the premises with regard to any trade secret he shall, unless the disclosure was made in the performance of his duty, be guilty of an offence.

(8) Nothing in this section authorises any person, except with the permission of the local authority under the Animal Health Act 1981, to enter any premises—

(a) in which an animal or bird affected with any disease to which that Act applies is kept; and

(b) which is situated in a place declared under that Act to be infected with such a disease.

(9) In the application of this section to Scotland, any reference to a justice of the peace includes a reference to the sheriff and to a magistrate.

DEFINITIONS
"authorised officer of a food authority": s.5(6).
"animal": s.53(1).
"business": s.1(3).
"contravention": s.53(1).
"enforcement authority": s.6(1).
"food business": s.1(3).
"functions": s.53(1).
"occupier": s.53(1).
"officer": s.53(1).
"premises": s.1(3).

GENERAL NOTE
This section brings together and extends the powers of entry which are set out in ss.87–89 and s.91 of the Food Act 1984 (see also s.36 of the Food and Drugs (Scotland) Act 1956). The opportunity has been taken to add to the previous powers in two important respects: firstly, s.32(1)(b) gives power to an authorised officer of an enforcement authority to enter business premises within or outwith the authority's area for the purpose of ascertaining evidence pertaining to a contravention within his own area (see *McNair* v. *Cave* [1903] 1 K.B. 24; *R* v. *Smith* [1896] 1 Q.B. 596, dealing with the old rules); secondly, the same provision would permit entry to premises to inspect food sources such as crops and live animals prior to their conversion into food. Along with ss.40 and 41, this section applies the E.C. Official Control of Foodstuffs Directive (89/397/EEC).

Subs. (1)
Paras. (a) and (b) relate to the powers of authorised officers of enforcement authorities, while para. (c) refers to an authorised officer of a food authority.
At all reasonable hours. See *Small* v. *Bickley* (1875) 32 L.T. 726; *Davies* v. *Winstanley* (1931) 144 L.T. 433.

Subs. (2)
Forcible entry without a warrant is not permitted: see *Robson* v. *Hallett* [1967] 2 Q.B. 939.

Subs. (5)
This is a new provision designed to deal with records kept in computerised form. Para. (b) allows the officer to require assistance in operating the computer and related material such as disks.

Subs. (6)
This is another new provision reflecting provisions which are found in other consumer protection legislation to seize and detain records which are needed for evidential purposes.

Subs. (7)

The precursor provision referred to *manufacturing process or trade secret*. Disclosure of a manufacturing process may be in the interests of public health. However, a *manufacturing process* may well be a *trade secret* and so may still be covered.

Obstruction etc. of officers

33.—(1) Any person who—
  (a) intentionally obstructs any person acting in the execution of this Act; or
  (b) without reasonable cause, fails to give to any person acting in the execution of this Act any assistance or information which that person may reasonably require of him for the performance of his functions under this Act.
shall be guilty of an offence.

  (2) Any person who, in purported compliance with any such requirement as is mentioned in subsection (1)(b) above—
  (a) furnishes information which he knows to be false or misleading in a material particular; or
  (b) recklessly furnishes information which is false or misleading in a material particular,
shall be guilty of an offence.

  (3) Nothing in subsection (1)(b) above shall be construed as requiring any person to answer any question or give any information if to do so might incriminate him.

DEFINITION
  "functions": s.53(1).

GENERAL NOTE
  This is a re-enactment with minor amendments of the existing rules (see s.91 of the Food Act 1984 and s.39 of the Food and Drugs (Scotland) Act 1956) in terms similar to those relating to the offence of obstruction, as in, for example, the Trade Descriptions Act 1968, the Weights and Measures Act 1985 and the Consumer Protection Act 1987. See *Soutar* v. *Kerr* 1907 S.C. 49; *French* v. *Card* (1909) 101 L.T. 428.

Subs. (1)
  Intentionally. This replaces *wilfully* in the precursor provision (s.91 of the Food Act 1984). *Wilfully* can be regarded as importing an element of *mens rea* (see, *e.g. Eaton* v. *Cobb* 114 J.P. 271), but in the context of wilful obstruction has been held not to imply *mens rea*, in the sense in which that term is used to mean that a person will only be guilty if he knowingly does a wrongful act, so that it is enough if a person intentionally and of his own free will causes the obstruction (*Arrowsmith* v. *Jenkins* [1963] 2 Q.B. 561). *Intentionally* should remove the need to prove *mens rea* in that sense.
  In the execution of this Act. The words *or of any regulation, byelaw, order or warrant made under it* appeared in the previous legislation but are otiose.

Offences

Time limit for prosecutions

34. No prosecution for an offence under this Act which is punishable under section 35(2) below shall be begun after the expiry of—
  (a) three years from the commission of the offence; or
  (b) one year from its discovery by the prosecutor,
whichever is the earlier.

GENERAL NOTE
  This is a re-enactment with minor amendments of s.95 of the Food Act 1984 (s.41 of the Food and Drugs (Scotland) Act 1956). These previous provisions stipulated that no prosecution could be commenced after the expiry of 28 days in the case of a sample of milk

and two months in other cases. As effective methods of refrigerated storage are now available these provisions have been removed. See *Daventry District Council* v. *Olins* [1990] 154 J.P. 478.

Punishment of offences

35.—(1) A person guilty of an offence under section 33(1) above shall be liable on summary conviction to a fine not exceeding level 5 on the standard scale or to imprisonment for a term not exceeding three months or to both.

(2) A person guilty of any other offence under this Act shall be liable—

    (a) on conviction on indictment, to a fine or to imprisonment for a term not exceeding two years or to both;

    (b) on summary conviction, to a fine not exceeding the relevant amount or to imprisonment for a term not exceeding six months or to both.

(3) In subsection (2) above "the relevant amount" means—

    (a) in the case of an offence under section 7, 8 or 14 above, £20,000;

    (b) in any other case, the statutory maximum.

(4) If a person who is—

    (a) licensed under section 1 of the Slaughterhouses Act 1974 to keep a slaughterhouse or knacker's yard;

    (b) registered under section 4 of the Slaughter of Animals (Scotland) Act 1980 in respect of any premises for use as a slaughterhouse; or

    (c) licensed under section 6 of that Act to use any premises as a knacker's yard,

is convicted of an offence under Part II of this Act, the court may, in addition to any other punishment, cancel his licence or registration.

DEFINITIONS

    "knacker's yard": s.53(1).
    "premises": s.1(3).
    "slaughterhouse": s.53(1).

GENERAL NOTE

Subs. (1)

    This sets out the punishment of the offences of obstruction or failure to give assistance or information. These offences are not triable on indictment. The current maximum fine (level 5) is £2,000. In England, proceedings will be in the Magistrates' Court and in Scotland will be in the District Court or the Sheriff Court (summary procedure).

Subs. (2)

    This deals with other offences under the Act. Conviction on indictment can result in an unlimited fine, up to two years' imprisonment or both. Summary conviction can result in a fine of up to £20,000 if the offence is under s.7 (rendering food injurious to health), s.8 (selling food not complying with food safety requirements) or s.14 (selling food not of the nature, substance or quality demanded). In other cases of summary conviction (for example, s.15—falsely describing or presenting food) the maximum fine is currently £2,000.

Subs. (3)

    Licensed or Registered persons may have, following conviction, the licence or registration revoked by the court.

Offences by bodies corporate

36.—(1) Where an offence under this Act which has been committed by a body corporate is proved to have been committed with the consent or connivance of, or to be attributable to any neglect on the part of—

(a) any director, manager, secretary or other similar officer of the body corporate; or

(b) any person who was purporting to act in any such capacity,

he as well as the body corporate shall be deemed to be guilty of that offence and shall be liable to be proceeded against and punished accordingly.

(2) In subsection (1) above "director", in relation to any body corporate established by or under any enactment for the purpose of carrying on under national ownership any industry or part of an industry or undertaking, being a body corporate whose affairs are managed by its members, means a member of that body corporate.

GENERAL NOTE

This is an exact re-enactment of s.94 of the Food Act 1984, designed to ensure that persons responsible for the commission of an offence cannot hide behind the corporate personality of their company or other body corporate.

Appeals

Appeals to magistrates' court or sheriff

37.—(1) Any person who is aggrieved by—

(a) a decision of an authorised officer of an enforcement authority to serve an improvement notice;

(b) a decision of an enforcement authority to refuse to issue such a certificate as is mentioned in section 11(6) or 12(8) above; or

(c) subject to subsection (2) below, a decision of such an authority to refuse, cancel, suspend or revoke a licence required by regulations under Part II of this Act,

may appeal to a magistrates' court or, in Scotland, to the sheriff.

(2) Subsection (1)(c) above shall not apply in relation to any decision as respects which regulations under Part II of this Act provide for an appeal to a tribunal constituted in accordance with the regulations.

(3) The procedure on an appeal to a magistrates' court under subsection (1) above, or an appeal to such a court for which provision is made by regulations under Part II of this Act, shall be by way of complaint for an order, and the Magistrates' Courts Act 1980 shall apply to the proceedings.

(4) An appeal to the sheriff under subsection (1) above, or an appeal to the sheriff for which provision is made by regulations under Part II of this Act, shall be by summary application.

(5) The period within which such an appeal as is mentioned in subsection (3) or (4) above may be brought shall be—

(a) one month from the date on which notice of the decision was served on the person desiring to appeal; or

(b) in the case of an appeal under subsection (1)(a) above, that period or the period specified in the improvement notice, whichever ends the earlier;

and, in the case of such an appeal as is mentioned in subsection (3) above, the making of the complaint shall be deemed for the purposes of this subsection to be the bringing of the appeal.

(6) In any case where such an appeal as is mentioned in subsection (3) or (4) above lies, the document notifying the decision to the person concerned shall state—

(a) the right of appeal to a magistrates' court or to the sheriff; and

(b) the period within which such an appeal may be brought.

DEFINITIONS
"enforcement authority": s.6(1).
"improvement notice": s.10(1).
"officer": s.53(1).

GENERAL NOTE
The right of appeal, which had been available under precursor legislation, has been
extended to cover appeals against the service of improvement notices and against failure to
lift a prohibition order (see s.11(6) above) or an emergency prohibition order (see s.12(7)
above). Appeals in respect of a decision by an enforcement authority to refuse, cancel,
suspend or revoke a licence can, by virtue of s.37(2), be made to a tribunal constituted in
accordance with the regulations.
The period within which appeals had to be brought under the previous legislation was 21
days (see, *e.g.* the Food Act 1984, s.104(2). S.37(5) replaces this with new time limits.

Appeals to Crown Court

38. A person who is aggrieved by—
   (a) any dismissal by a magistrates' court of such an appeal as is
       mentioned in section 37(3) above; or
   (b) any decision of such a court to make a prohibition order or an
       emergency prohibition order, or to exercise the power con-
       ferred by section 35(4) above,
may appeal to the Crown Court.

DEFINITIONS
"emergency prohibition order": s.12(2).
"prohibition order": s.11(5).

GENERAL NOTE
This provision does not apply to Scotland where appeals are dealt with by sheriff court
legislation and other rules.

Appeals against improvement notices

39.—(1) On an appeal against an improvement notice, the court may
either cancel or affirm the notice and, if it affirms it, may do so either in
its original form or with such modifications as the court may in the
circumstances think fit.
   (2) Where, apart from this subsection, any period specified in an
improvement notice would include any day on which an appeal against
that notice is pending, that day shall be excluded from that period.
   (3) An appeal shall be regarded as pending for the purposes of
subsection (2) above until it is finally disposed of, is withdrawn or is struck
out for want of prosecution.

DEFINITION
"improvement notice": s.10(1).

GENERAL NOTE
This provision deals with the court's powers on an appeal against an improvement notice.
The effect of subss. (2) and (3) is that the running of the time period for the improvement
notice is suspended until the appeal is dealt with.

PART IV

MISCELLANEOUS AND SUPPLEMENTAL

Powers of Ministers

Power to issue codes of practice

40.—(1) For the guidance of food authorities, the Ministers or the Minister may issue codes of recommended practice as regards the execution and enforcement of this Act and of regulations and orders made under it; and any such code shall be laid before Parliament after being issued.

(2) In the exercise of the functions conferred on them by or under this Act, every food authority—

    (a) shall have regard to any relevant provision of any such code; and

    (b) shall comply with any direction which is given by the Ministers or the Minister and requires them to take any specified steps in order to comply with such a code.

(3) Any direction under subsection (2)(b) above shall, on the application of the Ministers or the Minister, be enforceable by mandamus or, in Scotland, by an order of the Court of Session under section 45 of the Court of Session Act 1988.

(4) Before issuing any code under this section, the Ministers or the Minister shall consult with such organisations as appear to them or him to be representative of interests likely to be substantially affected by the code.

(5) Any consultation undertaken before the commencement of subsection (4) above shall be as effective, for the purposes of that subsection, as if undertaken after that commencement.

DEFINITIONS

    "food authority": s.5.
    "functions": s.53(1).
    "the Minister": s.4(1) and (2).
    "the Ministers": s.4(1).

GENERAL NOTE

This provision is designed to achieve *inter alia* consistency of enforcement of the Act by the various enforcement authorities. Moreover, control of enforcement work is necessary in order to comply with the E.C. Official Control of Foodstuffs Directive.

Subs. (4)

It is not yet clear which organisations will be consulted under this provision and the similar provision in s.48(4), but the words *who appear to them or him* confer discretion upon Ministers.

Subs. (5)

The Minister(s) may wish to carry out consultations prior to the coming into effect of s.40(4), and s.40(5) permits this to happen at any time after Royal Assent.

Power to require returns

41. Every food authority shall send to the Minister such reports and returns, and give him such information, with respect to the exercise of the functions conferred on them by or under this Act as he may require.

DEFINITIONS

    "food authority": s.5.
    "functions": s.53(1).
    "the Minister": s.4(1) and (2).

GENERAL NOTE
Surprisingly, previous legislation imposed no duty upon enforcement authorities to send reports and returns to the Minister. This provision gives a statutory basis for the supply of returns and will, along with s.40 above, ensure that the Act is being executed and enforced in a consistent manner by the various enforcement authorities.

Default powers

42.—(1) Where the Minister is satisfied that—

(a) a food authority (in this section referred to as "the authority in default") have failed to discharge any duty imposed by or under this Act; and

(b) the authority's failure affects the general interests of consumers of food,

he may by order empower another food authority (in this section referred to as "the substitute authority"), or one of his officers, to discharge that duty in place of the authority in default.

(2) For the purpose of determining whether the power conferred by subsection (1) above is exercisable, the Minister may cause a local inquiry to be held; and where he does so, the relevant provisions of the Local Government Act shall apply as if the inquiry were a local inquiry held under that Act.

(3) Nothing in subsection (1) above affects any other power exercisable by the Minister with respect to defaults of local authorities.

(4) The substitute authority or the Minister may recover from the authority in default any expenses reasonably incurred by them or him under subsection (1) above; and for the purpose of paying any such amount the authority in default may—

(a) raise money as if the expenses had been incurred directly by them as a local authority; and

(b) if and to the extent that they are authorised to do so by the Minister, borrow money in accordance with the statutory provisions relating to borrowing by a local authority.

(5) In this section "the relevant provisions of the Local Government Act" means subsections (2) to (5) of section 250 of the Local Government Act 1972 in relation to England and Wales and subsections (3) to (8) of section 210 of the Local Government (Scotland) Act 1973 in relation to Scotland.

DEFINITIONS
"food": s.1(1), (2) and (4).
"food authority": s.5.
"officer": s.53(1).
"the Minister": s.4(1) and (2).

GENERAL NOTE
It is necessary in an Act of this type that provision is made for the possibility of a food authority defaulting in its duties imposed by or under the Act. Powers have existed under the precursor legislation (ss.113 and 114 of the Food Act 1984; s.55 of the Food and Drugs (Scotland) Act 1956). As far as is known, the existing default powers have never been used, but the provisions in the Act are designed to introduce default powers which are less unwieldy than the present powers and closer to those which have existed for some time in relation to Scotland (see s.55 Food and Drugs (Scotland) Act 1956).

Protective provisions

Continuance of registration or licence on death

43.—(1) This section shall have effect on the death of any person who—

(a) is registered in respect of any premises in accordance with regulations made under Part II of this Act; or

(b) holds a licence issued in accordance with regulations so made.

(2) The registration or licence shall subsist for the benefit of the deceased's personal representative, or his widow or any other member of his family, until the end of—

(a) the period of three months beginning with his death; or

(b) such longer period as the enforcement authority may allow.

DEFINITION
"premises": s.53(1).

GENERAL NOTE
This is a straightforward provision allowing for the continuance of registration or a licence on death.

Protection of officers acting in good faith

44.—(1) An officer of a food authority is not personally liable in respect of any act done by him—

(a) in the execution or purported execution of this Act; and

(b) within the scope of his employment,

if he did that act in the honest belief that his duty under this Act required or entitled him to do it.

(2) Nothing in subsection (1) above shall be construed as relieving any food authority from any liability in respect of the acts of their officers.

(3) Where an action has been brought against an officer of a food authority in respect of an act done by him—

(a) in the execution or purported execution of this Act; but

(b) outside the scope of his employment,

the authority may indemnify him against the whole or a part of any damages which he has been ordered to pay or any costs which he may have incurred if they are satisfied that he honestly believed that the act complained of was within the scope of his employment.

(4) A public analyst appointed by a food authority shall be treated for the purposes of this section as being an officer of the authority, whether or not his appointment is a whole-time appointment.

DEFINITIONS
"food authority": s.5.
"officer": s.53(1).
"public analyst": s.27(1).

GENERAL NOTE
S.116 of the Food Act 1984 is largely re-enacted by this provision. S.44 gives protection to officers acting in good faith in Scotland, a matter which had been omitted from previous legislation.

The section applies to officers of food authorities (including a public analyst appointed by a food authority) rather than officers of enforcement authorities. Subs. (2) preserves the liability, including vicarious liability, of the authority for acts of its officers. Subs. (3) permits indemnity by the authority even where the officer had acted outside the scope of his employment. Action against individual officers is made less likely by the compensation provisions of s.9(7) and by the requirement that the most serious consequence of an enforcement officer's decision—closure under s.12—needs to be sanctioned by the court.

Financial provisions

Regulations as to charges

45.—(1) The Ministers may make regulations requiring or authorising charges to be imposed by enforcement authorities in respect of things done by them which they are required or authorised to do by or under this Act.

(2) Regulations under this section may include such provision as the Ministers see fit as regards charges for which the regulations provide and the recovery of such charges; and nothing in the following provisions shall prejudice this.

(3) Regulations under this section may provide that the amount of a charge (if imposed) is to be at the enforcement authority's discretion or to be at its discretion subject to a maximum or a minimum.

(4) Regulations under this section providing that a charge may not exceed a maximum amount, or be less than a minimum amount, may—

(a) provide for one amount, or a scale of amounts to cover different prescribed cases; and

(b) prescribe, as regards any amount, a sum or a method of calculating the amount.

DEFINITIONS
"enforcement authority": s.6(1)
"the Ministers": s.4(1).

GENERAL NOTE
Ministers may authorise charges under existing legislation in limited circumstances. This provision gives a general power to require or authorise charges, although it is expected that charges will be applied to a limited area of the activities of enforcement authorities and will not extend to routine matters such as inspection and sampling. Maximum and minimum charges, and scales of charges, may be set.

Expenses of authorised officers and county councils

46.—(1) Any expenses which are incurred under this Act by an authorised officer of a food authority in procuring samples, and causing samples to be analysed or examined, shall be defrayed by that authority.

(2) Any expenses incurred by a county council in the enforcement and execution of any provision of this Act, or of any regulations or orders made under it, shall, if the Secretary of State so directs, be defrayed as expenses for special county purposes charged on such part of the county as may be specified in the direction.

DEFINITIONS
"analysis": s.53(1).
"authorised officer of a food authority": s.5(6).
"examined": s.28(2).

GENERAL NOTE
S.129 of the Food Act 1984 is replaced by the simpler provision in s.46. Under subs. (2) the Secretary of State (normally for the Environment) may direct that expenses be charged on part of the county instead of on the whole county.

Remuneration of tribunal chairmen

47. There shall be paid out of money provided by Parliament to the chairman of any tribunal constituted in accordance with regulations under this Act such remuneration (by way of salary or fees) and such allowances as the Ministers may with the approval of the Treasury determine.

DEFINITION
"the Ministers": s.4(1).

GENERAL NOTE
This provision re-enacts s.43(4) and para. 6(2) of Pt. II of Sched. 4 of the Food Act 1984.

Instruments and documents

Regulations and orders

48.—(1) Any power of the Ministers or the Minister to make regulations or an order under this Act includes power—

(a) to apply, with modifications and adaptations, any other enactment (including one contained in this Act) which deals with matters similar to those being dealt with by the regulations or order;

(b) to make different provision in relation to different cases or classes of case (including different provision for different areas or different classes of business); and

(c) to provide for such exceptions, limitations and conditions, and to make such supplementary, incidental, consequential or transitional provisions, as the Ministers or the Minister considers necessary or expedient.

(2) Any power of the Ministers or the Minister to make regulations or orders under this Act shall be exercisable by statutory instrument.

(3) Any statutory instrument containing—

(a) regulations under this Act; or

(b) an order under this Act other than an order under section 60(3) below,

shall be subject to annulment in pursuance of a resolution of either House of Parliament.

(4) Before making—

(a) any regulations under this Act, other than regulations under section 17(2) or 18(1)(c) above; or

(b) any order under Part I of this Act,

the Ministers shall consult with such organisations as appear to them to be representative of interests likely to be substantially affected by the regulations or order.

(5) Any consultation undertaken before the commencement of subsection (4) above shall be as effective, for the purposes of that subsection, as if undertaken after that commencement.

DEFINITIONS
"the Minister": s.4(1) and (2).
"the Ministers": s.4(1).

GENERAL NOTE
This provision is largely a re-enactment of previous legislation with the exception of subs. (5), which is new. Subss. (1) and (4) are derived from s.118 of the Food Act 1956, while subss. (2) and (3) are drawn from s.120 of that Act. Statutory instruments apart from orders made under s.60(3) are to be subject to the negative resolution procedure, giving 40 days after which the instrument has been laid before Parliament for a Member of the House of Commons or the House of Lords to pray against the instrument.

Subs. (4)
Consultation is not required for orders made other than under Pt. 1 of the Act, for example, emergency control orders made under s.13(1) in Pt. II or orders under s.25; nor is consultation required for regulations made under s.17(2) or s.18(1)(c). Consultation is required for other regulations, including those under s.16(1)(c) which will introduce irradiation.

Subs. (5)
The Ministers may wish to carry out consultations prior to the coming into effect of s.48(4). S.48(5) permits this to happen prior to commencement of subs. (4). This means that an order can be made *inter alia* under s.5(4) in order to allocate enforcement responsibilities.

Form and authentication of documents

49.—(1) The following shall be in writing, namely—

    (a) all documents authorised or required by or under this Act to be given, made or issued by a food authority; and

    (b) all notices and applications authorised or required by or under this Act to be given or made to, or to any officer of, such an authority.

(2) The Ministers may by regulations prescribe the form of any document to be used for any of the purposes of this Act and, if forms are so prescribed, those forms or forms to the like effect may be used in all cases to which those forms are applicable.

(3) Any document which a food authority are authorised or required by or under this Act to give, make or issue may be signed on behalf of the authority—

    (a) by the proper officer of the authority as respects documents relating to matters within his province; or

    (b) by any officer of the authority authorised by them in writing to sign documents of the particular kind or, as the case may be, the particular document.

(4) Any document purporting to bear the signature of an officer who is expressed—

    (a) to hold an office by virtue of which he is under this section empowered to sign such a document; or

    (b) to be duly authorised by the food authority to sign such a document or the particular document,

shall for the purposes of this Act, and of any regulations and orders made under it, be deemed, until the contrary is proved, to have been duly given, made or issued by authority of the food authority.

(5) In this section—

    "proper officer", in relation to any purpose and to any food authority or any area, means the officer appointed for that purpose by that authority or, as the case may be, for that area;

    "signature" includes a facsimile of a signature by whatever process reproduced.

DEFINITIONS
"food authority": s.5.
"the Ministers": s.4(1).
"officer": s.53(1).

GENERAL NOTE
A re-enactment of existing legislation, this provision provides that certain documents, notices and applications shall be in writing, and gives the Ministers power to prescribe, by regulations, the form of any document to be used for the purposes of the Act. It also deals with the authority of officers to sign documents.

Service of documents

50.—(1) Any document which is required or authorised by or under this Act to be given to or served on any person may, in any case for which no other provision is made by this Act, be given or served either—

    (a) by delivering it to that person;

    (b) in the case of any officer of an enforcement authority, by leaving it, or sending it in a prepaid letter addressed to him, at his office;

    (c) in the case of an incorporated company or body, by delivering it to their secretary or clerk at their registered or principal office, or by sending it in a prepaid letter addressed to him at that office; or

    (d) in the case of any other person, by leaving it, or sending it in a prepaid letter addressed to him, at his usual or last known residence.

(2) Where a document is to be given to or served on the owner or the occupier of any premises and it is not practicable after reasonable inquiry to ascertain the name and address of the person to or on whom it should be given or served, or the premises are unoccupied, the document may be given or served by addressing it to the person concerned by the description of "owner" or "occupier" of the premises (naming them) and

(a) by delivering it to some person on the premises; or
(b) if there is no person on the premises to whom it can be delivered, by affixing it, or a copy of it, to some conspicuous part of the premises.

DEFINITIONS
"enforcement authority": s.6(1).
"occupier": s.53(1).
"premises": s.1(3).

GENERAL NOTE
This provision simplifies the previous rules contained in s.125 of the Food Act 1984 and is in similar terms to s.5 of the Control of Food Premises (Scotland) Act 1977. It sets out the procedure for the service of documents which are required or authorised under the Act to be given or served. There is no requirement for personal delivery, postal service of documents being permitted.

Amendments of other Acts

Contamination of food: emergency orders

51.—(1) Part I of the Food and Environment Protection Act 1985 (contamination of food) shall have effect, and shall be deemed always to have had effect, subject to the amendments specified in subsection (2) below.

(2) The amendments referred to in subsection (1) above are—

(a) in subsection (1) of section 1 (power to make emergency orders), the substitution for paragraph (a) of the following paragraph—

"(a) there exist or may exist circumstances which are likely to create a hazard to human health through human consumption of food;";

(b) in subsection (2) of that section, the omission of the definition of "escape";

(c) the substitution for subsection (5) of that section of the following subsection—

"(5) An emergency order shall refer to the circumstances or suspected circumstances in consequence of which in the opinion of the designating authority making it food such as is mentioned in subsection (1)(b) above is, or may be, or may become, unsuitable for human consumption; and in this Act 'designated circumstances' means the circumstances or suspected circumstances to which an emergency order refers in pursuance of this subsection.";

(d) in section 2(3) (powers when emergency order has been made), the substitution for the words "a designated incident" of the words "designated circumstances";

(e) in paragraph (a) of subsection (1) of section 4 (powers of officers), the substitution for the words "an escape of substances" of the words "such circumstances as are mentioned in section 1(1) above"; and

(f) in paragraph (b) and (c) of that subsection, the substitution for the words "the designated incident" of the words "the designated circumstances".

DEFINITIONS
"food": s.1(1), (2) and (4).
"human consumption": s.53(1).

GENERAL NOTE
The purpose of this provision is to amend Pt. I of the Food and Environment Protection Act 1985. Pt. I provides for emergency orders to be made where "there has been or may have been an escape of substances of such description and in such quantities as are likely to create a hazard to human health through human consumption of food" (s.(1)(1)). Orders have been made to deal with a number of problems, including the movement and slaughter of sheep following the Chernobyl disaster, and controls on livestock and animal products after lead had been discovered in cattle feedstuffs. However, the key phrase "escape of substances" is capable of application only to a restricted range of circumstances and so s.51(2)(a) of this Act permits emergency orders in a wider range of food contamination incidents by applying where "there are or may exist circumstances which are likely to create a hazard to human health through human consumption of food." The other amendments to the 1985 Act are consequential upon this change. The words *shall be deemed always to have had effect* give the amendment retrospective effect.

Markets, sugar beet and cold storage

52. In the Food Act 1984 (in this Act referred to as "the 1984 Act")—
    (a) Part III (markets); and
    (b) Part V (sugar beet and cold storage),
shall have effect subject to the amendments specified in Schedule 2 to this Act.

GENERAL NOTE
This provision is designed to ensure that in the future consolidation measures can be enacted, dealing with markets and with sugar beet and cold storage (see also Sched. 2).

Supplemental

General interpretation

53.—(1) In this Act, unless the context otherwise requires—
    "the 1984 Act" means the Food Act 1984;
    "the 1956 Act" means the Food and Drugs (Scotland) Act 1956;
    "advertisement" includes any notice, circular, label, wrapper, invoice or other document, and any public announcement made orally or by any means of producing or transmitting light or sound, and "advertise" shall be construed accordingly;
    "analysis" includes microbiological assay and any technique for establishing the composition of food, and "analyse" shall be construed accordingly;
    "animal" means any creature other than a bird or fish;
    "article" does not include a live animal or bird, or a live fish which is not used for human consumption while it is alive;
    "container" includes any basket, pail, tray, package or receptacle of any kind, whether open or closed;
    "contravention", in relation to any provision, includes any failure to comply with that provision;
    "cream" means that part of milk rich in fat which has been separated by skimming or otherwise;
    "equipment" includes any apparatus;
    "exportation" and "importation" have the same meanings as they have for the purposes of the Customs and Excise Management

Act 1979, and "export" and "import" shall be construed accordingly;

"fish" includes crustaceans and molluscs;

"functions" includes powers and duties;

"human consumption" includes use in the preparation of food for human consumption;

"knacker's yard" means any premises used in connection with the business of slaughtering, flaying or cutting up animals the flesh of which is not intended for human consumption;

"milk" includes cream and skimmed or separated milk;

"occupier", in relation to any ship or aircraft of a description specified in an order made under section 1(3) above or any vehicle, stall or place, means the master, commander or other person in charge of the ship, aircraft, vehicle, stall or place;

"officer" includes servant;

"preparation", in relation to food, includes manufacture and any form of processing or treatment, and "preparation for sale" includes packaging, and "prepare for sale" shall be construed accordingly;

"presentation", in relation to food, includes the shape, appearance and packaging of the food, the way in which the food is arranged when it is exposed for sale and the setting in which the food is displayed with a view to sale, but does not include any form of labelling or advertising, and "present" shall be construed accordingly;

"proprietor", in relation to a food business, means the person by whom that business is carried on;

"ship" includes any vessel, boat or craft, and a hovercraft within the meaning of the Hovercraft Act 1968, and "master" shall be construed accordingly;

"slaughterhouse" means a place for slaughtering animals, the flesh of which is intended for sale for human consumption, and includes any place available in connection with such a place for the confinement of animals while awaiting slaughter there or for keeping, or subjecting to any treatment or process, products of the slaughtering of animals there;

"substance" includes any natural or artificial substance or other matter, whether it is in solid or liquid form or in the form of a gas or vapour;

"treatment", in relation to any food, includes subjecting it to heat or cold.

(2) The following Table shows provisions defining or otherwise explaining expressions used in this Act (other than provisions defining or explaining an expression used only in the same section)—

authorised officer of a food authority	section 5(6)
business	section 1(3)
commercial operation	section 1(3) and (4)
contact material	section 1(3)
emergency control order	section 13(1)
emergency prohibition notice	section 12(1)
emergency prohibition order	section 12(2)
enforcement authority	section 6(1)
examination and examine	section 28(2)
food	section 1(1), (2) and (4)
food authority	section 5
food business	section 1(3)
food premises	section 1(3)

food safety requirements and related	
expressions	section 8(2)
food source	section 1(3)
improvement notice	section 10(1)
injury to health and injurious to	
health	section 7(3)
the Minister	section 4(1) and (2)
the Ministers	section 4(1)
premises	section 1(3)
prohibition order	section 11(5)
public analyst	section 27(1)
sale and related expressions	section 2
unfit for human consumption	section 8(4)

(3) Any reference in this Act to regulations or orders made under it shall be construed as a reference to regulations or orders made under this Act by the Ministers or the Minister.

(4) For the purposes of this Act, any class or description may be framed by reference to any matters or circumstances whatever, including in particular, in the case of a description of food, the brand name under which it is commonly sold.

(5) Where, apart from this subsection, any period of less than seven days which is specified in this Act would include any day which is—

(a) a Saturday, a Sunday, Christmas Day or Good Friday; or

(b) a day which is a bank holiday under the Banking and Financial Dealings Act 1971 in the part of Great Britain concerned;

that day shall be excluded from that period.

GENERAL NOTE

Many of the definitions of terms appear in s.132(1) of the Food Act 1984 (s.58 of the Food and Drugs (Scotland) Act 1956). Terms the definitions of which have been amended are listed below.

Analysis. In the Food Act 1984 *analysis* was defined as "includes micro-biological assay but no other form of biological assay . . . ." The new definition includes "any technique for establishing the composition of food."

Animal. The Food Act 1984 stated that "*'animal'* does not include bird or fish." The new definition *any creature other than a bird or fish* would make it clear that for example an insect is included.

Article. It was necessary to include live fish which are commonly used for human consumption (*i.e.* oysters and elvers) within the new legislation and the definition of article in the Food Act 1984 has been amended accordingly.

Contravention. This term was undefined in the precursor legislation.

Equipment. This term was undefined in the precursor legislation, but definition is necessary in the Act because of the use of the term "equipment" in s.11 (dealing with prohibition orders) and in Sched. 1, para. 5.

Exportation and *importation.* The latter term is as defined in the Food Act 1984 but the definition of the former is new and has, as it were, been imported from the Customs and Excise Management Act 1979.

Fish. Fish was not defined in the previous legislation and the purpose of the present definition is to ensure that crustacea and molluscs are included so that the term "fish" includes shellfish such as oysters. Molluscs, that is lamellibranchs, gastropods (*e.g.* snails) and cephalopods (*e.g.* cuttle fish) are included.

Milk. The 1984 Act's definition of milk excluded dried milk and condensed milk. These are not excluded by the new definition.

Occupier. A new definition, relating to orders made under s.1(3) and to vehicle, stall or place. (See also s.50(2) on service of documents).

Preparation. The words *processing or* have been added to the previous definition. Several sections of the Act refer to "process": see, *e.g.* ss.7(1)(d); 11(2)(a); 16(1)(c); and Sched. 1, para. 4.

Presentation. This term was not defined in the earlier legislation. Definition is necessary in relation to ss.15(3) and 16(1)(e).

Proprietor. This is a new definition, necessary because of the numerous references to proprietors in the Act.

Ship. "Ship" and "vessel" were defined separately in the Food Act 1984, the latter term being used to mean "a receptacle of any kind, whether open or closed." The term "container" now includes such receptacles, and "vessel" is thus limited to its nautical meaning. E.C. regulations applicable to fishing vessels can now be made under powers which refer to a "ship," *e.g.* under s.(1)(3).

Substance. In the 1984 Act the definition stated simply that substance "includes a liquid." The new definition is intended to give as wide a meaning as possible to substance and is in line with the definition of that term in other legislation, *e.g.* Consumer Protection Act 1987.

Treatment. This is a new definition, designed to ensure that use of cold treatments, *e.g.* (freezing) are treatments as well as heat treatments (*e.g.* pasteurisation).

Application to Crown

54.—(1) Subject to the provisions of this section, the provisions of this Act and of regulations and orders made under it shall bind the Crown.

(2) No contravention by the Crown of any provision of this Act or of any regulations or order made under it shall make the Crown criminally liable; but the High Court or, in Scotland, the Court of Session may, on the application of an enforcement authority, declare unlawful any act or omission of the Crown which constitutes such a contravention.

(3) Notwithstanding anything in subsection (2) above, the provisions of this Act and of regulations and orders made under it shall apply to persons in the public service of the Crown as they apply to other persons.

(4) If the Secretary of State certifies that it appears to him requisite or expedient in the interests of national security that the powers of entry conferred by section 32 above should not be exercisable in relation to any Crown premises specified in the certificate, those powers shall not be exercisable in relation to those premises; and in this subsection "Crown premises" means premises held or used by or on behalf of the Crown.

(5) Nothing in this section shall be taken as in any way affecting Her Majesty in her private capacity; and this subsection shall be construed as if section 38(3) of the Crown Proceedings Act 1947 (interpretation of references in that Act to Her Majesty in her private capacity) were contained in this Act.

DEFINITIONS

"enforcement authority": s.6(1).
"premises": s.1(3).

GENERAL NOTE

Previous food legislation did not apply to the Crown, and as a result the supply of food in, for example, a hospital or the Houses of Parliament was outwith the legislation. In 1986 (National Health Service (Amendment) Act 1986 ss.1 and 2) hospitals were brought within the legislation. These provisions are not affected by the new provision, which seeks (in subs. (2)) to strike a balance between the unacceptability of imposing criminal liability on the Crown and the need for food problems in Crown premises to be subject to some control. As a matter of convention, the Crown complies with declarations of the type mentioned in the subsection made by the courts. Subs. (3) brings persons in the public service of the Crown within the legislation in the same way as other persons. *Persons* would include legal persons, such as companies, which are in the public service of the Crown. Subs. (4) permits the exemption of certain premises from the powers of entry given to authorised officers under s.32, and in practice will be used in relation to such premises as defence establishments.

Water supply: England and Wales

55.—(1) Nothing in Part II of this Act or any regulations or order made under that Part shall apply in relation to the supply of water to any premises, whether by a water undertaker or by means of a private supply (within the meaning of Chapter II of Part II of the Water Act 1989).

(2) In the following provisions of that Act, namely—
    section 52 (duties of water undertakers with respect to water quality);

section 53 (regulations for preserving water quality); and

section 64 (additional powers of entry for the purposes of Chapter II),

for the words "domestic purposes", wherever they occur, there shall be substituted the words "domestic or food production purposes".

(3) In subsection (2) of section 56 of that Act (general functions of local authorities in relation to water quality), for the words "domestic purposes" there shall be substituted the words "domestic or food production purposes" and for the words "those purposes" there shall be substituted the words "domestic purposes".

(4) In subsection (1) of section 57 of that Act (remedial powers of local authorities in relation to private supplies), for the words "domestic purposes", in the first place where they occur, there shall be substituted the words "domestic or food production purposes".

(5) In subsection (1) of section 66 of that Act (interpretation etc. of Chapter II), after the definition of "consumer" there shall be inserted the following definition—

" 'food production purposes' shall be construed in accordance with subsection (1A) below;".

(6) After that subsection there shall be inserted the following subsection—

"(1A) In this Chapter references to food production purposes are references to the manufacturing, processing, preserving or marketing purposes with respect to food or drink for which water supplied to food production premises may be used; and in this subsection 'food production premises' means premises used for the purposes of a business of preparing food or drink for consumption otherwise than on the premises."

DEFINITIONS
"food": s.1(1), (2) and (4).
"premises": s.1(3).

GENERAL NOTE
The effect of this provision is that the supply of water to premises is governed by other legislation (principally the Water Act 1989) rather than this Act. Subss. (2)–(6) ensure that water for food production purposes meets the same standards as water for domestic purposes.

Water supply: Scotland

56.—(1) Nothing in Part II of this Act or any regulations or order made under that Part shall apply in relation to the supply of water to any premises, whether by a water authority (within the meaning of section 3 of the Water (Scotland) Act 1980) or by means of a private supply (within the meaning of Part VIA of that Act).

(2) In the following provisions of that Act, namely—

section 76A (duties of water authorities with respect to water quality); and

section 76B (regulations for preserving water quality),

for the words "domestic purposes", wherever they occur, there shall be substituted the words "domestic or food production purposes".

(3) In subsection (2) of section 76F of that Act (general functions of local authorities in relation to water quality), for the words "domestic purposes" there shall be substituted the words "domestic or food production purposes" and for the words "those purposes" there shall be substituted the words "domestic purposes".

(4) In subsection (1) of section 76G of that Act (remedial powers of local authorities in relation to private supplies), for the words "domestic

purposes", in the first place where they occur, there shall be substituted the words "domestic or food production purposes".

(5) In subsection (1) of section 76L of that Act (interpretation etc. of Part VIA), after the definition of "analyse" there shall be inserted the following definition—

" 'food production purposes' shall be construed in accordance with subsection (1A) below;".

(6) After that subsection there shall be inserted the following subsection—

"(1A) In this Part references to food production purposes are references to the manufacturing, processing, preserving or marketing purposes with respect to food or drink for which water supplied to food production premises may be used; and in this subsection 'food production premises' means premises used for the purposes of a business of preparing food or drink for consumption otherwise than on the premises."

DEFINITIONS
"food": s.1(1), (2) and (4).
"premises": s.1(3).

GENERAL NOTE
This has the same effect as s.55, but in relation to Scotland. The Water (Scotland) Act was also amended by Sched. 22 to the Water Act 1989.

Scilly Isles and Channel Islands

57.—(1) This Act shall apply to the Isles of Scilly subject to such exceptions and modifications as the Ministers may by order direct.

(2) Her Majesty may by Order in Council direct that any of the provisions of this Act shall extend to any of the Channel Islands with such exceptions and modifications (if any) as may be specified in the Order.

GENERAL NOTE
Similar powers appear in other legislation and they are designed to ensure that the provisions of the Act can be extended as mentioned in the section.

Territorial waters and the continental shelf

58.—(1) For the purposes of this Act the territorial waters of the United Kingdom adjacent to any part of Great Britain shall be treated as situated in that Part.

(2) An Order in Council under section 23 of the Oil and Gas (Enterprise) Act 1982 (application of civil law) may make provision for treating for the purposes of food safety legislation—

(a) any installation which is in waters to which that section applies; and

(b) any safety zone around any such installation.

as if they were situated in a specified part of the United Kingdom and for modifying such legislation in its application to such installations and safety zones.

(3) Such an Order in Council may also confer on persons of a specified description the right to require, for the purpose of facilitating the exercise of specified powers under food safety legislation—

(a) conveyance to and from any installation, including conveyance of any equipment required by them; and

(b) the provision of reasonable accommodation and means of subsistence while they are on any installation.

(4) In this section—

"food safety legislation" means this Act and any regulations and
orders made under it and any corresponding provisions in
Northern Ireland;
"installation" means an installation to which subsection (3) of the
said section 23 applies;
"safety zone" means an area which is a safety zone by virtue of Part
III of the Petroleum Act 1987; and
"specified" means specified in the Order in Council.

DEFINITION
"equipment": s.53.

GENERAL NOTE

Subs. (1)
This is designed to clarify which enforcement authorities have jurisdiction in respect of
which areas of the territorial waters.

Subs. (2)
Previous food legislation has not applied to oil and gas installations and safety zones. This
provision permits the extension and modification of the legislation to such installations and
safety zones.

Subs. (3)
This is designed to ensure that enforcement officers are afforded adequate means of
carrying out their duties on any installation.

Amendments transitional provisions, savings and repeals

59.—(1) The enactments mentioned in Schedule 3 to this Act shall have
effect subject to the amendments there specified (being minor amendments
and amendments consequential on the preceding provisions of this Act).

(2) The Ministers may by order make such modifications of local Acts,
and of subordinate legislation (within the meaning of the Interpretation
Act 1978), as appear to them to be necessary or expedient in consequence
of the provisions of this Act.

(3) The transitional provisions and savings contained in Schedule 4 to
this Act shall have effect; but nothing in this subsection shall be taken as
prejudicing the operation of sections 16 and 17 of the said Act of 1978
(which relate to the effect of repeals).

(4) The enactments mentioned in Schedule 5 to this Act (which include
some that are spent or no longer of practical utility) are hereby repealed
to the extent specified in the third column of that Schedule.

DEFINITION
"the Ministers": s.4(1).

GENERAL NOTE
This section brings in the minor and consequential amendments (Sched. 3), transitional
provisions and savings (Sched. 4) and repeals (Sched. 5).

Short title, commencement and extent

60.—(1) This Act may be cited as the Food Safety Act 1990.

(2) The following provisions shall come into force on the day on which
this Act is passed, namely—
    section 13;
    section 51; and
    paragraphs 12 to 15 of Schedule 2 and, so far as relating to those
        paragraphs, section 52.

(3) Subject to subsection (2) above, this Act shall come into force on such day as the Ministers may by order appoint, and different days may be appointed for different provisions or for different purposes.

(4) An order under subsection (3) above may make such transitional adaptations of any of the following, namely—

    (a) the provisions of this Act then in force or brought into force by the order; and

    (b) the provisions repealed by this Act whose repeal is not then in force or so brought into force,

as appear to the Ministers to be necessary or expedient in consequence of the partial operation of this Act.

(5) This Act, except—

    this section;

    section 51,

    section 58(2) to (4); and

    paragraphs 7, 29 and 30 of Schedule 3 and, so far as relating to those paragraphs, section 59(1),

does not extend to Northern Ireland.

DEFINITION
    "the Ministers": s.4(1).

GENERAL NOTE
    Powers to deal with emergencies (see ss.13 and 51) come into effect on the day on which the Act was passed, as do powers to gather information about sugar beet (paras. 12–15, Sched. 2 and s.52).

SCHEDULES

Section 16(3)   SCHEDULE 1

PROVISIONS OF REGULATIONS UNDER SECTION 16(1)

Composition of food

1. Provision for prohibiting or regulating—

    (a) the sale, possession for sale, or offer, exposure or advertisement for sale, of any specified substance, or of any substance of any specified class, with a view to its use in the preparation of food; or

    (b) the possession of any such substance for use in the preparation of food.

Fitness etc. of food

2.—(1) Provision for prohibiting—

    (a) the sale for human consumption; or

    (b) the use in the manufacture of products for sale for such consumption,

of food derived from a food source which is suffering or has suffered from, or which is liable to be suffering or to have suffered from, any disease specified in the regulations.

(2) Provision for prohibiting or regulating, or for enabling enforcement authorities to prohibit or regulate—

    (a) the sale for human consumption; or

    (b) the offer, exposure or distribution for sale for such consumption,

of shellfish taken from beds or other layings for the time being designated by or under the regulations.

3.—(1) Provision for regulating generally the treatment and disposal of any food—

    (a) which is unfit for human consumption; or

    (b) which, though not unfit for human consumption, is not intended for, or is prohibited from being sold for, such consumption.

(2) Provision for the following, namely—

    (a) for the registration by enforcement authorities of premises used or proposed to be used for the purpose of sterilising meat to which sub-paragraph (1) above applies, and for prohibiting the use for that purpose of any premises which are not registered in accordance with the regulations; or

(b) for the issue by such authorities of licences in respect of the use of premises for the purpose of sterilising such meat, and for prohibiting the use for that purpose of any premises except in accordance with a licence issued under the regulations.

Processing and treatment of food

4. Provision for the following, namely—
    (a) for the giving by persons possessing such qualifications as may be prescribed by the regulations of written opinions with respect to the use of any process or treatment in the preparation of food, and for prohibiting the use for any such purpose of any process or treatment except in accordance with an opinion given under the regulations; or
    (b) for the issue by enforcement authorities of licences in respect of the use of any process or treatment in the preparation of food, and for prohibiting the use for any such purpose of any process or treatment except in accordance with a licence issued under the regulations.

Food hygiene

5.—(1) Provision for imposing requirements as to—
    (a) the construction, maintenance, cleanliness and use of food premises, including any parts of such premises in which equipment and utensils are cleaned, or in which refuse is disposed of or stored;
    (b) the provision, maintenance and cleanliness of sanitary and washing facilities in connection with such premises; and
    (c) the disposal of refuse from such premises.

(2) Provision for imposing requirements as to—
    (a) the maintenance and cleanliness of equipment or utensils used for the purposes of a food business; and
    (b) the use, for the cleaning of equipment used for milking, of cleaning agents approved by or under the regulations.

(3) Provision for requiring persons who are or intended to become involved in food businesses, whether as proprietors or employees or otherwise, to undergo such food hygiene training as may be specified in the regulations.

6.—(1) Provision for imposing responsibility for compliance with any requirements imposed by virtue of paragraph 5(1) above in respect of any premises—
    (a) on the occupier of the premises; and
    (b) in the case of requirements of a structural character, on any owner of the premises who either—
        (i) lets them for use for a purpose to which the regulations apply; or
        (ii) permits them to be so used after notice from the authority charged with the enforcement of the regulations.

(2) Provision for conferring in relation to particular premises, subject to such limitations and safeguards as may be specified, exemptions from the operation of specified provisions which—
    (a) are contained in the regulations; and
    (b) are made by virtue of paragraph 5(1) above,
while there is in force a certificate of the enforcement authority to the effect that compliance with those provisions cannot reasonably be required with respect to the premises or any activities carried on in them.

Inspection etc. of food sources

7.—(1) Provision for securing the inspection of food sources by authorised officers of enforcement authorities for the purpose of ascertaining whether they—
    (a) fail to comply with the requirements of the regulations; or
    (b) are such that any food derived from them is likely to fail to comply with those requirements.

(2) Provision for enabling such an officer, if it appears to him on such an inspection that any food source falls within sub-paragraph (1)(a) or (b) above, to give notice to the person in charge of the food source that, until a time specified in the notice or until the notice is withdrawn—
    (a) no commercial operations are to be carried out with respect to the food source; and
    (b) the food source either is not to be removed or is not to be removed except to some place so specified.

(3) Provision for enabling such an officer, if on further investigation it appears to him, in the case of any such food source which is a live animal or bird, that there is present in the animal or bird any substance whose presence is prohibited by the regulations, to cause the animal or bird to be slaughtered.

DEFINITIONS
"advertisement": s.53(1).
"animal": s.53(1).
"commercial operation": s.1(3) and (4).
"enforcement authority": s.6(1).
"equipment": s.53(1).
"food": s.1(1), (2) and (4).
"food business": s.1(3).
"food premises": s.1(3).
"food source": s.1(3).
"human consumption": s.53(1).
"occupier": s.53(1).
"officer": s.53(1).
"premises": s.1(3).
"preparation": s.53(1).
"proprietor": s.53(1).
"sale and related expressions": s.2.
"substance": s.53(1).
"treatment": s.53(1).
"unfit for human consumption": s.8(4).

GENERAL NOTE
This Schedule details the areas which can be provided for in regulations under s.16(1) above. New areas include para. 4(a), dealing with prohibition of use of a process or treatment unless it is carried out in accordance with the written opinion of an expert; para. 4(b) on licensing of processes and treatments (such as irradiation); and para. 5(3) on provision of training for food handlers.

Section 52   SCHEDULE 2

AMENDMENTS OF PARTS III AND V OF 1984 Act

Amendments of Part III

1. Part III of the 1984 Act (markets) shall be amended in accordance with paragraphs 2 to 11 below.

2.—(1) In subsection (1) of section 50 (establishment or acquisition of markets), for the words "The council of a district" there shall be substituted the words "A local authority" and for the words "their district", in each place where they occur, there shall be substituted the words "their area".

(2) In subsection (2) of that section, for the words "the district" there shall be substituted the words "the authority's area".

(3) For subsection (3) of that section there shall be substituted the following subsection—

"(3) For the purposes of subsection (2), a local authority shall not be regarded as enjoying any rights, powers or privileges within another local authority's area by reason only of the fact that they maintain within their own area a market which has been established under paragraph (a) of subsection (1) or under the corresponding provision of any earlier enactment".

3. In section 51(2) (power to sell to local authority), the word "market" shall cease to have effect.

4.—(1) In subsection (1) of section 53 (charges by market authority), the words "and in respect of the weighing and measuring of articles and vehicles" shall cease to have effect.

(2) For subsection (2) of that section there shall be substituted the following subsection—

"(2) A market authority who provide—
        (a) a weighing machine for weighing cattle, sheep or swine; or
        (b) a cold air store or refrigerator for the storage and preservation of meat and other articles of food,

may demand in respect of the weighing of such animals or, as the case may be, the use of the store or refrigerator such charges as they may from time to time determine."

(3) In subsection (3)(b) of that section, the words "in respect of the weighing of vehicles, or, as the case may be," shall cease to have effect.

5. For subsection (2) of section 54 (time for payment of charges) there shall be substituted the following subsection—

"(2) Charges payable in respect of the weighing of cattle, sheep or swine shall be paid in advance to an authorised market officer by the person bringing the animals to be weighed."

6. In section 56(1) (prohibited sales in market hours), for the word "district" there shall be substituted the word "area".

7. In section 57 (weighing machines and scales), subsection (1) shall cease to have effect.

8. After that section there shall be inserted the following section—
"Provision of cold stores.

57A.—(1) A market authority may provide a cold air store or refrigerator for the storage and preservation of meat and other articles of food.

(2) Any proposal by a market authority to provide under this section a cold air store or refrigerator within the area of another local authority requires the consent of that other authority, which shall not be unreasonably withheld.

(3) Any question whether or not such a consent is unreasonably withheld shall be referred to and determined by the Ministers.

(4) Subsections (1) to (5) of section 250 of the Local Government Act 1972 (which relate to local inquiries) shall apply for the purposes of this section as if any reference in those subsections to that Act included a reference to this section."

9. Section 58 (weighing of articles) shall cease to have effect.

10. In section 60 (market byelaws), after paragraph (c) there shall be inserted the following paragraph—

"(d) after consulting the fire authority for the area in which the market is situated, for preventing the spread of fires in the market."

11. In section 61 (interpretation of Part III), the words from "and this Part" to the end shall cease to have effect and for the definition of "market authority" there shall be substituted the following definitions—

"'fire authority' means an authority exercising the functions of a fire authority under the Fire Services Act 1947;

'food' has the same meaning as in the Food Safety Act 1990;

'local authority' means a district council, a London borough council or a parish or community council;

'market authority' means a local authority who maintain a market which has been established or acquired under section 50(1) or under the corresponding provisions of any earlier enactment."

Amendments of Part V

12. Part V of the 1984 Act (sugar beet and cold storage) shall be amended in accordance with paragraphs 13 to 16 below.

13.—(1) In subsections (1) and (2) of section 68 (research and education), for the word "Company", wherever it occurs, there shall be substituted the words "processors of home-grown beet".

(2) After subsection (5) of that section there shall be inserted the following subsection—

"(5A) An order under this section shall be made by statutory instrument which shall be subject to annulment in pursuance of a resolution of either House of Parliament.".

(3) In subsection (6) of that section, for the definition of "the Company" and subsequent definitions there shall be substituted—

"'year' means a period of 12 months beginning with 1st April;

and in this section and sections 69 and 69A 'home-grown beet' means sugar beet grown in Great Britain".

14. In subsection (3) of section 69 (crop price), for the words "'home-grown beet' means sugar beet grown in Great Britian; and" there shall be substituted the words "and section 69A".

15. After that section there shall be inserted the following section—
"Information

69A.—(1) For the purpose of facilitating—

(a) the making of a determination under section 69(1); or

(b) the preparation or conduct of discussions concerning Community arrangements for or relating to the regulation of the market for sugar,

the appropriate Minister may serve on any processor of home-grown beet a notice requiring him to furnish in writing, within such period as is specified in the notice, such information as is so specified.

(2) Subject to subsection (3), information obtained under subsection (1) shall not be disclosed without the previous consent in writing of the person by whom the information was furnished; and a person who discloses any information so obtained in contravention of this subsection shall be liable—

(a) on conviction on indictment, to a fine or to imprisonment for a term not exceeding two years or to both;

(b) on summary conviction, to a fine not exceeding the statutory maximum or to imprisonment for a term not exceeding three months or to both.

(3) Nothing in subsection (2) shall restrict the disclosure of information to any of the Ministers or the disclosure—

(a) of information obtained under subsection (1)(a)—

    (i) to a person designated to make a determination under section 69(1); or

    (ii) to a body which substantially represents the growers of home-grown beet; or

(b) of information obtained under subsection (1)(b), to the Community institution concerned.

(4) In this section "the appropriate Minister" means—

(a) in relation to England, the Minister of Agriculture, Fisheries and Food; and

(b) in relation to Scotland or Wales, the Secretary of State."

16. Section 70 (provision of cold storage) shall cease to have effect.

GENERAL NOTE

The purpose of this Schedule is to list the amendments required for the purposes of s.52 above.

Section 59(1)   SCHEDULE 3

MINOR AND CONSEQUENTIAL AMENDMENTS

The Public Health Act 1936 (c.49)

1. An order made by the Secretary of State under section 6 of the Public Health Act 1936 may constitute a united district for the purposes of any functions under this Act which are functions of a food authority in England and Wales.

The London Government Act 1963 (c.33)

2. Section 54(1) of the London Government Act 1963 (food, drugs, markets and animals) shall cease to have effect.

The Agriculture Act 1967 (c.22)

3. In section 7(3) of the Agriculture Act 1967 (labelling of meat in relation to systems of classifying meat), the words from "and, without prejudice" to the end shall cease to have effect.

4.—(1) In subsection (2) of section 25 of that Act (interpretation of Part I), for the definition of "slaughterhouse" there shall be substituted the following definition—

"'slaughterhouse' has, in England and Wales, the meaning given by section 34 of the Slaughterhouses Act 1974 and, in Scotland, the meaning given by section 22 of the Slaughter of Animals (Scotland) Act 1980;".

(2) In subsection (3) of that section, for the words from "Part II" to "1955" there shall be substituted the words "secton 15 of the Slaughterhouses Act 1974 or section 1 of the Slaughter of Animals (Scotland) Act 1980".

The Farm and Garden Chemicals Act 1967 (c.50)

5. In section 4 of the Farm and Garden Chemicals Act 1967 (evidence of analysis of products)—

(a) in subsection (3), for the words "section 76 of the Food Act 1984" there shall be substituted the words "section 27 of the Food Safety Act 1990"; and

(b) in subsection (7)(c), the words from "for the reference" to "1956" shall cease to have effect.

The Trade Descriptions Act 1968 (c.29)

6. In section 2(5)(a) of the Trade Descriptions Act 1968 (certain descriptions to be deemed not to be trade descriptions), for the words "the Food Act 1984, the Food and Drugs (Scotland) Act 1956" there shall be substituted the words "the Food Safety Act 1990".

7. In section 22 of that Act (admissibility of evidence in proceedings for offences under Act), in subsection (2), the paragraph beginning with the words "In this subsection" shall cease to have effect, and after that subsection there shall be inserted the following subsection—

"(2A) In subsection (2) of this section—
'the food and drugs laws' means the Food Safety Act 1990, the Medicines Act 1968 and the Food (Northern Ireland) Order 1989 and any instrument made thereunder;
'the relevant provisions' means—
(i) in relation to the said Act of 1990, section 31 and regulations made thereunder;
(ii) in relation to the said Act of 1968, so much of Schedule 3 to that Act as is applicable to the circumstances in which the sample was procured; and
(iii) in relation to the said Order, Articles 40 and 44.
or any provisions replacing any of those provisions by virtue of section 17 of the said Act of 1990, paragraph 27 of Schedule 3 to the said Act of 1968 or Article 72 or 73 of the said Order."

The Medicines Act 1968 (c.67)

8. In section 108 of the Medicines Act 1968 (enforcement in England and Wales)—
(a) for the words "food and drugs authority", in each place where they occur, there shall be substituted the words "drugs authority"; and
(b) after subsection (11) there shall be inserted the following subsection—
"(12) In this section 'drugs authority' means—
(a) as respects each London borough, metropolitan district or non-metropolitan county, the council of that borough, district or county; and
(b) as respects the City of London (including the Temples), the Common Council of that City."

9. In section 109 of that Act (enforcement in Scotland)—
(a) paragraph (c) of subsection (2) shall cease to have effect; and
(b) after that subsection there shall be inserted the following subsection—
"(2A) Subsection (12) of section 108 of this Act shall have effect in relation to Scotland as if for paragraphs (a) and (b) there were substituted the words "an islands or district council".

10. After section 115 of that Act there shall be inserted the following section—
"Facilities for microbiological examinations.
115A. A drugs authority or the council of a non-metropolitan district may provide facilities for microbiological examinations of drugs."

11. In section 132(1) of that Act (interpretation), the definition of "food and drugs authority" shall cease to have effect and after the definition of "doctor" there shall be inserted the following definition—
"'drugs authority' has the meaning assigned to it by section 108(12) of this Act;".

12. In paragraph 1(2) of Schedule 3 to that Act (sampling) for the words from "in relation to England and Wales" to "Food and Drugs (Scotland) Act 1956" there shall be substituted the words "except in relation to Northern Ireland, has the meaning assigned to it by section 27 of the Food Safety Act 1990".

The Transport Act 1968 (c.73)

13. In Schedule 16 to the Transport Act 1968 (supplementary and consequential provisions), in paragraph 7(2), paragraphs (d) and (e) shall cease to have effect.

The Tribunals and Inquiries Act 1971 (c.62)

14.—(1) In Schedule 1 to the Tribunals and Inquiries Act 1971 (tribunals under supervision of Council on Tribunals), paragraph 15 shall cease to have effect and after paragraph 6B there shall be inserted the following paragraph—

"Food	6C. Tribunals consituted in accordance with regulations under Part II of the Food Safety Act 1990."

(2) In that Schedule, paragraph 40 shall cease to have effect and after paragraph 36 there shall be inserted the following paragraph—

"Food	36A. Tribunals constituted in accordance with regulations under Part II of the Food Safety Act 1990 being tribunals appointed for Scotland."

The Agriculture (Miscellaneous Provisions) Act 1972 (c.62)

15.—(1) In subsection (1) of section 4 of the Agriculture (Miscellaneous Provisions) Act 1972 (furnishing by milk marketing board of information derived from tests of milk)—
- (a) for the words "appropriate authority" there shall be substituted the words "enforcement authority"; and
- (b) for the words from "Milk and Dairies Regulations" to "1956" there shall be substituted the words "regulations relating to milk, dairies or dairy farms which were made under, or have effect as if made under, section 16 of the Food Safety Act 1990."

(2) In subsection (2) of that section, for the definition of "appropriate authority" there shall be substituted the following definition—

"'enforcement authority' has the same meaning as in the Food Safety Act 1990;".

(3) Subsection (3) of that section shall cease to have effect.

The Poisons Act 1971 (c.66)

16. In section 8(4)(a) of the Poisons Act 1972 (evidence of analysis in proceedings under Act) for the words "section 76 of the Food Act 1984, or section 27 of the Food and Drugs (Scotland) Act 1956" there shall be substituted the words "section 27 of the Food Safety Act 1990".

The Local Government Act 1972 (c.70)

17. In section 259(3) of the Local Government Act 1972 (compensation for loss of office)—
- (a) in paragraph (b), for the words "food and drugs authority, within the meaning of the Food Act 1984" there shall be substituted the words "food authority within the meaning of the Food Safety Act 1990";
- (b) in paragraph (c), for sub-paragraphs (i) and (ii) there shall be substituted the words "which are incorporated or reproduced in the Slaughterhouses Act 1974 or the Food Safety Act 1990"; and
- (c) the words "section 129(1) of the Food and Drugs Act 1955" shall cease to have effect.

The Slaughterhouses Act 1974 (c.3)

18. In the following provisions of the Slaughterhouses Act 1974, namely—
- (a) section 2(2)(a) (requirements to be complied with in relation to slaughterhouse licences);
- (b) section 4(2)(a) (requirements to be complied with in relation to knacker's yard licences);
- (c) section 12(2) (regulations with respect to slaughterhouses and knackers' yards to prevail over byelaws); and
- (d) section 16(3) (regulations with respect to public slaughterhouses to prevail over byelaws),

for the words "section 13 of the Food Act 1984" there shall be substituted the words "section 16 of the Food Safety Act 1990".

The Licensing (Scotland) Act 1976 (c.66)

19. In section 23(4) of the Licensing (Scotland) Act 1976 (application for new licence), for the words "section 13 of the Food and Drugs (Scotland) Act 1956" there shall be substituted "section 16 of the Food Safety Act 1990".

The Weights and Measures &c. Act 1976 (c.77)

20.—(1) In subsection (1) of section 12 of the Weights and Measures &c. Act 1976 (shortages of food and other goods), for paragraphs (a) and (b) there shall be substituted the following paragraph—

"(a) section 16 of the Food Safety Act 1990 ('the 1990 Act');".

(2) In subsection (9) of that section—

    (a) for paragraph (a) there shall be substituted the following paragraph—

        "(a) where it was imposed under the 1990 Act—

            (i) the Minister of Agriculture, Fisheries and Food and the Secretary of State acting jointly in so far as it was imposed in relation to England and Wales; and

            (ii) the Secretary of State in so far as it was imposed in relation to Scotland;"; and

    (b) in paragraph (c), the words "the 1956 Act or" shall cease to have effect.

21. In Schedule 6 to that Act (temporary requirements imposed by emergency orders), for paragraphs 2 and 3 there shall be substituted the following paragraph—

"Food Safety Act 1990 (c.16)

2.—(1) This paragraph applies where the relevant requirement took effect under or by virtue of the Food Safety Act 1990.

(2) The following provisions of that Act—

    (a) Part I (preliminary);

    (b) Part III (administration and enforcement); and

    (c) sections 40 to 50 (default powers and other supplemental provisions),

shall apply as if the substituted requirements were imposed by regulations under section 16 of that Act."

The Hydrocarbon Oil Duties Act 1979 (c.5)

22. In Schedule 5 to the Hydrocarbon Oil Duties Act 1979 (sampling) in paragraph 5(d) for the words "section 76 of the Food Act 1984, section 27 of the Food and Drugs (Scotland) Act 1956" there shall be substituted the words "section 27 of the Food Safety Act 1990".

The Slaughter of Animals (Scotland) Act 1980 (c.13)

23. In section 19(2) of the Slaughter of Animals (Scotland) Act 1980 (enforcement) for the words "section 13 of the Food and Drugs (Scotland) Act 1956" there shall be substituted the words "section 16 of the Food Safety Act 1990" and for the words "secton 36 of the said Act of 1956" there shall be substituted the words "section 32 of the said Act of 1990".

24. In section 22 of that Act (interpretation)—

    (a) for the definition of "knacker's yard" there shall be substituted the following definition—

      "'knacker's yard' means any premises used in connection with the business of slaughtering, flaying or cutting up animals the flesh of which is not intended for human consumption; and 'knacker' means a person whose business it is to carry out such slaughtering, flaying or cutting up"; and

    (b) for the definition of "slaughterhouse" there shall be substituted the following definition—

      "'slaughterhouse' means a place for slaughtering animals, the flesh of which is intended for human consumption, and includes any place available in connection with such a place for the confinement of animals while awaiting slaughter there or keeping, or subjecting to any treatment or process, products of the slaughtering of animals there; and 'slaughterman' means a person whose business is to carry out such slaughtering".

The Civic Government (Scotland) Act 1982 (c.45)

25. In section 39 of the Civic Government (Scotland) Act 1982 (street traders' licences)—

    (a) in subsection (3)(b), for the words "section 7 of the Milk and Dairies (Scotland) Act 1914" there shall be substituted the words "regulations made under section 19 of the Food Safety Act 1990"; and

    (b) in subsection (4)—

        (i) for the words "regulations made under sections 13 and 56 of the Food and Drugs (Scotland) Act 1956", there shall be substituted the words "section 1(3) of the Food Safety Act 1990";

        (ii) for the words "islands or district council" there shall be substituted the words "food authority (for the purposes of section 5 of the Food Safety Act 1990)"; and

(iii) for the words "sections 13 and 56 of the Food and Drugs (Scotland) Act 1956", there shall be substituted the words "section 16 of the Food Safety Act 1990".

The Public Health (Control of Disease) Act 1984 (c.22)

26. In section 3(2) of the Public Health (Control of Disease) Act 1984 (jurisdiction and powers of port health authority), for paragraph (a) there shall be substituted the following paragraph—

"(a) of a food authority under the Food Safety Act 1990;".

27. In section 7(3) of that Act (London port health authority), for paragraph (d) there shall be substituted the following paragraph—

"(d) of a food authority under any provision of the Food Safety Act 1990."

28.—(1) In subsection (1) of section 20 of that Act (stopping of work to prevent spread of disease), in paragraph (b) for the words "subsection (1) of section 28 of the Food Act 1984" there shall be substituted "subsection (1A) below".

(2) After that subsection there shall be inserted the following subsection—

"(1A) The diseases to which this subsection applies are—

(a) enteric fever (including typhoid and paratyphoid fevers);

(b) dysentery;

(c) diphtheria;

(d) scarlet fever;

(e) acute inflammation of the throat;

(f) gastro-enteritis; and

(g) undulant fever."

The Food and Environmental Protection Act 1985 (c.48)

29. In section 24(1) of the Food and Environment Protection Act 1985 (interpretation)—

(a) in the definition of "designated incident", for the words "designated incident" there shall be substituted the words "designated circumstances";

(b) the definition of "escape" shall cease to have effect; and

(c) for the definition of "food" there shall be substituted—

"'food' has the same meaning as in the Food Safety Act 1990."

30. In section 25 of that Act (Northern Ireland) after subsection (4) there shall be inserted the following subsection—

"(4A) Section 24(1) above shall have effect in relation to Northern Ireland as if for the definiton of 'food' there were substituted the following definition—

'"food" has the meaning assigned to it by Article 2(2) of the Food (Northern Ireland) Order 1989, except that it includes water which is bottled or is an ingredient of food;'."

The Local Government Act 195 (c.51)

31. In paragraph 15 of Schedule 8 to the Local Government Act 1985 (trading standards and related functions)—

(a) sub-paragraph (2) shall cease to have effect; and

(b) at the end of sub-paragraph (6) there shall be added the words "or section 5(1) of the Food Safety Act 1990".

The Weights and Measures Act 1985 (c.72)

32. In section 38 of the Weights and Measures Act 1985 (special powers of inspectors), subsection (4) (exclusion for milk) shall cease to have effect.

33. In section 93 of that Act (powers under other Acts with respect to marking of food) for the words "Food Act 1984" there shall be substituted the words "Food Safety Act 1990".

34. In section 94(1) of that Act (interpretation), in the definition of "drugs" and "food" for the words "Food Act 1984, or, in Scotland, the Food and Drugs (Scotland) Act 1956" there shall be substituted the words "Food Safety Act 1990".

The Agriculture Act 1986 (c.49)

35. In section 1(6) of the Agriculture Act 1986 (provision of agricultural goods and services), in the definition of "food", for the words "Food Act 1984" there shall be substituted "Food Safety Act 1990".

The National Health Service (Amendment) Act 1986 (c.66)

36.—(1) In subsection (2) of section 1 of the National Health Service (Amendment) Act 1986 (application of food legislation to health authorities and health service premises)—
(a) for the words "appropriate authority" there shall be substituted the word "Ministers"; and
(b) for the word "authority" there shall be substituted the word "Ministers".
(2) For subsection (7) of that section there shall be substituted—
"(7) In this section—
'the Ministers' has the same meaning as in the Food Safety Act 1990;
'the food legislation' means the Food Safety Act 1990 and any regulations or orders made (or having effect as if made) under it;
'health authority'—
(a) as respects England and Wales, has the meaning assigned to it by section 128 of the 1977 Act; and
(b) as respects Scotland, means a Health Board constituted under section 2 of the 1978 Act, the Commmon Services Agency constituted under section 10 of that Act or a State Hospital Management Committee constituted under section 91 of the Mental Health (Scotland) Act 1984."

The Consumer Protection Act 1987 (c.43)

37. In section 19(1) of the Consumer Protection Act 1987 (interpretation of Part II), in the definition of "food" for the words "Food Act 1984" there shall be substituted "Food Safety Act 1990".

The Road Traffic Offenders Act 1988 (c.53)

38. In section 16(7) of the Road Traffic Offenders Act 1988 (meaning of "authorised analyst" in relation to proceedings under Act), for the words "section 76 of the Food Act 1984, or section 27 of the Food and Drugs (Scotland) Act 1956" there shall be substituted the words "section 27 of the Food Safety Act 1990".

GENERAL NOTE

Minor and consequential amendments include: amendment to the Medicines Act 1968 to clarify references to drug authorities; amendment to the Transport Act 1968 so as to remove the prohibition upon an officer of a food authority from detaining a railway vehicle which contains food; and amendment of the Weights and Measures Act 1976 so as to permit the Minister to modify or except the relevant provisions of the Food Safety Act 1990 from an emergency order made under the 1976 Act (for example, to modify food safety standards in times of emergency such as shortage of food).

Section 59(3)   SCHEDULE 4

TRANSITIONAL PROVISIONS AND SAVINGS

Ships and aircraft

1. In relation to any time before the commencement of the first order under section 1(3) of this Act—
(a) any ship which is a home-going ship within the meaning of section 132 of the 1984 Act or section 58 of the 1956 Act (interpretation) shall be regarded as premises for the purposes of this Act; and
(b) the powers of entry conferred by section 32 of this Act shall include the right to enter any ship or aircraft for the purpose of ascertaining whether there is in the ship or aircraft any food imported as part of the cargo in contravention of the provisions of regulations made under Part II of this Act;
and in this Act as it applies by virtue of this paragraph "occupier", in relation to any ship or aircraft, means the master, commander or other person in charge of the ship or aircraft.

Regulations under the 1984 Act

2.—(1) In so far as any existing regulations made, or having effect as if made, under any provision of the 1984 Act specified in the first column of Table A below have effect in relation to England and Wales, they shall have effect, after the commencement of the relevant repeal, as if made under provisions of this Act specified in relation to that provision in the second column of that Table, or such of those provisions as are applicable.

(2) In this paragraph and paragraphs 3 and 4 below "existing regulations" means—

(a) any regulations made, or having effect as if made, under a provision repealed by this Act; and

(b) any orders having effect as if made under such regulations,

which are in force immediately before the coming into force of that repeal; and references to the commencement of the relevant repeal shall be construed accordingly.

TABLE A

Provision of the 1984 Act	Provision of this Act
section 4 (composition etc. of food)	sections 16(1)(a), (c) and (f) and (3) and 17(1)
section 7 (describing food)	section 16(1)(e)
section 13 (food hygiene)	section 16(1)(b), (c), (d) and (f), (2) and (3)
section 33 (milk and dairies)	section 16(1)(b), (c), (d) and (f), (2) and (3)
section 34 (registration), so far as relating to dairies or dairy farms	section 19
section 38 (milk: special designations)	section 18(2)
section 73(2) (qualification of officers)	section 5(6)
section 76(2) (public analysts)	section 27(2)
section 79(5) (form of certificate)	section 49(2)
section 119 (Community provisions)	section 17(2)

Regulations under the 1956 Act

3. Any existing regulations made, or having effect as if made, under any provision of the 1956 Act specified in the first column of Table B below shall have effect, after the commencement of the relevant repeal, as if made under the provisions of this Act specified in relation to that provision in the second column of that Table, or such of those provisions as are applicable.

TABLE B

Provision of the 1956 Act	Provision of this Act
section 4 (composition etc. of food)	sections 16(1)(a), (c) and (f) and (3) and 17(1)
section 7 (describing food)	section 16(1)(e)
section 13 (food hygiene)	sections 5(6) and 16(1)(b), (c), (d) and (f), (2) and (3)
section 16(2) (regulations as to milk)	section 18(2)
section 27(2) (public analysts)	section 27(2)
section 29(3) (form of certificate)	section 49(2)
section 56A (Community provisions)	section 17(2)

Other regulations

4. In so far as any existing regulations made under section 1 of the Importation of Milk Act 1983 have effect in relation to Great Britain, they shall have effect, after the commencement of the relevant repeal, as if made under section 18(1)(b) of this Act.

Orders with respect to milk in Scotland

5.—(1) Any existing order made under section 12(2) of the Milk and Dairies (Scotland) Act 1914 (orders with respect to milk) shall have effect, after the commencement of the relevant repeal, as if it were regulations made under section 16(1)(b), (d) and (f) and (2) of this Act.

(2) Any existing order made under section 3 of the Milk and Dairies (Amendment) Act 1922 (sale of milk under special designations) shall have effect, after the commencement of the relevant repeal, as if it were regulations made under section 18(2) of this Act.

(3) In this paragraph "existing order" means any order made under a provision repealed by this Act which is in force immediately before the coming into force of that repeal; and references to the commencement of the relevant repeal shall be construed accordingly.

Disqualification orders

6. The repeal by this Act of section 14 of the 1984 Act (court's power to disqualify caterers) shall not have effect as respects any order made, or having effect as if made, under that section which is in force immediately before the commencement of that repeal.

Food hygiene byelaws

7.—(1) The repeal by this Act of section 15 of the 1984 Act (byelaws as to food) shall not have effect as respects any byelaws made, or having effect as if made, under that section which are in force immediately before the commencement of that repeal.

(2) In so far as any such byelaws conflict with any regulations made, or having effect as if made, under Part II of this Act, the regulations shall prevail.

Closure orders

8. The repeal by this Act of section 21 of the 1984 Act or section 1 of the Control of Food Premises (Scotland) Act 1977 (closure orders) shall not have effect as respects any order made, or having effect as if made, under that section which is in force immediately before the commencement of that repeal.

Section 59(4)   SCHEDULE 5

REPEALS

Chapter	Short title	Extent of repeal
1914 c.46.	The Milk and Dairies (Scotland) Act 1914.	The whole Act.
1922 c.54.	The Milk and Dairies (Amendment) Act 1922.	The whole Act.
1934 c.51.	The Milk Act 1934.	The whole Act.
1949 c.34.	The Milk (Special Designations) Act 1949.	The whole Act.
1956 c.30.	The Food and Drugs (Scotland) Act 1956.	The whole Act.
1963 c.33.	The London Government Act 1963.	Section 54(1).
1967 c.22.	The Agriculture Act 1967.	In section 7(3), the words from "and, without prejudice" to the end.
1967 c.50.	The Farm and Garden Chemicals Act 1967.	In section 4(7)(c), the words from "for the reference" to "1956".
1968 c.29.	The Trade Descriptions Act 1968.	In section 22(2), the paragraph beginning with the words "In this subsection".
1968 c.67.	The Medicines Act 1968.	In section 132(1), the definition of "food and drugs authority". In Schedule 5, paragraph 17.
1968 c.73.	The Transport Act 1968.	In Schedule 16, in paragraph 7(2), paragraphs (d) and (e).
1971 c.62.	The Tribunals and Inquiries Act 1971.	In Schedule 1, paragraphs 15 and 40.
1972 c.66.	The Agriculture (Miscellaneous Provisions) Act 1972.	Section 4(3).
1972 c.68.	The European Communities Act 1972.	In Schedule 4, paragraph 3(2)(c).
1976 c.77.	The Weights and Measures &c. Act 1976.	In section 12(9)(c), the words "the 1956 Act or".
1977 c.28.	The Control of Food Premises (Scotland) Act 1977.	The whole Act.
1983 c.37.	The Importation of Milk Act 1983.	The whole Act.
1984 c.30.	The Food Act 1984.	Parts I and II. In section 51(2), the word "market".

Chapter	Short title	Extent of repeal
		In section 53, in subsection (1) the words "and in respect of the weighing and measuring of articles and vehicles", and in subsection (3)(b) the words "in respect of the weighing of vehicles, or as the case may be,"
		Section 57(1).
		Section 58.
		In section 61, the words from "and this Part" to the end.
		Part IV.
		Sections 70 to 92.
		In section 93, in subsection (2), paragraphs (b) to (d) and, in subsection (3), paragraphs (a) to (e) and (h) to (l).
		In section 94, subsection (1) except as regards offences under Part III of the Act, and subsection (2).
		In section 95, subsections (2) to (8).
		Sections 96 to 109.
		Sections 111 to 120.
		In section 121, subsections (2) and (3).
		Sections 122 to 131.
		In section 132, subsection (1) except the words "In this Act, unless the context otherwise requires" and the definitions of "animal" and "the Minister".
		Sections 133 and 134.
		In section 136, in subsection (2), paragraphs (b) and (c).
		Schedules 1 to 11.
1985 c.48.	The Food and Environment Protection Act 1985.	In section 1(2), the definition of "escape". In section 24(1), the definition of "escape".
1985 c.51.	The Local Government Act 1985.	In Schedule 8, paragraph 15(2).
1985 c.72.	The Weights and Measures Act 1985.	Section 38(4).

DEFINITIONS
   "food": s.1(1), (2) and (4).
   "contravention": s.53(1).
   "milk": s.53(1).
   "ship": s.53(1).

GENERAL NOTE
   Much of the Food Safety Act 1990 is concerned with the making of regulations or orders and it is of course necessary that savings are made and that transitional provisions operate (such as orders made under the previous food legislation) so as to ensure a smooth changeover in the applicable legislation.

INDEX

References are to sections

AUSTRALIAN CONSTITUTION (PUBLIC RECORD COPY) ACT 1990

(1990 c. 17)

An Act to exclude one of the record copies of the Commonwealth of Australia Constitution Act 1900 from the public records to which the Public Records Act 1958 applies.   [29th June 1990]

PARLIAMENTARY DEBATES
Hansard: H.C. Vol. 171, col. 1223; H.L. Vol. 519, col. 665; Vol. 520, col. 603; Vol. 520, col. 1617.

INTRODUCTION
The government of the Commonwealth of Australia requested that the record copy of the Commonwealth of Australia Constitution Act 1900, which is currently on loan, be allowed to remain in the keeping of the Commonwealth. The government in the U.K. supported this request and in response enacted the following piece of legislation, excluding the 1900 Act from the public records to which the Public Records Act 1958 applies.

Release of record copy of Australian Constitution

1. The copy of the Commonwealth of Australia Constitution Act 1900 which at the passing of this Act is on loan to the Commonwealth of Australia shall cease to be included in the public records to which the Public Records Act 1958 applies.

Short title

2. This Act may be cited as the Australian Constitution (Public Record Copy) Act 1990.

INDEX

References are to sections

AUSTRALIA,
Commonwealth of, 1

COMMONWEALTH of AUSTRALIA CONSTITUTION
ACT 1900, 1

PUBLIC RECORDS,
exclusion from, 1

PUBLIC RECORDS ACT 1958, 1

COMPUTER MISUSE ACT 1990*

(1990 c. 18)

An Act to make provision for securing computer material against unauthorised access or modification; and for connected purposes.

[29th June 1990]

PARLIAMENTARY DEBATES
   Hansard: H.C. Vol. 164, col. 390; Vol. 166, col. 1134; Vol. 171, col. 1287; H.L. Vol. 519, col. 230.

INTRODUCTION

Background to the Legislation
   The Computer Misuse Act 1990 gives effect, with some modifications, to various changes to the law recommended by the Law Commission's Report No. 186, *Computer Misuse*, Cm. 819, published in October 1989. The Commission undertook an investigation of this area of law in the light of public concern over "the misuse of computers or computer systems by parties other than those entitled to use or control those computers, either by simply seeking access to the computers, or by going further and using the computers or amending the information in them for what may be a wide range of ulterior motives" (Law Com. No. 186, para. 1.1). The Report followed the publication of a Report by the Scottish Law Commission in 1987, which advocated the creation of a new offence in Scotland, of "obtaining unauthorised access to a computer": *Report on Computer Crime* (Scot. Law Com. No. 106, Cm. 174). During the period of the English Law Commission's deliberations, however, further urgency was given to the matter when the House of Lords confirmed the decision of the Court of Appeal quashing the convictions of the two defendants in *R.* v. *Gold; R.* v. *Schifreen* [1988] A.C. 1063, a case in which a freelance computer journalist and an accountant had taken advantage of slack computer security arrangements to gain unauthorised access to the Prestel system, a computerised public information service. They gained access to the system on numerous occasions, altered files, and left various messages in the

---

* Annotations by Martin Wasik, LL.B., Barrister, Senior Lecturer in Law, Manchester University.

electronic mailboxes of subscribers to the system. Their prosecution for forgery under the Forgery and Counterfeiting Act 1981 ultimately failed since, according to Lord Brandon in that case, it had been a "Procrustean attempt" to force the facts of the case within the language of a statute which had never been designed to fit them.

The Law Commission, accordingly, recommended the creation of three new criminal offences to cater for different aspects of computer misuse, together with changes to existing provisions conferring jurisdiction on the courts of England and Wales, Scotland, and Northern Ireland, in so far as they would affect the prosecution of computer misuse cases. The suggested jurisdictional changes were in line with those advocated by the Commission in respect of fraud offences in their Report, published in April 1989, on *Jurisdiction over Offences of Fraud and Dishonesty with a Foreign Element* (Law Com. No. 180). A Private Member's Bill, sponsored by Mr Michael Colvin, was designed to give effect to the Law Commission's recommendations and this Bill, with some amendments, now takes the form of the Computer Misuse Act 1990.

Arrangement of the Act

The Act, by ss.1–3, creates three new criminal offences.

The first new offence, that of "unauthorised access to computer material" is triable summarily and is designed to criminalise the activity of computer "hacking", though the offence is drafted in such a way as to cover both the "remote" hacker, working from a distance, who endeavours to gain access to a program or to data held in a computer and the "insider", such as an employee, who may have limited authorisation to use the computer but knowingly exceeds that authority.

The second new offence, triable summarily or on indictment, is an aggravated form of the first, in that it consists of the commission of conduct sufficient to establish the first offence, together with an intention to commit or facilitate the commission of one of a range of further, more serious, offences. This new offence is designed to cover a range of situations, such as the case where a person gains unauthorised access to computer material in order to commit theft by redirecting funds to his own bank account, or where a person gains unauthorised access to confidential information held in a computer in order to facilitate a blackmail scheme.

The third new offence, also triable either way, is that of causing an unauthorised modification of the contents of any computer. The offence is designed to cover cases of deliberate erasure or corruption of programs or data, including the introduction of a "worm" or "virus" into a computer.

Later sections of the Computer Misuse Act 1990 make provision in respect of the territorial scope of offences under the Act, extradition for those offences, and arrangements for proceedings in Scotland and Northern Ireland. There is also provision, inserted into the Bill at a late stage, and the subject of considerable debate in Parliament, for the issuing of search warrants in respect of the unauthorised access to computer material offence.

Computer misuse of offences

Unauthorised access to computer material

1.—(1) A person is guilty of an offence if—
   (a) he causes a computer to perform any function with intent to secure access to any program or data held in any computer;
   (b) the access he intends to secure is unauthorised; and
   (c) he knows at the time when he causes the computer to perform the function that that is the case.

(2) The intent a person has to have to commit an offence under this section need not be directed at—
   (a) any particular program or data;
   (b) a program or data of any particular kind; or
   (c) a program or data held in any particular computer.

(3) A person guilty of an offence under this section shall be liable on summary conviction to imprisonment for a term not exceeding six months or to a fine not exceeding level 5 on the standard scale or to both.

DEFINITIONS
   "program or data held in a computer": s.17(6).
   "secure access": s.17(2), (3) and (4).

"unauthorised": s.17(5).

References to a program include references to part of a program: s.17(10).

The terms "computer", "data" and "program" are not defined in the Act and should, therefore, be given their ordinary meaning (see note to s.17).

GENERAL NOTE

S.1 creates a new offence triable summarily in a magistrates' court in England (for proceedings in England see s.11; for arrangements for Scotland see s.13 and for Northern Ireland see s.16).

The *actus reus* of the offence requires the defendant to "cause a computer to perform any function". This is intended to exclude mere physical contact with a computer and the scrutiny of data without any interaction with a computer (thus the reading of confidential computer output, the reading of data displayed on the screen, or "computer eavesdropping", are not covered). On the other hand it does not require that the defendant must succeed in obtaining access to the program or data, or be successful in subverting computer security measures in place. A remote hacker would, thus, "cause a computer to perform any function" if he gained access to it remotely and the computer responded, such as by activating a computer security device or by offering a log-on menu. An employee would "cause a computer to perform any function" as soon as he switched on the computer, and would be guilty of the offence if the requisite *mens rea* could also be proved. The substantive offence is thus drafted in such a way as to include conduct which might usually be thought to fall within the scope of the law of attempt.

There are two limbs to the *mens rea* of the offence. The first limb is the "intent to secure access to any program or data held in any computer". The word "any" makes it clear that the intent need not relate to the computer which the defendant is at that time operating. Subs. (2) makes it clear that the defendant's intent need not be directed at any particular program or data, so as to include the hacker who gains access to a computer without any clear idea of what he will find there. Recklessness is insufficient; still less would careless or inattentive gaining of access to the computer suffice for liability. The second limb is that the defendant must know at the time when he causes the computer to perform the function that the access which he intends to secure is unauthorised. The prosecution must prove both limbs.

Since this offence is summary only, there can be no charge of an attempt in respect of it. There is, however, the possibility of secondary liability arising in accord with the Magistrates' Courts Act 1980, s.44(1), where, for example, a person supplies a hacker with information which would assist him, such as a confidential computer password. The operator of a computer hacker "bulletin board" might, therefore, come within the reach of such an offence.

Penalties

The Law Commission recommended (para. 3.45), that the penalties available in respect of this offence should be three months' imprisonment and a fine of up to Level 4 on the standard scale (*i.e.* £1,000), but these penalties were doubled when the Bill was first introduced by Mr Colvin. The Law Commission also drew attention to the courts' general powers to award compensation under the Powers of Criminal Courts Act 1973, s.35, as amended by the Criminal Justice Acts 1982 and 1988, and the courts' powers to forfeit property used or intended for use in committing offences (*e.g.* hacking equipment) under Criminal Justice Act 1988, s.69(1).

Unauthorised access with intent to commit or facilitate commission of further offences

2.—(1) A person is guilty of an offence under this section if he commits an offence under section 1 above ("the unauthorised access offence") with intent—

(a) to commit an offence to which this section applies; or

(b) to facilitate the commission of such an offence (whether by himself or by any other person);

and the offence he intends to commit or facilitate is referred to below in this section as the further offence.

(2) This section applies to offences—

(a) for which the sentence is fixed by law; or

(b) for which a person of twenty-one years of age or over (not

18–3

previously convicted) may be sentenced to imprisonment for a term of five years (or, in England and Wales, might be so sentenced but for the restrictions imposed by section 33 of the Magistrates' Courts Act 1980).

(3) It is immaterial for the purposes of this section whether the further offence is to be committed on the same occasion as the unauthorised access offence or on any future occasion.

(4) A person may be guilty of an offence under this section even though the facts are such that the commission of the further offence is impossible.

(5) A person guilty of an offence under this section shall be liable—

(a) on summary conviction, to imprisonment for a term not exceeding six months or to a fine not exceeding the statutory maximum or to both; and

(b) on conviction on indictment, to imprisonment for a term not exceeding five years or to a fine or to both.

DEFINITIONS

"secure access": s.17(2), (3) and (4).
"unauthorised": s.17(5).
"program or data held in a computer": s.17(6).
References to a program include references to part of a program: s.17(10).
The terms "computer", "data" and "program" are not defined in the Act and should, therefore, be given their ordinary meaning (see note to s.17).

GENERAL NOTE

S.2 creates an offence triable either way, of committing the unauthorised access offence under s.1 with intent to commit or facilitate the commission of a more serious "further" offence. It is not necessary to prove that the intended further offence has actually been committed. The offences in ss.1 and 2 are hierarchical, with the s.2 offence catering for the defendant who gains unauthorised access to computer-held material with serious criminal intentions. Where a charge is brought under s.2, a conviction may be returned for the s.1 offence if this further intention is not proved: see s.12.

A person will be guilty of the s.2 offence in a range of situations. Obtaining the unauthorised access may, for example, be done with the intention of committing theft, such as by diverting funds which are in the course of an electronic funds transfer, to the defendant's own bank account, or to the bank account of an accomplice. It would also cover the case where the defendant gained unauthorised access to sensitive information held on computer with a view to blackmailing the person to whom that information related.

Subs. (2)

This subsection explains what qualifies as a further offence for the purposes of the s.2 offence. The main example of an offence the sentence for which is fixed by law is murder (life imprisonment). Most offences of fraud and dishonesty are punishable with at least five years' imprisonment. Such offences are "arrestable offences" for the purposes of the Police and Criminal Evidence Act 1984 and attract prescribed powers of arrest, search and seizure. See further the note to s.14.

Subs. (3)

It is made clear by this subsection that the defendant may intend to commit the further offence on the same occasion as the unauthorised access offence (as in the theft example just given) or on a future occasion (as in the blackmail example).

Subs. (4)

This makes it possible to convict a person who intended to commit the further offence even if, on the facts, that would be impossible (*e.g.* where the intended blackmail victim was, unknown to the defendant, dead). This rule is analogous to that in Criminal Attempts Act 1981, s.1(2), as applied in *R.* v. *Shivpuri* [1987] A.C. 1.

Penalties

The penalties available in respect of this offence are in accord with the Law Commission's recommendation. The Law Commission also drew attention to the courts' general powers to award compensation under the Powers of Criminal Courts Act 1973, s.35, as amended by the Criminal Justice Acts of 1982 and 1988, and to the courts' powers to forfeit property used or intended for use in committing offences (*e.g.* hacking equipment) under the Criminal Justice Act 1988, s.69(1). Since this offence is punishable on indictment with imprisonment for a term of five years, the offence is an arrestable offence for the purposes of the Police and Criminal Evidence Act 1984: see note to s.14.

Unauthorised modification of computer material

3.—(1) A person is guilty of an offence if—
- (a) he does any act which causes an unauthorised modification of the contents of any computer; and
- (b) at the time when he does the act he has the requisite intent and the requisite knowledge.

(2) For the purposes of subsection (1)(b) above the requisite intent is an intent to cause a modification of the contents of any computer and by so doing—
- (a) to impair the operation of any computer;
- (b) to prevent or hinder access to any program or data held in any computer; or
- (c) to impair the operation of any such program or the reliability of any such data.

(3) The intent need not be directed at—
- (a) any particular computer;
- (b) any particular program or data or a program or data of any particular kind; or
- (c) any particular modification or a modification of any particular kind.

(4) For the purposes of subsection (1)(b) above the requisite is knowledge that any modification he intends to cause is unauthorised.

(5) It is immaterial for the purposes of this section whether an unauthorised modification or any intended effect of it of a kind mentioned in subsection (2) above is, or is intended to be, permanent or merely temporary.

(6) For the purposes of the Criminal Damage Act 1971 a modification of the contents of a computer shall not be regarded as damaging any computer or computer storage medium unless its effect on that computer or computer storage medium impairs its physical condition.

(7) A person guilty of an offence under this section shall be liable—
- (a) on summary conviction, to imprisonment for a term not exceeding six months or to a fine not exceeding the statutory maximum or to both; and
- (b) on conviction on indictment, to imprisonment for a term not exceeding five years or to a fine or to both.

DEFINITIONS
  "modification of the contents of any computer": s.17(7).
  "program or data held in a computer": s.17(6).
  References to a program include references to part of a program: s.17(10).
  The terms "computer", "data" and "program" are not defined in the Act and should, therefore, be given their ordinary meaning (see note to s.17).

GENERAL NOTE
  S.3 creates an offence triable either way. When read in the context of s.17, it is clear that a wide range of different forms of conduct are included within its scope. It would cover all cases involving deliberate (recklessness is insufficient) alteration or erasure of any program or data held on a computer (s.17(7)(a)), where the defendant intended thereby to impair a computer's operation, hinder access to computer material by a legitimate user or impair the operation or reliability of computer-held material, and where he knew that the intended modification was unauthorised. It does not have to be proved that the defendant had any specific target computer, program or data in mind.

The section would also extend to a case where the defendant intentionally introduced a computer "worm" program into a computer system. A "worm" is a self-replicating program which rapidly uses up all the spare capacity on the computer by adding programs or data to the computer's contents (s.17(7)(b)), thereby impairing its operation (s.3(2)(a)). A likely effect of the introduction of a "worm" is to prevent or hinder access to a legitimate user (s.3(2)(b)).

Also within the scope of the section is the intentional introduction of a computer "virus" into a computer system. A "virus" is a program designed to corrupt or erase computer-held material. Where X deliberately introduces into circulation a floppy disk contaminated with a computer "virus" and Y, an innocent party, uses the disk on his computer, impairing its operation, it seems that X would be guilty of the offence at the time he introduced the disk into circulation, since s.17(7) states that any act which contributes towards causing such a modification shall be regarded as causing it. The liability of X would be unaffected by Y passing the disk, unused, to another innocent party, Z, who uses the disk and impairs the operation of Z's computer, since X's intent need not be directed at any particular computer, program or data (s.3(3)).

The offence under s.3 would also cater for a case where the defendant intentionally causes an unauthorised modification of the contents of a computer, intending thereby to prevent or hinder access by legitimate users to any data or program held on the computer (see, *e.g.* *Turner* (1984) 13 CCC (3d) 430, where a hacker placed a "locking device" on computer-held data, rendering the data inaccessible to users). By s.3(5) it is immaterial whether this modification or its intended effect is, or is intended to be, permanent or temporary.

The terms "virus" and "worms" are not used, and are hence undefined, in the Act.

Subs. (6)

This deals with the relationship between this offence and the offence of criminal damage under the Criminal Damage Act 1971. In *Cox* v. *Riley* (1986) 83 Cr.App.R. 54 the defendant deliberately erased the programs from a printed circuit card, which was used to operate a computerised machine, and he was convicted of criminal damage. His conviction was approved by the Divisional Court, on the basis that the card itself had been damaged (the programs themselves, being intangible property, fell outside the scope of the Criminal Damage Act, by virtue of s.10(1)). S.3(6) now declares that the scope of the 1971 Act in computer cases is confined to circumstances where the physical condition of the computer or computer storage medium has been impaired. The intended effect of this, it seems, is that were the facts of *Cox* v. *Riley* (1986) 83 Cr.App.R. 54 to recur, the defendant would not now be guilty of criminal damage, but would be guilty of the offence under s.3 of the Computer Misuse Act. It seems surprising that this change to the law was not achieved by amendment to the 1971 Act.

Penalties

The penalties for this offence are the same as for the offence under s.2. See the note on penalties in relation to s.2.

Jurisdiction

Territorial scope of offences under this Act

4.—(1) Except as provided below in this section, it is immaterial for the purposes of any offence under section 1 or 3 above—

    (a) whether any act or other event proof of which is required for conviction of the offence occurred in the home country concerned; or

    (b) whether the accused was in the home country concerned at the time of any such act or event.

(2) Subject to subsection (3) below, in the case of such an offence at least one significant link with domestic jurisdiction must exist in the circumstances of the case for the offence to be committed.

(3) There is no need for any such link to exist for the commission of an offence under section 1 above to be established in proof of an allegation to that effect in proceedings for an offence under section 2 above.

    (4) Subject to section 8 below, where—

(a) any such link does in fact exist in the case of an offence under section 1 above; and
(b) commission of that offence is alleged in proceedings for an offence under section 2 above;

section 2 above shall apply as if anything the accused intended to do or facilitate in any place outside the home country concerned which would be an offence to which section 2 applies if it took place in the home country concerned were the offence in question.

(5) This section is without prejudice to any jurisdiction exercisable by a court in Scotland apart from this section.

(6) References in this Act to the home country concerned are references—
(a) in the application of this Act to England and Wales, to England and Wales;
(b) in the application of this Act to Scotland, to Scotland; and
(c) in the application of this Act to Northern Ireland, to Northern Ireland.

DEFINITIONS
"home country": s.4(6).
"significant link with domestic jurisdiction": s.5(2) and (3).

GENERAL NOTE
The purpose of this section, taken together with ss.5–9 and s.16, is to introduce new rules whereby courts in the United Kingdom will have jurisdiction over the offences of computer misuse set out in ss.1–3 of this Act, whether that computer misuse originates from this country or is directed against a computer or computers located within it. The changes to jurisdiction are in accord with the recommendation of the Law Commission's Report No. 186, *Computer Misuse*, 1989, para. 4.2, and are in line with wider recommendations in respect of extending the jurisdiction of courts within the United Kingdom to cater for offences of fraud and dishonesty which have a foreign element (Law Commission Report No. 180, *Jurisdiction Over Offences of Fraud and Dishonesty With a Foreign Element*, 1989). These wider proposals have not yet been acted upon.

Subs. (3)
This subsection provides that jurisdiction to prosecute an offence under s.2 is not dependent on the existence of a significant link for the unauthorised access offence under s.1 (the offences under ss.1 and 2 are hierarchical). It is sufficient that the accused intended to carry out the further offence in that home country and that there would be jurisdiction under the current rules to try that offence. This would be relevant when unauthorised access to a computer is achieved abroad with the intent to commit the further offence in that home country, for example to carry out a fraud.

Subs. (4)
An offence under s.2 will be triable in a home country where the accused committed an offence under s.1 within that home country with intent to commit an act abroad which would have amounted to the further offence if it had been committed in that home country. Thus an offence under s.2 would be triable in England where an accused hacked into a computer in England in order to obtain information with a view to blackmailing someone in the United States. This provision is subject to the "double criminality" test in s.8(1).

Subs. (5)
The common law jurisdiction of the courts in Scotland already extends to offences of fraud which take place partly in one country and partly in another, provided that a significant part of the conduct takes place in Scotland. For the avoidance of doubt, however, ss.4 and 5 are extended to Scotland.

Significant links with domestic jurisdiction

5.—(1) The following provisions of this section apply for the interpretation of section 4 above.

(2) In relation to an offence under section 1, either of the following is a significant link with domestic jurisdiction—

(a) that the accused was in the home country concerned at the time when he did the act which caused the computer to perform the function; or

(b) that any computer containing any program or data to which the accused secured or intended to secure unauthorised access by doing that act was in the home country concerned at that time.

(3) In relation to an offence under section 3, either of the following is a significant link with domestic jurisdiction—

(a) that the accused was in the home country concerned at the time when he did the act which caused the unauthorised modification; or

(b) that the unauthorised modification took place in the home country concerned.

DEFINITIONS
"home country": s.4(6).
"secures access": s.17(2), (3) and (4).
"unauthorised modification": s.17(8).
References to a "program" include references to a part of a program: s.17(10).

GENERAL NOTE
This section determines, for the purposes of the offences under ss.1 and 3 of this Act, what constitutes a "significant link" with a home country. The test for founding jurisdiction is, in the case of an offence under s.1 if *either* the accused was in that country when he secured unauthorised access to a computer *or* if any computer to which the accused secured or intended to secure unauthorised access was in the home country at that time and, in the case of an offence under s.3, if *either* the accused was in the home country concerned when he did the act which caused the unauthorised modification *or* if any computer whose contents were modified was in the home country at that time.

Territorial scope of inchoate offences related to offences under this Act

6.—(1) On a charge of conspiracy to commit an offence under this Act the following questions are immaterial to the accused's guilt—

(a) the question where any person became a party to the conspiracy; and

(b) the question whether any act, omission or other event occurred in the home country concerned.

(2) On a charge of attempting to commit an offence under section 3 above the following questions are immaterial to the accused's guilt—

(a) the question where the attempt was made; and

(b) the question whether it had an effect in the home country concerned.

(3) On a charge of incitement to commit an offence under this Act the question where the incitement took place is immaterial to the accused's guilt.

(4) This section does not extend to Scotland.

GENERAL NOTE
This section, together with s.7, makes changes to the jurisdictional rules relating to conspiracy, attempt and indictment in respect of the offences under ss.1 and 3 of this Act, which are parallel to the changes made by ss.4 and 5 in respect of the substantive offences. S.6 deals with cases where the conduct takes place abroad but is targeted on a computer situated in a home country (or takes place in one home country and is targeted on a computer in a different home country). Conduct which takes place in a home country and which is targeted on a computer situated abroad is catered for in s.7. These changes are in line with the Law Commission recommendation in its *Report on Computer Misuse*, para. 4.3.

Subs. (2)

This subsection is confined to an attempt to commit the offence under s.3 of the Act, whilst subss. (1) and (3) apply to all three offences. This is because the offences under ss.1 and 2 are already drafted in such a way as to penalise attempts to gain unauthorised access.

Subs. (4)

This section does not extend to Scotland because the jurisdiction of the Scottish courts over inchoate offences flows from their jurisdiction over the substantive offences. See note to s.4(5).

Territorial scope of inchoate offences related to offences under external law corresponding to offences under this Act

7.—(1) The following subsections shall be inserted after subsection (1) of section 1 of the Criminal Law Act 1977—

"(1A) Subject to section 8 of the Computer Misuse Act 1990 (relevance of external law), if this subsection applies to an agreement, this Part of this Act has effect in relation to it as it has effect in relation to an agreement falling within subsection (1) above.

(1B) Subsection (1A) above applies to an agreement if—

(a) a party to it, or a party's agent, did anything in England and Wales in relation to it before its formation; or

(b) a party to it became a party in England and Wales (by joining it either in person or through an agent); or

(c) a party to it, or a party's agent, did or omitted anything in England and Wales in pursuance of it;

and the agreement would fall within subsection (1) above as an agreement relating to the commission of a computer misuse offence but for the fact that the offence would not be an offence triable in England and Wales if committed in accordance with the parties' intentions.".

(2) The following subsections shall be inserted after subsection (4) of that section—

"(5) In the application of this Part of this Act to an agreement to which subsection (1A) above applies any reference to an offence shall be read as a reference to what would be the computer misuse offence in question but for the fact that it is not an offence triable in England and Wales.

(6) In this section "computer misuse offence" means an offence under the Computer Misuse Act 1990.".

(3) The following subsections shall be inserted after section 1(1) of the Criminal Attempts Act 1981—

"(1A) Subject to section 8 of the Computer Misuse Act 1990 (relevance of external law), if this subsection applies to an act, what the person doing it had in view shall be treated as an offence to which this section applies.

(1B) Subsection (1A) above applies to an act if—

(a) it is done in England and Wales; and

(b) it would fall within subsection (1) above as more than merely preparatory to the commission of an offence under section 3 of the Computer Misuse Act 1990 but for the fact that the offence, if completed, would not be an offence triable in England and Wales.".

(4) Subject to section 8 below, if any act done by a person in England and Wales would amount to the offence of incitement to commit an offence under this Act but for the fact that what he had in view would not be an offence triable in England and Wales—

(a) what he had in view shall be treated as an offence under this Act for the purposes of any charge of incitement brought in respect of that act; and

(b) any such charge shall accordingly be triable in England and Wales.

GENERAL NOTE

This section provides for the prosecution of an inchoate offence in England and Wales to commit elsewhere the equivalent of the computer misuse offences. These provisions are subject to the principle of "double criminality" established in s.8(1). These provisions apply to Northern Ireland by virtue of s.16 of the Act, but not to Scotland.

Subss. (1) and (2)

These subsections relate to conspiracy and amend s.1 of the Criminal Law Act 1977. Subject to the double criminality principle (s.8(1)), they provide that every party to a conspiracy to perform abroad an act, which if performed here would constitute a computer misuse offence, will be triable in England and Wales if at least one conspirator became a party to it in England and Wales, or if he did anything there relating to the conspiracy or in pursuance of it.

Subs. (3)

This subsection relates to attempt and amends s.1 of the Criminal Attempts Act 1981. Subject to the double criminality principle (s.8(1), below), it provides that every attempt in England and Wales to perform abroad an act, which if performed in England and Wales would be an offence under s.3, will be triable in England and Wales. This subsection is confined to an attempt to commit the offence under s.3 of the Act, whilst subss. (1), (2) and (4) apply to all three offences. This is because the offences under ss.1 and 2 are already drafted in such a way as to penalise attempts to gain unauthorised access.

Subs. (4)

This subsection makes similar provision for the law of incitement, and is similarly subject to the double criminality principle (s.8(1), below).

Relevance of external law

8.—(1) A person is guilty of an offence triable by virtue of section 4(4) above only if what he intended to do or facilitate would involve the commission of an offence under the law in force where the whole or any part of it was intended to take place.

(2) A person is guilty of an offence triable by virtue of section 1(1A) of the Criminal Law Act 1977 only if the pursuit of the agreed course of conduct would at some stage involve—

(a) an act or omission by one or more of the parties; or

(b) the happening of some other event;

constituting an offence under the law in force where the act, omission or other event was intended to take place.

(3) A person is guilty of an offence triable by virtue of section 1(1A) of the Criminal Attempts Act 1981 or by virtue of section 7(4) above only if what he had in view would involve the commission of an offence under the law in force where the whole or any part of it was intended take place.

(4) Conduct punishable under the law in force in any place is an offence under that law for the purposes of this section, however it is described in that law.

(5) Subject to subsection (7) below, a condition specified in any of subsections (1) to (3) above shall be taken to be satisfied unless not later than rules of court may provide the defence serve on the prosecution a notice—

(a) stating that, on the facts as alleged with respect to the relevant conduct, the condition is not in their opinion satisfied;

(b) showing their grounds for that opinion; and

(c) requiring the prosecution to show that it is satisfied.

(6) In subsection (5) above "the relevant conduct" means—

(a) where the condition in subsection (1) above is in question, what the accused intended to do or facilitate;
(b) where the condition in subsection (2) above is in question, the agreed course of conduct; and
(c) where the condition in subsection (3) above is in question, what the accused had in view.

(7) The court, if it thinks fit, may permit the defence to require the prosecution to show that the condition is satisfied without the prior service of a notice under subsection (5) above.

(8) If by virtue of subsection (7) above a court of solemn jurisdiction in Scotland permits the defence to require the prosecution to show that the condition is satisfied, it shall be competent for the prosecution for that purpose to examine any witness or to put in evidence any production not included in the lists lodged by it.

(9) In the Crown Court the question whether the condition is satisfied shall be decided by the judge alone.

(10) In the High Court of Justiciary and in the sheriff court the question whether the condition is satisfied shall be decided by the judge or, as the case may be, the sheriff alone.

GENERAL NOTE

This section applies to those cases where, under the provisions of the Act, a court in a home country would have jurisdiction to try someone for acts which took place in the home country but which were directed at committing the computer misuse offence abroad. As we have seen, if there is a significant link with the domestic jurisdiction the offence is triable in the relevant home country. Where, however, in respect of an offence under s.2 the offence is triable in the home country (ss.4(3)(4)), or where the offence charged is a conspiracy, attempt or incitement to commit a computer misuse offence abroad (s.7), s.8 provides that, in addition, any such offence can only be prosecuted in the home country if, in respect of the s.2 offence, the further offence contemplated, if carried out, would be both punishable in the home country and in the relevant country abroad, or, in respect of an inchoate offence to commit a computer misuse offence abroad, that any such inchoate offence can only be prosecuted in the home country if the acts contemplated would be punishable both in the home country and in the relevant country abroad if carried out. These provisions apply to England and Wales, Scotland and, by virtue of s.16, to Northern Ireland.

Subss. (1) to (3)

Subs. (1) applies the double criminality principle to cases where an accused is charged with a s.2 offence triable by virtue of s.4(4). Subss. (2) and (3) apply the double criminality principle to cases where an accused is charged with conspiracy, attempt or incitement to commit a computer misuse offence abroad.

Subs. (4)

While several foreign countries have enacted computer misuse offences, their existence is not universal. Subs. (4) provides that if the conduct is punishable in the foreign country in question, it is not relevant how the offence is described in that law.

Subss. (5) to (9)

These subsections provide that it should be presumed that the condition of double criminality is satisfied unless the defence serves a notice on the prosecution stating that, in their opinion, the contrary is true, setting out the associated procedural matters.

British citizenship immaterial

9.—(1) In any proceedings brought in England and Wales in respect of any offence to which this section applies it is immaterial to guilt whether or not the accused was a British citizen at the time of any act, omission or other event proof of which is required for conviction of the offence.

(2) This section applies to the following offences—
(a) any offence under this Act;
(b) conspiracy to commit an offence under this Act;

(c) any attempt to commit an offence under section 3 above; and
(d) incitement to commit an offence under this Act.

GENERAL NOTE
Under this Act, jurisdiction is not limited to those who hold British citizenship, since the offences are designed to include computer misuse which takes place abroad but is targeted at a computer in this country. Subs. (2)(c) is confined to an attempt to commit the offence under s.3 of the Act since offences under ss.1 and 2 are already drafted in such a way as to penalise attempts to gain unauthorised access. It does not apply to Scotland as the Scottish courts have jurisdiction at common law to try any person charged with an offence triable in a Scottish court.

Miscellaneous and general

Saving for certain law enforcement powers

10. Section 1(1) above has effect without prejudice to the operation—
(a) in England and Wales of any enactment relating to powers of inspection, search or seizure; and
(b) in Scotland of any enactment or rule of law relating to powers of examination, search of seizure.

GENERAL NOTE
A number of enactments provide various authorities with powers of access, under certain circumstances, to computer records, for example the Police and Criminal Evidence Act 1984, ss.19 and 20, Finance Act 1985, s.10, and Children Act 1989, s.63. Where these authorities gain access to a computer in pursuance of their statutory powers, they, by virtue of s.10 of this Act, commit no offence.

Proceedings for offences under section 1

11.—(1) A magistrates' court shall have jurisdiction to try an offence under section 1 above if—
(a) the accused was within its commission area at the time when he did the act which caused the computer to perform the function; or
(b) any computer containing any program or data to which the accused secured or intended to secure unauthorised access by doing that act was in its commission area at that time.
(2) Subject to subsection (3) below, proceedings for an offence under section 1 above may be brought within a period of six months from the date on which evidence sufficient in the opinion of the prosecutor to warrant the proceedings came to his knowledge.
(3) No such proceedings shall be brought by virtue of this section more than three years after the commission of the offence.
(4) For the purposes of this section, a certificate signed by or on behalf of the prosecutor and stating the date on which evidence sufficient in his opinion to warrant the proceedings came to his knowledge shall be conclusive evidence of that fact.
(5) A certificate stating that matter and purporting to be so signed shall be deemed to be so signed unless the contrary is proved.
(6) In this section "commission area" has the same meaning as in the Justices of the Peace Act 1979.
(7) This section does not extend to Scotland.

GENERAL NOTE
In respect of the offence under s.1 of the Act, s.11 provides that a magistrates' court shall have jurisdiction if either the accused or the affected computer was in its commission area at the relevant time. The section also defines the time limits for prosecution for this offence. An exception is made here to the normal rule, set out in the Magistrates' Courts Act 1980, s.127, that a prosecution for a summary offence must be brought within six months of the date of commission of the offence. Instead, for this offence, summary prosecution must be

brought within six months of the date on which evidence sufficient in the opinion of the prosecutor to justify prosecution came to his knowledge and, in any event, not later than three years after the offence was allegedly committed. Corresponding provisions for Scotland are contained in s.13.

Conviction of an offence under section 1 in proceedings for an offence under section 2 or 3

12.—(1) If on the trial on indictment of a person charged with—
  (a) an offence under section 2 above; or
  (b) an offence under section 3 above or any attempt to commit such an offence;
the jury find him not guilty of the offence charged, they may find him guilty of an offence under section 1 above if on the facts shown he could have been found guilty of that offence in proceedings for that offence brought before the expiry of any time limit under section 11 above applicable to such proceedings.

(2) The Crown Court shall have the same powers and duties in relation to a person who is by virtue of this section convicted before it of an offence under section 1 above as a magistrates' court would have on convicting him of the offence.

(3) This section is without prejudice to section 6(3) of the Criminal Law Act 1967 (conviction of alternative indictable offence on trial on indictment).

(4) This section does not extend to Scotland.

GENERAL NOTE

In many cases the commission of an offence under ss.2 or 3 of this Act will entail commission of an offence under s.1. This section provides for the possibility of conviction of an offence under s.1 where the accused is found not guilty of an offence under ss.2 or 3, or an attempt to commit an offence under s.3. Special provision is made for this in s.12, since the general provision in the Criminal Law Act 1967, s.6(3) enabling an alternative conviction to be returned is inapplicable where offences are triable only summarily. If, by s.12, the offender is convicted of a s.1 offence in the Crown Court, the court is restricted to the powers of a magistrates' court when dealing with such a case. The normal time limits for prosecution of an offence under s.1 (see s.11) will not operate to debar conviction of a s.1 offence on a charge brought for an offence under ss.2 or 3. Corresponding provisions for Scotland are set out in s.13.

Proceedings in Scotland

13.—(1) A sheriff shall have jurisdiction in respect of an offence under section 1 or 2 above if—
  (a) the accused was in the sheriffdom at the time when he did the act which caused the computer to perform the function; or
  (b) any computer containing any program or data to which the accused secured or intended to secure unauthorised access by doing that act was in the sheriffdom at that time.

(2) A sheriff shall have jurisdiction in respect of an offence under section 3 above if—
  (a) the accused was in the sheriffdom at the time when he did the act which caused the unauthorised modification; or
  (b) the unauthorised modification took place in the sheriffdom.

(3) Subject to subsection (4) below, summary proceedings for an offence under section 1, 2 or 3 above may be commenced within a period of six months from the date on which evidence sufficient in the opinion of the procurator fiscal to warrant proceedings came to his knowledge.

(4) No such proceedings shall be commenced by virtue of this section more than three years after the commission of the offence.

(5) For the purposes of this section, a certificate signed by or on behalf of the procurator fiscal and stating the date on which evidence sufficient

in his opinion to warrant the proceedings came to his knowledge shall be conclusive evidence of that fact.

(6) A certificate stating that matter and purporting to be so signed shall be deemed to be so signed unless the contrary is proved.

(7) Subsection (3) of section 331 of the Criminal Procedure (Scotland) Act 1975 (date of commencement of proceedings) shall apply for the purposes of this section as it applies for the purposes of that section.

(8) In proceedings in which a person is charged with an offence under section 2 or 3 above and is found not guilty or is acquitted of that charge, he may be found guilty of an offence under section 1 above if on the facts shown he could have been found guilty of that offence in proceedings for that offence commenced before the expiry of any time limit under this section applicable to such proceedings.

(9) Subsection (8) above shall apply whether or not an offence under section 1 above has been libelled in the complaint or indictment.

(10) A person found guilty of an offence under section 1 above by virtue of subsection (8) above shall be liable, in respect of that offence, only to the penalties set out in section 1.

(11) This section extends to Scotland only.

GENERAL NOTE

This section makes provision in respect of proceedings in Scotland very similar to that made by ss.11 and 12 in respect of proceedings in England. See notes on ss.11 and 12.

Search warrants for offences under section 1

14.—(1) Where a circuit judge is satisfied by information on oath given by a constable that there are reasonable grounds for believing—
   (a) that an offence under section 1 above has been or is about to be committed in any premises; and
   (b) that evidence that such an offence has been or is about to be committed is in those premises;
he may issue a warrant authorising a constable to enter and search the premises, using such reasonable force as is necessary.

(2) The power conferred by subsection (1) above does not extend to authorising a search for material of the kinds mentioned in section 9(2) of the Police and Criminal Evidence Act 1984 (privileged, excluded and special procedure material).

(3) A warrant under this section—
   (a) may authorise persons to accompany any constable executing the warrant; and
   (b) remains in force for twenty-eight days from the date of its issue.

(4) In executing a warrant issued under this section a constable may seize an article if he reasonably believes that it is evidence that an offence under section 1 above has been or is about to be committed.

(5) In this section "premises" includes land, buildings, movable structures, vehicles, vessels, aircraft and hovercraft.

(6) This section does not extend to Scotland.

GENERAL NOTE

This section provides the police in England and Wales with a power, on obtaining a search warrant from a Circuit Judge, to enter and search premises and seize evidence (though not extending to privileged, excluded and special procedure material under the Police and Criminal Evidence Act 1984) if there are reasonable grounds to show that an offence under s.1 has been committed or is about to be committed. A power of search in respect of a summary offence is unusual, though a similar power is provided by s.109 of the Copyright, Designs and Patents Act 1988. The computer misuse offences under ss.2 and 3 of the Act are arrestable offences, being punishable with five years' imprisonment on indictment, so that a power of search already exists in relation to them, by virtue of ss.17 and 18 of the

Police and Criminal Evidence Act 1984 and in some circumstances under s.8 where an arrestable offence qualifies as a "serious arrestable offence" within the meaning of s.116(2) (Police and Criminal Evidence Act 1984).

This section does not apply to Scotland, since common law powers of search in Scotland may extend to any offence and can be invoked by a warrant.

Extradition where Schedule 1 to the Extradition Act 1989 applies

15. The offences to which an Order in Council under section 2 of the Extradition Act 1870 can apply shall include—
  (a) offences under section 2 or 3 above;
  (b) any conspiracy to commit such an offence; and
  (c) any attempt to commit an offence under section 3 above.

GENERAL NOTE

The Extradition Act 1989 provides that conduct is extraditable if it is both an offence here and in the other country and the conduct would, on conviction, attract a maximum sentence of 12 months or more in custody. The offences under ss.2 and 3 of the Computer Misuse Act are, therefore, extraditable on those grounds. The 1989 Act, however, by Sched. 1, retains in force the 1870 extradition regime which continues to apply in respect of countries with which Britain has negotiated extradition treaties. These are given effect by Orders in Council made under s.2 of the 1870 Act. S.15 of the Computer Misuse Act brings the offences under ss.2 and 3 within the ambit of that Schedule. It also includes conspiracy in relation to a s.2 or s.3 offence and an attempt to commit an offence under s.3 (There is no specific reference to an attempt to commit an offence under s.2 since that offence is defined in such a way as to include attempt). Incitement is not included in the offences listed in Sched. 1.

Application to Northern Ireland

16.—(1) The following provisions of this section have effect for applying this Act in relation to Northern Ireland with the modifications there mentioned.

(2) In section 2(2)(b)—
  (a) the reference to England and Wales shall be read as a reference to Northern Ireland; and
  (b) the reference to section 33 of the Magistrates' Courts Act 1980 shall be read as a reference to Article 46(4) of the Magistrates' Courts (Northern Ireland) Order 1981.

(3) The reference in section 3(6) to the Criminal Damage Act 1971 shall be read as a reference to the Criminal Damage (Northern Ireland) Order 1977.

(4) Subsections (5) to (7) below apply in substitution for subsections (1) to (3) of section 7; and any reference in subsection (4) of that section to England and Wales shall be read as a reference to Northern Ireland.

(5) The following paragraphs shall be inserted after paragraph (1) of Article 9 of the Criminal Attempts and Conspiracy (Northern Ireland) Order 1983—

"(1A) Subject to section 8 of the Computer Misuse Act 1990 (relevance of external law), if this paragraph applies to an agreement, this Part has effect in relation to it as it has effect in relation to an agreement falling within paragraph (1).

(1B) Paragraph (1A) applies to an agreement if—
  (a) a party to it, or a party's agent, did anything in Northern Ireland in relation to it before its formation;
  (b) a party to it became a party in Northern Ireland (by joining it either in person or through an agent); or
  (c) a party to it, or a party's agent, did or omitted anything in Northern Ireland in pursuance of it;

and the agreement would fall within paragraph (1) as an agreement relating to the commission of a computer misuse offence but for the fact that the offence would not be an offence triable in Northern Ireland if committed in accordance with the parties' intentions.".

(6) The following paragraph shall be inserted after paragraph (4) of that Article—

"(5) In the application of this Part to an agreement to which paragraph (1A) applies any reference to an offence shall be read as a reference to what would be the computer misuse offence in question but for the fact that it is not an offence triable in Northern Ireland.

(6) In this Article "computer misuse offence" means an offence under the Computer Misuse Act 1990.".

(7) The following paragraphs shall be inserted after Article 3(1) of that Order—

"(1A) Subject to section 8 of the Computer Misuse Act 1990 (relevance of external law), if this paragraph applies to an act, what the person doing it had in view shall be treated as an offence to which this Article applies.

(1B) Paragraph (1A) above applies to an act if—

(a) it is done in Northern Ireland, and

(b) it would fall within paragraph (1) as more than merely preparatory to the commission of an offence under section 3 of the Computer Misuse Act 1990 but for the fact that the offence, if completed, would not be an offence triable in Northern Ireland.".

(8) In section 8—

(a) the reference in subsection (2) to section 1(1A) of the Criminal Law Act 1977 shall be read as a reference to Article 9(1A) of that Order; and

(b) the reference in subsection (3) to section 1(1A) of the Criminal Attempts Act 1981 shall be read as a reference to Article 3(1A) of that Order.

(9) The references in sections 9(1) and 10 to England and Wales shall be read as references to Northern Ireland.

(10) In section 11, for subsection (1) there shall be substituted—

"(1) A magistrates' court for a county division in Northern Ireland may hear and determine a complaint charging an offence under section 1 above or conduct a preliminary investigation or preliminary inquiry into an offence under that section if—

(a) the accused was in that division at the time when he did the act which caused the computer to perform the function; or

(b) any computer containing any program or data to which the accused secured or intended to secure unauthorised access by doing that act was in that division at that time.";

and subsection (6) shall be omitted.

(11) The reference in section 12(3) to section 6(3) of the Criminal Law Act 1967 shall be read as a reference to section 6(2) of the Criminal Law Act (Northern Ireland) 1967.

(12) In section 14—

(a) the reference in subsection (1) to a circuit judge shall be read as a reference to a county court judge; and

(b) the reference in subsection (2) to section 9(2) of the Police and Criminal Evidence Act 1984 shall be read as a reference to Article 11(2) of the Police and Criminal Evidence (Northern Ireland) Order 1989.

GENERAL NOTE
    While the foregoing provisions of the Act apply to Northern Ireland, s.16 modifies them in a number of ways in respect of their application to Northern Ireland.

Interpretation

17.—(1) The following provisions of this section apply for the interpretation of this Act.

(2) A person secures access to any program or data held in a computer if by causing a computer to perform any function he—

(a) alters or erases the program or data;

(b) copies or moves it to any storage medium other than that in which it is held or to a different location in the storage medium in which it is held;

(c) uses it; or

(d) has it output from the computer in which it is held (whether by having it displayed or in any other manner);

and references to access to a program or data (and to an intent to secure such access) shall be read accordingly.

(3) For the purposes of subsection (2)(c) above a person uses a program if the function he causes the computer to perform—

(a) causes the program to be executed; or

(b) is itself a function of the program.

(4) For the purposes of subsection (2)(d) above—

(a) a program is output if the instructions of which it consists are output; and

(b) the form in which any such instructions or any other data is output (and in particular whether or not it represents a form in which, in the case of instructions, they are capable of being executed or, in the case of data, it is capable of being processed by a computer) is immaterial.

(5) Access of any kind by any person to any program or data held in a computer is unauthorised if—

(a) he is not himself entitled to control access of the kind in question to the program or data; and

(b) he does not have consent to access by him of the kind in question to the program or data from any person who is so entitled.

(6) References to any program or data held in a computer include references to any program or data held in any removable storage medium which is for the time being in the computer; and a computer is to be regarded as containing any program or data held in any such medium.

(7) A modification of the contents of any computer takes place if, by the operation of any function of the computer concerned or any other computer—

(a) any program or data held in the computer concerned is altered or erased; or

(b) any program or data is added to its contents;

and any act which contributes towards causing such a modification shall be regarded as causing it.

(8) Such a modification is unauthorised if—

(a) the person whose act causes it is not himself entitled to determine whether the modification should be made; and

(b) he does not have consent to the modification from any person who is so entitled.

(9) References to the home country concerned shall be read in accordance with section 4(6) above.

(10) References to a program include references to part of a program.

GENERAL NOTE

It will be noticed that there is no definition of "computer", "program" or "data" in this Act, since it was felt that the pace of technological change would soon render such definitions outdated. This is in accord with the recommendation of the Law Commission.

Citation, commencement etc.

18.—(1) This Act may be cited as the Computer Misuse Act 1990.

(2) This Act shall come into force at the end of the period of two months beginning with the day on which it is passed.

(3) An offence is not committed under this Act unless every act or other event proof of which is required for conviction of the offence takes place after this Act comes into force.

INDEX

References are to section numbers

NATIONAL HEALTH SERVICE AND COMMUNITY CARE ACT 1990*

(1990 c. 19)

ARRANGEMENT OF SECTIONS

PART I

THE NATIONAL HEALTH SERVICE: ENGLAND AND WALES

Local management

---

* Annotations by Joseph M. Jacob, Senior Lecturer in Law, London School of Economics, and Colin McKay, Legal Advisor, Scottish Society for the Mentally Handicapped.

An Act to make further provision about health authorities and other bodies
constituted in accordance with the National Health Service Act 1977; to
provide for the establishment of National Health Service trusts; to make
further provision about the financing of the practices of medical practitioners; to amend Part VII of the Local Government (Scotland) Act 1973
and Part III of the Local Government Finance Act 1982; to amend the
National Health Service Act 1977 and the National Health Service (Scotland) Act 1978; to amend Part VIII of the Mental Health (Scotland) Act
1984; to make further provision concerning the provision of accommodation and other welfare services by local authorities and the powers of the
Secretary of State as respects the social services functions of such authorities; to make provision for and in connection with the establishment of a
Clinical Standards Advisory Group; to repeal the Health Services Act
1976; and for connected purposes.

[June 29, 1990]

PARLIAMENTARY DEBATES
   Hansard, H.C. Vol. 163, cols. 498, 691; Vol. 169, cols. 178, 267, 547; Vol. 175, 318; H.L.
Vol. 517, cols. 9, 1255; Vol. 518, cols. 112, 440, 671, 779, 1140, 1239, 1473; Vol. 519, cols. 11,
1515; Vol. 520, cols. 158, 414, 509, 1325, 1381, 1729.
   This Bill was considered in Standing Committee E from December 19, 1989–February 27,
1990.

INTRODUCTION AND GENERAL NOTE

This Act is in five discrete Parts: one on the health service and one on community care. For England (and Wales), that is Parts I and III respectively, and for Scotland (Parts II and IV); in addition, Part V makes a number of legally important changes to the health service. In places the Act amends other legislation; elsewhere it stands on its own. So far as the general structure of the health service is concerned see Sweet and Maxwell's *The Encyclopedia of Health Services and Medical Law*, and as regards community care, see *Local Government Encyclopedia* and *The Social Services Encyclopedia*. As appears below, it is however necessary to read the Act together with a wealth of non-legal reforms, some of which are discussed in the notes that follow. Although the pace of the implementation of the reforms is likely to be gradual, the Act makes changes to both the health service and to social services as fundamental at least in legal terms as any of the post-War era. The most important of these changes is the shift in day-to-day control from a hierarchical bureaucratic system in which professionals are trusted to practice their rather arcane skills, to one based in relatively autonomous units dealing with each other by means of arrangements specifying not just quantity but quality of service. For an assessment written in anticipation of this change, see J.M. Jacob, *Doctors and Rules*, Routledge, 1988.

Part I of the Act reconstitutes regional and district health authorities, renames and reconstitutes Family Practitioner Committees as Family Health Service Authorities now under the control of the RHAs (ss.1, 2, 12 and 13 and Sched. 1). It also makes provision for arrangements between health service bodies to be known as "NHS contracts" (ss.3 and 4), and for the creation of autonomous institutions, to be called "NHS trusts" (s.5 and Scheds. 2 and 3). It establishes "fund holding practices" which will manage their funds independently (ss.14–17) and gives other practices "indicative amounts" to be fixed by the FHSA within which they should operate. The Audit Commission for Local Authorities is renamed the Audit Commission for Local Authorities and the National Health Service and its jurisdiction is correspondingly expanded (s.20 and Sched. 4). Following the establishment of NHS trusts, the "self-insurance" scheme for third party liability (*e.g.* in respect of malpractice actions) previously run within the NHS, is now to be the subject of regulations (s.21). Other provisions expand the Secretary of State's control over the Medical Practices Committee and the distribution of GPs (ss.22–23), place certain limits on dental practice and transfer the Secretary of State's powers over private practice to District Authorities. Corresponding provision is made for Scotland in Part II.

Part III deals with "Community Care" (defined in s.46(3)), but in places its provisions go wider, including "social service functions" (defined in the 1970 Local Authority Social Services Act) and places some duties on health authorities. Ss.42–45 make new provision for accommodation and welfare services, including (if regulations so determine) a requirement that District Health Authorities must consent to the provision of residential accommodation with nursing services under s.21 of the National Assistance Act 1948, as amended. They also effect a range of other amendments concerning residential accommodation to the 1948 Act. Provision is made for local authorities to prepare and publish a community care plan (s.46) and to make individual assessment of needs for community care services in addition to those required under the Disabled Persons (Services, Consultation and Representation) Act 1986 and the Children Act 1989. The Secretary of State is given the power to inspect premises used for community care (s.49). S.50 contains a series of important additions to the Local Authority Social Services Act 1970. The Secretary of State is given power to issue a direction to re-enforce guidance as to social service functions, and power to establish a complaints procedure. He has also new powers in relation to inquiries and defaults. Corresponding provision is made for Scotland in Part IV.

Part V removes Crown immunities from health authorities (s.60) but exempts them from income and corporation tax (s.61). It also establishes a Clinical Standards Advisory Group (s.62).

The background to the Act includes a large number of official publications. Among the more important of these are the two White Papers *Working for Patients* (1989 Cm. 555) and *Caring for People: Community Care in the next decade and beyond* (1989 Cm. 849); and Sir Roy Griffiths's Report *Community Care: Agenda for Action*, 1988.

Among the publications of the Department of Health are: *Contracts for Health Services: Operational Principles*; *Funding and Contracts for Hospital Services*; *Self-Governing Hospitals—an Initial Guide*; *Funding General Practice: Working for Patients; Indicative Prescribing Budgets for General Medical Practitioners*.

Prior to these there were: the Eighth Report from the Social Services Committee, Session 1988–89; Researching the National Health Service: the Government's plans for the future of the National Health Service (House of Commons Paper No. 214–III, 1988–89); the Government's reply to that Report (Cm. 851); the Second Report from the Social Services Committee, Session 1984–85; Community Care with special reference to adult mentally ill and mentally handicapped people (House of Commons Paper No. 13–I 1984–85); the Government's reply to that Report (Cm. 9674).

The Public Accounts Committee has produced a series of reports: *Financial Management in the National Health Service*; *Hospital Building in England*; *The National Health Service: Coronary Heart Disease*; *Use of Operating Theatres in the National Health Service*; *Quality of Clinical Care in National Health Service Hospitals*; *Competitive Tendering for Support Services in the National Health Service*; *NHS: Control over Professional and Technical Manpower*; and *The National Health Service: Control of Nursing Manpower*. There is in addition *NHS and Independent Hospitals*, a report by the National Audit Office.

The Parliamentary Under-Secretary of State for Health, Mr Roger Freeman, explained that the Act (*Hansard*, H.C. Vol. 169, col. 724): "is based on five key principles. First, it is based above all on the need to provide better patient care. The patient comes first and last. . . . Secondly, the NHS will continue to be financed . . . by the taxpayer and it will be largely free at the point of delivery. . . . [the] third principle behind the Bill, is better value for money. . . . The fourth principle is that we need to provide . . . greater choice for patients, not only in the selection of their general practitioners but in elective surgery and in the hospital to which they go, which may not be their own local hospital. The agreement and approval of the patient is required before he travels to another hospital, but it is humane and sensible to offer him the chance to do so because that will reduce waiting times for others, at hospitals which are not so fortunate. . . . The fifth and last general principle concerns the delegation of authority in the National Health Service. . . . We are talking about delegation not to, but from, the Secretary of State—to the National Health Service trusts, to general practice fund holders and to smaller, more businesslike district health authorities".

The Parliamentary Under-Secretary of State for the Department of Health, Baroness Hooper, added (*Hansard*, H.L. Vol. 517, col. 1256): "In many ways they are a direct descendant of the introduction of general management following the report by Sir Roy Griffiths in 1983 . . . The legislation . . . is merely a further step to complement the non-legislative action taken, for example, to introduce a more effective contract for general practitioners, to introduce medical audit in the hospital and family doctor services, to increase the number of consultants, to delegate functions from regional and district health authority headquarters to the operational level and to provide guidance to local authorities in improving their management of community care services. The legislation does not stand apart from all these other changes, but it does provide the motor which will allow these benefits to be fully realised in the future".

The then Conservative backbench member, Sir George Young, commented (*Hansard*, H.C. Vol. 163, col. 527): "The parallels between reforms in this [Act] and those in the Education Reform Act are striking. . . . For example, the proposals for grant-maintained schools are replicated by those for self-governing hospitals, giving a measure of independence and local autonomy within the state-funded sector. Those for local management of schools are replicated by those for general practitioners to become fund holders, allocating resources as closely as possible to the point of consumption. The proposals for open enrolment and funds following the pupil are paralleled by those that facilitate switching one's GP and greater reliance on capitation, so rewarding popular provision and making the system more responsive to the consumer. National curriculum and assessment are paralleled by the proposals for medical audit to try to measure output and value for money, to raise standards and to determine where improvements might be made".

In line with reforms in other sectors, the Act greatly extends three modern mechanisms of administration. First, in England as regards the NHS ss.3 and 4 and, as regards community care, s.42, impose a new reliance on negotiated arrangements both between health service bodies themselves, between the DHAs and the FHSAs and local government bodies, and between such bodies and voluntary and other organisations of the private sector. These are to be one of the main methods of ensuring efficiency and quality. Secondly, there is an increased scope for the issue of ministerial directions in both the NHS and local government. By s.18(1) of the 1977 NHS Act, in terms which show scant regard for the purposes of the Statutory Instruments Act 1946 or for constitutional propriety, "directions" may be given "either by regulations or by an instrument in writing". Under the new legislation, the potential of these directions has been greatly increased, perhaps particularly as regards local government by s.7A of the Local Government Act 1970, inserted by s.50 of this Act, and there are many other sections of this Act giving a power of direction. The Baroness in Waiting, Baroness Blatch, said (*Hansard*, H.L. Vol. 520, col. 483): "guidance is stronger than guidelines . . . if an authority did not take note of guidance, the Secretary of State has the power to make directions . . . guidance is expected to be followed. In the absence of it being followed and there being breaches, the Secretary of State can use powers so to direct" (see note to s.7A(2) under s.50 below).

In other words, the administrative scheme will be that the central departments will issue guidelines and guidance and, where the latter is disobeyed, may seek to enforce it by directions (it is to be noted that in relation to social service functions this statute specifically mentions the use of mandamus—see s.7D of the Local Government Act 1970 inserted by s.50 of this

Act—but there seems no reason why, except for this specific mention, this remedy would not also lie against a recalcitrant health authority): things may be required to be done by directions as well as by legislation and regulations.

The third modern mechanism of administration used under the Act, is audit and the setting of "performance criteria". Thus, as noted, the jurisdiction of the Audit Commission is extended to the NHS (s.20) and, by circular, there is to be a greater use of the new concept of "medical audit." In addition, both the setting of funds for "fund holding practices" (ss.14–7) and the establishment of "indicative prescribing amounts" (s.18) will also entail similar accountancy.

Despite ministerial hopes, as with the reforms made in local government and education, the new emphasis on "the consumer," on autonomous units and institutions responsible for the management of their own funds, and on the use of "contracts" to monitor efficiency and quality, is almost bound to lead to a new litigious atmosphere. The only sure restraint on a growth in litigation is that many of the arrangements will be made between parties anxious to maintain quasi-commercial relationships. But even here rather different considerations from those of the ordinary world of business may well apply because the public sector bodies will be under a duty to balance their accounts within each year and, at least in regard to the NHS, cross-subsidies between contracts are to be discouraged.

The notes to s.4(3) suggest that the draftsman might not have been altogether successful at excluding the jurisdiction of the court as regards the new "NHS contract". What is, however, clear is that so far as the arrangements are between the public and private sectors, they will be susceptible to ordinary litigation and so far as they are within the public sector, to judicial review.

The other area in which we may expect increased use of judicial review is against the "directions" which the minister may issue. In *R.* v. *Secretary of State*, ex p. *Khan* [1985] 1 All E.R. 40 it was held that a failure to apply the terms of a circular may be a misdirection so that here any direction would have to be within the terms of the guidance. Glanville Williams once wrote of statutes having "their prolific families of children" ("Sub-delegation and Circulars", 12 (1949) M.L.R. 37). A more appropriate simile would be to say the whole process must be like a Russian doll—the guidance must be within the statute and the directions within the guidance. So also it has been held that a circular—which is, it may be supposed, both guidance and guidelines—may set the relevant matters for *Wednesbury* reasonableness in the use of discretions by both health service and local government bodies (see *Bristol District Council* v. *Clark* [1975] 1 W.L.R. 1443, *per* Scarman L.J.).

In *Patchett* v. *Leathem* (1949) 65 T.L.R. 69 at 70, Streatfield J. spoke of circulars being "cursed" because they have not been to Parliament, they are unpublished, they may be "a jumble of provisions, legislative, administrative, or directive", and they are not in the precise language of a statute. In relation to this Act, the curse is doubled because many of the Departmental communications were issued before Royal Assent and may refer to matters which were the subject of amendment by Parliament. Cursed or not, there is no doubt that many of them contain guidance which satisfies this Russian doll effect. This applies to many of the official publications set out above.

On the relation of circulars to statute, see *R.* v. *The Secretary of State for Social Services*, ex p. *Stitt* (February 21, 1990); *Laker Airways* v. *Department of Trade* [1977] Q.B. 643 and more generally, on the constitutional aspects, Baldwin and Houghton, "Circular Arguments: The Status and Legitimacy of Administrative Rules" [1986] P.L. 239, 267 *et seq.* and G. Ganz, *Quasi-Legislation: Recent Developments in Secondary Legislation*, 1987, Sweet and Maxwell.

The central management of the health service remains on a non-statutory footing—the new constitutions of regional and district health authorities begin to make some mention of those with executive responsibility. The Parliamentary Under-Secretary of State for the Department of Health, Baroness Hooper, explained (*Hansard*, H.L. Vol. 519, col. 1526): "The National Health Service management executive has the responsibility on behalf of . . . the Secretary of State to monitor and review the implementation of policy by National Health Service bodies, including the implementation of legislation. There are already mechanisms in place to achieve this. . . . Each year objectives are agreed with the regional health authorities in the light of Ministers' policies and priorities and progress is kept under review. The regions are required to produce programmes and reports which focus on the key objectives that they have been set. The process culminates in a yearly meeting, chaired by the National Health Service Chief Executive at which progress is considered and fresh objectives set for the year ahead. A further ministerial meeting may be held if that appears necessary. Copies of the letters sent to each region at the end of this annual process are placed in the Libraries of both Houses". As regards the National Health Service management executive generally and its relation to the new Clinical Standards Advisory Group, see also note to s.62. As regards Advisory Committees, scc s.6 at the 1977 Act and S.I.s 1981 No. 101 and 597.

Regarding research, she said (*Hansard*, H.L. Vol. 518, col. 455): "we have decided that the Director of Research and Development should sit as a full member of the National Health

Service management executive" and (*Hansard*, H.L. Vol. 519, col. 1568): "We have . . . said in our White Paper response to [the House of Lords] Select Committee that [he] will, as necessary, convene advisory groups on the development of the programme in specific areas. We also said that the Director will wish to involve himself in the Medical Research Council, for example, and in scientific committees and advisory bodies. We expect [him] to consult widely and to maintain close contact with the research community. Further powers already exist to create advisory arrangements. For example, the existing Standing Medical Advisory Committee and the Standing Nursing and Midwifery Advisory Committee have been created under the discretionary powers in Section 6(3) of the National Health Service Act 1977. Those committees, while discretionary, have remained in force since 1949. If the need is identified to have an advisory council, we can use these powers to appoint one. Such a standing committee would have a duty to advise the Secretary of State on research as it saw fit, as well as on request".

The notes that follow record many of the undertakings given by ministers concerning their intent with regard to the use of their powers to make regulations, give directions and offer guidance and guidelines. They also contain many of the undertakings given in the semi-published Notes on Clauses issued at the commencement of the proceedings in the second chamber, the House of Lords.

A Commencement Order (No. 1—S.I. 1990 No. 1329 (C.37)) has been made under s.67.

PART I

THE NATIONAL HEALTH SERVICE: ENGLAND AND WALES

Local management

Regional and District Health Authorities

1.—(1) In the National Health Service Act 1977 (in this Part of this Act referred to as "the principal Act"), in section 8 (Regional and District Health Authorities etc.)—

(a) in subsection (1) for the words "Schedule 5 to this Act" there shall be substituted "Schedule 1 to the National Health Service and Community Care Act 1990";

(b) any reference to an area or an Area Health Authority shall be omitted; and

(c) subsection (5) (consultation before making orders under subsection (2)) shall be omitted.

(2) Part I of Schedule 1 to this Act shall have effect in place of Part I of Schedule 5 to the principal Act (membership of health authorities etc.).

(3) Part III of Schedule 5 to the principal Act (supplementary provisions as to authorities) shall be amended in accordance with Part III of Schedule 1 to this Act.

(4) Subject to subsection (5) below, at the end of the day appointed for the coming into force of this subsection,—

(a) any person who became a member of a Regional or District Health Authority under Part I of Schedule 5 to the principal Act shall cease to be such a member; and

(b) any person who, by virtue of an order under section 11 of the principal Act, became a member of a special health authority which is a relevant authority for the purposes of paragraph 9(1) of Schedule 5 to that Act (as amended by Part III of Schedule 1 to this Act) shall cease to be such a member.

(5) Subsection (4) above does not apply to a person holding office as chairman of a Regional, District or Special Health Authority.

DEFINITIONS

"District Health Authority": ss.8 and 128 of the National Health Service Act 1977, as amended by this Act and Sched. 1 to this Act.

"health authority": s.128 of the National Health Service Act 1977.

"officer": s.128 of the National Health Service Act 1977.

"prescribed": s.128 of the National Health Service Act 1977, as amended by this Act.

"principal Act": subs. (1).

"Regional Health Authority": ss.8 and 128 of the National Health Service Act 1977, as amended by this Act and Sched. 1 to this Act.

"regulations": ss.126 and 128 of the National Health Service Act 1977, as amended by this Act.

"special health authority": s.11 of the National Health Service Act 1977, as amended by this Act and Sched. 1 to this Act.

GENERAL NOTE

Subs. (1)(a)

S.8 of the 1977 Act referred to Pt. I of its Sched. 5. That made provision for the constitutions of regional and district health authorities. The new constitutions are to be found in Sched. 1 to this Act, which should be read with this section. See note to subs.(2).

Subs. (1)(b)

The only area health authorities still existing were in Wales. These now become district authorities. Of more importance than this mere change of name is the remark of the Parliamentary Under-Secretary of State for Health, Mr Roger Freeman (Comm. (SCE) col. 156) that: "there is a ... proposal in Wales to align boundaries of CHCs with those of district health authorities. But no automatic step would be taken to align CHC and DHA boundaries. We may well have to take into account arguments and considerations against automatic alignment in the event of two or three districts being merged".

Subs. (1)(c)

Under the new procedure for merging or changing district boundaries, Parliamentary control through the negative resolution procedure is maintained (s.8(2) of the 1977 Act) but the previous duty on the Secretary of State to consult with officers who might be transferred and with other bodies who might be concerned is removed. The Parliamentary Under-Secretary of State for Health, Mr Roger Freeman, said (Comm. (SCE) col. 155): "Comprehensive and proper consultation will be organised by the RHA if there are proposals to merge districts or to change district boundaries. It will be responsible for consulting widely, including with community health councils, before a proposal is submitted to Ministers". His counterpart in the House of Lords, Baroness Hooper, added (*Hansard*, H.L. Vol. 518, col. 131): "It should not be seen as a green light for widescale district health authority mergers ... The regional health authority will be expected to consult widely at local level before putting proposals to the Secretary of State. He will consider them only where there is a compelling case for a change".

Subs. (2)

As noted above, Pt. I of Sched. 1 makes provision for the new constitutions of regional and district health authorities. Ministers explained that "health authorities have never been able to make up their minds whether they are a kind of local government committee or a decision-making executive body for the health authority" (Secretary of State for Health, Mr Clarke, *Hansard*, H.C. Vol. 163, col. 506); "There is confusion in district and regional health authorities. Their members do not know whether they are on representative forums, councils or management bodies charged with running the National Health Service" (Parliamentary Under-Secretary of State for Health, Mr Roger Freeman, Comm. (SCE) col. 75); and, more elaborately: "The problem at present is that many health authority members tend to regard themselves as representatives of the body which nominated them or, in the case of some district health authority members, the local council which appointed them. This has led to fundamental confusion as to whether health authorities are representative or management bodies" (Parliamentary Under-Secretary of State for the Department of Health, Baroness Hooper, *Hansard*, H.L. Vol. 518, col. 119).

The intention is that they should be, and be seen to be, management bodies under the supervision of the Secretary of State. For a fuller discussion, see *The Encyclopedia of Health Services and Medical Law, Introduction*.

Beyond the important removal of Crown immunities (under s.60 of this Act), there is no formal change in the constitutional position of health authorities. Thus, the Parliamentary Under-Secretary of State for Health, Mr Roger Freeman, said (Comm. (SCE) col. 102): "No change is proposed ... to alter the present position of joint planning and joint finance" with local authorities (under s.22 of the 1977 Act). See also s.20 and Sched. 4 (and notes thereto) extending the remit and changing the name of the Audit Commission for Local Authorities.

Sched. 1, Pt. I defines the composition of regional health authorities, district health authorities and district health authorities in Wales. In each case the Chairman is to be appointed by the Secretary of State, there are to be a "prescribed" number of members appointed in the case of a regional health authority by the Secretary of State, and in the case of a district by the region (except in Wales where, in the absence of a region, the appointment is to be made by the Secretary of State). So also are the chief officer and such other officers as may be prescribed to be members of the authority. Regional health authorities and "prescribed" districts (presumably those containing a teaching hospital, but there must be some doubt whether a district will be prescribed if all its such hospitals are NHS trusts) will be bound to include a member with a post in a University with a medical or dental school.

The Notes on Clauses indicated that it was the intention to prescribe five non-officer members (including, in the case of a region, a chairman of a FHSA), to prescribe the chief finance officer as a member and to prescribe three other officers.

It may be helpful to recite the guidance given during the passage of the Bill concerning other matters relating to who is likely to be appointed. Following a recommendation of the Acheson Report on public health, the Parliamentary Under-Secretary of State for Health, Mr Roger Freeman, said (Comm. (SCE) col. 141): "we expect that the director of public health will be a member—we are not prescriptive about that . . .—and also, perhaps, a representative of the nursing profession"—previously these directors of public health were called community physicians and, before that, medical officers of health (as to other responsibilities, see also note to s.3).

Regarding the non-executive members, the Parliamentary Under-Secretary of State for the Department of Health, Baroness Hooper, added (*Hansard*, H.L. Vol. 518, col. 199) "in practice all health authorities contain a medical practitioner representative at present. I have no doubt that most health authorities, if not all, will continue that practice in the future. There is nothing to prevent that process continuing". In the Commons, the Parliamentary Under-Secretary of State for Health, Mr Roger Freeman, qualified this by saying (Comm. (SCE) col. 141): "but not, of course, from the consultants and doctors working in that authority".

The Parliamentary Under-Secretary of State for the Department of Health, Baroness Hooper, said (*Hansard*, H.L. Vol. 518, col. 126): "There is . . . nothing to prevent current members of health authorities being considered for reappointment as non-executive members of the reconstituted health authorities; indeed, we expect that a number of them will be. That is certainly in the interests of continuity . . . GPs will only be excluded from membership of district health authorities if they are practice fund holders . . . The appointment of the non-executive members of district health authorities will be a matter for the appropriate regional health authority acting within the terms of the new legislation, . . . but it will also be subject to departmental guidance". She added (*Hansard*, H.L. Vol. 518, col. 151) "In Wales, where the structure of the health service is different and there is no regional tier, all nine districts will have a university member".

As regards the other non-officer members, the Parliamentary Under-Secretary of State for the Department of Social Security, Lord Henley, said (*Hansard*, H.L. Vol. 518, col. 191): "Some will undoubtedly be drawn from the business world, but others will be drawn from a wide variety of backgrounds. In general they will all have links with the local community through either residence or work and will therefore be sensitive to its needs . . . suggestions for membership will be welcomed from all quarters. They will no doubt include people who . . . will be local councillors".

A mere general commercial interest in the health service will not disqualify an individual, but the Parliamentary Under-Secretary of State for the Department of Health, Baroness Hooper, warned (*Hansard*, H.L. Vol. 518, col. 207), echoing her colleague in the Commons, Mr Roger Freeman (Comm. (SCE) col. 141): "The membership and procedure regulations for both health authorities and FHSAs [*i.e.* currently S.I. 1983 No. 315] make it very clear that a chairman or member of a health authority is required to declare any pecuniary interest, direct or indirect, in a contract or any other matter that is the subject of consideration by the health authority. He or she may not then take part in any consideration or discussion of the contract or other matter or vote on any question in respect of it. . . . The membership and procedure regulations empower the Secretary of State to terminate the appointment of a chairman or member who has not declared a pecuniary interest as required under the regulations. These provisions will be retained in the revised membership and procedure regulations". Later the Parliamentary Under-Secretary of State for the Department of Health, Baroness Hooper, added (*Hansard*, H.L. Vol. 519, col. 1554): "[they] will be supplemented by guidance when necessary".

Subs. (3)

This subsection amends Pt. III of Sched. 5 of the principal Act (supplementary provisions as to health authorities and FHSAs). The main changes are that:

(1) all the non-officer members instead of only the Chairman can be paid (para. 7(1)) (the Secretary of State, Mr Kenneth Clarke, said (*Hansard*, H.C. Vol. 163, col. 787): "we expect to

make very modest payments, such as those that would be made to the non-executive director of a substantial board in the private sector");

(2) the Secretary of State can issue directions concerning the pay and conditions of a class of officer or an individual officer (para. 8);

(3) regulations can be made concerning the appointment and tenure of members of committees of an authority (para. 9(a));

(4) regulations can be made to suspend automatically from membership of an authority an officer (that is, executive) member who is suspended from his post of employment with the authority (para. 9(b)). Similar provision is made in relation to NHS trusts. It would almost certainly be unlawful for any suspension of an employee member to be for reasons connected with his membership of the authority: it would have to relate to matters arising in the employment;

(5) regulations can be made to make provision for officers to be employed on a job-sharing basis. The Notes on Clauses referred to officer members but the paragraph as enacted speaks of the "chief officer or any other officer"—a term broad enough to include all staff. Be that as it may, the intention announced by the Notes is that regulations will provide that, in relation to officer members, joint holders will count as one.

The Notes on Clauses also declared the intention to make new Membership and Procedure Regulations:

(1) to empower authorities to establish committees of non-members to undertake some functions presently carried out by members, *e.g.* hearing appeals to the DHA under the Mental Health Act;

(2) to require committees of FHSAs to have a majority of lay members (this would apply to its Service Committees under the NHS (Service Committees and Tribunal) Regulations S.I. 1974 No. 455 as amended);

(3) to give effect to Sched. 1, para. 9(b);

(4) to limit the persons who can be appointed by preventing the appointment of chairmen and members to more than one authority (except for the chairmen of FHSAs appointed to a region), by excluding from any appointment employees of a trade union with members in the NHS, and by excluding GP practice fund holders from RHA and DHA membership.

Other matters

The Baroness in Waiting, Baroness Blatch, said (*Hansard*, H.L. Vol. 519, col. 1636): "the department will be issuing guidance to health authorities on their new membership and the basic procedures they will need to follow in conducting their meetings". Later, more specifically, she said, (*Hansard*, H.L. Vol. 520, cols. 1332–3): "It is my department's intention to put in the guidance that all health authorities should [be willing to have the names and addresses of their members made public] . . . trusts [under s.5] will have an annual public meeting at which their accounts and plans will be discussed. It is a step forward from the present situation, where no management meetings at unit level are open to the public". See also HC 81/6.

Subs. (4)(a)

The Notes on Clauses explained: "There will be a gap of a few weeks between the day appointed under [the subsection] on which the terms of office of [then] current RHA members are brought to an end, and that on which the appointments of [then] DHA members are terminated. The gap will allow the chairman and non-executive members of the RHAs to appoint their officer members and the RHAs to then appoint the non-officer members of their DHAs. In each case, the new non-officer members will take up their appointments as soon as the existing members' terms come to an end".

Subs. (4)(b)

"*Relevant authority*". The Notes on Clauses explained that this would apply to the special health authorities for the London post-graduate teaching hospitals.

The Parliamentary Under-Secretary of State for the Department of Health, Baroness Hooper, added (*Hansard*, H.L. Vol. 518, col. 214) "The terms of office of all the current members of the special health authorities for the London postgraduate teaching hospitals will be brought to an end . . . and a new constitution order will then be laid under the terms of which the new members will be appointed". In addition (*Hansard*, H.L. Vol. 518, col. 153), "the special health authority for Hammersmith, as the special health authority for all the London postgraduate teaching hospitals, will have a non-executive member drawn from the relevant postgraduate institute of the university".

Family Health Services Authorities

2.—(1) On and after the day appointed for the coming into force of this subsection—

(a) each existing Family Practitioner Committee shall be known as a Family Health Services Authority; and

(b) any reference in any enactment to a Family Practitioner Committee shall be construed as a reference to a Family Health Services Authority;

and the generality of this subsection is not affected by any express amendment made by this Act.

(2) In subsection (1) above "enactment" means—

(a) an enactment passed before the day appointed for the coming into force of subsection (1) above; and

(b) an enactment comprised in subordinate legislation made before that day.

(3) In section 10 of the principal Act (Family Health Services Authorities)—

(a) for the words "Schedule 5 to this Act" there shall be substituted "Schedule 1 to the National Health Service and Community Care Act 1990"; and

(b) subsection (7) (consultation before making orders under subsection (4)) shall be omitted.

(4) Part II of Schedule 1 to this Act shall have effect in place of Part II of Schedule 5 to the principal Act (membership of Family Practitioner Committees).

(5) At the end of the day appointed for the coming into force of this subsection, any person who became a member of a Family Practitioner Committee under Part II of Schedule 5 to the principal Act (including a person holding office as chairman of such a committee) shall cease to be a member and, accordingly, in the case of a chairman, shall also cease to be chairman.

(6) Nothing in this section shall cause a Family Health Services Authority to be included in the expression "health authority," as defined in the principal Act.

DEFINITIONS

"enactment": subs. (2).

"Family Health Services Authority": s.10 of the National Health Service Act 1977 and Sched. 1 to this Act.

"health authority": s.128 of the National Health Service Act 1977.

"officer": s.128 of the National Health Service Act 1977.

"principal Act": s.1 of this Act.

"prescribed": s.128 of the National Health Service Act 1977, as amended by this Act.

GENERAL NOTE

The section should be read with ss.12–18 and ss.22–24.

Subs. (1)

The Secretary of State for Health, Mr Kenneth Clarke (Comm. (SCE) col. 163), expressed his hope "that changing the name will make it easier for the public to recognise the new body," and went on, "it will also reflect the substantial change that we are making ... In future, the family health services authorities ... will have responsibility for assessing the needs of the local population for good family health services, for planning service development and for ensuring that the contracts of all contractors are so managed that services are provided in the most effective possible way. They will have important duties monitoring cash limits and so on, for premises improvements and for other uses. They will still be responsible for important parts of the disciplinary procedure and for hearing complaints from the public. The more we can do to strengthen the authorities and give them greater responsibility, the more effectively they should be able to undertake that duty ... the authorities should combine encouraging the development of the best practice with chasing up examples of bad practice in their patch and ensuring that either GPs are made to raise their standards or effective action is taken".

Later, the Parliamentary Under-Secretary of State for the Department of Health, Baroness Hooper, added (*Hansard*, H.L. Vol. 518, col. 794): "The White Paper ... *Promoting Better Health* set out our proposals for simplifying and streamlining complaints procedures, which came into operation on 2 April. The new procedures provide for FPCs to accept oral complaints from people unable to make complaints in writing. Complaints received by health authorities within the time limits are also now acceptable. The time limit within which complaints may be accepted has also been extended from eight to thirteen weeks. In addition, all FPCs are required to provide an informal procedure to patients who may not wish to pursue more formal procedures. . . . We expect complaints that are handled informally to be resolved within four weeks". See also the Minister of State for the Department of Health, Mrs Virginia Bottomley at Comm. (SCE) col. 187.

Subs. (3)(a)
S.10 of the 1977 Act referred to Pt. II of its Sched. 5. That Part provided the constitution of what were then called Family Practitioner Committees. The new constitution is to be found in Sched. 1 to this Act, which should be read with this section.
See note to subs. (4).

Subs. (3)(b)
See note to s.1(1)(c).

Subs. (4)
The new constitutions of the FHSAs are similar to the new ones for regional and district health authorities (see s.1). Sched. 1, Pt. II defines the new composition of the authorities. In each case the Chairman is to be appointed by the Secretary of State and there are to be a "prescribed" number of members appointed by the region (except in Wales where, in the absence of a region, the appointment is to be made by the Secretary of State). So also, the chief officer, such other officers as may be prescribed and a prescribed number of other officers are to be members of the authority. The changes reflect the shift to avoid the confusion between a representative and executive body. See also s.12(1)(2), amending the 1977 Act to give the regions power over the FHSAs.

Subs. (5)
The Notes on Clauses said: "The reconstitution of FHSAs will depend on the timing of the reconstitution of new-style RHAs. As soon as the new RHAs have met and appointed the non-officer members of FHSAs in England, the terms of office of the existing FPC chairmen and members of FPCs will be brought to an end . . . and the new chairmen and members will take up their appointments".

Subs. (6)
The Parliamentary Under-Secretary of State for the Department of Social Security, Lord Henley, explained (*Hansard*, H.L. Vol. 519, col. 1532): "The term 'health authority' is used in [the 1977 Act] to differentiate between FPCs and other types of authorities. The distinction is needed, for example, in defining authorities which may make staff and facilities available to local authorities covered by s.26, or in defining doctors who work in hospitals as opposed to those who provide general medical services". Generally this is indeed true but in Sched. 5, Pt. III of the 1977 Act para. 8 joins them all in one term "authority".

Primary and other functions of health authorities etc. and exercise of functions

3.—(1) Any reference in this Act to the primary functions of a Regional, District or Special Health Authority is a reference to those functions for the time being exercisable by the authority by virtue of directions under section 11, section 13 or section 14 of the principal Act; and any reference in this Act to the primary functions of a Family Health Services Authority is a reference to the functions for the time being exercisable by the authority by virtue of this Act or section 15 of the principal Act.

(2) In addition to carrying out its primary functions, a Regional, District or Special Health Authority or a Family Health Services Authority may, as the provider, enter into an NHS contract (as defined in section 4 below) under which the goods or services to be provided are of the same description as goods or services which the authority already provides or could provide for the purposes of carrying out its primary functions.

(3) In section 16 of the principal Act (exercise of functions), in subsection (1) for the words from "an Area", in the first place where they occur, to

"Health Authority" in the second place where those words occur, there shall be substituted "a Regional or District Health Authority, or exercisable by a Regional or District Health Authority by virtue of any prescribed provision of this or any other Act, or exercisable by a Family Health Services Authority under Part I of the National Health Service and Community Care Act 1990".

(4) In section 17 of the principal Act (directions as to exercise of functions), in subsection (1) after the words "sections 13 to 16 above" there shall be inserted "and may also give directions with respect to the exercise by health authorities or Family Health Services Authorities of functions under the National Health Service and Community Care Act 1990".

(5) Nothing in this section or in the principal Act affects the power of a Regional, District or Special Health Authority at any time to provide goods or services under the principal Act for the benefit of an individual where—

  (a) the provision of those goods or services is neither within the primary functions of the authority nor carried out pursuant to an NHS contract; but

  (b) the condition of the individual is such that he needs those goods or services and, having regard to his condition, it is not practicable before providing them to enter into an NHS contract for their provision.

(6) In any case where—

  (a) a Regional, District or Special Health Authority provides goods or services for the benefit of an individual as mentioned in subsection (5) above, and

  (b) the provision of those goods or services is within the primary functions of another health authority or is a function of a health board,

the authority providing the goods or services shall be remunerated in respect of that provision by that other health authority or health board.

(7) The rate of any remuneration payable by virtue of subsection (6) above shall be calculated in such manner or on such basis as may be determined by the Secretary of State.

(8) In any case where—

  (a) a Regional, District or Special Health Authority provides goods or services for the benefit of an individual, and

  (b) the provision of those goods or services is not pursuant to an NHS contract, and

  (c) the individual is resident outside the United Kingdom and is of a description (being a description associating the individual with another country) specified for the purposes of this subsection by a direction made by the Secretary of State,

the authority shall be remunerated by the Secretary of State in respect of the provision of the goods or services in question at such rate or rates as he considers appropriate.

DEFINITIONS

"District Health Authority": ss.8 and 128 of the National Health Service Act 1977, as amended by this Act, and Sched. 1 to this Act.

"goods": s.26.

"health authority": s.128 of the National Health Service Act 1977.

"prescribed": s.128 of the National Health Service Act 1977, as amended by this Act.

"health board": National Health Service (Scotland) Act 1978.

"primary functions": s.128 of the National Health Service Act 1977, as inserted by this Act and subs. (1).

"principal Act": s.1.

"the provider": s.4.

"Regional Health Authority": ss.8 and 128 of the National Health Service Act 1977 as amended by this Act and Sched. 1 to this Act.

"services": s.26.

"special health authority": s.11 of the National Health Service Act 1977 as amended by this Act and Sched. 1 to this Act.

GENERAL NOTE

This section and s.4 attempt to create what has been called the "internal market"; see further notes to subs. (2) and s.4.

This section assumes that the funding of the health service will be moved from giving cash to Districts which supply services to what is called "residency funding". Under the new regime, the purchase and provision of services will be split. This shift alone did not require legislation but it has consequences which are reflected in this section, in the next, and in regulations to be made. As regards these new funding arrangements, the Parliamentary Under-Secretary of State for Wales, Mr Ian Grist, explained (*Hansard*, H.C. Vol. 163, col. 578): "the authorities will be funded on the basis of their resident population. They will have a clear duty to ensure that the health needs of that local population are properly met. Each health authority will need to carry out a systematic assessment of the health status and needs of its local population. The director of public health medicine in each district will be responsible for carrying out that assessment, in consultation with clinicians in hospitals, with general practitioners and with other interests. Their task will be to identify local needs and priorities and to ensure that people have access to a comprehensive range of high quality, value-for-money services from the hospitals and units judged best able to deliver them. Complementary to that will be the duty that we intend to place on social service authorities to produce social service plans in collaboration with health authorities, voluntary bodies and the users of services and their representatives. They must set out how they intend to ensure the provision of quality social care for people in their homes and their communities. Taken together, [the] proposals will lead to a systematic assessment of people's health and social needs and the planning of comprehensive services to meet those needs. Central to [the] approach is the need to devolve responsibility for the day-to-day provision of services to local unit level, thereby freeing district health authorities to concentrate on their principal task of assessing the needs of those for whom they are responsible and ensuring that those needs are met by service providers". See also the Parliamentary Under-Secretary of State for the Department of Health, Baroness Hooper at *Hansard*, H.L. Vol. 518, col. 203.

The Parliamentary Under-Secretary of State for Health, Mr Roger Freeman, said (Comm. (SCE) col. 230) "Some of the shire districts, which send patients into London, will see their allocations rise significantly. However, the basis of changing to residency funding will not change the nature of services provided, at least in the first year. Higher allocations will flow out from the district to the hospitals and to the districts where patients are being looked after outside their own district. It is a change in the basis of funding. Weighted capitation is the basis of allocating the real amount of funds available for those who live in a district, but that system will come in over a number of years as districts move to a fairer and more sensible system of resource allocation. The new basis of allocating funds will commence on 1 April 1991."

The Parliamentary Under-Secretary of State for the Department of Health, Baroness Hooper, said (*Hansard*, H.L. Vol. 520, col. 1340): "Contracts are the mechanism which will give effect to districts' assessments of their residents' health care needs. I should emphasise ... the impact of the new distinction between health care acquirers and providers. As acquirers districts will be able to set out in more detail their service requirements. Having accepted those requirements in the terms of NHS contracts, providers of services will be held to them. The contractual system puts the needs of the patient at the centre of health care delivery. Providers will need to meet contractual terms and not allow themselves to be put off course by the short-term operational problems encountered in delivering services ... regulations [to be] made under [this section] will specify districts' primary function as providing a comprehensive health service for all its resident population—children, adults and elderly people ... if it proves necessary that will be spelled out in guidance".

The Parliamentary Under-Secretary of State for the Department of Social Security, Lord Henley, added (*Hansard*, H.L. Vol. 519, col. 1627): "Under the new arrangements a CHC's remit will relate to all services purchased by its DHA for that district's resident population, regardless of whether the services are provided by a district managed unit, an NHS trust, or the private sector. The Government expects that NHS management will take account of the consumers' interest in all its activities, and the views of CHCs should be sought, along with those of other interested parties, on the strategic provision of services which districts are required to commission for their residents, especially taking account of such factors as the accessibility and convenience of services being commissioned by the DHA".

During consideration in Committee the information which will be required in order to administer the contracts was explained as follows (Comm. (SCE) col. 329): "First, minimum data must be set—namely, the minimum amount of data which a hospital will have to generate under contracting. It is necessary to know where the patient lives because we are funding the

DHAs on the basis of residence. It must be known under which contract a patient will be cared for and one has to know the provider—the DHA that will provide the cost of the particular patient care, excluding, of course, accident and emergency provision. This and other information is largely available already in the hospital system. It must be pulled together, however, and the easiest way in which to do that is through information technology and the patient administration systems".

The Department has issued much guidance concerning the content of these "contracts", see, *e.g. Contracts for Health Services: Operational Principles* and *Funding and Contracts for Hospital Services*, and their associated papers. Essential to the scheme is the fact that these contracts will contain increasingly detailed specifications of quality, including, at an early stage, such matters as waiting times. Two things are to be noted: first, there is not much doubt that in drawing these contracts authorities will be bound to obey the usual public law principles applicable to local authority contracting, so that for example they will have a general fiduciary duty to place contracts with the most advantageous provider (although not necessarily the cheapest) and must not have regard to irrelevant considerations. Secondly, the "remedies" for breach of these contracts seem obscure (see s.4(3) and note thereto).

Subs. (1)

The section refers to the functions of health authorities and FHSAs exercisable by directions under ss.11, 13, 14 and 15 of the 1977 Act. S.11 makes general provision for the establishment and functions of special health authorities; see *The Encyclopedia of Health Services and Medical Law* for the orders made under the section. S.13 permits the Secretary of State to direct regions in England and districts in Wales to perform his functions under the Act. S.14 permits regions, if directed by the Secretary of State, to direct districts to perform functions it is their duty to perform. S.15(a) requires FHSAs to administer the general medical services, etc. under Pt. II of the Act (ss.29–56). S.15(b) requires them to perform such other functions as may be prescribed. These functions are now to be known as "primary functions". (As to the fulfilment of these functions, see note to subs. (2)). At the time of the passage of the Act they were partly defined in the NHS (Directions to Authorities and Administration Arrangements) Regulations 1989 S.I. 1989 No. 51. But further requirements are imposed, *e.g.* by HC 88(64) which, following the Acheson report, requires each district to produce an annual health report to be written by the district director of public health or by HC (89)5 and its accompanying booklet on *The Discharge of Patients from Hospital* giving guidance on the arrangements to be made on discharge to ensure the appropriate continuity of care (see s.46 of this Act on community care plans, and especially note to s.46(2)(a)).

The Parliamentary Under-Secretary of State for Health, Mr Roger Freeman, explained these provisions and anticipated directions to be made in the following terms: (Comm. (SCE) col. 226–8): "We shall lay similar regulations under the negative resolution procedure ... setting out further duties on DHAs to provide a comprehensive range of services ... the DHAs will be obliged to serve all those who live within their catchment area ... some services undeniably need local access for residents in the authorities' catchment areas. But we do not define local access as access within a DHA's boundary. ... In some places such as in London's spatially small districts local access can be discharged by contiguous authorities ... decisions about services that require local access and the initial definition of core services in and for a district health authority must be made by the DHA ... A DHA has a responsibility to ensure that health care needs of its resident population are assessed ... [DHAs] have a responsibility to plan for the comprehensive health care of their residents".

He continued (Comm. (SCE) col. 229): "For accident and emergency services we shall require the DHA to provide an accident and emergency service for all comers, whether they are resident in this country or abroad. That service will be funded as a whole by the local DHA. If accident and emergency patients have to be admitted to a ward, the Secretary of State will prescribe the rates of charge by the inpatient wards for the services rendered to the district in which the patient is usually resident. That will be laid in regulations or in an administrative circular. If the patient is resident in this country, standard costs will be charged to the district and paid automatically. If the patient is resident abroad, the Secretary of State for Health will discharge that financial obligation direct to the hospital providing the service [see s.3(8)(c)]. The regulations ... will state that accident and emergency services are to be provided to all comers. The regulations will also change the basis of obligation from services within a district boundary to an obligation on the health authority to care for the health needs of its residents. That is a sharp change in function which requires a change in the regulations ... We shall consider how best to express the implicit duty to assess in regulations that will be laid before Parliament" (Comm. (SCE) col. 256).

He said (Comm. (SCE) col. 257): "We believe that non-clinical registration data collected by ... family health service authorities should be available to DHAs for the planning of health care for their catchment populations".

The Baroness in Waiting, Baroness Blatch, added (*Hansard*, H.L. Vol. 520, col. 270): "The White Paper *Promoting Better Health* also lays a specific responsibility on family practitioner committees to assess the health needs of all their residents and actively to develop services to meet those needs. In areas where there are homeless people they will need to take account of their special requirements. . . . The [Act] gives district health authorities specific responsibility for the provision of a comprehensive range of high quality services for all their population. That will, of course, include homeless people".

Subs. (2)

As can be seen, the "primary functions" of a health authority defined in subs. (1) largely relate to its own activities on behalf of its resident population. It will be able to secure the fulfilment of these functions in four ways: first, by simply doing what it has done before, that is, providing health care; secondly, by making arrangements (sometimes and misleadingly called a contract) with its own directly managed units; thirdly, by making arrangements with another health service body to do the work for it (what s.4 calls a NHS contract); and, similarly, fourthly, by making arrangements with a body outside the health service. No legislative change was required for the first, second and fourth of these: it is, however, to be noted that the second, the arrangements with its own directly-managed units, is a management device and has no meaning in law, partly because a body cannot contract with itself even through its servants or agents. The second and third methods relate to the so-called "internal market".

Subs. (2) is directed to a different matter. It is reciprocal with the third method by which health authorities may discharge their functions. A health service body (s.4(1) uses the term "the acquirer") may make an NHS contract with another such body (s.4(1) uses the term "the provider") whereby the second will carry out some particular task or tasks for the first on which the obligation is placed. This subsection empowers the second to carry out the contract.

The Parliamentary Under-Secretary of State for the Department of Social Security, Lord Henley, said (*Hansard*, H.L. Vol. 518, col. 496): "every DHA will publish a list of the services for which it has contracted, whether from its own directly managed units or from other providers. This is in line with the requirement, announced in the . . . guidance document *Operating Contracts*, that all contracts for health services should be publicly available".

The Parliamentary Under-Secretary of State for the Department of Social Security, Lord Henley, said (*Hansard*, H.L. Vol. 519, col. 1632): "Ambulances or other forms of hospital transport will continue to be provided free of charge for all patients for whom this is medically necessary. Guidance has already been issued on the way in which these transport services will fit into the contractual system. The most appropriate approach is likely to be for health care providers to arrange transport in support of their services. This will make it easier to integrate transport services into the overall package of patient care. Help with travelling expenses will also continue to be provided through the hospital travel costs scheme" (see the NHS (Travelling Expenses and Remission of Charges) Regulations 1988 (S.I. 1988 No. 551)).

The Baroness in Waiting, Baroness Blatch, said (*Hansard*, H.L. Vol. 519, col. 1586): "I expect district health authorities, when they are negotiating contracts, to specify that they require an integrated children's health service. It will then be for the providers to take the necessary organisational and management measures to deliver an integrated service. They will also need to demonstrate that they have effective liaison arrangements with local authority staff working in social services and education departments to implement provisions for the planning and assessment of need under [sections 46 and 47 of this Act] and Part III of the Children Act [1989]".

The Parliamentary Under-Secretary of State for the Department of Health, Baroness Hooper, confirmed (*Hansard*, H.L. Vol. 519, col. 1625): the "comprehensive range of services" will include speech therapy.

As regards the self-referral services, the Parliamentary Under-Secretary of State for the Department of Social Security, Lord Henley, said (*Hansard*, H.L. Vol. 519, col. 1610): "Guidance on contractual funding has already stressed the need for health authorities to [give] particular consideration to services which patients use on [this] basis . . . It is . . . a matter of ensuring that the contractual arrangements for self-referral services secure open access and confidentiality . . . In the case of genito-urinary medicine, *Contracts for Health Services: Operating Contracts* made it clear that, unless alternative arrangements are agreed with RHAs, DHAs will be expected to provide funding in the same way as for accident and emergency services; that is, by placing contracts which cover all patients who present themselves for the service regardless of district of residence. The guidance has also suggested that this may be an appropriate model for other self-referral services since it avoids the need for a contract or exchange of information with the patient's own DHA. However, different considerations may apply to different services in different districts and we believe it is important to allow proper scope for local decision-making. Generally, therefore, we expect DHAs to decide themselves the most appropriate arrangements for funding self-referral services used by their residents. In view of the particular importance of these services, however, *Operating Contracts* places a specific responsibility on the regions for ensuring that satisfactory arrangements for both confidentiality and access are made". Baroness Blatch added (*Hansard*, H.L. Vol. 520, col. 1357): "The important point on confidentiality is that treatment will begin and end in one local authority. There will not be a cross-boundary flow of information back to the home authority of the patient who is receiving services".

Complaints
The new position as regards complaints was outlined in committee as follows: (Comm. (SCE) col. 322) "First a complaint should be made to the patient's DHA; the DHA is answerable to residents in the sense that they should take up complaints with it. Secondly, if negligence occurs, it will be open to patients to pursue the matter directly with the DHAs and, if necessary, through the courts. Thirdly, it is important to take up issues of concern with the CHC, which should be an independent body—the voice of the patient. Fourthly, access to the Health Service Commissioner remains". For the new complaints procedure in general practice, see note to s.2(1).
As regards malpractice, the Act makes no change to either the basis or types of liability that may arise, but s.21 does establish the possibility of a scheme to share expenses and liabilities. Where a service is improperly performed, potentially (1) the practitioners may be liable; (2) the provider of the service may be directly liable and vicariously liable for the acts of its staff; and (3) the acquiring authority which placed the contract with that provider will have a duty to place an adequate contract in terms of the specification of standards and possibly a duty to monitor its performance with an authority which it reasonably believed could carry it out. To an extent, this last becomes a novel form of responsibility, but it is surmised that the old cases on the liability of a hospital for its independent contractor hospital consultants will be relevant (see *Hillyer* v. *St. Bartholomew's Hospital* [1909] 2 K.B. 820). Of course, a patient will not be able to sue on the contract itself, mainly because of the terms of s.4(3) but partly because of the doctrine of privity. However, the suggested head of liability lies outside contract although the terms of the arrangement will be relevant in determining the extent of the duty.

Subs. (3)
S.16 of the 1977 Act permits regulations to be made to allow a function of a health authority to be exercised by other bodies.

Subs. (4)
S.17 of the 1977 Act permits the Secretary of State and the regions to give directions as to the functions of the regions and districts.

Subs. (5)
As noted above, subs. (2) empowers a health service body to contract with another such body whereby the second will carry out some particular task or tasks for the first on which the obligation is placed. This subsection empowers a health service body to provide goods or services for an individual effectively in an emergency where it is not practicable to make a contract. The matter can be seen most clearly in relation to the obligations of a district. The obligation to provide the services is placed on the district of residence. The subsection allows another district to provide services even in the absence of a NHS contract.
Thus contingency reserves, designed in discussion with local GPs, will be maintained in order to enable GPs to refer patients to non-contract hospitals when judged necessary on clinical, social or other grounds; this contingency reserve must be administered in a simple, quick and non-bureaucratic way (*Hansard*, H.L. Vol. 519, col. 1603).

NHS contracts

4.—(1) In this Act the expression "NHS contract" means an arrangement under which one health service body ("the acquirer") arranges for the provision to it by another health service body ("the provider") of goods or services which it reasonably requires for the purposes of its functions.
(2) In this section "health service body" means any of the following, namely,—
(a) a health authority;
(b) a health board;
(c) the Common Services Agency for the Scottish Health Service;
(d) a Family Health Services Authority;

   (e) an NHS trust;

   (f) a recognised fund-holding practice;

   (g) the Dental Practice Board or the Scottish Dental Practice Board;

   (h) the Public Health Laboratory Service Board; and

   (i) the Secretary of State.

(3) Whether or not an arrangement which constitutes an NHS contract would, apart from this subsection, be a contract in law, it shall not be regarded for any purpose as giving rise to contractual rights or liabilities, but if any dispute arises with respect to such an arrangement, either party may refer the matter to the Secretary of State for determination under the following provisions of this section.

(4) If, in the course of negotiations intending to lead to an arrangement which will be an NHS contract, it appears to a health service body—

   (a) that the terms proposed by another health service body are unfair by reason that the other is seeking to take advantage of its position as the only, or the only practicable, provider of the goods or services concerned or by reason of any other unequal bargaining position as between the prospective parties to the proposed arrangement, or

   (b) that for any other reason arising out of the relative bargaining position of the prospective parties any of the terms of the proposed arrangement cannot be agreed,

that health service body may refer the terms of the proposed arrangement to the Secretary of State for determination under the following provisions of this section.

(5) Where a reference is made to the Secretary of State under subsection (3) or subsection (4) above, the Secretary of State may determine the matter himself or, if he considers it appropriate, appoint a person to consider and determine it in accordance with regulations.

(6) By his determination of a reference under subsection (4) above, the Secretary of State or, as the case may be, the person appointed under subsection (5) above may specify terms to be included in the proposed arrangement and may direct that it be proceeded with; and it shall be the duty of the prospective parties to the proposed arrangement to comply with any such directions.

(7) A determination of a reference under subsection (3) above may contain such directions (including directions as to payment) as the Secretary of State or, as the case may be, the person appointed under subsection (5) above considers appropriate to resolve the matter in dispute; and it shall be the duty of the parties to the NHS contract in question to comply with any such directions.

(8) Without prejudice to the generality of his powers on a reference under subsection (3) above, the Secretary of State or, as the case may be, the person appointed under subsection (5) above may by his determination in relation to an arrangement constituting an NHS contract vary the terms of the arrangement or bring it to an end; and where an arrangement is so varied or brought to an end—

   (a) subject to paragraph (b) below, the variation or termination shall be treated as being effected by agreement between the parties; and

   (b) the directions included in the determination by virtue of subsection (7) above may contain such provisions as the Secretary of State or, as the case may be, the person appointed under subsection (5) above considers appropriate in order satisfactorily to give effect to the variation or to bring the arrangement to an end.

(9) In subsection (2) above "NHS trust" includes—

   (a) such a trust established under the National Health Service (Scotland) Act 1978; and

   (b) a body established in Northern Ireland and specified by an order made by statutory instrument by the Secretary of State as equivalent to an NHS trust established under this Part of this Act.

"Dental Practice Board": s.37(1) of the National Health Service Act 1977.

"goods": s.26.

"Family Health Services Authority": s.10 of the National Health Service Act 1977 and Sched. 1 to this Act.

"health authority": s.128 of the National Health Service Act 1977.

"health board": s.2 and Sched. 1, Pt. I to the National Health Service (Scotland) Act 1978.

"health service body": subs. (2).

"NHS contract": subs. (1) and s.128 of the National Health Service Act 1977, as inserted by this Act.

"NHS trust": s.128 of the National Health Service Act 1977, as inserted by this Act; and s.5 of this Act; see also National Health Service (Scotland) Act 1978 as amended by this Act.

"Public Health Laboratory Service Board": s.5 and Sched. 3 to the National Health Service Act 1977.

"regulations": ss.126 and 128 of the National Health Service Act 1977, as amended by this Act.

"services": s.26.

GENERAL NOTE

With s.3 (and see notes thereto) this section is directed to establishing an "internal market" within the health service. The Parliamentary Under-Secretary of State for Health, Mr Roger Freeman, said (Comm. (SCE) cols. 323–4): "The contracts have two great advantages. First, they separate clearly the rôles and responsibilities of the acquirers and providers of health care, and that goes to the root of the Bill. Secondly, of course, responsibilities are formally set out and targets are set for the delivery not only of the quantity but the quality of health care". The Parliamentary Under-Secretary of State, Department of Health, Baroness Hooper (*Hansard*, H.L. Vol. 519, col. 1580), linking the contractual arrangements with the establishment of the Clinical Standards Advisory Group under s.62, argued that "the contractual process will focus attention on quality of care, on areas where improvements in health standards are needed and on outcome measures and objectives".

The Secretary of State for Health, Mr Kenneth Clarke, said (*Hansard*, H.C. Vol. 169, col. 608): "In future, services will be provided locally in pursuance of an agreement between the district health authority or general practitioner and hospitals and community units. Those who want services provided for residents will stipulate what they want—not just their quantity and cost, but most importantly their quality which they can specify and how they will measure it when the service is delivered. In exchange, those who work in the units and deliver the services will sign up to a given level of quality, explain how they propose to measure it, and deliver it in exchange for the resources that they have agreed to receive ... doctors and nurses to look at the contract to see what they think about it for their particular service. Many doctors and nurses may not like the way in which the quality of service is described. In that case the royal colleges must lay down how they would like their service to be judged and describe the quality to which they aspire. In that way they will help us to produce good contracts with which they can feel content because they are being asked to deliver something sensible that they should like to achieve and by which they are content to be measured in exchange for the resources that they require".

However, at least initially the importance of this section can be over-emphasised because it will only apply to arrangements involving more than one health service body. In addition, many of the contracts introduced in April 1991 will be in relatively simple block form, and there will be little difference from existing patterns of service. They will be the starting point, and the process will develop and evolve from there (*Hansard*, H.L. Vol. 520, col. 181).

Nevertheless, as will be seen in the notes to subs. (3), at least as far as the law is concerned, the concept of an "internal market" amounts to a contradiction in terms. A market implies access to the courts and where that happens by definition it is not "internal". Further, in so far as arrangements are to be made between health service bodies, they will be made in the shadow of the possibility of the body with the primary function (the purchaser; subs. (1) uses the term "the acquirer") making more efficient arrangements with bodies outside the health service: the arrangements between health service bodies will be conditioned by the general, external market.

Subs. (1)

"*The purposes of its functions*". It would seem that this expression is wider than "primary functions" so that NHS contracts will be able to cover other functions as well as the primary functions, that is, the discharge of obligations to the resident population and to any victims of accidents in their locality. These other functions themselves could be acquired by a NHS contract—subcontracting is allowed.

Subs. (2)
The list includes all potential NHS purchasers of health care.

Subs. (3)
"*Either party may refer the matter to the Secretary of State*". There seems no obstacle to the parties agreeing to private arbitration with an arbitrator of their choice; see *Contracts for Health Services: Operating Contracts*, para. 5.31. It is presumed that such an award would itself take effect on a further NHS contract and that *Callisher* v. *Bischoffsheim* (1870) L.R. 5 Q.B. 449 is some authority (but this view depends on likening an NHS contract to an ordinary contract and in particular importing notions of consideration). *Operating Contracts* also suggested, para. 4.33, that RHAs would act as conciliators.

"*Determination under the following provisions of this section*". See subss. (5), (7) and (8). Almost in accord with the idea of contracts being a private matter solely between the parties, the Secretary of State has no powers under the section to intervene nor does a third party have any powers to refer that dispute to him.

The Notes on Clauses said: "[the subsection] makes clear that NHS contracts shall not be regarded as being enforceable by law, nor as giving rise to any rights or liabilities in law". The Secretary of State, Mr Kenneth Clarke, said (Comm. (SCE) col. 349): "it is not intended that those contracts, as we call them, should be subject to litigation in courts of law. . . . I trust that no member of the Committee seriously contemplates different parts of the NHS commencing legal actions against other parts to enforce the terms of a contract. That would be a lawyer's charter and paradise, but of little benefit to patients. It is intended that the contracts be binding inside the Health Service and be adhered to by the parties". See also Comm. (SCE) col. 332 and the Parliamentary Under-Secretary of State for Health, Mr Roger Freeman, at Comm. (SCE) col. 323.

The extra-legal expressions of intent are plain enough. The question that remains is whether the statute has prevented litigation (or could, for the courts are very suspicious of Parliamentary attempts to exclude their jurisdiction). There are five reasons why it is doubtful if the intention to exclude the courts has been adequately expressed. First, assuming that the statutory scheme works as intended, there is no doubt that determinations of the Secretary of State will be subject to judicial review so that the whole range of matters which could have been argued had the action lain in contract can be brought to the court.

Secondly, the subsection refers to "an arrangement which . . . shall not be regarded for any purpose as giving rise to contractual rights and liabilities". There is nothing to prevent rights and liabilities arising from outside contract from being sued upon. Put simply, requested work done has to be paid for even in the absence of contract. The action lies in *assumpsit* for a *quantum meruit* (*cf.* the Australian case, *Pavey Matthews* v. *Paul* (1987) 69 A.L.R. 577, noted by Beatson 104 (1988) *Law Quarterly Review* 13, where there was a successful action on an oral agreement where statute required a written contract; see also *Scott* v. *Pattison* [1923] 2 K.B. 723). As Wilson J. put it two hundred years ago in *Shiells and Thorne* v. *Blackburne* (1789) 1 H.Bl. 158: "Where money has been paid for the performance of certain acts, the person receiving it is, by law, answerable for any degree of neglect on his part . . . and this rule has few exceptions".

Thirdly, and related to this, it appears likely that the draftsman has mistaken the legal nature of the obligation assumed by authorities (and practitioners) within orthodox medicine. That obligation rests without more on the fact of their occupation and the extent of their undertaking. For example, in *Barnett* v. *Chelsea and Kensington Hospital Management Committee* [1969] 1 Q.B. 428, a hospital had a casualty department (that is, held itself out as having one) and was accordingly bound to see and examine all patients who presented themselves. In that case, there was no question for example of there being any need for the contractual concept of "consideration". There seems no reason why, merely because the *content* of the obligation (and of the occupation) of health authorities is defined by an arrangement under whatever name or regulations made under statute (see note to s.3(1)), that the *basis* of the obligation should be altered.

The Encyclopedia of Health Services and Medical Law argues that the source of the malpractice action against an individual practitioner is what it calls "situation liability". It arises out of the public interest in the occupation and the assumption of the occupation by the practitioner. In all material respects it makes the practice of medicine by both individual practitioners and health authorities a "common calling". On this basis, the liability for failure to perform an NHS contract is not only a contractual liability (which the subsection excludes) but also a liability arising out of the situation determined by the undertaking (which the subsection does not exclude).

Fourthly, subs. (6) and (7) provide that "it shall be the *duty* of the parties" (emphasis supplied) to comply with any directions given as a result of arbitration proceedings under the section. It would seem odd that a duty should arise only after proceedings, because normally arbitration *determines* what rights and liabilities the parties have: it does not *create* them.

Fifthly, the Departmental guidance as to the content of these NHS contracts in effect insists that the only difference between them and an arrangement enforceable as a contract in the courts is that both parties are health service bodies: an identical arrangement with a non-health service body, *e.g.* a private hospital, is of course enforceable. The language of the Act and the language of the guidance is of commerce, albeit between parties who expect long term relationships, and thus the emphasis is on arbitration rather than litigation. For example, quality and standards are to be defined in the arrangement. So also cross-subsidies between one contract and another are to be discouraged (see *Contracts for Health Services: Operating Contracts*, para. 4.2, and EL(90)MB/26 "Contract Pricing: Cost Allocation Principles").

Subs. (4)
The subsection is aimed at the abuse of monopoly power by a provider within the health service—the abuse of monopoly power by bodies outside the health service would seem to fall under the general law of monopolies. If the DHA believes that there is an abuse of monopoly power by [a] provider . . . it has the power to refer the matter, after conciliation by the RHA, to the Secretary of State for arbitration (Comm. (SCE) cols. 327–8).

Subs. (6)
As noted above, the section imposes a duty on the parties to comply with the arbitral award. It makes no mention of how that duty shall be enforced and one may surmise that the general public and private law will apply.

Subs. (7)
See note to subs. (6).

National Health Service trusts

NHS trusts

5.—(1) Subject to subsection (2) or, as the case may be, subsection (3) below the Secretary of State may by order establish bodies, to be known as National Health Service trusts (in this Act referred to as NHS trusts),—

    (a) to assume responsibility, in accordance with this Act, for the ownership and management of hospitals or other establishments or facilities which were previously managed or provided by Regional, District or Special Health Authorities; or

    (b) to provide and manage hospitals or other establishments or facilities.

(2) In any case where the Secretary of State is considering whether to make an order under subsection (1) above establishing an NHS trust and the hospital, establishment or facility concerned is or is to be situated in England, he shall direct the relevant Regional Health Authority to consult, with respect to the proposal to establish the trust,—

    (a) the relevant Community Health Council and such other persons or bodies as may be specified in the direction; and

    (b) such other persons or bodies as the Authority considers appropriate; and, within such period (if any) as the Secretary of State may determine, the relevant Regional Health Authority shall report the results of those consultations to the Secretary of State.

(3) In any case where the Secretary of State is considering whether to make an order under subsection (1) above establishing an NHS trust and the hospital, establishment or facility concerned is or is to be situated in Wales, he shall consult the relevant Community Health Council and such other persons and bodies as he considers appropriate.

(4) In subsections (2) and (3) above—

    (a) any reference to the relevant Regional Health Authority is a reference to that Authority in whose region the hospital, establishment or other facility concerned is, or is to be, situated; and

    (b) any reference to the relevant Community Health Council is a reference to the Council for the district, or part of the district, in which that hospital, establishment or other facility is, or is to be, situated.

(5) Every NHS trust—

(a) shall be a body corporate having a board of directors consisting of a chairman appointed by the Secretary of State and, subject to paragraph 5(2) of Schedule 2 to this Act, executive and non-executive directors (that is to say, directors who, subject to subsection (7) below, respectively are and are not employees of the trust); and

(b) shall have the functions conferred on it by an order under subsection (1) above and by Schedule 2 to this Act.

(6) The functions specified in an order under subsection (1) above shall include such functions as the Secretary of State considers appropriate in relation to the provision of services by the trust for one or more health authorities.

(7) The Secretary of State may by regulations make general provision with respect to—

(a) the qualifications for and the tenure of office of the chairman and directors of an NHS trust (including the circumstances in which they shall cease to hold, or may be removed from, office or may be suspended from performing the functions of the office);

(b) the persons by whom the directors and any of the officers are to be appointed and the manner of their appointment;

(c) the maximum and minimum numbers of the directors;

(d) the circumstances in which a person who is not an employee of the trust is nevertheless, on appointment as a director, to be regarded as an executive rather than a non-executive director;

(e) the proceedings of the trust (including the validation of proceedings in the event of a vacancy or defect in appointment); and

(f) the appointment, constitution and exercise of functions by committees and sub-committees of the trust (whether or not consisting of or including any members of the board) and, without prejudice to the generality of the power, any such regulations, may make provision to deal with cases where the post of any officer of an NHS trust is held jointly by two or more persons or where the functions of such an officer are in any other way performed by more than one person.

(8) Part I of Schedule 2 to this Act shall have effect with respect to orders under subsection (1) above; Part II of that Schedule shall have effect, subject to subsection (9) below, with respect to the general duties and the powers and status of NHS trusts; the supplementary provisions of Part III of that Schedule shall have effect; and Part IV of that Schedule shall have effect with respect to the dissolution of NHS trusts.

(9) The specific powers conferred by paragraphs 14 and 15 in Part II of Schedule 2 to this Act may be exercised only to the extent that—

(a) the exercise will not interfere with the duties of the trust to comply with directions under paragraph 6 of that Schedule; and

(b) the exercise will not to any significant extent interfere with the performance by the trust of its obligations under any NHS contract or any obligations imposed by an order under subsection (1) above.

(10) The Secretary of State may by order made by statutory instrument confer on NHS trusts specific powers additional to those contained in paragraphs 10 to 15 of Schedule 2 to this Act.

DEFINITIONS

"Community Health Council": s.20 of the National Health Service Act 1977.

"District Health Authority": ss.8 and 128 of the National Health Service Act 1977, as amended by this Act, and Sched. 1 to this Act.

"executive director": subs. (5).

"functions": s.128 of the National Health Service Act 1977.

"hospital": s.128 of the National Health Service Act 1977.

"NHS contract": ss.3 and 26 of this Act and 128 of the National Health Service Act 1977, as inserted by this Act.

"non-executive director": subs. (5).

"Regional Health Authority": ss.8 and 128 of the National Health Service Act 1977, as amended by this Act, and Sched. 1 to this Act.

"regulations": ss.126 and 128 of the National Health Service Act 1977, as amended by this Act.

"services": s.26.

"special health authority": s.11 of the National Health Service Act 1977, as amended by this Act, and Sched. 1 to this Act.

GENERAL NOTE

This section, together with Sched. 2, ss.6, 7, 8 and 9 (and Schedule 3), and ss.10 and 11 make provision for the establishment of NHS trusts. They were foreshadowed in *Self-Governing Hospitals: an Initial Guide*. Whilst it is anticipated that possibly the initial majority of NHS trusts will be hospitals, the words "other establishments or facilities" in subs. (1)(a) and (b) cover any activity. The Parliamentary Under-Secretary of State, Department of Social Security, Lord Henley, pointed out (*Hansard*, H.L. Vol. 518, col. 137–8): "we are prepared to recognise that it may make sense for the full range of services in a district to become self-governing. We do not wish to prescribe that, nor do we wish to rule it out. The Government will certainly consider applications from whole districts, using benefit to patients as the key criterion ... any unit of whatever kind can apply. Its eligibility for National Health Service trust status will be considered on its merits ... it might make sense for the full range of services in a district to become NHS trusts. However, that will only relate to the services in the district. The DHA's other rôles, that is, planning, purchasing and public health—must be kept separate". He argued (*Hansard*, H.L. Vol. 518, col. 676): "Management freedom of NHSTs will enable them to respond more effectively to patient needs and improve the quality of services. Freedoms available to NHSTs will include the freedom to employ staff, retain surpluses, borrow money and acquire, own and dispose of assets. Most important, NHSTs will be an integral part of the National Health Service and will be accountable to the National Health Service Management Executive".

The freedoms granted to these NHS trusts are not total. As the Parliamentary Under-Secretary of State for Health, Mr Roger Freeman, pointed out (Comm. (SCE) col. 227): "NHS trusts that are also hospitals may have to be limited in their ability to eliminate or reduce the provision of certain services if guaranteed local access is required ... but [the Act] and regulations following it, will give the Secretary of State ultimate power to determine the minimum range of core services that must be provided". See also subs. (8), s.6 and notes thereto, ss.7–11 and Scheds. 2 and 3.

The legal position of these new institutions is *sui generis*. Certainly, they are not "trusts" or "charitable trusts" in the usual legal sense of the words (see s.11 and note thereto). On the other hand, it is reasonable to surmise that they will be subjected to similar fiduciary obligations as those that attach to local authorities (see *Bromley London Borough Council* v. *Greater London Council* [1983] 1 A.C. 768) or possibly even companies under the Companies Acts. As now with other health authorities (see s.60), they are not servants or agents of the Crown (Sched. 2, para. 18). In some ways, as stated in Committee, "trusts can be likened to nationalised industries". This applies both to their financial obligations and to their subjection to ministerial regulation and direction (Comm. (SCE) col. 389).

As regards the application process, the Minister of State for the Department of Health, Mrs Virginia Bottomley, said (Comm. (SCE) col. 414–5): "Health Service trusts ... will produce a prospectus document. The document will deal with the overall aims of the trusts, their progress in arranging contracts, the way in which they will develop their services, the quality that will be assured, their leadership and management arrangements, personnel issues, information systems, finance and estates. ... The fundamental criteria that ... the Secretary of State will consider when he is deciding whether to make an order are whether there is strong and effective leadership and personnel management and the extent to which senior professional staff are involved in the management of the hospitals. It is clear throughout our proposals that we look to have NHS trusts where there is a measure of cooperation and agreement and an ability to work together. When the NHS trust is accepting contracts, relations with the local community and the local DHA will, of course be extremely important, and there are several areas where collaboration and a spirit of goodwill are of great significance". See also note to subss. (2), (3) and (4).

The Parliamentary Under-Secretary of State for the Department of Health, Baroness Hooper, said (*Hansard*, H.L. Vol. 518, col. 727): "Because of the importance which we attach to undergraduate medical education and research, we shall specifically recognise it in the establishment orders of teaching trusts ... National Health Service trusts will be directly accountable to the Secretary of State, who will wish to satisfy himself not only that a trust has undertaken to provide adequate facilities for teaching and research and has made the necessary arrangements for collaboration, but, above all, that these undertakings have been met in practice. NHS trusts will be expected to include an outline of the provision which they intend to make for teaching and research in their annual reports and forward business plans. I am confident that this process and the process of monitoring a contract by district health authorities will ensure that the Secretary of State has ample early warning of problems . . . Section 51 of the National Health Service Act 1977 . . . requires the Secretary of State for the whole National Health Service to make available such facilities as are reasonably required by a university medical school for clinical research. That section will remain in force. But it is a duty which bites on the Secretary of State. As far as National Health Service Trusts are concerned, the Secretary of State will ensure that his duty is met by the process of careful scrutiny of plans and performance and, if necessary, use of reserve powers". See also note to subs. (5).

Subs. (1)

An order under the subsection is to be made by statutory instrument (Sched. 2, para. 2). The subsection should be read with subss. (5) and (6). As to the content of the order establishing or varying an NHS trust, see Sched. 2, para. 3(1). The Notes on Clauses explained that this order "will specify the valuation of the net assets of the trust and the division of the originating capital debt into amounts to be held respectively as interest-bearing debt and public dividend capital; the minimum value of an asset whose disposal the Secretary of State may prevent. [These matters are described in s.9.] The order may also make provision regarding paragraphs 3(2), 4(1) and 5 of Schedule 2".

Subss. (2), (3) and (4)

The Parliamentary Under-Secretary of State for the Department of Health, Baroness Hooper, explained (*Hansard*, H.L. Vol. 519, cols. 1639–40): "We have always been clear that we want wide consultation but that there should be flexibility to allow the consultation to be tailored to the circumstances of the individual application. The range of interests to be consulted on an application from a major teaching hospital, for example, may be very different from that concerned with an application from a community unit or an ambulance service . . . the White Paper and subsequent published documents [make clear] the criteria that applications for trust status will have to satisfy. First, management must be able to demonstrate the skills and capacity to run the unit, including strong and effective leadership, sufficient financial and personnel management expertise and adequate information systems. Secondly, senior professional staff, especially consultants, must be involved in the management of the unit. Thirdly, we shall want potential trusts to demonstrate the benefits which trust status will bring to patients and to demonstrate their financial viability. The amendment would therefore require the Secretary of State to issue guidance which would duplicate what already exists".

Subs. (5)

The Parliamentary Under-Secretary of State for the Department of Health, Baroness Hooper, said (*Hansard*, H.L. Vol. 518, cols. 717–8): "in the majority of cases the executive directors will include a senior nurse manager and medical director, and we shall provide for this in regulations . . . membership . . . will take account of their teaching rôle where appropriate. Each teaching trust will contain a non-executive member drawn from the university or medical or dental school. This member could also be an employee of the trust" (see also Sched. 2, para. 3(3)). This apparently includes an academic holding an honorary contract with the hospital which would otherwise have made him ineligible to be a non-executive director.

Subs. (7)

The Notes on Clauses said: "in any case where the post of an executive director is shared by more than one person, regulations will provide that both the people concerned may attend meetings of the trust board but they will have only one vote and count as one member for the purpose of achieving a quorum".

Subs. (7)(a)

"*Qualifications*": It is assumed that this word, here and in Sched. 2, para. 6(2), means formal qualifications rather than "characteristics". That paragraph also uses the expression "qualifications and experience".

The Notes on Clauses indicated that regulations will ensure that the non-executive directors will include at least two drawn from the local community; where a trust is designated as having a significant teaching commitment, one of the non-executive directors (in Wales, at least one) will be drawn from the relevant medical or dental school or university. The executive directors will include the chief officer of the trust, the finance director, and up to three other executives (usually the medical director and the senior nurse manager). The following will be excluded from appointment as non-executive directors: general medical or dental practitioners and their employees; the employees of any health service body; and the employees of a trade union with members who work in the NHS. In addition, similar provision will be made to that under the Membership and Procedure Regulations S.I. 1983 No. 315, barring certain people on account of bankruptcy.

Subs. (7)(b)
Non-executive chairmen will be appointed by the Secretary of State. In England two non-executive directors will be appointed by the RHA in which the trust is located and the remainder by the Secretary of State. In Wales, they all will be. Where applicable, the non-executive director drawn from a medical or dental school or university will be appointed by the Secretary of State after consulting the trust chairman. The chief officer will be appointed by the chairman and non-executive directors; the other executive directors will be appointed by the chairman and non-executive directors acting with the chief officer.

Subs. (7)(c)
NHS trust boards will comprise a non-executive chairman and up to 10 directors. There will be an equal number of executive and non-executive directors on all trust boards.

Subs. (7)(d)
The Notes on Clauses indicated that "there will be provisions relating to the proceedings of trust boards on the lines" of Sched. 1 of the Membership and Procedure Regulations S.I. 1983 No. 315.

Subs. (7)(e)
The Notes on Clauses indicated that "there will be provision for trusts to establish committees or sub-committees consisting of different classes of members, non-members or a mixture of both for carrying out some of its functions".

Subs. (8)
The Secretary of State for Health, Mr Kenneth Clarke, said (*Hansard*, H.C. Vol. 163, col. 510): "[The Schedule sets] out the freedoms of the NHSTs ... They include the freedom to employ their own staff, to conduct research and to provide facilities for medical education and other forms of training. NHSTs will have the same income-generation powers as other health authorities. The Schedule also contains safeguards in the form of specific powers of direction which the Secretary of State will have over the trusts. These powers will allow me and my successors to direct all trusts on matters of safety or ethics where a common policy will be pursued throughout the Health Service and, in exceptional circumstances, to direct an individual trust where there is justified cause for concern.
The Minister of State for the Department of Health, Mrs Virginia Bottomley, said (*Hansard*, H.C. Vol. 169, col. 573): "NHS trusts must follow our guidance regarding junior doctors' hours—they are not without the scheme and the guidance. . . . Paragraph 6(2)(e) of Schedule 2 gives the Secretary of State powers to direct NHS trusts to comply with the guidance".
It is of particular note that staff of NHS trusts will remain eligible for distinction awards administered by the advisory council in the same way as at present (Sched. 2(6)(f)). It is not clear how these will be funded except out of the ordinary revenue of the trust.

Subs. (9)
Para. 14 of Sched. 2 relates to making accommodation and services available at a charge; *cf.* ss.63 and 65 of the 1977 Act. The Minister of State, the Scottish Office, said (*Hansard*, H.L. Vol. 518, col. 751): "all National Health Service hospitals must conform to a detailed code of practice on the provision of [such services]. Similar . . . safeguards will apply to National Health Service trusts . . . the Secretary of State will be able to direct [them] on any aspects of their provision of pay and amenity beds if that appears necessary . . . under the [Act] the Secretary of State can direct trusts to comply with any guidance issued to health boards. We intend that National Health Service trusts should comply with the code of practice which I have already mentioned". Para. 15 of Sched. 2 makes reference to s.7(2) of the Health and Medicines Act 1988, which spells out powers for making more money available for improving the health service. Probably (although the matter is not free from doubt) the paragraph should be read subject to the provision in s.7(1) of that Act that the section does not authorise the disregard of "any enactment or rule of law" or the overriding of "any person's contractual or propriety rights".

Subs. (10)
No indication has been given of the use of the powers under this subsection.

Transfer of staff to NHS trusts

6.—(1) Subject to subsection (5) below, this section applies to any person who, immediately before an NHS trust's operational date—

(a) is employed by a health authority to work solely at, or for the purposes of, a hospital or other establishment or facility which is to become the responsibility of the trust; or

(b) is employed by a health authority to work at, or for the purposes of, such a hospital, establishment or facility and is designated for the purposes of this section by a scheme made by the health authority specified as mentioned in paragraph 3(1)(f) of Schedule 2 to this Act.

(2) A scheme under this section shall not have effect unless approved by the Secretary of State.

(3) Subject to section 7 below, the contract of employment between a person to whom this section applies and the health authority by whom he is employed shall have effect from the operational date as if originally made between him and the NHS trust.

(4) Without prejudice to subsection (3) above—

(a) all the health authority's rights, powers, duties and liabilities under or in connection with a contract to which that subsection applies shall by virtue of this section be transferred to the NHS trust on its operational date; and

(b) anything done before that date by or in relation to the health authority in respect of that contract or the employee shall be deemed from that date to have been done by or in relation to the NHS trust.

(5) In any case where—

(a) an order under section 5(1) above provides for the establishment of an NHS trust with effect from a date earlier than the operational date of the trust, and

(b) on or after that earlier date but before its operational date the NHS trust makes an offer of employment by the trust to a person who at that time is employed by a health authority to work (whether solely or otherwise) at, or for the purposes of, the hospital or other establishment or facility which is to become the responsibility of the trust, and

(c) as a result of the acceptance of the offer, the person to whom it was made becomes an employee of the NHS trust,

subsections (3) and (4) above shall have effect in relation to that person's contract of employment as if he were a person to whom this section applies and any reference in those subsections to the operational date of the trust were a reference to the date on which he takes up employment with the trust.

(6) Subsections (3) and (4) above are without prejudice to any right of an employee to terminate his contract of employment if a substantial change is made to his detriment in his working conditions; but no such right shall arise by reason only of the change in employer effected by this section.

(7) A scheme under this section may designate a person either individually or as a member of a class or description of employees.

DEFINITIONS
"health authority": s.128 of the National Health Service Act 1977.
"hospital": s.128 of the National Health Service Act 1977.
"NHS trust": ss.5 and 26 of this Act and 128 of the National Health Service Act 1977, as inserted by this Act.
"officer": s.128 of the National Health Service Act 1977.
"operational date": s.128 of the National Health Service Act 1977, as inserted by this Act.

GENERAL NOTE
This section should be read with s.7. The Minister of State for the Department of Health, Mrs Virginia Bottomley, explained (Comm. (SCE) col. 486): "Those employees who transfer

to an NHS trust will retain their existing contracts and all rights arising from them, subject to technical amendments and changes such as the substitution of the new employer and so on. It is for the trust to introduce changes in the existing contracts at any time after the transfer and to determine the pay and conditions of their staff. Consultants will be treated no differently from any other member of a professional team in an NHS trust". But (Comm. (SCE) cols. 466–7): "There will be uncertainty during the transition, but staff will not lose out by being transferred to NHS trust employment .... We intend that transfers should conform with good employment practices .... NHS trusts will be free to conduct their own industrial relations and to determine the machinery for doing so. That includes resolving questions relating to the recognition of staff organisations and trades unions. The power of NHS trusts to change terms and conditions of service, including staff pay, will be an important part of their greater freedom". Also, later (Comm. (SCE) cols. 480–1): "The NHS trusts will have to make such decisions for themselves, taking account of their circumstances, skill mixes and projections of manpower requirements, but they will be expected to honour any commitments that were made to individual members of staff before the transfer to trust employment about participating in training courses".

She added (Comm. (SCE) cols. 469–70): "The employees of NHS trusts will be free to remain in the NHS superannuation scheme or to join an alternative scheme offered by a trust. The trusts will contribute to the NHS superannuation scheme in the same way as health authorities ... the regulations will be amended to allow NHS trust staff to receive benefits under the [NHS injury scheme regulations] ... rights to maternity pay under the existing NHS terms will be protected on transfer ... Legislation and guidance on health and safety, ethical matters and good practice, and especially equal opportunities, will apply to NHS trusts ... NHS trusts will be obliged to follow guidance that applies to the NHS, including that on equal opportunities".

The Parliamentary Under-Secretary of State for the Department of Health, Baroness Hooper, argued (*Hansard*, H.L. Vol. 520, col. 171): "It is important to draw a distinction between statutory continuity of employment, which governs rights such as appeal to industrial tribunals, and recognition of service for purposes such as the calculation of leave entitlement. There is no statutory continuity of employment between health authorities, nor will there be between authorities and trusts. However, the recognition of NHS service is laid down in Whitley Council handbooks. If amendments to those agreements and handbooks are needed to recognise service with a trust when an employee moves back to a health authority, that will be a matter for negotiation in the Whitley forum".

Subs. (5)

The Parliamentary Under-Secretary of State for the Department of Health, Baroness Hooper, explained (*Hansard*, H.L. Vol. 520, col. 158): "a small number of key staff may need to transfer to trust employment earlier than that; that is, between a trust's establishment date and the operational date. Such staff will typically include the future chief officer of the trust and a few senior staff who are needed to carry out important preparatory work; for instance, negotiating National Health Service contracts and preparing for the transfer of staff and the ownership by the trust of its own assets ... [the subsection ensures] that such staff receive the same protection as all other National Health Service trust staff will enjoy on transfer".

Supplementary provisions as to transfer of staff

7.—(1) In the case of a person who falls within section 6(1)(b) above, a scheme under that section may provide that, with effect from the NHS trust's operational date, his contract of employment (in this section referred to as "his original contract") shall be treated in accordance with the scheme as divided so as to constitute—

(a) a contract of employment with the NHS trust; and

(b) a contract of employment with the health authority by whom he was employed before that date (in this section referred to as "the transferor authority").

(2) Where a scheme makes provision as mentioned in subsection (1) above,—

(a) the scheme shall secure that the benefits to the employee under the two contracts referred to in that subsection, when taken together, are not less favourable than the benefits under his original contract;

(b) section 6 above shall apply in relation to the contract referred to in subsection (1)(a) above as if it were a contract transferred under that section from the transferor authority to the NHS trust;

(c) so far as necessary to preserve any rights and obligations, the contract referred to in subsection (1)(b) above shall be regarded as a continuation of the employee's original contract; and

(d) for the purposes of section 146 of and Schedule 13 to the Employment Protection (Consolidation) Act 1978, the number of hours normally worked, or, as the case may be, the hours for which the employee is employed in any week under either of those contracts shall be taken to be the total of the hours normally worked or, as the case may be, for which he is employed under the two contracts taken together.

(3) Where, as a result of the provisions of section 6 above, by virtue of his employment during any period after the operational date of the NHS trust,—

(a) an employee has contractual rights against an NHS trust to benefits in the event of his redundancy, and

(b) he also has statutory rights against the trust under Part VI of the Employment Protection (Consolidation) Act 1978 (redundancy payments),

any benefits provided to him by virtue of the contractual rights referred to in paragraph (a) above shall be taken as satisfying his entitlement to benefits under the said Part VI.

DEFINITIONS
"health authority": s.128 of the National Health Service Act 1977.
"NHS trust": ss.5 and 26 of this Act and 128 of the National Health Service Act 1977, as inserted by this Act.
"operational date": s.128 of the National Health Service Act 1977, as inserted by this Act.
"original contract": subs. (1).
"transferor authority": subs. (1).

GENERAL NOTE

Subs. (1)
This subsection provides for the splitting of contracts of employees who work at two or more sites, one of which is transferred to an NHS trust.

Transfer of property, rights and liabilities to NHS trust

8.—(1) The Secretary of State may by order transfer or provide for the transfer to an NHS trust, with effect from such date as may be specified in the order, of such of the property, rights and liabilities of a health authority or of the Secretary of State as, in his opinion, need to be transferred to the trust for the purpose of enabling it to carry out its functions.

(2) An order under this section may create or impose such new rights or liabilities in respect of what is transferred or what is retained by a health authority or the Secretary of State as appear to him to be necessary or expedient.

(3) Nothing in this section affects the power of the Secretary of State or any power of a health authority to transfer property, rights or liabilities to an NHS trust otherwise than under subsection (1) above.

(4) Stamp duty shall not be chargeable in respect of any transfer to an NHS trust effected by or by virtue of an order under this section.

(5) Where an order under this section provides for the transfer—

(a) of land held on lease from a third party, that is to say, a person other than the Secretary of State or a health authority, or

(b) of any other asset leased or hired from a third party or in which a third party has an interest,

the transfer shall be binding on the third party notwithstanding that, apart from this subsection, it would have required his consent or concurrence.

(6) Any property, rights and liabilities which are to be transferred to an NHS trust shall be identified by agreement between the trust and a health authority or, in default of agreement, by direction of the Secretary of State.

(7) Where, for the purpose of a transfer pursuant to an order under this section, it becomes necessary to apportion any property, rights or liabilities, the order may contain such provisions as appear to the Secretary of State to be appropriate for the purpose; and where any such property or rights fall within subsection (5) above, the order shall contain such provisions as appear to the Secretary of State to be appropriate to safeguard the interests of third parties, including, where appropriate, provision for the payment of compensation of an amount to be determined in accordance with the order.

(8) In the case of any transfer made by or pursuant to an order under this section, a certificate issued by the Secretary of State that any property specified in the certificate or any such interest in or right over any such property as may be so specified, or any right or liability so specified, is vested in the NHS trust specified in the order shall be conclusive evidence of that fact for all purposes.

(9) Without prejudice to subsection (4) of section 126 of the principal Act, an order under this section may include provision for matters to be settled by arbitration by a person determined in accordance with the order.

DEFINITIONS
"health authority": s.128 of the National Health Service Act 1977.
"NHS trust": ss.5 and 26 of this Act and 128 of the National Health Service Act 1977, as inserted by this Act.
"officer": s.128 of the National Health Service Act 1977.
"principal Act": s.1.
"property": s.128 of the National Health Service Act 1977.

GENERAL NOTE

Subs. (8)
This subsection seeks to ensure that all property which the Secretary of State transfers is properly registered with the Land Registry on transfer.

Originating capital debt of, and other financial provisions relating to NHS trusts

9.—(1) Each NHS trust shall have an originating capital debt of an amount specified in an order made by the Secretary of State, being an amount representing, subject to subsection (2) below, the excess of the valuation of the assets which, on or in connection with the establishment of the trust, are or are to be transferred to it (whether before, on or after its operational date) over the amounts of the liabilities which are or are to be so transferred.

(2) In determining the originating capital debt of an NHS trust, there shall be left out of account such assets or, as the case may be, liabilities as are, or are of a class, determined for the purposes of this section by the Secretary of State, with the consent of the Treasury.

(3) An NHS trust's originating capital debt shall be deemed to have been issued out of moneys provided by Parliament and shall constitute an asset of the Consolidated Fund.

(4) In accordance with an order under subsection (1) above, an NHS trust's originating capital debt shall be divided between—
(a) a loan on which interest shall be paid at such variable or fixed rates and at such times as the Treasury may determine; and
(b) public dividend capital.

(5) The loan specified in subsection (4)(a) above is in this Part of this Act referred to as an NHS trust's "initial loan" and a rate of interest on the initial loan shall be determined as if section 5 of the National Loans Act 1968 had effect in respect of it and subsections (5) to (5B) of that section shall apply accordingly.

(6) Subject to subsections (4)(a) and (5) above, the terms of the initial loan shall be such as the Secretary of State, with the consent of the

Treasury, may determine; and, in the event of the early repayment of the initial loan, the terms may require the payment of a premium or allow a discount.

(7) With the consent of the Treasury, the Secretary of State may determine the terms on which any public dividend capital forming part of an NHS trust's originating capital debt is to be treated as having been issued, and, in particular, may determine the dividend which is to be payable at any time on any public dividend capital.

(8) An order under subsection (1) above shall be made—
(a) with the consent of the Treasury; and
(b) by statutory instrument.

(9) Schedule 3 to this Act shall have effect with respect to—
(a) borrowing by NHS trusts;
(b) the limits on their indebtedness;
(c) the payment of additional public dividend capital to them; and
(d) the application of any surplus funds of NHS trusts.

DEFINITIONS
"initial loan": subs. (5).
"NHS trust": ss.5 and 26 of this Act and 128 of the National Health Service Act 1977, as inserted by this Act and s.5 of this Act.
"operational date": s.128 of the National Health Service Act 1977, as inserted by this Act.
"originating capital debt": subs. (1).

GENERAL NOTE
The section should be read with s.10 (see also note to that section), s.64 and Sched. 3. The Notes on Clauses to s.5 anticipated that the order under this section will be the same as the establishing order under subs. (1) of that section; see note to that subsection.

The Parliamentary Under-Secretary of State for Health, Mr Roger Freeman, explained (Comm. (SCE) col. 489): "For directly-managed hospitals and other units that are not NHS trusts, we intend to introduce a capital charge regime. . . . [That] scheme . . . was spelt out clearly in the working paper. . . . With NHS trusts—especially hospitals—the provisions are different from those for directly-managed hospitals, but the net effect is the same. . . . The NHS trusts must appreciate their assets; they must also make a 6 per cent. real return on average assets in addition to the depreciation, which they keep. They may or may not distribute the 6 per cent. return through interest or public dividend capital. Directly-managed hospitals will pay a capital charge to the RHA—capital charge is a combination of depreciation and return—and the RHA will recirculate the capital charge to the districts which purchase services".

Subs. (1)
"Which, or in connection with the establishment of the trust". The Minister of State for the Scottish Office, Lord Sanderson of Bowden, explained (*Hansard*, H.L. Vol. 518, col. 762): "[These words make] it clear that the originating capital debt to a National Health Service trust takes account of the value of any assets transferred to the trust irrespective of whether the transfer takes place under an order under . . . [this section] . . . and irrespective of whether the transfer takes place before, on or after the operational date of the trust".

Subs. (2)
The Parliamentary Under-Secretary of State for Health, Mr Roger Freeman, explained (Comm. (SCE) col. 490): "I put on record that we do not intend that [gifted] assets [such as scanners] form part of the base on which we expect hospitals to make a return. They will, of course, have to be depreciated because hospitals will have to make provision for a replacement after the gift. I give . . . an absolute assurance that although such assets will be on the asset register, they will certainly not form part of the obligation to earn a return on either NHS trusts or, indeed directly-managed hospitals". The Baroness in Waiting, Baroness Blatch, added (*Hansard*, H.L. Vol. 520, col. 175): "the reserve power could be used . . . to exclude other assets or liabilities".

Subs. (9)
Despite the considerable independence of the activities of NHS trusts, the Schedule makes some inroads into their financial freedoms. Para. 7 is of particular note. Subject to the Secretary of State and the Treasury, it says: "An NHS trust may not invest any money held by it

except in securities of the Government of the United Kingdom". In health service jargon, the term *free moneys* is used to denote money not provided by the Treasury. This type of money is subject to the Charities Act 1960 and at least previously to the Trustee Investment Act 1961. It would appear that the terms of the paragraph are broad enough to place additional restraint on investment policy beyond the 1961 Act. So long as an investment remains as property and is not converted into cash, the paragraph does not apply. If money is held by trustees appointed under an order made under s.11, it may be that it is not "held by the trust" (see para. 11(3)) so that this para. 7 does not apply.

Financial obligations of NHS trusts

10.—(1) Every NHS trust shall ensure that its revenue is not less than sufficient, taking one financial year with another, to meet outgoings properly chargeable to revenue account.

(2) It shall be the duty of every NHS trust to achieve such financial objectives as may from time to time be set by the Secretary of State with the consent of the Treasury and as are applicable to it; and any such objectives may be made applicable to NHS trusts generally, or to a particular NHS trust or to NHS trusts of a particular description.

DEFINITION
"NHS trust": ss.5 and 26 of this Act and 128 of the National Health Service Act 1977, as inserted by this Act, and s.5 of this Act.

GENERAL NOTE
See also notes to ss.9 and 19. The Parliamentary Under-Secretary of State for Health, Mr Roger Freeman, said (Comm. (SCE) col. 1197–8): "NHS trusts would take over ... those liabilities that a hospital would incur in the ordinary course of its business for example, liabilities for the supply of equipment, drugs or hospital supplies ... NHS trusts will have an external financing limit set by the Government, and the limit for each year is their gross capital expenditure less the amount of cash that they have to pay for it. That cash is clearly the surplus before providing for depreciation, which is a non cash charge, but after payment of interest on public debt and any public dividend capital".

He explained (Comm. (SCE) col. 492): "The capitalisation of the NHS trust upon establishment will be split between interest bearing debt and public dividend capital. ... There will be an obligation upon the trusts to make a 6 per cent. return on the average assets, before any payment of interest and before any public dividend capital. That is 6 per cent. in real terms and equivalent to 6 per cent. on current values. ... Payment will be made to meet that return both for interest payments on the initial debt and dividend payments on the public dividend capital which may or may not be waived according to the financial needs and circumstances of the trusts. ... The obligation ... of taking one year with another to break even occurs after depreciation charges and interest payments but not the principal repayments on the debt, which is capital in nature, not interest. It is also after dividend payments on public dividend capital. That is an obligation. If there is a surplus above that, with agreement that surplus can be ploughed back into the further development of the hospital. ... The public gilt rate, the access to public sector borrowing, will almost invariably be cheaper and therefore financing for the development of trusts will come from the Treasury and not from the City. However, there may be instances for example, short term debt or where there is a particularly attractive source of capital at cheaper rates than the Government can borrow when trusts go to the City. For most borrowings that will have to be sanctioned, and there will be an external financing limit in aggregate and for each individual trust. The external financing limit will clearly be gross capital expenditure agreed less the depreciation flow and any surplus generated by the hospital".

He added (Comm. (SCE) col. 493): "[if the NHS trust does not make a 6 per cent. return, or if it makes a loss] clearly, the hospital will need to increase its charges and adjust its services of staffing levels. Like any other enterprise, it must break even. The hospital must ensure that the income entering the trust matches its expenditure". Presumably if it fails to "break even", it will be wound up under Sched. 2, paras. 29–32.

Trust funds and trustees for NHS trusts

11.—(1) The Secretary of State may by order made by statutory instrument provide for the appointment of trustees for an NHS trust; and any trustees so appointed shall have power to accept, hold and administer any property on trust for the general or any specific purposes of the NHS trust (including the purposes of any specific hospital or other establishment or facility which is owned and managed by the trust) or for all or any purposes relating to the health service.

(2) An order under subsection (1) above may—

(a) make provision as to the persons by whom trustees are to be appointed and generally as to the method of their appointment;

(b) make any appointment subject to such conditions as may be specified in the order (including conditions requiring the consent of the Secretary of State);

(c) make provision as to the number of trustees to be appointed, including provision under which that number may from time to time be determined by the Secretary of State after consultation with such persons as he considers appropriate; and

(d) make provision with respect to the term of office of any trustee and his removal from office.

(3) Where, under subsection (1) above, trustees have been appointed for an NHS trust, the Secretary of State may by order made by statutory instrument provide for the transfer of any trust property from the NHS trust to the trustees so appointed.

(4) In section 91 of the principal Act (private trusts for hospitals) in subsection (3) (definition of "the appropriate hospital authority") after paragraph (a) there shall be inserted the following paragraphs—

"(aa) where the hospital is owned and managed by an NHS trust and trustees have been appointed for the NHS trust, those trustees;

(ab) where the hospital is owned and managed by an NHS trust and neither paragraph (a) nor paragraph (aa) above applies, the NHS trust.";

(5) In section 92 of the principal Act (further transfers of trust property)—

(a) in subsection (1) after the word "hospital" there shall be inserted "or other establishment or facility" and for the words "or special trustees", in each place where they occur, there shall be substituted "NHS trust, special trustees or trustees for an NHS trust";

(b) in subsections (2) to (4), after the word "authorities", in each place where it occurs, there shall be inserted "or NHS trusts";

(c) in subsection (2) after the word "authority", there shall be inserted "or NHS trust"; and

(d) at the end of the section there shall be added the following subsection—

"(6) If it appears to the Secretary of State at any time that—

(a) the functions of any special trustees should be discharged by the trustees for an NHS trust, or

(b) the functions of the trustees for an NHS trust should be discharged by special trustees,

then, whether or not there has been any such change as is mentioned in subsection (1) above, he may, after consulting the special trustees and the trustees for the NHS trust, by order provide for the transfer of all trust property from or to the special trustees to or from the trustees for the NHS trust."

(6) In section 96 of the principal Act (trusts: supplementary provisions)—

(a) any reference to sections 90 to 95 of the principal Act includes a reference to subsections (1) to (3) above; and

(b) after subsection (1) there shall be inserted the following subsection—

"(1A) Where any transfer of property by virtue of those sections is of, or includes,—

(a) land held on lease from a third party, that is to say, a person other than the Secretary of State or a health authority, or

(b) any other asset leased or hired from a third party or in which a
      third party has an interest,
the transfer shall be binding on the third party notwithstanding that,
apart from this subsection, it would have required his consent or
concurrence."

(7) In section 98(1) of the principal Act (accounts and audit) after
paragraph (d) there shall be inserted—

   "(dd) any trustees for an NHS trust appointed in pursuance of
           section 11 of the National Health Service and Community
           Care Act 1990; and".

DEFINITIONS

"NHS trust": ss.5 and 26 of this Act and 128 of the National Health Service Act 1977, as
inserted by this Act, and s.5 of this Act.

"the health service": s.128 of the National Health Service Act 1977.

"hospital": s.128 of the National Health Service Act 1977.

"principal Act": s.1.

GENERAL NOTE

In this Act, an "NHS trust" is a term of art and not ordinarily a trust in its usual legal
meaning. In this section the word "trust" when used without the adjectival phrase, does take
that usual meaning, so also does "trustee".

This section enables the Secretary of State to appoint trustees to manage trust property held
by NHS trusts and to determine their number, method and conditions of appointment. It
empowers him to transfer trust property from NHS trusts to such trustees. It also extends ss.91
and 92 of the 1977 Act which relate to trust property and its management and his power to
transfer such property, to take account of NHS trusts.

Family Health Services Authorities

Functions of Family Health Services Authorities

12.—(1) In section 15 of the principal Act (duty of Family Health Services
Authority)—

   (a) in subsection (1), after the word "regulations" there shall be inserted
         "and subject to any directions from the relevant Regional Health
         Authority";

   (b) in paragraph (b) of that subsection, after the words "perform such"
         there shall be inserted "management and"; and

   (c) at the end of that subsection there shall be inserted the following
         subsections—

         "(1A) In relation to a Family Health Services Authority for a
         locality in England, any reference in this Act or the National Health
         Service and Community Care Act 1990 to the relevant Regional
         Health Authority is a reference to that Authority in whose region lies
         the whole or the greater part of the Authority's locality.

         (1B) In relation to a medical practitioner, any reference in this Act
         or the National Health Service and Community Care Act 1990 to the
         relevant Family Health Services Authority shall be construed as
         follows,—

            (a) if he practices in partnership with other medical practitioners,
                  the relevant Authority is that Authority on whose medical list
                  the members of the practice are included and, if some are
                  included on one Authority's medical list and some on anoth-
                  er's or if any of the members is included in the medical lists of
                  two or more Authorities, the relevant Authority is that
                  Authority in whose locality resides the largest number of
                  individuals who are on the lists of patients of the members of
                  the practice; and

            (b) in any other case, the relevant Authority is that Authority on whose medical list he is included and, if there is more than one, that one of them in whose locality resides the largest number of individuals who are on his list of patients."

(2) In section 17 of the principal Act (directions as to exercise of functions), in subsection (1) before the words "by a District Health Authority", there shall be inserted "(a)" and at the end of the subsection there shall be added "and

    (b) by a Family Health Services Authority in relation to which it is the relevant Regional Health Authority, of any functions exercisable by the Family Health Services Authority by virtue of section 15 above or the National Health Service and Community Care Act 1990."

(3) In section 42 of the principal Act (regulations as to pharmaceutical services), in subsection (3)—

    (a) in paragraph (d) for the words following "approved by" there shall be substituted "reference to prescribed criteria by the Family Health Services Authority in whose locality those premises are situated; and"; and

    (b) in paragraph (e) for the words "the prescribed body" there shall be substituted "that Family Health Services Authority".

(4) In section 44 of the principal Act (recognition by Secretary of State of certain local committees), in subsection (1)—

    (a) for the words from "the Secretary of State" to "is representative" there shall be substituted "a Family Health Services Authority is satisfied that a committee formed for its locality is representative"; and

    (b) for the word "he" there shall be substituted "the Family Health Services Authority";

and in subsection (2) of that section, for the words "Secretary of State's approval" there shall be substituted "approval of the Family Health Services Authority".

(5) Section 55 of the principal Act (reference of certain disputes affecting Family Practitioner Committees to the Secretary of State) shall cease to have effect.

DEFINITIONS

"District Health Authority": ss.8 and 128 of the National Health Service Act 1977, as amended by this Act, and Sched. 1 to this Act.

"Family Health Services Authority": s.10 of the National Health Service Act 1977 and Sched. 1 to this Act.

"medical list": s.29(2)(a) of the National Health Service Act 1977; see also the General Medical and Pharmaceutical Regulations S.I. 1974 No. 160, reg. 4.

"medical practitioner": s.15(1B) inserted by subs. (1) of this section; see also s.128 of the National Health Service Act 1977 and Medical Act 1983.

"pharmaceutical services": ss.41 and 128 of the National Health Service Act 1977.

"principal Act": s.1.

"Regional Health Authority": ss.8 and 128 of the National Health Service Act 1977, as amended by this Act, and Sched. 1 to this Act.

GENERAL NOTE

The Secretary of State, Mr Kenneth Clarke, explained the purposes of the section (Comm. (SCE) col. 166): "for the first time regional health authorities will be given overall responsibility for FHSAs. The FHSAs will be accountable to their regions in the way that district health authorities have been. That change has been broadly welcomed by most people because it stops an over sharp division developing between the hospital and community services, the family health services". The Notes on Clauses indicated that the functions of the Rural Dispensing Committee established by S.I. 1983 No. 312 (as amended) under the General Medical and Pharmaceutical Regulations S.I. 1974 No. 160 (as amended), regs. 26A and 30E–30G, will be transferred to the relevant RHA. More generally, the section reflects the enhanced management rôle of FHSAs for the family practitioner services in their area with the introduction of medical audit (by circular), indicative prescribing (see s.18) and GP fund holding (ss.14–15).

Financial duties in relation to Family Health Services Authorities

13.—(1) Section 97A of the principal Act (financial duties of health authorities) shall be amended in accordance with subsections (2) to (4) below.

(2) In subsection (1) for the words from "the expenditure attributable" to the end of the subsection there shall be substituted—

"(a) the expenditure attributable to the performance by the Regional Health Authority of its functions in that year, and

(b) the expenditure attributable to the performance by the District Health Authorities whose districts are in the region of their functions in that year, and

(c) the expenditure attributable to the performance by each Family Health Services Authority in relation to which the Regional Health Authority is the relevant Regional Health Authority of the Family Health Services Authority's functions in that year, other than expenditure falling within section 97(1)(aa) above,

does not exceed the aggregate of—

(i) the amounts allotted to the Regional Health Authority for that year under section 97(1)(a) above;

(ii) any other sums received under this Act, other than under section 97(1)(aa) above, in that year by the Regional Health Authority or by the District Health Authorities or Family Health Services Authorities concerned; and

(iii) any sums received otherwise than under this Act in that year by any of those Authorities for the purpose of enabling them to defray any such expenditure."

(3) In subsection (2)—

(a) for the words "Area Health Authority and every District Health Authority" there shall be substituted "District Health Authority and every Family Health Services Authority";

(b) in paragraph (a) of that subsection after the word "above" there shall be inserted "other than section 97(1)(aa)".

(4) In subsection (4) after the words "health authority" there shall be inserted "or Family Health Services Authority".

(5) In section 97B of the principal Act, in subsection (1)—

(a) for the words "Family Practitioner Committee" there shall be substituted "Family Health Services Authority whose locality is in Wales"; and

(b) at the end there shall be added the words "and any reference in subsections (2) and (4) below to a Family Health Services Authority is a reference to an Authority whose locality is in Wales".

DEFINITIONS

"District Health Authority": ss.8 and 128 of the National Health Service Act 1977, as amended by this Act, and Sched. 1 to this Act.

"Family Health Services Authority": s.10 of the National Health Service Act 1977 and Sched. 1 to this Act.

"functions": s.128 of the National Health Service Act 1977.

"health authority": s.128 of the National Health Service Act 1977.

"principal Act": s.1.

"Regional Health Authority": ss.8 and 128 of the National Health Service Act 1977, as amended by this Act, and Sched. 1 to this Act.

GENERAL NOTE

The section is consequent on s.12. See note to that section.

Fund-holding practices

Recognition of fund-holding practices of doctors

14.—(1) Any one or more medical practitioners who are providing general medical services in accordance with arrangements under section 29 of the principal Act may apply to the relevant Regional Health Authority for recognition as a fund-holding practice.

(2) The relevant Regional Health Authority shall not grant recognition as a fund-holding practice unless the medical practitioner or, as the case may be, each of the medical practitioners concerned fulfils such conditions as may be prescribed.

(3) Subject to subsection (4) below, in relation to a medical practitioner, any reference in this Part of this Act to the relevant Regional Health Authority is a reference to that Authority which, in relation to the practitioner's relevant Family Health Services Authority, is the relevant Regional Health Authority.

(4) Where two or more medical practitioners wish to make an application under subsection (1) above and, apart from this subsection, the relevant Family Health Services Authority in respect of one or more of them would be different from that in respect of the other or others, then, for the purposes of this section and any other provisions relating to fund-holding practices, the relevant Family Health Services Authority for each of them shall be determined as if they were all practising in a single partnership.

(5) In the application of this section to any medical practitioner whose relevant Family Health Services Authority has a locality in Wales, for any reference to the relevant Regional Health Authority there shall be substituted a reference to the Secretary of State.

(6) Regulations may make provision with respect to—

(a) the making of applications under subsection (1) above;

(b) the granting and refusal of recognition as a fund-holding practice;

(c) the conditions to be fulfilled for obtaining and continuing to be entitled to such recognition;

(d) appeals against any refusal of such recognition by a Regional Health Authority;

(e) withdrawing from, or becoming a member of, an existing recognised fund-holding practice;

(f) the continuity or otherwise of a recognised fund-holding practice in the event of the death or withdrawal of a member or the addition of a new member; and

(g) the operation of this section in a case where one or more of the medical practitioners wishing to make an application under subsection (1) above is also on the medical list of a health board;

and regulations making the provision referred to in paragraph (g) above may make such modifications of the preceding provisions of this section as the Secretary of State considers appropriate.

DEFINITIONS

"Family Health Services Authority": s.15 of the National Health Service Act 1977, as amended by s.13 of this Act.

"fund holding practice": subs. (1).

"general medical services": s.29 of the National Health Service Act 1977.

"health board": National Health Service (Scotland) Act 1978.

"medical practitioner": s.128 of the National Health Service Act 1977 and Medical Act 1983.

"principal Act": s.1.

"Regional Health Authority": ss.8 and 128 of the National Health Service Act 1977, as amended by this Act, and Sched. 1 to this Act.

"regulations": ss.126 and 128 of the National Health Service Act 1977, as amended by this Act.

"relevant Family Health Services Authority": s.15 of the National Health Service Act 1977, as amended by s.13 of this Act.

"relevant Regional Health Authority": s.15 of the National Health Service Act 1977, as amended by s.13 of this Act.

GENERAL NOTE

This section should be read with ss.15–17 (and notes thereto). It is to be noted that s.18 (indicative prescribing amounts) does not apply to practice fund holders (see note to that section). The accounts of practice budgets will be audited by the Audit Commission for Local Authorities and the National Health Service as part of its audit of FHSA and RHA accounts; see s.20 and Sched. 4, para. 2 (inserting new sections into the Local Government Finance Act 1982).

It is important to note that the status of a fund-holding practice is supplemental to the status as a general practitioner within the health service, so that the Terms of Service contained in Sched. 1 to the General Medical and Pharmaceutical Regulations S.I. 1974 No. 160 (as amended) continue to apply. In particular, all practices will have to produce annual reports. The Secretary of State for Health, Mr Kenneth Clarke, justified the possible new status (*Hansard*, H.C. Vol. 163, col. 513): "The proposals for fund holding general practitioners will give those who choose to develop it the opportunity to provide the patients in their practices with high quality care. It will give GPs much greater control over the resources they deploy in any event in their referral patterns and much more influence than they have ever had over the development of the local services used by their patients". The Parliamentary Under-Secretary of State for the Department of Health, Baroness Hooper, added (*Hansard*, H.L. Vol. 518, col. 832): "this is a voluntary scheme and any doctor or practice which becomes involved in it has the right to withdraw from it if it should so wish. The relevant provisions are contained in section 16".

The Parliamentary Under-Secretary of State for Health, Mr Roger Freeman, said (Comm. (SCE) col. 583): "Regulations will be made under [sections 14 and 15] to specify the precise categories of valid expenditure by fund holders and also how surpluses may be spent. . . . the regulations will outline in great detail, without trying to be inflexible, the correct way in which fund holders may proceed". The Notes on Clauses to s.15 said that regulations will make provision for the procedures to be followed by practices in applying to become fund holders and by RHAs in considering these applications. The criteria for acceptance will be defined. These, the Notes said, "are likely to include the size of the practice, their ability to manage the fund (as assessed by the RHA), adequate computer support and the commitment of all the practitioners involved. Practices with 11,000 or more patients will be eligible, and those with between 9,000 and 11,000 . . . will be considered on an individual basis". The obligations of practice fund holders will be determined in regulations: these "might include requirements to submit reports and accounts to the FHSA at regular intervals and not to accept "topping up" money from patients who want to be treated in private hospitals" (Notes on Clauses). Regulations will also make provision for appeals to the Secretary of State in England (but obviously not in Wales where there is no regional authority from which to appeal) and for GPs joining or leaving a fund holding practice: "the size of the fund may need to be adjusted or fund holding status removed or renounced".

The Parliamentary Under-Secretary of State for the Department of Health, Baroness Hooper, explained (*Hansard*, H.L. Vol. 520, col. 204): "the regulations . . . will be supplemented as necessary by detailed guidance . . . On recognition, our intention is that a practice must demonstrate that all the partners wish to join the scheme, that it has the ability to manage a practice fund and that it possesses an adequate computer support system. That system will enable GPs to manage their funds by keeping track of activity and expenditure. The hospital element of the fund will be set primarily on the basis of past usage of hospital services. Working with regional health authorities and family health services authorities, practices will need to provide details of past referral and treatment patterns in order for the budget to be set and contracts to be made with hospitals". Later she added, referring to Pt. VIII of the General Medical and Pharmaceutical Regulations S.I. 1974 No. 160 (*Hansard*, H.L. Vol. 518, col. 833): "If fund holders are at present dispensing doctors, they will continue to be dispensing doctors, but there are no plans to allow all fund holders to dispense".

The Parliamentary Under-Secretary of State for Health, Scottish Office, Mr Michael Forsyth, added (*Hansard*, H.C. Vol. 169, col. 686): "[the position for] a fund holder who had exceeded his budget would be that he [would] no longer be a fund holder. He would then revert to the status quo. . . . a GP's budget will be determined by his past expenditure and the profile of his patients [under the provisions for indicative amounts in section 18]. If a GP exceeds his budget, patient care will not in any way be threatened or diminished".

Subs. (6)(c)

The Parliamentary Under-Secretary of State for the Department of Social Security, Lord Henley, undertook that (*Hansard*, H.L. Vol. 518, col. 844): "Regulations . . . will make it a requirement that to continue to receive recognition as a fund holding practice, a practice should not allow 'topping up' of its fund in money or in kind".

Subs. (6)(d)
The reference to the RHA is to the Secretary of State in Wales, subs. (5).

Subs. (6)(e)
See s.16.

Subs. (6)(f)
Probably, although the point is not free from doubt, the paragraph enables regulations to be made to cover the erasure, suspension, or conditional registration of a practitioner by the G.M.C.

Subs. (6)(g)
"Health board". This refers to Scottish health authorities.

Payments to recognised fund-holding practices

15.—(1) In respect of each financial year, every Regional Health Authority shall be liable to pay to the members of each recognised fund-holding practice in relation to which it is the relevant Regional Health Authority a sum determined in such manner and by reference to such factors as the Secretary of State may direct (in this section referred to as an "allotted sum").

(2) In respect of each financial year, the Secretary of State shall be liable to pay to the members of each recognised fund-holding practice whose relevant Family Health Services Authority has a locality in Wales a sum determined in such manner and by reference to such factors as the Secretary of State may direct (in this section referred to as an "allotted sum").

(3) The liability to pay an allotted sum under subsection (1) or subsection (2) above may be discharged, in whole or in part, in either of the following ways—
   (a) by making payments on account of the allotted sum at such times and in such manner as the Secretary of State may direct; and
   (b) by discharging liabilities of the members of the practice to any other person (including, in particular, liabilities under NHS contracts);
and any reference in the following provisions of this Part of this Act to payment of or of a part of an allotted sum includes a reference to the discharge, in accordance with this subsection, of the whole or part of the liability to pay that sum.

(4) In any case where—
   (a) a Regional Health Authority makes a payment of or of any part of an allotted sum to the members of a recognised fund-holding practice, and
   (b) some of the individuals on the list of patients of any of the members of the practice reside in the region of another Regional Health Authority, or in Wales, or in the area of a Health Board,
the Authority making the payment shall be entitled to recover from that other Authority or, as the case may be, from the Secretary of State or that Health Board an amount equal to such portion of the payment as may be determined in accordance with directions given by the Secretary of State.

(5) In any case where—
   (a) the Secretary of State makes a payment of or of any part of an allotted sum to the members of a recognised fund-holding practice, and
   (b) some of the individuals on the list of patients of any of the members of the practice reside in the region of a Regional Health Authority,
the Secretary of State shall be entitled to recover from that Authority an amount equal to such portion of the payment as may be determined in accordance with directions given by the Secretary of State.

(6) The members of a recognised fund-holding practice may apply an allotted sum only for purposes specified in regulations under subsection (7) below.

(7) Regulations shall make provision with respect to the purposes for which allotted sums are to be or may be applied and may make provision generally with respect to the operation of recognised fund-holding practices in relation to allotted sums; and the regulations may, in particular,—

(a) require the members of a practice to pay to the relevant Regional Health Authority out of allotted sums paid to them an amount determined in accordance with the regulations as the basic cost of the drugs, medicines and listed appliances supplied pursuant to orders given by or on behalf of members of the practice;

(b) provide that the goods and services, other than general medical services, which may be purchased by or on behalf of the members of a practice out of allotted sums for the individuals on the lists of patients of the members of the practice shall be such as may be specified in a list approved for the purpose under the regulations; and

(c) impose a limit on the amount which may be spent out of an allotted sum on the provision of goods and services for any one individual, being a limit above which the cost of any goods and services for that individual in the financial year in question will fall to be met by the District Health Authority whose primary functions include the provision of goods and services (not necessarily the goods and services in question) to the individual concerned.

(8) In the application of subsection (7) above to the members of a practice whose relevant Family Health Services Authority has a locality in Wales, for the reference in paragraph (a) of that subsection to the relevant Regional Health Authority there shall be substituted a reference to the Secretary of State.

(9) In accordance with directions under section 17 of the principal Act, the relevant Family Health Services Authority shall monitor the expenditure of the members of a recognised fund-holding practice and may institute an audit and review in any case where the Authority consider it necessary to do so.

DEFINITIONS

"allotted sum": subss. (1), (2) and (3).

"District Health Authority": ss.8 and 128 of the National Health Service Act 1977, as amended by this Act, and Sched. 1 to this Act.

"general medical services": s.29 of the National Health Service Act 1977.

"goods": s.26.

"health board": National Health Service (Scotland) Act 1978.

"NHS contract": ss.3 and 26 of this Act and 128 of the National Health Service Act 1977, as inserted by this Act.

"primary functions": s.128 of the National Health Service Act 1977, as inserted by this Act, and s.3 of this Act.

"recognised fund holding practice": s.14.

"Regional Health Authority": ss.8 and 128 of the National Health Service Act 1977, as amended by this Act, and Sched. 1 to this Act.

"regulations": ss.126 and 128 of the National Health Service Act 1977, as amended by this Act.

"relevant Family Health Services Authority": s.15 of the National Health Service Act 1977, as amended by s.13 of this Act.

"services": s.26.

GENERAL NOTE

It may be useful to recite the explanations given by ministers concerning the way in which funds will be set: the Parliamentary Under-Secretary of State for the Department of Social Security, Lord Henley, said (*Hansard*, H.L. Vol. 518, col. 837): "the Secretary of State . . . will issue directions to the regional health authority on what factors need to be taken into account . . . by the regional health authorities or health boards when setting the fund". Later he said

(*Hansard*, H.L. Vol. 520, col. 206): "Practice funds will be set on an individual basis . . . after detailed discussions with each practice interested in participating in the scheme. Obviously a wide range of factors will be taken into account by the regional health authorities. Previous hospital treatment and prescribing patterns will be examined. Account will be taken of such matters as the age and sex composition of a practice's list, the number of chronically sick and disabled people and other potentially high cost patients that it may have. The Secretary of State will issue directions on the factors which need to be taken into account by the RHA when setting the fund".

The Parliamentary Under-Secretary of State for the Department of Health, Baroness Hooper, put it as follows (*Hansard*, H.L. Vol. 518, col. 824): "In setting the level of the fund, regions and health boards will take account of a wide range of factors. They will need to examine the previous hospital treatment and prescribing patterns of the practice and take account of the nature of the practice list. This will include such things as the age and sex composition of the list, the number of chronically sick and disabled people and other potentially high cost patients. If during the year a practice considers that the fund is likely to be insufficient because of, for example, an influx of new patients to the practice or an increase in patients requiring expensive drugs it will be able to discuss this with the FHSA and if necessary the fund can be increased. Regional health authorities and health boards will be required to hold adequate reserves to deal with this possibility . . . *Working for Patients* and [elsewhere] we said that overspends of up to five per cent. would be recouped in the following year. This will not now happen . . . the Government will make provision in directions given by the Secretary of State for the regional health authority and the health board to meet that overspend".

The Minister of State for the Department of Health, Mrs Virginia Bottomley, said (Comm. (SCE) col. 545): "If there were an influx on to the list of patients who required very costly drugs or special treatments, it would be open to the fund holders to discuss the matter with the family health service authority, and if necessary the budget could be increased". See also subs. (7)(c). Later she added (Comm. (SCE) col. 565): "Consideration will be given to patients with chronic complaints, and the DHA will bear the cost of hospital treatment, if it is more than 5,000".

As regards overspends, the Parliamentary Under-Secretary of State for Health, Mr Roger Freeman, explained (Comm. (SCE) col. 583): "Let us consider an overspend that is identified only after the year has ended and when there is no suggestion that patient services will be halted during the year because of a prospective overspend. An overspend can fall into one of two categories. If the overspend is valid, for example, if the RHA, on the advice of the FHSA, genuinely did not allocate enough to the budget it will be rolled on. It will be consolidated into a higher base for the next year. As for an overspend that is not valid, the budget holder will start in year two with the original base, as adjusted for other appropriate reasons because the demography or patient list may have changed. There is no suggestion that the money will be recovered from the fund holder. If there were persistent overspending, the sanction . . . would be to withdraw the fund".

The Parliamentary Under-Secretary of State for the Department of Health, Baroness Hooper, said (*Hansard*, H.L. Vol. 518, col. 842): "We shall expect RHAs to maintain contingency funds to enable additional payments to be made to fund holding practices if the fund needs to be increased in year. [This section] and its associated directions will allow for these funds to be held back and for their subsequent allocation".

As regards savings, the Parliamentary Under-Secretary of State for Health, Mr Roger Freeman, said (Off. Rep. St.Cm. E Col. 581–2): "although in practice staff reimbursement and improvements are cash limited at the FHSA level, expenditure on drugs is not cash limited . . . There will be no interruption in the flow of medical services by a fund in the course of a year. If a GP fund holding practice needs to prescribe drugs and to provide medical services, it will be able to do so, and we will look at the overspend after the end of the year. If the increase that is agreed at the beginning of the year is legitimate, it will be rolled into a higher base for the next year. . . . we shall . . . be drafting regulations to allow for the moneys that result from underspending to be kept by a fund holder and the items that the underspend may be used for. . . . Our regulations will specify precisely what the money can be spent on. . . . It is true that of the categories of expenditure appropriate for GP fund holders which we shall specify in regulations and further directives by the Secretary of State virement is possible. That means that practices can move expenditure from head to head between staff, improvements, drug prescribing, hospital services, diagnosis and so on".

The Parliamentary Under-Secretary of State for the Department of Social Security, Lord Henley, explained (*Hansard*, H.L. Vol. 518, col. 827): "Savings can only be spent after a practice's accounts have been completed and audited, and then only on specified purposes. Practices will be able to use savings for any of the purposes of the fund; that is, hospital services and prescribing costs and practice staff. In addition they will be able to spend savings in improvements to the practice which will benefit patients. These might include buying diagnostic equipment, funding health education campaigns and providing more and better facilities for

patients. Savings cannot be used for the direct personal benefit of the members of the practice
... RHAs will have overall responsibility for the scheme, but FHSAs will be given the
responsibility of monitoring fund holding practices. Practices will be required to submit
monthly and annual reports to the FHSA which will give details of how the fund is being used.
The FHSA will be in a position to recognise if practices are unnecessarily overspending or
indeed underspending. If there is any cause for concern, the practice will be required to take
remedial action".

Subs. (6)

The Minister of State for the Department of Health, Mrs Virginia Bottomley, said (Comm.
(SCE) col. 566): "We are aware of the potential danger of abuses in spending practice funds.
That is why [subs. (6) allows] any sums illegitimately spent on cars or foreign holidays, for
example, to be recovered from general practitioners rather than from the practice fund".

Subs. (7)

As regards expenditure not authorised by regulations under this subsection, see s.16(6)(7)
and notes thereto.

Subs. (7)(b)

The Baroness in Waiting, Baroness Blatch, explained (*Hansard*, H.L. Vol. 518, col. 849):
"GPs in a fund holding practice will be able to purchase for their patients certain hospital
inpatient and day care treatment as well as a majority of outpatient services and diagnostic
tests. The cost of prescriptions will also be met from the fund. The services covered by this
scheme will be specified in a list in regulations under [this paragraph]. The list will also
incorporate those treatments for which GPs can directly refer their patients rather than go
through a consultant. The direct access services at the start of the scheme will be physioth-
erapy, occupational therapy and speech therapy. The range of treatments covered by the
scheme can be reviewed in the light of experience".

The Parliamentary Under-Secretary of State for the Department of Health, Baroness
Hooper, added (*Hansard*, H.L. Vol. 520, col. 217): "It is not our intention to allow fund
holding GPs access to treatments for their patients which are not available to the patients of
non fund holding GPs ... Nevertheless, if ... the Secretary of State, under the powers given to
him in Section 3 of the [1977 Act] should decide to have specified complementary therapies
provided under the National Health Service, then the matter can of course be reconsidered.
This may prove necessary as a result of the [draft European Community directive on
homoeopathic medicine] ... The other issue of difficulty is that of clinical responsibility. ...
any GP is entitled to provide natural therapies for his patients either himself or through a
member of his practice staff. Under the new doctors' contract it will be open to FHSAs to
contribute to the costs of such a member of staff. In this case the GP himself remains clinically
responsible for his patients' treatment".

Renunciation and removal of recognition as a fund-holding practice and withholding of funds

16.—(1) Regulations may make provision as to the circumstances in
which the members of a recognised fund-holding practice may renounce
that status and such regulations may, in particular, make provision as to—
  (a) the notice to be given and the number of members of the practice by
     whom it is to be given;
  (b) the procedure to be followed; and
  (c) the consequences of such a renunciation.

(2) Regulations may make provision as to the circumstances in which and
the grounds on which the relevant Regional Health Authority or, as the case
may be, the Secretary of State may remove recognition from the members
of a fund-holding practice,—
  (a) with immediate effect; or
  (b) with effect from the end of a particular financial year; or
  (c) with effect from such other date as may be specified by the Regional
     Health Authority or, as the case may be, the Secretary of State.

(3) Where provision is made as mentioned in subsection (2) above,
regulations shall make provision with respect to—
  (a) the procedure for the removal of recognition;
  (b) appeals against the removal of recognition by a Regional Health
     Authority; and

(c) the consequences of the removal of recognition.

(4) Without prejudice to the generality of the powers conferred by subsection (3) above, regulations making provision as mentioned in paragraph (c) of that subsection—

  (a) may provide for the transfer of rights and obligations from the members of the fund-holding practice to one or more District Health Authorities determined in accordance with the regulations;
  (b) may provide for the recovery of sums from the members of the practice; and
  (c) may require the members of the practice to furnish such information as may reasonably be required by the Regional Health Authority or, as the case may be, the Secretary of State.

(5) The bringing of an appeal against the removal of recognition by a Regional Health Authority shall not be regarded as preserving the recognised status of the members of the fund-holding practice and, accordingly, subject to the outcome of the appeal, the relevant Regional Health Authority shall not be required, after the removal takes effect, to make any (or, as the case may be, any further) payment to the members of the practice of any part of the allotted sum for the financial year in question or, as the case may be, to determine and pay any allotted sum for a future financial year.

(6) Where any part of an allotted sum has been applied by the members of a recognised fund-holding practice (or any one or more of them) for purposes other than those specified in regulations under section 15(7) above, regulations may make provision for and in connection with the recovery by the relevant Regional Health Authority or, as the case may be, the Secretary of State of an amount equal to that part.

(7) Where provision is made as mentioned in subsection (6) above, regulations shall make provision with respect to appeals against the recovery of any amount by a Regional Health Authority.

DEFINITIONS
"allotted sum": s.15(1) of this Act.
"District Health Authority": ss.8 and 128 of the National Health Service Act 1977, as amended by this Act, and Sched. 1 to this Act.
"recognised fund holding practice": s.14.
"Regional Health Authority": ss.8 and 128 of the National Health Service Act 1977, as amended by this Act, and Sched. 1 to this Act.
"regulations": ss.126 and 128 of the National Health Service Act 1977, as amended by this Act.
"relevant Regional Health Authority": s.15 of the National Health Service Act 1977, as amended by s.13 of this Act.

GENERAL NOTE
"In normal circumstances, the practice would be expected to complete the year to which it was committed. Regulations will provide for exceptional circumstances under which a practice could close" (Minister of State for the Department of Health, Mrs Virginia Bottomley (Comm. (SCE) col. 545)).

Subs. (2)
The Notes on Clauses said that the grounds to be specified in the regulations "will vary slightly depending on the amount of time before withdrawal. Such grounds might include situations where it appeared that patient care was being adversely affected or where a practice had broken up".

Subs. (5)
This subsection makes provision for what is to happen to recognition during the currency of an appeal. Although the matter is not without doubt, it would appear that it does not preclude the court in a proper case from making a prohibitory order against the RHA preventing it from removing the recognised status.

Subs. (6)
The Notes on Clauses said: "It is intended that regulations . . . should deal with cases where

practice funds have been misspent. It would be restricted to cases where the misappropriation of the fund or of savings was clear".

Transfer of functions relating to recognised fund-holding practices

17.—(1) If the Secretary of State by regulations so provides, such of the functions of a Regional Health Authority or, in Wales, the Secretary of State under sections 14 to 16 above as are specified in, or determined in accordance with, the regulations shall become functions of a Family Health Services Authority with effect from such date as may be prescribed.

(2) Regulations under this section shall make provision for determining the Family Health Services Authority which is to exercise any of the functions concerned in relation to the members of any existing recognised fund-holding practice and in relation to any medical practitioners wishing to apply for recognition.

(3) Without prejudice to the generality of section 126(4) of the principal Act, regulations under this section may make such incidental and consequential modifications of the principal Act and of sections 14 to 16 above as appear to the Secretary of State to be necessary or expedient in consequence of the transfer of functions effected by the regulations.

DEFINITIONS
"Family Health Services Authority": s.10 of the National Health Service Act 1977 and Sched. 1 to this Act.
"functions": s.128 of the National Health Service Act 1977.
"medical practitioner": s.128 of the National Health Service Act 1977 and Medical Act 1983.
"modifications": s.128 of the National Health Service Act 1977.
"principal Act": s.1 of this Act.
"recognised fund holding practice": s.14.
"Regional Health Authority": ss.8 and 128 of the National Health Service Act 1977, as amended by this Act, and Sched. 1 to this Act.
"regulations": ss.126 and 128 of the National Health Service Act 1977, as amended by this Act.

Indicative amounts

Indicative amounts for doctors' practices

18.—(1) Subject to subsection (2) below, for each financial year, every Family Health Services Authority shall, by notice in writing given to each practice in relation to the members of which it is the relevant Family Health Services Authority, specify an amount of money (in this Act referred to as an "indicative amount") representing the basic price of the drugs, medicines and listed appliances which, in the opinion of the Authority, it is reasonable to expect will be supplied in that year pursuant to orders given by or on behalf of the members of that practice.

(2) Subsection (1) above does not apply with respect to a practice which is or forms part of a fund-holding practice recognised under section 14 above.

(3) For the purposes of this section, a "practice" means—
(a) a single medical practitioner who practises otherwise than in partnership; or
(b) any two or more medical practitioners who practise in partnership; and any reference to the members of a practice shall be construed accordingly.

(4) The members of a practice shall seek to secure that, except with the consent of the relevant Family Health Services Authority or for good cause, the orders for drugs, medicines and listed appliances given by them or on their behalf are such that the basic price of the items supplied pursuant to those orders in any financial year does not exceed the indicative amount notified to the practice for that year under subsection (1) above.

(5) For the purpose of measuring the extent to which a practice is operating within the indicative amount notified to it under subsection (1)

above for any financial year, a Family Health Services Authority shall set against that indicative amount an amount equal to the basic price of the drugs, medicines and listed appliances supplied in that year pursuant to orders given by or on behalf of members of the practice.

(6) For the purposes of this section, regulations may make provision as to the specification of, or means of calculating, the basic price of any drugs, medicines or listed appliances.

(7) If, in the case of any practice, a member is on the medical list of a Health Board constituted under section 2 of the National Health Service (Scotland) Act 1978 (as well as on that of a Family Health Services Authority), any question whether this section applies in relation to the members of the practice shall be determined in accordance with regulations made by the Secretary of State; and any such regulations may modify the preceding provisions of this section in their application to such a practice.

DEFINITIONS
"basic price": subs. (6).
"Family Health Services Authority": s.10 of the National Health Service Act 1977 and Sched. 1 to this Act.
"fund holding practice": s.14.
"listed appliance": s.41 of the National Health Service Act 1977.
"medical list": National Health Service (Scotland) Act 1978.
"medicine": ss.41 and 128 of the National Health Service Act 1977.
"indicative amount": subs. (1).
"practice": subs. (3).
"regulations": ss.126 and 128 of the National Health Service Act 1977, as amended by this Act.
"relevant Family Health Services Authority": s.15 of the National Health Service Act 1977, as amended by s.13 of this Act.

GENERAL NOTE
At a very late stage in the Bill's passage the Government accepted amendments to change what were called, in all the earlier documentation, "indicative drug budgets" to "indicative drug amounts". In the notes that follow that change has been made to the quotations.

The Minister of State for the Department of Health, Mrs Virginia Bottomley, said (Comm. (SCE) col. 641): "The indicative drug [amount] is a management tool and a way of monitoring precisely what is happening". As the Secretary of State for Health, Mr Kenneth Clarke, said (Comm. (SCE) col. 659): "Nothing in [the section] will affect the availability under the NHS of drugs or appliances of any kind": that continues to be governed by the Terms of Service whereby a GP is required to prescribe any drug or appliance that is needed for a patient. As the Parliamentary Under-Secretary of State for Wales, Mr Ian Grist, remarked (*Hansard*, H.C. Vol. 163, col. 575): "Indicative [amounts] are not cash limited and the [Act] exactly replicates existing provision about cash limiting expenditure in the family practitioner services". See also subs. (4) and note thereto.

The Parliamentary Under-Secretary of State for Health, Mr Roger Freeman, explained the difference between the way in which charging is proposed for indicative amounts and for GP fund holders (Comm. (SCE) col. 585): "What will be charged to the indicative [amount] is what we call the basic price. That is spelt out in ... *Funding General Practice: Working for Patients*. ... The basic price of a drug—it will be essentially a tariff, and I use the word advisedly—will exclude the cost of the container and the negotiated discounts that the pharmacist and the dispensing GP may negotiate. It is a basic price, standard throughout the country and it relates to the drug itself. When the indicative [amounts] are fixed by the family health services authorities they will take into account the prescribing needs of the patients on a doctor's list. The system for the GP fund holders is a different concept, namely, the true cost to the NHS. To the basic price—the tariff for the various drugs that doctors will prescribe and some will dispense—will be added the cost of the container, because fund holders will need to take it into account. The average discount that prevails throughout England will be subtracted. We can calculate the average discount because that discount, negotiated by the pharmacist, is passed on to the NHS and to the taxpayer. That represents the actual cost of dispensing the drug to the patient".

The Minister of State for the Department of Health, Mrs Virginia Bottomley, undertook (Comm. (SCE) col. 565): "No VAT will be charged on GP practice funds, nor will they have to charge it. Similarly, tax on savings made by a practice will not be regarded as taxable income.

The proceeds from those savings are to be used for patient care, not for the personal remuneration of any who are working in the practice. . .. when resources have been ploughed into the premises for patients' benefit, a liability for capital gains tax may arise when the premises are to be sold. We are seeking guidance from the Inland Revenue on that subject".

Subs. (1)
   The Minister of State for the Department of Health, Mrs Virginia Bottomley, said (Comm. (SCE) col. 641): "We hope that the family health services authorities will all have their own independent adviser working with local family practitioners, improving standards and ensuring that the practice is running well and that prescribing is appropriate". She added (Comm. (SCE) col. 652): "I can give . . . a clear assurance that there will be consultation with the local family health services authority about the way in which the size of the budget may move in future. The issues to be debated are the characteristics and demography of the practice, whether it has a GP with an interest in a particular speciality, whether a home may be opening up nearby with residents who have particular needs, and the arrival on the list of patients who need particularly costly drugs".

Subs. (4)
   The Parliamentary Under-Secretary of State for Health, Mr Roger Freeman, explained (Comm. (SCE) col. 634): "The only four elements of a GP's funds that are cash limited cover about 7 per cent. of family practitioner services expenditure. These are practice staff from 1 April 1990, expenditure on the cost rent scheme and the improvement grant scheme, the computer expenses and the management allowance to fund holders".

Subs. (6)
   The Notes on Clauses said: "The regulations will specify what is meant by the basic price of the item dispensed with reference to the rules outlined in the Drug Tariff and those for dispensing doctors contained in the Statement of Fees and Allowances". They will come into force on April 1, 1990.

Funding, audit and liabilities

Amendments relating to funding of health authorities etc.

19.—(1) Section 97 of the principal Act (means of meeting expenditure of health authorities out of public funds) shall be amended in accordance with this section.
   (2) In subsection (1) (payments to health authorities etc. by the Secretary of State)—
   (a) at the end of paragraph (a) there shall be added "including, in the case of a Regional Health Authority, its functions with respect to such expenditure of Family Health Services Authorities in relation to which it is the relevant Regional Health Authority as—
        (i) is attributable to the reimbursement of expenses of persons providing services in pursuance of Part II of this Act and is of a description specified in the allotment, and
        (ii) is attributable to the performance by the Family Health Services Authority of their functions in that year,";
   (b) after paragraph (a) there shall be inserted the following paragraph—
      "(aa) to each Regional Health Authority sums equal to any such expenditure of Family Health Services Authorities in relation to which it is the relevant Regional Health Authority as is attributable to the remuneration of persons providing services in pursuance of Part II of this Act and is not of a description specified as mentioned in paragraph (a) above"; and
   (c) in paragraph (b) for the words "Family Practitioner Committee" there shall be inserted "Family Health Services Authority whose locality is in Wales".
   (3) In subsection (2) (payments by Regional Health Authorities) for the words following "each financial year" there shall be substituted—
        "(a) to each District Health Authority whose district is included in the region sums not exceeding the amount allotted by the

Regional Health Authority to the District Health Authority for that year towards meeting the expenditure attributable to the performance by the District Health Authority of their functions in that year; and

(b) to each Family Health Services Authority in relation to which it is the relevant Regional Health Authority—

    (i) sums equal to the expenditure referred to in subsection (1)(aa) above; and

    (ii) sums not exceeding the amount allotted by the Regional Health Authority to the Family Health Services Authority for that year towards meeting other expenditure attributable to the reimbursement of expenses of persons providing services in pursuance of Part II of this Act and to the performance by the Family Health Services Authority of their functions in that year."

(4) In subsection (3) (directions of Secretary of State)—

(a) after the word "directions" there shall be inserted "(a),";

(b) after the word "Regional" there shall be inserted "or Special" and for the words "Practitioner Committee" there shall be substituted "Health Services Authority whose locality is in Wales"; and

(c) at the end of the subsection there shall be added "and

    (b) to a District Health Authority in England with respect to the payment of sums by them to the Regional Health Authority in respect of charges or other sums referable to the valuation or disposal of assets; and

    (c) to a Regional Health Authority with respect to the application of sums received by them by virtue of paragraph (b) above or by virtue of section 15(7)(a) of the National Health Service and Community Care Act 1990."

(5) In subsection (4) (directions of Regional Health Authorities) for the words from "an Area Health Authority" onwards there shall be substituted "a District Health Authority whose district is included in the region or a Family Health Services Authority in relation to which it is the relevant Regional Health Authority with respect to the application of any sum paid out of those sums to the District Health Authority or the Family Health Services Authority under subsection (2) above."

DEFINITIONS

"District Health Authority": ss.8 and 128 of the National Health Service Act 1977, as amended by this Act, and Sched. 1 to this Act.

"functions": s.128 of the National Health Service Act 1977.

"Family Health Services Authority": s.10 of the National Health Service Act 1977 and Sched. 1 to this Act.

"health authority": s.128 of the National Health Service Act 1977.

"principal Act": s.1.

"Regional Health Authority": ss.8 and 128 of the National Health Service Act 1977, as amended by this Act, and Sched. 1 to this Act.

"relevant Regional Health Authority": s.15 of the National Health Service Act 1977, as amended by s.13 of this Act.

"special health authority": s.11 of the National Health Service Act 1977, as amended by this Act, and Sched. 1 to this Act.

GENERAL NOTE

Subs. (4)

This deceptively short subsection enables considerable changes to take place in the accounting procedures of health authorities. The Parliamentary Under-Secretary of State for Health, Mr Roger Freeman, explained (Comm. (SCE) col. 693): "how . . . the capital change will be calculated. . . . the capital charge is made up of two elements: depreciation and a rate of return. Depreciation will be on current value of assets on a value which is assigned to an asset taking into account its remaining life, which may be substantial if it is a well constructed hospital. It is based on the open market value, assuming existing use; so it does not assume . . . that a district general hospital can be sold for housing redevelopment, in which case the values might be considerably higher. It assumes continued use of the site for hospital services, which puts a substantial restraint upon the valuation. . . . The capital charge will include not only an element for depreciation but also a return of six per cent. on the current value of land and buildings and equipment, so this is a six per cent. rate of return on the aggregate of the land and buildings on current values. It is a real rate of return, and the six per cent. rate can and, no doubt will, change over the years. The rate is equivalent to the Treasury rate of return needed on nonpublic trading organisations".

He explained (Comm. (SCE) col. 692): "The definition of a gifted asset is essentially an asset that has been gifted since vesting day, 1948, and for which public subscription or voluntary or charitable organisations' funds have paid. . . . the proportion that is paid for publicly will be part of the capital charges scheme and the voluntary gifted part will not. Part assets as well as whole assets will count".

He said further (Comm. (SCE) cols. 693–4): "districts which have higher land and building values, such as inner London, will be compensated for those higher values. . . . the system will start by the commissioning authorities being fully compensated for the higher values of the land and buildings within their district which they use for their local residents. In other words, to start with we shall make sure that the higher costs inevitably involved in, for example, central London are reflected in the amount of funds allocated to the DHAs. . . . over time, we intend to move to a full system of weighted capitation for the allocation of RHAs to DHAs, including the element of recycled funds for capital charges". But (Comm. (SCE) col. 696) "over a fairly extended period, it must be right for inner London DHAs to consider placing some of their contracts for elective surgery in hospitals that are further outside their district boundaries than they would otherwise do".

He also emphasised (Comm. (SCE) cols. 698–700): "The point is that private hospitals, even if they account on historic cost, will price on current cost. There is a difference between book keeping and the reality of the market place, which is pricing. . . . We are not transferring surplus land or buildings to trusts. There will be a lean transfer in which we shall take out any assets and land that could be sold over the next two or three years. We shall capitalise the trusts, therefore, at that opening value, and divide it between interest bearing debt and private dividend capital. . . . We are introducing a significant change in that for the first time in the public sector, capital will truly be differentiated from revenue. That means that when capital expenditure considerations are analysed and considered, those who plan the building of new hospitals and facilities will, for the first time, have to take into account the revenue consequences of their actions. . . . I forecast that with the introduction of capital charges, one or two new hospital building programmes will be reconsidered and that the refurbishment and modernisation of existing hospitals will become more appropriate".

Subs. (5)
This parallels the provision in relation to RHAs' power of direction over DHAs.

Extension of functions etc. of Audit Commission to cover the health service

20.—(1) Part III of the Local Government Finance Act 1982 (the Audit Commission for Local Authorities in England and Wales—in this section referred to as "the Commission") shall have effect subject to the amendments in Schedule 4 to this Act, being amendments—

(a) to extend the functions of the Commission to cover health authorities and other bodies established under this Act or the principal Act;

(b) to alter the title and constitution of the Commission to reflect its wider role; and

(c) to make provision consequential on or supplemental to the amendments referred to in paragraphs (a) and (b) above.

(2) In section 98 of the principal Act (accounts and audit),—

(a) in subsection (1), in the words following paragraph (e) for the words from "appointed" to "Comptroller" there shall be substituted "appointed by the Audit Commission for Local Authorities and the National Health Service in England and Wales and the Comptroller";

(b) after subsection (2A) of that section there shall be inserted the following subsection—

"(2B) So far as relates to allotted sums paid to the members of a fund-holding practice—

    (a) accounts shall be kept in such form as the Secretary of State may with the approval of the Treasury direct;

    (b) the Comptroller and Auditor General may examine the accounts and the records relating to them and any report of the auditor on them;

    (c) in respect of each financial year, annual accounts in such form as the Secretary of State may with the approval of the Treasury direct shall be prepared and submitted to the relevant Family Health Services Authority; and

    (d) in respect of each financial year, each Family Health Services Authority shall prepare, in such form as the Secretary of State may with the approval of the Treasury direct, and include in its own accounts, a summarised version of the accounts submitted to the Authority under paragraph (c) above.";

  (c) subsection (3) (regulations of the Secretary of State with respect to audit) shall be omitted; and

  (d) after subsection (4) there shall be inserted—

    "(5) In subsection (2B) above "recognised fund-holding practice" and "allotted sum" have the same meaning as in section 15 of the National Health Service and Community Care Act 1990."

(3) If the person who is for the time being the auditor, within the meaning of Part III of the Local Government Finance Act 1982, in relation to the accounts of a health service body, within the meaning of that Part, has reason to believe that the body, or any officer of the body,—

  (a) is about to make, or has made, a decision which involves or would involve the incurring of expenditure which is unlawful, or

  (b) is about to take, or has taken, a course of action which, if pursued to its conclusion, would be unlawful and likely to cause a loss or deficiency,

he shall refer the matter forthwith to the Secretary of State.

(4) It shall be the duty of the Commission to make, by such date as the Secretary of State may determine, an offer of employment by the Commission to each person employed in the civil service of the State in connection with the audit of the accounts of any of the bodies specified in section 98(1) of the principal Act whose name is notified to the Commission by the Secretary of State for the purposes of this subsection; and the terms of the offer must be such that they are, taken as a whole, not less favourable to the person to whom the offer is made than the terms on which he is employed on the date on which the offer is made.

(5) An offer made in pursuance of subsection (4) above shall not be revocable during the period of three months beginning with the date on which it is made.

(6) Where a person becomes an officer or servant of the Commission in consequence of subsection (4) above, then, for the purposes of the Employment Protection (Consolidation) Act 1978, his period of employment in the civil service of the State shall count as a period of employment by the Commission and the change of employment shall not break the continuity of the period of employment.

(7) Where a person ceases to be employed as mentioned in subsection (4) above—

  (a) on becoming an officer or servant of the Commission in consequence of an offer made in pursuance of that subsection, or

  (b) having unreasonably refused such an offer,

he shall not, on ceasing to be so employed, be treated for the purposes of any scheme under section 1 of the Superannuation Act 1972 as having been retired on redundancy.

(8) Without prejudice to any express amendment made by this Act, on and after the day appointed for the coming into force of this subsection, any

reference in any enactment (including an enactment comprised in subordinate legislation) to the Audit Commission for Local Authorities in England and Wales shall be construed as a reference to the Audit Commission for Local Authorities and the National Health Service in England and Wales.

DEFINITIONS
  "the Commission": subs. (1).
  "fund holding practice": s.14.
  "health authority": s.128 of the National Health Service Act 1977.
  "Family Health Services Authority": s.10 of the National Health Service Act 1977 and Sched. 1 to this Act.
  "health service body": s.12 of the Local Government Finance Act 1982, as amended by Sched. 4 to this Act, applying s.98(1) of the National Health Service Act 1977.
  "officer of the body": s.128 of the National Health Service Act 1977.
  "principal Act": s.1.
  "relevant Family Health Services Authority": s.15 of the National Health Service Act 1977, as amended by s.13 of this Act.

GENERAL NOTE
  This section and Sched. 4 allow the Audit Commission to take over the statutory audit of Health Service bodies from the Department of Health and the Welsh Office.

Subs. (1)
  The amendments to the Local Government Finance Act effected by the Schedule make many of its audit provisions applicable to health service bodies, including fund holding practices. Since, as ministers continually stressed during the passage of the Bill, the constitutional position of local government and health authorities is different, it seems particularly inappropriate that audit should be carried out by the same body acting under an act still beginning its title with "local government". A separate body, if need be with the same personnel, would have helped, *cf.* the Parliamentary Commissioner for the Administration and the Health Service Commissioner (the latter's jurisdiction was originally in the 1973 NHS Reorganisation Act defined by reference to the Act governing the former, but was usefully consolidated in the 1977 NHS Act).
  Para. 2 of the Schedule amends s.12 of the 1982 Act and includes a new regulation-making power. The Notes on Clauses said that regulations to be made under the new s.12(3B) would provide that "the requirement for an annual audit certificate and opinion on the accounts of individual GP fund holding practices shall be satisfied by such a certificate and opinion on the accounts of a FHSA which include summaries of those of the fund holding practices concerned. The Code of Audit Practice will provide for the individual detailed audit of fund holding practices on a cyclical basis".
  As regards para. 3, the Minister of State for the Scottish Office, Lord Sanderson of Bowden, said (*Hansard*, H.L. Vol. 520, cols. 266–7): "In general, we do not think it will be necessary for the auditor to do a detailed audit of the relevant accounts of each fund holder more frequently than once every three years because the accounts of every fund holder will be summarised and included in the accounts of the relevant FHSA or health board . . . But we also want to allow the auditor, if he is concerned about the financial affairs of an individual fund holding practice, to do a detailed audit more frequently than once every three years". These are the "circumstances" referred to in the new s.12(3B).
  Para. 3(2) is transitional to enable existing staff of the Department of Health and Welsh Office to be transferred to the Audit Commission.
  Para. 22 of the Schedule amends s.33 of the 1982 Act and includes a new regulation-making power. The Notes on Clauses said it was proposed to introduce the new arrangements for NHS audit on October 1, 1990. It will, the Notes said, "also be necessary to save the existing statutory provisions by regulations under s.33 to enable accounts for the 1990/91 financial year to be completed".
  Generally, the Parliamentary Under-Secretary of State for the Department of Social Security, Lord Henley, explained (*Hansard*, H.L. Vol. 520, col. 265): "In relation to local government, the commission has two distinct powers on value for money. One is contained in Section 26 of the Local Government Finance Act 1982. This requires the commission to undertake or promote studies into economy, efficiency and effectiveness. The [Act] applies this provision in full to the commission's new rôle in the National Health Service. The other power is the one in Section 27 of the 1982 Act which allows the commission to report on the impact of statutes, directions and guidance. Initially, we simply excluded this provision from

the new arrangements for NHS audit because of the major difference between the accountability of local authorities to their electorates and the position in the NHS where it is Parliament which holds the Government to account on its policies. But ... we [have accepted] that we could strengthen the commission's hand by making it explicit that it could take full account of the implementation of statutes, directions and guidance, subject to its not questioning the policy objectives of the Secretary of State. That is the provision contained in paragraph 19 of Schedule 4. It also mirrors professional audit practice. It is the auditor's rôle to report on regularity and value for money in the implementation of policy rather than dispute the underlying objectives".

If s.27 were to apply in full, the Parliamentary Under-Secretary of State for the Department of Social Security, Lord Henley, argued (*Hansard*, H.L. Vol. 518, col. 1162–3): "[it would] duplicate a departmental function. ... health authorities are managed by the NHS Management Executive, which has the responsibility for managing the impact of health policy. The executive is responsible to the policy board, chaired by the Secretary of State, and the latter is responsible to Parliament for policy and management of the NHS. The chain of command leading to public accountability is therefore complete in itself".

Schemes for meeting losses and liabilities etc. of certain health service bodies

21.—(1) The Secretary of State may by regulations made with the consent of the Treasury establish a scheme whereby any of the bodies specified in subsection (2) below may make provision to meet—

(a) expenses arising from any loss of or damage to their property; and

(b) liabilities to third parties for loss, damage or injury arising out of the carrying out of the functions of the bodies concerned.

(2) The bodies referred to in subsection (1) above are—

(a) health authorities;

(b) NHS trusts; and

(c) the Public Health Laboratory Service Board;

but a scheme under this section may limit the class or description of bodies which are eligible to participate in it.

(3) Without prejudice to the generality of the power conferred by subsection (1) above, a scheme under this section may—

(a) provide for the scheme to be administered by the Secretary of State or by a health authority or NHS trust specified in the scheme;

(b) require any body which participates in the scheme to make payments in accordance with the scheme; and

(c) provide for the making of payments for the purposes of the scheme by the Secretary of State.

(4) Without prejudice to any other power of direction conferred on the Secretary of State,—

(a) if the Secretary of State so directs, a body which is eligible to participate in a scheme shall do so; and

(b) where a scheme provides for it to be administered by the Secretary of State, a health authority or NHS trust shall carry out such functions in connection with the administration of the scheme by the Secretary of State as he may direct.

(5) Neither the Secretary of State nor any health authority or NHS trust administering a scheme under this section shall, by virtue of their activities under the scheme, be regarded as carrying on insurance business for the purposes of the Insurance Companies Act 1982.

DEFINITIONS

"functions": s.128 of the National Health Service Act 1977.

"health authority": s.128 of the National Health Service Act 1977.

"NHS trust": ss.5 and 26 of this Act and 128 of the National Health Service Act 1977, as inserted by this Act.

"property": s.128 of the National Health Service Act 1977.

"Public Health Laboratory Service Board": s.5, and Sched. 3 to the National Health Service Act 1977.

"regulations": ss.126 and 128 of the National Health Service Act 1977, as amended by this Act.

General Note
See HC(89)34, *Claims of Medical Negligence Against NHS Hospital and Community Doctors and Dentists.* See also the note to s.3(2), on complaints.

The Baroness in Waiting, Baroness Blatch, explained the purpose of this section as flowing (*Hansard*, H.L. Vol. 520, col. 268): "essentially from the establishment of National Health Service trusts. [It] will give the Secretary of State power to make regulations to enable him, or regions acting under delegated powers, to meet the liabilities of trusts or other defined health service bodies . . . health authorities currently bear their own risks and do not insure. Many regions run arrangements whereby the costs of particularly large clinical negligence claims are met from funds held back by the regions, thus spreading the cost between districts. In Scotland and Wales pooling arrangements to share the costs of high value liabilities are operated by the Secretary of State. These arrangements will, in all probability, take on more significance in future as health authorities will be responsible for meeting liabilities arising from the medical negligence of their employees".

The Parliamentary Under-Secretary of State for Health, Mr Roger Freeman, said (Comm. (SCE) col. 1314): "It should be voluntary and not compulsory . . . Expressed simply, the idea is that risks up to a certain threshold in any one year would be collectively insured by the 10, 14 or greater numbers of districts in a region, with individual districts picking up risks above that threshold. It is a sensible, workmanlike idea that should be pursued, and I shall take appropriate steps to take it up with regional chairmen and general managers".

Further amendments of the principal Act

The Medical Practices Committee

22.—(1) Section 7 of the principal Act (the Medical Practices Committee) shall be amended in accordance with this section.

(2) At the beginning of subsection (1) there shall be inserted "Subject to subsection (1A) below".

(3) After subsection (1) there shall be inserted the following subsection—

"(1A) The Secretary of State may by order make such modifications as he considers appropriate of paragraphs (a) and (b) of subsection (1) above."

(4) At the end of the section there shall be added the following subsection—

"(4) After consulting the Medical Practices Committee, the Secretary of State may give the Committee directions with respect to the exercise of its functions; and it shall be the duty of the Committee to comply with any such directions."

Definition
"principal Act": s.1 of this Act.

General Note
The section should be read with ss.7, 33 and 34 of the 1977 Act and with s.23 of this Act; see note to that section.

The Secretary of State for Health, Mr Kenneth Clarke, said (Comm. (SCE) col. 736): "I do not contemplate the immediate use of the new powers in [this section] largely because at the moment I am satisfied with the way in which the MPC for England and Wales, . . . is carrying out its functions in the NHS. Nevertheless, it is a long standing anomaly that the powers and constitution of the MPCs are carefully delineated in primary legislation. At the moment, the Secretary of State has no ability to modify their constitution and no power to issue directions about how they should exercise their judgment. The Secretary of State has that power over every other statutory body in the NHS".

Distribution of general medical services

23.—(1) In section 33 of the principal Act (distribution of general medical services) after subsection (1) there shall be inserted the following subsections—

"(1A) The Secretary of State may by order specify—

(a) the maximum number of medical practitioners with whom, in any year, all the Family Health Services Authorities for localities in England, taken as a whole, may enter into arrangements under section 29 above for the provision of general medical services; and

(b) the maximum number of medical practitioners with whom, in any year, all the Family Health Services Authorities for localities in Wales, taken as a whole, may enter into such arrangements.

(1B) An order under subsection (1A) above may contain such incidental and consequential provisions (including provisions amending this Part of this Act) as appear to the Secretary of State to be appropriate including, in particular, provisions as to the basis on which the Medical Practices Committee are to refuse applications under section 30 above in order to secure that any maximum number specified in the order is not exceeded."

(2) At the beginning of subsection (2) of that section (the Medical Practices Committee to select the persons whose applications are to be granted) there shall be inserted "Subject to subsection (2A) below" and after that subsection there shall be inserted the following subsection—

"(2A) If, in the opinion of the Medical Practices Committee, a medical practitioner is required for a particular part of the locality of a Family Health Services Authority, then, in such circumstances as may be prescribed,—

(a) the Authority (instead of the Committee) shall, in accordance with regulations, select the medical practitioner whose application they wish to be considered by the Committee; and

(b) the Committee shall not consider any application from a medical practitioner who is not so selected; and

(c) any medical practitioner who has made an application but is not so selected may appeal to the Secretary of State on a point of law;

and if the Secretary of State allows an appeal under paragraph (c) above he shall remit the application to the Authority for reconsideration."

(3) In subsection (4) of that section (applications under section 30 may be granted subject to certain conditions), after the word "but" there shall be inserted—

"(a) in granting an application shall specify, by reference to one or more prescribed conditions relating to hours or the sharing of work, the provision of general medical services for which the applicant will be entitled to be remunerated; and

(b) ";

and at the end of the subsection there shall be inserted the words "and an order under subsection (1A) above may make provision as to the extent to which account is to be taken under the order of medical practitioners whose ability to carry out remunerated work is limited by virtue of conditions imposed under paragraph (a) above".

(4) In subsection (5) of that section (appeals to the Secretary of State) for the words "such conditions" there shall be substituted "conditions under paragraph (a) or paragraph (b) of subsection (4) above" and for the words following "Secretary of State," in the first place where those words occur, there shall be substituted "on a point of law; and, if the Secretary of State allows such an appeal, he shall remit the application to the Medical Practices Committee for reconsideration".

(5) Subsection (7) of that section (directions on a successful appeal) shall be omitted.

(6) In subsection (8) of that section (matters to be taken into account) for the words from the beginning to "in any such case" there shall be substituted

"In any case where medical practitioners have to be selected from a number of applicants, the Medical Practices Committee or, where subsection (2A) above applies, the Family Health Services Authority shall".

(7) In section 34 of the principal Act (regulations for Medical Practices Committee)—

(a) in paragraph (b)(ii) after the words "under section 33 above" there shall be inserted "and where such an appeal is allowed, the reconsideration of any application"; and

(b) at the end of the section there shall be added the following subsection—

"(2) Regulations under this section may make provision for, and in connection with, the variation of any condition imposed under subsection (4) or subsection (5) of section 33 above, including provision for appeals to the Secretary of State on a point of law."

(8) In the case of a medical practitioner who, on the day appointed for the coming into force of this section, is providing general medical services in accordance with arrangements under section 29 of the principal Act, regulations may make transitional provisions by virtue of which those services shall be treated for the purposes of that Act as provided subject to such of the prescribed conditions referred to in section 33(4)(a) of that Act as are determined under the regulations and, accordingly, for enabling any such condition to be varied in accordance with regulations under section 34(2) of that Act.

DEFINITIONS

"Family Health Services Authority": s.10 of the National Health Service Act 1977 and Sched. 1 to this Act.

"general medical services": s.29 of the National Health Service Act 1977.

"medical practitioner": s.128 of the National Health Service Act 1977 and Medical Act 1983.

"prescribed": s.128 of the National Health Service Act 1977, as amended by this Act.

"principal Act": s.1.

"regulations": ss.126 and 128 of the National Health Service Act 1977, as amended by this Act.

GENERAL NOTE

The Parliamentary Under-Secretary of State for the Department of Health, Baroness Hooper, explained (*Hansard*, H.L. Vol. 518, col. 1217): "the Medical Practices Committee and its Scottish equivalent . . . are charged with responsibility for determining the distribution of GPs throughout Great Britain. The Government believe it right that, should a national ceiling be set, they should be free to control the distribution of GPs within it, subject only to any directions that the Secretary of State may give on specific matters. I emphasise that the direction making power itself will not allow the Secretary of State to impose local ceilings". The Secretary of State, Mr Kenneth Clarke, said (Comm. (SCE) cols. 740–1): "In [sections 22 and 23] I seek .. powers which any health Minister, past or future, would regard as welcome additions to the potential armoury of a Secretary of State if ever the planning of medical manpower began to be out of line with what was considered to be the proper development of the service. . . . Any Secretary of State needs power to ensure that there is a proper balance of medical manpower throughout the NHS between, for example, the manpower needs of the hospital and community health services on the one hand, and the GP services on the other".

Subs. (2)

The Parliamentary Under-Secretary of State for the Department of Social Security, Lord Henley, explained (*Hansard*, H.L. Vol. 518, col. 1219): "[the subsection] provides that in future FHSAs rather than the MPC shall select the doctor who is to succeed to a GP practice vacancy. These will be singlehanded vacancies. In our view it is sensible for the people locally who are responsible for running the services to make these decisions in accordance with regulations and guidance on proper procedures. Since the inception of the National Health Service unsuccessful candidates for practice vacancies have had a right of appeal to the Secretary of State against the refusal of their applications by the MPC. We have no wish to deny the right of appeal but, in the light of our decisions to devolve decision making to FHSAs, it seems sensible for appeals against these decisions to lie with the MPC. We also intend that all job-related appeals by GPs shall in future focus on procedural matters to stop second guessing, unnecessary delays and the pretence that central bodies can make a properly informed judgment on the merits of rival candidates.

"If an appeal is successful, the selection will be remitted to the body below for reconsideration. But there are practical difficulties involved in giving the MPC an appellate rôle on matters of procedure. The committee has no experience in this area and so has been unable to develop the necessary expertise. There will also need to be a substantial legal input which the committee does not at present possess and which would be costly to create. In addition, it is not a matter that the committee could readily delegate to officers. So the members themselves could become disproportionately involved in their appellate function. We do not want to deflect the committee in this way nor to create bureaucratic difficulties for them. We have therefore . . . [kept] the appellate rôle on practice vacancies with the Secretary of State, subject to the requirement that these concern procedural matters".

The Baroness in Waiting, Baroness Blatch, made it clear (*Hansard*, H.L. Vol. 520, col. 278): "when the regulations are made they will define FHSAs' powers and will specifically exclude partnership vacancies".

Subs. (3)

The Parliamentary Under-Secretary of State for the Department of Health, Baroness Hooper, explained (*Hansard*, H.L. Vol. 518, col. 1220): "The new arrangements for part time working and job sharing for GPs in Great Britain stem from . . . the White Paper Promoting Better Health and subsequent discussions with GP representatives. . . . Our intention is to provide more flexibility in working patterns, and open up new opportunities for doctors in general practice. The [Act] . . . defines the rôle of the two MPCs (Medical Practices Committees) in relation to that, building on their existing responsibilities for admissions to the medical lists of FHSAs [under s.29 of the 1977 Act] and health boards [in Scotland]. We want to ensure that GPs are admitted to the medical list . . . on conditions that are both appropriate and sensitive to their choice of working and that all parties know where they stand. The [Act] provides for that and also allows the MPCs to vary conditions relating to working hours if a doctor's circumstances should change.

"[The subsection seeks] to clarify and improve the new provisions. First, [it makes] it clear that all doctors will need to be admitted to medical lists on one basis or another, full time, part time or job sharing. Secondly, [it spells] out that regulations can include provision for appeals to the Secretary of State on procedural matters against decisions of the MPC to refuse to vary the conditions on which a GP has been admitted. This is consistent with GPs' existing rights of appeal against other decisions of the MPC. Thirdly, they allow regulations to be made to safeguard the position of GPs already working on a part time basis under locally agreed arrangements. We have sought to respond positively to the wishes of an increasing number of doctors to work on a more flexible basis—I believe that that applies very much in particular to women doctors—and to put the new arrangements on a proper footing through the good offices of the Medical Practices Committee".

The Notes on Clauses said that the new categories of flexible working hours which the MPC may approve are "likely to comprise three quarter time (19 hours), half time working (13 hours) and job sharing, where two doctors jointly must work 26 hours".

Limitations on right to be included on list of dental practitioners

24.—(1) Section 36 of the principal Act (regulations as to arrangements for general dental services) shall be amended in accordance with this section.

(2) In subsection (1)(b) (regulations to include provision conferring a right, subject to certain qualifications, to be entered on a list of dental practitioners providing general dental services) for the words "subsection (2)" there shall be substituted "subsections (2) and (3)".

(3) At the end of the section there shall be added the following subsection—

"(3) Regulations may make the exercise of the right conferred by virtue of paragraph (b) of subsection (1) above subject to any provision made by or under the regulations, and, in such cases as may be prescribed, may confer a right of appeal to a prescribed body in respect of a refusal to include a dental practitioner on such a list as is referred to in paragraph (a) of that subsection."

Definitions
Definitions
    "dental practitioner": s.128 of the National Health Service Act 1977 and the Dentists Act 1984.
    "general dental services": s.35 of the National Health Service Act 1977.
    "prescribed": s.128 of the National Health Service Act 1977 as amended by this Act.
    "principal Act": s.1 of this Act.
    "regulations": ss.126 and 128 of the National Health Service Act 1977 as amended by this Act.

General Note

Subs. (3)
    "Regulations will prescribe the minimum age for entitlement to these benefits and that in return for benefits under the scheme a practitioner will withdraw his name from the dental list held by the FHSA. To prevent such practitioners from being re-included in the dental list of any FHSA, regulations will provide that a dental practitioner who withdraws his name from the dental list having accepted early retirement shall not thereafter be entitled to have his name included on the dental list kept by any FHSA" (Notes on Clauses).
    The Secretary of State for Health, Mr Kenneth Clarke, said (Comm. (SCE) col. 747): "The only purpose of clauses 32 and 36 which we have in mind is to facilitate the introduction of the early retirement scheme, which is part of the new contract which we negotiated with the BDA".

Transfer to DHA of certain functions relating to private patients

    25.—(1) Section 65 of the principal Act (accommodation and services for private patients) shall be amended in accordance with this section.
    (2) In subsection (1) (power of Secretary of State to authorise accommodation and services at hospitals to be made available for private patients etc.)—
    (a) for the words from the beginning to "as he may determine," in the first place where those words occur, there shall be substituted "Subject to the provisions of this section, to such extent as they may determine, a District or Special Health Authority may make available at a hospital or hospitals for which they have responsibility accommodation and services";
    (b) for any subsequent reference to the Secretary of State in the words preceding paragraph (a) there shall be substituted a reference to the District Health Authority or Special Health Authority, as the case may require; and
    (c) in paragraph (a) for the words "him of any duty imposed on him by" there shall be substituted "the Authority of any function conferred on the Authority under",
    (3) After subsection (1) there shall be inserted the following subsection—
        "(1A) Before determining to make any accommodation or services available as mentioned in subsection (1) above, a District or Special Health Authority shall consult organisations representative of the interests of persons likely to be affected by the determination."
    (4) In subsection (2)—
    (a) for the words "The Secretary of State" there shall be substituted "A District or Special Health Authority"; and
    (b) for the words from "to which an authorisation" to "made available" there shall be substituted "which are made available under subsection (1) above to be so made available."
    (5) For subsection (3) of that section there shall be substituted the following subsection—
        "(3) The Secretary of State may give directions to a District or Special Health Authority in relation to the exercise of its functions under this section; and it shall be the duty of an authority to whom directions are so given to comply with them."

DEFINITIONS
"District Health Authority": ss.8 and 128 of the National Health Service Act 1977, as amended by this Act, and Sched. 1 to this Act.
"hospital": s.128 of the National Health Service Act 1977.
"principal Act": s.1.
"special health authority": s.11 of the National Health Service Act 1977, as amended by this Act, and Sched. 1 to this Act.

GENERAL NOTE
The Secretary of State, Mr Kenneth Clarke, set out the so called "six principles" for the grant of private patient facilities in the Green Book (Comm. (SCE) cols. 753–4): (1) the provision of [the] facilities does not significantly prejudice non paying patients; (2) subject to clinical considerations, earlier private consultation should not lead to earlier NHS admission; (3) a common waiting list should be used for urgent or seriously ill patients; (4) after admission, access to diagnostic and treatment facilities is governed by clinical considerations; (5) standards of clinical care and services are the same for all patients; and (6) single rooms are not held vacant for potential private patients.

He explained that the purpose of this section (Comm. (SCE) col. 749): "is to transfer to local level some of the powers which in the past have been exercisable by the Secretary of State centrally on improving the extension of private health in the NHS hospitals. . . . The intention is not to encourage the growth of private sector provision in NHS hospitals in ways that compromise their ability to provide NHS services to patients. . . . We expect DHAs and others to remember the need to ensure, when considering an application for more private practice to be undertaken in a hospital for whose management they are responsible, that the application should not proceed if it would seriously damage the hospital's ability to provide the highest quality NHS provision. Long and well established principles govern the applications to extend private practice. The Green Book will need to be revised when the Bill is enacted. Revision will remove the duty to consult other private hospitals in the area before extending private practice. It seems illogical to consult competitors about whether to undertake more private practice. Nevertheless, carefully followed procedures will ensure that proper consultation takes place and that no decision is taken to extend the range of private practice in a manner that might damage the NHS. An extension of private practice would have advantages for NHS hospitals and their authorities in some circumstances. They would include the ability to raise revenue, improved cooperation between private and public sectors which we consider beneficial to health care generally and the presence of consultants a great part whose private practice is on the premises of NHS hospitals with which they had a contract. . . . The Green Book requires DHAs to consult professional advisory machinery, hospital staff interests, CHAs, FPCs and other interested health authorities".

Subs. (5)
"It is intended that directions made under [the power granted by the subsection] will be used to ensure that health authorities abide by the so-called six principles set out above" (Notes on Clauses).

Interpretation

Interpretation of Part I

26.—(1) Subsection (2) below has effect with respect to the interpretation of this Part of this Act and the National Health Service Act 1977 (the principal Act).
(2) In section 128 of the principal Act, in subsection (1)—
(a) after the words "this Act" there shall be inserted "and Part I of the National Health Service and Community Care Act 1990";
(b) for the definition beginning "Area Health Authority" there shall be substituted—
" "District Health Authority" means the authority for a district, whether or not its name incorporates the word "District" ";
(c) in the definition of "health service hospital" after the words "this Act" there shall be inserted "or vested in an NHS trust";
(d) after the definition of "modifications" there shall be inserted—
" "NHS contract" has the meaning assigned by section 4(1) of the National Health Service and Community Care Act 1990;

"National Health Service trust" has the meaning assigned by section 5 of the National Health Service and Community Care Act 1990 and "NHS trust" shall be construed accordingly";

(e) after the definition of "officer" there shall be inserted—
" "operational date", in relation to an NHS trust, shall be construed in accordance with paragraph 3(1)(e) of Schedule 2 to the National Health Service and Community Care Act 1990";

(f) after the definition of "patient" there shall be inserted—
" "pharmaceutical services" has the meaning assigned by section 41 of this Act";

(g) in the definition of "prescribed" after the words "this Act" there shall be inserted "or Part I of the National Health Service and Community Care Act 1990";

(h) after the definition of "prescribed" there shall be inserted—
" "primary functions" shall be construed in accordance with section 3 of the National Health Service and Community Care Act 1990"; and

(i) in the definition of "regulations" after the words "this Act" there shall be inserted "or Part I of the National Health Service and Community Care Act 1990".

(3) In this Part of this Act—
"goods" includes accommodation;
"health board" means a Health Board constituted under section 2 of the National Health Service (Scotland) Act 1978 or a Health and Social Services Board constituted under the Health and Personal Social Services (Northern Ireland) Order 1972; and
"services" includes services of any description, whether or not being services under the principal Act.

DEFINITIONS
"principal Act": s.1 of this Act.

PART II

THE NATIONAL HEALTH SERVICE: SCOTLAND

Health Boards and other bodies

Health Boards, the Common Services Agency and state hospitals

27.—(1) Subject to subsection (2) below, at the end of the day appointed for the coming into force of this subsection, any person who is a member of—

(a) a Health Board;

(b) the management committee of the Common Services Agency for the Scottish Health Service; or

(c) a State Hospital Management Committee within the meaning of the Mental Health (Scotland) Act 1984,

shall cease to be such a member.

(2) Subsection (1) above does not apply to a person holding office as chairman of a Health Board or of a committee mentioned in subsection (1)(b) or (c) above.

(3) Schedule 1 (Health Boards) and Schedule 5 (Common Services Agency) to the National Health Service (Scotland) Act 1978 (in this Part of this Act referred to as "the 1978 Act") and Schedule 1 to the Mental Health (Scotland) Act 1984 (State Hospital Management Committees) shall be amended in accordance with Schedule 5 to this Act.

DEFINITIONS
"the 1978 Act": subs. 3.

This section changes the composition of Health Boards, the Common Services Agency and the Management Committee of the State Hospital at Carstairs from a date to be appointed.

Subss. (1) and (2)
All current members will lose their places apart from the Chairman. The termination of the office of existing board members was stated by the Parliamentary Under-Secretary to be a "one-off opportunity to reduce the size of the Health Boards" (Comm. (SCE) col. 209, January 16, 1990).

Subs. 3
This gives effect to Sched. 5, which amends the Schedules to the 1978 Act and the Mental Health (Scotland) Act 1984 dealing with the membership and staffing of these bodies. Unlike England and Wales, all appointments to Health Boards are made by the Secretary of State after consultation with interested bodies, and no change is made to this. The only specification as to membership is that, for prescribed Health Boards, at least one member must hold a post in a University with a medical or dental school (Sched. 5, para. 2).

Sched. 5 removes the nomination rights of Health Boards to the Management Committee of the Common Services Agency (para. 9). It also extends the power of the Secretary of State to remunerate the Chairmen of Health Boards and the Management Committee to include other members as may be prescribed (paras. 3 and 10). Powers are given to the Secretary of State to deal with the transfer of employees (paras. 5, 6, 11, 12 and 13).

Special Health Boards

28. In section 2 (Health Boards) of the 1978 Act—
(a) in subsection (1)—
> (i) after the words "Secretary of State" there shall be inserted the word "(a)"; and
> (ii) after the words "Health Boards" there shall be inserted— "and
>> (b) subject to subsections (1A) and (1C), may by order constitute boards, either for the whole of Scotland or for such parts of Scotland as he may so determine, for the purpose of exercising such of his functions under this Act as he may so determine; and those boards shall, without prejudice to subsection (1B), be called Special Health Boards.";
(b) after subsection (1) there shall be inserted the following subsections—
> "(1A) An order made under subsection (1)(b) may determine an area for a Special Health Board constituted under that subsection which is the same as the areas determined—
>> (a) for any other Special Health Board; or
>> (b) for any Health Board or Health Boards constituted by an order or orders made under subsection (1)(a).
>
> (1B) An order under subsection (1)(b) may specify the name by which a board constituted by the order shall be known.
>
> (1C) The Secretary of State may by order provide that such of the provisions of this Act or of any other enactment, or of any orders, regulations, schemes or directions made under or by virtue of this Act or of any other enactment, as apply in relation to Health Boards shall, subject to such modifications and limitations as may be specified in the order, so apply in relation to any Special Health Board so specified."; and
(c) in subsection (2), for the word "(1)" there shall be substituted the word "(1)(a)."

"the 1978 Act": s.27.

The Secretary of State is empowered to create Special Health Boards over all or part of

Scotland. The Special Health Boards may exercise such of the Secretary of State's functions under the 1978 Act as he may determine. The stated purpose of this section is to enable the creation of a new body with responsibilities for health education and promotion throughout Scotland, to replace the Scottish Health Education Group, which was part of the Common Services Agency (*Hansard*, H.C. Vol. 169, cols. 180–182).

Scottish advisory bodies

29.—(1) Section 5 of the 1978 Act (Scottish Health Service Planning Council) shall cease to have effect.

(2) Section 6 of that Act (national consultative committees) shall cease to have effect.

(3) In section 7 of that Act (local health councils)—

(a) in subsection (2), the words from "by local authorities" to "and for the appointment" shall cease to have effect;

(b) in subsection (9)(d), after the words "Health Board" there shall be inserted "and from any NHS trust in their area or district"; and

(c) in subsection (9)(e), after the words "Health Board" there shall be inserted "and establishments in their area or district administered by NHS trusts".

(4) In section 8(1) of that Act (university liaison committees)—

(a) after the words "those Boards" where they first occur there shall be inserted "and any NHS trusts in the area or combined areas";

(b) for the words "the area or combined" there shall be substituted "that area or those"; and

(c) after the words "those Boards" in the second place where they occur there shall be inserted ", any such NHS trust."

(5) In section 9 of that Act (local consultative committees)—

(a) for the words from "after consultation" to "is representative" in each of subsections (1), (3) and (4) there shall be substituted "a Health Board is satisfied that a committee formed for its area is representative";

(b) for the words "Secretary of State" in the second place where they occur in subsection (1) there shall be substituted "Health Board"; and

(c) for the word "he" in each of subsections (3) and (4) there shall be substituted "the Board".

DEFINITIONS
"NHS Trusts": s.31.
"the 1978 Act": s.27.

GENERAL NOTE

Subss. (1) and (2)
The Scottish Health Service Planning Council, whose duty was to advise the Secretary of State on the exercise of its functions under the 1978 Act is abolished under subs. (1).

Subsequently the Secretary of State is relieved of his duty to recognise committees representing health professionals, committees the function of which had been to advise the Scottish Health Service Planning Control, and to give them the status of national consultative committees. See, however, s.62 for the creation of a new Clinical Standards Advisory Group.

Subs. (3)
The constitution and remit of local health councils, established under s.7 of the 1978 Act, to represent the interests of the public, is amended by removing the right of local authorities to appoint members to the councils; and allowing all appointments to be made by the relevant health board. The councils may, by regulation, be given power to obtain information from and visit establishments run by NHS trusts.

Subs. (4)
University Liaison Committees, which advise health boards on clinical teaching and research, are also to be allowed the opportunity to give advice to local NHS trusts.

Local consultative committees represent health professionals in a particular area, and advise the health board on medical, dental, nursing and midwifery, pharmacy and ophthalmic aspects of the provision of services by the health board. This subsection substitutes recognition by the local health board for recognition by the Secretary of State.

NHS contracts

30. After section 17 of the 1978 Act there shall be inserted the following sections—

"**NHS contracts**
17A.—(1) The persons or bodies mentioned in paragraphs (a) to (e) of subsection (2) may, for the purpose of carrying out their functions under any enactment, and without prejudice to any other power they may have in that regard, enter into arrangements for the provision of goods or services to or by them with—
(a) one another; or
(b) any of the persons or bodies mentioned in paragraphs (f) to (m) of that subsection.
(2) The persons and bodies referred to in subsection (1) are—
(a) Health Boards;
(b) the Agency;
(c) the Scottish Dental Practice Board;
(d) a State Hospital Management Committee constituted under section 91 of the Mental Health (Scotland) Act 1984;
(e) NHS trusts established under section 12A;
(f) health authorities within the meaning of section 128(1) (interpretation) of the National Health Service Act 1977;
(g) the Dental Practice Board;
(h) the Public Health Laboratory Service Board;
(i) Family Health Services Authorities within the meaning of section 10 of the National Health Service Act 1977;
(j) recognised fund-holding practices;
(k) NHS trusts established under section 5 of the National Health Service and Community Care Act 1990;
(l) Health and Social Services Boards constituted under the Health and Personal Social Services (Northern Ireland) Order 1972; and
(m) the Secretary of State.
(3) In subsection (1)—
(a) "goods" includes accommodation; and
(b) "services" includes services of any description,
and in this Act an arrangement falling within that subsection is referred to as an "NHS contract."
(4) Whether or not an arrangement which constitutes an NHS contract would, apart from this subsection, be a contract in law, it shall not be regarded for any purpose as giving rise to contractual rights or liabilities, but if any dispute arises with respect to such an arrangement, either party may refer the matter to the Secretary of State for determination under the following provisions of this section.
(5) If, in the course of negotiations intending to lead to an arrangement which will be an NHS contract, it appears to either of the prospective parties that—
(a) the terms proposed by the other party are unfair by reason that that party is seeking to take advantage of its position as the only, or the only practicable, provider of the goods or services concerned or by reason of any other unequal bargain-

ing position as between the prospective parties to the proposed arrangement; or

(b) for any other reason arising out of the relative bargaining
positions of the prospective parties any of the terms of the
proposed arrangements cannot be agreed,

that party may refer the terms of the proposed arrangement to the
Secretary of State for determination under the following provisions
of this section.

(6) Where a reference is made to the Secretary of State under
subsection (4) or (5), the Secretary of State may determine the
matter himself or, if he considers it appropriate, appoint a person to
consider and determine it in accordance with regulations.

(7) By his determination of a reference under subsection (5), the
Secretary of State or, as the case may be, the person appointed by
him under subsection (6) may specify terms to be included in the
proposed arrangement and may direct that it be proceeded with; and
it shall be the duty of the prospective parties to the proposed
arrangement to comply with any such directions.

(8) A determination of a reference under subsection (4) may
contain such directions (including directions as to payment) as the
Secretary of State or, as the case may be, the person appointed under
subsection (6) considers appropriate to resolve the matter in dispute;
and it shall be the duty of the parties to the NHS contract in question
to comply with any such directions.

(9) Without prejudice to the generality of his powers on a reference under subsection (4), the Secretary of State or, as the case may
be, the person appointed by him under subsection (6) may by his
determination in relation to an arrangement constituting an NHS
contract vary the terms of the arrangement or bring it to an end; and
where the arrangement is so varied or brought to an end—

(a) subject to paragraph (b), the variation or termination shall be
treated as being effected by agreement between the parties;
and

(b) directions included in the determination by virtue of subsection (8) may contain such provisions as the Secretary of
State or, as the case may be, the person appointed by him
under subsection (6) considers appropriate in order satisfactorily to give effect to the variation or to bring the arrangement to an end.

Reimbursement of Health Boards' costs

17B.—(1) Where a Health Board provide goods or services under
this Act for an individual for whose health care it is not their function
to provide by virtue of section 2(1), in circumstances where the
condition of the individual is such that he needs those goods or
services and, having regard to his condition, it is not practicable,
before providing them, to enter into an NHS contract for their
provision, that Health Board shall be remunerated in respect of that
provision by the Health Board or Health and Social Services Board
which has the function, or the District or Special Health Authority
which has the primary functions, of providing those goods or services
to that individual.

(2) The rate of any remuneration payable by virtue of subsection
(1) shall be calculated in such manner or on such basis as may be
determined by the Secretary of State.

(3) In any case where—

(a) a Health Board provide goods or services for the benefit of an
individual; and

(b) the provision of those goods and services is not pursuant to an NHS contract; and

(c) the individual is resident outside the United Kingdom and is of a description (being a description associating the individual with another country) specified for the purposes of this subsection by a direction made by the Secretary of State,

the Health Board shall be remunerated by the Secretary of State in respect of the provision of the goods or services at such rate or rates as he considers appropriate.

(4) In subsection (1), "Health and Social Services Board" means such a Board constituted under the Health and Personal Social Services (Northern Ireland) Order 1972."

DEFINITIONS

"goods": subs. (3) of s.17A.
"Health and Social Services Board": subs. (4) of s.17B.
"NHS contract": subs. (3) of s.17A.
"NHS Trust": s.31.
"the 1978 Act": s.27.

GENERAL NOTE

Two new sections are added to the 1978 Act.

Section 17A empowers Health Boards, the Common Services Agency, the Scottish Dental Practice Board, the State Hospital Management Committee and NHS Trusts to enter into arrangements for the provision of goods or services to or by any of the health services bodies listed in subs. (2). These will not be contracts in the normal legal sense and the Secretary of State may determine disputes arising out of these NHS contracts (subs. (4)) varying or terminating the disputed contracts (subs. (9)). Where negotiations for a proposed contract are unsuccessful, and an abuse of bargaining power is alleged, the Secretary of State may specify the terms (subss. (5) and (7)) acting himself or through a representative (subs. (6)). The equivalent provision for England and Wales is s.4.

Section 17B: under s.17A a health board may contract to provide treatment for a patient who is the responsibility of another board. Where such treatment is provided in an emergency, the board shall be entitled to be remunerated by the health board or English or Welsh health authorities or Northern Ireland Health and Social Services Board (subs. (1)). The basis of remuneration is determined by the Secretary of State (subs. (2)) with special provision for the reimbursement of boards for the treatment of foreign patients (subs. (3)).

National Health Service trusts

National Health Service trusts

31. After section 12 of the 1978 Act there shall be inserted the following sections—

"National Health Service trusts

12A.—(1) Subject to subsection (2), the Secretary of State may by order establish bodies, to be known as National Health Service trusts (in this Act referred to as "NHS trusts")—

(a) to assume responsibility, in accordance with this Act, for the ownership and management of hospitals or other establishments or facilities which were previously managed or provided by Health Boards or the Agency; or

(b) to provide and manage hospitals or other establishments or facilities.

(2) The Secretary of State shall by regulations provide for such consultation as may be so prescribed to be carried out by a Health Board or the Agency, before he makes an order under subsection (1).

(3) Every NHS trust—

(a) shall be a body corporate having a board of directors consist-

ing of a chairman appointed by the Secretary of State and,
subject to paragraph 5(2) of Schedule 7A, executive and
non-executive directors (that is to say, directors who, subject
to subsection (5), respectively are and are not employees of
the trust); and

(b) shall have the functions conferred on it by an order under
subsection (1) and by Schedule 7A.

(4) The functions specified in an order under subsection (1) shall
include such functions as the Secretary of State considers appropriate in relation to the provision of services by the trust for one or
more of the following—

(a) Health Boards; and
(b) the Agency.

(5) Regulations may make general provision with respect to—

(a) the qualifications for and the tenure of office of the chairman
and directors of an NHS trust (including the circumstances in
which they shall cease to hold, or may be removed from, office
or may be suspended from performing the functions of the
office);
(b) the persons by whom the directors and any of the officers are
to be appointed and the manner of their appointment;
(c) the maximum and minimum numbers of the directors;
(d) the circumstances in which a person who is not an employee of
the trust is nevertheless, on appointment as a director, to be
regarded as an executive rather than as a non-executive
director;
(e) the proceedings of the trust (including the validation of proceedings in the event of a vacancy or defect in appointment);
(f) the appointment, constitution and exercise of functions by
committees and sub-committees of the trust (whether or not
consisting of or including any members of the board); and
(g) the application of the seal of the trust and the constitution and
proof of instruments.

(6) Part I of Schedule 7A shall have effect with respect to orders
under subsection (1); Part II of that Schedule shall have effect,
subject to subsection (7), with respect to the general duties and the
powers and status of NHS trusts; the supplementary provisions of
Part III of that Schedule shall have effect; and Part IV of that
Schedule shall have effect with respect to the dissolution of NHS
trusts.

(7) The specific powers conferred by paragraphs 14 and 15 in Part
II of Schedule 7A may be exercised only to the extent that the
exercise will not—

(a) interfere with the duty of the trust to comply with directions
under paragraph 6 of that Schedule; and
(b) to any significant extent interfere with the performance by the
trust of its obligations under any NHS contract or any obligations imposed by an order under subsection (1).

(8) The Secretary of State may by order confer on NHS trusts
specific powers additional to those contained in paragraphs 10 to 15
of Schedule 7A.

Transfer of staff to NHS trusts
12B.—(1) Subject to subsection (5), this section applies to any
person who, immediately before an NHS trust's operational date—

(a) is employed by a Health Board or the Agency (in this section
and section 12C referred to as a "transferor authority") to
work solely at, or for the purposes of, a hospital or other

19–63

establishment or facility which is to become the responsibility of the trust; or

(b) is employed by a transferor authority to work at, or for the purposes of, any such hospital, establishment or facility and is designated for the purposes of this section by a scheme made by the body specified as mentioned in paragraph 3(1)(f) of Schedule 7A.

(2) A scheme under this section shall not have effect unless approved by the Secretary of State.

(3) Subject to section 12C, the contract of employment between a person to whom this section applies and the transferor authority shall have effect from the operational date as if originally made between him and the NHS trust.

(4) Without prejudice to subsection (3)—

(a) all the transferor authority's rights, powers, duties and liabilities under or in connection with a contract to which that subsection applies shall by virtue of this section be transferred to the NHS trust on its operational date; and

(b) anything done before that date by or in relation to the transferor authority in respect of that contract or the employee shall be deemed from that date to have been done by or in relation to the NHS trust.

(5) In any case where—

(a) an order under section 12A(1) provides for the establishment of an NHS trust with effect from a date earlier than the operational date of the trust; and

(b) on or after that earlier date but before its operational date the NHS trust makes an offer of employment by the trust to a person who at that time is employed by a Health Board or the Agency to work, whether solely or otherwise, at, or for the purposes of, the hospital or other establishment or facility which is to become the responsibility of the trust; and

(c) as a result of the acceptance of the offer, the person to whom it was made becomes an employee of the NHS trust, subsections (3) and (4) shall have effect in relation to that person's contract of employment as if he were a person to whom this section applies and any reference in those subsections to the operational date of the trust were a reference to the date on which he takes up employment with the trust.

(6) Subsections (3) and (4) are without prejudice to any right of an employee to terminate his contract of employment if a substantial change is made to his detriment in his working conditions; but no such right shall arise by reason only of the change in employer effected by this section.

(7) A scheme under this section may designate a person either individually or as a member of a class or description of employees.

Supplementary provisions as to transfer of staff

12C.—(1) In the case of a person who falls within subsection (1)(b) of section 12B, a scheme under that section may provide that, with effect from the NHS trust's operational date, his contract of employment (in this section referred to as "his original contract") shall be treated in accordance with the scheme as divided so as to constitute—

(a) a contract of employment with the NHS trust; and

(b) a contract of employment with the transferor authority by whom he was employed before that date.

(2) Where a scheme makes provision as mentioned in subsection (1)—

  (a) the scheme shall secure that the benefits to the employee under the two contracts referred to in that subsection, when taken together, are not less favourable than the benefits under his original contract;
  (b) section 12B shall apply in relation to the contract referred to in subsection (1)(a) as if it were a contract transferred under that section from the transferor authority to the NHS trust;
  (c) so far as necessary to preserve any rights and obligations, the contract referred to in subsection (1)(b) shall be regarded as a continuation of the employee's original contract; and
  (d) for the purposes of section 146 of and Schedule 13 to the Employment Protection (Consolidation) Act 1978, the number of hours normally worked, or, as the case may be, the hours for which the employee is employed in any week under either of those contracts shall be taken to be the total of the hours normally worked or, as the case may be, for which he is employed under the two contracts taken together.

(3) Where, as a result of the provisions of section 12B, by virtue of his employment during any period after the NHS trust's operational date—

  (a) an employee has contractual rights against an NHS trust to benefits in the event of his redundancy, and
  (b) he also has statutory rights against the NHS trust under Part VI of the Employment Protection (Consolidation) Act 1978 (redundancy payments),

any benefits provided to him by virtue of the contractual rights referred to in paragraph (a) shall be taken as satisfying his entitlement to benefits under Part VI of that Act.

Transfer of property rights and liabilities to NHS trusts

12D.—(1) The Secretary of State may by order provide for the transfer to an NHS trust, with effect from such date as may be specified in the order, of such of the property, liabilities and obligations of a Health Board, the Agency or the Secretary of State as, in his opinion, need to be transferred to the NHS trust for the purpose of enabling it to carry out its functions.

(2) An order under this section may create or impose, or provide for the creation or imposition of, such new rights, liabilities or obligations in respect of what is transferred or what is retained by a Health Board or the Agency as appear to the Secretary of State to be necessary or expedient.

(3) Nothing in this section affects the power of the Secretary of State or any power of a Health Board or the Agency to transfer property, liabilities or obligations to an NHS trust otherwise than under subsection (1).

(4) Stamp duty shall not be chargeable in respect of any transfer to an NHS trust effected by virtue of an order under this section.

(5) Where an order under this section provides for the transfer—

  (a) of land held on lease from a third party, that is to say, a person other than the Secretary of State; or
  (b) of any other asset leased or hired from a third party or in which a third party has an interest,

the transfer shall be binding on the third party notwithstanding that, apart from this subsection, it would have required his consent or concurrence, or would have required to be intimated to him.

(6) Any property, liabilities and obligations which are to be transferred to an NHS trust shall be identified by agreement between, on the one hand, the NHS trust and, on the other hand, a Health Board or the Agency; or, in default of agreement, by direction of the Secretary of State.

(7) Where, for the purpose of a transfer pursuant to an order under this section, it becomes necessary to apportion any property, liabilities and obligations, the order may contain such provisions as appear to the Secretary of State to be appropriate for the purpose; and where any such property falls within subsection (5), the order shall contain such provisions as appear to the Secretary of State to be appropriate to safeguard the interests of third parties, including, where appropriate, provision for the payment of compensation of an amount to be determined in accordance with the order.

(8) Without prejudice to section 105(7), an order under this section may include provision for matters to be settled by arbitration by a person determined in accordance with the order.

Originating capital debt of, and other financial provisions relating to NHS trusts

12E.—(1) Each NHS trust shall have an originating capital debt of an amount specified in an order made by the Secretary of State with the consent of the Treasury, being an amount representing, subject to subsection (2), the excess of the valuation of the assets which, on or in connection with the establishment of the trust, are or are to be transferred to it (whether before, on or after its operational date) over the amounts of the liabilities which are or are to be so transferred.

(2) In determining the originating capital debt of an NHS trust, there shall be left out of account such assets or, as the case may be, such liabilities as are, or are of a class, determined for the purposes of this section by the Secretary of State, with the consent of the Treasury.

(3) An NHS trust's originating capital debt shall be deemed to have been issued out of moneys provided by Parliament and shall constitute an asset of the Consolidated Fund.

(4) In accordance with an order under subsection (1), an NHS trust's originating capital debt shall be divided between—

  (a) a loan on which interest shall be paid at such variable or fixed rates and at such times as the Treasury may determine; and

  (b) public dividend capital.

(5) The loan specified in subsection (4)(a) is in this Part of this Act referred to as an NHS trust's "initial loan" and a rate of interest on the initial loan shall be determined as if section 5 of the National Loans Act 1968 had effect in respect of it and subsections (5) to (5B) of that section shall apply accordingly.

(6) Subject to subsections (4)(a) and (5), the terms of the initial loan shall be such as the Secretary of State, with the consent of the Treasury, may determine; and, in the event of the early repayment of the initial loan, the terms may require the payment of a premium or allow a discount.

(7) With the consent of the Treasury, the Secretary of State may determine the terms on which any public dividend capital forming part of an NHS trust's originating capital debt is to be treated as having been issued, and, in particular, may determine the dividend which is to be payable at any time on any public dividend capital.

(8) Schedule 7B shall have effect with respect to—

  (a) borrowing by NHS trusts;

(b) the limits on their indebtedness;
(c) the payment of additional public dividend capital to them; and
(d) the application of any surplus funds of NHS trusts.

Financial obligations of NHS trusts

12F.—(1) Every NHS trust shall ensure that its revenue is not less than sufficient, taking one financial year with another, to meet outgoings properly chargeable to revenue account.

(2) It shall be the duty of every NHS trust to achieve such financial objectives as may from time to time be set by the Secretary of State with the consent of the Treasury and as are applicable to it; and any such objectives may be made applicable to NHS trusts generally, or to a particular NHS trust or to NHS trusts of a particular description."

DEFINITIONS
"NHS Trusts": subs. (1) of s.12A.
"the 1978 Act": s.27.

GENERAL NOTE
National Health Service Trusts are intended to be independent organisations established by the Secretary of State to own and manage hospitals and other facilities previously managed by health boards. The provisions in this section are virtually identical to the provisions for England and Wales found in ss.5 to 10 of this Act. (See GENERAL NOTES to these sections.)
S.12A corresponds to s.5. The duty to consult Community Health Councils with regard to the establishment of NHS trusts in s.5(2) is not replicated for Scottish Local Health Councils in s.12A(2).
S.12B corresponds to s.6. Under s.12B, employees may be transferred from the Common Services Agency, as well as individual health boards.
Ss.12C, 12D, 12E and 12F correspond to ss.7, 8, 9 and 10 respectively.
The provisions relating to NHS trusts came into force in Scotland on July 24, 1990 (S.I. 1520/1990).

Further provision relating to NHS trusts

32. After Schedule 7 to the 1978 Act there shall be inserted the Schedules set out in Schedule 6 to this Act.

DEFINITIONS
"the 1978 Act": s.27.

GENERAL NOTE
Sched. 6 makes detailed provision for NHS trusts by inserting two new schedules into the 1978 Act.

Sched. 7A
Paras. 1 to 16: these correspond with paras. 1 to 16 of Sched. 2 for England and Wales.
Paras. 17 to 19: these deal with the transfer of staff between local authorities and NHS trusts in connection with Community Care Services. Together with Sched. 5, paras. 6 and 11, which deal with health board staff and Common Services Agency staff respectively, they are similar in effect to s.49 in England and Wales.
Paras. 20 to 23 correspond to paras. 17 to 20 of Sched. 2; para. 24 corresponds to para. 27 of Sched. 2; paras. 25 to 28 correspond to paras. 29 to 32 of Sched. 2.

Sched. 7B
This corresponds to Sched. 3 for England and Wales. The maximum indebtedness in para. 3 is set at between £500,000 and £1,000,000, which is one tenth of the English and Welsh maxima.

Trust property of NHS trusts

33. After section 12F of the 1978 Act (as inserted by section 31 of this Act) there shall be inserted the following section—

"Trust property of NHS trusts

12G.—(1) Subject to subsection (2), an NHS trust shall have power to accept, hold and administer any property on trust for purposes relating to any service which it is their function to make arrangements for, administer or provide.

(2) The Secretary of State may by order make such provision as he thinks appropriate in relation to the appointment of trustees in respect of an NHS trust for the purpose of holding in trust any property which is to be so held on behalf of the trust; and any such order may include provision as to the persons by whom, the manner in which, the conditions on which and the time within which, such trustees are to be appointed.

(3) Where—

(a) section 82 applies in relation to any endowment or property which is held on trust by a Health Board; and

(b) that endowment or property is, by virtue of an order under section 12D, transferred to an NHS trust,

section 82 shall apply to the use of that endowment or property by the trust as it applied to the use thereof by the Health Board.

(4) Trustees appointed by virtue of subsection (2) shall cause proper accounts to be kept of the capital, income and expenditure vested in, received by and expended by them; and shall cause such accounts to be audited and an abstract thereof to be published in such manner as the Secretary of State may approve."

DEFINITIONS
 "NHS Trusts": s.31.
 "the 1978 Act": s.27.

GENERAL NOTE
 This section is similar in purpose to s.11 for England and Wales. It is intended to permit NHS trusts to benefit from existing and future endowments and charitable donations. Such funds will be held in a separate trust, with audited accounts. Under s.12D, inserted to the 1978 Act by s.31, existing endowments may be transferred to NHS trusts.

Subs. (3)
 Where s.82 of the 1978 Act requires the health board to ensure that the original objects of any trust fund are not prejudiced, the trustees of the NHS trust will be similarly bound on the transfer of such a fund.

Fund-holding practices

Fund-holding practices

34. After section 87 of the 1978 Act there shall be inserted the following sections—

"Fund-holding practices

Recognition of fund-holding practices of doctors

87A.—(1) Any one or more medical practitioners who are providing general medical services in accordance with arrangements under section 19 may apply to the relevant Health Board for recognition as a fund-holding practice.

(2) The relevant Health Board shall not grant recognition as a fund-holding practice unless the medical practitioner or, as the case may be, each of the medical practitioners concerned fulfils such conditions as may be prescribed.

(3) Where two or more medical practitioners who wish to make an application under subsection (1) are not partners in a single part-

nership, section 19(8)(a) (construction of "relevant Health Board") shall apply as if the medical practitioners were practising in a single partnership.

(4) Regulations may make provision with respect to—

(a) the making of applications under subsection (1);

(b) the granting and refusal of recognition as a fund-holding practice;

(c) the conditions to be fulfilled for obtaining and continuing to be entitled to such recognition;

(d) appeals against any refusal of such recognition by a Health Board;

(e) withdrawing from, or becoming a member of, an existing recognised fund-holding practice;

(f) the continuity or otherwise of a recognised fund-holding practice in the event of the death or withdrawal of a member or the addition of a new member; and

(g) the operation of this section in a case where one or more of the medical practitioners wishing to make an application under subsection (1) is also on the medical list of a Family Health Services Authority established under section 10 of the National Health Service Act 1977,

and regulations making the provision referred to in paragraph (g) may make such modifications of the preceding provisions of this section as the Secretary of State considers appropriate.

Payments to recognised fund-holding practices

87B.—(1) In respect of each financial year, every Health Board shall be liable to pay to the members of each recognised fund holding practice in relation to which it is the relevant Health Board a sum determined in such manner and by reference to such factors as the Secretary of State may direct (in this section referred to as an "allotted sum").

(2) The liability to pay an allotted sum under subsection (1) may be discharged, in whole or in part, in either of the following ways—

(a) by making payments on account of the allotted sum at such times and in such manner as the Secretary of State may direct; and

(b) by discharging liabilities of the members of the practice to any other person (including, in particular, liabilities under NHS contracts);

and any reference in this section and section 87C to payment of or of a part of an allotted sum includes a reference to the discharge, in accordance with this subsection, of the whole or part of the liability to pay that sum.

(3) In any case where—

(a) a Health Board makes a payment of, or of any part of, an allotted sum to the members of a recognised fund-holding practice, and

(b) some of the individuals on the lists of patients of any of the members of the practice reside in the area of another Health Board, or in the region of a Regional Health Authority established under section 8 of the National Health Service Act 1977,

the Board making the payment shall be entitled to recover from that other Board or the Authority an amount equal to such portion of the payment as may be determined in accordance with directions given by the Secretary of State.

(4) The members of a recognised fund-holding practice may apply allotted sums only for purposes specified in regulations under subsection (5).

(5) Regulations shall make provision with respect to the purposes for which allotted sums are to be or may be applied and may make provision generally with respect to the operation of recognised fund-holding practices in relation to allotted sums; and the regulations may, in particular,—

(a) require the members of a practice to pay to the relevant Health Board out of allotted sums paid to them an amount determined in accordance with the regulations as the basic cost of the drugs, medicines and listed appliances supplied pursuant to orders given by or on behalf of members of the practice;

(b) provide that the goods and services, other than general medical services, which may be purchased by or on behalf of the members of such a practice out of allotted sums for the individuals on the lists of patients of the members of the practice shall be such as may be specified in a list approved for the purpose under the regulations; and

(c) impose a limit on the amount which may be spent out of an allotted sum on the provision of goods and services for any one individual, being a limit above which the cost of any goods and services for that individual in the financial year in question will fall to be met by the Health Board whose functions include the provision of goods and services (not necessarily the goods and services in question) to the individual concerned.

(6) In accordance with directions given by the Secretary of State, the relevant Health Board shall monitor the expenditure of the members of a recognised fund-holding practice and may institute an audit and review in any case where the Board consider it necessary to do so.

Renunciation and removal of recognition as a fund-holding practice and withholding of funds

87C.—(1) Regulations may make provision as to the circumstances in which the members of a recognised fund- holding practice may renounce that status and such regulations may, in particular, make provision as to—

(a) the notice to be given and the number of members of the practice by whom it is to be given;

(b) the procedure to be followed; and

(c) the consequences of such a renunciation.

(2) Regulations may make provision as to the circumstances in which and the grounds on which the relevant Health Board may remove recognition from the members of a fund-holding practice,—

(a) with immediate effect; or

(b) with effect from the end of a particular financial year; or

(c) with effect from such other date as may be specified by the Health Board.

(3) Where provision is made as mentioned in subsection (2), regulations shall make provision with respect to—

(a) the procedure for removal of recognition;

(b) appeals against the removal of recognition by a Health Board; and

(c) the consequences of the removal of recognition.

(4) Without prejudice to the generality of the powers conferred by subsection (3), regulations making provision as mentioned in paragraph (c) of that subsection may—

(a) provide for the transfer of rights and obligations from the members of the fund-holding practice to one or more Health Boards determined in accordance with the regulations;

(b) provide for the recovery of sums from members of the practice; and

(c) require the members of the practice to furnish such information as may reasonably be required by the Health Board.

(5) The bringing of an appeal against the removal of recognition by a Health Board shall not be regarded as preserving the recognised status of the members of the fund-holding practice and, accordingly, subject to the outcome of the appeal, the relevant Health Board shall not be required, after the removal takes effect, to make any (or, as the case may be, any further) payment to the members of the practice of any part of the allotted sum for the financial year in question or, as the case may be, to determine and pay any allotted sum for a future financial year.

(6) Where any part of an allotted sum has been applied by the members of a recognised fund-holding practice (or any one or more of them) for purposes other than those specified in regulations under section 87B(5), regulations may make provision for and in connection with the recovery by the relevant Health Board of an amount equal to that part.

(7) Where provision is made as mentioned in subsection (6), regulations shall make provision with respect to appeals against the recovery of any amount by a Health Board."

DEFINITIONS
  "allotted sum": s.87B(1).
  "the 1978 Act": s.27.

GENERAL NOTE
  This provides for the recognition of fund-holding practices of GPs. It does this by inserting three new sections into the 1978 Act. The responsibilities of family health service authorities, district health authorities and regional health authorities with regard to fund-holding practices in England and Wales, are all, in Scotland, invested in health boards. Otherwise the provisions are virtually identical to those in England and Wales. (See General Notes to ss.14–16.)
  S.87A corresponds to s.14. Subs. 3 is slightly different from the corresponding s.14(4). S.19A(a) of the 1978 Act referred to in subs. (3) is inserted by s.37 of this Act.
  S.87B corresponds to s.15. Unlike s.15(4), subs. (3) makes no provision for recovery of funds in respect of patients living in Wales who are on the list of the Scottish Fund-Holding Practice, presumably since such a situation is not anticipated.
  S.87C corresponds to s.16.

Indicative amounts

Indicative amounts for doctors' practices

35. After the sections inserted in the 1978 Act by section 34 above there shall be inserted the following section—

"Indicative amounts

Indicative amounts for doctors' practices

87D.—(1) Subject to subsection (2), for each financial year every Health Board shall, by notice in writing given to each practice in relation to the members of which it is the relevant Health Board, specify an amount of money (in this Act referred to as an "indicative amount") representing the basic price of the drugs, medicines and listed appliances which, in the opinion of the Board, it is reasonable to expect will be supplied in that year pursuant to orders given by or on behalf of the members of that practice.

(2) Subsection (1) does not apply with respect to a practice which is or forms part of a fund-holding practice recognised under section 87A.

(3) For the purposes of this section, a "practice" means—

(a) a single medical practitioner who practises otherwise than in partnership; or

(b) any two or more medical practitioners who practise in partnership;

and any reference to the members of a practice shall be construed accordingly.

(4) The members of a practice shall seek to secure that, except with the consent of the relevant Health Board or for good cause, the orders for drugs, medicines and listed appliances given by them or on their behalf are such that the basic price of the items supplied pursuant to those orders in any financial year does not exceed the indicative amount notified to the practice for that year under subsection (1).

(5) For the purpose of measuring the extent to which a practice is operating within the indicative amount notified to it under subsection (1) for any financial year, a Health Board shall set against that indicative amount an amount equal to the basic price of the drugs, medicines and listed appliances supplied in that year pursuant to orders given by or on behalf of members of the practice.

(6) For the purposes of this section, regulations may make provision as to the specification of, or means of calculating, the basic price of any drugs, medicines and listed appliances.

(7) If, in the case of any practice, a member is on the medical list of a Family Health Services Authority established under section 10 of the National Health Service Act 1977 (as well as on that of a Health Board), any question whether this section applies in relation to the members of the practice shall be determined in accordance with regulations; and any such regulations may modify the preceding provisions of this section in their application to such a practice."

DEFINITIONS

"indicative amount": subs. (1).

"practice": subs. (3).

"the 1978 Act": s.27.

GENERAL NOTE

Health boards will now be obliged to notify GP practices of the amount of money which it is reasonable to expect the practice to spend on drugs, medicines and listed appliances in any year. It obliges practices to seek to ensure that the amount is not exceeded without consent or good cause. See also General Note to s.18 for England and Wales.

Audit

Accounts and audit of NHS trusts and fund-holding practices

36.—(1) The enactments specified in Schedule 7 to this Act shall have effect subject to the amendments set out in that Schedule being amendments—

(a) to extend the functions of the Commission for Local Authority Accounts in Scotland (in this section referred to as "the Commission") to cover Health Boards and other bodies established under the 1978 Act, the Mental Welfare Commission for Scotland and State Hospital Management Committees constituted under the Mental Health (Scotland) Act 1984;

(b) to alter the title and constitution of the Commission to reflect its wider role; and

(c) to make provision consequential on or supplemental to the amendments referred to in paragraphs (a) and (b) above.

(2) Section 86 of the 1978 Act (keeping and audit of accounts of certain Scottish health bodies) shall be amended in accordance with the following provisions of this section.

(3) In subsection (1), for the words from the beginning to "Agency" there shall be substituted—

"(1) The following bodies, that is to say—

(a) every Health Board;
(b) the Agency; and
(c) every NHS trust,".

(4) After subsection (1) there shall be inserted the following subsections—

"(1A) So far as relates to allotted sums paid to the members of a recognised fund-holding practice—

(a) accounts shall be kept in such form as the Secretary of State may with the approval of the Treasury direct and shall be audited by auditors appointed by the Secretary of State;
(b) the Comptroller and Auditor General may examine the accounts and the records relating to them and any report of the auditor on them;
(c) in respect of each financial year, annual accounts in such form as the Secretary of State may with the approval of the Treasury direct shall be prepared and submitted to the relevant Health Board; and
(d) in respect of each financial year, each Health Board shall prepare, in such form as the Secretary of State may with the approval of the Treasury direct, and include in its own accounts, a summarised version of the accounts submitted to the Board under paragraph (c).

(1B) In preparing its annual accounts in pursuance of subsection (1), an NHS trust shall comply with any directions given by the Secretary of State with the approval of the Treasury as to—

(a) the methods and principles according to which the accounts are to be prepared; and
(b) the information to be given in the accounts."

(5) Until the day appointed for the coming into force of paragraph 14 of Schedule 7 to this Act, in subsection (2)—

(a) for the words "subsection (1)" there shall be substituted "subsections (1) and (1A),";
(b) for the words "Health Board or the Agency" there shall be substituted "body mentioned in paragraphs (a) to (c) of subsection (1) or a recognised fund-holding practice"; and
(c) for the words "Board or the Agency" there shall be substituted "body or practice."

(6) In subsection (3), for the words "Health Board and the Agency" there shall be substituted "body mentioned in paragraphs (a) to (c) of subsection (1)."

(7) In subsection (4), for the words "Health Boards and the Agency" there shall be substituted "bodies mentioned in paragraphs (a) to (c) of subsection (1)."

(8) After subsection (4) there shall be added the following subsection—

"(5) In this section "recognised fund-holding practice" and "allotted sum" have the same meaning as in section 87B."

DEFINITIONS
"allotted sum": s.34 (s.87B).
"NHS Trust": s.31.

"recognised Fund-Holding Practice": s.34 (s.87B).
"the Commission": subs. (1)(a).
"the 1978 Act": s.27.

GENERAL NOTE

Subs. (1)

The Commission for Local Authority Accounts in Scotland (equivalent to the Audit Commission in England and Wales) is to be renamed the "Accounts Commission for Scotland" and its rôle is extended to cover Health Boards, the Common Services Agency, NHS Trusts, Fund-Holding Practices, the Mental Welfare Commission and the State Hospital Management Committee. Sched. 7 makes detailed changes to the Local Government (Scotland) Act 1973 to give effect to this. The minimum and maximum membership of the Commission are increased from nine to 11 and 12 to 15 respectively (para. 3(2)).

Civil servants currently employed in the auditing of the Health Service will be transferred to the employment of the Commission (para. 6).

The Controller of Audit's responsibility to make reports to the Commission in matters of concern regarding accounts is also extended to the above Health Service bodies (para. 9).

Any expenditure which is or is likely to be unlawful must be reported to the Secretary of State (para. 11).

Subss. (2) and (3)

These extend to NHS Trusts the requirements of s.86 of the 1978 Act to keep accounts in the form directed by the Secretary of State, subject to audit by auditors appointed by the Secretary of State (to be replaced by the Accounts Commission for Scotland when subs. (1) comes into force).

Subs. (4)

Fund-Holding Practices will also be subject to public audit, in respect of the allotted sums paid by the Health Board, and NHS Trust accounts must be in the form directed by the Secretary of State.

Subs. (5)

This anticipates a staged implementation of the new accounting arrangements. Initially, the current Civil Service audits will be extended to the new bodies created by the Act and at a later date the extended rôle of the Accounts Commission for Scotland in subs. (1) will be implemented. In the transitional period, s.86(2) of the 1978 Act will allow regulations to be made with respect to the audit of accounts of Health Boards, the Common Services Agency, Fund-Holding Practices and NHS Trusts.

Subs. (6)

NHS Trusts will also be required to transmit accounts to the Secretary of State.

Subs. (7)

The Secretary of State will prepare summarised accounts of NHS Trusts, which shall be certified by the Comptroller and Auditor General and laid before Parliament.

Miscellaneous

Relationship of Health Boards and medical practitioners

37. After subsection (7) of section 19 of the 1978 Act (arrangements and regulations for general medical services) there shall be inserted the following subsection—

> "(8) In relation to a medical practitioner, any reference in this Act to the relevant Health Board shall be construed as follows—
> (a) if he practises in partnership with other medical practitioners, the relevant Health Board is the Board on whose medical list the members of the practice are included and, if some are included on one Board's medical list and some on another's or if any of the members is included on the medical lists of two or more Boards, the relevant Health Board is the Board in whose area resides the largest number of individuals who are on the lists of patients of members of the practice; and

(b) in any other case, the relevant Health Board is the Board on whose medical list he is included and, if there is more than one, the Board in whose area resides the largest number of individuals who are on his list of patients."

DEFINITIONS
"the 1978 Act": s.27.

GENERAL NOTE
The "relevant Health Board" in any area will be the board responsible for recognising and administering Fund-Holding Practices and setting out indicative prescribing budgets. Normally this will be the Board on whose medical list the practice or individual GP is included, but where the practice or GP is on more than one list, the relevant Health Board will be the Board from whose area come the majority of the patients of the practice or GP.

Scottish Medical Practices Committee

38.—(1) In section 3 of the 1978 Act (the Scottish Medical Practices Committee), after subsection (1) there shall be inserted the following subsection—

"(1A) After consulting the Medical Practices Committee, the Secretary of State may give the Committee directions with respect to the exercise of its functions; and it shall be the duty of the Committee to comply with any such directions."

(2) In Schedule 2 to the 1978 Act (constitution etc of Scottish Medical Practices Committee), after paragraph 2 there shall be inserted—

"2A. The Secretary of State may by order make such modifications as he considers appropriate of paragraphs 1 and 2."

DEFINITIONS
"the 1978 Act": s.27.

GENERAL NOTE
The Scottish Medical Practices Committee controls the distribution of GPs in Scotland, seeking to ensure that the supply of general medical services is adequate throughout the country. This section gives the Secretary of State greater power to control the exercise of the Committee's functions, and to modify the composition of the Committee. The equivalent provision for England and Wales is s.22.

Distribution of general medical services

39.—(1) In section 23 of the 1978 Act (distribution of general medical services), after subsection (1) there shall be inserted the following subsections—

"(1A) The Secretary of State may by order specify the maximum number of medical practitioners with whom, in any year, all Health Boards taken as a whole may enter into arrangements under section 19 for the provision of general medical services.

(1B) An order under subsection (1A) may contain such incidental and consequential provisions (including provisions amending this Part of this Act) as appear to the Secretary of State to be appropriate including, in particular, provisions as to the basis on which the Medical Practices Committee are to refuse applications under section 20 in order to secure that any maximum number specified in the order is not exceeded."

(2) At the beginning of subsection (2) of that section (the Medical Practices Committee to select the person whose applications are to be granted) there shall be inserted "Subject to subsection (2A)" and after that subsection there shall be inserted the following subsection—

"(2A) If, in the opinion of the Medical Practices Committee, a medical practitioner is required for a particular part of the area of a Health Board, then, in such circumstances as may be prescribed,—

(a) the Board shall, in accordance with regulations, select the medical practitioner whose application they wish to be considered by the Committee; and

(b) the Committee shall not consider any application from a medical practitioner who is not so selected; and

(c) any medical practitioner who has made an application but is not so selected may appeal to the Secretary of State on a point of law;

and if the Secretary of State allows an appeal under paragraph (c) he shall remit the application to the Board for reconsideration."

(3) In subsection (4) of that section (applications under section 20 may be granted subject to certain conditions), after the word "but" there shall be inserted—

"(a) in granting an application shall specify, by reference to one or more prescribed conditions relating to hours or the sharing of work, the provision of general medical services for which the applicant will be entitled to be remunerated; and

(b),"

and at the end of the subsection there shall be inserted the words "and an order under subsection (1A) may make provision as to the extent to which account is to be taken under the order of medical practitioners whose ability to carry out remunerated work is limited by virtue of conditions imposed under paragraph (a)."

(4) In subsection (5) of that section (appeals to the Secretary of State) for the words "such conditions" there shall be substituted "conditions under paragraph (a) or (b) of subsection (4)" and for the words following "Secretary of State," in the first place where those words occur, there shall be substituted "on a point of law; and, if the Secretary of State allows such an appeal, he shall remit the application to the Medical Practices Committee for reconsideration."

(5) Subsection (7) of that section (directions on a successful appeal) shall be omitted.

(6) In subsection (8) of that section (matters to be taken into account) for the words from the beginning to "in any such case" there shall be substituted "In any case where medical practitioners have to be selected from a number of applicants, the Medical Practices Committee or, where subsection (2A) applies, the Health Board shall."

(7) In section 24 of the 1978 Act (regulations for Medical Practices Committee)—

(a) in paragraph (b)(ii) after the words "under section 23" there shall be inserted "and, where such an appeal is allowed, the reconsideration of any application"; and

(b) at the end of the section there shall be added the following subsection—

"(2) Regulations under this section may make provision for, and in connection with, the variation of any condition imposed under subsection (4) or (5) of section 23 including provision for appeals to the Secretary of State on a point of law.

(8) In the case of a medical practitioner who, on the day appointed for the coming into force of this section, is providing general medical services in accordance with arrangements under section 19 of the 1978 Act, regulations may make transitional provisions by virtue of which those services shall be treated for the purposes of that Act as provided subject to such of the prescribed conditions referred to in section 23(4)(a) of that Act as are determined under the regulations and, accordingly, for enabling any such condition to be varied in accordance with regulations under section 24(2) of that Act.

DEFINITIONS
"the 1978 Act": s.27.

GENERAL NOTE
Subss. (1) and (2)
Subs. (1) gives the Secretary of State powers to restrict the number of general practitioners, to prevent an imbalance between GPs and other doctors, whilst subs. (2) gives the Health Board a right of nomination of GPs to be considered by the Medical Practices Committee in prescribed circumstances, subject to a right of appeal.

Subs. (3)
This varies the conditions which may be imposed by the Scottish Medical Practices Committee.

Subss. (4) to (8)
These alter the appeal procedure, and make consequential amendments. The effect of this section is identical to s.23 for England and Wales.

Limitations on right to be included on list of dental practitioners

40.—(1) Section 25 of the 1978 Act (arrangements for general dental services) shall be amended in accordance with this section
(2) In subsection (2)(b) (regulations to include provision conferring a right, subject to certain qualifications, to be entered on a list of dental practitioners providing general dental services) for the words "subsection (2A)" there shall be substituted "subsections (2A) and (2B)."
(3) After subsection (2A) there shall be inserted the following subsection—

"(2B) Regulations may make the exercise of the right conferred by virtue of paragraph (b) of subsection (2) subject to any provision made by or under the regulations, and, in such cases as may be prescribed, may confer a right of appeal to a prescribed body in respect of a refusal to include a dental practitioner on such a list as is referred to in paragraph (a) of that subsection."

DEFINITIONS
"the 1978 Act": s.27.

GENERAL NOTE
This gives the Secretary of State power to make regulations controlling or restricting the right of dentists to be admitted to a Health Board's dental list. See also s.24 for the corresponding provision for England and Wales.

Schemes for meeting losses and liabilities etc. of certain health service bodies

41. After section 85A of the 1978 Act there shall be inserted the following section—

"**Schemes for meeting losses and liabilities etc. of certain health service bodies**
85B.—(1) The Secretary of State may by regulations made with the consent of the Treasury establish a scheme service whereby any of the bodies mentioned in subsection (2) may make provision to meet—
(a) expenses arising from any loss of or damage to their property; and
(b) liabilities to third parties for loss, damage (including solatium) or injury arising out of the carrying out of the functions of the bodies concerned.
(2) The bodies referred to in subsection (1) are—
(a) Health Boards;

(b) the Agency;

(c) a State Hospital Management Committee constituted under section 91 of the Mental Health (Scotland) Act 1984; and;

(d) NHS trusts,

but a scheme under this section may limit the class or description of bodies which are eligible to participate in it.

(3) Without prejudice to the generality of the power conferred by subsection (1), a scheme under this section may—

(a) provide for the scheme to be administered by the Secretary of State, the Agency, or a Health Board or NHS trust specified in the scheme;

(b) require any body which participates in the scheme to make payments in accordance with the scheme; and

(c) provide for the making of payments for the purposes of the scheme by the Secretary of State.

(4) Without prejudice to any other power of direction conferred on the Secretary of State,—

(a) if the Secretary of State so directs, any body which is eligible to participate in a scheme shall do so; and

(b) where a scheme provides for it to be administered by the Secretary of State, the Agency or a Health Board or NHS trust shall carry out such functions in connection with the administration of the scheme as the Secretary of State may direct.

(5) Neither the Secretary of State nor any body administering a scheme under this section shall, by virtue of their activities under the scheme, be regarded as carrying on insurance business for the purposes of the Insurance Companies Act 1982."

DEFINITIONS
"the 1978 Act": s.27.

GENERAL NOTE
The Secretary of State is empowered to make special arrangements to meet losses and liabilities of previous Health Boards, including NHS Trusts. These arrangements are likely to include provision to deal with large legal claims, which might be too large for an individual body to sustain. See also s.21.

PART III

COMMUNITY CARE: ENGLAND AND WALES

Provision of accommodation and welfare services

Provision of accommodation and welfare services: agency arrangements

42.—(1) In section 21(1) of the National Assistance Act 1948 (duties of local authorities to provide accommodation for persons aged 18 or over who are in need of care and attention by reason of age, infirmity or other circumstances)—

(a) in paragraph (a) for the word "infirmity" there shall be substituted "illness, disability"; and

(b) at the end of that paragraph there shall be added "and

(aa) residential accommodation for expectant and nursing mothers who are in need of care and attention which is not otherwise available to them."

(2) For subsections (1) and (1A) of section 26 of that Act (arrangements for provision of accommodation in premises maintained by voluntary organisations, etc.) there shall be substituted—

"(1) Subject to subsection (1A) of this section, arrangements under section 21 of this Act may include arrangements with any

voluntary organisation or other person, being an organisation or
person who—
  (a) manages a residential care home within the meaning of Part I
      of the Registered Homes Act 1984, and
  (b) is registered under that Part in respect of the home or is not
      required to be so registered by virtue of the home being a
      small home or being managed or provided by an exempt body,
for the provision of accommodation in that home.
  (1A) Arrangements under section 21 of this Act for the provision
of residential accommodation where nursing care is provided must
be arrangements made with a voluntary organisation or other person, being an organisation or person managing premises—
  (a) in respect of which the organisation or other person is regis-
      tered under Part II of the Registered Homes Act 1984, or
  (b) which do not fall within the definition of a nursing home in
      section 21 of that Act by reason only of being maintained or
      controlled by an exempt body,
for the provision of accommodation in those premises.
  (1B) Subject to subsection (1C) below no such arrangements as
mentioned in subsection (1A) of this section may be made by an
authority for the accommodation of any person without the consent
of such District Health Authority as may be determined in accordance with regulations.
  (1C) Subsection (1B) above does not apply to the making by an
authority of temporary arrangements for the accommodation of any
person as a matter of urgency; but, as soon as practicable after any
such temporary arrangements have been made, the authority shall
seek the consent required by subsection (1B) above to the making of
appropriate arrangements for the accommodation of the person
concerned.
  (1D) No arrangements may be made by virtue of this section with
a person who has been convicted of an offence under any provision
of the Registered Homes Act 1984 (or any enactment replaced by
that Act) or regulations made under section 16 or section 26 of that
Act (or under any corresponding provisions of any such
enactment)."
  (3) At the end of subsection (2) of that section (under which the arrangements must provide for the local authority to make payments in respect of
accommodation provided) there shall be added "and subject to subsection
(3A) below the local authority shall recover from each person for whom
accommodation is provided under the arrangements the amount of the
refund which he is liable to make in accordance with the following provisions of this section."
  (4) At the beginning of subsection (3) of that section (liability of persons
for whom accommodation is provided to make refunds to the local
authority) there shall be inserted "Subject to subsection (3A) below" and
after that subsection there shall be inserted the following subsection—
  "(3A) Where accommodation in any premises is provided for any
person under arrangements made by virtue of this section and the
local authority, the person concerned and the voluntary organisation
or other person managing the premises (in this subsection referred to
as "the provider") agree that this subsection shall apply—
  (a) so long as the person concerned makes the payments for which
      he is liable under paragraph (b) below, he shall not be liable to
      make any refund under subsection (3) above and the local
      authority shall not be liable to make any payment under
      subsection (2) above in respect of the accommodation pro-
      vided for him;

(b) the person concerned shall be liable to pay to the provider such sums as he would otherwise (under subsection (3) above) be liable to pay by way of refund to the local authority; and

(c) the local authority shall be liable to pay to the provider the difference between the sums paid by virtue of paragraph (b) above and the payments which, but for paragraph (a) above, the authority would be liable to pay under subsection (2) above."

(5) At the end of subsection (7) of that section (interpretation) there shall be added " "small home" means an establishment falling within section 1(4) of the Registered Homes Act 1984 and "exempt body" means an authority or body constituted by an Act of Parliament or incorporated by Royal Charter."

(6) In section 30(1) of that Act (under which a local authority may employ certain voluntary organisations as their agents for the provision of welfare services for disabled persons) for the words from "any voluntary organisation" onwards there shall be substituted "any voluntary organisation or any person carrying on, professionally or by way of trade or business, activities which consist of or include the provision of services for any of the persons to whom section 29 above applies, being an organisation or person appearing to the authority to be capable of providing the service to which the arrangements apply."

(7) In section 45(3) of the Health Services and Public Health Act 1968 (under which a local authority may employ certain voluntary organisations as their agents for promoting the welfare of old people) for the words from "any voluntary organisation" onwards there shall be substituted "any voluntary organisation or any person carrying on, professionally or by way of trade or business, activities which consist of or include the provision of services for old people, being an organisation or person appearing to the authority to be capable of promoting the welfare of old people."

DEFINITIONS

"disability": s.64 of the National Assistance Act 1948.

"District Health Authority": ss.8 and 128 of the National Health Service Act 1977, as amended by this Act, and Sched. 1 to this Act.

"small home": subs. (7).

"voluntary organisation": s.64 of the National Assistance Act 1948; see also ss.23 and 128 of the National Health Service Act 1977.

GENERAL NOTE

The Secretary of State for Health, Mr Kenneth Clarke, explained (Comm. (SCE) col. 814): "For the future, we shall convert to the purchaser provider arrangement. . . . Each resident will be entitled to income support in the ordinary way, not at the registered home rate, dependent on needs. Each resident will have the ordinary entitlement to housing benefit which is more sensitive to the actual cost of the residential element of the care than income support. The local authority, which is the responsible agency to which we are passing the prime responsibility with almost universal support, will be able to act as a purchaser on behalf of residents. It will negotiate the right rate for all whom it assesses for residential home care, and will pay it". The Parliamentary Under-Secretary of State for Wales, Mr Ian Grist, said (Comm. (SCE) col. 778): "We propose to have registration and inspection units in the local authorities, under the control of the director of social services, and quite separate from the running of local authority homes. The director of the unit would be advised by an advisory committee made up of representatives from various other sectors: the voluntary sector, the private sector, and so on. The unit's actions would be moderated by the knowledge and experience of the members of the advisory committee".

The Parliamentary Under-Secretary of State for the Department of Social Security, Lord Henley, explained (*Hansard*, H.L. Vol. 518, col. 1299): "The provisions of Sections 21 and 26 of the National Assistance Act 1948, as amended by [this section] and of Section 22 of the same Act, as amended by [s.43 of this Act] have the effect that a local authority which arranges residential or nursing home care for someone must charge that person the full amount he is assessed as being able to pay in accordance with regulations the Secretary of State will be making under Section 22(5) of the 1948 Act [see note to s.44]. The effect of this will be to leave the person with an amount, also to be prescribed in regulations, for personal expenses. The financial assessment provisions will be prescribed in regulations and will be legally binding on local authorities, with the aim of securing equality of treatment for people in residential care and nursing homes across the country and obliging local authorities to collect the full amount legally payable by such people".

Subs. (1)
The Baroness in Waiting, Baroness Blatch, said (*Hansard*, H.L. Vol. 520, col. 419): "we deliberately cast the definition of the people for whom local authorities may provide these services very broadly in order to be as inclusive as possible . . . The provisions of Section 21 [of the 1948 Act] as [amended by this section] are subject to approval and directions by the Secretary of State, and it is in giving such approvals and directions that the attention can be drawn to any group, such as people with drug and alcohol dependency, which it is felt needs a special mention . . . We have ascertained that local authorities could provide services for drug and alcohol misusers under paragraph (2) of Schedule 8 to the National Health Service Act 1977. That deals with the care of the ill, the aftercare of those who have been ill and the prevention of illness. Before that can be done the approval of the Secretary of State is required. That was given in a circular issued [in] 1974 as regards another Act and that will be repeated in new guidance which we propose to issue in connection with the new community care arrangements".
She confirmed (*Hansard*, H.L. Vol. 518, col. 1512–3) that disabled people, including people with communicative disorders (blindness and deafness), those mentally disordered or substantially handicapped by illness, injury or congenital deformity and any other illness were included within the terms of the National Assistance Act 1948; also (*Hansard*, H.L. Vol. 520, col. 422) that HIV and AIDS conditions also be included in guidance. As regards drug and alcohol misusers, see the new s.7E of the Local Authority Social Services Act 1970, inserted by s.50 of this Act. The Parliamentary Under-Secretary of State for the Department of Health, Baroness Hooper, said (*Hansard*, H.L. Vol. 520, col. 443): "the Secretary of State for Health has made clear that he will require local authorities to include services for drug and alcohol misusers in their community care plans" under s.46.
The Minister of State for the Scottish Office, Lord Sanderson of Bowden, explained (*Hansard*, H.L. Vol. 520, col. 455): "how [the Government's] proposals will ensure that there is quality control for domiciliary services. Local authorities making arrangements with individuals or organisations to provide domiciliary services will be able to do so under contract. Contracts of this kind will, wherever possible, include standard specifications and provisions for monitoring. The most effective safeguard against substandard privately provided services will be the frequency and intensity of local authority inspections. And the ultimate sanction of cancelling a contract will be a powerful incentive for agencies to deliver a proper standard of service. Finally, any dissatisfied clients will be free to use the new complaints procedures which we will establish under [s.7B of the Local Authority Social Services Act 1970, as inserted by s.50 of this Act and their Scottish equivalents]. We are anxious to see these procedures well publicised so as to provide a clear avenue for consumer reporting". Reg. 17 of the Residential Care Home Regulations 1984 (S.I. 1984 No. 1345) requires a registered person to inform every resident in writing how a complaint about the home can be made and to ensure that such information is available at all times to residents and their representatives.

Subs. (2)
This replaces subs. (1)(1A) of s.26 of the 1948 Act with new subs. (1) (1D).

Subs. (1A) of the s.26 of the 1948 Act
The Parliamentary Under-Secretary of State for the Department of Health, Baroness Hooper, explained (*Hansard*, H.L. Vol. 518, col. 1286): "at present there are two ways involving a district health authority in which a person may enter a nursing home. Under the first, the authority advises a hospital inpatient that he is ready for discharge from hospital but will need nursing home care. The patient and his family then arrange such care, and if they require help from public funds to meet the fees the patient claims income support. The second way is for the health authority itself to enter into a contractual arrangement with the nursing home. Under that the hospital is responsible for the full cost of the place in the home. The patient moves into the nursing home but remains a hospital inpatient which means that he cannot be charged for his care or accommodation and that his entitlement to social security benefits is very limited.
"When the new community care arrangements come into effect, patients leaving hospital will no longer be able to claim a special rate of income support to meet the fees in nursing homes (unless they have preserved entitlement to income support at the registered homes

rate). Thus, if they are unable to meet the fees themselves, such patients will need to seek help from the local authority. The local authority will assess their needs for community care in accordance with [section 47] . . . and if it decides their care needs call for the provision by the authority of nursing home care, the authority will proceed to arrange that in accordance with the new Section 26(1A) of the National Assistance Act 1948. The local authority will in effect be giving its consent to provision of nursing home care by agreeing to arrange it. It will also need to seek the consent of the health authority before making arrangements, in accordance with the new Subsection 1B to Section 26 of the 1948 Act. . . . Thus, provisions [in the Act] mean that a person cannot enter a nursing home for which a local authority will have to pay without that authority being closely involved in the process and consenting to the move. . . . The key to this is in the preparation of community care plans under [section 46] . . . . Local authorities will be advised, in accordance with the White Paper *Caring for People*, that plans should include planning agreements with district health authorities. One such agreement should cover the need for nursing home places arranged by the local authority and the criteria for admission to them. The assessment and placing of individual patients in these places will then take place in the context of that planning agreement".

Subs. (1B) of s.26 of the 1948 Act
   The Baroness in Waiting, Baroness Blatch, explained (*Hansard*, H.L. Vol. 518, col. 1289): "[the Government's] intention is that in England and Wales no one should enter a nursing home at the public expense until the health authority which continues to have responsibility for providing continuing nursing care to that person has given its consent. The health authority will normally give its consent through a process of multi-disciplinary assessment. These . . . regulations will set out those for whom district health authorities are responsible. . . . the policy is that district health authorities will be responsible for providing health services to . . . people living within their districts. It is important that [this new subsection] (1B) of Section 126 of the National Assistance Act 1948 should correspond with the regulations made under [the NHS provisions of s.3(1) of this Act] so that the consent of the right district health authority can be obtained. It is for that reason that [there will be] . . . a power to make regulations which will set out which district health authority is to give consent. Such a provision is needed to cope with the overlapping responsibilities of health and local authorities". The Parliamentary Under-Secretary of State for the Department of Health, Baroness Hooper, added (*Hansard*, H.L. Vol. 519, col. 73): "What we are planning to do in the [Act] on plans [in s.46] and assessment [in s.47] is to reinforce the good practice which already exists and in which hospital social workers already play an important part. Their rôle is of especial value at the interface between health and social care, as has been said, where people leaving care in the acute sector may need substantial support as they return to their homes or another community setting".

Subs. (1C) of s.26 of the 1948 Act
   The reference to "authority" is to local government authority. The Parliamentary Under-Secretary of State for the Department of Health, Baroness Hooper, explained (*Hansard*, H.L. Vol. 520, col. 425): "[the subsection clarified] that services could be provided in cases of urgency without the need either to seek the consent of the health authority as required by the new Section 26(1B) of the National Assistance Act 1948 . . . or the need to carry out an assessment in accordance with s.47 of this Act". See further s.47(4)(5) and the note thereto.

Subs. (1D) of s.26 of the 1948 Act
   The Parliamentary Under-Secretary of State, Baroness Hooper, confirmed (*Hansard*, H.L. Vol. 520, col. 1754): "it was the intention to make regulations under the Registered Homes Act requiring applicants to disclose criminal convictions". She also announced (*Hansard*, H.L. Vol. 520, col. 1751): "The Association of Chief Police Officers has . . . agreed to participate in administrative arrangements which would . . . help safeguard residents of homes. . . . it has . . . been agreed that work should start at once on detailed preparation for a scheme that will cover applicants for registration under the Registered Homes Act 1984; that is, managers and owners of residential care and nursing homes and managers of local authority run residential care homes. It is not intended that people who are already registered should be subject to retrospective checks, but checks will be made on all new managers in established care homes. That will apply to changes of management as well as to the setting up of new homes. The arrangements will be put in place as soon as possible. Our firm intention is that they should be up and running by 1st April 1991".

Subs. (4)
   The Parliamentary Under-Secretary of State for the Department of Social Security, Lord Henley, explained (*Hansard*, H.L. Vol. 520, cols. 437–8): "[the new subsection provides] an

alternative method of payment for use where the local authority, the provider of the accommodation and the user agree. Under the alternative arrangement the user will pay the part of the
cost of the accommodation he can meet from his resources, including income support and
housing benefit, direct to the provider. The local authority will then pay the balance of the cost,
rather than the full cost which it would otherwise be liable to pay under Section 26(2) of the
1948 Act. The local authority will work out what the user should pay using the same rules as it
would use to work out what a user would pay it if it were paying the full cost of the
accommodation. Thus both the user and the local authority will pay the same in both instances.
However, instead of the local authority meeting the full cost and the user paying his share to
the authority, the local authority and user will both pay their shares direct to the provider. This
alternative arrangement will permit the provider and user to form a normal landlord/tenant
relationship. We have discussed this with the Housing Corporation which has confirmed that,
if that is so, the funding will not be endangered". He confirmed that housing association grant
will be available for providing such homes. (See *Hansard*, H.L. Vol. 520, col. 439.)

Subs. (6)
"*Any person carrying on, professionally or by way of trade or business, activities which
consist of or include the provision of services for any of the persons to whom section 29 above
applies*". The Parliamentary Under-Secretary of State for the Department of Health, Baroness
Hooper, explained that (*Hansard*, H.L. Vol. 520, col. 439): "The Government's intention
always was that local authorities should only make arrangements for the provision of services
for payment with persons professionally engaged in providing those services or otherwise
providing them by way of business or trade. It was never [the] intention that local authorities
should be able to pay people who would have provided these services on a non commercial
basis and [these words make this] clear. [They] are needed to protect local authorities from
pressure to use their powers to make arrangements with private providers in ways in which the
Government never intended".

Subs. (7)
"*Any person carrying on, professionally or by way of trade or business, activities which
consist of or include the provision of services for old people*". See the note to subs. (6).

Exclusion of powers to provide accommodation in certain cases

43. After section 26 of the National Assistance Act 1948 there shall be
inserted—

> **"Exclusion of powers to provide accommodation under this Part in
> certain cases**
> 26A.—(1) Subject to subsection (3) of this section no accommo-
> dation may be provided under section 21 or 26 of this Act for any
> person
> who immediately before the date on which this section comes into
> force was ordinarily resident in relevant premises.
> (2) In subsection (1) "relevant premises" means—
> (a) premises in respect of which any person is registered under the
>   Registered Homes Act 1984;
> (b) premises in respect of which such registration is not required
>   by virtue of their being managed or provided by an exempt
>   body;
> (c) premises which do not fall within the definition of a nursing
>   home in section 21 of that Act by reason only of their being
>   maintained or controlled by an exempt body; and
> (d) such other premises as the Secretary of State may by reg-
>   ulations prescribe;
> and in this subsection "exempt body" has the same meaning as in
> section 26 of this Act.
> (3) The Secretary of State may by regulations provide that, in such
> cases and subject to such conditions as may be prescribed, subsection
> (1) of this section shall not apply in relation to such classes of persons
> as may be prescribed in the regulations.
> (4) The Secretary of State shall by regulations prescribe the
> circumstances in which persons are to be treated as being ordinarily

resident in any premises for the purposes of subsection (1) of this section.

(5) This section does not affect the validity of any contract made before the date on which this section comes into force for the provision of accommodation on or after that date or anything done in pursuance of such a contract."

DEFINITIONS
"exempt body": s.26 of the National Assistance Act 1948, as amended by s.42(5) of this Act.
"relevant premises": s.26A(2), as inserted by this Act.

GENERAL NOTE
See note to s.42 also.

S.26A(1) of the 1948 Act
The Parliamentary Under-Secretary of State for the Department of Social Security, Lord Henley, explained (*Hansard*, H.L. Vol. 518, col. 1329): "The opening words . . . specify that local authorities are debarred . . . from helping people with the provision of accommodation under Sections 21 or 26 of the National Assistance Act 1948. Those sections deal with the provision of accommodation. If a person leaves residential care or a nursing home to live independently he or she will be able to apply for local authority help with day or domiciliary care on the same basis as anyone else. These services are provided under a different legal provision from residential and nursing home care and local authorities are not debarred from providing this help to people with preserved entitlement".

S.26A(2)(d) of the 1948 Act
The Notes on Clauses indicated that the powers under this paragraph "will be used to make regulations bringing other types of homes, for instance, residential care homes with three beds or less . . . in circumstances in which income support is payable at the registered home rates" within the scope of this section.

S.26A(3) of the 1948 Act
These powers are likely to exempt (1) people at present supported by local authorities in private and voluntary homes, either under s.26 of the 1948 Act or Sched. 8, para. 2(2) to the 1977 Act; (2) other people under pension age, as well as people over pension age, who had been supported by local authorities under their previous powers or exempted for at least two years before reaching that age, *e.g.* those in nursing homes and in residential homes; (3) people over pension age who in the opinion of the local authority would be in danger of homelessness (Notes on Clauses).

S.26A(4) of the 1948 Act
The powers conferred by this subsection will be used to make regulations limiting the expression "ordinarily resident" to exclude people who might not be so regarded for income support purposes and thus would not have a preserved right to claim income support at the registered homes rates (*e.g.* people who at that time were being provided with respite care in a home on a temporary basis) (Notes on Clauses).

Charges for accommodation provided by local authorities

44.—(1) Section 22 of the National Assistance Act 1948 (charges for accommodation provided under Part III of that Act to be made at a standard rate fixed by the local authority subject to a minimum weekly rate prescribed under subsection (3)) shall have effect subject to the amendments specified in subsections (2) to (6) below.

(2) In subsection (1) (which relates to a person's liability to pay for accommodation) for the words from the beginning to "the accommodation" there shall be substituted "Subject to section 26 of this Act, where a person is provided with accommodation under this Part of this Act the local authority providing the accommodation shall recover from him the amount of the payment which he is liable to make."

(3) In subsection (2) (which requires the authority managing premises to fix the standard rate) after the word "payment" there shall be inserted

"which a person is liable to make" and at the end of that subsection there shall be added the words "and that standard rate shall represent the full cost to the authority of providing that accommodation."

(4) In subsection (3) (which makes provision for people who are unable to pay at the standard rate)—
(a) the words "(disregarding income support)," and
(b) the words from "Provided that" to the end of the subsection,
shall be omitted.

(5) After subsection (4) (under which the Secretary of State may prescribe the minimum sum assumed to be required for a resident's personal needs in determining the rate payable by him) there shall be inserted—
"(4A) Regulations made for the purposes of subsection (4) of this section may prescribe different sums for different circumstances."

(6) In subsection (5A) (under which a local authority managing premises in which accommodation is provided for a person may limit the payments required from him for a certain period to the minimum rate prescribed under subsection (3)) for the words "the minimum weekly rate prescribed under subsection (3) above" there shall be substituted "such amount as appears to them reasonable for him to pay."

(7) In section 29 of that Act (under subsection (4)(c) of which arrangements may be made for the provision of hostels where persons for whom welfare services are provided under that section may live) after subsection (4) there shall be inserted—
"(4A) Where accommodation in a hostel is provided under paragraph (c) of subsection (4) of this section—
(a) if the hostel is managed by a local authority, section 22 of this Act shall apply as it applies where accommodation is provided under section 21;
(b) if the accommodation is provided in a hostel managed by a person other than a local authority under arrangements made with that person, subsections (2) to (4A) of section 26 of this Act shall apply as they apply where accommodation is provided under arrangements made by virtue of that section; and
(c) sections 32 and 43 of this Act shall apply as they apply where accommodation is provided under sections 21 to 26;
and in this subsection references to "accommodation" include references to board and other services, amenities and requisites provided in connection with the accommodation, except where in the opinion of the authority managing the premises or, in the case mentioned in paragraph (b) above, the authority making the arrangements their provision is unnecessary."

GENERAL NOTE
The Minister for Health, Mrs Virginia Bottomley, said (Comm. (SCE) col. 907): "Under the future regime, the local authority will have to purchase the place in the private home for the individual and to make good the difference between what is returned in housing benefit and income support, having deducted the personal allowance. The local authority will need not only to purchase the place but to make a contribution to it when the individual's means require that . . . We are determined that under our arm's-length inspection unit local authority and private sector homes will have to meet the same high standards. There will be more pressure to take a rational decision on whether domiciliary or day care might be more appropriate than placing individuals in a local authority home". Also (Comm. (SCE) cols. 910–1): "It will be a managed system in which contracts will be placed. It will be important to maintain quality by monitoring contracts and to have some check and follow-up through case management of those who are placed in private homes. . . . It may be part of the contract that sufficient staff should have been trained".

The Parliamentary Under-Secretary of State for the Department of Social Security, Lord Henley, explained (*Hansard*, H.L. Vol. 518, cols. 1342–3): "It may be helpful if I explain how residential care in homes under local authority management will be funded under the new community care arrangements. Basically this will be in the same way as at present. The local authority will be responsible for the costs of providing the care and will charge residents what they can afford. In that respect it is on the same lines as the system now proposed for public support in independent homes. Residents will be allowed to keep a sum, to be specified in regulations, for their personal expenses. That figure will be the same for all comparable types of accommodation, which means that the allowance for people in local authority homes will be brought up to the level for people in independent homes at a cost of £10 million a year. Thus, so far as the amount residents are allowed to keep for the personal expenses goes, there will be no difference between residents in local authority homes and those in independent homes. Where the difference comes is in the amount that the local authority may be able to charge a resident. Residents in local authority homes will not be able to claim housing benefit and will only be able to claim income support at a special low rate equivalent to the standard rate of retirement pension. Thus, the amount that a resident who qualifies for income support will be able to pay will be much less at a local authority home compared with an independent home.

"We want to give local authorities every incentive to use independent sector provision to improve choice for potential residents and their carers. But clearly as a result there will be a need for local authorities to review their residential accommodation. However, we do not expect there to be any rush to privatise homes. Authorities will need to proceed slowly, considering how they can strike the best balance between residential provision (of all types) in their areas and other forms of community care and avoid the creation of local monopolies . . . [ss.26 and 29 as amended by this section] provide that the local authority will negotiate the cost of the place with the providers of the accommodation and pay the full cost to them. The authority will then charge the person what he can afford to pay and the person is required to pay over this amount subject to an allowance for personal expenses, prescribed in regulations. That is in fact the same system as will apply to all independent residential care and nursing homes. The important change is being made in the corresponding social security and housing benefit regulations. This will enable people in such accommodation to claim housing benefit and to receive income support based on the standard applicable amount and any premiums for which they are qualified. It will apply to people in hostels under Section 29 as well and they will accordingly be in exactly the same position in any event as other people in independent sector homes".

The Notes on Clauses provided an elaborate and useful account of the intended use of regulations under s.22(5) of the 1948 National Assistance Act. It is worth while to set it out in full:

"1. The regulation-making powers in section 22 of the National Assistance Act 1948 will be used to set up the arrangements for local authorities to work out how much the people for whom they arrange residential or nursing home care should contribute towards the cost of their accommodation and care. As paragraph 3.7.6. of the White Paper, *Caring For People* explains, local authorities will be responsible for meeting in full agreed charges for places they arrange in private and voluntary homes and will be under a duty to require residents to make a contribution covering up to full cost according to their financial circumstances.

2. Treatment of income capital. A resident's ability to contribute will be assessed on the basis of his or her personal resources only. The same assessment rules will apply whether a person is in a local authority home or a private or a voluntary home although entitlement to social security benefits is more limited in local authority homes. There will be no family means test. The contribution of a married resident will initially be calculated on the basis of his or her own resources. However, because under section 43 of the National Assistance Act 1948, married couples have a legal liability to support each other, his or her spouse will be asked to defray as much of the balance of the cost to the authority as he or she is reasonably able to meet. The income support rules will be applied to residents' income. All forms of income, including income support and housing benefit, will be taken into account in full with the exception of mobility allowance, war pensions, earnings and such income as Victoria and George Cross and similar annuities, for which full or partial disregards will be specified. The national insurance Christmas bonus and other occasional gifts will also be disregarded in full.

3. The income support rules will also be applied to residents' capital assets. Residents with capital in excess of the upper limit will be expected to meet the full cost of their place in the home until their capital falls to below this level.

4. The value of any property owned by residents will normally be counted as a capital asset but provision will be made for it to be wholly or partly disregarded in specified circumstances. Where the capital value of a property is disregarded any income from the property (such as rent) will be taken into account. Local authorities will also have the power to disregard the value of unoccupied property until it has been decided that the resident will need to reside permanently in residential or nursing home care.

5. Sections 21 and 24 of the Health and Social Services and Social Security Adjudications Act 1983 as amended by [this Act] will be brought into effect at the same time to empower local authorities to take effective action against residents who deliberately attempt to avoid paying charges.

6. *Personal expenses allowances.* The local authority will be required to allow residents to retain sums to be specified in regulations for personal expenses. These sums will be inalienable. The basic amount will be set at the level of the allowance for personal expenses for income support claimants in residential care or nursing homes.

7. *Contributions to enable a resident to meet fees in a particular home.* In some circumstances, relatives may choose to contribute to fees to enable a resident to stay in a home of his or her choice when the local authority is not prepared to meet the fees of that home in full (see paragraph 3.7.8 of the White Paper). Local authorities will have powers to disregard such payments up to the amount of the difference between the fee payable and the level the local authority would be prepared to meet.

8. *Basis of charges.* Amendments in [this Act] to sections 21 and 22 of the National Assistance Act will mean that local authorities will have to base their charges on the full cost of arranging a place in a private or voluntary home or providing accommodation and care in a home under their own management. They will also be able to include the cost of any other service required by the resident outside the home such as day care. Authorities will be obliged to collect as much of this amount from the resident as he or she can afford to pay, subject to the disregards set out above".

The Notes on Clauses provided a chart of support for people in homes before and after the commencement of the Act, showing the main provisions.

		"PRIVATE AND VOLUNTARY HOMES	LOCAL AUTHORITY HOMES including people over pension age placed in private and voluntary residential care by local authorities under s.26 of the 1948 Act ("sponsorship")
Existing Provision [Pre-Act]	(a) Nature of Funds	i. Income Support (to bring income—including attendance allowance—up to level of charge (or national limit if lower) plus retirement expenses).	(a)(i) Income Support (only paid to residents with total resources less than standard rate of pension).
			(ii) Personal Resources (including National Insurance benefit)
		ii. Personal Resources (including National Insurance benefit)	(iii) Local authority support (to meet balance of cost not met by resident from resources less an allowance for personal expenses).
		iii. Charitable payments (may be disregarded if given to help pay fees above income support limits)	
		iv. Help from relatives (may be similarly disregarded)	
		v. Local authority support "topping up" (people under pension age in residential care homes only)	
		vi. Attendance allowance	
	(b) Source of Funds	i. Central Government	(b)(i) Central Government
		ii. Central Government and private sources	(ii) Central Government and private sources
		iii. Charities	(iii) Local Social Services Authorities
		iv. Relatives	
		v. Local Social Services authorities	
		vi. Central Government	
	(c) Responsibility of LA for care needs assessment	None. Except where local authority are providing procedures support where the procedure for admission to LA homes may be followed	(c) Authorities have discretion over admission procedures.
Future of existing clients: proposed provision		Preserved entitlement to Income Support. Attendance Allowance remains payable. Other income as above. Local Authority support in accordance with [section 44]—people already receiving support will continue to get it.	As below (All Residents Change to New Regime but no new sponsorship—see notes to [section 44]

New clients when new scheme in operation: proposed provisions:	(a) Nature of Funds	i. Income Support (standard applicable amounts plus any premium)	(a)(i) Income Support (paid as above)
		ii. Housing Benefit	(ii) Personal resources (including National Insurance Benefits)
		iii. Personal resources (including National Insurance and other Benefits)	(iii) Local authority support (to meet balance of cost not met by resident from resources less an allowance for personal expenses—the personal allowances and assessment of income from capital will be aligned with those under the income support scheme. This will mean that most residents will contribute less and the local authority correspondingly more.
		iv. Local Authority support (to meet balance of cost of place negotiated by local authority not met by residents from resources less allowance for personal expenses)	
	(b) Source of Funds	i. Central Government	(b)(i) Central Government (as [Pre-Act] provision)
		ii. Local Housing Authorities (largely reimbursed by central Government)	(ii) Central Government and private sources (also as [Pre-Act] provision)
		iii. Central Government and private sources	(iii) Local Social Services Authorities
		iv. Local Social Services Authorities	
	(c) Responsibility of LA for care needs assessment	Care needs assessment to be carried out by the local authority before care at the public expense is arranged	(c) Local authority care needs assessment required before admission. Local authorities will have the responsibility of ensuring that placement in one of their homes is the appropriate type of care".

Recovery of charges due to local authorities for accommodation

45.—(1) In section 21 of the Health and Social Services and Social Security Adjudication Act 1983 (recovery of sums due to local authority where persons in residential accommodation have disposed of assets) after subsection (3) there shall be inserted—

"(3A) If the Secretary of State so directs, subsection (1) above shall not apply in such cases as may be specified in the direction."

(2) In sections 22 and 23 of that Act (which make provision as to arrears of contributions charged on interests in land in England and Wales and in Scotland respectively) after subsection (2) there shall be inserted—

"(2A) In determining whether to exercise their power under subsection (1) above and in making any determination under subsection (2) above, the local authority shall comply with any directions given to them by the Secretary of State as to the exercise of those functions."

(3) In section 24 of that Act (interest on sums charged on or secured over interests in land) for subsection (2) there shall be substituted—

"(2) The rate of interest shall be such reasonable rate as the Secretary of State may direct or, if no such direction is given, as the local authority may determine."

GENERAL NOTE

The section is concerned with recovery of money from people in local authority homes who have deliberately deprived themselves of resources so as to avoid paying for accommodation.

Subs. (2)

The Minister for Health, Mrs Virginia Bottomley, said (Comm. (SCE) col. 919): "Directions will be drawn up under the [subsection] to ensure a more ameliorating result from using the provision to take a charge [on land] against an individual. For example, if it will cause hardship, although there are some adverse circumstances, we would issue the directions. There has been a long-term intention to implement this provision, but it has not been possible to do so because of the lack of a direction-making power".

General provisions concerning community care services

Local authority plans for community care services

46.—(1) Each local authority—

(a) shall within such period after the day appointed for the coming into force of this section as the Secretary of State may direct, prepare and publish a plan for the provision of community care services in their area;

(b) shall keep the plan prepared by them under paragraph (a) above and any further plans prepared by them under this section under review; and

(c) shall, at such intervals as the Secretary of State may direct, prepare and publish modifications to the current plan, or if the case requires, a new plan.

(2) In carrying out any of their functions under paragraphs (a) to (c) of subsection (1) above, a local authority shall consult—

(a) any District Health Authority the whole or any part of whose district lies within the area of the local authority;

(b) any Family Health Services Authority the whole or any part of whose locality lies within the area of the local authority;

(c) in so far as any proposed plan, review or modifications of a plan may affect or be affected by the provision or availability of housing and the local authority is not itself a local housing authority, within the meaning of the Housing Act 1985, every such local housing authority whose area is within the area of the local authority;

(d) such voluntary organisations as appear to the authority to represent the interests of persons who use or are likely to use any community care services within the area of the authority or the interests of private carers who, within that area, provide care to persons for whom, in the exercise of their social services functions, the local authority have a power or a duty to provide a service.

(e) such voluntary housing agencies and other bodies as appear to the local authority to provide housing or community care services in their area; and

(f) such other persons as the Secretary of State may direct.

(3) In this section—

"local authority" means the council of a county, a metropolitan district or a London borough or the Common Council of the City of London;

"community care services" means services which a local authority may provide or arrange to be provided under any of the following provisions—

(a) Part III of the National Assistance Act 1948;

(b) section 45 of the Health Services and Public Health Act 1968;

(c) section 21 of and Schedule 8 to the National Health Service Act 1977; and

(d) section 117 of the Mental Health Act 1983; and

"private carer" means a person who is not employed to provide the care in question by any body in the exercise of its functions under any enactment.

DEFINITIONS

"community care services": subs. (3).

"District Health Authority": ss.8 and 128 of the National Health Service Act 1977, as amended by this Act, and Sched. 1 to this Act.

"Family Health Services Authority": s.10 of the National Health Service Act 1977 and Sched. 1 to this Act.

"local authority": subs. (3).

"private carer": subs. (3).

"social service functions": ss.2, 3 and 15 and Sched. 1 to the Local Authority Social Services Act 1970.

"voluntary organisation": s.64 of the National Assistance Act 1948; see also ss.23 and 128 of the National Health Service Act 1977.

GENERAL NOTE

The section should be read with the provisions relating to assessment in s.47 and the corresponding sections of the Disabled Persons (Services Consultation and Representation) Act 1986 and the Children Act 1989. It is to be noted that s.47 of the National Assistance Act 1948 relating to the compulsory removal of people unable to look after themselves remains in force.

The "community care functions" under this Part of this Act become "social services functions" by virtue of the provisions of para. 11 of Sched. 9, amending Sched. 1 of the Local Authority Social Services Act 1970. S.7 of the 1970 Act requires local authorities to have regard to general guidance given by the Secretary of State when carrying out their social services functions. By making community care functions social services functions these too are brought within the scope of the general powers of direction and inquiries, of the complaints procedure and of the default action set out in addition to the 1970 Act effected by s.50 of this Act.

As regards this section, the Minister for Health, Mrs Virginia Bottomley, said (Comm. (SCE) col. 974): "social care plans should be prepared and published by social services authorities. They will be expected to produce the plans jointly with health authorities and [family health service authorities] and in consultation with representatives of voluntary and private sectors, housing authorities and housing associations . . . . If the need arises the Secretary of State will be able to direct district health authorities and social services departments to collaborate or make planning agreements if there is any failure to comply with guidance". The Parliamentary Under-Secretary of State for the Department of Social Security, Lord Henley, added (*Hansard*, H.L. Vol. 518, cols. 1477–8): "These plans are a cornerstone of our policy. They are designed to enable local authorities to set out and publish the needs of the community they serve, their objectives for the arrangement of services to meet those needs within the resources available to them, and to set out targets which they are setting themselves to develop and improve the services available in their areas. We shall also require local authorities in drawing up their care plans to consult local statutory, voluntary and other agencies to ensure that the approach to community care becomes much more user driven rather than fitting clients into existing services . . . It may well be that as authorities develop their plans over time they may wish publicly to state the standards and specifications which they may require from service providers, including their own directly-managed provision".

The Baroness in Waiting, Baroness Blatch, said (*Hansard*, H.L. Vol. 520, col. 645) "everyone is ordinarily resident in the area of some local authority. If a person has no fixed abode he is reckoned to be ordinarily resident in the place where he happens to be when the need for services arises" and cited Lord Scarman in *Shah* v. *Barnet London Borough Council* [1983] 2 A.C. 309, " 'ordinarily resident' refers to a man's abode . . . which he has adopted voluntarily . . . for the time being, whether of short or long duration". She continued: "Therefore, even a short stay in a particular area can qualify as a place of ordinary residence. . . . Under the new community care arrangements the local authority where a person is ordinarily resident, . . . will be responsible for assessing and arranging community care services. This will entail the local authority entering into agreements with the providers of appropriate facilities. Thus it does not matter how few users the local authority has in any particular care category; it will still have to make arrangements to meet their care needs in the most appropriate way. This means that voluntary organisations will have to deal with the local authorities which place people with them. If they wish to admit a user who will need local authority support to remain in the facility they must contact the local authority in whose area the user is ordinarily resident. In the case of a homeless person who arrives and applies for admission that could well be the authority within whose areas the facility is situated".

Subs. (1)

The Minister for Health, Mrs Virginia Bottomley, argued (Comm. (SCE) col. 950): "[the] community care plan . . . will be an important tool and will provide a great deal of information about the services and how the planning has been undertaken. In addition, [under later sections local authorities] will have to make the arrangements for assessment . . . and for complaints procedures".

Some difficulty appears in the construction of this subsection because it is not entirely clear what the Secretary of State "may direct". Grammatically those words could apply merely to the "day appointed", thus limiting the scope of the Secretary of State's powers. However, s.67(2) makes general provision for making commencement orders and it would be surprising to find a specific power here. It would appear that the words "may direct" in para. (a) operate on the words "each local authority"; see also para. (c). It is not clear how far even this power of direction goes. Does it simply give him power over the period for the preparation of the plan or does it give him power to issue guidance (a word the section does not use) or direction (which, somewhat ambiguously, it does) over the content? Perhaps the resolution of the problem lies in the very wide powers contained in the new s.7A of the Local Authority Social Services Act 1970, inserted by s.50 of this Act.

In relation to this section, the Government's intention was fairly plain from the debates, but intentions are one thing and the expression of them in an Act quite another. The Baroness in Waiting, Baroness Blatch, explained (*Hansard*, H.L. Vol. 518, col. 1512): "community care plans will have to be comprehensive of the totality of need which the local authority has to address and the totality of the service provision it aims to provide within the resources available to it. . . . that also means working together with other agencies on the preparation of the care plan to ensure that all the resources at the disposal of the local community are brought to bear on both identifying the needs and then seeking out the most effective services to meet those needs, which will be further refined by the assessment process . . . Our guidance on community care plans will make clear that we are talking about the totality of potential provision for all client groups which the local authority serves", including "services for drug and alcohol misusers".

Baroness Blatch added (*Hansard*, H.L. Vol. 518, cols. 1537–8): "We will be issuing more detailed guidance on the interface between health and social service authorities. Essentially we want them to agree on how they will handle arrangements for the care of people in whom they have a mutual interest. . . . it is important that both social service and health authorities are allowed the freedom to determine the detailed arrangements about how they will consult one another and work jointly to ensure that a seamless community care service is available which covers both health and social needs. . . . the naming of an individual as a case manager is something that we accept would be good in practice. As such it is the type of practice that we would expect the social services inspectorate to include in advice to all local authorities . . . the [Act is] . . . designed to provide a framework for good practice, given that it is a framework and that the actual operational practice will be dealt with in guidelines".

Subs. (2)(a)

The Parliamentary Under-Secretary of State for the Department of Health, Baroness Hooper, said (*Hansard*, H.L. Vol. 520, cols. 489–90): "because we recognise the need for a seamless services for patients being discharged from hospital and in particular the special needs of those who have had treatment for a mental disorder, we have taken steps to address the situation. First, we have issued guidance on discharge planning for all patients. [See HC(89)5 and its accompanying booklet *The Discharge of Patients from Hospital*.] It covered the care of patients released after a short spell in hospital as well as of those who have received long-term care. Secondly, our draft guidance on community care planning . . . specifically mentions discharge procedures as an area on which health and local authorities should make planning agreements. As part of such agreements, health and local authorities will need to reach agreement on assessing the needs for care services provided by local authorities. Thirdly, in relation to mentally ill people, we have made it clear that mentally ill people discharged into the community should have a precise plan drawn up for their aftercare. This should help both to prevent inappropriate discharge and also lessen the risk of people losing touch with the caring services at a later stage. We have recently issued for consultation with local authorities, district health authorities and other interested bodies draft guidance on care programmes for mentally ill people . . . Fourthly, section 117 of the Mental Health Act 1983 already imposes a duty on district health authorities and local authorities to provide, in collaboration with voluntary agencies, aftercare services for certain categories of mentally disordered patients who have ceased to be detained and who leave hospital. The duty on the authority is to provide such aftercare services until they are satisfied that the person concerned is no longer in need of them". See also the note to s.3.

Subs. (2)(d)

A local authority shall, when preparing its community care plan, consult with organisations representing all carers of people for whom it has a duty or a power to provide any service.

Subs. (3)

Most services for mentally disordered people are already covered; see references to Pt. III of the National Assistance Act 1948 and s.21 and Sched. 8 to the National Health Service Act 1977. Section 117 of the Mental Health Act 1983 also gives an additional duty to local authorities to provide aftercare services for people leaving hospital after a period of compulsory detention under the terms of the Act. See also the note to s.47(1). Further, note the repeal of s.124 of the Mental Health Act 1983, which contains default powers which are rendered redundant by the general default powers in s.7D of the Local Authority Social

Services Act 1970, inserted by s.50 of this Act, in existing statutes which empower local authorities to provide services.

Assessment of needs for community care services

47.—(1) Subject to subsections (5) and (6) below, where it appears to a local authority that any person for whom they may provide or arrange for the provision of community care services may be in need of any such services, the authority—

(a) shall carry out an assessment of his needs for those services; and

(b) having regard to the results of that assessment, shall then decide whether his needs call for the provision by them of any such services.

(2) If at any time during the assessment of the needs of any person under subsection (1)(a) above it appears to a local authority that he is a disabled person, the authority—

(a) shall proceed to make such a decision as to the services he requires as is mentioned in section 4 of the Disabled Persons (Services, Consultation and Representation) Act 1986 without his requesting them to do so under that section; and

(b) shall inform him that they will be doing so and of his rights under that Act.

(3) If at any time during the assessment of the needs of any person under subsection (1)(a) above, it appears to a local authority—

(a) that there may be a need for the provision to that person by such District Health Authority as may be determined in accordance with regulations of any services under the National Health Service Act 1977, or

(b) that there may be a need for the provision to him of any services which fall within the functions of a local housing authority (within the meaning of the Housing Act 1985) which is not the local authority carrying out the assessment,

the local authority shall notify that District Health Authority or local housing authority and invite them to assist, to such extent as is reasonable in the circumstances, in the making of the assessment; and, in making their decision as to the provision of the services needed for the person in question, the local authority shall take into account any services which are likely to be made available for him by that District Health Authority or local housing authority.

(4) The Secretary of State may give directions as to the manner in which an assessment under this section is to be carried out or the form it is to take but, subject to any such directions and to subsection (7) below, it shall be carried out in such manner and take such form as the local authority consider appropriate.

(5) Nothing in this section shall prevent a local authority from temporarily providing or arranging for the provision of community care services for any person without carrying out a prior assessment of his needs in accordance with the preceding provisions of this section if, in the opinion of the authority, the condition of that person is such that he requires those services as a matter of urgency.

(6) If, by virtue of subsection (5) above, community care services have been provided temporarily for any person as a matter of urgency, then, as soon as practicable thereafter, an assessment of his needs shall be made in accordance with the preceding provisions of this section.

(7) This section is without prejudice to section 3 of the Disabled Persons (Services, Consultation and Representation) Act 1986.

(8) In this section—

"disabled person" has the same meaning as in that Act; and

"local authority" and "community care services" have the same meanings as in section 46 above.

DEFINITIONS
"community care services": s.46(3).
"disabled person: subs. (8) and the Disabled Persons (Services, Consultation and Representation) Act 1986.
"District Health Authority": ss.8 and 128 of the National Health Service Act 1977, as amended by this Act, and Sched. 1 to this Act.
"Family Health Services Authority": s.10 of the National Health Service Act 1977 and Sched. 1 to this Act.
"local authority": s.46(3).
"regulations": ss.126 and 128 of the National Health Service Act 1977, as amended by this Act.

GENERAL NOTE
See also the Disabled Persons (Services, Consultation and Representation) Act 1986.
Despite the limited express terms of this section, it is envisaged that assessment will lead to action. This need for action can be enforced under the new s.7A of the Local Authority Social Services Act 1970, inserted by s.50 of this Act.
The White Paper stated that the aim of assessment "is first to review the possibility of enabling the individual to continue to live at home even if this means arranging to move to different accommodation within the local community". The Parliamentary Under-Secretary of State for the Department of Health, Baroness Hooper, said (*Hansard*, H.L. Vol. 520, col. 491): "a named individual or key worker should, as a matter of practice, play an integral part in case management".

Subs. (1)
As regards complaints, see the note to s.7B(2), inserted by s.50 of this Act. As with that general section, whether a person is someone for whom an authority may provide community care services is a matter of law, and if assessment is refused, such a decision is open to challenge in the courts. This will apply equally to cases where the plan is inadequate or to, *e.g.* discharge from hospital without a plan. It is, however, to be noted that it is doubtful if a carer *per se* would have *locus standi* to bring such an action, or even for that matter to complain that his views had been ignored or disregarded. As with other sections of the Act, the Government did not anticipate litigation. For example, the Parliamentary Under-Secretary of State for the Department of Social Security, Lord Henley, argued (*Hansard*, H.L. Vol. 520, col. 614): "there are two safeguards. First, local authorities will have to publish their arrangements for assessment as part of their community care plans. Those arrangements should make it clear how the views of users and carers will be taken into account. If these plans are published and are the subject of consultation . . . there is ample opportunity for local debate about the arrangements and for local voluntary organisations and users and carers to see that there are sufficient opportunities for views to be taken into account".
The Baroness in Waiting, Baroness Blatch, said (*Hansard*, H.L. Vol. 520, col. 519): "Our guidance on assessment will advise local authorities on the advisability of setting up some sort of initial scrutiny. Such a procedure would be quite proper since the [section] leaves the form of the assessment to be decided by the local authority. An initial sift would have two purposes: first, to identify the people for whom no more detailed assessment is required, which would include those making unreasonable or vexatious requests; and, secondly, to decide the most appropriate form of assessment for those cases clearly needing further investigation".
She also explained (*Hansard*, H.L. Vol. 518, cols. 1538–9): "Assessment will identify needs for services. However, [the subsection] requires that, following assessment, local authorities must decide, having regard to the results of the assessment, whether there is a need for them to provide services. Therefore, the local authority is required to decide which of the needs it will meet taking into account duties under Section 2 of the Chronically Sick and Disabled Persons Act 1970. Apart from that, it is not obliged to meet all needs and will wish to take into account its priorities and resources". See also the note to s.46(3).
The Parliamentary Under-Secretary of State for the Department of Health, Baroness Hooper, said (*Hansard*, H.L. Vol. 518, cols. 1568–9): "Clearly . . . the local authority will need to bring in outside expertise. The White Paper states: 'all agencies and professions involved with the individual and his or her problems should be brought into the assessment procedure when necessary' and goes on to list a wide range of people, some from the social services department and some from other agencies who may need to be involved. The White Paper lists: 'social workers, GPs, community nurses, hospital staff such as consultants in geriatric medicine, psychiatry, rehabilitation and other hospital specialities, nurses, physiotherapists, occupational therapists, continence advisors, community psychiatric nurses, staff involved

with vision and hearing impairment, housing officers, the Employment Department's resettlement officers and its employment rehabilitation service, home helps, home care assistants and voluntary workers'".

Various undertakings were given as to the content of guidance to be issued—guidance which could eventually become enforceable under the powers in the new s.7A of the Local Authority Social Services Act 1970, inserted by s.50 of this Act. These included (1) the administrative procedures to be followed, but also the more professional aspect of carrying out assessments (*Hansard*, H.L. Vol. 520, col. 6245); (2) the need for assessments to be carried out without undue delay (*Hansard*, H.L. Vol. 520, col. 519); (3) the need for assessments to be in writing (*Hansard*, H.L. Vol. 518, col. 1576, and see *Hansard*, H.L. Vol. 520, col. 520); (4) the review at regular intervals to be agreed with the client and carers at the initial assessment (*Hansard*, H.L. Vol. 518, col. 1577); (5) the need for the person concerned and any carers to be fully involved both in the assessment of care needs and in the subsequent decision about what services should be provided (*Hansard*, H.L. Vol. 520, col. 614, and see s.8 of the Disabled Persons (Services, Consultation and Representation) Act 1986); and (6) a possible desire by local authorities to contract out to voluntary bodies some of the more specialised aspects of assessment. It was expressed that this would be particularly appropriate for people suffering from conditions of which local authority staff have little experience and where a great deal of knowledge and understanding of the condition is to be found in a voluntary organisation, *e.g.* drug and alcohol misusers (*Hansard*, H.L. Vol. 520, col. 628).

Baroness Blatch added (*Hansard*, H.L. Vol. 520, col. 654): "One of the great hopes of the new system as opposed to the old one is that, where a local authority feels that it makes economic sense . . . it will be forced to consider respite care more seriously as a provision. I recognise that respite care can play an important part not only in helping someone to remain in the community most of the time but also in giving his or her carer a much needed break. I agree that it should be available when needed . . . The outcome of the needs-based assessment should be the provision of services which best meet those needs. The statutory requirement to provide day and domiciliary care is enhanced to reinforce this and not to restrict the range of care offered by authorities . . . this point [will be] brought out in our guidance".

Subs. (2)

It is perhaps convenient in this note to set out what the Parliamentary Under-Secretary of State for the Department of Health, Baroness Hooper, said as regards the implementation of the Disabled Persons (Services, Consultation and Representation) Act 1986 (*Hansard*, H.L. Vol. 518, cols. 1580–1): "Four important sections, Sections 4, 8(1), 9 and 10, were implemented on 1 April 1987. They require local authorities to assess need on request, to have regard to the abilities of carers, to provide additional information and to consult organisations representing disabled people when making appointments. Progress continued with the implementation on 1 February 1988 of Sections 5 and 6, which impose duties on local authorities to identify and assess the needs of young disabled people when they leave school. Recently, at the end of 1989, Section 11 was brought into force, with the laying of a report on community care for mentally ill and mentally handicapped people . . . We announced in . . . *Caring for People* that we do not now intend to implement Section 7, which would impose statutory obligations on health and social service authorities to identify and assess the needs of people leaving hospital after receiving treatment for six months or more for a mental disorder. That decision was taken in the light of new proposals to improve the provision of services for mentally ill people including, from 1991, the preparation of care programmes. The need to implement Section 7 will of course be reconsidered in the light of several years' experience of the introduction of the care programmes.

"Sections 1, 2 and 3 of the Act concern the appointment and rights of authorised representatives of disabled people and their rights to make representations about their needs. They are the most complex and potentially the most expensive of all the Act's provisions. I reconfirm statements that have been made previously that no decisions on their implementation can be made until we have established their cost. Following preliminary consideration of their resource and service implications, an official approach was made to the local authority associations in February this year seeking their views on these issues. Further action will depend on the outcome of those consultations".

Subss. (5) and (6)

The Parliamentary Under-Secretary of State for the Department of Health, Baroness Hooper, explained (*Hansard*, H.L. Vol. 520, cols. 425–6): "[the subsections] cover not only the emergency provision of nursing home care but also the provision of other community care services by the local authority . . . [they] mean that a voluntary organisation providing community care services would need to come to some arrangement with a local authority regarding the provision of urgent treatment. But, equally, the local authority itself will need—and, indeed will have a duty—to come to arrangements with providers in order to meet the need of their local communities. Therefore, there is nothing to stop a voluntary organisation and a local authority agreeing together for the provision of temporary care without any formalities in order to cope with situations where care is required urgently. [They] provide a mechanism for such arrangements and we shall certainly be advising and encouraging local authorities to make them in order to supplement the consultations that they will also need to make with voluntary sector and other interested parties in preparing their community care plans [under s.47]".

Inspection of premises used for provision of community care services

48.—(1) Any person authorised by the Secretary of State may at any reasonable time enter and inspect any premises (other than premises in respect of which any person is registered under the Registered Homes Act 1984) in which community care services are or are proposed to be provided by a local authority, whether directly or under arrangements made with another person.

(2) Any person inspecting any premises under this section may—

(a) make such examination into the state and management of the premises and the facilities and services provided therein as he thinks fit;

(b) inspect any records (in whatever form they are held) relating to the premises, or any person for whom community care services have been or are to be provided there; and

(c) require the owner of, or any person employed in, the premises to furnish him with such information as he may request.

(3) Any person exercising the power to inspect records conferred by subsection (2)(b) above—

(a) shall be entitled at any reasonable time to have access to, and inspect and check the operation of, any computer and any associated apparatus or material which is or has been in use in connection with the records in question; and

(b) may require—

(i) the person by whom or on whose behalf the computer is or has been so used; or

(ii) any person having charge of or otherwise concerned with the operation of the computer, apparatus or material,

to give him such reasonable assistance as he may require.

(4) Any person inspecting any premises under this section—

(a) may interview any person residing there in private—

(i) for the purpose of investigating any complaint as to those premises or the community care services provided there, or

(ii) if he has reason to believe that the community care services being provided there for that person are not satisfactory; and

(b) may examine any such person in private.

(5) No person may—

(a) exercise the power conferred by subsection (2)(b) above so as to inspect medical records; or

(b) exercise the power conferred by subsection (4)(b) above,

unless he is a registered medical practitioner and, in the case of the power conferred by subsection (2)(b) above, the records relate to medical treatment given at the premises in question.

(6) Any person exercising the power of entry under subsection (1) above shall, if so required, produce some duly authenticated document showing his authority to do so.

(7) Any person who intentionally obstructs another in the exercise of that power shall be guilty of an offence and liable on summary conviction to a fine not exceeding level 3 on the standard scale.

(8) In this section "local authority" and "community care services" have the same meanings as in section 46 above.

DEFINITIONS
"community care services": s.46(3).
"local authority": s.46(3).
"registered medical practitioner": s.128 of the National Health Service Act 1977 and Medical Act 1983.

GENERAL NOTE
The Minister for Health, Mrs Virginia Bottomley (Comm. (SCE) col. 1076) linked this section with contractual arrangements to be set up under the National Assistance Act s.26, as amended by s.42 of this Act (under which there will be mechanisms for monitoring and for ensuring quality control), with assessment under s.42 of this Act, and with the complaints procedures under s.7B of the Local Authority Social Services Act, inserted by s.50 of this Act. She suggested that in total they will safeguard quality. This section, she said, "gives the Secretary of State powers to inspect premises where community care is being undertaken, particularly those premises that are not safeguarded by existing legislation", including, as the Parliamentary Under-Secretary of State for the Department of Health, Baroness Hooper, said (Hansard, H.L. Vol. 519, col. 37): "private and voluntary services with which the local authorities have made contracts [and] it does not exclude smaller homes" under the Registered Homes Act.

The Baroness in Waiting, Baroness Blatch, explained the purpose of this clause as (Hansard, H.L. Vol. 519, cols. 41–2): "to provide persons authorised by the Secretary of State with the power to inspect certain premises. The persons authorised will normally be members of the social service inspectorate or nursing and medical staff of the Department of Health in England and their opposite numbers in Wales. . . . The purpose of the power is to enable the authorised persons to inspect both the services provided and the way the local authority is exercising its community care functions. We would expect such inspections to form part of the investigation of serious complaints and other major irregularities. They may also be used in conjunction with monitoring of local authorities' performance. In any event we do not expect that it will be necessary to make a great deal of use of them. The main inspection and monitoring function in respect of private and voluntary facilities with which local authorities have made arrangements will fall to the authorities themselves. They do not need special legislative provision for this and will be expected to include in contracts the arrangements for access and inspection. It may happen, especially in small houses, that the residents' doctors may decide to keep case notes on the premises. Medical records held on other premises such as day centres may contain details of care or treatment provided elsewhere. Given the general purpose of these provisions, we do not feel that it would be right for such records to be open to inspection, nor do we see any need for them to be".

The Parliamentary Under-Secretary of State, Baroness Hooper, added (Hansard, H.L. Vol. 520, col. 1394): "the persons authorised by the Secretary of State to carry out the inspections . . . will be drawn for the most part from the social services inspectorate and from other members of the staff of the Department of Health. When such people are not doctors they are almost certain to be qualified in one or other of the caring professions—for instance, nurses, social workers or therapists. Such people would be bound by their own professional codes of conduct which place clear limits on the unauthorised disclosure of information gained in the course of professional activities. Even where this might not be the case the people concerned would still be covered by the codes of conduct covering the use made by civil servants of information gained in the course of their employment".

Subs. (4)(a)
The paragraph is drawn surprisingly tightly. It would appear to exclude an express power, in the absence of a complaint, to interview any person (staff are compelled to provide information under subs. (2)(c)) unless there is reason to believe that that person is not receiving satisfactory community care services.

Subs. (4)(b)
Presumably any examination by a doctor (see subs. (5)) under the section which involves a "trespass to the person", that is, a physical touching, must be with the consent of the person involved.

Transfer of staff from health service to local authorities

49.—(1) In connection with arrangements relating to community care services made by virtue of this Part of this Act, the Secretary of State may make regulations with respect to the transfer to employment by a local authority of persons previously employed by a National Health Service body.

(2) Regulations under this section may also make provision with respect to the return to employment by a National Health Service body of a person to whom the regulations previously applied on his transfer (whether from that or another National Health Service body) to employment by a local authority.

(3) Without prejudice to the generality of subsections (1) and (2) above, regulations under this section may make provision with respect to—
   (a) the terms on which a person is to be employed by a local authority or National Health Service body;
   (b) the period and continuity of a person's employment for the purposes of the Employment Protection (Consolidation) Act 1978;
   (c) superannuation benefits; and
   (d) the circumstances in which, if a person declines an offer of employment made with a view to such a transfer or return as is referred to in subsection (1) or subsection (2) above and then ceases to be employed by a National Health Service body or local authority, he is not to be regarded as entitled to benefits in connection with redundancy.

(4) In this section—
   (a) "local authority" and "community care services" have the same meaning as in section 46 above; and
   (b) "National Health Service body" means a Regional, District or Special Health Authority or a National Health Service trust.

(5) Regulations under this section may make different provision with respect to different cases or descriptions of case, including different provision for different areas.

DEFINITIONS
   "community care services": subs. (4) and s.46(3).
   "local authority": subs. (4) and s.46(3).
   "National Health Service body": subs. (4).

GENERAL NOTE
   The Parliamentary Under-Secretary of State for the Department of Health, Baroness Hooper, explained (*Hansard*, H.L. Vol. 519, cols. 45–6): "The issue which this [section] addresses is one which was raised in the Griffiths Report, that is the question of ensuring that the skills of staff employed in long-stay hospitals are not lost when responsibility for their patients passes to another authority. As the report pointed out, such staff will have direct personal knowledge of individual former patients and their needs, as well as a wide range of skills which are equally valuable in a community setting . . . At present staff who transfer to the employment of the local authority at the same time as their former patients move to local authority care would not be regarded as continuously employed for various statutory purposes. They will finish one employment and begin another. That means that, unless the NHS could offer them a suitable alternative job, they would become redundant and be entitled to compensation. Furthermore, they would have to work for the local authority for two years if they were full time in order to acquire statutory rights in their new employment.
   "[The section] therefore empowers the Secretary of State to make regulations providing for the transfer of such staff. In particular, that would allow a person's service with the NHS and local authorities to be treated as continuous employment. That means that statutory rights, such as access to an industrial tribunal, would be protected and that NHS service would continue to be counted for the purposes of calculating any future redundancy payments or compensation for unfair dismissal. The purpose of the [section] is straightforward but the detailed definition of the circumstances to which it should apply requires some care. It is important that proper account is taken of the views of those immediately involved, including health and local authorities and representatives of the NHS staff. That points to a regulation-making power as the best way of proceeding because there can be detailed consultation about the terms of the regulations, and that is what we intend".

Powers of the Secretary of State as respects social services functions of local authorities

50. After section 7 of the Local Authority Social Services Act 1970 (local authorities to exercise social services functions under guidance of the Secretary of State) there shall be inserted the following sections—

"Directions by the Secretary of State as to exercise of social services functions

7A.—(1) Without prejudice to section 7 of this Act, every local authority shall exercise their social services, functions in accordance with such directions as may be given to them under this section by the Secretary of State.

(2) Directions under this section—

(a) shall be given in writing; and

(b) may be given to a particular authority, or to authorities of a particular class, or to authorities generally.

Complaints procedure

7B.—(1) The Secretary of State may by order require local authorities to establish a procedure for considering any representations (including any complaints) which are made to them by a qualifying individual, or anyone acting on his behalf, in relation to the discharge of, or any failure to discharge, any of their social services functions in respect of that individual.

(2) In relation to a particular local authority, an individual is a qualifying individual for the purposes of subsection (1) above if—

(a) the authority have a power or a duty to provide, or to secure the provision of, a service for him; and

(b) his need or possible need for such a service has (by whatever means) come to the attention of the authority.

(3) A local authority shall comply with any directions given by the Secretary of State as to the procedure to be adopted in considering representations made as mentioned in subsection (1) above and as to the taking of such action as may be necessary in consequence of such representations.

(4) Local authorities shall give such publicity to any procedure established pursuant to this section as they consider appropriate.

Inquiries

7C.—(1) The Secretary of State may cause an inquiry to be held in any case where, whether on representations made to him or otherwise, he considers it advisable to do so in connection with the exercise by any local authority of any of their social services functions (except in so far as those functions relate to persons under the age of eighteen).

(2) Subsections (2) to (5) of section 250 of the Local Government Act 1972 (powers in relation to local inquiries) shall apply in relation to an inquiry under this section as they apply in relation to an inquiry under that section.

Default powers of Secretary of State as respects social services functions of local authorities

7D.—(1) If the Secretary of State is satisfied that any local authority have failed, without reasonable excuse, to comply with any of their duties which are social services functions (other than a duty imposed by or under the Children Act 1989), he may make an order declaring that authority to be in default with respect to the duty in question.

(2) An order under subsection (1) may contain such directions for the purpose of ensuring that the duty is complied with within such period as may be specified in the order as appear to the Secretary of State to be necessary.

(3) Any such direction shall, on the application of the Secretary of State, be enforceable by mandamus.

Grants to local authorities in respect of social services for the mentally ill

7E. The Secretary of State may, with the approval of the Treasury, make grants out of money provided by Parliament towards any expenses of local authorities incurred in connection with the exercise of their social services functions in relation to persons suffering from mental illness."

DEFINITIONS
  "functions": s.15 of the Local Authority Social Services Act 1970.
  "social service functions": ss.2, 3 and 15 and Sched. 1 to the Local Authority Social Services Act 1970.

GENERAL NOTE

S.7A of the 1970 Act
  Directions are different from orders and regulations, which are to be made under s.65 and which are subject to parliamentary approval: directions do not have the approval of Parliament (see the Parliamentary Under-Secretary of State for Health, Mr Roger Freeman, Comm. (SCE) col. 1085, and GENERAL NOTE to this Act). The Notes on Clauses added: "Generally it is intended that this power should be used infrequently and only to the extent necessary to safeguard the interests of users of services and their carers".

S.7A(1) of the 1970 Act
  The Parliamentary Under-Secretary of State for the Department of Health, Baroness Hooper, explained (*Hansard*, H.L. Vol. 519, col. 95–6): "The reference to 'social services' therefore as opposed to 'community care' simply uses the terminology of the 1970 Act and refers to 'social services functions'. Enactments conferring social services functions on local authorities' social services committees are listed in Schedule 1 to the 1970 Act. They include Acts other than those referred to in the definition of community care services in [section 46]. In regard to the use of direction-making powers, we have so far said that powers of direction will be used to reinforce community care guidance. We have no plans at this stage to use them in other ways".

S.7A(2) of the 1970 Act
  The Parliamentary Under-Secretary of State for Health, Mr Roger Freeman, explained (Comm. (SCE) col. 1088): "The powers of specific direction are to correct abuses". Also: "General directions could be embodied in circulars, although we do not intend to issue circulars as directions. Most of the content of circulars would be guidance. It is important to appreciate the sequence of using the various powers under the [section] which could be general directions on how social services are to be provided, in the sense of drawing up care plans and assessment, perhaps an inquiry if there is a problem, perhaps a specific direction to correct the errors discovered in an inquiry, and then perhaps a default order under" s.7D. He said (Comm. (SCE) cols. 1085–6): "The substance of general directions should relate to how we should expect local authorities to prepare programmes of care in the community by social services departments. That would cover how they should consult, draw up plans and the extent of such plans, the assessment procedures to be followed, who should be consulted and who else should be involved in assessing the care needs of, for example, frail elderly people who may or may not be able to continue living in their own homes. Those are two clear examples of general directions. Secondly, unlike specific directions, general directions do not introduce any new principle ... under sections 21 and 29 of the National Assistance Act 1948 ... the Executive have powers of general direction. There are also powers of general direction under section 45 of the Health Services and Public Health Act 1968". He added, "by direction, the Secretary of State cannot upset the purpose of primary legislation and therefore the principles of clause 37, which call for mixed care for the elderly in local authority residential accommodation and, in the independent sector, voluntary and private sector accommodation".

He then went on to describe the way they will be drawn up (Comm. (SCE) cols. 1986–7): "we shall prepare draft guidelines on how to draw up a care plan and make an assessment. We shall then consult the local authority associations and the British Association of Social Workers and others to ensure that the guidelines are workable and sensible and in accordance with the spirit and the letter of the Act. When we have consulted, we shall issue the guidelines in the form of general directions. The purpose of the power is to give the guidelines, after proper consultation and coordination, the effective force that they need". Having explained that under existing legislation the Secretary of State has no powers to say that responsibilities under statute are not being discharged nor to set up inquiries himself and follow them with directions, he continued: "The local authority, sometimes with encouragement from central Government, is responsible for setting up an inquiry and putting its own house in order. It is important to complete the legislative circle and to give the Secretary of State powers to make specific directions ... [the new section] gives the Secretary of State power to set up inquiries, which is new, and section [7D] gives him power to make specific directions in the event of default. Sections 7A and 7B have to be read together. It would be illogical to have sections 7B and [7D] without having the power to follow up the consequences of inquiries and defaults". One could well add that the new s.7C completes the statutory arsenal.

S.7B of the 1970 Act

"*Qualifying individual*". The Government view was that a decision by a local authority that a person is not a person for whom they may provide services is a matter of law to be decided by the court. It is not appropriate for a complaints procedure to be established under the new section (the Baroness in Waiting, Baroness Blatch (*Hansard*, H.L. Vol. 520, col. 1396). However, organisations or carers can bring complaints or make representations on behalf of other service users. The term *person* includes a body of persons corporate or incorporate, so that organisations can make representations on behalf of a client (see the Baroness in Waiting, Baroness Blatch, *Hansard*, H.L. Vol. 519, col. 100). Presumably such a decision is also open to challenge via the Local Government Commission.

The Parliamentary Under-Secretary of State for the Department of Social Security, Lord Henley, said (*Hansard*, H.L. Vol. 520, col. 622) "In our guidance associated with [the] requirement [in this new subsection] we shall make it clear that local authorities must be able to deal properly with complaints, and, while we are not recommending a separate structure for complaints against assessment, such complaints could be considered by the mechanisms that the local authority would be required to set up. Our guidance also makes it clear that the final stage in the complaints procedure must bring in an independent element on lines similar to that which local authorities will be required to have under the Children Act 1989".

S.7D of the 1970 Act

The Parliamentary Under-Secretary of State for the Department of Health, Baroness Hooper, explained (*Hansard*, H.L. Vol. 519, col. 103): "We expect the default procedures in this [section] to work in the following way. The first stage will be when it comes to the Secretary of State's attention that an authority is failing to discharge its functions. This may come from a number of directions—the work of the social services inspectorate, information received from organisations representing disabled people or by direct representations to the Secretary of State by users of services. The first thing the Secretary of State needs to do is to satisfy himself that the authority has failed without reasonable excuse to exercise its functions. This will entail some form of further investigation or inquiry and may, if the Secretary of State feels it would be useful, include using the general powers of direction to direct the authority to exercise its functions in a particular way.

It will only be after these processes have been exhausted and work with the authorities through the social services inspectorate has failed to secure any improvement in the situation that the use of the default powers will be considered ... When these powers are used the Secretary of State first has to issue an order then, if it is not complied with, he can seek an order from the court to enforce it".

S.7E of the 1970 Act

This section was added at the latest possible Parliamentary stage (the Lords' consideration of the Commons response to the Lords Amendments). At an earlier stage, the Parliamentary Under-Secretary of State for the Department of Health, Baroness Hooper, gave undertakings which still probably indicate Government intentions (*Hansard*, H.L. Vol. 520, col. 679): "we shall be issuing a guidance to local authorities on the provision of services for this group. It will include approval by the Secretary of State of schemes to provide residential care under Section 21 of the National Assistance Act 1948 and non-residential welfare services under Schedule 8 to the National Health Service Act 1977. This will be the first time that we have issued such comprehensive guidance to local authorities. Secondly, we shall be directing local authorities to include services for drug addicts and alcoholics in their community care plans and thus they will be required to translate our guidance into specific proposals for their areas". See also s.46(2).

PART IV

COMMUNITY CARE: SCOTLAND

Power of Secretary of State to give directions

51. After subsection (1) of section 5 (powers of Secretary of State) of the Social Work (Scotland) Act 1968 (in this Part of this Act referred to as "the 1968 Act") there shall be inserted the following subsection—

"(1A) Without prejudice to subsection (1) above, the Secretary of State may issue directions to local authorities, either individually or collectively, as to the manner in which they are to exercise any of their functions under this Act or any of the enactments mentioned in section 2(2) of this Act; and a local authority shall comply with any direction made under this subsection."

GENERAL NOTE

The Secretary of State has the power under s.5 of the Social Work (Scotland) Act 1968 to issue general guidance on the Social Work functions of local authorities and to make regulations in relation to the performance of these functions. This section adds a new power to issue binding directions to local authorities as to the manner in which they are to exercise their social work functions. Directions may relate to all local authorities or selected authorities. There is no restriction as to the form these directions might take, even to the extent of the equivalent provision in England and Wales (s.50)', which requires directions to be in writing. While this power potentially puts social work departments virtually under the control of the Secretary of State, Ministers have stressed that it is a reserve power to be used sparingly (*Hansard*, H.L. Vol. 520, col. 687). The Under-Secretary of State stated that the clause provides for powers that may be necessary to ensure the Government's policy on the mixed economy of care is carried out (Comm. (SCE) col. 1164). The direction-making power is not restricted to community care but extends to all social work functions.

Local authority plans for, and complaints in relation to, community care services in Scotland

52. After section 5 of the 1968 Act there shall be inserted the following sections—

"**Local authority plans for community care services**

5A.—(1) Within such period after the day appointed for the coming into force of this section as the secretary of State may direct, and in accordance with the provisions of this section, each local authority shall prepare and publish a plan for the provision of community care services in their area.

(2) Each local authority shall from time to time review any plan prepared by them under subsection (1) above, and shall, in the light of any such review, prepare and publish—

(a) any modifications to the plan under review; or

(b) if the case requires, a new plan.

(3) In preparing any plan or carrying out any review under subsection (1) or, as the case may be, subsection (2) above the authority shall consult—

(a) any Health Board providing services under the National Health Service (Scotland) Act 1978 in the area of the authority;

(b) in so far as the plan or, as the case may be, the review may affect or be affected by the provision or availability of housing, every district council in the area of the authority;

(c) such voluntary organisations as appear to the authority to represent the interests of persons who use or are likely to use any community care services within the area of the authority or the interests of private carers who, within that area, provide care to persons for whom, in the exercise of their functions under this Act or any of the enactments mentioned in section 2(2) of this Act, the local authority have a power or a duty to provide, or to secure the provision of, a service;

(d) such voluntary housing agencies and other bodies as appear to the authority to provide housing or community care services in their area; and

(e) such other persons as the Secretary of State may direct.

(4) In this section—

"community care services" means services, other than services for children, which a local authority are under a duty or have a power to provide, or to secure the provision of, under Part II of this Act or section 7 (functions of local authorities), 8 (provision of after-care services) or 11 (training and occupation of the mentally handicapped) of the Mental Health (Scotland) Act 1984; and

"private carer" means a person who is not employed to provide the care in question by any body in the exercise of its functions under any enactment.

Complaints procedure

5B.—(1) Subject to the provisions of this section, the Secretary of State may by order require local authorities to establish a procedure whereby a person, or anyone acting on his behalf, may make representations (including complaints) in relation to the authority's discharge of, or failure to discharge, any of their functions under this Act, or any of the enactments referred to in section 2(2) of this Act, in respect of that person.

(2) For the purposes of subsection (1) of this section, "person" means any person for whom the local authority have a power or a duty to provide, or to secure the provision of, a service, and whose need or possible need for such a service has (by whatever means) come to the attention of the authority.

(3) An order under subsection (1) of this section may be commenced at different times in respect of such different classes of person as may be specified in the order.

(4) In relation to a child, representations may be made by virtue of subsection (1) above by the child, or on his behalf by—

(a) his parent;

(b) any person having parental rights in respect of him;

(c) any local authority foster parent; or

(d) any other person appearing to the authority to have a sufficient interest in the child's wellbeing to warrant his making representations on the child's behalf.

(5) In this section—

"child" means a child under the age of 18 years; and

"parent" and "parental rights " have the same meaning as in section 8 (interpretation) of the Law Reform (Parent and Child) (Scotland) Act 1986.

(6) A local authority shall comply with any directions given by the Secretary of State as to the procedure to be adopted in considering representations made as mentioned in subsection (1) of this section and as to the taking of such action as may be necessary in consequence of such representations.

(7) Every local authority shall give such publicity to the procedure established under this section as they consider appropriate."

DEFINITIONS
"child": s.5B(5).
"community care services": s.5A(4).
"parent": s.5B(5).
"parental rights": s.5B(5).
"person": s.5B(2).
"the 1968 Act": s.51.

GENERAL NOTE
This section inserts two new sections into the 1968 Act. S.5A introduces a new planning procedure which, along with the assessment procedure introduced by s.55, is one of the key legislative components of the new community care provisions.

S.5A

Subss. (1) and (2)
Each local authority (meaning a Regional or Islands Council: 1968 Act, s.1(2)) must prepare, and from time to time review or replace, a plan for the provision of community care services. It is intended that the plans should cover a three-year period and be reviewed annually (*Caring for People*, para. 10.8). The content of the plans will be a matter for guidance from the Secretary of State. The first plans are to be published by April 1, 1992.

Subs. (3)
(a) Local health boards must always be consulted in the preparation and review of community care plans;
(b) District Councils must be consulted only in so far as a plan or a review may affect or be affected by housing issues;
(c) and (d) the voluntary sector may be consulted both as representatives of those who use community care services and their carers, and as providers of those services. Housing Associations are covered by (d), as are private sector providers of housing and care services.
There is no requirement to consult the Secretary of State. Indeed, he has no formal responsibility to monitor, approve or even receive the plans, although the draft guidance on community care planning indicates that he will take an interest in them.

Subs. (4)
"*Community care services*". This definition is extremely important and requires careful consideration. Under Pt. II of the 1968 Act, local authorities have a general duty to "promote social welfare" by making available "advice, guidance and assistance" including assistance in kind (and in restricted circumstances in cash) to children and persons in need. This includes providing and arranging for the provision of residential establishments and, when s.56 is implemented, arranging for the provision of nursing homes. It also includes domiciliary services (s.14, as amended by Sched. 9, para. 10(6)) and the specific duties imposed by the Chronically Sick and Disabled Persons (Scotland) Act 1972.
S.7 of the Mental Health (Scotland) Act 1984 empowers local authorities, with the approval of the Secretary of State, to provide residential accommodation for persons suffering from mental disorder, to exercise statutory guardianship functions, to provide ancillary or supplementary services, and to supervise persons suffering from mental handicap who are not liable to detention or subject to guardianship. S.8 obliges local authorities to provide after-care services to persons suffering from mental disorder and s.11 requires them to provide training and occupation for mentally handicapped people over school age.
The exclusion of "services for children" is not as clear as it might appear. It could mean "services specifically provided for children" or "any social work service received by an individual child". If the latter meaning is correct, in the absence of a statutory definition of children, it must be assumed that anyone under 18 is a child for the purposes of this definition. However, many people, certainly from the age of 16, will be receiving what are effectively adult services (*e.g.* adult training centres, supported hostels) and it would seem anomalous to exclude these from community care. If the former meaning is correct, such services would be included in community care, but the borderline may be more difficult to draw.
Although subs. (3) requires wide consultation, the definition of community care services makes it clear that the plan will not deal with the totality of community care in a region, which would include health, housing, education, etc., but only those aspects which are the responsibility of the social work department. Health boards will be instructed to prepare separate plans for their element of community care, and it is intended that there will be planning agreements to ensure that the two plans are complementary (*Caring for People*, para. 10.17).

"Private carer". The definition serves to exclude trade unions and professional associations representing carers employed by statutory agencies from the right to be consulted.

S.5B

Subs. (1)
  This makes provision for a new complaints procedure, which will apply to all social work functions, and not only community care services. Anyone acting on behalf of a person may make representations, including friends, relatives, carers and representative organisations. The reference to "functions" rather than "services" means that an assessment may be the subject of representation (but see subs. (2)). The new procedure is to be implemented from April 1, 1991.

Subs. (2)
  This defines who may be the subject of a complaint. Concern has been expressed about the position of carers. Although they may make representations on behalf of the person in need of care, they have no right to complain on their own behalf, unless they can establish that they themselves may need a service from the local authorities. Another problem with this definition concerns people refused a service from the local authority. The local authority could argue that, because no power or duty exists to provide the person with a service, the person has no right to complain, even though the complaint concerns the local authority's interpretation of its powers and duties. However, it seems that the Government does not interpret the provision in this way and the intention is that people should always have the right to complain if they feel they have been wrongly denied a service (*Hansard*, H.L. Vol. 520, col. 513).

Subss. (4) and (5)
  These would appear to limit, for children, the provision in subs. (1) that anyone may represent a person with a right to complain. Why this should be done is unclear, and the equivalent section for England and Wales (s.50) makes no such provision.

Subs. (6)
  Given the terms of s.51, this appears to be superfluous.

Inspection of premises providing accommodation

53.—(1) Section 6 of the 1968 Act (supervision of establishments and places providing accommodation etc.) shall be amended as follows.
  (2) In subsection (1) after "place" insert "the facilities and services provided therein."
  (3) In subsection (1), for the words "required to be kept therein" there shall be substituted "(in whatever form they are held) relating to the place or to any person for whom services have been or are provided there."
  (4) After subsection (2) there shall be inserted the following subsections—
  "(2A) Any such person may require the owner of, or any person employed in, the establishment or place in question to furnish him with such information as he may request.
  (2B) In exercising the power to inspect records and registers under this section a person—
    (a) shall be entitled at any reasonable time to have access to, and inspect and check the operation of, any computer and any associated apparatus or material which is or has been in use in connection with the records or register in question; and
    (b) may require—
      (i) the person by whom or on whose behalf the computer is or has been so used; or
      (ii) any person having charge of or otherwise concerned with the operation of the computer, apparatus or material,
  to give him such reasonable assistance as he may require.
  (2C) In exercising the power to inspect places under this section a person—
    (a) may interview any person residing there in private—

(i) for the purpose of investigating any complaint as to that place or the services provided there; or
(ii) if he has reason to believe that the services being provided there for that person are not satisfactory; and
(b) may examine any such person in private.
(2D) No person may—
(a) exercise the power to inspect records or registers under subsection (1) or (2) above so as to inspect medical records; or
(b) exercise the power conferred by subsection (2C)(b) above, unless he is a registered medical practitioner and, in the case of the power conferred by subsection (1) or (2) above, the records or register relate to medical treatment given at the place in question."

DEFINITIONS
"the 1968 Act": s.51.

GENERAL NOTE

Subs. (1)
S.6 of the 1968 Act empowers authorised officers of the Secretary of State to enter and inspect registered residential establishments and other premises where care is provided, including those where care is provided for children. This widens and clarifies the officer's powers.

Subs. (2)
This makes it clear that facilities and services may be inspected, as well as the state and management of the place, and the condition and treatment of residents.

Subs. (3)
This gives powers to inspect all relevant records, and not only those required to be kept by virtue of the 1968 Act.

Subs. (4)
Powers to require information to be provided, to check computerised information systems and to interview and examine residents are ensured. In respect of medical records, the power can only be exercised by a medical practitioner.

Inquiries
54. After section 6 of the 1968 Act there shall be inserted the following section—

"Inquiries
6A.—(1) The Secretary of State may cause an inquiry to be held into the functions of a local authority under this Act or any of the enactments mentioned in section 2(2) of this Act, except in so far as those functions relate to persons under the age of 18.
(2) The Secretary of State may, before an inquiry is commenced, direct that it shall be held in private, but where no such direction has been given the person holding the inquiry may if he thinks fit hold it or any part of it in private.
(3) Subsections (2) to (8) of section 210 of the Local Government (Scotland) Act 1973 (powers in relation to local inquiries) shall apply in relation to an inquiry under this section as they apply in relation to a local inquiry under that section."

DEFINITIONS
"the 1968 Act": s.51.

GENERAL NOTE
The Secretary of State is empowered to initiate enquiries into the social work functions of a

local authority. The new power does not cover social work functions in respect of children, where a power to hold enquiries already exists under the Children Act 1975.

Duty of local authority to make assessment of needs

55. After section 12 of the 1968 Act there shall be inserted the following section—

> **"Duty of local authority to make assessment of needs**
> 12A.—(1) Subject to the provisions of this section, where it appears to a local authority that any person for whom they are under a duty or have a power to provide, or to secure the provision of, community care services may be in need of any such services, the authority—
> > (a) shall make an assessment of the needs of that person for those services; and
> > (b) having regard to the results of that assessment, shall then decide whether the needs of that person call for the provision of any such services.
>
> (2) Before deciding, under subsection (1)(b) of this section, that the needs of any person call for the provision of nursing care, a local authority shall consult a medical practitioner.
>
> (3) If, while they are carrying out their duty under subsection (1) of this section, it appears to a local authority that there may be a need for the provision to any person to whom that subsection applies—
> > (a) of any services under the National Health Service (Scotland) Act 1978 by the Health Board—
> > > (i) in whose area he is ordinarily resident; or
> > > (ii) in whose area the services to be supplied by the local authority are, or are likely, to be provided; or
> > (b) of any services which fall within the functions of a housing authority (within the meaning of section 130 (housing) of the Local Government (Scotland) Act 1973) which is not the local authority carrying out the assessment,
>
> the local authority shall so notify that Health Board or housing authority, and shall request information from them as to what services are likely to be made available to that person by that Health Board or housing authority; and, thereafter, in carrying out their said duty, the local authority shall take into account any information received by them in response to that request.
>
> (4) Where a local authority are making an assessment under this section and it appears to them that the person concerned is a disabled person, they shall—
> > (a) proceed to make such a decision as to the services he requires as is mentioned in section 4 of the Disabled Persons (Services, Consultation and Representation) Act 1986 without his requesting them to do so under that section; and
> > (b) inform him that they will be doing so and of his rights under that Act.
>
> (5) Nothing in this section shall prevent a local authority from providing or arranging for the provision of community care services for any person without carrying out a prior assessment of his needs in accordance with the preceding provisions of this section if, in the opinion of the authority, the condition of that person is such that he requires those services as a matter of urgency.
>
> (6) If, by virtue of subsection (5) of this section, community care services have been provided for any person as a matter of urgency, then, as soon as practicable thereafter, an assessment of his needs

shall be made in accordance with the preceding provisions of this section.

(7) This section is without prejudice to section 3 of the said Act of 1986.

(8) In this section—

"community care services" has the same meaning as in section 5A of this Act;

"disabled person" has the same meaning in the said Act of 1986; and

"medical practitioner" means a fully registered person within the meaning of section 55 (interpretation) of the Medical Act 1983."

DEFINITIONS

"community care services": s.52.
"disabled person": subs. (8).
"housing authority": subs. (3)(b).
"medical practitioner": subs. (8).
"the 1968 Act": s.51.

GENERAL NOTE

Before services are provided by a social work department assessments must be held as determined in the Act. It is intended that this will come into force on April 1, 1993 and the details of the assessment procedure will be the subject of guidance from the Secretary of State.

Subs. (1)

An assessment will be necessary before the provision of any community care service, subject to subs. (5). The assessment will be a two-stage process. The first stage is to assess the person's needs, which should be considered regardless of the ability of the local authority to meet the need. The second stage is to decide what services shall be provided by the local authorities. At the second stage, the availability of resources will come into consideration. The Act does not introduce any new duty to meet all those needs which are uncovered by the assessment process. However, in identifying need, the process may identify existing duties which would oblige the local authority to act. Any discrepancy between the level of need and the availability of resources should be fed into the planning process introduced by s.52.

Subs. (2)

The power to arrange for the provision of nursing care is introduced by s.56, but is here qualified by the requirement to consult a medical practitioner.

Subs. (3)

The assessment, strictly speaking, is for community care services, which are only those services which are the responsibility of the local social work authority (see note to s.52). Clearly, other needs for health care and housing provision may become apparent in an assessment. The Government rejected attempts to introduce a full multi-disciplinary assessment procedure into the legislation, arguing that it would be unnecessarily prescriptive. The subsection requires health boards and housing authorities to be notified of apparent need, and the social work department to consider their response in making an assessment of what they can provide. The equivalent provision for England and Wales, s.47(3), contains a duty to invite the other bodies to assist in the assessment which is not reproduced here.

Subs. (4)

The Disabled Persons (Services, Consultation and Representation) Act 1986 has already introduced an assessment procedure for social work services to a disabled person. This subsection ensures that a community care assessment of a disabled person will incorporate the procedure set out in the 1986 Act.

Subss. (5) and (6)

Services can be provided in an emergency without a formal assessment, provided that one takes place as soon as practicable.

Subs. (7)

S.3 of the 1986 Act introduced rights to disabled people and their representatives to make representations in connection with assessments of need for social work services. It has not yet been implemented.

Residential accommodation with nursing and provision of care and after-care

56. After section 13 of the 1968 Act there shall be inserted the following sections—

"Residential accommodation with nursing

Residential accommodation with nursing
13A.—(1) Without prejudice to section 12 of this Act, a local authority shall make such arrangements as they consider appropriate and adequate for the provision of suitable residential accommodation where nursing is provided for persons who appear to them to be in need of such accommodation by reason of infirmity, age, illness or mental disorder, dependency on drugs or alcohol or being substantially handicapped by any deformity or disability.
(2) The arrangements made by virtue of subsection (1) above shall be made with a voluntary or other organisation or other person, being an organisation or person managing premises which are—
  (a) a nursing home within the meaning of section 10(2)(a) of the Nursing Homes Registration (Scotland) Act 1938 in respect of which that organisation or person is registered or exempt from registration under that Act; or
  (b) a private hospital registered under section 12 of the Mental Health (Scotland) Act 1984,
for the provision of accommodation in those premises.
(3) The provisions of section 6 of this Act apply in relation to premises where accommodation is provided for the purposes of this section as they apply in relation to establishments provided for the purposes of this Act.

Provision of care and after-care

Provision of care and after-care
13B.—(1) Subject to subsection (2) below, a local authority may with the approval of the Secretary of State, and shall, if and to the extent that the Secretary of State so directs, make arrangements for the purpose of the prevention of illness, the care of persons suffering from illness, and the after-care of such persons.
(2) The arrangements which may be made under subsection (1) above do not include arrangements in respect of medical, dental or nursing care, or health visiting."

DEFINITIONS
"the 1968 Act": s.51.

GENERAL NOTE

S.13A
Subs. (1)
  Local authorities previously had the power to provide or arrange for residential accommodation, but no power to provide homes where specialised nursing care is provided. This gives them a power to arrange for the provision of such accommodation.

Subs. (2)
  This makes it clear that the nursing homes may not be provided directly by the local authority, but by arrangement with other bodies, who will be paid by the local authority. The registration of private and voluntary nursing homes and private hospitals will remain the responsibility of the health board and Secretary of State respectively.

Subs. (3)
This extends the Secretary of State's power of inspection to homes funded by the local authority under this new section.

S.13B
This is not a new provision and was formerly found in s.27 of the National Health Service (Scotland) Act 1947. It has been re-enacted in the 1968 Act as a consolidation measure.

Exclusion of powers to provide accommodation in certain cases

57. After section 86 of the 1968 Act there shall be inserted the following section—

> **"Exclusion of powers to provide accommodation in certain cases**
> 86A.—(1) Subject to subsection (3) below, no accommodation may be provided under this Act for any person who immediately before the date on which this section comes into force, was ordinarily resident in relevant premises.
> (2) In subsection (1) above "relevant premises" means—
> (a) any establishment in respect of which a person is registered under section 62 of this Act;
> (b) any nursing home within the meaning of the Nursing Homes Registration (Scotland) Act 1938 in respect of which a person is registered or exempt from registration under that Act;
> (c) any private hospital registered under section 12 of the Mental Health (Scotland) Act 1984; and
> (d) such other premises as the Secretary of State may by regulations prescribe.
> (3) The Secretary of State may by regulations provide that in such cases and subject to such conditions as may be prescribed subsection (1) above shall not apply in relation to such classes of persons as may be prescribed in the regulations.
> (4) The Secretary of State shall by regulations prescribe the circumstances in which persons are to be treated as being ordinarily resident in any premises for the purposes of subsection (1) above.
> (5) This section does not affect the validity of any contract made before the date on which this section comes into force for the provision of accommodation on or after that date or anything done in pursuance of such a contract."

DEFINITIONS
"relevant premises": subs. (2).
"the 1968 Act": s.51.

GENERAL NOTE
Once the community care provisions are fully implemented (currently set for April 1, 1993), people moving into private or voluntary residential or nursing care will no longer receive high levels of Income Support. The primary responsibility for meeting the care costs will pass to local authorities. Those who are already in residential or nursing care on the implementation date will receive transitional protection of the social security benefits. This section prevents local authorities from financially supporting the costs of accommodation of those who receive this transitional protection. However, regulations may waive this restriction. Anyone below pensionable age in a nursing home or residential care home is likely to be exempted (Comm. (SCE) col. 865), since their care costs are often so high that local authorities must "top up" even the high levels of income support.

Power of Secretary of State to make grants

58. After section 92 of the 1968 Act there shall be inserted the following section—

"Power of the Secretary of State to make grants
92A. The Secretary of State may, with the approval of the Treasury, make grants out of money provided by Parliament towards any expenses of local authorities in respect of their functions under—
(a) Part II of this Act; and
(b) sections 7 and 8 of the Mental Health (Scotland) Act 1984, in relation to persons suffering from mental illness."

DEFINITIONS
"the 1968 Act": s.51.

GENERAL NOTE
Although the Government rejected Sir Roy Griffith's idea of a specific "ring-fenced" grant to local authorities for community care, this section makes provision for such a grant for services for people with mental illness. It is not intended that this grant should fund *all* mental illness services but that it should "help accelerate the development of community based services for people with a mental illness" (*Caring for People*, para. 10.29). The first grants will be payable from April 1, 1991.

PART V

MISCELLANEOUS AND GENERAL

Parliamentary disqualification

59.—(1) In Schedule 1 to the House of Commons Disqualification Act 1975 (offices disqualifying for membership of the House of Commons), in Part III for the entry which begins "Chairman in receipt of remuneration of any Regional Health Authority" there shall be substituted the following entry—
"Chairman or any member, not being also an employee, of any Regional Health Authority, District Health Authority, Family Health Services Authority or special health authority which is a relevant authority for the purposes of paragraph 9(1) of Schedule 5 to the National Health Service Act 1977."
(2) In the said Part III there shall be inserted (at the appropriate place) the following entry—
"Chairman or non-executive member of a National Health Service trust established under the National Health Service and Community Care Act 1990 or the National Health Service (Scotland) Act 1978."
(3) In the said Part III—
(a) in the entry which begins "Paid Chairman of a Health Board," for the words "Paid Chairman" there shall be substituted "Chairman or any member, not being also an employee,";
(b) in the entry which begins "Chairman of the Management Committee of the Common Services Agency" after the word "Chairman" there shall be inserted "or any member, not being also an employee,"; and
(c) in the entry relating to the Chairman of a committee constituted under section 91 of the Mental Health (Scotland) Act 1984, after the word "Chairman" there shall be inserted "or any member, not being also an employee."

DEFINITIONS
"District Health Authority": ss.8 and 128 of the National Health Service Act 1977, as amended by this Act, and Sched. 1 to this Act.
"Family Health Services Authority": s.10 of the National Health Service Act 1977 and Sched. 1 to this Act.
"non-executive member": s.5 of this Act; see also Sched. 1.
"Regional Health Authority": ss.8 and 128 of the National Health Service Act 1977, as amended by this Act, and Sched. 1 to this Act.

"special health authority": s.11 of the National Health Service Act 1977, as amended by this Act, and Sched. 1 to this Act.

Removal of Crown immunities

60.—(1) Subject to the following provisions of this section, on and after the day appointed for the coming into force of this subsection, no health service body shall be regarded as the servant or agent of the Crown or as enjoying any status, immunity or privilege of the Crown; and so far as concerns land in which the Secretary of State has an interest, at any time when—

(a) by virtue of directions under any provision of the National Health Service Act 1977, the Mental Health (Scotland) Act 1984 or the Health and Medicines Act 1988 or by virtue of orders under section 2 or section 10 of the National Health Service (Scotland) Act 1978, powers of disposal or management with respect to the land are conferred on a health service body, or

(b) the land is otherwise held, used or occupied by a health service body, the interest of the Secretary of State shall be treated for the purposes of any enactment or rule of law relating to Crown land or interests as if it were an interest held otherwise than by the Secretary of State (or any other emanation of the Crown).

(2) In Schedule 8 to this Act—

(a) Part I has effect to continue certain exemptions for health service bodies and property held, used or occupied by such bodies;

(b) the amendments in Part II have effect, being amendments consequential on subsection (1) above; and

(c) the transitional provisions in Part III have effect in connection with the operation of subsection (1) above.

(3) Where, as a result of the provisions of subsection (1) above, by virtue of his employment during any period after the day appointed for the coming into force of that subsection—

(a) an employee has contractual rights against a health service body to benefits in the event of his redundancy, and

(b) he also has statutory rights against the health service body under Part VI of the Employment Protection (Consolidation) Act 1978 (redundancy payments),

any benefits provided to him by virtue of the contractual rights referred to in paragraph (a) above shall be taken as satisfying his entitlement to benefits under the said Part VI.

(4) Nothing in subsection (1) above affects the extent of the expression "the services of the Crown" where it appears in—

(a) Schedule 1 to the Registered Designs Act 1949 (provisions as to the use of registered designs for the services of the Crown etc.); and

(b) sections 55 to 59 of the Patents Act 1977 (use of patented inventions for the services of the Crown);

and, accordingly, services provided in pursuance of any power or duty of the Secretary of State under Part I of the National Health Service Act 1977 or Part I or Part III of the National Health Service (Scotland) Act 1978 shall continue to be regarded as included in that expression, whether the services are in fact provided by a health service body, a National Health Service trust or any other person.

(5) The Secretary of State may by order made by statutory instrument provide that, in relation to any enactment contained in a local Act and specified in the order, the operation of subsection (1) above shall be excluded or modified to the extent specified in the order.

(6) No order shall be made under subsection (5) above unless a draft of it has been laid before, and approved by a resolution of, each House of Parliament.

(7) In this section "health service body" means—
(a) a health authority, within the meaning of the National Health Service Act 1977;
(b) a Health Board or Special Health Board constituted under section 2 of the National Health Service (Scotland) Act 1978;
(c) a State Hospital Management Committee constituted under section 91 of the Mental Health (Scotland) Act 1984;
(d) a Family Health Services Authority;
(e) the Common Services Agency for the Scottish Health Service;
(f) the Dental Practice Board;
(g) the Scottish Dental Practice Board; and
(h) the Public Health Laboratory Service Board.

DEFINITIONS
"Dental Practice Board": s.37 of the National Health Service Act 1977.
"Family Health Services Authority": s.10 of the National Health Service Act 1977 and Sched. 1 of this Act.
"health service body": subs. (7).
"Public Health Laboratory Service Board": s.5 and Sched. 3 to the National Health Service Act 1977.

GENERAL NOTE
Previously, health authorities were regarded as part of the Crown because they were carrying out functions of the Crown imposed on the Secretary of State by s.1 of the 1977 Act (see *Encyclopedia of Health Services and Medical Law, Introduction* and the note to s.12 of the 1977 Act), notwithstanding that Sched. 5, para. 12(1) required them to be treated "in all respects . . . as a principal". In particular, it has been held, in, *e.g. Wood* v. *Leeds Area Health Authority (Training)* [1974] I.C.R. 535, that the rule of interpretation whereby a statute did not bind the Crown unless it was especially mentioned applied to health authorities. The trend in recent years (perhaps starting with the Crown Proceedings Act 1947) has been more and more to equate the Crown with a "subject", see, *e.g.* the National Health Service (Amendment) Act 1986 (now repealed by this Act). This section continues that policy.

Subs. (1)
The words in the subsection "status, immunity or privilege" are very wide but it is possible that they can lead to difficulties. They have in common that each of them had to be especially pleaded. They do not apply to rules of law or discretions which the court could take of its own motion and it is not certain that all these have been removed. It is presumed that the draftsman has considered that the removal of Crown "status" has removed the rule of law concerning the need for express mention of a statute to bind the Crown.

Subs. (2)(a)
This paragraph continues certain exemptions for the health service, *viz.* it retains Crown immunity under: (1) the Employers' Liability (Compulsory Insurance) Act 1969, so that the health service does not have to carry insurance against injury or disease sustained as a result of employment. It is concerned only with insurance and not liability (see also s.21 above and note thereto); (2) the Vehicles (Excise) Act 1971, so that a road fund licence is not required by health service vehicles, and the Road Traffic Act 1988, so that third party insurance is not required. Under s.23 of the 1977 Act, the Secretary of State may lend a vehicle to any person, including a voluntary organisation, to enable it to provide a service under that Act. The NHS (Vehicles) Order S.I. 1974 No. 168 has been made under that section, whereby such vehicles are also exempt. It continues in force; (3) the Copyright, Designs and Patents Act 1988, s.48, so that NHS copyright material remains part of the Crown's copyright.

Subs. (2)(b)
This paragraph makes specific provision consequent on subs. (1), *viz.*: under the Town and Country Planning Acts, planning permission is required in order to change the use of consecrated land or land consisting of a burial ground; see also Sched. 8, para. 16 (and, as regards Scotland, para. 17) making more general transitional provision.
Under the Value Added Tax Act health service bodies continue to be eligible to claim refunds of VAT on certain services. Health authorities are given the same protection against compulsory purchase of the land as the statutory undertakers such as British Telecom and British Gas under the Acquisition of Land Act 1971. Under the Housing Acts the health

service must seek a repossession court in respect of property let in consequence of a tenant's employment, but see also Sched. 8, para. 19 (and, as regards Scotland, para. 20), making more general transitional provision.

Subs. (2)(c)

This paragraph makes transitional provision to various statutes. Of especial note is the provision relating to the Medicines Act 1968, by which where a health service body or NHS trust had made an application for a clinical trial or animal test certificate before April 1, 1991 it shall be treated as having had a licence. See also the notes to subs.(2)(b) above.

Subs. (3)

This subsection prevents any entitlement to both contractual and statutory redundancy payments.

Subs. (4)

The Parliamentary Under-Secretary of State for the Department of Social Security, Lord Henley, explained (*Hansard*, H.L. Vol. 519, col. 137) "the use of registered designs, copyright, or patent material where the removal of Crown immunity is one area which would or could cost the NHS money without bringing any benefits to patients or staff". He went on: "Legislation covering these areas has consistently recognised the value to the general public of maintaining a Crown or public service exemption for the use of such material without the permission of the owner of the intellectual property in the material. These provisions are used sparingly. But on occasions the public interest in patient care is best served by invoking them. There was, for example, a recent case relating to lithotripter machines, where, without the use of these powers, NHS patients would have been deprived of the benefit of this equipment pending the outcome of litigation relating to the patents in the equipment. These provisions do not allow the Crown simply to use others' ideas without payment. When these powers in relation to the use of patents and registered designs are invoked there is provision for compensation of the owner of the intellectual property. In the case of copyright the power is not a wide one and is indeed one of the many cases where use can be made of copyright material without infringement. Any diversion of effort or funds from patient care which does not bring an offsetting benefit in the form of higher standards is to be avoided. The public interest in patient care will remain even when Crown immunity has in general been removed from the NHS".

Health service bodies: taxation

61.—(1) In Part XII of the Income and Corporation Taxes Act 1988 (special classes of companies and business: miscellaneous businesses and bodies) after section 519 there shall be inserted the following section—

> **"Health service bodies**
>   519A.—(1) A health service body—
>   (a) shall be exempt from income tax in respect of its income, and
>   (b) shall be exempt from corporation tax,
> and, so far as the exemption from income tax conferred by this subsection calls for repayment of tax, effect shall be given thereto by means of a claim.
>   (2) In this section "health service body" means—
>   (a) a health authority, within the meaning of the National Health Service Act 1977;
>   (b) a National Health Service trust established under Part I of the National Health Service and Community Care Act 1990;
>   (c) a Family Health Services Authority;
>   (d) a Health Board or Special Health Board, the Common Services Agency for the Scottish Health Service and a National Health Service trust respectively constituted under sections 2, 10 and 12A of the National Health Service (Scotland) Act 1978;
>   (e) a State Hospital Management Committee constituted under section 91 of the Mental Health (Scotland) Act 1984;
>   (f) the Dental Practice Board;
>   (g) the Scottish Dental Practice Board; and

(h) the Public Health Laboratory Service Board."

(2) In section 149B of the Capital Gains Tax Act 1979 (miscellaneous exemptions from tax) in subsection (3) after the words "section 519 of the Taxes Act 1988" there shall be inserted "and a health service body, within the meaning of section 519A of that Act."

(3) Where any conveyance, transfer or lease is made or agreed to be made to a National Health Service trust established under Part I of the National Health Service and Community Care Act 1990 or the National Health Service (Scotland) Act 1978, no stamp duty shall be chargeable by virtue of any of the following headings in Schedule 1 to the Stamp Act 1891—

(a) "Conveyance or Transfer on Sale,"
(b) "Conveyance or Transfer of any kind not hereinbefore described,"
(c) "Lease or Tack,"

on the instrument by which the conveyance, transfer or lease, or the agreement for it, is effected.

(4) At the end of section 27 of the Value Added Tax Act 1983 (application to Crown) there shall be added the following subsection—

"(5) For the purposes of subsection (4) above a National Health Service trust established under Part I of the National Health Service and Community Care Act 1990 or the National Health Service (Scotland) Act 1978 shall be regarded as a body of persons exercising functions on behalf of a Minister of the Crown."

(5) At the end of Schedule 3 to the Inheritance Tax Act 1984 (gifts for national purposes) there shall be added—

"A health service body, within the meaning of section 519A of the Income and Corporation Taxes Act 1988."

DEFINITIONS
"Dental Practice Board": s.37 of the National Health Service Act 1977.
"Family Health Services Authority": s.10 of the National Health Service Act 1977 and Sched. 1 to this Act.
"health authority": s.128 of the National Health Service Act 1977.
"health service body": subs. (1) of this Act, inserting s.519A of the Income and Corporation Taxes Act 1988.
"National Health Service trust": ss.5 and 26 of this Act and 128 of the National Health Service Act 1977, as inserted by this Act and s.5 of this Act.
"Public Health Laboratory Service Board": s.5 and Sched. 3 to the National Health Service Act 1977.

Clinical Standards Advisory Group

62.—(1) There shall be established in accordance with this section a Clinical Standards Advisory Group (in this section referred to as "the Advisory Group") which shall have the following functions—

(a) in accordance with a request made by the Health Ministers or any one of them, to provide advice on the standards of clinical care for, and the access to and availability of services to, national health service patients and, in this connection, to carry out such investigations into such matters (if any) and to make such reports in relation thereto as the Health Ministers may require;

(b) in accordance with a request made by one or more health service bodies, to provide advice on, to carry out investigations into and to report on the standards of clinical care for, and the access to and availability of services to, national health service patients for whom services are or are to be provided by or on behalf of the body or bodies concerned; and

(c) such other functions as may be prescribed by regulations.

(2) The Advisory Group shall consist of a chairman and other members appointed by the Health Ministers and regulations may—

(a) require that one or more members of the Advisory Group shall be appointed from persons nominated by such body or bodies as may be specified in the regulations; and

(b) provide that one or more of the members who are not appointed from persons so nominated must fulfil such conditions or hold such posts as may be so specified.

(3) Regulations may make provision as to—

(a) the appointment, tenure and vacation of office of the chairman and members of the Advisory Group;

(b) the appointment of and the exercise of functions by committees and sub-committees of the Advisory Group (including committees and sub-committees consisting wholly or partly of persons who are not members of the Advisory Group);

(c) the procedure of the Advisory Group and any committees or sub-committees thereof; and

(d) the attendance at meetings of the Advisory Group or any committee or sub-committee thereof of persons appointed by the Health Ministers and the extent of their participation in such meetings.

(4) Proceedings of the Advisory Group, or of any committee or sub-committee of the Advisory Group, shall not be invalidated by any vacancy in membership or by any defect in a member's appointment or qualifications.

(5) The Health Ministers—

(a) may pay to the chairman and members of the Advisory Group, or of any committee or sub-committee of the Advisory Group or any persons appointed as mentioned in subsection (3)(d) above, such sums by way of remuneration and travelling and other allowances as the Health Ministers, with the consent of the Treasury, may determine;

(b) shall make available to the Advisory Group and to any committee or sub-committee thereof such staff and other services or facilities as are necessary to enable them to carry out their functions; and

(c) shall defray such expenditure as is reasonably incurred by the Advisory Group in carrying out their functions.

(6) Where the Advisory Group carry out an investigation or make a report in accordance with a request made by a health service body, that body shall reimburse, in such manner as the Health Ministers may determine, so much of the expenditure incurred by them under paragraphs (a) and (c) of subsection (5) above as they certify as being attributable to the carrying out of that investigation or the making of that report.

(7) In this section—

"clinical care" means any action which is taken in connection with the diagnosis of illness or the care or treatment of a patient, and which is taken solely in consequence of the exercise of clinical judgment;

"the Health Ministers" means the Secretaries of State respectively concerned with health in England, in Wales and in Scotland;

"health service body" means—

(i) a health authority, within the meaning of the National Health Service Act 1977,

(ii) a Health Board or Special Health Board constituted under section 2 of the National Health Service (Scotland) Act 1978,

(iii) a State Hospital Management Committee constituted under section 91 of the Mental Health (Scotland) Act 1984,

(iv) the Common Services Agency for the Scottish Health Service,

(v) a National Health Service trust constituted under Part I of this Act or under the National Health Service (Scotland) Act 1978, and

        (vi) a Family Health Services Authority;
"national health service patient" means any person for whom any services are or are to be provided by or on behalf of a health service body;
"regulations" means regulations made by the Health Ministers and any such regulations may make different provision for different cases or descriptions of case, including different provision for different areas; and
"services" means services provided—

(a) in England and Wales, by virtue of directions under section 13 or section 14 of the National Health Service Act 1977 or section 5 of this Act; or

(b) in Scotland, by a health service body under Part I or Part III of the National Health Service (Scotland) Act 1978; or

(c) pursuant to an NHS contract, as defined in section 4(1) of this Act or section 17A of the National Health Service (Scotland) Act 1978.

DEFINITIONS
"Advisory Group": subs. (1).
"clinical care": subs. (7).
"Family Health Services Authority": s.10 of the National Health Service Act 1977 and Sched. 1 to this Act.
"the Health Ministers": subs. (7).
"health service body": subs. (7).
"NHS contract": ss.3 and 26 of this Act and 128 of the National Health Service Act 1977, as inserted by this Act.
"national health service patient": subs. (7).
"National Health Service trust": ss.5 and 26 of this Act and 128 of the National Health Service Act 1977, as inserted by this Act and s.5 of this Act.
"regulations": subs. (7).
"services": subs. (7).

GENERAL NOTE
This section was inserted by the House of Lords and provides a somewhat rare example in the statute book of a provision which necessitated a change in the Long Title.
The Parliamentary Under-Secretary of State for the Department of Health, Baroness Hooper, located the constitutional position of the Group (see also the note to s.3 above) (*Hansard*, H.L. Vol. 520, cols. 699–700): "The NHS management executive is responsible to the Secretary of State for the quality of services in the NHS generally. That includes all aspects of quality from portering services and the food that patients receive right through to standards of clinical care. The different aspects of quality are naturally the responsibility of different management executive directors. Clinical standards, for example, are an important part of the remit of the medical and nursing directors; but they all combine to influence the overall quality of service that the patient receives. It would surely be wrong to separate the clinical side of quality and place it in the hands of a different body.
"The Clinical Standards Advisory Group will play a key rôle in guaranteeing and improving standards of clinical care . . . its rôle will be to provide forthright and independent advice on clinical standards to the Secretary of State and the NHS management executive. It will not be accountable to him for those standards. . . .
"At the highest level the National Health Service policy board supervises the work of the management executive under the chairmanship of the Secretary of State. It includes members with a wealth of experience both of the health service and of the management of other large organisations who provide valuable advice at both strategic and working levels on all aspects of its work, including quality improvement. The management executive itself has a membership with in-depth experience of the National Health Service as well as members drawn from outside the public sector . . . The management executive already has a large range of independent advisers to consult in its everyday work. Directors are in regular contact with regional chairmen and general managers, both informally and through the established review procedures. It is a reflection of the importance of quality in these contacts that it features on the agenda of all the reviews of regional health authorities' performance undertaken by the management executive last year . . . Equally important, the management executive has established effective working relationships with independent bodies. These can provide a valuable source of advice and support in specific areas of work, including quality. A good

example is medical audit, where the management executive has allocated funds to a number of bodies, including the Royal College of General Practitioners and the College of Anaesthetists' quality of care unit to help in the development of a nationwide audit system".

Earlier she had said (*Hansard*, H.L. Vol. 520, col. 245): "It might be helpful if I set out in some detail the way in which we envisage the Clinical Standards Advisory Group operating. The Group will consist of a lay chairman, members appointed on the nomination of medical, dental and nursing royal colleges and the chairmen of the standing medical, dental and nursing advisory committees. It will have a wide remit to provide advice, carry out studies and submit reports at the request of the Secretaries of State on issues relating to standards of clinical care nationally, regionally or locally. In addition, the Group will be able to provide advice on specific local issues at the request of health service bodies. That will enable it to provide valuable help to districts seeking to monitor the quality of service obtained through a particular pattern of National Health Service contracts or to help a National Health Service trust looking for independent advice on aspects of the services which it provides. The Group's programme of work will be settled between it and the Secretaries of State. They will consider together proposals for studies, including those from health service bodies and other organisations; for example, the royal colleges. It will also give priority to those which they consider to be of the greatest value to the health service as a whole."

She added (*Hansard*, H.L. Vol. 520, cols. 246–8): "as regards the independence of the Group . . . the expertise of its members will enable it to become a respected source of advice on clinical quality, complementing the drive to improve standards in the National Health Service both locally and nationally. . . . there will be nothing to prevent the Group initiating activity, though we would largely expect it to respond to requests".

Also (*Hansard*, H.L. Vol. 520, col. 257): "the Group's activities will be able to extend to the quality of clinical care in the community health services . . . The [section] makes clear that that includes the questions of access to and availability of high standards of clinical care . . . this field [is left] to the Group, leaving other more general aspects of care—for example, the quality of hospital food, . . . to be tackled through the NHS management executives' continuing programme of quality improvement . . . the Group's activities will be fully funded and [the] appropriate staffing support will be provided. The Group will have the ability to look at access to services as well as at the services themselves . . . and therefore the Group will be able to look at excessive waiting times".

Subs. (1)
"Under this subsection . . . the Group has powers to advise on standards of clinical care, access to services and, in addition, availability of services. A break in continuity which adversely affected the quality of treatment of a patient would certainly fall within the scope of an investigation into standards of clinical care; a discontinuity in treatment could well be the result of restricted access to, or, alternatively, availability of a service" (*Hansard*, H.L. Vol. 520, col. 695).

Repeal of remaining provisions of Health Services Act 1976

63.—(1) Part III (control of hospital building outside National Health Service) and Part IV (supplementary and general) of the Health Services Act 1976 shall cease to have effect.

(2) Notwithstanding the repeal of Part III of the Health Services Act 1976 by this Act,—

  (a) that Part shall continue to have effect in relation to any authorisation granted by the Secretary of State under section 13(2) of that Act which is in force when that repeal takes effect; and

  (b) the amendment made by section 19(4)(b) of that Act shall continue to have effect.

GENERAL NOTE

Subs. (2)
The Parliamentary Under-Secretary of State for Health, Mr Roger Freeman, said (Comm. (SCE) col. 1181): "Only one permission has been granted under the legislation that we seek to annul".

Financial provisions

64.—(1) There shall be paid out of moneys provided by Parliament—

(a) any sums required by the Secretary of State for making loans to a National Health Service trust;
(b) any sums required by the Secretary of State for fulfilling a guarantee of a sum borrowed by a National Health Service trust;
(c) any amount paid as public dividend capital under paragraph 5 of Schedule 3 to this Act;
(d) any expenses of the Secretary of State under this Act; and
(e) any increase attributable to this Act in the sums so payable under any other enactment.

(2) Any sums received by the Secretary of State under this Act shall be paid into the Consolidated Fund.

DEFINITIONS
"National Health Service trust": ss.5 and 26 of this Act and 128 of the National Health Service Act 1977, as inserted by this Act and s.5 of this Act.

GENERAL NOTE
See notes to ss.5–10 and 19. When a trust is established, its initial capitalisation will equal the net assets transferred by the Secretary of State to the trust. The net assets are assets at proper valuation of land and buildings less liabilities. No surplus assets are to be transferred. As opening capitalisation is equal to transferred assets, then technically a trust cannot over-borrow from the state (Comm. (SCE) col. 1199).

Regulations, orders and directions

65.—(1) Any power to make regulations conferred by this Act shall be exercisable by statutory instrument, and any such statutory instrument shall be subject to annulment in pursuance of a resolution of either House of Parliament.

(2) In section 126 of the National Health Service Act 1977 (orders and regulations and directions) in each of subsections (2) to (4) after the words "this Act" there shall be inserted "or Part I of the National Health Service and Community Care Act 1990" and at the end of that section there shall be added the following subsection—

"(5) Without prejudice to the generality of subsection (4) above, any power which may be exercised as mentioned in paragraphs (a) and (b) of that subsection may make different provision for different areas."

Amendments and repeals

66.—(1) Schedule 9 to this Act, which contains minor amendments and amendments consequential on the provisions of this Act, shall have effect.

(2) The enactments specified in Schedule 10 to this Act, which include some that are spent, are hereby repealed to the extent specified in the third column of that Schedule.

Short title, commencement and extent

67.—(1) This Act may be cited as the National Health Service and Community Care Act 1990.

(2) This Act, other than this section, shall come into force on such day as the Secretary of State may by order made by statutory instrument appoint, and different days may be so appointed for different provisions or for different purposes and for different areas or descriptions of areas.

(3) An order under subsection (2) above may contain such transitional provisions and savings (whether or not involving the modification of any statutory provision) as appear to the Secretary of State necessary or expedient in connection with the provisions brought into force.

(4) Part I of this Act, other than section 15(4), does not extend to Scotland; Part II, other than section 34, and Part IV of this Act do not

extend to England and Wales; and Part III of this Act, other than subsections (3) and (4) of section 42, subsections (1) and (3) to (6) of section 44
and section 45, does not extend to Scotland.

(5) This Act, other than sections 59 and 61, does not extend to Northern
Ireland.

(6) The Secretary of State may by order made by statutory instrument
provide that so much of this Act as extends to England and Wales shall
apply to the Isles of Scilly with such modifications, if any, as are specified in
the order and, except as provided in pursuance of this subsection, Parts I
and III of this Act do not apply to the Isles of Scilly.

SCHEDULES

Sections 1 and 2   SCHEDULE 1

HEALTH AUTHORITIES AND FAMILY HEALTH SERVICES AUTHORITIES

PART I

MEMBERSHIP OF REGIONAL AND DISTRICT HEALTH AUTHORITIES

Regional health authorities

1.—(1) A Regional Health Authority shall consist of—
(a) a chairman appointed by the Secretary of State;
(b) a prescribed number of members appointed by him;
(c) the chief officer of the authority;
(d) such other officers as may be prescribed; and
(e) not more than a prescribed number of other officers of the authority appointed by the
chairman and the members specified in paragraphs (b) and (c) above.

(2) Except in so far as regulations otherwise provide, no person who is an officer of the
authority may be appointed under sub-paragraph (1)(b) above; and, without prejudice to any
provision made by virtue of paragraph 12(a) of Schedule 5 to the principal Act (regulations as to
appointment and tenure)—
(a) at least one of the persons appointed under sub-paragraph (1)(b) above must hold a post
in a university with a medical or dental school; and
(b) regulations may provide that all or any of the other persons appointed under sub-
paragraph (1)(b) above must fulfil prescribed conditions or hold posts of a prescribed
description.

District health authorities

2.—(1) A District Health Authority for a district in England shall consist of—
(a) a chairman appointed by the Secretary of State;
(b) a prescribed number of members appointed by the Regional Health Authority whose
region includes the district in question;
(c) the chief officer of the authority;
(d) such other officers as may be prescribed; and
(e) not more than a prescribed number of other officers of the authority appointed by the
chairman and the members specified in paragraphs (b) and (c) above.

(2) Except in so far as regulations otherwise provide, no person who is an officer of the
authority may be appointed under sub-paragraph (1)(b) above; and, without prejudice to any
provision made by virtue of paragraph 12(a) of Schedule 5 to the principal Act (regulations as
to appointment and tenure), but subject to sub-paragraph (3) below, regulations may provide
that all or any of the persons appointed under sub-paragraph (1)(b) above must fulfil
prescribed conditions or hold posts of a prescribed description.

(3) In the case of a prescribed authority, at least one of the persons appointed under
sub-paragraph (1)(b) above must hold a post in a university with a medical or dental school.

3.—(1) A District Health Authority for a district in Wales shall consist of—
(a) a chairman appointed by the Secretary of State;
(b) a prescribed number of members appointed by him;
(c) the chief officer of the authority;
(d) such other officers as may be prescribed; and

(e) not more than a prescribed number of other officers of the authority appointed by the chairman and the members specified in paragraphs (b) and (c) above.

(2) Sub-paragraphs (2) and (3) of paragraph 2 above apply in relation to sub-paragraph (1) above as they apply in relation to sub-paragraph (1) of that paragraph.

PART II

MEMBERSHIP OF FAMILY HEALTH SERVICES AUTHORITIES

4.—(1) A Family Health Services Authority in England shall consist of—
(a) a chairman appointed by the Secretary of State;
(b) a prescribed number of members appointed by the Regional Health Authority which (in accordance with Section 15(1A) of the principal Act) is the relevant Regional Health Authority in relation to the family Health Services Authority; and
(c) the chief officer of the Authority;
(d) such other officers as may be prescribed;
and, if the Secretary of State so directs, the Authority shall also include not more than a prescribed number of other officers of the Authority appointed by the chairman and the members appointed under paragraphs (b) and (c) above.

(2) No person who is an officer of the Authority may be appointed under sub-paragraph (1)(b) above; and, without prejudice to any provision made by virtue of paragraph 12(a) of Schedule 5 to the principal Act (regulations as to appointment and tenure), regulations may provide that all or any of the persons appointed under sub-paragraph (1)(b) above must fulfil prescribed conditions or hold posts of a prescribed description.

5.—(1) A Family Health Services Authority in Wales shall consist of—
(a) a chairman appointed by the Secretary of State;
(b) a prescribed number of members appointed by him; and
(c) the chief officer of the Authority;
(d) such other officers as may be prescribed;
and, if the Secretary of State so directs, the Authority shall also include not more than a prescribed number of other officers of the Authority appointed by the chairman and the members appointed under paragraphs (b) and (c) above.

(2) Sub-paragraph (2) of paragraph 4 above applies in relation to sub-paragraph (1) above as it applies in relation to sub-paragraph (1) of that paragraph.

PART III

AMENDMENTS OF PART III OF SCHEDULE 5 TO THE PRINCIPAL ACT

6. In paragraph 8 of Schedule 5, (corporate status) the words "Area Health Authority" shall be omitted.

7.—(1) In paragraph 9 of that Schedule (pay and allowances), in sub-paragraph (1) after the words "chairman of an authority" there shall be inserted "and to any member of a relevant authority who is appointed by the Secretary of State or a Regional Health Authority."

(2) At the end of the paragraph there shall be added the following sub-paragraph—
    "(7) In sub-paragraph (1) above "relevant authority" means—
    (a) a Regional Health Authority, a District Health Authority or a Family Health Services Authority; or
    (b) any special health authority which is specified in Schedule 1 to the Authorities for London Post-Graduate Teaching Hospitals (Establishment and Constitution) Order 1982, in the Board of Governors of the Eastman Dental Hospital (Establishment and Constitution) Order 1984 or in any other provision of an order under this Act which specifies an authority for the purposes of this sub-paragraph."

8. In paragraph 10 of that Schedule (staff at the end of sub-paragraph (1A) there shall be added the words "and a direction under that sub-paragraph may relate to a particular officer or class of officer specified in the direction."

9. In paragraph 12 of that Schedule (regulations as to tenure of office, committees and sub-committees and procedure etc. of authorities)—
    (a) at the end of paragraph (a) there shall be added the words "and any members of a committee or sub-committee of an authority who are not members of the authority";
    (b) after paragraph (a) there shall be inserted the following paragraph—
        "(aa) the circumstances in which a member of an authority who is (or is to be regarded as) an officer of the authority may be suspended from performing his functions as a member"; and

(c) in paragraph (b) after the word "appointment" there shall be inserted "and constitution."

10. After paragraph 12 of that Schedule there shall be inserted the following paragraph—

"12A. Regulations made by virtue of this Schedule or Schedule 1 to the National Health Service and Community Care Act 1990 may make provision (including provision modifying those Schedules) to deal with cases where the post of chief officer or any other officer of an authority is held jointly by two or more persons or where the functions of such an officer are in any other way performed by more than one person."

Section 5   SCHEDULE 2

NATIONAL HEALTH SERVICE TRUSTS

PART I

ORDERS UNDER SECTION 5(1)

1.—(1) Any reference in this Part of this Schedule to an order is a reference to an order under section 5(1) of this Act establishing an NHS trust or any subsequent order under that provision amending or revoking a previous order.

(2) An order shall be made by statutory instrument.

2. The provisions made by an order shall be in conformity with any general provision made by regulations under section 5(7) of this Act.

3.—(1) Without prejudice to any amendment made by a subsequent order, the first order to be made in relation to any NHS trust shall specify—

(a) the name of the trust;

(b) the functions of the trust;

(c) the number of executive directors and non-executive directors;

(d) where the trust is to be regarded as having a significant teaching commitment, a provision to secure the inclusion in the non-executive directors referred to in paragraph (c) above of a person appointed from a university with a medical or dental school specified in the order;

(e) the operational date of the trust, that is to say, the date on which the trust is to begin to undertake the whole of the functions conferred on it; and

(f) if a scheme is to be made under section 6 of this Act, the health authority which is to make the scheme.

(2) For the purposes of sub-paragraph (1)(d) above, an NHS trust is to be regarded as having a significant teaching commitment in the following cases—

(a) if the trust is established to assume responsibility for the ownership and management of a hospital or other establishment or facility which, in the opinion of the Secretary of State, has a significant teaching and research commitment; and

(b) in any other case, if the Secretary of State so provides in the order.

(3) In a case where the order contains a provision made by virtue of sub-paragraph (1)(d) above and a person who is being considered for appointment by virtue of that provision—

(a) is employed by the university in question, and

(b) would also, apart from this sub-paragraph, be regarded as employed by the trust,

his employment by the trust shall be disregarded in determining whether, if appointed, he will be a non-executive director of the trust.

(4) An order shall specify the accounting date of the trust.

4.—(1) An order may require a Regional, District or Special Health Authority to make staff, premises and other facilities available to an NHS trust pending the transfer or appointment of staff to or by the trust and the transfer of premises or other facilities to the trust.

(2) An order making provision under this paragraph may make provision with respect to the time when the Regional, District or Special Health Authority's functions under the provision are to come to an end.

5.—(1) An order may provide for the establishment of an NHS trust with effect from a date earlier than the operational date of the trust and, during the period between that earlier date and the operational date, the trust shall have such limited functions for the purpose of enabling it to begin to operate satisfactorily with effect from the operational date as may be specified in the order.

(2) If an order makes the provision referred to in sub-paragraph (1) above, then, at any time during the period referred to in that sub-paragraph, the NHS trust shall be regarded as properly constituted (and may carry out its limited functions accordingly) notwithstanding that, at that time, all or any of the executive directors have not yet been appointed.

(3) If an order makes the provision referred to in sub-paragraph (1) above, the order may require a Regional, District or Special Health Authority to discharge such liabilities of the NHS trust as—

(a) may be incurred during the period referred to in that sub-paragraph; and

(b) are of a description specified in the order.

PART II

DUTIES, POWERS AND STATUS

Specific duties

6.—(1) An NHS trust shall carry out effectively, efficiently and economically the functions for the time being conferred on it by an order under section 5(1) of this Act and by the provisions of this Schedule and, with respect to the exercise of the powers conferred by section 5(10) of this Act and paragraphs 10 to 15 below, shall comply with any directions given to it by the Secretary of State, whether of a general or a particular nature.

(2) An NHS trust shall comply with any directions given to it by the Secretary of State with respect to all or any of the following matters—

(a) the qualifications of persons who may be employed as officers of the trust;

(b) the employment, for the purpose of performing functions specified in the direction, of officers having qualifications or experience of a description so specified;

(c) the manner in which officers of the trust are to be appointed;

(d) prohibiting or restricting the disposal of, or of any interest in, any asset which, at the time the direction is given, the Secretary of State reasonably considers to have a value in excess of such sum as may be specified in an order under section 5(1) of this Act and in respect of which the Secretary of State considers that the interests of the National Health Service require that the asset should not be disposed of;

(e) compliance with guidance or directions given (by circular or otherwise) to health authorities, or particular descriptions of health authorities; and

(f) the implementation of awards relating to the distinction or merit of medical practitioners or dental practitioners or any class or classes of such practitioners.

7.—(1) For each accounting year an NHS trust shall prepare and send to the Secretary of State an annual report in such form as may be determined by the Secretary of State.

(2) At such time or times as may be prescribed, an NHS trust shall hold a public meeting at which its audited accounts and annual report and any report on the accounts made pursuant to subsection (3) of section 15 of the Local Government Finance Act 1982 shall be presented.

(3) In such circumstances and at such time or times as may be prescribed, an NHS trust shall hold a public meeting at which such document as may be prescribed shall be presented.

8. An NHS trust shall furnish to the Secretary of State such reports, returns and other information, including information as to its forward planning, as, and in such form as, he may require.

9.—(1) An NHS trust shall be liable to pay—

(a) to the chairman and any non-executive director of the trust remuneration of an amount determined by the Secretary of State, not exceeding such amount as may be approved by the Treasury;

(b) to the chairman and any non-executive director of the trust such travelling and other allowances as may be determined by the Secretary of State with the approval of the Treasury;

(c) to any member of a committee or sub-committee of the trust who is not also a director such travelling and other allowances as may be so determined.

(2) If an NHS trust so determines in the case of a person who is or has been a chairman of the trust, the trust shall be liable to pay such pension, allowances or gratuities to or in respect of him as may be determined by the Secretary of State with the approval of the Treasury.

(3) Different determinations may be made under sub-paragraph (1) or sub-paragraph (2) above in relation to different cases or descriptions of cases.

Specific powers

10. In addition to carrying out its other functions, an NHS trust may, as the provider, enter into NHS contracts.

11. An NHS trust may undertake and commission research and make available staff and provide facilities for research by other persons.

12. An NHS trust may—

(a) provide training for persons employed or likely to be employed by the trust or otherwise in the provision of services under the principal Act; and

19–122

(b) make facilities and staff available in connection with training by a university or any other body providing training in connection with the health service.

13. An NHS trust may enter into arrangements for the carrying out, on such terms as seem to the trust to be appropriate, of any of its functions jointly with any Regional, District or Special Health Authority, with another NHS trust or with any other body or individual.

14. According to the nature of its functions, an NHS trust may make accommodation or services or both available for patients who give undertakings (or for whom undertakings are given) to pay, in respect of the accommodation or services (or both) such charges as the trust may determine.

15. For the purpose of making additional income available in order better to perform its functions, an NHS trust shall have the powers specified in section 7(2) of the Health and Medicines Act 1988 (extension of powers of Secretary of State for financing the Health Service).

General powers

16.—(1) Subject to Schedule 3 to this Act, an NHS trust shall have power to do anything which appears to it to be necessary or expedient for the purpose of or in connection with the discharge of its functions, including in particular power—
(a) to acquire and dispose of land and other property;
(b) to enter into such contracts as seem to the trust to be appropriate;
(c) to accept gifts of money, land or other property, including money, land or other property to be held on trust, either for the general or any specific purposes of the NHS trust or for all or any purposes relating to the health service; and
(d) to employ staff on such terms as the trust thinks fit.
(2) The reference in sub-paragraph (1)(c) above to specific purposes of the NHS trust includes a reference to the purposes of a specific hospital or other establishment or facility which is owned and managed by the trust.

17.—(1) Without prejudice to the generality of paragraph 16 above, for or in respect of such of its employees as it may determine, an NHS trust may make such arrangements for providing pensions, allowances or gratuities as it may determine; and such arrangements may include the establishment and administration, by the trust or otherwise, of one or more pension schemes.
(2) The reference in sub-paragraph (1) above to pensions, allowances or gratuities to or in respect of employees of an NHS trust includes a reference to pensions, allowances or gratuities by way of compensation to or in respect of any of the trust's employees who suffer loss of office or employment or loss or diminution of emoluments.

Status

18. An NHS trust shall not be regarded as the servant or agent of the Crown or, except as provided by this Act, as enjoying any status, immunity or privilege of the Crown; and an NHS trust's property shall not be regarded as property of, or property held on behalf of, the Crown.

PART III

SUPPLEMENTARY PROVISIONS

Re-imbursement for health services work carried out otherwise than under NHS contract

19.—(1) In any case where an NHS trust provides goods or services for the benefit of an individual and—
(a) the provision of those goods or services is not pursuant to an NHS contract, and
(b) the condition of the individual is such that he needs those goods or services and, having regard to his condition, it is not practicable before providing them to enter into an NHS contract for their provision, and
(c) the provision of those goods or services is within the primary functions of a District Health Authority or is a function of a health board,
the trust shall be remunerated by that Authority or health board in respect of the provision of the goods or services in question.
(2) The rate of any remuneration payable by virtue of sub-paragraph (1) above shall be calculated in such manner or on such basis as may be determined by the Secretary of State.

20. In any case where an NHS trust provides goods or services for the benefit of an individual and—
(a) the provision of those goods or services is not pursuant to an NHS contract, and

(b) the individual is resident outside the United Kingdom and is of a description (being a description associating the individual with another country) specified for the purposes of this paragraph by a direction made by the Secretary of State,
the trust shall be remunerated by the Secretary of State in respect of the provision of the goods or services in question at such rate or rates as he considers appropriate.

Supply of goods and services by local authorities

21. In section 28 of the principal Act (supply of goods and services by local authorities) in subsection (3) after the words "health authorities," in each place where they occur, there shall be inserted "and NHS trusts," and at the end there shall be added "and the National Health Service and Community Care Act 1990."

Making of charges

22. In each of sections 81 (charges for more expensive supplies) and 82 (charges for repairs and replacement necessitated by an act or omission of the person supplied etc.) of the principal Act, in paragraph (a)—
(a) after the words "Secretary of State" there shall be inserted "or an NHS trust"; and
(b) after the word "him" there shall be inserted "or, as the case may be, by the trust."

Power to raise money by appeals etc.

23.—(1) In section 96A of the principal Act (power of health authorities etc. to raise money etc. by appeals, collections etc.) in subsection (1), after the word "authority," in each place where it occurs, there shall be inserted "or NHS trust."
(2) In subsections (3), (4) and (7) to (9) of that section, for the words "authority or Board," in each place where they occur, there shall be substituted "authority, NHS trust or Board."
(3) In subsection (5), of that section, for the words from "Area or District" onwards there shall be substituted "body responsible for the hospital if that body and the special trustees agree; and in this subsection the body responsible for a hospital is,—
(a) in the case of a hospital vested in a NHS trust, that trust; and
(b) in any other case, the District Health Authority exercising functions on behalf of the Secretary of State in respect of the hospital."
(4) After subsection (5) of that section there shall be inserted the following subsection—
"(5A) Where property is given in pursuance of this section on trust for any purposes of an NHS trust for which trustees have been appointed under section 11(1) of the National Health Service and Community Care Act 1990, then, if those trustees and the NHS trust agree, the property may be held, administered and applied by those trustees instead of by the NHS trust."
(5) In subsection (6) of that section for the words "or to special trustees" there shall be substituted to an NHS trust or to special trustees or trustees for an NHS trust."

Accounts and audit

24.—(1) In section 98 of the principal Act (accounts and audit), in subsection (1) after paragraph (bb) there shall be inserted—
"(bbb) every NHS trust."
(2) After subsection (2A) of that section there shall be inserted—
"(2B) in preparing its annual accounts in pursuance of subsection (2) above, an NHS trust shall comply with any directions given by the Secretary of State with the approval of the Treasury as to—
(a) the methods and principles according to which the accounts are to be prepared; and
(b) the information to be given in the accounts."

Protection of members and officers

25. In section 125 of the principal Act (protection of members and officers of health authorities etc.)—
(a) for paragraph (b) there shall be substituted—
"(b) an NHS trust"; and
(b) at the end there shall be added "and the National Health Service and Community Care Act 1990."

Compulsory acquisition

26.—(1) An NHS trust may be authorised to purchase land compulsorily for the purposes of its functions by means of an order made by the trust and confirmed by the Secretary of State.

(2) Subject to sub-paragraph (3) below, the Acquisition of Land Act 1981 shall apply to the compulsory purchase of land under this paragraph.

(3) No order shall be made by an NHS trust under Part II of the Acquisition of Land Act 1981 with respect to any land unless the proposal to acquire the land compulsorily—

(a) has been submitted to the Secretary of State in such form and together with such information as he may require; and

(b) has been approved by him.

Use and development of consecrated land and burial grounds

27. Section 128 of the Town and Country Planning Act 1971 (use and development of consecrated land and burial grounds) applies to consecrated land and land comprised in a burial ground, within the meaning of that section, which an NHS trust holds for any of its purposes as if—

(a) that land had been acquired by the trust as mentioned in subsection (1) of that section; and

(b) the trust were a statutory undertaker, within the meaning of that Act.

Instruments etc.

28.—(1) The fixing of the seal of an NHS trust shall be authenticated by the signature of the chairman or of some other person authorised either generally or specially by the trust for that purpose and of one other director.

(2) Any document purporting to be a document duly executed under the seal of an NHS trust shall be received in evidence and shall, unless the contrary is proved, be deemed to be so executed.

(3) A document purporting to be signed on behalf of an NHS trust shall be received in evidence and shall, unless the contrary is proved, be deemed to be so signed.

PART IV

DISSOLUTION

29.—(1) The Secretary of State may by order made by statutory instrument dissolve an NHS trust.

(2) An order under this paragraph may be made—

(a) on the application of the NHS trust concerned; or

(b) if the Secretary of State considers it appropriate in the interests of the health service.

(3) Except where it appears to the Secretary of State necessary to make an order under this paragraph as a matter of urgency, no such order shall be made until after the completion of such consultation as may be prescribed.

30.—(1) If an NHS trust is dissolved under this Part of this Schedule, the Secretary of State may by order transfer or provide for the transfer to—

(a) the Secretary of State, or

(b) a health authority, or

(c) another NHS trust,

of such of the property, rights and liabilities of the NHS trust which is dissolved as in his opinion is appropriate; and any such order may include provisions corresponding to those of section 8 of this Act.

(2) An order under this paragraph may make provision in connection with the transfer of staff employed by or for the purposes of the NHS trust which is dissolved; and such an order may include provisions corresponding to those of sections 6 and 7 of this Act, including provision for the making of a scheme by such health authority or other body as may be specified in the order.

(3) No order shall be made under this paragraph until after completion of such consultation as may be prescribed.

31. Without prejudice to the generality of paragraph 30 above, if an NHS trust is dissolved under this Part of this Schedule, the Secretary of State or such other NHS trust or health authority as he may direct shall undertake the responsibility for the continued payment of any such pension, allowances or gratuities as, by virtue of paragraph 9(2) or paragraph 17 above, would otherwise have been the responsibility of the trust which has been dissolved.

32. An NHS trust may not be dissolved or wound up except in accordance with this Part of this Schedule.

Section 9

SCHEDULE 3

FINANCIAL PROVISIONS RELATING TO NHS TRUSTS

Borrowing

1.—(1) Subject to the provisions of this paragraph and to any limit imposed under the following provisions of this Schedule, for the purpose of its functions an NHS trust may borrow (both temporarily, by way of overdraft, and longer term) from the Secretary of State or from any other person.

(2) An NHS trust may not mortgage or charge any of its assets or in any other way use any of its assets as security for a loan.

(3) Except with the consent of the Secretary of State, an NHS trust may not borrow in any currency other than sterling; and the Secretary of State shall not give his consent to any such borrowing except with the approval of the Treasury.

(4) Interest on any sums borrowed from the Secretary of State by an NHS trust shall be paid at such variable or fixed rates and at such times as the Treasury may determine.

(5) A rate of interest under sub-paragraph (4) above shall be determined as if section 5 of the National Loans Act 1968 had effect in respect of it and subsections (5) to (5B) of that section shall apply accordingly.

(6) Subject to sub-paragraphs (4) and (5) above, the terms on which any sums are borrowed from the Secretary of State by an NHS trust shall be such as he may determine; and, in the event of the early repayment of any sums so borrowed, such terms may require the payment of a premium or allow a discount.

Guarantees of borrowing

2.—(1) The Secretary of State may guarantee, in such manner and on such conditions as, with the approval of the Treasury, he considers appropriate, the repayments of the principal of and the payment of interest on any sums which an NHS trust borrows from a person other than the Secretary of State.

(2) Immediately after a guarantee is given under this paragraph, the Secretary of State shall lay a statement of the guarantee before each House of Parliament.

(3) Where any sum is issued for fulfilling a guarantee so given, the Secretary of State shall lay before each House of Parliament a statement relating to that sum as soon as possible after the end of each financial year beginning with that in which the sum is issued and ending with that in which all liability in respect of the principal of the sum and in respect of interest on it is finally discharged.

(4) If any sums are issued in fulfilment of a guarantee given under this paragraph, the NHS trust concerned shall make to the Secretary of State, at such times and in such manner as the Secretary of State may from time to time direct,—

  (a) payments of such amounts as the Secretary of State with the consent of the Treasury so directs in or towards repayment of the sums so issued; and

  (b) payments of interest, at such rates as the Secretary of State with the consent of the Treasury so directs, on what is outstanding for the time being in respect of sums so issued.

Limits on indebtedness

3.—(1) The aggregate of all sums borrowed by NHS trusts established to assume responsibility for the ownership and management of, or to provide and manage, hospitals or other establishments or facilities which are situated in England shall not exceed £5,000 million or such other sum not exceeding £10,000 million as may be specified by order made by the Secretary of State with the consent of the Treasury.

(2) The aggregate of all sums borrowed by NHS trusts established to assume responsibility for the ownership and management of, or to provide and manage, hospitals or other establishments or facilities which are situated in Wales shall not exceed £300 million or such other sum not exceeding £600 million as may be specified by order made by the Secretary of State with the consent of the Treasury.

(3) The references in sub-paragraphs (1) and (2) above to sums borrowed do not include a reference to NHS trusts' initial loans.

4. Any power to make an order under paragraph 3 above shall be exercisable by statutory instrument which shall be subject to annulment in pursuance of a resolution of the House of Commons.

Additional public dividend capital

5.—(1) If the Secretary of State, with the consent of the Treasury, considers it appropriate to do so, he may, instead of making a loan to an NHS trust under paragraph 1 above, pay an amount to the trust as public dividend capital.

(2) Section 9 of this Act shall apply to public dividend capital paid to an NHS trust under this paragraph as it applies to public dividend capital forming part of the trust's originating capital debt.

Surplus funds

6. If it appears to the Secretary of State that any amount standing in the reserves of an NHS trust is surplus to its foreseeable requirements, the trust shall, if the Secretary of State with the approval of the Treasury and after consultation with the trust so directs, pay that amount into the Consolidated Fund.

Investment

7. An NHS trust may not invest any money held by it except in securities of the Government of the United Kingdom or in such other manner as the Secretary of State may with the consent of the Treasury approve.

Section 20   SCHEDULE 4

AMENDMENTS OF PART III OF THE LOCAL GOVERNMENT FINANCE ACT 1982

1.—(1) In section 11 (establishment of Audit Commission), in subsection (1) after the words "Local Authorities" there shall be inserted "and the National Health Service."

(2) In subsection (2) of that section—
(a) for the word "thirteen" there shall be substituted "fifteen";
(b) for the word "seventeen" there shall be substituted "twenty"; and
(c) for paragraphs (a) and (b) there shall be substituted the words "such organisations and other bodies as appear to him to be appropriate."

2.—(1) In section 12 (accounts subject to audit), in subsection (2) after paragraph (e) there shall be inserted—
      "(ea) a body specified in section 98(1) of the National Health Service Act 1977."

(2) After subsection (3) of that section there shall be inserted the following subsections—
      "(3A) This section also applies to the accounts of the members of a recognised fund-holding practice so far as they relate to allotted sums paid to them, and subject to subsection (3B) and section 16(1A) below, any reference in this Part of this Act to the accounts of a body shall be construed, in relation to the members of a fund-holding practice, as a reference to such of their accounts as relate to allotted sums so paid.

      (3B) In such circumstances and to such extent as regulations made by the Secretary of State so provide, this Part of this Act shall not apply to the accounts for any year of the members of a recognised fund-holding practice if those accounts are submitted to a Family Health Services Authority and summarised in that Authority's accounts.

      (3C) In subsection (3A) above "allotted sums" has the same meaning as in section 15 of the National Health Service and Community Care Act 1990."

(3) After subsection (4) of that section there shall be inserted the following subsection—
      "(5) Any reference in this Part of this Act to a health service body is a reference to a body specified in section 98(1) of the National Health Service Act 1977 or to the members of a recognised fund-holding practice as mentioned in subsection (3A) above."

3.—(1) In section 13 (appointment of auditors), in each of subsections (3) and (4), after the word "body," in the first place where it occurs, there shall be inserted "other than a health service body."

(2) In subsection (5) of that section after the words "Secretary of State" there shall be inserted "or is a person for the time being approved by the Secretary of State, acting on the recommendation of the Commission."

(3) After subsection (5) of that section there shall be inserted the following subsection—

"(5A) The Secretary of State shall not approve any person for the purposes of subsection (5) above after March 31, 1996 but, subject to the withdrawal of his approval after that date, any person who is so approved immediately before that date shall continue to be so approved after that date."

4.—(1) In section 14 (code of audit practice), at the end of subsection (1) there shall be added "and a different code may be prepared with respect to the audit of the accounts of health service bodies as compared with the code applicable to the accounts of other bodies."

(2) At the end of the section there shall be added the following subsection—

"(7) In the application of subsection (6) above to a code which relates to the accounts of health services bodies,—

(a) if the code relates only to those accounts, the reference to associations of local authorities shall be construed as a reference to organisations connected with the health service, within the meaning of the National Health Service Act 1977; and

(b) if the code relates also to the accounts of other bodies, that reference shall be construed as including a reference to such organisations."

5. In section 15 (general duties of auditors), in subsection (1)(a) after the words "section 23 below" there shall be inserted "or, in the case of a health service body, directions under subsection (2) or subsection (2B) of section 98 of the National Health Service Act 1977."

6. In section 16 (auditor's rights to obtain documents and information) after subsection (1) there shall be inserted the following subsection—

"(1A) In the case of a recognised fund-holding practice the reference in subsection (1) above to documents includes a reference to documents relating to all the accounts and records of the members of the practice, whether or not relating to the allotted sum, within the meaning of that section."

7. In section 17 (public inspection of accounts and right of challenge), in subsection (1) after the words "Part of this Act" there shall be inserted "other than the audit of the accounts of a health service body."

8. In section 18 (auditor's reports), in subsection (4) after the word "Commission" there shall be inserted "and, in the case of a health service body, to the Secretary of State."

9. In section 19 (declaration that item of account is unlawful), in subsection (1) after the words "Part of this Act" there shall be inserted "other than the audit of the accounts of a health service body."

10. In section 20 (recovery of amount not accounted for etc.), in subsection (1) after the words "Part of this Act" there shall be inserted "other than the audit of the accounts of a health service body."

11. In section 21 (fees for audit), after subsection (2) there shall be inserted the following subsection—

"(2A) In the application of subsection (2) above to the audit of the accounts of a health service body, the reference to associations of local authorities shall be construed as a reference to organisations connected with the health service."

12.—(1) In section 22 (extraordinary audit), at the beginning of each of subsections (1) and (3) there shall be inserted "Subject to subsection (4A) below."

(2) After subsection (4) of that section there shall be inserted the following subsection—

"(4A) Subsection (1)(a) above does not apply in relation to the accounts of a health service body; and in the application of subsection (3) above to an extraordinary audit of any such accounts for the words "15 to 20 above, except subsections (1) and (2) of section 17" there shall be substituted "15, 16, and 18 above." "

13. In section 23 (regulations as to accounts), in subsection (1) after the words "this Part of this Act" there shall be inserted "other than health service bodies."

14. In section 24 (right of local government elector to inspect accounts etc.), in subsection (1) after the words "Part of this Act" there shall be inserted "other than a health service body."

15. At the end of section 25 (audit of accounts of officers) there shall be inserted the following subsection—

"(2) In the application of subsection (1) above to an officer of a health service body for the words "15 to 24" there shall be substituted "15, 16, 18, 21 and 22." "

16. In section 25A (power of auditor to issue prohibition order), in subsection (1) after the words "Part of this Act," in the first place where they occur, there shall be inserted "other than a health service body."

17. In section 25D (power of auditor to apply for judicial review), in subsection (1) after the word "body," in the first place where it occurs, there shall be inserted "other than a health service body."

18.—(1) In section 26 (studies for improving economy etc. in services), at the end of subsection (3) there shall be added "and, in the case of studies relating to a health service body, shall, on request, furnish to the Comptroller and Auditor General, all material relevant to the studies."

(2) At the end of subsection (4) of that section there shall be added "and, in the case of any health service bodies, the Commission shall also consult the Secretary of State and the Comptroller and Auditor General."

19.—(1) In section 27 (reports on impact of statutory provisions etc.), in subsection (1) after the words "Part of this Act" there shall be inserted "other than health service bodies."

(2) At the end of that section there shall be added the following subsection—

"(6) Notwithstanding that the services provided by health service bodies are excluded from the scope of studies under this section, in undertaking or promoting studies under section 26(1) above relating to a health service body, the Commission may take into account the implementation by the body of—

(a) any particular statutory provision or provisions, and

(b) any directions or guidance given by the Secretary of State (whether pursuant to any such provision or otherwise),

but the power conferred by this subsection shall not be construed as entitling the Commission to question the merits of the policy objectives of the Secretary of State."

20.—(1) In section 29 (miscellaneous functions of Commission), at the end of subsection (2) there shall be added "or, in the case of a health service body, such other organisations as appear to the body to be appropriate."

(2) At the end of subsection (3) of that section there shall be added "or the National Health Service."

21. In section 30 (restriction on disclosure of information), in subsection (1)(b) after the words "Part of this Act" there shall be inserted "or, in the case of a health service body, for the purposes of the functions of the Secretary of State and the Comptroller and Auditor General under the National Health Service Act 1977."

22.—(1) In section 33 (commencement and transitional provisions) after subsection (4) there shall be inserted the following subsection—

"(4A) The Secretary of State may by regulations provide for any statutory provision not contained in this Part of this Act to continue to apply on and after the day appointed for the coming into force of paragraph 22 of Schedule 4 to the National Health Service and Community Care Act 1990 in relation to accounts for any period beginning before that day of health service bodies, with such modifications, additions and omissions as may be prescribed by the regulations; and different provision may be made by such regulations in relation to the accounts of bodies of different descriptions and in relation to the accounts for different periods.

(2) In subsection (5) of that section (provision of working capital to the Commission) for the words "second appointed day," in the second place where they occur, there shall be substituted "day appointed for the coming into force of paragraph 22 of Schedule 4 to the National Health Service and Community Care Act 1990" and at the end of the subsection there shall be added the words "with respect to its functions in relation to health service bodies."

23. In section 36 (interpretation), in subsection (1),—

(a) in the definition of "the Commission" after the words "Local Authorities" there shall be inserted "and the National Health Service"; and

(b) after that definition there shall be inserted—

"health service body" has the meaning assigned by section 12(5) above;

"recognised fund-holding practice" shall be construed in accordance with section 14 of the National Health Service and Community Care Act 1990."

24.—(1) In Schedule 3 (provisions as to the Commission), in paragraph 3(3) for the word "and," in the last place where it occurs, there shall be substituted "or, as the case may require, such organisations connected with the health service as appear to him to be appropriate and (in either case)."

(2) At the beginning of paragraph 9 there shall be inserted "Subject to sub-paragraph (2) below" and at the end of the paragraph there shall be inserted—

"(2) Sub-paragraph (1) above shall apply separately with respect to the functions of the Commission in relation to health service bodies and its functions in relation to other bodies."

Section 27   SCHEDULE 5

HEALTH BOARDS, THE COMMON SERVICES AGENCY AND STATE HOSPITALS

Health Boards

1. Schedule 1 to the 1978 Act shall be amended in accordance with paragraphs 2 to 7 below.

2. After paragraph 2 of that Schedule (membership of Health Boards) there shall be inserted the following paragraph—
    "2A. In the case of a prescribed Health Board at least one of the persons appointed under paragraph 2 above must hold a post in a university with a medical or dental school."

3. In paragraph 4 of that Schedule (remuneration), after the words "Health Board" there shall be inserted "and to such other members of a Health Board as may be prescribed."

4. At the end of paragraph 5A of that Schedule there shall be added the words "and a direction under that paragraph may relate to a particular officer or servant or class of officer or servant specified in the direction."

5. After paragraph 7 of that Schedule there shall be inserted the following paragraphs—
    "7A. Regulations may provide for the transfer of officers and servants from a Health Board to—
    (a) another Health Board;
    (b) the Agency; or
    (c) a state hospital,
    and for arrangements under which the services of an officer or servant of a Health Board are placed at the disposal of a body mentioned in sub-paragraphs (a) to (c).
    7B. Directions may be given by the Secretary of State—
    (a) to a Health Board to place services of any of its officers or servants at the disposal of a body mentioned in sub-paragraphs (a) to (c) of paragraph 7A; and
    (b) to any such body to employ as an officer or servant any person who is or was employed by a Health Board and is specified in the direction,
    and a Board or body to which such directions are given shall comply with the directions.
    7C. Before making regulations under paragraph 7A or 8A, the Secretary of State shall consult such bodies and organisations as appear to him to be concerned."

6. After paragraph 8 of that Schedule there shall be inserted the following paragraph—
    "8A. In connection with arrangements relating to community care services (within the meaning of section 5A(4) (local authority plans for community care services) of the Social Work (Scotland) Act 1968), regulations may make provision with respect to—
    (a) the transfer to employment by a local authority of officers or servants employed by a Health Board; and
    (b) the transfer to employment by a National Health Service body of officers and servants transferred to employment by a local authority by virtue of this paragraph,
    and for the purposes of this paragraph "National Health Service body" means a Health Board, the Agency or an NHS trust.".

7. In paragraph 11(b) of that Schedule (delegation to committees etc.), for the words "composed, as to a majority, by members of Health Boards" there shall be substituted "constituted in accordance with the regulations."

Common Services Agency

8. Schedule 5 to the 1978 Act shall be amended in accordance with paragraphs 9 to 12 below.

9. In paragraph 3 of that Schedule (appointment of chairman and members) for the words from "other members appointed" to the end there shall be substituted "such other members as the Secretary of State may, after consultation with the Health Boards, appoint."

10. In paragraph 3A of that Schedule (remuneration), after the words "management committee" there shall be inserted "and to such other members of the management committee as may be prescribed."

11. After paragraph 7A of that Schedule there shall be inserted the following paragraphs—
    "7B. Regulations may provide for the transfer of officers and servants from the Agency to a Health Board or state hospital, and for arrangements under which the services of an officer or servant of the Agency are placed at the disposal of a Health Board or state hospital.
    7C. Directions may be given by the Secretary of State—
    (a) to the Agency to place services of any of its officers or servants at the disposal of a Health Board or state hospital; and
    (b) to a Health Board or state hospital to employ as an officer or servant any person who is or was employed by the Agency and is specified in the direction,
    and it shall be the duty of the Agency, a Health Board or a state hospital to comply with any such directions given to it."

12. After paragraph 8 of that Schedule there shall be inserted the following paragraphs—
    "8A. In connection with arrangements relating to community care services (within the meaning of section 5A(4) (local authority plans for community care services) of the Social Work (Scotland) Act 1968), regulations may make provision with respect to—
    (a) the transfer to employment by a local authority of officers or servants employed by the Agency; and
    (b) the transfer to employment by a National Health Service body of officers and servants transferred to employment by a local authority by virtue of this paragraph,
    and for the purposes of this paragraph "National Health Service body" means the Agency, a Health Board or an NHS trust.
    8B. Before making regulations under paragraph 7B or 8A, the Secretary of State shall consult such bodies and organisations as appear to him to be concerned.".

State hospitals

13. In Schedule 1 to the Mental Health (Scotland) Act 1984 (State Hospital Management Committees)—
    (a) in paragraph 6(b) (delegation to committees etc.), for the words "composed, as to a majority, of members of a State Hospital Management Committee" there shall be substituted "constituted in accordance with the regulations"; and
    (b) in paragraph 8 (application of provisions of the 1978 Act) the word "and" at the end of sub-paragraph (d) shall be omitted and after sub-paragraph (e) there shall be inserted—
        "; and
        (f) paragraphs 7A to 7C and 8A of Schedule 1 (which relate to the transfer of staff)."

Section 32   SCHEDULE 6

SCHEDULES TO BE INSERTED AFTER SCHEDULE 7 TO THE NATIONAL HEALTH SERVICE (SCOTLAND) ACT 1978

"SCHEDULE 7A

NATIONAL HEALTH SERVICE TRUSTS

PART I

ORDERS ESTABLISHING NHS TRUSTS ETC.

1. Any reference in this Part of this Schedule to an order is a reference to an order under section 12A(1) establishing an NHS trust or any subsequent order under that provision amending or revoking a previous order.

2. The provisions made by an order shall be in conformity with any general provision made by regulations under section 12A(5).

3.—(1) Without prejudice to any amendment made by a subsequent order, the first order to be made in relation to any NHS trust shall specify—
    (a) the name of the trust;
    (b) the functions of the trust;
    (c) the number of executive directors and non-executive directors;
    (d) where the trust is to be regarded as having a significant teaching commitment, a provision to secure the inclusion in the non-executive directors referred to in paragraph (c) of a person appointed from a university with a medical or dental school specified in the order;
    (e) the operational date of the trust, that is to say, the date on which the trust is to begin to undertake the whole of the functions conferred on it; and
    (f) if a scheme is to be made under section 12B, the body (being a Health Board or the Agency) which is to make the scheme.

(2) For the purposes of sub-paragraph (1)(d), an NHS trust is to be regarded as having a significant teaching commitment in the following cases—
    (a) if the trust is established to assume responsibility for the ownership and management of a hospital or other establishment or facility which, in the opinion of the Secretary of State, has a significant teaching and research commitment; and

(b) in any other case, if the Secretary of State so provides in the order.

(3) In a case where the order contains a provision made by virtue of sub-paragraph (1)(d) and a person who is being considered for appointment by virtue of that provision—

(a) is employed by the university in question; and

(b) would also, apart from this sub-paragraph, be regarded as employed by the trust,

his employment by the trust shall be disregarded in determining whether, if appointed, he will be a non-executive director of the trust.

(4) An order shall specify the accounting date of the trust.

4.—(1) An order may require a Health Board and the Agency to make staff, premises and other facilities available to an NHS trust pending the transfer or appointment of staff to or by the trust and the transfer of premises or other facilities to the trust.

(2) An order making provision under this paragraph may make provision with respect to the time when the Health Board's functions under the provision are to come to an end.

5.—(1) An order may provide for the establishment of an NHS trust with effect from a date earlier than the operational date of the trust and, during the period between that earlier date and the operational date, the trust shall have such limited functions for the purposes of enabling it to begin to operate satisfactorily with effect from the operational date as may be specified in the order.

(2) If an order makes the provision referred to in sub-paragraph (1), then, at any time during the period referred to in that sub-paragraph, the NHS trust shall be regarded as properly constituted (and may carry out its limited functions accordingly) notwithstanding that, at that time, all or any of the executive officers have not yet been appointed.

(3) If an order makes the provision referred to in sub-paragraph (1) above, the order may require a Health Board to discharge such liabilities of the NHS trust as—

(a) may be incurred during the period referred to in that sub-paragraph; and

(b) are of a description specified in the order.

PART II

DUTIES, POWERS AND STATUS OF NHS TRUSTS

Specific duties

6.—(1) An NHS trust shall carry out effectively, efficiently and economically the functions for the time being conferred on it by an order under section 12A(1) and by the provisions of this Schedule and, with respect to the exercise of the powers conferred by an order under section 12A(8) or paragraphs 10 to 15, shall comply with any directions given to it by the Secretary of State, whether of a general or a particular nature.

(2) An NHS trust shall comply with any directions given to it by the Secretary of State with respect to all or any of the following matters—

(a) the qualifications of persons who may be appointed as officers of the trust;

(b) the employment, for the purpose of performing functions specified in the direction, of officers having qualifications or experience of a description so specified;

(c) the manner in which officers of the trust are to be appointed;

(d) prohibiting or restricting the disposal of, or of any interest in, any asset which, at the time the direction is given, the Secretary of State reasonably considers to have a value in excess of such sum as may be specified in an order under section 12A(1) and in respect of which the Secretary of State considers that the interests of the National Health Service require that the asset should not be disposed of;

(e) compliance with guidance or directions given (by circular or otherwise) to Health Boards or particular descriptions of Health Boards, or the Agency; and

(f) the implementation of awards relating to the distinction or merit of medical practitioners or dental practitioners or any class or classes of such practitioners.

7.—(1) For each accounting year an NHS trust shall prepare and send to the Secretary of State an annual report in such form as may be determined by the Secretary of State.

(2) At such time or times as may be prescribed, an NHS trust shall hold a public meeting at which its audited accounts, its annual report, and such other documents as may be prescribed shall be presented.

(3) In such circumstances and at such time or times as may be prescribed, an NHS trust shall hold a public meeting at which such documents as may be prescribed shall be presented.

8. An NHS trust shall furnish to the Secretary of State such reports, returns and other information, including information as to its forward planning as, and in such form as, he may require.

9.—(1) An NHS trust shall be liable to pay—

(a) to the chairman and any non-executive director of the trust—

(i) remuneration of an amount determined by the Secretary of State, not exceeding such amount as may be approved by the Treasury; and

(ii) such travelling and other allowances as may be determined by the Secretary of State with the approval of the Treasury; and

(b) to any member of a committee or sub-committee of the trust who is not also a director such travelling and other allowances as may be so determined.

(2) If an NHS trust so determines in the case of a person who is or has been a chairman of the trust, the trust shall be liable to pay such pension, allowances or gratuities to or in respect of him as may be determined by the Secretary of State with the approval of the Treasury.

(3) Different determinations may be made under sub-paragraph (1) or (2) in relation to different cases or description of cases.

Specific powers

10. An NHS trust may enter into NHS contracts.

11. An NHS trust may undertake and commission research and make available staff and provide facilities for research by other persons.

12. An NHS trust may—
(a) provide training for persons employed or likely to be employed by the trust or otherwise in the provision of services under this Act; and
(b) make facilities and staff available in connection with training by a university or any other body providing training in connection with the health service.

13. An NHS trust may enter into arrangements for the carrying out, on such terms as seem to it to be appropriate, of any of its functions jointly with any Health Board, with the Agency, with another NHS trust or with any other body or individual.

14. According to the nature of its functions, an NHS trust may make accommodation or services or both available for patients who give undertakings (or for whom undertakings are given) to pay, in respect of the accommodation or services (or both) such charges as the trust may determine.

15. For the purpose of making additional income available in order better to perform its functions, an NHS trust shall have the powers specified in section 7(2) of the Health and Medicines Act 1988 (extension of powers of Secretary of State for financing the Health Service).

General powers

16. Subject to Schedule 7B, an NHS trust shall have power to do anything which appears to it to be necessary or expedient for the purpose of or in connection with the discharge of its functions, including in particular power—
(a) to acquire and dispose of land and other property;
(b) to enter into such contracts as seem to the trust to be appropriate;
(c) to accept gifts of money, land or other property, including money, land or other property to be held on trust, for purposes relating to any service which it is their function to provide, administer, or make arrangements for, which purposes shall include any purposes relating to a hospital or other establishment or facility which is provided or managed by the trust; and
(d) to employ staff on such terms as the trust thinks fit.

17. In connection with arrangements relating to community care services (within the meaning of section 5A(4) (local authority plans for community care services) of the Social Work (Scotland) Act 1968), the Secretary of State may by regulations make provision with respect to—
(a) the transfer to employment by a local authority of staff employed by an NHS trust; and
(b) the transfer to employment by a National Health Service body of staff transferred to employment by a local authority by virtue of this paragraph,

and for the purposes of this paragraph "National Health Service body" means an NHS trust, a Health Board or the Agency.

18. Regulations made under paragraph 17 may make such incidental and consequential provision in relation to staff transferred by virtue of that paragraph as may be made in relation to officers and servants of a Health Board transferred by virtue of regulations made under paragraph 8A of Schedule 1.

19. Before making regulations under paragraph 17, the Secretary of State shall consult such bodies and organisations as appear to him to be concerned.

20.—(1) Without prejudice to the generality of paragraph 16, to or in respect of such of its employees as it may determine, an NHS trust may make such arrangements for providing pensions, allowances or gratuities as it may determine; and such arrangements may include the establishment and administration, by the trust or otherwise, of one or more pension schemes.

(2) The reference in sub-paragraph (1) to pensions, allowances or gratuities to or in respect of employees of an NHS trust includes a reference to pensions, allowances or gratuities by way of compensation to or in respect of any of the trust's employees who suffer loss of office or employment or loss or diminution of emoluments.

Status

21. An NHS trust shall not be regarded as the servant or agent of the Crown or, except as provided by this Act, as enjoying any status, immunity or privilege of the Crown; and an NHS trust's property shall not be regarded as property of, or property held on behalf of, the Crown.

PART III

SUPPLEMENTARY PROVISIONS

Reimbursement for health services work carried out otherwise than under contract

22.—(1) In any case where an NHS trust provides goods or services for the benefit of an individual and—
   (a) those goods or services are not provided pursuant to an NHS contract; and
   (b) the condition of the individual is such that he needs those goods or services and, having regard to his condition, it is not practicable before providing them to enter into an NHS contract for their provision, and
   (c) the provision of those goods or services is a function of a Health Board or is within the primary functions of a District Health Authority within the meaning of the National Health Service Act 1977,
the trust shall be remunerated by that Board or Authority in respect of the provision of the goods or services in question.

(2) The rate of any remuneration payable by virtue of sub-paragraph (1) shall be calculated in such manner or on such basis as may be determined by the Secretary of State.

23. In any case where an NHS trust provides goods or services for the benefit of an individual and—
   (a) paragraph 22(1)(a) applies but paragraph 22(1)(c) does not apply; and
   (b) the individual is resident outside the United Kingdom and is of a description (being a description associating the individual with another country) specified for the purposes of this paragraph by a direction made by the Secretary of State,
the trust shall be remunerated by the Secretary of State in respect of the provision of the goods or services in question at such rate or rates as he considers appropriate.

Use and development of land used for religious purposes and burial grounds

24. Where land consisting of a church or other building used or formerly used for religious worship, or the site thereof, or a burial ground, within the meaning of section 118 of the Town and Country Planning (Scotland) Act 1972 (provisions as to churches and burial grounds), is held by an NHS trust for any of its purposes, that section applies to the land as if—
   (a) the land had been acquired by the trust as mentioned in subsection (1) of that section; and
   (b) the trust were a statutory undertaker, within the meaning of that Act.

PART IV

DISSOLUTION

25.—(1) The Secretary of State may by order dissolve an NHS trust.

(2) An order under this paragraph may be made—
   (a) on the application of the NHS trust concerned; or
   (b) if the Secretary of State considers it appropriate in the interests of the health service as a whole.

(3) Except where it appears to the Secretary of State necessary to make an order under this paragraph as a matter of urgency, no such order shall be made until after the completion of such consultation as may be prescribed.

26.—(1) If an NHS trust is dissolved under this Part of this Schedule, the Secretary of State may by order transfer or provide for the transfer to—
   (a) the Secretary of State, or

(b) a Health Board, or
(c) the Agency, or
(d) another NHS trust,
of such of the property, rights and liabilities of the NHS trust which is dissolved as in his opinion is appropriate and any such order may include provisions corresponding to those of section 12D.

(2) An order under this paragraph may make provision in connection with the transfer of staff employed by or for the purposes of the NHS trust which is dissolved; and such an order may include provisions corresponding to those of sections 12B and 12C, including provision for the making of a scheme by such body (being a Health Board or the Agency) as may be specified in the order.

(3) No order shall be made under this paragraph until after completion of such consultation as may be prescribed.

27. If an NHS trust is dissolved under this Part of this Schedule, the Secretary of State or such other NHS trust or Health Board as he may direct or, if he so directs, the Agency shall undertake the responsibility for the continued payment of any such pension, allowances or gratuities as, by virtue of paragraph 9(2) or paragraph 20 above, would otherwise have been the responsibility of the trust which has been dissolved.

28. An NHS trust may not be dissolved or wound up except in accordance with this Part of this Schedule.

SCHEDULE 7B

FINANCIAL PROVISIONS RELATING TO NHS TRUSTS

Borrowing

1.—(1) Subject to the provisions of this paragraph and to any limit imposed under the following provisions of this Schedule, for the purpose of its functions an NHS trust may borrow (both temporarily, by way of overdraft, and longer term) from the Secretary of State or from any other person.

(2) An NHS trust may not grant any security over any of its assets or in any other way use any of its assets as security for a loan.

(3) Except with the consent of the Secretary of State, an NHS trust may not borrow in any currency other than sterling; and the Secretary of State shall not give his consent to any such borrowing except with the approval of the Treasury.

(4) Interest on any sums borrowed from the Secretary of State by an NHS trust shall be paid at such variable or fixed rates and at such times as the Treasury may determine.

(5) A rate of interest under sub-paragraph (4) shall be determined as if section 5 of the National Loans Act 1968 had effect in respect of it and subsections (5) to (5B) of that section shall apply accordingly.

(6) Subject to sub-paragraphs (4) and (5), the terms on which any sums are borrowed from the Secretary of State by an NHS trust shall be such as he may determine; and, in the event of the early repayment of any sums so borrowed, such terms may require the payment of a premium or allow a discount.

Guarantees of borrowing

2.—(1) The Secretary of State may guarantee, in such manner and on such conditions as, with the approval of the Treasury, he considers appropriate, the repayments of the principal of and the payment of interest on any sums which an NHS trust borrows from a person other than the Secretary of State.

(2) Immediately after a guarantee is given under this paragraph, the Secretary of State shall lay a statement of the guarantee before each House of Parliament.

(3) Where any sum is issued for fulfilling a guarantee so given, the Secretary of State shall lay before each House of Parliament a statement relating to that sum as soon as possible after the end of each financial year beginning with that in which the sum is issued and ending with that in which all liability in respect of the principal of the sum and in respect of interest on it is finally discharged.

(4) If any sums are issued in fulfilment of a guarantee given under this paragraph, the NHS trust concerned shall make to the Secretary of State, at such times and in such manner as the Secretary of State may from time to time direct,—
(a) payments of such amounts as the Secretary of State with the consent of the Treasury so directs in or towards repayment of the sums so issued; and
(b) payments of interest, at such rates as the Secretary of State with the consent of the

Treasury so directs, on what is outstanding for the time being in respect of sums so issued.

Limits on indebtedness

3.—(1) The aggregate of all sums borrowed by NHS trusts established to assume responsibility for the ownership and management of, or to provide and manage, hospitals or other establishments or facilities which are situated in Scotland shall not exceed £500 million or such other sum not exceeding £1,000 million as may be specified by order made by the Secretary of State with the consent of the Treasury.

(2) The reference in sub-paragraph (1) to sums borrowed does not include a reference to the initial loan of NHS trusts.

4. Any power to make an order under paragraph 3 shall be exercisable by statutory instrument which shall be subject to annulment in pursuance of a resolution of the House of Commons.

Additional public dividend capital

5.—(1) If the Secretary of State, with the consent of the Treasury, considers it appropriate to do so, he may, instead of making a loan to an NHS trust under paragraph 1, pay an amount to the trust as public dividend capital.

(2) Section 12E shall apply to public dividend capital paid to an NHS trust under this paragraph as it applies to public dividend capital forming part of the trust's originating capital debt.

Surplus funds

6. If it appears to the Secretary of State that any amount standing in the reserves of an NHS trust is surplus to its foreseeable requirements, the trust shall, if the Secretary of State with the approval of the Treasury and after consultation with the trust so directs, pay that amount into the Consolidated Fund.

Investment

7. An NHS trust may not invest any money held by it except in securities of the Government of the United Kingdom or in such other manner as the Secretary of State may with the consent of the Treasury approve.

Section 36   SCHEDULE 7

AMENDMENTS RELATING TO AUDIT OF ACCOUNTS OF SCOTTISH HEALTH SERVICE BODIES

The Local Government (Scotland) Act 1973

1. Part VII of the Local Government (Scotland) Act 1973 (finance) shall be amended in accordance with paragraphs 2 to 13 below.

2. In section 96 (accounts and audit of local authorities), in subsection (4), for the words "Commission for Local Authority Accounts" there shall be substituted "Accounts Commission for Scotland."

3.—(1) Section 97 (establishment of Commission for Local Authority Accounts in Scotland) shall be amended as follows.

(2) In subsection (1)—

(a) for the words "Commission for Local Authority Accounts in Scotland" there shall be substituted "Accounts Commission for Scotland";

(b) for the word "twelve" there shall be substituted "fifteen";

(c) for the word "nine" there shall be substituted "eleven"; and

(d) after the word "authorities" there shall be inserted "and such organisations connected with the health service."

(3) In subsection (2)—

(a) in paragraph (a)—

    (i) after the words "accounts of" there shall be inserted "(i)," and

    (ii) after the word "authorities" there shall be inserted the following sub-paragraphs—

      "(ii) the bodies mentioned in section 86(1)(a) to (c) of the National Health Service (Scotland) Act 1978;

(iii) the members of every recognised fund-holding practice;

(iv) the Mental Welfare Commission for Scotland; and

(v) any State Hospital Management Committee constituted under section 91 of the Mental Health (Scotland) Act 1984,";

(b) in paragraph (c), after the word "authorities" there shall be inserted "or, as the case may be, health service bodies"; and

(c) in paragraph (d), after the word "authorities" there shall be inserted "or health service bodies."

(4) After subsection (2) there shall be inserted the following subsections—

"(2A) Subject to section 100(1A) of this Act, in relation to the members of a recognised fund-holding practice, any reference in this Part of this Act to their accounts is a reference only to the accounts relating to allotted sums paid to them.

(2B) In this Part of this Act—

"health service body" means a body referred to in subsection (2)(a)(ii) to (v) above; and

"recognised fund-holding practice" and "allotted sum" have the same meanings as in section 87B of the National Health Service (Scotland) Act 1978."

(5) In subsection (3), after the word "authorities" there shall be inserted "and such organisations connected with the health service."

(6) After subsection (4) there shall be inserted the following subsections—

"(4A) It shall be the duty of the Commission to make, by such date as the Secretary of State may determine, an offer of employment by the Commission to each person employed in the civil service of the State in connection with the audit of the accounts of any health service body whose name is notified to the Commission by the Secretary of State for the purposes of this subsection; and the terms of the offer must be such that they are, taken as a whole, not less favourable to the person to whom the offer is made than the terms on which he is employed on the date on which the offer is made.

(4B) An offer made in pursuance of subsection (4A) above shall not be revocable during the period of three months beginning with the date on which it is made.

(4C) Where a person becomes an officer of the Commission in consequence of subsection (4A) above, then, for the purposes of the Employment Protection (Consolidation) Act 1978, his period of employment in the civil service of the State shall count as a period of employment by the Commission and the change of employment shall not break the continuity of the period of employment.

(4D) Where a person ceases to be employed as mentioned in subsection (4A) above—

(a) on becoming an officer of the Commission in consequence of an offer made in pursuance of that subsection; or

(b) having unreasonably refused such an offer,

he shall not, on ceasing to be so employed, be treated for the purposes of any scheme under section 1 of the Superannuation Act 1972 as having been retired on redundancy."

(7) At the end of subsection (6) there shall be added—

"or a person who is, within the period of five years beginning with the relevant date, approved by the Secretary of State, acting on the recommendation of the Commission and whose approval is not (whether during that period or after its expiry) withdrawn by the Secretary of State acting on such recommendation.

(6A) In subsection (6) above, "the relevant date" means the date appointed for the coming into force of paragraph 3(3) of Schedule 7 to the National Health Service and Community Care Act 1990."

4.—(1) Section 97A (studies for improving economy etc. in services) shall be amended as follows.

(2) At the end of subsection (2) there shall be added "and, in the case of studies relating to a health service body, shall, on request, furnish to the Comptroller and Auditor General all material relevant to the studies."

(3) At the end of subsection (3) there shall be added "and, in the case of a health service body, the Commission shall also consult the Secretary of State and the Comptroller and Auditor General."

5.—(1) Section 98 (expenses and accounts of Commission) shall be amended as follows.

(2) In subsection (1)—

(a) in paragraph (b), after the word "Commission" where it first occurs there shall be inserted "relating to their functions with respect to local authorities"; and

(b) at the end of paragraph (b) there shall be inserted the following paragraph—

"(c) such part of the expenses of the Commission relating to their functions with respect to health service bodies as is not met by grants under paragraph (a) above shall be met by health service bodies in accordance with regulations made by the

Secretary of State after consultation with such organisations connected with the health service as appear to him to be concerned."

(3) In subsection (2), after "(b)" there shall be inserted "or (c)."

6. In section 99 (general duties of auditors)—

(a) after the word "authority" in both places where it occurs there shall be inserted "or health service body; and

(b) in paragraph (a), after the word "Act" there shall be inserted "or, in the case of a health service body, directions under section 86(3) of the National Health Service (Scotland) Act 1978."

7.—(1) Section 100 (auditor's right of access to documents) shall be amended as follows.

(2) In subsection (1)—

(a) after the word "authority" where it first occurs there shall be inserted "or health service body"; and

(b) after the word "authority" in the second place where it occurs there shall be inserted "or body."

(3) After subsection (1) there shall be inserted the following subsection—

"(1A) In the case of a recognised fund-holding practice, the reference in subsection (1) above to documents includes a reference to documents relating to all the accounts and records of the members of the practice, whether or not relating to an allotted sum."

(4) In subsection (2), after the word "authority" there shall be inserted "and health service body."

8. In section 101 (completion of audit), after subsection (4) there shall be added the following subsection—

"(5) Within 14 days of the completion of the audit of the accounts of a health service body the auditor shall place on any abstract of those accounts prepared by the health service body by virtue of section 86 of the National Health Service (Scotland) Act 1978 a certificate, in such form as the Commission may direct, to the effect that he has audited the accounts in accordance with the provisions of this Part of this Act; and the auditor shall, on so certifying, forthwith send copies of the abstract of the accounts to the Commission, the Secretary of State and the health service body."

9.—(1) Section 102 (reports to Commission by Controller of Audit) shall be amended as follows.

(2) In subsection (1)—

(a) after the word "authorities" there shall be inserted "and health service bodies"; and

(b) after the word "authority" there shall be inserted "or health service body."

(3) After subsection (4) there shall be added the following subsection—

"(5) Without prejudice to subsection (1) above and section 104A(2) of this Act, the Controller of Audit may make a report to the Commission on any matters arising out of or in connection with the accounts of a health service body and shall send a copy of any report so made to any health service body which is named in that report and to the Secretary of State."

10. In section 103 (action by Commission on reports by Controller of Audit), after the word "Audit" there shall be inserted "with respect to the accounts of any local authority."

11. After section 104 there shall be inserted the following section—

"Audit of accounts of health service bodies: special provisions

104A.—(1) Where the auditor of the accounts of a health service body has reason to believe that the body, or any officer of the body—

(a) has made a decision which involves the incurring of expenditure which is unlawful; or

(b) has taken a course of action which, if pursued to its conclusion, would be unlawful and likely to cause a loss or deficiency,

he shall forthwith make a report to the Controller of Audit.

(2) On receipt of a report under subsection (1) above the Controller of Audit—

(a) shall forthwith send a copy of the report to the Commission and to the Secretary of State; and

(b) may, if he thinks fit, send to the Commission and to the Secretary of State any observations which he may have on the report.

(3) The Commission may make a report to the Secretary of State on any matters arising out of or in connection with the accounts of a health service body."

12. After subsection (2) of section 106 (application of sections 93 to 105 to bodies other than local authorities and to officers) there shall be added the following subsection—

"(3) In the application of subsection (2) above to an officer of a health service body, for the words from "96" to "section 105" there shall be substituted "97 to 104A".""

13. In Schedule 8 (provisions as to the Commission), for the words "Commission for Local Authority Accounts in Scotland" in both places where they occur there shall be substituted "Accounts Commission for Scotland."

The National Health Service (Scotland) Act 1978

14.—(1) Section 86 of the National Health Service (Scotland) Act 1978 (keeping and audit of accounts of certain Scottish health bodies) shall be amended as follows.

(2) In subsections (1) and (1A), for the words "by auditors appointed by the Secretary of State" there shall be substituted "in accordance with Part VII of the Local Government (Scotland) Act 1973 by auditors appointed by the Accounts Commission for Scotland."

(3) After subsection (1B) there shall be inserted the following subsection—

"(1C) In such circumstances and to such extent as regulations made by the Secretary of State so provide, the requirement in subsection (1A)(a) to have accounts audited shall not apply to the accounts for any year of a recognised fund-holding practice if those accounts are submitted to a Health Board and summarised in the Board's accounts."

(4) Subsection (2) shall cease to have effect.

General amendment

15. Without prejudice to any express amendment made by this Act, for any reference in any enactment (including an enactment comprised in subordinate legislation) to the Commission for Local Authority Accounts in Scotland there shall be substituted a reference to the Accounts Commission for Scotland.

Section 60   SCHEDULE 8

PROVISIONS ARISING OUT OF REMOVAL OF CROWN IMMUNITIES FROM HEALTH SERVICE BODIES

PART I

AMENDMENTS CONTINUING CERTAIN STATUTORY EXEMPTIONS

The Employers' Liability (Compulsory Insurance) Act 1969

1. In section 3 of the Employers' Liability (Compulsory Insurance) Act 1969 (employers exempted from insurance), in subsection (2) after the words "subsection (1)(a) above" there shall be inserted—

"(a) a health service body, as defined in section 60(7) of the National Health Service and Community Care Act 1990, and a National Health Service trust established under Part I of that Act or the National Health Service (Scotland) Act 1978; and

(b) ."

The Vehicles (Excise) Act 1971

2. In section 7 of the Vehicles (Excise) Act 1971 (miscellaneous exemptions from duty), after subsection (4) there shall be inserted the following subsection—

"(4A) A mechanically propelled vehicle shall not be chargeable with any duty under this Act at a time when it is used or kept on a road by a health service body, as defined in section 60(7) of the National Health Service and Community Care Act 1990 or a National Health Service trust established under Part I of that Act or the National Health Service (Scotland) Act 1978."

The Copyright, Designs and Patents Act 1988

3. At the end of section 48 of the Copyright, Designs and Patents Act 1988 (material communicated to the Crown in the course of public business) there shall be added the following subsection—

"(6) In this section "the Crown" includes a health service body, as defined in section 60(7) of the National Health Service and Community Care Act 1990, and a National Health Service trust established under Part I of that Act or the National Health Service (Scotland) Act 1978; and the reference in subsection (1) above to public business shall be construed accordingly."

The Road Traffic Act 1988

4. In section 144 of the Road Traffic Act 1988 (exceptions from requirement of third-party insurance or security) in subsection (2) after paragraph (d) there shall be inserted the following paragraphs—

"(da) to a vehicle owned by a health service body, as defined in section 60(7) of the National Health Service and Community Care Act 1990, at a time when the vehicle is being driven under the owner's control,

(db) to an ambulance owned by a National Health Service trust established under Part I of the National Health Service and Community Care Act 1990 or the National Health Service (Scotland) Act 1978, at a time when a vehicle is being driven under the owner's control."

PART II

CONSEQUENTIAL AMENDMENTS

The Acquisition of Land (Authorisation Procedure) (Scotland) Act 1947

5. In the First Schedule to the Acquisition of Land (Authorisation Procedure) (Scotland) Act 1947 (procedure for authorising compulsory purchases), after paragraph 10 there shall be inserted the following paragraph—

"10A. In paragraphs 9 and 10 of this Schedule "statutory undertakers" include—

(a) a health service body, as defined in section 60(7) of the National Health Service and Community Care Act 1990; and

(b) a National Health Service trust established under Part I of that Act or the National Health Service (Scotland) Act 1978;

but in relation to a health service body, as so defined, any reference in those paragraphs to land acquired or available for acquisition by the statutory undertakers shall be construed as a reference to land acquired or available for use by the Secretary of State for use or occupation by that body."

The Town and Country Planning Act 1971

6. In section 128 of the Town and Country Planning Act 1971 (use and development of consecrated land and burial grounds) after subsection (4) there shall be inserted the following subsection—

"(4A) In the case of land—

(a) which has been acquired by the Secretary of State under subsection (1) of section 87 of the National Health Service Act 1977 or to which, by virtue of subsection (6) of that section, this section applies as if it had been so acquired, and

(b) which is held, used or occupied by a health service body, as defined in section 60(7) of the National Health Service and Community Care Act 1990,

subsection (1) or, as the case may be, subsection (4) above shall apply with the omission of paragraph (a) and, in paragraph (b), of the words "in any other case"."

The Town and Country Planning (Scotland) Act 1972

7. In section 118 of the Town and Country Planning (Scotland) Act 1972 (provisions as to churches and burial grounds), after subsection (1) there shall be inserted the following subsection—

"(1A) In the case of land—

(a) which has been acquired by the Secretary of State under section 79(1) of the National Health Service (Scotland) Act 1978; and

(b) which is held, used or occupied by a health service body, as defined in section 60(7) of the National Health Service and Community Care Act 1990),

subsection (1) of this section shall apply with the omission of paragraph (a) and, in paragraph (b), of the words "in any other case"."

The Acquisition of Land Act 1981

8.—(1) At the end of section 16 of the Acquisition of Land Act 1981 (statutory undertakers' land excluded from compulsory purchase) there shall be added the following subsection—

"(3) In the preceding provisions of this section "statutory undertakers" include—

(a) a health service body, as defined in section 60(7) of the National Health Service and Community Care Act 1990; and

(b) a National Health Service trust established under Part I of that Act or the National Health Service (Scotland) Act 1978;

but in relation to a health service body, as so defined, any reference in those provisions to land acquired or available for acquisition by the statutory undertakers shall be construed as a reference to land acquired or available for acquisition by the Secretary of State for use or occupation by that body."

(2) In section 17 of that Act (local authority and statutory undertakers' land) at the end of subsection (2) there shall be inserted the following subsection—

"(2A) Subsection (3) of section 16 above applies in relation to subsections (1) and (2) above as it applies in relation to the preceding provisions of that section."

The Value Added Tax Act 1983

9. In section 27 of the Value Added Tax Act 1983 (application to Crown), in subsection (4) after the words "Minister of the Crown" there shall be inserted the words "including a health service body, as defined in section 60(7) of the National Health Service and Community Care Act 1990."

The Housing Act 1988

10. In Schedule 2 to the Housing Act 1988 (grounds for possession of dwelling-houses let on assured tenancies), at the end of Ground 16 (dwelling-house let in consequence of employment by the landlord) there shall be added the following paragraph—

"For the purposes of this ground, at a time when the landlord is or was the Secretary of State, employment by a health service body, as defined in section 60(7) of the National Health Service and Community Care Act 1990, shall be regarded as employment by the Secretary of State."

The Housing (Scotland) Act 1988

11. In Schedule 5 to the Housing (Scotland) Act 1988 (grounds for possession of houses let on assured tenancies) at the end of Ground 17 (house let in consequence of employment by the landlord) there shall be added the following paragraph—

"For the purposes of this ground, at a time when the landlord is or was the Secretary of State, employment by a health service body, as defined in section 60(7) of the National Health Service and Community Care Act 1990, shall be regarded as employment by the Secretary of State."

PART III

TRANSITIONAL PROVISIONS

12. In this Part of this Schedule—

(a) "the appointed day" means the day appointed for the coming into force of subsection (1) of section 60 of this Act;

(b) "functional health service land" means land which for the time being falls within paragraph (a) or paragraph (b) of that subsection;

(c) "health service body" has the same meaning as in that section; and

(d) "NHS trust" means such a trust established under Part I of this Act or the National Health Service (Scotland) Act 1978.

The Building (Scotland) Act 1959

13.—(1) Notwithstanding section 60(1) of this Act, where, on or after the appointed day, relevant work is carried out by or on behalf of a health service body or an NHS trust—

(a) in relation to a building which is, immediately before the appointed day, a Crown building within the meaning of section 26(3) of the Building (Scotland) Act 1959 (application to the Crown); or

(b) in constructing a building which, if it had been constructed before the appointed day, would have been a Crown building within the meaning of that provision,

Part II of that Act shall apply to the relevant work as if it were being carried out before the appointed day.

(2) In sub-paragraph (1) above, "relevant work" means work in respect of which, before the appointed day, a health service body has granted a certificate that the detail design has been completed.

The Medicines Act 1968

14.—(1) In any case where—
(a) before the appointed day, a health service body or an NHS trust has made an application for a licence under Part II of the Medicines Act 1968 or any such application as is referred to in section 36 of that Act (applications for clinical trial and animal test certificates), and
(b) the application was accompanied by a declaration under paragraph (a) or paragraph (b) of sub-paragraph (2) below, and
(c) the application has not been determined before the appointed day,
then, on and after the appointed day and until the application is determined, the health service body or NHS trust concerned shall be treated for all purposes as if it held a licence or, as the case may be, a certificate of the description applied for.
(2) The declarations referred to in sub-paragraph (1)(b) above are,—
(a) in the case of a health service body, that, at the date of the application, the body was carrying on activities which, after the appointed day, it would be unlawful to carry on except in accordance with a licence or certificate of the description applied for; and
(b) in the case of an NHS trust, that the trust has been established to assume responsibility for the ownership and management of a hospital or other establishment of facility and, at the date of the application, a health service body was carrying on at that hospital, establishment or facility activities which it is unlawful for the NHS trust to carry on except in accordance with a licence or certificate of the description applied for.
(3) For the purposes of sub-paragraph (1) above, an application is determined when the licensing authority—
(a) grant a licence or, as the case may be, certificate to the applicant (whether or not in accordance with the application); or
(b) notify the applicant of their refusal to grant a licence or certificate on the application.
(4) Expressions used in sub-paragraphs (1) to (3) above have the same meaning as in sections 18 to 22 of the Medicines Act 1968 (applications for, and grant of, licences), including, where applicable, any of those sections as applied by subsection (3) of section 36 of that Act in relation to applications falling within subsection (1) of that section.

The Fire Precautions Act 1971

15.—(1) Without prejudice to the continuing validity on and after the appointed day of any fire certificate issued before that day in accordance with subsection (3) of section 40 of the Fire Precautions Act 1971 (certain functions in relation to premises occupied or owned by the Crown exercisable by a fire inspector instead of by the fire authority), any application made, notice issued or other thing done before the appointed day to or by a fire inspector in relation to premises held, used or occupied by a health service body, shall be treated on and after that day as if made, issued or done to or by a fire authority.
(2) Expressions used in sub-paragraph (1) above have the same meaning as in the Fire Precautions Act 1971.

The Town and Country Planning Act 1971

16.—(1) This paragraph applies if—
(a) before the appointed day, notice of any proposed development has been given to a local planning authority in accordance with arrangements relating to development by government departments; and
(b) the development relates to land which notice was given, was functional health service land; and
(c) the proposed development has not been carried out before the appointed day.
(2) So far as relates to the carrying out of the development of which notice was given as mentioned in sub-paragraph (1)(a) above, for the purposes of the arrangements referred to in that paragraph and of the Town and Country Planning Act 1971,—
(a) the carrying out of the development shall continue to be regarded as being by or on behalf of the Crown; and
(b) so long as the interest of the Secretary of State in the land referred to in sub-paragraph (1)(b) above continues on and after the appointed day to be held in fact by the Secretary of State or an NHS trust, that interest shall be regarded as continuing to be an interest of, or held on behalf of, the Crown.

(3) Subject to paragraph 12 above, expressions used in sub-paragraphs (1) and (2) above have the same meaning as in the Town and Country Planning Act 1971.

The Town and Country Planning (Scotland) Act 1972

17.—(1) This paragraph applies if—
(a) before the appointed day, notice of any proposed development has been given to a planning authority in accordance with arrangements relating to development by government departments; and
(b) the development relates to land which, at the time the notice was given, was functional health service land; and
(c) the proposed development has not been carried out before the appointed day.

(2) So far as relates to the carrying out of the development of which notice was given as mentioned in sub-paragraph (1)(a) above, for the purposes of the arrangements referred to in that paragraph and of the Town and Country Planning (Scotland) Act 1972—
(a) the carrying out of the development shall continue to be regarded as being by or on behalf of the Crown; and
(b) so long as the interest of the Secretary of State in the land referred to in sub-paragraph (1)(b) above continues on and after the appointed day to be held in fact by the Secretary of State or an NHS trust, that interest shall be regarded as continuing to be an interest of, or held on behalf of, the Crown.

(3) Subject to paragraph 12 above, expressions used in sub-paragraphs (1) and (2) above have the same meaning as in the Town and Country Planning (Scotland) Act 1972.

The Building Act 1984

18.—(1) If, immediately before the appointed day, approved work is proposed to be carried out by or on behalf of a Crown authority (whether or not in relation to a Crown building) the fact that, on or after the appointed day, the work may be carried out by or on behalf of a health service body or an NHS trust shall not prevent it continuing to be regarded for the purposes of Part I of the Building Act 1984 as work carried out by a Crown authority.

(2) Subject to sub-paragraph (3) below, expressions used in sub-paragraph (1) above have the same meaning as in section 44 of the Building Act 1984 (application of Part I to Crown).

(3) Any reference in sub-paragraph (1) above to approved work is a reference to work in respect of which, before the appointed day, either a contract for carrying it out was entered into or all necessary design certificates were signed in accordance with arrangements relating to compliance with the substantive requirements of building regulations by Regional and District Health Authorities and certain Special Health Authorities.

The Housing Act 1988 and the Rent Act 1977

19.—(1) This paragraph applies to a tenancy—
(a) which was entered into before the appointed day; and
(b) which is of land in England or Wales which, immediately before the appointed day, was functional health service land.

(2) If and so long as the interest of the landlord under a tenancy to which this paragraph applies continues on and after the appointed day to belong in fact either to the Secretary of State or to an NHS trust, it shall be taken to belong to a government department for the purposes of—
(a) paragraph 11 of Schedule 1 to the Housing Act 1988 (Crown tenancies entered into after the commencement of Part I of that Act not to be assured tenancies); or
(b) section 13 of the Rent Act 1977 (earlier Crown tenancies not to be protected tenancies).

(3) Expressions used in sub-paragraphs (1) and (2) above have the same meaning as in Part I of the Housing Act 1988 or, as the case may require, the Rent Act 1977.

The Housing (Scotland) Act 1988 and the Rent (Scotland) Act 1984

20.—(1) This paragraph applies to a tenancy—
(a) which was entered into before the appointed day; and
(b) which is of land in Scotland which, immediately before the appointed day, was functional health service land.

(2) If and so long as the interest of the landlord under a tenancy to which this paragraph applies continues on and after the appointed day to belong in fact either to the Secretary of State or to an NHS trust, it shall be taken to belong to a government department for the purposes of—

(a) paragraph 10 of Schedule 4 to the Housing (Scotland) Act 1988 (Crown tenancies entered into after the commencement of that Schedule not to be assured tenancies); or

(b) section 4 of the Rent (Scotland) Act 1984 (earlier Crown tenancies not to be protected tenancies).

(3) Expressions used in sub-paragraphs (1) and (2) above have the same meaning as in Part II of the Housing (Scotland) Act 1988 or, as the case may be, the Rent (Scotland) Act 1984.

Section 66(1)   SCHEDULE 9

MINOR AND CONSEQUENTIAL AMENDMENTS

The Public Health (Scotland) Act 1897

1.—(1) In section 54 of the Public Health (Scotland) Act 1897 (removal of infected persons without proper lodging to hospital), after the words "Secretary of State" in both places where they occur, there shall be inserted the words "or to any hospital managed by a National Health Service trust established under section 12A of the National Health Service (Scotland) Act 1978."

(2) In section 55(1) of that Act (detention of infected persons without proper lodging in hospital) after the word "hospital," where it first appears, there shall be inserted the words "vested in the Secretary of State or managed by a National Health Service trust established under section 12A of the National Health Service (Scotland) Act 1978."

(3) In section 55(3) of that Act, after the words "vested in the Secretary of State" there shall be inserted the words "or managed by a National Health Service trust established under section 12A of the National Health Service (Scotland) Act 1978."

(4) In section 96 of that Act (power of local authority to remove sick persons to hospital), after the words "Secretary of State" there shall be inserted the words "or managed by a National Health Service trust established under section 12A of the National Health Service (Scotland) Act 1978."

The Voluntary Hospitals (Paying Patients) Act 1936

2. In section 1 of the Voluntary Hospitals (Paying Patients) Act 1936 (definitions)—

(a) in the definition of "voluntary hospital," after the words "of the rates" there shall be inserted "or which is vested in an NHS trust"; and

(b) after the definition of "committee of management" there shall be inserted—

" "NHS trust" means a National Health Service trust established under Part I of the National Health Service and Community Care Act 1990."

The Nursing Homes Registration (Scotland) Act 1938

3. In section 10(3)(a) (interpretation) of the Nursing Homes Registration (Scotland) Act 1938, after the words "local authority" there shall be inserted the words "or a National Health Service trust established under section 12A of the National Health Service (Scotland) Act 1978."

The Public Health (Scotland) Act 1945

4. In section 1(3) of the Public Health (Scotland) Act 1945 (regulations with regard to treatment and prevention of spread of certain diseases)—

(a) after the words "Health Boards" there shall be inserted the words "or National Health Service trusts established under section 12A of the National Health Service (Scotland) Act 1978"; and

(b) in the proviso to that subsection, after the word "Board" there shall be inserted the words "National Health Service trust,"

The National Assistance Act 1948

5.—(1) At the beginning of subsection (4) of section 21 of the National Assistance Act 1948 (accommodation provided under section 21 to be provided in premises managed by a local authority) there shall be inserted "Subject to the provisions of section 26 of this Act."

(2) For paragraphs (b) and (c) of subsection (7) of that section (which enable health services to be provided on premises where accommodation is provided under that section) there shall be substituted—

"(b) make arrangements for the provision on the premises in which the accommoda-

tion is being provided of such other services as appear to the authority to be
required."

(3) At the end of subsection (8) of that section (which excludes from that section provision
required to be made by a local authority under other enactments) there shall be inserted "or
authorised or required to be provided under the National Health Service Act 1977."

(4) In section 24 of that Act (authority liable for provision of accommodation)—

(a) in subsection (6) for the words from "patient" to "shall" there shall be substituted
"patient in a hospital vested in the Secretary of State or an NHS trust shall"; and

(b) at the end there shall be added—

"(7) In subsection (6) above "NHS trust" means a National Health Service trust
established under Part I of the National Health Service and Community Care Act 1990
or under the National Health Service (Scotland) Act 1978."

(5) In section 26 of that Act (provision of accommodation in premises maintained by
voluntary organisations etc.)—

(a) in subsection (2) the words "subsection (1) of" shall be omitted;

(b) after subsection (4) there shall be inserted—

"(4A) Section 21(5) of this Act shall have effect as respects accommodation provided
under arrangements made by virtue of this section with the substitution for the
reference to the authority managing the premises of a reference to the authority making
the arrangements.";

(c) in subsection (5) the words "subsection (1) of" shall be omitted.

(6) Subsections (2) and (3) of section 35 of that Act (duty of authorities to exercise functions
under Part III of that Act in accordance with regulations) shall cease to have effect.

(7) Section 36 of that Act (default powers of Minister) shall cease to have effect.

(8) Section 54 of that Act (which enables inquiries to be held for the purposes of that Act)
shall cease to have effect.

(9) In paragraph (f) of section 65 of that Act (application to Scotland)—

(a) the words "Part IV of" shall cease to have effect;

(b) at the end there shall be inserted "or section 7 (functions of local authorities) of the
Mental Health (Scotland) Act 1984,".

The Public Records Act 1958

6. In Schedule 1 to the Public Records Act 1958 (definition of public records), in the Table in
Part I, in the entry relating to the Department of Health, in the second column—

(a) after the words "National Health Service Authorities" there shall be inserted "including
National Health Service trusts"; and

(b) for the words "National health service hospitals" there shall be substituted "health
service hospitals, within the meaning of the National Health Service Act 1977."

The Human Tissue Act 1961

7. In section 1 of the Human Tissue Act 1961 (removal of parts of bodies for medical
purposes)—

(a) in subsection (4A)(b) after the words "health authority" there shall be inserted "or NHS
trust"; and

(b) at the end of subsection (10) there shall be added "and "NHS trust" means a National
Health Service trust established under the National Health Service and Community
Care Act 1990 or the National Health Service (Scotland) Act 1978."

The Abortion Act 1967

8. In section 1 of the Abortion Act 1967 (medical termination of pregnancy), in subsection
(3) after the words "National Health Service (Scotland) Act 1978" there shall be inserted "or in
a hospital vested in a National Health Service trust."

The Leasehold Reform Act 1967

9. In section 28 of the Leasehold Reform Act 1967 (retention or resumption of land required
for public purposes)—

(a) in subsection (5)(d) for the words "and any special health authority" there shall be
substituted "any special health authority and any National Health Service trust"; and

(b) in subsection (6)(c) for the words "or special health authority" there shall be substituted
"special health authority or National Health Service trust."

The Social Work (Scotland) Act 1968

10.—(1) The Social Work (Scotland) Act 1968 shall be amended as follows.

(2) In section 2 (the social work committee), in subsection (2) after paragraph (k) there shall be inserted—

"(l) sections 21 to 23 of the Health and Social Services and Social Security Adjudications Act 1983;

(m) the Access to Personal Files Act 1987."

(3) In section 4 (provisions relating to performance of functions by local authorities), after the word "Act," there shall be inserted the words "or section 7 (functions of local authorities) or 8 (provision of after-care services) of the Mental Health (Scotland) Act 1984,".

(4) In section 6 (supervision of establishments), in—

(a) subsection (1)—

(i) for the words "duly authorised officer of," there shall be substituted the words "person duly authorised by"; and

(ii) after the words "of this Act," where they first occur, there shall be inserted the words "or section 7 (functions of local authorities) or 8 (provision of after-care services) of the Mental Health (Scotland) Act 1984";

(b) subsection (1)(a), at the end there shall be inserted "or section 7 or 8 of the said Act of 1984,";

(c) subsection (2)—

(i) for the word "officer" there shall be substituted the word "person"; and

(ii) after the words "of this Act" there shall be inserted the words "or section 7 or 8 of the said Act of 1984";

(d) subsection (3), for the word "officer" there shall be substituted the words "authorised person"; and

(e) subsection (4), for the words "An officer" there shall be substituted the words "A person."

(5) In section 12 (general social welfare services of local authorities) at the end there shall be inserted—

"(6) For the purposes of subsection (2) of this section 'person in need' includes a person who is in need of care and attention arising out of drug or alcohol dependency or release from prison or other form of detention."

(6) In section 14 (home help), for the words—

(a) "home help," where they first occur there shall be substituted the words "domiciliary services";

(b) "help is," there shall be substituted the words "services are"; and

(c) "home help is," there shall be substituted the words "domiciliary services are."

(7) In section 59(1) (provision of residential and other establishments), at the beginning there shall be inserted the words "Subject to section 13A of this Act,".

(8) In section 61(1A) (definition of "establishment")—

(a) after the word "include" there shall be inserted "(a)"; and

(b) at the end of the definition of "establishment" there shall be inserted—

"; or

(b) any establishment providing residential accommodation with nursing falling within section 13A of this Act;".

(9) In subsection (1) of section 67 (inspection of establishments by local authorities)—

(a) for the words "duly authorised officer of" there shall be substituted the words "person duly authorised by";

(b) for the words "required to be kept therein by virtue of this Part of this Act" there shall be substituted the words "(in whatever form they are held) relating to the place or to any person for whom services have been or are provided there by virtue of this Act or section 7 (functions of local authorities) or 8 (provision of after-care services) of the Mental Health (Scotland) Act 1984";

(c) after the words "subsections (2)," there shall be inserted the words "to (2D)";

(d) for the words "an officer," where they first occur, there shall be substituted the words "a person"; and

(e) for the words "an officer of" there shall be substituted the words "a person authorised by."

(10) In subsection (2) of the said section 67, for the word "officer," in both places where it occurs, there shall be substituted the word "person."

(11) In subsection (1)(d) of section 86 (adjustments between authority providing accommodation etc., and authority of area of residence), at the end there shall be inserted—

"or

   (e) in the provision of accommodation, services or facilities for persons ordinarily so resident under section 7 (functions of local authorities) or 8 (provision of after-care services) of the Mental Health (Scotland) Act 1984.";

(12) In subsection (3) of the said section 86, after the words "1978" there shall be inserted the words "or in a hospital managed by a National Health Service trust established under Part I of the National Health Service and Community Care Act 1990 or section 12A of the National Health Service (Scotland) Act 1978."

(13) In section 87 (charges for services and accommodation),—

   (a) in subsection (1), after the words "under this Act," there shall be inserted the words "or section 7 (functions of local authorities) or 8 (provision of after-care services) of the Mental Health (Scotland) Act 1984";

   (b) in subsection (1A), after the words "under this Act," there shall be inserted the words "or section 7 or 8 of the said Act of 1984";

   (c) in subsections (2), (3) and (4), after the words "under this Act," there shall be inserted the words "or section 7 of the said Act of 1984;" and

   (d) in subsection (4), after the word "organisation" there shall be inserted the words "or any other person or body."

(14) In subsection (1) of section 94 (interpretation),—

   (a) after the definition of "contributor" there shall be inserted the following definition—
   " "domiciliary services" means any services, being services provided in the home, which appear to a local authority to be necessary for the purpose of enabling a person to maintain as independent an existence as is practicable in his home;"; and

   (b) in the definition of "hospital," after the words "1978" there shall be inserted—
   "(aa) any hospital managed by a National Health Service trust established under section 12A of the National Health Service (Scotland) Act 1978;.""

The Local Authority Social Services Act 1970

11. In Schedule 1 to the Local Authority Social Services Act 1970 (enactments conferring functions assigned to social services committee)—

   (a) in the entry relating to the Children Act 1989, in the second column after the words "health authorities" there shall be inserted "National Health Service trusts";

   (b) for the entry relating to section 6 of the Local Authority Social Services Act 1970 there shall be substituted—

"Sections 6 and 7B of this Act	Appointment of director of social services, etc; provision and conduct of complaints procedure."; and

   (c) at the end of that Schedule there shall be inserted—

"National Health Service and Community Care Act 1990 (c. 19)	
Section 46	Preparation of plans for community care services.
Section 47	Assessment of needs for community care services."

The Chronically Sick and Disabled Persons Act 1970

12. In section 2(1) of the Chronically Sick and Disabled Persons Act 1970, the words from "to the provisions" in the first place where they occur, to "the purpose) and" shall be omitted and after the words "Secretary of State)" there shall be inserted "and to the provisions of section 7A of that Act (which requires local authorities to exercise their social services functions in accordance with directions given by the Secretary of State)."

The Local Government Act 1972

13. In section 113 of the Local Government Act 1972 (placing of staff at disposal of other bodies),—

   (a) in subsection (1A) after the words "special health authority," in each place where they occur, there shall be inserted "or NHS trust"; and

   (b) at the end there shall be added the following subsection—
   "(4) In subsection (2A) above "NHS trust" means a National Health Service trust established under Part I of the National Health Service and Community Care Act 1990."

The Criminal Procedure (Scotland) Act 1975

14. In section 462 (interpretation) of the Criminal Procedure (Scotland) Act 1975, in paragraph (a) of the definition of "hospital," after the words "Secretary of State" there shall be inserted the words "or in a National Health Service trust."

The Child Benefit Act 1975

15. In section 3 of the Child Benefit Act 1975 (meaning of "person responsible for child") in subsection (3) (certain days of absence disregarded) in paragraph (c) for the words following "under" there shall be substituted "section 21 of the National Assistance Act 1948, the Children Act 1989 or the Social Work (Scotland) Act 1968."

The Children Act 1975

16. In section 99(1)(b) of the Children Act 1975 (inquiries in Scotland) the words "paragraph (a) of section 1(4) and" shall cease to have effect and after the word "(h)" there shall be inserted "to (k)."

The Adoption Act 1976

17. In section 2 of the Adoption Act 1976 (local authorities' social services) in paragraph (a) (as set out in paragraph 1 of Schedule 10 to the Children Act 1989) after the words "health authorities" there shall be inserted "National Health Service trusts."

The National Health Service Act 1977

18.—(1) In section 41 of the National Health Service Act 1977 (arrangements for pharmaceutical services)—
(a) for the words "supply to persons who are in that locality" there shall be substituted "provision to persons who are in that locality of";
(b) in paragraph (b) after the words "health authority" there shall be inserted "or an NHS trust" and the word "and" at the end of the paragraph shall be omitted; and
(c) after paragraph (c) there shall be inserted "and
(d) such other services as may be prescribed."

(2) At the end of section 43 of that Act (persons authorised to provide pharmaceutical services) there shall be added the following subsection—
"(3) No arrangements for the provision of pharmaceutical services falling within section 41(d) above shall be made with persons other than those who are registered pharmacists or are of a prescribed description."

(3) In section 63 of that Act (hospital accommodation on part payment) after subsection (1) there shall be inserted the following subsection—
"(1C) References in subsection (1) above to a health service hospital do not include references to a hospital vested in an NHS trust."

(4) At the end of section 65 of that Act (accommodation and services for private patients) there shall be added the following subsection—
"(4) References in the preceding provisions of this section to a health service hospital do not include references to a hospital vested in an NHS trust."

(5) In section 83A of that Act (remission and repayment of charges and payment of travelling expenses) in subsection (1)—
(a) in paragraph (b) after the words "Secretary of State" there shall be inserted "or an NHS trust" and at the end there shall be added "and," and
(b) after paragraph (b) there shall be inserted the following paragraph—
"(c) for the reimbursement by a District Health Authority to an NHS trust and, in such cases as may be prescribed to another District Health Authority, of payments made by virtue of exercising the functions conferred under paragraph (b) above."

(6) In section 84 of that Act (inquiries) at the end of subsection (1) there shall be added the words "or Part I of the National Health Service and Community Care Act 1990."

(7) In section 85 of that Act (default powers)—
(a) in subsection (1), for paragraph (e) there shall be substituted the following paragraph—
"(e) an NHS trust";
and in the words following paragraph (g) after the words "this Act" there shall be inserted "or Part I of the National Health Service and Community Care Act 1990";

(b) in subsection (2), for the words from the beginning to "body shall" there shall be substituted "The members of the body in default shall";

(c) subsections (3) and (4) shall be omitted.

(8) In section 86 of that Act (emergency powers) after the words "this Act," in the first place where they occur, there shall be inserted "or Part I of the National Health Service and Community Care Act 1990" and after the words "this Act," in the second place where they occur, there shall be inserted "or that Part."

(9) At the end of section 103 of that Act (special arrangement as to payment of remuneration) there shall be inserted the following subsection—

"(3) If the Secretary of State by order so provides with respect to remuneration in respect of such pharmaceutical services as may be specified in the order,—

(a) an NHS trust determined in accordance with the order shall have the function of paying sums so determined to the Family Health Services Authority which, under Part II of this Act, has the function of paying that remuneration; and

(b) nothing in subsection (2) above shall apply with respect to that remuneration."

(10) In section 109 of that Act, after paragraph (d) there shall be inserted—

"(da) NHS trusts."

(11) In section 110 of that Act (investigations for England and for Wales), after paragraph (b) there shall be inserted—

"(ba) an NHS trust which is managing a hospital or other establishment or facility which is in Wales."

(12) In section 122 of that Act (recovery of charges), in subsection (1) after the words "this Act," in the second place where they occur, there shall be inserted "or Part I of the National Health Service and Community Care Act 1990."

(13) In Schedule 7 to that Act (additional provisions as to Community Health Councils), in paragraph 2—

(a) in sub-paragraph (d) after the word "by" there shall be inserted "Regional Health Authorities, NHS trusts"; and

(b) in sub-paragraph (e) for the words from "such Authorities," in the first place where those words appear, to the end of the sub-paragraph there shall be inserted "Regional and District Health Authorities, NHS trusts or relevant Family Health Services Authorities, and the right of members of Councils to enter and inspect premises controlled by such health authorities or NHS trusts."

(14) In Schedule 8 to that Act (local social services authorities' functions)—

(a) in paragraph 1 (care of mothers) after the word "mothers" there shall be inserted "(other than for the provision of residential accommodation for them)";

(b) in paragraph 2 (prevention, care and after-care)—

(i) sub-paragraphs (1)(a) and (4) (which make provision respectively for the provision by authorities of residential accommodation and for regulations to be made conferring powers of inspection of certain premises provided under that paragraph) shall cease to have effect; and

(ii) after sub-paragraph (4A) there shall be inserted—

"(4AA) No authority is authorised or may be required under this paragraph to provide residential accommodation for any person."

The National Health Service (Scotland) Act 1978

19.—(1) In section 2 of the National Health Service (Scotland) Act 1978 (Health Boards), in subsection (5) after the words "subsection (1)" there shall be inserted "and in exercising any function otherwise conferred on them by or under this Act."

(2) In subsection (5) of section 11 (Scottish Hospital Trust) of that Act, after the words "and shall cause" there shall be inserted the words "such accounts to be audited and."

(3) In section 12 of that Act (Scottish Hospital Endowments Research Trust), after subsection (4) there shall be inserted the following subsections—

"(4A) The Research Trust shall have power to engage in activities intended to stimulate the giving of money or other property to assist them in carrying out the purpose aforesaid.

(4B) Subject to any directions of the Secretary of State excluding specified activities or descriptions of activity, the activities authorised by subsection (4A) include public appeals or collections, and the soliciting of sponsorship, donations, legacies, bequests and gifts."

(4) In section 13 of that Act (co-operation between Health Boards and other authorities), after the word "Boards," there shall be inserted "NHS trusts,".

(5) In subsection (1)(a) of section 13A of that Act (co-operation in planning of services for disabled persons, the elderly and others) for the words from "being" to the end there shall be

substituted the words "by Health Boards and such of the authorities mentioned in that section as may be concerned;".

(6) For paragraph (b) of subsection (2) of section 25 of that Act (arrangements for provision of general dental services) there shall be substituted the following paragraph—

"(b) for conferring a right, subject to—
   (i) subsection (2A);
   (ii) the provisions of this Part relating to the disqualification of persons providing services; and
   (iii) section 8 (persons over retiring age) of the Health and Medicines Act 1988 and regulations made under that section,
on any dental practitioner who wishes to be included in any such list to be so included;".

(7) In section 27 of that Act (arrangements for provision of pharmaceutical services)—
(a) in subsection (1)—
   (i) for the word "supply" there shall be substituted "provision";
   (ii) in paragraph (b), after the word "Board" there shall be inserted "or by an NHS trust";
   (iii) at the end of paragraph (c) there shall be inserted—
   "; and
   (d) such services as may be prescribed,"; and
   (iv) for the words "services provided in accordance with the arrangements are" there shall be substituted "provision of drugs, medicines, appliances and services in accordance with the arrangements is";
(b) in subsection (2), after the word "mentioned" in the second place where it occurs there shall be inserted ", or to whom services mentioned in subsection (1)(d) are to be provided,";
(c) in subsections (3)(b), (c) and (d) and (4), before the word "services" in each place where it occurs there shall be inserted "pharmaceutical"; and
(d) in subsection (4)(d) for the words "a prescribed criterion" there shall be substituted "prescribed criteria".

(8) In section 28(2) of that Act (persons authorised to provide pharmaceutical services)—
(a) after the word "medicines" in the first place where it occurs there shall be inserted "or the provision of pharmaceutical services";
(b) after the word "undertake" there shall be inserted "(a)";
(c) for the word "supplied" there shall be substituted "provided"; and
(d) after the word "dispensed" there shall be inserted—
   ", and
   (b) that all services mentioned in section 27(1)(d) provided by them under those arrangements shall be provided,".

(9) In section 55(1) (hospital accommodation on part payment) of that Act, after the word "hospital" there shall be inserted the words "vested in the Secretary of State".

(10) In section 57(1) (accommodation and services for private patients), after the word "hospital" where it first occurs there shall be inserted "vested in the Secretary of State".

(11) In section 73 of that Act (charges for more expensive supplies) at the end there shall be inserted—

"(c) by a National Health Service trust in respect of the supply by them of any appliance or vehicle which is, at the request of the person supplied, of a more expensive type than the prescribed type, or in respect of the replacement or repair of any such appliance, or the replacement of any such vehicle.".

(12) In section 74 of that Act (charges for repairs and replacement in certain cases), after paragraph (b) there shall be inserted—
   "or
   (c) by an NHS trust in respect of the replacement or repair of any appliance or vehicle supplied by them,".

(13) In section 75A of that Act (remission and repayment of charges and payment of travelling expenses)—
(a) in subsection (1), at the end there shall be inserted—
   "and
   (d) for the payment by the Secretary of State to NHS trusts of such sums as will reimburse them for any sums paid by them as travelling expenses in such cases as may be prescribed"; and
(b) in subsection (2), for the words "or (c)" there shall be substituted the words ", (c) or (d)".

(14) In section 77 of that Act (default powers), after paragraph (a) of subsection (1) there shall be inserted—

"(aa) an NHS trust".

(15) In section 79 of that Act (purchase of land and moveable property)—

(a) in subsection (1), after the word "Act" where it first appears there shall be inserted the words "and may take any such property or land on lease,"; and

(b) in subsection (2), after the word "(1)," there shall be inserted the words "other than on lease".

(16) In section 84 of that Act (power of trustees to make payments to Health Boards)—

(a) in subsection (1), after the words "Health Board" where they—

(i) second occur, there shall be inserted the words "or an NHS trust"; and

(ii) third occur, there shall be inserted the words "or NHS trust";

(b) in subsection (2)—

(i) after the words "Health Board" there shall be inserted the words "or NHS trust"; and

(ii) after the word "Boards" there shall be inserted the words "or NHS trusts"; and

(c) in subsection (3), after the words "Health Board" there shall be inserted the words "or an NHS trust".

(17) In section 84A of that Act (power to raise money by appeals etc.)—

(a) in subsection (1), after the word "Board" there shall be inserted "or NHS trust"; and

(b) in subsections (3) to (7), after the word "Board" in each place where it occurs there shall be inserted ", NHS trust".

(18) In section 93(1) of that Act (bodies subject to investigation by Health Service Commissioner for Scotland), after paragraph (b) there shall be inserted—

"(bb) NHS trusts."

(19) In section 101 of that Act (protection of health bodies and their officers), after the word "Board" there shall be inserted ", an NHS trust".

(20) In section 102(1) of that Act (management of state hospitals), for the word "90(2)" there shall be substituted "91(2)".

(21) In section 105 of that Act (orders, regulations and directions)—

(a) after subsection (1) there shall be inserted the following subsection—

"(1A) Subsection (1) does not apply to orders made under section 12D(1) or paragraph 26(1) of Schedule 7A.";

(b) in subsection (4), after the words " 10(3) to (5)" there shall be inserted the words "12A(1), 12A(8), 12E(1), 12G(2),"; and

(c) at the end of the said subsection (4) there shall be inserted the words "paragraph 25(1) of Schedule 7A and paragraph 3 of Schedule 7B."

(22) In section 108(1) of that Act (interpretation)—

(a) in the definition of "Health Board", for the word "board" there shall be substituted the words "Health Board";

(b) at the end of the definition of "health service hospital" there shall be added "or vested in an NHS trust";

(c) after the definition of "modifications" there shall be inserted—

" "National Health Service trust" has the meaning indicated by section 12A and "NHS trust" shall be construed accordingly"; and

"NHS contract" has the meaning indicated by section 17A(3)";

(d) after the definition of "officer" there shall be inserted—

" "operational date", in relation to an NHS trust, shall be construed in accordance with paragraph 3(1)(e) of Schedule 7A;"; and

(e) after the definition of "the Research Trust" there shall be inserted—

" "Special Health Board" means a Special Health Board constituted under section 2;".

(23) In section 110 of that Act (citation, extent and commencement)—

(a) in subsection (2), for the words "subsection (3)" there shall be substituted "subsections (2A) and (3)"; and

(b) after subsection (2) there shall be inserted—

"(2A) Section 87B(3) extends also to England and Wales."

(24) In Schedule 6 to that Act (the Hospital Trust)—

(a) in paragraph 4(c), after the words "Health Boards" there shall be inserted the words "and NHS trusts";

(b) after paragraph 4(e) there shall be inserted—

"(ea) power to accept from any NHS trust for investment and management on behalf of the trust any property held on behalf of the trust by trustees appointed by virtue of section 12G(2), and any endowments or accumulated income otherwise held by the trust;";

(c) in paragraph 4(f)—

(i) after the words "paragraph (e)" there shall be inserted the words "or, as the case may be, paragraph (ea)"; and

(ii) after the words "Health Board" there shall be inserted the words "or, as the case may be, by an NHS Trust";

(d) in paragraph 6(2), after the words "Health Boards" there shall be inserted the words "or NHS trusts";

(e) in paragraph 7(1), after the words "Health Boards" there shall be inserted the words ", NHS trusts";

(f) in paragraph 7(2), after the words "Health Boards" there shall be inserted the words ", NHS trusts"; and

(g) in paragraph 7(3), at the end there shall be inserted—
"(c) in so far as it is distributed among NHS trusts, being used by that trust for any purpose for which the trust was established."

The Employment Protection (Consolidation) Act 1978

20. In the Employment Protection (Consolidation) Act 1978, in section 29 (time off for public duties) in subsection (1)(d) after the words "member of" there shall be inserted "a National Health Service trust or".

The Overseas Development and Co-operation Act 1980

21. In the Overseas Development and Co-operation Act 1980, in Schedule 1 (statutory bodies with powers under section 2(1))—

(a) in Part II, in the heading, after the words "NATIONAL HEALTH SERVICE ACT 1977" there shall be inserted "AND THE NATIONAL HEALTH SERVICE AND COMMUNITY CARE ACT 1990";

(b) at the end of that Part there shall be inserted "National Health Service trusts"; and

(c) at the end of Part IV (bodies constituted under the National Health Service (Scotland) Act 1978), there shall be inserted "National Health Service trusts".

The Education Act 1981

22. In the Education Act 1981, in section 10 (duty of health authority to notify parents)—

(a) in subsection (1), after the words "Health Authority" there shall be inserted "or a National Health Service trust"; and

(b) after the words "the Authority", in each place where they appear, there shall be inserted "or trust".

The Acquisition of Land Act 1981

23. In the Acquisition of Land Act 1981, in section 17 (local authority and statutory undertakers' land), in subsection (4), in the definition of "statutory undertakers" after paragraph (a) there shall be inserted—
"(aa) a National Health Service trust established under Part I of the National Health Service and Community Care Act 1990, and".

The Mental Health Act 1983

24.—(1) In section 12 of the Mental Health Act 1983 (general provisions as to medical recommendations), in subsection (3) after the words "National Health Service Act 1977" there shall be inserted "or paragraph 14 of Schedule 2 to the National Health Service and Community Care Act 1990."

(2) In section 19 of that Act (regulations as to transfer of patients), in subsection (3)—

(a) after the words "such a hospital" there shall be inserted "or in a hospital vested in a National Health Service trust", and

(b) for the words from "for which the managers" to "also the managers", there shall be substituted "which is managed by the managers of, or is vested in the National Health Service trust for, the first-mentioned hospital".

(3) In section 23 of that Act (discharge of patients)—

(a) in subsection (3) after the words "a contract with a" there shall be inserted "National Health Service trust", and after the words "by that" there shall be inserted "trust or", and

(b) in subsection (4), after the word "exercised" there shall be inserted "subject to subsection (5) below" and after the word "authority", in each place in which it occurs, there shall be inserted "trust", and

(c) after subsection (4) there shall be inserted the following subsection—

"(5) The reference in subsection (4) above to the members of an authority, trust or body or the members of a committee or sub-committee of an authority, trust or body,—

(a) in the case of a District or Special Health Authority or a committee or sub-committee of such an authority, is a reference only to the chairman of the authority and such members (of the authority, committee or sub-committee, as the case may be) as are not also officers of the authority, within the meaning of the National Health Service Act 1977; and

(b) in the case of a National Health Service trust or a committee or sub-committee of such a trust, is a reference only to the chairman of the trust and such directors or (in the case of a committee or sub-committee) members as are not also employees of the trust."

(4) In section 24 of that Act (visiting and examination of patients), in subsection (3) after the words "District Health Authority" there shall be inserted "National Health Service trust"; and in paragraph (a) of that subsection after the word "authority" there shall be inserted "or trust".

(5) In section 32 of that Act (regulations for purposes of Part II), in subsection (3) after the words "District Health Authorities" there shall be inserted "National Health Service trusts" and for the words "and authorities" there shall be inserted "authorities and trusts".

(6) In section 117 of that Act (after-care) in subsection (3) for the words "the District Health Authority for the district" there shall be substituted "such District Health Authority as may be determined in accordance with regulations made by the Secretary of State".

(7) In section 139 of that Act (protection for acts done in pursuance of the Act), at the end of subsection (4) there shall be inserted "or against a National Health Service trust established under the National Health Service and Community Care Act 1990".

(8) In section 140 of that Act (notification of hospitals having arrangements for reception of urgent cases) after the words "administered by" there shall be inserted "or otherwise available to".

(9) In section 145(1) of that Act (definitions) in the definition of "the managers", after paragraph (b) there shall be inserted the following paragraph—

"(bb) in relation to a hospital vested in a National Health Service trust, the directors of the trust".

The Health and Social Services and Social Security Adjudications Act 1983

25.—(1) In section 17 of the Health and Social Services and Social Security Adjudications Act 1983 (charges for local authority services in England and Wales) after paragraph (e) of subsection (2) (services to which that section applies) there shall be inserted "other than the provision of services for which payment may be required under section 22 or 26 of the National Assistance Act 1948".

(2) In subsection (8) of section 21 of that Act (recovery of sums due to local authority where persons in residential accommodation have disposed of assets), at the end there shall be inserted the words "or section 7 (functions of local authorities) of the Mental Health (Scotland) Act 1984,".

The Public Health (Control of Disease) Act 1984

26.—(1) In section 13 of the Public Health (Control of Disease) Act 1984 (regulations for control of certain diseases), in subsection (4), in paragraph (a) after the words "District Health Authorities" there shall be inserted "National Health Service trusts".

(2) In section 37 of that Act (removal to hospital of person with notifiable disease), in subsection (1)—

(a) in paragraph (c) after the words "Secretary of State" there shall be inserted "or, pursuant to arrangements made by a District Health Authority (whether under an NHS contract or otherwise), in a suitable hospital vested in a NHS trust or other person"; and

(b) in the words following paragraph (c) for the words from "responsible" to "the hospital" there shall be substituted "in whose district lies the area, or the greater part of the area, of the local authority".

(3) In section 41 of that Act (removal to hospital of inmate of common lodging-house with notifiable disease), in subsection (1)—

(a) in paragraph (c) after the words "Secretary of State" there shall be inserted "or, pursuant to arrangements made by a District Health Authority (whether under an NHS contract or otherwise) in a suitable hospital vested in an NHS trust or any other person"; and

(b) in the words following paragraph (c) for the words from "responsible" to "of the hospital" there shall be substituted "in whose district lies the area, or the greater part of the area, of the local authority".

(4) In section 7A of that Act (definitions) after the definition of "London port health authority" there shall be inserted—

     " "NHS trust" and "NHS contract" have the same meaning as in Part I of the National Health Service and Community Care Act 1990 or, as the case may require, the National Health Service (Scotland) Act 1978".

The Registered Homes Act 1984

27. In section 21 of the Registered Homes Act 1984 (meaning of "nursing home") in subsection (3)(a) (premises excluded from the definition) for the words "hospital or" there shall be substituted "health service hospital, within the meaning of the National Health Service Act 1977, or any".

The Mental Health (Scotland) Act 1984

28.—(1) In subsection (2)(e) of section 3 (functions and duties of the Mental Welfare Commission) of the Mental Health (Scotland) Act 1984 after the words "Health Board"—

(a) where they first occur, there shall be inserted the words ", a National Health Service trust established under section 12A of the National Health Service (Scotland) Act 1978"; and

(b) where they second occur, there shall be inserted the words ", the National Health Service trust".

(2) In subsection (2)(a) of section 12 (registration of private hospitals) of that Act, after the words "Secretary of State" there shall be inserted the words "or managed by a National Health Service trust established under section 12A of the National Health Service (Scotland) Act 1978."

(3) In section 20(1)(c) (medical recommendations: hospital) of that Act—

(a) for the words "or 58 of" there shall be substituted the words "of, or paragraph 14 of Schedule 7A to,"; and

(b) for the word "relates" there shall be substituted the word "relate".

(4) In subsection (1) of section 125 (interpretation) of that Act—

(a) in the definition of "hospital", after paragraph (a) there shall be inserted—

     "(aa) any hospital managed by a National Health Service trust established under section 12A of the said Act of 1978;";

(b) in the definition of "managers of a hospital", after paragraph (a) there shall be inserted—

     "(aa) in relation to a hospital managed by a National Health Service trust established under section 12A (National Health Service trusts) of the said Act of 1978, the directors of the trust;".

The Hospital Complaints Procedure Act 1985

29. After section 1 of the Hospital Complaints Procedure Act 1985 there shall be inserted—

     "1A. It shall also be the duty of the Secretary of State to give directions under paragraph 6(2)(e) of Schedule 2 to the National Health Service and Community Care Act 1990 and paragraph 6(2)(e) of Schedule 7A to the National Health Service (Scotland) Act 1978, to any NHS trust which is responsible for the management of a hospital, to comply with directions under section 1 above."

The Disabled Persons (Services, Consultation and Representation) Act 1986

30.—(1) In section 2 of the Disabled Persons (Services, Consultation and Representation) Act 1986 (rights of authorised representatives of disabled persons), in subsection (5) (by virtue of which a disabled person's authorised representative may visit and interview him in various categories of accommodation)—

(a) in paragraph (a) (hospital accommodation) after the words "the 1977 Act" there shall be inserted "or by a National Health Service trust established under the provisions of the National Health Service and Community Care Act 1990" and after the words "the 1978 Act" there shall be inserted "or by a National Health Service trust established under that Act";

(b) in paragraph (c) (accommodation provided by a voluntary organisation in accordance with arrangements made under section 26 of the National Assistance Act 1948) after the word "organisation", in the first place where it occurs, there shall be inserted the words "or other person"; and

(c) in paragraph (cc) (which is inserted by paragraph 59(4) of Schedule 13 to the Children Act 1989) after the word "organisation" there shall be inserted the words "or other person".

(2) In section 7 of that Act (persons discharged from hospital), in subsection (9), in the definition of "managers" the word "and" at the end of paragraph (c) shall be omitted and after that paragraph there shall be inserted—

"(cc) in relation to a hospital vested in a National Health Service trust means the directors of that trust; and".

The Education (No. 2) Act 1986

31. In section 7 of the Education (No. 2) Act 1986 (appointment of representative governors) in subsection (2), for the words following "provide" there shall be substituted—
"(a) in the case of a hospital vested in the Secretary of State, for one governor to be appointed by the District Health Authority; and
(b) in the case of a hospital vested in a National Health Service trust, for one governor to be appointed by that trust."

The AIDS (Control) Act 1987

32.—(1) Section 1 of the AIDS (Control) Act 1987 (periodical reports on matters relating to AIDS and HIV) shall be amended as follows—
(a) in subsection (1), in paragraph (b) the word "and" at the end of sub-paragraph (ii) shall be deleted and at the end of sub-paragraph (iii) there shall be inserted—
"and
(iv) each NHS trust";
(b) in subsection (2) after the words "District Health Authority" in the first place where they occur, there shall be inserted "an NHS trust";
(c) in subsection (3) after the words "District Health Authority" there shall be inserted "NHS trust" and after the words "by the Authority" there shall be inserted "trust"; and
(d) at the end there shall be added—
"(10) In this section "NHS trust" means a National Health Service trust established under Part I of the National Health Service and Community Care Act 1990 or, as the case may be, under the National Health Service (Scotland) Act 1978."
(2) In the Schedule to that Act (contents of reports), after the word "Authority", in each place in which that word appears, there shall be inserted "NHS trust".

The Community Health Councils (Access to Information) Act 1988

33. In section 1 of the Community Health Councils (Access to Information) Act 1988 (access to meetings and documents of Community Health Councils), in subsection (6)(a) after the words "exercises functions" there shall be inserted "or any National Health Service trust which is established under Part I of the National Health Service and Community Care Act 1990 and carries on any of its activities from premises in the area of the authority".

The Health and Medicines Act 1988

34. In section 7 of the Health and Medicines Act 1988 (extension of powers for financing the health service) in subsection (2), after the word "powers," in the second place where it occurs, there shall be inserted "(exercisable outside as well as within Great Britain)".

The Road Traffic Act 1988

35. In section 161 of the Road Traffic Act 1988 (interpretation) in subsection (1), in the definition of "hospital" for the word "on", in the first place where it occurs, there shall be substituted "any health service hospital, within the meaning of the National Health Service Act 1977 or the National Health Service (Scotland) Act 1978 and any other".

The Children Act 1989

36.—(1) In section 21 of the Children Act 1989 (provision of accommodation for children in police protection etc.), in subsection (3) after the words "vested in the Secretary of State" shall be inserted the words "or otherwise made available pursuant to arrangements made by a District Health Authority".

(2) In section 24 of that Act (advice and assistance for certain children)—

(a) at the end of subsection (2)(d)(ii) there shall be added the words "or in any accommodation provided by a National Health Service trust"; and

(b) at the end of subsection (12)(c) there shall be added the words "or any accommodation provided by a National Health Service trust".

(3) In section 29 of that Act (recoupment of cost of providing services etc.), at the end of paragraph (c) of subsection (8) there shall be added the words "or any other hospital made available pursuant to arrangements made by a District Health Authority".

(4) In section 80 of that Act (inspection of children's homes etc.)—

(a) in subsection (1)(d) after the words "health authority" there shall be inserted "or National Health Service trust"; and

(b) in subsection (5)(e) after the words "health authority" there shall be inserted "National Health Service trust".

(5) In section 85 of that Act (children accommodated by health authorities and local education authorities), in subsection (1) after the words "health authority" there shall be inserted "National Health Service trust".

The Opticians Act 1989

37. In section 27 of the Opticians Act 1989 (sale and supply of optical appliances), at the end of subsection (4)(b)(i) there shall be inserted "or the National Health Service and Community Care Act 1990".

Section 66(2)   SCHEDULE 10

Enactments Repealed

Chapter	Short title	Extent of repeal
1 & 2 Geo. 6 c. 73.	The Nursing Homes Registration (Scotland) Act 1938.	Section 1(3)(bb) and (bc).
11 & 12 Geo. 6 c. 29.	The National Assistance Act 1948.	In section 21(8) the words from the beginning to "subsection". Section 22(7). In section 26, in subsections (2) and (5) the words "subsection (1) of". Section 35(2) and (3). Section 36. In section 41(1) the words "the Mental Health Act 1959, or" Section 54.
7 & 8 Eliz. 2 c. 72.	The Mental Health Act 1959.	In section 8, subsection (1), in subsection (2) the words from the beginning to "description; and" and the words "accommodation or" in the second place where they occur and subsection (3).
1968 c. 46.	The Health Services and Public Health Act 1968.	Section 44(1). In section 45, in subsection (5), in paragraph (b) the word "36" and in paragraph (c) the word "54".
1968 c. 49.	The Social Work (Scotland) Act 1968.	In section 1, in subsection (4)(b), the word "and" and subsection (4)(c).
1970 c. 44.	The Chronically Sick and Disabled Persons Act 1970.	In section 2(1) the words from "to the provisions" in the first place where they occur, to "the purpose) and".
1971 c. 40.	The Fire Precautions Act 1971.	In section 40, subsections (2)(c) and (10).

Chapter	Short title	Extent of repeal
1972 c. 70.	The Local Government Act 1972.	In Schedule 23, in paragraph 2, in sub-paragraph (3) the words from "in sub-section (1)" to "whereby" and" and "of that section" and sub-paragraph (7), and paragraph 9(1).
1973 c. 32.	The National Health Service Reorganisation Act 1973.	In Schedule 4, paragraph 45.
1975 c. 14.	The Social Security Act 1975.	In section 35(6)(a) the words from "paragraph 2" to "1977".
1975 c. 22.	The Children Act 1975.	In section 99(1)(b) the words "paragraph (a) of section 1(4) and".
1976 c. 83.	The Health Services Act 1976.	The whole Act.
1977 c. 49.	The National Health Service Act 1977.	In section 8, in subsection (1) the word "areas", in each place where it occurs, and in paragraph (b) the word "or", where it first appears; subsection (1A) (b); in subsection (2) the words "area or" (and "Area or"), in each place where they occur; in subsection (3) the words "areas or" and "area or"; subsection (5). Section 10(7). In section 11(1) the words "Area or". In section 12(a) the words "Area Health Authorities". In section 13(1) the words "an Area Health Authority of which the area is Wales". In section 14 the words "Area or" and "area or" in each place where they occur. In section 16, in subsection (1) the words "Area or" where they occur in paragraphs (c) and (d); in subsection (2) the words "an Area Health Authority", in the first place where they occur and the words "an Area Health Authority and a District Health Authority are equivalent to each other". In section 18(3) the words "Area or". Section 33(7). In section 41(b) the final word "and". Section 55. Section 85(1)(e), (3) and (4). In section 91(3)(b) the words "Area or". In section 97(6) the word "Area". In section 98, subsections (1)(b) and (3). Section 99(1)(b). In Schedule 5, Parts I and II in paragraph 8 the words "Area Health Authority" and paragraph 15(2). In Schedule 8, in paragraph 2, sub-paragraph (1)(a), in sub-paragraph (3) the words "residential accommodation or", and sub-paragraph (4). In Schedule 14, in paragraph 13(1)(b) the word "44". In Schedule 15, paragraphs 5, 24(1), 63 and 67.

Chapter	Short title	Extent of repeal
1978 c. 29.	The National Health Service (Scotland) Act 1978.	Section 2(9). Sections 5 and 6. In section 7(2), the words from "by local authorities" to "and for the appointment". In section 10, in subsection (4), the words "the Planning Council", and subsection (9). Section 13A(1)(c). Section 13B. Section 23(7). Section 57(3). Section 85(1)(a). Section 86(2). In section 108(1), the definitions of "the national consultative committees" and "the Planning Council". Schedul 3. In Schedule 15, in paragraph 10(b) "82" and paragraph 15.
1978 c. 44.	The Employment Protection (Consolidation) Act 1978.	In section 99, in subsection (1), paragraph (c) and the word "or" immediately preceding it. In section 111(1)(a) the words "or paragraph (c)". Section 138(5). Section 149(1)(d). Schedule 5.
1980 c. 53.	The Health Services Act 1980.	Sections 12 to 15. Section 22. In Schedule 1, paragraph 5; in paragraph 78, sub-paragraphs (2) to (6); paragraph 79. In Schedule 2, paragraphs 1 to 6. Schedule 3. In Schedule 4, paragraph 7(b).
1983 c. 20.	The Mental Health Act 1983.	Section 124. In section 135(6) the words from "or under" to "1977".
1983 c. 41.	The Health and Social Services and Social Security Adjudications Act 1983.	In section 30, in subsection (3), paragraph (a) and in the words following paragraph (b) the words "2(1) and" and "respectively".
1984 c. 22.	The Public Health (Control of Disease) Act 1984.	In section 37(1) the words "Area or". In section 41(1) the words "Area or".
1984 c. 23.	The Registered Homes Act 1984.	Section 25(1)(d) and (e).
1984 c. 36.	The Mental Health (Scotland) Act 1984.	Section 13(1)(c).
1984 c. 48.	The Health and Social Security Act 1984.	In Schedule 3, paragraphs 6(a) and 12.
1986 c. 33.	The Disabled Persons (Services, Consultation and Representation) Act 1986.	In section 2(5)(b), the words "or Schedule 8 to the 1977 Act".
1986 c. 50.	The Social Security Act 1986.	In Schedule 10, paragraph 32(2).
1986 c. 66.	The National Health Service (Amendment) Act 1986.	Sections 1 and 2.
1988 c. 9.	The Local Government Act 1988.	In Schedule 1, in paragraph 2(4)(b) the words from "Schedule 8" to "1977".

Chapter	Short title	Extent of repeal
1988 c. 41.	The Local Government Finance Act 1988.	In Schedule 1, in paragraph 9(2)(b) the words from "or paragraph" to "1977".
1988 c. 49.	The Health and Medicines Act 1988.	In Schedule 2, paragraph 11.
1989 c.42.	The Local Government and Housing Act 1989.	In section 184, subsections (1) and (3).
1990 c. 19.	The National Health Service and Community Care Act 1990.	Section 36(5).

INDEX

References are to section numbers but see the rubrics under the headings 'Community Care:
Scotland' and 'National Health Service: Scotland'

ENTERTAINMENTS (INCREASED PENALTIES) ACT 1990

(1990 c. 20)

An Act to increase the penalties for certain offences under enactments relating to the licensing of premises or places used for dancing, music or other entertainments of a like kind.

[13th July 1990]

PARLIAMENTARY DEBATES
Hansard, H.C. Vol. 168, col. 1110; Vol. 171, col. 650; H.L. Vol. 520, cols. 1007, 1619, 2019. The Bill was considered in Standing Committee G on March 29, 1990.

INTRODUCTION
Legislation which affects both public and private entertainment already exists to provide for the licensing of places which are used for music, dancing or other similar entertainment; offences and penalties are included within these provisions. This Act is intended to amend the existing sections which prescribe the penalties to be incurred, by introducing a new maximum penalty of a fine of £20,000, six months' imprisonment, or both, for each of certain offences contained within these sections.

Offences under the Local Government Act 1963 (c.33), Sched. 12 (current penalty: fine at level 5 on the standard scale (£2,000), three months' imprisonment, or both), the Private Places of Entertainment (Licensing) Act 1967 (c.19), s.4 (current penalty: fine at level 4 on the standard scale (£1,000), three months' imprisonment, or both), the Local Government (Miscellaneous Provisions) Act 1982 (c.30), Sched. 1 (current penalty: fine at level 5 on the standard scale (£2,000) and the Civic Government (Scotland) Act 1982 (c.45), s.7 are all susceptible to changes under the new legislation.

For the three Acts which relate to England and Wales the relevant offences are those concerning the use of a place for an entertainment when either no licence has been granted or activity is being undertaken in breach of any terms or conditions relating to the limitation of the number of people who may be present; for the Scottish Act the relevant offences are those relating to failure to have a public entertainments licence or failure to comply with conditions limiting admittance.

The Act is not intended to affect directly public finance or public service manpower.

Increase of penalties: England and Wales

1.—(1) For sub-paragraph (3) of paragraph 10 of Schedule 12 to the London Government Act 1963 (licensing of public entertainments in Greater London) there shall be substituted the following sub-paragraphs—

"(3) Any person guilty of an offence under sub-paragraph (1) or (2) of this paragraph shall be liable on summary conviction—

(a) in the case of an offence to which sub-paragraph (3A) of this paragraph applies, to a fine not exceeding £20,000 or to imprisonment for a term not exceeding six months or to both;

(b) in any other case, to a fine not exceeding level 5 on the standard scale or to imprisonment for a term not exceeding three months or to both.

(3A) This sub-paragraph applies to—

(a) any offence under sub-paragraph (1) of this paragraph where the entertainment provided is entertainment in respect of which a licence is required under paragraph 1 of this Schedule; and

(b) any offence under sub-paragraph (2) of this paragraph where the licence held is a licence granted under that paragraph and the term, condition or restriction which is contravened imposes a limit on the number of persons who may be present at the entertainment,

but excluding (in each case) any offence which would not be an offence if section 3 of the Greater London Council (General Powers) Act 1978

20–1

(premises used for public entertainment consisting wholly or partly of human posing deemed to be premises used for public dancing) had not been enacted."

(2) For subsection (3) of section 4 of the Private Places of Entertainment (Licensing) Act 1967 there shall be substituted the following subsections—
"(3) Any person guilty of an offence under this section shall be liable on summary conviction—
    (a) in the case of an offence to which subsection (3A) of this section applies, to a fine not exceeding £20,000 or to imprisonment for a term not exceeding six months or to both;
    (b) in any other case, to a fine not exceeding level 4 on the standard scale or to imprisonment for a term not exceeding three months or to both.
(3A) This subsection applies to—
    (a) any offence under subsection (1) of this section; and
    (b) any offence under subsection (2) of this section where the terms, conditions or restrictions which are contravened or not complied with include one which imposes a limit on the number of persons who may be present at the entertainment."

(3) In paragraph 12 of Schedule 1 to the Local Government (Miscellaneous Provisions) Act 1982 (licensing of public entertainments outside Greater London)—
    (a) in sub-paragraphs (1) and (2) the words "and liable on summary conviction to a fine not exceeding level 5 on the standard scale" shall be omitted; and
    (b) after sub-paragraph (2) there shall be inserted the following sub-paragraphs—
"(2A) Any person guilty of an offence under sub-paragraph (1) or (2) above shall be liable on summary conviction—
    (a) in the case of an offence to which sub-paragraph (2B) below applies, to a fine not exceeding £20,000 or to imprisonment for a term not exceeding six months or to both;
    (b) in any other case, to a fine not exceeding level 5 on the standard scale.
(2B) This sub-paragraph applies to—
    (a) any offence under sub-paragraph (1) above where the entertainment provided is entertainment to which paragraph 1 or 3 above applies; and
    (b) any offence under sub-paragraph (2) above where the licence in force is a licence under paragraph 1 or 4 above and the terms, conditions or restrictions which are contravened or not complied with include one which imposes a limit on the number of persons who may be present at the entertainment."

Increase of penalties: Scotland

2.—(1) In subsection (1) of section 7 of the Civic Government (Scotland) Act 1982 (maximum penalty for not having a required licence), after the word "conviction" there shall be inserted the words—
    "(a) in a case where the licence so required is a public entertainment licence, to a fine not exceeding £20,000 or to imprisonment for a term not exceeding six months or to both; and
    (b) in any other case,".
(2) In subsection (2) of that section (maximum penalty for non-compliance with licence condition) after the word "conviction" there shall be inserted the words—

"(a) in a case where the licence is a public entertainment licence and the condition is attached under section 41(3)(b) of this Act, to such fine or imprisonment as is mentioned in subsection (1)(a) above (or to both); and

(b) in any other case,".

Short title, saving and extent

3.—(1) This Act may be cited as the Entertainments (Increased Penalties) Act 1990.

(2) Nothing in this Act shall have effect in relation to offences committed before the coming into force of this Act.

(3) This Act does not extend to Northern Ireland.

INDEX

References are to section numbers

LICENSING (LOW ALCOHOL DRINKS) ACT 1990

(1990 c. 21)

An Act to amend the definition of "intoxicating liquor" in the Licensing Act 1964 and "alcoholic liquor" in the Licensing (Scotland) Act 1976 with respect to alcohol in low alcohol drinks.

[13th July 1990]

PARLIAMENTARY DEBATES
Hansard, H.C. Vol. 165, col. 1241; Vol. 170, col. 1673; H.L. Vol. 520, cols. 1107, 1798. The Bill was considered in Standing Committee C on February 28, 1990.

INTRODUCTION
The definition of "intoxicating liquor" contained in the Licensing Act 1964 (c.26), s.201, and the Licensing (Scotland) Act 1976 (c.66), s.139, (both as amended) indicates that liquor of a strength not greater than 1.2 per cent. is excluded from this classification. This Act amends these interpretations by making provision to substitute a strength of 0.5 per cent. as the level under which alcohol will not be classified as intoxicating.

Low alcohol liquor not to be intoxicating liquor for the purposes of the Licensing Act 1964

1. In the definition of "intoxicating liquor" in section 201(1) of the Licensing Act 1964, for paragraph (a) (exclusion of any liquor which, whether made on the premises of a brewer for sale or elsewhere, is found on analysis of a sample thereof at any time to be of an original gravity not exceeding 1016° and of a strength not exceeding 1.2 per cent.) there shall be substituted the following—

"(a) any liquor which is of a strength not exceeding 0.5 per cent at the time of the sale or other conduct in question;".

Corresponding provision for Scotland

2. In the definition of "alcoholic liquor" in section 139(1) of the Licensing (Scotland) Act 1976 (which contains the same exclusion) for the words from "on analysis of" to the words "1.2%" there shall be substituted the words "is of a strength not exceeding 0.5%".

Short title commencement and extent

3.—(1) This Act may be cited as the Licensing (Low Alcohol Drinks) Act 1990.

(2) This Act shall come into force on such day as the Secretary of State may by order made by statutory instrument appoint; but if and to the extent that it has not come into force before January 1, 1994 it shall come into force automatically on that date.

(3) This Act does not extend to Northern Ireland.

INDEX

References are to section numbers

TERM AND QUARTER DAYS (SCOTLAND) ACT 1990*

(1990 c. 22)

An Act to regulate, in relation to Scotland, the dates of Whitsunday, Martinmas, Candlemas and Lammas; and for connected purposes.

[13th July 1990]

PARLIAMENTARY DEBATES

Hansard, H.L. Vol. 520, col. 373.
The Bill was considered in Second Scottish Standing Committee on May 2, 1990.

INTRODUCTION AND GENERAL NOTE

This Act gives effect to the proposals in the Report on the Scottish Term and Quarter Days by the Scottish Law Commission, which was published in October 1987 (Scot. Law Com. No. 108). Consideration of the issue by the Commission was prompted by the Scottish Landowners' Federation in 1986, and the Report was preceded by a Consultation Paper which was published in July 1986.

Whitsunday, Martinmas, Candlemas and Lammas are the only expressions currently used in Scottish legal practice to denote specific dates. They are most commonly encountered in the context of leases, particularly of agricultural subjects. Collectively they are referred to as the quarter days because they divide the legal year into four parts. Whitsunday and Martinmas are also referred to as term days because they are employed in leases to denote terms or days on which a tenant takes entry to or removes from leased subjects. Various definitions of the term and quarter days have developed, some at common law and some as a result of statutory provisions. There have also been significant local variations, all of which has caused considerable confusion, which this Act is intended to resolve.

Term days of Whitsunday and Martinmas

The ecclesiastical definition of Whitsunday was (and remains) the seventh Sunday after Easter. As Easter is a moveable date (being the first Sunday after the full moon which falls on or after the vernal equinox, presumed to be March 21, and accordingly capable of variation from March 22 to April 25), Whitsunday was also subject to significant variation. This caused problems regarding its use as a term date, particularly in the context of removings where the date could fall so late as to result in an outgoing tenant obtaining the benefit of early pasture. To resolve these problems, an Act of 1690, cap. 39, defined Whitsunday as May 15. This definition, originally restricted to the legal term of removing, was extended for all legal purposes by the Removings Act 1693. No such problem attended the definition of Martinmas which, at common law, was regarded as November 11 (Rankin, *The Law of Leases in Scotland* (3rd ed., 1916, p. 341)).

These definitions were, however, complicated by local variations resulting from the effect of the Calendar (New Style) Act 1750 which, in order to effect a change from the Julian to the Gregorian calendar, omitted eleven days between September 2 and September 14, 1752. In some localities, the definitions of Whitsunday and Martinmas were adjusted to May 26 and November 22 respectively to take into account the "missing" days, a practice sanctioned, probably accidentally, by transitional provisions in the 1750 Act.

Certain post-1693 statutes contain, in effect although not necessarily explicitly, definitions of the term days, usually for the restricted purposes of the particular statute. The Removal Terms (Scotland) Act 1886, s.4, the Agricultural Holdings (Scotland) Act 1949, s.93(1), and the Crofters (Scotland) Act 1955, s.37(1), specify May 28 and November 28; the Sheriff Courts (Scotland) Act 1907, s.37, specifies May 15 and November 11. Many difficulties surround the definitions in the Agricultural Holdings (Scotland) Act 1949, which (contrary to widespread belief) only apply to that Act and, unless the context otherwise requires, with the result that different dates can apply for different purposes in the same lease. Furthermore, it is always possible for the parties to an agreement (particularly a lease) to specify their own conventional definitions, and such definitions are frequently encountered in practice.

To resolve these problems, the 1990 Act defines Whitsunday and Martinmas as May 28 and November 28 respectively and the phrase "term days" as, unless the contexts otherwise requires, May 28 and November 28 (s.1(1)(a) and (c)).

Quarter days of Candlemas and Lammas

The other Scottish quarter days (Whitsunday and Martinmas being both term days and

---

*Annotations by D.C. Coull, LL.B., Ph.D., Solicitor.

quarter days) are Candlemas (the Feast of the Purification of the Virgin Mary) and Lammas (the Feast of First Fruits) which have established common law definitions of February 2 and August 1 respectively. The principal significance of the quarter days is in regard to the payment of rent, but the problem which they present is that, no matter which definitions of Whitsunday and Martinmas are adopted, the four quarter days fail to divide the year into equal portions. The Scottish Law Commission felt that the opportunity presented by defining Martinmas and Whitsunday should be extended by redefining Candlemas and Lammas in such a manner as to provide quarters of nearly equal duration, notwithstanding that the latter terms had established common law definitions. If Candlemas and Lammas are defined as February 28 and August 28 respectively, then, with the recommended new dates for Whitsunday and Martinmas, the year divides into three terms each of 92 days and one term of 89 days (90 days in a leap year) which is as near equal as can be achieved. Accordingly the 1990 Act defines Candlemas and Lammas as February 28 and August 28 respectively and the phrase "quarter days" as, unless the context otherwise requires, February 28, May 28, August 28 and November 28 (s.1(1)(b) and (d)).

Scope of the definitions
The changes effected by the 1990 Act apply solely for legal purposes and do not apply, for example, to any ecclesiastical definition of the term days (s.1(2) and (3)). It is not possible to contract out of the new definitions, but where in a lease or other document one of the traditional expressions is used followed by a specific date other than the statutory one (*e.g.* "Whitsunday (May 15)"), the specific date will prevail and the traditional expression shall be disregarded (s.1(7)).

Transitional provisions
Difficulties may arise when a deed executed before the 1990 Act comes into force uses one of the traditional terms but does not stipulate a specific date because, in the absence of such specification, the new definition will apply (s.1(4)). In order to allow parties to such deeds, and in particular commercial landlords, who may be very significantly affected, to reach agreement as to how such difficulties are to be resolved (*e.g.* by entering into a separate agreement stipulating the dates which will apply), the Act does not come into force until the end of the period of 12 months beginning with the date upon which it received the Royal Assent (*i.e.* on July 13, 1991 (s.3(2)). Where agreement cannot be reached, any party having an interest may make a summary application to the sheriff, within the said 12 month period, for a declaration to the effect that the date inserted by the parties to the deed was a specific date other than the statutory date. The decision of the sheriff is final (s.1(5) and (6)). Furthermore, as a period prescribed by a notice (*e.g.* a notice to quit) could span the date of commencement of the Act, it is provided that where any notice given before the date upon which the Act comes into force uses one of the traditional expressions, that expression should be construed as if the Act had not been passed (s.2(1)). To avoid the Act having retrospective effect, it is expressly provided that the Act shall not affect any right or obligation which is enforceable before it comes into force (s.2(2)).

Application
The Act extends to Scotland only.

Whitsunday, Martinmas, Candlemas and Lammas

1.—(1) For the purposes mentioned in subsection (2) below—
(a) Whitsunday and Martinmas mean May 28 and November 28 respectively;
(b) Candlemas and Lammas mean February 28 and August 28 respectively;
(c) the term days shall, unless the context otherwise requires, be May 28 and November 28; and
(d) the quarter days shall, unless the context otherwise requires, be February 28, May 28, August 28 and November 28.
(2) The purposes referred to in subsection (1) above are the purposes of—
(a) any enactment or rule of law;
(b) any lease, agreement or undertaking which is entered into or given, or any document which is executed, after this subsection comes into force.
(3) In this Act—

(a) any reference to a lease, agreement or undertaking is a reference to a lease, agreement or undertaking, whether written or oral;

(b) any reference to a document is a reference to a document intended to have legal effect.

(4) Subject to subsection (5) below, where in a lease, agreement or undertaking which is subsisting when, or in a document which has been executed before, this subsection comes into force there is a reference to any of the following—

(a) Whitsunday, Martinmas, Candlemas or Lammas; or

(b) a term or quarter day,

without further specification as to date or month, the date applicable to the reference shall be the date prescribed therefor in paragraph (a), (b), (c) or (d) of subsection (1) above.

(5) Subsection (4) above shall not apply if the sheriff (on a summary application made within the period of 12 months beginning with the date of the passing of this Act) on being satisfied that the date intended in the lease, agreement, undertaking or document was a specific date other than the date so prescribed, makes a declaration accordingly.

(6) The decision of the sheriff on a summary application under subsection (5) above shall be final.

(7) Where in a lease, agreement or undertaking which is entered into or given, or in a document which is executed, after this subsection comes into force there is a reference such as is mentioned in subsection (4)(a) or (b) above and a date is specified therefor which is a date other than the date prescribed therefor in paragraph (a), (b), (c) or (d) of subsection (1) above, the date so specified shall have effect and the reference shall be disregarded.

Subs. (1)(c) and (d)
There have not hitherto been statutory definitions of the expressions "term days" and "quarter days" although the latter expression has conventionally been taken to denote Candlemas, Whitsunday, Lammas and Martinmas collectively. The expression "term days" is commonly encountered in leases with no further specification, although it may be possible to deduce the meaning from other parts of the deed. The definitions now prescribed will apply unless the context otherwise requires. For the effect on subsisting agreements, see subs. (4); for the result when a date other than a statutory date is specified, see subs. (7).

Subss. (2) and (3)
The statutory definitions apply for legal purposes only. They extend to oral as well as written agreements and to common law as well as statutory provisions. However, they do not apply for the purpose of allocating holidays, religious festivals, or other ecclesiastical purposes.

Subss. (4) and (7)
Where in an agreement (or other document), whether entered into or executed before or after the Act comes into force, there is a reference to a term or quarter day and the parties have expressly stipulated the specific date which is to apply, that date will prevail and the statutory definition will have no effect.

Subss. (5) and (6)
Entitlement to make application to the sheriff is not restricted to the parties to the agreement; accordingly any party having an interest may apply, *e.g.* a heritable creditor who has entered into possession of leased subjects. Application to the sheriff may be made at any time within the period of 12 months after the date of the passing of the Act, *i.e.* up to July 12, 1991. The statutory definitions will not apply unless the sheriff has disposed of the application, even if that is outwith the 12 month period (see s.3(3)).

Saving provisions and repeal

2.—(1) Any notice which—

(a) is given in relation to any lease, agreement, undertaking or document before this section comes into force (other than a notice given in accordance with a declaration of the sheriff under section 1(5) of this Act); and

22–3

    (b) contains a reference (expressly or by implication) to Whitsunday, Martinmas, Candlemas or Lammas, or to a term day or quarter day, shall, without further specification as to date or month, have effect and be enforceable as if this Act had not been passed.

    (2) Nothing in this Act shall affect—

    (a) any right; or

    (b) any obligation,

which is enforceable before this section comes into force.

    (3) The Removings Act 1693 is hereby repealed.

Subs. (1)

    But for this subsection, the statutory definitions would apply to any notice given before the Act comes into force, even if the parties had provided their own definitions of the term or quarter days. This would be patently unfair and accordingly the statutory definitions will not apply to such a notice, unless the notice has been given in accordance with a declaration by a sheriff in terms of s.1(5).

Subs. (2)

    This subsection is intended to remove any suggestion that the Act operates in a retrospective manner. The legislation does not affect rights and obligations arising under an agreement entered into, and enforceable before, the Act comes into force.

Subs. (3)

    The Removings Act 1693 (Act 1693, cap. 40) preserved and extended the definition of Whitsunday as May 15 contained in the Act 1690, cap. 39.

Short title, commencement and extent

    3.—(1) This Act may be cited as the Term and Quarter Days (Scotland) Act 1990.

    (2) This Act (except section 1(5) and (6) and this section) shall come into force at the end of the period of 12 months beginning with the date on which it is passed.

    (3) This Act (except section 1(5) and (6) and this section) shall not apply to a lease, agreement, undertaking or document in relation to which a summary application under section 1(5) of this Act is pending until the application has been disposed of.

    (4) This Act extends to Scotland only.

Subs. (2)

    This subsection is designed to allow parties to subsisting agreements to consider the effect which the new definitions will have on their rights and obligations, to attempt to reach private agreements in order to resolve difficulties or to apply to the sheriff in the event of failure so to do, to adjust collection records, and, especially in the case of commercial landlords, to take account of any disruption to cash flow.

Subs. (3)

    See note on s.1(5) and (6).

INDEX

References are to section numbers

ACCESS TO HEALTH RECORDS ACT 1990

(1990 c. 23)

ARRANGEMENT OF SECTIONS

Preliminary

An Act to establish a right of access to health records by the individuals to whom they relate and other persons; to provide for the correction of inaccurate health records and for the avoidance of certain contractual obligations; and for connected purposes.

[13th July 1990]

PARLIAMENTARY DEBATES
Hansard, H.C. Vol. 167, col. 1227; H.L. Vol. 520, col. 1206.
The Bill was considered in Standing Committee B on May 23, 1990.

INTRODUCTION
   Since the introduction of the Data Protection Act 1984 (c.35), patients have been entitled to access to their computerised health records. This Act is aimed at providing the equivalent right of access to information which is recorded in manually held health records. Regulations are made as to who is entitled to have access to such records and in what form they will be presented.
   An application may be made by either the patient or, in certain circumstances, by another on his or her behalf and applications must be answered within specified time limits, as determined within the Act, depending on the proximity of the treatment.
   A number of exceptions are made as to entitlement to see records; a child, or in Scotland a pupil, will be denied access unless it can be established that he or she is "capable of understanding the nature of the application"; a parent or guardian can not procure the records on his or her behalf unless the patient consents or is seen to be incapable of understanding the nature of the application but it is deemed to be in his or her best interest to gain such access. Any condition or term in a contract which purports to require an individual to supply someone else with a copy or part of his or her health record, as made available under this Act, will subsequently be held as void.
   The emphasis thus seems to be on an individual's control of personal and private information.
   Access to health files will not only allow people to examine exactly what has been recorded about them, satisfying personal curiosity, but, perhaps more importantly, will allow for mistakes to be noted and rectified; s.6 provides for the correction of any inaccuracies found in records.
   Several exceptions are created which curb the actual scope of access; no pre-commencement material can be shown unless necessary for the full understanding of a part which has already been released; if the holder of the information is of the opinion that disclosure of the information requested would result in either serious physical or mental harm to the patient, or to another, access can be denied; if the disclosure would allow the identification of an individual other than the patient, or a health professional who provided information contained

in the record, the information will be withheld (in this case consent may be gained from the said individual). In addition, if the request for information is made by anyone other than the patient, no material will be released that the patient would not have expected to be released.

The Secretary of State can also make regulations to add to these exceptions.

Provision is made in order to enable an applicant to enforce compliance with a request. An order may be made by either the High Court or county court in England, or the Court of Sessions or the sheriff in Scotland, requiring compliance by the holder of the record; the court has the jurisdiction to request access to the record, or part, in question during deliberations over entitlement but the information will not be disclosed to the applicant before a determination that access should be granted is made. The Secretary of State may prescribe arrangements for dealing with complaints about non-compliance to be made by the holders, and in these circumstances the court can not hear an application for redress until such channels have been utilised.

Preliminary

"Health record" and related expressions

1.—(1) In this Act "health record" means a record which—

(a) consists of information relating to the physical or mental health of an individual who can be identified from that information, or from that and other information in the possession of the holder of the record; and

(b) has been made by or on behalf of a health professional in connection with the care of that individual;

but does not include any record which consists of information of which the individual is, or but for any exemption would be, entitled to be supplied with a copy under section 21 of the Data Protection Act 1984 (right of access to personal data).

(2) In this Act "holder", in relation to a health record, means—

(a) in the case of a record made by, or by a health professional employed by, a general practitioner—

(i) the patient's general practitioner, that is to say, the general practitioner on whose list the patient is included; or

(ii) where the patient has no general practitioner, the Family Practitioner Committee or Health Board on whose medical list the patient's most recent general practitioner was included;

(b) in the case of a record made by a health professional for purposes connected with the provision of health services by a health service body, the health service body by which or on whose behalf the record is held;

(c) in any other case, the health professional by whom or on whose behalf the record is held.

(3) In this Act "patient", in relation to a health record, means the individual in connection with whose care the record has been made.

Health professionals

2.—(1) In this Act "health professional" means any of the following, namely—

(a) a registered medical practitioner;

(b) a registered dentist;

(c) a registered optician;

(d) a registered pharmaceutical chemist;

(e) a registered nurse, midwife or health visitor;

(f) a registered chiropodist, dietician, occupational therapist, orthoptist or physiotherapist;

(g) a clinical psychologist, child psychotherapist or speech therapist;

(h) an art or music therapist employed by a health service body; and

(i) a scientist employed by such a body as head of a department.

(2) Subsection (1)(a) above shall be deemed to include any person who is provisionally registered under section 15 or 21 of the Medical Act 1983 and is engaged in such employment as is mentioned in subsection (3) of that section.

(3) If, after the passing of this Act, an order is made under section 10 of the Professions Supplementary to Medicine Act 1960, the Secretary of State may by order make such consequential amendments of subsection (1)(f) above as may appear to him to be necessary or expedient.

(4) The provisions of this Act shall apply in relation to health professionals in the public service of the Crown as they apply in relation to other health professionals.

Main Provisions

Right of access to health records

3.—(1) An application for access to a health record, or to any part of a health record, may be made to the holder of the record by any of the following, namely—

(a) the patient;

(b) a person authorised in writing to make the application on the patient's behalf;

(c) where the record is held in England and Wales and the patient is a child, a person having parental responsibility for the patient;

(d) where the record is held in Scotland and the patient is a pupil, a parent or guardian of the patient;

(e) where the patient is incapable of managing his own affairs, any person appointed by a court to manage those affairs; and

(f) where the patient has died, the patient's personal representative and any person who may have a claim arising out of the patient's death.

(2) Subject to section 4 below, where an application is made under subsection (1) above the holder shall, within the requisite period, give access to the record, or the part of a record, to which the application relates—

(a) in the case of a record, by allowing the applicant to inspect the record or, where section 5 below applies, an extract setting out so much of the record as is not excluded by that section;

(b) in the case of a part of a record, by allowing the applicant to inspect an extract setting out that part or, where that section applies, so much of that part as is not so excluded; or

(c) in either case, if the applicant so requires, by supplying him with a copy of the record or extract.

(3) Where any information contained in a record or extract which is so allowed to be inspected, or a copy of which is so supplied, is expressed in terms which are not intelligible without explanation, an explanation of those terms shall be provided with the record or extract, or supplied with the copy.

(4) No fee shall be required for giving access under subsection (2) above other than the following, namely—

(a) where access is given to a record, or part of a record, none of which was made after the beginning of the period of 40 days immediately preceding the date of the application, a fee not exceeding the maximum prescribed under section 21 of the Data Protection Act 1984; and

(b) where a copy of a record or extract is supplied to the applicant, a fee not exceeding the cost of making the copy and (where applicable) the cost of posting it to him.

(5) For the purposes of subsection (2) above the requisite period is—
(a) where the application relates to a record, or part of a record, none of which was made before the beginning of the period of 40 days immediately preceding the date of the application, the period of 21 days beginning with that date;
(b) in any other case, the period of 40 days beginning with that date.
(6) Where—
(a) an application under subsection (1) above does not contain sufficient information to enable the holder of the record to identify the patient or, in the case of an application made otherwise than by the patient, to satisfy himself that the applicant is entitled to make the application; and
(b) within the period of 14 days beginning with the date of the application, the holder of the record requests the applicant to furnish him with such further information as he may reasonably require for that purpose,
subsection (5) above shall have effect as if for any reference to that date there were substituted a reference to the date on which that further information is so furnished.

Cases where right of access may be wholly excluded

4.—(1) Where an application is made under subsection (1)(a) or (b) of section 3 above and—
(a) in the case of a record held in England and Wales, the patient is a child; or
(b) in the case of a record held in Scotland, the patient is a pupil,
access shall not be given under subsection (2) of that section unless the holder of the record is satisfied that the patient is capable of understanding the nature of the application.
(2) Where an application is made under subsection (1)(c) or (d) of section 3 above, access shall not be given under subsection (2) of that section unless the holder of the record is satisfied either—
(a) that the patient has consented to the making of the application; or
(b) that the patient is incapable of understanding the nature of the application and the giving of access would be in his best interests.
(3) Where an application is made under subsection (1)(f) of section 3 above, access shall not be given under subsection (2) of that section if the record includes a note, made at the patient's request, that he did not wish access to be given on such an application.

Cases where right of access may be partially excluded

5.—(1) Access shall not be given under section 3(2) above to any part of a health record—
(a) which, in the opinion of the holder of the record, would disclose—
(i) information likely to cause serious harm to the physical or mental health of the patient or of any other individual; or
(ii) information relating to or provided by an individual, other than the patient, who could be identified from that information; or
(b) which was made before the commencement of this Act.
(2) Subsection (1)(a)(ii) above shall not apply—
(a) where the individual concerned has consented to the application; or
(b) where that individual is a health professional who has been involved in the care of the patient;
and subsection (1)(b) above shall not apply where and to the extent that, in the opinion of the holder of the record, the giving of access is necessary in order to make intelligible any part of the record to which access is required to be given under section 3(2) above.

(3) Where an application is made under subsection (1)(c), (d), (e) or (f) of section 3 above, access shall not be given under subsection (2) of that section to any part of the record which, in the opinion of the holder of the record, would disclose—

(a) information provided by the patient in the expectation that it would not be disclosed to the applicant; or

(b) information obtained as a result of any examination or investigation to which the patient consented in the expectation that the information would not be so disclosed.

(4) Where an application is made under subsection (1)(f) of section 3 above, access shall not be given under subsection (2) of that section to any part of the record which, in the opinion of the holder of the record, would disclose information which is not relevant to any claim which may arise out of the patient's death.

(5) The Secretary of State may by regulations provide that, in such circumstances as may be prescribed by the regulations, access shall not be given under section 3(2) above to any part of a health record which satisfies such conditions as may be so prescribed.

Correction of inaccurate health records

6.—(1) Where a person considers that any information contained in a health record, or any part of a health record, to which he has been given access under section 3(2) above is inaccurate, he may apply to the holder of the record for the necessary correction to be made.

(2) On an application under subsection (1) above, the holder of the record shall—

(a) if he is satisfied that the information is inaccurate, make the necessary correction;

(b) if he is not so satisfied, make in the part of the record in which the information is contained a note of the matters in respect of which the information is considered by the applicant to be inaccurate; and

(c) in either case, without requiring any fee, supply the applicant with a copy of the correction or note.

(3) In this section "inaccurate" means incorrect, misleading or incomplete.

Duty of health service bodies etc. to take advice

7.—(1) A health service body or Family Practitioner Committee shall take advice from the appropriate health professional before they decide whether they are satisfied as to any matter for the purposes of this Act, or form an opinion as to any matter for those purposes.

(2) In this section "the appropriate health professional", in relation to a health service body (other than a Health Board which is the holder of the record by virtue of section 1(2)(a) above), means—

(a) where, for purposes connected with the provision of health services by the body, one or more medical or dental practitioners are currently responsible for the clinical care of the patient, that practitioner or, as the case may be, such one of those practitioners as is the most suitable to advise the body on the matter in question;

(b) where paragraph (a) above does not apply but one or more medical or dental practitioners, are available who, for purposes connected with the provision of such services by the body, have been responsible for the clinical care of the patient, that practitioner or, as the case may be, such one of those practitioners as was most recently so responsible; and

(c) where neither paragraph (a) nor paragraph (b) above applies, a health professional who has the necessary experience and qualifications to advise the body on the matter in question.

(3) In this section "the appropriate health professional", in relation to a Family Practitioner Committee or a Health Board which is the holder of the record by virtue of section 1(2)(a) above, means—

(a) where the patient's most recent general practitioner is available, that practitioner; and

(b) where that practitioner is not available, a registered medical practitioner who has the necessary experience and qualifications to advise the Committee or Board on the matter in question.

Supplemental

Applications to the court

8.—(1) Subject to subsection (2) below, where the court is satisfied, on an application made by the person concerned within such period as may be prescribed by rules of court, that the holder of a health record has failed to comply with any requirement of this Act, the court may order the holder to comply with that requirement.

(2) The court shall not entertain an application under subsection (1) above unless it is satisfied that the applicant has taken all such steps to secure compliance with the requirement as may be prescribed by regulations made by the Secretary of State.

(3) For the purposes of subsection (2) above, the Secretary of State may by regulations require the holders of health records to make such arrangements for dealing with complaints that they have failed to comply with any requirements of this Act as may be prescribed by the regulations.

(4) For the purpose of determining any question whether an applicant is entitled to be given access under section 3(2) above to any health record, or any part of a health record, the court—

(a) may require the record or part to be made available for its own inspection; but

(b) shall not, pending determination of that question in the applicant's favour, require the record or part to be disclosed to him or his representatives whether by discovery (or, in Scotland, recovery) or otherwise.

(5) The jurisdiction conferred by this section shall be exercisable by the High Court or a county court or, in Scotland, by the Court of Session or the sheriff.

Avoidance of certain contractual terms

9. Any term or condition of a contract shall be void in so far as it purports to require an individual to supply any other person with a copy of a health record, or of an extract from a health record, to which he has been given access under section 3(2) above.

Regulations and orders

10.—(1) Regulations under this Act may make different provision for different cases or classes of cases including, in particular, different provision for different health records or classes of health records.

(2) Any power to make regulations or orders under this Act shall be exercisable by statutory instrument.

(3) Any statutory instrument containing regulations under this Act or an order under section 2(3) above shall be subject to annulment in pursuance of a resolution of either House of Parliament.

Interpretation

11. In this Act—

"application" means an application in writing and "apply" shall be construed accordingly;

"care" includes examination, investigation, diagnosis and treatment;

"child" means an individual who has not attained the age of 16 years;

"general practitioner" means a medical practitioner who is providing general medical services in accordance with arrangements made under section 29 of the National Health Service Act 1977 or section 19 of the National Health Service (Scotland) Act 1978;

"Health Board" has the same meaning as in the National Health Service (Scotland) Act 1978;

"health service body" means—

    (a) a health authority within the meaning of the National Health Service Act 1977;

    (b) a Health Board;

    (c) a State Hospital Management Committee constituted under section 91 of the Mental Health (Scotland) Act 1984; or

    (d) a National Health Service trust first established under section 5 of the National Health Service and Community Care Act 1990 or section 12A of the National Health Service (Scotland) Act 1978;

"information", in relation to a health record, includes any expression of opinion about the patient;

"make", in relation to such a record, includes compile;

"parental responsibility" has the same meaning as in the Children Act 1989.

Short title, commencement, and extent

12.—(1) This Act may be cited as the Access the Health Records Act 1990.

(2) This Act shall come into force on November 1, 1991.

(3) This Act does not extend to Northern Ireland.

INDEX

References are to section numbers

RIGHTS OF WAY ACT 1990*

(1990 c. 24)

An Act to amend the law relating to rights of way and the disturbance and restoration of the surface of land over which rights of way pass; to keep the line of rights of way clear of crops; to enable local authorities to act in connection therewith; and for connected purposes.

[13th July 1990]

PARLIAMENTARY DEBATES
Hansard, H.C. Vol. 167, col. 1180; Vol. 171, col. 1340; Vol. 175, col. 1257; H.L. Vol. 519, col. 1485; Vol. 520, cols. 1000, 1691, 2018.
The Bill was considered in Standing Committee C on April 25, 1990.

INTRODUCTION
This Act establishes a new legal regime for rights of way over cultivated arable land. It originated in a Private Member's Bill entitled the *Rights of Way (Agricultural Land) Bill*, introduced by Mr Edward Leigh M.P.

ABBREVIATIONS
1980 Act: the Highways Act 1980.

Amendment of Part IX of Highways Act 1980

1.—(1) Part IX of the Highways Act 1980 (lawful and unlawful interference with highways and streets) is amended as follows.
(2) After section 131 insert the following—

"Disturbance of surface of certain highways

131A.—(1) A person who, without lawful authority or excuse, so disturbs the surface of—
 (a) a footpath,
 (b) a bridleway, or
 (c) any other highway which consists of or comprises a carriageway other than a made-up carriageway,
as to render it inconvenient for the exercise of the public right of way is guilty of an offence and liable to a fine not exceeding level 3 on the standard scale.
(2) Proceedings for an offence under this section shall be brought only by the highway authority or the council of the non-metropolitan district, parish or community in which the offence is committed; and, without prejudice to section 130 (protection of public rights) above, it is the duty of the highway authority to ensure that where desirable in the public interest such proceedings are brought."
(3) For section 134 (ploughing of footpath or bridleway) substitute—

"Ploughing etc. of footpath or bridleway

134.—(1) Where in the case of any footpath or bridleway (other than a field-edge path) which passes over a field or enclosure consisting of agricultural land, or land which is being brought into use for agriculture—

---

* Annotations by Malcolm Forster, Director, Centre for Environmental Law, Faculty of Law, University of Southampton.

(a) the occupier of the field or enclosure desires in accordance with the rules of good husbandry to plough, or otherwise disturb the surface of, all or part of the land comprised in the field or enclosure, and

(b) it is not reasonably convenient in ploughing, or otherwise disturbing the surface of, the land to avoid disturbing the surface of the path or way so as to render it inconvenient for the exercise of the public right of way,

the public right of way shall be subject to the condition that the occupier has the right so to plough or otherwise disturb the surface of the path or way.

(2) Subsection (1) above does not apply in relation to any excavation or any engineering operation.

(3) Where the occupier has disturbed the surface of a footpath or bridleway under the right conferred by subsection (1) above he shall within the relevant period, or within an extension of that period granted under subsection (8) below,—

(a) so make good the surface of the path or way to not less than its minimum width as to make it reasonably convenient for the exercise of the right of way; and

(b) so indicate the line of the path or way on the ground to not less than its minimum width that it is apparent to members of the public wishing to use it.

(4) If the occupier fails to comply with the duty imposed by subsection (3) above he is guilty of an offence and liable to a fine not exceeding level 3 on the standard scale.

(5) Proceedings for an offence under this section in relation to a footpath or bridleway shall be brought only by the highway authority or the council of the non-metropolitan district, parish or community in which the offence is committed.

(6) Without prejudice to section 130 (protection of public rights) above, it is the duty of the highway authority to enforce the provisions of this section.

(7) For the purposes of this section "the relevant period",—

(a) where the disturbance of the surface of the path or way is the first disturbance for the purposes of the sowing of a particular agricultural crop, means fourteen days beginning with the day on which the surface of the path or way was first disturbed for those purposes; or

(b) in any other case, means twenty-four hours beginning with the time when it was disturbed.

(8) On an application made to the highway authority before the disturbance or during the relevant period, the authority may grant an extension of that period for an additional period not exceeding twenty-eight days.

(9) In this section "minimum width", in relation to a highway, has the same meaning as in Schedule 12A to this Act."

(4) For section 135 (temporary diversion of path or way ploughed under section 134) substitute—

"Authorisation of other works disturbing footpath or bridleway

135.—(1) Where the occupier of any agricultural land, or land which is being brought into use for agriculture, desires to carry out in relation to that land an excavation or engineering operation, and the excavation or operation—

(a) is reasonably necessary for the purposes of agriculture, but

(b) will so disturb the surface of a footpath or bridleway which passes over that land as to render it inconvenient for the exercise of the public right of way, he may apply to the highway authority for an order that the public right of way shall be subject to the condition that he has the right to disturb the surface by that excavation or operation during such period, not exceeding three months, as is specified in the order ("the authorisation period").

(2) The highway authority shall make an order under subsection (1) above if they are satisfied either—

(a) that it is practicable temporarily to divert the path or way in a manner reasonably convenient to users; or

(b) that it is practicable to take adequate steps to ensure that the path or way remains sufficiently convenient, having regard to the need for the excavation or operation, for temporary use while it is being carried out.

(3) An order made by a highway authority under subsection (1) above—

(a) may provide for the temporary diversion of the path or way during the authorisation period, but shall not divert it on to land not occupied by the applicant unless written consent to the making of the order has been given by the occupier of that land, and by any other person whose consent is needed to obtain access to it;

(b) may include such conditions as the authority reasonably think fit for the provision, either by the applicant or by the authority at the expense of the applicant, of facilities for the convenient use of any such diversion, including signposts and other notices, stiles, bridges, and gates;

(c) shall not affect the line of a footpath or bridleway on land not occupied by he applicant;

and the authority shall cause notices of any such diversion, together with a plan showing the effect of the diversion and the line of the alternative route provided, to be prominently displayed throughout the authorisation period at each end of the diversion.

(4) An order made by a highway authority under subsection (1) above may include such conditions as the authority reasonably think fit—

(a) for the protection and convenience during the authorisation period of users of the path or way;

(b) for making good the surface of the path or way to not more than its minimum width before the expiration of the authorisation period;

(c) for the recovery from the applicant of expenses incurred by the authority in connection with the order.

(5) An order under this section shall not authorise any interference with the apparatus or works of any statutory undertakers.

(6) If the applicant fails to comply with a condition imposed under subsection (3)(b) or (4)(a) or (b) above he is guilty of an offence and liable to a fine not exceeding level 3 on the standard scale.

(7) Proceedings for an offence under this section in relation to a footpath or bridleway shall be brought only by the highway authority or (with the consent of the highway authority) the council of the non-metropolitan district, parish or community in which the offence is committed.

(8) Without prejudice to section 130 (protection of public rights) above, it is the duty of the highway authority to enforce the provisions of this section.

(9) In this section "minimum width", in relation to a highway, has the same meaning as in Schedule 12A to this Act."

(5) After section 137 insert the following—

"Interference by crops

137A.—(1) Where a crop other than grass has been sown or planted on any agricultural land the occupier of the land shall from time to time take such steps as may be necessary—

(a) to ensure that the line on the ground of any relevant highway on the land is so indicated to not less than its minimum width as to be apparent to members of the public wishing to use the highway; and

(b) to prevent the crop from so encroaching on any relevant highway, whether passing over that or adjoining land, as to render it inconvenient for the exercise of the public right of way.

(2) For the purposes of subsection (1) above, a crop shall be treated as encroaching on a highway if, and only if, any part of the crop grows on, or otherwise extends onto or over, the highway in such a way as to reduce the apparent width of the highway to less than its minimum width.

(3) For the purposes of the application of subsection (1) above in the case of a particular crop, the crop shall be treated as grass if, and only if—

(a) it is of a variety or mixture commonly used for pasture, silage, or haymaking, whether or not it is intended for such a use in that case; and

(b) it is not a cereal crop.

(4) If the occupier fails to comply with the duty imposed by subsection (1) above he is guilty of an offence and liable to a fine not exceeding level 3 on the standard scale.

(5) Without prejudice to section 130 (protection of public rights) above, it is the duty of the highway authority to enforce the provisions of this section.

(6) In this section—

"minimum width", in relation to a highway, has the same meaning as in Schedule 12A to this Act; and

"relevant highway" means—

(a) a footpath,

(b) a bridleway, or

(c) any other highway which consists of or comprises a carriageway other than a made-up carriageway."

(6) After section 160 insert the following—

"Further powers of highway authorities and district councils in relation to highways.

160A. Schedule 12A to this Act shall have effect."

DEFINITIONS

"agricultural": s.329(1) of the 1980 Act.

"agriculture": s.329(1) of the 1980 Act.

"bridleway": s.328 of the 1980 Act.

"carriageway": s.329(1) of the 1980 Act.

"field-edge path": ss.2 and 329(1) of the 1980 Act.

"footpath": s.329(1) of the 1980 Act.

"highway": s.328 of the 1980 Act.

"highway authority": s.1 of the 1980 Act.

"made-up carriageway": s.329(1) of the 1980 Act.

"minimum width": ss.1(2), 4: s.139A(9) and Sched. 12A of the 1980 Act.

"relevant period": s.1(2); s.139A(7) of the 1980 Act.

Subs. 2

This subsection introduces specifically a new s.113A into the 1980 Act. The section as a whole provides that it is to be a criminal offence for any person, without lawful excuse, to disturb the surface of a footpath, bridleway or any other unmade-up highway so as to "render it inconvenient for the exercise of the public rights of way".

This provision provides the sub-stratum for the limited exceptions which follow in what are now ss.134 and 135 of the 1980 Act. Note that this section is cast in general terms and is not confined to farmers ploughing up paths across fields, but could be applied to any interference with the surface—*e.g.* if a golf club place a new bunker across the line of a footpath. In fact, the main reason for the enactment of the section was the loss of field-edge paths running across the headlands of ploughed fields.

Note that there is a restriction on the right to prosecute for non-compliance with the duty, in that only highway or local authorities can bring a prosecution. This restriction is, however, balanced by an obligation on highway authorities to prosecute "where desirable in the public interest".

Note also that the "default power" provisions of the new Sched. 12A (see below) apply where this section has been contravened.

Level 3 on the standard scale is currently £400.

Subs. 3

This subsection substitutes a new s.134 of the 1980 Act, dealing with the ploughing up of footpaths and bridleways.

The purpose of the new section is to strike a fair and workable balance between the interests of the farming community and walkers and horsemen and horsewomen using the footpath or bridleway. The section provides that, where a footpath or bridleway passes over a field and the occupier of the field wishes, "in accordance with the rules of good husbandry" to plough the field and he can not do so without so disturbing the surface of the path so as to render it inconvenient for the exercise of the public rights of way, those rights shall be subject to the occupier's right to so disturb the surface.

Note that there is no right to disturb the surface of a field-edge path, *i.e.* one which follows the sides or headlands of a field; see s.2 (s.329(1) of the 1980 Act). Note also that the right only applies to *public* rights of way. Disturbance of the surface over which a private right of way is enjoyed may expose the farmer to a private action for interference with the easement.

Plough or otherwise disturb the surface. The former s.134 was unsatisfactory in practice in a number of ways. It only conferred a right to plough the land crossed by the footpath or bridleway, and this restricted right gave rise to much debate, *e.g.* as to whether hoeing, ridging up, harrowing, etc. fell within the provisions of the section. Note that this section only deals with disturbances caused by crop-related operations. Disturbance from excavations and engineering operations are the subject of the new s.135—see s.1(3)(2) (s.134(2) of the 1980 Act).

The preconditions

Good husbandry. The section does not confer a right to plough paths indiscriminately, far less as a means of hindering their use. The right conferred by the section can only be exercised when the principles and rules of good husbandry prevail. "Good husbandry" is a familiar concept in agricultural law, more readily recognised than defined. For a broad statement of what is entailed in good husbandry, see s.11 of the Agriculture Act 1947.

The farming community had manifested some concern about their obligations in respect of land taken out of arable production under the "set-aside" scheme. Although "set-aside" does not involve the growing of crops (indeed quite the opposite), it does require that the land entered in the scheme be worked from time to time. The Countryside Commission, in its advice to farmers on this point, stresses that the right conferred by this section extends to "set-aside" land, but, more importantly, so does the duty to make good the surface of the path (see below).

Not reasonably convenient to avoid disturbance. The right given by the section is to be seen as a last resort. If the land can be worked in a reasonably convenient manner without disturbing the surface of the footpath or bridleway, the farmer must adopt that course. If he does not, he may commit an offence under the new s.131A. This is, effectively, a reversal of the terms of the previous s.134, which provided that paths could be ploughed if "convenient".

Subs. (3)(3)

Having availed himself of the right conferred by the new s.134(1), however, the occupier must then restore the surface of the path or bridleway to not less than a minimum width so as to enable rights to be exercised with reasonable convenience and he must also indicate the line of the path or way (also indicating its minimum width) so that it is apparent to members of the public wishing to use it.

Making good. In view of the varying nature of the works which may have to be done to restore paths on differing soil types in different parts of the country, the Act does not try to spell out in any detail the kind of steps which a farmer must take to make good a path whose surface has been disturbed. Case-law under the earlier versions of this section would suggest that the standard to be expected of the farmer would depend, at least in part, on the use to which the path or way had been put. Thus, a path which is used by villagers to go from one side of the village to another wearing ordinary clothes and footwear may have to be restored to a standard higher than a remote hill-path normally only used by hikers wearing walking boots. Note that the duty to make good does not refer to the pre-existing condition of the path. Thus, it would appear that a farmer may have to restore a path which prior to the disturbance was in a poor condition to a state in which the rights over it can be exercised with reasonable convenience, thus effectively "improving" the path.

Marking the route on the ground. This is a new requirement imposed by the 1990 Act, to obviate the previous frustrations felt by walkers and riders who were unable to discern the line of the path or way on the ground. Not only the line of the path, but also its minimum width (see below) must be marked out. It should not be thought that the farmer is thus obliged to erect elaborate way-marks (such as those used by National Park Authorities or the National Trust). The Countryside Commission has suggested that, in some cases, it might be sufficient to mark the line with tractor-tracks or markers at 100–150 metre intervals.

Relevant period. See subs. (7).

Subs. (3)(4)

This section makes it clear that it is the occupier's responsibility to ensure that the section is complied with. The previous version of the section fixed criminal liability on "a person" who contravened it, with the result that there was doubt about the farmer's liability when he had employed independent contractors. The doubt on this point is now removed, and therefore occupiers should take care to satisfy themselves that contractors employed by them are competent to make good and mark paths and ways disturbed by them.

Subs. (3)(5),(6)

Note that, here also, there is a restriction on the right to prosecute for non-compliance with the duty, in that only highway or local authorities can bring a prosecution. In this case, however, the highway authority (but not other authorities) is under a duty to enforce the section.

Subs. (3)(7)

Paths and ways must be restored within 14 days from the first ploughing, where the disturbance is created by the sowing of an agricultural crop, and within 24 hours in any other case. Note that there is a new 14-day period for each new crop.

Minimum widths are one metre for a footpath and two metres for a bridleway—see below.

Subs. (3)(8)

There is no prescribed form of application for an extension. Applications should be made before the relevant period in question has expired, otherwise the farmer will be in breach of the Act as soon as the 14 days or 24 hours elapse.

Subs. (4)

S.134 does not apply to excavations or engineering operations, but these are covered by a new s.135 introduced by the 1990 Act. If an occupier of land crossed by a footpath or bridleway wishes to undertake excavations or engineering works which will interfere with the path or way, but which are reasonably necessary for the purposes of agriculture (a common example being the construction of field drains), he may not simply undertake those works. Instead, he must apply to the highway authority for an order subjecting the right of way to interruption for the period specified in the order (which shall not exceed three months). Before making such an order, the highway authority must satisfy itself that it is practicable temporarily to divert the right of way in a manner reasonably convenient to users (or that the right of way can still be used reasonably conveniently while the works are being carried out). Such orders may also be made subject to conditions relating to, *e.g.* the protection of users and making good the surface to the statutory minimum width during the currency of the notice.

Although it looks rather restrictive, this section in fact confers a new right on farmers. Though not uncommon for farmers to disturb paths and ways in the course of these operations, there was in fact no legal right to do so (it not being "ploughing" within the meaning of the former s.134). Now, a farmer who makes a s.135 application has an inconvertible right to break up the surface of a path or way.

Note that the order is limited in time to the duration of the works. It is not, therefore, a form of "back-door" diversion.

Subs. (4)(3)

Note that, although notices of the order must be posted when it has been made, there are no obligations as to publication of the application, nor any provision for representations to be made by those using the path or way.

Subs. (4)(7),(8)

Failure to comply with the section is a criminal offence, but, once again, prosecutions can only be instituted by the highway authority or the local authority. As with s.134, however, the highway authority (but not other authorities) is under a duty to enforce the section.

Subs. (5)

This section introduces a new obligation on occupiers to ensure that growing crops do not so encroach upon a footpath, bridleway or any other unmade-up highway as to render it inconvenient for use. The section is introduced as a result of a marked increase in obstructions of this sort, many being exacerbated by the spread of crops such as oil-seed rape which have a tendency to "flop" over onto paths, etc.

There are two aspects to the new duty, first, to ensure that the line of the way remains visible throughout the crop-cycle, and, secondly to prevent the encroachment of crops. Crops "encroach" for this purpose if they reduce the apparent width of the highway to less than its statutory minimum. This provision does not apply to grass crops, *i.e.* crops (other than cereals) of a variety of mixture "commonly used for pasture, silage or hay-making".

Subs. (5)

In contrast to s.131A, 134 and 135, any person (including a private individual) may bring a prosecution for contravention of this section.

Amendment of s.329(1) of Highways Act 1980

2. In section 329(1) (further provision as to interpretation) of the Highways Act 1980 insert immediately before the definition of "financial year"—
" 'field-edge path' means a footpath or bridleway that follows the sides or headlands of a field or enclosure;".

GENERAL NOTE

There was no such definition in s.329(1) of the 1980 Act as originally drawn, although s.134(2) made it clear that there was no right to plough field-edge paths. The repeal of that version of s.134 by this Act made this section necessary.

Amendment of s.333 of Highways Act 1980

3. In section 333 (saving for rights and liabilities as to interference with highways) of the Highways Act 1980, number the existing provision as subsection (1) and insert at the end—
"(2) Nothing in section 134 or 135 above relating to disturbance of the surface of a highway in any manner is to be taken as affecting any right existing apart from this Act to disturb its surface in that manner."

GENERAL NOTE

In some cases, farmers may be able to establish "common law rights to plough" over paths, etc. In such cases, it may be that, when the landowner dedicated the path, he did so on the conditions that he should have the right to plough the land over which it ran and that the public, rather that the landowner, should restore its surface—see, *e.g. Mercer* v. *Woodgate* (1869) L.R. 5 Q.B. 26.

Such rights are now extremely difficult to establish, but this section preserves those which can be proved.

Insertion of new Schedule 12A to Highways Act 1980

4. After Schedule 12 to the Highways Act 1980 insert—

"SCHEDULE 12A

FURTHER POWERS OF HIGHWAY AUTHORITIES AND COUNCILS IN RELATION TO INTERFERENCE WITH HIGHWAYS

Interpretation

1.—(1) For the purposes of this Schedule the "minimum width" and "maximum width" of a highway shall be determined in accordance with sub-paragraphs (2) and (3) below.

(2) In any case where the width of the highway is proved, that width is both the "minimum width" and the "maximum width".

(3) In any other case—
  (a) the "minimum width" is—
     (i) as respects a footpath which is not a field-edge path, 1 metre,
     (ii) as respects a footpath which is a field-edge path, 1.5 metres,
     (iii) as respects a bridleway which is not a field-edge path, 2 metres, or
     (iv) as respects any other highway, 3 metres; and
  (b) the "maximum width" is—
     (i) as respects a footpath, 1.8 metres,
     (ii) as respects a bridleway, 3 metres, or
     (iii) as respects any other highway, 5 metres.

Competent authorities

2. For the purposes of this Schedule each of the following shall be a competent authority in relation to a highway—
  (a) the highway authority; and
  (b) in the case of a highway maintained by a district council under section 42 or 50 of this Act, that council.

Power to carry out works

3.—(1) Where the surface of—
  (a) a footpath,
  (b) a bridleway, or
  (c) any other highway which consists of or comprises a carriageway other than a made-up carriageway,
has been so disturbed as to render it inconvenient for the exercise of the public right of way, a competent authority may make good the surface to an extent not less than the minimum width nor greater than the maximum width.

(2) Where the surface of a footpath or bridleway ws disturbed under the right conferred by section 134(1) of this Act, the power conferred by sub-paragraph (1) above shall not become exercisable until the expiration of the period which is the relevant period for the purposes of section 134 or an extension of that period granted under subsection (8) of that section.

(3) Where the surface of a footpath or bridleway was disturbed under an order made by virtue of section 135 of this Act, the power conferred by sub-paragraph (1) above shall not become exercisable until the expiration of the period which is the authorisation period for the purposes of section 135.

4.—(1) Where the occupier of any land fails to carry out the duty imposed on him by section 134(3)(b) or 137A(1) of this Act in relation to a highway, a competent authority may carry out such works as may be necessary or expedient for the purpose of rectifying the default.

(2) Sub-paragraph (1) above does not authorise the carrying out of works to an extent greater than the maximum width of the highway.

(3) Where the surface of a footpath or bridleway was disturbed under the right conferred by section 134(1) of this Act, the power conferred by sub-paragraph (1) above shall not become exercisable until the expiration of the period which is the relevant period for the purposes of section 134, or an extension of that period granted under subsection (8) of that section.

5. If the applicant fails to comply with a condition imposed under section 135(3)(b) or (4)(a) or (b) of this Act, a competent authority may carry out such works as may be necessary or expedient for the purpose of rectifying the default.

6. Paragraphs 7 to 9 below have effect in relation to the carrying out by a competent authority of work under paragraphs 3 to 5 above in relation to a highway which passes over any land ("the relevant land").

Entry on land

7. Subject to paragraph 8 below, any person duly authorised in writing by the authority may enter on the relevant land, or any other land the authorty reasonably believe to be in the same occupation, for any purpose connected with the carrying out of the work; and may take with him on to the land such vehicles, machinery and other equipment as may be requisite.

8.—(1) Except in the case of entry, solely for the purpose of obtaining information, on land other than a building or structure, before entering on any land the authority shall give the occupier not less than twenty-four hours' notice of their intention to do so; and the notice shall—

(a) identify the highway to which it relates; and

(b) specify the work to be carried out and the equipment to be used for that purpose; and

(c) identify the line or lines of passage over the land in question, if any, that may need to be used for access to the site of the work; and

(d) state the date and time when the power to enter on the land becomes exercisable.

(2) Without prejudice to section 322 (service of notices etc.) of this Act, if after reasonable enquiry the authority are satisfied that it is not practicable to ascertain the name and address of the occupier, a notice under this paragraph may be given by addressing it to him as "The Occupier" of the land (describing it) and affixing copies of the notice to some conspicuous object—

(a) at each end of so much of the highway as is referred to in the notice; and

(b) at such other points in the vicinity of that highway as the authority may consider suitable; and

(c) if appropriate, at a point adjacent to a highway comprising a made-up carriageway from which access is required for equipment.

(3) A notice shall not be given under this paragraph before the power referred to in paragraph 3, 4 or 5 above has become exercisable.

Financial

9.—(1) Subject to sub-paragraph (2) below, a competent authority may recover the amount of any expenses reasonably incurred by the authority in, or in connection with, the carrying out of the work—

(a) in a case falling within paragraph 3(1) above, from the occupier of the relevant land or the person who disturbed the surface of the highway; and

(b) in any other case, from the occupier of the relevant land.

(2) A person—

(a) is not liable under paragraph (a) of sub-paragraph (1) above if he shows that he had any lawful authority or excuse for disturbing the surface of the highway; and

(b) is not liable under that paragraph as an occupier of land if he shows that the surface of the highway was not disturbed by him or with his consent ."

GENERAL NOTE

This section contains a new code enabling highway authorities and district councils to take action themselves when a farmer is in default of his obligations under the various preceding sections of the Act.

The drafting of the 1980 Act was somewhat unsatisfactory in this respect. Highway and other authorities were obliged in practice to rely upon proceedings for obstruction, which were often drawn-out and which provided no immediate remedy. Also, there was frequently inconsistency among different magistrates' courts as to whether, *e.g.* growing crops, constituted an obstruction. The 1980 Act as originally drawn was also unclear as to whether, when authorities had themselves taken action to clear a blocked path or way, they could recover their costs.

The new Schedule seeks to put these matters beyond doubt.

Expenses

5. There shall be paid out of moneys provided by Parliament any increase attributable to the provisions of this Act in the sums payable out of moneys so provided under any other Act.

Short title, commencement, consequential repeals and extent

6.—(1) This Act may be cited as the Rights of Way Act 1990.

(2) This Act shall come into force at the end of the period of one month beginning with the day on which it is passed.

(3) Nothing in this Act shall affect the application of sections 134 and 135 of the Highways Act 1980 in relation to any ploughing of a footpath or bridleway begun before the commencement of this Act.

(4) Section 61 of the Wildlife and Countryside Act 1981 and section 21 of the Agriculture Act 1986 (which amend sections 134 and 135 of the Highways Act 1980) are hereby repealed.

(5) In paragraph 25 of Schedule 4 to the Local Government Act 1985, the words "134(7) and (10)(a)," are hereby repealed.

(6) This Act extends to England and Wales only.

INDEX

References in roman type are to section numbers of this Act. References in italic are to section numbers of Part IX or to Schedule 12A of the Highways Act 1980 (as amended)

BRIDLEWAY,
  disturbance of, 1(2), *131A*
    temporary, 1(4), *135*
  ploughing, 1(3), *134*

COMMENCEMENT, 6(2), (3)
COMPETENT AUTHORITIES, 4, *Sched. 12A.2*
  entry on land, right of, 4, *Sched. 12A.7, 8*
  power to carry out works, 4, *Sched. 12A.3 to 6*
  recovery of expenses, 4, *Sched. 12A.9*
  see also HIGHWAY AUTHORITY
CROPS, INTERFERENCE BY, 1(5), *137A*
  grass, 1(5), *137A.–(3)*

DISTURBANCE OF RIGHT OF WAY, 1(2), *131A*
  making good by competent authority, 4, *Sched. 12A.3 to 6*
  temporary, 1(4), *135*

ENGINEERING OPERATION, 1(3), *134.–(2)*
  authorisation of, 1(4), *135*
ENTRY ON LAND, 4, *Sched. 12A.7, 8*
EXCAVATION, 1(3), *134.–(2)*
  authorisation of, 1(4), *135*
EXPENSES, 5
EXTENT, 6(6)

FOOTPATH,
  disturbance of, 1(2), *131A*
    temporary, 1(4), *135*
  ploughing, 1(3), *134*

HIGHWAY (OTHER THAN MADE-UP HIGHWAY),
  disturbance of, 2(1), *131A.–(1)(c)*

HIGHWAY AUTHORITY,
  further powers, 1(6), *329(1)*, *Sched. 12*
  proceedings by, 1(2), *131A.–(2)*, 1(3), *134.–(5)*, 1(5), *137A.–(5)*
  see also COMPETENT AUTHORITIES

MAXIMUM WIDTH, 4, *Sched. 12A.1*
MINIMUM WIDTH, 1(3), 1(4), 1(5), *134(99)*, *135 (9)*, *137A.–(2),(6)*, *Sched. 12A.1*

OFFENCES,
  allowing interference by crops, 1(5), *137A*
  disturbing surface, 1(2), *131A.–(1)*
  failing to comply with temporary diversion order, 1(4), *135(6)*
  failing to make good, 1(3), *134.–(4)*

PLOUGHING OF RIGHT OF WAY, 1(3), *134*
  making good, 1(3), *134.–(3)*
    relevant period for, 1(3), *134(7),(8)*
  right of occupier, 1(3), *134.–(1)*

REPEALS, 6(4), (5)

SAVING, 3, *333*
SHORT TITLE, 6(1)

TEMPORARY DIVERSIONS, 1(4), *135*

24–11

HORSES (PROTECTIVE HEADGEAR FOR YOUNG RIDERS) ACT 1990

(1990 c. 25)

An Act to secure the wearing of protective headgear by children while horse riding; to prescribe offences and penalties; and for connected purposes. [13th July 1990]

PARLIAMENTARY DEBATES
  Hansard, H.C. Vol. 170, col. 1733; Vol. 171, col. 666; Vol. 175, col. 1272; H.L. Vol. 520, cols. 77, 975, 1516, 2075.
  The Bill was considered in Standing Committee C on April 4, 1990.

INTRODUCTION
  The Act is aimed at ensuring the safety of any minor who during the course of work or recreation is involved with horse riding ("horse" is defined broadly in s.3(1)). The onus is on parents, employers or any other person supervising or otherwise connected with the minor or the charge of the horse to secure the wearing of protective headgear by the rider and failure to do so may result in prosecution under one of the offences detailed in this Act (s.1). Specific reference is made to the Children and Young Persons Act 1933 (c.12) and the Children and Young Persons (Scotland) Act 1937 (c.37) in relation to defining a person who has responsibility for a child, or, who has custody, charge or care of the child, respectively, and to the relevant section of the Children Act 1989 (c.41) which is not yet in force. An indication as to the level of fine which would be imposed if found guilty is contained in s.1(3).
  There is also scope for the Secretary of State to make further regulations to prescribe the type of headgear deemed acceptable and any circumstance in which a minor would be permitted to ride without such protection.

Causing or permitting child under 14 to ride on road without protective headgear

1.—(1) Except as provided by regulations, it is an offence for any person to whom this subsection applies to cause or permit a child under the age of 14 years to ride a horse on a road unless the child is wearing protective headgear, of such description as may be specified in regulations, in such manner as may be so specified.
  (2) Subsection (1) above applies to the following persons—
  (a) any person who—
      (i) for the purposes of Part I of the Children and Young Persons Act 1933, has responsibility for the child; or
      (ii) for the purposes of Part II of the Children and Young Persons (Scotland) Act 1937, has custody, charge or care of the child;
  (b) any owner of the horse;
  (c) any person other than its owner who has custody of or is in possession of the horse immediately before the child rides it; and
  (d) where the child is employed, his employer and any other person to whose orders the child is subject in the course of his employment.
  (3) A person guilty of an offence under subsection (1) above is liable on summary conviction to a fine not exceeding level 1 on the standard scale.
  (4) Until the coming into force of paragraph 5 of Schedule 13 to the Children Act 1989, subsection (2)(a)(i) above shall have effect as if for "responsibility for the child" there were substituted "custody, charge or care of the child".

Regulations

2.—(1) The Secretary of State may by regulations made by statutory instrument—

(a) provide that section 1 of this Act shall not apply in relation to children of any prescribed description, or in relation to the riding of horses in such circumstances as may be prescribed;

(b) prescribe for the purposes of that section (by reference to shape, construction or any other quality) the descriptions of protective headgear to be worn by children of any prescribed description in prescribed circumstances; and

(c) prescribe for those purposes the manner in which such headgear is to be worn.

(2) Before making any regulations under this section the Secretary of State shall consult such representative organisations as he thinks fit.

(3) Any statutory instrument containing regulations under this section shall be subject to annulment in pursuance of a resolution of either House of Parliament.

Interpretation

3.—(1) In this Act—

"horse" includes pony, mule, donkey or other equine animal;

"regulations" means regulations under section 2 of this Act; and

"road" does not include a footpath or bridleway but, subject to that, has—

(a) in England and Wales the meaning given by section 192(1) of the Road Traffic Act 1988; and

(b) in Scotland the meaning given by section 151(1) of the Roads (Scotland) Act 1984.

(2) For the purposes of the definition of "road" in subsection (1) above—

(a) "footpath" means a way—

(i) over which the public have a right of way or, in Scotland, of passage on foot only; and

(ii) which is not associated with a carriageway; and

(b) "bridleway" means a way over which the public have the following, but no other, rights of way: a right of way on foot and a right of way on horseback or leading a horse, with or without a right to drive animals of any description along the way.

Corresponding provision for Northern Ireland

4. An Order in Council under paragraph 1(1)(b) of Schedule 1 to the Northern Ireland Act 1974 (legislation for Northern Ireland in the interim period) which states that it is made only for purposes corresponding to those of this Act—

(a) shall not be subject to paragraph 1(4) and (5) of that Schedule (affirmative resolution of both Houses of Parliament); but

(b) shall be subject to annulment in pursuance of a resolution of either House of Parliament.

Short title, commencement and extent

5.—(1) This Act may be cited as the Horses (Protective Headgear for Young Riders) Act 1990.

(2) This Act, apart from section 4 and this section, shall not come into force until such day as the Secretary of Sate may by order made by statutory instrument appoint.

(3) Section 4 and this section extend to Northern Ireland, but otherwise this Act does not extend there.

INDEX

References are to section numbers

GAMING (AMENDMENT) ACT 1990*

(1990 c. 26)

An Act to amend the provisions of the Gaming Act 1968 relating to premises licensed or registered under Part II of that Act.

[13th July 1990]

PARLIAMENTARY DEBATES
Hansard, H.L. Vol. 515, col. 1502; Vol. 517, col. 1103; H.C. Vol. 175, col. 1305.

INTRODUCTION AND GENERAL NOTE
This Act introduces minor amendments to the Gaming Act 1968. Its most important provision gives effect to a recommendation of the Royal Commission on Gambling (1978: Cm. 7200, paras. 19.31–19.37), giving power to the Gaming Board for Great Britain to vet any person who becomes the controller of a body corporate which holds a certificate of consent to apply for a gaming licence. Hitherto the Board has had power only to revoke a certificate if the conduct of the premises was effectively controlled by someone other than the holder; in the event of a take-over, the holder remains the same legal entity. This has led on occasion to some abuse of the legislation.
  The Act was sponsored by Lord Allen of Abbeydale and was supported by the Gaming Board for Great Britain, the British Casino Association and the Government.
  The Act does not extend to Northern Ireland.

COMMENCEMENT
This Act comes into force on September 13, 1990, but paras. 3 and 4 of the Schedule shall come into force on such day as the Secretary of State may appoint.

ABBREVIATION
The 1968 Act: Gaming Act 1968.

Amendments of Gaming Act 1968

1. Part II of the Gaming Act 1968 and Schedules 2 to 4 to that Act shall have effect with the amendments specified in the Schedule to this Act, being amendments the principal purpose of which is—
  (a) to make new provision with respect to the keeping and production of records in connection with club premises licensed under that Part;
  (b) to require the payment of fees when certificates of consent under Schedule 2 are applied for;
  (c) to require an application for the continuance of a certificate of consent to be made where the certificate is held by a body corporate and there is a change in a controller of that body; and
  (d) to require a public company which is the holder of a licence to notify changes in the holding of its shares.

Subs. 1(a)
  By the new s.22(1)(c) of the 1968 Act, the Secretary of State may make regulations requiring licence-holders to keep on their premises copies of the records concerning cheque transactions which, under s.22(1)(b), they are required to make and retain. Where the records are kept by means of computer, legible and visible print-outs must be available. S.43 of the 1968 Act is amended to give an inspector or constable power to take such print-outs from the premises.

Subs. 1(b)
  This imposes fees of £5,000 and £2,500 respectively upon applicants for certificates of consent to apply for and to transfer a licence under the 1968 Act. Where the licence is restricted to the playing of bingo, the fees are £1,500 and £500 respectively.

---

* Annotations by Dr David Miers, Senior Lecturer in Law, Cardiff Law School.

Subs. 1(c)

Where the holder of a certificate of consent to his applying for the grant of a licence under the 1968 Act is a body corporate, or a licence is transferred to a body corporate, and any person has, since the grant of the certificate of consent or the certificate of consent to transfer, become a "controller" of the holder, the holder shall make an application to the Board for the continuance of the certificate. This application is subject to the same criteria as apply to any first-time application for a certificate (Sched. 2, para. 4 of the 1968 Act). A controller means a person who alone, or with associates, is entitled to exercise 15 per cent. or more of the body corporate's voting power. These provisions do not apply to bingo club licences.

Subs. 1(d)

This imposes a duty on public companies to notify the Gaming Board of any change in shareholding which, by Pt. VI of the Companies Act 1985, the company is required to make. This currently means a change of 5 per cent. or more. This provision does not apply to bingo club licences.

Short title, commencement and extent

2.—(1) This Act may be cited as the Gaming (Amendment) Act 1990.

(2) Subject to subsection (3) below, this Act shall come into force at the end of the period of two months beginning with the day on which it is passed.

(3) Paragraphs 3 and 4 of the Schedule to this Act shall come into force on such day as the Secretary of State may appoint by an order made by statutory instrument; and different days may be appointed for different provisions or for different purposes.

(4) Paragraphs 3 and 4 of that Schedule do not affect applications made before they come into force.

(5) Paragraph 5 of that Schedule applies to certificates of consent issued before as well as after it comes into force.

(6) This Act does not extend to Northern Ireland.

DEFINITION

"Secretary of State": one of Her Majesty's Principal Secretaries of State; Interpretation Act 1978, Sched. I.

Section 1   SCHEDULE

AMENDMENTS OF GAMING ACT 1968

Keeping and production of records

1. After paragraph (b) of subsection (1) of section 22 there shall be inserted—
   "(c) during such period as may be so prescribed—
      (i) to keep those records or (if the regulations so provide) copies of them on the premises; or
      (ii) where those records are kept by means of a computer, to secure that the records are accessible from the premises and that the information comprised in those records can readily be produced in a form in which it can be taken away and in which it is visible and legible."

2.—(1) Section 43 shall be amended as follows.

(2) For subsection (2) there shall be substituted—
   "(2) Any inspector or constable may at any reasonable time enter any premises in respect of which a licence under this Act is for the time being in force, and while on the premises may—
      (a) inspect the premises and any machine or other equipment on the premises, and any book or document on the premises, which he reasonably requires to inspect for the purpose of ascertaining whether a contravention of this Act or of any regulations made under it is being or has been committed;
      (b) take copies of any such book or document or of any entry in it; and
      (c) if any information reasonably required by him for that purpose is contained in a computer and is accessible from the premises, require it to be produced in a form in which it can be taken away and in which it is visible and legible."

(3) After paragraph (c) of subsection (3) there shall be inserted—
"(ca) fails without reasonable excuse to comply with a requirement imposed in relation to those premises under subsection (2)(c) of this section; or".

(4) In subsection (5) the word "and" at the end of paragraph (a) shall be omitted and after that paragraph there shall be inserted—
"(aa) if he has reasonable cause to believe that any information which is contained in a computer and is accessible from the premises may be required for those purposes, require it to be produced in a form in which it can be taken away and in which it is visible and legible; and".

(5) After subsection (5) there shall be inserted—
"(5A) The holder of a licence under this Act in respect of any premises shall be guilty of an offence if he, or any person acting on his behalf, fails without reasonable excuse to comply with a requirement imposed in relation to those premises under subsection (5)(aa) of this section."

(6) In subsection (9) after the words "paragraphs (c)" there shall be inserted ",(ca)".

(7) After subsection (10) there shall be inserted—
"(11) In this section "document" has the same meaning—
(a) in England and Wales, as in Part I of the Civil Evidence Act 1968 and any reference to a copy of a document shall be construed in accordance with section 10(2) of that Act; and
(b) in Scotland, as in the Civil Evidence (Scotland) Act 1988 and any reference to a copy of a document shall be construed in accordance with section 6(2) of that Act."

Fees

3.—(1) Section 48 shall be amended as follows.

(2) In subsection (3) for the words "Except as provided by subsection (4)" there shall be substituted the words "Except as provided by subsections (4) and (4A)".

(3) After paragraph (c) of that subsection there shall be inserted—
"(ca) in respect of an application for a certificate consenting to the making of an application for the grant of a licence under this Act, a fee of £5,000;
(cb) in respect of an application for a certificate consenting to the making of an application for the transfer of such a licence, a fee of £2,500;".

(4) After subsection (4) there shall be inserted—
"(4A) Where the licence to which the certificate relates is to be, or is, subject to the restrictions mentioned in subsection (4) above, the fee to be charged under paragraph (ca) of subsection (3) of this section shall be £1,500 or £500 instead of £5,000 or £2,500."

(5) In subsection (5) for the words "subsection (3) or subsection (4)" there shall be substituted the words "subsection (3), (4) or (4A)".

(6) In subsection (6) for the words "fees charged in accordance with paragraph (f) or paragraph (g)" there shall be substituted the words "fees charged in accordance with paragraph (ca), (cb), (f) or (g)".

4. After paragraph 63 of Schedule 2 (payment of fees) there shall be inserted—
"63A. No application for a certificate of consent under this Schedule shall be treated as duly made until the appropriate fee has been paid to the Board."

Application for continuance of consent certificate

5. After paragraph 35 of Schedule 2 there shall be inserted—
"*Application for continuance of certificate following change of controller of body corporate.*

35A.—(1) Where the holder of a certificate of consent to his applying for the grant of a licence under this Act (other than a certificate limited to a bingo club licence) is a body corporate and at any time while the certificate is in force any person becomes a controller of the holder—
(a) the holder shall make an application to the Board for the continuance of the certificate in accordance with this paragraph; and
(b) on such an application the Board shall continue the certificate in force unless they determine to revoke it under the subsequent provisions of this paragraph.

(2) An application under this paragraph shall contain such particulars as the holder of the certificate can reasonably provide of the controller in question and of the nature and extent of his interest in the holder of the certificate and in any body corporate of which the holder is a subsidiary.

(3) An application under this paragraph shall be made within five weeks of the time when the person in question becomes a controller of the holder of the certificate but the Board may, in any particular case, entertain an application made later if—

(a) they are satisfied that the failure to make it before the end of that period was due to inadvertence; and

(b) the application is made before the end of such extended period as the Board may in that case allow.

(4) The Board may on an application under this paragraph revoke the certificate to which the application relates if it appears to them that, if the holder were then applying for such a certificate under paragraph 4 of this Schedule, they would in accordance with sub-paragraphs (5) and (6) of that paragraph determine not to issue it; and the Board may also revoke a certificate if the holder fails to make an application in respect of it in accordance with this paragraph in a case in which this paragraph requires him to do so.

(5) Where a licence (other than a bingo club licence) is transferred to a body corporate and—

(a) a person has become a controller of that body corporate at any time between the issuing of a certificate consenting to the application for the transfer and the transfer of the licence; or

(b) a person becomes a controller of that body corporate at any subsequent time, sub-paragraphs (1) to (4) above shall apply to that body corporate as they apply to the holder of the certificate by virtue of which the application for the licence was originally made except that the period of five weeks mentioned in sub-paragraph (3) shall, in a case within paragraph (a) above, run from the date on which the licence was transferred.

(6) Where on an application under this paragraph the Board continue a certificate in force they shall serve on the applicant a notice stating that they have done so; and sub-paragraphs (4), (5) and (6) of paragraph 35 of this Schedule shall have effect in relation to the revocation of a certificate by virtue of this paragraph as they have effect in relation to the revocation of a certificate by virtue of that paragraph.

(7) In this paragraph "controller", in relation to a body corporate, means a person who, either alone or with any associate or associates, is entitled to exercise, or control the exercise of, 15 per cent. or more of the voting power at any general meeting of the body corporate or of another body corporate of which it is a subsidiary.

(8) In sub-paragraph (7) above "associate", in relation to a person entitled to exercise or control the exercise of voting power in relation to a body corporate means—

(a) the wife or husband or son or daughter of that person;

(b) any company of which that person is a director;

(c) any person who is an employee or partner of that person;

(d) if that person is a company—

    (i) any director of that company;

    (ii) any subsidiary of that company;

    (iii) any director or employee of any subsidiary; and

(e) if that person has with any other person an agreement or arrangement with respect to the acquisition, holding or disposal of shares or other interests in that body corporate or under which they undertake to act together in exercising their voting power in relation to it, that other person.

(9) In this paragraph "subsidiary" has the same meaning as in the Companies Act 1985."

Notification of change in shareholding in public company

6. After paragraph 64 of Schedule 2 there shall be inserted—

"Notification of change in shareholding in public company

64A.—(1) Where the holder of a licence under this Act (other than a bingo club licence) is a public company, then, if at any time the company receives any notification under Part VI of the Companies Act 1985, the company shall send a copy of the notification to the Board as soon as reasonably practicable after that time.

(2) A company which fails to comply with sub-paragraph (1) of this paragraph shall be guilty of an offence and shall be liable on summary conviction to a fine not exceeding level 3 on the standard scale.

(3) In this paragraph "public company" has the meaning given by section 1(3) of the said Act of 1985."

Other amendments

7. In paragraph 4(6)(b) of Schedule 2 for the words ", the club to which the consent application relates" there shall be substituted the words "in respect of any club, that club".

8. In paragraph 56(4)(b) for the word "maintained" there shall be substituted the word "managed".

9. In paragraph 63(2), for the words "liable under section 21 of the Licensing (Scotland) Act 1959 to" there shall be substituted the word "who".

10.—(1) In Schedule 3 after paragraph 3(a) there shall be inserted—
    "(aa) the reference in paragraph 5(3) to the Board, and".
  (2) In paragraph 4 of that Schedule after the words "references to" there shall be inserted the words "the Board,".
  (3) In paragraph 3(3) of Schedule 4 the words "the Board," shall be omitted.

INDEX

References in roman type are to sections of this Act. References in italic are to paragraphs of the Schedule

SOCIAL SECURITY ACT 1990*

(1990 c. 27)

An Act to amend the law relating to social security and to occupational and personal pension schemes; to establish and confer functions on a Pensions Ombudsman and a Registrar of Occupational and Personal Pension

---

* Annotations by John Mesher, B.A., B.C.L., LL.M., Barrister, Reader in Law, Simmons & Simmons Research Fellow in Pension Law, University of Sheffield.

Schemes; to make provision for the payment of grants for the improvement of energy efficiency in certain dwellings; and for purposes connected therewith. [July 13, 1990]

PARLIAMENTARY DEBATES
Hansard, H.C. Vol. 165, col. 625; Vol. 170, cols. 495, 547, 1077; Vol. 176, cols. 72, 79; H.L. Vol. 518, col. 234; Vol. 520, cols. 10, 97, 113, 1273, 1691, 1893; Vol. 521, col. 279.
The Bill was considered in Standing Committee G from February 1–March 8, 1990.

INTRODUCTION AND GENERAL NOTE
A Social Security Act has become at least an annual event over the last ten years or so. Most of them contain a mixture of fundamental changes, tidying-up, corrections, reversal of inconvenient decisions and "lawyer's law." The 1990 Act is no exception. Although it is not a massive piece of legislation and does not introduce radical changes, it does contain a number of important innovations and developments of existing policy over a wide area.

The Government described the Act as having three strategic objectives (*Hansard*, H.C. Vol. 170, col. 1137, April 3, 1990 (Tony Newton); *Hansard*, H.L. Vol. 518, col. 234, April 20, 1990 (Lord Henley)), which are clearly regarded as the most important from the viewpoint of policy. These are (1) to continue the development of a more coherent structure of benefits for the disabled; (2) to strengthen the arrangements for the maintenance of lone parents and their children; and (3) to introduce greater protection for members of occupational pension schemes. The rest of the Act may be classified as covering (4) other changes to specific social security benefits, to contributions and to adjudication; (5) changes to the scheme for recovering social security benefits from payments of compensation for personal injury; and (6) the introduction of a new scheme of home insulation grants.

(1) Benefits for the disabled
Ss.1 to 4 are concerned with benefits for the disabled. S.1 introduces from October 1, 1990 a special rule for the terminally ill on a claim for attendance allowance. The normal six-month qualifying period is removed and a "fast track" for decision-making is to be introduced. This is in fulfilment of a commitment made in the House of Lords during the passage of the Social Security Act 1989.

Ss.2 to 4 form part of a package unveiled in the Government's document *The Way Ahead—Benefits for Disabled People* (Cm. 917, January 1990), which is described as helping to produce a fairer pattern of income maintenance for those who are unable to work as a result of disability. S.2 introduces an age-related addition to the non-contributory Severe Disablement Allowance at the same rates as the Invalidity Allowance attached to the contributory Invalidity Pension. This has been brought into effect from December 3, 1990. S.3 abolishes the Reduced Earnings Allowance within the Industrial Injuries scheme for accidents and diseases occurring after October 1, 1990. REA is regarded as overlapping anomalously with Invalidity Benefit. S.4 will remove the future build-up after April 1991 of the earnings-related Additional Pension payable with the basic Invalidity Pension. The AP is regarded as inhibiting the growth of occupational cover for long-term sickness. Overall, the aim of the package is to shift the emphasis of social security coverage towards those disabled people who have never been able to work or who have been disabled early in their working lives and to reduce the advantages held by those whose disablement is work-related. The way in which the package produces this result will be explored in the annotations to the individual sections.

(2) Maintenance for lone parents and their children
S.8 inserts (from October 15, 1990) two new sections into the Social Security Act 1986 and makes some other consequential amendments. First, where the lone parent on Income Support is not married to the other parent, and so is only entitled to maintenance for the child(ren), a court may include in an order obtained by the DSS an amount in respect of the income support paid to the claimant herself. Second, the DSS may transfer an order which it has obtained to the lone parent on her coming off income support. Third, the DSS is given power to enforce orders obtained by a lone parent on income support. The Government has made radical proposals concerning the whole system of maintenance in a White Paper, *Children Come First* (Cm. 1264, October 1990), but these changes are regarded as suitable for immediate introduction.

(3) Greater protection for members of occupational pension schemes
The relevant provisions are ss.11 to 14 and Scheds. 2 to 4. The amendments are far-reaching and detailed. They stem from the report of the Occupational Pensions Board *Protecting Pensions—Safeguarding Benefits in a Changing Environment* (Cm. 573, February 1989). The OPB had been asked to consider the issues in the report by the then Secretary of State for Social Security in April 1988 and almost all of its recommendations were accepted by the current

Secretary of State in November 1989. Although there have been some alterations as the legislation went through Parliament, the framework is still that proposed by the OPB. The 1990 Act operates by amendment of the Social Security Pensions Act 1975.

S.11 with Sched. 2 requires all final salary occupational pension schemes to increase pensions earned by service after a date to be specified once they come into payment. The required annual increase is to be in line with price increases up to a limit of five per cent. Schemes whose fund has a surplus will be required to provide increases to pensions earned by service before the specified date. At the moment increases of pensions in payment in many schemes are discretionary.

S.12 with Sched. 3 provides for the appointment from October 1, 1990 of a Pensions Ombudsman, with power to investigate disputes of fact or law between individuals and the trustees or managers of schemes or employers, to investigate claims of maladministration causing injustice and to make binding awards. The Ombudsman is perhaps the most innovative feature of the Act. The OPB recommended a Pensions Tribunal, rather than an Ombudsman. The implications of the change will be explored in the annotations to Sched. 3 (which contains the substance of the Ombudsman scheme). But all were agreed that an alternative to the High Court was essential.

S.13 provides for a registration scheme for occupational and personal pension schemes.

S.14 with Sched. 4 carries out what are described as miscellaneous amendments. The most important provisions require the appointment of an independent trustee when the employer becomes insolvent, make any deficiency in the assets of a scheme on its winding-up a debt due from the employer, place restrictions on schemes investing in employer-related assets and require the revaluation of preserved pensions earned by service before 1985 as well as those earned by service after 1984.

(4) Other social security changes

S.5 provides that s.165A of the Social Security Act 1975 (requiring a claim to be made before there can be entitlement to benefit) has retrospective effect.

S.6 provides special rules for late claims for widow's benefits where it is difficult to establish the husband's death.

S.9 will have effect once the new system giving financial responsibility for new residents in residential care and nursing homes to local authorities (originally planned for April 1991, but now postponed) comes into operation. It requires the Secretary of State, when prescribing the maximum rates for remaining income support beneficiaries, to take into account the amount which local authorities have agreed to pay.

S.10 gives the Secretary of State additional powers to make regulations and give directions about the social fund, following a series of judicial review decisions.

S.16 takes industrial injuries benefits out of the list of benefits paid out of the National Insurance Fund.

S.17 imposes new penalties for non-payment of social security contributions.

Sched. 6 contains a variety of amendments, particularly on the procedure for making regulations and on restricting the entitlements of other claimants when a person wins a test case against the DSS.

(5) Recovery of benefits from compensation payments

Sched. 1, implemented by s.7, makes some important changes in the scheme set up by the Social Security Act 1989 and beginning on September 3, 1990.

(6) Home insulation grants

S.15 empowers the Secretary of State to set up a scheme for home insulation grants by regulations and to give the decision-making power to an agency.

ABBREVIATIONS

A Day	: appointed day
AO	: adjudication officer
AP	: Additional Pension
DSS	: Department of Social Security
ESC	: earlier service component
GMP	: guaranteed minimum pension
IVB	: invalidity benefit
LPI	: limited price-indexing
LSC	: later service component
MAT	: Medical Appeal Tribunal
MIB	: Motor Insurers' Bureau
1975 Act	: Social Security Act 1975

OPAS	: Occupational Pensions Advisory Service
OPB	: Occupational Pensions Board
PCA	: Parliamentary Commissioner for Administration
REA	: Reduced Earnings Allowance
RPI	: Retail Price Index
SDA	: severe disablement allowance
SERPS	: State Earnings-Related Pension Scheme
SFO	: Social Fund Officer
SSAT	: Social Security Appeal Tribunal
The Way Ahead	: The Way Ahead—Benefits for Disabled People (Cm. 917, January 1990)

Benefits

Attendance allowance for the terminally ill

1.—(1) In section 35 of the principal Act (attendance allowance) after subsection (2A) there shall be inserted—

"(2B) If a terminally ill person makes a claim expressly on the ground that he is such a person, then—

  (a) he shall be taken for the purposes of subsection (2) above—

    (i) to satisfy, or to be likely to satisfy, both of those conditions for the remainder of his life, beginning with the date of the claim or, if later, the date determined under section 105 or 106 below as the first date on which he is terminally ill; and

    (ii) to have satisfied those conditions for the period of six months immediately preceding that date (so however that no allowance shall be payable by virtue of this sub-paragraph for any period preceding that date); and

  (b) the period specified in a certificate issued by virtue of paragraph (*a*) above shall be the remainder of the person's life, beginning with that date.

(2C) for the purposes of subsection (2B) above—

  (a) a person is "terminally ill" at any time if at that time he suffers from a progressive disease and his death in consequence of that disease can reasonably be expected within 6 months; and

  (b) where a person purports to make a claim for an attendance allowance by virtue of that subsection on behalf of another, that other shall be regarded as making the claim, notwithstanding that it is made without his knowledge or authority."

(2) In subsection (4) of that section, after the words "otherwise provide" there shall be inserted the words "and subject to subsection (2B) above."

(3) In section 105(3) of that Act (questions to be determined by the Attendance Allowance Board) after the words "whether a person" there shall be inserted "(a)" and for the words "section 35(1) of this Act" there shall be substituted the words—

"subsection (1) of section 35 above;

  (b) suffers, or has at any time suffered, from renal failure, for the purposes of subsection (2A) of that section; or

  (c) is or has at any time been terminally ill, within the meaning of subsection (2B) of that section.";

(4) In section 106 of that Act (review of, and appeal from, Board's decisions) at the beginning of subsection (1) there shall be inserted the words "Subject to the following provisions of this section" and after paragraph (*a*) of that subsection there shall be inserted—

"(aa) at any time review a determination of theirs under section 105(3) above or this subsection of any question whether a person is or was at any time terminally ill, within the meaning of section 35(2B) above, if there has been a change in medical

opinion with respect to his condition or his reasonable expectation of life.";
(5) After that subsection there shall be inserted—
"(1A) No determination under section 105(3) or subsection (1) above
shall be reviewed on the ground that the person in question is or was at
any time terminally ill, within the meaning of section 35(2B) above,
unless an application for review is made expressly on that ground
either—
(a) by the person himself; or
(b) by any other person purporting to act on his behalf, whether
or not that other person is acting with his knowledge or authority;
and a determination may be so reviewed on such an application, notwithstanding that no claim under section 35(2B) above has been made."
(6) In section 165A of that Act (making of claim a condition of entitlement) there shall be added at the end—
"(3) Where a person purports to make a claim for an attendance
allowance by virtue of section 35(2B) above on behalf of another, that
other shall be regarded for the purposes of this section as making the
claim, notwithstanding that it is made without his knowledge or
authority."
(7) It shall be the duty of the Secretary of State to publish a draft of the first
form to be used by terminally ill persons for claiming an attendance allowance, to invite comments on the draft from interested persons and organisations and to consider any such comments received within one month of
that invitation before ordering the printing of the form.

COMMENCEMENT
October 1, 1990 (Social Security Act 1990 (Commencement No. 1) Order 1990 (S.I. 1990 No.
1446), art. 2(h) and Sched., Part II).

DEFINITION
"the principal Act": s.20.

GENERAL NOTE
This section introduces a new alternative qualification for the higher rate of attendance
allowance. Normally a person must show that they need frequent attention or continual
supervision and that they have done so for six months before entitlement can start (Social
Security Act 1975, s.35(2)). This waiting period is due to be reduced to three months in 1992
when the new disability allowance, encompassing both attendance allowance and mobility
allowance, is introduced (*The Way Ahead*, para. 4.15). However, in fulfilment of an undertaking given while the Social Security Act 1989 was going through Parliament, a special rule has
been introduced for the terminally ill, with no waiting period. For many years there have been
complaints that the most seriously afflicted claimants frequently died before they could qualify
for the allowance. It is estimated that 58,000 people per year will benefit from it (*Hansard*, H.L.
Vol. 518, col. 235, April 20, 1990) and that the cost will rise from about £20 million in 1991 to
£35 million per year by 1992–3 (Standing Committee G, col. 10, February 1, 1990).
The success of the new rule will depend crucially on the definition of terminal illness, about
which much doubt was expressed in Parliament, and on the speed and sensitivity of decision-
making. On the latter point, a special unit is to be set up with 125 staff years allocated in the first
year and extra numbers to follow (Standing Committee G, col. 57, February 6, 1990, as
corrected in a letter quoted at col. 160 (February 15, 1990)). The aim is that decisions should be
made within two weeks of the date of claim (Standing Committee G, col. 11, February 1, 1990).
The major amendment is that carried out by subs. (1). The other amendments mainly deal
with issues of procedure.

Subs. (1)
Two new subsections are inserted into s.35 of the 1975 Act. The new subs. (2B) provides that
if a terminally ill person makes a claim expressly on the ground that he is such a person, he is
deemed to satisfy the medical conditions for the higher rate of allowance from the date of claim
(or the date that he meets the definition of terminally ill, if later) for the rest of his life (although
see the amendment made by subs. (4)). He does not have to show the need for any attention or
supervision. Subs. (2C) then provides the definition of terminally ill and starts a chain of
provisions about how claims can be made.

"Terminally ill". Under the new subs. (2C)(a) a person must be suffering from a progressive disease and his death in consequence of that disease must reasonably be expected within six months. He is terminally ill at any date on which those conditions are satisfied. The requirement that a person is suffering from a disease introduces a limitation. Although in the context of s.17 of the 1975 Act a disease has been described as "a departure from health identifiable by its signs and symptoms, an abnormality of some sort" (*CS 221/49*), it seems that the victims of accidents or those afflicted by disablements of various kinds could not be said to be suffering from a disease for that reason alone. The disease then has to be progressive. This seems to indicate that the disease in its nature is one which tends to worsen or is not curable by treatment. Mr Nicholas Scott, the Minister for Social Security, said in Committee that, "A progressive disease is one where the basic disease process is a continuing one. The examples that I gave earlier—HIV infection, MND [motor neurone disease] and cancer—are the three most common that come into that category. They are diseases in which the pathological changes are finite: it has to be a continuous process" (Standing Committee G, col. 34, February 1, 1990). This does not seem helpful in identifying any particular principle and it is suggested that the authorities will have to look to the ordinary meaning of the words used.

If there is a progressive disease, death in consequence must reasonably be expected within six months. First, it must be the case that the progressive disease need not be the sole cause of the predicted death. It must be enough that it is a significant operative cause, an effective cause. However, the question of what degree of likelihood of death from that cause within six months amounts to a reasonable expectation is one of judgment for the Attendance Allowance Board. Various alternatives were suggested, such as lengthening the period or making it more indeterminate, but none were acceptable to the Government. However, it was accepted that the formula was a difficult one and eventually a commitment was given that the provision would be monitored to see how satisfactorily the formula works (*Hansard*, H.L. Vol. 520, col. 1895, July 2, 1990). The period of six months was chosen not simply because of the length of the normal waiting period (so that there are no plans to change it in 1992) but because the Government was advised that the majority of those diagnosed as terminally ill die within three months (Standing Committee G, cols. 20 and 34, February 1, 1990). There may of course be a reluctance to diagnose terminal illness, and certainly in some circumstances to communicate the diagnosis to the patient or his family. Some attempt to meet these difficulties is made in the provisions on claims, discussed below.

The process envisaged is that the claimant's own doctor will attach a statement to the claim giving the claimant's medical condition, the treatment prescribed and the prognosis. The Attendance Allowance Board, through one of its delegated medical practitioners, will then determine whether the claimant is terminally ill or not (Standing Committee G, col. 11, February 1, 1990).

Claims. By virtue of the opening words of the new s.35(2B) the new rule only applies where the claimant expressly says that he is terminally ill. A person in that position may not know of the terminal diagnosis or may not be capable of claiming. Thus under the new s.35(2C)(b), whenever a person purports to claim attendance allowance under s.35(2B) for another, that other is regarded as making the claim even though he does not know about or authorise the claim (and see the amendment carried out by subs. (6)). This sidesteps the usual rules about appointees where a person is incapable of managing their own affairs. It means that a member of the family or the claimant's doctor or even some organisation (since under the Interpretation Act 1978 "person" includes corporate and incorporate bodies, unless the context is to the contrary) may make the claim, and the claimant or family need not know that the claim has been made. The decision on the claim and any order book for payment will be sent to the claimant directly, but without any reference to terminal illness (*Hansard*, H.C. Standing Committee G, col. 43, February 6, 1990). It was argued that the claimant could not then deduce that he was terminally ill from the receipt of the attendance allowance, but it is highly unlikely that someone still in possession of their faculties would not be suspicious when an order book for a benefit they had never claimed suddenly arrived.

If a claim made under s.35(2B) fails it should be considered as a claim for attendance allowance under the normal conditions.

Awards. Since the certificate issued under the new s.35(2B)(b) will be for life, the award of allowance will be for life. It does not in itself matter that the claimant does not die within six months from the date of the award. Entitlement will continue. But if the claimant ceases to meet the definition of "terminally ill" the award of the allowance is to be reviewed. See subs. (4).

Subss. (2) and (3)

These are simply consequential on subs. (1).

Subs. (4)

Although an award under the new s.35(2B) will be for life that does not mean that the award cannot be reviewed. Under the existing provisions of s.106(1) of the 1975 Act, the Attendance Allowance Board may at any time review one of its determinations if there has been a relevant change of circumstances or if the original decision was made in ignorance of, or was based on, a mistake as to a material fact. If, for instance, the claimant's condition unexpectedly improves, that would be a relevant change of circumstances. If the original diagnosis was revealed to be mistaken, that would reveal a mistake as to a material fact. The conditions for review would be met. The Attendance Allowance Board would then have to determine, on review, whether the original decision ought to be changed. There is authority for concluding that the conditions for review in such circumstances are not met merely by the obtaining of another medical opinion; there must be shown to be some mistake or change in the claimant's actual condition (see *R(S) 6/78* and *R(S) 4/86*). The new s.106(1)(aa) triggers review merely where there is a change in medical opinion about the claimant's condition or his reasonable expectation of life. This formulation raises problems. Whose medical opinion is at issue? How much of a change is necessary? The second question may be academic, since a review need not result in the revision of the determination, but the first question may be a controversial one.

Where the review in issue is of a determination which was unfavourable to the claimant's entitlement, see subs. (5) below.

Subs. (5)

The effect of the new s.106(1A) is that where an unfavourable determination has been made, whether following a s.35(2B) claim or not, a review on the ground of terminal illness will only be carried out on an express application on that ground by the claimant or anyone purporting to act on his behalf.

Subs. (6)

See subs. (1).

Subs. (7)

Because of the sensitivity of questions about terminal illness, there was concern that there should be the widest consultation about leaflets and claim forms. The Minister for Social Security accepted the amendment inserting this subsection at Committee stage (Standing Committee G, col. 70, February 6, 1990). Many organisations were consulted, but it appears that the claim form had been sent to the printers well before the Act received Royal Assent (*Hansard*, H.L. Vol. 519, col. 617, May 21, 1990).

Severe disablement allowance: age related addition

2.—(1) After section 36 of the principal Act (severe disablement allowance) there shall be inserted the following section—

"Severe disablement allowance: age related addition

36A.—(1) If a person was under the age of 60 on the day on which he qualified for severe disablement allowance, the weekly rate of his severe disablement allowance shall be increased by an age related addition at whichever of the weekly rates specified in the second column of paragraph 2A of Part III of Schedule 4 to this Act is applicable in his case, that is to say—

(a) the higher rate, if he was under the age of 40 on the day on which he qualified for severe disablement allowance;

(b) the middle rate, if he was between the ages of 40 and 50 on that day; or

(c) the lower rate, if he was between the ages of 50 and 60 on that day.

(2) Subject to subsection (4) below, for the purposes of this section the day on which a person qualified for severe disablement allowance is his first day of incapacity for work in the period of not less than 196 consecutive days mentioned in section 36(2)(b) or (3)(b) above, as the case may be, which preceded the first day in his current period of entitlement.

(3) For the purposes of this section, a person's "current period of entitlement" is a current period—

    (a) which consists of one or more consecutive days on which he is or has been entitled to a severe disablement allowance; and

    (b) which begins immediately after the last period of one or more consecutive days for which he was not entitled to such an allowance.

(4) Regulations—

    (a) may prescribe cases where a person is to be treated for the purposes of this section as having qualified for severe disablement allowance on a prescribed day earlier than the day ascertained in accordance with subsection (2) above;

    (b) may provide for days which are not days of incapacity for work in relation to a person to be treated as days of incapacity for work for the purpose of determining under this section the day on which he qualified for severe disablement allowance; and

    (c) may make provision for disregarding prescribed days in computing any period of consecutive days for the purposes of subsection (3) above."

(2) In Part III of Schedule 4 to that Act, after paragraph 2 (weekly rate of severe disablement allowance) there shall be inserted the following—

"2A. Age related addition (section 36A).	(a) Higher rate	10.00
	(b) Middle rate	6.20
	(c) Lower rate	3.10
	(the appropriate rate being determined in accordance with section 26A(1))".	

(3) In consequence of subsections (1) and (2) above, in section 34(1)(b) of that Act (which specifies severe disablement allowance as one of the non-contributory benefits under Chapter II of Part II of that Act) after the word "(with" there shall be inserted the words "age related addition and."

COMMENCEMENT

December 3, 1990 (Social Security Act 1990 (Commencement No. 2) Order 1990 (S.I. 1990 No. 1942), art. 2(e) and Sched.

DEFINITION

"the principal Act": s.20.

GENERAL NOTE

Severe disablement allowance is a non-contributory benefit paid to those who have been incapable of work and have also satisfied an additional condition of severe disability for a continuous period of 196 days. Claimants with a sufficient contribution record are entitled to invalidity benefit, consisting of an invalidity pension and an age-related invalidity allowance, on satisfying the test of long-term incapacity for work alone. Invalidity pension is paid at a higher rate than severe disablement allowance.

S.2, in inserting a new s.36A into the 1975 Act, introduces the equivalent of the invalidity allowance for severe disablement allowance. The higher rate goes to those who qualify below the age of 40, with lower rates to those who qualified below the age of 60. This improvement is the first part of the package of amendments to the balance of income maintenance benefits set out in Chapter 6 of *The Way Ahead*, designed to work in favour of those disabled early in life. The other parts are in ss.3 and 4 of this Act. Para. 6.7 of *The Way Ahead* estimated that some 245,000 SDA recipients would be entitled to the new age-related addition, although recognising that for many the increase would simply result in a corresponding decrease in means-tested benefits such as income support or housing benefit. The net additional cost is estimated at £16 million in 1991 and about £50 million per year thereafter (*Hansard*, H.C., Vol. 165, col. 630, January 22, 1990). The Social Security Advisory Committee, in its report *Benefits for Disabled People: a Strategy for Change* (1989), recommended that the rates of SDA should be raised progressively until they were equal to those of invalidity benefit. In the Commons, the Minister for Social Security would give no promises about any further alignment of the rates of the two benefits, mainly on the grounds of cost (about an extra £100 million per year for full alignment) but also on the basis that there ought to be a difference between a non-contributory benefit and one earned by contributions (Standing Committee G, cols. 97–8, February 8, 1990). However, in the House of Lords Baroness Blatch described the Government as "agreeable in principle to the particular recommendation of the Committee, as and when practicable" and said that s.2 was "a positive first stage in that process" (*Hansard*, H.L. Vol. 519, col. 633, May 21, 1990).

The new s.36A operates in much the same way as s.16 of the 1975 Act on invalidity allowance. Note that the upper age limit for qualification is 60 for both sexes, rather than pensionable age. The crucial date for identifying the appropriate rate of addition is that of the first day in the period of at least 196 consecutive days which preceded the first day of the *current* period of entitlement. The effect of s.36A(3) is that, subject to regulations which might be made under subs. (4), any break in entitlement to SDA results in a new current period beginning with a new qualifying date.

Reduced earnings allowance and retirement allowance

3.—(1) In subsection (1) of section 59A of the principal Act (conditions of entitlement to reduced earnings allowance) after paragraph (b) there shall be added the words—

"but a person shall not be entitled to reduced earnings allowance to the extent that the relevant loss of faculty results from an accident happening on or after the appointed day."

(2) After that subsection there shall be inserted—

"(1A) A person—

(a) who immediately before the appointed day is entitled to reduced earnings allowance in consequence of the relevant accident, but

(b) who subsequently ceases to be entitled to that allowance for one or more days,

shall not again be entitled to reduced earnings allowance in consequence of that accident; but this subsection does not prevent the making at any time of a claim for, or an award of, reduced earnings allowance in consequence of that accident for a period which commences not later than the day after that on which the claimant was last entitled to that allowance in consequence of that accident.

(1B) For the purposes of subsection (1A) above—

(a) a person who, apart from section 57(4) above, would have been entitled to reduced earnings allowance immediately before the appointed day shall be treated as entitled to that allowance on any day (including a Sunday) on which he would have been entitled to it apart from that provision;

(b) regulations may prescribe other circumstances in which a person is to be treated as entitled, or as having been entitled, to reduced earnings allowance on any prescribed day."

(3) In paragraph (b) of subsection (6) of that section (further awards) after the words "for such further period" there shall be inserted the words ", commencing as mentioned in subsection (1A) above,."

(4) After subsection (10A) of that section there shall be inserted—

"(10B) In this section" the appointed day "means the day on which section 3 of the Social Security Act 1990 comes into force."

(5) In section 59B of that Act (retirement allowance) the following provisions shall cease to have effect—

(a) in subsection (1) (circumstances in which a beneficiary ceases to be entitled to reduced earnings allowance and in which he may become entitled to it again) the words from "and may become" onwards;

(b) in subsection (3) (retirement allowance payable for life, unless beneficiary returns to regular employment etc) the words "Unless he returns to regular employment"; and

(c) subsection (4) (entitlement to retirement allowance to cease on return to regular employment etc).

(6) That section shall have effect, and be taken at all times on and after January 1, 1990 to have had effect, with the addition of the following subsection after subsection (8)—

"(9) "Day of interruption of employment" has the same meaning for the purposes of this section as it has for the purposes of provisions of this Act relating to unemployment benefit, sickness benefit or invalidity benefit."

(7) In section 77(2)(a) of that Act (regulations modifying provisions relating to certain benefits in their application to prescribed diseases and injuries) after the words "disablement benefit" there shall be inserted the words "or reduced earnings allowance."

(8) The following provisions shall cease to have effect—

(a) in section 2 of the Social Security Act 1988, the subsection (8) originally enacted (restriction on entitlement to reduced earnings allowance); and

(b) in Schedule 1 to the 1989 Act, paragraph 8(7) (which substitutes for that subsection a subsection (8) and a subsection (8A)).

COMMENCEMENT
Subs. (6), July 13, 1990 (s.23(3)); remainder, October 1, 1990 (Social Security Act 1990 (Commencement No. 1) Order 1990 (S.I. 1990 No. 1446), art. 2(h) and Sched., Part II).

DEFINITION
"the principal Act": s.20.

GENERAL NOTE
Reduced earnings allowance replaced special hardship allowance on October 1, 1986. There is entitlement if a person is entitled to disablement benefit under the industrial injuries scheme, or would be entitled but for his disablement being assessed at less than 14 per cent., and is unable to follow his regular occupation or an alternative of equivalent standard. The allowance tops up the claimant's current earnings to their previous level, subject to a maximum of 40 per cent. of the maximum rate of disablement benefit. There is no equivalent of REA for those disabled otherwise than as a result of an industrial accident or a prescribed disease. It is thus part of the "industrial preference".

The Way Ahead (paras. 6.12–14) proposed to end the acquisition of new entitlements to REA. There was said to be "an anomalous overlap" between REA and "the main earnings-replacement benefit, IVB [invalidity benefit]," because the majority of REA recipients who are not working also receive invalidity benefit. There is of course no overlap when the claimant is still working but has reduced earnings. The change was estimated to reduce expenditure by £1 million in 1990–1, £15 million in 1991–2 and £40 million in 1992–3. The reason for the build-up is that existing entitlements continue and it is only the acquisition of new entitlements (currently 14,500 per year) which is prevented. For this reason the annual savings predicted by 2001–2 are approximately £130 million (see the figures quoted at *Hansard*, H.C. Vol. 170, col. 1100, April 3, 1990). It was therefore perhaps disingenuous for the Minister for Social Security to describe the change as "a limited adjustment to the balance within a provision for people who are disabled" (Standing Committee G, col. 120, February 13, 1990). There were naturally strong objections from the Opposition that the long-term reductions in expenditure from this change and that carried out by s.4 far outweighed the extra spending under s.2 and that the result was an unacceptable levelling down. It also emerged that the Industrial Injuries Advisory Council had expressed its opposition to the proposal on REA (*ibid.*, col. 130). Nevertheless, the change was defended on the basis that REA is not directed to those within the whole population suffering the most severe disabilities and that there are higher priorities within the overall pattern of benefits (*ibid.*, cols. 116, 130). The estimates in *The Way Ahead* were that when all its proposals (some of the most far-reaching of which are not in this Act) are implemented in 1993–4 there will be net additional spending on benefits for people who are long-term sick and disabled, of £300 million per year (para. 7.5). It was also argued that following the phasing out of REA, occupational sickness and disability schemes might be encouraged to include provision for reduced earnings.

Subs. (1)
This is the main operative part of the amendment. There can be no entitlement to REA in relation to a loss of faculty (*i.e.* the loss of function of a part of the body) resulting from an accident happening after September 30, 1990. The "appointed day" is defined in the new s.59A(10B) (inserted by subs. (4)) as the day on which s.3 of this Act comes into force. Although the amendment only refers to accidents, the effect of Sched. 2 to the Social Security (Industrial Injuries) (Prescribed Diseases) Regulations 1985 (S.I. 1985 No. 967) is that that

reference includes prescribed diseases and the date of onset of the disease is the equivalent of the date of the accident.

It will immediately be seen that the cut-off is not in terms of the date of claim, but in terms of the date of the accident or the onset of a prescribed disease. There is special provision made for those entitled or deemed to be entitled to REA immediately before October 1, 1990 (see subs. (2)), but new claims may arise for many years in relation to pre-October 1990 accidents. The circumstances of the claimant may change so that a loss of earning capacity resulting from an accident 40 years before comes into being, which was not there before. Or a claimant may simply be late in making a claim for REA. Indeed, given the terms of the new s.59A(1A) and (1B) inserted by subs. (2), it is better for the claimant not to establish an entitlement until after September 30, 1990.

Subs. (2)

The new subss. (1A) and (1B) of s.59A contain important transitional provisions. Under subs. (1A), where a person is entitled to REA immediately before October 1, 1990 (presumably this includes an entitlement established after September 30, 1990, *e.g.* on appeal or review or by establishing good cause for a late claim) and subsequently ceases to be entitled, he cannot again be entitled to REA in relation to the same accident or prescribed disease. For instance, the claimant's earnings or earning capacity may increase sufficiently firmly to lead to non-entitlement on a renewal claim. If there is a subsequent deterioration there cannot be entitlement to REA again. It is said that if the rule were otherwise it "would be anomalous in relation to other cases where accident or disease occurred after the Bill becomes law" (Standing Committee G, col. 141, February 13, 1990). However, the new rule seems to be anomalous in relation to new claims relying on pre-October 1990 accidents. There can be breaks in entitlement where that entitlement did not start until after September 30, 1990. The exception to the new rule is where entitlement is established following on immediately from the end of a previous period of entitlement, which has expired.

Under s.59A(1B)(a) a person is deemed to be entitled to REA during the 90 day period following the accident or the onset of the prescribed disease during which there can be no entitlement to disablement benefit, if they would have been entitled but for the 90 day rule.

Subs. (3)

This amendment is consequential on subs. (2).

Subs. (4)

The "appointed day" is October 1, 1990.

Subs. (5)

Retirement allowance under s.59B of the 1975 Act is a benefit created by the Social Security Act 1988 which is paid when a current REA beneficiary gives up regular employment after pensionable age. It is intended to compensate for the fact that the reduction in the claimant's earning capacity will also have reduced his capacity to earn a pension. As entitlement to REA is phased out so will be entitlement to retirement allowance.

The present amendments secure that if a claimant becomes entitled to retirement allowance he cannot become re-entitled to REA on resuming regular employment.

Subs. (6)

This is a technical correction.

Subs. (7)

This amendment is necessary to authorise regulations to modify the effect of the provisions of the 1975 Act on REA on prescribed diseases.

Subs. (8)

These repealed provisions have not yet come into operation.

Computation of additional pension for purposes of invalidity pension etc.

4.—(1) In section 14 of the Pensions Act (which provides for the rate of an invalidity pension under section 15 of the principal Act to be calculated in accordance with section 6 of the Pensions Act, in similar manner to a Category A retirement pension, but with modifications) for the words from "taking the reference" onwards there shall be substituted the words "but with the substitution for subsection (6) of that section of the following—

"(6) In the application of this section for the purpose of determining the weekly rate of a person's invalidity pension for any period of interruption of employment—

(a) "relevant year" means any tax year, being neither earlier than the tax year 1978–79 nor later than the tax year 1990–91, in the period which—

(i) begins with the tax year in which the invalidity pensioner attained the age of 16; and

(ii) ends with the tax year immediately preceding the tax year which includes or included the first day of entitlement to the pension in respect of that period of interruption of employment; and

(b) "final relevant year" means the last tax year which is a relevant year in relation to the invalidity pensioner." "

(2) In section 15 of the Pensions Act, in subsection (4) (determination of weekly rate of widow's invalidity pension by reference to notional rates of widow's pension) after paragraph (b) there shall be added the words—

"but, in calculating the weekly rate of a widow's pension for the purposes of paragraph (a) above, or the weekly rate of a widow's pension without reduction, for the purposes of paragraph (b) above, any additional pension by virtue of section 6 above as it applies for the purposes of section 13 above shall be determined without reference to any surpluses in her late husband's earnings factors for tax years after 1990–91."

(3) In section 16 of that Act (invalidity pension for widowers) for subsection (4) there shall be substituted—

"(4) The weekly rate mentioned in paragraph (b) of subsection (3) above is a rate determined in the manner specified in section 6 above for a Category A retirement pension, but with the modifications that—

(a) where the man's wife was over pensionable age when she died, references in that section to the pensioner shall be taken as references to the wife;

(b) where the man's wife was under pensionable age when she died, references in that section to the pensioner and the tax year in which he attained pensionable age shall be taken as references to the wife and the tax year in which she died; and

(c) any additional pension shall be determined without reference to any surpluses in her earnings factors for tax years after 1990–91."

COMMENCEMENT
To be confirmed. Intended for April 1991.

DEFINITIONS
"the Pensions Act": s.20.
"the principal Act": *ibid.*

GENERAL NOTE
Section 4 is concerned with the additional pension payable with invalidity pension since 1979. As the opening lines of subs. (1) make clear, s.14 of the Social Security Pensions Act 1975 provides for an invalidity pension for someone under pensionable age to be calculated in the same way as a retirement pension as at the date entitlement to invalidity pension starts. S.6 of the Pensions Act provides for a retirement pension to consist of a basic component (which converts to the basic rate of invalidity pension) and an earnings-related component (which converts to the additional pension). The earnings-related component depends on earnings in tax years from 1978–9 onwards and reaches its full value after 20 years' build-up.

The Government's proposals are well-described in *The Way Ahead* (paras. 6.8–9):

"Secondly, we think it right, in the context of expanding occupational cover, to act to restrain the build-up of earnings-related Additional Pension (AP) entitlement, over and above the basic Invalidity Pension, that would otherwise be in prospect over the next decade.

The average amount of such AP is just over £9, with a maximum of over £41, at a total cost of £450 million a year. But these amounts will increase to an average of £21 and a maximum of £84, at a total cost of £1.6 billion [1989–90 prices] a year by 1998. A continuing commitment on this scale would have been likely not only to inhibit the growth of occupational cover but also, through the constraints inevitably imposed on Government's ability to do more for those with no such entitlement, to have widened yet further the gap between those who have been able to work and those who have not.

"We want to ensure that both now and in the future we can give proper emphasis to the needs of the most vulnerable disabled people who are least able to make financial provision for themselves. The forthcoming Social Security Bill will therefore include powers to provide that no new rights to AP should accrue in respect of earnings which fall after April 1991 when the new legislation comes into force. The change will reduce benefits expenditure by £5 million in 1992/3 rising by the end of the century to about £350 million. Spending on AP will, nonetheless, continue to rise to over £1.3 billion by 2000–1."

It was confirmed that all accrued entitlements to AP would be preserved and revalued in the future. Since the age-related invalidity allowance will remain and AP is currently offset against any invalidity allowance entitlement, some claimants will experience no difference in total invalidity benefit.

The Parliamentary discussion made little advance on these arguments. Most of the same arguments held about s.3 were also deployed here, particularly on the long-term balance between savings on benefits for those who have worked and expenditure on new benefits for those who have not. There was also dispute about the extent and nature of coverage by occupational sick pay schemes. For the fullest statement of the Opposition view on the report by IFF Research Ltd. (DHSS, 1988) see Mr Paul Flynn (Standing Committee G, cols. 170–2, February 15, 1990) and for the Government view see Lord Henley (*Hansard*, H.L. Vol. 519, cols. 682–3, May 21, 1990). In answer to questions as to why s.4 would operate from April 1991, while the new disability allowance and disability employment credit were not planned to start until April 1992, the Minister for Social Security explained that earnings in one tax year could influence the rate of benefit for claims starting in the following tax year (Standing Committee G, col. 168, February 15, 1990). Thus if earnings in the tax year 1991–2 had been allowed to count for AP they would have influenced the level of benefit in 1992–3 and there would have been an overlap.

Subs. (1)

The substance of the amendment is achieved by substituting a new s.6(6) in the Social Security Pensions Act 1975 for invalidity pension purposes which limits the years from which earnings factors are relevant to the calculation of additional pension to those between and including 1978–9 and 1990–1.

Subss. (2) and (3)

These amendments achieve the same result for invalidity pension payable to widows and widowers on their deceased spouse's contributions and earnings.

Retrospective effect of section 165A of the principal Act

5.—(1) The following section shall be inserted after section 165A of the principal Act—

> **"Retrospective effect of section 165A of the principal Act**
> 165B.—(1) This section applies where a claim for benefit is made or treated as made at any time on or after September 2, 1985 (the date on which section 165A above, as originally enacted, came into force) in respect of a period the whole or any part of which falls on or after that date.
> (2) Where this section applies, any question arising as to—
> (a) whether the claimant is or was at any time (whether before, on or after September 2, 1985) entitled to the benefit in question, or to any other benefit on which his entitlement to that benefit depends, or
> (b) in a case where the claimant's entitlement to the benefit depends on the entitlement of another person to a benefit, whether that other person is or was so entitled,

shall be determined as if section 165A above, as in force at the time of the claim referred to in subsection (1) above, and any regulations made under or referred to in that section as so in force, had also been in force, with any necessary modifications, at all times relevant for the purpose of determining the entitlement of the claimant, and, where applicable, of the other person, to the benefit or benefits in question (including the entitlement of any person to any benefit on which that entitlement depends, and so on).

(3) In any case where—

(a) a claim for benefit was made or treated as made (whether before, on or after September 2, 1985, and whether by the same claimant as the claim referred to in subsection (1) above or not), and benefit was awarded on that claim, in respect of a period falling wholly or partly before that date, but

(b) that award would not have been made had the current requirements applied in relation to claims for benefit, whenever made, in respect of periods before that date, and

(c) entitlement to the benefit claimed as mentioned in subsection (1) above depends on whether the claimant or some other person was previously entitled or treated as entitled to that or some other benefit,

then, in determining whether the conditions of entitlement to the benefit so claimed are satisfied, the person to whom benefit was awarded as mentioned in paragraphs (a) and (b) above shall be taken to have been entitled to the benefit so awarded, notwithstanding anything in subsection (2) above.

(4) In subsection (3) above "the current requirements" means—

(a) the provisions of section 165A above, as in force at the time of the claim referred to in subsection (1) above, and any regulations made under or referred to in that section as so in force, with any necessary modifications; and

(b) subsection (1) (with the omission of the words following "at any time") and subsection (2) above.

(5) Any reference in any enactment to section 165A of this Act (but not a reference to any specific provision of that section) shall be taken to include a reference to this section.

(6) This section shall be taken to have come into force on September 2, 1985."

(2) In Schedule 20 to the principal Act (glossary of expressions), the entry relating to "entitled" and cognate expressions—

(a) shall be taken at all times on or after September 2, 1985 but before the passing of this Act to have had effect with the substitution, in the second column, of the words "sections 165A and 165B" for the words "section 165A"; and

(b) shall have effect as from the passing of this Act with the substitution for those words of the words "sections 165A to 165D."

(3) Section 32(4) of the Social Security Act 1985 (which made similar provision to that made by subsection (3) of the section inserted by subsection (1) above) shall be deemed never to have been enacted.

(4) In paragraph 48 of Schedule 10 to the 1986 Act (which applies sections 87 and 165A(1) of the principal Act to income-related benefits) in paragraph (b), for the words "section 165A(1)" there shall be substituted the words "sections 165A(1) and 165B."

(5) Paragraph 48 of Schedule 10 to the 1986 Act shall have effect, and be taken always to have had effect, as if it had originally been enacted with the amendment made by subsection (4) above.

COMMENCEMENT
July 13, 1990 (s.23(3)(a)).

"the principal Act": s.20.

GENERAL NOTE
S.165A was added to the Social Security Act 1975 from September 2, 1985 (and a new form was substituted from April 6, 1987). Its introduction was precipitated by the decision of the House of Lords in *Insurance Officer* v. *McCaffery* [1984] 1 W.L.R. 1353 that (subject to an express provision to the contrary) a person was entitled to benefit if he met the conditions of entitlement even though he had not made a claim for that benefit. Claiming went to payability, not entitlement. This was contrary to the long-standing assumption of the DSS. S.165A accordingly provides that in general no-one can be entitled to a benefit without claiming it.

However, there are a number of benefits where entitlement can depend on whether a person was entitled to a benefit at some earlier date (*e.g.* on reaching pensionable age). While s.165A clearly governed such questions from September 2, 1985 onwards, it was arguable that in relation to earlier dates the *McCaffery* principle had to be applied. In June 1989 a Social Security Commissioner in a decision referred to in Parliament under the name of Cartwright decided that this argument was correct. The insertion of s.165B is to reverse the effect of that decision and to do so retrospectively back to September 2, 1985.

The form of the new s.165B is complex and the retrospective effects are difficult to work out. It only applies to claims made or treated as made on or after September 2, 1985 (subs. (1)). Thus very late appeals or very long good causes for late claims might not be affected. Then on any such claim, if a question of entitlement at any other date arises, (including dates before September 2, 1985) that question is to be decided according to the principle of s.165A (subs. (2)). The only exception to this occurs when for any period benefit has been awarded following a claim. The beneficiary is treated as entitled to that benefit even though under the current s.165A requirements he would not be (subs. (3)).

Subss. (2) to (5) of s.5 ensure that all statutory references to s.165A or s.165A(1) are taken also to include a reference to s.165B.

Late claims for widowhood benefits where death is difficult to establish

6.—(1) In section 165A of the principal Act (no entitlement to benefit without claim)—

(a) in subsection (1), after the words "Except in such cases as may be prescribed" there shall be inserted the words "and subject to section 165C below"; and

(b) in subsection (2), after paragraph (b) there shall be inserted the words—
"except as provided by section 165C below."

(2) After the section 165B of that Act inserted by section 5 above there shall be inserted—

"Late claims for widowhood benefits where death is difficult to establish

165C.—(1) This section applies where a woman's husband has died, or may be presumed to have died, and the circumstances are such that—

(a) more than twelve months have elapsed since the date of death (whether he died, or is presumed to have died, before or after the coming into force of this section);

(b) either—
(i) the husband's body has not been discovered or identified or, if it has been discovered and identified, the woman does not know that fact, or
(ii) less than twelve months have elapsed since she first knew of the discovery and identification of the body; and

(c) no claim for any of the widowhood benefits, that is to say—
(i) widow's benefit,
(ii) an invalidity pension under section 15 of the Pensions Act, or
(iii) a Category A retirement pension by virtue of subsection (5) of that section,

was made or treated as made in respect of the death by the woman before the coming into force of this section.

(2) Where this section applies, notwithstanding that any time prescribed for making a claim for a widowhood benefit in respect of the death has elapsed, then—

(a) in any case falling within paragraph (b)(i) of subsection (1) above where it has been determined—

(i) under subsection (1)(b) of section 98 above on a claim made by the woman, or

(ii) under subsection (2A) of that section on the submission of a question by her,

that the husband has died or is presumed to have died, or

(b) in any case falling within paragraph (b)(ii) of subsection (1) above where the identification was made not more than twelve months before the woman first knew of the discovery and identification of the body,

such a claim may be made or treated as made at any time before the expiration of the period of twelve months beginning with the date on which that determination was made or, as the case may be, the date on which she first knew of the discovery and identification.

(3) If, in a case where a claim for a widowhood benefit is made or treated as made by virtue of this section, the claimant would, apart from subsection (2) of section 165A above, be entitled to—

(a) a widow's payment in respect of the husband's death more than twelve months before the date on which the claim is made or treated as made, or

(b) any other widowhood benefit in respect of his death for a period more than twelve months before that date,

then, notwithstanding anything in that section, she shall be entitled to that payment or, as the case may be, to that other benefit (together with any increase under section 41(4) above)."

(3) In section 104 of that Act, after subsection (5) (regulations restricting the arrears of benefit payable in consequence of a review etc) there shall be inserted—

"(6) Regulations under subsection (5)(b) above shall not restrict the payment to or for a woman of so much of—

(a) any widow's benefit, any invalidity pension under section 15 of the Pensions Act or any Category A or Category B retirement pension, or

(b) any increase of such a benefit or pension,

as falls to be paid by reason of a review which takes place by virtue of subsection (1)(a) or (b) above in consequence of a claim for a widowhood benefit, within the meaning of section 165C below, which is made or treated as made by virtue of that section."

(4) The Social Security (Widow's Benefit) Transitional Regulations 1987 shall have effect with the insertion in regulation 2, at the end of paragraph (b), of the words—

"; and

(c) any reference in section 165C of the 1975 Act to widow's payment included a reference to widow's allowance, together with any increase under section 41(2)(e) of that Act."

(5) The amendment by subsection (4) above of a provision contained in regulations shall not be taken to have prejudiced any power to make further regulations revoking or amending that provision.

COMMENCEMENT
July 13, 1990 (s.23(3)(a)).

DEFINITION
    "the principal Act": s.20.

GENERAL NOTE
    The new s.165C of the Social Security Act 1975 applies to benefits to which widows are entitled on their late husband's contributions, where the claim is made after July 12, 1990. If there is a delay in discovering or identifying the husband's body or the widow has to rely on the presumption of death, s.165C can operate to allow entitlement to be backdated beyond the normal 12 months under s.165A.
    If the husband's body has not to the knowledge (actual, not reasonably to be expected) of the widow been discovered and identified and his death or presumption of death has been determined in an AO's decision (subss. (1)(b)(i) and (2)(a)) a claim may be made within 12 months of that determination. Then there can be entitlement to the date or presumed date of death, even though that goes back more than 12 months before the date of claim (subs. (3)). Where the widow does know of the discovery and identification of her husband's body she may claim within 12 months of acquiring that knowledge (subss. (1)(b)(ii) and (2)), with the same element of backdating (subs. (3)). However, if more than 12 months elapse between the actual identification and the widow's coming to know of it, she cannot rely on s.165C (subs. (2)(b)) if she has not already done so under subs. (1)(b)(i).

Recovery from damages etc. of sums equivalent to benefit: further provisions

7. The enactments specified in Schedule 1 to this Act shall have effect with the amendments specified in that Schedule.

COMMENCEMENT
    July 13, 1990 (s.23(3)(a)).

GENERAL NOTE
    See annotations to Sched. 1.

Liability to maintain dependants

8.—(1) After section 24 of the 1986 Act (recovery of expenditure on benefit from person liable for maintenance) there shall be inserted—

"**Recovery of expenditure on income support: additional amounts and transfer of orders**
    24A.—(1) In any case where—
    (a) the claim for income support referred to in subsection (1) of section 24 above is or was made by the parent of one or more children in respect of both himself and those children, and
    (b) the other parent is liable to maintain those children but, by virtue of not being the claimant's husband or wife, is not liable to maintain the claimant,
    the sum which the court may order that other parent to pay under subsection (4) of that section may include an amount, determined in accordance with regulations, in respect of any income support paid to or for the claimant by virtue of such provisions as may be prescribed.
    (2) Where the sum which a court orders a person to pay under section 24(4) above includes by virtue of subsection (1) above an amount (in this section referred to as a "personal allowance element") in respect of income support by virtue of paragraph 1(2) of Schedule 2 to the Income Support (General) Regulations 1987 (personal allowance for lone parent) the order shall separately identify the amount of the personal allowance element.
    (3) In any case where—
    (a) there is in force an order under subsection (4) of section 24 above made against a person ("the liable parent") who is the parent of one or more children, in respect of the other parent or the children, and
    (b) payments under the order fall to be made to the Secretary of State by virtue of subsection (6)(a) of that section, and
    (c) that other parent ("the dependent parent") ceases to claim income support,

27–17

the Secretary of State may, by giving notice in writing to the court which made the order and to the liable parent and the dependent parent, transfer to the dependent parent the right to receive the payments under the order, exclusive of any personal allowance element, and to exercise the relevant rights in relation to the order, except so far as relating to that element.

(4) Notice under subsection (3) above shall not be given (and if purportedly given, shall be of no effect) at a time when there is in force a maintenance order made against the liable parent—

(a) in favour of the dependent parent or one or more of the children; or

(b) in favour of some other person for the benefit of the dependent parent or one or more of the children;

and if such a maintenance order is made at any time after notice under that subsection has been given, the order under section 24(4) above shall cease to have effect.

(5) Except as provided by subsections (7) and (8) below, where the Secretary of State gives notice under subsection (3) above, he shall cease to be entitled—

(a) to receive any payment under the order in respect of any personal allowance element, or

(b) to exercise the relevant rights, so far as relating to any such element,

notwithstanding that the dependent parent does not become entitled to receive any payment in respect of that element or to exercise the relevant rights so far as so relating.

(6) If, in a case where the Secretary of State gives notice under subsection (3) above, a payment under the order is or has been made to him wholly or partly in respect of the whole or any part of the period beginning with the day on which the transfer takes effect and ending with the day on which the notice under subsection (3) above is given to the liable parent, the Secretary of State shall—

(a) repay to or for the liable parent so much of the payment as is referable to any personal allowance element in respect of that period or, as the case may be, the part of it in question; and

(b) pay to or for the dependent parent so much of any remaining balance of the payment as is referable to that period or part;

and a payment under paragraph (b) above shall be taken to discharge, to that extent, the liability of the liable parent to the dependent parent under the order in respect of that period or part.

(7) If, in a case where the Secretary of State has given notice under subsection (3) above, the dependent parent makes a further claim for income support, then—

(a) the Secretary of State may, by giving a further notice in writing to the court which made the order and to the liable parent and the dependent parent, transfer back from the dependent parent to himself the right to receive the payments and to exercise the relevant rights; and

(b) that transfer shall revive the Secretary of State's right to receive payment under the order in respect of any personal allowance element and to exercise the relevant rights so far as relating to any such element.

(8) A transfer under subsection (3) or (7) above does not transfer or otherwise affect the right of any person—

(a) to receive a payment which fell due to him at a time before the transfer took effect; or

(b) to exercise the relevant rights in relation to any such payment;

and, where notice is given under subsection (3), subsection (5) above does not deprive the Secretary of State of his right to receive such a payment in respect of any personal allowance element or to exercise the relevant rights in relation to such a payment.

(9) For the purposes of this section—

(a) a transfer under subsection (3) above takes effect on the day on which the dependent parent ceases to be in receipt of income support in consequence of the cessation referred to in paragraph (c) of that subsection, and

(b) a transfer under subsection (7) above takes effect on—

(i) the first day in respect of which the dependent parent receives income support after the transfer under subsection (3) above took effect, or

(ii) such later day as may be specified for the purpose in the notice under subsection (7),

irrespective of the day on which notice under the subsection in question is given.

(10) Any notice required to be given to the liable parent under subsection (3) or (7) above shall be taken to have been given if it has been sent to his last known address.

(11) In this section—

"child" means a person under the age of 16, notwithstanding section 26(3)(d) below;

"court" shall be construed in accordance with section 24 above;

"maintenance order"—

(a) in England and Wales, means—

(i) any order for the making of periodical payments or for the payment of a lump sum which is, or has at any time been, a maintenance order within the meaning of the Attachment of Earnings Act 1971;

(ii) any order under Part III of the Matrimonial and Family Proceedings Act 1984 (overseas divorce) for the making of periodical payments or for the payment of a lump sum;

(b) in Scotland, has the meaning given by section 106 of the Debtors (Scotland) Act 1987, but disregarding paragraph (h) (alimentary bond or agreement);

"the relevant rights," in relation to an order under section 24(4) above, means the right to bring any proceedings, take any steps or do any other thing under or in relation to the order which the Secretary of State could have brought, taken or done apart from any transfer under this section.

Reduction of expenditure on income support: certain maintenance orders to be enforceable by the Secretary of State

24B.—(1) This section applies where—

(a) a person ("the claimant") who is the parent of one or more children is in receipt of income support either in respect of those children or in respect of both himself and those children; and

(b) there is in force a maintenance order made against the other parent ("the liable person")—

(i) in favour of the claimant or one or more of the children; or

(ii) in favour of some other person for the benefit of the claimant or one or more of the children;

and in this section "the primary recipient" means the person in whose favour that maintenance order was made.

(2) If, in a case where this section applies, the liable person fails to comply with any of the terms of the maintenance order—

    (a) the Secretary of State may bring any proceedings or take any other steps to enforce the order that could have been brought or taken by or on behalf of the primary recipient; and

    (b) any court before which proceedings are brought by the Secretary of State by virtue of paragraph (a) above shall have the same powers in connection with those proceedings as it would have had if they had been brought by the primary recipient.

(3) The Secretary of State's powers under this section are exercisable at his discretion and whether or not the primary recipient or any other person consents to their exercise; but any sums recovered by virtue of this section shall be payable to or for the primary recipient, as if the proceedings or steps in question had been brought or taken by him or on his behalf.

(4) The powers conferred on the Secretary of State by subsection (2)(a) above include power—

    (a) to apply for the registration of the maintenance order under—

        (i) section 17 of the Maintenance Orders Act 1950;

        (ii) section 2 of the Maintenance Orders Act 1958; or

        (iii) the Civil Jurisdiction and Judgments Act 1982; and

    (b) to make an application under section 2 of the Maintenance Orders (Reciprocal Enforcement) Act 1972 (application for enforcement in reciprocating country).

(5) Where this section applies, the prescribed person shall in prescribed circumstances give the Secretary of State notice of any application—

    (a) to alter, vary, suspend, discharge, revoke, revive, or enforce the maintenance order in question; or

    (b) to remit arrears under that maintenance order;

and the Secretary of State shall be entitled to appear and be heard on the application.

(6) Where, by virtue of this section, the Secretary of State commences any proceedings to enforce a maintenance order, he shall, in relation to those proceedings, be treated for the purposes of any enactment or instrument relating to maintenance orders as if he were a person entitled to payment under the maintenance order in question (but shall not thereby become entitled to any such payment).

(7) Where, in any proceedings under this section in England and Wales, the court makes an order for the whole or any part of the arrears due under the maintenance order in question to be paid as a lump sum, the Secretary of State shall inform the Legal Aid Board of the amount of that lump sum if he knows—

    (a) that the primary recipient either—

        (i) received legal aid under the Legal Aid Act 1974 in connection with the proceedings in which the maintenance order was made, or

        (ii) was an assisted party, within the meaning of the Legal Aid Act 1988, in those proceedings; and

    (b) that a sum remains unpaid on account of the contribution required of the primary recipient—

        (i) under section 9 of the Legal Aid Act 1974 in respect of those proceedings, or

        (ii) under section 16 of the Legal Aid Act 1988 in respect of the costs of his being represented under Part IV of that Act in those proceedings,

    as the case may be.

(8) In this section "maintenance order" has the same meaning as it has in section 24A above, but does not include any such order for the payment of a lump sum."

(2) Until such time as there comes into force an amendment of Schedule 1 to the Attachment of Earnings Act 1971 (maintenance orders to which the Act applies) which has the effect of including among the orders specified in that Schedule any order for periodical or other payments made or having effect as if made under Schedule 1 to the Children Act 1989, the definition of "maintenance order" in subsection (11) of the section 24A of the 1986 Act inserted by subsection (1) above shall have effect as if, in paragraph (a), after sub-paragraph (ii) there were inserted—

"(iii) any order under paragraph 1(2)(a), (b) or (c) of Schedule 1 to the Children Act 1989 (financial provision for children against their parents).";

(3) In section 26 of the 1986 Act, in subsection (3) (definitions for purposes of sections 24, 25 and 26) after the words "section 24" there shall be inserted "24A, 24B."

COMMENCEMENT
October 15, 1990 (Social Security Act 1990 (Commencement No. 1) Order 1990 (S.I. 1990 No. 1446), art. 2(i)).

DEFINITION
"the 1986 Act": s.20.

GENERAL NOTE
These new provisions now form one of the central strategic objectives of the Act (*Hansard*, H.C. Vol. 170, col. 1137, April 3, 1990 (Tony Newton); *Hansard*, H.L. Vol. 518, col. 234, April 20, 1990 (Lord Henley)), but were only introduced at the Report stage in the Commons. They therefore received relatively little Parliamentary discussion due to the operation of the guillotine. The Government is carrying out a general review of the maintenance system, based on a survey of work in U.K. courts and DSS offices and study of overseas systems, and has produced radical proposals in the White Paper, *Children Come First* (Cm. 1264, October 1990). Action had already been taken to tighten up the assessment of an absent parent's ability to pay maintenance for his family on income support. The current provisions are regarded as desirable in the short term to improve the effectiveness of the present system, pending more radical reform (*Hansard*, H.C. Vol. 170, col. 566, March 28, 1990).

S.8 inserts two new sections into the Social Security Act 1986. The new s.24A contains two elements. The first relates to the situation where a lone parent is receiving income support, but the absent parent of the child(ren) is not liable to maintain the parent under s.26(3) of the 1986 Act because the parents are not or are no longer married. Where the DSS seeks its own order against the absent parent, courts are empowered to take into account income support relating to the lone parent in calculating the amount to be paid for the child(ren) and the DSS may of course take this into account in negotiating voluntary agreements. The second is to allow a DSS order to be transferred to the lone parent when that person comes off income support, rather than the lone parent having to obtain a separate private maintenance order. The new s.24B allows the DSS to enforce a lone parent's private maintenance order where the parent is on income support.

There was a general welcome for the second element of s.24A, but some opposition to the other elements on the basis that their aim was more to reduce social security expenditure than to assist lone parents. The Secretary of State predicted that the amount of maintenance recovered by the DSS in respect of lone parents on income support would rise to about £260 million in 1990–91, having gone up from £155 million in 1988–89 to £180 million in 1989–90 (*ibid.*, col. 571). The predicted increase was partly based on the provisions in s.8 and partly on giving greater priority and resources to such work, with changes in the administrative guidance. These changes are to point out the need to stress to lone parents on benefits the advantages of reflecting the absent parent's proper responsibilities in the maintenance arrangements from the outset and also to indicate that the "normal expectation" should be that a lone parent will co-operate in establishing where responsibility lies. It is, however, recognised that there may be circumstances in which lone parents will not wish to name the father of a child. *Children Come First* (para. 5.33) proposes reductions in the lone parent's benefit for non-co-operation.

Section 24A.

Subss. (1) and (2). These provisions comprise the first element identified above. They apply when both conditions (a) and (b) in subs. (1) are satisfied. Under (a), s.24(1) of the 1986 Act gives the DSS power to obtain an order against a person who is liable to maintain a claimant of income support or a person included in the family for claiming purposes. S.26(3) defines liability to maintain for this purpose. There is a liability to maintain a spouse and any children. Under s.26(3)(d) "child" includes a person aged 16 to 18 (inclusive) who is still a member of the claimant's family for income support purposes (*e.g.* because still in full-time education). However, s.24A(11) provides that for the purposes of s.24A "child" is restricted to a person under the age of 16. Thus, lone parent claimants whose children are all over 15 will fall outside this new provision. Under (b) the absent parent must not be married to the lone parent, so that the obligation to maintain under s.26(3) is only in respect of the child(ren). If both these conditions are met, a court may include whatever amount the regulations determine in respect of the income support paid for the lone parent. The Income Support (Liable Relatives) Regulations 1990 (S.I. 1990 No. 1777) specify in all cases the children's personal allowances, family premium, lone parent premium and disabled child premium for a child whom the absent parent is liable to maintain and the carer premium for such a child (reg. 2(1)).

The intention was that the regulation-making power "will be used to specify that once having looked at the allowances and premiums that are paid because there are children, the court should also have regard to the income support personal allowance paid for the mother" (*Hansard*, H.C. Vol. 170, col. 567, March 28, 1990).

The Liable Relatives Regulations (reg. 2(2)) provide that if the absent parent has the means to pay in addition to the amounts specified in reg. 2(1), a court order may include some or all of the dependent parent's personal allowance. It is said that in a private maintenance order for children the court can take account of the parent's care costs and that social security law is thus being brought into line with family law. However, there is nothing as specific as s.24A in family law. The existing power of the court is quite wide. Under s.24(4) it may order payment of such sum as it considers appropriate. The assumption seems to be that not only could the personal allowance for a child under 16 be considered under this provision, but also the family premium (paid to all claimants with a child or young person (16–18) in the family) and the additional lone parent premium. If such amounts can be considered under the existing law (and they might be considered to reflect the care costs of the lone parent) there seems no reason why the court could not also consider some part of the parent's personal allowance if that was considered "appropriate." However, the new s.24A(1) and the regulations will make the position clear, which should be an advantage. It is notable that the court retains a discretion as to what amounts to consider, and that the overriding factor under s.24(4) is what is appropriate. Under para. 1 of Sched. 2 to the Income Support (General) Regulations 1987 (S.I. 1987 No. 1967) the personal allowance for a lone parent aged under 18 or over 24 is the same as for a single person with no dependants. There is only a difference (currently £7.90 p.w.) for those aged 18 to 24.

Subs. (2) provides that if the lone parent's personal allowance under Sched. 2 is covered by the order, this element must be separately identified. This has no bearing on subs. (1), but is relevant to the procedure set up by subss. (3) to (10).

Subss. (3) to (10). These provisions contain the important procedure allowing the transfer of a DSS order to the lone parent on coming off income support. The conditions for transfer under subs. (3) are that in such a case (remembering that "child" is defined to cover only those under 16 (subs. 11)) the Secretary of State gives notice to the court which made the order and to both the parents. Then the right to enforce or apply for variation of the order (apart from any personal allowance element identified under subs. (2)) is transferred to the lone parent (known as "the dependent parent"). Thus, the personal allowance element, which is of no net benefit to the lone parent while she is on income support, is removed at the point when its value would actually be felt by the lone parent. The DSS can no longer enforce the personal allowance element of the order (subs. (5)). Under subs. (9)(a) the transfer takes effect on the day on which the dependent parent ceases to receive income support in consequence of ceasing to claim. This is a peculiar way of putting things. If the dependent parent's circumstances change (*e.g.* her capital goes over the cut-off limit or she starts full-time work) her entitlement to income support may be terminated on review by the AO under s.104 of the Social Security Act 1975. She may well then choose not to claim income support again, as it would be a useless exercise. The dependent parent could, with some strain, be said to cease to claim income support and so to satisfy subs. (3)(c), but the cessation of receipt of income support is not in consequence of the cessation of claiming but of the review and revision by the AO.

Subs. (3) is not to apply if a private maintenance order (see subs. (11) for definition) is in existence, and if the dependent parent obtains one after a transfer the right to enforce the DSS order disappears (subs. (4)).

If, after a transfer, the dependent parent makes another claim for income support (presumably only while still maintaining children under 16), the Secretary of State may, by giving notice to all parties re-transfer to the DSS the right to enforce the order and revive the personal allowance element on the dependent parent becoming entitled to income support (subss. (7) and (9)(b)). Presumably the revival of the personal allowance element requires the conditions of subss. (1) and (2) to be met at the date of revival.

Section 24B.
S.24B enables the DSS to enforce certain private maintenance orders in favour of lone parent claimants of income support. Only lone parents are covered by subs. (1)(a), and not mere separated spouses, but the maintenance order may be in favour either of the parent or the child(ren) or both. The Secretary of State may at his discretion and without the consent of the lone parent take steps (including those specified in subs. (5)) to enforce the order as if he were the person entitled to payment under the order (subss. (2), (3) and (6)). But any sums recovered are payable to the primary recipient under the order (subss. (3) and (6)). Under subs. (5) regulations may specify who has to inform the DSS of applications to vary, suspend, etc. the private order or to remit arrears. Reg. 3 of the Liable Relatives Regulations specifies various court officials. The Secretary of State is given the right to be heard on any such application, but has no power to make such an application, *e.g.* to increase the amount of an order. This is because subs. (2) only operates when there is a failure to comply with the terms (*i.e.* the existing terms) of the order.
Subs. (7) requires the Secretary of State to inform the Legal Aid Board when a lump sum of arrears is to be paid when the Board might be able to recover a contribution out of the lump sum.
Overall s.24B is a powerful weapon for the DSS to enforce the payment of maintenance orders. If the lone parent has her own order, which is not being paid, income support will make up the shortfall. There is thus no great incentive for the lone parent to go through all the hassle of enforcement, and there may be other circumstances making her reluctant to take action. The DSS will have no such inhibitions.

Income support in respect of accommodation charges for certain persons in residential care and nursing homes

9.—In section 22 of the 1986 Act (calculation of income-related benefits) after subsection (2) there shall be inserted—
  "(2A) In prescribing, for the purposes of income support amounts under subsection (1) above in respect of accommodation in any area for qualifying persons in cases where prescribed conditions are fulfilled, the Secretary of State shall take into account information provided by local authorities or other prescribed bodies or persons with respect to the amounts which they have agreed to pay for the provision of accommodation in relevant premises in that area.
  (2B) In subsection (2A) above—
    "accommodation" includes any board or care;
    "local authority"—
      (a) in relation to areas in England and Wales, has the same meaning as it has in Part III of the National Assistance Act 1948; and
      (b) in relation to areas in Scotland, has the meaning given by section 1(2) of the Social Work (Scotland) Act 1968;
    "qualifying person" means any person who falls within—
      (a) subsection (1) of section 26A of the National Assistance Act 1948 (which is inserted by the National Health Service and Community Care Act 1990 and relates to persons ordinarily resident in residential care or nursing homes immediately before the commencement of that section); or
      (b) subsection (1) of section 86A of the Social Work (Scotland) Act 1968 (the corresponding provision for Scotland),
    or who would fall within either of those subsections apart from any regulations under subsection (3) of the section in question;

"relevant premises"—
- (a) in relation to areas in England and Wales, has the meaning given by section 26A(2) of the National Assistance Act 1948; and
- (b) in relation to areas in Scotland, has the meaning given by section 86A(2) of the Social Work (Scotland) Act 1968."

COMMENCEMENT
To be confirmed. Originally intended for April 1991, but now probably deferred to April 1993.

DEFINITION
"the 1986 Act": s.20.

GENERAL NOTE
The new subsections of s.22 of the Social Security Act 1986 inserted by this section are closely bound up with the Government's community care reforms. After those reforms come into force new residents in residential care and nursing homes will be supported by local authorities, who will negotiate prices with voluntary organisations and home owners in order to make contracts for places. However, existing residents will continue to be supported through the income support system, so that the maximum amounts set in Sched. 4 of the Income Support (General) Regulations 1987 (S.I. 1987 No. 1967) will continue to be of relevance. The effect of the new subs. (2A) is that in making the amending regulations the Secretary of State must take into account information about the prices agreed with local authorities, although there is no legal obligation to keep the income support limit in line with market levels.

The community care reforms under the National Health Service and Community Care Act 1990 were intended to come into force in April 1991, but after the passage of the Social Security Act 1990, it was announced that they would not come into effect until April 1993. Thus these amendments will also have to be delayed until after that date. It was indicated by the Secretary of State that any information available from local authorities before April 1991 would be used in making his judgments, and research was to be commissioned on the true costs of running residential care and nursing homes (*Hansard*, H.C. Vol. 170, cols. 606–7, March 28, 1990). Such information might be used in advance of April 1993, during which time there will have to be several upratings, but it is likely to be on an informal rather than a statutory basis.

Amendments relating to the social fund

10.—(1) In section 32 of the 1986 Act, after subsection (8D) there shall be inserted—

"(8E) The Secretary of State may give general directions to social fund officers or groups of social fund officers, or to any class of social fund officers, with respect to the control and management by social fund officers or groups of social fund officers of the amounts allocated to them under subsections (8A) to (8D) above."

(2) In subsection (10) of that section (power to nominate a social fund officer to issue guidance to other officers in his area on specified matters) for the words "to issue" there shall be substituted the words "who shall issue."

(3) In section 33 of that Act, after subsection (10) (questions to be determined in accordance with general directions) there shall be inserted—

"(10ZA) Without prejudice to the generality of subsection (10) above, the Secretary of State may issue directions under that subsection for the purpose of securing that a social fund officer or group of social fund officers shall not in any specified period make awards of any specified description which in the aggregate exceed the amount, or a specified portion of the amount, allocated to that officer or group of officers under section 32(8A) to (8D) above for payments under awards of that description in that period."

(4) In subsection (10A) of that section (which specifies certain matters with respect to which directions may be given) after paragraph (e) there shall be inserted—

"(f) that a social fund payment such as is mentioned in section 32(2)(b) above shall only be awarded to a person if either—

(i) he is in receipt of a benefit under the benefit Acts which is specified in the direction and the circumstances are such as are so specified; or

(ii) in a case where the conditions specified in sub-paragraph (i) above are not satisfied, the circumstances are such as are specified in the direction.";

(5) At the end of that section there shall be added—

"(13) The Secretary of State may by regulations—

(a) make provision with respect to the time at which an application for a social fund payment such as is mentioned in section 32(2)(b) above is to be treated as made;

(b) prescribe conditions that must be satisfied before any determination in connection with such an application may be made or any award of such a payment may be paid;

(c) prescribe circumstances in which such an award becomes extinguished."

COMMENCEMENT
July 13, 1990 (s.23(3)(a)).

DEFINITION
"the 1986 Act": s.20.

GENERAL NOTE
All of these amendments relate to the controversial social fund scheme, and several stem from the first challenges under the judicial review procedure to the administration of the scheme.

Subs. (1)
S.32(2)(b) of the Social Security Act 1986 provides that payments may be made out of the social fund "to meet other needs [than for maternity or funeral expenses under head (a)] in accordance with directions given or guidance issued by the Secretary of State." Directions are binding on the social fund officers (SFOs) who make decisions under the scheme (s.33(10)). In *R.* v. *Secretary of State for Social Security*, ex p. *Stitt* it was argued that under subs. (2)(b) the Secretary of State was only empowered to give directions as to how payments should be made from the fund and not to specify categories of need which could not be met. In the Divisional Court (*The Times*, February 23, 1990) it was held that since s.32(5) put the maintenance of the social fund under the control and management of the Secretary of State, he was empowered to give "such directions as can reasonably be regarded as being necessary for the proper control and management of the Social Fund so as to enable that fund to meet the needs of applicants which cannot be met out of their other resources" (Woolf L.J.). Such a power was not expressly given by s.32(5), and the new s.32(8E) may be regarded as an express confirmation of what was previously implied. The Court of Appeal decision in *Stitt* (*The Times*, July 4, 1990) suggests that the power to give directions limiting the categories of need to be met was not limited by the "control and management" criterion. This certainly was the approach of Butler-Sloss L.J. and Sir Patrick Connor, although all the judges expressed their surprise, at the least, at the extent of the powers given to the Secretary of State. Thus, the insertion of s.32(8E) will not detract from the generality of the powers granted.

The Minister for Social Security said that he envisaged that directions issued under subs. (8E) will "cover the requirement to plan the expenditure from the local allocation through profiles of anticipated expenditure and recoveries and levels of priorities of needs that can be sustained from the allocation. They will require social fund officers to have regard to such factors in reaching decisions in individual cases. They will also require the area social fund officer—normally the local office manager . . .—to keep the profiles and levels of priorities under review and revise them in the light of changing circumstances" (*Hansard*, H.C. Vol. 170, col. 579, March 28, 1990).

Subs. (2)
The amendment to s.32(10) requires the area social fund officer to give guidance on matters specified by the Secretary of State.

Subs. (3)

S.33(9) of the 1986 Act lists one of the factors to which a SFO must have regard in determining whether to make an award or not as "any relevant allocation under section 32(8A) to (8D)", *i.e.* the local budget. But subs. (9) is subject to subs. (10), which requires SFOs to comply with directions issued by the Secretary of State and to take account of guidance given by him. No directions were issued requiring SFOs not to make awards which would result in the local budget being exceeded, but several paragraphs of the guidance contained in the Social Fund Manual were to this effect. The Divisional Court in *R.* v. *Social Fund Inspector and Secretary of State for Social Security*, ex p. *Roberts* (*The Times*, February 23, 1990) struck down these paragraphs as unlawful. For guidance to be proper it must be expressed in the language of guidance and not in the language of direction. Therefore the SFO was left with the necessity to have regard to the local budget, as well as all the circumstances of the case and the other specified factors, under subs. (9).

The intention of the new subs. (10ZA) of s.33 was described by the Minister for Social Security as follows (*Hansard*, H.C. Vol. 170, col. 580, March 28, 1990):

"[It] is essential to the successful operation of the fund that its resources are managed so as not to exceed the amounts allocated for payments. Under the present legislation, it would be possible to issue directions on matters relating to the control of the budget. I have already mentioned the power that we are taking in respect of directions for the management and control of local budgets. The additional power that we are taking under the new clause will reinforce the effect of those directions by giving the Secretary of State explicit power to issue directions requiring social fund officers to keep within their allocations. Such directions will, therefore, preclude a social fund officer, or a group of social fund officers, from making any award that would result in the sums allocated to that officer or group of officers being exceeded. This must be right if the scheme is to operate within the strict monetary limits, as Parliament originally intended, and as was recognised by the court."

It is clear that subs. (10ZA) will authorise such directions, which could anyway have been made under the general power of subs. (10).

An extra £12.3 million has been put into the 1990–91 budget to make up for the extra expenditure incurred as a result of the judgment in *Roberts*. The Secretary of State has also issued directions under the new power in subs. (10ZA) (*The Guardian*, September 4, 1990).

Subs. (4)

S.33(10A) lists some matters on which the Secretary of State may issue directions, without prejudicing the generality of subs. (10). This provision adds to the list the power to direct that payments may only be made from the fund either if the applicant is in receipt of a particular social security benefit or if the circumstances are as specified in the direction. Once again, such a power already existed under subs. (10), but has now been made explicit. The aim is to draw the line between community care grants and budgeting loans, which are only available to people on, or shortly to be on, income support, and crisis loans, where receipt of benefit is not a qualifying condition.

Subs. (5)

The new s.33(13) gives power to make regulations on three procedural matters. The Social Fund (Miscellaneous Provisions) Regulations 1990 (S.I. 1990 No. 1788) amend the Social Fund (Applications) Regulations to specify that an application for a payment from the social fund is treated as made on the day on which the application is received in the local office. Under the second category, the 1990 Regulations provide that a condition on which an award is made (*e.g.* discharge from residential care) must actually occur before payment is made. Finally, regulations provide that an award is to be extinguished if the applicant dies before it is paid or a giro is not cashed within 12 months of its issue. (See reg. 3(b) of the 1990 Regulations).

Occupational and personal pensions etc.

Annual increase of certain occupational pensions

11.—(1) The following section shall be inserted after section 58 of the Pensions Act—

"**Annual increase in rate of pension, other than guaranteed minimum pension or money purchase benefit**

58A.—(1) This section applies in relation to any pensions. occupational pension scheme—

    (a) which is neither a public service pension scheme nor a money purchase scheme; and

(b) whose rules do not require the annual rate of every pension which commences or has commenced under the scheme to be increased each year by at least an amount equal to the appropriate percentage of that rate.

(2) On and after the appointed day, Schedule 3A to this Act shall have effect for the purpose of requiring the provision by schemes to which this section applies of annual increases in the annual rates of pensions under those schemes.

(3) In this section—

"annual rate," in relation to a pension, means the annual rate of the pension, as previously increased under the rules of the scheme or under Schedule 3A to this Act;

"the appointed day" means the day on which this section and Schedule 3A to this Act come into force;

"the appropriate percentage," in relation to an increase in the annual rate of a pension, means the percentage specified in the last revaluation order made before the increase is to take effect as the revaluation percentage for the last revaluation period of twelve months;

"money purchase scheme" means a pension scheme under which all the benefits that may be provided are money purchase benefits;

"pension" does not include—

(a) a guaranteed minimum pension or any increase in such a pension under section 37A above; or

(b) any money purchase benefit;

"revaluation order," "revaluation percentage" and "revaluation period" shall be construed in accordance with section 52A above."

(2) After Schedule 3 to the Pensions Act there shall be inserted the Schedule set out in Schedule 2 to this Act.

(3) In the case of an occupational pension scheme—

(a) such as is mentioned in subsection (1) of section 58A of the Pensions Act, and

(b) which is constituted by trust deed,

no payment shall be made out of the resources of the scheme to or for a person who is or has been the employer of persons in the description or category of employment to which the scheme relates until such time as provision has been made by the scheme for every pension which commences or has commenced under it to be increased as mentioned in paragraph (b) of that subsection.

(4) Nothing in subsection (3) above applies in relation to payments made to or for a person by virtue of his or any other person's membership of the scheme in question.

(5) Expressions used in this section and the Pensions Act have the same meaning in this section as they have in that Act.

(6) The provisions of subsection (3) above override any provision of a scheme to the extent that it conflicts with them.

COMMENCEMENT

Subss. (3) to (6): August 17, 1990 (Social Security Act 1990 (Commencement No. 1) Order 1990 (S.I. 1990 No. 1446), art. 2(g)); remainder: to be confirmed, intended for January 1, 1992.

DEFINITIONS

"occupational pension scheme": Social Security Pensions Act 1975, s.66(1).
"resources": *ibid.*
"the Pensions Act": s.20.

GENERAL NOTE

Subss. (1) and (2)

The new s.58A of, and Sched. 3 to the Social Security Pensions Act 1975 constitute the first general requirement on private sector pension schemes to increase the amounts of pensions once payment has commenced. The new s.58A establishes the framework and is discussed here. The details are in the new Sched. 3 (Sched. 2 to this Act) and are discussed in the notes to that Schedule.

Background

The problem of the erosion of the real value of pensions by inflation first emerged in the years of and immediately following World War I (Hannah, *Inventing Retirement*, p. 112). While this period saw the first legislation for increases in public service pensions, the problem was seen as an exceptional consequence of wartime. Since the late 1940s inflation has been persistent and accelerating, particularly in the 1970s. By then complete index-linking had been established in the public sector, either by legislation or the terms of schemes. But in 1979 almost no private sector schemes provided complete index-linking. Only approximately 20 per cent. of members enjoyed guaranteed increases of about three per cent., 40 per cent. of members had received no increase in the previous year and only five per cent. received an increase of more than two-thirds of the inflation rate (Government Actuary, *Occupational Pension Schemes: 1979: Sixth Survey*, 1981, pp. 56–8). The disparity between the public and private sector was a cause of criticism. The Scott Committee, set up in 1980 to enquire into the valuation of the inflation-proofing of pensions, declared it to be "a highly desirable social objective that the standard of living of those in retirement should be protected" and made no recommendation to reduce the public sector provision (*Inquiry into the Value of Pensions*, Cm. 8147, 1981, para. 6).

The inflation problem was also addressed by the Occupational Pensions Board in its report, *Greater Security for the Rights and Expectations of Members of Occupational Pension Schemes*, Cm. 8649, 1982, since it was the overwhelming concern of the evidence submitted by individuals. The OPB's recommendation was that all schemes should aim as far as possible to maintain the real value of the retired member's pension income, but rejected a mandatory requirement. This was mainly because of the costs of pension increases at a time of economic difficulties, but also because it was thought that voluntary action could achieve progress if the revaluation of the preserved pensions of early leavers was introduced. The OPB did, however, point out that the real cost of providing benefits not linked to inflation would increase considerably if there were to be an end to inflation, with a corresponding reduction in interest rates. It is also the case that the structure of contracted-out pensions introduced from 1978 by the Social Security Pensions Act 1975 provides some inflation-proofing. Pensions payable under the State Earnings-Related Pension Scheme (SERPS) are fully inflation-proofed once in payment. For an occupational scheme to contract-out of SERPS it must pay at least the guaranteed minimum pension (GMP), roughly the equivalent of the SERPS entitlement. Once the GMP comes into payment it is deducted from the individual's SERPS entitlement. At the outset of the scheme, the GMP was flat-rate, so that the protection of the real value of the individual's GMP comes through the SERPS entitlement. (From April 1988 GMPs in payment must be increased in line with the Retail Price Index (RPI) up to a maximum of three per cent.). The GMP element will be significant for lower earners, but only once entitlements have built towards the maximum from 1998.

This is the background to the OPB's 1989 report, *Protecting Pensions—Safeguarding Benefits in a Changing Environment*, Cm. 573. Statistics from the Government Actuary for 1987, which were probably available to the OPB, showed that the proportion of members receiving no increase in the previous year had only gone down to 20 per cent., while most of the increases received by the other 80 per cent. were in the three to five per cent. range (*Hansard*, H.C. Vol. 170, col. 549, March 28, 1990). The OPB highlighted the drawbacks of relying on discretionary increases in pensions, particularly where the management of a company changes through takeover or merger. They say "We put on record our view that time is running out for a structure of fully discretionary payments. Although this has worked satisfactorily in many cases, we believe that in future years it will seem extraordinary that generations of pensioners should have been so exposed to uncertainty as to their standard of living from one year to another, and so dependent on the decisions of company managers whose main preoccupations and responsibilities were, necessarily, elsewhere" (para. 11.10). The aim expressed in the 1982 Report was reaffirmed, but the OPB recommended that schemes should voluntarily introduce guarantees of what they called limited price-indexing (LPI), *i.e.* increases in line with the RPI up to a maximum of five per cent. Their view was that the financial risk of guarantees as against discretionary increases is often over-estimated and that the five per cent. limit would prevent undue strains in times of high inflation. If schemes did not guarantee LPI or better, there should be a "pensioner's option" of replacing the scheme pension by a lower initial pension incorporating a guarantee of LPI, probably as an extension of good practice (para. 11.28). Reaction from the pensions industry to maintaining the voluntary extension of good practice was generally favourable, although not by any means unanimous (see Incomes Data Services, *Uprating Pensions in Payment*, 1989, Chap. 3). Initially the Secretary of State, Tony Newton, accepted this approach, because of the funding difficulties of statutorily required increases, but went beyond the OPB's recommendations in introducing a requirement to revalue *all* present and future pensions in payment up to five per cent. where a scheme is wound up (*Hansard*, H.C. Vol. 159, col. 529 (written answers), November 7, 1989).

The form of s.11 included in the Bill when introduced in the Commons reflected this intention, which was maintained through the Committee stage. The criticism from the Opposition was on the basis that limiting increases to five per cent. meant that the real value of pensions would not be maintained, let alone keep pace with increases in earnings, and that protection ought to extend to all circumstances, not just winding-up. From the pensions industry, the criticism was that the imposition of LPI on pensions earned by any past service imposed large potential liabilities on winding-up that would not have been catered for by past levels of contributions. At the Report stage the Secretary of State announced that in view of all these considerations the Government had concluded that a better balance between the different aims of pension policy would be achieved by applying the general requirements about increases to schemes that are continuing as well as those that are being wound up. "We will seek to avoid forcing employers to put new money into schemes to fund commitments to past service. . . . The new clause makes two requirements. First, schemes will have to pay annual increases to members for pension rights which they build up after an appointed day. For those rights derived from future service, members should be guaranteed increases in line with the retail prices index up to a maximum of five per cent. a year." The second requirement is that "schemes will have to use surpluses to pay increases to members for pension rights which they have already built up. That should include pensions which are now in payment. The guaranteed rate of increase that each scheme will have to pay will depend on the surplus in the pension fund, but the target rate of increase for schemes will be the rise in RPI up to five per cent. a year. . . . In other words, schemes that have surpluses will have to use them to guarantee increases at target level before taking a contribution holiday or a refund" (*Hansard*, H.C. Vol. 170, cols. 548–9, March 28, 1990). In order to allow time for consultation on methods of calculating surpluses and the increases available from them, the new requirements would not bite until 1992.

There has continued to be disquiet about the new provision, particularly that the five per cent. limit is too low or too high, although it is generally agreed to be a considerable improvement on the original version. The Government's view is that it is not good enough that 20 per cent. of members are getting no increase at a time when good investment performances have continued to yield surpluses (*ibid.*). However, these members are most likely to be in smaller schemes where the cost impact is likely to be greatest. The answer is that the overall benefit structure of such a scheme may have to be adjusted so that the initial level of pension is lower (*Hansard*, H.L. Vol. 519, col. 840, May 22, 1990; *Protecting Pensions*, para. 11.14). It remains to be seen whether this, or the withdrawal of employers from final salary schemes, will result from the effect of the new s.58A and other provisions increasing the costs of schemes (see, *e.g.* para. 4 of Sched. 4 extending the revaluation of preserved pension rights to those referable to service before January 1, 1985 and the effects of the E.C.J. judgment in *Barber* v. *Guardian Royal Exchange Assurance Group* [1990] 2 All E.R. 660) or whether the Government have found the right balance between security for members and cost.

S.58A.

Subs. (1) first excludes public service pension schemes and money purchase schemes. "Public service pension scheme" is defined in s.66(1) of the Social Security Pensions Act 1975. Such schemes have their benefits index-linked under the Pensions (Increase) Act 1971 and so do not need s.58A. Members of money purchase schemes (defined in subs. (3), referring on to s.66(1) of the Pensions Act for the definition of "money purchase benefits", therefore covering schemes in which *all* benefits are money purchase benefits) will be entitled to a lump sum to be converted into an annuity. They may choose whether to buy a flat-rate annuity or one with guaranteed increases at various levels. The question of pension increases in personal pension schemes used for contracting out of SERPS will be considered as part of the review of the terms for contracting out in the quinquennium starting in April 1993 (*Hansard*, H.L. Vol. 519, col. 826, May 22, 1990). Secondly, schemes which already guarantee at least LPI on the whole of every existing and future pension are excluded. The "appropriate percentage" referred to in subs. (1)(b) is defined in subs. (3) by reference to revaluation orders under s.52A of the Pensions Act for the purposes of revaluation of preserved pension rights, where a limit of five per cent. compound per year is imposed (s.52A(9)). Schemes have to guarantee LPI on pensions referable to service before the appointed day as well as those referable to service after that day in order to fall outside s.58A.

Subs. (2) then applies the detailed rules of the new Sched. 3 (set out in Sched. 2 to the 1990 Act and annotated there) to non-excluded occupational pension schemes from the appointed day (expected to be January 1, 1992). However, see the immediate effect of s.11(3) of the 1990 Act.

Note that the new provisions apply to "pensions" under schemes. This word is defined in subs. (3) to exclude the GMP element as increased under s.37A of the Pensions Act. This is because of the index-linking provided through SERPS under s.29 of the Pensions Act, described above. Money purchase benefits are also excluded from the definition. This is necessary because a scheme may provide some benefits not on a money purchase basis and thus not be excluded entirely as a money purchase scheme.

Subs. (3)

Although the main provisions under Sched. 3 requiring the use of surpluses to provide increases in pensions referable to service before January 1, 1992 will not come into force until that date, subs. (3) prohibits the return of surplus to an employer from August 17, 1990. The prohibition applies only to schemes to which s.58A(1) of the Pensions Act applies; public service and money purchase schemes are thus excluded. The great majority of occupational pension schemes are constituted by trust deed in order to meet the conditions for "exempt approval" under ss.590 and 591 of the Income and Corporation Taxes Act 1988, but schemes within the definition in s.66(1) of the Pensions Act might be constituted by purely contractual arrangements or possibly by implied trusts. Such schemes are not subject to subs. (3). If subs. (3) applies, no payment can be made to a person (which includes corporate bodies: Interpretation Act 1978) who is or has been an employer of a member of the scheme until the scheme guarantees LPI on all pensions in payment. That full guarantee must by definition not currently exist for the scheme to come within s.58A(1). "Resources" is defined in s.66(1). Subs. (3) overrides the scheme rules (subs. (6)).

Scheme rules rarely allow a repayment to the employer while the scheme is continuing, although amendments may be possible to achieve that end, but on winding-up the return of any funds remaining after the benefits of members and their dependants have been secured and possibly augmented is standard. Indeed, the existence of a provision in the rules to that effect is a condition of Inland Revenue approval (Occupational Pension Schemes: Notes on approval under the Finance Act 1970 as amended by the Finance Act 1971 (IR 12), para. 15.4). Subs. (3) is in quite general terms and seems to apply to a scheme although it is being wound up. The result is that from August 17, 1990 the funds of such a scheme must be applied to guaranteeing LPI to all existing and future pensioners before any surplus returns to the employer, regardless of what the scheme rules say.

The Occupational Pension Schemes (Transitional Provisions and Savings) Regulations 1990 (S.I. 1990 No. 1530) exempt from the application of subs. (3) certain payments to employers from schemes which were established before August 17, 1990. Most of the kinds of payments specified are straightforward, but the list includes loans and investments of scheme funds, providing that they show a reasonable commercial return (reg. 2(2)(c)), and payments for which a proposal was received by the Inland Revenue for approval before July 17, 1990 (reg. 2(2)(f)).

The Pensions Ombudsman

12.—(1) The Pensions Act shall have effect with the amendments made by Schedule 3 to this Act, which are made for the purpose of establishing, conferring functions on, and making general provision in connection with, a commissioner to be known as the Pensions Ombudsman.

(2) In the Tribunals and Inquiries Act 1971—

(a) in paragraph 23 of Schedule 1 (certain tribunals concerned with pensions to be under the general supervision of the Council) there shall be added at the end of the second column—

"(e) the Pensions Ombudsman established under Part IVA of the Social Security Pensions Act 1975 (c. 60) in respect of his functions under or by virtue of section 59C(2) of that Act."; and

(b) in section 8(2) (which specifies the paragraph numbers of the tribunals which are excepted from the requirement of concurrence to the removal of members) after "22" there shall be inserted "23(e)."

COMMENCEMENT
October 1, 1990 (Social Security Act 1990 (Commencement No. 1) Order 1990 (S.I. 1990 No. 1446), art. 2(e) and (h)); July 18, 1990 for authorising the making of regulations (art. 2(d)).

DEFINITION
"the Pensions Act": s.20.

GENERAL NOTE

Subs. (1)
This provision simply enacts Sched. 3 on the Pensions Ombudsman. Full annotations follow that Schedule.

Subs. (2)
The effect of this provision is that the element of the Pensions Ombudsman's jurisdiction covering the investigation and determination of disputes of fact or law between the trustees or managers of a scheme, or an employer, and an authorised complainant is put within the remit of the Council on Tribunals. The Council then has certain statutory powers in relation to that jurisdiction. When the Pensions Ombudsman is investigating and determining complaints of injustice in consequence of maladministration he is outside the Council's remit. This emphasises the strange mixture of functions given to the Pensions Ombudsman, who has nearly all the powers usually associated with a tribunal.

Registration of occupational and personal pension schemes

13.—(1) At the beginning of Part V of the Pensions Act there shall be inserted the following section—

"Registration of occupational and personal pension schemes
59K.—(1) The Secretary of State may by regulations make provision—
(a) for the compilation and maintenance of a register of occupational and personal pension schemes ("the register");
(b) for the appointment of a Registrar of Occupational and Personal Pension Schemes ("the registrar"); and
(c) for conferring on the registrar such functions relating to the compilation and maintenance of the register as may be specified in the regulations.
(2) The regulations—
(a) may make provision with respect to any of the following matters, that is to say—
(i) the remuneration and expenses, and any pensions, allowances or gratuities, or compensation for loss of office, payable to or in respect of the registrar;
(ii) the staff and other facilities that are to be available to the registrar;
(iii) the other terms and conditions upon which the registrar is to hold office; and
(iv) the removal of the registrar from office; and
(b) may confer upon the registrar power to appoint an agent to perform any of his functions on his behalf.
(3) The register—
(a) may consist of one or more parts, as may be prescribed;
(b) shall be organised in such manner, and contain such information relating to occupational and personal pension schemes, as may be prescribed; and
(c) subject to the regulations, may be kept in such manner and form as the registrar may think fit.
(4) The regulations may make provision—
(a) for the register, or for extracts from the register, or for copies

of the register or of extracts from the register, to be open to inspection by, and

(b) for copies of the register, or of extracts from it, to be supplied to,

such persons, in such manner, at such times, upon payment of such fees, and subject to such other terms and conditions, as may be prescribed.

(5) The regulations may require—

(a) any person who is or has been—

(i) a trustee or manager of an occupational or personal pension scheme or an administrator of a public service pension scheme, or

(ii) the employer in relation to employment of any description or category to which an occupational pension scheme relates, and

(b) such other persons as may be prescribed,

to provide the registrar with such information for the purposes of the register in such form and within such time as may be prescribed.

(6) The Secretary of State, the Inland Revenue and the Occupational Pensions Board may provide the registrar with such information as he may request for the purposes of the register; and no obligation as to secrecy or confidentiality imposed by statute or otherwise on—

(a) persons employed in the Department of Social Security,

(b) persons employed in relation to the Inland Revenue, or

(c) the staff of the Occupational Pensions Board,

shall prevent them from disclosing to the registrar such information as is necessary for the purposes of the register.

(7) The Secretary of State may direct the registrar to submit to him, in such form and at such intervals as may be specified in the direction, such statistical and other reports as the Secretary of State may require; and the Secretary of State may determine at his discretion whether or not to publish a report submitted to him under this subsection.

(8) In this section "employer," in relation to a pension scheme, includes a person who is or has been treated under section 66(3) below as an employer in relation to the scheme for the purposes of Part III or IV of this Act.

(9) Subsections (2) to (5) above are without prejudice to the generality of subsection (1) above and nothing in subsection (5) or (6) above shall be taken to imply that the Occupational Pensions Board may not be appointed as the registrar."

(2) The following provisions of the Pensions Act (which make provision with respect to the registration of occupational pension schemes and which are set out in Schedule 2 to the Social Security Act 1985 and have not all been brought into force) shall cease to have effect—

(a) sections 56B to 56D;

(b) section 56E(1)(c);

(c) sections 56F to 56K;

(d) section 56L(1)(b), (5)(b) and (9); and

(e) sections 56M and 56N.

COMMENCEMENT

July 18, 1990 (Social Security Act 1990 (Commencement No. 1) Order 1990 (S.I. 1990 No. 1446), art. 2(a)).

DEFINITION

"the Pensions Act": s.20.

The statutory framework for a registrar of occupational pension schemes inserted into the
Social Security Pensions Act 1975 by the Social Security Act 1985 was never brought into force.
That framework envisaged the registrar having extensive functions for the collection of scheme
documentation. The OPB in *Protecting Pensions: Safeguarding Benefits in a Changing Environment*, Cm. 573, 1989, instead recommended the simplified proposals it had originally proposed
in 1981. These were for the compulsory registration of all pension schemes with a registry which
would be essentially a tracing agency. The OPB also recommended that a trustees' annual
report should be filed with the registrar (para. 13.6). It was envisaged that fees paid by schemes
for registration would finance an information and conciliation service and a pensions tribunal.
The Government has accepted the essentials of the OPB's recommendation for a tracing
agency, but without any wider functions.

Subs. (1)
Subs. (1) inserts a new s.59K into the Social Security Pensions Act 1975, which mainly gives
authority for the making of regulations which will constitute the registration scheme. Under
s.59K(1) the register will cover both occupational pension schemes and personal pension
schemes. There is power under subs. (3) for regulations to prescribe any information about
schemes which must be provided, but the intention is to limit the scheme to a means of tracing
the name and address of the company responsible for dealing with pensions under particular
schemes. "We are not attempting to provide a much more comprehensive information service
about pension schemes, along the lines of that which is provided for in the 1985 Act. There
would be all kinds of operational problems if we tried to do so. There are more than 100,000
pension schemes. It would be a vast undertaking and would involve a massive library of pension
scheme reports, alongside the tracing registry" (Standing Committee G, col. 294, February 27,
1990). Once the scheme was traced, a member could then ask for a copy of any annual report
under the Occupational Pension Schemes (Disclosure of Information) Regulations 1986.
S.59K(4) allows fees to be prescribed for inspection of the register. The Government has in
mind a "nominal" fee of about £1. There is no fee for registration, but there is a separate
provision (see Sched. 4, para. 12) for a levy on schemes to finance the tracing registry, the
information and conciliation service and the Pensions Ombudsman.
Under s.59K(6) the DSS, the OPB and the Inland Revenue are authorised to provide
information to the registrar. The Secretary of State may require the registrar to produce
reports, which he may then publish.
It was announced on September 6, 1990 that the OPB is to be the registrar and that schemes
will have to provide information for the first time early in 1991.

Subs. (2)
The provisions of the Pensions Act setting up the framework for a more extensive registration
system are repealed.

Miscellaneous amendments relating to pensions

14.—(1) The enactments mentioned in Schedule 4 to this Act (which
relate to occupational and personal pensions) shall have effect with the
amendments there specified.

(2) Regulations may modify the provisions inserted into the Pensions Act
by paragraph 2 of that Schedule in any manner which the Secretary of State
thinks appropriate with a view to securing the orderly implementation of
those provisions and to obtaining general compliance with them.

COMMENCEMENT
Various dates: see Sched. 4.

DEFINITIONS
"the Pensions Act": s.20.
"regulations": *ibid.*

GENERAL NOTE
Subs. (1) enacts the amendments in Sched. 4. See the annotations to that Schedule. Subs. (2)
gives the Secretary of State very wide powers to make regulations to modify the application of
the new s.58B of the Social Security Pensions Act 1975 inserted by para. 2 of Sched. 4
(deficiency of assets of scheme on winding-up to be a debt due from the employer).

27–33

Energy efficiency in certain dwellings etc.

Grants for the improvement of energy efficiency in certain dwellings etc.

15.—(1) The Secretary of State may make or arrange for the making of grants—

    (a) towards the cost of carrying out work—

        (i) for the purpose of improving the thermal insulation of dwellings, or

        (ii) otherwise for the purpose of reducing or preventing the wastage of energy in connection with space or water heating in dwellings; and

    (b) where any such work is, or is to be, carried out, towards the cost of providing persons with advice relating to thermal insulation or to the economic and efficient use of domestic appliances or of facilities for lighting, or for space or water heating, in dwellings;

but no grants shall be made under this section except in accordance with regulations made by the Secretary of State.

(2) The regulations may make provision with respect to—

    (a) the descriptions of dwelling and work in respect of which a grant under subsection (1)(a) above may be made;

    (b) the nature and extent of the advice with respect to the provision of which grants under subsection (1)(b) above may be made;

    (c) the descriptions of person from whom an application for a grant under subsection (1)(a) or (b) above may be entertained;

    (d) the persons to whom such an application is to be made;

    (e) the payment of such grants to persons other than the applicant;

    (f) the conditions on which such a grant may be made.

(3) The regulations—

    (a) may specify or make provision for determining the amount or maximum amount of any grant under this section; and

    (b) may include provision requiring work to comply with standards of materials and workmanship (whether prescribed standards, or standards otherwise laid down from time to time by a prescribed person) if it is to be eligible for a grant under subsection (1)(a) above.

(4) Subsections (1) to (3) above shall apply in relation to any building in multiple occupation as they apply in relation to a dwelling; and for this purpose "building in multiple occupation" means a building which is occupied by persons who do not form a single household, exclusive of any part of the building which is occupied as a separate dwelling by persons who form a single household.

(5) The Secretary of State may delegate any of his functions in relation to grants under this section to such persons or bodies of persons as he may determine, and may pay to any person or body of persons to whom functions are so delegated, or upon whom functions are otherwise conferred under or by virtue of this section, such fees as may be agreed.

(6) Without prejudice to the generality of the powers conferred by this section, the regulations may make provision for any of the following matters, that is to say—

    (a) for appointing for any particular area a person or body of persons (an "administering agency") to perform in that area such functions as the Secretary of State may confer upon that person or body for the purposes of, or otherwise in connection with, this section (whether those functions are prescribed, or specified otherwise than in regulations);

    (b) for the administering agency for any area to select, in accordance with criteria (whether prescribed criteria, or criteria otherwise laid down from time to time by a prescribed person), and register as the network installer for any particular locality within their area, a person or body of persons capable of carrying out, or arranging for the carrying out of, work in respect of which grants under subsection (1)(a) above may be made, to perform in that locality such functions as the Secretary of State or that agency may confer upon that person or body for the purposes of, or otherwise in connection with, this section (whether those functions are prescribed, or specified otherwise than in regulations);

(c) for the allocation by the Secretary of State to an administering agency of the sums which are to be available to that agency in any period for the purpose of making grants under this section in that period, and for the re-allocation of any sums so allocated;

(d) for the allocation by an administering agency to a network installer of an amount which represents the total amount of grant under this section which the agency determines is, or is to be, available for any period in respect of work carried out, and advice given, by that installer and any sub-contractors of his in that period, and for the re-allocation of any amount so allocated.

(7) The provision that may be made in regulations by virtue of subsection (6) above includes provision—

(a) for the making of appointments, or the conferring of functions, under that subsection to be effected in whole or in part by or under a contract made between prescribed persons and for requiring any such contract to contain prescribed terms and conditions or terms and conditions with respect to prescribed matters;

(b) for terminating any appointment as an administering agency or any registration as a network installer;

(c) for conferring upon network installers the exclusive right to apply for grants by virtue of subsection (4) above;

(d) for conferring upon administering agencies functions relating to the general oversight of network installers and the verification of claims made, and information supplied, by them.

(8) The power to make regulations under this section shall be exercisable by statutory instrument made with the consent of the Treasury; and any statutory instrument containing regulations under this section shall be subject to annulment in pursuance of a resolution of the House of Commons.

(9) Regulations under this section—

(a) may make different provision with respect to any labour involved, materials used or other items comprised in the carrying out of work; and

(b) may make different provision for different cases and different areas.

(10) In this section—

"functions" means powers and duties and includes the exercise of a discretion with respect to any matter;

"prescribed" means specified in, or determined in accordance with, regulations under this section.

(11) Sections 252 and 253 of the Housing (Scotland) Act 1987 (grants for thermal insulation) shall cease to have effect.

COMMENCEMENT
Apart from subs. (11) (not yet known), July 13, 1990 (s.23(3)(a)).

DEFINITION
"regulations": s.20.

GENERAL NOTE
S.15 sets up the statutory framework for a scheme to replace the present energy grants scheme, which has provided funds for draught-proofing in low-income households. That scheme has relied on the community programme, which is now inadequate for the purpose. The

new scheme will be introduced and run by the Department of Energy. The intention is that administering agencies will be appointed in particular localities. These will receive applications and determine whether they meet the criteria set out in the regulations and will be provided with funds by the Secretary of State. The agencies may also provide advice on insulation and the efficient use of energy in dwellings. A consultation exercise on the structure to be adopted was carried out while the Act was going through Parliament.

The cost is estimated to be £12 million in 1990–91 and £30 million in a full year.

S.15 itself merely contains a series of authorisations for the making of regulations, which may set out the criteria for making grants and provide for a maximum level of grant.

Financial provisions

Removal of certain liabilities from the National Insurance Fund

16.—(1) In section 1 of the principal Act (outline of the contributory system) at the end of paragraph (a) of subsection (1) there shall be added the word "and" and paragraph (c) of that subsection (benefit under the Old Cases Act to be provided by means of contributions etc) shall cease to have effect.

(2) At the end of that subsection there shall be added the words "together with the additions under subsection (4A) below" and after subsection (4) there shall be inserted—

"(4A) For the financial year beginning with April 1, 1990 and for each subsequent financial year, there shall, by way of addition to contributions, be paid out of money provided by Parliament, in such manner and at such times as the Treasury may determine, amounts the total of which for any such year is equal to the aggregate of all statutory sick pay and statutory maternity pay paid by employers and others in that year, as estimated by the Government Actuary."

(3) In section 134 of that Act (destination of contributions etc) after subsection (2) there shall be inserted—

"(2A) The additions paid under section 1(4A) above shall be paid, in accordance with any directions given by the Treasury, into the National Insurance Fund."

(4) In section 135 of that Act, at the end of subsection (2) (which specifies the benefits which are to be paid out of money provided by Parliament instead of out of the National Insurance Fund) there shall be added—

"(h) industrial injuries benefit."

(5) In subsection (5) of that section (Consolidated Fund to be reimbursed out of National Insurance Fund in respect of certain administrative expenses, but excluding those specified in the paragraphs of that subsection) after paragraph (a) there shall be inserted—

"(aa) expenses attributable to the carrying into effect of the Old Cases Act; and ."

(6) In section 137(1) and (2) of that Act (Government Actuary's periodical reviews of the working of the principal Act and the Old Cases Act with a view to ascertaining likely demands on the National Insurance Fund) the words "and the Old Cases Act" shall cease to have effect.

(7) In section 159 of that Act, in subsection (4) (certain payments in respect of pre-1948 cases to be made out of the National Insurance Fund) for the words "the National Insurance Fund" there shall be substituted the words "money provided by Parliament."

(8) In the Old Cases Act—

(a) in sections 2(1) and 5(1) (schemes under those provisions to be financed out of the National Insurance Fund) for the words "the National Insurance Fund" there shall be substituted the words "money provided by Parliament";

(b) in section 4(4)(e) (provision for the repayment to the National Insurance Fund of payments subsequently found not to have been due) for the words "the National Insurance Fund" there shall be substituted the words "the Secretary of State"; and

(c) section 13 (reciprocal arrangements with Northern Ireland in relation to payments out of the respective National Insurance Funds) shall cease to have effect.

(9) Section 46(3) of the 1982 Act and section 85(4)(a) of the 1986 Act (which provide for the payment of sums out of the National Insurance Fund into the Consolidated Fund in respect of estimated administrative expenses relating to statutory sick pay and statutory maternity pay) shall cease to have effect.

(10) Subsections (1) and (4) to (8) above shall be taken to have come into force on April 1, 1990.

COMMENCEMENT
Subss. (1), (4) to (8) and (10), July 13, 1990 (s.23(3)(a)); subss. (2), (3) and (9), July 18, 1990 (Social Security Act 1990 (Commencement No. 1) Order 1990 (S.I. 1990 No. 1446), art. 2(a)).

DEFINITIONS
"the 1982 Act": s.20.
"the 1986 Act": *ibid*.
"the Old Cases Act": *ibid*.
"the principal Act": *ibid*.

GENERAL NOTE
The overall effect of s.16 is to remove the cost of providing industrial injuries benefits (including those under the Industrial Injuries and Diseases (Old Cases) Act 1975), statutory sick pay and statutory maternity pay from the National Insurance Fund and to transfer it to general taxation. The reasoning is that entitlement to these benefits does not depend on having paid any contributions (Standing Committee G, col. 388, March 6, 1990).

Note that by virtue of subs. (10) the amendments made by subss. (1) and (4) to (8) are taken to have been in force since April 1, 1990.

Interest and penalties in respect of certain contributions

17.—(1) In section 9 of the principal Act, in subsection (5) (Inland Revenue to pay to the Secretary of State the Class 4 contributions collected by them) after the words "pay to him" there shall be inserted "(a)" and at the end of that subsection there shall be added the words "and

(b) so much of any interest recovered by the Inland Revenue by virtue of paragraph 7 of Schedule 2 to this Act as remains after the deduction by them of any administrative costs attributable to its recovery."

(2) In subsection (6) of that section (estimated Class 4 contributions collected from persons in Northern Ireland to be paid over to the Northern Ireland Department) after the word "collected" there shall be inserted the words ", or interest in respect of such contributions recovered,".

(3) In section 134 of that Act (destination of contributions etc) after the subsection (2A) inserted by section 16 above there shall be inserted—

"(2B) The sums paid to the Secretary of State by the Inland Revenue under section 9(5)(b) of this Act and paragraphs 5(3)(b) and 5A(7) of Schedule 1 to this Act in respect of interest and penalties recovered by them in connection with contributions of any class shall, subject to section 9(6) of this Act, be paid, in accordance with any directions given by the Treasury, into the National Insurance Fund."

(4) In section 135 of that Act (general financial arrangements) after subsection (6) there shall be added—

"(7) Any expenditure in respect of the payment of interest or repayment supplements under or by virtue of paragraph 5 of Schedule 1 to this Act or paragraph 7 of Schedule 2 to this Act shall be defrayed out of the National Insurance Fund in accordance with any directions given by the Treasury."

(5) In paragraph 5 of Schedule 1 to that Act (power to combine collection of contributions with collection of tax) after sub-paragraph (1) there shall be inserted—

"(1A) Without prejudice to the generality of sub-paragraph (1) above, the provision that may be made by virtue of paragraph (a) of that sub-paragraph includes, in relation to Class 1 contributions—

(a) provision for requiring the payment of interest on sums due in respect of Class 1 contributions which are not paid by the due date, for determining the date (being not less than 14 days after the end of the tax year in respect of which the sums are due) from which such interest is to be calculated and for enabling the repayment or remission of such interest;

(b) provision for requiring the payment of interest on sums due in respect of Class 1 contributions which fall to be repaid and for determining the date (being not less than one year after the end of the tax year in respect of which the sums are due) from which such interest is to be calculated;

(c) provision for, or in connection with, the imposition and recovery of penalties in relation to any returns required to be made which relate to Class 1 contributions, but subject to sub-paragraph (2) and paragraph 5A below;

and any reference to contributions or income tax in paragraph (b) or (c) of sub-paragraph (1) above shall be construed as including a reference to any interest or penalty in respect of contributions or income tax, as the case may be.

(1B) The rate of interest applicable for any purpose of this paragraph shall be the rate from time to time prescribed for that purpose under section 178 of the Finance Act 1989.

(1C) Regulations under this paragraph may require the payment of interest on sums due in respect of contributions, notwithstanding that a question arising in relation to the contributions has not been determined under section 93 of this Act by the Secretary of State, except that where—

(a) any such question arises which affects a person's liability for, or the amount of, any such interest, and

(b) either—

(i) that person requires the question to be determined under section 93, or

(ii) a question of law arising in connection with the determination of the question is, or is to be, referred to a court under section 94 of this Act,

the regulations shall not require the payment of any such interest until the question has been determined under section 93 by the Secretary of State or the reference has been finally disposed of under section 94, as the case may be; but, subject to that, this paragraph is without prejudice to sections 93, 94 and 96 of this Act."

(6) In sub-paragraph (3) of that paragraph (payment of receipts to Secretary of State) after the words "pay to him" there shall be inserted "(a)" and at the end of that sub-paragraph there shall be added the words "and

(b) so much of any interest recovered by the Inland Revenue by virtue of this paragraph as remains after the deduction by them of any administrative costs attributable to its recovery."

(7) After that paragraph there shall be inserted the provisions set out in Schedule 5 to this Act, which relate to the imposition and recovery of certain penalties.

(8) In paragraph 7 of Schedule 2 to the principal Act (which provides for the charging of interest under section 88 of the Taxes Management Act 1970 in respect of Class 4 contributions, but precludes the charging of interest

under section 86 of that Act in respect of overdue contributions) and in paragraph 7 of Schedule 2 to the Social Security (Northern Ireland) Act 1975 (which reproduces those provisions)—

(a) for the words "Section 88(1)" there shall be substituted the words "(1) Sections 86 and 88(1)";

(b) after the word "(interest" there shall be inserted the words "on amounts overdue, and";

(c) for the words "it applies" there shall be substituted the words "they apply"; and

(d) for the words from "but section 86" to "shall not apply" there shall be substituted the words "and section 824 of the Income and Corporation Taxes Act 1988 (repayment supplements) shall, with the necessary modifications, apply in relation to Class 4 contributions as it applies in relation to income tax."

(9) In each of those Acts, at the end of paragraph 7 of Schedule 2 there shall be added—

"(2) The Inland Revenue shall have the same powers under section 1 of the Taxes Management Act 1970 (general functions of care and management) in relation to the remission of interest payable under section 86 or 88 of that Act by virtue of this paragraph as they have in relation to the remission of interest payable under either of those sections on tax."

(10) In section 178 of the Finance Act 1989 (rates of interest) in subsection (2), after paragraph (g) there shall be inserted—

"(gg) paragraph 5 of Schedule 1 to the Social Security Act 1975,".

COMMENCEMENT

Subs. (7), July 18, 1990 (Social Security Act 1990 (Commencement No. 1) Order 1990 (S.I. 1990 No. 1446), art. 2(a)); remainder, not known at date of publication.

DEFINITION

"the principal Act": s.20.

GENERAL NOTE

The amendments in subss. (1) to (4) and (6) provide that any interest and penalties on contributions collected by the Inland Revenue are to be paid into the National Insurance Fund, which is also to bear the cost of interest on the repayment of contributions. Subss. (5) and (8) to (10) provide for the extension of the power to require the payment of interest on late paid contributions. Sub. (7) enacts Sched. 5, which gives power for regulations to impose penalties on the late payment of contributions.

General financial provisions

18.—(1) There shall be paid out of money provided by Parliament—

(a) any expenses incurred under this Act by a Minister of the Crown; and

(b) any increase attributable to the provisions of this Act in the sums payable out of such money under any other Act.

(2) There shall be paid out of the National Insurance Fund into the Consolidated Fund, at such times and in such manner as the Treasury may direct, such sums as the Secretary of State may estimate (in accordance with any directions given by the Treasury) to be the amount of the administrative expenses incurred by him under sections 4, 6 and 17, Schedules 1 and 5 and paragraphs 1 to 3, 5, 9, 26 and 27 of Schedule 6 excluding any category of expenses or payments which the Treasury may direct, or any enactment may require, to be excluded from the Secretary of State's estimates under this subsection.

(3) There shall be paid into the Consolidated Fund any increase by virtue of this Act in the sums so payable by virtue of any other Act.

COMMENCEMENT

July 13, 1990 (s.23(3)(a)).

General and supplementary provisions

Regulations and orders

19.—(1) Subject to the following provisions of this section, subsections (1) to (3A) of section 166 of the principal Act shall apply in relation to any power conferred by any provision of this Act, other than section 15, to make regulations or an order as they apply in relation to any power conferred by that Act to make regulations or an order, but as if for references to that Act there were substituted references to this Act.

(2) A statutory instrument—

(a) which contains (whether alone or with other provisions) any regulations or orders under this Act, other than regulations under section 15 above or orders under section 23 below, and

(b) which is not subject to any requirement that a draft of the instrument be laid before and approved by a resolution of each House of Parliament,

shall be subject to annulment in pursuance of a resolution of either House of Parliament.

(3) A power conferred by this Act to make any regulations or an order, where the power is not expressed to be exercisable with the consent of the Treasury, shall if the Treasury so direct be exercisable only in conjunction with them.

COMMENCEMENT
July 13, 1990 (s.23(3)(a)).

DEFINITIONS
"the principal Act": s.20.
"regulations": *ibid*.

Interpretation

20. In this Act, unless the context otherwise requires—
"the 1973 Act" means the Social Security Act 1973;
"the 1982 Act" means the Social Security and Housing Benefits Act 1982;
"the 1986 Act" means the Social Security Act 1986;
"the 1989 Act" means the Social Security Act 1989;
"the Old Cases Act" means the Industrial Injuries and Diseases (Old Cases) Act 1975;
"the Pensions Act" means the Social Security Pensions Act 1975;
"prescribe," except in section 15, means prescribe by regulations;
"the principal Act" means the Social Security Act 1975;
"regulations" means regulations made by the Secretary of State.

COMMENCEMENT
July 13, 1990 (s.23(3)(a)).

Minor and consequential amendments and repeals

21.—(1) The enactments mentioned in Schedule 6 to this Act shall have effect with the amendments there specified (being minor amendments and amendments consequential on provisions of this Act).

(2) The enactments mentioned in Schedule 7 to this Act (which include some that are spent or of no further practical utility) are repealed to the extent specified in the third column of that Schedule.

(3) The Secretary of State may by regulations make—
(a) such transitional provision,

(b) such consequential provision, or
(c) such savings,
as he considers necessary or expedient in preparation for or in connection with the coming into force of any provision of this Act or the operation of any enactment repealed or amended by a provision of this Act during any period when the repeal or amendment is not wholly in force.

COMMENCEMENT
Subss. (1) and (2), various dates (see Scheds. 6 and 7); subs. (3), July 13, 1990 (s.23(3)(a)).

Provision for Northern Ireland

22.—(1) An Order in Council under paragraph 1(1)(b) of Schedule 1 to the Northern Ireland Act 1974 (legislation for Northern Ireland in the interim period) which states that it is made only for purposes corresponding to those of this Act—
(a) shall not be subject to paragraph 1(4) and (5) of that Schedule (affirmative resolution of both Houses of Parliament); but
(b) shall be subject to annulment in pursuance of a resolution of either House of Parliament.
(2) Subject to any Order made after the passing of this Act by virtue of subsection (1)(a) of section 3 of the Northern Ireland Constitution Act 1973, the matters specified in subsection (3) below shall not be transferred matters for the purposes of that Act but shall for the purposes of subsection (2) of that section be treated as specified in Schedule 3 to that Act.
(3) The matters referred to in subsection (2) above are the matters dealt with—
(a) by the section 59B inserted into the Pensions Act by Schedule 3 to this Act, other than subsections (4) and (5)(b) of that section; and
(b) by subsections (1), (2), other than paragraph (a)(ii), (3), (4) and (9) of the section 59K inserted into that Act by section 13(1) of this Act.

COMMENCEMENT
July 13, 1990 (s.23(3)(a)).

DEFINITION
"the Pensions Act": s.20.

Short title, commencement and extent

23.—(1) This Act may be cited as the Social Security Act 1990; and this Act, other than section 15, and the Social Security Acts 1975 to 1989 may be cited together as the Social Security Acts 1975 to 1990.
(2) Apart from the provisions specified in subsection (3) below, this Act shall not come into force until such day as the Secretary of State may by order appoint; and different days may be so appointed for different provisions or different purposes of the same provision.
(3) The provisions referred to in subsection (2) above are the following—
(a) sections 3(6), 5, 6, 7, 10, 15, other than subsection (11), 16(1), (4) to (8) and (10), 18, 19, 20, 21(3), 22 and this section;
(b) Schedule 1;
(c) paragraphs 6, 8, 9 and 15 of Schedule 4 (and section 14 so far as relating to those provisions);
(d) paragraphs 2 to 9, 12 to 15, 17, 18, 19, 21, 26, 27 and 30 of Schedule 6 (and section 21 so far as relating to those provisions);
(e) the amendments in that Schedule to the extent that they are consequential on any provision specified in paragraphs (a) to (d) above (and section 21 so far as relating to any such amendments); and
(f) the repeals in Schedule 7 to the extent that they are consequential on

any provision specified in paragraphs (a) to (e) above (and section 21 so far as relating to those repeals).

(4) Where any enactment repealed or amended by this Act extends to any part of the United Kingdom, the repeal or amendment extends to that part.

(5) The following provisions of this Act extend to Northern Ireland, namely—

(a) section 13(1), so far as it amends the Pensions Act by the insertion of section 59K(1), (2), other than paragraph (a)(ii), (3), (4) and (9);

(b) section 22 above and this section;

(c) paragraph 5(1) and (3) of Schedule 1;

(d) Schedule 3, so far as it amends the Pensions Act by the insertion of section 59B, other than subsections (4) and (5)(b), and section 12(1) so far as relating to that amendment;

and paragraph 5(4) of Schedule 1 extends to Northern Ireland only.

(6) Except as provided by this section, this Act does not extend to Northern Ireland.

COMMENCEMENT
July 13, 1990 (subs. (3)(a)).

SCHEDULES

Section 7   SCHEDULE 1

AMENDMENTS RELATING TO THE RECOVERY FROM DAMAGES ETC OF SUMS EQUIVALENT TO BENEFIT

Payments under compensation schemes for motor accidents

1.—(1) In the definition of "compensation payment" in section 22(3) of the 1989 Act—

(a) at the beginning of paragraph (b) there shall be inserted the words "either (i)" and at the end of that paragraph there shall be inserted the words "or

(ii) in pursuance of a compensation scheme for motor accidents,"; and

(b) for the words following that paragraph there shall be substituted the words—

"but does not include benefit or an exempt payment or so much of any payment as is referable to costs incurred by any person;".

(2) After that definition there shall be inserted—

" "compensation scheme for motor accidents" means any scheme or arrangement under which funds are available for the payment of compensation in respect of motor accidents caused, or alleged to have been caused, by uninsured or unidentified persons;".

(3) In consequence of the amendment made by sub-paragraph (1)(b) above, in the definition of "relevant period" in the said section 22(3), the words from "whether or not" onwards shall be omitted.

(4) In paragraph 13 of Schedule 4 to that Act, after sub-paragraph (2) there shall be inserted—

"(2A) A person who makes any payment (whether a compensation payment or not) on behalf of himself or another—

(a) in consequence of any accident, injury or disease suffered, or any damage to property sustained, by any other person, or

(b) which is referable to any costs, or, in Scotland, expenses, incurred by any such other person by reason of such an accident, injury, disease or damage,

shall, if the Secretary of State so requests him in writing, furnish the Secretary of State with such particulars relating to the size and composition of the payment as may be specified in the request."

Payments into court

2.—(1) In paragraph 12 of Schedule 4 to that Act, in sub-paragraph (2)(b) (payments into court: compensator not liable to make relevant payment etc until he is notified that the money has been paid out to the other party) after the words "notified that" there shall be inserted the words "the whole or any part of."

(2) In sub-paragraph (5) of that paragraph (special provision where payment into court is paid out to or for the other party within 21 days) for the words "paid out of court to or for" there shall be substituted the words "accepted by" and for the words "was made" there shall be substituted the words "(or, if there were two or more such payments, the last of them) was made; but where the payment into court is not so accepted, then—

    (a) the relevant period as respects that compensator shall end on the day on which he is notified that the payment has been paid out of court to or for that other party; and

    (b) in determining the amount of the relevant payment, that compensator shall be treated as if his payment into court had been made on that day."

(3) In sub-paragraph (6) of that paragraph (the initial period) after the words "payment into court" there shall be inserted the words "(or, if there were two or more such payments, the last of them)."

(4) After that sub-paragraph there shall be inserted—

    "(6A) Where a payment into court is paid out wholly to or for the party who made the payment (otherwise than to or for the other party to the action) the making of the payment into court shall cease to be regarded as the making of a compensation payment."

Appeals: special time limit for provisional damages

3. In paragraph 17 of that Schedule, in sub-paragraph (3) (which provides a special time limit for appeals in cases where provisional damages are awarded) for paragraph (a) there shall be substituted—

    "(a) an award of damages ("provisional damages") has been made under or by virtue of—

        (i) section 32A(2)(a) of the Supreme Court Act 1981,

        (ii) section 12(2)(a) of the Administration of Justice Act 1982, or

        (iii) section 51(2)(a) of the County Courts Act 1984, and."

Appeal to Commissioner by Secretary of State on point of law

4. In sub-paragraph (11) of that paragraph (appeal on point of law from decision of social security appeal tribunal or medical appeal tribunal) after the words "at the instance of" there shall be inserted the words "the Secretary of State,".

Interaction with the Northern Ireland scheme

5.—(1) At the beginning of Part IV of that Schedule (which, among other things, relates to cases where the compensator is not resident in Great Britain) there shall be inserted the following—

"Persons in Northern Ireland

20A.—(1) Where, immediately before making a compensation payment to or in respect of a victim, the compensator—

    (a) is not resident and does not have a place of business in Great Britain, but

    (b) is resident or has a place of business in Northern Ireland,

the Great Britain provisions shall apply as if at that time he were resident or had a place of business in the relevant part of Great Britain.

(2) Where, immediately before making a Northern Ireland compensation payment to or in respect of a Northern Ireland victim, the Northern Ireland compensator—

    (a) is not resident and does not have a place of business in Northern Ireland, but

    (b) is resident or has a place of business in any part of Great Britain,

the Northern Ireland provisions shall apply as if at that time he were resident or had a place of business in Northern Ireland.

(3) Where an address in Northern Ireland is the first address notified in writing to the compensator by or on behalf of the victim as his residence (or, if the victim has died, by or on behalf of the intended recipient as the victim's last residence) then—

    (a) the compensator shall apply, as a Northern Ireland compensator, for a Northern Ireland certificate in accordance with the Northern Ireland provisions (and shall not make any separate application for a certificate of total benefit);

    (b) any Northern Ireland certificate which is issued to the compensator in relation to the victim and the accident, injury or disease in question—

        (i) shall contain a statement that it is to be treated as including a certificate of total benefit so issued by the Secretary of State and that any relevant payment required to be made to him by reference thereto is to be paid to the Northern Ireland Department as his agent; and

(ii) shall be taken to include such a certificate of total benefit; and

(c) any payment made by the compensator to the Northern Ireland Department in pursuance of such a Northern Ireland certificate shall be applied—

(i) first towards discharging his liability under the Northern Ireland provisions, and

(ii) then, as respects any remaining balance, towards discharging his liability under the Great Britain provisions,

in respect of the relevant victim and that accident, injury or disease.

(4) Where an address in any part of Great Britain is the first address notified in writing to the Northern Ireland compensator by or on behalf of the Northern Ireland victim as his residence (or, if the Northern Ireland victim has died, by or on behalf of the Northern Ireland intended recipient as the Northern Ireland victim's last residence) then—

(a) the Northern Ireland compensator shall apply, as a compensator, for a certificate of total benefit in accordance with the Great Britain provisions (and shall not make any separate application for a Northern Ireland certificate);

(b) any certificate of total benefit which is issued to the Northern Ireland compensator in relation to the Northern Ireland victim and the accident, injury or disease in question—

(i) shall contain a statement that it is to be treated as including a Northern Ireland certificate so issued by the Northern Ireland Department and that any Northern Ireland relevant payment required to be made to that Department by reference thereto is to be paid to the Secretary of State as its agent; and

(ii) shall be taken to include such a Northern Ireland certificate; and

(c) any payment made by the Northern Ireland compensator to the Secretary of State in pursuance of such a certificate shall be applied—

(i) first towards discharging his liability under the Great Britain provisions, and

(ii) then, as respects any remaining balance, towards discharging his liability under the Northern Ireland provisions, in respect of the relevant victim and that accident, injury or disease.

(5) For the purposes of sub-paragraph (1) above, "the relevant part of Great Britain," in relation to a compensator, means—

(a) if the compensator has been notified in writing—

(i) by or on behalf of the victim, or

(ii) where the victim has died, by or on behalf of the intended recipient,

that the victim is or was at any time resident at an address in any part of Great Britain, that part of Great Britain (or, if more than one such notification has been given, the part in which he was so notified that the victim was most recently so resident); or

(b) in any other case, such part of Great Britain as the Secretary of State may determine in accordance with regulations.

(6) In this paragraph—

"the Great Britain provisions" means the recoupment provisions, other than this paragraph;

"Northern Ireland certificate" means a certificate of total benefit, within the meaning of the Northern Ireland provisions;

"Northern Ireland compensation payment" means a compensation payment, within the meaning of the Northern Ireland provisions;

"Northern Ireland compensator" means a compensator, within the meaning of the Northern Ireland provisions;

"the Northern Ireland Department" has the same meaning as it has in the principal Act;

"the Northern Ireland intended recipient" means the intended recipient, within the meaning of the Northern Ireland provisions, in relation to a Northern Ireland compensation payment;

"the Northern Ireland provisions" means any legislation corresponding to the recoupment provisions (other than this paragraph) and having effect in Northern Ireland;

"Northern Ireland relevant payment" means a relevant payment, within the meaning of the Northern Ireland provisions;

"Northern Ireland victim" means a person who is the victim, within the meaning of the Northern Ireland provisions, in relation to a Northern Ireland compensation payment;

"the relevant victim" means the person who is the victim or the Northern Ireland victim (or both), as the case may be.

(7) This paragraph extends to Northern Ireland."

(2) In paragraph 21 of that Schedule (which makes provision for cases where the compensator is not resident and does not have a place of business in Great Britain) for the words "Great Britain" there shall be substituted the words "any part of the United Kingdom."

(3) In section 33(6) of that Act (provisions extending to Northern Ireland) after the words "and this section" there shall be inserted the words "and paragraph 20A of Schedule 4."

(4) In consequence of sub-paragraph (1) above—

(a) in Article 59(10) of the Social Security (Northern Ireland) Order 1986 (definition of "the recoupment provisions") after the words "Order 1989" there shall be inserted the words "and paragraph 20A of Schedule 4 to the Social Security Act 1989"; and

(b) in the definition of "the recoupment provisions" in paragraph 1(1) of Schedule 4 to the Social Security (Northern Ireland) Order 1989, after the word "Schedule" there shall be inserted the words "and paragraph 20A of Schedule 4 to the Social Security Act 1989."

Interest on damages: reductions in respect of relevant payments

6. After paragraph 23 of that Schedule there shall be added—

"Interest on damages: reductions in respect of relevant payments

24. In assessing the amount of interest payable in respect of an award of damages, the amount of the award shall be treated as reduced by a sum equal to the amount of the relevant payment (if any) required to be made in connection with the payment of the damages and—

(a) in England and Wales, if both special and general damages are awarded, any such reductions shall be treated as made first against the special damages and then, as respects any remaining balance, against the general damages; and

(b) in Scotland, if damages are awarded both for patrimonial loss and for solatium, any such reductions shall be treated as made first against the damages for patrimonial loss and then, as respects any remaining balance, against the damages for solatium."

Law Reform (Personal Injuries) Act 1948 (c. 41)

7. In section 2(1) of the Law Reform (Personal Injuries) Act 1948 (half of certain benefits to be brought into account in assessing damages) for the word "him" there shall be substituted the words "the injured person."

COMMENCEMENT
July 13, 1990 (s.23(3)(b)).

DEFINITION
"the 1989 Act": s.20.

GENERAL NOTE
Sched. 1 makes amendments to s.22 of and Sched. 4 to the Social Security Act 1989 on the recoupment of social security benefits from payments made in compensation for personal injury. Those provisions came into operation on September 3, 1990 in relation to payments made from that date for injuries or diseases from January 1, 1989.

Para. 1
Para. 1 covers two important changes to the recoupment scheme.

The first is to ensure that all payments from the Motor Insurers' Bureau (MIB) come under the scheme. The MIB is set up by agreement among motor insurers and funded out of motor insurance premiums to compensate those suffering personal injury by negligence in a road accident who are unable to get compensation through compulsory third party insurance. Thus under para. 1(1)(a) and (2) payments in the two areas covered by the MIB scheme—uninsured drivers and untraced drivers—are included in the definition of "compensation payment" in s.22(3) of the 1989 Act. Since the previous definition required the payment to be made by or on behalf of a person liable or alleged to be liable for the injury, the untraced drivers part of the MIB scheme seemed to fall outside the definition. There may even have been doubt about the uninsured drivers scheme. It was objection to this aspect of Sched. 1 which led the House of

Lords to vote to remove the entire Schedule from the Act. It was restored by the House of Commons on July 9, 1990. The MIB had apparently initially approached the DSS to argue that all payments from the scheme should be exempted from recoupment as are all payments from the Criminal Injuries Compensation Board (s.22(4)(f)).

The second change under para. 1 is to exclude from the definition of "compensation payment" any part of a payment which is referable to costs. The previous definition expressly included costs and the original intention of Sched. 1 was to ensure that payments direct to solicitors were caught. When Sched. 1 was restored by the House of Commons the Government had been convinced by the arguments of the Law Society and particularly Lord Byron. The Parliamentary Under-Secretary of State, Lord Henley, described the process following the removal of Sched. 1 without the discussion of any amendments. "I have since met the noble Lords, together with representatives from the Law Society, and we had an interesting and fruitful discussion on the issues. I am sure the House will warmly welcome the amendments to Sched. 1 which address an important concern articulated by the noble Lord, Lord Byron, in his amendments. Principally, we have now excluded costs from the definition of compensation payment in the 1989 Act. We were concerned about the scope for manipulation but we have listened to the convincing arguments put forward and we are now satisfied that any scope for manipulation is slight" (*Hansard*, H.L. Vol. 521, col. 295, July 11, 1990). The protection against manipulation is in the provision inserted into Sched. 4 to the 1989 Act by para. 1(4), which allows the Secretary of State to request a breakdown of any payment including costs, whether the payment counts as a compensation payment or not (*e.g.* because it comes under £2,500).

Paras. 2 to 4
These provisions contain technical amendments or corrections.

Para. 5
This paragraph links the Great Britain scheme in the 1989 Act with the Northern Ireland scheme under the equivalent legislation. The intention is described by the Parliamentary Under-Secretary of State, Mrs Gillian Shephard. "It is not uncommon for a compensator whose place of business is in Great Britain to pay compensation to a Northern Ireland resident. Equally, it is not uncommon for a person to have received benefits from both Great Britain and Northern Ireland. Therefore, it makes sense to link the two schemes to make life simpler for compensators. Paragraph 5 provides that a compensator will deal only with one recovery unit depending on the latest address of the victim—Belfast if it is in Northern Ireland; Newcastle if it is in Great Britain. Similarly, only one certificate will be issued which will include any benefits paid in both parts of the U.K. Thus, the problems of dealing with two different organisations will be avoided. Officials have discussed this approach with the private sector, which has been favourably disposed" (Standing Committee G, col. 235, February 22, 1990).

Para. 6
The new para. 24 provides that interest is not payable on the element of damages repaid to the DSS under the recoupment provisions.

Para. 7
This is a correction of sexist language.

Section 11(2)   SCHEDULE 2

SCHEDULE TO BE INSERTED AS SCHEDULE 3A TO THE PENSIONS ACT

Section 58A.   "SCHEDULE 3A

ANNUAL INCREASE IN RATE OF CERTAIN OCCUPATIONAL PENSIONS

Interpretation

1. In this Schedule—
    "annual rate," in relation to a pension or the later or earlier service component of a pension, means the annual rate of the pension or component, as previously increased under the rules of the scheme or this Schedule;
    "the appointed day" means the day on which this Schedule and section 58A of this Act come into force;

"the appropriate percentage," in relation to an increase in the annual rate of a pension or a component of a pension, means the percentage specified in the last revaluation order made before the increase is to take effect as the revaluation percentage for the last revaluation period of twelve months;

"earlier service component" means so much (if any) of the annual rate of the pension as is attributable to pensionable service before the appointed day;

"later service component" means so much (if any) of the annual rate of the pension as is attributable to pensionable service on or after the appointed day;

"pension," in relation to a scheme, means any pension which commences or has commenced under the scheme but does not include—

(a) a guaranteed minimum pension or any increase in such a pension under section 37A above; or

(b) any money purchase benefit;

"pensionable service" has the meaning given by paragraph 3 of Schedule 16 to the 1973 Act;

"qualifying scheme" means a scheme to which section 58A of this Act applies;

"revaluation order," "revaluation percentage" and "revaluation period" shall be construed in accordance with section 52A above.

Annual increase of later service component

2.—(1) If, apart from this Schedule, the annual rate of a pension under a qualifying scheme would not be increased as mentioned in section 58A(1)(b) of this Act, the annual rate of its later service component shall be increased annually by at least an amount equal to the appropriate percentage of the annual rate of that component as applicable immediately before the increase takes effect.

(2) The first increase by virtue of this paragraph in the rate of a pension shall take effect not later than the first anniversary of the commencement of the pension and subsequent increases shall take effect at intervals of not more than twelve months thereafter.

(3) This paragraph is subject to paragraphs 4 to 7 below.

Annual increase of earlier service component where scheme is in surplus

3.—(1) If on any valuation day the value of a qualifying scheme's assets, as determined in accordance with regulations, exceeds the value of its liabilities, as so determined, the amount of the excess (the "valuation surplus") shall be applied in accordance with the following provisions of this paragraph in providing for annual increases, up to the aggregate referred to in sub-paragraph (6) below, in the annual rate of the earlier service component of each pension under the scheme that would not, apart from this Schedule, be increased as mentioned in section 58A(1)(b) of this Act.

(2) The amount of each annual increase to be provided in pursuance of this paragraph in consequence of a valuation surplus shall be an amount equal to the appropriate percentage of the annual rate of the earlier service component of the pension in question as applicable immediately before that annual increase takes effect.

(3) Except in a case where regulations otherwise provide, the days which are "valuation days" for the purposes of this paragraph are—

(a) the appointed day; and

(b) each subsequent day as at which the assets and liabilities of the scheme in question are actuarially valued for any purpose.

(4) Where, in consequence of a valuation surplus, this paragraph requires provision to be made for annual increases in the annual rate of the earlier service component of a pension, the first of those increases shall take effect not later than the first anniversary of the later of—

(a) the valuation day as at which the valuation was made which disclosed the valuation surplus; or

(b) the commencement of the pension;

and subsequent increases shall take effect at intervals of not more than twelve months thereafter.

(5) In any case where—

(a) a valuation of the assets and liabilities of a qualifying scheme discloses a valuation surplus, but

(b) the amount of the surplus is insufficient to provide in full for the annual increases otherwise required by this paragraph in pensions under the scheme,

the valuation surplus shall be applied in providing for the increases so required, but only at the percentage rate that would apply year by year in relation to those increases if, for the maximum percentage of 5 per cent. specified in section 52A(9)(a) above, there were substituted such lower percentage as represents the greatest maximum percentage, as determined in accordance with regulations, by reference to which the valuation surplus is sufficient to provide for annual increases in the earlier service component of the pensions in question.

(6) If a valuation surplus is disclosed on a valuation at any time when either—

(a) provision has already been made by the scheme for the annual rate of the earlier service component of every such pension as is mentioned in sub-paragraph (1) above to be increased annually in the aggregate by at least the appropriate percentage of that rate, or

(b) the application of part only of the valuation surplus would be sufficient to secure that result,

this paragraph does not require that valuation surplus or, as the case may be, the remaining part of it, to be applied in the provision of increases under this paragraph.

(7) The powers conferred by sub-paragraphs (1) and (5) above to make regulations include, respectively, power to provide that the valuation of the scheme's assets or liabilities is to be calculated and verified, or the percentage in question is to be determined,—

(a) in such manner as may, in the particular case, be approved—
(i) by a prescribed person;
(ii) by a person with prescribed professional qualifications or experience; or
(iii) by a person approved by the Secretary of State;

(b) in accordance with guidance prepared by a prescribed body;

(c) in accordance with prescribed principles and requirements; or

(d) in accordance with principles determined by the person who performs the duties of calculation and verification.

(8) This paragraph is subject to paragraphs 4 to 7 below.

Proportional increases where first period is less than 12 months

4.—(1) Where a pension commenced to be paid less than twelve months before the date on which its first increase under paragraph 2 above is to take effect, the amount of that first increase shall be determined by the application of the formula—

$$\frac{M \times I}{12}$$

where—

    M is the number of complete months in the period beginning with the commencement of the pension and ending immediately before that date; and

    I   is the amount of the increase that would have been required by that paragraph, apart from this sub-paragraph.

(2) This paragraph shall apply in relation to the first increase of a pension by virtue of paragraph 3 above in consequence of each successive valuation surplus as it applies in relation to the first increase of a pension under paragraph 2 above.

Restriction on increases where member is under 55

5.—(1) No increase under paragraph 2 or 3 above is required to be paid to or for a member of a scheme whose pension has commenced but who has not attained the age of 55 at the time when the increase takes effect, unless—

(a) he is permanently incapacitated by mental or physical infirmity from engaging in regular full-time employment, or

(b) he has retired on account of mental or physical infirmity from the office or employment in respect of which, or on retirement from which, the pension is payable,

in which case the pension shall be payable at the annual rate at which it would have been payable apart from this sub-paragraph.

(2) The rules of a scheme may provide that if, in a case where a pension has been paid to or for a member under the age of 55 at an increased rate in consequence of paragraph (a) or (b) of sub-paragraph (1) above, the member—

(a) ceases to suffer from the infirmity in question before he attains the age of 55, but

(b) continues to be entitled to the pension,

any increases subsequently taking effect under paragraph 2 or 3 above in the annual rate of the pension shall not be paid or shall not be paid in full.

(3) In any case where—

(a) by virtue only of sub-paragraph (1) or (2) above, increases are not paid to or for a member or are not paid in full, but

(b) the member attains the age of 55 or, in a case falling within sub-paragraph (2) above, again satisfies the conditions set out in paragraph (a) or (b) of sub-paragraph (1) above,

his pension shall thereupon become payable at the annual rate at which it would have been payable apart from sub-paragraph (1) or (2) above.

Application of Schedule to pensions not attributable to pensionable service

6. Regulations may provide that this Schedule (other than this paragraph) shall apply in relation to any pension under a qualifying scheme as if so much of the annual rate of the pension as would not otherwise be attributable to pensionable service were attributable in accordance with the regulations—
(a) to pensionable service before the appointed day;
(b) to pensionable service on or after that day; or
(c) partly to pensionable service before, and partly to pensionable service on or after, that day;
and any reference to the earlier or later service component of the pension shall be construed accordingly.

Regulations

7.—(1) The Secretary of State may by regulations direct that section 58A of this Act and this Schedule shall have effect, in such cases as he may specify in the regulations, subject to such modifications as he may specify.
(2) In sub-paragraph (1) above "modification," without prejudice to the generality of that sub-paragraph, includes addition, omission and amendment.

Overriding effect of the increase provisions

8. The provisions of section 58A of this Act, this Schedule and any regulations made under it override any provision of a qualifying scheme, other than a protected provision (within the meaning of paragraph 7 of Schedule 1A to this Act), to the extent that it conflicts with them."

COMMENCEMENT
To be confirmed. Intended for January 1, 1992.

GENERAL NOTE
Sched. 2 inserts a new Sched. 3A into the Social Security Pensions Act 1975. It contains the detailed provisions for the compulsory increase of private sector pensions imposed by the new s.58A inserted by s.11. See the annotations to s.11 for the background and the general statutory framework. The annotations here deal with additional points of detail. S.58A defines the types of scheme and of pensions to which the obligation applies. It applies not just to the pensions paid to members themselves, but to anyone else (*e.g.* spouses, children and dependants) under the scheme.
Note at the outset that the provisions of the new Sched. 3A override scheme rules (para. 8) and that the Secretary of State has very wide powers to modify the effect of s.58A and Sched. 3A by regulations (para. 7).

Para. 1
Most of these definitions simply repeat those in s.58A(3).
The definitions of "earlier service component" (ESC) and "later service component" (LSC) are important to the nature of the obligation to increase pensions. The distinction between these different elements of a pension depends on whether the service to which the rate of pension is attributable is before or after the appointed day (A Day). There may often be cases where the rate of a pension cannot be attributed in this simple way. For instance, a scheme may base the level of pension on potential service or may provide for a flat rate of pension. In these sorts of cases, regulations to be made under para. 6 will have to provide answers. There may also be a need to deal with service under another scheme from which the member has transferred rights to the scheme from which his pension is paid. The definition of "pensionable service" adopts that in para. 3 of Sched. 16 to the Social Security Act 1973, which is in terms of a particular scheme and applies only to actual service in employment to which the scheme relates. An example would be if a person has 20 years' service under the scheme of employer X, then the day after A Day changes employment to employer Y and a transfer payment entitles him to count 20 years' service in employer Y's scheme. It remains to be seen whether, in the absence of regulations, the pension earned by that 20 years' service is not attributable to pensionable service before A Day or whether it will be permissible to argue that if that element of pension is attributable to pensionable service before A Day, even though in a different scheme, it is part of the ESC.

Para. 2

Under sub-para. (1), if a scheme within the scope of s.58A(1) does not already guarantee at least limited price increases (LPI), *i.e.* in line with prices up to five per cent., in which case it is excluded by s.58A(1)(b), the LSC must from A Day enjoy at least LPI. In effect, pension earned by service after A Day must be increased by the percentage specified in the last revaluation order before the increase takes effect. The revaluation order applies LPI. Sub-para. (2) requires the first increase to take place within a year of the commencement of payment of the pension and for subsequent increases to be at no greater intervals. If a scheme chooses to make the first increase under para. 2 earlier than 12 months after a pension starts (this will usually be the case because a scheme will wish to increase all pensions on a uniform date), an apportionment is to be made under para. 4. If a scheme chooses to make a subsequent increase less than a year after the last one, it appears that the full annual increase must be applied. All this of course only applies if the scheme rules do not guarantee LPI.

Note the exclusion of pensioners under 55 by para. 5.

Para. 3

While the obligation in relation to pension earned by service after A Day is clear, the obligation in relation to pension earned by service before A Day (ESC) is a particularly complex matter. The general structure is that if on any "valuation day" there is a "valuation surplus", an increase of as close to LPI as can be funded from the valuation surplus is to be applied within a year and on a continuing basis thereafter.

The first valuation day is to be A Day (sub-para. (3)(a)). This would seem to require vast numbers of schemes to obtain actuarial valuations as at the same day, and regardless of whether there had been a valuation only a few months before. Therefore it is likely that regulations under sub-para. (3) or para. 7 will modify this requirement. Any subsequent day on which the assets and liabilities of the scheme are actuarially valued counts as a valuation day (sub-para. (3)(b)). Under reg. 8(3) of the Occupational Pension Schemes (Disclosure of Information) Regulations 1986 (S.I. 1986 No. 1046) an actuarial valuation must be obtained at least every three years and six months, and scheme rules may oblige the trustees to obtain valuations at other intervals. There is some doubt about the application of para. 3 where a scheme commences to be wound up, since this may not necessarily involve an actuarial valuation of rights and liabilities.

On every valuation day it must be considered whether there is a valuation surplus. Regulations are to be made under para. 7 about how the valuation is to be carried out. Discussions are in progress with the actuarial profession to determine the appropriate methods and assumptions for calculating the size of scheme surpluses and the guaranteed increases that would flow from them (on which see sub-para. (5)) (*Hansard*, H.C. Vol. 170, col. 549, March 28, 1990). If there is a valuation surplus on any valuation day, then it is to be applied in providing increases to the ESC (sub-para. (1)). If the surplus is large enough, annual increases at the rate of LPI are to be provided (sub-para. (2)). If the surplus is not large enough to secure that level of increase, the largest annual increase that can be sustained is to be applied (sub-para. (5)). If application of the whole of the surplus would take the increases over the level of LPI, either initially or because of the applications of earlier surpluses, only that part necessary to provide LPI has to be applied (sub-para. (6)). These provisions could result in very small increases being required, and it may be that regulations will lift the obligation to provide such amounts, in order to avoid disproportionate administrative expense.

The first increase following the disclosure of a surplus must take effect within a year of the valuation date and annually thereafter (sub-para. (4)). Para. 4 applies where the first increase takes effect within less than a year, in order to allow schemes to maintain their regular date for increases.

Note the exception of increases for the under-55s in para. 5.

Para. 4

See notes to paras. 2 and 3.

Para. 5

No increase needs to be provided under Sched. 3A where the pension is payable to a member of the scheme under the age of 55 who is not affected by mental or physical infirmity (sub-para. (1)). Once the member reaches 55 he is to be paid at the rate that would have been applicable if increases had been applied. This exception does not apply to pensions paid under the scheme to people other than the member, *e.g.* a spouse, children or dependants.

The intention is that schemes should only be statutorily required to pay increases to individuals who might be considered to have retired. In occupations where the normal retirement age is quite young, it is said that the individual will probably not consider himself retired and will look for other employment (*Hansard*, H.L. Vol. 519, cols. 853–4, May 22, 1990). There is an equivalent rule for public service pension schemes, and s.1 of the Pensions (Miscellaneous

Provisions) Act 1990 is removing the right of female members under 55 with dependants to increases under the Pensions (Increase) Act 1971.

Para. 6
  See the notes to para. 1.

Para. 7
  The power to make regulations to modify s.58A and this Schedule appears unlimited.

Section 12(1)   SCHEDULE 3

THE PENSIONS OMBUDSMAN

After Part IV of the Pensions Act there shall be inserted the following—

"PART IVA

THE PENSIONS OMBUDSMAN

The Pensions Ombudsman

  59B.—(1) for the purpose of conducting investigations in accordance with this Part of this Act or any corresponding legislation having effect in Northern Ireland there shall be a commissioner, to be known as the Pensions Ombudsman.

  (2) The Pensions Ombudsman shall be appointed by the Secretary of State and shall hold office upon such terms and conditions as the Secretary of State may think fit.

  (3) The Pensions Ombudsman may at any time—

  (a) be removed from office by notice in writing given to him by the Secretary of State; or

  (b) resign his office by giving such notice to the Secretary of State.

  (4) The Secretary of State may make available such staff and other facilities as he thinks fit for the Pensions Ombudsman and any function of the Pensions Ombudsman, other than the determination of complaints made and disputes referred under this Part of this Act, may be performed by any member of that staff who is authorised for that purpose by the Pensions Ombudsman.

  (5) The Secretary of State may—

  (a) pay to or in respect of the Pensions Ombudsman such amounts by way of remuneration, compensation for loss of office, pension, allowances and gratuities, or by way of provision for any such benefits, as the Secretary of State may determine with the approval of the Treasury; and

  (b) reimburse him in respect of any expenses incurred by him in the performance of his functions.

  (6) The Pensions Ombudsman shall prepare a report on the discharge of his functions for the period ending with March 31, following the coming into force of this section, and for each subsequent financial year, and shall submit it to the Secretary of State as soon as practicable thereafter.

  (7) The Secretary of State shall arrange for the publication of each report submitted to him under subsection (6) above.

Functions of the Pensions Ombudsman

  59C.—(1) The Pensions Ombudsman may investigate and determine any complaint made to him in writing by or on behalf of an authorised complainant who alleges that he has sustained injustice in consequence of maladministration in connection with any act or omission of the trustees or managers of an occupational or personal pension scheme.

  (2) The Pensions Ombudsman may also investigate and determine any dispute of fact or law which arises in relation to such a scheme between—

  (a) the trustees or managers of the scheme, and

  (b) an authorised complainant in relation to the scheme,

and which is referred to him in writing by or on behalf of the authorised complainant.

  (3) The Secretary of State may by regulations provide that, subject to any modifications or exceptions specified in the regulations, this Part of this Act shall apply in relation to—

  (a) the employer in relation to any description or category of employment to which an occupational pension scheme relates or has related, or

(b) any prescribed person or body of persons concerned with the financing or administration of, or the provision of benefits under, any occupational or personal pension scheme,

as it applies in relation to the trustees or managers of such a scheme.

(4) The Pensions Ombudsman may investigate a complaint or dispute notwithstanding that it arose, or relates to a matter which arose, before the coming into force of this Part of this Act.

(5) The Pensions Ombudsman shall not investigate or determine a complaint or dispute—

(a) if, before the making of the complaint or the reference of the dispute, proceedings have been commenced in any court in respect of the matters which would be the subject of the investigation;

(b) if the scheme is of a description which is excluded from the jurisdiction of the Pensions Ombudsman by regulations under this subsection; or

(c) if and to the extent that the complaint or dispute, or any matter arising in connection with the complaint or dispute, is of a description which is excluded from the jurisdiction of the Pensions Ombudsman by regulations under this subsection.

(6) The persons who, for the purposes of this Part of this Act, are "authorised complainants" in relation to a scheme are—

(a) a member of the scheme,

(b) the widow or widower, or any surviving dependant, of a deceased member of the scheme;

(c) where the complaint or dispute relates to the question—

    (i) whether a person who claims to be such a person as is mentioned in paragraph (a) or (b) above is such a person, or

    (ii) whether a person who claims to be entitled to become a member of the scheme is so entitled,

the person so claiming.

(7) In this Part of this Act—

"employer," in relation to a pension scheme, includes a person—

    (a) who is or has been an employer in relation to the scheme, or

    (b) who is or has been treated under section 66(3) below as an employer in relation to the scheme for the purposes of Part III or IV of this Act, or under Article 2(4) of the Social Security Pensions (Northern Ireland) Order 1975 as an employer in relation to the scheme for the purposes of Part IV or V of that Order;

"member," in relation to a pension scheme, includes a person—

    (a) who is or has been in pensionable service under the scheme, as defined in paragraph 3 of Schedule 16 to the 1973 Act or paragraph 3 of Schedule 3 to the Social Security Pensions (Northern Ireland) Order 1975, or

    (b) who is or has been treated under section 66(4) below as a member in relation to the scheme for the purposes of Part III or IV of this Act, or under Article 2(5) of the Social Security Pensions (Northern Ireland) Order 1975 as a member in relation to the scheme for the purposes of Part IV or V of that Order;

"Northern Ireland public service pension scheme" means a public service pension scheme, within the meaning of Article 2(2) of that Order;

"trustees or managers," in relation to a pension scheme which is a public service pension scheme or a Northern Ireland public service pension scheme, includes the scheme's administrators.

Death, insolvency or disability of authorised complainant

59D.—(1) Where an authorised complainant dies or is a minor or is otherwise unable to act for himself, then, unless subsection (3) below applies—

(a) any complaint or dispute (whenever arising) which the authorised complainant might otherwise have made or referred under this Part of this Act may be made or referred by the appropriate person, and

(b) anything in the process of being done by or in relation to the authorised complainant under or by virtue of this Part of this Act may be continued by or in relation to the appropriate person,

and any reference in this Part of this Act, except this section, to an authorised complainant shall be construed as including a reference to the appropriate person.

(2) For the purposes of subsection (1) above "the appropriate person" means—

(a) where the authorised complainant has died, his personal representatives; or

(b) in any other case, a member of the authorised complainant's family, or some body or individual suitable to represent him.

(3) Where a person is acting as an insolvency practitioner in relation to an authorised complainant, investigations under this Part of this Act shall be regarded for the purposes of the Insolvency Act 1986 and the Bankruptcy (Scotland) Act 1985 as legal proceedings.

(4) In this section "acting as an insolvency practitioner" shall be construed in accordance with section 388 of the Insolvency Act 1986, but disregarding subsection (5) of that section (exclusion of official receiver).

Staying court proceedings where a complaint is made or a dispute is referred

59E.—(1) This section applies where—

(a) a complaint has been made or a dispute referred to the Pensions Ombudsman; and

(b) any party to the investigation subsequently commences any legal proceedings in any court against any other party to the investigation in respect of any of the matters which are the subject of the complaint or dispute.

(2) In England and Wales, where this section applies any party to the legal proceedings may at any time after acknowledgment of service, and before delivering any pleadings or taking any other step in the proceedings, apply to that court to stay the proceedings.

(3) In Scotland, where this section applies any party to the legal proceedings may—

(a) if the proceedings are in the Court of Session, at any time—

    (i) after appearance has been entered but before defences have been lodged or any other step in the proceedings has been taken; or

    (ii) (in procedure by petition) after intimation and service but before answers have been lodged or any other step in the proceedings has been taken; and

(b) if the proceedings are in the sheriff court, at any time—

    (i) after notice has been given of intention to defend but before defences have been lodged or any other step in the proceedings has been taken; or

    (ii) (in summary cause procedure) after appearance has been made, or notice of intention to appear has been lodged, but before any defence has been stated or any other step in the proceedings has been taken,

apply to the court for a sist of process.

(4) On an application under subsection (2) or (3) above the court may make an order staying or, in Scotland, sisting the proceedings if it is satisfied—

(a) that there is no sufficient reason why the matter should not be investigated by the Pensions Ombudsman; and

(b) that the applicant was at the time when the legal proceedings were commenced, and still remains, ready and willing to do all things necessary to the proper conduct of the investigation.

(5) for the purposes of this section the parties to an investigation are—

(a) the authorised complainant in question;

(b) the trustees or managers of the scheme in question;

(c) any person against whom allegations are made in the complaint or reference; and

(d) any person claiming under a person falling within paragraphs (a) to (c) above.

Procedure on an investigation

59F.—(1) Where the Pensions Ombudsman proposes to conduct an investigation into a complaint made or dispute referred under this Part of this Act, he shall afford to the trustees and managers of the scheme concerned, and any other person against whom allegations are made in the complaint or reference, an opportunity to comment on any allegations contained in the complaint or reference.

(2) The Secretary of State may by statutory instrument make rules with respect to the procedure which is to be adopted in connection with the making of complaints, the reference of disputes, and the investigation of complaints made and disputes referred, under this Part of this Act.

(3) The rules may include provision—

(a) requiring any oral hearing held in connection with an investigation under this Part of this Act to take place in public, except in such cases as may be specified in the rules; and

(b) as to the persons entitled to appear and be heard on behalf of parties to an investigation, as defined in section 59E(5) above.

(4) Subject to any provision made by the rules, the procedure for conducting an investigation under this Part of this Act shall be such as the Pensions Ombudsman

considers appropriate in the circumstances of the case; and he may, in particular, obtain information from such persons and in such manner, and make such inquiries, as he thinks fit.

Investigations: further provisions

59G.—(1) For the purposes of an investigation under this Part of this Act or under any corresponding legislation having effect in Northern Ireland, the Pensions Ombudsman may require any trustee or manager of the scheme concerned, or any other person who, in his opinion, is able to furnish information or produce documents relevant to the investigation, to furnish any such information or produce any such documents.

(2) For the purposes of any such investigation, the Pensions Ombudsman shall have the same powers as the court in respect of the attendance and examination of witnesses (including the administration of oaths and affirmations and the examination of witnesses abroad) and in respect of the production of documents.

(3) No person shall be compelled for the purposes of any such investigation to give any evidence or produce any document which he could not be compelled to give or produce in civil proceedings before the court.

(4) If any person without lawful excuse obstructs the Pensions Ombudsman in the performance of his functions or is guilty of any act or omission in relation to an investigation under this Part which, if that investigation were a proceeding in the court, would constitute contempt of court, the Pensions Ombudsman may certify the offence to the court.

(5) Where an offence is certified under subsection (4) above, the court may inquire into the matter and after hearing any witnesses who may be produced against or on behalf of the person charged with the offence, and after hearing any statement that may be offered in defence, deal with him in any manner in which the court could deal with him if he had committed the like offence in relation to the court.

(6) To assist him in an investigation, the Pensions Ombudsman may obtain advice from any person who in his opinion is qualified to give it and may pay to any such person such fees or allowances as he may determine with the approval of the Treasury.

(7) The Pensions Ombudsman may refer any question of law arising for determination in connection with a complaint or dispute to the High Court or, in Scotland, the Court of Session.

(8) In this section "the court" means—

(a) in England and Wales, a county court;

(b) in Scotland, the sheriff.

(9) Subsections (4) and (5) above shall be construed, in their application to Scotland, as if contempt of court were in Scots law categorised as an offence.

Determinations of the Pensions Ombudsman

59H.—(1) Where the Pensions Ombudsman has conducted an investigation under this Part of this Act, he shall send a written statement of his determination of the complaint or dispute in question—

(a) to the authorised complainant in question; and

(b) to the trustees or managers of the scheme in question;

and any such statement shall contain the reasons for his determination.

(2) Where the Pensions Ombudsman makes a determination under this Part of this Act or under any corresponding legislation having effect in Northern Ireland, he may direct the trustees or managers of the scheme concerned to take, or refrain from taking, such steps as he may specify in the statement referred to in subsection (1) above or otherwise in writing.

(3) Subject to subsection (4) below, the determination by the Pensions Ombudsman of a complaint or dispute, and any direction given by him under subsection (2) above, shall be final and binding on—

(a) the authorised complainant in question;

(b) the trustees or managers of the scheme concerned; and

(c) any person claiming under them respectively.

(4) An appeal on a point of law shall lie to the High Court or, in Scotland, the Court of Session from a determination or direction of the Pensions Ombudsman at the instance of any person falling within paragraphs (a) to (c) of subsection (3) above.

(5) Any determination or direction of the Pensions Ombudsman shall be enforceable—

(a) in England and Wales, in a county court as if it were a judgment or order of that court, and

(b) in Scotland, by the sheriff, as if it were a judgment or order of the sheriff and whether or not the sheriff could himself have granted such judgment or order.

(6) If the Pensions Ombudsman considers it appropriate to do so in any particular case, he may publish in such form and manner as he thinks fit a report of any investigation under this Part of this Act and of the result of that investigation.

(7) For the purposes of the law of defamation, the publication of any matter by the Pensions Ombudsman—

(a) in submitting or publishing a report under section 59B(6) or subsection (6) above, or

(b) in sending to any person a statement under subsection (1) above or a direction under subsection (2) above, shall be absolutely privileged.

Power to make special county court rules

59J.—(1) The Secretary of State may by statutory instrument make rules—

(a) regulating the practice, and the forms of proceedings, which are to be followed in county courts in any proceedings under or by virtue of this Part of this Act; and

(b) prescribing the scales of costs to be paid in connection with any such proceedings.

(2) Without prejudice to the generality of subsection (1) above, rules under this section may to any extent, and with or without modifications, apply any county court rules to proceedings under or by virtue of this Part of this Act."

COMMENCEMENT
October 1, 1990 (Social Security Act 1990 (Commencement No. 1) Order 1990 (S.I. 1990 No. 1446), art. 2(e)).

DEFINITION
"the Pensions Act": s.20.

GENERAL NOTE
Sched. 3 inserts eight new sections into the Social Security Pensions Act 1975 to establish the Pensions Ombudsman scheme.

Background
One of the central elements of the OPB's recommendations on helping individuals in their report *Protecting Pensions: Safeguarding Benefits in a Changing Environment*, Cm. 573 (1989) was for setting up a body to adjudicate in disputes between the individual and a pension scheme or provider. A substantial majority of respondents to the OPB who expressed a view saw a need for such a body, because the ultimate recourse to the High Court was unrealistic in most cases and did not provide an expeditious remedy (para. 13.3). Although the link was not explicitly made, it seems likely that the recommendation that trust law should continue as the legal basis of pension schemes, rather than being replaced by a statutory basis (para. 8.15), was conditional to some extent on a more effective means of enforcing individuals' rights being introduced.

The OPB considered three alternatives: a pensions ombudsman; an arbitration procedure; and a pensions tribunal. They did not consider that an ombudsman system would be suitable for three reasons. Such a system was best suited to dealing with disputes between a large organisation and an individual, whereas in the pensions field disputes might arise between two sets of trustees or between a trustee body and some other organisation. Secondly, a body which included members from the legal, actuarial and accounting professions could function more efficiently than an ombudsman with advisers. Thirdly, very large sums might be involved in disputes between two bodies and an ombudsman would not be the best method of resolving such disputes (para. 13.12). Arbitration was rejected because a compulsory system was necessary. The conclusion was that a body with the legal standing of a tribunal, with statutorily defined powers of enforcement, but able to conduct hearings without the formal atmosphere of a court of law, would be the best solution. It was recommended that there should be one tribunal for the whole country. The membership might be variable, but should consist of pensions experts with a lawyer chairman. It would deal with all types of occupational or personal pension provision. The costs would be met from the registration fees for the registry (paras. 13.14–16).

The OPB's analysis of the alternatives was not particularly penetrating, although there was a general welcome for an alternative to the High Court. The response from the Government in Mr Tony Newton's speech to the Society of Pension Consultants on November 7, 1989 was in these terms (see *SPC News*, No. 6).

"My view is that we should concentrate the new service on the types of problem that individuals, rather than schemes, can face. Disputes involving trustees, concerning large sums of money, are likely to end up in the courts in any case. That is not really our concern here. I believe therefore that the Ombudsman concept, which has become well-established and well-respected, is the right one. There are clear parallels with other Ombudsmen who adjudicate between individuals and large organisations. In the financial sector I am thinking particularly of the Banking and the Building Societies Ombudsmen. It is an adaptable concept that can be tailor-made to suit the particular characteristics of a certain situation, or industry.

"I propose therefore to have discussions with the pensions industry about the operation and financing of a statutory Ombudsman scheme—that is a statutory requirement on pension schemes to belong to the Ombudsman scheme and to abide by the decisions. Of course, if either party to the proceedings was unhappy with the Ombudsman's decision they would still have the right of appeal to the High Court."

Thus there was no intention to provide a mechanism covering all possible disputes concerning pensions, but an avenue for individuals which would combine legally binding rulings with the investigative powers not normally associated with a tribunal. The Parliamentary Under-Secretary of State, Lord Henley, said that a "tribunal would only be able to listen to arguments put to it, whereas an ombudsman is able to take the initiative and investigate the complaints. That is of great benefit to the individual." In addition, while it is agreed that the system should be financed from fees paid by the pensions industry, this would not be possible with a tribunal. Finally, a single Ombudsman can cover the whole of the U.K., but there might have to be separate tribunals for Scotland and Northern Ireland (*Hansard*, H.L. Vol. 519, col. 857, May 22, 1990; and see Standing Committee G, col. 245, February 22, 1990). Since there is no problem about a system of social security appeal tribunals and medical appeal tribunals covering the whole of the U.K., the other reasons seem more compelling.

The Building Societies Ombudsman is perhaps the closest analogy, since that scheme is set up by statute (the Building Societies Act 1986, Sched. 12), although its decisions need not be complied with. The decisions of the Banking Ombudsman and the Insurance Ombudsman are binding on members of the scheme, but membership of the scheme is voluntary. Therefore, the Pensions Ombudsman proposal was a unique combination of elements, and as will be seen, the terms of reference bring it much closer to the traditional powers of a tribunal.

S.59B

S.59B provides for the appointment of the Pensions Ombudsman by the Secretary of State. If a tribunal had been set up, presumably the appointment would have had to have been made by the Lord Chancellor. No qualifications of any kind are specified for the appointee. At the date of publication no public advertisement inviting applications for the post had appeared and there was no indication of how the appointment would be made.

Under subs. (4) the provision of staff for the Ombudsman is a matter for the Secretary of State. The power for the Ombudsman to delegate functions, apart from the determination of complaints and disputes, to such staff is in line with the powers of the Health Service Ombudsman. The Ombudsman is obliged to provide an annual report to the Secretary of State, who is bound to have it published (subss. (6) and (7)). The contents of the report are up to the Ombudsman, and may therefore contain details of determinations made during the year. The Ombudsman has an independent power to publish reports of each investigation (s.59H(6)). See also s.59H(7) for absolute privilege in defamation.

S.59C

Subss. (1) and (2) set out the two elements of the Pensions Ombudsman's jurisdiction.

Under subs. (1) he may (not "shall") investigate and determine a complaint by an "authorised complainant" that he has sustained injustice in consequence of maladministration in connection with any act or omission of the trustees or managers of an occupational or personal pension scheme. Thus both occupational and personal pension schemes (defined in s.66(1) of the Pensions Act and s.84(1) of the Social Security Act 1986) are covered. Public service schemes are covered, but see subs. (5)(b). Under subs. (3) regulations may extend the parties against whom complaints may be made to include employers and other bodies concerned with the scheme. "Authorised complainant" is defined exhaustively in subs. (6) (referring on to subs. (7)) to cover members or ex-members of the scheme in question, surviving spouses and dependants of deceased members, and those claiming to be or to be entitled to be members.

The central element is the meaning of "injustice in consequence of maladministration." This phrase appears in the legislation setting up the Parliamentary Ombudsman and the Local Government Ombudsman (Parliamentary Commissioner Act 1967, ss.5(1)(a) and 10(3); Local Government Act 1974, s.31(1)). In neither Act is the phrase defined, and each Ombudsman has had to work out what limitations it imposes. "Injustice" requires some personal injustice suffered by the complainant, rather than some grievance felt by the community or a part of it. Whether some present or reasonably anticipated material damage is required is more controversial. There is evidence that the Local Government Ombudsman has included the causing of anxiety (Lewis *et al.*, *Complaints Procedures in Local Government* (1987), Vol. 1, para. 2.12). Since matters like unreasonable delay or rudeness will be prime examples of maladministration, there is pressure to adopt a flexible approach to injustice. Conversely, if material injustice has occurred there is some pressure to infer that it resulted from maladministration.

"Maladministration" is a concept which fits more happily in the Civil Service or local government context than in pensions, but it has a wide meaning, perhaps wider than the Government realised. For instance, in resisting an Opposition amendment to include expressly within the Ombudsman's jurisdiction the exercise of any discretionary power by the trustees or managers, the Parliamentary Under-Secretary of State, Mrs Gillian Shephard, said this.

"What is important is that trustees abide by the law of the land and by the scheme rules, but we see no justification for the suggestion that they should be made accountable for their decisions to the pensions ombudsman. The way in which a decision is reached may constitute maladministration, and that is clearly a matter for the ombudsman, but the decision is a matter for the trustees. Trustees of schemes may of course translate what are discretionary decisions into rights within the rules of the scheme if they choose to do so, but that is their responsibility and duty as trustees under the law."

While the way in which a decision is reached may constitute the central focus of maladministration, other ombudsmen have not restricted themselves to that narrow focus.

A useful list of examples of maladministration is given following an analysis of the determinations of the Parliamentary Ombudsman by Gregory and Hutchesson (*The Parliamentary Ombudsman*, 1975, p. 281):

    (1) assorted mistakes, errors and oversights;
    (2) failing to impart information or provide adequate explanations;
    (3) giving inaccurate information and misleading advice;
    (4) misapplication of departmental rules and instructions;
    (5) peremptory or inconsiderate behaviour on the part of officials;
    (6) unjustifiable delay;
    (7) not treating, so far as possible, like cases alike.

To this list they add in relation to discretionary decisions (p. 309) "failure to take account of all the circumstances", with which must go taking into account irrelevant considerations. All of these headings can apply with the appropriate adjustments in the pensions context, and many could apply to the process of coming to a discretionary decision. Proper investigations and consistency of decision-making will be of prime importance. Investigation of these issues may require examination of the substance of discretionary decisions. Although under the law of trusts trustees are not bound to give reasons for the way in which they exercise discretions, this rule may not apply in the statutory jurisdiction of the Ombudsman. See the notes to the new s.59G for his powers of investigation. In addition, a pattern of the results of individual decisions may suggest that like cases are not treated alike. However, another matter which has become more prominent since 1975 may impinge more directly on discretionary decisions. This is the emergence of the approach that the correct application of a rule which produces injustice may involve maladministration if proper steps have not been taken to consider how the injustice might be avoided or whether the rule should be changed. If this approach were to be adopted by the Pensions Ombudsman, and it must be stressed that it is for each Ombudsman to work out his own approach, it could lead to considerable investigation of the merits of the exercise of discretions. It should also be noted that providing injustice in consequence of maladministration is raised in the complaint, an investigation may follow and the Ombudsman's determination need not be in terms of the statutory language.

Under subs. (2) the Ombudsman may investigate disputes of fact or law arising between the same parties, again on the complaint of an "authorised complainant" (subss. (6) and (7)). Such a dispute is more straightforward to identify and constitutes what was envisaged as falling within the jurisdiction of a tribunal, if one had been set up. Disputes of fact presumably include not only disputes about "primary" facts (*e.g.* what is a person's medical condition) but also disputes about conclusions of fact (*e.g.* is that person as a result of his medical condition incapable of work). A great many issues as to the trustees' and the employer's powers and duties will be raised under disputes of law.

Subs. (4) confirms that the Ombudsman may investigate complaints or disputes although they arose before Pt. IVA of the Pensions Act came into force on October 1, 1990.

Subs. (5) contains important exclusions. Under head (a) the Ombudsman may not investigate a matter if proceedings relating to it have been commenced in any court before the making of the complaint or reference. The timing of a complaint or reference is in the hands of the authorised complainant, as is the starting of an action against the trustees. So the route to the High Court remains open at the authorised complainant's option. But if the trustees apply to the Court for directions on the true meaning of the trust deed or on the exercise of a power or duty under the scheme (Rules of the Supreme Court, Ord. 85, r. 2), does this amount to the commencement of proceedings? See s.59E for the situation where proceedings are started after the complaint or reference is made.

Under head (b) regulations may exclude certain descriptions of scheme from investigation. Some one-person schemes and schemes where the members are also the trustees (better known as small self-administered schemes) might be excluded. Public service schemes will probably be excluded from the jurisdiction over disputes of fact or law, at least at first, because appeal mechanisms already exist (Standing Committee G, col. 283, February 27, 1990). Under head (c) regulations may exclude certain types of complaints or disputes. The Government is considering excluding complaints and references where the potential award is over a certain figure (*ibid.*).

Note the fairly expansive definitions in subss. (6) and (7).

S.59D

This section provides for complaints and references to be made or continued when the authorised complainant dies, is a minor or is unable to act for himself.

S.59E

Where a party commences court proceedings after a complaint or reference has been made to the Ombudsman, any party may apply to the court to stay the proceedings. The parties are defined in subs. (5). The court may make an order if satisfied that there is no sufficient reason why the matter should not be investigated by the Ombudsman and the applicant is ready to co-operate in the investigation (subs. (4)). There is no statutory power to stop the Ombudsman's investigation, but the Ombudsman has a discretion under s.59C whether to investigate a complaint or reference or not.

S.59F

On an investigation the Ombudsman may make any inquiries he thinks fit and obtain any information he thinks fit. Powers in these matters are supplied by s.59G. But these powers are subject to the necessity to give the persons complained against an opportunity to comment on the allegations made against them (subs. (1)) and to follow any procedure laid down by regulations (subss. (2) and (3)).

S.59G

Under subss. (1) to (5) the Ombudsman has power to require the production of documents or information, with enforcement powers as if he were a court. He may require witnesses to attend and give evidence and to produce documents, but not beyond what a court could require. It is not clear whether the power to require the furnishing of information under subs. (1) is free of this restriction. It has been suggested that the principle laid down in *The Marquess of Londonderry's Settlement, Re* [1965] Ch. 918, that trustees are not bound to disclose as trust documents documents showing the reasons for the exercise of a discretion, will limit the way in which the Ombudsman can investigate that area. But it was stressed in *Londonderry, Re* that the Court of Appeal there was not considering an action by a beneficiary for alleged breach of trust. In that circumstance, any documents relevant to the issue before the court would have to be disclosed. Thus, there are circumstances in which trustees or managers can be compelled to produce such documents, which should therefore be available to the Ombudsman. The power of the Ombudsman to go out and collect the evidence and information he thinks necessary is what marks out such an institution from a tribunal, however inquisitorial.

Under subs. (6) the Ombudsman may employ experts to assist him.

Under subs. (7) the Ombudsman may refer any question of law arising in connection with a complaint or dispute to the High Court or the Court of Session. It remains to be seen how much use the Ombudsman makes of this power, in the light of the right of appeal on a point of law from his determinations.

S.59H

On the completion of an investigation the Ombudsman must send a copy of his determination of the complaint or dispute with his reasons to the parties (subs. (1)). The determination may include a direction to the trustees or managers or employer to take or refrain from taking specified steps (subs. (2)). It appears that a determination or direction cannot be made until the investigation is completed, so that there is no power to make any interim orders. At the Committee stage in the Commons the Government undertook to monitor carefully the speed and effects of the Ombudsman's decisions and to consider interim orders if there proved to be difficulties in practice (Standing Committee G, col. 287, February 27, 1990).

Determinations and directions are binding on the authorised complainant, the trustees or managers (or employer) concerned and any person claiming under them and may be enforced as though they were court orders (subss. (3) and (5)). The binding nature of determinations differentiates the Pensions Ombudsman from any of the other statutory ombudsmen. Some commentators wished the award not to be binding on the complainant, so that he would have the choice of enforcing the award or going to court, but this was firmly rejected. Although only the particular complainant is bound, it may be that the Ombudsman will investigate groups of complaints from individuals together and so define the rights of a group. It is possible that this effect could stem from the binding effect on the trustees or managers, especially if the Ombudsman directed that they were to treat any person in the same position as the authorised complainant in the same way.

Subs. (4) establishes a right of appeal on a point of law to the High Court or the Court of Session at the instance of any person on whom a determination or direction is binding. Since there is no appeal on the facts and a determination is final under subs. (3), there is no mechanism for correcting a decision made in ignorance of material facts. But note that it is an error of law to come to a conclusion based on no evidence or to give inadequate reasons. All relevant issues of fact or law which are raised must be dealt with and the losing party must be able to see why he has lost. Often decisions on the facts can be attacked through one of these mechanisms.

The court is given no specific powers if it finds an error of law. Presumably if sufficient facts have been determined, the court may give the decision which the Ombudsman ought to have given, or if that is not the case, must remit the complaint or dispute to the Ombudsman with directions on the law.

Under subs. (5) the Ombudsman may publish any report of an investigation and the result in any form he thinks fit. It is up to the Ombudsman whether to report all investigations or a selection or none at all, and whether to anonymise the reports. He is also obliged to produce an annual report under s.59B(6). The Ombudsman has absolute privilege in the law of defamation in publishing any report (subs. (7)).

Section 14   SCHEDULE 4

OCCUPATIONAL AND PERSONAL PENSION SCHEMES

PART I

PROTECTING PENSIONS

Occupational pensions: independent trustee where employer insolvent etc

1. The following sections shall be inserted after the section 57B of the Pensions Act inserted by paragraph 11 below—

"Requirement for independent trustee where employer becomes insolvent etc.

57C.—(1) This section applies in relation to an occupational pension scheme which is constituted by trust deed—
  (a) if a person ("the practitioner") commences to act as an insolvency practitioner in relation to a company which, or an individual who, is the employer of persons in the description or category of employment to which the scheme relates; or
  (b) if the official receiver becomes—
      (i) the liquidator or provisional liquidator of a company which is the employer of any such persons, or
      (ii) the receiver and the manager, or the trustee, of the estate of a bankrupt who is the employer of any such persons.
  (2) If and so long as this section applies to a scheme, it shall be the duty of the practitioner or official receiver—
  (a) to satisfy himself that at all times at least one of the trustees of the scheme is an independent person; and
  (b) if at any time he is not so satisfied, to appoint under this paragraph, or to secure the appointment of, an independent person as a trustee of the scheme;
but this subsection is subject to subsection (5) below.
  (3) For the purposes of subsection (2) above a person is "independent" only if—
  (a) he has no interest in the assets of the employer or of the scheme, otherwise than as trustee of the scheme;
  (b) he is neither connected with, nor an associate of—
      (i) the employer;
      (ii) any person for the time being acting as an insolvency practitioner in relation to the employer; or
      (iii) the official receiver, acting in any of the capacities mentioned in sub-section (1)(b) above in relation to the employer; and

(c) he satisfies such other requirements as may be prescribed;
and any reference in this section or section 57D below to an "independent trustee" shall
be construed accordingly.

(4) Sections 249 and 435 of the Insolvency Act 1986 (connected and associated
persons) shall apply for the purposes of paragraph (b) of subsection (3) above as they
apply for the purposes of that Act; and section 74 of the Bankruptcy (Scotland) Act 1985
(associated persons) shall apply for the purposes of that paragraph as that section applies
for the purposes of the said Act of 1985.

(5) Where, apart from this subsection, the duties imposed by subsection (2) above in
relation to a scheme would fall to be discharged at the same time by two or more persons
acting in different capacities, those duties shall be discharged—

(a) if the employer is a company, by the person or persons acting as the company's
liquidator, provisional liquidator or administrator; or

(b) if the employer is an individual, by the person or persons acting as his trustee in
bankruptcy or interim receiver of his property or as permanent or interim trustee
in the sequestration of his estate.

(6) If the practitioner or official receiver neglects or refuses to discharge any duty
imposed upon him by subsection (2) above in relation to a scheme, any member of the
scheme may apply to the appropriate court for an order requiring him to discharge his
duties under that subsection.

(7) Where this section applies in relation to a scheme, it shall cease to do so—

(a) if some person other than the employer mentioned in subsection (1) above
becomes the employer of persons in the description or category of employment to
which the scheme relates; or

(b) if at any time neither the practitioner nor the official receiver is acting in relation
to the employer;
but nothing in this subsection affects the application of this section in relation to the
scheme on any subsequent occasion when the conditions specified in subsection (1)(a) or
(b) above are satisfied in relation to the scheme.

(8) In this section—

"acting as an insolvency practitioner" and "official receiver" shall be construed in
accordance with sections 388 and 399 of the Insolvency Act 1986;

"the appropriate court", in relation to an application for an order under subsection (6) above, means—

(a) if the employer in question is a company—

(i) where a winding up order has been made or a provisional
liquidator appointed, the court which made the order or appointed
the liquidator;

(ii) in any other case, any court having jurisdiction to wind up the
company; and

(b) in any other case—

(i) in England and Wales, the court as defined in section 385 of the
Insolvency Act 1986; or

(ii) in Scotland, where sequestration has been awarded or, by
virtue of the proviso to section 13(1) of the Bankruptcy 1985 (Scotland) Act 1985 (petition presented by creditor or trustee acting under
trust deed) an interim trustee appointed, the court which made the
award or appointment and, if no such award or appointment has been
made, any court having jurisdiction under section 9 of that Act;

"bankrupt" has the meaning given by section 381 of the Insolvency Act 1986;

"company" means a company within the meaning given by section 735(1) of the
Companies Act 1985 or a company which may be wound up under Part V of
the Insolvency Act 1986 (unregistered companies);

"interim trustee" and "permanent trustee" have the same meaning as they have
in the Bankruptcy (Scotland) Act 1985.

(9) References in this section to an individual include, except where the context
otherwise requires, references to a partnership and to any debtor within the meaning of
the Bankruptcy (Scotland) Act 1985.

Independent trustees: further provisions

57D.—(1) If and so long as section 57C above applies in relation to a scheme, no
independent trustee of the scheme shall be removed from being a trustee by virtue only
of any provision of the scheme.

(2) If a trustee appointed under subsection (2)(b) of that section ceases to be an
independent trustee, then—

(a) he shall forthwith give written notice of that fact to the practitioner or official receiver by whom the duties under that provision fall to be discharged; and

(b) he shall cease to be a trustee of the scheme, unless the circumstances are such that upon his cessation there would be no other trustee of the scheme, in which case he shall not cease by virtue of this subsection to be a trustee until such time as another trustee is appointed.

(3) A trustee appointed under subsection (2)(b) of that section shall be entitled to be paid out of the scheme's resources his reasonable fees for acting in that capacity and any expenses reasonably incurred by him in doing so, and to be so paid in priority to all other claims falling to be met out of the scheme's resources.

(4) If, immediately before the appointment of an independent trustee under subsection (2)(b) of that section, there is no trustee of the scheme other than the employer, the employer shall cease to be a trustee upon the appointment of the independent trustee.

(5) If and so long as section 57C above applies in relation to a scheme—

(a) any power vested in the trustees or managers of the scheme and exercisable at their discretion shall be exercisable only by the independent trustee; and

(b) any power—

    (i) which the scheme confers on the employer (otherwise than as trustee or manager of the scheme), and

    (ii) which is exercisable by him at his discretion but only as trustee of the power,

shall be exercisable only by the independent trustee; but if, in either case, there is more than one independent trustee, the power shall also be exercisable with the consent of at least half of those trustees by any person who could exercise it apart from this subsection.

(6) Notwithstanding anything in section 155 of the Insolvency Act 1986 (court orders for inspection etc), if and so long as section 57C above applies in relation to a scheme, it shall be the duty of the practitioner or official receiver to provide the trustees of the scheme, as soon as practicable after the receipt of a request, with any information which the trustees may reasonably require for the purposes of the scheme.

(7) Any expenses incurred by the practitioner or official receiver in complying with a request under subsection (6) above shall be recoverable by him as part of the expenses incurred by him in the discharge of his duties; and he shall not be required under that subsection to take any action which involves expenses that cannot be so recovered, unless the trustees of the scheme undertake to meet them.

(8) The provisions of section 57C above and this section, and of any regulations made under that section or this section, override any provision of a scheme to the extent that it conflicts with them.

(9) The Secretary of State may make regulations modifying section 57C above and this section in their application—

(a) to any occupational pension scheme which applies to earners in employments under different employers;

(b) to any occupational pension scheme of which there are no members who are in pensionable service under the scheme, as defined in paragraph 3 of Schedule 16 to the 1973 Act; or

(c) to any case where a partnership is the employer, or one of the employers, in relation to an occupational pension scheme.

(10) Section 57C above and this section (other than this subsection) shall not apply in relation to an occupational pension scheme of a prescribed description."

Employer to make good deficiencies on winding up

2. The following section shall be inserted into the Pensions Act after the section 58A inserted by section 11 of this Act—

Deficiencies in the assets of a scheme on winding up

58B.—(1) If, in the case of an occupational pension scheme which is not a money purchase scheme, the value at the applicable time of the scheme's liabilities, as determined in accordance with regulations, exceeds the value of its assets, as so determined, then—

(a) an amount equal to the excess shall be treated as a debt due from the employer to the trustees of the scheme; and

(b) if that debt has not been discharged before the default time then, for the purposes of the law relating to winding up, bankruptcy or sequestration as it applies in relation to the employer, it shall be taken to arise at the default time.

(2) In this section—
    "the applicable time" means the earlier of—
        (a) any time when the scheme is being wound up which falls before the default time; or
        (b) the default time;
    "the default time" means—
        (a) in England and Wales—
            (i) where the employer is a company, immediately before the company goes into liquidation, within the meaning of section 247(2) of the Insolvency Act 1986; or
            (ii) where the employer is an individual, immediately before the commencement of his bankruptcy, within the meaning of section 278 of that Act; or
        (b) in Scotland—
            (i) where the employer is a company, immediately before the commencement of the company's being wound up, within the meaning of section 129 of that Act; or
            (ii) where the employer is a debtor, within the meaning of the Bankruptcy (Scotland) Act 1985, immediately before the date of sequestration as defined in section 12(4) of that Act;
    "the employer" means the employer of persons in the description or category of employment to which the scheme relates;
    "money purchase scheme" has the same meaning as it has in section 58A above.
(3) The power to make regulations conferred by subsection (1) above includes power to provide—
    (a) that, in calculating the value of the scheme's liabilities, any provision of the scheme which limits the amount of its liabilities by reference to the amount of its assets is to be disregarded;
    (b) that the value of the scheme's liabilities or assets is to be calculated and verified in such manner as may, in the particular case, be approved—
        (i) by a prescribed person,
        (ii) by a person with prescribed professional qualifications or experience, or
        (iii) by a person approved by the Secretary of State,
    or that their value is to be calculated and verified in accordance with guidance prepared by a prescribed body.
(4) This section is without prejudice to any other right or remedy which the trustees may have in respect of the deficiency.
(5) A debt due by virtue only of this section shall be regarded neither as a preferential debt for the purposes of the Insolvency Act 1986 nor as a preferred debt for the purposes of the Bankruptcy (Scotland) Act 1985.
(6) The Secretary of State may make regulations modifying this section in its application—
    (a) to any occupational pension scheme which applies to earners in employments under different employers;
    (b) to any case where a partnership is the employer, or one of the employers, in relation to an occupational pension scheme;
    (c) to any occupational pension scheme of which there are no members who are in pensionable service under the scheme, as defined in paragraph 3 of Schedule 16 to the 1973 Act; or
    (d) to any case where the assets and liabilities of the scheme are transferred to another occupational pension scheme.
(7) The provisions of this section and of any regulations made under it override any provision of a scheme to the extent that it conflicts with this section or those regulations."

Investment of scheme's resources

3. After section 57 of the Pensions Act there shall be inserted the following section—

"Restrictions on investment of scheme's resources in employer-related assets
    57A.—(1) An occupational pension scheme shall comply with such restrictions as may be prescribed with respect to the proportion of its resources that may at any time be invested in, or in any description of, employer-related investments.
    (2) In this section—
        "employer-related investments" means—

(a) shares or other securities issued by the employer or by any person who is connected with, or an associate of, the employer;

(b) land which is occupied or used by, or subject to a lease in favour of, the employer or any such person;

(c) property (other than land) which is used for the purposes of any business carried on by the employer or any such person;

(d) loans to the employer or any such person;

"the employer" means the employer of persons in the description or category of employment to which the scheme in question relates;

"securities" means any asset, right or interest falling within paragraph 1, 2, 4 or 5 of Schedule 1 to the Financial Services Act 1986.

(3) If and to the extent that any sums due and payable by a person to the trustees or managers of a scheme remain unpaid, those sums shall be regarded for the purposes of this section as loans made to that person by the trustees or managers, and resources of the scheme shall be regarded as invested accordingly.

(4) Sections 249 and 435 of the Insolvency Act 1986 (connected and associated persons) shall apply for the purposes of this section as they apply for the purposes of that Act; and section 74 of the Bankruptcy (Scotland) Act 1985 shall apply for the purposes of this section as that section applies for the purposes of the said Act of 1985."

Revaluation of preserved pensions

4.—(1) for the definition of "qualifying pensionable service" in paragraph 2(3) of Schedule 1A to the Pensions Act (which precludes revaluation of accrued rights referable to service before January 1, 1985) there shall be substituted—

" "qualifying pensionable service" means—

(a) where the termination of pensionable service occurs after the coming into force of this paragraph of this definition, the whole of the member's pensionable service, as defined in this sub-paragraph; and

(b) in any other case, so much of any such service as falls on or after January 1, 1985."

(2) In paragraph 3 of that Schedule (average salary benefits) in sub-paragraph (5) (definition of "salaries") for the words from "means" to "terminated" there shall be substituted the words "means, subject to sub-paragraph (5A) below, the member's salaries for the period between the date when his pensionable service commenced and the date when it terminated."

(3) After that sub-paragraph there shall be inserted—

"(5A) Where the member's pensionable service terminated before the coming into force of this sub-paragraph, sub-paragraph (5) above shall have effect with the substitution for the words from "means" to "terminated" of the words "means the member's salaries for the period between January 1, 1985 and the date when his pensionable service terminated.""

Part II

Miscellaneous Amendments

Preservation of rights for persons opting out of schemes

5.—(1) In Schedule 16 to the 1973 Act, in sub-paragraph (1) of paragraph 6 (short service benefit where member's service in relevant employment terminates before normal pension age etc) for the words "service in relevant employment" there shall be substituted the words "pensionable service."

(2) At the end of that paragraph there shall be added—

"(6) In any case where—

(a) the pensionable service of a member of a scheme terminated during the period beginning with April 6, 1988 and ending immediately before the coming into force of this sub-paragraph, otherwise than on the termination of his service in relevant employment, and

(b) during that period no payments in discharge of his rights under the scheme were made in consequence of that termination,

sub-paragraph (1) above shall be taken at all times on and after April 6, 1988 (the date on which section 15 of the Social Security Act 1986 came into force) to have had effect in relation to that member and his rights under the scheme with the amendment made by paragraph 5(1) of Schedule 4 to the Social Security Act 1990 (which substituted the words "pensionable service" for the words "service in relevant employment")."

(3) In paragraph 15(4) of that Schedule (commutation of widow's, widower's or dependant's benefit by the beneficiary) for the words "by the beneficiary" there shall be substituted the words "of that benefit".

(4) In consequence of the amendment made by sub-paragraph (1) above—

(a) in paragraph 2(b) of that Schedule (definition of "long service benefit") after the words "remains in relevant employment" there shall be inserted the words ", and continues to render service which qualifies him for benefits,";

(b) in paragraph 17(1)(b) of that Schedule, for the words "relevant employment" there shall be substituted the words "pensionable service";

(c) in Schedule 1A to the Pensions Act (revaluation of pensions and transfer values)—

   (i) in paragraphs 1(1)(b), 2(2)(d) and 11(1)(b), sub-paragraph (ii) and the word "or" immediately preceding it shall cease to have effect;

   (ii) in paragraphs 1(4) and 11(2), the words "relevant employment" shall be omitted; and

   (iii) paragraph 12(1)(b) and the word "or" immediately preceding it shall cease to have effect.

Contracting-out conditions: age at which pension or annuity is to commence under a money purchase scheme

6.—(1) In section 32 of the Pensions Act, in subsection (2B) (modifications of Schedule 1 to the 1986 Act in its application for the purpose of determining whether a money purchase scheme can be contracted-out) after paragraph (d)(ii) there shall be inserted—

"(iii) for the references in sub-paragraphs (3)(a) and (7)(a)(i) to the date on which the member attains pensionable age there shall be substituted a reference to a date not earlier than that on which he attains the age of 60 nor later than that on which he attains the age of 65; and".

(2) The amendment made by sub-paragraph (1) above shall be taken to have come into force on May 17, 1990.

Contracting-out conditions: guaranteed minimum for married women and widows paying reduced rate contributions

7.—(1) In section 33 of the Pensions Act, in subsection (1A) (special conditions in the case of married women and widows paying reduced rate contributions) in paragraph (a) after the words "if she attains pensionable age" there shall be inserted the words "and does not have a guaranteed minimum under section 35 below".

(2) In section 35 of that Act, after subsection (2) (calculation of guaranteed minimum by reference to earnings factors derived from earnings on which primary Class 1 contributions have been paid) there shall be added—

"(2ZA) In determining the guaranteed minimum in a case where—

(a) earnings such as are mentioned in subsection (1) above have been paid to a married woman or widow who is liable to pay primary Class 1 contributions at a reduced rate by virtue of section 3 of this Act, and

(b) the tax week in which those earnings are paid falls in the tax year 1991–92 or any subsequent tax year,

the married woman or widow shall be treated for the purposes of this section as having such earnings factors derived from those earnings as she would have had if primary Class 1 contributions had been payable, and paid, upon them otherwise than at a reduced rate."

(3) If, immediately before the coming into force of this paragraph, there is in force in relation to an occupational pension scheme a contracting-out certificate under Part III of the Pensions Act then, to the extent that the rules of the scheme are inconsistent with any provision made by sub-paragraph (1) or (2) above, they shall be overridden by that provision.

Protection of earner's and widow's pensions

8.—(1) Sections 41A and 41B of the Pensions Act (protection of earner's and widow's pension) shall have effect, and be taken at all times on and after July 21, 1989 to have had effect, with the amendments made by sub-paragraphs (2) to (7) below, which are in substitution for the amendments made by paragraphs 6 and 7 of Schedule 6 to the 1989 Act; and those paragraphs shall be taken never to have come into force.

(2) In section 41A of the Pensions Act, in subsection (1C) (which defines the "relevant aggregate") after paragraph (c) there shall be added the words "and

(d) where the scheme provides that part of the earner's pension shall accrue after the termination of employment date by reason of employment after that date, the later earnings addition."

(3) After subsection (2) of that section there shall be inserted—

"(2A) In this section "the later earnings addition" means the amount (if any) by which (R2 - G2) exceeds (R1 - G1), where—

R1 is the relevant sum;

G1 is the earner's guaranteed minimum on the day after his termination of employment date;

R2 is the amount that would have been the relevant sum, had the weekly rate of the benefit which determines that sum been calculated by reference to the earner's later earnings level; and

G2 is that amount which bears to R2 the proportion which G1 bears to R1.

(2B) For the purposes of subsection (2A) above, the earner's "later earnings level" is the level of earnings by reference to which the weekly rate of the benefit which determines the relevant sum would have been calculated, had the termination of employment date fallen on the earlier of—

(a) the commencement of payment date, or

(b) the date on which the earner ceased to be in pensionable service under the scheme."

(4) In subsection (11) of that section (definitions) for the words " "short service benefit" is" there shall be substituted the words " "pensionable service" and "short service benefit" are".

(5) In section 41 B of the Pensions Act, in subsection (1A) (which defines the "relevant aggregate") after paragraph (c) there shall be added the words "and

(d) where the scheme provides that part of the widow's pension shall accrue after the termination of employment date by reason of the earner's employment after that date, the later earnings addition."

(6) After subsection (3) of that section there shall be inserted—

"(3A) In this section "the later earnings addition" "means the amount (if any) by which (R2 - G2) exceeds (R1 - G1), where—

R1 is the relevant sum;

G1 is one half of the earner's guaranteed minimum on the day after his termination of employment date;

R2 is the amount that would have been the relevant sum, had the weekly rate of the pension which determines that sum been calculated by reference to the earner's later earnings level; and

G2 is that amount which bears to R2 the proportion which G1 bears to R1.

(3B) For the purposes of subsection (3A) above, the earner's "later earnings level" is the level of earnings by reference to which the weekly rate of the pension which determines the relevant sum would have been calculated, had the earner's termination of employment date fallen on the earlier of—

(a) the earner's commencement of payment date, or

(b) the date on which the earner ceased to be in pensionable service under the scheme."

(7) After subsection (5) of that section, there shall be added—

"(6) In this section "pensionable service" shall be construed in accordance with Schedule 16 to the Social Security Act 1973."

(8) In section 41A of that Act, in subsection (1), for the words "relevant date" there shall be substituted the words "commencement of payment date" and subsections (1A) and (1B) shall cease to have effect.

(9) In consequence of this paragraph, regulation 2(1) and (2) of the Occupational Pension Schemes (Transitional Provisions and Savings) Regulations 1989 shall be deemed never to have been made.

(10) If, before July 21, 1989, an earner ceased to be in contracted-out employment by reference to an occupational pension scheme other than a money purchase contracted-out scheme, sections 41A and 41B of the Pensions Act shall apply in relation to the earner and the earner's widow or widower as if neither this paragraph nor paragraphs 6 and 7 of Schedule 6 to the 1989 Act had been enacted.

(11) Expressions used in sub-paragraph (10) above and the Pensions Act have the same meaning in that sub-paragraph as they have in that Act.

Provisions for the suspension or forfeiture of pensions

9.—(1) In section 41C(3) of the Pensions Act—

(a) in paragraph (a), sub-paragraph (ii) shall be omitted and for the word "or" immediately preceding it there shall be substituted the word "and", and

(b) in paragraph (d) (provisions about commutation of pensions to be included among the provisions which are not overridden by sections 41A and 41B of that Act) for the word "commutation" there shall be substituted the words "the commutation, suspension or forfeiture".

(2) After that paragraph there shall be inserted—

"and

(e) any provision of a scheme whereby, as respects so much of a widow's or widower's pension as exceeds the guaranteed minimum pension—

(i) no pension, or a pension at a reduced rate, is payable if the earner and the widow or widower married not more than six months before the earner's death;

(ii) the whole or any part of the pension is not paid to the widow or widower, but instead comparable benefits are provided for one or more dependants of the deceased earner; or

(iii) no pension, or a pension at a reduced rate, is payable to the widow or widower (or, where a provision such as is mentioned in sub-paragraph (ii) above operates, to another dependant of the deceased earner) who was more than ten years younger than the deceased earner."

(3) In paragraph 7(4) of Schedule 1A to the Pensions Act, in paragraph (a) (adaptations of section 41C(3) in its application for certain purposes to schemes which are not contracted-out) after sub-paragraph (iii) there shall be added—

"(iv) from paragraph (e), the words from "as respects" to "guaranteed minimum pension" ";

and paragraph (b) (which made, in relation to schemes which are not contracted- out, similar provision to that made by sub-paragraph (2) above as modified by this sub-paragraph) shall be omitted.

(4) The amendments made by sub-paragraph (1) above shall be deemed to have come into force on November 1, 1986 (the date on which certain amendments relating to commutation, suspension and forfeiture took, or are deemed to have taken, effect).

The insurance companies which may take transfer values

10. In section 52C of the Pensions Act (extinguishment of scheme's liability for pensions appropriately secured by insurance policies or annuity contracts) in subsection (4) (meaning of "appropriately secured") for paragraph (a) there shall be substituted—

"(a) the insurance company with which it is or was taken out or entered into—

(i) is, or was at the relevant time, carrying on ordinary long- term insurance business in the United Kingdom or any other member State, and

(ii) satisfies, or satisfied at the relevant time, prescribed requirements; and".

Grants by the Occupational Pensions Board to advisory bodies

11. The following section shall be inserted after the section 57A of the Pensions Act inserted by paragraph 3 above—

"Grants by the Board to advisory bodies etc.

57B.—(1) The Occupational Pensions Board may make grants on such terms and conditions as they think fit to any person or body of persons providing advice or assistance, or carrying out other prescribed functions, in connection with occupational or personal pensions.

(2) The Secretary of State may pay to the Occupational Pensions Board such sums as he may think fit towards any expenditure of theirs in making grants under this section."

Levy towards meeting cost of the Pensions Ombudsman, the Registry and certain grants made by the Board

12. After section 60 of the Pensions Act there shall be inserted the following section—

"Levies towards meeting certain expenditure under this Act

60ZA.—(1) For the purpose of meeting some or all of the expenditure under section 57B, Part IVA, and section 59K of this Act, regulations may make provision for imposing a levy in respect of such occupational or personal pension schemes as may be prescribed.

(2) Any levy imposed under this section shall be payable to the Secretary of State by or on behalf of—

(a) the administrators of such public service pension schemes as may be prescribed,

(b) the trustees or managers of such other occupational or personal pension schemes as may be prescribed, or

(c) such other persons as may be prescribed,

at such rates and at such times as may be prescribed.

(3) The amount payable by any person on account of the levy shall be a debt due from him to the Secretary of State and shall be recoverable accordingly.

(4) Regulations under this section may include provision relating to the collection and recovery of amounts payable by way of levy under this section, but this subsection is without prejudice to the generality of subsection (1) above."

Extension of certain pension scheme provisions to Northern Ireland

13. In section 68(4) of the Pensions Act (provisions which extend to Northern Ireland) for the words "Section 57 of this Act extends" there shall be substituted the words "The following provisions of this Act, namely, sections 57, 59B, other than subsections (4) and (5)(b), and 59K(1), (2), other than paragraph (a)(ii), (3), (4) and (9) extend".

Revaluation: extension of certain provisions to widowers

14. In section 9(4) of the 1986 Act, in paragraph (i) (which was inserted by paragraph 16(b) of Schedule 6 to the 1989 Act and which specifies certain provisions in Schedule 1A to the Pensions Act which are to be construed as if "widow" included "widower") after the word "paragraphs" there shall be inserted "2(2)(e),".

Overriding effect of certain 1989 Act amendments

15.—(1) In paragraph 19 of Schedule 6 to the 1989 Act (which made minor amendments to the requirements specified in Schedule 1 to the 1986 Act which appropriate schemes must satisfy) after sub-paragraph (2) there shall be added—

"(3) If immediately before the passing of the Social Security Act 1990 there is in force in relation to an occupational or personal pension scheme either—

(a) a contracting-out certificate under Part III of the Pensions Act which states that the scheme is contracted-out by virtue of section 32(2A) of that Act, or

(b) an appropriate scheme certificate under Part I of the 1986 Act,

then, to the extent that the rules of the scheme are inconsistent with any provision made by sub-paragraph (1) or (2) above, they shall be overridden by that provision."

(2) In paragraph 20 of Schedule 6 to the 1989 Act (amendments relating to the manner of giving effect to protected rights) after sub-paragraph (3) there shall be added—

"(4) If immediately before the passing of the Social Security Act 1990 there is in force in relation to an occupational or personal pension scheme either—

(a) a contracting-out certificate under Part III of the Pensions Act which states that the scheme is contracted-out by virtue of section 32(2A) of that Act, or

(b) an appropriate scheme certificate under Part I of the 1986 Act,

then, to the extent that the rules of the scheme are inconsistent with any provision made by sub-paragraphs (1) to (3) above, they shall be overridden by that provision."

COMMENCEMENT

Paras. 6, 8, 9 and 15, July 13, 1990 (s.23(3)(c)); paras. 12 to 14, July 18, 1990 (Social Security Act 1990 (Commencement No. 1) Order 1990 (S.I. 1990 No. 1446), art. 2(a)); para. 11, October 1, 1990 (Social Security Act 1990 (Commencement No. 2) Order 1990 (S.I. 1990 No. 1942), art. 2(a) and Sched.); para. 1, November 12, 1990 (*ibid.*, art. 2(d)); para. 3, December 3, 1990 (*ibid.*, art. 2(e)); para. 4, January 1, 1991 (*ibid.*, art. 2(f)); remainder, to be confirmed.

DEFINITIONS

"the 1973 Act": s.20.

"the 1986 Act": *ibid.*

"the 1989 Act": *ibid.*

"the Pensions Act": *ibid.*

GENERAL NOTE

Para. 1

Para. 1 inserts new ss.57C and 57D into the Social Security Pensions Act 1975 relating to the appointment of an independent trustee when an employer goes into liquidation. The OPB in their report *Protecting Pensions: Safeguarding Benefits in a Changing Environment*, Cm. 573, 1989, concluded that further steps were needed in this area. They recommended (para. 10.13)—

"(i) The insolvency practitioner should be required within a specified period after his appointment to appoint an independent trustee chosen from a panel of approved individuals and organisations.

(ii) If the employer had been the sole trustee the independent trustee should become the sole trustee.

(iii) If the employer had not been the sole trustee, the independent trustee could act together with those of the existing trustees willing to do so. If none of them was willing to continue, the independent trustee should become the sole trustee.

(iv) The insolvency practitioner should be required to provide within a specified timetable such information to the trustees as they required for the efficient winding-up of the scheme.

(v) The fees of the independent trustee should rank level with those of the insolvency practitioner."

These recommendations are implemented by ss.57C and 57D with effect from November 12, 1990.

Note first that these provisions override any contrary provisions in the scheme (s.57D(8)). Then s.57C applies to occupational pension schemes constituted by trust deed (subs. (1)). Thus public service schemes set up by or under statute are excluded, as are purely contractual schemes. Under s.57D(10) regulations may exclude descriptions of scheme from the operation of s.57C and 57D. The initial proposal was to exclude money purchase schemes and small self-administered schemes where all the members are also trustees. In such cases there is no possibility of trustees acting to benefit the employer when their duties were to act in the interest of the beneficiaries (Standing Committee G, col. 312, March 1, 1990, and DSS consultative paper). Reg. 6 of the Occupational Pension Schemes (Independent Trustees) Regulations 1990 (S.I. 1990 No. 2075) excludes these kinds of schemes and also schemes which provide death-in-service benefits only or under which all benefits are secured by earmarked insurance policies. The other condition for the application of s.57C is that either an insolvency practitioner begins to act in relation to the employer or the official receiver becomes the liquidator or receiver. It appears from the tense that if either of these things has happened before the section comes into force it does not apply. This is confirmed by reg. 7 of the Independent Trustees Regulations.

If s.57C applies, one of the trustees of the scheme must be an independent trustee within the meaning of subs. (3) and the insolvency practitioner or the official receiver must appoint an independent person as necessary. This duty can be enforced by court order (subs. (6)). To be independent the person must have no interest in the assets of the employer or the pension scheme, otherwise than as a trustee of the scheme, and must not be connected or associated (see subs. (4)) with the employer, the insolvency practitioner who is acting or the official receiver who is acting. This prescription excludes employees. If the employer is a large quoted company many people may be excluded as shareholders, possibly as trustees of other schemes. Regulations may prescribe other requirements for independence. Reg. 2 of the Independent Trustees Regulations prescribes two other conditions. The first (reg. 2(2)) is that the person has not in the three years before the triggering of s.57C provided services to the trustees or managers, or an employer under the scheme. "Services" will include advice. The second condition (reg. 2(3)) is that the person is not connected or associated with a person who has an interest in the assets of the employer or the scheme, other than as a scheme trustee, or with a person to whom reg. 2(2) applies. No requirements about adequate indemnity insurance have been imposed.

While s.57C applies no independent trustee may be removed under the rules of the scheme (s.57D(1)) and any discretionary powers vested in the trustees or managers of the scheme or the employer shall be exercisable only by the independent trustee, or with the consent of at least half their number if there are more than one (s.57D(5)). If the employer had previously been the sole trustee he ceases to be a trustee as soon as the independent trustee is appointed (s.57D(4)). These provisions will avoid the problem encountered in *Icarus (Hertford)* v. *Driscoll* (unreported, December 4, 1989, Aldous J.) and *Mettoy Pension Trustees* v. *Evans* (*Financial Times*, February 9, 1990, Warner J.), where the power of liquidators to exercise fiduciary powers of the employer was at issue. In *Icarus* it was held that the liquidator could decide whether to exercise the power to augment benefits on winding-up, whereas in *Mettoy* it was held that the liquidator could not do so because of the conflict between his duties to the beneficiaries under the pension scheme and his duties to the employer's creditors.

Under s.57D(6) the insolvency practitioner or the receiver is under a duty to supply reasonably required information to the trustees.

The operation of the two sections may be modified by regulations in the circumstances set out in s.57D(9). Head (a) covers what are known as centralised schemes, which cover a number of different employers. By virtue of reg. 3(2) of the Independent Trustees Regulations, s.57C only applies where an employer under the scheme who has the power to appoint or remove trustees or is himself a trustee becomes insolvent. In most cases, this will be the principal employer under the scheme. If such an employer is not insolvent, it does not seem to matter that the employers under the scheme are associated with one another. If such an employer is insolvent then the references in ss.57C and 57D to "the employer" are to that employer. Under head (b), where a scheme is paid-up, s.57C applies only if the employer has the power to appoint or remove trustees or is himself a trustee (reg. 4). The right to be paid the surplus on a wind-up does not bring in s.57C. Under head (c), s.57C only applies to a partnership in England and Wales when the partnership is insolvent (reg. 5). The insolvency of an individual partner does not, contrary to the initial proposal, trigger s.57C. There is no modification at all for Scottish partnerships.

Para. 2

The OPB in *Protecting Pensions* expressed some concern at the ability of an employer to benefit shareholders at the expense of pension scheme members by winding up the scheme, giving members only their strict legal rights and taking the resulting surplus. Although they did not find evidence of widespread use of the power to wind up for such a purpose in the U.K. they made a series of recommendations. One was that if a scheme was wound up, whether on the insolvency of the employer or with the employment continuing, any deficiency in the scheme (taking account of its new liabilities to improve preserved pensions under Sched. 1A to the Pensions Act) should be a debt due from the employer (paras. 10.6 and 10.17).

The new s.58B inserted into the Pensions Act implements this recommendation and over-rides scheme rules (subs. (7)). It applies to occupational pension schemes other than money purchase schemes. Assets always equal liabilities in money purchase schemes. Then the section bites if the value of the scheme's liabilities exceeds its assets at "the applicable time." The applicable time is defined in subs. (3). It is the earlier of the beginning of the winding-up of the scheme or the going into liquidation or bankruptcy of the employer ("the default time"). Thus it seems that if the scheme has begun to be wound up or the employer has become insolvent before s.58B is brought into force the section does not apply. If there is a deficiency, applying the methods and assumptions to be prescribed under subs. (5), its amount becomes a debt due to the scheme from the employer (subs. (1)). The debt is not a preferential debt for the purposes of the Insolvency Act 1986 (subs. (5)).

Under subs. (6) regulations may modify the application of s.58B in specified circumstances. Under head (a) on centralised schemes, the DSS's initial proposal was that regulations should make each employer liable for the proportion of the deficiency that the liabilities for that employer's employees and ex-employees bear to the total liabilities of the scheme, regardless of whether the employers are associated or not. This proposal has been severely criticised by the Association of Pension Lawyers, and it seems that a different solution might come forward for non-associated employers and employers who have ceased to participate in the scheme before the applicable time. Under head (b) on partnerships presumably the same approach will be taken as under s.57D. For paid-up schemes under head (c) it is proposed that regulations will modify the definition of "the applicable time" to make it the earlier of the last member ceasing to be in pensionable service and the default time. Under head (d) it is proposed that where a scheme is wound up so that its assets and liabilities can be transferred to another scheme, s.58B should not apply, since it is assumed that the employer will be responsible for any deficiency in the receiving scheme. However, there is no power to modify s.58B where the employer goes into voluntary liquidation as part of a corporate reconstruction and there is no intention to wind up the scheme, which is to be continued by a different employer.

Para. 3

The new s.57A of the Pensions Act deals with self-investment, *i.e.* investment in a scheme's sponsoring employer or investment closely connected with that employer, such as an invest-ment in a property occupied by the employer. The National Association of Pension Funds in their June 1988 report *Self-Investment by Pension Funds* concluded that "the potential for conflicts of interest, irresolvable pressures and argument is so great that self-investment is an unhelpful and undesirable practice." The OPB in *Protecting Pensions* did not accept the sweep of that conclusion given the diversity of cases and circumstances brought to their notice and the fact that a holding of the sponsoring employer's shares may form part of a balanced portfolio. In addition, an employer, by keeping funding levels low, may in practice achieve the same effect as an investment of pension funds with the employer. However, if carried to extremes, self-investment can gravely weaken security, so that a maximum level of self-investment should be set, with the possibility of temporarily exceeding that limit. The recommendation was that in schemes other than small self-administered schemes, if assets net of self-investment did not cover winding-up liabilities, there should normally be a maximum of five per cent. of scheme assets (paras. 15.14–16).

The initial response of the Government was to go further and impose a limit of five per cent. on all occupational pension schemes. S.57A would allow such an approach, because it leaves the restrictions on "employer-related investments" (defined in subs. (2)) to be prescribed by regulations. However, as a result of representations about the effect on small self-administered schemes, it was announced that the restrictions would not apply to such schemes where all the members are 20 per cent. directors and all investment decisions are taken unanimously (see Standing Committee G, col. 336, March 1, 1990). The approach to the regulations as a whole was described as follows (*ibid.*):

"Many representations have continued to be received from employers, whose pension schemes are not covered by that exemption, outlining the possible effects on their business and pension scheme if their pension scheme is required to dispose too quickly of assets held in the company. At the same time, the recently published National Association of Pension Funds survey for 1989 shows an increase in the number of self-investing schemes—38 per cent. up from 23 per cent. the previous year—and this despite a code of good practice aimed at reducing the practice substantially.

"The position is clearly more serious than was originally thought when we framed our proposals, and this is yet another example of a developing situation. Therefore, we intend to arrange for a survey to be carried out, which will provide up-to-date information on the extent of self-investment, which sectors it is concentrated in and what the particular problems will be in restricting it. We will be asking for the report by this summer so that we can maintain our intention of introducing regulations as soon as practicable after Royal Assent.

"The report will guide us to the appropriate limits and time scale which we should adopt. In the meantime, I would not want anyone to take the view, or get the impression, that the Government have changed their intention to restrict self-investment. It is very much our intention to reduce that practice, but it is equally important that we do so in a responsible and informed way that does not turn the potential double risk to jobs and pensions entailed in self-investment into reality."

Para. 4

Para. 4 implements the OPB's recommendation that for persons becoming entitled to preserved benefits on or after an Appointed Day, the revaluation provisions introduced by the Social Security Act 1985 should apply to the whole of the non-GMP pension and not only to that part deemed to have been earned from January 1, 1985 (*Protecting Pensions*, para. 9.13). The OPB considered that this extension would help to meet the widely perceived need for better protection on wind-up or bulk transfer and, given that it was unlikely to start before January 1991, would only apply to members with at least six years' pensionable service at that date. The extra cost was therefore calculated for an average scheme at one-quarter of one per cent. of payroll for 15 years (paras. 9.9–10). The Appointed Day has been confirmed as January 1, 1991.

The revaluation required is the LPI (in line with the retail price index subject to a maximum of five per cent.) specified in the annual revaluation orders, which will also define the required increase in pensions in payment under the new s.58A. The provisions appear to fit together nicely, but a number of gaps remain. The first is that those whose entitlement to preserved benefits began or begin before January 1, 1991 will only be entitled to an increase on the element of pension attributable to service from January 1, 1985. Here the OPB recommended that as a matter of good practice, employers and trustees should extend the principle of the legislative amendment to as wide a range of individuals as resources permit (para. 9.15). Many schemes already apply increases to preserved pensions earned by pre-1985 service. The second gap is that by virtue of para. 1(2)(b) of Sched. 1A to the Pensions Act revaluation is only applied to benefits payable to persons other than the member himself if the member dies after reaching normal pension age. If the member dies after leaving service but before reaching normal pension age, the pension payable to the surviving spouse and children does not have to have been revalued since the date of leaving service. Once the pension comes into payment it must be increased under s.58A.

Para. 5

These are technical changes and corrections.

Para. 6

In order for a money purchase scheme to be used to contract out of SERPS the benefits must become payable at a unisex age between 60 and 65. This is in reaction to the decision of the European Court of Justice in *Barber* v. *Guardian Royal Exchange Assurance Group* [1990] 2 All E.R. 660 that pensions paid to members of contracted-out occupational pension schemes are "pay" within the meaning of Article 119 of the Treaty of Rome (equal pay for equal work). Thus for a scheme to provide benefits to men and women at different ages, *e.g.* by reference to the differential state pensionable age, even though required for contracting-out, article 119 will be breached. The amended condition is deemed to have been in force from May 17, 1990, the date of the decision in *Barber*.

No change has yet been made in the conditions for a final salary scheme to contract out of SERPS, although the GMP must be provided at different ages for men and women.

Paras. 7 to 10
These are mainly technical amendments.

Para. 11
The new s.57B of the Pensions Act authorises the OPB to make grants to bodies or persons providing advice and assistance in connection with occupational or personal pensions. This is the implementation cf the OPB recommendation to set up such a body, based on the existing work of the Occupational Pensions Advisory Service (OPAS) (*Protecting Pensions*, para. 13.9). OPAS is a registered charity financed by voluntary donations. The new service will be financed out of the levy on schemes under s.60ZA. OPAS is restricted to occupational schemes. The new body will also cover problems with personal pensions.

Para. 12
The new s.60ZA of the Pensions Act authorises the making of regulations to impose a levy on occupational and personal pension schemes in order to meet some or all of the costs of the advice and conciliation service, the Pensions Ombudsman and the pensions registry.

Paras. 13 to 15
These are technical amendments.

Section 17(7)   SCHEDULE 5

SPECIAL PENALTIES IN THE CASE OF CERTAIN RETURNS

The provisions referred to in section 17(7) of this Act are as follows—

"*Special penalties in the case of certain returns*

5A.—(1) This paragraph applies where regulations under paragraph 5 above make provision requiring any return which is to be made in accordance with a specified provision of regulations under that paragraph (the "contributions return") to be made—
   (a) at the same time as any specified return required to be made in accordance with a provision of regulations made by the Inland Revenue under section 203(2) (PAYE) or 566(1) (sub- contractors) of the Income and Corporation Taxes Act 1988 to which section 98A of the Taxes Management Act 1970 applies (the "tax return"); or
   (b) if the circumstances are such that the return mentioned in paragraph (a) above does not fall to be made, at a time defined by reference to the time for making that return, had it fallen to be made;
and, in a case falling within paragraph (b) above, any reference in the following provisions of this paragraph to the tax return shall be construed as a reference to the return there mentioned.
   (2) Where this paragraph applies, regulations under paragraph 5 above may provide that section 98A of the Taxes Management Act 1970 (penalties for late, fraudulent or negligent returns) shall apply in relation to any specified provision of regulations in accordance with which the contributions return is required to be made; and where they so provide then, subject to the following provisions of this paragraph—
   (a) that section shall apply in relation to the contributions return as it applies in relation to the tax return; and
   (b) sections 100 to 100D and 102 to 104 of that Act shall apply in relation to a penalty under section 98A of that Act to which a person is liable by virtue of this sub-paragraph as they apply in relation to any other penalty under that section.
   (3) Where a person is liable to a penalty under paragraph (a) of subsection (2) of section 98A of that Act (first twelve months' default) in consequence of a failure in

respect of a tax return, he shall not also be liable to a penalty under that paragraph in respect of any failure in respect of the associated contributions return.

(4) In any case where—

(a) a person is liable to a penalty under subsection (2)(b) or (4) of that section (tax-related penalties) in respect of both a tax return and its associated contributions return, and

(b) an officer of the Inland Revenue authorised for the purposes of section 100 of that Act has determined that a penalty is to be imposed under that provision in respect of both returns,

the penalty so imposed shall be a single penalty of an amount not exceeding the limit determined under sub-paragraph (5) below.

(5) The limit mentioned in sub-paragraph (4) above is an amount equal to the sum of—

(a) the maximum penalty that would have been applicable under subsection (2)(b) or (4) of that section (as the case may be) for a penalty in relation to the tax return only; and

(b) the maximum penalty that would have been so applicable in relation to the associated contributions return only.

(6) So much of any single penalty imposed by virtue of sub-paragraph (4) above as is recovered by the Inland Revenue shall, after the deduction of any administrative costs of the Inland Revenue attributable to its recovery, be apportioned between the Inland Revenue and the Secretary of State in the ratio T:C, where—

T is the maximum penalty that could have been imposed under the provision in question in relation to the tax return only; and

C is the maximum penalty that could have been so imposed in relation to the associated contributions return only.

(7) The Inland Revenue shall, at such times and in such manner as the Treasury may direct, account to the Secretary of State for, and pay to him—

(a) the amounts apportioned to him under sub-paragraph (6) above in respect of such penalties as are there mentioned; and

(b) so much of any penalty otherwise imposed by virtue of this paragraph and recovered by the Inland Revenue as remains after the deduction by them of any administrative costs attributable to its recovery.

(8) Sub-paragraphs (6) and (7) above shall have effect notwithstanding any provision which treats a penalty under section 98A of that Act as if it were tax charged in an assessment and due and payable.

(9) In the application of section 98A of that Act by virtue of this paragraph, any reference to a year of assessment shall be construed, in relation to a contributions return, as a reference to the tax year corresponding to that year of assessment.

(10) In the application of section 100D of that Act (court proceedings for penalties in cases of fraud) by virtue of this paragraph—

(a) subsection (2) shall have effect with the omission of the words "or Northern Ireland" and paragraph (c); and

(b) subsection (3) shall have effect with the omission of the words from "and any such proceedings instituted in Northern Ireland" onwards.

(11) In the application of section 103 of that Act (time limit for recovery) by virtue of this paragraph—

(a) any reference in subsection (1) to tax shall be taken to include a reference to Class 1 contributions;

(b) any penalty by virtue of sub-paragraph (4) above shall be regarded as a penalty in respect of the tax return in question; and

(c) where, by virtue of subsection (2) (death), subsection (1)(b) does not apply in relation to a penalty under section 98A(2)(b) or (4) of that Act in respect of a tax return, it shall also not apply in relation to a penalty so imposed in respect of the associated contributions return.

(12) A penalty under section 98A of that Act as it applies by virtue of this paragraph may be imposed notwithstanding that a question arising in relation to contributions has not been determined under section 93 of this Act by the Secretary of State, except that where—

(a) any such question arises which affects a person's liability for, or the amount of, the penalty, and

(b) either—

(i) that person requires the question to be determined under section 93, or

(ii) a question of law arising in connection with the determination of the question is, or is to be, referred to a court under section 94 of this Act, the penalty shall not be imposed until the question has been determined under section 93 by the Secretary of State or the reference has been finally disposed of under section 94, as the case may be; but subject to that, this paragraph is without prejudice to sections 93, 94 and 96 of this Act.

(13) for the purposes of this paragraph—
(a) "contributions return" and "tax return" shall be construed in accordance with sub-paragraph (1) above; and
(b) a contributions return and a tax return are "associated" if the contributions return is required to be made—
    (i) at the same time as the tax return, or
    (ii) where sub-paragraph (1)(b) above applies, at a time defined by reference to the time for making the tax return."

COMMENCEMENT
July 18, 1990 (Social Security Act 1990 (Commencement No. 1) Order 1990 (S.I. 1990 No. 1446), art. 2(a)).

GENERAL NOTE
These provisions are inserted into Sched. 1 of the Social Security Act 1975 by s.17(7) and provide for penalties for late payment of contributions or returns.

Section 21(1)   SCHEDULE 6

MINOR AND CONSEQUENTIAL AMENDMENTS

Orders increasing contributions

1.—(1) In subsection (6K) of section 4 of the principal Act (certain orders relating to contributions to be subject to the effect of subsequent orders under that section) after the word "under" there shall be inserted the words "Part IV of this Act or".
(2) The words "section 4 above or this Part of this Act" shall be substituted—
(a) in section 121(3) of the principal Act, for the words "that section or section 122 below";
(b) in section 123(3) of that Act, for the words "that section or under section 120 above"; and
(c) in section 123A(8) of that Act, for the words "this section".

Contributions of registered dock workers

2.—(1) In section 4(7) of the principal Act (reduced contributions for certain persons) the reference to section 145 of the Employment Protection (Consolidation) Act 1978 (which related to registered dock workers and which was repealed by the Dock Work Act 1989 as from July 3, 1989) shall be omitted.
(2) Notwithstanding the repeal of section 145 of the said Act of 1978 or of the reference to it in section 4(7) of the principal Act, regulation 133 of the Contributions Regulations (reduced rate of contributions for registered dock workers) shall continue to have effect, and be taken to have continued to have had effect at all times on and after July 3, 1989, in relation to earnings paid or treated as paid before April 6, 1988 as it had effect by virtue of regulation 4 of the 1988 Regulations (which continues in force accordingly).
(3) Nothing in this paragraph shall be taken to have prejudiced any power to amend or revoke the regulations to which it refers.
(4) In this paragraph—
    "the Contributions Regulations" means the Social Security (Contributions) Regulations 1979; and
    "the 1988 Regulations" means the Social Security (Contributions) Amendment Regulations 1988.

Restriction on dependency increases

3.—(1) In section 33 of the principal Act, in subsection (3) (which requires benefit payable by virtue of that section where the contribution conditions are only partially satisfied to be paid at a reduced rate) after the words "conditions are satisfied" there shall be inserted the words "(and may be nil)".
(2) In section 47A of that Act (rate of adult dependency increases to be determined in accordance with regulations in certain cases where the associated retirement pension is attributable to reduced contributions) after the words "pension is determined" there shall be inserted "(a)" and at the end of that section there shall be added the words "and
    (b) the regulations shall not provide for any such increase in a case where the

retirement pension by reference to which the rate of the said benefit or invalidity pension is determined—

       (i) would have been payable only by virtue of section 33 above; and

       (ii) would, in consequence of a failure to satisfy a contribution condition, have contained no basic pension."

(3) In section 8 of the Social Security (Miscellaneous Provisions) Act 1977, in subsection (1) (which precludes any increase on account of a child in the amount of certain pensions payable by virtue of section 33(2) of the principal Act where a contribution condition is not satisfied) after the words "on account of a child" there shall be inserted the words "or an adult, or under section 28(7) of the principal Act (invalidity),".

(4) In subsection (2) of that section (which contains a similar restriction in relation to unemployment or sickness benefit where entitlement to a retirement pension would have arisen only by virtue of section 33) after the words "on account of a child" there shall be added the words "or an adult or under section 28(7) of the principal Act (invalidity)."

Regulations relating to industrial injuries and diseases

4.—(1) In section 76 of the principal Act, after subsection (4) (power to make regulations for determining, among other things, the time at which a person is to be treated as having developed a prescribed injury or disease) there shall be inserted—

"(4A) Notwithstanding any other provision of this Act, the power conferred by subsection (4)(a) above includes power to provide that the time at which a person shall be treated as having developed a prescribed disease or injury shall be the date on which he first makes a claim which results in the payment of benefit by virtue of this Chapter in respect of that disease or injury."

(2) In section 77 of that Act, at the end of subsection (2) (power to modify provisions relating to disablement benefit and its administration) there shall be added the words—

"and for the purposes of this subsection the provisions of this Act which relate to the administration of disablement benefit or reduced earnings allowance shall be taken to include section 165A and any provision which relates to the administration of both the benefit in question and other benefits."

(3) Regulations 6(2)(c), 25 and 36 of the Social Security (Industrial Injuries) (Prescribed Diseases) Regulations 1985 (onset of occupational deafness and time for claiming in respect of occupational deafness or occupational asthma), any former regulations which they directly or indirectly re-enact with or without amendment, shall be taken to be, and always to have been, validly made.

Certain officers in Northern Ireland to be eligible for appointment as adjudication officers for Great Britain

5.—(1) In section 97 of the principal Act, in subsection (1) (appointment of adjudication officers) after the words "and may include" there shall be inserted "(a)" and at the end of that subsection there shall be added the words "or

  (b) officers of the Northern Ireland Department appointed with the concurrence of that Department."

(2) In section 56 of the 1986 Act (legal proceedings) after subsection (4A) there shall be inserted—

"(4B) Any proceedings in respect of any act or omission of an adjudication officer which, apart from this subsection, would fall to be brought against a person appointed by virtue of section 97(1)(b) of the Social Security Act 1975 who is resident in Northern Ireland, other than proceedings for an offence, may instead be brought against the Chief Adjudication Officer; and, for the purposes of any proceedings so brought, the acts or omissions of the adjudication officer shall be treated as the acts or omissions of the Chief Adjudication Officer."

Adjudication

6.—(1) In section 100 of the principal Act (appeal to social security appeal tribunal) there shall be added at the end—

"(8) In any case where—

  (a) an adjudication officer has decided any claim or question under Chapter IV or V of Part II of this Act, and

  (b) the right to benefit under those Chapters of any person other than the claimant is or may be, under Schedule 9 to this Act, affected by that decision,

that other person shall have the like right of appeal to a social security appeal tribunal as the claimant.

(9) Subsection (2) above shall apply to a person with a right of appeal under subsection (7) or (8) above as it applies to a claimant."

(2) In section 101 of that Act, in subsection (2) (persons at whose instance an appeal lies from a social security appeal tribunal to a Commissioner on a point of law) the following paragraph shall be inserted after paragraph (b)—

"(bb) in a case relating to industrial injuries benefit, a person whose right to benefit is or may be, under Schedule 9 to this Act, affected by the decision appealed against;".

(3) In subsection (3) of that section, in paragraph (c) (appeal at the instance of a trade union where the claimant was a member of the union) after the words "the claimant" there shall be inserted the words "or, in relation to industrial death benefit, the deceased".

(4) The amendments made by this paragraph shall be deemed to have come into force on the day on which paragraph 2 of Schedule 1 to the Social Security Act 1988 came into force.

Restrictions on entitlement to benefit in certain cases of error

7.—(1) In section 104 of the principal Act (reviews), after the subsection (6) inserted by section 6(3) of this Act, there shall be inserted—

"(7) Subsection (8) below applies in any case where—

(a) on the determination, whenever made, of a Commissioner or the court (the "relevant determination"), a decision made by an adjudicating authority is or was found to have been erroneous in point of law, and

(b) in consequence of that determination, any other decision—

(i) which was made before the date of that determination, and

(ii) which is referable to a claim made or treated as made by any person for any benefit,

falls (or would, apart from subsection (8) below fall) to be revised on a review carried out under subsection (1A) above after the coming into force of this subsection.

(8) Where this subsection applies, any question arising on the review referred to in subsection (7)(b) above, or on any subsequent review of a decision which is referable to the same claim, as to any person's entitlement to, or right to payment of, any benefit—

(a) in respect of any period before the date of the relevant determination, or

(b) in the case of widow's payment, in respect of a death occurring before that date,

shall be determined as if the decision referred to in subsection (7)(a) above had been found by the Commissioner or court in question not to have been erroneous in point of law.

(9) In determining whether a person is entitled to benefit in a case where his entitlement depends on his having been entitled to the same or some other benefit before attaining a particular age, subsection (8) above shall be disregarded for the purpose only of determining the question whether he was so entitled before attaining that age.

(10) for the purposes of subsections (7) to (9) above—

(a) "adjudicating authority" and "the court" have the same meaning as they have in section 165D below;

(b) any reference to—

(i) a person's entitlement to benefit, or

(ii) a decision which is referable to a claim,

shall be construed in accordance with subsection (5) of that section; and

(c) the date of the relevant determination shall, in prescribed cases, be determined in accordance with any regulations made under subsection (6) of that section."

(2) After the section 165C of that Act inserted by section 6(2) of this Act there shall be inserted the following section—

"Restrictions on entitlement to benefit in certain cases of error

165D.—(1) This section applies where—

(a) on the determination, whenever made, of a Commissioner or the court (the "relevant determination"), a decision made by an adjudicating authority is or was found to have been erroneous in point of law; and

(b) after both the coming into force of this section and the date of the relevant determination, a claim which falls, or which would apart from this section fall, to be decided in accordance with the relevant determination is made or treated under section 51B(1) of the Social Security Act 1986 as made by any person for any benefit.

(2) Where this section applies, any question which arises on, or on the review of a decision which is referable to, the claim mentioned in subsection (1)(b) above and which relates to the entitlement of the claimant or any other person to any benefit—

(a) in respect of a period before the relevant date, or

(b) in the case of a widow's payment, in respect of a death occurring before that date,

shall be determined as if the decision referred to in subsection (1)(a) above had been found by the Commissioner or court in question not to have been erroneous in point of law.

(3) In determining whether a person is entitled to benefit in a case where—

(a) his entitlement depends on his having been entitled to the same or some other benefit before attaining a particular age, and

(b) he attained that age—

    (i) before both the date of the relevant determination and the date of the claim referred to in subsection (1)(b) above, but

    (ii) not before the earliest day in respect of which benefit could, apart from this section, have been awarded on that claim,

subsection (2) above shall be disregarded for the purpose only of determining the question whether he was entitled as mentioned in paragraph (a) above.

(4) In this section—

"adjudicating authority" means—

(a) an adjudication officer, the Attendance Allowance Board, a social security appeal tribunal or a medical appeal tribunal;

(b) any of the following former bodies or officers, that is to say, the National Assistance Board, the Supplementary Benefits Commission, a benefit officer, an insurance officer or a supplement officer; or

(c) any of the officers who, or tribunals or other bodies which, in Northern Ireland correspond to those mentioned in paragraph (a) or (b) above;

"the court" means the High Court, the Court of Appeal, the Court of Session, the High Court or Court of Appeal in Northern Ireland, the House of Lords or the Court of Justice of the European Community;

"the relevant date" means whichever is the latest of—

(a) the date on which the relevant determination was made;

(b) the date which falls twelve months before the date on which the claim referred to in subsection (1)(b) above is made or treated under section 51B(1) of the Social Security Act 1986 as made; and

(c) the earliest date in respect of which the claimant would, apart from this section, be entitled on that claim to the benefit in question.

(5) For the purposes of this section—

(a) any reference in this section to entitlement to benefit includes a reference to entitlement—

    (i) to any increase in the rate of a benefit; or

    (ii) to a benefit, or increase of benefit, at a particular rate; and

(b) any reference to a decision which is "referable to" a claim is a reference to—

    (i) a decision on the claim,

    (ii) a decision on a review of the decision on the claim, or

    (iii) 3 decision on a subsequent review of the decision on the review, and so on.

(6) The date of the relevant determination shall, in prescribed cases, be determined for the purposes of this section in accordance with any regulations made for that purpose."

(3) In paragraph 48 of Schedule 10 to the 1986 Act (which applies sections 87 and 165A(1) of the principal Act to income-related benefits) at the end of paragraph (b) there shall be inserted the words "and

(c) section 165D (restrictions on entitlement in certain cases of error)."

Parliamentary control of regulations and orders

8.—(1) In section 67 of the principal Act (Parliamentary control of orders and regulations) for subsections (2) to (4) there shall be substituted—

"(2) Subsection (1) above does not apply to a statutory instrument by reason only that it contains—

(a) regulations under section 129 which the instrument states are made for the purpose of making provision consequential on the making of an order under section 4, 120, 122, 123A or 134;

(b) regulations under powers conferred by any provision mentioned in paragraph

(a) of that subsection which are to be made for the purpose of consolidating regulations to be revoked in the instrument;

(c) regulations which, in so far as they are made under powers so conferred, only replace provisions of previous regulations with new provisions to the same effect.

(3) A statutory instrument—

(a) which contains (whether alone or with other provisions) orders or regulations made under this Act by the Secretary of State, other than orders under section 30(6), 120 or 122, and

(b) which is not subject to any requirement that a draft of the instrument be laid before and approved by a resolution of each House of Parliament,

shall be subject to annulment in pursuance of a resolution of either House of Parliament.

(4) A statutory instrument—

(a) which contains (whether alone or with other provisions) regulations made under this Act by the Lord Chancellor, and

(b) which is not subject to any requirement that a draft of the instrument be laid before and approved by a resolution of each House of Parliament,

shall be subject to annulment in pursuance of a resolution of either House of Parliament."

(2) In section 62 of the Pensions Act, for subsections (1) and (2) there shall be substituted—

"(1) Section 167 of the principal Act shall have effect as if, in subsection (1) (statutory instruments requiring affirmative parliamentary procedure), there were included in paragraph (a) a reference to regulations made by virtue of section 3 above.

(2) Subsection (3) of the said section 167 (statutory instruments subject to annulment) shall have effect as if in paragraph (a), after the words "other than" there were inserted the words "an order which, under any provision of the Pensions Act, is required to be laid before Parliament after being made or."

(3) In section 22 of the Child Benefit Act 1975, for subsections (3) to (5) there shall be substituted—

"(3) Subject to subsection (4) below, a statutory instrument containing (whether alone or with other provisions) any regulations under section 5 or 17(1) above shall not be made unless a draft of the instrument has been laid before and approved by a resolution of each House of Parliament.

(4) Subsection (3) above does not apply to a statutory instrument by reason only that it contains regulations under powers conferred by any provision mentioned in that subsection which are to be made for the purpose of consolidating regulations to be revoked in the instrument.

(5) A statutory instrument—

(a) which contains (whether alone or with other provisions) any regulations under this Act, and

(b) which is not subject to any requirement that a draft of the instrument be laid before and approved by a resolution of each House of Parliament,

shall be subject to annulment in pursuance of a resolution of either House of Parliament."

(4) In section 24(5) of the Social Security (Miscellaneous Provisions) Act 1977 for the words "containing regulations" there shall be substituted—

"(a) which contains (whether alone or with other provisions) any regulations, and

(b) which is not subject to any requirement that a draft of the instrument be laid before and approved by a resolution of each House of Parliament,".

(5) In section 5(4) of the Social Security (No.2) Act 1980—

(a) at the beginning there shall be inserted the words "A statutory instrument containing (whether alone or with other provisions)"; and

(b) for the words "a draft of the regulations" there shall be substituted the words "a draft of the instrument."

(6) In section 7 of that Act, for subsection (4) there shall be substituted—

"(4) A statutory instrument—

(a) which contains (whether alone or with other provisions) any regulations under this Act, and

(b) which is not subject to any requirement that a draft of the instrument be laid before and approved by a resolution of each House of Parliament,

shall be subject to annulment in pursuance of a resolution of either House of Parliament."

(7) In section 45 of the 1982 Act, for subsection (2) there shall be substituted—

"(2) Any power of the Secretary of State to make orders or regulations under this Act shall be exercisable by statutory instrument; and any statutory instrument—

(a) which contains (whether alone or with other provisions) any such orders or regulations, other than an order under section 48(3) of this Act, and

(b) which is not subject to any requirement that a draft of the instrument be laid before and approved by a resolution of each House of Parliament,

shall be subject to annulment in pursuance of a resolution of either House of Parliament."

(8) Section 27(3) and (4) of the Social Security Act 1985 (which relate to parliamentary control of statutory instruments and which are spent) shall cease to have effect.

(9) In section 83 of the 1986 Act, for subsection (4) there shall be substituted—

"(4) A statutory instrument—

(a) which contains (whether alone or with other provisions) orders or regulations under this Act, other than orders under section 88 below, and

(b) which is not subject to any requirement that a draft of the instrument be laid before and approved by a resolution of each House of Parliament,

shall be subject to annulment in pursuance of a resolution of either House of Parliament."

(10) After section 15 of the Social Security Act 1988 there shall be inserted the following section—

"Regulations and orders etc.

15A.—(1) Section 166(1) to (3A) of the Social Security Act 1975 (regulations and orders: general provisions) shall apply in relation to any power conferred by any provision of this Act to make orders or regulations under this Act as they apply in relation to any power conferred by that Act to make orders or regulations, but as if for references to that Act there were substituted references to this Act.

(2) A statutory instrument—

(a) which contains (whether alone or with other provisions) any orders or regulations under this Act, other than orders under section 18 below, and

(b) which is not subject to any requirement that a draft of the instrument be laid before and approved by a resolution of each House of Parliament,

shall be subject to annulment in pursuance of a resolution of either House of Parliament.

(3) In this Act—

"prescribe" means prescribe by regulations: and

"regulations" means regulations made under this Act by the Secretary of State."

(11) In consequence of sub-paragraph (10) above, the following provisions of that Act shall cease to have effect—

(a) section 13(7) and (8);

(b) in section 18(3) and (4) the words "made by statutory instrument";

(c) section 18(7) and (8).

(12) In section 29 of the 1989 Act, for subsection (3) there shall be substituted—

"(3) A statutory instrument—

(a) which contains (whether alone or with other provisions) any regulations or orders under this Act, other than orders under section 33 below, and

(b) which is not subject to any requirement that a draft of the instrument be laid before and approved by a resolution of each House of Parliament,

shall be subject to annulment in pursuance of a resolution of either House of Parliament.";

and, in consequence, subsection (4) shall cease to have effect.

Return of Class 2 contributions paid by low-earners

9. In Schedule 1 to the principal Act (contributions: supplementary provisions) in paragraph 6(1) (matters for which regulations may provide) after the paragraph (gg) inserted by section 2 of the 1989 Act there shall be inserted—

"(gh) for the repayment, on the making of an application in the prescribed manner and within the prescribed time, of Class 2 contributions paid by a person in respect of a period which consists of, or falls within, a tax year for which his earnings from employment as a self-employed earner were, or were such as to be treated by regulations under subsection (5) of section 7 of this Act as being, at a lower rate than the one specified in that subsection for that year;

(gj) for excepting a person from liability for contributions repaid by virtue of paragraph (gh) above, to the extent that he would not have been so excepted by virtue of section 7(5) of this Act;".

Maternity allowance: contribution conditions for women paid otherwise than weekly

10.—(1) In Schedule 3 to the principal Act, at the beginning of paragraph 3 (contribution conditions for maternity allowance) there shall be inserted the words—
    "(1) Subject to sub-paragraph (2) below,".
(2) At the end of that paragraph there shall be added—
    "(2) In the case of a claimant who is or has been paid otherwise than weekly, any week—
        (a) in respect of which she did not pay contributions of a relevant Class, but
        (b) for which her earnings were such that, had she been paid weekly she would have been required to pay primary Class 1 contributions in respect of that week, and
        (c) for which no such election as is mentioned in section 3(2)(a) of the Pensions Act (contributions at a reduced rate) was in force in her case,
    shall be treated for the purposes of sub-paragraph (1) above as a week in respect of which she actually paid such contributions otherwise than at a reduced rate.
    (3) For the purposes of sub-paragraph (2) above, the amount of the claimant's earnings for any week shall be determined in accordance with regulations."

Tax years

11. In Schedule 20 to the principal Act (glossary of expressions) in the entry relating to "tax year," the following paragraph shall be added at the end of the second column—
    "The expression "1978–79" means the tax year beginning with April 6, 1978, and any correspondingly framed reference to a pair of successive years shall be construed as a reference to the tax year beginning with April 6th in the earlier of them."

Old Cases Act schemes: changes in parliamentary control

12. In section 4 of the Old Cases Act, for subsection (8) (schemes to be made by statutory instrument subject to affirmative procedure, unless made for the purpose only of replacing provisions of previous schemes with provisions to the same effect or of making provision consequential on certain orders or regulations, and if made for that purpose only, to be subject to negative procedure) there shall be substituted—
    "(8) The power to make a scheme shall be exercisable by statutory instrument, and an instrument—
        (a) which contains such a scheme (whether alone or with other provisions), and
        (b) which is not subject to any requirement that a draft of the instrument be laid before and approved by a resolution of each House of Parliament,
    shall be subject to annulment in pursuance of a resolution of either House of Parliament."

Re-establishment courses and resettlement units

13.—(1) In Schedule 5 to the Supplementary Benefits Act 1976, paragraph 1 (power to provide re-establishment courses and facilities for persons attending them) shall cease to have effect.
(2) For paragraph 4 of that Schedule (power of Secretary of State to make contributions to voluntary organisations which provide re-establishment courses or resettlement units) there shall be substituted—

"Grants for voluntary organisations providing places

4.—(1) The Secretary of State may, upon such terms and subject to such conditions as he may determine, give assistance by way of grant to any local authority or voluntary organisation which provides places for purposes similar to the purposes for which resettlement units are provided by the Secretary of State.
    (2) In this paragraph "local authority" means the council of a county, a district, a region, an islands area or a London borough, or the Common Council of the City of London."

Mobility allowance for certain persons eligible for invalid carriages: pre-consolidation amendment.

14. The amendments of paragraph (a) of section 13(3) of the Social Security (Miscellaneous Provisions) Act 1977 by the National Health Service Act 1977 and the National Health Service

(Scotland) Act 1978 shall be deemed never to have been made and that paragraph shall accordingly have effect and be deemed at all times to have had effect as originally enacted.

Statutory sick pay: alterations to the rates of payment

15.—(1) In subsection (1A) of section 7 of the 1982 Act (rates of statutory sick pay: power by regulations to substitute alternative provisions for subsection (1)(a) to (c) and to make consequential amendments)—
   (a) for the word "regulations" there shall be substituted the word "order"; and
   (b) in paragraph (a), for the words "subsection (1)(a) to (c) above" there shall be substituted the words "the paragraphs of subsection (1) above."

(2) In subsection (1B) of that section (regulations under subsection (1A) to be subject to affirmative parliamentary procedure) for the word "regulations" there shall be substituted the words "an order."

Statutory sick pay for NHS staff with divided contracts

16. In section 26 of the 1982 Act (interpretation) after subsection (5) (which confers power to treat two or more contracts of employment as one) there shall be inserted—
   "(5A) Where, in consequence of the establishment of one or more National Health Service trusts under Part I of the National Health Service and Community Care Act 1990 or the National Health Service (Scotland) Act 1978, a person's contract of employment is treated by a scheme under that Part or Act as divided so as to constitute two or more contracts, regulations may make provision enabling him to elect for all of those contracts to be treated as one contract for the purposes of this Part of this Act or of such provisions of this Part of this Act as may be prescribed; and any such regulations may prescribe—
      (a) the conditions that must be satisfied if a person is to be entitled to make such an election;
      (b) the manner in which, and the time within which, such an election is to be made;
      (c) the persons to whom, and the manner in which, notice of such an election is to be given;
      (d) the information which a person who makes such an election is to provide, and the persons to whom, and the time within which, he is to provide it;
      (e) the time for which such an election is to have effect;
      (f) which one of the person's employers under the two or more contracts is to be regarded for the purposes of statutory sick pay as his employer under the one contract;
   and the powers conferred by this subsection are without prejudice to any other power to make regulations under this Part of this Act."

Income support and trade disputes etc: "the relevant sum"

17.—(1) Section 23 of the 1986 Act (income support and trade disputes etc) shall be amended in accordance with sub-paragraphs (2) and (3) below.

(2) For subsection (6) (meaning of "relevant sum") there shall be substituted—
      "(6) Subject to subsection (7) below, "the relevant sum" for the purposes of subsection (5) above shall be £19.50."

(3) For paragraph (a) of subsection (7) (annual increase of the relevant sum by reference to the percentage increase in applicable amounts under the up-rating order) there shall be substituted—
      "(a) increasing that sum by the percentage by which the personal allowance under paragraph 1(1) of Part I of Schedule 2 to the Income Support (General) Regulations 1987 for a single person aged not less than 25 has been increased by the order; and".

Certain housing benefit to be paid as rent allowance instead of rent rebate

18. In section 28 of the 1986 Act, in subsection (1)(b) (housing benefit in respect of certain payments to housing authorities to take the form of a rent rebate) after the words "rent rebate" there shall be inserted the words ",or, in prescribed cases, of a rent allowance," and after subsection (5) of that section there shall be inserted—
      "(5A) The cases that may be prescribed under subsection (1)(b) above do not include any case where the payment in respect of which the housing benefit is granted

is a payment in respect of a dwelling which, within the meaning of Part VI of the Local Government and Housing Act 1989, is a house or other property of an authority within the authority's Housing Revenue Account."

Housing benefit finance

19.—(1) In section 30 of the 1986 Act (housing benefit finance), after subsection (2) there shall be inserted—
"(2ZA) Nothing in this section shall be taken to imply that any such addition or deduction as is mentioned in subsection (2)(a) or (b) above may not be determined by reference to—
(a) an authority's expenditure in respect of any housing benefit, or in respect of any rebate or allowance within the meaning of the Social Security and Housing Benefits Act 1982, granted during any previous year; or
(b) any subsidy under this section or that Act paid to an authority in respect of any previous year."
(2) In subsection (2A) of that section (things which the Secretary of State may do by reference to determinations of rent officers)—
(a) after the words "the Secretary of State—" there shall be inserted—
"(za) may provide for any calculation under paragraph (a) of subsection (2) above to be made,"; and
(b) in paragraph (a), for the words "paragraph (a) of subsection (2) above" there shall be substituted the words "that paragraph".

Community charge benefit in the form of reduction of charge in subsequent year

20. In section 31A(1)(b) and (2)(b) of the 1986 Act (which provides that community charge benefit may take the form of a reduction in the amount of the charge which a person is liable to pay in respect of the relevant chargeable financial year)—
(a) for the words "is liable" there shall be substituted the words "is or becomes liable"; and
(b) after the word "relevant" there shall be inserted the words ",or any subsequent,".

Community charge benefit finance

21.—(1) In section 31F of the 1986 Act, for subsection (3) (amount by reference to which community charge benefit subsidy is to be calculated) there shall be substituted—
"(3) Any calculation under subsection (2) above shall be made by reference to the total amount of the community charge benefits allowed by the authority during the year with any additions specified in the order but subject to any deductions so specified."
(2) After subsection (5) of that section there shall be inserted—
"(5A) Nothing in this section shall be taken to imply that any such addition or deduction as is mentioned in subsection (3) or (4) above may not be determined by reference to—
(a) an authority's expenditure in respect of community charge benefits allowed during any previous year, or
(b) any subsidy paid under this section to an authority in respect of any previous year."
(3) For subsection (6) of that section (conditions for payment of community charge benefit subsidy) there shall be substituted the following—
"(6) Subsidy under this section shall be payable by the Secretary of State at such time and in such manner as the Treasury may direct; and subsections (8A) to (8F) of section 30 above shall apply in relation to a charging authority or a levying authority and subsidy under this section as they apply in relation to a rating authority, a housing authority or a local authority and subsidy under that section."

Statutory maternity pay for NHS staff with divided contracts

22. In section 50 of the 1986 Act (interpretation) after subsection (2) (which confers power to treat two or more contracts of employment as one) there shall be inserted—
"(2A) Where, in consequence of the establishment of one or more National Health Service trusts under Part I of the National Health Service and Community Care Act 1990 or the National Health Service (Scotland) Act 1978, a woman's contract of employment is treated by a scheme under that Part or Act as divided so as to constitute two or more contracts, regulations may make provision enabling her to elect for all of

those contracts to be treated as one contract for the purposes of this Part of this Act or of such provisions of this Part of this Act as may be prescribed; and any such regulations may prescribe—
  (a) the conditions that must be satisfied if a woman is to be entitled to make such an election;
  (b) the manner in which, and the time within which, such an election is to be made;
  (c) the persons to whom, and the manner in which, notice of such an election is to be given;
  (d) the information which a woman who makes such an election is to provide, and the persons to whom, and the time within which, she is to provide it;
  (e) the time for which such an election is to have effect;
  (f) which one of the woman's employers under the two or more contracts is to be regarded for the purposes of statutory maternity pay as her employer under the one contract;
and the powers conferred by this subsection are without prejudice to any other power to make regulations under this Part of this Act."

Functions of the Deputy Government Actuary

23. In section 63(11) of the 1986 Act (report of Government Actuary on likely effect of annual up-rating order on National Insurance Fund) for the words "giving the latter's opinion" there shall be substituted the words "or the Deputy Government Actuary, giving that Actuary's opinion."

Income support: implementation of increases due to attainment of particular ages

24. After section 64A of the 1986 Act (effect of alteration in component rates of income support) there shall be inserted the following section—

"Implementation of increases in income support due to attainment of particular ages
  64B.—(1) This section applies where—
  (a) an award of income support is in force in favour of a person ("the recipient"); and
  (b) there is a component which becomes applicable, or applicable at a particular rate, in his case if he or some other person attains a particular age.
  (2) If, in a case where this section applies, the recipient or other person attains the particular age referred to in paragraph (b) of subsection (1) above and in consequence—
  (a) the component in question becomes applicable, or applicable at a particular rate, in the recipient's case (whether or not some other component ceases, for the same reason, to be applicable, or applicable at a particular rate, in his case), and
  (b) after taking account of any such cessation, the recipient becomes entitled to an increased amount of income support,
then, except as provided by subsection (3) below, as from the day on which he becomes so entitled, the amount of income support payable to or for him under the award shall be that increased amount, without any further decision of an adjudication officer, and the award shall have effect accordingly.
  (3) Subsection (2) above does not apply in any case where, in consequence of the recipient or other person attaining the age in question, some question arises in relation to the recipient's entitlement to any benefit under the benefit Acts, other than—
  (a) the question whether the component concerned, or any other component, becomes or ceases to be applicable, or applicable at a particular rate, in his case; and
  (b) the question whether, in consequence, the amount of his income support falls to be varied.
  (4) In this section "component", in relation to a person and his income support, means any of the sums specified in regulations under section 22(1) above.

Statutory maternity pay for servicewomen

25. Section 79(5) of the 1986 Act (which precludes the payment of statutory maternity pay to women members of HM forces) shall cease to have effect.

Christmas bonus for pensioners

26.—(1) In Schedule 6 to the 1986 Act, in paragraph 3 (Christmas bonus for pensioners: circumstances in which a person is to be treated as entitled to a qualifying benefit in a relevant week) the following provisions shall cease to have effect—

(a) sub-paragraph (2)(a)(ii) and (iii) (persons otherwise not entitled to a qualifying benefit in consequence of the former limit on pensioners' earnings or the requirement to claim the qualifying benefit); and
(b) sub-paragraph (3)(d) (couples: members otherwise not entitled to an increase in respect of the other member in consequence of the requirement to claim the benefit).

(2) This paragraph shall be deemed to have come into force on October 1, 1989.

Benefits for women widowed before April 11, 1988

27.—(1) The Social Security (Widow's Benefit and Retirement Pensions) Amendment Regulations 1987 shall have effect, and be taken always to have had effect, with the substitution for regulations 3 and 4 (transitional provisions about widowed mother's allowance where the husband died before April 11, 1988, which were retrospectively amended by section 6(2) of the 1989 Act, and savings) of the following—

"3. Regulation 16(1) of the principal Regulations shall apply to a widow whose late husband died before April 11, 1988 as if regulation 2(6) above had not been made."

(2) In any case where—
(a) a claim for a widow's pension or a widowed mother's allowance is made, or treated as made, before the passing of this Act, and
(b) the Secretary of State has made a payment to or for the claimant on the ground that if the claim had been received immediately after its passing she would have been entitled to that pension or allowance, or entitled to it at a higher rate, for the period in respect of which the payment is made,
the payment so made shall be treated as a payment of that pension or allowance; and, if and to the extent that an award of the pension or allowance, or an award at a higher rate, is made for the period in respect of which the payment was made, the payment shall be treated as made in accordance with that award.

(3) Where, in consequence of regulation 2(6) of the Social Security (Widow's Benefit and Retirement Pensions) Amendment Regulations 1987 (deemed entitlement to child allowance for purposes of widowed mother's allowance etc), an adjudicating authority has decided before the passing of this Act that a widow whose husband died before April 11, 1988 either—
(a) is not entitled to a benefit under section 25 or 26 of the principal Act, or
(b) is entitled to such a benefit at a particular rate,
an adjudication officer may review that decision, notwithstanding anything in section 104 of the principal Act.

(4) In any case where—
(a) it is determined on such a review that the widow in question was entitled to a benefit under section 25 or 26 of the principal Act, or was entitled to such a benefit at a higher rate, and
(b) the application for the review was made before the end of the period of twelve months beginning with the passing of this Act,
the decision on the review may take effect on April 11, 1988 or any later date, notwithstanding any provision of any Act or instrument restricting the payment of any benefit or increase of benefit to which a person would otherwise be entitled by reason of a review in respect of any period before the review.

(5) Subsection (4) of section 104 of the principal Act (appeals from reviews) shall apply in relation to a review under this paragraph as it applies in relation to a review under that section.

(6) In this paragraph "adjudicating authority" means—
(a) an adjudication officer;
(b) a social security appeal tribunal;
(c) a Commissioner, as defined in Schedule 20 to the principal Act.

(7) The amendment by sub-paragraph (1) above of provisions contained in regulations shall not be taken to have prejudiced any power to make further regulations revoking or amending those provisions.

(8) Nothing in this paragraph shall be taken to prejudice section 16 or 17 of the Interpretation Act 1978 (effect of repeals, substitutions etc).

Unauthorised disclosure or information relating to particular persons

28.—(1) In section 19 of the 1989 Act, in subsection (7) (construction of references to government departments) after the word "include" there shall be inserted "(a)" and at the end there shall be added the words "and
(b) the Scottish Courts Administration."

(2) In subsection (9)(d) of that section (lawful authority: court proceedings) after the words "this Act" there shall be inserted the words "or in any corresponding enactment having effect in Northern Ireland".

(3) In subsection (10) of that section—

(a) in paragraph (b) (mental health receivers) for the words "or any corresponding enactment having effect in Northern Ireland" there shall be substituted the words "or a controller appointed under Article 101 of the Mental Health (Northern Ireland) Order 1986";

(b) in paragraph (d)(i), for the words "or any similar appointee in Northern Ireland" there shall be substituted the words "or sub-paragraph (a) of rule 38(1) of Order 109 of the Rules of the Supreme Court (Northern Ireland) 1980";

(c) in paragraph (d)(ii), for the words from "that rule" onwards there shall be substituted the words "the said rule 41(1) or a controller ad interim appointed under sub-paragraph (b) of the said rule 38(1)"; and

(d) in the words following paragraph (d), after the word "receiver," there shall be inserted the word "controller".

(4) In Schedule 2 to that Act (persons employed in social security adjudication or administration) for the entry in Part I relating to the Inland Revenue there shall be substituted—

"Other public departments and offices

A member or officer of the Commissioners of Inland Revenue.
A civil servant in the Scottish Courts Administration."

(5) In that Part, after the entry "An insurance officer" there shall be inserted—
"A supplement officer."

(6) In Part II of that Schedule (construction of references to government departments etc) paragraph 1(2) (definitions) shall be omitted and for paragraph 3 (which relates to the Lord Chancellor's Department) there shall be substituted—

"3. Any reference in Part I of this Schedule to the Lord Chancellor's Department or the Scottish Courts Administration is a reference to that Department or Administration only to the extent that the functions carried out by persons in its employ are, or are connected with—

(a) functions of the Chief, or any other, Social Security Commissioner; or

(b) functions of the Council on Tribunals or the Scottish Committee of that Council which relate to social security or to occupational or personal pension schemes or to war pensions."

(7) In paragraph 4 of that Part (the Inland Revenue) in paragraph (b), the words "as defined in paragraph 1(2) above" shall be omitted and after that paragraph there shall be inserted—

"5. In this Part of this Schedule—

"occupational pension scheme" has the meaning given by section 66(1) of the Pensions Act;

"personal pension scheme" has the meaning given by section 84(1) of the 1986 Act;

"war pension" has the meaning given by section 25(4) of this Act."

Employment related schemes for pensions or other benefits: equal treatment for men and women

29. In Schedule 5 to that Act, in paragraph 5 (unfair maternity provisions) in sub-paragraph (2)(a), after the word "women" there shall be inserted the word "members".

Incapacity for work: councillor's allowances and expenses

30.—(1) In Schedule 8 to that Act, paragraph 2 (which makes provision with respect to local authority councillors and incapacity for work) shall be amended in accordance with sub-paragraphs (2) to (4) below.

(2) In sub-paragraph (2) (certain benefits to be reduced by the excess of the councillor's allowance over the earnings limit specified in regulation 3(3) of the Social Security (Unemployment, Sickness and Invalidity Benefit) Regulations 1983, which was £35 at the passing of this Act) for the words "the amount of councillor's allowance" there shall be substituted the words "the net amount of councillor's allowance".

(3) In the definition of "councillor's allowance" in sub-paragraph (6), the following shall be omitted—

(a) in the paragraph (a) substituted by paragraph 113 of Schedule 11 to the Local Government and Housing Act 1989, the words "or in section 18(2) of that Act of 1989"; and

(b) in the paragraph (b) so substituted, the words "other than such an allowance as is mentioned in section 18(2) of that Act of 1989".

(4) In that sub-paragraph, after the definition of "incapacity benefit" there shall be inserted—

" "net amount", in relation to any councillor's allowance to which a person is entitled, means the aggregate amount of the councillors allowance or allowances to which he is entitled for the week in question, reduced by the amount of any expenses incurred by him in that week in connection with his membership of the council or councils in question;".

(5) In section 36(7) of the principal Act (regulations relating to severe disablement allowance), in paragraph (cc) (which was inserted by paragraph 2(5) of Schedule 8 to the 1989 Act and authorises the reduction of benefit by the excess of the amount of councillor's allowance over a prescribed sum) for the words "the amount of councillor's allowance" there shall be substituted the words "the net amount of councillor's allowance".

Joint citations

31. In the following enactments, for the words "the Social Security Acts 1975 to 1989" in each place where they occur there shall be substituted the words "the Social Security Acts 1975 to 1990"—

(a) section 6(1) of the National Insurance Act 1974;
(b) sections 9(7) and 18(1) of the Social Security Act 1980;
(c) section 4(5) of the Forfeiture Act 1982;
(d) section 5(1)(a) of the Social Security Act 1985;
(e) paragraph (b) of the definition of "the benefit Acts" in section 84(1) of the 1986 Act.

DEFINITIONS
"the 1982 Act": s.20.
"the 1986 Act": *ibid.*
"the 1989 Act": *ibid.*
"the Old Cases Act": *ibid.*
"the Pensions Act": *ibid.*
"the principal Act": *ibid.*

GENERAL NOTE
Only selected provisions are annotated.

Para. 3
These amendments deal with cases where a person receives only a SERPS pension or a graduated retirement benefit, with no basic pension. It has never been the policy intention that an adult dependency increase or an invalidity addition should be paid to such a person. This is put beyond doubt by these amendments. See *Hansard*, H.C., Standing Committee G, cols. 394–5, March 6, 1990.

Para. 4
Sub-para. (1) authorises the making of regulations to deem the date of onset of an industrial disease to be the date on which a claim is made for benefit in respect of that disease. At the moment the Prescribed Diseases Regulations (see sub-para. (3)) refer to the first day on which the claimant suffered a loss of faculty, or July 5, 1948, if later.

Sub-para. (2) reverses the effect of the Court of Appeal's decision in *McKiernan* v. *Secretary of State for Social Security* (*The Times*, November 1, 1989) that the regulations mentioned were invalid. Those regulations purported to exclude the ordinary rule allowing the back-dating of a claim for benefit where good cause is proved in cases of occupational deafness and occupational asthma. They purported to apply absolute time limits for claiming. The Court of Appeal held that there was no power in the 1975 Act to make these regulations because a power to modify a statute had to be expressly given, not implied. Sub-para. (2) declares the regulations always to have been validly made, thus reversing the effect of *McKiernan*, not just for other claimants, but, as pointed out in Parliament, for Mr McKiernan himself (*Hansard*, H.C. Vol. 176, cols. 76, 78, July 9, 1990).

Para. 6
These amendments secure that with effect from the date of the repeal of Sched. 9 of the Social Security Act 1975 for deaths after April 11, 1988, where an adjudication officer's (AO's) decision under the industrial injuries scheme might affect another person's right to industrial death benefit under Sched. 9, that other person has all the usual rights of appeal from that decision.

Para. 7
Sub-para. (1) inserts new subss. (7) to (10) in s.104 of the Social Security Act 1975 (review) and sub-para. (2) inserts a new s.165D on claims. The aim is that where an established

interpretation of the law is overturned by a decision of a Social Security Commissioner or a higher court, effect can only be given to the new interpretation for other claimants on review or a fresh claim with effect from the date of that decision (the decision is referred to below as the J decision and the date as the J Day).

Background

The general rule on claims for benefit is that there can be no entitlement for a period more than 12 months before the actual date of claim, however good the cause for delay in claiming (1975 Act, s.165A(2)). Thus, if a possible entitlement is revealed by the J decision and the person has not previously claimed, that limit applies. If the person has already had a decision and applies for a review of that decision based on the new interpretation, again there is a general limit of 12 months before the date of the request for review (Social Security (Adjudication) Regulations 1986, regs. 65 and 69–71). However, there is an exemption from this limit under reg. 72(1) of the Adjudication Regulations where, among other things, the decision to be reviewed was erroneous by reason of a mistake made by an adjudication officer (AO). Acting on a mistaken view of the law could obviously come within reg. 72(1) (although doubt is apparently cast on this view by *CSSB 308/1989*), so that a revision on review triggered by the J decision could go back to the date of the original decision. Alarm about this effect led to the insertion of reg. 72(2) from September 1, 1987, which provided that reg. 72 should not apply where review is on the ground that the original decision was erroneous in law by reason of the J decision. The result is that in such cases the normal 12 month limit applies. The argument that the original decision is not erroneous *by reason of* the J decision, but is simply revealed to have been erroneous all along, was rejected in *R(SB) 11/89*.

In an investigation by the Parliamentary Commissioner for Administration (the Ombudsman) into the decision of the Secretary of State about how extensively to trawl back for past entitlements following a Commissioner's decision on the offsetting of payments of occupational pension against dependency additions to invalidity benefit, the Ombudsman raised the effect of reg. 72(2) of the Adjudication Regulations (Case No. C191/88, Fourth Report of the PCA for 1989–90). He was concerned that the longer the delay in identifying a claimant's case as requiring review, the more benefit was lost, because of the absolute time limit recently reintroduced. He was not convinced that this effect was brought to Ministers' attention. In the course of responding to that point the DSS said that it would introduce a common start date for entitlement on review in such cases, but gave no indication of what sort of date would be chosen. The provisions in the 1990 Act are said to be in fulfilment of this undertaking. See *Hansard*, H.L. Vol. 519, cols. 684–6, May 21, 1990 (Lord Henley).

The new provisions

The new provisions on review (s.104) and claims (s.165D) apply where "on a determination, whenever made, of a Commissioner or the court . . ., a decision made by an adjudicating authority is or was found to have been erroneous in point of law". Note that appeals from initial decisions (including reviews or refusals to review) which are not affected by the new rules are themselves clear of the new rules. An adjudicating authority is an AO or any of his legislative predecessors, a SSAT, MAT, the Attendance Allowance Board, the Supplementary Benefits Commission or the National Assistance Board. The court includes everything above the Commissioner (s.165D(4)). Then, if any earlier decision falls to be revised on review carried out on or after July 13, 1990 "in consequence of that determination" (s.104(7)(b)), entitlement before J Day is to be determined as if the adjudicating authority's decision had been found not to be erroneous in point of law (s.104(8)). Alternatively, if a new claim is made after J Day, entitlement before that date is to be decided on the same assumption (s.165D(2)). These provisions do not seem to achieve the intended aim, and give rise to a number of problems.

The problems

The aim of the provisions is clear—a common start date for revising other claimants' entitlements when an appeal overturns the previously accepted DSS interpretation of the law. The main political argument against them was that the start date was placed unacceptably and unfairly late at J Day. Since reg. 72(2) still exists, there is only a common start date when the review takes place within 12 months of J Day, so that the primary aim is not met. But the form of the new provisions raises more fundamental problems.

The argument is as follows. For the new rules to apply, a Commissioner or higher court must have found an adjudicating authority's decision to be erroneous in point of law. Thus, if a SSAT adopts the AO's view of the law and the Commissioner holds the SSAT to have made an error of law, the new rules apply. But if a SSAT differs from the AO and the Commissioner holds that the SSAT has not made an error of law, the condition in s.104(7)(a) and s.165D(1)(a) is not met. The Commissioner's jurisdiction is only to determine whether the *SSAT* has made an error of law. Although the reasons for his determination may include an indication that the AO's decision was erroneous in point of law, this is not something which is "found" "on the determination". A similar point can be made if the AO's view is accepted by the SSAT and the Commissioner, but the Court of Appeal finds the Commissioner to have been in error of law. The Commissioner is not within the definition of "adjudicating authority". The Court of Appeal will not have "found" an adjudicating authority's decision to be erroneous in point of law and the new rules do not apply. On this view, there seems to be no point to the inclusion of an AO in the definition of "adjudicating authority", but this merely points out the confused drafting. If this argument is correct, the new rules apply capriciously, depending on the precise history of the appeal before the J decision. This situation could not be allowed to continue, but while it did it would enable the effect of the new rules to be avoided in some cases.

There are some other difficulties. If the new rules apply, the decision of the relevant adjudicating authority is to be assumed not to have been erroneous in point of law. What if the AO decides according to the accepted DSS interpretation, the SSAT reaches the same result but for peculiar and different reasons and the Commissioner decides that a third approach is correct? It appears to be the *SSAT* decision which must be assumed not to be erroneous in law, thus incorporating its reasons rather than the DSS interpretation. Similarly, if the SSAT decision is erroneous in several respects, only one of which is the matter which would trigger the review, it appears that all the errors must be assumed not to be errors. This is linked with the problem of identifying which J decisions have as a consequence that other decisions should be revised on review. AOs commonly do not carry out reviews if a single Commissioner's decision goes against the DSS view, especially if an appeal is being taken to the Court of Appeal. If the Court of Appeal then confirms the Commissioner's decision, the J Day ought to be the date of the Commissioner's decision. But if there are a series of equally authoritative decisions, which one establishes the J Day? If it is the earliest one, then review and revision of decisions made after its date are free of the new rules, because the new s.104(7)(b)(i) applies those rules only to decisions made *before* J Day which are reviewed after J Day. The new s.165D will apply to claims made or treated as made after J Day and after July 12, 1990. It will not be unusual for a claim to be made before J Day and the decision to be made after J Day.

Finally, the new provisions are almost certainly ineffective in relation to rulings of the European Court of Justice, which is included within the definition of "court" in s.165D(4). If the ECJ has ruled that the law is such and such, for a national legislature to remove a person's entitlement based on that ruling would be a breach of the obligation to provide an adequate remedy (see *Von Colson* [1984] E.C.R. 1891).

See generally on these sections, M. Rowland, *Legal Action*, October 1990, p. 21, and J. Mesher, *The Adviser*, September 1990, p. 9.

Para. 8

This amendment harmonises a number of similarly worded provisions in social security legislation relating to the Parliamentary control of orders and regulations. It introduces a common terminology to show whether a statutory instrument is subject to affirmative or negative procedures.

Para. 10

The qualifying contribution condition for maternity allowance is that the claimant must have paid contributions of a relevant class in respect of at least 26 weeks in the 52 weeks immediately preceding the 14th week before the expected week of confinement. Difficulties can arise when the claimant is not paid weekly and the period of employment is very close to or is exactly 26 weeks. For instance, a monthly-paid employee whose employment begins or ends in the middle of a month might not pay contributions in the first or last month because her earnings were below the monthly lower earnings limit. However, she might have earned enough in the weeks in which she worked to have paid contributions if she had been paid on a weekly basis. This amendment provides that such weeks may be treated as weeks in which contributions were actually paid. See *Hansard*, H.L. Vol. 519, col. 1034, May 24, 1990.

Para. 13

Sched. 5 to the Supplementary Benefits Act 1976 formerly authorised the DSS to run re-establishment centres for people in need of re-establishment through lack of regular occupation or lack of instruction or training. See Mesher, *CPAG's Supplementary Benefit and Family Income Supplement: the Legislation* (1987 ed.), p. 34. Resettlement units were places at which "persons without a settled way of living" were afforded temporary board and lodging "with a view to influencing them to lead a more settled life" (Sched. 5, para. 2).

Para. 16

These amendments allow regulations to provide transitional protection for employees with separate contracts of employment with both a health authority and a NHS trust to treat those as one contract for the purposes of statutory sick pay. See para. 22 on statutory maternity pay. They fulfil a commitment given during the passage of the National Health Service and Community Care Act. See *Hansard*, H.L. Vol. 519, col. 1035, May 24, 1990.

Para. 17
The "relevant sum" is the amount automatically deducted from the income support of a claimant who is caught by the trade dispute disqualification. This provision updates the amount expressly mentioned in s.23(6) of the 1986 Act and alters the method of increasing the amount.

Para. 22
See para. 16.

Para. 24
The new s.64B of the 1986 Act provides that where the amount of income support increases on a person reaching a particular age, effect is to be given to that increase automatically without the need for an AO's decision.

Para. 26
To qualify for the Christmas bonus a person can be treated as entitled to a benefit if he would be entitled to it if he made a claim for it. When the retirement conditions for retirement pension were abolished in October 1989 this brought people who had deliberately not claimed retirement pension in order to earn increments on the pension into entitlement to the bonus. This amendment takes them out again with effect from October 1989. See *Hansard*, H.C. Standing Committee G, col. 406, March 6, 1990.

Para. 30
These amendments establish the intention of the provision made by the Social Security Act 1989 that the net amount of a councillor's attendance allowance after deducting reasonable expenses incurred in council duties should be set against the therapeutic earnings limit for sickness or invalidity benefit.

Section 21(2)   SCHEDULE 7

REPEALS

Chapter	Short title	Extent of repeal
1975 c. 14.	Social Security Act 1975.	Section 1(1)(c) and the word "and" immediately preceding it. In section 4(7), the words "145". In section 59B— (a) in subsection (1), the words from "and may become" onwards; (b) in subsection (3), the words "Unless he returns to regular employment"; (c) subsection (4); (d) in subsection (7)(b), the words "or returned to"; and (e) in subsection (8), the words "or as not having returned to", "as having returned to, or" and "or returned to". In section 135(5), the word "and" at the end of paragraph (a). In section 137(1) and (2), the words "and the Old Cases Act". In section 152(6), the words "the Treasury supplements and".
1975 c. 16.	Industrial Injuries and Diseases (Old Cases) Act 1975.	Section 13.
1975 c. 60.	Social Security Pensions Act 1975.	In section 32(2B)(d)(i), the word "and". In section 33(2), the words "and (4)".

Chapter	Short title	Extent of repeal
		Section 41A(1A) and (1B).
		Section 41C(3)(a)(ii).
		Sections 56B to 56D.
		Section 56E(1)(c).
		Sections 56F to 56K.
		In section 56L—
		(a) in subsection (1), in paragraph (a), the words "or (c)" and paragraph (b);
		(b) in subsection (5), paragraph (b) and, in paragraph (c) the words "or the registrar"; and
		(c) subsection (9).
		Sections 56M and 56N.
		In Schedule 1A—
		(a) in paragraphs 1(1)(b), 2(2)(d) and 11(1)(b), sub-paragraph (ii) and the word "or" immediately preceding it;
		(b) in paragraphs 1(4) and 11(2), the words " "relevant employment" ";
		(c) in paragraph 7(4), in paragraph (a), the word "and" immediately preceding sub-paragraph (iii), and paragraph (b); and
		(d) paragraph 12(1)(b) and the word "or" immediately preceding it.
1976 c. 71.	Supplementary Benefits Act 1976.	In Schedule 5, paragraph 1.
1977 c. 5.	Social Security (Miscellaneous Provisions) Act 1977.	Section 1(7)(b).
1977 c. 49.	National Health Service Act 1977.	In Schedule 15, paragraph 71.
1978 c. 29.	National Health Service (Scotland) Act 1978.	In Schedule 16, paragraph 44.
1979 c. 18.	Social Security Act 1979.	Section 4(2)(b).
1980 c. 30.	Social Security 1980.	In Schedule 1, paragraph 15.
		In Schedule 2, in Part I, paragraph 31(b), (c) and (h).
1982 c. 24.	Social Security and Housing Benefits Act 1982.	Section 46(3).
1985 c. 53.	Social Security Act 1985.	Section 27(3) and (4).
		Section 31(1).
		Section 32(4).
		In Schedule 5, paragraphs 12, 22 and 35.
1986 c. 50.	Social Security Act 1986.	In section 33(10A), the word "and" immediately preceding paragraph (e).
		In section 79, in subsection (4), the words "Subject to subsection (5) below" and subsection (5).
		Section 85(4)(a).
		In Schedule 6—
		(a) in paragraph 3, sub-paragraphs (2)(a)(ii) and (iii); and
		(b) in sub-paragraph (3), paragraph (d) and the word "or" immediately preceding it.
		In Schedule 10, paragraphs 68(1), 78 and 89.
1987 c. 26.	Housing (Scotland) Act 1987.	Section 252 and 253.
1988 c. 7.	Social Security Act 1988.	Section 2(8) and (8A).
		Section 13(7) and (8).
		In section 18, in subsections (3) and (4), the words "made by statutory instrument"

Chapter	Short title	Extent of repeal
1989 c. 24.	Social Security Act 1989.	and subsections (7) and (8). Section 6(2). In section 22(3), in the definition of "relevant period", the words from "whether or not" onwards. Section 29(4). In Schedule 1, paragraph 8(3), (4) and (7). In Schedule 2, in Part II, paragraph 1(2) and in paragraph 4(b) the words "as defined in paragraph 1(2) above". In Schedule 3, paragraph 16. In Schedule 6, paragraphs 6, 7 and 8(1)(a). In Schedule 8, in paragraph 2(6), in the definition of "councillor's allowance, in the paragraph (a) substituted by paragraph 113 of Schedule 11 to the Local Government and Housing Act 1989 the words "or in section 18(2) of that Act of 1989" and, in the paragraph (b) so substituted, the words "other than such an allowance as is mentioned in section 18(2) of that Act of 1989" and paragraph 8(2). In Schedule 9, the entry relating to section 41C(3)(a)(ii) of the Pensions Act.

COMMENCEMENT

See s.23(3)(f) and the Social Security Act 1990 (Commencement No. 2) Order 1990 (S.I. 1990 No. 1942).

INDEX

References in roman type are to section numbers of the Act. References in italic are to the Schedules

APPROPRIATION ACT 1990

(1990 c. 28)

An Act to apply a sum out of the Consolidated Fund to the service of the year ending on 31st March 1991, to appropriate the supplies granted in this Session of Parliament, and to repeal certain Consolidated Fund and Appropriation Acts.

[26th July 1990]

PARLIAMENTARY DEBATES
Hansard, H.C. Vol. 176, col. 261.

INTRODUCTION
   The Act provides for the annual setting aside of sums of public money, to be issued out of the Consolidated Fund, for particular and specifically noted heads of expenditure, *e.g.* defence, administration of justice, fixing the appropriate sum to be made available. Authorisation is given by virtue of this Act to allow money to be borrowed up to the total sum appropriated in anticipation of revenue.

GRANT OUT OF THE CONSOLIDATED FUND

Issue out of the Consolidated Fund for the year ending 31st March 1991

1. The Treasury may issue out of the Consolidated Fund of the United Kingdom and apply towards making good the supply granted to Her Majesty for the service of the year ending on 31st March 1991 the sum of £81,111,939,000·00.

APPROPRIATION OF GRANTS

Appropriation of sums voted for supply services

2. All sums granted by this Act and the other Acts mentioned in Schedule (A) annexed to this Act out of the said Consolidated Fund towards making good the supply granted to Her Majesty amounting, as appears by the said schedule, in the aggregate, to the sum of £148,286,800,965.82 are appropriated, and shall be deemed to have been appropriated as from the date of the passing of the Acts mentioned in the said Schedule (A), for the services and purposes expressed in Schedule (B) annexed hereto.
   The abstract of the schedules annexed hereto, with the notes (if any) to such schedules, shall be deemed to be part of this Act in the same manner as if they had been contained in the body thereof.
   In addition to the said sums granted out of the Consolidated Fund, there may be applied out of any money directed, under section 2 of the Public Accounts and Charges Act 1891, to be applied as appropriations in aid of the grants for the services and purposes specified in Schedule (B) annexed hereto the sums respectively set forth in the last column of the said schedule.

Repeals

3. The enactments mentioned in Schedule (C) annexed to this Act are hereby repealed.

Short title

4. This Act may be cited as the Appropriation Act 1990.

ABSTRACT
OF
SCHEDULES (A) and (B) to which this Act refers

Section 2   SCHEDULE (A)

Grants out of the Consolidated Fund .... £148,286,800,965·82

C.L. STATS. (6)—13

Section 2   SCHEDULE (B)—Appropriation of Grants

	Supply Grants	Appropriations in Aid
	£	£
1988–89 and 1989–90		
Part 1. Defence and Civil (Excesses), 1988–89	10,336,965·82	9,203,606·55
Part 2. Supplementary, 1989–90	7,833,325,000·00	851,636,000·00
1990–91		
Part 3. Class I	21,232,060,000·00	1,937,943,000·00
Part 4. Class II	2,535,006,000·00	143,814,000·00
Part 5. Class III	698,045,000·00	1,257,251,000·00
Part 6. Class IV	2,182,685,000·00	769,104,000·00
Part 7. Class V	3,164,623,000·00	465,733,000·00
Part 8. Class VI	3,209,701,000·00	932,829,000·00
Part 9. Class VII	3,713,800,000·00	217,319,000·00
Part 10. Class VIII	28,268,192,000·00	1,613,712,000·00
Part 11. Class IX	6,118,178,000·00	120,883,000·00
Part 12. Class X	1,249,169,000·00	407,777,000·00
Part 13. Class XI	6,658,773,000·00	1,398,524,000·00
Part 14. Class XII	494,193,000·00	14,000·00
Part 15. Class XIII	19,051,266,000·00	5,936,607,000·00
Part 16. Class XIV	23,368,764,000·00	1,202,125,000·00
Part 17. Class XV	7,612,235,000·00	869,445,000·00
Part 18. Class XVI	4,211,635,000·00	281,779,000·00
Part 19. Class XVII	1,683,518,000·00	6,063,000·00
Part 20. Class XVIII	4,532,303,000·00	1,125,061,000·00
Part 21. Class XIX	288,827,000·00	22,438,000·00
Part 22. Class XIXA	37,666,000·00	336,000·00
Part 23. Class XIXB	32,500,000·00	4,200,000·00
Total	140,443,139,000·00	18,712,957,000·00
Grand Total	148,286,800,965·82	19,573,796,606·55

SCHEDULE (A)

Grants out of the Consolidated Fund

	£
For the service of the year ended 31st March 1989—	
Under Act 1990 c.4	10,336,965·82
For the service of the year ended 31st March 1990—	
Under Act 1989 c.46	2,881,928,000·00
Under Act 1990 c.4	4,951,397,000·00
For the service of the year ending on 31st March 1991—	
Under Act 1989 c.46	58,271,200,000·00
Under Act 1990 c.4	1,060,000,000·00
Under this Act	81,111,939,000·00
Total	148,286,800,965·82

SCHEDULE (B).—Part 1

Defence and Civil (Excesses), 1988–89 ——————

DEFENCE AND CIVIL (EXCESSES), 1988–1989

SUMS granted, and sums which may be applied as appropriations in aid in addition thereto, to make good excesses on certain grants for defence and civil services for the year ended 31st March 1989, viz.:—

	Supply Grants	Surplus receipts available to be applied as Appropriations in Aid
	£	£
Vote		
CLASS I		
4. Defence accommodation services etc.	8,999,754·60	—
CLASS VII		
7. Department of Employment Training programmes	1,000·00	—
CLASS VIII		
6. Sale of Shares in British Airways plc		
For Expenditure by the Department of Transport in connection with the sale of surplus shares in British Airways including the costs of maintaining the register of shareholders and to meet the residual costs of privatisation	56,461·98	—
CLASS IX		
2. Miscellaneous housing administration and grants	1,000·00	—
CLASS XI		
5. Administration of Justice: England and Wales (Lord Chancellor's Department)	1,000·00	—
CLASS XVI		
12. Police Grant, Legal Aid and Criminal Injuries Compensation, Scotland	89,611·37	14,630·26
16. Student awards, Scotland.	1,187,137·87	—
CLASS XX		
19. Civil accommodation services and administration etc. (Property Services Agency of the Department of the Environment)	1,000·00	9,188,976·29
Total, Defence and Civil (Excesses) 1988–89 . . .	10,336,965·82	9,203,606·55

SCHEDULE (B).—Part 2

Supplementary, 1989–90

Supplementary, 1989–90

Schedule of Supplementary Sums granted, and of the sums which may be applied as appropriations in aid in addition thereto, to defray the charges for the Services herein particularly
mentioned, for the year ended 31st March 1990, including provision for numbers of personnel
as set out hereunder, viz.:—

	Supply Grants	Appropriations in Aid
	£	£
Vote		
Class I		
1. For expenditure by the Ministry of Defence on personnel costs etc., of the Armed Forces and their Reserves and Cadet Forces etc. (including provision for the Royal Air Force Reserve to an additional number not exceeding 3,800); personnel costs etc., of Defence Ministers and of certain civilian staff employed by the Ministry of Defence; on movements; certain stores; supplies and services; plant and machinery; charter of ships; certain research; lands and buildings; sundry grants; payments abroad including contributions and subscriptions to international organisations; and grants in aid...............	130,282,000	*—15,540,000
2. For expenditure by the Procurement Executive of the Ministry of Defence in operating its Headquarters and Establishments and for its other common services; for research etc. by contract; for lands and buildings; for development by contract, production, repair etc., and purchases for sale abroad of sea systems, land systems, air systems and associated equipment; for payment to Harland and Wolff plc; for certain contingent liabilities, and for sundry other Procurement Executive services including those on repayment terms to non-exchequer customers...........	260,842,000	*—46,964,000
3. For expenditure by the Ministry of Defence on retired pay, pensions, etc.	9,606,000	168,000
4. For expenditure including loans by the Property Services Agency of the Department of the Environment on public building work and certain accommodation services, etc. for defence purposes	52,518,000	*—4,095,000
5. For expenditure by the Ministry of Defence on the refit and repair of ships, on associated capital facilities, on contractors' redundancy costs and on administration	43,858,000	1,461,000
Class II		
1. For expenditure by the Foreign and Commonwealth Office on its salaries, building and other accommodation services, and administration, and those of HM Diplomatic Service, official information services, sundry services and loans and a grant in aid for catering services........	24,242,000	—
2. For expenditure by the Foreign and Commonwealth Office on grants and subscriptions, etc., to certain international organisations, certain		

	Supply Grants	Appropriations in Aid
	£	£

CLASS II—continued

Vote

grants in aid, special payments and assistance, scholarships, military aid and sundry other grants and services . . . .

| | 3,074,000 | 821,000 |

4. For expenditure by the Foreign and Commonwealth Office on a grant in aid of the British Council . . . .

| | 285,000 | — |

5. For expenditure by the Foreign and Commonwealth Office: Overseas Development Administration on the official United Kingdom Aid Programme and other payments made under the Overseas Development and Cooperation Act 1980, including financial aid, grants in aid and technical cooperation to governments, institutions, voluntary agencies and individuals; loans to the Commonwealth Development Corporation; pensions and allowances in respect of overseas service including contributions to pension funds; capital and other subscriptions and contributions, including grants in aid and payments under guarantee, to multilateral development banks and other international and regional bodies; emergency, refugee and other relief; assistance to Eastern Europe; running costs and other administrative costs . . . .

| | 137,323,000 | 340,000 |

CLASS IV

1. For expenditure by the Intervention Board for Agricultural Produce in giving effect in the United Kingdom to the agricultural support provisions of the Common Agricultural Policy of the European Community and for other services . . .

| | 1,000 | — |

2. For expenditure by the Intervention Board for Agricultural Produce on central administration and miscellaneous services . . . .

| | 1,000 | *—92,000* |

3. For expenditure by the Ministry of Agriculture, Fisheries and Food on market support, grants and loans for capital and other improvements, support for agriculture in special areas and compensation to sheep producers, animal health, arterial drainage, flood and coast protection, and certain other services . . . .

| | 10,368,000 | *—1,769,000* |

4. For expenditure by the Ministry of Agriculture, Fisheries and Food on commissioned research and development and advice, education and training services, botanical services, assistance to production, marketing and processing, and certain alternative land uses, support for the fishing industry, emergency and strategic food services, protective, agency and other services, including grants in aid and international subscriptions . . . .

| | 300,000 | — |

CLASS V

1. For expenditure by the Department of Trade and Industry on regional development grants, regional selective assistance, selective assistance to individual industries, certain other services including UK contributions arising from its commitments under international commodity agree-

	Supply Grants	Appropriations in Aid
	£	£

CLASS V—*continued*

Vote

ments and a special payment to the International Tin Council, a strategic mineral stockpile, the film industry and on support for the aerospace, shipbuilding, steel and vehicle industries including loans, grants and the purchase of assets and assistance to redundant steel workers, and other payments.................................. | 1,000 | *—3,694,000

3. For expenditure by the Department of Trade and Industry on the regulation of trading practices, for special payments in connection with Barlow Clowes Gilt Managers Ltd. and Barlow Clowes International Ltd., and associated companies, on consumer protection, and on central and miscellaneous services including publicity, grants in aid, international subscriptions, grants to the fund for sub-postmasters and residual expenses arising from the sale of shares in British Telecommunications plc and in Rolls Royce plc........ | 160,593,000 | 106,000

6. For expenditure by the Export Credits Guarantee Department in connection with interest support to banks and other lenders of export finance, cover under the tender to contract/forward exchange supplement scheme, grants towards financing of exports to match foreign competition, cost escalation cover and residual commitments under discontinued guarantees offered to banks and external trade agencies .... | 89,699,000 | *—15,023,000

7. For expenditure by the Export Credits Guarantee Department in connection with export credits guarantees, other guarantees given in the national interest or to render economic assistance to overseas countries, and overseas investment insurance.................................... | 11,701,000 | 172,934,000

8. For expenditure by the Department of Trade and Industry in connection with the sale of shares in British Steel plc. and for the costs of collecting the second instalment...................... | 1,000 | *—3,001,000

CLASS VI

1. For expenditure by the Department of Energy on assistance to the coal industry including grants and loans to the British Coal Corporation and payments to mineworkers made redundant before 29th March 1987 .... | 3,748,000,000 | 12,100,000

3. For Expenditure by the Department of Energy on salaries and other administrative costs...... | 1,210,000 | 100,000

5. For payment of pensions, etc, to members of the United Kingdom Atomic Energy Authority's superannuation schemes and other related expenditure .... | 13,396,000 | *—13,396,000

7. For Expenditure by the Office of Electricity Regulation.................................... | 1,000 | *—324,000

CLASS VII

1. For expenditure by the Department of Employment on promoting and improving training, enterprise and services for small firms, providing programmes of youth and adult training, employ-

	Supply Grants	Appropriations in Aid
	£	£

CLASS VII—*continued*

Vote

ment rehabilitation services and voluntary projects, technical and vocational education, work related further education and the costs of the Skills Training Agency, on the administration of training and central and miscellaneous services including a grant in aid.....................

| | 2,000 | *—25,079,000 |

2. For expenditure by the Department of Employment on the promotion of skills and competence for work, help for unemployed people including programmes administered by the Employment Service, services for people with serious disabilities and the administration of the Employment Service, on the promotion of enterprise, tourism and services for small firms, including grants in aid and administration costs, compensation for persons disabled by pneumoconiosis, byssinosis and diffuse mesothelioma, on the improvement of industrial relations, including administration costs and a grant in aid, on training projects covered by payments from the European Communities; on refunds of payments to the European Communities, on National Dock Labour Board administration and contributions towards severance payments for registered dockers and for staff of the Board on an international subscription and central and miscellaneous services ....

| | 23,797,000 | *—125,000 |

5. For expenditure by the Department of Employment on the sale of the Skills Training Agency .

| | 809,000 | — |

CLASS VIII

1. For expenditure by the Department of Transport on the construction, improvement and maintenance of motorways and trunk roads, including the acquisition of land, scheme design and preparation, compensation, the purchase of maintenance vehicles and equipment and the maintenance and operation of the Woolwich Ferry ....

| | 87,833,000 | 17,891,000 |

2. For expenditure by the Department of Transport on assistance to shipping; civil aviation; roads and central administration; certain licensing and testing schemes; research and development; road safety and certain other transport services, including civil defence, grants in aid, international subscriptions, and residual expenses associated with the privatisation of transport industries ....

| | 4,657,000 | 700,000 |

3. For expenditure by the Department of Transport on support to nationalised transport industries and to ports; rebate of fuel duty to bus operators; and costs of the driver testing and training organisation ....

| | 105,600,000 | — |

4. For expenditure by the Department of Transport in connection with driver and vehicle registration and licensing, the collection of revenue and the

	Supply Grants	Appropriations in Aid
	£	£

CLASS VIII—*continued*

Vote

development and maintenance of information technology systems for other parts of the Department ....

	7,259,000	710,000

5. For expenditure by the Department of Transport on transport supplementary grants to Highway Authorities in England and certain other grants and payments in support of local roads and transport expenditure ....

	622,000	4,137,000

CLASS IX

1. For expenditure by the Department of the Environment on subsidies, improvements and investment, payments to the Housing Corporation and other sundry services ....

	272,888,000	2,750,000

2. For expenditure of the Department of the Environment on housing administration, including grant in aid to the Housing Corporation and Housing Action Trusts, housing management and mobility, housing, building and construction research; rent officers and Rent Assessment Panels; grants to home improvement agencies; and grants and payments for sundry housing services and projects.....................

	1,000	—

CLASS X

1. For expenditure by the Department of the Environment on grants to new towns, local authority and other environmental services (including recreation), town and country planning (including compensation), and other water supply, conservation and sewerage services ....

	10,130,000	—

2. For expenditure by the Department of the Environment on other environmental services including grants in aid and international subscriptions, on grants in aid to the Rural Development Commission, National Rivers Authority and British Waterways Board, on bridge works, on developing civil defence water services, on assistance to the environmental protection industry, on payments in connection with environmental research, on other water supply and sewerage services and on a contribution to the Hillsborough Disaster Appeal ....

	35,987,000	—

3. For expenditure by the Department of the Environment on derelict land reclamation, the Urban Programme, grants and other assistance to the private sector for urban regeneration, grants in aid for Urban Development Corporations, payments in connection with inner cities and urban land research and surveys and transitional grants for voluntary bodies.............

	111,900,000	—

4. For expenditure by the Department of the Environment on royal palaces, etc. (including administration), royal parks, etc. (including administration), historic buildings, ancient monuments and certain public buildings, the national heritage, on grants in aid and other grants, on payments to the Inland Revenue covering assets

	Supply Grants	Appropriations in Aid
	£	£

CLASS X—*continued*

Vote

	Supply Grants	Appropriations in Aid
accepted in lieu of tax, on an international subscription and on the resurvey of listed buildings	430,000	—
5. For expenditure by the Department of the Environment on central administration, including royal commissions, committees, etc.; payments in connection with research and surveys	5,996,000	2,346,000
9. For expenditure by the Department of the Environment for expenses incurred in connection with the sale of shares in the water holding companies; subscriptions for new shares in water holding companies; and to meet any criminal proceedings against the residuary water authorities	1,296,201,000	147,700,000
10. For expenditure by the Office of Water Services on administration and operational costs	1,105,000	—

CLASS XI

	Supply Grants	Appropriations in Aid
1. For expenditure by the Home Office on court services, compensation for criminal injuries, including a grant in aid, probation, police, community services and superannuation payments for police and fire services	6,277,000	*—1,984,000*
3. For expenditure by the Home Office on court services, other services related to crime, probation and after-care, police, fire, civil defence, control of immigration and nationality, issue of passports, etc., other protective and community services, certain broadcasting services, data protection, an inquiry into the Hillsborough Stadium disaster and other miscellaneous services including grants in aid and international subscriptions; and on administration (excluding prisons)	1,000	168,000
4. For expenditure by the Home Office on payment to the BBC for Home Broadcasting and payments in respect of the collection and enforcement of licence fees.	8,531,000	—
5. For expenditure by the Lord Chancellor's Department on the Court Service, the Law Commission, the Office of the Special Commissioners for Income Tax, the Office of the Social Security Commissioners, the V.A.T. tribunals, the Immigration Appellate Authorities, the Transport Tribunal, the Banking and Building Societies' Appeals Tribunals, the Public Trust Office, certain other legal services, including a grant-in-aid for the administration of legal aid, site acquisitions, the development and construction of court buildings and the refurbishment and adaptation of office and general accommodation.	15,798,000	1,500,000
6. For grants to the Legal Aid Fund and expenditure by the Lord Chancellor's Department on legal aid in criminal cases and costs paid from central funds.	10,000,000	—
8. For expenditure by the Northern Ireland Court Service on court services and certain other legal services including grants in aid	1,661,000	

	Supply Grants	Appropriations in Aid
	£	£

CLASS XI—*continued*

Vote

12. For expenditure by the Serious Fraud Office on administrative costs........................ | 300,000 | — |

13. For expenditure by the Crown Office on witnesses' expenses and other costs associated with crown prosecutions......................... | 500,000 | — |

14. For expenditure by the Lord Advocate's Departments on administrative costs including fees paid to temporary Procurators Fiscal and grants in aid | 1,000 | — |

CLASS XII

1. For expenditure by the Department of Education and Science on schools, assisted places scheme, City Technology Colleges, teacher training, adult education, youth services, and on miscellaneous educational services, including grants in aid and international subscriptions and the provision of a school in Armenia......................... | 2,778,000 | *—9,698,000 |

2. For expenditure by the Department of Education and Science on universities, polytechnics and colleges and certain other institutions, grants for higher and further education, payment of certain licence fees to the Home Office, grants in aid and international subscriptions................... | 1,026,000 | — |

3. For expenditure by the Department of Education and Science on student awards and fees, preparations for the establishment of a student top-up loans scheme, reimbursement of fees for qualifying European Community students and compensation payments to redundant teachers and staff of certain institutions .... | 36,600,000 | — |

4. For expenditure by the Department of Education and Science on administration................ | 3,420,000 | — |

5. For expenditure by the Department of Education and Science on grants in aid of the Agricultural and Food Research Council, the Medical Research Council, the Natural Environment Research Council, the Science and Engineering Research Council, the Economic and Social Research Council, the Royal Society, the Fellowship of Engineering and Centre for Exploitation of Science and Technology, and of the science policy studies programme of the Advisory Board for the Research Councils, including subscriptions to certain international organisations and the payment of certain fees to the Home Office | 1,000 | 1,597,000 |

6. For expenditure by the Department of Education and Science on teachers' superannuation ...... | 170,000,000 | *—70,822,000 |

CLASS XIII

2. For expenditure by the Office of Arts and Libraries on grants in aid to the Arts Council and other bodies; on grants to other institutions; on payments to the Inland Revenue for assets accepted in lieu of tax; on the Government Art Collection; and on international subscriptions and certain other services for the benefit of the arts .... | 9,978,000 | — |

4. For the expenditure by the Office of Arts and Libraries on administration .... | 61,000 | 4,000 |

	Supply Grants	Appropriations in Aid
	£	£
CLASS XIV		
Vote		
1. For expenditure by the Department of Health on hospital, community health and other services, England.	47,880,000	5,075,000
3. For expenditure by the Department of Health on administration, including certain expenditure on behalf of the Department of Social Security, on the national health service in England and on miscellaneous health, personal social and other services (some of which are administered on a United Kingdom basis), including family practitioner committee administration, mental health, medical, scientific and technical services, services for disabled persons, grants to voluntary organisations, etc., grants in aid and subscriptions to international organisations.	29,224,000	*—1,979,000*
CLASS XV		
6. For expenditure by the Department of Social Security on subsidies to housing, rating and local authorities towards the costs of administering the housing benefit scheme, to local authorities in Scotland towards the costs incurred in preparing for the introduction of and administration of the community charge rebate scheme, and to authorities towards the costs incurred in preparing to implement the changes to the housing benefit scheme and the community charge rebate scheme in respect of the treatment of poorer pensioners, certain 16-17 year olds, and hostel dwellers	3,000,000	—
7. For expenditure by the Department of Social Security on administration, for agency payments, and for certain other services including grants to local authorities, voluntary organisations, an international subscription, and major capital works projects for the Department of Health, including telecommunications capital.	13,770,000	16,876,000
CLASS XVI		
1. For expenditure by the Department of Agriculture and Fisheries for Scotland on market support, assistance for structural measures, support in special areas, compensation to sheep producers and certain other services including animal health	1,600,000	452,000
6. For expenditure by the Scottish Development Department on roads and certain associated services, including the acquisition of land, lighting, road safety and related services, including a grant in aid, on assistance to local transport, on support for transport services in the Highlands and Islands, piers and harbours and on certain other transport services and grants, on historic buildings and monuments (including administration) and on other central environmental services including a grant in aid.	1,881,000	740,000
7. For expenditure by the Scottish Development Department on assistance to local transport, and on piers and harbours, and on water, sewerage and other environmental services.	4,615,000	—

	Supply Grants	Appropriations in Aid
	£	£

Class XVI—*continued*

Vote

8. For expenditure by the Scottish Development Department on housing subsidies, grant in aid to Scottish Homes and a range of other Exchequer contributions and grants relating to housing, the capitalisation of certain housing specific grants and sundry other housing services including sites for travelling people   9,339,000   *—3,000

12. For expenditure by the Scottish Home and Health Department on legal aid and criminal injuries compensation (excluding administration), on police and fire services superannuation and police grant   6,790,000   —

13. For expenditure by the Scottish Courts Administration on costs and fees in connection with legal proceedings   4,000,000   —

14. For expenditure by the Scottish Home and Health Department on a grant in aid for legal aid administration; certain services relating to crime; prison services and the Parole Board for Scotland; fire and police services (excluding grants to local authorities and superannuation); civil defence (including grants); certain other services including a grant in aid; hospital and community health and other health services   2,000   *—11,792,000

15. For expenditure by the Scottish Education Department on: schools; higher and further education, including compensation payments; community education; curriculum development, educational services, training and research; sport; arts, libraries, museums and galleries, including purchase grants; community service for offenders, provision of secure accommodation for children and other social work grants including training and research; publicity; indemnities; administration; grants to local authorities, including the careers service; EC agency payments and grants-in-aid   162,000   —

16. For expenditure by the Scottish Education Department on awards to students receiving higher and further education and reimbursément of fees for qualifying European Community students   14,000,000   —

17. For expenditure by the Scottish Home and Health Department on the provision of services under the National Health Service in Scotland, on welfare food and certain other services   17,883,000   *—733,000

18. For the expenditure of the Scottish Record Office on administrative costs and grants   1,000   —

19. For expenditure of the General Register Office for Scotland on administrative and operational costs   50,000   —

20. For the expenditure of the Department of the Registers of Scotland on administrative costs . . .   1,000   523,000

21. For expenditure by the Scottish Office on administrative costs and the Royal Commission on the Ancient and Historical Monuments of Scotland.   1,014,000   82,000

	Supply Grants	Appropriations in Aid
	£	£

CLASS XVI—*continued*

Vote

22. For expenditure by the Scottish Office for revenue and rate support grants in Scotland ...... | 9,481,000 | *—16,418,000*

23. For expenditure by the Scottish Office on rate rebate grants to local authorities in Scotland ... | 3,038,000 | —

24. For expenditure by the Scottish Home and Health Department on superannuation allowances and gratuities etc, in respect of teachers, and the widows, widowers and dependants of deceased teachers .... | 12,388,000 | *—5,088,000*

27. For expenditure by the Scottish Home and Health Department on hospital and community health services [New Estimate] .... | 24,934,000 | 545,029,000

CLASS XVII

2. For expenditure by the Welsh Office on assistance to agricultural production, food processing and marketing, certain alternative land uses and other miscellaneous agricultural services including commissioned surveys; protective, agency and other support for the Welsh fishing industry; on industrial development and other activities undertaken by the Welsh Development Agency and the Development Board for Rural Wales including grants in aid; support for medium and small sized firms, employment and certain other services .... | 1,000 | —

5. For expenditure by the Welsh Office on tourism, roads and certain associated services including road safety, housing, historic buildings and ancient monuments, other environmental services including civil defence (including grants), education, libraries and museums, health and personal social services, grants in aid, EC agency payments, other grants and certain other services, including research .... | 2,000 | —

6. For expenditure by the Welsh Office on housing subsidies, grants to housing associations, a range of other Exchequer contributions and grants relating to housing (including home improvements); urban programme grants (including urban development grant), grants for urban investment, grant in aid to the Urban Development Corporation, grants in respect of water, sewerage, land availability studies, town and country planning, gypsy sites, other local services (including clean air grants), welfare food payments, certain EC agency payments, special grants to local authorities in natural emergencies and, certain other services .... | 16,524,000 | 1,218,000

7. For expenditure by the Welsh Office on family practitioner services under the National Health Service. .... | 996,000 | 358,000

8. For expenditure by the Welsh Office on hospital and community health services, supporting health services, family practitioner services, administration and related services, and services for the disabled .... | 5,001,000 | 3,351,000

	Supply Grants	Appropriations in Aid
	£	£

CLASS XVII—*continued*

Vote

9. For expenditure by the Welsh Office on central administration .... | 1,786,000 | —

12. For expenditure by the Welsh Office on rate rebate grants to local authorities in Wales ..... | 330,000 | —

13. For expenditure by the Welsh Office for expenses incurred in connection with the sale of shares in the water holding company; subscription for new shares in the water holding company; and to meet the costs of any criminal proceedings against the residuary water authority.................... | 276,001,000 | 14,303,000

CLASS XVIII

1. For expenditure by the Northern Ireland Office on central and miscellaneous services, services related to crime, police, prisons, training schools, probation and after-care etc., compensation schemes, Crown prosecutions, and other legal services, grants in aid and certain other grants.. | 12,660,000 | 87,000

2. For expenditure by the Northern Ireland Office on a grant in aid of the Northern Ireland Consolidated Fund and other transfers .... | 200,000,000 | —

CLASS XIX

1. For expenditure by the Central Office of Information on home and overseas publicity........ | 142,000 | 43,144,000

2. For expenditure by the Customs and Excise Department on administrative costs, both capital and current, including an international subscription .... | 21,768,000 | —

7. For expenditure by the Inland Revenue Department on the management and collection of the direct taxes; the provision of rating and valuation services; and services provided for other Departments..................................... | 27,600,000 | 16,000

8. For expenditure of the Inland Revenue Department on life assurance premium relief and mortgage interest relief......................... | 90,000,000 | —

11. For expenditure by Her Majesty's Treasury on economic and financial administration, and for certain other services including grants in aid to certain parliamentary bodies and others .... | 1,004,000 | 15,000

12. For expenditure by the Treasury in connection with the manufacture, and distribution of coinage in the United Kingdom...................... | 4,500,000 | —

13. For expenditure by the Central Computer and Telecommunications Agency (HM Treasury) in connection with computers and general telecommunications including an international subscription .... | 279,000 | —

15. For rates and contributions in lieu of rates paid by the Rating of Government Property Department in respect of property occupied by the Crown and premises occupied by representatives of Commonwealth and foreign countries and international organisations....................... | 15,130,000 | 3,000,000

18. For expenditure by the Central Statistical Office on the provision of national accounts and other statistics and on departmental administration,

	Supply Grants	Appropriations in Aid
	£	£
CLASS XIX—*continued*		
Vote		
including contributions on behalf of HM Government to international organisations	2,123,000	92,000
CLASS XX		
1. For the expenditure by the Office of the Minister for the Civil Service on the central management of the civil service, on the Office of the Parliamentary Counsel and certain other services including grants in aid.	2,098,000	215,000
7. For expenditure by the Ordnance Survey on the survey of Great Britain and other mapping services	2,067,000	—
10 For expenditure by the Department of Her Majesty's Most Honourable Privy Council on pay and administrative costs.	290,000	—
11. For expenditure by the Public Record Office on operational and administrative costs	238,000	—
12. For expenditure by the Office of Fair Trading on administrative and operational costs	125,000	—
14. For expenditure by the Office of Telecommunications on administrative and operational costs .	1,000	66,000
15. For expenditure by the Office of Population Censuses and Surveys on administration and operational costs, including a grant in aid.	1,515,000	685,000
16. For the expenditure of the Law Officers' Department and the Procurator General and Treasury Solicitor on administration costs.	293,000	115,000
17. For expenditure by the Department of the Procurator General and Treasury Solicitor on costs and fees for legal services.	4,621,000	108,000
18. For expenditure by the Property Services Agency of the Department of the Environment on acquisitions, public building work, accommodation services, administration and certain other services for civil purposes in the United Kingdom	11,725,000	96,172,000
TOTAL SUPPLEMENTARY 1989-90.	7,833,325,000	851,636,000

*Deficit

SCHEDULE (B).—PART 3

Class I 1990–91

CLASS I

SCHEDULE OF SUMS granted, and of the sums which may be applied as appropriations in aid in addition thereto, to defray the charges of the several Services herein particularly mentioned, which will come in course of payment during the year ending on 31st March 1991, including provision for numbers of personnel as set out hereunder, viz.:—

	Sums not exceeding	
	Supply Grants	Appropriations in Aid
	£	£
Vote		
1. For expenditure by the Ministry of Defence on personnel costs etc. of the Armed Forces and their Reserves and Cadet Forces etc., (including provision for Naval Service to a number not exceeding 66,800, provision for Army Service to a number not exceeding 172,550, for the Individual Reserves to a number not exceeding 109,805, for the Territorial Army to a number not exceeding 85,364, for the Home Service Force to a number not exceeding 4,596, and for the Ulster Defence Regiment to a number not exceeding 6,800, and provision for Air Force Service to a number not exceeding 95,240, for Royal Air Force Reserve to a number not exceeding 16,150, and for the Royal Auxiliary Air Force to a number not exceeding 2,550); personnel costs etc. of Defence Ministers and of certain civilian staff employed by the Ministry of Defence, movements, certain stores, supplies and services, plant and machinery, charter of ships, certain research, lands and buildings, sundry grants and payments abroad....................................	8,968,295,000	1,220,044,000
2. For expenditure by the Procurement Executive of the Ministry of Defence in operating its Headquarters and Establishments and for its other common services; for research etc. by contract; for lands and buildings; for development by contract, production, repair etc. and purchases for sale abroad of sea systems, land systems, air systems and associated equipment; for certain contingent liabilities, and for sundry other Procurement Executive services including those on repayment terms to non-exchequer customers (Including a Supplementary sum of £48,900,000)	8,531,208,000	528,506,000
3. For expenditure by the Ministry of Defence on retired pay, pensions and other payments etc...	1,407,570,000	1,496,000
4. For expenditure by the Ministry of Defence on new construction and maintenance works and related services at defence establishments on fees and some works costs for visiting forces (Including a Supplementary sum of £55,000,000)......	1,930,960,000	149,419,000
5. For expenditure by the Ministry of Defence on the refit and repair of ships, associated capital facilities, on contractors' redundancy costs and administration	494,027,000	38,478,000
TOTAL, CLASS............................ £	21,332,060,000	1,937,943,000

SCHEDULE (B).—PART 4

———————

CLASS II

SCHEDULE OF SUMS granted, and of the sums which may be applied as appropriations in aid in addition thereto, to defray the charges of the several Services herein particularly mentioned, which will come in course of payment during the year ending on 31st March 1991, viz:—

	Sums not exceeding	
	Supply Grants	Appropriations in Aid
	£	£
Vote		
1. For expenditure by the Foreign and Commonwealth Office on its salaries, building and other accommodation services and administration, and those of HM Diplomatic Service, official information services, sundry services and loans and payments in connection with catering services (Revised sum)	534,722,000	26,923,000
2. For expenditure by the Foreign and Commonwealth Office on grants and subscriptions, etc., to certain international organisations, grants etc. to non-governmental and statutory organisations, special payments and assistance, scholarships, military aid and sundry other grants and services (Including a Supplementary sum of £12,130,000)	176,019,000	16,855,000
3. For expenditure by the Foreign and Commonwealth Office on payments to the British Broadcasting Corporation for external broadcasting and monitoring services and for contractual services in connection with FCO relay stations .	139,920,000	2,608,000
4. For expenditure by the Foreign and Commonwealth Office on the British Council	74,433,000	24,325,000
5. For expenditure by the Foreign and Commonwealth Office: Overseas Development Administration under the Overseas Development and Co-operation Act 1980 on the official United Kingdom aid programme and for assistance to Eastern Europe; including financial and technical assistance to governments, institutions, voluntary agencies and individuals; pensions and allowances in respect of overseas service including contributions to pension funds; capital and other subscriptions and contributions, including payments under guarantee, to multilateral development banks and other international and regional bodies; emergency, refugee and other relief assistance; loans to the Commonwealth Development Corporation; running costs, related capital expenditure, and other administrative costs including for the Natural Resources Institute (an executive agency) (Including a Supplementary sum of £30,000,000)	1,471,654,000	71,924,000
6. For expenditure by the Foreign and Commonwealth Office (Overseas Development Adminis-		

| | Sums not exceeding | |
	Supply Grants	Appropriations in Aid
	£	£
Class II—*continued*		
Vote		
tration) on pension and superannuation payments etc., in respect of overseas service and sundry other services and expenses	138,258,000	1,179,000
Total, Class II........................ £	2,535,006,000	143,814,000

SCHEDULE (B).—PART 5

Class III 1990–91 ———————

CLASS III

SCHEDULE OF SUMS granted, and of the sums which may be applied as appropriations in aid in addition thereto, to defray the charges of the several Services herein particularly mentioned, which will come in course of payment during the year ending on 31st March, 1991, viz.:—

	Sums not exceeding	
	Supply Grants	Appropriations in Aid
	£	£
Vote		
1. For expenditure by the Intervention Board —Executive Agency in giving effect in the United Kingdom to the agricultural support provisions of the Common Agricultural Policy of the European Community and for other services (Revised sum)..............................	1,000	1,183,778,000
2. For expenditure by the Intervention Board— Executive Agency on central administration and miscellaneous services (Revised sum)...........	37,508,000	1,294,000
3. For expenditure by the Ministry of Agriculture, Fisheries and Food on market support, grants and loans for capital and other improvements, support for agriculture in special areas and compensation to sheep producers, animal health, arterial drainage, flood and coast protection, and certain other services	140,319,000	13,910,000
4. For expenditure by the Ministry of Agriculture, Fisheries and Food on commissioned research and development and advice, education and training services, botanical services, assistance to production, marketing and processing, and certain alternative land uses, support for the fishing industry, emergency and strategic food services, protective, agency and other services (Including a Supplementary sum of £2,411,000)	157,371,000	17,179,000
5. For expenditure by the Ministry of Agriculture, Fisheries and Food on departmental research, advisory services and administration and certain other services (Revised sum).................	285,096,000	40,740,000
6. For payments to Forestry Fund...............	77,750,000	350,000
TOTAL, CLASS III..........................£	698,045,000	1,257,251,000

Appropriation Act 1990

SCHEDULE (B).—Part 6

Class IV

Schedule of Sums granted, and of the sums which may be applied as appropriations in aid in addition thereto, to defray the charges of the several Services herein particularly mentioned, which will come in course of payment during the year ending on 31st March 1991, viz:—

	Sums not exceeding	
	Supply Grants	Appropriations in Aid
	£	£
Vote		
1. For expenditure by the Department of Trade and Industry on regional development grants, regional selective assistance, selective assistance to individual industries, certain other services including UK contributions arising from its commitments under international commodity agreements, a strategic mineral stockpile, and support for the film, aerospace, shipbuilding and steel industries including loans, grants and assistance to redundant steel workers, and other payments	371,385,000	105,889,000
2. For expenditure by the Department of Trade and Industry on central and miscellaneous services (including running costs, capital expenditure, consultancy advice, paid publicity, and grants to the fund for sub-postmasters), support for industry (including industrial research and development, civil aircraft research and demonstration, education, training, design, quality, marketing, management best practice and standards, and support for telecommunications), business development (including the Consultancy Initiatives and the Regional Enterprise Grant scheme), measurement and technology support, space technology programmes, protection of innovation, research establishments major works and other expenditure (including expenditure by the National Physical Laboratory, the National Enginering Laboratory, the National Weights and Measures Laboratory and the National Measurement Accreditation Service), miscellaneous support services, international trade (including export promotion, trade co-operation and international exhibitions), enterprise and job creation (the Inner Cities Initiative), the regulation of financial and trading practices, for special payments in connection with Barlow Clowes Gilt Managers Ltd., and Barlow Clowes International Ltd., and associated companies, consumer protection, Companies House Executive Agency, Radiocommunications Executive Agency, Warren Spring Laboratory Executive Agency, the Laboratory of the Government Chemist Executive Agency, English Industrial Estates Corporation, provision of land and buildings, loan, grants and other payments (Revised sum)	787,377,000	188,469,000
3. For Government support for British Shipbuil-		

	Sums not exceeding	
	Supply Grants	Appropriations in Aid
	£	£

CLASS IV—*continued*

Vote

ders, including the costs associated with the remedial measures in Sunderland, and grants from the shipbuilding intervention fund on residual contract obligations ....

4. For expenditure by the Export Credits Guarantee Department on administration ....

5. For expenditure by the Export Credits Guarantee Department in connection with interest support to banks and other lenders of export finance, cover under the tender to contract/forward exchange supplement scheme, grants towards financing of exports to match foreign competition; cost escalation cover; and residual commitments under discontinued guarantees offered to banks and external trade agencies (Including a Supplementary sum of £130,398,000).........

6. For expenditure by the Export Credits Guarantee Department in connection with export credits guarantees; other guarantees given in the national interest or to render economic assistance to overseas countries; overseas investment insurance and trading expenses ....

7. For the expenditure by the Office of Fair Trading on administrative and operational costs.......

8. For expenditure by the Office of Telecommunications on administrative and operational costs .

Description	Supply Grants	Appropriations in Aid
(residual contract obligations)	8,000,000	—
(4. administration)	40,749,000	1,601,000
(5. interest support)	372,200,000	79,349,000
(6. export credits guarantees)	581,320,000	393,620,000
(7. Office of Fair Trading)	14,790,000	76,000
(8. Office of Telecommunications)	6,864,000	100,000
TOTAL, CLASS IV............................£	2,182,685,000	769,104,000

SCHEDULE (B).—Part 7

Class V 1990–91

Class V

Schedule of Sums granted, and of the sums which may be applied as appropriations in aid in addition thereto, to defray the charges of the several Services herein particularly mentioned, which will come in course of payment during the year ending on 31st March 1991, viz.:—

	Sums not exceeding	
	Supply Grants	Appropriations in Aid
	£	£
Vote		
1. For expenditure by the Department of Energy on assistance to the coal industry including grants and loans to the British Coal Corporation and payments to mineworkers made redundant before 29 March 1987 (Including a Supplementary sum of £918,000,000)	2,800,100,000	316,058,000
2. For expenditure by the Department of Energy in connection with energy related programmes including research and development; energy efficiency; selective assistance to industry; promotion and security of oil and gas supplies; grants and certain other services, including payments to international organisations and the Piper Alpha Memorial Appeal, and expenditure in connection with the sale of shares in British Gas (Revised sum)	289,010,000	2,406,000
3. For expenditure by the Department of Energy on salaries and other administrative costs (Revised sum)......................................	39,317,000	4,752,000
4. For expenditure by the Department of Energy on refunds and repayments of petroleum licensing proceeds, and other payments connected with such proceeds............................	1,000	43,559,000
5. For payment of pensions, etc., to members of the United Kingdom Atomic Energy Authority's superannuation schemes and other related expenditure	22,486,000	62,643,000
6. For expenditure by the Department of Energy in connection with the privatisation of the electricity supply industry in England and Wales	1,000	35,500,000
7. For expenditure by the Office of Gas Supply on administrative costs.......................	1,573,000	15,000
8. For expenditure by the Office of Electricity Regulation (Including a Supplementary sum of £1,500,000)...............................	12,135,000	800,000
Total, Class V......................... £	3,164,623,000	465,733,000

SCHEDULE (B).—PART 8

CLASS VI

SCHEDULE OF SUMS granted, and of the sums which may be applied as appropriations in aid in addition thereto, to defray the charges of the several Services herein particularly mentioned, which will come in course of payment during the year ending on 31st March, 1991, viz.:—

	Sums not exceeding	
	Supply Grants	Appropriations in Aid
	£	£
Vote		
1. For expenditure by the Department of Employment on improving, promoting and disseminating training among individuals, small firms and employers, encouraging enterprise, running services for small firms, and the Enterprise Allowance Scheme, providing training programmes for young people and adults, providing employment rehabilitation services, technical and vocational education, work related further education and the costs of the Skills Training Agency until privatisation, on the administration of training and enterprise, and central and miscellaneous services (Revised sum)	2,467,308,000	423,321,000
2. For expenditure by the Department of Employment on the promotion of skills and competence for work, the promotion of enterprise, tourism and services for small firms; the improvement of industrial relations; industrial tribunals; compensation for persons disabled by certain industrial diseases; payments towards expenses of trade union ballots; on National Dock Labour Board administration, and residual expenses following the wind-up of the Board; administration, central and miscellaneous services..................	213,825,000	29,352,000
3. For expenditure by the Employment Service of the Department of Employment on help for the unemployed, support for services for people with disabilities, on research and publicity and on administration	393,976,000	462,431,000
4. Amount required in the year ending 31 March 1991 for expenditure by the Department of Employment on grants in aid to the Health and Safety Commission and to the Advisory, Conciliation and Arbitration Service	134,591,000	55,000
5. For expenditure by the Department of Employment on the sale of Skills Training Agency (Revised sum)	1,000	17,670,000
TOTAL, CLASS VI........................ £	3,209,701,000	932,829,000

SCHEDULE (B).—Part 9

Class VII 1990–91   ————————

Class VII

Schedule of Sums granted, and of the sums which may be applied as appropriations in aid in addition thereto, to defray the charges of the several Services herein particularly mentioned, which will come in course for payment during the year ending on 31st March 1991, viz.:—

	Sums not exceeding	
	Supply Grants	Appropriations in Aid
	£	£
Vote		
1. For expenditure by the Department of Transport on the construction, improvement and maintenance of motorways and trunk roads, including the acquisition of land, scheme design and preparation, compensation, the purchase of maintenance vehicles and equipment and the maintenance and operation of Woolwich Ferry .	1,808,062,000	98,384,000
2. For expenditure by the Department of Transport in connection with grants for freight facilities and travel concessions; shipping; civil aviation; roads and central administration; certain licensing and testing schemes; research and development; road safety and certain other transport services, including civil defence, and residual expenses associated with the privatisation of transport industries (Revised sum)	253,236,000	73,093,000
3. For expenditure by the Department of Transport on support to nationalised transport industries and to ports; rebate of fuel duty to bus operators; and costs of driver testing and training	1,252,075,000	552,000
4. For expenditure by the Department of Transport in connection with driver and vehicle registration and licensing, the collection of revenue, on compensation to, and payment towards the pensions of local authority staff employed in driver and vehicle licensing before the setting up of DVLC and the development and maintenance of information technology systems for other parts of the Department (Including a Supplementary sum of £3,005,000).	132,909,000	30,373,000
5. For expenditure by the Department of Transport on transport supplementary grants to Highway Authorities in England and certain other grants and payments in support of local roads and transport expenditure	267,518,000	14,917,000
Total, Class VII. . . . . £	3,713,800,000	217,319,000

SCHEDULE (B).—PART 10

Class VIII 1990–91

CLASS VIII

SCHEDULE OF SUMS granted, and of the sums which may be applied as appropriations in aid in addition thereto, to defray the charges of the several Services herein particularly mentioned, which will come in course of payment during the year ending on 31st March 1991, viz.:—

	Sums not exceeding	
	Supply Grants	Appropriations in Aid
	£	£
Vote		
1. For expenditure by the Department of the Environment on subsidies, improvements and investment, payments to the Housing Corporation and other sundry services (Revised sum)	6,029,484,000	2,500,000
2. For expenditure by the Department of the Environment on housing administration, including payment to the Housing Corporation and Housing Action Trusts; housing management and mobility; housing, building and construction research; rent officers and Rent Assessment Panels; grants to home improvement agencies; grants and payments for sundry housing services and projects (Revised sum)	98,032,000	172,000
3. For expenditure by the Department of the Environment on city grants to the private sector for urban regeneration, derelict land reclamation, city action teams, payments in connection with inner cities and urban land research, the Urban Programme, transitional grants for voluntary bodies and payments to urban development corporations....................................	989,342,000	7,176,000
4. For expenditure by the Department of the Environment on road infrastructure required for the development of new towns, gypsy sites, smoke control, planning redevelopment and other environmental services, on other water supply, conservation and sewerage services, and on town and country planning (including compensation)	47,200,000	97,000
5. For expenditure by the Department of the Environment on countryside, recreation and the environment, including research and assistance to the environmental protection industry, on payments to the Rural Development Commission, Sports Council, National Rivers Authority and British Waterways Board, on bridgeworks, on other water supply and sewerage services including civil defence and on national parks (Revised sum)......................................	357,896,000	95,000
6. For expenditure by the Department of the Environment on royal palaces, Historic Royal Palaces Agency (including administration), royal parks, royal armouries etc. (including administration), historic buildings, ancient monuments and certain public buildings, the national heritage, on payments to the Inland Revenue covering assets accepted in lieu of tax and on the assessment of possible listed buildings (Revised sum)	149,847,000	16,144,000

	Sums not exceeding	
	Supply Grants	Appropriations in Aid
	£	£

CLASS VIII—*continued*

Vote

7. For expenditure by the Department of the Environment (Property Holdings) on acquisitions, public building work, accommodation services, administration and certain other services for civil purposes in the United Kingdom (Revised sum)

| | 1,000 | 801,772,000 |

8. For expenditure by the Department of the Environment on central administration, including royal commissions, committees, etc.; and by the Building Research Establishment, including payments in connection with research and surveys .

| | 156,599,000 | 36,333,000 |

9. For expenditure by the Department of the Environment on revenue support grant, residual payments of rate support grants and community charge preparation costs grant and payment of national non-domestic rates to charging authorities in England, on a grant to certain authorities with low average rateable values, on payments to specified bodies and the Commission for Local Administration in England . . . .

| | 20,009,457,000 | 400,000 |

10. For expenditure by the Department of the Environment for expenses incurred in connection with the sale of shares in the water holding companies . . . .

| | 1,000 | 5,019,000 |

11. For expenditure by the Office of Water Services on administrative and operational costs. . . . .

| | 5,238,000 | — |

12. For expenditure by the Ordnance Survey on the survey of Great Britain and other mapping services . . . .

| | 16,436,000 | 46,028,000 |

13. For expenditure by PSA Services on works and similar services for other Government Departments and certain other clients and certain administration costs. . . . .

| | 29,658,000 | 697,402,000 |

14. For expenditure by the Department of the Environment on rate rebate grants and on community charge transitional relief grants to local authorities in England (Revised sum). . . . .

| | 379,000,000 | — |

15. For expenditure by the Department of the Environment (Property Holdings) on the sale of The Crown Suppliers (New Estimate) . . . .

| | 1,000 | 574,000 |

TOTAL, CLASS VIII. . . . . £

| | 28,268,192,000 | 1,613,712,000 |

SCHEDULE (B).—Part 11

Class IX

Schedule of Sums granted, and of the sums which may be applied as appropriations in aid in addition thereto, to defray the charges of the several Services herein particularly mentioned, which will come in course of payment during the year ending on 31st March 1991, viz.:—

	Sums not exceeding	
	Supply Grants	Appropriations in Aid
	£	£
Vote		
1. For expenditure by the Home Office on court services, compensation for criminal injuries, probation, police and superannuation payments for police and fire services	2,689,448,000	16,398,000
2. For expenditure by the Home Office in England and Wales on prisons (including central administration and other costs arising from the detention of prisoners), the Parole Board, the storage and maintenance of equipment (including certain civilian emergency equipment), and transport management..............................	1,294,715,000	36,785,000
3. For expenditure by the Home Office on police, civil defence, fire, the Football Licensing Authority, court services, other services related to crime, probation and after-care, certain broadcasting services, data protection and other miscellaneous services, prevention of drug abuse, control of immigration and nationality, issue of passports etc., community services; and on administration (excluding prisons) (Including a Supplementary sum of £2,302,000)............	758,925,000	67,680,000
4. For expenditure by the Home Office on payments to the British Broadcasting Corporation for home broadcasting and payments in respect of the collection and enforcement of licence fees	1,360,035,000	—
5. For the expenditure of the Charity Commission of England and Wales on administrative costs (Revised sum)	14,302,000	20,000
6. For expenditure by the Home Office in connection with the sale of the Independent Broadcasting Authority transmission system.........	753,000	—
Total, Class IX............................£	6,118,178,000	120,883,000

SCHEDULE (B).—Part 12

Class X 1990–91

Class X

Schedule of Sums granted, and of the sums which may be applied as appropriations in aid in addition thereto, to defray the charges of the several Services herein particularly mentioned, which will come in course of payment during the year ending on 31st March 1991, viz.:—

	Sums not exceeding	
	Supply Grants	Appropriations in Aid
	£	£
Vote		
1. For expenditure by the Lord Chancellor's Department on the Court Service, the Law Commission, the Office of the Special Commissioners for Income Tax, the Office of the Social Security Commissioners, the VAT tribunals, the Immigration Appellate Authorities, the Transport Tribunal, the Banking and Building Societies' Appeals Tribunals, the Statutory Publications Office, the Public Trust Office, certain other legal services, the administration of legal aid, site acquisitions, the development and construction of court buildings and the acquisition, disposal, refurbishment and adaptation of office and general accommodation (Including a Supplementary sum of £1,832,000)................	321,132,000	187,800,000
2. For grants to the Legal Aid Fund and for expenditure by the Lord Chancellor's Department on legal aid in criminal cases and costs paid from central funds.........................	619,565,000	1,000,000
3. For expenditure by the Northern Ireland Court Service on court services and certain other legal services..................................	16,360,000	6,959,000
4. For expenditure by the Northern Ireland Court Service on legal aid and court services........	13,084,000	—
5. For expenditure by the Crown Prosecution Service on administrative costs.................	130,668,000	189,000
6. For expenditure by the Director of Public Prosecutions on crown prosecutions and in connection with the confiscation of the proceeds of crime ..	63,800,000	14,500,000
7. For expenditure by the Serious Fraud Office on administrative costs........................	6,567,000	—
8. For expenditure by the Serious Fraud Office on investigations and prosecutions..............	6,946,000	260,000
9. For expenditure by the Legal Secretariat to the Law Officers and the Department of the Procurator General and Treasury Solicitor on Administration costs...........................	14,354,000	1,525,000
10. For expenditure by the Department of the Procurator General and Treasury Solicitor on costs and fees for legal services....................	4,897,000	1,063,000
11. For expenditure by the Land Registry on administrative costs	1,000	195,859,000
12. For expenditure by the Public Record Office on administrative and operational costs	19,823,000	562,000

	Sums not exceeding	
	Supply Grants	Appropriations in Aid
	£	£
CLASS X—*continued*		
Vote		
13. For expenditure by the Lord Advocate's Departments on administrative costs, including fees paid to temporary Procurators Fiscal	26,857,000	60,000
14. For expenditure by the Crown Office on witnesses' expenses and other costs associated with Crown prosecutions	5,115,000	—
TOTAL, CLASS X........................... £	1,249,169,000	407,777,000

SCHEDULE (B).—PART 13

Class XI, 1990–91 ————

CLASS XI

SCHEDULE OF SUMS granted, and of the sums which may be applied as appropriations in aid in addition thereto, to defray the charges of the several Services herein particularly mentioned, which will come in course of payment during the year ending on 31st March 1991, viz.:—

	Sums not exceeding	
	Supply Grants	Appropriations in Aid
	£	£
Vote		
1. For expenditure by the Department of Education and Science on the assisted places scheme, voluntary schools, City Technology Colleges, grant maintained schools, adult education, youth services, miscellaneous international and other educational services and research, including the provision of a school in Armenia and central government grants to local authorities. (Revised sum)...........................	653,341,000	53,222,000
2. For expenditure by the Department of Education and Science on universities, polytechnics and colleges and certain other institutions, grants for higher and further education, and payment of certain licence fees to the Home Office........	3,113,747,000	9,961,000
3. For expenditure by the Department of Education and Science on student awards and fees, student loans, access funds, reimbursement of fees for qualifying European Community students and compensation payments to redundant teachers and staff of certain institutions (Including a Supplementary sum of £9,080,000)	1,370,434,000	3,000
4. For expenditure by the Department of Education and Science on administration...............	90,923,000	3,392,000
5. For expenditure by the Department of Education and Science on payments to the Agricultural and Food Research Council, the Medical Research Council, the Natural Environment Research Council, the Science and Engineering Research Council, the Economic and Social Research Council, the Royal Society, the Fellowship of Engineering and the Centre for Exploitation of Science and Technology, and the Advisory Board for the Research Councils, and the payment of certain licence fees to the Home Office	897,147,000	4,322,000
6. For expenditure by the Department of Education and Science on superannuation allowances and gratuities, etc., in respect of teachers, and the widows, widowers, children and dependants of deceased teachers	533,181,000	1,327,624,000
TOTAL, CLASS XI........................... £	6,658,773,000	1,398,524,000

SCHEDULE (B).—PART 14

Class XII 1990–91   ―――――――

CLASS XII

SCHEDULE OF SUMS granted, and of the sums which may be applied as appropriations in aid in addition thereto, to defray the charges of the several Services herein particularly mentioned, which will come in course of payment during the year ending on 31st March 1991, viz.:—

	Sums not exceeding	
	Supply Grants	Appropriations in Aid
	£	£
Vote		
1. For expenditure by the Office of Arts and Libraries on payments to the national and other museums and galleries, to the Museums and Galleries Commission, to the Museum of London; and for related research, surveys and other services	181,532,000	—
2. For expenditure by the Office of Arts and Libraries on payments to the Arts Council and other bodies; on payments to the Inland Revenue for assets accepted in lieu of tax; on the Government Art Collection; and on certain other services for the benefit of the arts	199,025,000	5,000
3. For expenditure by the Office of Arts and Libraries on payment to the British Library and the Royal Geographical Society; on the British Library St. Pancras project and the Royal Commission on Historical Manuscripts; on payments in respect of Public Lending Right; and for a development incentive scheme.	111,834,000	—
4. For expenditure by the Office of Arts and Libraries on administration.......................	1,802,000	9,000
TOTAL, CLASS XII......................... £	494,193,000	14,000

SCHEDULE (B).—PART 15

Class XIII 1990–91

CLASS XIII

SCHEDULE OF SUMS granted, and of the sums which may be applied as appropriations in aid in addition thereto, to defray the charges of the several Services herein particularly mentioned, which will come in course of payment during the year ending on 31st March 1991, viz.:—

	Sums not exceeding	
	Supply Grants	Appropriations in Aid
	£	£
Vote		
1. For expenditure by the Department of Health on hospital, community health and related services, on family practitioner services and on family practitioner committees (Including a Supplementary sum of £178,800,000)	13,902,857,000	3,429,284,000
2. For expenditure by the Department of Health on family practitioner services, on medical treatment given to people from the United Kingdom in other countries of the European Community, and on welfare food	888,375,000	895,765,000
3. For expenditure by the Department of Health on administration, including certain expenditure on behalf of the Department of Social Security, on the national health service in England, on family practitioner administration and related services, on miscellaneous health, personal social and other services (some of which are administered on a United Kingdom basis), including mental health, medical, scientific and technical services, services for disabled persons, grants to voluntary organisations, etc., and payments to international organisations (Including a Supplementary sum of £1,531,000)	687,918,000	36,656,000
4. For expenditure by the Department of Health on family practitioner services	3,175,574,000	579,699,000
5. For expenditure by the Department of Health on pensions, allowances, gratuities, etc, to or in respect of persons engaged in health services or in other approved employment	347,844,000	967,565,000
6. For the expenditure of the Office of Population Censuses and Surveys on administrative and operational costs	48,698,000	27,638,000
TOTAL, CLASS XIII........................ £	19,051,266,000	5,936,607,000

SCHEDULE (B).—Part 16

Class XIV 1990–91

Class XIV

Schedule of Sums granted, and of the sums which may be applied as appropriations in aid in addition thereto, to defray the charges of the several Services herein particularly mentioned, which will come in course of payment during the year ending on 31st March 1991, viz.:—

	Sums not exceeding	
	Supply Grants	Appropriations in Aid
	£	£
Vote		
1. For expenditure by the Department of Social Security on non-contributory retirement pensions, Christmas bonus payments to pensioners, pensions, etc., for disablement or death arising out of war or service in the armed forces after 2 September 1939 and on sundry other services, on attendance allowances, invalid care allowance, severe disablement allowance, mobility allowance, and on the Independent Living Fund	3,641,000,000	1,614,000
2. For expenditure by the Department of Social Security on income support, supplementary benefit and transitional payments to hostels....	8,461,000,000	218,220,000
3. For expenditure by the Department of Social Security on child benefit, one-parent benefit and family credit................................	5,314,000,000	1,797,000
4. For sums payable into the social fund for expenditure on maternity expenses, funeral expenses, heating expenses in exceptionally cold weather and other needs..........................	152,000,000	—
5. For expenditure by the Department of Social Security on rent rebate, rent allowance, community charge benefit, community charge rebate and rate rebate subsidies, to housing, charging, levying and local authorities and residual expenditure on subsidies towards the administrative costs incurred by these authorities in operating the former housing benefit scheme, on transitional payments to help certain housing benefit claimants significantly affected by the changes to the housing benefit scheme and certain supplementary benefit claimants not entitled to benefit under the income support scheme and on payments to authorities in respect of completed enquiry forms returned to the Transitional Payments Unit (Including a Supplementary sum of £444,000,000).............................	3,980,041,000	200,000
6. For expenditure by the Department of Social Security on subsidies to housing and local authorities towards the costs of administering the housing benefit scheme, and to charging and levying authorities towards the cost of administering the community charge benefit scheme............	114,464,000	—
7. For expenditure by the Department of Social Security on administration, for agency payments, and for certain other services including grants to local authorities, voluntary organisations, and		

	Sums not exceeding	
	Supply Grants	Appropriations in Aid
	£	£
CLASS XIV—*continued*		
Vote		
major capital works projects for the Department of Health, including telecommunications capital (Including a Supplementary sum of £3,080,000)	1,706,259,000	980,294,000
TOTAL, CLASS XIV......................... £	23,368,764,000	1,202,125,000

SCHEDULE (B).—PART 17

Class XV 1990–91

CLASS XV

SCHEDULE OF SUMS granted, and of the sums which may be applied as appropriations in aid in addition thereto, to defray the charges of the several Services herein particularly mentioned, which will come in course of payment during the year ending on 31st March 1991, viz.:—

	Sums not exceeding	
	Supply Grants	Appropriations in Aid
	£	£
Vote		
1. For expenditure by the Department of Agriculture and Fisheries for Scotland on market support, assistance for structural measures, support in special areas, compensation to sheep producers and certain other services including animal health	51,411,000	12,707,000
2. For the expenditure by the Department of Agriculture and Fisheries for Scotland on educational and advisory services, botanical services, assistance to production, marketing and processing, and certain alternative land uses, assistance to crofting communities, administrative and land management services, assistance to the Scottish fishing industry, fishery protection and certain other services including research and development and special services	85,435,000	8,004,000
3. For expenditure by the Industry Department for Scotland on the Scottish Development Agency and the Highlands and Islands Development Board; on regional enterprise grants; on the promotion of tourism; on financial assistance to nationalised industries; on consumer protection; on Scottish Enterprise and Highlands and Islands Enterprise; and on sundry other services in connection with trade and industry, etc.	142,816,000	6,148,000
4. For expenditure by the Industry Department for Scotland on a contribution to the Department of Employment in relation to training activities in Scotland	267,285,000	—
5. For expenditure by the Industry Department for Scotland on regional development grants and regional selective assistance..................	103,965,000	6,780,000
6. For expenditure by the Scottish Development Department on roads and certain associated services, including the acquisition of land, lighting, road safety and related services, on assistance to local transport, on support for transport services in the Highlands and Islands, piers and harbours and on certain other transport services and grants, on historic buildings and monuments (including administration) and on other central and environmental services	251,542,000	9,458,000
7. For expenditure by the Scottish Development Department on assistance to local transport, on piers and harbours, on home insulation and sites for travelling people and on water, sewerage and		

	Sums not exceeding	
	Supply Grants	Appropriations in Aid
	£	£

CLASS XV—*continued*

Vote

    other environmental services..................

other environmental services..................	22,522,000	—

8. For expenditure by the Scottish Development Department on housing subsidies, funds for Scottish Homes, and a range of other Exchequer contributions and grants relating to housing.... | 306,983,000 | 7,000 |

9. For expenditure by the Industry Department for Scotland on grants to New Town Development Corporations in connection with housing and other services, on the urban programme and other urban regeneration initiatives and on expenses connected with the review of new towns wind up..................................... | 104,199,000 | — |

10. For expenditure by the Industry Department for Scotland in connection with the privatisation of the electricity supply in Scotland .... | 14,000,000 | — |

11. For expenditure by the Scottish Courts Administration on court services, the Scottish Law Commission and certain legal services, including a grant in aid .... | 42,665,000 | 8,653,000 |

12. For expenditure by the Scottish Home and Health Department on legal aid, criminal injuries compensation (excluding administration), police, police and fire services superannuation and welfare food .... | 313,428,000 | 690,000 |

13. For expenditure by the Scottish Courts Administration on costs and fees in connection with legal proceedings.......................... | 9,190,000 | — |

14. For expenditure by the Scottish Home and Health Department on legal aid administration; certain services relating to crime; prison services and the Parole Board for Scotland; fire and police services (excluding grants to local authorities and superannuation); civil defence (including grants), and other protective and miscellaneous services; and miscellaneous health services..... | 155,246,000 | 5,193,000 |

15. For expenditure by the Scottish Education Department on: schools, including establishment of self-governing schools; higher and further education, including compensation payments; special educational needs; community education; curriculum development, educational services, including support for School Boards, training and research; sport; arts, libraries, museums and galleries, including purchase grants and payments to Royal Society of Edinburgh, Royal Scottish Geographical Society and Scottish Film Production Fund; community service for offenders; provision of secure accommodation for children and other social work grants including training and research; Unemployed Voluntary Action Fund; publicity; indemnities; administration; central government grants to local authorities, including the Careers Service; and EC agency payments.. | 231,975,000 | 1,270,000 |

	Sums not exceeding	
	Supply Grants	Appropriations in Aid
	£	£

CLASS XV—*continued*

Vote

16. For expenditure by the Scottish Education Department on student loans including administration and related access funds, student awards and fees and reimbursement of fees for qualifying European Community students (Including a Supplementary sum of £675,000)................

	183,802,000	3,000

17. For expenditure by the Scottish Home and Health Department on the provision of services under the National Health Service in Scotland. .

	488,024,000	129,056,000

18. For expenditure of the Scottish Record Office on administrative costs and a grant ....

	2,967,000	660,000

19. For expenditure of the General Register Office for Scotland on administrative and operational costs......................................

	7,571,000	1,664,000

20. For the expenditure of the Department of the Registers of Scotland on administrative costs...

	1,000	22,841,000

21. For expenditure by the Scottish Office on administrative costs and the Royal Commission on the Ancient and Historical Monuments of Scotland.

	128,790,000	6,011,000

22. For expenditure by the Scottish Office for revenue and rate support grants in Scotland ....

	2,479,300,000	—

23. For expenditure by the Scottish Office on rate rebate grants and payments in connection with community charge transitional relief to local authorities in Scotland ....

	69,162,000	—

24. For expenditure by the Scottish Home and Health Department on superannuation allowances and gratuities, etc., in respect of teachers, and the widows, widowers and dependants of deceased teachers ....

	63,751,000	148,919,000

25. For expenditure by the Scottish Home and Health Department on pensions, allowances, gratuities, etc., to or in respect of persons engaged in health service or in other approved employment.............................

	29,743,000	145,279,000

26. For expenditure by the Scottish Development Department on adviser's fees and other costs in connection with the sale by the Scottish Transport Group of Scottish Bus operating subsidiaries......................................

	348,000	52,000

27. For expenditure by the Scottish Home and Health Department on hospital and community health, general medical services (part), and other health services, including central health services, training services for the disabled and civil defence (Including a Supplementary sum of £24,274,000)

	2,056,114,000	356,050,000

TOTAL, CLASS XV......................... £	7,612,235,000	869,445,000

SCHEDULE (B).—Part 18

Class XVI 1990–91

Class XVI

Schedule of Sums granted, and of the sums which may be applied as appropriations in aid in addition thereto, to defray the charges of the several Services herein particularly mentioned, which will come in course of payment during the year ending on 31st March 1991, viz.:—

	Sums not exceeding	
	Supply Grants	Appropriations in Aid
	£	£
Vote		
1. For expenditure by the Welsh Office on market support, grants for capital and other improvements, support for agriculture in special areas and compensation to sheep producers, animal health, arterial drainage, flood and coast protection and certain other services..............	38,321,000	9,633,000
2. For expenditure by the Welsh Office on assistance to agricultural production, food processing and marketing, certain alternative land uses and other miscellaneous agricultural services including commissioned surveys; protective, agency and other support for the Welsh fishing industry; on industrial development and other activities undertaken by the Welsh Development Agency and the Development Board for Rural Wales; support for medium and small sized firms, employment and certain other services (Revised sum).......................................	98,998,000	6,000
3. For expenditure by the Welsh Office on regional development grants, regional selective assistance, small firm measures, and housing subsidy for the Development Board for Rural Wales ...	104,604,000	8,150,000
4. For expenditure by the Welsh Office on a contribution to the Department of Employment in relation to training activities in Wales	144,324,000	—
5. For expenditure by the Welsh Office on tourism, roads and transport and certain associated services, housing, historic buildings and ancient monuments, other environment services (including civil defence), education, libraries and museums, health and personal social services, grants in aid, EC agency payments, other grants and certain other services, including research (Including a Supplementary sum of £495,000) ..	317,825,000	13,434,000
6. For expenditure by the Welsh Office on housing, other environmental services, welfare food payments, EC agency payments and certain other services (Revised sum)......................	583,343,000	4,827,000
7. For expenditure by the Welsh Office on family practitioner services under the National Health Service................................	274,898,000	74,710,000
8. For expenditure by the Welsh Office on hospital and community health services, general medical services (part), family practitioner services administration and related services, and other		

	Sums not exceeding	
	Supply Grants	Appropriations in Aid
	£	£
CLASS XVI—*continued*		
Vote		
health services (Including a Supplementary sum of £11,125,000)	962,838,000	168,680,000
9. For expenditure by the Welsh Office on central administration	51,748,000	1,838,000
10. For expenditure by the Welsh Office on revenue support grant, transitional relief grant and payment of national non-domestic rates income to local authorities in Wales, payments to specified bodies and payments following recalculations of rate support grant for prior years	1,604,300,000	—
11. For expenditure by the Welsh Office for national parks supplementary grant and transport grant to county councils in Wales	30,185,000	—
12. For expenditure by the Welsh Office on residual rate rebate grants to local authorities in Wales .	250,000	—
13. For expenditure by the Welsh Office for expenses incurred in connection with the sale of shares in the Welsh water holding company	1,000	501,000
TOTAL, CLASS XVI........................ £	4,211,635,000	281,779,000

Appropriation Act 1990

SCHEDULE (B).—Part 19

Class XVII 1990–91

_____

Class XVII

Schedule of Sums granted, and of the sums which may be applied as appropriations in aid in addition thereto, to defray the charges of the several Services herein particularly mentioned, which will come in course of payment during the year ending on 31st March 1991, viz.:—

	Sums not exceeding	
	Supply Grants	Appropriations in Aid
	£	£
Vote		
1. For expenditure by the Northern Ireland Office on central and miscellaneous services, services related to crime, police, prisons, training schools, probation and after-care etc, compensation schemes, crown prosecutions and other legal services and certain other grants............	683,518,000	6,063,000
2. For expenditure by the Northern Ireland Office on a grant of the Northern Ireland Consolidated Fund and other transfers	1,000,000,000	—
Total, Class XVII........................ £	1,683,518,000	6,063,000

SCHEDULE (B).—Part 20

Class XVIII 1990–91

Class XVIII

Schedule of Sums granted, and of the sums which may be applied as appropriations in aid in addition thereto, to defray the charges of the several Services herein particularly mentioned, which will come in course of payment during the year ending on 31st March 1991, viz.:—

	Sums not exceeding	
	Supply Grants	Appropriations in Aid
	£	£
Vote		
1. For expenditure by Her Majesty's Treasury on economic and financial administration; on computers and general telecommunications; payments to certain parliamentary bodies and the National Economic Development Council; and certain other services including general expenses of certain Pay Review Bodies, expenses in connection with Honours and Dignities, and expenditure in connection with the sale of shares in British Petroleum	77,531,000	34,587,000
2. For expenditure by Her Majesty's Treasury in connection with the manufacture, storage and distribution of coinage for use in the United Kingdom..................................	25,684,000	13,300,000
3. For expenditure of the Civil Service Catering Organisation (HM Treasury) in connection with the provision of catering services	1,000	20,374,000
4. For rates and contributions in lieu of rates paid by the Rating of Government Property Department in respect of property occupied by the Crown and premises occupied by representatives of Commonwealth and foreign countries and international organisations......................	215,300,000	501,300,000
5. For expenditure by Her Majesty's Treasury on the superannuation of civil servants, pensions, etc, in respect of former members of the Royal Irish Constabulary and other pensions and non-current payments; and for certain other services	1,499,400,000	319,000,000
6. For expenditure by the Customs and Excise Department on the administration of taxation, the operation of customs and revenue controls and other customs and excise work	640,926,000	19,469,000
7. For expenditure by the Inland Revenue Department on the management and collection of the direct taxes; the provision of rating and valuation services; and services provided for other Departments (Including a Supplementary sum of £29,000,000)...............................	1,377,913,000	62,401,000
8. For expenditure of the Inland Revenue Department on life assurance premium relief, mortgage interest relief and private medical insurance premium relief...............................	446,000,000	—
9. For expenditure of the Department for National Savings on administration and publicity costs...	174,169,000	1,044,000
10. For expenditure on administrative costs by the Registry of Friendly Societies on behalf of the		

	Sums not exceeding	
	Supply Grants	Appropriations in Aid
	£	£
CLASS XVIII—*continued*		
Vote		
Building Societies Commission and the Central Office of the Registry......................	2,205,000	3,412,000
11. For expenditure by the National Debt Office and Public Works Loan Commission on administrative costs..................................	1,000	1,551,000
12. For expenditure by the Paymaster General's Office on administrative costs...............	19,120,000	782,000
13. For expenditure by the Central Statistical Office on the provision of national accounts and other statistics and on departmental administration...	27,394,000	1,512,000
14. For expenditure by the Central Office of Information on home and overseas publicity........	1,084,000	142,711,000
15. For the expenditure of the Department of the Government Actuary on administrative costs...	482,000	3,368,000
16. For expenditure by the Controller of Her Majesty's Stationery Office to compensate the HMSO Trading Fund for the provision of reports of Parliamentary debates at less than full cost, and for the price concessions to public libraries.	2,544,000	—
17. For expenditure by the Controller of Her Majesty's Stationery Office on the reimbursement of the HMSO Trading Fund in respect of goods and services supplied to the Houses of Parliament and to United Kingdom members of the European Assembly...............................	21,259,000	250,000
18. For the salaries of the Crown Estate Commissioners and the expenses of their Office	1,132,000	—
19. For expenditure by HM Treasury to repay to the Contingencies Fund certain miscellaneous advances made during the year ended 31 March 1990 (New Estimate)	158,000	—
TOTAL, CLASS XVIII...................... £	4,532,303,000	1,125,061,000

SCHEDULE (B).—PART 21

Class XIX 1990–91

CLASS XIX

SCHEDULE OF SUMS granted, and of the sums which may be applied as appropriations in aid in addition thereto, to defray the charges of the several Services herein particularly mentioned, which will come in course of payment during the year ending on 31st March 1991, viz.:—

	Sums not exceeding	
	Supply Grants	Appropriations in Aid
	£	£
Vote		
1. For the expenditure by the Office of the Minister for the Civil Service on the central management of the civil service, on the Office of the Parliamentary Counsel and certain other services (Including a Supplementary sum of £978,000) ..	43,621,000	17,056,000
2. For the expenditure by the Cabinet Office, including the Chancellor of the Duchy of Lancaster, on administrative costs	21,918,000	5,049,000
3. For Her Majesty's foreign and other secret services	148,200,000	—
4. For expenditure of the Department of Her Majesty's Privy Council on administrative costs	1,670,000	23,000
5. For the expenditure of the Office of the Parliamentary Commissioner for Administration and the Health Service Commissioners for England, Scotland and Wales on administrative costs	3,090,000	—
6. For the expenditure of the House of Lords on Peers' expenses, administrative costs, staff pensions and security	17,320,000	310,000
7. For the expenditure of the House of Commons on Members' salaries, allowances, pensions, etc., financial assistance to Opposition parties and an Exchequer contribution to the Members' Fund .	53,008,000	—
TOTAL, CLASS XIX........................ £	288,827,000	22,438,000

Appropriation Act 1990

SCHEDULE (B).—Part 22

Class XIXA 1990–91

_____

Class XIXA

Schedule of Sums granted, and of the sums which may be applied as appropriations in aid in addition thereto, to defray the charges of the several Services herein particularly mentioned, which will come in course of payment during the year ending on 31st March 1991, viz.:—

	Sums not exceeding	
	Supply Grants	Appropriations in Aid
	£	£
Vote		
1. For expenditure by the House of Commons Commission	37,666,000	336,000
Total, Class XIXA........................ £	37,666,000	336,000

SCHEDULE (B).—Part 23

Class XIXB 1990–91

———

Class XIXB

Schedule of Sums granted, and of the sums which may be applied as appropriations in aid in addition thereto, to defray the charges of the several Services herein particularly mentioned, which will come in course of payment during the year ending on 31st March 1991, viz.:—

	Sums not exceeding	
	Supply Grants	Appropriations in Aid
	£	£
Vote 1. For expenditure of the National Audit Office ..	32,500,000	4,200,000
Total, Class XIXB.......................... £	32,500,000	4,200,000

SCHEDULE (C)

Enactments Repealed

Chapter	Short Title
1988 c.6	Consolidated Fund Act 1988
1988 c.38	Appropriation Act 1988

INDEX

References in roman type are to sections of the Act. References in italic type are to Schedule B; the relevant letter is followed by an Arabic numeral indicating the number of the Part, then follows a Roman numeral indicating the Class number and finally an Arabic number indicating the Vote number. Except where otherwise stated all italic references are to Supply Grants and Appropriations in Aid for the year ending March 31, 1991.

28–47

FINANCE ACT 1990*

(1990 c. 29)

---

*Annotations by Philip Baker, M.A., B.C.L., LL.M., Ph.D., Barrister, Christopher Cant, M.A., Barrister, Ian Ferrier, M.A., Barrister, David Goy, LL.M., John Shock, M.A., F.C.A., Barrister.

An Act to grant certain duties, to alter other duties, and to amend the law relating to the National Debt and the Public Revenue, and to make further provision in connection with Finance.

[26th July 1990]

PARLIAMENTARY DEBATES
Hansard, H.C. Vol. 171, col. 934; Vol. 176, cols. 692, 868; H.L. Vol. 521, cols. 869, 1128.
The Bill was considered in Committee on May 15 and 16, 1990 and in Standing Committee E from May 17 to July 3, 1990.

INTRODUCTION AND GENERAL NOTE

The Finance Act 1990 results from the first Budget of Mr John Major, who took office as Chancellor of the Exchequer after the sudden resignation of Mr Nigel Lawson in October 1989 following a dispute with Sir Alan Walters, the Prime Minister's personal economic adviser. The background to this dispute concerned the advisability and timing of British entry into the exchange rate mechanism (ERM) of the European monetary system (EMS) and at longer range the formation of a European monetary union (EMU), possibly with a single currency.

The more immediate problems affecting the Budget were the continuing high rate of inflation, approaching ten per cent., and a balance of payments deficit of £15 billion, which required strict corrective action in the form of a 15 per cent. base rate of interest. These circumstances gave Mr Major little room for manoeuvre. His most important initiative was to introduce various measures to encourage saving. These included the following: (1) various alterations to the regulations governing personal equity plans (PEPs), increasing the investment limits and relaxing some of the rules (see S.I. 1990 No. 678); (2) improving the attractiveness of employee share ownership plans (ESOPs) (ss.31–40); (3) abolishing the composite rate tax (CRT) on interest paid by banks and building societies (s.30 and Sched. 5). Following the introduction of the independent taxation of women from April 6, 1990, there are 14 million people who have savings income that does not merit taxation, but which is nevertheless taxed under the present system, because CRT cannot be reclaimed. From April 6, 1991, banks and building societies will be able to pay interest gross to such people; (4) introducing the tax exempt special savings account (TESSA) (s.28). This accords tax exemption to a five-year savings plan with a bank or building society, up to an overall limit of £9,000.

In addition to these specific measures, the Finance Act, as always, includes a number of detailed amendments to the fiscal code. The following are among the more important.

Charities (ss.24–27). Gifts to charity are further encouraged. In particular, charities may in future reclaim tax on donations out of income made by individuals or companies to a limit of £5m. in any one year.

Insurance companies (ss.41–50 and Scheds. 6–9). The system for taxing insurance companies is completely overhauled.

Oil industry (ss.60–62, 121). The tax treatment of abandonment costs on closing down North Sea oil and gas fields is improved.

Inland Revenue administration (ss.90–106). Further measures are introduced to improve the workings of the Inland Revenue, many of them in implementation of the report of the Keith Committee (Cmnd. 8822).

Stamp duty on shares (ss.107–111). The stamp duty on share transfers, introduced in 1714, is abolished, together with stamp duty reserve tax (S.D.R.T.), which was introduced in 1986 to buttress the stamp duty by imposing a charge on agreements to transfer securities which did not generate a stampable document. The abolition of the stamp duty and of S.D.R.T. will take effect on the introduction of the TAURUS system of paperless share trading on the Stock Exchange, expected at the end of 1991.

Ports privatisation levy (ss.115–120). A 50 per cent. tax is imposed on the proceeds of sales of shares by former public port authorities.

Football (ss.4 and 126). Following the Bradford and Hillsborough disasters, a contribution of £100m. over five years is made towards improving safety at football grounds. This is done by way of a reduction in pool betting duty, to be passed on by the pools promoters to the Football Trust.

ABBREVIATIONS

C.A.A. 1990	:	Capital Allowances Act 1990
C.G.T.A. 1979	:	Capital Gains Tax Act 1979
E.B.R.D.	:	European Bank for Reconstruction and Development
F.A. 1963	:	Finance Act 1963
F.A. 1988	:	Finance Act 1988
F.A. 1989	:	Finance Act 1989
I.C.T.A. 1970	:	Income and Corporation Taxes Act 1970
I.C.T.A. 1988	:	Income and Corporation Taxes Act 1988
PRT	:	Petroleum Revenue Tax
S.D.R.T.	:	Stamp Duty Reserve Tax
T.M.A. 1970	:	Taxes Management Act 1970
VED	:	Vehicle Excise Duty

PART I

CUSTOMS AND EXCISE AND VALUE ADDED TAX

CHAPTER I

CUSTOMS AND EXCISE

Rates of duty

Spirits, beer, wine, made-wine and cider

1.—(1) In section 5 of the Alcoholic Liquor Duties Act 1979 (spirits) for "£15·77" there shall be substituted "£17·35."

(2) In section 36 of that Act (beer) for "£0·90" there shall be substituted "£0.97."

(3) For the Table of rates of duty in Schedule 1 to that Act (wine and made-wine) there shall be substituted the Table in Schedule 1 to this Act.

(4) In section 62(1) of that Act (cider) for "£17·33" there shall be substituted "£18·66."

(5) This section shall be deemed to have come into force at 6 o'clock in the evening of 20th March 1990.

GENERAL NOTE

The duty on beer and wine is increased by seven per cent. and on spirits by ten per cent. The effect is to increase the price of a pint of beer by 2p, a bottle of table wine by 7p and a bottle of spirits by 54p. The higher increase on spirits reflects the fact that there has been a duty standstill since 1985. This was partly to encourage the Scotch whisky industry, 85 per cent. of whose output is exported.

Tobacco products

2.—(1) For the Table in Schedule 1 to the Tobacco Products Duty Act 1979 there shall be substituted—

"TABLE

1. Cigarettes	An amount equal to 21 per cent. of the retail price plus £34.91 per thousand cigarettes.
2. Cigars	£53.67 per kilogram.
3. Hand-rolling tobacco . .	£56.63 per kilogram.
4. Other smoking tobacco and chewing tobacco . . .	£24.95 per kilogram."

(2) This section shall be deemed to have come into force on 23rd March 1990.

GENERAL NOTE

After a year's standstill, the duty on cigarettes and cigars is increased by ten per cent., putting 10p on a packet of 20 cigarettes and 5p on a packet of five small cigars. The duty on pipe tobacco, considered less injurious to health, is unchanged.

Hydrocarbon oil

3.—(1) In section 6 of the Hydrocarbon Oil Duties Act 1979—

(a) in subsection (1), for "£0·2044" (duty on light oil) and "£0·1729" (duty on heavy oil) there shall be substituted "£0·2248" and "£0·1902" respectively; and

(b) subsection (2A) (special rate of duty on petrol below 4 star) shall cease to have effect.

(2) In section 11(1) of that Act, for "£0·0077" (rebate on fuel oil) and "£0·0110" (rebate on gas oil) there shall be substituted "£0·0083" and "£0·0118" respectively.

(3) In section 13A(1) of that Act (rebate on unleaded petrol), for "£0·0272" there shall be substituted "£0·0299."

(4) In section 14(1) of that Act (rebate on light oil for use as furnace fuel), for "£0·0077" there shall be substituted "£0·0083."

(5) In Part I of Schedule 3 to that Act, for paragraph 10A there shall be substituted—

"10A. Amending the definition of "aviation gasoline" in subsection (4) of section 6 of this Act."

(6) Subsections (1) to (4) above shall be deemed to have come into force at 6 o'clock in the evening of 20th March 1990.

GENERAL NOTE

Vehicle excise duty (VED) on cars and many other vehicles remains unchanged. To recoup the cost of this, the duty on petrol and derv is increased by ten per cent., rather more than strict revalorisation would justify. The effect is to add 9p to a gallon of derv and 11p to a gallon of leaded petrol. For unleaded petrol the increase is 9p per gallon, widening the tax differential in favour of unleaded petrol to 16p per gallon. The market share of unleaded petrol had increased fivefold to 30 per cent. since the changes in the previous Budget.

Pool betting duty

4.—(1) In section 7(1) of the Betting and Gaming Duties Act 1981 (which specifies 42½ per cent. as the rate of pool betting duty), for the words "42½ per cent." there shall be substituted the words "40 per cent.".

(2) This section shall apply in relation to bets made at any time by references to an event taking place on or after 6th April 1990.

GENERAL NOTE

Following disasters at Bradford and Hillsborough football grounds, there was widespread concern about the safety of spectators. This section implements a reduction in pool betting duty from 42.5 per cent. to 40 per cent., on a clear understanding that the full amount saved is passed by the pools promoters to the Football Trust and is used by it to improve the safety and comfort of spectators at English and Scottish football league grounds.

The reduction will yield £100m. in five years, in addition to the £75m. which the Football Trust had already said would be available over the next ten years. The duty reduction will be reviewed after five years.

For further consequential provisions, see s.126.

Vehicles excise duty

5.—(1) The Vehicles (Excise) Act 1971 ("the 1971 Act") and the Vehicles (Excise) Act (Northern Ireland) 1972 ("the 1972 Act") shall be amended as follows.

(2) In Schedule 3 to each Act (annual rates of duty on haulage vehicles)—
   (a) in paragraph 1 of Part I, for the words from "according" to the end there shall be substituted the words "be the rate specified in relation to vehicles of that description in the second column of that Part."; and
   (b) for the Table set out in Part II there shall be substituted the Table set out in Part I of Schedule 2 to this Act.

(3) Part II of Schedule 2 to this Act (which amends Part I of Schedule 4 to the 1971 Act) shall have effect.

(4) Part III of Schedule 2 to this Act (which amends Part I of Schedule 4 to the 1972 Act) shall have effect.

(5) For the Tables set out in Part II of Schedule 4 to the 1971 Act there shall be substituted the Tables set out in Part IV of Schedule 2 to this Act.

(6) The Tables set out in Part IV of Schedule 2 to this Act shall also be substituted for the Tables set out in Part II of Schedule 4 to the 1972 Act, but with the following modifications—
   (a) for the words "plated gross weight," in each place where they occur there shall be substituted the words "relevant maximum weight," and
   (b) for the words "plated train weight," in each place where they occur, there shall be substituted the words "relevant maximum train weight."

(7) In paragraph 2 of Schedule 4A to each Act (annual rates of duty on vehicles used for carrying or drawing exceptional loads) for "£3,100" there shall be substituted "£3,250."

(8) This section, except subsections (3) and (4), shall apply in relation to licences taken out after 20th March 1990.

(9) Subsections (3) and (4) above shall apply in relation to licences taken out after 30th September 1990.

GENERAL NOTE

The amendments to VED made by this section and Sched. 2 have the effect of simplifying the system by eliminating 188 different VED rates, following on the removal of 80 in F.A. 1989. Further progress is also made in aligning duty to road track costs, particularly by reducing the differential between rigid and articulated lorries.

Other provisions

Vehicles excise duty: exemptions

6.—(1) Section 4 of each of the Vehicles (Excise) Act 1971 and the Vehicles (Excise) Act (Northern Ireland) 1972 (exemptions) shall be amended as follows.

(2) In subsection (1) the following paragraph shall be inserted after paragraph (c)—

"(ca) veterinary ambulances;."

(3) In subsection (1) the following paragraphs shall be inserted after paragraph (k)—

"(ka) vehicles (other than mowing machines) neither constructed nor adapted for use nor used for the carriage of a driver or passenger;

(kb) vehicles (other than ambulances) used for the carriage of disabled persons by bodies for the time being recognised for the purposes of this paragraph by the Secretary of State;."

(4) The following subsections shall be inserted after subsection (1)—

"(1A) The Secretary of State shall recognise a body for the purposes of subsection (1)(kb) above if, on application made to him in such manner as he may specify, it appears to him that the body is concerned with the care of disabled persons.

(1B) The issue by the Secretary of State of a nil licence in respect of a mechanically propelled vehicle shall be treated, where the document is issued by virtue of paragraph (kb) of subsection (1) above, as recognition by him for the purposes of that paragraph of the body by reference to whose use of the vehicle the document is issued.

(1C) The Secretary of State may withdraw recognition of a body for the purposes of subsection (1)(kb) above if it appears to him that the body is no longer concerned with the care of disabled persons.

(1D) The reference in subsection (1B) above to the issue by the Secretary of State of a nil licence is a reference to the issue by him in accordance with regulations under this Act of a document which—

(a) is in the form of a vehicle licence, and

(b) has the word "NIL" marked in the space provided for indicating the amount of duty payable."

(5) In subsection (2) the following definitions shall be inserted before the definition of "road construction vehicle"—

" 'ambulance' means a vehicle which—

(a) is constructed or adapted for, and used for no other purpose than, the carriage of sick, injured or disabled persons to or from welfare centres or places where medical or dental treatment is given; and

(b) is readily identifiable as a vehicle used for the carriage of such persons by virtue of being marked "Ambulance," on both sides;

'disabled person' means a person suffering from a physical or mental defect or disability;

'veterinary ambulance' means a vehicle which—

(a) is used for no other purpose than the carriage of sick or injured animals to or from places where veterinary treatment is given; and

(b) is readily identifiable as a vehicle used for the carriage of such animals by virtue of being marked "Veterinary Ambulance" on both sides;."

(6) This section shall be deemed to have come into force on 21st March 1990.

GENERAL NOTE

The section extends and clarifies various exemptions from VED.

Subs. (2)

Exemption is extended to ambulances carrying animals as well as humans.

Subs. (3)

Exemption is extended to vehicles, other than mowing machines, not used for the carriage of a driver or passenger, and to vehicles, other than ambulances, used for the carriage of disabled persons by recognised bodies.

Subs. (4)

This provides for the recognition of such bodies by the Secretary of State.

Subs. (5)

This provides definitions of "ambulance", "veterinary ambulance" and "disabled person".

Entry of goods on importation

7. Schedule 3 to this Act (which amends the provisions of the Customs and Excise Management Act 1979 about initial and supplementary entries and postponed entry) shall have effect in relation to goods imported on or after the day on which this Act is passed.

GENERAL NOTE

Sched. 3 makes provision for the entry of goods on importation to be made by the agents of importers. See further the Note to Sched. 3.

Spirits methylated abroad

8.—(1) In section 4(1) of the Alcoholic Liquor Duties Act 1979, for the definition of "methylated spirits" there shall be substituted—
" "methylated spirits" means—
(a) spirits mixed in the United Kingdom with some other substance in accordance with regulations made under section 77 below; or
(b) spirits mixed outside the United Kingdom with some other substance if the spirits and other substance, and the proportions in which they are mixed, are such as are prescribed by those regulations for the production of methylated spirits in the United Kingdom;".
(2) This section shall come into force on 1st January 1991.

GENERAL NOTE

The manufacture of and dealing in methylated spirits is strictly regulated in view of the possible abuse of such spirits. The definition of "methylated spirits" is extended to include such spirits produced outside the U.K., but in accordance with the U.K. regulations.

Lodgings for officers in charge of distillery

9. In section 12 of the Alcoholic Liquor Duties Act 1979 (licence to manufacture spirits) subsections (6) to (9) (requirement that distiller provide lodgings for officers in charge of distillery) shall cease to have effect.

GENERAL NOTE

The provisions regarding lodgings for officers in charge of a distillery are repealed. These are redundant in view of the system of preparing records by the distillery itself rather than by an excise officer. The requirement to provide accommodation at a distiller's warehouse remains.

CHAPTER II

VALUE ADDED TAX

Registration

10.—(1) The Value Added Tax Act 1983 shall be amended as follows.

(2) For paragraph 1(1) to (3) of Schedule 1 (registration) there shall be substituted—

"(1) Subject to sub-paragraphs (3) to (5) below, a person who makes taxable supplies but is not registered becomes liable to be registered—

(a) at the end of any month, if the value of his taxable supplies in the period of one year then ending has exceeded £25,400; or

(b) at any time, if there are reasonable grounds for believing that the value of his taxable supplies in the period of thirty days then beginning will exceed £25,400.

(2) Where a business carried on by a taxable person is transferred to another person as a going concern and the transferee is not registered at the time of the transfer, then, subject to sub-paragraphs (3) to (5) below, the transferee becomes liable to be registered at that time if—

(a) the value of his taxable supplies in the period of one year ending at the time of the transfer has exceeded £25,400; or

(b) there are reasonable grounds for believing that the value of his taxable supplies in the period of thirty days beginning at the time of the transfer will exceed £25,400.

(3) A person does not become liable to be registered by virtue of sub-paragraph (1)(a) or (2)(a) above if the Commissioners are satisfied that the value of his taxable supplies in the period of one year beginning at the time at which, apart from this sub-paragraph, he would become liable to be registered will not exceed £24,400."

(3) In paragraph 1(4) of Schedule 1 after "(1)(a)" there shall be inserted "or (2)(a)."

(4) In paragraph 1(5) of Schedule 1 after "sub-paragraph (1)" there shall be inserted "or (2)."

(5) In paragraph 1(6) of Schedule 1 after "sub-paragraph (1)" there shall be inserted "or (2)."

(6) For paragraphs 3 and 4 of Schedule 1 there shall be substituted—

"3.—(1) A person who becomes liable to be registered by virtue of paragraph 1(1)(a) above shall notify the Commissioners of the liability within thirty days of the end of the relevant month.

(2) The Commissioners shall register any such person (whether or not he so notifies them) with effect from the end of the month following the relevant month or from such earlier date as may be agreed between them and him.

(3) In this paragraph "the relevant month," in relation to a person who becomes liable to be registered, means the month at the end of which he becomes liable to be registered.

4.—(1) A person who becomes liable to be registered by virtue of paragraph 1(1)(b) above shall notify the Commissioners of the liability before the end of the period by reference to which the liability arises.

(2) The Commissioners shall register any such person (whether or not he so notifies them) with effect from the beginning of the period by reference to which the liability arises.

4A.—(1) A person who becomes liable to be registered by virtue of paragraph 1(2) above shall notify the Commissioners of the liability within thirty days of the time when the business is transferred.

(2) The Commissioners shall register any such person (whether or not he so notifies them) with effect from the time when the business is transferred.

4B. Where a person becomes liable to be registered by virtue of paragraph 1(1)(a) above and by virtue of paragraph 1(1)(b) or 1(2) above at the same time, the Commissioners shall register him in accordance with paragraph 4(2) or 4A(2) above, as the case may be, rather than paragraph 3(2) above."

(7) Section 33(1A) (registration of transferee of business) shall cease to have effect.

(8) In consequence of the amendment of paragraph 1 of Schedule 1, in section 28(1) (registration of local authorities) for "1(a)(ii)" there shall be substituted "1(1)(a)."

(9) Subsections (2) to (5) and (8) above shall be deemed to have come into force on 21st March 1990.

(10) Subsections (6) and (7) above apply in relation to persons who become liable to be registered after 20th March 1990.

GENERAL NOTE

The registration threshold for value added tax is raised from £23,600 to £25,400, the maximum permissible under EEC regulations. Also, the requirement to register is related to actual turnover in the previous year or estimated turnover in the following month. The previous requirements related to quarterly turnover or to estimated turnover in the following year are abolished. Particularly in view of the severe penalties now attaching to failure to register, this provision is a considerable boon to small businesses.

Bad debts

11.—(1) Subsection (2) below applies where—
(a) on or after 1st April 1989 a person has supplied goods or services for a consideration in money and has accounted for and paid tax on the supply,
(b) the whole or any part of the consideration for the supply has been written off in his accounts as a bad debt, and
(c) a period of two years (beginning with the date of the supply) has elapsed.

(2) Subject to the following provisions of this section and to regulations under it the person shall be entitled, on making a claim to the Commissioners, to a refund of the amount of tax chargeable by reference to the outstanding amount.

(3) In subsection (2) above "the outstanding amount" means—
(a) if at the time of the claim the person has received no payment by way of the consideration written off in his accounts as a bad debt, an amount equal to the amount of the consideration so written off;
(b) if at that time he has received a payment or payments by way of the consideration so written off, an amount by which the payment (or the aggregate of the payments) is exceeded by the amount of the consideration so written off.

(4) A person shall not be entitled to a refund under subsection (2) above unless—
(a) the value of the supply is equal to or less than its open market value, and
(b) in the case of a supply of goods, the property in the goods has passed to the person to whom they were supplied or to a person deriving title from, through or under that person.

(5) Regulations under this section may—
(a) require a claim to be made at such time and in such form and manner as may be specified by or under the regulations;
(b) require a claim to be evidenced and quantified by reference to such records and other documents as may be so specified;
(c) require the claimant to keep, for such period and in such form and manner as may be so specified, those records and documents and a

record of such information relating to the claim and to subsequent payments by way of consideration as may be so specified;

(d) require the repayment of a refund allowed under this section where any requirement of the regulations is not complied with;

(e) require the repayment of the whole or, as the case may be, an appropriate part of a refund allowed under this section where the claimant subsequently receives any payment (or further payment) by way of the consideration written off in his accounts as a bad debt;

(f) include such supplementary, incidental, consequential or transitional provisions as appear to the Commissioners to be necessary or expedient for the purposes of this section;

(g) make different provision for different circumstances.

(6) The provisions which may be included in regulations by virtue of subsection (5)(f) above may include rules for ascertaining—

(a) whether, when and to what extent consideration is to be taken to have been written off in accounts as a bad debt;

(b) whether a payment is to be taken as received by way of consideration for a particular supply;

(c) whether, and to what extent, a payment is to be taken as received by way of consideration written off in accounts as a bad debt.

(7) The provisions which may be included in regulations by virtue of subsection (5)(f) above may include rules dealing with particular cases, such as those involving part payment or mutual debts; and in particular such rules may vary the way in which the following amounts are to be calculated—

(a) the outstanding amount mentioned in subsection (2) above, and

(b) the amount of any repayment where a refund has been allowed under this section.

(8) No claim for a refund may be made under subsection (2) above in relation to a supply as regards which a refund is claimed, whether before or after the passing of this Act, under section 22 of the Value Added Tax Act 1983 (existing provision for refund in cases of bad debts).

(9) Section 22 of that Act shall not apply in relation to any supply made after the day on which this Act is passed.

(10) Sections 4 and 5 of that Act shall apply for determining the time when a supply is to be treated as taking place for the purposes of construing this section.

(11) That Act shall be amended as follows—

(a) in section 39(1A)(b) after the word "above" there shall be inserted the words "or section 11 of the Finance Act 1990";

(b) in section 40(1)(f) after the words "section 22 above" there shall be inserted the words "or section 11 of the Finance Act 1990."

(12) In section 13(2) of the Finance Act 1985, the word "and" at the end of paragraph (b) shall be omitted and after paragraph (c) there shall be inserted the words "and

(d) a refund under section 11 of the Finance Act 1990,".

GENERAL NOTE

Under the Value Added Tax Act 1989, s.22, relief is available for bad debts on which VAT has been paid only where the debtor has been formally declared insolvent. This section allows instead relief for all debts that are over two years old and have been written off in the traders' accounts. The change will be worth about £150m. in tax relief to businesses next year.

Appropriate regulations may be made by the Customs and Excise governing the relief.

Domestic accommodation

12.—(1) Section 14 of the Value Added Tax Act 1983 (credit for input tax against output tax) shall be amended as follows.

(2) The following subsection shall be inserted after subsection (3) (definition of "input tax")—

"(3A) For the purposes of subsection (3) above, where goods or services supplied to, or goods imported by, a company are used or to be used in connection with the provision of accommodation by the company, they shall not be treated as used or to be used for the purpose of any business carried on by the company to the extent that the accommodation is used or to be used for domestic purposes by—

    (a) a director of the company, or

    (b) a person connected with a director of the company."

(3) The following subsection shall be inserted at the end—

"(11) For the purposes of this section "director" means—

    (a) in relation to a company whose affairs are managed by a board of directors or similar body, a member of that board or similar body;

    (b) in relation to a company whose affairs are managed by a single director or similar person, that director or person;

    (c) in relation to a company whose affairs are managed by the members themselves, a member of the company;

and a person is connected with a director if that person is the director's wife or husband, or is a relative, or the wife or husband of a relative, of the director or of the director's wife or husband."

(4) This section applies in relation to goods or services supplied, and goods imported, on or after the day on which this Act is passed.

GENERAL NOTE

Value added tax incurred by companies in the provision of accommodation for domestic purposes to their directors or their directors' relatives will no longer be allowed as input tax.

Goods shipped as stores

13.—(1) In section 16 of the Value Added Tax Act 1983 (zero-rating) the following subsection shall be inserted after subsection (6) (goods shipped for use as stores etc)—

"(6A) Subsection (6)(b) above shall not apply in the case of goods shipped for use as stores on a voyage or flight to be made by the person to whom the goods were supplied and to be made for a purpose which is private."

(2) This section applies in relation to supplies made after the day on which this Act is passed.

GENERAL NOTE

Zero-rating is accorded under the Value Added Tax Act 1983, s.16(6) to exports and goods shipped as stores or for sale en route on a voyage or flight to a destination abroad. To conform with the Eighteenth Council Directive (89/465/EEC) as adopted on July 18, 1989, which withdrew derogations 21 and 22 of Annex F to the Sixth Council Directive (77/388/EEC), zero-rating is now withdrawn from the supply of stores for private voyages or flights.

Supplies to groups

14.—(1) Section 29A of the Value Added Tax Act 1983 (supplies to groups) shall be amended as follows.

(2) In subsection (1) for "and (3)" there shall be substituted "to (3A)."

(3) The following subsection shall be inserted after subsection (3)—

"(3A) Subsection (4) below shall not apply to the extent that the chargeable assets consist of capital items in respect of which regulations made under section 15(3) and (4) above, and in force when the assets are transferred, provide for adjustment to the deduction of input tax."

(4) This section shall have effect in relation to transfers of assets made on or after 1st April 1990.

GENERAL NOTE

Under the Value Added Tax Act 1983, s.29A, inserted by the Finance Act 1987, s.15(1), a charge to tax arises in certain circumstances when assets are transferred to a partly exempt group as part of a transfer of a going concern. The provision treats the transaction as a supply to and by the group (a self-supply). The group is responsible for accounting for the tax due, and can recover such tax only to the extent that the assets are used to make taxable supplies.

Some capital items, *i.e.* computers and computer equipment worth £50,000 or more, and land and buildings, and certain extensions to buildings worth £250,000 or more, are now removed from the ambit of s.29A and dealt with under the Value Added Tax (General) (Amendment) (No. 4) Regulations 1989 (S.I. 1989 No. 2355). The regulations implement a "capital goods scheme" which will provide a permanent means of preventing tax avoidance on these items by partly exempt businesses.

The self-supply charge under s.29A will continue to apply to assets not covered by the capital goods scheme.

Power to assess

15.—(1) In paragraph 4(2) of Schedule 7 to the Value Added Tax Act 1983 after the words "so paid or credited," there shall be inserted the words "or which would not have been so paid or credited had the facts been known or been as they later turn out to be,".

(2) This section shall apply in relation to an amount paid or credited to a person after the day on which this Act is passed.

GENERAL NOTE

The amendment to the Value Added Tax Act 1983, Sched. 7, para. 4(2) clarifies the circumstances in which the Customs and Excise may raise an assessment to recover a repayment of tax which turns out to have been incorrect.

Interest on tax etc. recovered or recoverable by assessment

16.—(1) Section 18 of the Finance Act 1985 (interest on tax etc. recovered or recoverable by assessment) shall be amended as follows.

(2) In subsection (1) for the words from "that tax" to "rate" there shall be substituted the words "whole of the amount assessed shall carry interest at the prescribed rate from the reckonable date."

(3) In subsection (3) for the words from "that tax" to "rate" there shall be substituted the words "the whole of the amount paid shall carry interest at the prescribed rate from the reckonable date."

(4) Subsections (4) and (5) shall cease to have effect.

(5) In subsection (7) for "(4) and (5)" there shall be substituted "(1) and (3)."

(6) This section applies in relation to assessments made on or after the day on which this Act is passed.

GENERAL NOTE

The amendment to the Finance Act 1985, s.18, simplifies the procedure for charging interest on assessments by making it unnecessary for the Customs and Excise to apportion amounts to different parts of a period.

PART II

INCOME TAX, CORPORATION TAX AND CAPITAL GAINS TAX

CHAPTER I

GENERAL

Income tax rates and allowances

Rates and main allowances

17.—(1) Income tax shall be charged for the year 1990–91, and—

(a) the basic rate shall be 25 per cent.;
(b) the basic rate limit shall be £20,700;
(c) the higher rate shall be 40 per cent.; and
(d) section 1(4) of the Taxes Act 1988 (indexation of basic rate limit) shall not apply.

(2) In sections 1(5) and 257C(2) of the Taxes Act 1988, for the words from "between" to the end there shall be substituted the words "during the period beginning with 6th April and ending with 17th May in the year of assessment."

(3) In section 828 of that Act (orders and regulations), in subsection (4), for "257(11)" there shall be substituted "257C."

(4) Subsections (2) and (3) above shall have effect for the year 1990–91 and subsequent years of assessment.

GENERAL NOTE
The basic rate, higher rate, and level of income at which the higher rate applies remain unchanged.

There is no express provision in the Act increasing personal allowances save for s.18 which deals with the relief for blind persons. As a consequence I.C.T.A. 1988, s.257C, takes effect to increase the allowances by the rate of inflation between December 1988 and December 1989, an increase of 7·7 per cent. The allowances are:

(i) Personal allowance—£3,005;
(ii) Married couple's allowance—£1,720;
(iii) Age allowance (65 to 74)—£3,670;
(iv) Married age allowance (65 to 74)—£2,145;
(v) Age allowance (75 and over)—£3,820;
(vi) Married age allowance (75 and over)—£2,185.

Subsection (2) has the effect of delaying the date on which the new allowances take effect for the P.A.Y.E. systems from May 5, 1990, to May 18. In consequence payments under that system made before that date will be made using the 1989–90 tax tables.

Relief for blind persons

18. In section 265(1) of the Taxes Act 1988, for "£540" there shall be substituted "£1,080."

GENERAL NOTE
The doubling of the blind person's allowance is the one increase in personal allowances in excess of the indexation increase.

Corporation tax rates

Charge and rate of corporation tax for 1990

19. Corporation tax shall be charged for the financial year 1990 at the rate of 35 per cent.

GENERAL NOTE
The corporation tax rate remains constant at 35 per cent.

Small companies

20.—(1) For the financial year 1990—
(a) the small companies' rate shall be 25 per cent., and
(b) the fraction mentioned in section 13(2) of the Taxes Act 1988 (marginal relief for small companies) shall be one-fortieth.

(2) In section 13(3) of that Act (limits of marginal relief), in paragraphs (a) and (b)—
(a) for "£150,000" there shall be substituted "£200,000", and
(b) for "£750,000" there shall be substituted "£1,000,000."

(3) Subsection (2) above shall have effect for the financial year 1990 and subsequent financial years; and where by virtue of that subsection section 13

of the Taxes Act 1988 has effect with different relevant maximum amounts in relation to different parts of a company's accounting period, then for the purposes of that section those parts shall be treated as if they were separate accounting periods and the profits and basic profits of the company for that period shall be apportioned between those parts.

GENERAL NOTE
    The small companies rate of corporation tax remains unchanged at 25 per cent. but the limits applicable to the rate are changed. The lower rate now applies to companies with profits up to £200,000 rather than £150,000. The marginal relief applies to companies with profits between £200,000 and £1m (increased from £750,000).

Benefits in kind

Care for children

21.—(1) The following section shall be inserted after section 155 of the Taxes Act 1988—

"Care for children
    155A.—(1) Where a benefit consists in the provision for the employee of care for a child, section 154 does not apply to the benefit to the extent that it is provided in qualifying circumstances.
    (2) For the purposes of subsection (1) above the benefit is provided in qualifying circumstances if—
        (a) the child falls within subsection (3) below,
        (b) the care is provided on premises which are not domestic premises,
        (c) the condition set out in subsection (4) below or the condition set out in subsection (5) below (or each of them) is fulfilled, and
        (d) in a case where the registration requirement applies, it is met.
    (3) The child falls within this subsection if—
        (a) he is a child for whom the employee has parental responsibility,
        (b) he is resident with the employee, or
        (c) he is a child of the employee and maintained at his expense.
    (4) The condition is that the care is provided on premises which are made available by the employer alone.
    (5) The condition is that—
        (a) the care is provided under arrangements made by persons who include the employer,
        (b) the care is provided on premises which are made available by one or more of those persons, and
        (c) under the arrangements the employer is wholly or partly responsible for financing and managing the provision of the care.
    (6) The registration requirement applies where—
        (a) the premises on which the care is provided are required to be registered under section 1 of the Nurseries and Child-Minders Regulation Act 1948 or section 11 of the Children and Young Persons Act (Northern Ireland) 1968, or
        (b) any person providing the care is required to be registered under section 71 of the Children Act 1989 with respect to the premises on which it is provided;
and the requirement is met if the premises are so registered or (as the case may be) the person is so registered.
    (7) In subsection (3)(c) above the reference to a child of the employee includes a reference to a stepchild of his.
    (8) In this section—

> "care" means any form of care or supervised activity, whether or not
> provided on a regular basis, but excluding supervised activity
> provided primarily for educational purposes;
> "child" means a person under the age of eighteen;
> "domestic premises" means any premises wholly or mainly used as a
> private dwelling;
> "parental responsibility" has the meaning given in section 3(1) of the
> Children Act 1989."

(2) In section 154(2) of the Taxes Act 1988 for the words "section 155" there shall be substituted the words "sections 155 and 155A."

(3) This section applies for the year 1990–91 and subsequent years of assessment.

GENERAL NOTE

Under the previous law where an employer provided childcare facilities for an employee the cost of such provision was taxable under the benefit in kind rules in I.C.T.A. 1988, s.154, if the employee earned more than £8,500 p.a. or was a director. This section provides a relief from such charge for such provision.

In order to obtain the relief the various conditions set out in subs. (2) of the new s.155A must be met. The alternative conditions set out in subs. (4) or (5) enable relief to be available whether the childcare facility is provided by the employer alone, at its own premises, or alternatively if the employer pays for places at a nursery run by a third party so long as the employer is partly responsible for its finance and management.

It is important to note that this relief only excludes a charge under s.154. It does not prevent a charge if the employer provides an employee with cash or with some sort of voucher enabling the employee to make his or her own arrangements for the provision of childcare. It also provides no relief for mothers who out of their own earnings employ nannies to look after their children while they work.

Car benefits

22.—(1) In Schedule 6 to the Taxes Act 1988 (taxation of directors and others in respect of cars) for Part I (tables of flat rate cash equivalents) there shall be substituted—

PART I

TABLES OF FLAT RATE CASH EQUIVALENTS

TABLE A

Cars with an original market value up to £19,250 and having a cylinder capacity

Cylinder capacity of car in cubic centimetres	Age of car at end of relevant year of assessment	
	Under 4 years	4 years or more
1400 or less	£1,700	£1,150
More than 1400 but not more than 2000	£2,200	£1,500
More than 2000	£3,550	£2,350

TABLE B

Cars with an original market value up to £19,250 and not having a cylinder capacity

Original market value of car	Age of car at end of relevant year of assessment	
	Under 4 years	4 years or more
Less than £6,000	£1,700	£1,150
£6,000 or more but less than £8,500	£2,200	£1,500
£8,500 or more but not more than £19,250	£3,550	£2,350

TABLE C

Cars with an original market value of more than £19,250

Original market value of car	Age of car at end of relevant year of assessment	
	Under 4 years	4 years or more
More than £19,250 but not more than £29,000	£4,600	£3,100
More than £29,000	£7,400	£4,900

(2) This section shall have effect for the year 1990–91 and subsequent years of assessment.

GENERAL NOTE
   This section increases by 20 per cent. the scale charges for taxing employees on the value of their private use of company cars. These are the cash equivalents on which employees earning more than £8,500 p.a. and directors are taxable under I.C.T.A. 1988, s. 157.
   It should be noted that there is no increase in the charges for fuel provided for private motoring to which I.C.T.A. 1988, s.158, applies.

Mileage allowances

Limit on chargeable mileage profit

23. Schedule 4 to this Act (which contains provisions about sums paid in respect of travelling expenses) shall have effect.

Charities

Payroll deduction scheme

24.—(1) In section 202(7) of the Taxes Act 1988 (which limits to £480 the deductions attracting relief) for "£480" there shall be substituted "£600."
   (2) This section shall have effect for the year 1990–91 and subsequent years of assessment.

GENERAL NOTE
   The payroll deduction scheme allows for gifts to charities to be deducted from an employee's emoluments and to be treated as a deductible expense for Sched. E purposes. This section increases to £600 per annum (from £480 per annum) the maximum amount to which the scheme applies.

Donations to charity by individuals

25.—(1) For the purposes of this section, a gift to a charity by an individual ("the donor") is a qualifying donation if—
(a) it is made on or after 1st October 1990,
(b) it satisfies the requirements of subsection (2) below, and
(c) the donor gives an appropriate certificate in relation to it to the charity.
(2) A gift satisfies the requirements of this subsection if—
(a) it takes the form of a payment of a sum of money;
(b) it is not subject to a condition as to repayment;
(c) it is not a covenanted payment to charity;
(d) it does not constitute a sum falling within section 202(2) of the Taxes Act 1988 (payroll deduction scheme);
(e) neither the donor nor any person connected with him receives a benefit in consequence of making it or, where the donor or a person connected with him does receive a benefit in consequence of making it, the relevant value in relation to the gift does not exceed two and a half per cent. of the amount of the gift and the amount to be taken into account for the purposes of this paragraph in relation to the gift does not exceed £250;
(f) it is not conditional on or associated with, or part of an arrangement involving, the acquisition of property by the charity, otherwise than by way of gift, from the donor or a person connected with him;
(g) the sum paid is not less than £600;
(h) the sum paid does not, when aggregated with any other qualifying donations already made by the donor in the relevant year of assessment, exceed £5,000,000; and
(i) the donor is resident in the United Kingdom at the time the gift is made.
(3) The reference in subsection (1)(c) above to an appropriate certificate is a reference to a certificate which is in such form as the Board may prescribe and contains statements to the following effect—
(a) that the gift satisfies the requirements of subsection (2) above, and
(b) that, either directly or by deduction from profits or gains brought into charge to tax in the relevant year of assessment, the donor has paid or will pay to the Board income tax of an amount equal to income tax at the basic rate for the relevant year of assessment on the grossed up amount of the gift.
(4) For the purposes of subsections (2)(e) above and (5) below, the relevant value in relation to a gift is—
(a) where there is one benefit received in consequence of making it which is received by the donor or a person connected with him, the value of that benefit;
(b) where there is more than one benefit received in consequence of making it which is received by the donor or a person connected with him, the aggregate value of all the benefits received in consequence of making it which are received by the donor or a person connected with him.
(5) The amount to be taken into account for the purposes of subsection (2)(e) above in relation to a gift to a charity is an amount equal to the aggregate of—
(a) the relevant value in relation to the gift, and
(b) the relevant value in relation to each gift already made to the charity by the donor in the relevant year of assessment which is a qualifying donation for the purposes of this section.
(6) Where a gift is a qualifying donation, the Income Tax Acts, except Part IX of the Taxes Act 1988 (annual payments), shall have effect, in their

application to the donor, as if the making of the gift were the making of a covenanted payment to charity of an amount equal to the grossed up amount of the gift, being a payment falling to be made at the time the gift is made.

(7) Where the payment which the donor is treated by virtue of subsection (6) above as making would, if in fact made, be payable wholly or partly out of profits or gains brought into charge to income tax, they shall be assessed and charged with income tax on the donor without distinguishing the payment and in respect of so much of them as is equal to the payment and may be deducted in computing his total income the donor shall be charged at the appropriate rate.

(8) Where the payment which the donor is treated by virtue of subsection (6) above as making would, if in fact made, not be payable or not be wholly payable out of profits or gains brought into charge to income tax, the donor shall be assessable and chargeable with income tax at the appropriate rate on the payment, or on so much of it as would not be payable out of profits or gains brought into charge to income tax.

(9) For the purposes of subsections (7) and (8) above the appropriate rate is the basic rate for the year of assessment in which, in accordance with subsection (6) above, the payment falls to be made.

(10) The receipt by a charity of a gift which is a qualifying donation shall be treated for the purposes of the Tax Acts, in their application to the charity, as the receipt, under deduction of income tax at the basic rate for the relevant year of assessment, of an annual payment of an amount equal to the grossed up amount of the gift.

(11) Section 839 of the Taxes Act 1988 applies for the purposes of subsections (2) and (4) above.

(12) For the purposes of this section —
  (a) "charity" has the same meaning as in section 506 of the Taxes Act 1988 and includes each of the bodies mentioned in section 507 of that Act;
  (b) "covenanted payment to charity" has the meaning given by section 660(3) of the Taxes Act 1988;
  (c) "relevant year of assessment," in relation to a gift, means the year of assessment in which the gift is made;
  (d) references, in relation to a gift, to the grossed up amount are to the amount which after deducting income tax at the basic rate for the relevant year of assessment leaves the amount of the gift; and
  (e) references to profits or gains brought into charge to income tax are to profits or gains which are treated for the purposes of section 348 of the Taxes Act 1988 as brought into charge to income tax.

GENERAL NOTE

The relief given in respect of certain covenanted payments to charity is now extended by this section to also cover lump sum payments provided that the requirements of subs. (2) are satisfied. If they are, then the payment is treated as if it has had basic rate tax deducted from it and as if it has been made pursuant to a covenant. This means that the payment must be grossed up and treated as a deduction for higher rate of tax purposes.

The payment must be greater than £600 but not, when aggregated with other payments in the year of assessment, exceed £5 million. Payments made under the payroll deduction scheme are excluded.

No benefit must be received by the donor or a connected person in return for the payment which exceeds £250 or 2½ per cent. of the value of the payment. This will exclude, for example, gifts to a charity which is looking after, say, a child of the donor if the charity is so acting in consequence of the gift.

This section applies to payments made on or after October 1, 1970.

Company donations to charity

26.—(1) Section 339 of the Taxes Act 1988 (charges on income: donations to charity) shall be amended as follows.

(2) In subsection (1) after the word "payment" there shall be inserted the words "of a sum of money."

(3) In subsection (2) the words "and is not a close company" shall be omitted.

(4) The following subsections shall be inserted after subsection (3)—

"(3A) A payment made by a close company is not a qualifying donation if it is of a sum which leaves less than £600 after deducting income tax under subsection (3) above.

(3B) A payment made by a close company is not a qualifying donation if—

(a) it is made subject to a condition as to repayment, or

(b) the company or a connected person receives a benefit in consequence of making it and either the relevant value in relation to the payment exceeds two and a half per cent. of the amount given after deducting tax under section 339(3) or the amount to be taken into account for the purposes of this paragraph in relation to the payment exceeds £250.

(3C) For the purposes of subsections (3B) above and (3D) below, the relevant value in relation to a payment to a charity is—

(a) where there is one benefit received in consequence of making it which is received by the company or a connected person, the value of that benefit;

(b) where there is more than one benefit received in consequence of making it which is received by the company or a connected person, the aggregate value of all the benefits received in consequence of making it which are received by the company or a connected person.

(3D) The amount to be taken into account for the purposes of subsection (3B)(b) above in relation to a payment to a charity is an amount equal to the aggregate of—

(a) the relevant value in relation to the payment, and

(b) the relevant value in relation to each payment already made to the charity by the company in the accounting period in which the payment is made which is a qualifying donation within the meaning of this section.

(3E) A payment made by a close company is not a qualifying donation if it is conditional on, or associated with, or part of an arrangement involving, the acquisition of property by the charity, otherwise than by way of gift, from the company or a connected person.

(3F) A payment made by a company is not a qualifying donation unless the company gives to the charity to which the payment is made a certificate in such form as the Board may prescribe and containing—

(a) in the case of any company, a statement to the effect that the payment is one out of which the company has deducted tax under subsection (3) above, and

(b) in the case of a close company, a statement to the effect that the payment satisfies the requirements of subsections (3A) to (3E) above.

(3G) A payment made by a company is not a qualifying donation if the company is itself a charity."

(5) The following subsection shall be inserted after subsection (7)—

"(7A) In subsections (3B) to (3E) above references to a connected person are to a person connected with—

(a) the company, or

(b) a person connected with the company;

and section 839 applies for the purposes of this subsection."

(6) This section applies in relation to payments made on or after 1st October 1990.

GENERAL NOTE

I.C.T.A. 1988, s.339, permits companies which are not close companies to treat a lump sum gift to charity as a charge on its profits. This section now permits close companies to obtain the same relief subject to certain additional restrictions. These restrictions are similar to those imposed in respect of lump sum gifts to charity by individuals—for example any benefit received by the company or a connected person in consequence of the gift must not exceed £250 or 2½ per cent. of its value. Similarly, the gift must not be part of an arrangement under which the charity is to acquire property from the company or a connected person.

There are also certain changes introduced relating to all companies and not just close companies. These are:

(i) a payment will not qualify if it leaves less than £600 after deducting income tax;

(ii) the gift must be the payment of a sum of money;

(iii) the donor company must not be a charity;

(iv) a certificate in the prescribed form must be given to the charity by the company.

Section 27 contains provisions as to the maximum amount which may qualify for this relief.

Maximum qualifying company donations

27.—(1) In section 338 of the Taxes Act 1988 (allowance of charges on income and capital) in subsection (2) for the words "to section 339" there shall be substituted the words "to sections 339 and 339A."

(2) In section 339 of that Act (charges on income: donations to charity) subsection (5) shall be omitted and in subsection (9) for "(5)" there shall be substituted "(4)."

(3) The following section shall be inserted after section 339 of that Act—

"Maximum qualifying donations

339A.—(1) If in a particular accounting period of a company the company has no associated company, a qualifying donation made by the company in that period shall not be allowable under section 338 by virtue of subsection (2)(b) of that section to the extent that, when taken together with any qualifying donations already made by the company in that period, the amount given, after deducting income tax under section 339(3), exceeds £5 million.

(2) If in a particular accounting period of a company the company has one or more associated companies, a qualifying donation made by the company in that period shall not be allowable under section 338 by virtue of subsection (2)(b) of that section to the extent that, when taken together with any qualifying donations already made by the company in that period, the amount given, after deducting income tax under section 339(3), exceeds the appropriate fraction of £5 million.

(3) Subsection (1) or (2) above shall not apply where—

    (a) the company concerned is not a close company in the accounting period concerned, and

    (b) in that period the maximum amount allowable under section 338 by virtue of subsection (2)(b) of that section ("the allowable maximum") is (apart from this subsection) less than a sum equal to 3 per cent. of the dividends paid on the company's ordinary share capital in that period ("the relevant sum");

and in such a case the allowable maximum in that period shall be the relevant sum.

(4) For the purposes of subsection (2) above, the appropriate fraction is a fraction whose numerator is one and whose denominator is one plus the number of associated companies.

(5) In applying subsections (1) to (4) above to any accounting period of a company, an associated company shall be disregarded if—

    (a) it has not carried on any trade or business at any time in that accounting period (or, if an associated company during part only of that accounting period, at any time in that part of that accounting period), or

(b) it is a charity throughout that accounting period (or, if an associated company during part only of that accounting period, throughout that part of that accounting period).

(6) In determining for the purposes of this section how many associated companies a company has got in an accounting period or whether a company has an associated company in an accounting period, an associated company shall be counted even if it was an associated company for part only of the period, and two or more associated companies shall be counted even if they were associated companies for different parts of the period.

(7) For an accounting period of less than 12 months the figure of £5 million specified in subsections (1) and (2) above shall be proportionately reduced.

(8) For the purposes of this section a company is an associated company of another at a particular time if at that time one of the two has control of the other or both are under the control of the same person or persons; and in this subsection "control" shall be construed in accordance with section 416."

(4) This section applies in relation to accounting periods ending on or after 1st October 1990.

GENERAL NOTE

This section imposes an upper limit on the gifts made by companies which qualify for relief under I.C.T.A. 1988, s.339. In the case of close companies it is £5 million if the company has had no other associated companies during any part of the relevant accounting period, whilst in the case of companies which are not close companies it is three per cent. of the dividends paid on the company's ordinary share capital.

If there is an associated company for any part of the relevant accounting period then the maximum figure is reduced by a fraction being

$$\frac{1}{1 + \text{number of associated companies.}}$$

For these purposes certain associated companies are disregarded—those that have not carried on any trade or business during the accounting period or those that are charities.

In so far as a relevant accounting period is less than twelve months there will be a proportionate reduction of what would otherwise be the maximum amount.

Savings

Tax-exempt special savings accounts

28.—(1) After section 326 of the Taxes Act 1988 there shall be inserted—

"Tax-exempt special savings accounts

326A. —(1) Subject to the provisions of section 326B, any interest or bonus payable on a deposit account in respect of a period when it is a tax-exempt special savings account shall not be regarded as income for any income tax purpose.

(2) An account is a "tax-exempt special savings account" for the purposes of this section if the conditions set out in subsections (3) to (9) below and any further conditions prescribed by regulations made by the Board are satisfied when the account is opened; and subject to section 326B it shall continue to be such an account until the end of the period of five years beginning with the day on which it is opened, or until the death of the account-holder if that happens earlier.

(3) The account must be opened on or after 1st January 1991 by an individual aged 18 or more.

(4) The account must be with a building society or an institution authorised under the Banking Act 1987.

(5) The account must be identified as a tax-exempt special savings account and the account-holder must not simultaneously hold any other such account (with the same or any other society or institution).

(6) The account must not be a joint account.

(7) The account must not be held on behalf of a person other than the account-holder.

(8) The account must not be connected with any other account held by the account-holder or any other person; and for this purpose an account is connected with another if—

    (a) either was opened with reference to the other, or with a view to enabling the other to be opened on particular terms, or with a view to facilitating the opening of the other on particular terms, and

    (b) the terms on which either was opened would have been significantly less favourable to the holder if the other had not been opened.

(9) There must not be in force a notice given by the Board to the society or institution prohibiting it from operating new tax-exempt special savings accounts.

Loss of exemption for special savings accounts

326B.—(1) A tax-exempt special savings account shall cease to be such an account if at any time after it is opened any of the conditions set out in subsections (4) to (8) of section 326A, or any further condition prescribed by regulations made by the Board, is not satisfied, or if any of the events mentioned in subsection (2) below occurs.

(2) The events referred to in subsection (1) above are—

    (a) the deposit of more than £3,000 in the account during the period of 12 months beginning with the day on which it is opened, more than £1,800 in any of the succeeding periods of 12 months, or more than £9,000 in total;

    (b) a withdrawal from the account which causes the balance to fall below an amount equal to the aggregate of—

        (i) all the sums deposited in the account before the time of the withdrawal, and

        (ii) an amount equal to income tax at the basic rate on any interest or bonus paid on the account before that time (and for this purpose the basic rate in relation to any interest or bonus is the rate that was the basic rate when the interest or bonus was paid);

    (c) the assignment of any rights of the account-holder in respect of the account, or the use of such rights as security for a loan.

(3) If at any time an account ceases to be a tax-exempt special savings account by virtue of subsection (1) above, the Income Tax Acts shall have effect as if immediately after that time the society or institution had credited to the account an amount of interest equal to the aggregate of any interest and bonus payable in respect of the period during which the account was a tax-exempt special savings account.

Tax-exempt special savings accounts: supplementary

326C.—(1) The Board may make regulations—

    (a) prescribing conditions additional to those set out in section 326A which must be satisfied if an account is to be or remain a tax-exempt special savings account;

    (b) making provision for the giving by the Board to building societies and other institutions of notices prohibiting them from operating new tax-exempt special savings accounts, including provision about appeals against the giving of notices;

    (c) requiring building societies and other institutions operating or proposing to operate tax-exempt special savings accounts to give information or send documents to the Board or to make documents available for inspection;

(d) making provision as to the transfer of tax-exempt special savings accounts from one building society or institution to another;

(e) generally for supplementing the provisions of sections 326A and 326B.

(2) The reference in section 326A to a deposit account shall be taken to include a reference to a share account with a building society, and accordingly that section, section 326B and subsection (1) above shall apply to such an account with the necessary modifications."

(2) In the Table in section 98 of the Taxes Management Act 1970 (penalties for failure to comply with notices etc), in each column, before "regulations under section 333" there shall be inserted—

"regulations under section 326C;".

(3) In section 149B of the Capital Gains Tax Act 1979, for subsection (4) there shall be substituted.

"(4) Any bonus to which section 326 (certified contractual savings schemes) or 326A (tax-exempt special savings accounts) of the Taxes Act 1988 applies shall be disregarded for all purposes of the enactments relating to capital gains tax."

GENERAL NOTE

This section contains the legislative framework for a new form of saving scheme involving a Tax Exempt Special Savings Account or "Tessa" for short. Each adult is to be entitled to own one such account which can be either with a commercial bank or building society. Income earned from such an account will be tax-free so long as the capital in it, which cannot exceed specified limits, and an amount equal to income tax at the basic rate or any interest or bonus previously paid is untouched for five years from the opening of the account. Accounts can be opened on or after January 1, 1991.

The new ss.326A and 326B set out the basic conditions that have to be satisfied before tax-free income can be enjoyed. Section 326A sets out conditions relating to the nature of the account itself and by whom and with whom it can be held. The section stipulates that only adults can open accounts which must not be joint accounts, nor held on behalf of some other person nor in any way connected with any other account held by the account holder or any third person.

The amounts deposited in a Tessa cannot exceed (1) £3,000 in the first 12 months after it is opened; (2) more than £1,800 in any succeeding 12-month period; (3) more than £9,000 in total over the five-year period at the end of which such account ceases to qualify for relief. The aim is to encourage regular saving. Tax relief on income from the account is lost if any of the capital is withdrawn over the five-year period. Income from the account can be withdrawn without loss of exemption so long as the income is the net of tax income (s.326B(2)(b)(ii)). If too much capital is deposited in the account or any excessive withdrawal takes place any tax exemption previously enjoyed is lost by virtue of s.326B(3).

Extension of SAYE

29. In section 326 of the Taxes Act 1988 (income tax relief for SAYE)—

(a) in subsection (1), after paragraph (b) there shall be inserted the words "or

(c) in respect of money paid to an institution authorised under the Banking Act 1987,";

(b) in the subsection, for the words "be disregarded" onwards there shall be substituted the words "not be regarded as income for any income tax purpose.";

(c) in subsection (2), after the words "building society" there shall be inserted the words "or an institution authorised under the Banking Act 1987"; and

(d) after subsection (3) there shall be inserted—

"(4) In this section "certified contractual savings scheme" means, in relation to an institution authorised under the Banking Act 1987, a scheme—

(a) providing for periodical contributions by individuals for a specified period, and

(b) certified by the Treasury as corresponding to a scheme certified under subsection (2) above, and as qualifying for exemption under this section."

GENERAL NOTE
    Interest and terminal bonuses payable under contractual saving schemes ("Save As You Earn") are exempt from income tax under I.C.T.A. 1988, s.326. This section extends the definition of persons who can offer such schemes to include banks as opposed to only Building Societies and the Department of National Savings.

Building societies and deposit-takers

30. Schedule 5 to this Act (which contains provisions relating to building societies, deposit-takers and investors) shall have effect.

Employee share ownership trusts

Conditions for roll-over relief

31.—(1) Relief is available under section 33(1) below where each of the seven conditions set out in subsections (2) to (8) below is fulfilled.

(2) The first condition is that a person (the claimant) makes a disposal of shares, or his interest in shares, to the trustees of a trust which—

(a) is a qualifying employee share ownership trust at the time of the disposal, and

(b) was established by a company (the founding company) which immediately after the disposal was a trading company or the holding company of a trading group.

(3) The second condition is that the shares—

(a) are shares in the founding company,

(b) form part of the ordinary share capital of the company,

(c) are fully paid up,

(d) are not redeemable, and

(e) are not subject to any restrictions other than restrictions which attach to all shares of the same class or a restriction authorised by paragraph 7(2) of Schedule 5 to the Finance Act 1989.

(4) The third condition is that, at any time in the entitlement period, the trustees—

(a) are beneficially entitled to not less than 10 per cent. of the ordinary share capital of the founding company,

(b) are beneficially entitled to not less than 10 per cent. of any profits available for distribution to equity holders of the founding company, and

(c) would be beneficially entitled to not less than 10 per cent. of any assets of the founding company available for distribution to its equity holders on a winding-up.

(5) The fourth condition is that the claimant obtains consideration for the disposal and, at any time in the acquisition period, all the amount or value of the consideration is applied by him in making an acquisition of assets or an interest in assets (replacement assets) which—

(a) are, immediately after the time of the acquisition, chargeable assets in relation to the claimant, and

(b) are not shares in, or debentures issued by, the founding company or a company which is (at the time of the acquisition) in the same group as the founding company;

but the preceding provisions of this subsection shall have effect without the words ", at any time in the acquisition period," if the acquisition is made pursuant to an unconditional contract entered into in the acquisition period.

(6) The fifth condition is that, at all times in the proscribed period, there are no unauthorised arrangements under which the claimant or a person

connected with him may be entitled to acquire any of the shares, or an interest in or right deriving from any of the shares, which are the subject of the disposal by the claimant.

(7) The sixth condition is that no chargeable event occurs in relation to the trustees in—
  (a) the chargeable period in which the claimant makes the disposal,
  (b) the chargeable period in which the claimant makes the acquisition, or
  (c) any chargeable period falling after that mentioned in paragraph (a) above and before that mentioned in paragraph (b) above;

and "chargeable period" here means a year of assessment or (if the claimant is a company) an accounting period of the claimant for purposes of corporation tax.

(8) The seventh condition is that the disposal is made on or after 20th March 1990.

GENERAL NOTE

The Finance Act 1989 introduced qualifying employee share ownership schemes ("ESOP"), the main advantage of which is a statutory right to obtain deductions in computing profits for contributions towards such schemes. ESOPs have not proved popular particularly because of the restrictive conditions that must be met to obtain qualification. This and the following sections of the Act provide for a rollover relief from capital gains tax on a sale of shares to such schemes in the hope of encouraging their use. The relief requires, as with rollover relief on a sale of business assets, the reinvestment of the sale proceeds into new chargeable assets. The new assets can however be of any description so long as they are "chargeable".

The structure of the relief is set out in ss.31 to 35 whereas ss.36 to 38 contain provisions for recovery of the relief if the ESOP breaches certain rules for qualifying ESOPs and the deferred gain has not already been taxed. Ordinarily, as with the rollover relief available on the replacement of business assets, the gain rolled over will be brought into charge on a sale of the replacement assets.

The relief given by this group of sections is not available on a gift of shares but a hold over relief on such gift may be available under C.G.T.A. 1979, s.126.

In order to obtain the relief the basic conditions that must be satisfied are as follows:
  (1) there is a disposal of shares to the trustees of an ESOP which was established by a trading company or a holding company of a trading group at the time of the establishment;
  (2) the shares must be ordinary shares in the founding company, must be fully paid up, must not be redeemable, and must not be subject to restrictions other than those attaching to all shares of the same class;
  (3) the ESOP unit must own at least 10 per cent. of the founding company at some time in the period of 12 months commencing on the date of the sale;
  (4) the claimant must obtain consideration on his disposal and apply it in acquiring new "chargeable assets" within either six months from the date of the sale or the date the 10 per cent. stake is acquired, whichever is the later;
  (5) there must be no arrangements in the period between the date of disposal and acquisition permitting the claimant to reacquire the shares disposed of;
  (6) there must be no chargeable event as defined in F.A. 1989, s.69, in relation to the trustees of the ESOP concerned in the periods referred to in s.31(7);
  (7) the disposal must be made on or after March 20, 1990.

Conditions for relief: supplementary

32.—(1) This section applies for the purposes of section 31 above.

(2) The entitlement period is the period beginning with the disposal, and ending on the expiry of twelve months beginning with the date of the disposal.

(3) The acquisition period is the period beginning with the disposal, and ending on the expiry of six months beginning with—
  (a) the date of the disposal, or
  (b) if later, the date on which the third condition (set out in section 31(4) above) first becomes fulfilled.

(4) The proscribed period is the period beginning with the disposal, and ending on—
  (a) the date of the acquisition, or

(b) if later, the date on which the third condition (set out in section 31(4) above) first becomes fulfilled.

(5) All arrangements are unauthorised unless—

(a) they arise wholly from a restriction authorised by paragraph 7(2) of Schedule 5 to the Finance Act 1989, or

(b) they only allow one or both of the following as regards shares, interests or rights, namely, acquisition by a beneficiary under the trust and appropriation under an approved profit sharing scheme.

(6) An asset is a chargeable asset in relation to the claimant at a particular time if—

(a) at that time he is resident or ordinarily resident in the United Kingdom, and

(b) were the asset to be disposed of at that time, a gain accruing to him would be a chargeable gain.

(7) An asset is also a chargeable asset in relation to the claimant at a particular time if, were it to be disposed of at that time, any gain accruing to him on the disposal would be a chargeable gain—

(a) in respect of which he would be chargeable to capital gains tax under section 12(1) of the Capital Gains Tax Act 1979 (non-resident with United Kingdom branch or agency), or

(b) which would form part of his chargeable profits for corporation tax purposes by virtue of section 11(2)(b) of the Taxes Act 1988 (non-resident companies).

(8) But an asset is not a chargeable asset in relation to the claimant at a particular time if, were he to dispose of the asset at that time, he would fall to be regarded for the purposes of any double taxation relief arrangements as not liable in the United Kingdom to tax on any gains accruing to him on the disposal; and "double taxation relief arrangements" means arrangements having effect by virtue of section 788 of the Taxes Act 1988 (as extended to capital gains tax by section 10 of the Capital Gains Tax Act 1979).

(9) The question whether a trust is at a particular time a qualifying employee share ownership trust shall be determined in accordance with Schedule 5 to the Finance Act 1989; and "chargeable event" in relation to trustees has the meaning given by section 69 of that Act.

(10) The expressions "holding company," "trading company" and "trading group" have the meanings given by paragraph 1 of Schedule 20 to the Finance Act 1985; and "group" (except in the expression "trading group") shall be construed in accordance with section 272 of the Taxes Act 1970.

(11) "Ordinary share capital" in relation to the founding company means all the issued share capital (by whatever name called) of the company, other than capital the holders of which have a right to a dividend at a fixed rate but have no other right to share in the profits of the company.

(12) Schedule 18 to the Taxes Act 1988 (group relief: equity holders and profits or assets available for distribution) shall apply for the purposes of section 31(4) above as if—

(a) the trustees were a company,

(b) the references to section 413(7) to (9) of that Act were references to section 31(4) above,

(c) the reference in paragraph 7(1)(a) to section 413(7) of that Act were a reference to section 31(4) above, and

(d) paragraph 7(1)(b) were omitted.

GENERAL NOTE

This section defines various terms used in s.31.

The relief

33.—(1) In a case where relief is available under this subsection the

claimant shall, on making a claim in the period of two years beginning with the acquisition, be treated for the purposes of the 1979 Act—
  (a) as if the consideration for the disposal were (if otherwise of a greater amount or value) of such amount as would secure that on the disposal neither a gain nor a loss accrues to him, and
  (b) as if the amount or value of the consideration for the acquisition were reduced by the excess of the amount or value of the actual consideration for the disposal over the amount of the consideration which the claimant is treated as receiving under paragraph (a) above.
(2) Relief is available under subsection (3) below where—
  (a) relief would be available under subsection (1) above but for the fact that part only of the amount or value mentioned in section 31(5) above is applied as there mentioned, and
  (b) all the amount or value so mentioned except for a part which is less than the amount of the gain (whether all chargeable gain or not) accruing on the disposal is so applied.
(3) In a case where relief is available under this subsection the claimant shall, on making a claim in the period of two years beginning with the acquisition, be treated for the purposes of the 1979 Act—
  (a) as if the amount of the gain accruing on the disposal were reduced to the amount of the part mentioned in subsection (2)(b) above, and
  (b) as if the amount or value of the consideration for the acquisition were reduced by the amount by which the gain is reduced under paragraph (a) above.
(4) Nothing in subsection (1) or (3) above shall affect the treatment for the purposes of the 1979 Act of the other party to the disposal or of the other party to the acquisition.
(5) The provisions of the 1979 Act fixing the amount of the consideration deemed to be given for a disposal or acquisition shall be applied before the preceding provisions of this section are applied.
(6) In this section "the 1979 Act" means the Capital Gains Tax Act 1979.

GENERAL NOTE
  This section contains the relief applicable if the conditions contained in s.31 are met. The relief is a rollover relief similar to that available on a replacement of business assets where relief under C.G.T.A. 1979, s.115, is available. The main difference between the two is that the relief given by this clause is available whatever type of replacement asset is acquired so long as it is a "chargeable" asset.
  As with s.115 the relief is available whether the whole or part of the consideration is applied in acquiring a new asset. If only part is acquired, however, the part not applied must be less than the gain otherwise arising. The effect of the relief is to reduce the cost of acquisition of the new asset for C.G.T. purposes, thereby leaving a crystallisation of the charge that would otherwise have arisen on a disposal of the shares concerned until a disposal of the new asset.

Dwelling-houses: special provision

34.—(1) Subsection (2) below applies where—
  (a) a claim is made under section 33 above,
  (b) immediately after the time of the acquisition mentioned in section 31(5) above and apart from this section, any replacement asset was a chargeable asset in relation to the claimant,
  (c) the asset is a dwelling-house or part of a dwelling-house or land, and
  (d) there was a time in the period beginning with the acquisition and ending with the time when section 33(1) or (3) above falls to be applied such that, if the asset (or an interest in it) were disposed of at that time, it would be within section 101(1) of the Capital Gains Tax Act 1979 (relief on disposal of private residence) and the individual there mentioned would be the claimant or the claimant's spouse.

(2) In such a case the asset shall be treated as if, immediately after the time of the acquisition mentioned in section 31(5) above, it was not a chargeable asset in relation to the claimant.

(3) Subsection (4) below applies where—

(a) the provisions of section 33(1) or (3) above have been applied,

(b) any replacement asset which, immediately after the time of the acquisition mentioned in section 31(5) above and apart from this section, was a chargeable asset in relation to the claimant consists of a dwelling-house or part of a dwelling-house or land, and

(c) there is a time after section 33(1) or (3) above has been applied such that, if the asset (or an interest in it) were disposed of at that time, it would be within section 101(1) of the Capital Gains Tax Act 1979 and the individual there mentioned would be the claimant or the claimant's spouse.

(4) In such a case—

(a) the asset shall be treated as if, immediately after the time of the acquisition mentioned in section 31(5) above, it was not a chargeable asset in relation to the claimant and adjustments shall be made accordingly, but

(b) any gain treated as accruing in consequence of the application of paragraph (a) above shall be treated as accruing at the time mentioned in subsection (3)(c) above or, if there is more than one such time, at the earliest of them.

(5) Subsection (6) below applies where—

(a) a claim is made under section 33 above,

(b) immediately after the time of the acquisition mentioned in section 31(5) above and apart from this section, any replacement asset was a chargeable asset in relation to the claimant,

(c) the asset was an option to acquire (or to acquire an interest in) a dwelling-house or part of a dwelling-house or land,

(d) the option has been exercised, and

(e) there was a time in the period beginning with the exercise of the option and ending with the time when section 33(1) or (3) above falls to be applied such that, if the asset acquired on exercise of the option were disposed of at that time, it would be within section 101(1) of the Capital Gains Tax Act 1979 and the individual there mentioned would be the claimant or the claimant's spouse.

(6) In such a case the option shall be treated as if, immediately after the time of the acquisition mentioned in section 31(5) above, it was not a chargeable asset in relation to the claimant.

(7) Subsection (8) below applies where—

(a) the provisions of section 33(1) or (3) above have been applied,

(b) any replacement asset which, immediately after the time of the acquisition mentioned in section 31(5) above and apart from this section, was a chargeable asset in relation to the claimant consisted of an option to acquire (or to acquire an interest in) a dwelling-house or part of a dwelling-house or land,

(c) the option has been exercised, and

(d) there is a time after section 33(1) or (3) above has been applied such that, if the asset acquired on exercise of the option were disposed of at that time, it would be within section 101(1) of the Capital Gains Tax Act 1979 and the individual there mentioned would be the claimant or the claimant's spouse.

(8) In such a case—

(a) the option shall be treated as if, immediately after the time of the acquisition mentioned in section 31(5) above, it was not a chargeable asset in relation to the claimant and adjustments shall be made accordingly, but

(b) any gain treated as accruing in consequence of the application of paragraph (a) above shall be treated as accruing at the time mentioned in subsection (7)(d) above or, if there is more than one such time, at the earliest of them.

(9) References in this section to an individual include references to a person entitled to occupy under the terms of a settlement.

GENERAL NOTE

As mentioned in the commentary to s.31, the rollover relief given by s.33 is available whatever the nature of the new assets acquired, so long as they are "chargeable assets" immediately after the time of acquisition. A dwelling-house occupied as a main residence by a taxpayer immediately after its acquisition would not be a "chargeable asset" because C.G.T.A. 1979, s.101, would preclude a gain accruing on its disposal being a chargeable gain. Nevertheless, without more provision dwelling-houses which subsequently became main residences would still qualify as "chargeable assets" if only the time immediately after acquisition were looked at. If this were so it would enable a rollover of the gain arising on the disposal of the shares into a tax free asset. This section attempts to stop this being possible. By subss. (1) and (2) if a dwelling house becomes occupied as a main residence prior to the time a claim is made under s.33 the asset is treated as not being a chargeable asset immediately after the time of acquisition so as to preclude the relief. Where subsequent to the claim being made a house becomes occupied as a main residence by the claimant the relief is once again lost as a result of subss. (3) and (4). The chargeable gain accruing is only treated as accruing, however, at the time the circumstances occur giving rise to the loss of relief.

Subss. (5) to (8) contain similar provisions to subss. (1) to (4) save that they deal with the case where the new asset is an option to acquire a house where the option is subsequently examined and the house becomes occupied as the main residence of the claimant.

Shares: special provision

35.—(1) Subsection (2) below applies where—
(a) a claim is made under section 33 above,
(b) immediately after the time of the acquisition mentioned in section 31(5) above and apart from this section, any replacement asset was a chargeable asset in relation to the claimant,
(c) the asset consists of shares, and
(d) in the period beginning with the acquisition and ending when section 33(1) or (3) above falls to be applied relief is claimed under Chapter III of Part VII of the Taxes Act 1988 (business expansion scheme) in respect of the asset.

(2) In such a case the asset shall be treated as if, immediately after the time of the acquisition mentioned in section 31(5) above, it was not a chargeable asset in relation to the claimant.

(3) Subsection (4) below applies where—
(a) the provisions of section 33(1) or (3) above have been applied,
(b) any replacement asset which, immediately after the time of the acquisition mentioned in section 31(5) above and apart from this section, was a chargeable asset in relation to the claimant consists of shares, and
(c) after section 33(1) or (3) above has been applied relief is claimed under Chapter III of Part VII of the Taxes Act 1988 in respect of the asset.

(4) In such a case the asset shall be treated as if, immediately after the time of the acquisition mentioned in section 31(5) above, it was not a chargeable asset in relation to the claimant and adjustments shall be made accordingly.

GENERAL NOTE

Section 35 deals with a similar situation to s.34 in that it is contemplating a case where an asset is acquired which on acquisition is a chargeable asset but which ceases to be so after the time of acquisition. The new asset relevant to s.35 is shares qualifying for BES relief, a disposal of which qualifies for C.G.T. relief by virtue of C.G.T.A. 1979, s.149C. In effect this section precludes a rollover into shares qualifying for such relief.

Chargeable event when replacement assets owned

36.—(1) Subsection (3) below applies where—
(a) the provisions of section 33(1) or (3) above are applied,
(b) a chargeable event occurs in relation to the trustees on or after the date on which the disposal is made (and whether the event occurs before or after the provisions are applied or the passing of this Act),
(c) the claimant was neither an individual who died before the chargeable event occurs nor trustees of a settlement which ceased to exist before the chargeable event occurs, and
(d) the condition set out below is fulfilled.

(2) The condition is that, at the time the chargeable event occurs, the claimant or a person then connected with him is beneficially entitled to all the replacement assets.

(3) In a case where this subsection applies, the claimant or connected person (as the case may be) shall be deemed for all purposes of the Capital Gains Tax Act 1979—
(a) to have disposed of all the replacement assets immediately before the time when the chargeable event occurs, and
(b) immediately to have reacquired them,
at the relevant value.

(4) The relevant value is such value as secures on the deemed disposal a chargeable gain equal to—
(a) the amount by which the amount or value of the consideration mentioned in section 33(1)(b) above was treated as reduced by virtue of that provision (where it applied), or
(b) the amount by which the amount or value of the consideration mentioned in section 33(3)(b) above was treated as reduced by virtue of that provision (where it applied).

(5) In a case where subsection (3) above would apply if "all" read "any of" in subsection (2) above, subsection (3) shall nevertheless apply, but as if—
(a) in subsection (3)(a) "all the replacement assets" read "the replacement assets concerned," and
(b) the relevant value were reduced to whatever value is just and reasonable.

(6) Subsection (7) below applies where—
(a) subsection (3) above applies (whether or not by virtue of subsection (5) above), and
(b) before the time when the chargeable event occurs anything has happened as regards any of the replacement assets such that it can be said that a charge has accrued in respect of any of the gain carried forward by virtue of section 33(1) or (3) above.

(7) If in such a case it is just and reasonable for subsection (3) above to apply as follows, it shall apply as if—
(a) the relevant value were reduced (or further reduced) to whatever value is just and reasonable, or
(b) the relevant value were such value as secures that on the deemed disposal neither a gain nor a loss accrues (if that is just and reasonable);
but paragraph (a) above shall not apply so as to reduce the relevant value below that mentioned in paragraph (b) above.

(8) For the purposes of subsection (6)(b) above the gain carried forward by virtue of section 33(1) or (3) above is the gain represented by the amount which by virtue of either of those provisions falls to be deducted from the expenditure allowable in computing a gain accruing on the disposal of

replacement assets (that is, the amount found under subsection (4)(a) or (b) above, as the case may be).

(9) In this section "chargeable event" in relation to trustees has the meaning given by section 69 of the Finance Act 1989.

GENERAL NOTE

This and the next two sections contain charging provisions if an ESOP breaches the rules for qualifying ESOPs and such breach occurs before the gain rolled over has been taxed. This section deals with the simple case of where the breach occurs before the new assets have been sold. Section 37 deals with the case of where the new assets have been disposed of but the gain rolled over under C.G.T.A. 1979, s.115. Section 31 deals with the case of where the new assets were shares and have been disposed of in consideration of the receipt of qualifying corporate bonds in circumstances where no disposal and thus no crystallisation of charge is regarded as taking place.

A breach of the ESOP rules occurs when a chargeable event, as defined in F.A. 1989, s.69, takes place. It includes, for example, a retention by the trustees of shares for longer than seven years. Where a breach occurs, in a case where relief under s.33 has been obtained, it results in the claimant facing the charge to C.G.T. which but for the relief he would have faced on the disposal to the ESOP concerned. As an anti-avoidance measure a like charge can arise when the replacement asset is owned by a person "connected" with the claimant. Thus a gift from husband to wife would not prevent the clawback of the relief, such a gift not of itself crystallising a charge. Where a connected person has acquired the replacement assets in circumstances where the disposal to him crystallised the deferred charge, the charge on him should be reduced by virtue of the provisions in ss.(6) and (9).

Chargeable event when replacement property owned

37.—(1) Subsection (3) below applies where—
(a) paragraphs (a) to (c) of section 36(1) above are fulfilled, and
(b) the condition set out below is fulfilled.
(2) The condition is that—
(a) before the time when the chargeable event occurs, all the gain carried forward by virtue of section 33(1) or (3) above was in turn carried forward from all the replacement assets to other property on a replacement of business assets, and
(b) at the time the chargeable event occurs, the claimant or a person then connected with him is beneficially entitled to all the property.
(3) In a case where this subsection applies, the claimant or connected person (as the case may be) shall be deemed for all purposes of the 1979 Act—
(a) to have disposed of all the property immediately before the time when the chargeable event occurs, and
(b) immediately to have reacquired it,
at the relevant value.
(4) The relevant value is such value as secures on the deemed disposal a chargeable gain equal to—
(a) the amount by which the amount or value of the consideration mentioned in section 33(1)(b) above was treated as reduced by virtue of that provision (where it applied), or
(b) the amount by which the amount or value of the consideration mentioned in section 33(3)(b) above was treated as reduced by virtue of that provision (where it applied).
(5) In a case where subsection (3) above would apply if "all the" in subsection (2) above (in one or more places) read "any of the," subsection (3) shall nevertheless apply, but as if—
(a) in subsection (3)(a) "all the property" read "the property concerned," and
(b) the relevant value were reduced to whatever value is just and reasonable.
(6) Subsection (7) below applies where—

(a) subsection (3) above applies (whether or not by virtue of subsection (5) above), and

(b) before the time when the chargeable event occurs anything has happened as regards any of the replacement assets, or any other property, such that it can be said that a charge has accrued in respect of any of the gain carried forward by virtue of section 33(1) or (3) above.

(7) If in such a case it is just and reasonable for subsection (3) above to apply as follows, it shall apply as if—

(a) the relevant value were reduced (or further reduced) to whatever value is just and reasonable, or

(b) the relevant value were such value as secures that on the deemed disposal neither a gain nor a loss accrues (if that is just and reasonable);

but paragraph (a) above shall not apply so as to reduce the relevant value below that mentioned in paragraph (b) above.

(8) For the purposes of subsections (2) and (6)(b) above the gain carried forward by virtue of section 33(1) or (3) above is the gain represented by the amount which by virtue of either of those provisions falls to be deducted from the expenditure allowable in computing a gain accruing on the disposal of replacement assets (that is, the amount found under subsection (4)(a) or (b) above, as the case may be).

(9) For the purposes of subsection (2) above a gain is carried forward from assets to other property on a replacement of business assets if, by one or more claims under sections 115 to 121 of the 1979 Act, the chargeable gain accruing on a disposal of the assets is reduced, and as a result an amount falls to be deducted from the expenditure allowable in computing a gain accruing on the disposal of the other property.

(10) In this section "the 1979 Act" means the Capital Gains Tax Act 1979.

GENERAL NOTE

This section contains similar provisions to s.36 but deals with the case where the new assets acquired have been disposed of before a chargeable event occurs but in circumstances where the gain on such disposal has been rolled over under C.G.T.A. 1979, s.115.

Chargeable event when bonds owned

38.—(1) Subsection (3) below applies where—

(a) paragraphs (a) to (c) of section 36(1) above are fulfilled, and

(b) the condition set out below is fulfilled.

(2) The condition is that—

(a) all the replacement assets were shares (new shares) in a company or companies,

(b) there has been a transaction to which paragraph 10(1) of Schedule 13 to the Finance Act 1984 applies and as regards which all the new shares constitute the old asset and qualifying corporate bonds constitute the new asset, and

(c) at the time the chargeable event occurs, the claimant or a person then connected with him is beneficially entitled to all the bonds.

(3) In a case where this subsection applies, a chargeable gain shall be deemed to have accrued to the claimant or connected person (as the case may be); and the gain shall be deemed to have accrued immediately before the time when the chargeable event occurs and to be of an amount equal to the relevant amount.

(4) The relevant amount is an amount equal to the lesser of—

(a) the first amount, and

(b) the second amount.

(5) The first amount is—

(a) the amount of the chargeable gain that would be deemed to accrue under paragraph 10(1)(b) of Schedule 13 to the Finance Act 1984 if

there were a disposal of all the bonds at the time the chargeable event
occurs, or
(b) nil, if an allowable loss would be so deemed to accrue if there were
such a disposal.
(6) The second amount is an amount equal to—
(a) the amount by which the amount or value of the consideration mentioned in section 33(1)(b) above was treated as reduced by virtue of
that provision (where it applied), or
(b) the amount by which the amount or value of the consideration mentioned in section 33(3)(b) above was treated as reduced by virtue of
that provision (where it applied).
(7) In a case where subsection (3) above would apply if "all the" in
subsection (2) above (in one or more places) read "any of the," subsection
(3) shall nevertheless apply, but as if—
(a) in subsection (5) above "all the bonds" read "the bonds concerned,"
(b) the second amount were reduced to whatever amount is just and
reasonable, and
(c) the relevant amount were reduced accordingly.
(8) Subsection (9) below applies where—
(a) subsection (3) above applies (whether or not by virtue of subsection
(7) above), and
(b) before the time when the chargeable event occurs anything has happened as regards any of the new shares, or any of the bonds, such that
it can be said that a charge has accrued in respect of any of the gain
carried forward by virtue of section 33(1) or (3) above.
(9) If in such a case it is just and reasonable for subsection (3) above to
apply as follows, it shall apply as if—
(a) the second amount were reduced (or further reduced) to whatever
amount is just and reasonable, and
(b) the relevant amount were reduced (or further reduced) accordingly
(if the second amount is less than the first amount).
(10) But nothing in subsection (9) above shall have the effect of reducing
the second amount below nil.
(11) For the purposes of subsection (8)(b) above the gain carried forward
by virtue of section 33(1) or (3) above is the gain represented by the amount
which by virtue of either of those provisions falls to be deducted from the
expenditure allowable in computing a gain accruing on the disposal of
replacement assets (that is, the amount found under subsection (6)(a) or (b)
above, as the case may be).

GENERAL NOTE
This section contains further provisions similar to s.36 but dealing with the case where the
new assets were shares and have been disposed of in consideration of the receipt of qualifying
corporate bonds in circumstances where no crystallisation of the rolled over gain has occurred.

Information

39.—(1) An inspector may by notice in writing require a return to be made
by the trustees of an employee share ownership trust in a case where—
(a) a disposal of shares, or an interest in shares, has at any time been
made to them, and
(b) a claim is made under section 33(1) or (3) above.
(2) Where he requires such a return to be made the inspector shall specify
the information to be contained in it.
(3) The information which may be specified is information the inspector
needs for the purposes of sections 36 to 38 above, and may include information about—
(a) expenditure incurred by the trustees;
(b) assets acquired by them;

(c) transfers of assets made by them.

(4) The information which may be required under subsection (3)(a) above may include the purpose of the expenditure and the persons receiving any sums.

(5) The information which may be required under subsection (3)(b) above may include the persons from whom the assets were acquired and the consideration furnished by the trustees.

(6) The information which may be required under subsection (3)(c) above may include the persons to whom assets were transferred and the consideration furnished by them.

(7) In a case where section 33(1) or (3) above has been applied, the inspector shall send to the trustees of the employee share ownership trust concerned a certificate stating—

(a) that the provision concerned has been applied, and

(b) the effect of the provision on the consideration for the disposal or on the amount of the gain accruing on the disposal (as the case may be).

(8) For the purposes of this section, the question whether a trust is an employee share ownership trust shall be determined in accordance with Schedule 5 to the Finance Act 1989.

(9) In the Table in section 98 of the Taxes Management Act 1970 (penalties for failure to comply with notices etc.) at the end of the first column there shall be inserted—

"Section 39 of the Finance Act 1990."

GENERAL NOTE

This section gives the Revenue power to obtain information from trustees of an ESOP where a claim for relief has been made under s.33.

Other enactments

40.—(1) Section 117 of the 1979 Act (roll-over relief: depreciating assets) shall be amended as mentioned in subsections (2) to (4) below.

(2) In subsection (1) after "116 above" there shall be inserted "and section 33 of the Finance Act 1990."

(3) The following subsection shall be inserted after subsection (2)—

"(2A) Where section 33 of the Finance Act 1990 has effect subject to the provisions of this section, subsection (2)(b) above shall have effect as if it read—

"(b) section 36(3) of the Finance Act 1990 applies as regards asset No.2 (whether or not by virtue of section 36(5)), or."

(4) In subsection (3) for "and so claims" there shall be substituted "and claims."

(5) Where a charge can be said to accrue by virtue of section 36 or 37 above in respect of any of the gain carried forward by virtue of section 33(1) or (3) above, so much of the gain charged shall not be capable of being carried forward (from assets to other property or from property to other property) under sections 115 to 121 of the 1979 Act on a replacement of business assets.

(6) For the purpose of construing subsection (5) above—

(a) what of the gain has been charged shall be found in accordance with what is just and reasonable;

(b) section 37(8) and (9) above shall apply.

(7) In a case where—

(a) section 38 above applies in the case of bonds,

(b) subsequently a disposal of the bonds occurs as mentioned in paragraph 10(1)(b) of Schedule 13 to the Finance Act 1984, and

(c) a chargeable gain is deemed to accrue under paragraph 10(1)(b),

the chargeable gain shall be reduced by the relevant amount found under section 38 above or (if the amount exceeds the gain) shall be reduced to nil.

(8) The relevant amount shall be apportioned where the subsequent disposal is of some of the bonds mentioned in subsection (7)(a) above; and subsection (7) shall apply accordingly.

(9) In this section "the 1979 Act" means the Capital Gains Tax Act 1979.

GENERAL NOTE
This section contains various consequential amendments resulting from the relief given by s.33.

Insurance companies and friendly societies

Apportionment of income etc.

41. Schedule 4 to this Act (which makes provision about the apportionment of income etc. and related provision) shall have effect.

GENERAL NOTE
F.A. 1989 contained a number of provisions altering the taxation of life assurance companies. Ss.41 to 50 now introduce the second branch of those changes.

Schedule 6 contains a number of new provisions for the purpose of allocating income and gains between the different classes of business carried on by an insurance company.

Overseas life assurance business

42. Schedule 7 to this Act (which makes provision about the taxation of overseas life assurance business) shall have effect.

GENERAL NOTE
Schedule 7 contains a new tax regime for overseas life assurance business.

Deduction for policy holders' tax

43.—(1) In section 82(1)(a) of the Finance Act 1989 (computation of profits on Case I basis), for the words ", in respect of the period, are allocated to or expended on behalf of policy holders or annuitants" there shall be substituted the words "are allocated to, and any amounts of tax or foreign tax which are expended on behalf of, policy holders or annuitants in respect of the period."

(2) In section 436(3) of the Taxes Act 1988 (modified application of section 82 in relation to computations of profits of general annuity business or pension business), the words "and of the words "tax or" in section 82(1)(a)" shall be added at the end of paragraph (a).

(3) The Finance Act 1989 shall be deemed always to have had effect with the amendment made by subsection (1) above, and the amendment made by subsection (2) above shall have the same effect as, by virtue of section 84(5)(b) of that Act, it would have had if it had been made by Schedule 8 to that Act.

GENERAL NOTE
F.A. 1989, s.82, applies if the profits of an insurance company from life assurance business are computed under the Sched. D, Case I basis. In making the necessary computations it is permissible to deduct as an expense the amounts allocated to policyholders or annuitants (bonuses, reversionary bonuses and reductions in premium). In addition to amounts allocated to policyholders or annuitants any amounts expended on behalf of them by the company use are also to be deductible. This section now limits the later deductions to tax (including foreign tax) paid by the company on behalf of policyholders or annuitants.

This amendment is to be treated as if it had always been included in F.A. 1989, s.82.

Subs. (2) applies in respect of the computation of profits for the general annuity and pension business of a company. In that case the deductions in respect of expenditure are limited to foreign tax.

Reinsurance commissions

44.—(1) In section 85(2) of the Finance Act 1989 (receipts excluded from charge under Case VI of Schedule D), after paragraph (c) there shall be inserted—

"(ca) any reinsurance commission; or."

(2) In section 86 of the Finance Act 1989 (spreading of relief for expenses), at the end of subsection (1) there shall be added the words "and less any reinsurance commissions falling within section 76(1)(ca) of that Act."

(3) In section 76(1) of the Taxes Act 1988 (treatment of expenses of management), after paragraph (c) there shall be inserted—

"(ca) there shall also be deducted from the amount treated as the expenses of management for any accounting period any reinsurance commission earned in the period which is referable to basic life assurance business; and."

(4) Sections 85 and 86 of the Finance Act 1989 shall be deemed always to have had effect with the amendments made by subsections (1) and (2) above, and section 76 of the Taxes Act 1988 shall have effect as if the amendment made by subsection (3) above had been included among those made by section 87 of the Finance Act 1989.

(5) Nothing in subsection (2) above applies to commissions in respect of the reinsurance of liabilities assumed by the recipient company in respect of insurances made before 14th March 1989, but without prejudice to the application of that subsection to any reinsurance commission attributable to a variation on or after that date in a policy issued in respect of such an insurance; and for this purpose the exercise of any rights conferred by a policy shall be regarded as a variation of it.

GENERAL NOTE

F.A. 1989, s.85, applies to the method of computing an insurance company's profits from life assurance business on the basis of investment income and gains less management expenses. Subs. (2) of that section excludes certain specified receipts from the computation. To that list is now added reinsurance commissions (subs. (1)) and this addition is to be treated as if it had been enacted in F.A. 1989.

Subs. (2) relates to the spreading of relief for acquisition (expenses of acquiring new life assurance business) (F.A. 1989, s.86). By virtue of that section such expenses are spread over a seven-year period. One of the classes of deductible expenses is commissions (other than commissions in respect of industrial life assurance). There is now to be deducted from the aggregate figure for commissions any reinsurance commission earned in the period which is referable to the basic life assurance business. This amendment is to be treated as having been originally enacted in F.A. 1989 save that it will not apply to reinsurance commissions earned on liabilities arising from a policy made before March 14, 1989 (unless subsequently varied).

Similarly, in computing the deductible expenses of management of a life assurance company using the Sched. D, Case I basis the aggregate of the commissions paid by the company is to be reduced by reinsurance commissions earned in the period which is referable to basic life assurance business.

Policy holders' share of profits etc.

45.—(1) In section 88 of the Finance Act 1989 (corporation tax: policy holders' fraction of profits), in subsection (1) for the words "the policy holders' fraction of its relevant profits for any accounting period shall" there shall be substituted the words—

"(a) the policy holders' share of the relevant profits for any accounting period, or

(b) where the business is mutual business, the whole of those profits,

shall."

(2) In subsection (4) of that section, for the word "fraction" there shall be substituted the word "share," and after the words "that period" there shall be inserted the words ", or where the business is mutual business the whole of those profits,".

(3) For section 89 of that Act (which defines the shareholders' and policy holders' fractions) there shall be substituted—

"Policy holders' share of profits
89. —(1) The references in section 88 above to the policy holders' share of the relevant profits for an accounting period of a company carrying on life assurance business are references to the amount arrived at by deducting from those profits the Case I profits of the company for the period in respect of the business, reduced in accordance with subsection (2) below.

(2) For the purposes of subsection (1) above, the Case I profits for a period shall be reduced by—

(a) the amount, so far as unrelieved, of any franked investment income arising in the period as respects which the company has made an election under section 438(6) of the Taxes Act 1988, and

(b) the shareholders' share of any other unrelieved franked investment income arising in the period from investments held in connection with the business.

(3) For the purposes of this section "the shareholders' share" in relation to any income is so much of the income as is represented by the fraction

$$\frac{A}{B}$$

where—

A is an amount equal to the Case I profits of the company for the period in question in respect of its life assurance business, and

B is an amount equal to the excess of the company's relevant non-premium income and relevant gains over its relevant expenses and relevant interest for the period.

(4) Where there is no such excess as is mentioned in subsection (3) above, or where the Case I profits are greater than any excess, the whole of the income shall be the shareholders' share; and (subject to that) where there are no Case I profits, none of the income shall be the shareholders' share.

(5) In subsection (3) above the references to the relevant non-premium income, relevant gains, relevant expenses and relevant interest of a company for an accounting period are references respectively to the following items as brought into account for the period, so far as referable to the company's life assurance business,—

(a) the company's investment income from the assets of its long-term business fund together with its other income, apart from premiums;

(b) any increase in the value (whether realised or not) of those assets;

(c) expenses payable by the company;

(d) interest payable by the company;

and if for any period there is a reduction in the value referred to in paragraph (b) above (as brought into account for the period), that reduction shall be taken into account as an expense of the period.

(6) Except in so far as regulations made by the Treasury otherwise provide, in this section "brought into account" means brought into account in the revenue account prepared for the purposes of the Insurance Companies Act 1982; and where the company's period of account does not coincide with the accounting period, any reference to an amount brought into account for the accounting period is a reference to the corresponding amount brought into account for the period of account in which the accounting period is comprised, proportionately

reduced to reflect the length of the accounting period as compared with the length of the period of account.

(7) In this section "Case I profits" means profits computed in accordance with the provisions of the Taxes Act 1988 applicable to Case I of Schedule D.

(8) For the purposes of this section franked investment income is "unrelieved" if—

    (a) it has not been excluded from charge to tax by virtue of any provision,

    (b) no tax credit comprised in it has been paid, and

    (c) no relief has been allowed against it by deduction or set-off."

(4) In subsection (3) of section 434 of the Taxes Act 1988 (franked investment income etc.)—

    (a) for the words "policy holders' fraction" in both places where they occur there shall be substituted the words "policy holders' share";

    (b) in paragraph (a), after the word "income" there shall be inserted the words "from investments held in connection with the company's life assurance business";

    (c) in paragraph (b), for the words "only to the shareholders' fraction of that income" there shall be substituted the words "to that income excluding the amount within paragraph (a) above."

(5) In subsection (3A) of that section, for the word "fraction" there shall be substituted the word "share."

(6) In subsection (6) of that section, for the word "therefrom" onwards there shall be substituted the words "the policy holders' share of the relevant profits."

(7) After subsection (6) of that section there shall be inserted—

    "(6A) For the purposes of this section—

        (a) "the policy holders' share" of any franked investment income is so much of that income as is not the shareholders' share within the meaning of section 89 of the Finance Act 1989, and

        (b) "the policy holders' share of the relevant profits" has the same meaning as in section 88 of that Act."

(8) In section 434A of the Taxes Act 1988—

    (a) in subsection (1), for the word "fraction" there shall be substituted the word "share," and

    (b) in subsection (2), for the words "the relevant profits" onwards there shall be substituted the words " "the policy holders' share of the relevant profits" has the same meaning as in section 88 of the Finance Act 1989."

(9) In section 438 of the Taxes Act 1988, in subsection (6) after the words "part of its" there shall be inserted the word "relevant," and after that subsection there shall be inserted—

    "(6A) In subsection (6) above "relevant franked investment income" means the shareholders' share of franked investment income within subsection (1) above, and for this purpose "shareholders' share" has the same meaning as for the purposes of section 89 of the Finance Act 1989."

(10) The Finance Act 1989 shall be deemed always to have had effect with the amendments made by subsections (1) to (3) above, and the amendments made by subsections (4) to (9) above shall have the same effect as, by virtue of section 84(5)(b) of that Act, they would have had if they had been made by Schedule 8 to that Act.

(11) Paragraphs 1 and 3(3) of Schedule 8 to the Finance Act 1989 shall be deemed never to have had effect.

GENERAL NOTE

    F.A. 1989, s.88, provides that the rate of corporation tax chargeable on the policyholder's share of the life assurance company's profits shall be the same as the basic rate for income tax. This amendment in subs. (1) applies the same rate to the whole of the profits of the life assurance business if it is a mutual business.

This section introduces a new s.89 in F.A. 1989 for determining the policyholder's share and the shareholder's share of the profits of a life assurance company arising from its life assurance business. It is only the former which has the benefit of the special rate of corporate tax (equivalent to the basic rate of income tax). The old rules in the unamended F.A. 1989, s.89, are wholly replaced as from the outset.

Instead of evenly dividing the profits of the life assurance business in accordance with a stated formula it is now necessary to carry out calculations to determine the policyholder's share of the profits and once this is determined the remainder will be the shareholder's share.

The policyholder's share will be the profits of the life assurance business less the trading profit calculated under Sched. D, Case I by which trading profits have been reduced by:

(i) any unrelieved franked investment income in respect of which an election under I.C.T.A. 1988, s.438(6), had been made (to forgo payment of pension business tax credit); and

(ii) the shareholder's share of any other unrelieved franked investment income arising from investments held in connection with the life assurance business.

For this purpose the shareholder's share is determined by the formula in subs. (3) being the proportion which the Case I profit bears to the excess of income and gains over expenses. These figures are to be ascertained on the basis of the insurance company's revenue account.

Annual deemed disposal of holdings of unit trusts etc.

46.—(1) Where at the end of an accounting period the assets of an insurance company's long term business fund include—

(a) rights under an authorised unit trust, or

(b) relevant interests in an offshore fund,

then, subject to the following provisions of this section and to section 47 below, the company shall be deemed for the purposes of corporation tax on capital gains to have disposed of and immediately re-acquired each of the assets concerned at its market value at that time.

(2) Subsection (1) above shall not apply to assets linked solely to pension business or to assets of the overseas life assurance fund, and in relation to other assets (apart from assets linked solely to basic life assurance business) shall apply only to the relevant chargeable fraction of each class of asset.

(3) For the purposes of subsection (2) above "the relevant chargeable fraction" in relation to linked assets is the fraction of which—

(a) the denominator is the mean of such of the opening and closing long term business liabilities as are liabilities in respect of benefits to be determined by reference to the value of linked assets, other than assets linked solely to basic life assurance business or pension business and assets of the overseas life assurance fund; and

(b) the numerator is the mean of such of the opening and closing liabilities within paragraph (a) above as are liabilities of business the profits of which are not charged to tax under Case I or Case VI of Schedule D (disregarding section 85 of the Finance Act 1989).

(4) For the purposes of subsection (2) above "the relevant chargeable fraction" in relation to assets other than linked assets is the fraction of which—

(a) the denominator is the aggregate of—

(i) the mean of the opening and closing long term business liabilities, other than liabilities in respect of benefits to be determined by reference to the value of linked assets and liabilities of the overseas life assurance business, and

(ii) the mean of the opening and closing amounts of the investment reserve; and

(b) the numerator is the aggregate of—

(i) the mean of such of the opening and closing liabilities within paragraph (a) above as are liabilities of business the profits of which are not charged to tax under Case I or Case VI of Schedule D (disregarding section 85 of the Finance Act 1989), and

(ii) the mean of the appropriate parts of the opening and closing amounts of the investment reserve.

(5) For the purposes of this section an interest is a "relevant interest in an offshore fund" if—

(a) it is a material interest in an offshore fund for the purposes of Chapter V of Part XVII of the Taxes Act 1988, or

(b) it would be such an interest if the shares and interests excluded by subsections (6) and (8) of section 759 of that Act were limited to shares or interests in trading companies.

(6) For the purposes of this section the amount of an investment reserve and the "appropriate part" of it shall be determined in accordance with section 432A(8) and (9) of the Taxes Act 1988.

(7) In this section—

"authorised unit trust" has the same meaning as in section 468 of the Taxes Act 1988;

"market value" has the same meaning as in the Capital Gains Tax Act 1979;

"trading company" means a company—

(a) whose business consists of the carrying on of insurance business, or the carrying on of any other trade which does not consist to any extent of dealing in commodities, currency, securities, debts or other assets of a financial nature, or

(b) whose business consists wholly or mainly of the holding of shares or securities of trading companies which are its 90 per cent. subsidiaries;

and in this section and section 47 below other expressions have the same meanings as in Chapter I of Part XII of the Taxes Act 1988.

(8) Schedule 8 to this Act (which contains transitional provisions relating to the charge imposed by this section) shall have effect.

(9) Subject to the provisions of Schedule 8, this section shall have effect in relation to accounting periods beginning on or after 1st January 1991 or, where the Treasury by order appoint a later day, in relation to accounting periods beginning on or after that day (and not in relation to any earlier accounting period, even if the order is made after 1st January 1991 and the period has ended before it is made).

General Note

There will be annual deemed disposals and reacquisitions at market value by insurance companies of holdings in authorised unit trusts and interests in offshore funds if they are assets of the company's long term business. Excluded from these assets are those linked solely to pension business or assets of the overseas life assurance fund.

A fraction of the class of asset only will be chargeable determined by subs. (3) if a linked asset and by subs. (4) if not.

Subject to the transitional provisions contained in Sched. 8 this will apply to accounting periods beginning on or after January 1, 1991 or a later date if appointed by Treasury order. The power to defer the date will be exercised if the date for abolishing stamp duty on transfer of securities is set at December 31, 1991. This is to enable insurance companies to exchange holdings in authorised unit trusts and similar offshore funds for assets which are not subject to charge under s.46 without incurring a stamp duty charge.

The charge to capital gains tax will be spread in accordance with the provisions of s.47.

Spreading of gains and losses under section 46

47.—(1) Any chargeable gains or allowable losses which would otherwise accrue on disposals deemed by virtue of section 46 above to have been made at the end of a company's accounting period shall be treated as not accruing to it, but instead—

(a) there shall be ascertained the difference ("the net amount") between the aggregate of those gains and the aggregate of those losses, and

(b) one seventh of the net amount shall be treated as a chargeable gain or, where it represents an excess of losses over gains, as an allowable loss accruing to the company at the end of the accounting period, and

(c) a further one seventh shall be treated as a chargeable gain or, as the case may be, as an allowable loss accruing at the end of each succeeding accounting period until the whole amount has been accounted for.

(2) For any accounting period of less than one year, the fraction of one seventh referred to in subsection (1)(c) above shall be proportionately reduced; and where this subsection has had effect in relation to any accounting period before the last for which subsection (1)(c) above applies, the fraction treated as accruing at the end of that last accounting period shall also be adjusted appropriately.

(3) Where—

(a) the net amount for an accounting period of an insurance company represents an excess of gains over losses,

(b) the net amount for one of the next six accounting periods (after taking account of any reductions made by virtue of this subsection) represents an excess of losses over gains,

(c) there is (after taking account of any such reductions) no net amount for any intervening accounting period, and

(d) within two years after the end of the later accounting period the company makes a claim for the purpose in respect of the whole or part of the net amount for that period,

the net amounts for both the earlier and the later period shall be reduced by the amount in respect of which the claim is made.

(4) Subject to subsection (5) below, where a company ceases to carry on long term business before the end of the last of the accounting periods for which subsection (1)(c) above would apply in relation to a net amount, the fraction of that amount that is treated as accruing at the end of the accounting period ending with the cessation shall be such as to secure that the whole of the net amount has been accounted for.

(5) Where there is a transfer of the whole or part of the long term business of an insurance company ("the transferor") to another company ("the transferee") in accordance with a scheme sanctioned by a court under section 49 of the Insurance Companies Act 1982, any chargeable gain or allowable loss which (assuming that the transferor had continued to carry on the business transferred) would have accrued to the transferor by virtue of subsection (1) above after the transfer shall instead be deemed to accrue to the transferee.

(6) Where subsection (5) above has effect, the amount of the gain or loss accruing at the end of the first accounting period of the transferee ending after the day when the transfer takes place shall be calculated as if that accounting period began with the day after the transfer.

(7) Where the transfer is of part only of the transferor's long term business, subsection (5) above shall apply only to such part of any amount to which it would otherwise apply as is appropriate.

(8) Any question arising as to the operation of subsection (7) above shall be determined by the Special Commissioners who shall determine the question in the same manner as they determine appeals; but both the transferor and transferee shall be entitled to appear and be heard or to make representations in writing.

GENERAL NOTE

Any gain or loss arising by reason of the deemed disposal at the end of an insurance company's accounting period in accordance with s.46 shall not accrue in full immediately. One-seventh (or a proportionately adjusted part if the accounting period is not a year) will accrue and then at the end of each of the next six accounting periods a further one-seventh shall accrue.

If a net gain is spread forward under this provision and a notional net loss arises in one of the next six accounting periods this loss can be set off against the earlier gain provided that:

(i) there are no unrelieved net gains or losses in the intervening period; and

(ii) a claim is made within two years of the end of the accounting period in which the notional loss arises.

In the event of any accounting period being for less than one year there will then be an adjustment.

If the company ceases to carry on long-term business then the outstanding amount will accrue at the end of the accounting period in which the cessation occurs.

If there is a transfer of the long-term business to another company then the transferee will have the outstanding fractions accrue to it. If the transfer is of a part only then there is an apportionment as is appropriate.

Transfers of long term business

48. Schedule 9 to this Act (which makes provision about the tax consequences of certain transfers of long term business by insurance companies) shall have effect.

GENERAL NOTE

Schedule 9 introduces a number of reliefs to place the transferee of a long-term insurance business acquired pursuant to Insurance Companies Act 1982, s.49, in the same tax position as the transferor.

The transfer of assets will (if the requirements are satisfied) be a no gain/no loss disposal. Unrelieved management expenses and losses will be capable of deduction by the transferee and capital allowances may be used by the transferee.

Friendly societies: increased tax exemption

49.—(1) In subsection (2) of section 460 of the Taxes Act 1988 (exemption from tax for profits of friendly society arising from life or endowment business), in paragraph (c)—

(a) in sub-paragraph (i), for "£100" there shall be substituted "£150"; and

(b) after that sub-paragraph there shall be inserted—

"(ia) where the profits relate to contracts made after 31st August 1987 but before 1st September 1990, of the assurance of gross sums under contracts under which the total premiums payable in any period of 12 months exceed £100;".

(2) In subsection (3) of that section, for the words "of subsection (2)(c)(i)" there shall be substituted the words "of subsection (2)(c)(i) or (ia)."

(3) In subsection (3) of section 464 of that Act (maximum benefits payable to members of friendly societies), for the words from "Kingdom)" to the end there shall be substituted the words "Kingdom)—

(a) contracts under which the total premiums payable in any period of 12 months exceed £150; or

(b) contracts made before 1st September 1990 under which the total premiums payable in any period of 12 months exceed £100,

unless all those contracts were made before 1st September 1987."

(4) In subsection (4) of that section, for the word "limit" there shall be substituted the word "limits."

(5) In paragraph 3(8)(b)(ii) of Schedule 15 to that Act (amount of premiums to be disregarded in determining whether a policy meets conditions for it to be a qualifying policy), after the word "premiums" there shall be inserted the words "or, where those premiums are payable otherwise than annually, an amount equal to 10 per cent. of those premiums if that is greater."

GENERAL NOTE

This section raises the limits on premiums by reference to which the exempt business of a friendly society is determined. The limit of £100 per annum has been increased to £150 with effect from September 1, 1990.

Friendly societies: application of enactments

50.—(1) Section 463 of the Taxes Act 1988 (application to life or endowment business of friendly societies of Corporation Tax Acts as they apply to mutual life assurance business) shall be renumbered as subsection (1) of that section.

(2) After that provision as so renumbered there shall be added—

"(2) The provisions of the Corporation Tax Acts which apply on the transfer of the whole or part of the long term business of an insurance company to another company shall apply in the same way—

(a) on the transfer of the whole or part of the business of a friendly society to another friendly society (and on the amalgamation of friendly societies), and

(b) on the transfer of the whole or part of the business of a friendly society to a company (and on the conversion of a friendly society into a company),

so however that the Treasury may by regulations provide that those provisions as so applied shall have effect subject to such modifications and exceptions as may be prescribed by the regulations.

(3) Regulations under this section may include provision having retrospective effect."

GENERAL NOTE

I.C.T.A. 1988, s.463, treats the non-exempt profits of the life or endowment business of a registered friendly society in the same manner as for mutual life assurance business.

Subs. (2) now deals with the transfer of the whole or part of the business of a friendly society to another or to a company or an amalgamation or conversion to a company. In any of these circumstances the provisions concerning the transfer of the whole or part of the long-term business of an insurance company to another shall apply subject to such modifications as may be contained in regulations made by the Treasury.

Sched. 9 contains rules concerning such transfer by insurance companies.

The Treasury may also by order make regulations applying the corporation tax rules, applicable to transfers of long term businesses between insurance companies, to transfers in which the transferee is a friendly society.

Unit and investment trusts etc.

Authorised unit trusts

51. The following sections shall be inserted immediately before section 469 of the Taxes Act 1988—

"Authorised unit trusts: corporation tax

468E.—(1) This section has effect as regards an accounting period of the trustees of an authorised unit trust ending after 31st December 1990.

(2) Subject to subsection (3) below, the rate of corporation tax for a financial year shall be deemed to be the rate at which income tax at the basic rate is charged for the year of assessment which begins on 6th April in the financial year concerned.

(3) Where the period begins before 1st January 1991, subsection (2) above shall only apply for the purpose of computing corporation tax chargeable for so much of the period as falls in the financial year 1991 and subsection (4) below shall apply for the purpose of computing corporation tax chargeable for so much of the period as falls in the financial year 1990.

(4) So much of the period as falls after 31st December 1990 and before 1st April 1991 shall be deemed to fall in a financial year for which the

rate of corporation tax is the rate at which income tax at the basic rate is charged for the year 1990–91.

(5) Subsections (3) and (4) above shall not apply where the authorised unit trust concerned is a certified unit trust as respects the period.

(6) Where the period begins after 31st December 1990, section 338 shall have effect as if any reference to interest of any description were a reference to interest of that description on borrowing of a relevant description.

(7) Where the authorised unit trust concerned is a certified unit trust as respects the period, subsection (6) above shall have effect without the words preceding "section 338."

(8) For the purposes of subsection (6) above borrowing is of a relevant description if it is borrowing in respect of which there has been no breach during the accounting period of the duties imposed on the manager of the scheme by regulations under section 81 of the Financial Services Act 1986 with respect to borrowing by the trustees of the scheme.

(9) The Treasury may by regulations provide that for subsection (8) above (as it has effect for the time being) there shall be substituted a subsection containing a different definition of what constitutes borrowing of a relevant description for the purposes of subsection (6) above.

(10) Regulations under subsection (9) above may contain such supplementary, incidental, consequential or transitional provision as the Treasury think fit.

(11) In this section "certified unit trust" means, as respects an accounting period, a unit trust scheme in the case of which—

    (a) an order under section 78 of the Financial Services Act 1986 is in force during the whole or part of that accounting period, and

    (b) a certificate under section 78(8) of that Act, certifying that the scheme complies with the conditions necessary for it to enjoy the rights conferred by the UCITS directive, has been issued before or at any time during that accounting period.

(12) In this section—

"authorised unit trust" has the same meaning as in section 468,

"the UCITS directive" means the directive of the Council of the European Communities, dated 20th December 1985, on the co-ordination of laws, regulations and administrative provisions relating to undertakings for collective investment in transferable securities (no.85/611/EEC), and

"unit trust scheme" has the same meaning as in section 469.

Authorised unit trusts: distributions

468F.—(1) Subsection (2) below applies where—

    (a) as regards a distribution period ending after 31st December 1990 a dividend is treated by virtue of section 468(2) as paid to a unit holder (whether or not income is in fact paid to the unit holder),

    (b) the dividend is treated as paid by the trustees of a unit trust scheme which is an authorised unit trust as respects the accounting period in which the distribution period falls, and

    (c) on the date of payment the unit holder is within the charge to corporation tax and not a dual resident.

(2) For the purpose of computing corporation tax chargeable in the case of the unit holder the payment shall be deemed—

    (a) to be an annual payment, and not a dividend or other distribution, and

    (b) to have been received by the unit holder after deduction of income tax at the basic rate, for the year of assessment in which the date of payment falls, from a corresponding gross amount.

(3) Subsection (2) above shall have effect subject to the following provisions of this section and to section 468G.

(4) Subsection (2) above shall not apply where the rights in respect of which the dividend is treated as paid are held by the trustees of a unit trust scheme which is an authorised unit trust as respects the accounting period (of that scheme) in which the date of payment falls.

(5) Where the unit holder is on the date of payment the manager of the scheme, subsection (2) above shall not apply in so far as the rights in respect of which the dividend is treated as paid are rights held by him in the ordinary course of his business as manager of the scheme.

(6) Subsection (2) above shall not apply to so much of the payment as is attributable to income of the trustees arising before 1st January 1991.

(7) Subsection (6) above shall not apply where—

    (a) the payment is treated as made as regards a distribution period falling in an accounting period as respects which the authorised unit trust is a certified unit trust, or

    (b) the authorised unit trust is on the date of payment a fund of funds.

(8) In this section—

"authorised unit trust" has the same meaning as in section 468,

"certified unit trust" has the same meaning as in section 468E,

"distribution period" has the same meaning as in section 468,

"dual resident" means a person who is resident in the United Kingdom and falls to be regarded for the purposes of any arrangements having effect by virtue of section 788 as resident in a territory outside the United Kingdom,

"fund of funds" means a unit trust scheme the sole object of which is to enable the unit holders to participate in or receive profits or income arising from the acquisition, holding, management or disposal of units in unit trust schemes, and

"unit trust scheme" has the same meaning as in section 469."

Dividends paid to investment trusts

468G.—(1) Section 468F(2) shall not apply in a case where—

    (a) the first condition set out below is fulfilled, and

    (b) if one or more of the second to fourth conditions set out below applies, the condition (or each of the conditions) which applies is fulfilled.

(2) The first condition is that—

    (a) the unit holder is a company which is an investment trust as respects the accounting period of the company that includes 20th March 1990, and

    (b) immediately before the end of 20th March 1990, not less than 90 per cent. by value of the company's investments consisted of units in a unit trust scheme which (or units in different unit trust schemes each of which) was an authorised unit trust on 20th March 1990.

(3) The second condition applies if the date of payment is included in an accounting period of the company which falls after the company's accounting period that includes 20th March 1990; and the condition is that the company is an investment trust as respects—

    (a) the accounting period of the company that includes the date of payment, and

    (b) each (if any) accounting period of the company which falls after the company's accounting period that includes 20th March 1990 and before the company's accounting period that includes the date of payment.

(4) The third condition applies if the company makes an investment after 20th March 1990, and on or before the date of payment, in units in a unit trust scheme which is an authorised unit trust on the date of payment; and the condition is that, immediately before the end of the date of payment, each unit held by the company in a unit trust scheme which is an authorised unit trust on that date is a unit in a unit trust scheme—
    (a) in which the company held units immediately before the end of 20th March 1990, and
    (b) which was an authorised unit trust on 20th March 1990.
(5) The fourth condition applies if—
    (a) the third condition applies, and
    (b) immediately before the end of 20th March 1990 the company held units in more than one unit trust scheme which was an authorised unit trust on that date;
and the condition is that the investments made by the company after 20th March 1990, and on or before the date of payment, were made in accordance with the requirements applicable to the investment of funds of the company on 20th March 1990.
(6) For the purposes of this section—
    (a) "authorised unit trust" has the same meaning as in section 468,
    (b) "unit trust scheme" has the same meaning as in section 469, and
    (c) a unit trust scheme is an authorised unit trust on a particular date if it is an authorised unit trust as respects the accounting period of the scheme that includes that date."

GENERAL NOTE

Since January 1, 1990, unit trusts which are freely marketable within the EEC have been charged to corporation tax at a rate equal to the basic rate of income tax. In addition these unit trusts get relief for management expenses and interest on permitted borrowings (see I.C.T.A. 1988, s.468B).

From January 1, 1991, this tax regime is to be extended to all authorised unit trusts (defined in I.C.T.A. 1988, s.468). This means that even if not freely marketable within the EEC they will now be chargeable at the basic rate of income tax rather than the main rate of corporation tax. Also the few authorised unit trusts not previously able to get relief for management expenses or interest (those investing in gilts or sterling deposits) will now be able to.

For accounting periods beginning before January 1, 1991, but ending after December 31, 1990, the basic rate charge will only apply to so much of the period as falls within the financial year 1991. So much of the period as falls between December 31, 1990 and April 1, 1991, shall be charged at the basic rate for the year 1990/91. These rules do not apply to a certified unit trust which is governed by I.C.T.A. 1988, ss.468A, B and C.

Section 468F treats any distributions to companies investing in authorised unit trusts as being an annual payment from which basic rate tax has been deducted unless the payment is made to either:
(a) another authorised unit trust; or
(b) a manager of the scheme holding the units in the ordinary course of its business.

This applies to distribution periods ending after December 31, 1990, save as regards income of the trustees arising before January 1, 1991.

The treatment provided for in s.468F will not apply to distributions made by an investment trust company which immediately before the end of March 20, 1990, had not less than 90 per cent. value of its assets invested in authorised unit trusts if one of the three conditions contained in s.468F(2) to (4) is satisfied.

The three conditions are
    (i) in each accounting period following March 20, 1990 (including the one in which the payment is made) the company has been an investment trust;
    (ii) the company makes an investment after March 20, 1990, but on or before the date of payment in units in a trust which is authorised at the date of payment provided that all units held at the date of payment were also held before the end of March 20, 1990 and were in authorised trusts.
    (iii) if (ii) above applies and before the end of March 20, 1990, the company held units in more than one authorised trust provided that any subsequent investments on or

before the payment date were made in accordance with requirements applicable
to the investment of funds of the company on March 20, 1990.

Unit trusts: repeals

52.—(1) The Taxes Act 1988 shall have effect subject to the following
provisions of this section.

(2) In section 468 (authorised unit trusts) subsection (5) shall not apply as
regards a distribution period beginning after 3lst December 1990.

(3) Where a particular distribution period is by virtue of subsection (2)
above the last distribution period as regards which section 468(5) applies in
the case of a trust, the trustees' liability to income tax in respect of any source
of income chargeable under Case III of Schedule D shall be assessed as if
they had ceased to possess the source of income on the last day of that
distribution period.

(4) But where section 67 of the Taxes Act 1988 applies by virtue of
subsection (3) above, it shall apply with the omission from subsection (1)(b)
of the words from "and shall" to "this provision."

(5) Section 468B (certified unit trusts: corporation tax) shall not apply as
regards an accounting period ending after 31st December 1990.

(6) Section 468C (certified unit trusts: distributions) shall not apply as
regards a distribution period ending after 3lst December 1990.

(7) Section 468D (funds of funds: distributions) shall not apply as regards
a distribution period ending after 3lst December 1990.

(8) In this section "distribution period" has the same meaning as in section
468 of the Taxes Act 1988.

GENERAL NOTE

I.C.T.A. 1988, s.468(5), provides that an authorised unit trust is not treated as a company for
tax purposes if the trustees may only invest in gilts or on the money market. As regards
distribution periods beginning after December 31, 1990, this rule no longer applies and so such
unit trusts will be subject to corporation tax in accordance with the provisions in I.C.T.A. 1988,
s.468.

In the last distribution period of a unit trust within subs. (5) the trustees will be taxed as if the
source of their income had ceased on the last day of the distribution period. The rules regarding
cessation contained in I.C.T.A. 1988, s.67, will apply so that the trustees will be charged to tax
on the actual income for the period. The tax on the income of the preceding period will not be
affected, however.

The special rules relating to certified unit trusts contained in ss.468B, C and D will not apply
as regards a distribution period ending after December 31, 1990.

Unit trust managers: exemption from bond-washing provisions

53.—(1) Section 732 of the Taxes Act 1988 (application of bond-washing
provisions to dealers in securities) shall have effect, and be deemed always
to have had effect, with the insertion of the following subsection after
subsection (5)—

"(5A) Subsection (1) above shall not apply if the securities are
rights in a unit trust scheme and the subsequent sale is carried
out by the first buyer in the ordinary course of his business as
manager of the scheme."

(2) Section 472 of the Taxes Act 1970 (corresponding provision of the old
law) shall be deemed always to have had effect with the insertion after
subsection (5) of the subsection set out in subsection (1) above.

GENERAL NOTE

I.C.T.A. 1988, s.732, contains the anti-bondwashing rules which are aimed at preventing
sales of securities with a view to converting income into capital. Managers of authorised unit
trusts are to be allowed to sell units back to persons who sold units prior to those units becoming
ex div. provided the transactions are undertaken by the manager in the ordinary course of

business. It applies to all accounting periods ending after April 5, 1970. It puts the managers in the same position as Stock Exchange market members.

Indexation: collective investment schemes

54.—(1) The provisions specified in subsection (2) below (which provide for an indexation allowance on the disposal of assets) shall not apply in the case of a disposal if each of the three conditions set out below is fulfilled.

(2) The provisions are—
(a) in the Finance Act 1982, sections 86(4) and 87 and, in Schedule 13, paragraphs 1 to 7, 8(2)(c) and 10(3), and
(b) in the Finance Act 1985, section 68(4) to (8) and, in Schedule 19, paragraphs 1(3), 2, 5, 7(3), 8(1)(b) and (c), 11 to 15, 18, 22 and 23.

(3) The first condition is that the disposal is of rights in property to which collective investment arrangements relate; and—
(a) collective investment arrangements are arrangements which constitute a collective investment scheme;
(b) "collective investment scheme" has the same meaning as in the Financial Services Act 1986.

(4) Subject to subsection (5) below, the second condition is that, at some time in the relevant ownership period, not less than 90 per cent. of the market value (at that time) of the investment property then falling within the arrangements was represented by—
(a) non-chargeable assets,
(b) shares in a building society, or
(c) such assets and such shares.

(5) In a case where—
(a) the arrangements are ones under which the contributions of the participants, and the profits or income out of which payments are to be made to them, are pooled in relation to separate parts of the property in question, and
(b) the disposal is of rights in property falling within a separate part,
subsection (4) above shall have effect as if the reference to the arrangements were to the separate part.

(6) For the purposes of subsection (4) above the relevant ownership period is the period which begins with the later of—
(a) the earliest date on which any relevant consideration was given for the acquisition of the rights, and
(b) 1st April 1982,
and ends with the day on which the disposal is made.

(7) For the purposes of subsection (4) above investment property is all property other than cash awaiting investment.

(8) For the purposes of subsection (4) above an asset is a non-chargeable asset if, were it to be disposed of—
(a) at the time the rights are disposed of, and
(b) by a person resident in the United Kingdom,
any gain accruing on the disposal would not be a chargeable gain.

(9) In subsection (4)(b) above "shares" and "building society" have the same meanings as in the Building Societies Act 1986.

(10) For the purposes of subsection (6) above relevant consideration is consideration which, assuming the application of Chapter II of Part II of the Capital Gains Tax Act 1979 to the disposal of the rights, would fall to be taken into account in determining the amount of the gain or loss accruing on the disposal, whether that consideration was given by or on behalf of the person making the disposal or by or on behalf of a predecessor in title of his whose acquisition cost represents (directly or indirectly) the whole or any part of the acquisition cost of the person making the disposal.

(11) The third condition is that the disposal is made on or after 20th March 1990.

GENERAL NOTE

This section removes the availability of the indexation allowance for capital gains tax from certain unit trusts so as to prevent the possibility of allowable losses being created by their application. This applies to funds which are invested as to not less than 90 per cent. in non-chargeable assets (such as deposit accounts or gilts) and building society shares or any combination of them. It affects unit trusts and offshore funds invested as gilt funds or sterling deposit funds.

Investment trusts

55.—(1) In section 842 of the Taxes Act 1988 (investment trusts) the following subsections shall be inserted after subsection (2)—

"(2A) Subsection (1)(e) above shall not apply as regards an accounting period if—

(a) the company is required to retain income in respect of the period by virtue of a restriction imposed by law, and

(b) the amount of income the company is so required to retain in respect of the period exceeds an amount equal to 15 per cent. of the income the company derives from shares and securities.

(2B) Subsection (2A) above shall not apply where—

(a) the amount of income the company retains in respect of the accounting period exceeds the amount of income it is required by virtue of a restriction imposed by law to retain in respect of the period, and

(b) the amount of the excess or, where the company distributes income in respect of the period, that amount together with the amount of income which the company so distributes is at least £10,000 or, where the period is less than 12 months, a proportionately reduced amount.

(2C) Paragraph (e) of subsection (1) above shall not apply as regards an accounting period if the amount which the company would be required to distribute in order to fall within that paragraph is less than £10,000 or, where the period is less than 12 months, a proportionately reduced amount."

(2) This section applies in relation to accounting periods ending on or after the day on which this Act is passed.

GENERAL NOTE

In order to be an investment trust the requirements set out in I.C.T.A. 1988, s.842, must be satisfied. One is that the company does not retain more than 15 per cent. of the income received from the shares and securities held by it. This can lead to a conflict if the general company law requires that it should be retained as a matter of prudence. The change introduced by this clause enables the 15 per cent. limit to be exceeded if it is required by a restriction imposed by law to do so. Similarly, if the amount distributed would not exceed £10,000, then it need not incur the administrative costs of making such a distribution.

Securities

Convertible securities

56. Schedule 10 to this Act (convertible securities) shall have effect.

Deep gain securities

57.—(1) In Schedule 11 to the Finance Act 1989 (deep gain securities) paragraph 1 (meaning of deep gain security) shall be amended as follows.

(2) The following sub-paragraph shall be inserted after sub-paragraph (3)—

"(3A) In the case of a security issued on or after 9th June 1989, for the purposes of sub-paragraph (2) above "redemption" does not include any redemption which may be made before maturity only if—

(a) the person who issued the security fails to comply with the duties imposed on him by the terms of issue,

(b) the person who issued the security becomes unable to pay his debts, or

(c) the security was issued by a company and a person gains control of the company in pursuance of the acceptance of an offer made by that person to acquire shares in the company."

(3) The amendment made by this section shall be deemed always to have had effect.

GENERAL NOTE

Sched. 11 of the Finance Act 1989 provides for the taxation of deep gain securities which is similar to that relating to deep discount securities.

One difficulty has been that an amount payable might be regarded as a deep gain no matter what the reason for the redemption of the security.

The following occurrences will not now cause the provisions of Sched. 11 to operate in the event of a redemption:

(i) a breach of duty by the user of the security;

(ii) the inability of the issuer to pay its debts; or

(iii) a take over of the issuer company.

Qualifying indexed securities

58.—(1) In Schedule 11 to the Finance Act 1989 (deep gain securities) paragraph 2 (qualifying indexed securities) shall be amended as follows.

(2) In sub-paragraph (2)(c) for the words from "the security" to "8th June 1989" there shall be substituted the words "the security was quoted in the official list of a recognised stock exchange at the time it was issued."

(3) The following sub-paragraphs shall be inserted after sub-paragraph (8)—

"(8A) If a security was issued before 9th June 1989, was not quoted in the official list of a recognised stock exchange at the time it was issued, but was quoted in such a list on 8th June 1989, for the purposes of sub-paragraph (2)(c) above it shall be deemed to have been quoted in that list at the time it was issued.

(8B) If a security was issued on or after 9th June 1989, and was quoted in the official list of a recognised stock exchange at a time after it was issued but before the end of the qualifying period, for the purposes of sub-paragraph (2)(c) above it shall be deemed to have been quoted in that list at the time it was issued; and the qualifying period is the period of one month beginning with the day on which the security was issued."

(4) The following sub-paragraph shall be inserted after sub-paragraph (11)—

"(11A) In a case where the terms of issue contain provision for the amount payable on redemption to be not less than a specified percentage of the issue price, the provision shall not prevent the fourth condition being fulfilled if the specified percentage is not greater than 10."

(5) The following sub-paragraph shall be inserted after sub-paragraph (12)—

"(12A) In a case where—

(a) the terms of issue contain provision for the amount payable on redemption in any of the qualifying circumstances (set out in sub-paragraph (13) below) to be not more than the issue price, and

(b) the security was issued on or after 9th June 1989,

the provision shall not prevent the fourth condition being fulfilled."

(6) In sub-paragraph (13)—

(a) for the words "and (12)" there shall be substituted the words ", (12) and (12A)," and

(b) in paragraph (d) the words "before 9th June 1989" shall be omitted.
(7) The amendments made by this section shall be deemed always to have had effect.

GENERAL NOTE
This section amends the meaning of the term "qualifying indexed securities" as used in the legislation concerning deep gain securities contained in F.A. 1989, Sched. 11. Such securities fall outside the legislation applicable to deep gain securities.

The first amendment is to exclude from the definition of deep gain securities, securities quoted at the time of issue (or within one month thereafter) and linked to a published index of share prices (see subss. (2) and (3)). Previously only such securities issued before June 9, 1989, were excluded. The further amendments made by subss. (4) and (5) are designed to exclude securities with nominal floors to their redemption value or with provisions for early redemption following the takeover of the issuer.

Deep discount securities

59.—(1) In Schedule 4 to the Taxes Act 1988 (deep discount securities) paragraph 1 (interpretation) shall be amended as follows.

(2) The following sub-paragraph shall be inserted after sub-paragraph (1A) (itself inserted by Schedule 10 to this Act)—

"(1B) Notwithstanding anything in sub-paragraph (1) above, for the purposes of this Schedule a security is not a deep discount security if—
    (a) it was issued on or after 1st August 1990, and
    (b) under the terms of issue, there is more than one date on which the holder will be entitled to require it to be redeemed by the company or the public body which issued it."

(3) This section shall come into force on 1st August 1990.

GENERAL NOTE
This section excludes from being deep discount securities, securities issued after August 1, 1990, if under the terms of issue there is more than one date on which the holder is entitled to require redemptions. Such a security will become subject to the provisions of F.A. 1989, Sched. 11 relating to deep gain securities.

Oil industry

Allowance for abandonment expenditure related to offshore machinery or plant

60. In section 62 of the Capital Allowances Act 1990 (treatment of demolition costs) in subsection (1)(b) after the words "machinery or plant" there shall be inserted "then, subject to section 62A"; and after that section there shall be inserted the following sections—

"Special allowance for demolition costs related to offshore machinery or plant

62A.—(1) Subject to subsection (3) below, this section applies to expenditure which, apart from this section, would fall within section 62(1)(b) and which is incurred—
    (a) by any person carrying on a ring fence trade; and
    (b) for the purposes of or in connection with the closing down of, or of any part of, an oil field, within the meaning of Part I of the Oil Taxation Act 1975; and
    (c) on the demolition of machinery or plant which has been brought into use for the purposes of that trade and which is or forms part of an offshore installation or a submarine pipe-line;
and in this section any such expenditure is referred to as "abandonment expenditure."

(2) In this section "ring fence trade" means activities which—

(a) fall within any of paragraphs (a) to (c) of subsection (1) of section 492 of the principal Act (treatment of oil extraction activities etc. for tax purposes); and

(b) constitute a separate trade (whether by virtue of that subsection or otherwise).

(3) In subsection (1)(c) above—

(a) the reference to demolition is a reference to demolition which is carried out, wholly or substantially, in order to comply with an abandonment programme, within the meaning of Part I of the Petroleum Act 1987, or with any condition to which the approval of such a programme is subject; and

(b) "offshore installation" and "submarine pipe-line" have the same meaning as in that Part.

(4) If the person incurring any abandonment expenditure so elects,—

(a) for the chargeable period related to the incurring of that expenditure there shall be made to that person an allowance equal to the excess of the abandonment expenditure to which the election relates over any moneys received for the remains of the machinery or plant concerned; and

(b) that excess shall not be taken into account to increase qualifying expenditure as mentioned in section 62(1)(b).

(5) An election under this section—

(a) shall specify the abandonment expenditure to which it relates and the amounts of any such moneys received as mentioned in subsection (4)(a) above;

(b) shall be made by notice in writing given to the inspector not later than two years after the end of the chargeable period related to the incurring of the abandonment expenditure; and

(c) shall be irrevocable.

(6) This section has effect where the chargeable period related to the incurring of the expenditure or its basis period ends after 30th June 1991.

Treatment of post-cessation abandonment expenditure related to offshore machinery or plant

62B.—(1) Subsection (2) below applies in any case where—

(a) a person (in this section referred to as "the former trader") ceases to carry on a ring fence trade; and

(b) after 30th June 1991 and within the period of three years immediately following the last day on which he carried on that trade, the former trader incurs expenditure (in this section referred to as "post-cessation expenditure") on the demolition of machinery or plant which falls within section 62A(1)(c); and

(c) the post-cessation expenditure would have been abandonment expenditure for the purposes of section 62A if the demolition had been carried out and the expenditure incurred before the cessation of the ring fence trade; and

(d) apart from this section, the post-cessation expenditure would not be deductible in computing the income of the former trader for any purpose of corporation tax or income tax.

(2) Where this subsection applies, the qualifying expenditure of the former trader for the chargeable period related to the cessation of his ring fence trade shall be treated for the purposes of sections 24 and 25 as increased by so much of the post-cessation expenditure as exceeds any moneys received in the three year period referred to in paragraph (b) of subsection (1) above for the remains of the machinery or plant referred to in that paragraph.

(3) Where subsection (2) above applies, any moneys received as mentioned in that subsection shall not constitute income of the former trader for any purpose of income tax or corporation tax.

(4) All such adjustments shall be made, whether by way of discharge or repayment of tax or otherwise, as may be required in consequence of the provisions of this section.

(5) In this section "ring fence trade" has the same meaning as in section 62A."

GENERAL NOTE

This section inserts two new sections in C.A.A. 1990 in connection with demolition costs. Section 62 of that Act provided, *inter alia*, that, where demolished machinery or plant is not replaced, the net cost of demolition is treated as qualifying expenditure for the purposes of *ibid.*, s.24 ("writing-down allowances and balancing adjustments") and s.25 ("qualifying expenditure").

New ss.62A and 62B are to be inserted in relation to "offshore" machinery or plant. They come into effect for chargeable (or basis) periods ending after June 30, 1991.

Under the proposed s.62A, a right of election is given to taxpayers where:

(a) the trade carried on is a "ring fence trade";
(b) the expenditure arises in connection with the closing down of all or part of an oil field; and
(c) the machinery or plant demolished has been brought into use for the purposes of the trade and is, or is part of, an off-shore installation or a submarine pipeline. Such demolition must be carried out wholly or substantially to comply with an "abandonment programme" or a condition of such a programme under the Petroleum Act 1987.

Where an election is made, any excess of "abandonment expenditure" over moneys received for the remains of the machinery or plant is not treated as qualifying expenditure under s.62(1)(b). Instead, an allowance equal to the excess is given in full for the chargeable period related to the incurring of the expenditure.

Carrying back of losses referable to allowance for abandonment expenditure

61. In section 393 of the Taxes Act 1988 (loss relief: losses other than terminal losses) after subsection (4) there shall be inserted the following subsections—

"(4A) Where a company carrying on a ring fence trade incurs a loss in that trade in an accounting period for which an allowance falls to be made to it under section 62A of the 1990 Act, subsections (2) and (3) above shall have effect in relation to so much of the loss as does not exceed that allowance as if were a period of three years ending immediately before the beginning of the accounting period in which the loss is incurred.

(4C) In subsections (4A) above "ring fence trade" has the same meaning as in section 62A of the 1990 Act."

GENERAL NOTE

Section 61 operates together with s.60 which introduced the new 100 per cent. allowance for demolition expenditure on the abandonment of an offshore installation or submarine pipe-line. A company receiving the new allowance may have insufficient profits to utilise this allowance in the year in which it is available. Section 61 therefore provides that the allowance may be set against trading income of the ring fence trade for accounting periods ending within three years preceding the beginning of the accounting period in which the abandonment expenditure was incurred. Where an accounting period falls partly within this three-year period and partly prior to that period, then the trading income must be apportioned and the allowance set only against income of that part which falls within the three-year period.

CT treatment of PRT repayment

62.—(1) In section 500 of the Taxes Act 1988 (deduction of PRT in computing income for corporation tax purposes), in subsection (4) (reduction or extinguishment of deduction where PRT repaid)—

(a) at the beginning there shall be inserted the words "Subject to the
following provisions of this section"; and

(b) for the words "accounting period" there shall be substituted "calendar year."

(2) For subsection (5) of that section there shall be substituted the following subsections—

"(5) If, in a case where paragraph 17 of Schedule 2 to the 1975 Act
applies, an amount of petroleum revenue tax in respect of which a
deduction has been made under subsection (1) above is repaid by virtue
of an assessment under that Schedule or an amendment of such an
assessment, then, so far as concerns so much of that repayment as
constitutes the appropriate repayment,—

(a) subsection (4) above shall not apply; and

(b) the following provisions of this section shall apply in relation to
the company which is entitled to the repayment.

(6) In subsection (5) above and the following provisions of this
section—

(a) "the appropriate repayment" has the meaning assigned by sub-
paragraph (2) of paragraph 17 of Schedule 2 to the 1975 Act;

(b) in relation to the appropriate repayment, a "carried back loss"
means an allowable loss which falls within sub-paragraph (1)(a)
of that paragraph and which (alone or together with one or more
other carried back losses) gives rise to the appropriate
repayment;

(c) in relation to a carried back loss, "the operative chargeable
period" means the chargeable period in which the loss accrued;
and

(d) in relation to the company which is entitled to the appropriate
repayment, "the relevant accounting period" means the accounting period in or at the end of which ends the operative chargeable
period or, if the company's ring fence trade is permanently
discontinued before the end of the operative chargeable period,
the last accounting period of that trade.

(7) In computing for corporation tax the amount of the company's
income arising in the relevant accounting period from oil extraction
activities or oil rights there shall be added an amount equal to the
appropriate repayment; but this subsection has effect subject to subsection (8) below in any case where—

(a) two or more carried back losses give rise to the appropriate
repayment; and

(b) the operative chargeable period in relation to each of the carried
back losses is not the same; and

(c) if subsection (6)(d) above were applied separately in relation to
each of the carried back losses there would be more than one
relevant accounting period.

(8) Where paragraphs (a) to (c) of subsection (7) above apply, the
appropriate repayment shall be treated as apportioned between each of
the relevant accounting periods referred to in paragraph (c) of that
subsection in such manner as to secure that the amount added by virtue
of that subsection in relation to each of those relevant accounting
periods is what it would have been if—

(a) relief for each of the carried back losses for which there is a
different operative chargeable period had been given by a separate assessment or amendment of an assessment under Schedule 2
to the 1975 Act; and

(b) relief for a carried back loss accruing in an earlier chargeable
period had been so given before relief for a carried back loss
accruing in a later chargeable period.

(9) Any additional assessment to corporation tax required in order to give effect to the addition of an amount by virtue of subsection (7) above may be made at any time not later than six years after the end of the calendar year in which is made the repayment of petroleum revenue tax comprising the appropriate repayment.

(10) In this section "allowable loss" and "chargeable period" have the same meaning as in Part I of the 1975 Act and "calendar year" means a period of twelve months beginning on 1st January."

(3) At the end of section 502(1) of the Taxes Act 1988 (defined expressions for Chapter V of Part XII) there shall be added "and

"ring fence trade" means activities which—

(a) fall within any of paragraphs (a) to (c) of subsection (1) of section 492; and

(b) constitute a separate trade (whether by virtue of that subsection or otherwise)."

GENERAL NOTE

Petroleum revenue tax is deductible in computing the corporation tax charge for the accounting period during which the PRT chargeable period ends. If PRT is subsequently repaid, then the repayment must be added back to the corporation tax computation. Under the former law, the repayment was added back to the accounting period in which the deduction was originally taken. This clause alters the law by providing that, where a repayment of PRT arises out of the carry-back of a loss to preceding PRT chargeable periods, the repayment is to be added to the corporation tax computation for the accounting period *in which the loss arose.*

Section 62 is closely linked with s.121 (below) which adds a new paragraph 17 to Sched. 2 to the Oil Taxation Act 1975 dealing with PRT repayments arising due to the carry back of losses incurred in subsequent PRT accounting periods (called an "appropriate repayment"). Where a company receives an appropriate repayment, this has to be added to the company's income from oil extraction activities or oil rights for the accounting period during which ends the PRT chargeable period in which the loss was incurred. If the loss arises after the company's ring fence trade has ended, then the repayment must be added to the income of the last accounting period of that trade.

New subs. 505(8) contains provisions dealing with the situation where two or more losses are carried back, so that the appropriate repayment has to be apportioned to different accounting periods.

Disposals of certain shares deriving value from exploration or exploitation assets or rights

63.—(1) In Schedule 8 to the Finance Act 1988 (capital gains: assets held on 31st March 1982) in paragraph 12 (certain disposals excluded from elections under section 96(5) of that Act), in sub-paragraph (2) at the end of paragraph (c) there shall be inserted "or

(d) shares which, on 31st March 1982, were unquoted and derived their value, or the greater part of their value, directly or indirectly from oil exploration or exploitation assets situated in the United Kingdom or a designated area or from such assets and oil exploration or exploitation rights taken together."

(2) After the said sub-paragraph (2) there shall be inserted the following sub-paragraphs—

"(2A) For the purposes of sub-paragraph (2)(d) above,—

(a) "shares" includes stock and any security, as defined in section 254(1) of the Taxes Act 1988; and

(b) shares (as so defined) were unquoted on 31st March 1982 if, on that date, they were neither quoted on a recognised stock exchange nor dealt in on the Unlisted Securities Market;

but nothing in this paragraph affects the operation, in relation to such unquoted shares, of sections 77 to 81 of the Capital Gains Tax Act 1979 (under which, on a reorganisation etc., a new holding may fall to be treated as the same asset as the original shares).

(2B) In sub-paragraph (2)(d) above—

"designated area" means an area designated by Order in Council under section 1(7) of the Continental Shelf Act 1964;

"oil exploration or exploitation assets" shall be construed in accordance with sub-paragraphs (2C) and (2D) below; and

"oil exploration or exploitation rights" means rights to assets to be produced by oil exploration or exploitation activities (as defined in sub-paragraph (2D) below) or to interests in or to the benefit of such assets.

(2C) For the purposes of sub-paragraph (2)(d) above an asset is an oil exploration or exploitation asset if either—

(a) it is not a mobile asset and is being or has at some time been used in connection with oil exploration or exploitation activities carried on in the United Kingdom or a designated area; or

(b) it is a mobile asset which has at some time been used in connection with oil exploration or exploitation activities so carried on and is dedicated to an oil field in which the company whose shares are disposed of by the disposal or a person connected with that company, within the meaning of section 839 of the Taxes Act 1988, is or has been a participator;

and, subject to sub-paragraph (2D) below, expressions used in paragraphs (a) and (b) above have the same meaning as if those paragraphs were included in Part I of the Oil Taxation Act 1975.

(2D) In the preceding provisions of this paragraph "oil exploration or exploitation activities" means activities carried on in connection with—

(a) the exploration of land (including the seabed and subsoil) in the United Kingdom or a designated area, as defined in sub-paragraph (2B) above, with a view to searching for or winning oil; or

(b) the exploitation of oil found in any such land;

and in this sub-paragraph "oil" has the same meaning as in Part I of the Oil Taxation Act 1975."

(3) The amendments made by subsections (1) and (2) above have effect with respect to disposals on or after 22nd January 1990.

(4) Notwithstanding that, apart from this subsection, an election under section 96(5) of the Finance Act 1988 is irrevocable, where—

(a) such an election has been made before 22nd January 1990, and

(b) apart from subsection (1) above, the assets to the disposal of which the election would apply include assets falling within paragraph 12(2) (d) of Schedule 8 to the Finance Act 1988 (as set out in subsection (1) above),

the election may be revoked by notice in writing given to the inspector before 1st January 1991 by the person by whom the election was made.

GENERAL NOTE

This section gives effect to the first of two changes restricting capital losses on North Sea oil assets which were outlined in a Press Release issued on January 22, 1990. The section adds to the list of assets for which no election can be made under F.A. 1988, s.96(5), unquoted shares which derive their value from oil exploration or exploitation assets or rights. It operates in conjunction with s.64 (below) which introduces a new regime for calculating the chargeable gain on the disposal of an "oil industry asset."

F.A. 1988, s.96(5), provides that a person may elect that s.96(3) shall not apply to any disposals of assets held by him on March 31, 1982. The effect is that all such assets are deemed to have been disposed of and reacquired on March 31, 1982, and the person need not be concerned with whether s.96(3) might otherwise apply (dealing with such situation where, *inter alia*, a smaller gain would have accrued had there been no rebasing).

Certain assets cannot, however, be the objects of an election under s.96(5)—these include plant and machinery on which capital allowances can be claimed, assets held in connection with working mineral deposits, or a petroleum production licence (see F.A. 1988, Sched. 8, para. 12(2)). S.63 adds to this list shares which were unquoted on March 31.

Limitation of losses on disposal of oil industry assets

64.—(1) This section applies to a disposal of an oil industry asset where the following conditions are fulfilled—

(a) the disposal occurs on or after 22nd January 1990;

(b) the person making the disposal held the asset on 31st March 1982 or, by virtue of paragraph 1 of Schedule 8 to the Finance Act 1988 (previous no gain/no loss disposals), is treated as having held the asset on that date for the purposes of section 96 of that Act (rebasing to 1982 of assets held on 31st March 1982);

(c) disregarding the following provisions of this section, for the purposes of capital gains tax, a loss would accrue on the disposal; and

(d) in the application of section 96 of the Finance Act 1988 to the disposal, subsection (2) of that section (the rebasing to 1982 values) does not apply because of the operation of subsection (3)(b) of that section (a smaller loss accrues if subsection (2) does not apply).

(2) For the purposes of this section, the following are "oil industry assets"—

(a) a licence under the Petroleum (Production) Act 1934 or the Petroleum (Production) Act (Northern Ireland) 1964;

(b) shares falling within sub-paragraph (2)(d) of paragraph 12 of Schedule 8 to the Finance Act 1988 (exclusion of certain disposals from elections under section 96(5) of the Finance Act 1988);

(c) oil exploration or exploitation assets, which expression shall be construed, subject to subsection (3) below, in accordance with sub-paragraphs (2C) and (2D) of the said paragraph 12; and

(d) any interest in an asset falling within paragraphs (a) to (c) above.

(3) In the application of sub-paragraph (2C)(b) of paragraph 12 of Schedule 8 to the Finance Act 1988 for the purposes of subsection (2)(c) above, for the words from "the company whose shares" to "that company" there shall be substituted "the person making the disposal or a person connected with him."

(4) Where this section applies to a disposal, there shall be determined for the purposes of this section the loss or gain which would accrue on the disposal on the following assumptions—

(a) that subsection (2) of section 96 of the Finance Act 1988 continues not to apply on the disposal; and

(b) that, in calculating the indexation allowance on the disposal, subsection (4) of section 68 of the Finance Act 1985 (indexation based on 1982 values) does not apply;

and in the following provisions of this section the loss or gain (if any) on the disposal, determined on those assumptions, is referred to as the non-rebased loss or, as the case may be, the non-rebased gain.

(5) If there is a non-rebased loss on a disposal to which this section applies and that loss is less than the loss which accrues on the disposal as mentioned in subsection (1)(c) above, it shall·be assumed for the purposes of capital gains tax that the loss which accrues on the disposal is the non-rebased loss.

(6) If there is a non-rebased gain on a disposal to which this section applies, it shall be assumed for the purposes of capital gains tax that the oil industry asset concerned was acquired by the person making the disposal for a consideration such that, on the disposal, neither a gain nor a loss accrues to him.

(7) If, on the determination referred to in subsection (4) above, there is neither a non-rebased loss nor a non-rebased gain on a disposal, subsection (6) above shall apply in relation to the disposal as if there were a non-rebased gain on the disposal.

GENERAL NOTE

This section contains the second of the changes necessary to implement the restriction of capital losses on North Sea oil assets promised in the Press Release of January 22, 1990. These changes have been introduced because of the relatively high value of such assets in March 1982 due to the high oil price at that time. The section provides that, on the disposal of such assets, indexation allowance will be calculated on the original acquisition cost and not on their March 1982 values.

The section applies to the disposal after January 22, 1990, of an "oil industry asset" which was held on March 31, 1982 (or is treated as having been then held). An oil industry asset is a petroleum exploitation licence, shares deriving their value, or the greater part of their value, from oil exploration or exploitation assets (as covered by s.63), or any share in any of these assets. Where a loss would arise on the disposal of such an asset, and a smaller loss or a gain would have arisen on the disposal but for the March 1982 rebasing, then the gain or loss must be recalculated with the indexation allowance based on the original acquisition cost (and not the March 1982 value). This recalculated loss or gain is called the "non-rebased loss or gain."

If there is a non-rebased loss which is less than the loss calculated on March 1982 values, then the person can only deduct the smaller, non-rebased loss. If there is a non-rebased gain, then the disposal is treated as a no gain/no loss disposal. Similarly, if there is neither a non-rebased loss or gain, then the disposal is deemed to be a no gain/no loss disposal.

International

Dual resident companies: capital gains

65.— (1) In section 267 of the Taxes Act 1970 (company reconstructions etc.) after subsection (2) there shall be inserted—
(2A) This section does not apply in relation to an asset if the company acquiring it, though resident in the United Kingdom,—
  (a) is regarded for the purposes of any double taxation arrangements having effect by virtue of section 788 of the Taxes Act 1988 as resident in a territory outside the United Kingdom, and
  (b) by virtue of the arrangements would not be liable in the United Kingdom to tax on a gain arising on a disposal of the asset occurring immediately after the acquisition."
(2) In section 273 of the Taxes Act 1970 (transfers within a group) in subsection (2), after paragraph (d) there shall be inserted "or
(e) a disposal to a company which, though resident in the United Kingdom,—
    (i) is regarded for the purposes of any double taxation arrangements having effect by virtue of section 788 of the Taxes Act 1988 as resident in a territory outside the United Kingdom, and
    (ii) by virtue of the arrangements would not be liable in the United Kingdom to tax on a gain arising on a disposal of the asset occurring immediately after its acquisition."
(3) In section 276 of the Taxes Act 1970 (replacement of business assets by members of a group) in subsection (1A) for the words following "a dual resident investing company" there shall be substituted the words "or a company which, though resident in the United Kingdom,—
  (a) is regarded for the purposes of any double taxation arrangements having effect by virtue of section 788 of the Taxes Act 1988 as resident in a territory outside the United Kingdom, and
  (b) by virtue of the arrangements would not be liable in the United Kingdom to tax on a gain arising on a disposal of, or of the interest in, the new assets occurring immediately after the acquisition;
and in this subsection "the old assets" and "the new assets" have the same meanings as in section 115 of the Capital Gains Tax Act 1979, and "dual resident investing company" has the same meaning as in section 404 of the Taxes Act 1988."
(4) Subsections (1) and (2) above shall apply to disposals on or after 20th March 1990.
(5) Subject to subsection (6) below, subsection (3) above shall apply where the disposal of, or of the interest in, the old assets or the acquisition

of, or of the interest in, the new assets (or both) takes place on or after 20th March 1990.

(6) Subsection (3) above shall not apply where the acquisition takes place before 20th March 1990 and the disposal takes place within the period of twelve months beginning with the date of the acquisition or such longer period as the Board may by notice in writing allow.

GENERAL NOTE

This section is the first of a trio of sections making amendments to the existing tax legislation to take account of dual resident companies. Specifically, these amendments are aimed at companies which, though regarded as resident in the U.K. for domestic taxation purposes, are regarded as resident in another country for the purposes of a double taxation agreement. This situation arises because of the operation of the "tie-breaker clauses" in double taxation agreements.

Where a company is regarded as resident in the U.K. for U.K. domestic purposes, and resident in the other treaty country for that country's domestic tax purposes, the treaty has to decide in which country the company will be regarded as resident for the purposes of the treaty. This issue is decided by the tie-breaker clause; in most of the U.K.'s treaties this is the country where the effective management is carried out. If the place of effective management is outside the U.K., the consequence is that the company will, in some cases, be protected by the treaty against U.K. taxation on capital gains.

While this situation of companies being resident in the U.K. for domestic purposes but resident elsewhere for treaty purposes could exist prior to 1988, F.A. 1988, s.66 (which provided that companies incorporated in the U.K. would be regarded as resident in this country), widened the scope for this situation very considerably. It became very easy to incorporate a company in the U.K. but ensure that its effective management was carried out in another country, being a country whose treaty provided a shelter against U.K. taxation on capital gains.

This section combats such a structure by denying three reliefs to a company which, though resident in the U.K. for domestic purposes, is resident in another country for the purposes of a treaty and, as a result, is protected by the treaty from U.K. taxation on its capital gains. The three reliefs which are denied to such dual resident companies are:

(i) transfer of the whole or part of a company's business to another company (I.C.T.A. 1970, s.267);

(ii) transfers of assets within a group of companies (I.C.T.A. 1970, s.273); and

(iii) replacement of business assets by another member of a group (I.C.T.A. 1970, s.276).

The first two restrictions apply to any disposals after March 20, 1990. The third restriction generally applies where the disposal of the old assets or the acquisition of the new assets take place after March 20, 1990. Since, however, it is possible for the relief in s.276 to apply where an acquisition takes place within 12 months *before* the disposal of the old assets, the restriction will not apply where the acquisition has taken place before March 20, 1990, and the disposal of the old assets takes place within 12 months (or such longer period as may be permitted) after the acquisition.

Dual resident companies: transfers of assets abroad

66.—(1) In sections 742(8) and 745(4) of the Taxes Act 1988, after the words "incorporated outside the United Kingdom" there shall be inserted the words ", or regarded for the purposes of any double taxation arrangements having effect by virtue of section 788 as resident in a territory outside the United Kingdom,".

(2) Subject to subsection (3) below, this section shall apply in relation to transfers of assets and associated operations on or after 20th March 1990.

(3) In so far as the amendment of subsection (4) of section 745 relates to subsections (3)(b) and (5) of that section, it shall come into force on that date.

GENERAL NOTE

This section, like s.65, also deals with problems created by dual resident companies; that is, companies resident in the U.K. for domestic tax purposes, but deemed to be resident in another country for the purposes of a double taxation agreement. Previously, such companies would be regarded as resident in the U.K. for the purposes of I.C.T.A. 1988, ss.739 and 740 (avoidance of income by transfer of assets abroad), even though they would enjoy an exemption from U.K. taxation by virtue of the treaty.

This section therefore provides that, for the purposes of ss.739 and 740, and for the purposes of the information power in s.745, a company which is regarded as resident in another territory under a treaty shall be regarded as not resident in the U.K.

Dual resident companies: controlled foreign companies

67.—(1) In section 749 of the Taxes Act 1988, after subsection (4) there shall be inserted—

"(4A) For the purposes of this Chapter, any company which, though resident in the United Kingdom, is regarded for the purposes of any double taxation arrangements having effect by virtue of section 788 as resident in a territory outside the United Kingdom shall be treated as if it were resident outside the United Kingdom (and not resident in the United Kingdom)."

(2) In section 751(2) of that Act, after paragraph (b) there shall be inserted—

"(bb) the company becomes, or ceases to be, a company in relation to which section 749(4A) has effect; or."

(3) In Schedule 25 to that Act—

(a) paragraphs 2(1)(c) and 4(1)(c) shall be omitted,

(b) after paragraph 2(1) there shall be inserted—

"(1A) A payment of dividend to a company shall not fall within sub-paragraph (1)(d) above unless it is taken into account in computing the company's income for corporation tax.", and

(c) after paragraph 4(1) there shall be inserted—

"(1A) A payment to a company shall not be a subsequent dividend within the meaning of sub-paragraph (1)(b) above unless it is taken into account in computing the company's income for corporation tax."

(4) Subsections (1) and (2) above shall apply on and after 20th March 1990 and subsection (3) above shall apply to dividends paid on or after that date.

GENERAL NOTE

This is the third of the trio of sections dealing with dual resident companies. This amendment relates to the legislation dealing with controlled foreign companies in I.C.T.A. 1988, s.747, *et seq*. Any company which, though resident in the U.K. for domestic tax purposes, is resident in another territory for treaty purposes, is to be regarded as resident outside the U.K. for the controlled foreign company legislation.

The section makes one other change to the controlled foreign company legislation. There is a defence to a charge under that legislation if the controlled foreign company follows an acceptable distribution policy by paying dividends (directly or indirectly) to the U.K. parent (see I.C.T.A. 1988, Sched. 25, paras. 2 and 4). The change now provides that the dividend must be taken into account in computing the recipient company's income for corporation tax purposes. Effectively, therefore, the recipient cannot enjoy protection from U.K. corporation tax (by virtue of a treaty or otherwise).

Movements of capital between residents of member States

68.—(1) In section 765 of the Taxes Act 1988 (certain transactions unlawful unless carried out with Treasury consent), in subsection (1), after the words "Subject to the provisions of this section" there shall be inserted the words "and section 765A."

(2) After that section there shall be inserted—

"Movements of capital between residents of member States

765A.—(1) Section 765(1) shall not apply to a transaction which is a movement of capital to which Article 1 of the Directive of the Council of the European Communities dated 24th June 1988 No. 88/361/EEC applies.

(2) Where if that Article did not apply to it a transaction would be unlawful under section 765(1), the body corporate in question (that is to say, the body corporate resident in the United Kingdom) shall—

(a) give to the Board within six months of the carrying out of the transaction such information relating to the transaction, or to persons connected with the transaction, as regulations made by the Board may require, and

(b) where notice is given to the body corporate by the Board, give to the Board within such period as is prescribed by regulations made by the Board (or such longer period as the Board may in the case allow) such further particulars relating to the transaction, to related transactions, or to persons connected with the transaction or related transactions, as the Board may require."

(3) In section 98 of the Taxes Management Act 1970 (penalties for failure to furnish information and for false information)—

(a) in subsection (1), after the words "Subject to" there shall be inserted the words "the provisions of this section and;"

(b) after subsection (4) there shall be inserted—

"(5) In the case of a failure to comply with section 765A(2)(a) or (b) of the principal Act, subsection (1) above shall have effect as if for "£300" there were substituted "£3,000" and as if for "£60" there were substituted "£600".";

(c) in the first column of the Table, after "section 755" there shall be inserted "section 765A(2)(b);"; and

(d) in the second column of the Table, after "section 639" there shall be inserted "section 765A(2)(a);".

(4) This section shall apply to transactions carried out on or after 1st July 1990.

GENERAL NOTE

This section provides that Treasury consent will no longer be necessary for any transaction falling within I.C.T.A. 1988, s.765(1)(c) or (d), where that transaction is a movement of capital within EEC Council Directive 88/361/EEC of June 24, 1988 (the Capital Movements Directive). The transactions to which this applies are the issue of shares or debentures by a non-resident company over which a resident company has control, or the transfer of shares or debentures in a non-resident company over which a resident company has control. This amendment has effect with respect to transactions taking place on or after July 1, 1990. A Press Release was issued at the time of publication of the Finance Bill (April 19, 1990) explaining this provision.

While Treasury consent is no longer necessary for a transaction falling within this provision, and it will no longer be a criminal offence to carry out such a transaction without consent, nevertheless the transaction must be reported to the Board of Inland Revenue within six months together with such information as the Board may by regulation provide. Reporting will only be required for transactions which would previously have required special Treasury consent—any transaction which is covered by the Treasury's general consents will not require to be reported. An initial penalty of £3,000 and a daily penalty of £600 is provided for failure to comply with the reporting requirement.

European Economic Interest Groupings

69. Schedule 11 to this Act (which makes provision about the taxation of income and gains in the case of European Economic Interest Groupings) shall have effect.

GENERAL NOTE

Section 69 introduces Sched. 11 concerning the taxation of European Economic Interest Groupings. This legislation is deemed to have come into effect on July 1, 1989 (see Sched. 11, para. 5) (the date on which the EEC Council Regulation on European Economic Interest Groupings became directly applicable).

Transfer of United Kingdom branch or agency

70.—(1) After section 273 of the Taxes Act 1970 there shall be inserted—

"Transfer of United Kingdom branch or agency

273A.—(1) Subject to subsections (3) and (4) below, subsection (2) below applies for the purposes of corporation tax on chargeable gains where—

(a) there is a scheme for the transfer by a company ("company A")—
  (i) which is not resident in the United Kingdom, but
  (ii) which carries on a trade in the United Kingdom through a branch or agency,
  of the whole or part of the trade to a company resident in the United Kingdom ("company B"),

(b) company A disposes of an asset to company B in accordance with the scheme at a time when the two companies are members of the same group, and

(c) a claim in relation to th asset is made by the two companies within two years after the end of the accounting period of company B during which the disposal is made.

(2) Where this subsection applies—

(a) company A and company B shall be treated as if the asset were acquired by company B for a consideration of such amount as would secure that neither a gain nor a loss would accrue to company A on the disposal, and

(b) section 127(3) of the Finance Act 1989 shall not apply to the asset by reason of the transfer.

(3) Subsection (2) above does not apply where—

(a) company B, though resident in the United Kingdom,—
  (i) is regarded for the purposes of any double taxation arrangements having effect by virtue of section 788 of the Taxes Act 1988 as resident in a territory outside the United Kingdom, and
  (ii) by virtue of the arrangements would not be liable in the United Kingdom to tax on a gain arising on a disposal of the asset occurring immediately after its acquisition, or

(b) company B is—
  (i) a dual resident investing company, within the meaning of section 404 of the Taxes Act 1988, or
  (ii) an investment trust, within the meaning of section 842 of that Act.

(4) Subsection (2) above shall not apply unless any gain accruing to company A—

(a) on the disposal of the asset in accordance with the scheme, or

(b) where that disposal occurs after the transfer has taken place, on a disposal of the asset immediately before the transfer,

would be a chargeable gain and would, by virtue of section 11(2)(b) of the Taxes Act 1988, form part of its profits for corporation tax purposes.

(5) In this section "company" and "group" have the meanings which would be given by section 272 above if subsections (1)(a) and (2) of that section were omitted."

(2) In section 272(1) of the Taxes Act 1970—

(a) for the word "For" there shall be substituted the words "Except as otherwise provided, for," and

(b) the words ", subject to section 280(7) below," shall be omitted.

(3) In section 275 of that Act for subsection (1) there shall be substituted—

"(1) Where there is a disposal of an asset acquired in relevant circumstances, section 34 of the Capital Gains Tax Act 1979 (restriction of losses by reference to capital allowances) shall apply in relation to capital allowances made to the person from which it was acquired (so far as not taken into account in relation to a disposal of the asset by that person), and so on as respects previous transfers of the asset in relevant circumstances.

(1A) In subsection (1) above "relevant circumstances" means circumstances in which section 273 or 273A above applied or in which section 273 above would have applied but for subsection (2) of that section.

(1B) Subsection (1) above shall not be taken as affecting the consideration for which an asset is deemed under section 273 or 273A to be acquired."

(4) In section 281(2) of that Act, after the words "section 273" there shall be inserted the words "or 273A."

(5) In section 126C(4) of the Capital Gains Tax Act 1979—

(a) after the words "section 273" there shall be inserted the words "or 273A,"

(b) for the words "that section applies" there shall be substituted the words "either of those sections applies," and

(c) for the words "that section does not apply" there shall be substituted the words "neither of those sections applies."

(6) In paragraph 10(2)(c) of Schedule 13 to the Finance Act 1984, after the words "section 273(1)" there shall be inserted the words "or 273A."

(7) In—

(a) section 68(7A)(b) of the Finance Act 1985, and

(b) paragraph 1(3)(b) of Schedule 8 to the Finance Act 1988, after "273," there shall be inserted "273A,".

(8) In paragraph 5 of Schedule 11 to the Finance Act 1988—

(a) for the words "of the Taxes Act 1970 (which treats" there shall be substituted the words "or 273A of the Taxes Act 1970 (which treat," and

(b) for the words "section 273(1)," in the second place where they occur, there shall be substituted the words "either of those sections."

(9) This section shall apply to disposals on or after 20th March 1990.

GENERAL NOTE

This section contains a new relief from the charge to tax on capital gains where a non-resident company incorporates the whole or part of a trade previously carried on by a U.K. branch. Such a transaction would otherwise constitute a disposal chargeable to tax under C.G.T.A. 1979, s.12, or F.A. 1989, s.127(3) (deemed disposal where a non-resident ceases to carry on a trade through a branch or agency in the U.K.). The new provisions operate to deem the assets to be acquired by the new company for a consideration such that no gain or loss would accrue on the disposal, and F.A. 1989, s.127(3), is excluded. The relief applies to disposals on or after March 20, 1990.

In order for the relief to apply the following conditions must be satisfied:

(i) the transferor company ("Company A") is not resident in the U.K. but carries on a trade in the U.K. through a branch or agency and is liable to corporation tax on a disposal of assets by virtue of I.C.T.A. 1988, s.11(2)(b);

(ii) the disposal is to a company which is resident in the U.K. ("Company B") and which is not deemed to be resident in another territory by virtue of a double taxation agreement, nor is it a dual resident investing company or an investment trust;

(iii) the disposal is in accordance with a scheme for the transfer of the whole or part of the trade from Company A to Company B;

(iv) at the time of the transfer Company A and Company B are members of a group of companies; for this purpose the definition of a group includes companies not resident in the U.K. (new s.273A(5));

(v) a claim to relief is made by the two companies within two years of the end of the accounting period of Company B in which the disposal took place.

Two points deserve attention. First, the relief only applies if Company B is already a member of the same group as Company A; the new U.K. company must therefore be set up prior to the transfer. Secondly, Company B must be a company resident in the U.K. (*i.e.* in most cases, one incorporated in the U.K.) another non-resident company which is in the same group as Company A cannot qualify.

Section 70 operates by the inclusion in I.C.T.A. 1970 of a new s.273A. This new section itself operates by analogy with I.C.T.A. 1970, s.273 (relief for transfer of assets within a group). Subss. (3)–(8) of s.70 make consequential amendments applying those provisions relating to s.273 to the new s.273A.

Miscellaneous

Relief for interest

71. For the year 1990–91 the qualifying maximum defined in section 367(5) of the Taxes Act 1988 (limit on relief for interest on certain loans) shall be £30,000.

GENERAL NOTE

The limit on loans for house purchase on which interest relief is available is maintained at the level of £30,000 which has obtained since 1983.

Capital gains: annual exempt amount for 1990–91

72. For the year 1990–91 section 5 of the Capital Gains Tax Act 1979 (annual exempt amount) shall have effect as if the amount specified in subsection (1A) were £5,000; and accordingly subsection (1B) of that section (indexation) shall not apply for that year.

GENERAL NOTE

The annual exempt amount for capital gains tax remains at £5,000 (£2,500 in the case of most trusts). With the introduction of independent taxation from April 6, 1990, husbands and wives will each be entitled to their separate £5,000 exemption.

Business expansion scheme: abolition of "locality rule"

73.—(1) In Schedule 4 to the Finance Act 1988 (business expansion scheme: private rented housing), in paragraph 13 (exclusion of expensive dwelling-houses)—
   (a) in sub-paragraph (2) (assumptions to be made in arriving at value at the relevant date), for paragraph (a) there shall be substituted—
      "(a) on the assumption that the dwelling-house was in the same state as at the valuation date;"; and
   (b) sub-paragraph (3) (which includes the assumption that the locality was in the same state as at the valuation date) shall be omitted.
   (2) This section shall apply where the valuation date is on or after 20th March 1990.

GENERAL NOTE

The effect of this amendment is to omit the "locality rule" for Business Expansion Scheme companies letting residential property. The scheme does not apply to dwelling-houses with a market value of more than £85,000 (£125,000 in the case of Greater London) at the time of issuing the shares or, if later, of acquiring the property. At the date of valuation, increases in value due to improvements in the amenities of the locality were not allowed for in establishing the market value at the relevant date. This discouraged investment in run-down inner city areas, a disincentive which is now removed.

Debts of overseas governments etc.

74. After section 88 of the Taxes Act 1988 there shall be inserted—

   "Debts of overseas governments etc.
      88A.—(1) For any period of account of a company overseas ending on or after 20th March 1990, section 88B shall have effect for the purpose of restricting the extent to which a debt to which subsection (2)

below applies may be estimated to be bad for the purposes of section 74(j); and—

  (a) any deduction which may fall to be made in computing the company's profits or gains for the period, and

  (b) any addition which may fall to be so made (for example because the relevant percentage of the debt for the period is smaller than the amount estimated to be bad for an earlier period),

shall be determined accordingly.

  (2) Subject to subsection (3) below, this subsection applies to any debt—

  (a) which is owed by an overseas State authority, or

  (b) payment of which is guaranteed by an overseas State authority, or

  (c) which is estimated to be bad for the purposes of section 74(j) wholly or mainly because due payment is or may be prevented, restricted or subjected to conditions—

> (i) by virtue of any law of a State or other territory outside the United Kingdom or any act of an overseas State authority, or

> (ii) under any agreement entered into in consequence or anticipation of such a law or act.

  (3) Subsection (2) above does not apply to interest on a debt or to a debt which represents the consideration for the provision of goods or services.

  (4) In this section "overseas State authority" means—

  (a) a State or other territory outside the United Kingdom,

  (b) the government of such a State or territory,

  (c) the central bank or other monetary authority of such a State or territory,

  (d) a public or local authority in such a State or territory, or

  (e) a body controlled by such a State, territory, government, bank or authority;

and for this purpose "controlled" shall be construed in accordance with section 840.

Section 88A debts: restriction on deductions under section 74(j)

88B.—(1) Where this section has effect in relation to a debt, no more than the relevant percentage of the debt shall be estimated to be bad for the purposes of section 74(j).

  (2) The relevant percentage of a debt for any period of account of the company is such percentage (which may be zero) as may be determined in accordance with regulations by reference to the position at the end of that period.

  (3) Subsection (2) above has effect subject to the following provisions of this section, and in those provisions—

  (a) "the base period" means the last period of account of the company ending before 20th March 1990, and

  (b) "the base percentage," in relation to a debt, means such percentage (which may be zero) as may be determined in accordance with regulations by reference to the position at the end of the base period.

  (4) If for any period of account of the company which ends less than two years after the base period the percentage provided for in subsection (2) above in relation to a debt is greater than the base percentage, the base percentage shall be the relevant percentage for the first-mentioned period.

  (5) If for any later period of account of the company the percentage provided for in subsection (2) above in relation to a debt is greater than

the base percentage increased by five percentage points for each complete year (except the first) that has elapsed between—

(a) the end of the base period, and

(b) the end of the later period in question,

then the base percentage as so increased shall be the relevant percentage for the later period.

(6) In relation to a company which had no periods of account ending before 20th March 1990, the relevant percentage in relation to a debt shall be the same as it would have been on the assumption that the company had had such periods of account (and that any notional periods of account before its first actual period of account had been of one year each).

(7) In this section "regulations" means regulations made by the Treasury; but the Treasury shall not make any regulations under this section unless a draft of them has been laid before and approved by a resolution of the House of Commons.

Section 88A debts: restriction on other deductions

88C.—(1) Where—

(a) on or after 20th March 1990 a company incurs in respect of a debt a loss which would be allowed as a deduction in computing the amount of the company's profits or gains under Case I or Case II of Schedule D,

(b) section 88A(2) applies to the debt,

(c) either—

(i) a deduction is made in respect of the debt in accordance with section 74(j) for any period of account of the company before that in which the loss is incurred, or

(ii) the debt was acquired by the company on or after 20th March 1990 for a consideration greater than the price which it might reasonably have been expected to fetch on a sale in the open market at the time of acquisition, and

(d) the amount of the loss is greater than 5 per cent. of the debt,

then, subject to subsection (3) below, only such part of the loss as equals 5 per cent. of the debt shall be allowed as a deduction for the period of account in which the loss is incurred; but further parts calculated in accordance with subsection (2) below may be allowed for subsequent periods until the loss is exhausted.

(2) The part of the loss allowed as a deduction for any period of account after that in which the loss is incurred shall not exceed such amount as, together with any parts allowed under this section for earlier periods, is equal to 5 per cent. of the debt for each complete year that has elapsed between—

(a) the beginning of the period in which the loss was incurred, and

(b) the end of the period in question.

(3) Subsections (1) and (2) above shall not apply to a loss incurred on a disposal of the debt to an overseas State authority if the State or territory by reference to which it is an overseas State authority is the same as that by reference to which section 88A(2) applies to the debt.

(4) References in subsections (1) and (2) above to the incurring of a loss in respect of a debt include references to the making of a deduction, otherwise than in accordance with section 74(j), in respect of a reduction in the value of a debt; and for the purposes of those subsections such a deduction shall be treated as made immediately before the end of the period of account for which it is made."

GENERAL NOTE

Over the past two decades the commercial banks have made very large loans to foreign governments, particularly in the Third World. It has become apparent that much of this debt may be either uncollectable or subject to considerable delay in repayment. The provisions of I.C.T.A. 1988, s.74(j), governing the deduction of bad debts are inadequate to deal with the problem and accordingly three new sections, 88A, B and C are inserted to cover this situation. The purpose of the legislation is to give greater certainty about tax deductions and smooth out future increases in the cost of relief to the Exchequer. The rules for calculating the amount of debt eligible for tax relief follow in broad terms the existing Bank of England guidelines, known as "the matrix".

Section 88A

This section introduces the new rules by providing that relief under I.C.T.A. 1988, s.74(j), is to be restricted by reference to s.88B. It also defines the borrowers to whom the provisions apply as "overseas state authorities". The term normally used to refer to these borrowings is "sovereign debt". The provisions do not apply to interest on debt or commercial debt.

Section 88B

The section provides for regulations to be issued by the Treasury governing the percentage of sovereign debt which may be claimed for tax relief in each year. The regulations, which will require approval by the House of Commons, will follow the criteria in the Bank of England's matrix and will prescribe scores for each criterion and provide tables to convert point scores into maximum percentages allowable for tax.

To smooth claims, the allowable amount will be restricted to that allowed in a company's actual or notional period of account ending before Budget day, for a period of two years. Thereafter, annual cumulative increases of up to five percentage points will be permitted.

Example

Megabank plc has lost £100m. to Ruritania. Up to 1989 relief has been given on £30m. and the allowable total using the Treasury formula is £48m. For subsequent years the figures are as follows:

	1990	1991	1992
		£m.	
Allowable amount for Treasury formula	50	52	60
Restricted allowable amount	48	52	58
Relief given	18	4	6

Section 88C

The smoothing provisions are extended to cases where banks dispose of sovereign debt and incur a loss. Write-off of such losses is restricted to instalments of a maximum of five per cent. of the principal amount.

Example

Megabank plc has already provided £40m. loss on its loan to Ruritania. It sells the debt for £50m., incurring a further £10m. loss. This will be allowed for tax in instalments of £5m.

However, if Megabank disposes of the loan to Ruritania itself, the loss will immediately be allowable in full. This is to facilitate debt reduction agreements with debtor countries.

Local enterprise agencies

75. In section 79(11) of the Taxes Act 1988 (contributions to local enterprise agencies made before 1st April 1992 to be deductible as expenses), for "1992" there shall be substituted "1995."

GENERAL NOTE

The relief given since 1982 for contributions by persons carrying on a trade, profession or vocation or by investment companies to an "approved local enterprise agency", *i.e.* a body for promoting industrial and commercial activity with particular reference to small businesses, had a cut-off date of 1992. This is now extended to 1995.

Training and enterprise councils and local enterprise companies

76. After section 79 of the Taxes Act 1988 there shall be inserted—

"Contributions to training and enterprise councils and local enterprise companies

79A.—(1) Notwithstanding anything in section 74, but subject to the provisions of this section, where a person carrying on a trade, profession or vocation makes any contribution (whether in cash or in kind) to a training and enterprise council or local enterprise company, any expenditure incurred by him in making the contribution may be deducted as an expense in computing the profits or gains of the trade, profession or vocation for the purposes of tax if it would not otherwise be so deductible.

(2) Where any such contribution is made by an investment company any expenditure allowable as a deduction under subsection (1) above shall for the purposes of section 75 be treated as expenses of management.

(3) Subsection (1) above does not apply in relation to a contribution made by any person if either he or any person connected with him receives or is entitled to receive a benefit of any kind whatsoever for or in connection with the making of that contribution, whether from the council concerned or from any other person.

(4) In any case where—

(a) relief has been given under subsection (1) above in respect of a contribution, and

(b) any benefit received in any chargeable period by the contributor or any person connected with him is in any way attributable to that contribution,

the contributor shall in respect of that chargeable period be charged to tax under Case I or Case II of Schedule D, or if he is not chargeable to tax under either of those Cases for that period under Case VI of Schedule D, on an amount equal to the value of that benefit.

(5) In this section—

(a) "training and enterprise council" means a body with which the Secretary of State has made an agreement (not being one which has terminated) under which it is agreed that the body shall carry out the functions of a training and enterprise council, and

(b) "local enterprise company" means a company with which an agreement (not being one which has terminated) under which it is agreed that the company shall carry out the functions of a local enterprise company has been made by the Scottish Development Agency, the Highlands and Islands Development Board, Scottish Enterprise or Highlands and Islands Enterprise.

(6) Section 839 applies for the purposes of subsections (3) and (4) above.

(7) This section applies to contributions made on or after 1st April 1990 and before 1st April 1995.

GENERAL NOTE

A new relief is introduced for contributions by persons carrying on a trade, profession or vocation or by investment companies to training and enterprise councils ("TECs"). TECs are local private sector bodies who will assume responsibility for delivery of Government training and enterprise programmes in their area, and have scope to develop their own initiatives. TECs will operate in England and Wales. In Scotland the relief will operate for contributions to local enterprise companies ("LECs") which will carry out similar functions.

Relief will be withdrawn if a contributor receives a benefit for or in connection with the making of the contribution. This is similar to a provision in relation to contributions to local enterprise agencies.

Expenses of entertainers

77. The following section shall be inserted after section 201 of the Taxes Act 1988—

"Expenses of entertainers

201A.—(1) Where emoluments of an employment to which this section applies fall to be charged to tax for a year of assessment for which this section applies, there may be deducted from the emoluments of the employment to be charged to tax for the year—

(a) fees falling within subsection (2) below, and

(b) any additional amount paid by the employee in respect of value added tax charged by reference to those fees.

(2) Fees fall within this subsection if—

(a) they are paid by the employee to another person,

(b) they are paid under a contract made between the employee and the other person, who agrees under the contract to act as an agent of the employee in connection with the employment,

(c) at each time any of the fees are paid the other person carries on an employment agency with a view to profit and holds a current licence for the agency,

(d) they are calculated as a percentage of the emoluments of the employment or as a percentage of part of those emoluments, and

(e) they are defrayed out of the emoluments of the employment falling to be charged to tax for the year concerned.

(3) For the purposes of subsection (2) above—

(a) "employment agency" means an employment agency within the meaning given by section 13(2) of the Employment Agencies Act 1973, and

(b) a person holds a current licence for an employment agency if he holds a current licence under that Act authorising him to carry on the agency.

(4) The amount which may be deducted by virtue of this section shall not exceed 17·5 per cent. of the emoluments of the employment falling to be charged to tax for the year concerned.

(5) This section applies to employment as an actor, singer, musician, dancer or theatrical artist.

(6) This section applies for the year 1990–91 and subsequent years of assessment."

GENERAL NOTE

From April 6, 1990 most actors working under Standard Equity Contracts will be treated as Sched. E employees, and their expenses will be subject to the stringent "wholly, exclusively and necessarily" rule. The new I.C.T.A. 1988, s.201A, makes it clear that they will be able to deduct agent's fees from their emoluments.

Waste disposal

78. The following sections shall be inserted after section 91 of the Taxes Act 1988—

"Waste disposal: restoration payments

91A.—(1) This section applies where on or after 6th April 1989 a person makes a site restoration payment in the course of carrying on a trade.

(2) Subject to subsection (3) below, for the purposes of income tax or corporation tax the payment shall be allowed as a deduction in computing the profits or gains of the trade for the period of account in which the payment is made.

(3) Subsection (2) above shall not apply to so much of the payment as—

(a) represents expenditure which has been allowed as a deduction in computing the profits or gains of the trade for any period of account preceding the period of account in which the payment is made, or

(b) represents capital expenditure in respect of which an allowance has been, or may be, made under the enactments relating to capital allowances.

(4) For the purposes of this section a site restoration payment is a payment made—

(a) in connection with the restoration of a site, or part of a site, and

(b) in order to comply with any condition of a relevant licence, or any condition imposed on the grant of planning permission to use the site for the carrying out of waste disposal activities, or any term of a relevant agreement.

(5) For the purposes of this section waste disposal activities are the collection, treatment, conversion and final depositing of waste materials, or any of those activities.

(6) For the purposes of this section a relevant licence is—

(a) a disposal licence under Part I of the Control of Pollution Act 1974 or Part II of the Pollution Control and Local Government (Northern Ireland) Order 1978, or

(b) a waste management licence under Part II of the Environmental Protection Act 1990 or any corresponding provision for the time being in force in Northern Ireland.

(7) For the purposes of this section relevant agreement is an agreement made under section 52 of the Town and Country Planning Act 1971, section 50 of the Town and Country Planning (Scotland) Act 1972 or section 106 of the Town and Country Planning Act 1990 (all of which relate to agreements regulating the development or use of land) or under any provision corresponding to section 106 of the Town and Country Planning Act 1990 and for the time being in force in Northern Ireland.

(8) For the purposes of this section a period of account is a period for which an account is made up.

Waste disposal: preparation expenditure

91B.—(1) This section applies where a person—

(a) incurs, in the course of carrying on a trade, site preparation expenditure in relation to a waste disposal site (the site in question),

(b) holds, at the time the person first deposits waste materials on the site in question, a relevant licence which is then in force,

(c) makes a claim for relief under this section in such form as the Board may direct, and

(d) submits such plans and other documents (if any) as the Board may require;

and it is immaterial whether the expenditure is incurred before or after the coming into force of this section.

(2) In computing the profits or gains of the trade for a period of account ending after 5th April 1989, the allowable amount shall be allowed as a deduction for the purposes of income tax or corporation tax.

(3) In relation to a period of account (the period in question) the allowable amount shall be determined in accordance with the formula—

$$(A - B) \times \frac{C}{C + D}$$

(4) A is the site preparation expenditure incurred by the person at any time before the beginning of, or during, the period in question—

(a) in relation to the site in question, and

(b) in the course of carrying on the trade;
but this subsection is subject to subsections (5) and (9) below.
  (5) A does not include any expenditure—
  (a) which has been allowed as a deduction in computing the profits
      or gains of the trade for any period of account preceding the
      period in question, or
  (b) which constitutes capital expenditure in respect of which an
      allowance has been, or may be, made under the enactments
      relating to capital allowances.
  (6) B is an amount equal to any amount allowed as a deduction under
this section, if allowed—
  (a) in computing the profits or gains of the trade for any period of
      account preceding the period in question, and
  (b) as regards expenditure incurred in relation to the site in question;
and if different amounts have been so allowed as regards different
periods, B is the aggregate of them.
  (7) C is the volume of waste materials deposited on the site in
question during the period in question; but if the period is one beginning before 6th April 1989 C shall be reduced by the volume of any
waste materials deposited on the site during the period but before that
date.
  (8) D is the capacity of the site in question not used up for the deposit
of waste materials, looking at the state of affairs at the end of the period
in question.
  (9) Where any of the expenditure which would be included in A
(apart from this subsection) was incurred before 6th April 1989, A shall
be reduced by an amount determined in accordance with the formula—

$$E \times \frac{F}{F + G}$$

  (10) For the purposes of subsection (9) above—
  (a) E is so much of the initial expenditure (that is, the expenditure
      which would be included in A apart from subsection (9) above) as
      was incurred before 6th April 1989,
  (b) F is the volume of waste materials deposited on the site in
      question before 6th April 1989, and
  (c) G is the capacity of the site in question not used up for the deposit
      of waste materials, looking at the state of affairs immediately
      before 6th April 1989.
  (11) For the purposes of this section—
  (a) a waste disposal site is a site used (or to be used) for the disposal
      of waste materials by their deposit on the site,
  (b) in relation to such a site, site preparation expenditure is expendi-
      ture on preparing the site for the deposit of waste materials (and
      may include expenditure on earthworks),
  (c) in relation to such a site, "capacity" means capacity expressed in
      volume,
  (d) "relevant licence" has the same meaning as in section 91A, and
  (e) a period of account is a period for which an account is made up."

GENERAL NOTE
  In *Rolfe* v. *Wimpey Waste Management* [1989] S.T.C. 454 the Court of Appeal affirmed that
all expenditure on preparing or making good a landfill site was capital. The new ss.91A and 91B
are designed to ensure that a revenue deduction will be available for such expenditures where
they do not qualify for capital allowances, as from April 6, 1989, the date of the Court of Appeal
decision.

Section 91A
  This permits the deduction of site restoration payments not otherwise allowable for tax. The

relief is confined to persons holding a disposal licence under the Control of Pollution Act 1974, s.5, or in future a waste management licence under the forthcoming Environment Protection Act 1990.

Section 91B

This allows expenditure on preparing a site to be deducted in calculating trading profits on a basis determined by the proportion of the site capacity filled with waste in that year. Again, the relief is confined to persons holding a relevant licence.

> *Example*
>
> Garbage Disposal plc had incurred by the end of 1990 £2m. in preparation expenditure on its North Quarry site, of which £1·5m. had already been allowed for tax. In that year it deposited one million cubic yards of waste at North Quarry, and capacity of four million cubic yards remained. Garbage Disposal will be allowed a deduction of £100,000, *i.e.* one-fifth of the unrelieved expenditure.

Relief under the section is confined to expenditure after its starting date of April 6, 1989.

Priority share allocations for employees etc.

79.—(1) In section 68 of the Finance Act 1988 (which provides for the benefits derived from priority rights in share offers to be disregarded in certain circumstances), after subsection (3) there shall be inserted—

"(3A) The fact that the allocations of shares in the company to which persons who are not directors or employees of the company are entitled are smaller than those to which directors or employees of the company are entitled shall not be regarded for the purposes of subsection (2)(b) above as meaning that they are not entitled on similar terms if—

(a) each of the first-mentioned persons is also entitled, by reason of his office or employment and in priority to members of the public, to an allocation of shares in another company or companies which are offered to the public (at a fixed price or by tender) at the same time as the shares in the company, and

(b) in the case of each of those persons the aggregate value (measured by reference to the fixed price or the lowest price successfully tendered) of all the shares included in the allocations to which he is entitled is the same, or as nearly the same as is reasonably practicable, as that of the shares in the company included in the entitlement of a comparable director or employee of the company."

(2) This section applies to offers made on or after the day on which this Act is passed.

GENERAL NOTE

The purpose of this section is to extend the relief from tax introduced by F.A. 1988, s.68, on priority share allocations to employees in a public offer of shares. The amendment deals with the circumstances in which employees are entitled to share allocations in two or more companies whose shares are offered for sale at the same time. When two or more such companies jointly own another company they may decide to encourage the employees of that subsidiary by offering them priority rights to shares in the companies. In such circumstances the employees might be offered fewer priority shares in any one company than are offered to the directors of that company.

The amendment allows such mixed priority rights to be taken into account in deciding whether the "similar terms" rule in F.A. 1988, s.68(2)(b), is satisfied. The aggregate value of shares offered to such an employee must be the same, or as nearly the same as is reasonably practicable, as the value of the entitlement of a comparable employee of any of the offered companies.

The extended relief is expected to be relevant in the forthcoming electricity privatisation.

Broadcasting: transfer of undertakings of Independent Broadcasting Authority and Cable Authority

80. Schedule 12 to this Act shall have effect.

GENERAL NOTE

Schedule 12 introduces provisions to prevent undesired tax liabilities from arising under the developments introduced by the forthcoming Broadcasting Act 1990, which include the replacement of the Independent Broadcasting Authority and the Cable Television Authority by new bodies. See further the GENERAL NOTE to Sched. 12.

Futures and options: exemptions

81.—(1) The following section shall be inserted after section 468 of the Taxes Act 1988—

"Authorised unit trusts: futures and options

468AA.—(1) Trustees shall be exempt from tax under Case I of Schedule D in respect of income if—
    (a) the income is derived from transactions relating to futures contracts or options contracts, and
    (b) the trustees are trustees of a unit trust scheme which is an authorised unit trust as respects the accounting period in which the income is derived.

(2) For the purposes of subsection (1) above a contract is not prevented from being a futures contract or an options contract by the fact that any party is or may be entitled to receive or liable to make, or entitled to receive and liable to make, only a payment of a sum (as opposed to a transfer of assets other than money) in full settlement of all obligations.

(3) In this section—

"authorised unit trust" has the same meaning as in section 468, and

"unit trust scheme" has the same meaning as in section 469."

(2) The following section shall be inserted at the end of Part XIV of the Taxes Act 1988 (pension schemes etc.)—

"Futures and options

659A.—(1) For the purposes of sections 592(2), 608(2)(a), 613(4), 614(3) and (4), 620(6) and 643(2)—
    (a) "investments" (or "investment") includes futures contracts and options contracts, and
    (b) income derived from transactions relating to such contracts shall be regarded as income derived from (or income from) such contracts,

and paragraph 7(3)(a) of Schedule 22 to this Act shall be construed accordingly.

(2) For the purposes of subsection (1) above a contract is not prevented from being a futures contract or an options contract by the fact that any party is or may be entitled to receive or liable to make, or entitled to receive and liable to make, only a payment of a sum (as opposed to a transfer of assets other than money) in full settlement of all obligations."

(3) In section 149B of the Capital Gains Tax Act 1979 (miscellaneous exemptions) the following subsections shall be inserted after subsection (9)—

"(10) In subsections (1)(g) and (h) and (2) above "investments" includes futures contracts and options contracts; and paragraph 7(3)(d) of Schedule 22 to the Taxes Act 1988 shall be construed accordingly.

(11) For the purposes of subsection (10) above a contract is not prevented from being a futures contract or an options contract by the fact that any party is or may be entitled to receive or liable to make, or entitled to receive and liable to make, only a payment of a sum (as opposed to a transfer of assets other than money) in full settlement of all obligations."

(4) Section 659 of the Taxes Act 1988 (financial futures and traded options) shall cease to have effect.

(5) Subsections (1) and (2) above apply in relation to income derived after the day on which this Act is passed.

(6) Subsection (3) above applies in relation to disposals made after the day on which this Act is passed.

(7) Insofar as section 659 of the Taxes Act 1988 relates to provisions of that Act, subsection (4) above applies in relation to income derived after the day on which this Act is passed.

(8) Insofar as section 659 of the Taxes Act 1988 relates to section 149B of the Capital Gains Tax Act 1979, subsection (4) above applies in relation to disposals made after the day on which this Act is passed.

GENERAL NOTE

The changes made by this section are to exempt from tax trading income from futures and options in the hands of pension schemes and authorised unit trusts. The purpose is to assist the growth of the futures and options market in the U.K. and to promote futures and options funds, a new kind of authorised unit trust which will be allowed once regulations governing their operation are made by the Department of Trade and Industry and the Securities and Investments Board.

The new I.C.T.A. 1988, s.468AA, applies these provisions in relation to authorised unit trusts and s.659A in relation to pension schemes; s.659 is repealed but an amendment to C.G.T.A. 1979, s.149B, preserves the existing exemption from capital gains tax conferred by that section.

Settlements: child's income

82.—(1) In section 663 of the Taxes Act 1988 (child's income treated as settlor's) in subsection (4) (exception for income not exceeding £5) for "£5" there shall be substituted "£100."

(2) This section shall have effect for the year 1991–92 and subsequent years of assessment.

GENERAL NOTE

Under I.C.T.A. 1988, s.663, income arising from settlements made by parents on their children while minors is treated as the income of the parent. The *de minimis* exclusion of £5 per annum has not been increased since the predecessor of s.663 was introduced in 1936. It is now revalorised to £100.

Loans to traders

83.—(1) Section 136 of the Capital Gains Tax Act 1979 (relief in respect of loans to traders) shall be amended as follows.

(2) The following subsections shall be inserted after subsection (5)—
    "(5A) Where—
    (a) an allowable loss has been treated under subsection (4) above as accruing to any person, and
    (b) the whole or any part of the amount of the payment mentioned in subsection (4)(b) is at any time recovered by him,
this Act shall have effect as if there had accrued to him at that time a chargeable gain equal to so much of the allowable loss as corresponds to the amount recovered.
    (5B) Where—
    (a) an allowable loss has been treated under subsection (3) above as accruing to a company (the first company), and
    (b) the whole or any part of the outstanding amount mentioned in subsection (3)(a) is at any time recovered by a company (the second company) in the same group as the first company,
this Act shall have effect as if there had accrued to the second company at that time a chargeable gain equal to so much of the allowable loss as corresponds to the amount recovered.

(5C) Where—
(a) an allowable loss has been treated under subsection (4) above as accruing to a company (the first company), and
(b) the whole or any part of the outstanding amount mentioned in subsection (4)(a), or the whole or any part of the amount of the payment mentioned in subsection (4)(b), is at any time recovered by a company (the second company) in the same group as the first company,
this Act shall have effect as if there had accrued to the second company at that time a chargeable gain equal to so much of the allowable loss as corresponds to the amount recovered."

(3) In subsection (6) for "subsection (5)" there shall be substituted "subsections (5) to (5C)."

(4) The following subsection shall be inserted after subsection (9)—
"(9A) For the purposes of subsections (5B) and (5C) above two companies are in the same group if they were in the same group when the loan was made or have been in the same group at any subsequent time."

(5) This section applies where an amount is recovered on or after 20th March 1990.

GENERAL NOTE
Various loopholes in C.G.T.A. 1979, s.136, are closed. The section allows relief from capital gains tax in relation to losses by lenders or guarantors in respect of loans to traders. The new provisions in s.136 are as follows:

Subs. (5A)
Where a guarantor recovers in respect of a payment for which he has been allowed relief, the repayment is charged to capital gains tax.

Subs. (5B)
A recovery of a loss by a company in the same group as the company which was allowed the loss is brought into charge to capital gains tax.

Subs. (5C)
The same principle applies in relation to recoveries of sums paid under guarantee, where one company is allowed the loss and another company in the same group makes the recovery.

Subs. (9A)
Subss. (5B) and (5C) apply whether the two companies were within the same group when the loan was made or at any subsequent time.

Qualifying corporate bonds: relief

84. The following sections shall be inserted after section 136 of the Capital Gains Tax Act 1979—

"Relief for qualifying corporate bonds
136A.—(1) In this section "a qualifying loan" means a qualifying loan in the case of which—
(a) the borrower's debt is a debt on a security as defined in section 82 above,
(b) but for that fact, the loan would be a qualifying loan within the meaning of section 136 above, and
(c) the security is a qualifying corporate bond.
(2) If, on a claim by a person who has made a qualifying loan, the inspector is satisfied that one of the following three conditions is fulfilled, this Act shall have effect as if an allowable loss equal to the allowable amount had accrued to the claimant when the claim was made.
(3) The first condition is that—
(a) the value of the security has become negligible,
(b) the claimant has not assigned his right to recover any outstanding amount of the principal of the loan, and

(c) the claimant and the borrower are not companies which have been in the same group at any time after the loan was made.

(4) The second condition is that—

(a) the security's redemption date has passed,

(b) all the outstanding amount of the principal of the loan was irrecoverable (taking the facts existing on that date) or proved to be irrecoverable (taking the facts existing on a later date), and

(c) subsection (3)(b) and (c) above are fulfilled.

(5) The third condition is that—

(a) the security's redemption date has passed,

(b) part of the outstanding amount of the principal of the loan was irrecoverable (taking the facts existing on that date) or proved to be irrecoverable (taking the facts existing on a later date), and

(c) subsection (3)(b) and (c) above are fulfilled.

(6) In a case where the inspector is satisfied that the first or second condition is fulfilled, the allowable amount is the lesser of—

(a) the outstanding amount of the principal of the loan;

(b) the amount of the security's acquisition cost;

and if any amount of the principal of the loan has been recovered the amount of the security's acquisition cost shall for this purpose be treated as reduced (but not beyond nil) by the amount recovered.

(7) In a case where the inspector is satisfied that the third condition is fulfilled, then—

(a) if the security's acquisition cost exceeds the relevant amount, the allowable amount is an amount equal to the excess;

(b) if the security's acquisition cost is equal to or less than the relevant amount, the allowable amount is nil.

(8) For the purposes of subsection (7) above the relevant amount is the aggregate of—

(a) the amount (if any) of the principal of the loan which has been recovered, and

(b) the amount (if any) of the principal of the loan which has not been recovered but which in the inspector's opinion is recoverable.

(9) Where an allowable loss has been treated under subsection (2) above as accruing to any person and the whole or any part of the relevant outstanding amount is at any time recovered by him, this Act shall have effect as if there had accrued to him at that time a chargeable gain equal to so much of the allowable loss as corresponds to the amount recovered.

(10) Where—

(a) an allowable loss has been treated under subsection (2) above as accruing to a company (the first company), and

(b) the whole or any part of the relevant outstanding amount is at any time recovered by a company (the second company) in the same group as the first company,

this Act shall have effect as if there had accrued to the second company at that time a chargeable gain equal to so much of the allowable loss as corresponds to the amount recovered.

(11) In subsections (9) and (10) above "the relevant outstanding amount" means—

(a) the amount of the principal of the loan outstanding when the claim was allowed, in a case where the inspector was satisfied that the first or second condition was fulfilled;

(b) the amount of the part (or the greater or greatest part) arrived at by the inspector under subsection (5)(b) above, in a case where he was satisfied that the third condition was fulfilled.

(12) This section applies if the security was—

(a) issued on or after 15th March 1989, or
(b) issued before 15th March 1989 but held on 15th March 1989 by the person who made the loan.

Section 136A: supplementary
136B.—(1) In section 136A above "qualifying corporate bond" has the same meaning as in section 64 of the Finance Act 1984.

(2) For the purposes of section 136A above a security's redemption date is the latest date on which, under the terms on which the security was issued, the company or body which issued it can be required to redeem it.

(3) For the purposes of section 136A above a security's acquisition cost is the amount or value of the consideration in money or money's worth given, by or on behalf of the person who made the loan, wholly and exclusively for the acquisition of the security, together with the incidental costs to him of the acquisition.

(4) For the purposes of section 136A(10) above two companies are in the same group if they have been in the same group at any time after the loan was made.

(5) Section 136(6) above shall apply for the purposes of section 136A(6) and (8) to (10) above as it applies for the purposes of section 136(5) above.

(6) Section 136(7), (9) and (10)(c) above shall apply for the purposes of section 136A above and of this section as they apply for the purposes of section 136, ignoring for this purpose the words following "lender" in section 136(9)."

GENERAL NOTE
Under F.A. 1984, s.64, as amended by F.A. 1989, s.139, most bonds issued by companies were exempted from capital gains tax. This meant, however, that losses on such bonds were not allowable for tax, so deterring investors from making such loans. The new sections inserted in the C.G.T.A. 1979 are designed to remedy this defect.

Section 136A
Losses on qualifying corporate bonds are allowed relief if one of the following three conditions is satisfied:
(a) the value of the bond has become negligible;
(b) the redemption date has passed and the whole loan is irrecoverable;
(c) the redemption date has passed and part of the loan is irrecoverable.
In each case there must not be any assignment of the right to recover and the claimant and the borrowers must not have been companies in the same group at any time after the loan was made.
In the first and second cases the *quantum* of relief is the difference between the outstanding principal and the acquisition cost, less any recoveries. In the third case it is the difference between acquisition cost and amounts recovered, or recoverable in the inspector's opinion.
Subsequent recoveries by the lender or by a company in the same group are brought into charge to capital gains tax.
The section applies as from March 15, 1989.

Section 136B
This contains interpretative provisions for the purposes of the new relief by applying appropriate definitions from F.A. 1984, s.64, and C.G.T.A. 1979, s.136.

Qualifying corporate bonds: reorganisations etc.

85.—(1) In Part II of Schedule 13 to the Finance Act 1984 (qualifying corporate bonds: reorganisations etc.) the following paragraph shall be inserted after paragraph 11—
    "12.—(1) This paragraph applies in a case where—
        (a) the new asset mentioned in paragraph 10 above is a qualifying corporate bond in respect of which an allowable loss is treated as accruing under section 136A(2) of the principal Act, and

(b) the loss is treated as accruing at a time falling after the relevant transaction but before any actual disposal of the new asset subsequent to the relevant transaction.

(2) For the purposes of paragraph 10 above, a subsequent disposal of the new asset shall be treated as occurring at (and only at) the time the loss is treated as accruing."

(2) This section applies whether the relevant transaction occurs before or on or after the day on which this Act is passed.

GENERAL NOTE

The new para. 12 of Sched. 13 to the Finance Act 1984 makes a necessary adaptation to the provisions relating to reorganisations, conversions and reconstructions affecting corporate bonds. Where a loss is allowed subsequent to such a reorganisation and there is a later disposal of the new asset this is treated as occurring at the time the loss is treated as accruing.

Groups of companies

86.—(1) In subsection (1F) of section 272 of the Taxes Act 1970 (application of Schedule 18 to Taxes Act 1988 for determining membership of groups for capital gains purposes), for the words "paragraph 7(1)(b) were omitted" there shall be substituted the words "paragraphs 5(3) and 7(1)(b) were omitted."

(2) Subject to subsection (3) below, the amendment made by subsection (1) above shall be deemed always to have had effect.

(3) If a company which (apart from this subsection) is the principal company of a group (within the meaning of section 272) at any time during the period beginning with 14th March 1989 and ending with 25th January 1990 so elects, in determining whether a company is a member of the group at any time during that period subsection (1F) of that section shall apply as if the amendment made by subsection (1) above did not have effect.

(4) An election under subsection (3) above shall be irrevocable and shall be made by notice in writing to the inspector at any time within two years after the end of the first accounting period of the principal company ending after 31st January 1990.

(5) There may be made any such adjustment, whether by way of discharge or repayment of tax, the making of an assessment or otherwise, as is appropriate in consequence of an election under subsection (3) above.

GENERAL NOTE

F.A. 1989, s.138, made certain amendments to the definition of groups of companies in I.C.T.A. 1970, s.272, to prevent these provisions being used for the avoidance of tax on capital gains. Among the amendments was one which, following I.C.T.A. 1988, Sched. 18, para. 5(3), applied the assumption that an arrangement under which rights to profits or assets of a subsidiary may be reduced in the future had already taken place. The legislation was not intended to have this effect, which could have adverse effects for some normal commercial arrangements. Accordingly para. 5(3) is left out of account for the definition of a group for capital gains purposes. Actual reductions of rights to profits or assets may still have the effect of causing a company to fail the capital gains group test and lead to tax charges.

The change is effective from Budget Day 1989, but groups may elect that it should only apply after January 25, 1990, when it was announced in a parliamentary written answer and Revenue press release.

Capital allowances: vehicles provided by employees

87.—(1) In section 27 of the Capital Allowances Act 1990 (professions, employments, vocations etc.) in subsection (1) for the words "and (3)" there shall be substituted the words "to (3)."

(2) The following subsections shall be inserted after subsection (2) of that section—

"(2A) In the case of machinery to which this subsection applies, subsection (2)(a) above shall have effect with the omission of the word "necessarily."

(2B) Subsection (2A) above applies to machinery if—
(a) it consists of a mechanically propelled road vehicle, and
(b) capital expenditure incurred on its provision is incurred partly for the purposes of the office or employment and partly for other purposes.

(2C) Section 24 in its application in accordance with this section to an office or employment shall have effect, where a person's qualifying expenditure consists of expenditure incurred on the provision of machinery to which subsection (2A) above applies, with the modifications set out in subsections (2D) and (2E) below.

(2D) In subsection (2)(b) for the word "whole" there shall be substituted the words "appropriate fraction."

(2E) The following subsection shall be inserted after subsection (2)—

"(2A) For the purposes of subsection (2)(b) above the appropriate fraction is—

$$\frac{A}{B}$$

where—
A is the number of chargeable periods in the case of which—
(a) the person has carried on the trade,
(b) the machinery or plant has belonged to him, and
(c) he has claimed an allowance falling to be made to him under this section by reference to expenditure incurred on the provision of the machinery or plant; and
B is the number of chargeable periods in the case of which—
(a) the person has carried on the trade,
(b) the machinery or plant has belonged to him, and
(c) an allowance falls to be made to him under this section by reference to expenditure incurred on the provision of the machinery or plant." "

(3) Where—
(a) at the beginning of the year 1990–91 machinery consisting of a mechanically propelled road vehicle is provided by a person for use in the performance of the duties of an office or employment held by him, and
(b) the machinery was also provided by him at the end of the year 1989–90 for use in the performance of the duties of that office or employment but without that provision being necessary,

Part II of the Capital Allowances Act 1990 shall have effect as if he had incurred capital expenditure on the provision of the machinery for the purposes of the office or employment in the year 1990–91, the amount of that expenditure being taken as the price which the machinery would have fetched if sold in the open market on 6th April 1990, and the machinery being treated as belonging to him in consequence of his having incurred that expenditure.

(4) This section shall apply for the year 1990–91 and subsequent years of assessment.

GENERAL NOTE

For 1990–91 and subsequent years certain amendments are made to C.A.A. 1990, s.27 ("Professions, employments, vocations, etc."). The operation of *ibid.*, s.24 ("writing-down allowances and balancing adjustments") is also affected by virtue of a new subs. (2C) inserted in s.27 (subs. (2)).

C.A.A. 1990, s.27(2)(a), required any machinery or plant to be "necessarily" provided for use in the performance of the duties of an office or employment if capital allowances were to be granted. This accorded with the usual requirement of "necessity" in relation to allowances under Sched. E (see GENERAL NOTE to I.C.T.A. 1988, s.198).

That requirement is now removed in relation to capital allowances on road vehicles provided in part only for the purposes of the office or employment and in part for other purposes. See new subss. 27(2A), (2B) of the C.A.A. 1990.

The new subss. 27(2C) to (2E) amend the operation of s.24(2)(b) by substituting a "relevant fraction" for the "whole" in computing the balancing allowance on the permanent discontinuance of the office or employment. The "relevant fraction" is defined in the new subs. 27(2E) which itself inserts a new subs. 2(A) in s.24. References are made therein to "the trade" but apply, by virtue of s.27(1)(a), to employments and offices.

Subs. (3) deals with the case where a road vehicle not previously eligible for capital allowances because it was not "necessarily" provided becomes eligible by virtue of this change in the law. It is treated as being provided at the open market value on April 6, 1990.

Capital allowances: miscellaneous amendments

88. Schedule 13 to this Act shall have effect.

Correction of errors in Taxes Act 1988

89. Schedule 14 to this Act shall have effect.

GENERAL NOTE
The mammoth task of preparing the 1988 consolidation of the Taxes Act was unfortunately not completed without minor errors. Many of these were corrected by F.A. 1988, s.146, and Sched. 13. A further instalment, mostly amending statutory references which were not updated, is contained in Sched. 14. See further the GENERAL NOTE to that Schedule.

CHAPTER II

MANAGEMENT

Returns and information

Income tax returns

90.—(1) The following sections shall be substituted for sections 8 and 9 of the Taxes Management Act 1970 (return of income)—

"Personal return
8.—(1) For the purposes of assessing a person to income tax, he may be required by a notice given to him by an inspector—
   (a) to make and deliver to the inspector within the time limited by the notice a return containing such information as may be required in pursuance of the notice, and
   (b) to deliver with the return such accounts and statements, relating to information contained in the return, as may be required in pursuance of the notice.
(2) Every return under this section shall include a declaration by the person making the return to the effect that the return is to the best of his knowledge correct and complete.
(3) A notice under this section may require different information, accounts and statements for different periods or in relation to different descriptions of source of income.
(4) Notices under this section may require different information, accounts and statements in relation to different descriptions of person.

Trustee's return
8A.—(1) For the purpose of assessing a trustee of a settlement, and the settlors and beneficiaries, to income tax an inspector may by a notice given to the trustee require the trustee—

(a) to make and deliver to the inspector within the time limited by the notice a return containing such information as may be required in pursuance of the notice, and

(b) to deliver with the return such accounts and statements, relating to information contained in the return, as may be required in pursuance of the notice;

and a notice may be given to any one trustee or separate notices may be given to each trustee or to such trustees as the inspector thinks fit.

(2) Every return under this section shall include a declaration by the person making the return to the effect that the return is to the best of his knowledge correct and complete.

(3) A notice under this section may require different information, accounts and statements for different periods or in relation to different descriptions of source of income.

(4) Notices under this section may require different information, accounts and statements in relation to different descriptions of settlement.

Partnership return

9.—(1) Where a trade or profession is carried on by two or more persons jointly, for the purposes of making an assessment to income tax in the partnership name an inspector may act under subsection (2) or (3) below (or both).

(2) An inspector may by a notice given to the partners require such person as is identified in accordance with rules given with the notice—

(a) to make and deliver to the inspector within the time limited by the notice a return containing such information as may be required in pursuance of the notice, and

(b) to deliver with the return such accounts and statements as may be required in pursuance of the notice.

(3) An inspector may by a notice given to any partner require the partner—

(a) to make and deliver to the inspector within the time limited by the notice a return containing such information as may be required in pursuance of the notice, and

(b) to deliver with the return such accounts and statements as may be required in pursuance of the notice;

and a notice may be given to any one partner or separate notices may be given to each partner or to such partners as the inspector thinks fit.

(4) Every return under this section shall include—

(a) a declaration of the names and residences of the partners;

(b) a declaration by the person making the return to the effect that the return is to the best of his knowledge correct and complete.

(5) A notice under this section may require different information, accounts and statements for different periods or in relation to different descriptions of source of income.

(6) Notices under this section may require different information, accounts and statements in relation to different descriptions of partnership."

(2) In section 12 of that Act (information about chargeable gains)—

(a) in subsection (1) for the words "Section 8" there shall be substituted the words "Sections 8 and 8A" and for the words "it applies" there shall be substituted the words "they apply";

(b) in subsection (2) after the words "section 8" there shall be inserted the words "or section 8A";

(c) in subsection (4) the words "of income of a partnership" shall be omitted.

(3) In section 93 of that Act (penalties) in subsection (1) for the words "9 of this Act (or either" there shall be substituted the words "8A or 9 of this Act (or any."

(4) In section 95 of that Act (penalties) in subsection (1)(a) for the words "9 of this Act (or either" there shall be substituted the words "8A or 9 of this Act (or any."

(5) This section applies where a notice to deliver a return was, or falls to be, given after 5th April 1990.

GENERAL NOTE

The process of updating the Taxes Management Act continues. This section introduces three new sections, 8, 8A and 9, dealing with personal, trust and partnership returns. The result is a considerable streamlining of the legislation.

Section 8

This section is reduced from nine subsections to four. The practical effect of the change is not likely to be great, although the more general terms of the new section may increase official powers. For example, a formal right to demand accounts and statements with the return is included, but it is already virtually impossible to refuse such demands where they are well-founded.

Section 8A

There was a specific provision previously in the T.M.A. regarding returns by trustees of settlement. This is now rectified and it is made clear that a return may be demanded from each and every trustee.

Section 9

The procedure in relation to partnership returns is slightly modified. The "precedent partner" disappears and is replaced by "such person as is identified in accordance with rules given with the notice." As before, the inspector can require a return from each and every one of the partners.

Corporation tax returns

91.—(1) Section 11 of the Taxes Management Act 1970 (return of profits) shall be amended as follows.

(2) In subsection (1), for the words from "the profits" to the end there shall be substituted the words "such information as may be required in pursuance of the notice together with such accounts, statements and reports as may be so required.

> "(1A) The information which a company may be required to supply under this section is information which is relevant to the application of the Corporation Tax Acts to the company; and the accounts, statements and reports which a company may be so required to supply are accounts, statements and reports which are so relevant."

(3) In subsection (2), for the words "of profits and losses arising in" there shall be substituted the word "for."

(4) In subsection (3) (return to include declaration that return is correct and complete)—

(a) after the word "declaration" there shall be inserted the words "by the person making the return"; and

(b) after the word "is" there shall be inserted the words "to the best of his knowledge."

(5) Subsection (7) shall cease to have effect.

(6) In subsection (8), the words from "or different" to the end shall be omitted.

(7) The following subsection shall be inserted after subsection (8)—

> "(8A) A return under this section shall be amended by the company delivering to the inspector a document in such form, containing such information and accompanied by such statements as the Board may require."

(8) Subsection (4) above shall apply with respect to any notice served on or after the day on which this Act is passed.

(9) Subsections (2), (3) and (5) to (7) above shall apply with respect to any notice served after the day appointed for the purposes of section 82 of the Finance (No.2) Act 1987.

GENERAL NOTE
All but one of the amendments made to T.M.A. 1970, s.11, are to take effect from the introduction of the "Pay and File" system for corporation tax, expected to be in 1993. As with ss.8 and 9, the amendments largely streamline the legislation. The new subsection (8A) provides for the amending of a return by the production of further information at the requirement of the Board.

Information powers relating to interest

92.—(1) Section 17 of the Taxes Management Act 1970 (interest paid or credited by banks etc. without deduction of income tax) shall be amended as mentioned in subsections (2) and (3) below.

(2) In subsection (1)—

(a) after the words "without deduction of income tax" there shall be inserted the words "or after deduction of income tax";

(b) after the words "the amount of the interest" there shall be inserted the words "actually paid or credited and (where the interest was paid or credited after deduction of income tax) the amount of the interest from which the tax was deducted and the amount of the tax deducted";

(c) paragraph (a) of the proviso shall be omitted.

(3) The following subsections shall be inserted after subsection (4)—

"(5) The Board may by regulations provide as mentioned in all or any of the following paragraphs—

(a) that a return under subsection (1) above shall contain such further information as is prescribed if the notice requiring the return specifies the information and requires it to be contained in the return;

(b) that a person required to make and deliver a return under subsection (1) above shall furnish with the return such further information as is prescribed if the notice requiring the return specifies the information and requires it to be so furnished;

(c) that if a person is required to furnish information under any provision made under paragraph (b) above, and the notice requiring the return specifies the form in which the information is to be furnished, the person shall furnish the information in that form;

(d) that a notice under subsection (1) above shall not require prescribed information; and in this subsection "prescribed" means prescribed by the regulations.

(6) Regulations under subsection (5) above—

(a) shall be made by statutory instrument subject to annulment in pursuance of a resolution of the House of Commons,

(b) may make different provision in relation to different cases or descriptions of case, and

(c) may include such supplementary, incidental, consequential or transitional provisions as appear to the Board to be necessary or expedient."

(4) Section 18 of that Act (interest paid without deduction of income tax) shall be amended as mentioned in subsections (5) and (6) below.

(5) In subsection (1)—

(a) after the words "without deduction of income tax" there shall be inserted the words "or after deduction of income tax";

(b) in paragraph (b) for the words "so paid or received" there shall be substituted the words "actually paid or received and (where the interest has been paid or received after deduction of income tax) the amount of the interest from which the tax has been deducted and the amount of the tax deducted";

(c) for the words "its amount" there shall be substituted the words "the amount actually received and (where the interest has been received after deduction of income tax) the amount of the interest from which the tax has been deducted and the amount of the tax deducted."

(6) The following subsections shall be inserted after subsection (3A)—

"(3B) The Board may by regulations provide as mentioned in all or any of the following paragraphs—

(a) that a person required to furnish information under subsection (1) above shall furnish at the same time such further information as is prescribed if the notice concerned specifies the information and requires it to be so furnished;

(b) that if a person is required to furnish information under subsection (1) above or under any provision made under paragraph (a) above, and the notice concerned specifies the form in which the information is to be furnished, the person shall furnish the information in that form;

(c) that a notice under subsection (1) above shall not require prescribed information;

and in this subsection "prescribed" means prescribed by the regulations.

(3C) Regulations under subsection (3B) above—

(a) shall be made by statutory instrument subject to annulment in pursuance of a resolution of the House of Commons,

(b) may make different provision in relation to different cases or descriptions of case, and

(c) may include such supplementary, incidental, consequential or transitional provisions as appear to the Board to be necessary or expedient."

(7) Subsections (1) to (3) above shall have effect as regards a case where interest is paid or credited in the year 1991–92 or a subsequent year of assessment.

(8) Subsections (4) to (6) above shall have effect as regards a case where interest is paid in the year 1991–92 or a subsequent year of assessment.

GENERAL NOTE

The present Revenue powers in T.M.A. 1970, ss.17 and 18, allow them to obtain information from banks, building societies and other deposit-takers regarding interest paid without deduction of tax. At present most interest is free of basic rate tax in the hands of the recipients because the institutions concerned account to the Revenue for composite rate tax (CRT), representing the tax due from their depositors. This is a tax on the institutions not the depositors.

With the abolition of CRT from April 6, 1991, the institutions will be required to deduct basic rate income tax at source from interest paid to depositors, unless the depositor concerned certifies that he is entitled to payment gross.

The amendments to ss.17 and 18 will allow the Revenue to require information regarding interest paid under deduction of income tax at the basic rate as well as interest paid gross. The detailed rules will be implemented by regulations made by the Revenue by statutory instrument after consultation with the institutions concerned.

Restrictions on Board's power to call for information

93.—(1) In section 20 of the Taxes Management Act 1970 (powers to call for information), after subsection (7) there shall be inserted—

"(7A) A notice under subsection (2) above is not to be given unless the Board have reasonable grounds for believing—

(a) that the person to whom it relates may have failed or may fail to comply with any provision of the Taxes Acts; and

(b) that any such failure is likely to have led or to lead to serious prejudice to the proper assessment or collection of tax."

(2) This section shall apply with respect to notices given on or after the day on which this Act is passed.

GENERAL NOTE

Demands for information by an inspector under T.M.A. 1970, s.20, require the prior approval of a general or special commissioner, but there is no such restriction on a demand by the Board. The Board's power subsists even while an appeal is in progress: *R.* v. *I.R.C.*, ex p. *Taylor (No. 2)* [1990] 2 All E.R. 409. A statutory restriction is now put on this power by requiring the Board to have reasonable grounds for believing that there has been a failure to comply with the provisions of the Taxes Acts leading to "serious prejudice" to the proper assessment or collection of tax.

Donations to charity: inspection powers

94.—(1) The Board may require a charity to produce for inspection by an officer of the Board all such books, documents and other records in the possession, or under the control, of the charity as contain information relating to payments made on or after 1st October 1990 and in respect of which the charity has made a claim to repayment of tax by virtue of section 339 of the Taxes Act 1988 (donations to charity by companies) or section 25 of this Act.

(2) For the purposes of subsection (1) above "charity" has the same meaning as in section 506 of the Taxes Act 1988 and includes—

(a) each of the bodies mentioned in section 507 of that Act, and

(b) any Association of a description specified in section 508 of that Act (scientific research organisations).

(3) In the second column in the Table in section 98 of the Taxes Management Act 1970 (penalty for failure to furnish information etc.) there shall be added at the end—

"Section 94(1) of the Finance Act 1990."

GENERAL NOTE

The very wide extension of relief for gifts to charity made by ss.25–27 carries obvious dangers of abuse. The Revenue is given a wide power to require charities to produce all information in their possession regarding such gifts on which they have claimed repayment of tax.

Corporation tax determinations

Determinations

95.—(1) The following sections shall be inserted after section 41 of the Taxes Management Act 1970—

"Corporation tax determinations

Determination procedure

41A.—(1) If an inspector is satisfied that a return under section 11 of this Act affords correct and complete information concerning an amount which is—

(a) required to be given in the return, and

(b) determinable under this section,

he shall determine the amount accordingly.

(2) If an inspector is not satisfied that a return under section 11 of this Act affords correct and complete information concerning an amount which is—

(a) required to be given in the return, and

(b) determinable under this section,

he may determine the amount to the best of his judgment.

(3) If a company is required to deliver a return under section 11 of this Act and fails to deliver the return within the time limited by that section, an inspector may determine any amount which is—

(a) required to be given in the return, and

(b) determinable under this section,

to the best of his judgment.

(4) An amount shall be treated as determined under this section when the inspector gives notice in writing of the determination to the company which makes, or is required to make, the return.

(5) After an amount has been determined under this section, the determination shall not be altered except in accordance with the express provisions of the Taxes Acts.

(6) Section 31 of this Act (except subsection (3)) shall apply in relation to a determination under this section as it applies in relation to an assessment to tax.

(7) A determination under this section which has become final shall be conclusive for the purposes of the Corporation Tax Acts, except sections 36(3), 41B and 43A of this Act.

(8) The power conferred by subsection (2) or (3) above includes power to determine that an amount is nil.

(9) In this section references to an amount which is determinable under this section are references to—

(a) the amount of losses incurred in a trade in an accounting period, computed in accordance with section 393(7) of the principal Act; or

(b) the amount for an accounting period which is available for surrender by way of group relief under section 403(3) (capital allowances), (4) (expenses of management) or (7) (charges on income) of the principal Act.

Reduction of determination

41B.—(1) Where an inspector discovers that an amount determined under section 41A of this Act is or has become excessive, he may issue a direction that the amount determined shall be reduced by an amount specified in the direction.

(2) A direction under this section in relation to a determination shall be treated as issued when the inspector gives notice in writing of the direction to the company given notice of the determination under section 41A of this Act.

(3) Section 31 of this Act (except subsection (3)) shall apply in relation to a direction under this section as it applies in relation to an assessment to tax.

(4) Section 41A(7) of this Act shall not apply to a determination at any time when a direction under this section has been issued in relation to the determination and has not become final.

(5) After a direction under this section has become final, the determination to which it relates shall have effect as if the amount determined were reduced by the amount specified in the direction.

(6) The power conferred by subsection (1) above includes power to issue a direction which would have the effect of reducing the amount determined to nil.

(7) In its application to a determination in relation to which a direction under this section has already been issued, subsection (1) above shall have effect with the insertion after the word "Act" of the words ", as reduced by the amount specified in any previous direction under this section in relation to the determination,".

Time limits
41C.—(1) A determination of an amount may be made under section 41A of this Act at any time not later than 6 years from the end of the period to which the amount relates.

(2) Subject to subsection (3) below, a direction in relation to a determination may be issued under section 41B of this Act at any time not later than 6 years from the end of the period to which the determination relates.

(3) A direction in relation to a determination may be issued under section 41B of this Act at any time not later than 20 years from the end of the period to which the determination relates if the excess by virtue of which the power conferred by that section is exercisable is attributable to the fraudulent or negligent conduct of—

(a) the company given notice of the determination under section 41A of this Act, or

(b) a person acting on its behalf."

(2) This section applies in relation to accounting periods ending after the day appointed for the purposes of section 10 of the Taxes Act 1988 (pay and file).

GENERAL NOTE
A power is given to the inspector to "determine" corporate losses and other amounts available for surrender as group relief in the same way as profits are determined by assessment. This will give companies greater certainty in relation to their tax affairs. The same right of appeal is given against a determination as against an assessment. The procedure will apply after the introduction of "Pay and File" in 1993.

Section 41A
This contains the power for an inspector to determine losses of a company either in accordance with its return or to the best of his judgment where the return is defective or has not been duly made. A determination, once made, has the definitive character of an assessment and can only be altered by the issue of a reduced determination under s.41B by agreement or through the appeal procedure under s.31.

Section 41B
If an inspector "discovers" that he has determined a loss in an excessive amount he may issue a direction reducing the determination which takes effect in the same way as the determination which it replaces.

Section 41C
The normal time-limits apply to determination. A determination under s.41A may be made within six years from the end of the period to which it relates. A direction under s.41B reducing a determination may be made within six years from the end of the period to which the determination relates. This deadline is extended to 20 years where there has been fraudulent or negligent conduct by the company or a person acting on its behalf.

Consequential group relief adjustments

96.—(1) This section applies where—
(a) a determination of an amount for an accounting period of a company ("the surrendering company") is made under section 41A of the Taxes Management Act 1970, and
(b) immediately after the determination, or a direction relating to it under section 41B of that Act, becomes final, the amount of relief of any description which the surrendering company consents to surrender by way of group relief for the period ("the surrendered amount") exceeds the amount which, in relation to relief of that description, is the relevant amount for the period.

(2) For the purposes of subsection (1) above, the amount which is, at any time, the relevant amount in relation to relief of any description for an accounting period of a company is—

(a) the amount of relief of that description available to the company for surrender by way of group relief for the period, less

(b) so much, if any, of that amount as represents relief given in an assessment on the surrendering company which has become final and conclusive.

(3) The surrendering company shall make whatever adjustment of the surrendered amount is necessary in consequence of the determination or direction ("the necessary adjustment") by reducing or withdrawing consent to surrender before the end of 30 days from the date on which the determination or direction becomes final.

(4) If the surrendering company fails to make the necessary adjustment within the period mentioned in subsection (3) above, it shall be made—

(a) except where paragraph (b) below applies, in such manner as may be specified by the inspector by notice in writing to the surrendering company and to the company or, if more than one, each company whose claim for group relief is affected by the adjustment, or

(b) where the surrendering company gives notice in writing to the inspector within the relevant period, in such manner as may be specified in the notice given by the surrendering company.

(5) For the purposes of subsection (4)(b) above the relevant period is the period of 30 days beginning with the day on which notice under subsection (4)(a) above is given to the surrendering company.

(6) The power to make an assessment under section 412(3) of the Taxes Act 1988 (power to assess where inspector discovers that group relief which has been given is or has become excessive) shall also be exercisable where group relief which has been given becomes excessive in consequence of the making of the necessary adjustment.

(7) Subsection (8) below applies where any tax to which a company ("the chargeable company") becomes liable in consequence of the making of the necessary adjustment has been assessed on the company and is unpaid at the end of 6 months from the date on which the assessment becomes final and conclusive ("the relevant date").

(8) Any other company which has obtained group relief by virtue of a surrender by the surrendering company for the accounting period to which the necessary adjustment relates may, within 2 years from the relevant date, be assessed and charged (in the name of the chargeable company) to an amount not exceeding the lesser of—

(a) the amount of the unpaid tax, and

(b) the amount of tax which the other company saves by virtue of the surrender.

(9) A company paying an amount of tax under subsection (8) above shall be entitled to recover from the chargeable company a sum equal to that amount together with any interest on that amount which it has paid under section 87A of the Taxes Management Act 1970.

(10) An assessment by virtue of subsection (6) above shall not be out of time if made within one year from the date on which the determination or direction giving rise to the making of the necessary adjustment becomes final.

(11) In subsection (1)(b) above, the reference to the amount of relief of any description which the surrendering company consents to surrender by way of group relief for the period includes a reference to the amount of relief of that description which the surrendering company consents to surrender for any assumed accounting period under section 409 of the Taxes Act 1988 (companies joining or leaving group or consortium) which is comprised in the period.

(12) In section 87A of the Taxes Management Act 1970 (interest on overdue corporation tax etc.) in subsection (3) after the words "1970" there shall be inserted the words ", section 96(8) of the Finance Act 1990."

GENERAL NOTE
    This deals with the situation where a determination of an amount available for group relief results in an amount surrendered being excessive, for instance because the company has already been given relief through an assessment. In such a case the surrendering company must reduce or withdraw its consent to surrender within 30 days. Alternatively, the adjustment may be made by the inspector in default of action by the company, or in accordance with a notice given by the company within 30 days of the inspector's adjustment. Where tax remains unpaid or is saved as a result of an adjustment it may be assessed on the company which obtained the group relief within two years after the end of six months from the date when the assessment reflecting the adjustment became final and conclusive. This latter assessment may be raised within one year of the date of the determination or direction giving rise to it. The other company is entitled to reimbursement of any tax or interest which it has paid on behalf of the surrendering company.

Claims by companies

Payment of tax credits
    97.—(1) Section 42 of the Taxes Management Act 1970 (claims) shall be amended as follows.
    (2) In subsection (5) (form of claims) there shall be inserted at the beginning the words "Subject to subsection (5A) below,".
    (3) The following subsection shall be inserted after subsection (5)—
        "(5A) A claim by a company for payment of a tax credit shall be made by being included in a return under section 11 of this Act."
    (4) The following subsection shall be inserted after subsection (10)—
        "(10A) In subsection (5A) above—
        (a) the reference to a claim for payment includes a reference to a claim resulting in payment; and
        (b) the reference to a claim being included in a return includes a reference to a claim being included by virtue of an amendment of the return."
    (5) This section applies in relation to claims relating to income of accounting periods ending after the day appointed for the purposes of section 10 of the Taxes Act 1988 (pay and file).

GENERAL NOTE
    The amendments to T.M.A. 1970, s.42, included here will allow companies to receive payments of tax credits before their profits are finally agreed. They will be entitled to receive payments of amounts which are not in dispute and to appeal to commissioners where there is a dispute over the amount to be paid.
    This procedure will become applicable when "Pay and File" comes into force in 1993.

Repayment of income tax deducted at source
    98.—(1) The Taxes Act 1988 shall be amended as follows.
    (2) In section 7(2) (set off against corporation tax of income tax deducted from payments received by resident companies) the words from "and accordingly" to the end shall be omitted.
    (3) The following subsections shall be inserted after section 7(5)—
        "(6) A claim for the purposes of subsection (5) above, so far as relating to subsection (2) above and section 11(3), shall be made by being included in a return under section 11 of the Management Act (corporation tax return) for the period to which the claim relates.
        (7) In subsection (6) above the reference to a claim being included in a return includes a reference to a claim being included by virtue of an amendment of the return."
    (4) In section 11(3) (set off against corporation tax of income tax deducted from payments received by non-resident companies) the words from "and accordingly" to the end shall be omitted.
    (5) This section applies in relation to income tax falling to be set off against corporation tax for accounting periods ending after the day appointed for the purposes of section 10 of the Taxes Act 1988 (pay and file).

GENERAL NOTE
The amendments to I.C.T.A. 1988, ss.7 and 11, included here will allow companies to receive repayments of income tax deducted at source before their profits are finally agreed. The procedure and its applicability is similar to that in relation to tax credits; see GENERAL NOTE to s.97.

Loss relief

99.—(1) The Taxes Act 1988 shall be amended as follows.

(2) In section 393 (relief for trading losses) in subsection (1) (carry forward of losses on the making of a claim)—

(a) for the words "the company may make a claim requiring that the loss" there shall be substituted the words "the loss shall," and

(b) for the words "on that claim" there shall be substituted the words "under this subsection"; and in subsection (11) (time limit for claims) the words from the beginning to "of six years; and" shall be omitted.

(3) In section 396 (relief for Case VI losses on the making of a claim)—

(a) in subsection (1) for the words "the company may make a claim requiring that the loss" there shall be substituted the words "the loss shall," and

(b) subsection (3) (time limit for claims) shall cease to have effect.

(4) This section applies in relation to accounting periods ending after the day appointed for the purposes of section 10 of the Taxes Act 1988 (pay and file).

GENERAL NOTE
Set-off of trading losses and losses arising under Case VI of Sched. D against future profits will be made automatically after the introduction of "Pay and File" in 1993 rather than by way of claim by the company.

Group relief: general

100.—(1) The Taxes Act 1988 shall be amended as follows.

(2) In section 412 (group relief: claims and adjustments) the following subsection shall be substituted for subsections (1) and (2)—

"(1) Schedule 17A to this Act (which makes provision with respect to claims for group relief shall have effect."

(3) The Schedule set out in Schedule 15 to this Act shall be inserted after Schedule 17.

(4) This section has effect as respects claims for group relief for accounting periods ending after the day appointed for the purposes of section 10 of the Taxes Act 1988 (pay and file).

GENERAL NOTE
The amendments made to the system for group relief, applicable from the introduction of "Pay and File" in 1993, are designed to give greater flexibility in obtaining this relief. See further the GENERAL NOTE to Sched. 15.

Group relief: relieved losses

101.—(1) The following section shall be inserted after section 41 1 of the Taxes Act 1988—

"Group relief by way of substitution for loss relief

411A.—(1) Group relief may be given in respect of a loss notwithstanding that relief has been given in respect of it under section 393(1).

(2) Where group relief in respect of a loss is given by virtue of subsection (1) above, all such assessments or adjustments of assessments shall be made as may be necessary to withdraw the relief in respect of the loss given under section 393(1).

(3) An assessment under subsection (2) above shall not be out of time if it is made within one year from the date on which the surrendering company gave the inspector notice of consent to surrender relating to the loss.

(4) For the purposes of this section relief under section 393(1) shall be treated as given for losses incurred in earlier accounting periods before losses incurred in later accounting periods."

(2) This section has effect as respects claims for group relief for accounting periods ending after the day appointed for the purposes of section 10 of the Taxes Act 1988 (pay and file).

GENERAL NOTE

The new I.C.T.A. s.411A, allows the granting of group relief for a loss notwithstanding that relief under s.393 has already been given for it.

The inspector can withdraw the previous s.393 relief by assessment within one year of the group relief claim being made.

For the purposes of the new section, s.393 relief will be withdrawn for earlier periods before later periods.

Capital allowances: general

102.—(1) The Capital Allowances Act 1990 shall be amended as follows.
(2) The following section shall be inserted after section 145—

   "Corporation tax allowances: claims
      145A. Schedule Al to this Act shall have effect."
(3) The Schedule set out in Schedule 16 to this Act shall be inserted before Schedule 1.
(4) This section has effect as respects claims for allowances falling to be made for accounting periods ending after the day appointed for the purposes of section 10 of the Taxes Act 1988 (pay and file).

GENERAL NOTE

This section introduces a number of changes to be made in the claiming of allowances by companies. T.M.A. 1970, s.42, will no longer apply. The details are set out in the notes to Sched. 16. The changes apply to claims for accounting periods ending after the day appointed by the Treasury under I.C.T.A. 1988, s.8(3), which is to be not before March 31, 1992 (see Finance (No. 2) Act 1987, s.95).

Capital allowances: assimilation to claims by individuals

103.—(1) Schedule 17 to this Act (which amends the Capital Allowances Act 1990 for the purpose of assimilating claims by companies to claims by individuals) shall have effect.
(2) This section has effect as respects allowances and charges falling to be made for chargeable periods ending after the day appointed for the purposes of section 10 of the Taxes Act 1988 (pay and file).

GENERAL NOTE

This section provides for the assimilation of claims by companies to those by individuals. It is to come into operation on the "appointed day" for I.C.T.A. 1988, s.10, which will not be before March 31, 1992.

The sections affected are set out in the GENERAL NOTE to Sched. 17.

Miscellaneous

Officers

104.—(1) In section 1 of the Taxes Management Act 1970 (appointment of inspectors etc.) the following subsections shall be inserted after subsection (2)—

"(2A) The Board may appoint a person to be an inspector or collector for general purposes or for such specific purposes as the Board think fit.

(2B) Where in accordance with the Board's administrative practices a person is authorised to act as an inspector or collector for specific purposes, he shall be deemed to have been appointed to be an inspector or collector for those purposes."

(2) In section 55 of that Act (recovery of tax not postponed)—

(a) in subsection (7) for the words "the inspector" there shall be substituted the words "an inspector";

(b) in subsection (10) for the words "this section," in the first place where they occur, there shall be substituted the words "subsection (3) above."

(3) The amendment made by subsection (1) above shall be deemed always to have had effect.

(4) The amendments made by subsection (2) above shall apply where notice of appeal is given on or after the day on which this Act is passed.

GENERAL NOTE

Since the earliest days of income tax, the assessment and collection of tax has been carried out by different officers. The amendments made by this will pave the way for experiments leading to a possible merger of the work of inspectors and collectors of taxes with a view to greater operational efficiency and improved service to taxpayers.

Recovery of excessive repayments of tax

105.—(1) In section 30 of the Taxes Management Act 1970 (recovery of excessive repayments of tax) the following subsection shall be inserted after subsection (1)—

"(1A) Subsection (1) above shall not apply where the amount of tax which has been repaid is assessable under section 29 of this Act."

(2) This section applies in relation to amounts of tax repaid on or after the day on which this Act is passed.

GENERAL NOTE

An assessment to recover an excessive repayment of tax under T.M.A. 1970, s.30, will not be raised where the repayment is itself assessable under the general assessing procedure in s.29.

Corporation tax: collection

106. In section 10 of the Taxes Act 1988 (time for payment of tax) the following subsection shall be substituted for subsection (2)—

"(2) Where by virtue of subsection (1)(a) above corporation tax for an accounting period of a company is due without the making of an assessment, the amount for the time being shown in a return by the company under section 11 of the Management Act (corporation tax return) as the corporation tax for the period shall be treated for the purposes of Part VI of the Management Act (collection and recovery) as tax charged and due and payable under an assessment on the company."

GENERAL NOTE

Where, under "Pay and File," a return, or amended return, shows the amount of tax which is correctly due at that time, the Revenue is given power to enforce collection of that tax without making an assessment. This does not affect the requirement on the inspector to make an assessment when the profits have been agreed.

PART III

STAMP DUTY AND STAMP DUTY RESERVE TAX

Repeals

Bearers: abolition of stamp duty

107.—(1) Stamp duty shall not be chargeable under the heading "Bearer Instrument" in Schedule 1 to the Stamp Act 1891.

(2) Subsection (1) above applies to an instrument which falls within section 60(1) of the Finance Act 1963 if it is issued on or after the abolition day.

(3) Subsection (1) above applies to an instrument which falls within section 60(2) of that Act if the stock constituted by or transferable by means of it is transferred on or after the abolition day.

(4) In subsection (2) above the reference to section 60(1) of the Finance Act 1963 includes a reference to section 9(1)(a) of the Finance Act (Northern Ireland) 1963 and in subsection (3) above the reference to section 60(2) of the former Act includes a reference to section 9(1)(b) of the latter.

GENERAL NOTE

In line with the general abolition of stamp duty on securities, the duty on bearer instruments is ended as from the abolition day, which is expected to be at the end of 1991.

F.A. 1963, s.60(1), relates to any bearer security except a "foreign loan security", which is covered by s.60(2). A foreign loan security is one which is issued outside the U.K. in a foreign currency and not offered for subscription in the U.K. directly or indirectly.

Transfer of securities: abolition of stamp duty

108.—(1) Where defined securities are transferred to or vested in a person by an instrument, stamp duty shall not be chargeable on the instrument.

(2) In this section "defined securities" means—

  (a) stocks, shares or loan capital,

  (b) interests in, or in dividends or other rights arising out of, stocks, shares or loan capital,

  (c) rights to allotments of or to subscribe for, or options to acquire or to dispose of, stocks, shares or loan capital, and

  (d) units under a unit trust scheme.

(3) In this section "loan capital" means—

  (a) any debenture stock, corporation stock or funded debt, by whatever name known, issued by a government or a body corporate or other body of persons (which here includes a local authority and any body whether formed or established in the United Kingdom or elsewhere);

  (b) any capital raised by a government, or by such a body as is mentioned in paragraph (a) above, if the capital is borrowed or has the character of borrowed money, and whether it is in the form of stock or any other form;

  (c) stock or marketable securities issued by a government.

(4) In this section "unit" and "unit trust scheme" have the same meanings as they had in Part VII of the Finance Act 1946 immediately before the abolition day.

(5) In this section references to a government include references to a government department, including a Northern Ireland department.

(6) In this section "government" means the government of the United Kingdom or of Northern Ireland or of any country or territory outside the United Kingdom.

(7) Subject to subsection (8) below, this section applies if the instrument is executed in pursuance of a contract made on or after the abolition day.

(8) In the case of an instrument—

(a) which falls within section 67(1) or (9) of the Finance Act 1986 (depositary receipts) or section 70(1) or (9) of that Act (clearance services), or

(b) which does not fall within section 67(1) or (9) or section 70(1) or (9) of that Act and is not executed in pursuance of a contract,

this section applies if the instrument is executed on or after the abolition day.

GENERAL NOTE

At the end of 1991 the Stock Exchange intends to introduce the TAURUS system of paperless share trading. This will make the present stamp duty on transfer of securities unviable, since stamp duty is a tax on documents. To allow planning for TAURUS to proceed, the government has made an advance decision not to charge tax on share transfers. The loss of revenue will amount to nearly £1 billion annually, but it is anticipated that the position of London as a securities market will be strengthened.

The stamp duty is abolished on all transfers after abolition day, unless in pursuance of a contract made before that day.

Stamp duty: other repeals

109.—(1) Section 83 of the Stamp Act 1891 (fine for certain acts relating to securities) shall not apply where an instrument of assignment or transfer is executed, or a transfer or negotiation of the stock constituted by or transferable by means of a bearer instrument takes place, on or after the abolition day.

(2) The following provisions (which relate to the cancellation of certain instruments) shall not apply where the stock certificate or other instrument is entered on or after the abolition day—

(a) section 109(1) of the Stamp Act 1891,

(b) section 5(2) of the Finance Act 1899,

(c) section 56(2) of the Finance Act 1946, and

(d) section 27(2) of the Finance (No. 2) Act (Northern Ireland) 1946.

(3) Section 67 of the Finance Act 1963 (prohibition of circulation of blank transfers) shall not apply where the sale is made on or after the abolition day; and section 16 of the Finance Act (Northern Ireland) 1963 (equivalent provision for Northern Ireland) shall not apply where the sale is made on or after the abolition day.

(4) No person shall be required to notify the Commissioners under section 68(1) or (2) or 71(1) or (2) of the Finance Act 1986 (depositary receipts and clearance services) if he first issues the receipts, provides the services or holds the securities as there mentioned on or after the abolition day.

(5) No company shall be required to notify the Commissioners under section 68(3) or 71(3) of that Act if it first becomes aware as there mentioned on or after the abolition day.

(6) The following provisions shall cease to have effect—

(a) section 56(1), (3) and (4) and section 57(2) to (4) of the Finance Act 1946 (unit trusts),

(b) section 27(1), (3) and (4) and section 28(2) to (4) of the Finance (No. 2) Act (Northern Ireland) 1946 (unit trusts),

(c) section 33 of the Finance Act 1970 (composition by financial institutions in respect of stamp duty),

(d) section 127(7) of the Finance Act 1976 (extension of composition provisions to Northern Ireland), and

(e) section 85 of the Finance Act 1986 (provisions about stock, marketable securities, etc.).

(7) The provisions mentioned in subsection (6) above shall cease to have effect as provided by the Treasury by order.

(8) An order under subsection (7) above—

(a) shall be made by statutory instrument;

(b) may make different provision for different provisions or different purposes;

(c) may include such supplementary, incidental, consequential or transitional provisions as appear to the Treasury to be necessary or expedient.

(9) Nothing in this section shall affect the application of section 56 of the Finance Act 1946 or section 27 of the Finance (No. 2) Act (Northern Ireland) 1946 by section 259 of the Inheritance Tax Act 1984.

GENERAL NOTE
This section contains further repeals of provisions which will be redundant after the abolition of the stamp duty on transfer of securities.

Stamp duty reserve tax: abolition

110.—(1) Stamp duty reserve tax shall cease to be chargeable.

(2) In relation to the charge to tax under section 87 of the Finance Act 1986 subsection (1) above applies where—
(a) the agreement to transfer is conditional and the condition is satisfied on or after the abolition day, or
(b) the agreement is not conditional and is made on or after the abolition day.

(3) In relation to the charge to tax under section 93(1) of that Act subsection (1) above applies where securities are transferred, issued or appropriated on or after the abolition day (whenever the arrangement was made).

(4) In relation to the charge to tax under section 96(1) of that Act subsection (1) above applies where securities are transferred or issued on or after the abolition day (whenever the arrangement was made).

(5) In relation to the charge to tax under section 93(10) of that Act subsection (1) above applies where securities are issued or transferred on sale, under terms there mentioned, on or after the abolition day.

(6) In relation to the charge to tax under section 96(8) of that Act subsection (1) above applies where securities are issued or transferred on sale, under terms there mentioned, on or after the abolition day.

(7) Where before the abolition day securities are issued or transferred on sale under terms mentioned in section 93(10) of that Act, in construing section 93(10) the effect of subsections (1) and (3) above shall be ignored.

(8) Where before the abolition day securities are issued or transferred on sale under terms mentioned in section 96(8) of that Act, in construing section 96(8) the effect of subsections (1) and (4) above shall be ignored.

GENERAL NOTE
Stamp duty reserve tax ("S.D.R.T.") was introduced in 1986 to buttress the stamp duty on transfers of securities by imposing a charge on agreements to transfer securities which did not generate a document which was stamped. The decision to discontinue the stamp duty on transfers of securities after the introduction of the TAURUS system of paperless trading on the Stock Exchange (expected at the end of 1991) means that S.D.R.T. will be redundant. It is accordingly prospectively abolished in relation to agreements effective after that time.

General

111.—(1) In sections 107 to 110 above "the abolition day" means such day as may be appointed by the Treasury by order made by statutory instrument.

(2) Sections 107 to 109 above shall be construed as one with the Stamp Act 1891.

GENERAL NOTE
The abolition day for stamp duty on transfers of securities and of S.D.R.T. is to be fixed by Treasury statutory instrument. It is expected to be at the end of 1991, when the TAURUS system on the Stock Exchange becomes operational.

Paired shares

Stamp duty

112.—(1) In section 143 of the Finance Act 1988 (paired shares) in subsection (1)(b) for the words "an equal number of" there shall be substituted the word "other."

(2) Subsection (1) above applies where—

(a) the offers referred to in section 143(1) are made, or are to be made, on or after the day on which this Act is passed, and

(b) before the offers are made, or are to be made, units comprising shares in the two companies concerned were offered (whether before or on or after the day on which this Act is passed) in circumstances where section 143 applied without the amendment made by subsection (1) above.

GENERAL NOTE

The arrangements for charging stamp duty on paired shares, *i.e.* shares in a U.K. company and a foreign company dealt in as a unit, only applied where equal numbers of units were offered in the U.K. and the foreign country. This restriction is now removed. F.A. 1988, s.143, was introduced with Eurotunnel in mind and the amendment reflects changes in the financing arrangements.

Stamp duty reserve tax

113.—(1) Section 99 of the Finance Act 1986 (stamp duty reserve tax: interpretation) shall be amended as follows.

(2) In subsection (6A) (paired shares) in paragraph (b) for the words "an equal number of" there shall be substituted the word "other."

(3) The following subsection shall be inserted after subsection (6A)—

"(6B) For the purposes of subsection (4) above, shares issued by a body corporate which is not incorporated in the United Kingdom ("the foreign company") are paired with shares issued by a body corporate which is so incorporated ("the UK company") where—

(a) the articles of association of the UK company and the equivalent instruments governing the foreign company each provide that no share in the company to which they relate may be transferred otherwise than as part of a unit comprising one share in that company and one share in the other, and

(b) the shares issued by the foreign company, and the shares issued by the UK company, are issued to give effect to an allotment of the shares (as part of such units) as fully or partly paid bonus shares."

(4) In subsection (9) for the words "subsection (6A)" there shall be substituted the words "subsections (6A) and (6B)."

(5) Subsection (2) above applies where—

(a) the offers referred to in section 99(6A) are made on or after the day on which this Act is passed, and

(b) before the offers are made, units comprising shares in the two companies concerned were offered (whether before or on or after the day on which this Act is passed) in circumstances where section 99(6A) applied without the amendment made by subsection (2) above.

(6) Subsections (3) and (4) above apply where—

(a) the shares referred to in section 99(6B) are issued on or after the day on which this Act is passed, and

(b) before they are issued, units comprising shares in the two companies concerned were offered (whether before or on or after the day on which this Act is passed) in circumstances where section 99(6A) applied without the amendment made by subsection (2) above.

    The removal of the restriction on paired shares for stamp duty purposes effected by s.112 is
applied for S.D.R.T. purposes. S.D.R.T. is extended to agreements to transfer bonus paired
shares.

International organisations

International organisations

114.—(1) In section 126 of the Finance Act 1984 (tax exemptions in
relation to designated international organisations) in subsection (3) the
following paragraph shall be inserted after paragraph (c)—
      "(d) no stamp duty reserve tax shall be chargeable under section 93
            (depositary receipts) or 96 (clearance services) of the Finance
            Act 1986 in respect of the issue of securities by the
            organisation."
    (2) Where an organisation or body is designated under section 126(1) or
(4) before the day on which this Act is passed, subsection (1) above applies
in relation to the issue of securities by the organisation or body on or after
that day.
    (3) Where an organisation or body is designated under section 126(1) or
(4) on or after the day on which this Act is passed, subsection (1) above
applies in relation to the issue of securities by the organisation or body after
the designation.

GENERAL NOTE
    The occasion for this section is the establishment in London of the European Bank for
Reconstruction and Development (EBRD), set up to help eastern European countries develop
market economies. The EBRD may wish to issue chargeable securities to a nominee for either a
depositary bank or a clearance service. The amendment removes the charge to S.D.R.T. on
such transactions.

PART IV

MISCELLANEOUS AND GENERAL

Ports levy

Levy on privatisation of certain ports

115.—(1) A levy shall be chargeable on the disposal of securities of a
company which is, or has control of, a successor company to a relevant port
authority if the disposal is made by—
    (a) the relevant port authority,
    (b) a company under the control of the relevant port authority, or
    (c) a person constituted under a private Act, the Bill for which was
         promoted by the relevant port authority.
    (2) For the purposes of this section and sections 116 to 120 below—
    (a) "securities," in relation to a company, includes shares, debentures,
         bonds and other securities of the company, whether or not constitut-
         ing a charge on the assets of the company;
    (b) "control" shall be construed in accordance with section 416 of the
         Taxes Act 1988;
    (c) a company is a successor company to a relevant port authority if the
         whole or any part of the authority's undertaking is transferred to it in
         accordance with the provisions of a private Act, the Bill for which was
         promoted by the authority;
    (d) a relevant port authority is an authority which is a harbour authority
         within the meaning of the Harbours Act 1964 or the Harbours Act
         (Northern Ireland) 1970 but not a company having a share capital or a
         local authority (within the meaning of section 842A of the Taxes Act
         1988); and
    (e) "shares" include stock;

and in sections 116 to 120 below "levy" means levy under subsection (1) above.

GENERAL NOTE
The reason for the ports levy is that there is a move towards privatisation of the "trust ports," the fifty or so harbours which are governed by port authorities. Government time was not available for a general privatisation measure, but private bills to this end were introduced by the Tees and Hartlepool port authority and the Clyde port authority. Privatisation will be achieved by transferring the assets of the authorities to companies whose shares will be sold. In line with the decision in the Trustee Savings Bank case, *Ross* v. *Lord Advocate* [1986] 1 W.L.R. 1077, it is considered that the assets of the trust ports belong to the state, and it was felt to be right that a levy should be made on the proceeds of the privatisation, in view of past state expenditure on the trust ports and to prevent the privatised ports from attaining an unduly large cash injection which might give them an unfair competitive advantage over other ports.
It is intended that the levy will be applied to further privatisations of trust ports, however these are structured.

Amount of levy

116.—(1) Subject to subsection (2) below, levy shall be charged at the rate of 50 per cent. on the consideration given for the securities disposed of.

(2) Where no consideration is given for the securities disposed of, or their market value at the time of the disposal is greater than the consideration given, levy shall be charged at the rate of 50 per cent. on that market value.

(3) There shall be allowed as a deduction from the amount on which levy would otherwise be chargeable any expenditure wholly and exclusively incurred for the purposes of the disposal by the person making the disposal, being—
(a) fees, commissions or remuneration paid for professional services,
(b) costs of transfer,
(c) costs of advertising, or
(d) expenses reasonably incurred in ascertaining the market value of the securities disposed of.

(4) Where—
(a) a scheme has been effected or arrangements have been made (whether before or after a disposal) whereby the value of securities disposed of has been materially reduced, and
(b) the aim or one of the aims of the scheme or arrangements is decreasing liability to levy,
the amount on which levy would be chargeable apart from this subsection shall be increased by such amount as appears to the Secretary of State to be appropriate.

(5) The market value of securities shall be determined for the purposes of this section as it would fall to be determined in accordance with sections 150(1) to (3) and 152 of the Capital Gains Tax Act 1979 for the purposes of tax on chargeable gains (but subject to section 117 below).

(6) The Treasury may substitute for the percentage for the time being specified in subsections (1) and (2) above such other percentage as they may prescribe by order made by statutory instrument.

(7) An order under subsection (6) above shall not be made unless a draft of the order has been laid before and approved by a resolution of the House of Commons.

GENERAL NOTE
The rate of levy is fixed at 50 per cent. of the proceeds of sale of the shares concerned, or of their market value if this is greater. Expenses of flotation are deductible. The Secretary of State for Transport may increase the amount subject to levy if a levy avoidance scheme has been operated.
The Treasury can vary the rate of levy by statutory instrument, subject to affirmative resolution of the House of Commons.

Levy on employee securities

117.—(1) This section applies where securities of a company are disposed of for no consideration, or for a consideration less than their market value, to—

(a) directors or employees of the company or of another company which is a wholly-owned subsidiary of the company,

(b) the trustees of a share option scheme or profit sharing scheme approved under Schedule 9 to the Taxes Act 1988, or

(c) the trustees of trusts to which section 86 of the Inheritance Tax Act 1984 applies and which do not permit any of the settled property to be applied otherwise than for the benefit of—

(i) persons of a class defined by reference to employment by, or the holding of office with, the company or another company which is a wholly-owned subsidiary of the company, or

(ii) persons of a class defined by reference to marriage or relationship to, or dependence on, persons of that class;

and in this subsection "wholly-owned subsidiary" shall be construed in accordance with section 736 of the Companies Act 1985.

(2) Where this section applies, the market value of the securities shall for the purposes of section 116 above be taken to be reduced—

(a) if no consideration is given for the securities, to nil, or

(b) otherwise, to the amount of the consideration given for the securities, or as nearly to nil, or that amount, as is permitted under subsection (3) below.

(3) A reduction under subsection (2) above shall not exceed the difference between—

(a) three per cent. of the aggregate of the amounts on which levy is chargeable (ignoring any reduction under subsection (2) above) in the case of the disposal in question and any other disposals of securities of the company made on or before the day of that disposal, and

(b) the amount of any reductions under subsection (2) above in the case of the other disposals.

GENERAL NOTE
Up to three per cent. of the shares may be disposed of on favourable terms to employees or for their benefit without triggering the provision in s.115 requiring the shares to be valued at market for levy purposes.

Payment of levy

118.—(1) Levy chargeable on a disposal shall be paid to the Secretary of State by the person by whom the disposal was made.

(2) The amount of the levy shall be assessed by the Secretary of State who shall serve a notice of assessment on the person by whom the disposal was made stating the date of issue of the notice of assessment and the effect of subsection (3) below.

(3) The amount assessed shall be payable within the period of three months beginning with the day on which the disposal was made or within the period of 30 days beginning with the date of the issue of the notice of assessment, if that period ends later.

(4) Where any levy payable by the person by whom the disposal was made is not paid within the period of six months beginning with the first day after the period within which it is payable, the Secretary of State may, within the period of three years beginning with that day, serve on the company whose securities were disposed of a notice stating—

(a) particulars of the levy assessed and the amount remaining unpaid,

(b) the date of issue of the notice, and

(c) the effect of subsection (5) below.

(5) The amount unpaid shall be payable to the Secretary of State by the company within the period of 30 days beginning with the date of issue of the notice under subsection (4) above.

(6) Any amount paid in accordance with subsection (5) above shall cease to be payable to the Secretary of State by the person who made the disposal but the company may recover it from that person.

(7) A person who is liable to make a payment of levy but does not make payment of the amount due during the period within which it is payable shall also pay to the Secretary of State interest on the unpaid levy at the rate applicable under section 178 of the Finance Act 1989 from the first day after the end of that period until payment of the levy is made; and the interest shall be paid without deduction of tax.

(8) In subsection (2) of that section, after paragraph (m) there shall be inserted "and

(n) section 118(7) of the Finance Act 1990."

GENERAL NOTE

Levy is to be assessed by the Transport Secretary on the person making the disposal and is payable within three months of the disposal or 30 days of the assessment, if later.

Levy unpaid within six months may be assessed on the company whose shares are concerned within the following three years, and is payable within 30 days. The company will have a right of recovery from the person making the disposal.

Interest on unpaid levy is chargeable at the rate provided by F.A. 1989, s.178.

Information for purposes of levy

119.—(1) A person who makes a disposal of securities on which levy is chargeable shall give to the Secretary of State, not later than 30 days after the day on which the disposal is made, written notification that he has made the disposal.

(2) The Secretary of State may by notice in writing require—

(a) a person who is or may be liable to levy,

(b) a person to whom there has been made a disposal of securities on which levy is chargeable, or

(c) a company whose securities have been the subject of such a disposal, to deliver to him documents, or to furnish to him particulars, to which subsection (3) below applies within such time, not less than 30 days after the date of the notice, as may be specified in the notice.

(3) This subsection applies to—

(a) documents specified or described in the notice under subsection (2) above which are in the possession or power of the person to whom the notice is given and which (in the opinion of the Secretary of State) contain, or may contain, information relevant to a liability to levy or to the amount of such a liability, and

(b) particulars specified or described in the notice which the Secretary of State may reasonably require as being relevant to, or to the amount of, such a liability.

(4) Where any person fails to give notification in accordance with sub-section (1) above or to comply with a notice under subsection (2) above, he shall be liable—

(a) to a penalty not exceeding £300, and

(b) if the failure continues after a penalty is imposed under paragraph (a) above, to a further penalty or penalties not exceeding £60 for each day on which the failure continues after the day on which the penalty under paragraph (a) above was imposed (but excluding any day for which a penalty under this paragraph has already been imposed).

(5) Where a person fraudulently or negligently furnishes any incorrect particulars in response to a notice under subsection (2) above he shall be liable to a penalty not exceeding £3,000.

(6) Proceedings for a penalty under this section shall be instituted by the Secretary of State before the High Court or, in Scotland, before the Court of Session, the Court of Exchequer in Scotland, and any penalty imposed by the court shall be paid to the Secretary of State.

(7) Proceedings within subsection (6) above may not be instituted later than six years after the date on which the penalty was incurred or began to be incurred.

(8) Any proceedings within subsection (6) above instituted in England and Wales shall be deemed to be civil proceedings by the Crown within the meaning of Part II of the Crown Proceedings Act 1947 and any such proceedings instituted in Northern Ireland shall be deemed to be civil proceedings within the meaning of that Part of that Act as for the time being in force in Northern Ireland.

GENERAL NOTE

Persons disposing of securities liable to levy must inform the Transport Secretary within 30 days.

The Secretary is given wide powers to require documents or information from the vendors or purchasers of shares or the company itself. Failure to comply or fraudulent or negligent replies attract penalties on the lines of T.M.A., s.98, enforceable by action in the courts.

Supplementary provisions relating to levy

120.—(1) The time when a disposal of securities is made shall be determined for the purposes of sections 115 to 119 above as it would fall to be determined in accordance with section 27 of the Capital Gains Tax Act 1979 for the purposes of tax on chargeable gains.

(2) A payment of levy by the person by whom a disposal is made shall be allowable as a deduction from the consideration in the computation under that Act of the gain accruing to the person on the disposal; but, subject to that, no payment of levy, interest on unpaid levy or penalty under section 119 above shall be allowed as a deduction in computing any income, profits or losses for any tax purposes.

(3) There shall be paid into the Consolidated Fund—

(a) all payments of levy received by the Secretary of State,

(b) all interest paid to the Secretary of State on unpaid levy, and

(c) all penalties paid to the Secretary of State under section 119 above.

(4) Any expenses of the Secretary of State incurred in consequence of any of sections 115 to 119 above or of this section shall be defrayed out of money provided by Parliament.

GENERAL NOTE

Levy is allowed as a deduction, but capital gains tax will be chargeable on the net proceeds at 35 per cent. Accordingly the privatised companies will retain about one third of the proceeds of the assets of the trust ports, in addition to the assets themselves.

It is noteworthy that no appeal procedure is made available in relation to this tax. Judicial review would appear to be the only avenue for challenging assessments.

Petroleum revenue tax

Limit on PRT repayment interest where loss carried back

121.—(1) Schedule 2 to the Oil Taxation Act 1975 (management and collection of PRT) shall be amended as follows.

(2) At the beginning of paragraph 16 (interest on repayments) there shall be inserted the words "Subject to paragraph 17 below."

(3) After that paragraph there shall be inserted the following paragraph—

"17.—(1) This paragraph applies where—

(a) an assessment made on a participator for a chargeable period or an amendment of such an assessment (in this paragraph referred to as "the relevant assessment or amendment") gives effect to relief under subsection (2) or subsection (3) of section 7 of this Act for one or more allowable losses accruing in a later chargeable period (in this paragraph referred to, in relation to the relevant assessment or amendment, as "the relief for losses carried back"); and

(b) the later chargeable period referred to in paragraph (a) above ends after 30th June 1991; and

(c) an amount of tax becomes repayable to the participator by virtue of the relevant assessment or amendment (whether wholly or partly by reason of giving effect to the relief for losses carried back).

(2) In the following provisions of this paragraph, so much of the repayment of tax referred to in sub-paragraph (1)(c) above as is attributable to giving effect to the relief for losses carried back is referred to as "the appropriate repayment."

(3) For the purpose of determining the amount of the appropriate repayment in a case where the relevant assessment or amendment not only gives effect to the relief for losses carried back but also takes account of any other matter (whether a relief or not) which goes to reduce the assessable profit of the period in question or otherwise to reduce the tax payable for that period, the amount of the repayment which is attributable to the relief for losses carried back is the difference between—

(a) the total amount of tax repayable by virtue of the relevant assessment or amendment; and

(b) the amount of tax (if any) which would have been so repayable if no account had been taken of the relief for losses carried back.

(4) Where this paragraph applies, the amount of interest which, by virtue of paragraph 16 above, is carried by the appropriate repayment shall not exceed the difference between—

(a) 85 per cent. of the allowable loss or losses referred to in sub-paragraph (1)(a) above; and

(b) the amount of the appropriate repayment."

GENERAL NOTE

This section, which is closely related to ss.60–62, is part of a package of measures designed to improve the tax treatment of future abandonment costs to be met by companies when North Sea oil and gas fields are closed down and the offshore installations removed.

Operating in conjunction with the new reliefs given by ss.60–62, the section puts a cap on the amount of interest paid to companies in respect of petroleum revenue tax (PRT) losses carried back to earlier chargeable periods. The cap ensures that for losses arising in any period after June 30, 1991, the PRT interest, when combined with the repayment to which it relates, does not exceed 85 per cent. of the PRT loss which is carried back to the earlier period.

Without this restriction it might be possible, where large PRT losses on abandonment are carried back for a number of periods, for the relief given for PRT (including the associated interest payment), when added to other tax relief, to approach or even exceed 100 per cent. of the expenditure concerned.

Variation, on account of fraudulent or negligent conduct, of decision on expenditure claim etc.

122.—(1) In the Oil Taxation Act 1975, in Schedule 5 (allowance of certain expenditure on a claim by the responsible person) paragraph 9 (variation of decision on a claim where the amount of expenditure allowed etc. was incorrectly stated in the notice of the decision) shall be amended in accordance with subsections (2) to (4) below.

(2) After sub-paragraph (1) there shall be inserted the following sub-paragraphs—

"(1A) In any case falling within sub-paragraph (1B) below, sub-paragraph (1) above shall have effect—

(a) with the substitution for the words "within the period of three years commencing with" of the words "at any time after"; and

(b) with the omission of the words "before the expiry of that period".

(1B) The cases referred to in sub-paragraph (1A) above are those where—
  (a) the incorrect statement of the relevant amount in the notice of the decision mentioned in sub-paragraph (1) above was an over-statement of that amount; and
  (b) that over-statement was, in whole or in part, referable to an error in a statement or declaration made in connection with the claim; and
  (c) at least one of the conditions in sub-paragraph (1C) below is fulfilled with respect to that error.

(1C) The conditions referred to in sub-paragraph (1B)(c) above are—
  (a) that the error was attributable, in whole or in part, to the fraudu-lent or negligent conduct of the responsible person or a person acting on his behalf;
  (b) that paragraph (a) above does not apply but, on the error coming to the notice of the person by whom the statement or declaration was made or a person acting on his behalf, the error was not remedied without unreasonable delay; and
  (c) that paragraph (a) above does not apply but, on the error coming to the notice of any person who subsequently becomes the res-ponsible person, the error was not remedied without unreason-able delay."

(3) After sub-paragraph (2) there shall be inserted the following sub-paragraph—
  "(2A) In any case where—
  (a) the relevant amount which was incorrectly stated is a part of any expenditure falling within paragraph (c) of sub-paragraph (2) above (in this sub-paragraph referred to as a "paragraph (c) amount"), and
  (b) under sub-paragraph (1B)(a) above the question arises whether the incorrect statement was an over-statement,
that question shall be determined by comparing the total amount which, in accordance with the notice of decision containing the incorrect statement, was brought into account under section 2(9)(b)(ii) of this Act with the total amount which would have been so brought into account if the paragraph (c) amounts stated in that notice had been correct."

(4) For sub-paragraph (11) there shall be substituted the following sub-paragraph—
  "(11) In a case falling within sub-paragraph (1B) above, this para-graph has effect in relation to notices of decisions of the Board under paragraph 3 above whenever given; and, in any other case, this para-graph has effect in relation to such notices given after 15th March 1983."

(5) In the Table set out in paragraph 2 of Schedule 6 to the Oil Taxation Act 1975 (which modifies Schedule 5 in its application to a claim under Schedule 6) in the second column relating to paragraph 9 of Schedule 5 there shall be inserted—
  "Omit sub-paragraph (1C)(c)."

(6) In the Table set out in paragraph 1(3) of Schedule 7 to the Oil Taxation Act 1975 (which modifies Schedule 5 in its application to Schedules 7 and 8), in the entry in the second column relating to paragraph 9 of Schedule 5,—
  (a) at the beginning insert "In sub-paragraph (1C) omit paragraph (c)"; and
  (b) after "(b) and (c)" insert "omit sub-paragraph (2A)."

GENERAL NOTE
Under the existing law, the Inland Revenue can only reopen its decisions on PRT expendi-

ture claims within three years of the decision, even where it transpires that the claim was made negligently or fraudulently. There is no similar time bar on adjustments to income for PRT purposes. Accordingly the time bar for reviewing expenditure claims is removed in cases of fraud or negligence by or on behalf of the claimant. The removal of the bar applies to past as well as future claim periods. The provision, which is consistent with other parts of the tax system, is expected to yield up to £20m. in 1990–91 and £10m. in 1991–92, depending on the number of cases identified.

Miscellaneous

Gas levy

123.—(1) Gas levy shall not be payable by any person in respect of any gas unless—

(a) the gas is purchased by that person under a tax-exempt contract or under terms comprised in an excluded oil document; or

(b) the gas is won by that person, and not sold by him under such a contract or under terms so comprised, and is gas to which subsection (2) below applies.

(2) This subsection applies to gas which the British Gas Corporation was on 23rd August 1986 obliged or entitled to purchase (whether immediately or at some future date) under a tax-exempt contract or under terms comprised in an excluded oil document.

(3) In determining whether any gas which is won at any time is gas to which subsection (2) above applies, no account shall be taken of—

(a) any future variation of rights and liabilities under a tax-exempt contract, or under terms comprised in an excluded oil document, other than one effected by the exercise of an existing option; or

(b) any future termination of such rights and liabilities other than one occurring before 5th March 1990.

(4) In this section—

"excluded oil document" means a document which on 1st April 1980 was treated for the purposes of paragraph (a) of subsection (1) of section 10 of the Oil Taxation Act 1975 as containing the whole or part of a contract for the sale of excluded oil as defined in that subsection;

"existing option" means an option granted before the commencement of this section;

"future," in relation to a variation or termination, means effected or occurring after that commencement;

"tax-exempt contract" has the same meaning as the Gas Levy Act 1981;

"termination" means any termination, whether occurring by effluxion of time, by the exercise of an existing option or otherwise.

(5) This section shall be deemed to have come into force on 24th August 1986.

GENERAL NOTE

Under the Oil Taxation Act 1975, s.10(1)(a), gas sold to the British Gas Corporation under a contract made before the end of June 1975 was excluded from the scope of petroleum revenue tax. By the Gas Levy Act 1981 a levy was imposed on the corporation in respect of that gas. By the Gas Act 1986 the assets of the corporation were transferred to British Gas plc on August 24, 1986, and the gas levy was widened to cover any person purchasing gas under such a contract. Gas levy also included in certain circumstances gas won by any person. The section provides that such gas is not subject to the levy if it was still covered by contract to the corporation when the Gas Act 1986 come into effect.

Inheritance tax: restriction on power to require information

124.—(1) In section 219 of the Inheritance Tax Act 1984 (power to require information), after subsection (1) there shall be inserted—

"(1A) A notice under this section is not to be given except with the consent of a Special Commissioner and the Commissioner is to give his consent only on being satisfied that in all the circumstances the Board are justified in proceeding under this section."

(2) This section shall apply with respect to notices given on or after the day on which this Act is passed.

GENERAL NOTE

A demand by the Revenue for information under I.H.T.A. 1984, s.219, is now subjected to the requirement of prior approval by a Special Commissioner. This brings the procedure into line with that for other taxes under T.M.A. 1970, s.20.

Information for tax authorities in other member States

125.—(1) Subsections (1) to (8) and (8C) to (9) of section 20 of the Taxes Management Act 1970 (powers to call for information relevant to liability to income tax, corporation tax or capital gains tax) shall have effect as if the references in those provisions to tax liability included a reference to liability to a tax of a member State other than the United Kingdom which is a tax on income or on capital for the purposes of the Directive of the Council of the European Communities dated 19th December 1977 No. 77/799/EEC.

(2) In their application by virtue of subsection (1) above those provisions shall have effect as if—

(a)   the reference in section 20(7A) to any provision of the Taxes Acts were a reference to any provision of the law of the member State in accordance with which the tax in question is charged.

(b)   the references in subsection (2) of section 20B to an appeal relating to tax were references to an appeal, review or similar proceedings under the law of the member State relating to the tax in question, and

(c)   the reference in subsection (6) of that section to believing that tax has or may have been lost to the Crown were a reference to believing that the tax in question has or may have been lost to the member State.

(3) Section 219 of the Inheritance Tax Act 1984 (power to require information for purposes of that Act) shall have effect as if the reference to that Act in subsection (1) of that section included a reference to any provision of the law of a member State other than the United Kingdom in accordance with which there is charged any tax—

(a)   which is of a character similar to that of inheritance tax or is chargeable on or by reference to death or gifts inter vivos, and

(b)   in relation to which the Directive mentioned in subsection (1) above has effect by virtue of any other Directive of the Council (whether adopted before or after the passing of this Act) extending that Directive.

(4) In its application by virtue of subsection (3) above section 219 shall have effect as if the reference to income tax in subsection (2) of that section included a reference to any tax of a member State other than the United Kingdom such as is mentioned in subsection (1) above.

(5) In section 77 of the Finance Act 1978 (disclosure of information to tax authorities of member States: obligation of secrecy) references to the Directive mentioned in subsection (1) above shall include a reference to that Directive as extended by any other Directive of the Council (whether adopted before or after the passing of this Act) to any taxes of a character similar to that of inheritance tax or chargeable on or by reference to death or gifts inter vivos.

(6) Subsections (1) and (2) above shall apply with respect to notices given on or after the day on which this Act is passed, subsections (3) and (4) above shall apply with respect to notices given on or after such day as the Treasury may by order made by statutory instrument appoint and subsection (5) above shall come into force on that day.

Under Directive 77/799 the EEC required member countries to provide each other on request with information about their taxpayers in relation to income and gains. The European Commission has been examining whether changes to the directive would be desirable in the light of the forthcoming liberalisation of capital movements to extend the use of the directive to taxes on gifts.

The Revenue considered that F.A. 1978, s.77, was sufficient to comply with the directive, but it now appears that the directive includes information which the Revenue does not have, and does not need, for its own purposes. The law is accordingly amended to cover the wider ambit of the directive and its possible extension to inheritance tax.

This provision represents another wide extension of the powers of the European Commission in Brussels in relation to the U.K.

Pools payments for football ground improvements

126.—(1) This section applies to any payment (including a payment made before the passing of this Act) which, in consequence of the reduction in pool betting duty effected by section 4 above, is made by a person liable to pay that duty in order to meet, directly or indirectly, capital expenditure incurred (whether by the person to whom it is made or any other person) in improving the safety or comfort of spectators at a ground to be used for the playing of association football.

(2) Where a person carrying on a trade makes a payment to which this section applies, the payment may be deducted in computing for tax purposes the profits or gains of the trade.

(3) A payment to which this section applies shall not be regarded as an annual payment.

(4) Section 153 of the Capital Allowances Act 1990 shall not apply to expenditure of the kind mentioned in subsection (1) above in so far as it has been or is to be met, directly or indirectly, out of a payment to which this section applies.

(5) Where a payment to which this section applies is made to trustees, the sum received by them and any assets representing it (but not any income or gains rising from them) shall not be relevant property for the purposes of Chapter III of Part III of the Inheritance Tax Act 1984.

Under s.4, pool betting duty is reduced from 42.5 per cent. to 40 per cent. on the clear understanding that the full amount saved is passed by the pools promoters to the Football Trust and is used by it to improve the safety and comfort of spectators at English and Scottish football league grounds.

This section is designed to ensure that the full amount can be so applied without any incidental charge to tax.

Definition of "local authority" for certain tax purposes

127.—(1) In the Taxes Act 1988 the following section shall be inserted after section 842—

"Local authorities

842A.—(1) Except so far as the context otherwise requires in the Tax Acts "local authority" means—
  (a) in relation to England and Wales, an authority of a description specified for the purposes of this paragraph,
  (b) in relation to Scotland, an authority of a description specified for the purposes of this paragraph, and
  (c) in relation to Northern Ireland, an authority of a description specified for the purposes of this paragraph,

(2) The following are the descriptions of authority specified for the purposes of paragraph (a) of subsection (1) above—
  (a) a charging authority for the purposes of the Local Government Finance Act 1988;

(b) a precepting authority for the purposes of that Act;
(c) a body having power by virtue of regulations under section 74 of that Act to issue a levy;
(d) a body having power by virtue of regulations under section 75 of that Act to issue a special levy;
(e) a combined police authority established by an amalgamation scheme under the Police Act 1964;
(f) a fire authority constituted by a combination scheme under the Fire Services Act 1947;
(g) an authority having power to make or determine a rate.
(3) The following are the descriptions of authority specified for the purposes of paragraph (b) of subsection (1) above—
(a) a regional council;
(b) an islands council;
(c) a district council;
(d) a joint board or committee within the meaning of the Local Government (Scotland) Act 1973;
(e) an authority having power to requisition any sum from an authority falling within any of paragraphs (a) to (c) above.
(4) The following are the descriptions of authority specified for the purposes of paragraph (c) of subsection (1) above—
(a) an authority having power to make or determine a rate;
(b) an authority having power to issue a precept, requisition or other demand for the payment of money to be raised out of a rate.
(5) In this section "rate" means a rate the proceeds of which are applicable for public local purposes and which is leviable by reference to the value of land or other property."
(2) In the Capital Gains Tax Act 1979, in section 155(1) (interpretation) the following definition shall be inserted after the definition of "land"—
" 'local authority' has the meaning given by section 842A of the Taxes Act 1988,".
(3) Schedule 18 to this Act (consequential amendments) shall have effect.
(4) This section shall be deemed to have come into force on 1st April 1990.

GENERAL NOTE
Under I.C.T.A. 1988, s.519, and C.G.T.A. 1979, s.149B(3), a "local authority" enjoys exemption from income tax, corporation tax and capital gains tax. "Local authority" was defined under I.C.T.A. 1988, s.519(4), in terms of powers in relation to the raising of rates. Under the Local Government Finance Act 1988 and the corresponding legislation for Scotland domestic rates were abolished and replaced by the community charge or "poll tax" and the administration of business rates was centralised. New definitions of "local authority" are accordingly required and are provided for England and Wales in subs. (2) and for Scotland in subs. (3) of the new s.842A.
The rating system continues in Northern Ireland and the previous definition is re-enacted in subss. (4) and (5).

Repayment of fees and charges

128.—(1) This section applies where at the beginning of the day on which this Act is passed—
(a) an enactment confers power to make provision for payment of a fee or charge (however described), and
(b) sums paid in pursuance of provision made in exercise of the power are payable into the Consolidated Fund.
(2) Subject to subsection (3) below, the enactment shall be treated as also conferring power to make provision about repayment of sums paid, or purported to be paid, in pursuance of provision made in exercise of the power.
(3) Subsection (2) above shall not apply if the fee or charge is one—
(a) repayment of which is prohibited or regulated by an enactment, or

(b) power to make provision about repayment of which is expressly conferred, or expressly negatived, to any extent.

(4) Without prejudice to the generality of the power conferred by virtue of subsection (2) above, the provision which may be made by virtue of that subsection includes provision—
  (a) that repayment shall be made only if a specified person is satisfied that specified conditions are met or in other specified circumstances;
  (b) that repayment shall be made in part only;
  (c) that, in the case of partial repayment, the amount repaid shall be a specified sum or determined in a specified manner; and
  (d) for repayment of different amounts in different circumstances.

(5) In subsection (4) above "specified" means specified in the instrument exercising the power.

(6) In determining for the purposes of this section whether sums are payable into the Consolidated Fund, section 3 of the Government Trading Funds Act 1973 (payments into a trading fund) shall be disregarded.

(7) In this section "enactment" includes Northern Ireland legislation as defined in section 24(5) of the Interpretation Act 1978.

(8) An Order in Council under paragraph l(l)(b) of Schedule 1 to the Northern Ireland Act 1974 (legislation for Northern Ireland in the interim period) which states that it is made only for purposes corresponding to those of this section—
  (a) shall not be subject to sub-paragraphs (4) and (5) of paragraph 1 of that Schedule (affirmative resolution of both Houses of Parliament); but
  (b) shall be subject to annulment in pursuance of a resolution of either House.

GENERAL NOTE
Most Government revenues are paid into the Consolidated Fund, established under the fiscal reforms carried out by Pitt the Younger at the end of the eighteenth century. This section confers power to make provision regarding repayment of fees and charges paid into the Fund.

Settlement of stock disputes by deputy registrars

129. In section 5 of the National Debt Act 1972 (settlement by Chief Registrar of friendly societies of disputes as to holdings on National Savings Stock Register)—
  (a) in subsection (1), after the words "Chief Registrar of friendly societies" there shall be inserted the words "or a deputy appointed by him,"
  (b) in subsection (2), after the words "Chief Registrar" there shall be inserted the words "or deputy,"
  (c) in subsection (3)(a), after the words "Chief Registrar of friendly societies" there shall be inserted the words "or a deputy appointed by him," and
  (d) subsection (3)(b) shall cease to have effect.

GENERAL NOTE
Disputes between the Director of Savings and holders of stock on the National Savings Stock Register are referred to the Chief Registrar of friendly societies for settlement. This section allows the Chief Registrar to appoint a deputy for this purpose.

Limit for local loans

130. In section 4(1) of the National Loans Act 1968 (which provides that the aggregate of any commitments of the Public Works Loan Commissioners in respect of undertakings to grant local loans and any amount outstanding in respect of the principal of such loans shall not exceed £42,000 million or such other sum not exceeding £50,000 million as the Treasury may specify by order) for the words "£42,000 million" and "£50,000 million" there shall be substituted respectively "£55,000 million" and "£70,000 million."

GENERAL NOTE

The limit for loans by the Public Works Loan Commissioners is raised to £55 billion, or such higher amount as the Treasury may specify by order up to £70 bn. The previous limits of £42 bn. and £50 bn. were set in 1986.

General

Interpretation etc.

131.—(1) In this Act "the Taxes Act 1970" means the Income and Corporation Taxes Act 1970 and "the Taxes Act 1988" means the Income and Corporation Taxes Act 1988.

(2) Chapter II of Part I of this Act shall be construed as one with the Value Added Tax Act 1983.

(3) Part II of this Act, so far as it relates to capital gains tax, shall be construed as one with the Capital Gains Tax Act 1979.

Repeals

132. The enactments specified in Schedule 19 to this Act (which include spent or unnecessary enactments) are hereby repealed to the extent specified in the third column of that Schedule, but subject to any provision at the end of any Part of that Schedule.

Short title

133. This Act may be cited as the Finance Act 1990.

SCHEDULES

Section 1   SCHEDULE 1

TABLE OF RATES OF DUTY ON WINE AND MADE-WINE

Description of wine or made-wine	Rates of duty per hectolitre
	£
Wine or made-wine of a strength not exceeding 2 per cent.	11.03
Wine or made-wine of a strength exceeding 2 per cent. but not exceeding 3 per cent.	18.38
Wine or made-wine of a strength exceeding 3 per cent. but not exceeding 4 per cent.	25.73
Wine or made-wine of a strength exceeding 4 per cent. but not exceeding 5 per cent.	33.09
Wine or made-wine of a strength exceeding 5 per cent. but not exceeding 5.5 per cent.	40.44
Wine or made-wine of a strength exceeding 5.5 per cent. but not exceeding 15 per cent. and not being sparkling	110.28
Sparkling wine or sparkling made-wine of a strength exceeding 5.5 per cent. but not exceeding 15 per cent.	182.10
Wine or made-wine of a strength exceeding 15 per cent. but not exceeding 18 per cent.	190.20
Wine or made-wine of a strength exceeding 18 per cent. but not exceeding 22 per cent.	219.40
Wine or made-wine of a strength exceeding 22 per cent.	219.40 plus £17.35 for every 1 per cent. or part of 1 per cent. in excess of 22 per cent.

GENERAL NOTE
This implements an increase of seven per cent. in the duties on wine and made-wine. See further the note to s.1.

Section 5   SCHEDULE 2

VEHICLES EXCISE DUTY: RATES

PART I

TABLE SUBSTITUTED IN PART II OF SCHEDULE 3 TO THE 1971 ACT AND THE 1972 ACT

Description of vehicle	Rate of duty £
1. Special machines	16.00
2. Haulage vehicles, being showmen's vehicles	90.00
3. Haulage vehicles, not being showmen's vehicles	330.00
4. Recovery vehicles	50.00

PART II

AMENDMENTS OF PART I OF SCHEDULE 4 TO THE 1971 ACT

1. Part I of Schedule 4 to the 1971 Act (annual rates of duty on goods vehicles: general provisions) shall be amended as follows.
2.—(1) Paragraph 1 (vehicles chargeable at the basic rate of duty) shall be amended as follows.
(2) In sub-paragraph (1)(a) for the words "does not exceed 7.5 tonnes" there shall be substituted the words "exceeds 3,500 kilograms but does not exceed 7,500 kilograms."
(3) In sub-paragraph (1)(b) for the words "an unladen weight which exceeds 1,525 kilograms" there shall be substituted the words "a design weight which exceeds 3,500 kilograms."
(4) In sub-paragraph (1)(c) for the words "an unladen weight which exceeds 1,525 kilograms" there shall be substituted the words "a plated gross weight exceeding 3,500 kilograms or, in the case of a vehicle which has no such weight, a design weight exceeding 3,500 kilograms."
3. In paragraph 2 for the words "7.5 tonnes" there shall be substituted the words "7,500 kilograms" and for the words "12 tonnes" there shall be substituted the words "12,000 kilograms."
4. In paragraph 3—
(a) in sub-paragraph (1) for the words "12 tonnes" there shall be substituted the words "12,000 kilograms"; and
(b) in sub-paragraph (2)(a) for the words "4 tonnes" there shall be substituted the words "4,000 kilograms."
5. In paragraph 4(1) for the words "12 tonnes" there shall be substituted the words "12,000 kilograms."
6.—(1) Paragraph 5 (special types of vehicle) shall be amended as follows.
(2) In sub-paragraph (1) for the words from "an unladen" to "plated train" there shall be substituted the words "a plated gross weight or plated train weight exceeding 3,500 kilograms or, in the case of a vehicle which has neither a plated gross weight nor a plated train weight, a design weight exceeding 3,500 kilograms; and
(a) which, in the case of a vehicle having a plated gross weight or plated train weight, has such a."
(3) In sub-paragraph (1)(b) for the words "42 of that Act" there shall be substituted the words "44 of the Road Traffic Act 1988."
(4) In sub-paragraph (3)—
(a) in paragraph (a), for the words "30 tonnes" there shall be substituted the words "30,000 kilograms" and for the words "30.49 tonnes" there shall be substituted the words "30,490 kilograms"; and
(b) in paragraph (b), for the words "37 tonnes" there shall be substituted the words "37,000 kilograms" and for the words "38 tonnes" there shall be substituted the words "38,000 kilograms."
7.—(1) Paragraph 6 (farmers' goods vehicles and showmen's goods vehicles) shall be amended as follows.
(2) In sub-paragraph (1)—

(a) for the word "unladen" there shall be substituted the word "design"; and

(b) for the words "1,525" there shall be substituted the words "3,500."

(3) In sub-paragraph (2) for the words "7.5 tonnes," in both places where they occur, there shall be substituted the words "7,500 kilograms" and for the words "12 tonnes," in both places where they occur, there shall be substituted the words "12,000 kilograms."

8. Paragraph 7 shall cease to have effect.

9. In paragraph 15(1) (interpretation) the following definition shall be inserted after the definition of "business"—

> " 'design weight' means the weight which a vehicle is designed or adapted not to exceed when in normal use and travelling on a road laden;".

Part III

Amendments of Part I of Schedule 4 to the 1972 Act

10. The amendments set out in paragraphs 2 to 9, except 6(2) and (3), above shall also be made in Part I of Schedule 4 to the 1972 Act (corresponding provision for Northern Ireland), but with the following modifications—

(a) for the words "plated gross weight," in each place where they occur, there shall be substituted the words "relevant maximum weight"; and

(b) for the words "plated train weight," in each place where they occur, there shall be substituted the words "relevant maximum train weight."

11. In paragraph 5(1) of Part I of Schedule 4 to the 1972 Act (special types of vehicle), for the words "an unladen weight exceeding 1,525" there shall be substituted the words "a relevant maximum weight or a relevant maximum train weight exceeding 3,500 kilograms or, in the case of a vehicle which has neither a relevant maximum weight nor a relevant maximum train weight, a design weight which exceeds 3,500."

Part IV

Tables Substituted in Part II of Schedule 4 to the 1971 Act and the 1972 Act

Table A

Rates of Duty on Rigid Goods Vehicles Exceeding 12,000 Kilograms Plated Gross Weight

General Rates

Plated gross weight of vehicle		Rate of duty		
(1) Exceeding	(2) Not Exceeding	(3) Two axle vehicle	(4) Three axle vehicle	(5) Four or more axle vehicle
kgs	kgs	£	£	£
12,000	13,000	450.00	470.00	340.00
13,000	14,000	630.00	470.00	340.00
14,000	15,000	810.00	470.00	340.00
15,000	17,000	1,280.00	470.00	340.00
17,000	19,000	—	820.00	340.00
19,000	21,000	—	990.00	340.00
21,000	23,000	—	1,420.00	490.00
23,000	25,000	—	2,160.00	800.00
25,000	27,000	—	—	1,420.00
27,000	29,000	—	—	2,240.00
29,000	30,490	—	—	3,250.00

TABLE A(1)

RATES OF DUTY ON RIGID GOODS VEHICLES EXCEEDING 12,000 KILOGRAMS
PLATED GROSS WEIGHT

RATES FOR FARMERS' GOODS VEHICLES

Plated gross weight of vehicle		Rate of duty		
(1)	(2)	(3)	(4)	(5) Four or more axle vehicle
Exceeding	Not Exceeding	Two axle vehicle	Three axle vehicle	
kgs	kgs	£	£	£
12,000	13,000	270.00	280.00	205.00
13,000	14,000	380.00	280.00	205.00
14,000	15,000	490.00	280.00	205.00
15,000	17,000	770.00	280.00	205.00
17,000	19,000	—	490.00	205.00
19,000	21,000	—	595.00	205.00
21,000	23,000	—	850.00	295.00
23,000	25,000	—	1,295.00	480.00
25,000	27,000	—	—	850.00
27,000	29,000	—	—	1,345.00
29,000	30,490	—	—	1,950.00

TABLE A(2)

RATES OF DUTY ON RIGID GOODS VEHICLES EXCEEDING 12,000 KILOGRAMS
PLATED GROSS WEIGHT

RATES FOR SHOWMEN'S GOODS VEHICLES

Plated gross weight of vehicle		Rate of duty		
(1)	(2)	(3)	(4)	(5) Four or more axle vehicle
Exceeding	Not Exceeding	Two axle vehicle	Three axle vehicle	
kgs	kgs	£	£	£
12,000	13,000	115.00	120.00	90.00
13,000	14,000	160.00	120.00	90.00
14,000	15,000	205.00	120.00	90.00
15,000	17,000	320.00	120.00	90.00
17,000	19,000	—	205.00	90.00
19,000	21,000	—	250.00	90.00
21,000	23,000	—	355.00	125.00
23,000	25,000	—	540.00	200.00
25,000	27,000	—	—	355.00
27,000	29,000	—	—	560.00
29,000	30,490	—	—	815.00

TABLE B

SUPPLEMENTARY RATES OF DUTY ON RIGID GOODS VEHICLES EXCEEDING 12,000
KILOGRAMS PLATED GROSS WEIGHT USED FOR DRAWING TRAILERS EXCEEDING
4,000 KILOGRAMS PLATED GROSS WEIGHT

GENERAL RATES

Plated gross weight of trailer		Duty supplement
Exceeding	Not exceeding	
kgs	kgs	£
4,000	8,000	130.00
8,000	10,000	130.00
10,000	12,000	130.00
12,000	14,000	360.00
14,000	—	360.00

TABLE B(1)

SUPPLEMENTARY RATES OF DUTY ON RIGID GOODS VEHICLES EXCEEDING 12,000
KILOGRAMS PLATED GROSS WEIGHT USED FOR DRAWING TRAILERS EXCEEDING
4,000 KILOGRAMS PLATED GROSS WEIGHT

RATES FOR FARMERS' GOODS VEHICLES

Plated gross weight of trailer		Duty supplement
Exceeding	Not exceeding	
kgs	kgs	£
4,000	8,000	130.00
8,000	10,000	130.00
10,000	12,000	130.00
12,000	14,000	360.00
14,000	—	360.00

TABLE B(2)

SUPPLEMENTARY RATES OF DUTY ON RIGID GOODS VEHICLES EXCEEDING 12,000
KILOGRAMS PLATED GROSS WEIGHT USED FOR DRAWING TRAILERS EXCEEDING
4,000 KILOGRAMS PLATED GROSS WEIGHT

RATES FOR SHOWMEN'S GOODS VEHICLES

Plated gross weight of trailer		Duty supplement
Exceeding	Not exceeding	
kgs	kgs	£
—	—	80.00

TABLE C

RATES OF DUTY ON TRACTOR UNITS EXCEEDING 12,000 KILOGRAMS PLATED
TRAIN WEIGHT AND HAVING ONLY 2 AXLES

GENERAL RATES

Plated train weight of tractor unit		Rate of duty		
(1)	(2)	(3)	(4)	(5)
		For a tractor unit to be used with semi-trailers with any number of axles	For a tractor unit to be used only with semi-trailers with not less than two axles	For a tractor unit to be used only with semi-trailers with not less than three axles
Exceeding	Not exceeding			
kgs	kgs	£	£	£
12,000	14,000	440.00	440.00	440.00
14,000	16,000	440.00	440.00	440.00
16,000	18,000	500.00	440.00	440.00
18,000	20,000	500.00	440.00	440.00
20,000	22,000	780.00	440.00	440.00
22,000	23,000	780.00	440.00	440.00
23,000	25,000	1,150.00	570.00	440.00
25,000	26,000	1,150.00	570.00	440.00
26,000	28,000	1,150.00	1,090.00	440.00
28,000	29,000	1,680.00	1,680.00	1,050.00
29,000	31,000	1,680.00	1,680.00	1,050.00
31,000	33,000	2,450.00	2,450.00	1,680.00
33,000	34,000	2,450.00	2,450.00	1,680.00
34,000	36,000	2,750.00	2,750.00	2,750.00
36,000	38,000	3,100.00	3,100.00	3,100.00

Finance Act 1990

Table C(1)

RATES OF DUTY ON TRACTOR UNITS EXCEEDING 12,000 KILOGRAMS PLATED
TRAIN WEIGHT AND HAVING ONLY 2 AXLES

RATES FOR FARMERS' GOODS VEHICLES

Plated train weight of tractor unit		Rate of duty		
(1)	(2)	(3)	(4)	(5)
		For a tractor unit to be used with semi-trailers with any number of axles	For a tractor unit to be used only with semi-trailers with not less than two axles	For a tractor unit to be used only with semi-trailers with not less than three axles
Exceeding	Not exceeding			
kgs	kgs	£	£	£
12,000	14,000	265.00	265.00	265.00
14,000	16,000	265.00	265.00	265.00
16,000	18,000	300.00	265.00	265.00
18,000	20,000	300.00	265.00	265.00
20,000	22,000	470.00	265.00	265.00
22,000	23,000	470.00	265.00	265.00
23,000	25,000	690.00	340.00	265.00
25,000	26,000	690.00	340.00	265.00
26,000	28,000	690.00	655.00	265.00
28,000	29,000	1,010.00	1,010.00	630.00
29,000	31,000	1,010.00	1,010.00	630.00
31,000	33,000	1,470.00	1,470.00	1,010.00
33,000	34,000	1,470.00	1,470.00	1,010.00
34,000	36,000	1,650.00	1,650.00	1,650.00
36,000	38,000	1,860.00	1,860.00	1,860.00

TABLE C(2)

RATES OF DUTY ON TRACTOR UNITS EXCEEDING 12,000 KILOGRAMS PLATED
TRAIN WEIGHT AND HAVING ONLY 2 AXLES

RATES FOR SHOWMEN'S GOODS VEHICLES

Plated train weight of tractor unit		Rate of duty		
(1)	(2)	(3)	(4)	(5)
		For a tractor unit to be used with semi-trailers with any number of axles	For a tractor unit to be used only with semi-trailers with not less than two axles	For a tractor unit to be used only with semi-trailers with not less than three axles
Exceeding	Not exceeding			
kgs	kgs	£	£	£
12,000	14,000	110.00	110.00	110.00
14,000	16,000	110.00	110.00	110.00
16,000	18,000	125.00	110.00	110.00
18,000	20,000	125.00	110.00	110.00
20,000	22,000	195.00	110.00	110.00
22,000	23,000	195.00	110.00	110.00
23,000	25,000	290.00	145.00	110.00
25,000	26,000	290.00	145.00	110.00
26,000	28,000	290.00	275.00	110.00
28,000	29,000	420.00	420.00	265.00
29,000	31,000	420.00	420.00	265.00
31,000	33,000	615.00	615.00	420.00
33,000	34,000	615.00	615.00	420.00
34,000	36,000	690.00	690.00	690.00
36,000	38,000	775.00	775.00	775.00

Finance Act 1990

TABLE D

RATES OF DUTY ON TRACTOR UNITS EXCEEDING 12,000 KILOGRAMS PLATED
TRAIN WEIGHT AND HAVING 3 OR MORE AXLES

GENERAL RATES

Plated train weight of tractor unit		Rate of duty		
(1)	(2)	(3)	(4)	(5)
		For a tractor unit to be used with semi-trailers with any number of axles	For a tractor unit to be used only with semi-trailers with not less than two axles	For a tractor unit to be used only with semi-trailers with not less than three axles
Exceeding	Not exceeding			
kgs	kgs	£	£	£
12,000	14,000	440.00	440.00	440.00
14,000	16,000	440.00	440.00	440.00
16,000	18,000	440.00	440.00	440.00
18,000	20,000	440.00	440.00	440.00
20,000	22,000	440.00	440.00	440.00
22,000	23,000	440.00	440.00	440.00
23,000	25,000	570.00	440.00	440.00
25,000	26,000	570.00	440.00	440.00
26,000	28,000	1,090.00	440.00	440.00
28,000	29,000	1,680.00	640.00	440.00
29,000	31,000	1,680.00	640.00	440.00
31,000	33,000	2,450.00	970.00	440.00
33,000	34,000	2,450.00	1,420.00	550.00
34,000	36,000	2,450.00	2,030.00	830.00
36,000	38,000	2,730.00	2,730.00	1,240.00

TABLE D(1)

RATES OF DUTY ON TRACTOR UNITS EXCEEDING 12,000 KILOGRAMS PLATED
TRAIN WEIGHT AND HAVING 3 OR MORE AXLES

RATES FOR FARMERS' GOODS VEHICLES

Plated train weight of tractor unit		Rate of duty		
(1)	(2)	(3)	(4)	(5)
		For a tractor unit to be used with semi-trailers with any number of axles	For a tractor unit to be used only with semi-trailers with not less than two axles	For a tractor unit to be used only with semi-trailers with not less than three axles
Exceeding	Not exceeding			
kgs	kgs	£	£	£
12,000	14,000	265.00	265.00	265.00
14,000	16,000	265.00	265.00	265.00
16,000	18,000	265.00	265.00	265.00
18,000	20,000	265.00	265.00	265.00
20,000	22,000	265.00	265.00	265.00
22,000	23,000	265.00	265.00	265.00
23,000	25,000	340.00	265.00	265.00
25,000	26,000	340.00	265.00	265.00
26,000	28,000	655.00	265.00	265.00
28,000	29,000	1,010.00	385.00	265.00
29,000	31,000	1,010.00	285.00	265.00
31,000	33,000	1,270.00	580.00	265.00
33,000	34,000	1,470.00	850.00	330.00
34,000	36,000	1,470.00	1,220.00	500.00
36,000	38,000	1,640.00	1,640.00	745.00

Finance Act 1990

TABLE D(2)

RATES OF DUTY ON TRACTOR UNITS EXCEEDING 12,000 KILOGRAMS PLATED
TRAIN WEIGHT AND HAVING 3 OR MORE AXLES

RATES FOR SHOWMEN'S GOODS VEHICLES

Plated train weight of tractor unit		Rate of duty		
(1)	(2)	(3)	(4)	(5)
Exceeding	Not exceeding	For a tractor unit to be used with semi-trailers with any number of axles	For a tractor unit to be used only with semi-trailers with not less than two axles	For a tractor unit to be used only with semi-trailers with not less than three axles
kgs	kgs	£	£	£
12,000	14,000	110.00	110.00	110.00
14,000	16,000	110.00	110.00	110.00
16,000	18,000	110.00	110.00	110.00
18,000	20,000	110.00	110.00	110.00
20,000	22,000	110.00	110.00	110.00
22,000	23,000	110.00	110.00	110.00
23,000	25,000	145.00	110.00	110.00
25,000	26,000	145.00	110.00	110.00
26,000	28,000	275.00	110.00	110.00
28,000	29,000	420.00	160.00	110.00
29,000	31,000	420.00	160.00	110.00
31,000	33,000	615.00	245.00	110.00
33,000	34,000	615.00	355.00	140.00
34,000	36,000	615.00	510.00	210.00
36,000	38,000	685.00	685.00	310.00

GENERAL NOTE

Pt. I rationalises the rates on haulage vehicles to a single rate, and implements an overall slight increase.

Pt. II substitutes kilograms for tonnes as the unit for measuring vehicle weights. It also reduces VED on all 200,000 goods vehicles under 3,500 kilograms.

Pt. III applies the changes made by Pt. II to the corresponding Northern Ireland legislation.

Pt. IV implements the substitution of kilograms for tonnes as the unit for measuring vehicle weights. It also continues the process of aligning duty to road track costs. In particular, the duty on the heaviest rigid goods vehicles is increased by 17 per cent.

Section 7   SCHEDULE 3

ENTRY OF GOODS ON IMPORTATION

1. The Customs and Excise Management Act 1979 shall be amended as follows.
2.—(1) Section 37A (initial and supplementary entries) shall be amended as follows.
(2) In subsection (1)(b), the word "may" shall be omitted.
(3) The following subsection shall be inserted after subsection (1)—
    "(1A) Without prejudice to section 37 above, a direction under that section may—
    (a) provide that where the importer is not authorised for the purposes of this section but a person who is so authorised is appointed as his agent for the purpose of entering the goods, the entry may consist of an initial entry made by the person so appointed and a supplementary entry so made; and
    (b) make such supplementary provision in connection with entries consisting of initial and supplementary entries made as mentioned in paragraph (a) above as the Commissioners think fit."

(4) In subsection (2), for the words from the beginning to "unpaid duty," there shall be substituted the words—
"(2) Where—
(a) an initial entry made under subsection (1) above has been accepted and the importer has given security by deposit of money or otherwise to the satisfaction of the Commissioners for payment of the unpaid duty, or
(b) an initial entry made under subsection (1A) above has been accepted and the person making the entry on the importer's behalf has given such security as is mentioned in paragraph (a) above,
the goods may."
(5) In subsection (3) after the words "initial entry" there shall be inserted the words "under subsection (1) above."
(6) The following subsection shall be inserted after subsection (3)—
"(3A) A person who makes an initial entry under subsection (1A) above on behalf of an importer shall complete the entry by delivering the supplementary entry within such time as the Commissioners may direct."
3.—(1) Section 37B (postponed entry) shall be amended as follows.
(2) The following subsection shall be inserted after subsection (1)—
"(1A) The Commissioners may, if they think fit, direct that where—
(a) such goods as may be specified in the direction are imported by an importer who is not authorised for the purposes of this subsection;
(b) a person who is authorised for the purposes of this subsection is appointed as his agent for the purpose of entering the goods;
(c) the person so appointed has delivered a document relating to the goods to the proper officer, in such form and manner, containing such particulars and accompanied by such documents as the Commissioners may direct; and
(d) the document has been accepted by the proper officer,
the goods may be delivered before an entry of them has been delivered or any duty chargeable in respect of them has been paid."
(3) The following subsections shall be inserted after subsection (3)—
"(3A) The Commissioners may, if they think fit, direct that where—
(a) such goods as may be specified in the direction are imported by an importer who is not authorised for the purposes of this subsection;
(b) a person who is authorised for the purposes of this subsection is appointed as his agent for the purpose of entering the goods;
(c) the goods have been removed from the place of importation to a place approved by the Commissioners for the clearance out of charge of such goods; and
(d) the conditions mentioned in subsection (3B) below have been satisfied,
the goods may be delivered before an entry of them has been delivered or any duty chargeable in respect of them has been paid.
(3B) The conditions are that—
(a) on the arrival of the goods at the approved place the person appointed as the agent of the importer for the purpose of entering the goods delivers to the proper officer a notice of the arrival of the goods in such form and containing such particulars as may be required by the directions;
(b) within such time as may be so required the person appointed as the agent of the importer for the purpose of entering the goods enters such particulars of the goods and such other information as may be so required in a record maintained by him at such place as the proper officer may require; and
(c) the goods are kept secure in the approved place for such period as may be required by the directions."
(4) In subsection (4), after "(3)(a)" there shall be inserted "or (3B)(a)."
(5) In subsection (5), for the words "this section" there shall be substituted the words "subsection (1) or (2) above."
(6) The following subsection shall be inserted after subsection (5)—
"(5A) No goods shall be delivered under subsection (1A) or (3A) above unless the person appointed as the agent of the importer for the purpose of entering the goods gives security by deposit of money or otherwise to the satisfaction of the Commissioners for the payment of any duty chargeable in respect of the goods which is unpaid."
(7) In subsection (6), for the words "this section" there shall be substituted the words "subsection (1) or (2) above."
(8) The following subsection shall be inserted after subsection (6)—
"(6A) Where goods of which no entry has been made have been delivered under subsection (1A) or (3A) above, the person appointed as the agent of the importer for the purpose of entering the goods shall deliver an entry of the goods under section 37(1) above within such time as the Commissioners may direct."

(9) In subsection (7)—

(a) in paragraph (a), after "(1)" there shall be inserted "or (1A)"; and

(b) after paragraph (b) there shall be inserted the words "and

(c) in the case of goods delivered by virtue of a direction under subsection (3A) above, on the date on which particulars of the goods were entered as mentioned in sub-section (3B)(b) above."

4.—(1) Section 37C (provisions supplementary to sections 37A and 37B) shall be amended as follows.

(2) In subsection (1)(a)—

(a) for the word "importer" there shall be substituted the word "person"; and

(b) for the words "or (2)" there shall be substituted the words ", (1A), (2) or (3A)."

(3) In subsection (1)(b), for the word "importer" there shall be substituted the word "person."

(4) In subsection (2)(a), for the word "importer" there shall be substituted the word "person."

GENERAL NOTE

The Schedule makes provision for the entry of goods on importation by the agents of importers.

Para. 2

This allows initial and supplementary entries to be made by such agents.

Para. 3

This makes similar provision with regard to postponed entry.

Para. 4

This provides for the authorisation of the agents by the Customs and Excise.

Section 23   SCHEDULE 4

LIMIT ON CHARGEABLE MILEAGE PROFIT

The following shall be inserted after section 197A of the Taxes Act 1988—

"Mileage allowances

Limit on chargeable mileage profit

197B.—(1) In a case where—

(a) in the year 1989-90 (the base year) sums paid to a person by reason of an employment held by him are paid in respect of expenses incurred by him in travelling, in the course of the duties of the employment, in a motor vehicle provided by him,

(b) in a subsequent year of assessment (the year concerned) he makes a mileage profit as respects an employment,

(c) the amount of the mileage profit he makes in the year concerned or, where he makes a mileage profit in that year as respects more than one employment, the aggregate of the mileage profits he makes in that year would (apart from this section) be greater than the maximum amount for the year,

(d) section 197E does not prevent this section from applying, and

(e) a claim is made for relief under this section,

the amount of the mileage profit he makes in the year concerned or, as the case may be, the aggregate of the mileage profits he makes in that year shall be treated as being equal to the maximum amount for the year.

(2) In a case where the employee's relevant mileage for the year concerned is more than his relevant mileage for the base year, the maximum amount for the year concerned shall be found by applying the formula—

$$\left(A \times \frac{B}{C} \right) + D$$

(3) In any other case, the maximum amount for the year concerned shall be found by applying the formula—

$$A + D$$

(4) A is the taxed mileage profit for the base year.

(5) B is the employee's relevant mileage for the year concerned.

(6) C is the employee's relevant mileage for the base year.

(7) D is—

(a) nil if the year concerned is 1990–91;

(b) an amount found by multiplying £1,000 by E if the year concerned is 1991–92 or a subsequent year of assessment.

(8) E is 1 if the year concerned is 1991–92, 2 if it is 1992–93, 3 if it is 1993–94, and so on (adding 1 for each succeeding year of assessment).

Definition of mileage profit

197C.—(1) This section applies for the purposes of section 197B.

(2) The employee makes a mileage profit in the year concerned as respects an employment if—

(a) by reason of the employment sums are paid to him in the year in respect of expenses incurred by him in travelling, in the course of the duties of the employment, in a motor vehicle provided by him, and

(b) subsection (3), (4) or (6) below applies.

(3) This subsection applies if all or part of the sums mentioned in subsection (2)(a) above fall to be treated as emoluments of the employment for the year in accordance with an administrative scheme (such as a fixed profit car scheme).

(4) This subsection applies if—

(a) subsection (3) above does not apply,

(b) the employment is employment to which Chapter II of this Part applies, and

(c) the amount of the sums mentioned in subsection (2)(a) above exceeds the aggregate deductible amount for the year concerned in relation to the employment.

(5) For the purposes of subsection (4) above the aggregate deductible amount for the year concerned in relation to the employment is the aggregate of the following—

(a) any expenses of travelling in a vehicle provided by the employee which fall to be deducted from the emoluments of the employment for the year under section 198(1), and

(b) the amount of any allowance which, by virtue of Part II of the 1990 Act, falls to be made to the employee for the year in respect of expenditure incurred on the provision of a vehicle for use in the performance of the duties of the employment.

(6) This subsection applies if—

(a) neither subsection (3) nor subsection (4) above applies, and

(b) all or part of the sums mentioned in subsection (2)(a) above fall to be treated as emoluments of the employment for the year.

(7) If subsection (3) or (6) above applies, the amount of the mileage profit made by the employee in the year concerned as respects the employment is the amount of the sums mentioned in subsection (2)(a) above which fall to be treated as emoluments of the employment for the year.

(8) If subsection (4) above applies, the amount of the mileage profit made by the employee in the year concerned as respects the employment is the amount of the excess mentioned in subsection (4)(c).

Definition of taxed mileage profit

197D.—(1) This section applies for the purposes of section 197B.

(2) Where in the base year the employee holds one employment to which this section applies, the taxed mileage profit for the year is the relevant amount for that employment determined in accordance with subsection (5) or (6) below.

(3) Where in the base year the employee holds more than one employment to which this section applies, the taxed mileage profit for the year shall be determined by—

(a) finding the relevant amount for each of those employments in accordance with subsection (5) or (6) below, and

(b) aggregating the amounts so found.

(4) In subsections (2) and (3) above the references to employment to which this section applies are to employment by reason of which in the base year the employee is paid sums (relevant sums) in respect of expenses incurred by him in travelling, in the course of the duties of the employment, in a motor vehicle provided by him.

(5) If—

(a) the employment is not employment to which Chapter II of this Part applies, or

(b) the relevant sums paid to the employee in the base year by reason of the employment are sums in respect of which his liability to tax is determined by reference to an administrative scheme (such as a fixed profit car scheme),

the relevant amount for the employment is the amount of such (if any) of the relevant sums paid to him in the base year by reason of the employment as are in fact treated as emoluments of the employment for that year.

(6) If—

(a) the employment is employment to which Chapter II of this Part applies, and

(b) the relevant sums paid to the employee in the base year by reason of the employment are not sums in respect of which his liability to tax is determined by reference to an administrative scheme (such as a fixed profit car scheme),

the relevant amount for the employment is an amount found by deducting G from F, except that it can never be less than nil.

(7) For the purposes of subsection (6) above F is the amount of such (if any) of the relevant sums paid to the employee in the base year by reason of the employment as are by virtue of section 153 in fact treated as emoluments of the employment for that year.

(8) For the purposes of subsection (6) above G is the aggregate of the following—

(a) any expenses of travelling in a vehicle provided by the employee in fact deducted from the emoluments of the employment for the base year under section 198(1), and

(b) the amount of any allowance in fact made to the employee for the year, by virtue of Chapter I of Part III of the Finance Act 1971, in respect of expenditure incurred on the provision of a vehicle for use in the performance of the duties of the employment.

Exception from section 197B

197E.—(1) If the sums paid to the employee in the year concerned in respect of expenses incurred by him in travelling, in the course of the duties of his employment or employments, in any motor vehicle provided by him exceed the sums paid to him in the base year in respect of expenses so incurred by him, section 197B shall not apply for the year concerned unless the whole of the excess can be justified by reference to allowable factors.

(2) For the purposes of this section the following are allowable factors—

(a) an increase in motoring costs;

(b) a change by any employer of his practices so as more fully to reimburse motoring costs;

(c) any change of vehicle;

(d) a change in the employee's relevant mileage.

Other interpretative provisions

197F.—(1) This section applies for the purposes of sections 197B to 197E.

(2) The employee's relevant mileage for a year of assessment is the number of miles by reference to which in that year he is paid sums in respect of expenses incurred by him in travelling, in the course of the duties of his employment or employments, in any motor vehicle provided by him.

(3) "Employment" means an office or employment the emoluments of which fall to be assessed under Schedule E; and related expressions shall be construed accordingly."

GENERAL NOTE

Mileage allowances paid to employees who use their own cars in the course of their employments are taxable under Sched. E to the extent that the amounts paid exceed the allowable costs incurred. To reduce the administrative burden involved in determining the "profit" received by employees by virtue of the receipt of such allowances the Revenue have for some time operated the "fixed profit car scheme" under which employees have been taxed by reference to certain fixed criteria. The Revenue now consider that this scheme has become too generous to taxpayers and has proposed changes to the system. In essence these changes will lead to a reduced tax free allowance being available to employees with a business mileage in excess of 4,000 miles. This schedule is concerned with giving transitional relief for those adversely affected by these changes. It seeks to ensure that nobody who received a mileage allowance from his employer in 1989–90 will pay any more tax in 1990–91. In subsequent years the additional amount taxable cannot exceed £1,000 p.a.

Section 30   SCHEDULE 5

BUILDING SOCIETIES AND DEPOSIT-TAKERS

Introduction

1. The Taxes Act 1988 shall be amended as mentioned in paragraphs 2 to 14 below.

Building societies

2.—(1) Section 476 (building societies: regulations for payment of tax) shall cease to have effect.

(2) This paragraph shall apply as regards the year 1991-92 and subsequent years of assessment.

3.—(1) Section 477 (investments becoming or ceasing to be relevant building society investments) shall cease to have effect.

(2) This paragraph shall apply as regards any time falling on or after 6th April 1991.

3.—(1) Section 477 (investments becoming or ceasing to be relevant building society investments) shall cease to have effect.

(2) This paragraph shall apply as regards any time falling on or after 6th April 1991.

4.—(1) The following section shall be inserted immediately before section 478—

"Building societies: regulations for deduction of tax

477A.—(1) The Board may by regulations make provision with respect to any year of assessment requiring any building society—

(a) in such cases as may be prescribed by the regulations to deduct out of any dividend or interest paid or credited in the year in respect of shares in, or deposits with or loans to, the society a sum representing the amount of income tax on it, and

(b) to account for and pay any amount required to be deducted by the society by virtue of this subsection.

(2) Regulations under subsection (1) above may—

(a) make provision with respect to the furnishing of information by building societies or their investors, including, in the case of societies, the inspection of books, documents and other records on behalf of the Board;

(b) contain such incidental and consequential provisions as appear to the Board to be appropriate, including provisions requiring the making of returns.

(3) For any year of assessment to which regulations under subsection (1) above apply, dividends or interest payable in respect of shares in, or deposits with or loans to, a building society shall be dealt with for the purposes of corporation tax as follows—

(a) in computing for any accounting period ending in the year of assessment the income of the society from the trade carried on by it, there shall be allowed as a deduction the actual amount paid or credited in the accounting period of any such dividends or interest, together with any amount of income tax accounted for and paid by the society in respect thereof;

(b) no part of any such dividends or interest paid or credited in the year of assessment shall be treated as a distribution of the society or as franked investment income of any company resident in the United Kingdom.

(4) Subsection (3)(a) above shall apply to any terminal bonus paid by the society under a certified contractual savings scheme as if it were a dividend on a share in the society.

(5) Notwithstanding anything in sections 64, 66 and 67, for any year of assessment to which regulations under subsection (1) above apply income tax chargeable under Case III of Schedule D shall, in the case of any relevant sum, be computed on the full amount of the income arising in the year of assessment.

(6) For the purposes of subsection (5) above a sum is relevant if it is a sum in respect of which a liability to deduct income tax—

(a) is imposed by regulations under subsection (1) above, or

(b) would be so imposed if a certificate were not supplied, in accordance with the regulations, to the effect that the person beneficially entitled to the sum is unlikely to be liable to pay any amount by way of income tax for the year of assessment in which the sum is paid.

(7) Notwithstanding anything in sections 348 to 350, for any year of assessment to which regulations under subsection (1) above apply income tax shall not be deducted upon payment to the society of any interest on advances, being interest payable in that year.

(8) Subsection (7) above shall not apply to any payment of relevant loan interest to which section 369 applies.

(9) In this section "dividend" has the meaning given by regulations under subsection (1) above, but any sum which is paid by a building society by way of dividend and which is not paid under deduction of income tax shall be treated for the purposes of Schedule D as paid by way of interest."

(2) This paragraph shall apply as regards the year 1991-92 and subsequent years of assessment.

Deposit-takers

5.—(1) Section 479 (interest paid on deposits with banks etc.) shall cease to have effect.

(2) This paragraph shall apply as regards interest paid or credited on or after 6th April 1991.

6.—(1) Section 480 (deposits becoming or ceasing to be composite rate deposits) shall cease to have effect.

(2) This paragraph shall apply as regards any time falling on or after 6th April 1991.

7.—(1) The following sections shall be inserted immediately before section 481—

"Relevant deposits: deduction of tax from interest payments

480A.—(1) Any deposit-taker making a payment of interest in respect of a relevant deposit shall, on making the payment, deduct out of it a sum representing the amount of income tax on it for the year of assessment in which the payment is made.

(2) Any payment of interest out of which an amount is deductible under subsection (1) above shall be a relevant payment for the purposes of Schedule 16 whether or not the deposit-taker making the payment is resident in the United Kingdom.

(3) Schedule 16 shall apply in relation to any payment which is a relevant payment by virtue of subsection (2) above—

(a) with the substitution for any reference to a company of a reference to a deposit-taker,

(b) as if paragraph 5 applied only in relation to payments received by the deposit-taker and falling to be taken into account in computing his income chargeable to corporation tax, and

(c) as if in paragraph 7 the reference to section 7(2) included a reference to sections 11(3) and 349(1).

(4) In relation to any deposit-taker who is not a company, Schedule 16 shall have effect as if—

(a) paragraph 5 were omitted, and

(b) references to accounting periods were references to periods for which the deposit-taker makes up his accounts.

(5) For the purposes of this section, crediting interest shall be treated as paying it.

Relevant deposits: exception from section 480A

480B.—(1) The Board may by regulations provide that section 480A(1) shall not apply as regards a payment of interest if such conditions as may be prescribed by the regulations are fulfilled.

(2) In particular, the regulations may include—

(a) provision for a certificate to be supplied to the effect that the person beneficially entitled to a payment is unlikely to be liable to pay any amount by way of income tax for the year of assessment in which the payment is made;

(b) provision for the certificate to be supplied by that person or such other person as may be prescribed by the regulations;

(c) provision about the time when, and the manner in which, a certificate is to be supplied;

(d) provision about the form and contents of a certificate.

(3) Any provision included under subsection (2)(d) above may allow the Board to make requirements, in such manner as they see fit, as to the matters there mentioned.

(4) for the purposes of this section, crediting interest shall be treated as paying it.

Relevant deposits: computation of tax on interest

480C. Notwithstanding anything in sections 64, 66 and 67, income tax chargeable under Case III of Schedule D on interest in respect of a relevant deposit shall be computed on the full amount of the income arising in the year of assessment."

(2) This paragraph shall apply as regards interest paid or credited on or after 6th April 1991.

8.—(1) Section 481 (definitions of relevant deposit etc.) shall be amended as follows.

(2) The following subsection shall be inserted after subsection (1)—

"(1A) In this section 'the relevant provisions' also means sections 480A and 480C."

(3) In subsection (2) the following shall be inserted after paragraph (c)—

"(ca) any local authority";

and paragraphs (d) and (e) shall be omitted.

(4) In subsection (6) after the word "sections" there shall be inserted the words "480A, 480C."

(5) Sub-paragraph (3) above shall apply as regards interest paid or credited on or after 6th April 1991.

9.—(1) Section 482 (supplementary provisions) shall be amended as follows.

(2) In subsection (6), in paragraph (b) of the definition of "qualifying certificate of deposit" for the words "less than seven days" there shall be substituted the words "more than five years."

(3) In subsection (6), the following paragraph shall be substituted for paragraph (a) of the definition of "qualifying time deposit"—

"(a) require repayment of the deposit at a specified time falling before the end of the period of five years beginning with the date on which the deposit is made;".

(4) In subsection (11) the following shall be inserted after paragraph (a)—

"(aa) with respect to the furnishing of information by depositors or deposit-takers, including, in the case of deposit-takers, the inspection of books, documents and other records on behalf of the Board; and."

(5) The following subsection shall be inserted after subsection (11)—

"(11A) In subsection (11)(aa) above the reference to depositors is to persons who are appropriate persons (within the meaning given by subsection (6) above) in relation to deposits."

(6) Sub-paragraphs (2) and (3) above shall apply as regards interest paid or credited on or after 6th April 1991.

General

10.—(1) Section 349 (annual interest etc.) shall be amended as follows.

(2) In subsection (3) after paragraph (d) there shall be inserted "or

(e) to any dividend or interest paid or credited in a relevant year of assessment in respect of shares in, or deposits with or loans to, a building society; or

(f) to any payment in respect of which a liability to deduct income tax is imposed by section 480A(1); or

(g) to any payment in respect of which a liability to deduct income tax would be imposed by section 480A(1) if conditions prescribed by regulations under section 480B were not fulfilled."

(3) The following subsection shall be inserted at the end—

"(4) In subsection (3)(e) above—

'dividend' has the same meaning as in section 477A, and

'relevant year of assessment' means a year of assessment to which regulations under subsection (1) of that section apply."

(4) This paragraph shall apply as regards a payment made on or after 6th April 1991.

11.—(1) In section 352(1) (certificates of deduction of tax) for the words "or 687" there shall be substituted the words ", 480A or 687 or by virtue of regulations under section 477A(1)."

(2) This paragraph shall apply as regards a payment made on or after 6th April 1991.

12.—(1) In section 483 (determination of reduced rate for building societies and composite rate for banks etc.) subsections (1) to (3) and (5) shall cease to have effect.

(2) This paragraph shall apply where the first year of assessment mentioned in section 483(1) is 1990-91 or a subsequent year of assessment.

13.—(1) In section 686 (liability to additional rate tax of certain income of discretionary trusts) subsection (5) shall cease to have effect.

(2) This paragraph shall apply as regards a sum paid or credited on or after 6th April 1991.

14.—(1) In section 687 (payments under discretionary trusts) in subsection (3) the words following paragraph (i) shall cease to have effect.

(2) This paragraph shall apply as regards an amount paid or credited on or after 6th April 1991.

Management

15. In the Table in section 98 of the Taxes Management Act 1970 (penalties for failure to comply with notices etc.) there shall be inserted in the first and second columns, after the entry relating to regulations under section 476(1) of the Taxes Act 1988—

"regulations under section 477A(1);".

Transitional provision

16.—(1) In its application to the year 1991-92, section 477A of the Taxes Act 1988 shall have effect with the following modifications.

(2) Regulations under subsection (1) may also require any building society to account for and pay, on transitional sums, an amount representing income tax calculated in part at the basic rate for the year 1990-91 and in part at the reduced rate determined for that year under section 483(1)(a) of the Taxes Act 1988.

(3) In sub-paragraph (2) above the reference to transitional sums is to such sums paid or credited after 28th February 1991 and before 6th April 1991 as may be determined in accordance with the regulations.

(4) In subsection (3)(a) for the words from "actual" to the end of the paragraph there shall be substituted the words "appropriate amount."

(5) The following subsection shall be inserted after subsection (3)—

"(3A) In subsection (3)(a) above the reference to the appropriate amount is to the actual amount paid or credited in the accounting period of any such dividends or interest together with—

(a) in the case of dividends or interest paid or credited in the year 1990-91, any amount accounted for and paid by the society in respect thereof as representing income tax, and

(b) in the case of dividends or interest paid or credited in the year 1991-92, any amount of income tax accounted for and paid by the society in respect thereof."

GENERAL NOTE

This Schedule abolishes composite rate tax from April 6, 1991. In its place building societies, banks and some other deposit takers will operate a system under which they will deduct tax at source from interest paid. This will have the beneficial effect as far as low income persons are concerned in enabling them to obtain repayment of the tax deducted. This is not possible under the composite rate system. It is intended that regulations will be made that will allow individuals who do not expect to pay tax to certify that this is so and thereby obtain payment gross, thus obviating the need for repayment claims.

Section 41　　　　　　　　　　　SCHEDULE 6

LIFE ASSURANCE: APPORTIONMENT OF INCOME ETC.

1.—(1) Section 431 of the Taxes Act 1988 shall be amended as follows.

(2) In subsection (2)—

(a) in the definition of "general annuity business," after the words "pension business" there shall be inserted the words "or overseas life assurance business"; and

(b) there shall be inserted in the appropriate places in alphabetical order—

" "basic life assurance business" means life assurance business other than general annuity business, pension business and overseas life assurance business";

" "closing" and "opening," in relation to a period of account, refer respectively to the position at the end and at the beginning of the period and, in relation to an accounting period, refer respectively to the position at the end and at the beginning of the period of account in which the accounting period falls";

" "closing liabilities" includes liabilities assumed at the end of the period of account concerned in consequence of the declaration of reversionary bonuses or a reduction in premiums";

" "industrial assurance business" has the same meaning as in the Insurance Companies Act 1982";

" "investment reserve," in relation to an insurance company, means the excess of the value of the assets of the company's long term business fund over the liabilities of the long term business";

" "liabilities," in relation to an insurance company, means the liabilities of the company estimated as for the purposes of its periodical return (excluding any that have fallen due or been reinsured and any not arising under or in connection with policies or contracts effected as part of the company's insurance business)";

" "linked assets" means assets of an insurance company which are identified in its records as assets by reference to the value of which benefits provided for under a policy or contract are to be determined";

" "long term business" has the meaning given by section 1(1) of the Insurance Companies Act 1982";

" "long term business fund" means the fund maintained by an insurance company in respect of its long term business or, where the company carries on both ordinary long term business and industrial assurance business, either or both (as the context may require) of the two funds so maintained";

" "ordinary long term business" and "ordinary life assurance business" mean respectively long term business and life assurance business that is not industrial assurance business";

" "overseas life assurance business"—

(a) in the case of life assurance business other than reinsurance business, means business with a policy holder or annuitant not residing in the United Kingdom the policy or contract for which was effected at or through a branch or agency outside the United Kingdom where life assurance business is carried on; and

(b) in the case of reinsurance business, means business the contract for which was effected at or through a branch or agency outside the United Kingdom where none, or no significant part, of the reinsurance business carried on relates to life assurance business with policy holders or annuitants residing in the United Kingdom";

" "overseas life assurance fund" shall be construed in accordance with Schedule 19AA";

" "value," in relation to assets of an insurance company, means the value of the assets as taken into account for the purposes of the company's periodical return";

" "with-profits liabilities" means liabilities in respect of policies or contracts under which the policy holders or annuitants are eligible to participate in surplus;".

(3) After subsection (2) there shall be inserted—

"(2A) Linked assets shall be taken to be linked solely to long term business of a particular category if, and only if, all (or all but an insignificant proportion) of the policies or contracts providing for the benefits concerned are policies or contracts the effecting of which constitutes the carrying on of business of that category."

(4) In subsection (3)(b), after the words "other annuity business" there shall be inserted the words "that is not overseas life assurance business."

2. After section 431 of the Taxes Act 1988 there shall be inserted—

"Amendment of Chapter etc.

431A. Where it is expedient to do so in consequence of the exercise of any power under the Insurance Companies Act 1982, the Treasury may by order amend the provisions of this Chapter and any other provision of the Tax Acts so far as relating to insurance companies."

3. In section 432(2) of the Taxes Act 1988—

(a) for the words "industrial life assurance" there shall be substituted the words "industrial assurance"; and

(b) after the words "section 76" there shall be inserted the words "and where appropriate the provisions of this Chapter."

4. After section 432 of that Act there shall be inserted—

"Apportionment of income and gains

432A.—(1) This section has effect where—

(a) an insurance company carries on in any period both ordinary long term business and industrial assurance business, or life assurance business and other long term business, or more than one class of life assurance business, and

(b) it is necessary for the purposes of the Corporation Tax Acts to determine in relation to the period what parts of—

(i) income arising from the assets of the company's long term business fund, or

(ii) gains or losses accruing on the disposal of such assets,

are referable to any of the categories of business in question.

(2) The classes of life assurance business referred to in subsection (1) above are—

(a) pension business;

(b) general annuity business;

(c) overseas life assurance business; and

(d) basic life assurance business.

(3) Income arising from, and gains or losses accruing on the disposal of, assets linked solely to ordinary long term business, industrial assurance business, life assurance business, long term business other than life assurance business, pension business or basic life assurance business shall be referable to the category of business concerned.

(4) Income arising from, and gains or losses accruing on the disposal of, assets of the overseas life assurance fund (and no other assets) shall be referable to overseas life assurance business.

(5) There shall be referable to any category of business (apart from overseas life assurance business) the relevant fraction of any income, gains or losses not directly referable to any of the appropriate categories of business.

(6) For the purposes of subsection (5) above "the relevant fraction," in relation to a category of business, is the fraction of which—

(a) the numerator is the aggregate of—

(i) the mean of the opening and closing liabilities of the category, reduced by the mean of the opening and closing values of any assets directly referable to the category, and

(ii) the mean of the appropriate parts of the opening and closing amounts of the investment reserve; and

(b) the denominator is the aggregate of—

(i) the mean of the opening and closing liabilities of the long term business, reduced by the mean of the opening and closing values of any assets directly referable to any of the appropriate categories of business, and

(ii) the mean of the opening and closing amounts of the investment reserve.

(7) For the purposes of subsections (5) and (6) above—

(a) references to appropriate categories of business—

(i) where the category of business in question is ordinary long term business or industrial assurance business, are references to those categories of business;

(ii) where the category of business in question is life assurance business or long term business other than life assurance business, are references to those categories of business; and

(iii) where the category of business in question is pension business, general annuity business or basic life assurance business, are references to pension business and basic life assurance business; and

(b) income, gains or losses are directly referable to a category of business if referable to the category by virtue of subsection (3) above and assets are directly referable to a category of business if income arising from the assets is, and gains or losses accruing on the disposal of the assets are, so referable.

(8) In subsection (6) above "appropriate part," in relation to the investment reserve, means—

(a) where all of the liabilities of the long term business are linked liabilities, the part of that reserve which bears to the whole the same proportion as the amount of the liabilities of the category of business in question bears to the whole amount of the liabilities of the long term business,

(b) where any of the liabilities of the long term business are not linked liabilities but none (or none but an insignificant proportion) are with-profits liabilities, the part of that reserve which bears to the whole the same proportion as the amount of the liabilities of the category of business in question which are not linked liabilities bears to the whole amount of the liabilities of the long term business which are not linked liabilities, and

(c) in any other case, the part of that reserve which bears to the whole the same proportion as the amount of the with-profits liabilities of the category of business in question bears to the whole amount of the with-profits liabilities of the long term business;

and in this subsection "linked liabilities" means liabilities in respect of benefits to be determined by reference to the value of linked assets.

(9) Where the category of business in question is a class of life assurance business, for the purposes of this section—

(a) "liabilities" does not include liabilities of the overseas life assurance business; and

(b) assets of the overseas life assurance fund and liabilities of the overseas life assurance business shall be left out of account in determining the investment reserve.

(10) Subsection (5) above shall not apply in relation to gains or losses accruing on disposals deemed to have been made by virtue of section 46 of the Finance Act 1990 except where it is necessary to determine what parts are referable to different categories of business within subsection (3)(b) of that section (and shall apply in that case subject to appropriate modifications).

Apportionment of receipts brought into account

432B.—(1) This section and sections 432C to 432E have effect where it is necessary in accordance with section 83 of the Finance Act 1989 to determine what parts of any items brought into account in the revenue account prepared for the purposes of the Insurance Companies Act 1982 are referable to life assurance business or any class of life assurance business.

(2) Where in addition to the revenue account prepared for the purposes of the Insurance Companies Act 1982 in respect of the whole of any business carried on by a company there are prepared for the purposes of that Act revenue accounts relating to parts of the business, amounts referred to in sections 432C to 432E shall, so far as they relate to those parts, be ascertained by reference to the latter accounts rather than by reference to the former.

(3) Sections 432C and 432D apply where the business with which an account is concerned ("the relevant business") relates exclusively to policies or contracts under which the policy holders or annuitants are not eligible to participate in surplus; and section 432E applies where the relevant business relates wholly or partly to other policies or contracts.

Section 432B apportionment: income of non-participating funds

432C.—(1) To the extent that the amount brought into account as income is attributable to assets linked solely to life assurance business, pension business or basic life assurance business, it shall be referable to the category of business concerned.

(2) To the extent that that amount is attributable to assets of the overseas life assurance fund, it shall be referable to overseas life assurance business.

(3) There shall be referable to any category of business (apart from overseas life assurance business) the relevant fraction of so much of the amount brought into account as income as is not directly referable to any of the appropriate categories of business.

(4) For the purposes of subsection (3) above "the relevant fraction," in relation to a category of business, is the fraction of which—

(a) the numerator is the mean of the opening and closing liabilities of the relevant business so far as referable to the category, reduced by the mean of the opening and closing values of any assets of the relevant business directly referable to the category; and

(b) the denominator is the mean of the opening and closing liabilities of the relevant business, reduced by the mean of the opening and closing values of any assets of the relevant business directly referable to any of the appropriate categories of business.

(5) For the purposes of subsections (3) and (4) above—

(a) references to appropriate categories of business—

(i) where the category of business in question is life assurance business, are references to that category of business and long term business other than life assurance business; and

(ii) where the category of business in question is pension business, general annuity business or basic life assurance business, are references to pension business and basic life assurance business; and

(b) the part of the amount brought into account as income which is directly referable to a category of business is the part referable to the category by virtue of subsection (1) above and assets are directly referable to a category of business if such part of the amount brought into account as income as is attributable to them is so referable.

(6) Where the category of business in question is a class of life assurance business, for the purposes of this section "liabilities" does not include liabilities of the overseas life assurance business.

Section 432B apportionment: value of non-participating funds

432D.—(1) To the extent that the amount brought into account as the increase or decrease in the value of assets is attributable to assets linked solely to life assurance business, pension business or basic life assurance business, or to assets of the overseas life assurance fund which are linked solely to overseas life assurance business, it shall be referable to the category of business concerned.

(2) There shall be referable to any category of business the relevant fraction of the amount brought into account as the increase or decrease in the value of assets except so far as the amount is attributable to assets which are directly referable to any of the appropriate categories of business.

(3) Subsections (4) and (5) (but not (6)) of section 432C shall apply for the purposes of this section as if—

(a) each of the references to a subsection of that section were a reference to the corresponding subsection of this section, and

(b) in subsection (5)—

(i) a reference to overseas life assurance business were included after each of the references to pension business in paragraph (a)(ii), and

(ii) each of the references in paragraph (b) to income were a reference to the increase or decrease in the value of assets.

Section 432B apportionment: participating funds

432E.—(1) The part of the net amount of the items referred to in subsection (1) of section 83 of the Finance Act 1989 (that is to say the income referred to in paragraph (a) of that subsection increased or reduced by the increase or reduction in the value referred to in paragraph (b)) which is referable to a particular category of business shall be—

(a) the amount determined in accordance with subsection (2) below, or

(b) the amount determined in accordance with subsection (3) below, whichever is the greater.

(2) For the purposes of subsection (1) above there shall be determined the amount which is such as to secure—

(a) in a case where the relevant business is mutual business, that

$$CAS = CS, \text{ and}$$

(b) in any other case, that

$$CS - CAS = (S - AS) \times \frac{CAS}{AS}$$

where—

S is the surplus of the relevant business;

AS is so much of that surplus as is allocated to persons entitled to the benefits provided for by the policies or contracts to which the relevant business relates;

CAS is so much of the surplus so allocated as is attributable to policies or contracts of the category of business concerned; and

CS is so much of the surplus of the relevant business as would remain if the relevant business were confined to business of the category concerned.

(3) For the purposes of subsection (1) above there shall also be determined the aggregate of—

(a) the applicable percentage of what is left of the mean of the opening and closing liabilities of the relevant business so far as referable to the category of business concerned after deducting from it the mean of the opening and closing values of any assets of the relevant business linked solely to that category of business, and

(b) the part of the net amount mentioned in subsection (1) above that is attributable to assets linked solely to that category of business.

(4) For the purposes of subsection (3) above "the applicable percentage," in any case, is such percentage as may be determined for that case by or in accordance with an order made by the Treasury.

(5) Where the part of the net amount referable to a particular category or categories of business ("the subsection (3) category or categories") is the amount determined in accordance with subsection (3) above, the amount determined in accordance with subsection (2) above in relation to any other category ("the relevant category") shall be reduced by—

$$\frac{XY}{Z}$$

where—

X is the excess of the amount determined in accordance with subsection (3) above in the case of the subsection (3) category (or each of them) over the amount determined in its case (or the case of each of them) in accordance with subsection (2) above;

Y is so much of the surplus of the relevant business as is allocated to persons entitled to the benefits provided for by policies or contracts of the relevant category; and

Z is so much of the surplus of the relevant business as is allocated to persons entitled to the benefits provided for by policies or contracts of the category (or each of the categories) which is not a subsection (3) category.

(6) Where the category of business concerned is overseas life assurance business—

(a) if the part of the income brought into account that is attributable to assets of the overseas life assurance fund not linked solely to overseas life assurance business is greater than the amount arrived at under subsection (3)(a) above, this section shall have effect as if that part of that income were the amount so arrived at; and

(b) the amount which, apart from this paragraph, would be the part of the net amount referable to that category of business shall be—

(i) reduced by the part of the net amount attributable to distributions of companies resident in the United Kingdom relating to assets of the company's overseas life assurance fund, and

(ii) increased by the amount which is income of the relevant business by virtue of section 441A."

5. In section 436 of the Taxes Act 1988, in subsection (3) for sub-paragraph (i) of paragraph (d) there shall be substituted—

"(i) group income so far as referable to pension business shall be deducted from the receipts to be taken into account,".

6. In section 437 of that Act, in subsection (2) for paragraph (a) there shall be substituted—

"(a) taxed income, group income and income attributable to offshore income gains, so far as referable to general annuity business, shall be deducted from the receipts to be taken into account;".

7. In section 439 of that Act, for the words from the beginning to "1982"; in subsection (5) there shall be substituted—

"(1) For the purposes of this Chapter restricted government securities shall be treated as linked solely to pension business.

(2) In this section."

8. For section 440 of that Act there shall be substituted—

"Transfers of assets etc.

440.—(1) If at any time an asset (or a part of an asset) held by an insurance company ceases to be within one of the categories set out in subsection (4) below and comes within another of those categories, the company shall for the purposes of corporation tax be deemed to have disposed of and immediately re-acquired the asset (or part) for a consideration equal to its market value at that time.

(2) Where—

(a) an asset is acquired by a company as part of the transfer to it of the whole or part of the business of an insurance company ("the transferor") in accordance with a scheme sanctioned by a court under section 49 of the Insurance Companies Act 1982, and

(b) the asset (or part of it) is within one of the categories set out in subsection (4) below immediately before the acquisition and is within another of those categories immediately afterwards,

the transferor shall for the purposes of corporation tax be deemed to have disposed of and immediately re-acquired the asset (or part) immediately before the acquisition for a consideration equal to its market value at that time.

(3) Where, apart from this subsection, section 273 or 274 of the 1970 Act (transfers within a group) would apply to a disposal or acquisition by an insurance company of an asset (or part of an asset) which, immediately before the disposal or (as the case may be) immediately after the acquisition, is within one of the categories set out in paragraphs (a) to (d) of subsection (4) below, that section shall not apply to the disposal or acquisition.

(4) The categories referred to in subsections (1) to (3) above are—

(a) assets linked solely to basic life assurance business;

(b) assets linked solely to pension business;

(c) assets of the overseas life assurance fund;

(d) assets of the long term business fund not within any of the preceding paragraphs;

(e) other assets.

(5) In this section "market value" has the same meaning as in the 1979 Act.

Securities

440A.—(1) Subsection (2) below applies where the assets of an insurance company include securities of a class all of which would apart from this section be regarded for the purposes of corporation tax on chargeable gains as one holding.

(2) Where this subsection applies—

(a) so many of the securities as are identified in the company's records as securities by reference to the value of which there are to be determined benefits provided for under policies the effecting of all (or all but an insignificant proportion) of which constitutes the carrying on of basic life assurance business shall be treated for the purposes of corporation tax as a separate holding linked solely to that business,

(b) so many of the securities as are identified in the company's records as securities by reference to the value of which there are to be determined benefits provided for under contracts the effecting of all (or all but an insignificant proportion) of which constitutes the carrying on of pension business shall be treated for those purposes as a separate holding linked solely to that business,

(c) so many of the securities as are included in the overseas life assurance fund shall be treated for those purposes as a separate holding which is an asset of that fund,

(d) so many of the securities as are included in the company's long term business fund but do not fall within any of the preceding paragraphs shall be treated for those purposes as a separate holding which is an asset of that fund (but not of any of the descriptions mentioned in those paragraphs), and

(e) any remaining securities shall be treated for those purposes as a separate holding which is not of any of the descriptions mentioned in the preceding paragraphs.

(3) Subsection (2) above also applies where the assets of an insurance company include securities of a class and apart from this section some of them would be regarded as a 1982 holding, and the rest as a new holding, for the purposes of corporation tax on chargeable gains.

(4) In a case within subsection (3) above—

(a) the reference in any paragraph of subsection (2) above to a separate holding shall be construed, where necessary, as a reference to a separate 1982 holding and a separate new holding, and

(b) the questions whether such a construction is necessary in the case of any paragraph and, if it is, how many securities falling within the paragraph constitute each of the two holdings shall be determined in accordance with paragraph 12 of Schedule 6 to the Finance Act 1990 and the identification rules applying on any subsequent acquisitions and disposals.

(5) Section 66 of the 1979 Act shall have effect where subsection (2) above applies as if securities regarded as included in different holdings by virtue of that subsection were securities of different kinds.

(6) In this section—

"1982 holding" has the meaning given by Part II of Schedule 19 to the Finance Act 1985;

"new holding" has the meaning given by Part III of that Schedule; and

"securities" has the same meaning as in section 65 of the 1979 Act."

9.—(1) In section 724 of the Taxes Act 1988, after subsection (1) there shall be inserted—

"(1A) If at any time securities held by an insurance company cease to be within one of the categories set out in section 440(4) and come within another of those categories, the company shall be treated for the purposes of sections 710 to 728 as transferring the securities to itself at that time."

(2) In section 711(6) of that Act, for the words "or 722(1) or (2)" there shall be substituted the words ", 722(1) or (2) or 724(1A)."

(3) In section 712(4) of that Act, for the words "and 722" there shall be substituted the words ", 722 and 724(1A)."

10. In section 58(10) of the Finance (No. 2) Act 1975, the definition of "trading stock" shall cease to have effect.

11.—(1) Paragraph 9 above shall be deemed to have come into force on 24th May 1990 but, subject to that,—

(a) in so far as it relates to determinations of profits in accordance with section 83 of the Finance Act 1989, this Schedule shall apply in relation to any period for which such a determination falls to be made, other than a period for which it falls to be made only by virtue of an election under section 83(5) of the Finance Act 1989, and

(b) in so far as it relates to section 432A of the Taxes Act 1988, this Schedule shall apply to income arising, and disposals occurring, on or after 1st January 1990.

(2) Subject to sub-paragraph (1) above, this Schedule shall be deemed to have come into force on 1st January 1990.

(3) The preceding provisions of this paragraph shall have effect subject to paragraph 12 below.

12.—(1) Where at the end of 1989 the assets of an insurance company include securities of a class some of which are regarded as a single 1982 holding, and the rest of which are regarded as a single new holding, for the purposes of corporation tax on chargeable gains—

(a) at the beginning of 1990 there shall be both a 1982 holding and a new holding of the description mentioned in any paragraph of section 440A(2) of the Taxes Act 1988 within which any of the securities fall at that time (whether or not there would be apart from this sub-paragraph), and

(b) the 1982 holding and the new holding of the description mentioned in any such paragraph shall at that time bear to one another the same proportions as the single 1982 holding and the single new holding at the end of 1989.

(2) For the period beginning with 1st January 1990 and ending with 19th March 1990, section 440(4) of the Taxes Act 1988 (as substituted by paragraph 8 of this Schedule) and section 440A(2) of that Act shall have effect with the omission of paragraph (d) (so that all assets not within paragraphs (a) to (c) fall within paragraph (e)).

(3) Sub-paragraph (4) below applies where—

(a) at the end of 19th March 1990 the assets of an insurance company include securities of a class some of which are regarded as a relevant 1982 holding, and others of which are regarded as a relevant new holding, for the purposes of corporation tax on chargeable gains, and

(b) some of the securities are included in the company's long term business fund but others are not;

and for the purposes of this sub-paragraph a holding is a "relevant" holding if it is not linked to pension business or basic life assurance business and is not an asset of the overseas life assurance fund.

(4) Where this sub-paragraph applies—

  (a) at the beginning of 20th March 1990 there shall be both a 1982 holding and a new holding of each of the descriptions mentioned in paragraphs (d) and (e) of section 440A(2) of the Taxes Act 1988 (whether or not there would be apart from this sub-paragraph), and

  (b) the 1982 holding and the new holding of each of those descriptions shall at that time bear to one another the same proportions as the 1982 holding and the new holding mentioned in sub-paragraph (3)(a) above at the end of 19th March 1990.

  (5) Except for the purposes of determining the assets of a company which are linked solely to basic life assurance business, the amendments made by this Schedule shall have effect in relation to a company with the omission of references to overseas life assurance business as respects any time before the provisions of Schedule 7 to this Act have effect in relation to the company.

  (6) Sub-paragraph (7) below applies where—

  (a) the first accounting period of an insurance company beginning on or after 1st January 1990 begins after 20th March 1990,

  (b) at some time during the accounting period the company carries on overseas life assurance business, and

  (c) immediately before the beginning of the accounting period the assets of the long term business fund of the company include both a relevant 1982 holding and a relevant new holding of securities of the same class;

and for the purposes of this sub-paragraph a holding is a "relevant" holding if it is not linked to pension business or basic life assurance business.

  (7) Where this sub-paragraph applies—

  (a) at the beginning of the accounting period there shall be both a 1982 holding and a new holding of each of the descriptions mentioned in paragraphs (c) and (d) of section 440A(2) of the Taxes Act 1988 (whether or not there would be apart from this sub-paragraph), and

  (b) the 1982 holding and the new holding of each of those descriptions shall at that time bear to one another the same proportions as the 1982 holding and the new holding mentioned in sub-paragraph (6)(c) above immediately before the beginning of the period.

  (8) No disposal or re-acquisition shall be deemed to occur by virtue of section 440 of the Taxes Act 1988 (as substituted by paragraph 8 of this Schedule) by reason only of the coming into force (in accordance with the provisions of paragraph 11 of this Schedule and this paragraph) of any provision of section 440A of that Act.

  (9) The substitution made by paragraph 8 of this Schedule shall not affect—

  (a) the operation of section 440 of the Taxes Act 1988 (as it has effect before the substitution) before 20th March 1990, or

  (b) the operation of subsections (6) and (7) of that section (as they have effect before the substitution) in relation to the disposal of an asset which has not been deemed to be disposed of by virtue of section 440 (as it has effect after the substitution) before the time of the disposal.

  (10) In this paragraph—

    "1982 holding" has the meaning given by Part II of Schedule 19 to the Finance Act 1985;

    "new holding" has the meaning given by Part III of that Schedule; and

    "securities" has the same meaning as in section 65 of the Capital Gains Tax Act 1979.

GENERAL NOTE

This Schedule contains a number of amendments making provision for the allocation of the income and gains of an insurance company between the various types of business carried on by it.

Para. 2

There is now power to make amendments by regulations.

Para. 4

  (i) S.432A.   This provision operates if an insurance company carries on:

  (a) ordinary long-term business;

  (b) industrial assurance business; or

  (c) life assurance and other classes of business and different classes of life assurance.

Any income arising from or gains accruing on the disposal of an asset which is linked in the company's records to a particular type of business will be apportioned to that business.

If it relates to the assets of the overseas life assurance fund then it is referable to the overseas life assurance business.

In all other cases there must be an apportionment in accordance with the fraction set out in sub-para. (6). This apportions on the basis of the liabilities to the company of each type of business. In doing so account is taken of the differences between with-profits and without-profits business. To achieve this the long-term business investment reserve is divided amongst the different types of business.

The division is to be made in accordance with the following rules:

(a) if there is nothing but linked liabilities then the investment reserve is divided in accordance with the liabilities;

(b) if there are some non-linked liabilities but none are with-profits liabilities then the relevant part of the investment reserve is divided in accordance with the non-linked liabilities;

(c) in any other case by reference to the with-profits liabilities. The part of the reserve apportioned to each class of business is then added to the liabilities of that class in determining the relevant fraction.

(ii) S.432B. This section and ss.432C to 432E will govern the allocation of receipts and value. In doing so any accounts relating to particular types of business will be used rather than the general accounts of the company.

(iii) S.432C. The following rules apply regarding the allocation of receipts in respect of non-participating business:

(a) if the receipts arise from assets solely linked to a particular class of business then the receipts are allocated to that business;

(b) if attributable to assets of the overseas life assurance fund then it is referable to the overseas business;

(c) other receipts are allocated between the different classes of business in accordance with the relevant fraction which apportions the receipt by reference to the proportions of the liabilities of the relevant businesses reduced by the value of the assets (if any) backing those liabilities.

(iv) S.432D. Similar rules to those set out in (ii) above apply to the allocation of the value of assets between different classes of non-participating business.

(v) S.432E. This section contains the rules concerning the allocation of investment income and the increase or decrease of the value of assets. There are two calculations to be carried out and it is the greater which is used. This section applies to businesses concerning contracts or policies which are not non-participating.

Para. 5

In computing the profits of a pension business instead of leaving out of account group income in full that part referable to pension business will be taken into account.

Para. 6

In computing the profits of a general annuity business taxed income, group income and income attributable to offshore income gains will now be taken into account so far as referable to general annuity business.

Para. 7

The income and gains arising from certain issues of Treasury Stock will only be allocated to the pension business of an insurance company (I.C.T.A. 1988, s.439). Due to the new sections it has been possible to simplify this section.

Para. 8

Assets which are moved from one class of business to another class will be subject to a deemed disposal. Similarly if as a result of a transfer of long-term business an asset is held by the transferee as part of a different class of business from that for which it was held by the transferor there will again be a deemed disposal. It will in both cases be a disposal at market value.

The securities held by an insurance company shall not be treated as one holding but as separate holdings in accordance with s.440A by reference to the separate classes of business carried on by it.

Para. 9

This paragraph applies the accrued income scheme introduced by F.A. 1989 to transfers of securities with accrued interest rights by a company between different categories of its businesses. Such a transfer will give rise to a charge on the investment income. It is intended to prevent internal bond washing.

Para. 11

This paragraph sets out the dates at which the various provisions take effect.

(i) the determination of profits in accordance with F.A. 1989, s.83, the Schedule applies to any period for which such determination falls to be made unless an election is made to substitute March 14, 1989 for January 1, 1990.

(ii) as regards I.C.T.A. 1988, s.432A, the Schedule applies to income arising and disposals occurring after December 31, 1989;

(iii) otherwise the commencement date is January 1, 1990.
Para. 12 contains transitional provisions applying
(a) to companies holding securities of a class some of which are a 1982 holding and some a single new holding;
(b) to companies carrying on overseas life assurance business and not having an accounting period beginning between December 31, 1989 and March 21, 1990.

Section 42   SCHEDULE 7

OVERSEAS LIFE ASSURANCE BUSINESS

1. In section 76(1)(d) of the Taxes Act 1988, for the words "or pension business" there shall be substituted the words ", pension business or overseas life assurance business."
2. In section 231(1) of that Act, for the words "and 247" there shall be substituted the words ", 247 and 441A."
3. For section 441 of that Act there shall be substituted—

"Overseas life assurance business
    441.—(1) This section and section 441A shall apply for an accounting period of an insurance company resident in the United Kingdom if during the period the company carries on overseas life assurance business.
    (2) Subject to the provisions of this section and section 441A, profits arising to the company from the overseas life assurance business shall be treated as income within Schedule D, and be chargeable under Case VI of that Schedule, and for that purpose—
    (a) that business shall be treated separately, and
    (b) subject to paragraph (a) above, the profits from it shall be computed in accordance with the provisions of this Act applicable to Case I of Schedule D.
    (3) Subsection (2) above shall not apply if the company is charged to corporation tax in accordance with the provisions applicable to Case I of Schedule D in respect of the profits of its life assurance business.
    (4) In making the computation referred to in subsection (2) above—
    (a) sections 82(1), (2) and (4) and 83 of the Finance Act 1989 shall apply with the necessary modifications and in particular with the omission of the words "tax or" in section 82(1)(a), and
    (b) there may be set off against the profits any loss, to be computed on the same basis as the profits, which has arisen from overseas life assurance business in any previous accounting period beginning on or after 1st January 1990.
    (5) Section 396 shall not be taken to apply to a loss incurred by a company on overseas life assurance business.
    (6) Nothing in section 128 or 399(1) shall affect the operation of this section.
    (7) Notwithstanding section 337(2), there shall be deductible in computing the profits arising to a company from overseas life assurance business—
    (a) interest payable by the company under a liability of the long term business, so far as referable to overseas life assurance business, and
    (b) annuities payable by the company, so far as so referable.
    (8) Gains accruing on the disposal by a company of assets of its overseas life assurance fund shall not be chargeable gains.

Section 441: distributions
    441A.—(1) Section 208 shall not apply to a distribution in respect of any asset of an insurance company's overseas life assurance fund.
    (2) Subject to subsection (3) below, an insurance company shall not be entitled under section 231 to a tax credit in respect of such a distribution.
    (3) A company shall be entitled to such a tax credit if and to the extent that, were the recipient an individual resident in the territory in which the relevant branch or agency is situated, he would be entitled to the credit under arrangements having effect by virtue of section 788.
    (4) For the purposes of subsection (3) above the relevant branch or agency, in the case of a tax credit in respect of a distribution, is—
    (a) where the relevant asset is linked solely to overseas life assurance business—
            (i) the branch or agency at or through which the company has effected policies or contracts the benefits under which are to be determined by reference to the value of the asset, or
            (ii) in a case where there is more than one such branch or agency, the branches to which different parts of it are allocated by the company in accordance with subsection (5) below;

(b) subject to paragraph (a) above, where the management of the relevant asset is under the control of a person whose normal place of work is at a branch or agency, that branch or agency; and

(c) in any other case, the branch or agency to which it is allocated by the company.

(5) Where policies or contracts the benefits under which are to be determined by reference to the value of an asset within subsection (4)(a) above have been effected at or through more than one branch or agency, different parts of the asset shall be allocated to them so as to secure as far as practicable that the part allocated to each is proportionate to the part of the liabilities in respect of those benefits represented by liabilities under policies or contracts effected at or through it.

(6) Where the overseas life assurance business carried on at or through a branch or agency in a territory includes—

(a) reinsurance business which consists of the reinsurance of liabilities of a person resident in another territory, or

(b) retrocession business,

the amount of any tax credit in relation to which the branch or agency is the relevant branch or agency shall be reduced by the proportion which the liabilities of that reinsurance business bear to all the liabilities of the overseas life assurance business carried on at or through the branch or agency.

(7) Where a company is entitled to an amount of tax credit by virtue of this section the company may claim to have that amount paid to it.

(8) No franked investment income shall be used under Chapter V of Part VI of this Act to frank a company's distributions if the tax credit (or any part of the tax credit) comprised in it is payable to the company under subsection (7) above."

4. In section 724 of that Act—

(a) in subsection (3), for the words after "insurance company" there shall be substituted the words "to the extent that the securities transferred are immediately before the transfer referable to a business the profits of which are computed in accordance with section 436 or 441.", and

(b) in subsection (4), for the words after "apply," in the first place where it occurs, there shall be substituted the words "if the transferee is an insurance company to the extent that the securities transferred are immediately after the transfer referable to a business the profits of which are computed in accordance with section 436 or 441."

5. After section 804 of that Act there shall be inserted—

"Overseas life assurance business: restriction of credit

804A.—(1) Subsection (2) below applies where credit for tax which is payable under the laws of a territory outside the United Kingdom and computed otherwise than wholly by reference to profits arising in that territory is to be allowed (in accordance with this Part) against corporation tax charged by virtue of section 441 in respect of the profits of a company's overseas life assurance business for an accounting period.

(2) Where this subsection applies, the amount of the credit shall not exceed the greater of—

(a) any such part of the tax payable under the laws of the territory outside the United Kingdom as is charged by reference to profits arising in that territory, and

(b) the shareholders' share of the tax so payable.

(3) For the purposes of subsection (2) above the shareholders' share of tax payable under the laws of a territory outside the United Kingdom is so much of that tax as is represented by the fraction.

$$\frac{A}{B}$$

where—

A is an amount equal to the profits of the company for the period which are chargeable to tax under section 441; and

B is an amount equal to the excess of—

(a) the amount taken into account as receipts of the company in computing those profits, apart from premiums and sums received by virtue of a claim under a reinsurance contract, over

(b) the amounts taken into account as expenses and interest in computing those profits.

(4) Where there is no such excess as is mentioned in subsection (3) above, or where the profits are greater than any excess, the whole of the tax payable under the laws of the territory outside the United Kingdom shall be the shareholders' share; and (subject to that) where there are no profits, none of it shall be the shareholders' share.

(5) Where, by virtue of this section, the credit for any tax payable under the laws of a territory outside the United Kingdom is less than it otherwise would be, section 795(2)(a) shall not prevent a deduction being made for the difference in computing the profits of the overseas life assurance business.

6. After Schedule 19 to the Taxes Act 1988 there shall be inserted—

Section 431   "SCHEDULE 19AA

OVERSEAS LIFE ASSURANCE FUND

1.—(1) This Schedule shall have effect for determining for the purposes of this Chapter the assets of a company which are the assets of its overseas life assurance fund.

(2) The Treasury may by order amend any of the following provisions of this Schedule.

2.—(1) Assets of a company at the end of a period of account which—

(a) were assets of the overseas life assurance fund at the end of the immediately preceding period of account, and

(b) are assets of the long term business fund of the company throughout the period,

shall be assets of the overseas life assurance fund throughout the period.

(2) Where in a period of account assets of a company which were assets of the overseas life assurance fund at the end of the immediately preceding period of account are disposed of by the company, or otherwise cease to be assets of the long term business fund of the company, they shall be assets of the overseas life assurance fund from the beginning of the period until they are disposed of or, as the case may be, they cease to be assets of the long term business fund.

(3) Where—

(a) in any period of account assets are acquired by a company as assets of the long term business fund, or otherwise become assets of that fund,

(b) the assets are disposed of by the company, or otherwise cease to be assets of that fund, later in the same period,

(c) throughout the part of the period during which the assets are assets of the long term business fund they are either—

(i) linked solely to the overseas life assurance business of the company, or

(ii) assets within paragraph 5(5)(c) below, and

(d) it is appropriate having regard to all the circumstances (including a comparison between the relationship of the value of the assets of the overseas life assurance fund and the liabilities of the overseas life assurance business and that of the value of the assets of the long term business fund and the liabilities of the company's long term business) that they be assets of the overseas life assurance fund,

they shall be assets of the overseas life assurance fund for the part of the period during which they are assets of the long term business fund.

3.—(1) Where the value of the assets mentioned in paragraph 2(1) above at the end of the period is less than the amount mentioned in paragraph 4 below (or where there are no assets within paragraph 2(1)), assets which—

(a) are assets of the long term business fund of the company at the end of the period,

(b) have a value at that time equal to the difference (or to that amount), and

(c) are designated in accordance with paragraph 5 below,

shall become assets of the overseas life assurance fund at the relevant time.

(2) In sub-paragraph (1) above "the relevant time" means—

(a) where the asset is not an asset of the long term business fund of the company throughout the period, the time when it became such an asset, and

(b) in any other case, the end of the period.

(3) Where the value of the assets mentioned in paragraph 2(1) above at the end of the period is greater than the amount mentioned in paragraph 4 below, assets which—

(a) are assets of the long term business fund of the company at the end of the period,

(b) have a value at that time equal to the difference, and

(c) are designated in accordance with paragraph 5 below,

shall cease to be assets of the overseas life assurance fund at the end of the period.

4.—(1) The amount referred to in paragraph 3 above is the aggregate of—

(a) the liabilities of the company's overseas life assurance business at the end of the period of account, and

(b) the appropriate part of the investment reserve at that time.

(2) In sub-paragraph (1)(b) above the "appropriate part," in relation to the investment reserve, means—

(a) where all of the liabilities of the long term business are linked liabilities, the part of that reserve which bears to the whole the same proportion as the amount of the liabilities of the overseas life assurance business bears to the whole amount of the liabilities of the long term business,

(b) where any of the liabilities of the long term business are not linked liabilities but none (or none but an insignificant proportion) are with-profits liabilities, the part of that reserve which bears to the whole the same proportion as the amount of the liabilities of the overseas life assurance business which are not linked liabilities bears to the whole amount of the liabilities of the long term business which are not linked liabilities, and

(c) in any other case, the part of that reserve which bears to the whole the same proportion as the amount of the with-profits liabilities of the overseas life assurance business bears to the whole amount of the with-profits liabilities of the long term business;

and in this sub-paragraph "linked liabilities" means liabilities in respect of benefits to be determined by reference to the value of linked assets.

5.—(1) Any designation of assets required for the purposes of paragraph 3 above shall be made by a company in accordance with the following provisions of this paragraph.

(2) When designating assets for the purposes of paragraph 3(1) above, a company shall not designate an asset falling within any paragraph of sub- paragraph (5) below unless it designates all assets falling within each of the preceding paragraphs of that sub-paragraph.

(3) When designating assets for the purposes of paragraph 3(3) above, a company shall not designate an asset falling within any paragraph of sub- paragraph (5) below unless it designates all assets falling within each of the succeeding paragraphs of that sub-paragraph.

(4) When an asset falls within more than one paragraph of sub- paragraph (5) below, it shall be taken for the purposes of this paragraph to fall only within the first of them.

(5) The categories of assets referred to in sub-paragraphs (2) and (3) above are—

(a) assets linked solely to overseas life assurance business;

(b) so many of any assets denominated in an overseas currency, other than any non-overseas linked assets, as have a value at the end of the period not exceeding the amount of the company's liabilities in respect of benefits expressed in that currency so far as referable to overseas life assurance business;

(c) assets the management of which is under the control of a person whose normal place of work is at a branch or agency at or through which the company carries on overseas life assurance business;

(d) securities issued by the Treasury with a FOTRA condition and securities to which section 581 of this Act applies;

(e) assets not within paragraph (f) below;

(f) shares in companies resident in the United Kingdom;

but assets linked solely to pension business or basic life assurance business are not within any paragraph of this sub-paragraph (and may not be designated for the purposes of paragraph 3 above).

(6) For the purposes of sub-paragraph (5)(b) above assets are "non-overseas linked assets" if they are linked assets and none of the policies or contracts providing for the benefits concerned are policies or contracts the effecting of which constitutes the carrying on of overseas life assurance business.

(7) For the purposes of sub-paragraph (5)(d) above securities are issued with a FOTRA condition if—

(a) they are issued with the condition that the interest on the securities shall not be liable to income tax so long as it is shown, in a manner directed by the Treasury, that the securities are in the beneficial ownership of persons who are not ordinarily resident in the United Kingdom, or

(b) they are issued with the condition mentioned in section 22(1) of the finance (No. 2) Act 1931 whether or not modified by virtue of section 60(1) of the Finance Act 1940."

7. In paragraph 3(4) of Schedule 28 to the Taxes Act 1988, for the words from "life assurance business," to "the unindexed gain," there shall be substituted the words "life assurance business,—

(a) a profit arising from general annuity business and attributable to a material disposal falls (or would but for the reference to offshore income gains in section 437(2) fall) to be taken into account in the computation under section 436, or

(b) a profit arising from overseas life assurance business and attributable to a material disposal falls to be taken into account in the computation under section 441,

the unindexed gain,".

8. In section 84(1) of the Finance Act 1989, for the words "and pension business" there shall be substituted the words ", pension business and overseas life assurance business."

9. In section 28 of the Capital Allowances Act 1990—

(a) in subsection (1), after the words "subsection (2)" there shall be inserted the words "or (2A),"

(b) in subsection (2), the words "Subject to subsection (2A) below," shall be inserted at the beginning,

(c) after subsection (2) there shall be inserted—

"(2A) Where a company carrying on the business of life assurance is charged to tax under section 441 of the principal Act in respect of the profits of the overseas life assurance business for an accounting period—

(a) any allowance in respect of expenditure on the provision of machinery or plant for use for the management of the overseas life assurance business which falls to be made for the period by virtue of this section shall be given effect by treating it as an expense of that business for that period, and

(b) any charge in respect of such expenditure which falls to be so made shall be given effect by treating it as a receipt of that business for that period;

and sections 73, 144 and 145, and section 75(4) of the principal Act, shall not apply.", and

(d) in subsection (5), after the words "subsection (2)" there shall be inserted the words "or (2A)."

10.—(1) This Schedule shall apply for accounting periods beginning on or after 1st January 1990; and paragraph 9 above shall apply for accounting periods beginning on or after that date and ending on or before 5th April 1990 as well as for later accounting periods.

(2) In relation to the first period of account of an insurance company beginning on or after 1st January 1990, the assets of the company which—

(a) are assets of the long term business fund of the company at the beginning of the period,

(b) have a value at that time equal to the amount mentioned in paragraph 4 of Schedule 19AA to the Taxes Act 1988, and

(c) are designated in accordance with paragraph 5 of that Schedule (on the same basis as a designation required for the purposes of paragraph 3(1) of that Schedule),

shall be treated for the purposes of sub-paragraphs (1) and (2) of paragraph 2 of that Schedule as if they were the assets of the overseas life assurance fund at the end of the immediately preceding period of account.

GENERAL NOTE

This Schedule introduces new rules in place of the old for the tax treatment of life assurance business done through overseas branches of U.K. resident companies. These new rules apply for accounting periods beginning on or after January 1, 1990.

Taxation of overseas life business (s.441)

Unless the profits are already taxable in accordance with Sched. D, Case I a charge under Sched. D, Case VI will be made. For this purpose the business will be treated as separate from the other businesses carried on by the company. In computing the profits the Case I rules will apply.

Losses incurred on the overseas life assurance business may be utilised.

The company will not be chargeable to capital gains tax on disposals of assets in the overseas life assurance fund.

The avoidance rules relating to dealings in commodity futures will not apply.

Distributions

(i) A distribution in respect of an asset in the overseas life assurance fund will not be free from charge to corporation tax as other distributions are due to I.C.T.A. 1988, s.208.

(ii) There will be no tax credit available in such a distribution unless the recipient were an individual, resident where the relevant branch or agency is situated, in which case a credit would be available by reason of double taxation arrangements pursuant to I.C.T.A. 1988, s.788.

If a company is entitled to a tax credit then it is entitled to have it paid to it.

Restriction on credit for tax paid

The restriction introduced in s.804A operates if foreign tax is paid which is not computed wholly by reference to the profits arising in the territory in which the charge to tax is made.

In such circumstances the amount of that foreign tax which can be set off against corporation tax by reason of I.C.T.A. 1988, s.441, shall not exceed the greater of two amounts either:

(a) the part of the tax charged on profits arising in the territory; or

(b) the shareholder's share which is calculated in accordance with subs. (3).

Assets of overseas life assurance fund

The new Schedule 19A governs the allocation of assets to a company's overseas life assurance fund ("o.l.a.f."). These provisions may be amended by statutory instrument.

These rules include the following:

(i) if the assets were in the "o.l.a.f." in the preceding accounting period and are at the

end of the relevant accounting period then they will be treated as having been in the "o.l.a.f." throughout that period;
(ii) if the assets were included in the "o.l.a.f." at the end of the previous accounting period and are disposed of, then from the end of that previous period to the disposal they are treated as being in the "o.l.a.f.";
(iii) assets acquired and disposed of in the same accounting period which are then linked to the "o.l.a.f." or controlled at the overseas branch or agency will form part of the "o.l.a.f." provided that it is appropriate to do so;
(iv) if at the end of an accounting period the assets of the "o.l.a.f." at the end of the previous accounting period which satisfy para. 2(1) are less than the liabilities of the "o.l.a.f." and the appropriate part of the investment reserve, then this difference shall be made up with assets from the company's long-term business fund, which are designated in accordance with para. 5. There is an order of priority for classes of assets laid down in para. 5(5).

Section 46   SCHEDULE 8

INSURANCE COMPANIES: HOLDINGS OF UNIT TRUSTS ETC.

General

1. In this Schedule—
(a) "section 46 assets" means rights under authorised unit trusts and relevant interests in offshore funds which are assets of a company's long term business fund;
(b) "linked section 46 assets" means section 46 assets which are linked assets;
(c) "relevant linked liabilities," in relation to a company, means such of the liabilities of its basic life assurance business as are liabilities in respect of benefits under pre-commencement policies, being benefits to be determined by reference to the value of linked assets;
(d) "pre-commencement policies" means policies issued in respect of insurances made before 1st April 1990, but excluding policies varied on or after that date so as to increase the benefits secured or to extend the term of the insurance (any exercise of rights conferred by a policy being regarded for this purpose as a variation).

Exemption for certain linked assets

2.—(1) Where within two years after the end of an accounting period an insurance company makes a claim for the purpose in relation to the period, section 46(1) of this Act shall not apply at the end of the period to so much of any class of linked assets as it would otherwise apply to and as represents relevant linked liabilities.
(2) For the purposes of sub-paragraph (1) above assets of any class shall be taken to represent relevant linked liabilities only to the extent that their value does not exceed the fraction set out in sub-paragraph (3) below of such of the company's relevant linked liabilities as are liabilities in respect of benefits to be determined by reference to the value of assets of that class.
(3) The fraction referred to in sub-paragraph (2) above is—

$$\frac{A \times C \times 110}{B \times D \times 100}$$

where—
A is the amount at the end of 1989 of such of the company's relevant linked liabilities as are liabilities in respect of benefits to be determined by reference to the value of linked section 46 assets;
B is the amount of the company's relevant linked liabilities at that time;
C is the amount of the company's relevant linked liabilities at the end of the accounting period for which the claim is made;
D is the amount at the end of that period of such of the company's relevant linked liabilities as are liabilities in respect of benefits to be determined by reference to the value of linked section 46 assets.

Replacement of assets

3.—(1) Subject to sub-paragraph (2) below, paragraph 4 below applies where—
(a) after the end of 1989 an insurance company exchanges section 46 assets ("the old assets") for other assets ("the new assets") to be held as assets of the long term business fund,
(b) the new assets are not section 46 assets but are assets on the disposal of which any gains accruing would be chargeable gains,

(c) both the old assets and the new assets are linked solely to basic life assurance business, or both are neither linked solely to basic life assurance business or pension business nor assets of the overseas life assurance fund, and

(d) the company makes a claim for the purpose within two years after the end of the accounting period in which the exchange occurs.

(2) Sub-paragraph (1) above shall have effect in relation to old assets only to the extent that their amount, when added to the amount of any assets to which paragraph 4 below has already applied and which are assets of the same class, does not exceed the aggregate of—

(a) the amount of the assets of the same class included in the long term business fund at the beginning of 1990, other than assets linked solely to pension business and assets of the overseas life assurance fund, and

(b) 110 per cent. of the amount of the assets of that class which represents any subsequent increases in the company's relevant linked liabilities in respect of benefits to be determined by reference to the value of assets of that class.

(3) The reference in sub-paragraph (2)(b) above to a subsequent increase in liabilities is a reference to any amount by which the liabilities at the end of an accounting period ending after 31st December 1989 exceed those at the beginning of the period (or at the end of 1989 if that is later); and for the purposes of that provision the amount of assets which represents an increase in liabilities is the excess of—

(a) the amount of assets whose value at the later time is equivalent to the liabilities at that time, over

(b) the amount of assets whose value at the earlier time is equivalent to the liabilities at that time.

4. Where this paragraph applies, the insurance company (but not any other party to the exchange) shall be treated for the purposes of corporation tax on capital gains as if the exchange had not involved a disposal of the old assets or an acquisition of the new, but as if the old and the new assets were the same assets acquired as the old assets were acquired.

5. References in paragraphs 3 and 4 above to the exchange of assets include references to the case where the consideration obtained for the disposal of assets (otherwise than by way of an exchange within paragraph 3(1)) is applied in acquiring other assets within six months after the disposal; and for the purposes of those paragraphs the time when an exchange occurs shall be taken to be the time when the old assets are disposed of.

Supplementary

6.—(1) This paragraph applies where at any time after the end of 1989 there is a transfer of long term business of an insurance company ("the transferor") to another company ("the transferee") in accordance with a scheme sanctioned by a court under section 49 of the Insurance Companies Act 1982.

(2) Where the transfer is of the whole of the long term business of the transferor, the preceding provisions of this Schedule shall have effect in relation to the assets of the transferee as if that business had at all material times been carried on by him.

(3) Where the transfer is of part of the long term business of the transferor, those provisions shall have effect in relation to assets of the transferor and the transferee to such extent as is appropriate.

(4) Any question arising as to the operation of sub-paragraph (3) above shall be determined by the Special Commissioners who shall determine the question in the same manner as they determine appeals; but both the transferor and the transferee shall be entitled to appear and be heard or to make representations in writing.

GENERAL NOTE

Section 46 introduces deemed disposal of holdings in unit trusts and offshore funds at the end of each accounting period of an insurance company.

Linked assets

If assets held by the company are linked to insurances made before April 1, 1990, then provided that the company makes a claim those assets will not be chargeable to capital gains tax under the provisions of s.46, save and to the extent that the liabilities secured by the asset cease to exist.

Replacements

Roll over relief is available if an insurance company transfers its holdings in unit trusts or offshore funds for other types of chargeable asset and they are linked solely to basic life assurance business or neither are solely so linked. A claim must be made by the company within two years of the end of the accounting period in which the transaction takes place. The new assets will have the same acquisition costs as the old assets. This covers not just exchanges but also sales when the consideration is applied within six months in the acquisition of the new assets.

In the case of a transfer of long-term business pursuant to the Insurance Companies Act 1982, s.49, then the transferee will be entitled to the reliefs contained in this Schedule as if the business had been carried on by one person at all material times.

Section 48   SCHEDULE 9

INSURANCE COMPANIES: TRANSFERS OF LONG TERM BUSINESS

Capital gains

1. After section 267 of the Taxes Act 1970 there shall be inserted—

"Insurance companies: transfers of business
        267A.—(1) This section applies where there is a transfer of the whole or part of the long term business of an insurance company ("the transferor") to another company ("the transferee") in accordance with a scheme sanctioned by a court under section 49 of the Insurance Companies Act 1982.
        (2) Subject to subsection (3) below, where this section applies section 267 above shall not be prevented from having effect in relation to any asset included in the transfer by reason that—
            (a) the transfer is not part of a scheme of reconstruction or amalgamation,
            (b) the condition in paragraph (c) of subsection (1) of that section is not satisfied, or
            (c) the asset is within subsection (2) of that section;
and where section 267 above applies by virtue of paragraph (a) above the references in subsection (3A) of that section to the reconstruction or amalgamation shall be construed as references to the transfer.
        (3) Section 267 above shall not have effect in relation to an asset by virtue of subsection (2) above unless—
            (a) any gain accruing to the transferor—
                (i) on the disposal of the asset in accordance with the scheme, or
                (ii) where that disposal occurs after the transfer of business has taken place, on a disposal of the asset immediately before that transfer, and
            (b) any gain accruing to the transferee on a disposal of the asset immediately after its acquisition in accordance with the scheme,
would be a chargeable gain which would form part of its profits for corporation tax purposes (and would not be a gain on which, under any double taxation arrangements having effect by virtue of section 788 of the Taxes Act 1988, it would not be liable to tax)."
2. In section 127 of the Finance Act 1989, after subsection (3) (deemed disposal and reacquisition where a person ceases to carry on trade in the United Kingdom through branch or agency) there shall be inserted—
        "(3A) Subsection (3) above shall not apply to an asset by reason of a transfer of the whole or part of the long term business of an insurance company to another company if section 267 of the Taxes Act 1970 has effect in relation to the asset by virtue of section 267A of that Act."

Accounting periods

3. In section 12 of the Taxes Act 1988, after subsection (7) there shall be inserted—
        "(7A) Notwithstanding anything in subsections (1) to (7) above, where there is a transfer of the whole or part of the long term business of an insurance company to another company in accordance with a scheme sanctioned by a court under section 49 of the Insurance Companies Act 1982, an accounting period of the company from which the business is transferred shall end with the day of the transfer."

Expenses of management and losses

4. The following section shall be inserted after section 444 of the Taxes Act 1988—

"Transfers of business
        444A.—(1) Subject to the following provisions of this section, this section applies where there is a transfer of the whole or part of the long term business of an insurance company

("the transferor") to another company ("the transferee") in accordance with a scheme sanctioned by a court under section 49 of the Insurance Companies Act 1982.

(2) Any expenses of management which (assuming the transferor had continued to carry on the business transferred after the transfer) would have been deductible by the transferor under sections 75 and 76 in computing profits for an accounting period following the period which ends with the day on which the transfer takes place shall, instead, be treated as expenses of management of the transferee (and deductible in accordance with those sections, as modified in the case of acquisition expenses by section 86(6) to (9) of the Finance Act 1989 and in the case of expenses to which subsection (6) or (7) of section 87 of that Act applies by that subsection).

(3) Any loss which (assuming the transferor had continued to carry on the business transferred after the transfer)—

(a) would have been available under section 436(3)(c) to be set off against profits of the transferor for the accounting period following that which ends with the day on which transfer takes place, or

(b) where in connection with the transfer the transferor also transfers the whole or part of any overseas life assurance business, would have been so available under section 441(4)(b),

shall, instead, be treated as a loss of the transferee (and available to be set off against profits of the same class of business as that in which it arose).

(4) Where acquisition expenses are treated as expenses of management of the transferee by virtue of subsection (2) above, the amount deductible for the first accounting period of the transferee ending after the transfer takes place shall be calculated as if that accounting period began with the day after the transfer.

(5) Where the transfer is of part only of the transferor's long term business, subsection (2) or (3) above shall apply only to such part of any amount to which it would otherwise apply as is appropriate.

(6) Any question arising as to the operation of subsection (5) above shall be determined by the Special Commissioners who shall determine the question in the same manner as they determine appeals; but both the transferor and transferee shall be entitled to appear and be heard or to make representations in writing.

(7) Subject to subsection (8) below, this section shall not apply unless the transfer is effected for bona fide commercial reasons and does not form part of a scheme or arrangements of which the main purpose, or one of the main purposes, is avoidance of liability to corporation tax.

(8) Subsection (7) above shall not affect the operation of this section in any case where, before the transfer, the Board have, on the application of the transferee, notified the transferee that the Board are satisfied that the transfer will be effected for bona fide commercial reasons and will not form part of any scheme or arrangements such as are mentioned in that subsection; and subsections (2) to (5) of section 88 of the 1979 Act shall have effect in relation to this subsection as they have effect in relation to subsection (1) of that section."

Capital allowances

5. After section 152 of the Capital Allowances Act 1990 there shall be inserted—

"Insurance companies: transfers of business
152A.—(1) This section applies where assets are transferred as part of or in connection with, a transfer of the whole or part of the long term business of an insurance company ("the transferor") to another company ("the transferee") in accordance with a scheme sanctioned by a court under section 49 of the Insurance Companies Act 1982.

(2) Where this section applies—

(a) there shall be made, in accordance with this Act, to or on the transferee (instead of the transferor) any such allowances and charges as would have fallen to be made to or on the transferor; and

(b) the amount of any such allowance or charge shall be computed as if everything done to or by the transferor had been done to or by the transferee (but so that no sale or transfer of assets which is made to the transferee by the transferor shall be treated as giving rise to any such allowance or charge)."

Transfer to friendly society

6. In section 460 of the Taxes Act 1988, after subsection (10) there shall be inserted—

"(10A) Where at any time there is a transfer of the whole or part of the long term business of an insurance company to a friendly society in accordance with a scheme sanctioned by a court under section 49 of the Insurance Companies Act 1982, any life or endowment business which relates to contracts included in the transfer shall not thereafter be tax exempt life or endowment business for the purposes of this Chapter."

Commencement

7. This Schedule shall apply to transfers of business taking place on or after 1st January 1990; and (subject to that) the amendment made by paragraph 5 of this Schedule shall apply in relation to accounting periods ending on or before 5th April 1990 as well as in relation to later accounting periods.

GENERAL NOTE
This Schedule contains provisions replacing the extra-statutory concession announced in the Press Release dated October 17, 1988. It applies when the transfer is pursuant to a scheme approved by a Court under the Insurance Companies Act 1982, s.49. The intention is that the successor will step into the shoes of the transferor for tax purposes.

Capital gains tax
There will be a no gain/no loss disposal if the requirements of I.C.T.A. 1988, s.267, are satisfied, other than that there is a scheme of reconstruction or amalgamation and the asset is trading stock.

Management expenses
Unrelieved expenses of management incurred in connection with the transferred business will be deductible by the transferee subject to the spreading provisions of F.A. 1989, s.86.

Losses
Unrelieved losses arising from pension business or general annuity business may be set off against profits of the same class of business of the successor. Similarly if the transfer involves overseas life assurance business then unrelieved losses arising from it may be used by the successor.

Capital allowances
Allowances relating to plant, machinery and industrial building transferred will be allowed to the transferor up to the date of transfer and to the transferee after that date.
These provisions apply to transfers after December 31, 1989.

Friendly society
On a transfer to a friendly society the tax exemption previously enjoyed by life or endowment business will be lost.

Section 56   SCHEDULE 10

CONVERTIBLE SECURITIES

PART I

INTRODUCTION

Qualifying provision for redemption

1. For the purposes of this Schedule a qualifying provision for redemption, in relation to a security, is a provision which—
   (a) provides for redemption before maturity only at the option of the person holding the security for the time being,
   (b) provides for such redemption on one occasion only,
   (c) provides for such redemption to occur on the last day of an income period, and
   (d) is such that the amount payable on redemption on exercise of the option is fixed (as opposed to variable), is determined at the time the security becomes subject to the provision, and constitutes a deep gain.

Qualifying convertible securities

2.—(1) For the purposes of this Schedule a security is a qualifying convertible security at the time of its issue if—

(a) it fulfils each of the first eight conditions mentioned below, and
(b) it fulfils the ninth condition mentioned below (where it applies) or it fulfils the ninth and tenth conditions mentioned below (where they apply).

(2) The first condition is that the security was issued by a company on or after 9th June 1989.

(3) The second condition is that the security—
(a) is not a share in a company,
(b) is redeemable, and
(c) was not issued in circumstances such that, by virtue of section 209(2)(c) of the Taxes Act 1988, it (or part of it) constituted or fell within a distribution of a company.

(4) The third condition is that at the time the security was issued it was quoted in the official list of a recognised stock exchange.

(5) The fourth condition is that under the terms of issue—
(a) the security can be converted into ordinary share capital in the company which issued it,
(b) the security either carries no right to interest, or carries a right to interest at a rate which is fixed (as opposed to variable) and determined at the time of issue, and
(c) any amount payable on redemption (at any time), and any amount payable by way of interest, is payable in the currency in which the issue price is denominated.

(6) The fifth condition is that at the time of issue of the security it is subject to one (and one only) qualifying provision for redemption.

(7) The sixth condition is that the yield to redemption for the relevant redemption period represents no more than a reasonable commercial return; and the relevant redemption period is the redemption period which ends with the day on which the occasion for redemption under the qualifying provision for redemption falls.

(8) The seventh condition is that the security—
(a) is a deep discount security but would not be one if it were not for the qualifying provision for redemption, or
(b) is a deep gain security but would not be one if it were not for the qualifying provision for redemption;

and paragraph 21 of Schedule 4 to the Taxes Act 1988, and paragraph 22B(1) of Schedule 11 to the Finance Act 1989, shall be ignored in construing paragraphs (a) and (b) above.

(9) The eighth condition is that the obtaining of a tax advantage by any person was not the main benefit, or one of the main benefits, that might be expected to accrue from issuing the security.

(10) The ninth condition applies where the security carries a right to interest, and is that—
(a) the first (or only) interest payment day falls on a day which bears the same date in the month as the day of issue bears, but which occurs in the sixth month after the month in which that day falls, or
(b) the first (or only) interest payment day falls on the first anniversary of the day of issue.

(11) The tenth condition applies where there is more than one interest payment day, and is that—
(a) if sub-paragraph (10)(a) above applies, each interest payment day (other than the first) falls on a day which bears the same date in the month as the interest payment day immediately preceding it bears, but which occurs in the sixth month after the month in which that day falls;
(b) if sub-paragraph (10)(b) above applies, each interest payment day (other than the first) falls on the first anniversary of the interest payment day immediately preceding it.

(12) If a security is quoted in the official list of a recognised stock exchange at a time after it was issued but before the end of the qualifying period, for the purposes of sub-paragraph (4) above it shall be deemed to have been quoted in that list at the time it was issued; and the qualifying period is the period of one month beginning with the day on which the security was issued.

Events after issue

3.—(1) A security which was a qualifying convertible security at the time of its issue shall continue to be a qualifying convertible security for the purposes of this Schedule.

(2) But sub-paragraph (1) above shall have effect subject to paragraphs 4(2) and 5(2) below.

Securities becoming subject to later options

4.—(1) This paragraph applies where—
(a) a security becomes at any time (the time in question) subject to a qualifying provision for redemption (the new provision), and
(b) immediately before that time it was a qualifying convertible security.

(2) If the relevant requirement is not satisfied, the security shall cease to be a qualifying convertible security for the purposes of this Schedule at the time in question.

(3) For the purposes of this paragraph the relevant requirement is satisfied if—
(a) the security becomes subject to the new provision on or after the relevant day but not after the day on which the occasion for redemption under the old provision falls,
(b) the person who issued the security did not indicate, at any time falling before the relevant day, that the security might become subject to a qualifying provision for redemption (in addition to any other such provision or provisions),
(c) the day on which the occasion for redemption under the new provision falls is not less than one year after the day on which the occasion for redemption under the old provision falls,
(d) the amount payable on redemption on exercise of the option for which the new provision provides is not less than the amount payable on redemption on exercise of the option for which the old provision provides,
(e) the yield to redemption for the relevant redemption period represents no more than a reasonable commercial return, and
(f) the obtaining of a tax advantage by any person is not the main benefit, or one of the main benefits, that might be expected to accrue from the new provision.
(4) For the purposes of this paragraph the relevant day is the day falling 30 days before the day on which the occasion for redemption under the old provision falls.
(5) For the purposes of this paragraph the old provision is—
(a) if the security became subject to one other qualifying provision for redemption before the time in question, that provision, or
(b) if the security became subject to more than one qualifying provision for redemption before the time in question, the one to which it last became subject.
(6) For the purposes of this paragraph the relevant redemption period is the redemption period which ends with the day on which the occasion for redemption under the new provision falls.

Other later events in relation to securities

5.—(1) This paragraph applies where—
(a) a prohibited event occurs in relation to a security at any time (the time in question), and
(b) immediately before that time it was a qualifying convertible security.
(2) The security shall cease to be a qualifying convertible security for the purposes of this Schedule at the time in question.
(3) For the purposes of this paragraph, a prohibited event occurs in relation to a security if—
(a) it ceases to be quoted in the official list of a recognised stock exchange,
(b) it becomes subject to a provision under which it carries a right to interest at a rate which is variable or falls to be determined at a time other than issue (or both),
(c) it becomes subject to a provision under which any amount payable on redemption (at any time) is payable in a currency different from that in which the issue price is denominated,
(d) it becomes subject to a provision under which any amount payable by way of interest is payable in a currency different from that in which the issue price is denominated,
(e) it becomes subject to a provision which would be a qualifying provision for redemption but for the fact that one or more of sub-paragraphs (b) to (d) of paragraph 1 above is (or are) not fulfilled as regards the provision, or
(f) there is a time when more than 10 per cent. of the securities issued under the relevant prospectus are held by companies which are linked companies at that time.
(4) For the purposes of sub-paragraph (3)(f) above the relevant prospectus is the prospectus under which the security concerned was issued.
(5) For the purposes of sub-paragraph (3)(f) above, the question whether companies are linked companies at a particular time shall be determined in accordance with paragraph 4 of Schedule 11 to the Finance Act 1988.

Deep gain

6.—(1) For the purposes of this Schedule the amount payable on redemption, on exercise of the option under a provision for redemption (the provision concerned), constitutes a deep gain if it constitutes such a gain by virtue of sub-paragraph (2) or (4) below (or both).
(2) The amount payable on redemption (on exercise of the option under the provision concerned) constitutes a deep gain if the issue price of the security is less than the amount so payable, and the amount by which it is less represents more than—
(a) 15 per cent. of the amount so payable, or
(b) half Y per cent. of the amount so payable, where Y is the number of complete years between the day of issue and the day on which the occasion for redemption under the provision concerned falls.

(3) Sub-paragraph (4) below applies where the security became subject to—
- (a) a qualifying provision for redemption (the prior provision), or
- (b) qualifying provisions for redemption (the prior provisions),

before it became subject to the provision concerned.

(4) The amount payable on redemption (on exercise of the option under the provision concerned) constitutes a deep gain if the base amount is less than the amount so payable, and the amount by which it is less represents more than—
- (a) 15 per cent. of the amount so payable, or
- (b) half Y per cent. of the amount so payable, where Y is the number of complete years between the base day and the day on which the occasion for redemption under the provision concerned falls.

(5) For the purposes of sub-paragraph (4) above—
- (a) the base amount is the amount payable on redemption on exercise of the option provided for by the prior provision (if there is only one) or the last of the prior provisions (if there are two or more), and
- (b) the base day is the day on which the occasion for redemption falls under the prior provision (if there is only one) or the last of the prior provisions (if there are two or more).

(6) For the purposes of sub-paragraph (5) above the last of the prior provisions is the one to which the security last became subject.

Income period

7.—(1) This paragraph applies for the purposes of this Schedule.

(2) In relation to a security which carries a right to interest each of the following is an income period—
- (a) the period beginning with the day of issue and ending with the first (or only) interest payment day, and
- (b) any period beginning with the day after one interest payment day and ending with the next interest payment day.

(3) In relation to a security which does not carry a right to interest each of the following is an income period—
- (a) the period beginning with the day of issue and ending with the first relevant day, and
- (b) the period beginning with the day after one relevant day and ending with the next relevant day.

(4) For the purposes of sub-paragraph (3) above each day on which an anniversary of the day of issue falls is a relevant day.

Redemption period

8.—(1) For the purposes of this Schedule each of the following is a redemption period in relation to a security—
- (a) the period beginning with the day of issue and ending with the day on which the first (or only) relevant redemption occasion falls, and
- (b) any period beginning with the day after the day on which one relevant redemption occasion falls and ending with the day on which the next relevant redemption occasion falls.

(2) For the purposes of sub-paragraph (1) above a relevant redemption occasion is an occasion for redemption under a qualifying provision for redemption.

Yield to redemption

9.—(1) For the purposes of this Schedule the yield to redemption for a redemption period is a rate (expressed as a percentage) such that if a sum equal to the relevant amount were to be invested at that rate on the assumption that—
- (a) the rate would be applied on a compounding basis at the end of each relevant income period, and
- (b) the amount of any interest payable in respect of a relevant income period would be deducted after applying the rate,

the value of that sum on the relevant redemption day would be equal to the amount payable on redemption of the security on that day under the relevant redemption provision.

(2) For the purposes of this paragraph the relevant amount is the issue price, in a case where the redemption period concerned is the period falling within paragraph 8(1)(a) above.

(3) For the purposes of this paragraph the relevant amount is the amount payable on redemption on the last relevant occasion, in a case where the redemption period concerned is

one falling within paragraph 8(1)(b) above; and the last relevant occasion is the occasion for redemption, under a qualifying provision for redemption, last occurring before the redemption period begins.

(4) For the purposes of this paragraph—

(a) a relevant income period is any income period which consists of or falls within the redemption period,

(b) the relevant redemption day is the last day of the redemption period, and

(c) the relevant redemption provision is the qualifying provision for redemption providing for redemption on that day.

Transfer etc.

10.—(1) This paragraph applies for the purposes of this Schedule.

(2) "Transfer," in relation to a security, means transfer by way of sale, exchange, gift or otherwise.

(3) But (notwithstanding sub-paragraph (2) above) "transfer" does not include a transfer made on a conversion of a security into ordinary share capital in a company.

(4) Where an agreement for the transfer of a security is made, it is transferred, and the person to whom it is agreed to be transferred becomes entitled to it, when the agreement is made and not on a later transfer made pursuant to the agreement; and "entitled," "transfer" and cognate expressions shall be construed accordingly.

(5) A person holds a security at a particular time if he is entitled to it at the time.

(6) A person acquires a security when he becomes entitled to it.

(7) If an agreement is conditional (whether on the exercise of an option or otherwise) for the purposes of sub-paragraph (4) above it is made when the condition is satisfied.

Miscellaneous

11.—(1) This paragraph applies for the purposes of this Schedule.

(2) In relation to a security—

(a) the amount payable (or paid) on redemption does not include any amount payable (or paid) by way of interest,

(b) the day of issue is the day on which the security is issued, and

(c) an interest payment day is a day on which interest is payable under the security.

(3) A deep discount security is a security which is a deep discount security for the purposes of Schedule 4 to the Taxes Act 1988.

(4) A deep gain security is a security which is a deep gain security for the purposes of Schedule 11 to the Finance Act 1989.

(5) Ordinary share capital, in relation to a company, means any share capital (by whatever name called) of the company, other than capital the holders of which have a right to a dividend at a fixed rate but have no other right to share in the profits of the company.

(6)"Tax advantage" has the meaning given by section 709(1) of the Taxes Act 1988.

PART II

CHARGE TO TAX

The charge

12.—(1) For the purposes of this Part of this Schedule a chargeable event occurs if, on or after 9th June 1989, there is a transfer of a security and at the time of the transfer the security—

(a) is a qualifying convertible security, and

(b) is subject to at least one qualifying provision for redemption under which the occasion for redemption has not arrived.

(2) For the purposes of this Part of this Schedule a chargeable event also occurs if—

(a) a person holding a security redeems it on or after 9th June 1989,

(b) immediately before the redemption the security is a qualifying convertible security, and

(c) the redemption is made in exercise of the option for redemption under a qualifying provision for redemption to which the security is subject.

(3) For the purposes of this Part of this Schedule the chargeable person is the person making the transfer or exercising the option (as the case may be).

(4) Where a chargeable event occurs—

(a) the chargeable amount shall be treated as income of the chargeable person,

(b) the income shall be chargeable to tax under Case III or Case IV (as the case may be) of Schedule D,

(c) the income shall be treated as arising in the year of assessment in which the chargeable event occurs, and

(d) notwithstanding anything in sections 64 to 67 of the Taxes Act 1988, the tax shall be computed on the income arising in the year of assessment for which the computation is made.

Chargeable amount

13.—(1) For the purposes of paragraph 12 above the chargeable amount is—

(a) the amount obtained on transfer or redemption, in a case where that amount is equal to or less than the total income element;

(b) so much of the amount obtained on transfer or redemption as is equal to the total income element, in a case where that amount is greater than that element.

(2) For the purposes of this paragraph the amount obtained on transfer or redemption is the amount obtained, in respect of the transfer or redemption, by the person making the transfer or (as the case may be) the person who was entitled to the security immediately before redemption.

(3) For the purposes of sub-paragraph (2) above the person concerned shall be treated as obtaining in respect of the transfer or redemption—

(a) any amount he actually obtains in respect of it, and

(b) any amount he is entitled to obtain, but does not obtain, in respect of it.

(4) Sub-paragraph (3) above shall not apply where paragraph 16, 17 or 18(2) below applies.

Total income element

14.—(1) The total income element for the purposes of paragraph 13 above shall be determined by—

(a) finding the income element for each income period (if any) the whole of which consists of or falls within the ownership period, and

(b) finding the partial income element for each income period (if any) a part of which consists of or falls within the ownership period.

(2) The aggregate of the income elements and the partial income elements so found is the total income element.

(3) The ownership period is the period which—

(a) begins with the day on which the chargeable person acquired the security, and

(b) ends with the day on which the chargeable event occurs.

Income elements

15.—(1) This paragraph has effect for the purposes of paragraph 14 above.

(2) The income element for an income period shall be determined in accordance with the formula—

$$\frac{A \times B}{100} - C$$

(3) For the purposes of sub-paragraph (2) above—

(a) A is the adjusted issue price of the security,

(b) B is the figure included in the percentage representing the yield to redemption for the redemption period which consists of the income period or in which the income period falls, and

(c) C is the amount of interest (if any) payable in respect of the income period.

(4) The partial income element for an income period a part of which consists of or falls within the ownership period shall be determined in accordance with the formula—

$$D \times \frac{E}{F}$$

(5) For the purposes of sub-paragraph (4) above—

(a) D is the income element for the income period (determined in accordance with the formula mentioned in sub-paragraph (2) above),

(b) E is the number of days in the income period which consist of or fall within the ownership period, and

(c) F is the number of days in the income period.

(6) The adjusted issue price of a security, in relation to a particular income period, is the aggregate of the issue price of the security and the income elements for all previous income periods of the security (determined in accordance with the formula mentioned in sub-paragraph (2) above).

Death

16.—(1) Where an individual who is entitled to a security dies, for the purposes of this Part of this Schedule he shall be treated as—
  (a) transferring it immediately before his death, and
  (b) obtaining in respect of the transfer an amount equal to the market value of the security at the time of the transfer.

(2) Where a security is transferred by personal representatives to a legatee, for the purposes of paragraph 13 above they shall be treated as obtaining in respect of the transfer an amount equal to the market value of the security at the time of the transfer.

(3) In sub-paragraph (2) above "legatee" includes any person taking (whether beneficially or as trustee) under a testamentary disposition or on an intestacy or partial intestacy, including any person taking by virtue of an appropriation by the personal representatives in or towards satisfaction of a legacy or other interest or share in the deceased's property.

Market value

17.—(1) This paragraph applies where a security is transferred from one person to another and—
  (a) they are connected with each other,
  (b) the transfer is made for a consideration which consists of or includes consideration not in money or money's worth, or
  (c) the transfer is made otherwise than by way of a bargain made at arm's length.

(2) For the purposes of paragraph 13 above the person making the transfer shall be treated as obtaining in respect of it an amount equal to the market value of the security at the time of the transfer.

(3) Section 839 of the Taxes Act 1988 (connected persons) shall apply for the purposes of this paragraph.

Underwriters

18.—(1) An underwriting member of Lloyd's shall be treated for the purposes of this Part of this Schedule as absolutely entitled as against the trustees to the securities forming part of his premiums trust fund, his special reserve fund (if any) and any other trust fund required or authorised by the rules of Lloyd's, or required by the underwriting agent through whom his business or any part of it is carried on, to be kept in connection with the business.

(2) Where a security forms part of a premiums trust fund at the end of 31st December of any relevant year, for the purposes of this Part of this Schedule—
  (a) the trustees of the fund shall be treated as transferring the security at that time, and
  (b) they shall be treated as obtaining in respect of the transfer an amount equal to the market value of the security at the time of the transfer;
and for this purpose relevant years are 1989 and subsequent years.

(3) Where a security forms part of a premiums trust fund at the beginning of 1st January of any relevant year, for the purposes of this Part of this Schedule the trustees of the fund shall be treated as acquiring the security at that time; and for this purpose relevant years are 1990 and subsequent years.

(4) Sub-paragraph (5) below applies where the following state of affairs exists at the beginning of 1st January of-any year or the end of 31st December of any year—
  (a) securities have been transferred by the trustees of a premiums trust fund in pursuance of an arrangement mentioned in section 129(1) or (2) of the Taxes Act 1988,
  (b) the transfer was made to enable another person to fulfil a contract or to make a transfer,
  (c) securities have not been transferred in return, and
  (d) section 129(3) of that Act applies to the transfer made by the trustees.

(5) The securities transferred by the trustees shall be treated for the purposes of sub-paragraphs (2) and (3) above as if they formed part of the premiums trust fund at the beginning of 1st January concerned or the end of 31st December concerned (as the case may be).

(6) Paragraph 16(1) above shall not apply where—
  (a) the individual concerned is an underwriting member of Lloyd's, and
  (b) the security concerned forms part of a premiums trust fund, a special reserve fund or any other trust fund required or authorised by the rules of Lloyd's, or required by the underwriting agent through whom the individual's business or any part of it is carried on, to be kept in connection with the business.

(7) In a case where an amount treated as income chargeable to tax by virtue of paragraph 12 above constitutes profits or gains mentioned in section 450(1) of the Taxes Act 1988—

(a) section 450(1)(b) shall apply, and

(b) paragraph 12(4)(c) above shall not apply.

(8) For the purpose of computing income tax for the year 1987-88 sub-paragraph (7) above shall have effect as if—

(a) the reference to section 450(1) of the Taxes Act 1988 were to paragraph 2 of Schedule 16 to the finance Act 1973, and

(b) the reference to section 450(1)(b) were to paragraph 2(b) of that Schedule.

(9) In this paragraph "business" and "premiums trust fund" have the meanings given by section 457 of the Taxes Act 1988.

Trustees

19.—(1) Where on a transfer or redemption of a security by trustees an amount is treated as income chargeable to tax by virtue of paragraph 12 above, the rate at which it is chargeable shall be a rate equal to the sum of the basic rate and the additional rate for the year of assessment in which the transfer or redemption is made.

(2) Where the trustees are trustees of a scheme to which section 469 of the Taxes Act 1988 applies, sub-paragraph (1) above shall not apply if or to the extent that the amount is treated as income in the accounts of the scheme.

Receipts in United Kingdom

20.—(1) Sub-paragraph (2) below applies where—

(a) by virtue of paragraph 12(4) above an amount is treated as income of a person and as chargeable to tax under Case IV of Schedule D, and

(b) the person satisfies the Board, on a claim in that behalf, that he is not domiciled in the United Kingdom, or that (being a Commonwealth citizen or a citizen of the Republic of Ireland) he is not ordinarily resident in the United Kingdom.

(2) In such a case—

(a) any amounts received in the United Kingdom in respect of the amount treated as income shall be treated as income arising in the year of assessment in which they are so received, and

(b) paragraph 12(4) above shall have effect with the substitution of paragraph (a) above for paragraph 12(4)(c).

(3) For the purposes of sub-paragraph (2) above—

(a) there shall be treated as received in the United Kingdom all amounts paid, used or enjoyed in, or in any manner or form transmitted or brought to, the United Kingdom, and

(b) subsections (6) to (9) of section 65 of the Taxes Act 1988 shall apply as they apply for the purposes of subsection (5) of that section.

Charities

21.—(1) In a case where—

(a) paragraph 12 above would apply (apart from this paragraph) in the case of a transfer or redemption of a security,

(b) immediately before the transfer or redemption was made the security was held by a charity, and

(c) the amount which would (apart from this paragraph) be treated as income by virtue of paragraph 12 above is applicable and applied for charitable purposes,

that paragraph shall not apply in the case of the transfer or redemption.

(2) In this paragraph "charity" has the same meaning as in section 506 of the Taxes Act 1988.

Retirement benefit schemes

22. In a case where—

(a) paragraph 12 above would apply (apart from this paragraph) in the case of a transfer or redemption of a security, and

(b) immediately before the transfer or redemption was made the security was held for the purposes of an exempt approved scheme (within the meaning of Chapter I of Part XIV of the Taxes Act 1988),

that paragraph shall not apply in the case of the transfer or redemption.

Stock lending

23. In a case where—
(a) a security is the subject of a transfer which falls within section 129(3) of the Taxes Act 1988, and
(b) paragraph 12 above would apply in the case of the transfer (apart from this paragraph),
that paragraph shall not apply in the case of the transfer.

Identification of securities

24. Section 88 of the Finance Act 1982 shall apply to the identification, for the purposes of this Part of this Schedule, of qualifying convertible securities transferred or redeemed as it applies to the identification, for the purposes of capital gains tax, of deep discount securities disposed of.

PART III

THE ISSUING COMPANY

25.—(1) In a case where—
(a) a qualifying convertible security is redeemed, and
(b) the circumstances are such that paragraph 12 above applies in the case of the redemption,
sub-paragraph (2) below shall apply in relation to the company which issued the security.
(2) For the purposes of sections 338 and 494 of the Taxes Act 1988 (allowance of charges on income) the relevant amount shall be treated as if it were interest—
(a) falling within section 338(3)(b), and
(b) paid by the company in the accounting period in which the redemption occurs (and not as mentioned in the words of section 338(3) which follow paragraph (b)).
(3) In this paragraph "the relevant amount" means so much of the amount paid on the redemption as exceeds the issue price of the security.

PART IV

AMENDMENTS

(1) Deep discount securities

26.—(1) Schedule 4 to the Taxes Act 1988 (deep discount securities) shall be amended as follows.
(2) In paragraph 1 (interpretation) the following sub-paragraph shall be inserted after sub-paragraph (1)—
"(1A) Notwithstanding anything in sub-paragraph (1) above, for the purposes of this Schedule a security is not a deep discount security if—
(a) it was issued by a company on or after 1st August 1990, and
(b) under the terms of issue it can be converted into share capital in a company (whether or not the company is the one which issued the security)."
(3) The following shall be inserted after paragraph 20—

"Convertible securities: special rules

21. In a case where—
(a) a security is a qualifying convertible security, for the purposes of Schedule 10 to the Finance Act 1990, at the time of its issue, and
(b) apart from this paragraph it would be a deep discount security at that time,
the security shall be treated, at the time of its issue and at all subsequent times, as not being a deep discount security."

(2) Deep gain securities

27.—(1) Schedule 11 to the Finance Act 1989 (deep gain securities) shall be amended as follows.
(2) In paragraph 4 (meaning of transfer etc.) the following sub-paragraph shall be inserted after sub-paragraph (2)—
"(2A) But (notwithstanding sub-paragraph (2) above) "transfer" does not include a transfer made on a conversion of a security into share capital in a company."
(3) The following shall be inserted after paragraph 22—

"Convertible securities: special rules (1)

22A.—(1) Sub-paragraph (2) below applies where—
(a) a security is a qualifying convertible security, for the purposes of Schedule 10 to the Finance Act 1990, at the time of its issue,
(b) apart from paragraph 21 of Schedule 4 to the Taxes Act 1988, it would be a deep discount security at that time, and
(c) at a later time it ceases to be a qualifying convertible security for the purposes of Schedule 10 to the Finance Act 1990.
(2) As regards any event occurring in relation to the security after the time mentioned in sub-paragraph (1)(c) above, paragraphs 5 to 19 above shall have effect as if—
(a) the security were a deep gain security, and
(b) it had been acquired as such (whatever the time it was acquired).
(3) For the purposes of sub-paragraph (2) above events, in relation to a security, include anything constituting a transfer or acquisition for the purposes of this Schedule.

Convertible securities: special rules (2)

22B.—(1) In a case where—
(a) a security is a qualifying convertible security, for the purposes of Schedule 10 to the Finance Act 1990, at the time of its issue, and
(b) apart from this sub-paragraph it would be a deep gain security at that time,
then (subject to sub-paragraph (3) below) the security shall be treated, at the time of its issue and at all subsequent times, as not being a deep gain security.
(2) Sub-paragraph (3) below applies where—
(a) sub-paragraph (1) above applies in the case of a security, and
(b) at a time after its issue it ceases to be a qualifying convertible security for the purposes of Schedule 10 to the Finance Act 1990.
(3) As regards any event occurring in relation to the security after the time mentioned in sub-paragraph (2)(b) above, paragraphs 5 to 19 above shall have effect as if—
(a) the security were a deep gain security, and
(b) it had been acquired as such (whatever the time it was acquired).
(4) For the purposes of sub-paragraph (3) above events, in relation to a security, include anything constituting a transfer or acquisition for the purposes of this Schedule."

(3) Corporate bonds

28.—(1) Section 64 of the Finance Act 1984 (qualifying corporate bonds) shall be amended as follows.
(2) The following subsection shall be inserted after subsection (3C)—
"(3D) For the purposes of this section "corporate bond" also includes a security—
(a) which is not included in the definition in subsection (2) above, and
(b) which, by virtue of paragraph 22A(2) or 22B(3) of Schedule 11 to the Finance Act 1989, falls to be treated as a deep gain security as mentioned in the paragraph concerned."
(3) The following subsection shall be inserted after subsection (5C)—
"(5D) Subject to subsection (6) below, for the purposes of this section and Schedule 13 to this Act a corporate bond which falls within subsection (3D) above is a qualifying corporate bond as regards a disposal made after the time mentioned in paragraph 22A(1)(c) or 22B(2)(b) (as the case may be) of Schedule 11 to the Finance Act 1989."

PART V

APPLICATION OF SCHEDULE

29.—(1) The amendment made by paragraph 27(2) above shall be deemed always to have had effect.
(2) Paragraph 28 above shall have effect in relation to disposals after the relevant time (and, in relation to such disposals, shall be regarded as always having had effect).
(3) In sub-paragraph (2) above "the relevant time" means the time referred to, as regards the security concerned, in section 64(5D) of the Finance Act 1984.
(4) Subject to sub-paragraphs (1) to (3) above, this Schedule shall be deemed to have come into force on 9th June 1989.

GENERAL NOTE
A consultative document was published on October 27, 1989, by the Inland Revenue entitled

"Convertible and Indexed Securities", which concerned the possible tax treatment of certain convertible securities which fell within the rules introduced by the Finance Act 1989 applicable to "deep gain securities." The provisions of this Schedule are a result of that Consultative Document and the consultations that followed and introduce new tax rules applicable to "qualifying convertible securities." Where they apply, the legislation concerning "deep gain securities" and "deep discount securities" is inoperative.

The broad outline of the Schedule is as follows. Part I contains the definition provisions describing a "qualifying convertible security." Part II provides for the charges to tax that may arise as regards such a security. Part III gives tax relief to the issuing company when it redeems such a security. Part IV contains amendments to other legislation which operate in particular to oust the rules otherwise applicable to deep gain and deep discount securities.

Part I sets out the various conditions that need to be satisfied before the security can qualify as a qualifying convertible security. The principal ones are as follows:
 (i) the securities must be convertible into the ordinary share capital of the company which issued it;
 (ii) they must be quoted on a recognised stock exchange;
 (iii) the yield to redemption must represent no more than a reasonable commercial return;
 (iv) the security must give the investor one, but only one, option to require redemption before maturity ("the qualifying provision for redemption");
 (v) the security must be either a deep discount or deep gain security but would not be either were it not for the terms of the qualifying provision for redemption.
The tax treatment applicable to these securities is broadly as follows:
 (a) on a transfer of a security or redemption under the qualifying provision for redemption the "total income element" (as defined in para. 14) is taxable as income (see para. 12(3)). Any gain in excess of such element will be subject to tax as a chargeable gain;
 (b) any transfer after the qualifying provision for redemption has ceased to apply, or a redemption after such time, will give rise to a chargeable gain alone;
 (c) conversion of a security into shares will not crystallise any charge. The gain otherwise arising will be rolled over into the shares and will be taxable on the share sale.
Para. 25 provides a tax relief for the issuing company where para. 12 creates a charge on a redemption. It is noteworthy that the amount treated as interest by that provision is only treated as paid in the accounting period in which the redemption occurs. This is to be contrasted with the position of deep discount securities where a deduction is available prior to payment (see I.C.T.A. 1988, Sched. 4, para. 5.).

Section 69   SCHEDULE 11

EUROPEAN ECONOMIC INTEREST GROUPINGS

Taxation

1. After section 510 of the Taxes Act 1988 there shall be inserted—

"European Economic Interest Groupings
    510A.—(1) In this section "grouping" means a European Economic Interest Grouping formed in pursuance of Council Regulation (EEC) No. 2137/85 of 25th July 1985, whether registered in Great Britain, in Northern Ireland, or elsewhere.
    (2) Subject to the following provisions of this section, for the purposes of charging tax in respect of income and gains a grouping shall be regarded as acting as the agent of its members.
    (3) In accordance with subsection (2) above—
    (a) for the purposes mentioned in that subsection the activities of the grouping shall be regarded as those of its members acting jointly and each member shall be regarded as having a share of its property, rights and liabilities; and
    (b) for the purposes of charging tax in respect of gains a person shall be regarded as acquiring or disposing of a share of the assets of the grouping not only where there is an acquisition or disposal of assets by the grouping while he is a member of it, but also where he becomes or ceases to be a member of a grouping or there is a change in his share of the property of the grouping.
    (4) Subject to subsection (5) below, for the purposes of this section a member's share of any property, rights or liabilities of a grouping shall be determined in accordance with the contract under which the grouping is established.

(5) Where the contract does not make provision as to the shares of members in the property, rights or liabilities in question a member's share shall be determined by reference to the share of the profits of the grouping to which he is entitled under the contract (and if the contract makes no provision as to that, the members shall be regarded as having equal shares).

(6) Subject to subsection (7) below, where any trade or profession is carried on by a grouping it shall be regarded for the purposes of charging tax in respect of income and gains as carried on in partnership by the members of the grouping.

(7) Sections 111 and 114(4) shall not apply to the members of a grouping and section 112 shall have effect in relation to the members of a grouping as if the second reference in subsection (2) to the firm were a reference to the members and subsection (3) were omitted.

(8) Notwithstanding subsection (7) above, where a trade or profession is carried on by a grouping, the amount on which the members are chargeable to income tax in respect of it shall be computed (but not assessed) jointly."

Management

2. After section 12 of the Taxes Management Act 1970 there shall be inserted—

"European Economic Interest Groupings

European Economic Interest Groupings
12A.—(1) In this section "grouping" means a European Economic Interest Grouping formed in pursuance of Council Regulation (EEC) No. 2137/85 of 25th July 1985 ("the Council Regulation"), whether registered in Great Britain, in Northern Ireland, or elsewhere.

(2) For the purposes of making assessments to income tax, corporation tax and capital gains tax on members of a grouping, an inspector may act under subsection (3) or (4) below.

(3) In the case of a grouping which is registered in Great Britain or Northern Ireland or has an establishment registered in Great Britain or Northern Ireland, an inspector may by a notice given to the grouping require the grouping—
   (a) to make and deliver to the inspector within the time limited by the notice a return containing such information as may be required in pursuance of the notice, and
   (b) to deliver with the return such accounts and statements as may be required in pursuance of the notice.

(4) In the case of any other grouping, an inspector may by a notice given to any member of the grouping resident in the United Kingdom, or if none is to any member of the grouping, require the member—
   (a) to make and deliver to the inspector within the time limited by the notice a return containing such information as may be required in pursuance of the notice, and
   (b) to deliver with the return such accounts and statements as may be required in pursuance of the notice,
and a notice may be given to any one of the members concerned or separate notices may be given to each of them or to such of them as the inspector thinks fit.

(5) Every return under this section shall include a declaration by the grouping or member making the return to the effect that the return is to the best of the maker's knowledge correct and complete.

(6) A notice under this section may require different information, accounts and statements for different periods, in relation to different descriptions of income or gains or in relation to different descriptions of member.

(7) Notices under this section may require different information, accounts and statements in relation to different descriptions of grouping.

(8) Subject to subsection (9) below, where a notice is given under subsection (3) above, everything required to be done shall be done by the grouping acting through its manager or, where there is more than one, any of them; but where the manager of a grouping (or each of them) is a person other than an individual, the grouping shall act through the individual, or any of the individuals, designated in accordance with the Council Regulation as the representative of the manager (or any of them).

(9) Where the contract for the formation of a grouping provides that the grouping shall be validly bound only by two or more managers acting jointly, any declaration required by subsection (5) above to be included in a return made by a grouping shall be given by the appropriate number of managers."
3.—(1) After section 98A of the Taxes Management Act 1970 there shall be inserted—

"European Economic Interest Groupings

98B.—(1) In this section "grouping" means a European Economic Interest Grouping formed in pursuance of Council Regulation (EEC) No. 2137/85 of 25th July 1985, whether registered in Great Britain, in Northern Ireland, or elsewhere.

(2) Subject to subsections (3) and (4) below, where a grouping or member of a grouping required by a notice given under section 12A above to deliver a return or other document fails to comply with the notice, the grouping or member shall be liable—

(a) to a penalty not exceeding £300; and

(b) if the failure continues after a penalty is imposed under paragraph (a) above, to a further penalty or penalties not exceeding £60 for each day on which the failure continues after the day on which the penalty under paragraph (a) above was imposed (but excluding any day for which a penalty under this paragraph has already been imposed).

(3) No penalty shall be imposed under subsection (2) above in respect of a failure at any time after the failure has been remedied.

(4) If a grouping to which, or member to whom, a notice is given proves that there was no income or chargeable gain to be included in the return, the penalty under subsection (2) above shall not exceed £100.

(5) Where a grouping or member fraudulently or negligently delivers an incorrect return, accounts or statement, or makes an incorrect declaration in a return delivered, under section 12A above, the grouping or member shall be liable to a penalty not exceeding £3000 multiplied by the number of members of the grouping at the time of delivery."

(2) In section 100(2) of that Act (penalties which are imposed by Commissioners), after paragraph (d) there shall be inserted "or

(e) section 98B(2)(a) above."

4.—(1) At the end of section 36 of the Taxes Management Act 1970 (extension of time for assessment in case of fraudulent or negligent conduct), there shall be added—

"(4) Any act or omission such as is mentioned in section 98B below on the part of a grouping (as defined in that section) or member of a grouping shall be deemed for the purposes of subsection (1) above to be the act or omission of each member of the grouping."

(2) At the end of section 40 of that Act (extension of time for assessment in case of fraudulent or negligent conduct of person who has died), there shall be added—

"(4) Any act or omission such as is mentioned in section 98B below on the part of a grouping (as defined in that section) or member of a grouping shall be deemed for the purposes of subsection (2) above to be the act or omission of each member of the grouping."

Commencement

5. This Schedule shall be deemed to have come into force on 1st July 1989.

Section 80 SCHEDULE 12

BROADCASTING: TRANSFER OF UNDERTAKINGS OF INDEPENDENT BROADCASTING AUTHORITY AND CABLE AUTHORITY

Transfer of IBA's transmission activities to nominated company: corporation tax

1.—(1) Subject to sub-paragraph (2), the following provisions shall apply for the purposes of the Corporation Tax Acts, namely—

(a) the part of the trade carried on by the IBA which is transferred to the nominated company under the Broadcasting Act 1990 ("the principal Act") shall be treated as having been, at the time when it began to be carried on by the IBA and at all times since that time, a separate trade carried on by that company;

(b) the trade carried on by that company after the transfer date shall be treated as the same trade as that which, by virtue of paragraph (a) above, it is treated as having carried on before that date;

(c) all property, rights and liabilities of the IBA which are transferred under the principal Act to that company shall be treated as having been, at the time when they became vested in the IBA and at all times since that time, property, rights and liabilities of that company; and

(d) anything done by the IBA in relation to any such property, rights and liabilities as are mentioned in paragraph (c) above shall be deemed to have been done by that company.

(2) There shall be apportioned between the IBA and the nominated company—

(a) the unallowed tax losses of the IBA, and

(b) any expenditure which they have incurred before the transfer date and by reference to which capital allowances may be made,

in such manner as is just and reasonable having regard—

    (i) to the extent to which such losses and expenditure are attributable to the part of the trade carried on by them which is transferred to that company under the principal Act, and

    (ii) as respects the apportionment of such expenditure, to the division of their assets between the relevant transferees which is effected under that Act.

(3) In this paragraph—

    "the IBA's final accounting period" means the last complete accounting period of the IBA ending before the transfer date;

    "unallowed tax losses" means losses, allowances or amounts which, as at the end of the IBA's final accounting period, are tax losses within the meaning given by section 400(2) of the Taxes Act 1988, excluding losses which are allowable capital losses within the meaning of paragraph 6 below.

(4) This paragraph shall have effect in relation to accounting periods beginning after the IBA's final accounting period.

Transfer of IBA's assets to Commission and Radio Authority: chargeable gains

2.—(1) For the purposes of the Capital Gains Tax Act 1979 ("the 1979 Act") the transfer under the principal Act of any asset from the IBA to the Commission or the Radio Authority shall be deemed to be for a consideration such that no gain or loss accrues to the IBA; and Schedule 5 to that Act (assets held on 6th April 1965) shall have effect in relation to an asset so transferred as if the acquisition or provision of it by the IBA had been the acquisition or provision of it by the Commission or (as the case may be) by the Authority.

(2) In paragraph 1(3) of Schedule 8 to the Finance Act 1988 (capital gains: assets held on 31st March 1982), there shall be added after paragraph (g) "; and

    (h) paragraph 2(1) of Schedule 12 to the Finance Act 1990."

(3) Where the benefit of any debt in relation to which the IBA are, for the purposes of section 134 of the 1979 Act (debts), the original creditor is transferred under the principal Act to the Commission or the Radio Authority, the Commission or (as the case may be) the Radio Authority shall be treated for those purposes as the original creditor in relation to the debt in place of the IBA.

Disposal by IBA of DBS assets to DBS programme contractor: chargeable gains

3.—(1) For the purposes of the 1979 Act the disposal under the principal Act of any relevant asset by the IBA to a DBS programme contractor shall be deemed to be for a consideration such that no gain or loss accrues to the IBA.

(2) In this paragraph—

(a) "relevant asset" means any equipment or other asset (of whatever description) which has been used or held by the IBA in connection with the transmission of DBS services; and

(b) "DBS programme contractor" and "DBS service" have the meaning given by section 37(3) of the Cable and Broadcasting Act 1984.

Transfer of Cable Authority's assets to Commission: chargeable gains

4. For the purposes of the 1979 Act the transfer by the principal Act of any asset from the Cable Authority to the Commission shall be deemed to be for a consideration such that no gain or loss accrues to that Authority.

Transfer of shares from Commission to Channel 4 company: chargeable gains

5.—(1) For the purposes of the 1979 Act the transfer by the principal Act of shares in the Channel 4 company from the Commission to the Channel Four Television Corporation shall be deemed to be for a consideration such that no gain or loss accrues to the Commission.

(2) In sub-paragraph (1) "the Channel 4 company" means the body corporate referred to in section 12(2) of the Broadcasting Act 1981.

Apportionment of unallowed capital losses between relevant transferees

6.—(1) The unallowed capital losses of the IBA shall be apportioned between the relevant transferees in such manner as is just and reasonable having regard to the purposes, or principal purposes, for which the relevant assets were respectively used or held by the IBA and the activities which are to be carried on by those transferees respectively as from the transfer date.

(2) Any unallowed capital losses of the IBA which are apportioned to one of the relevant transferees under sub-paragraph (1) shall be treated as allowable capital losses accruing to that transferee on the disposal of an asset on the transfer date.

(3) In this paragraph—
"allowable capital losses" means losses which are allowable for the purposes of the 1979 Act;
"relevant assets," in relation to unallowed capital losses of the IBA, means the assets on whose disposal by the IBA those losses accrued;
"unallowed capital losses," in relation to the IBA, means allowable capital losses which have accrued to the IBA before the transfer date, in so far as they have not been allowed as deductions from chargeable gains.

Roll-over relief in connection with nominated company

7. Where the IBA have before the transfer date disposed of (or of their interest in) any assets used, throughout the period of ownership, wholly or partly for the purposes of the part of their trade transferred to the nominated company under the principal Act, sections 115 to 119 of the 1979 Act (roll-over relief on replacement of business assets) shall have effect in relation to that disposal as if the IBA and the nominated company were the same person.

Disputes as to apportionments etc.

8.—(1) This paragraph applies where any apportionment or other matter arising under the foregoing provisions of this Schedule appears to be material as respects the liability to tax (for whatever period) of two or more relevant transferees.

(2) Any question which arises as to the manner in which the apportionment is to be made or the matter is to be dealt with shall be determined, for the purposes of the tax of both or all of the relevant transferees concerned—
(a) in a case where the same body of General Commissioners have jurisdiction with respect to both or all of those transferees, by those Commissioners, unless those transferees agree that it shall be determined by the Special Commissioners;
(b) in a case where different bodies of Commissioners have jurisdiction with respect to those transferees, by such of those bodies as the Board may direct, unless those transferees agree that it shall be determined by the Special Commissioners; and
(c) in any other case, by the Special Commissioners.

(3) The Commissioners by whom the question falls to be determined shall make the determination in like manner as if it were an appeal except that both or all of the relevant transferees concerned shall be entitled to appear and be heard by the Commissioners or to make representations to them in writing.

Securities of nominated company

9.—(1) Any share issued by the nominated company to the Secretary of State in pursuance of the principal Act shall be treated for the purposes of the Corporation Tax Acts as if it had been issued wholly in consideration of a subscription paid to that company of an amount equal to the nominal value of the share.

(2) Any debenture issued by the nominated company to the Secretary of State in pursuance of the principal Act shall be treated for the purposes of the Corporation Tax Acts as if it had been issued—
(a) wholly in consideration of a loan made to that company of an amount equal to the principal sum payable under the debenture; and
(b) wholly and exclusively for the purposes of the trade carried on by that company.

Interpretation

10.—(1) In this Schedule—
"the 1979 Act" means the Capital Gains Tax Act 1979;
"the Commission" means the Independent Television Commission;
"the IBA" means the Independent Broadcasting Authority;
"the nominated company" and "the transfer date" have the same meaning as in the provisions of the principal Act relating to the transfer of the undertakings of the IBA and the Cable Authority;

"the principal Act" means the Broadcasting Act 1990;
"the relevant transferees" means the Commission, the Radio Authority and the nominated company.
(2) References in this Schedule to things transferred under the principal Act are references to things transferred in accordance with a scheme made under that Act.

GENERAL NOTE

Under the Broadcasting Act 1990 the Independent Broadcasting Authority ("IBA") and the Cable Television Authority give way to new bodies—the Independent Television Commission, the Radio Authority and a new transmission company. The Schedule is designed to assure fiscal neutrality for the consequent transactions.
Para. 1 permits the IBA's transmission activities to be treated as having been always carried on by the new transmission company. Losses carried forward are to be apportioned on a just and reasonable basis.
Para. 2 precludes a charge to capital gains tax boom arising on the transfer of assets of IBA to the Independent Television Commission or the Radio Authority.
Paras. 3, 4 and 5 have similar effect in relation to disposals by the IBA of direct broadcasting by satellite ("DBS") assets to DBS programme contractors, by the Cable Authority of assets to the Independent Television Commission, and by the Commission of shares in the Channel 4 company to the Channel Four Television Corporation.
Para. 6. Unallowed capital losses of the IBA are to be apportioned among the recipient bodies on a just and reasonable basis.
Para. 7. Roll-over relief on assets disposed of by the IBA before the transfer date will be carried over to the transmission company.
Para. 8. Disputes arising out of the Schedule's provisions will be decided by General or Special Commissioners as may be appropriate.
Para. 9. No tax charge will arise in relation to shares or debentures by the transmission company to the Government.
Para. 10 contains definitions.

Section 88   SCHEDULE 13

CAPITAL ALLOWANCES: MISCELLANEOUS AMENDMENTS

Hotels in enterprise zones: initial allowances

1.—(1) In section 1(2) of the Capital Allowances Act 1990, after the words "shall include a reference to" there shall be inserted the words "a qualifying hotel and to."
(2) In section 7(1) of that Act, for the words "this Part, except Chapter I," there shall be substituted the words "this Chapter and Chapter III as it applies for the purposes of this Chapter."
(3) This paragraph shall apply in relation to any chargeable period or its basis period ending on or after 6th April 1990.

Scientific research allowance: writing off of expenditure

2.—(1) In section 8(5)(b) of that Act, for the words "ceases to be used by the person in question for scientific research connected with the trade" there shall be substituted the words "ceases to belong to the person in question."
(2) This paragraph shall apply where an asset ceases to belong to a person on or after 6th April 1990.

Disposal value of machinery or plant after succession to trade

3.—(1) In section 78 of that Act, after subsection (2) there shall be inserted—
"(2A) Where the disposal value of any machinery or plant in relation to which an election under subsection (2) above has effect falls to be ascertained in accordance with section 26, that section shall apply as if the person mentioned in subsection (2) of that section were the deceased."
(2) This paragraph shall apply to machinery or plant in relation to which an election under section 78(2) is made on or after 6th April 1990.

Non-resident companies: use of allowances

4.—(1) In section 149 of that Act, subsection (2) shall be omitted.

(2) This paragraph shall apply in relation to chargeable periods beginning on or after 6th April 1990.

Contributions: machinery and plant

5.—(1) In section 154(2) of that Act, for the words from "as if" to "and for" there shall be substituted the words "as if—
(a) the reference to expenditure in respect of which an allowance would have been made under Part I included a reference to expenditure in respect of which a first-year allowance would have been made under Part II or which would have been taken into account in determining qualifying expenditure for the purpose of any allowance or charge under section 24; and
(b) the reference to the making to the contributor to expenditure on the provision of an asset of such initial and writing-down allowances as would have been made to him if his contribution had been expenditure on the provision of a similar asset included a reference to his being treated under Part II as if his contribution had been expenditure on the provision of that asset;
and for."
(2) This paragraph shall apply to contributions made on or after 6th April 1990.

Sale of machinery or plant

6.—(1) In section 161(10) of that Act, the words "and of subsection (8)" shall be omitted.
(2) This paragraph shall apply in relation to a sale of an asset when both the time of completion and the time when possession of the asset is given are on or after 6th April 1990.

Assured tenancies allowance

7.—(1) In section 832(1) of the Taxes Act 1988, in the definition of "the Capital Allowances Acts," the words ", but excluding Part III of that Act" shall be omitted.
(2) This paragraph shall apply for chargeable periods beginning on or after 6th April 1990.

GENERAL NOTE
A number of amendments to the C.A.A. 1990 are made under this Schedule by s.75, to be effective on or after April 6, 1990.
Para. 1 brings qualifying hotels in enterprise zones within the 100 per cent. initial allowance provisions (C.A.A. 1990, s.1).
Para. 2 amends C.A.A. 1990, s.8, dealing with the time at which allowances are written off. Scientific research allowances under C.A.A. 1990, s.138 ("Assets ceasing to belong to traders"), are to be treated as written off when the asset ceases to belong to the person in question and not, as in *ibid.*, s.8(5)(b), when it ceases to be used for research connected with that person's trade.
A new subs. (2A) is inserted in C.A.A. 1990, s.78, by para. 3. Subs. 78(2) provides that a person inheriting a trade under a will or intestacy may, in certain circumstances, elect that machinery or plant acquired by him with the trade will be treated as having been sold to him at the open market price or, if it is less, the written down value. Where the written down value is taken, the disposal value of the machinery or plant is, under the new subs. (2A), to be limited to the capital expenditure incurred by the deceased.
Under para. 4, the operation of C.A.A. 1990, s.149 is extended. This section split up, for certain capital allowance purposes, the income of a non-resident company liable to corporation tax and that liable to income tax. This did not previously extend to allowances on machinery or plant or to scientific research allowance under subs. 149(2). That subsection is to be omitted.
Para. 5 amends the provisions relating to allowances on contributions made to the cost of machinery or plant in C.A.A. 1990, s.154. The effect of the amended subs. 154(2) is the same as that of the original subsection, *i.e.* that capital allowances are given on the amount of the contribution as though it had been expenditure on the provision of machinery or plant.
Para. 6 extends the operation of C.A.A. 1990, s.161(8) which defines the time of a sale as the earlier of the time of completion and the time when possession is given. This did not previously apply to machinery or plant but is now to do so by an amendment to subs. 161(10).
I.C.T.A. 1990, s.832(1), defining "the Capital Allowances Acts", is incorporated in C.A.A. 1990, Sched. 1, para. 8(36). This excluded Pt. III of C.A.A. 1990 ("Dwelling Houses Let on Assured Tenancies"). That exclusion is to be omitted by para. 7. Allowances within Pt. III will thus be allowable for a claim for group relief.

SCHEDULE 14

AMENDMENTS CORRECTING ERRORS IN THE TAXES ACT 1988

PART I

AMENDMENTS OF THE TAXES ACT 1988

1. The Taxes Act 1988 shall have effect, and shall be deemed always to have had effect, subject to the amendments made by this Part of this Schedule.

2. In section 37(1)—

(a) for the words "subsection (2) below" there shall be substituted the words "subsection (2) or (3) below";

(b) for the words "this subsection" there shall be substituted the words "subsection (2) or (3) below"; and

(c) for the words "the amount of that tax" there shall be substituted the words "that amount."

3. In section 213(6), for "(3)(1)(a)" there shall be substituted "(3)(a)."

4.—(1) In sections 322(1)(a) and (2) and 323(1), after the words "a British Dependent Territories citizen" there shall be inserted the words ", a British National (Overseas)."

(2) In section 323(7), after the words "British Dependent Territories citizens" there shall be inserted the words ", British Nationals (Overseas)."

5. In section 326(2)(a), for the words from "12" to "1969" there shall be substituted the words "11 of the National Debt Act 1972."

6. In section 377(1)(b), for "(5)" there shall be substituted "(8)."

7. In section 393(2), for "492(2)" there shall be substituted "492(3)."

8. In section 478(3), for the words "section (2)" there shall be substituted the words "subsection (2)."

9. In section 751(1)(a), for the words "the persons" there shall be substituted the word "persons."

10. In section 757(7), before the words "the earliest date" there shall be inserted the words "any time on or after."

11. In section 761(1), for the words "and Schedule" there shall be substituted the words "or Schedule."

12. In section 773(2), for the words "this section" there shall be substituted the words "section 770."

13. In paragraph 4(1) of Schedule 16, for "(4)" there shall be substituted "(3)."

PART II

AMENDMENTS OF OTHER ENACTMENTS

The Taxes Management Act 1970 (c. 9)

14. In section 31(3) of the Taxes Management Act 1970, for the words "Part XV or XVI" there shall be substituted the words "any of sections 660 to 685 and 695 to 702."

15. In section 98 of that Act, in the first column of the Table, in the entry relating to Schedule 9 to the Taxes Act 1988, for the words "paragraphs 6 and 25" there shall be substituted the words "paragraph 6."

The Oil Taxation Act 1975 (c. 22)

16. In paragraph 5(2) of Schedule 3 to the Oil Taxation Act 1975, for the words "section 17 of this Act" and the words "the said section 17" there shall be substituted the words "section 500 of the Taxes Act."

The Capital Gains Tax Act 1979 (c. 14)

17. In section 149C of the Capital Gains Tax Act 1979—

(a) in subsection (2), after the word "given" there shall be inserted the words "to him"; and

(b) in subsection (7), after the words "shares" there shall be inserted the words "issued after 18th March 1986."

The Finance Act 1981 (c. 35)

18. In section 83(3) of the Finance Act 1981, for the words "section 45(2)(b) above" there shall be substituted the words "section 740(2)(b) of the Taxes Act."

Commencement

19.—(1) Subject to the following provisions of this paragraph, the amendments made by this Part of this Schedule shall be treated for the purposes of their commencement as if they had been made by the Taxes Act 1988.

(2) An individual may elect that in relation to him the amendment made by paragraph 17(b) of this Schedule shall not have effect with respect to exchanges (and similar events) taking place before 1st January 1990.

(3) An election under sub-paragraph (2) above shall be irrevocable and shall be made by notice in writing to the inspector at any time before 6th April 1991.

(4) There may be made any such adjustment, whether by way of discharge or repayment of tax, the making of an assessment or otherwise, as is appropriate in consequence of the amendment made by paragraph 17(b) of this Schedule or an election under sub-paragraph (2) above.

GENERAL NOTE

Most of the changes made by this Schedule are to correct very minor oversights in the preparation of the 1988 Consolidation Act, such as the updating of statutory references.

Para. 17, however, does make a possibly material change by applying the provisions of C.G.T.A. 1979, s.149C(7), only to shares issued after March 18, 1986. In this case the taxpayer is given a right to elect by notice given before April 6, 1991, that the change shall not apply in relation to events occurring before January 1, 1990.

Otherwise the amendments take effect as if they had been in the original consolidation.

Section 100   SCHEDULE 15

CLAIMS FOR GROUP RELIEF

Section 412   "SCHEDULE 17A

GROUP RELIEF: CLAIMS

Introductory

1.—(1) This Schedule has effect as respects claims for group relief.

(2) Section 42 of the Management Act (procedure for making claims) shall not apply to such claims.

Time limits

2.—(1) No claim for an accounting period of a company may be made if—

(a) the company has been assessed to corporation tax for the period, and

(b) the assessment has become final and conclusive.

(2) Sub-paragraph (1) above shall not apply in the case of a claim made before the end of 2 years from the end of the period.

(3) This paragraph applies to the withdrawal of a claim as it applies to the making of a claim.

3.—(1) No claim for an accounting period of a company may be made after the end of 6 years from the end of the period, except under paragraph 5 below.

(2) This paragraph applies to the withdrawal of a claim as it applies to the making of a claim.

4. Where under paragraph 2 or 3 above a claim may not be made after a certain time, it may be made within such further time as the Board may allow.

5.—(1) A claim for an accounting period of a company may be made after the end of 6 years from the end of the period if—

(a) the company has been assessed to corporation tax for the period before the end of 6 years from the end of the period,

(b) the company has appealed against the assessment, and

(c) the assessment has not become final and conclusive.

(2) No claim for an accounting period of a company may be made under this paragraph after the end of 6 years and 3 months from the end of the period.

Method of making claim

6.—(1) A claim shall be made by being included in a return under section 11 of the Management Act (corporation tax return) for the period for which the claim is made.

(2) In sub-paragraph (1) above the reference to a claim being included in a return includes a reference to a claim being included by virtue of an amendment of the return.

(3) This paragraph applies to the withdrawal of a claim as it applies to the making of a claim.

Nature of claim

7. A claim may be made for less than the full amount available.

8. A claim, other than one under paragraph 5 above, shall be for an amount which is quantified at the time the claim is made.

9.—(1) A claim under paragraph 5 above shall be expressed to be conditional, as to the amount claimed, on, and only on, the outcome of one or more relevant matters specified in the claim.

(2) For the purposes of this paragraph a matter is relevant if it is relevant to the determination of the assessment of the claimant company to corporation tax for the period for which the claim is made.

Consent to surrender

10.—(1) A claim shall require the consent of the surrendering company.

(2) A consortium claim shall require the consent of each member of the consortium in addition to the consent of the surrendering company.

(3) Consent to surrender shall be of no effect unless, at or before the time the claim is made, notice of consent is given by the consenting company to the inspector to whom the surrendering company makes its returns under section 11 of the Management Act.

(4) Notice of consent to surrender, in the case of consent by the surrendering company, shall be of no effect unless it contains the following particulars—

(a) the name of the surrendering company;
(b) the name of the company to which relief is being surrendered;
(c) the amount of relief being surrendered;
(d) the accounting period of the surrendering company to which the surrender relates;
(e) the tax district references of the surrendering company and the company to which relief is being surrendered.

(5) Where notice of the surrendering company's consent to surrender is given to the inspector after the surrendering company has made a return under section 11 of the Management Act for the period to which the relief being surrendered relates, the notice shall be of no effect unless the surrendering company at the same time amends the return.

(6) Where consent to surrender relates to a loss in respect of which relief has been given under section 393(1), notice of consent to surrender, in the case of the surrendering company, shall be of no effect unless, at the same time as giving the notice to the inspector, the company amends its return under section 11 of the Management Act for the period, or, if more than one, each of the periods, in which relief for the loss has been given under section 393(1).

(7) For the purposes of sub-paragraph (6) above relief under section 393(1) shall be treated as given for losses incurred in earlier accounting periods before losses incurred in later accounting periods.

(8) A claim shall require to be accompanied by a copy of the notice of consent to surrender given for the purposes of this paragraph by the surrendering company.

(9) A consortium claim shall in addition require to be accompanied by a copy of the notice of consent to surrender given for the purposes of this paragraph by each member of the consortium.

11.—(1) This paragraph applies in relation to claims under paragraph 5 above.

(2) In the case of consent to surrender by the surrendering company, consent which relates to relief which is the subject of more than one claim under paragraph 5 above shall be of no effect unless it specifies an order of priority in relation to the claims.

Adjustments

12.—(1) All such assessments or adjustments of assessments shall be made as may be necessary to give effect to a claim or the withdrawal of a claim.

(2) An assessment under this paragraph shall not be out of time if it is made—

(a) in the case of a claim, within one year from the date on which an assessment of the claimant company to corporation tax for the period for which the claim is made becomes final and conclusive, and
(b) in the case of the withdrawal of a claim, within one year from the date on which the claim is withdrawn."

GENERAL NOTE

The new Sched. 17A to the I.C.T.A. 1988, applicable from the introduction of "Pay and File" in 1993, is designed to give greater flexibility in obtaining group relief.

Para. 1

The claims procedure under the T.M.A. 1970, s.42, will no longer apply to claims for group relief.

Paras. 2–5

The normal time-limit for making, varying or withdrawing claims to group relief will be two years after the date that the profits and losses for the period are determined, subject to an overall time-limit of six years. The time-limit of six years may be extended by three months if there is an open appeal against an assessment at that time. It may also be extended if the Board so allow. The Revenue has stated that its policy will be to admit only those claims which, for reasons beyond the company's control, could not have been made within the statutory time limit.

Para. 6

A claim will be made by virtue of being included in a return or amended return under the T.M.A. 1970, s.11, rather than by the separate procedure under *ibid.*, s.42.

Paras. 7–9

As before, claims need not be for the full amount available. However, they must be quantified at the time the claim is made, except in the case where it is made not later than three months after the end of the statutory period where there is an open appeal. In this case the *quantum* will be conditional on the outcome of the appeal.

Paras. 10–12

Claims will require the consent of the surrendering company, as before, and must identify with some particularity the surrendering company, the receiving company, the amount surrendered and other relevant details. This reverses the decision in *Gallic Leasing Ltd.* v. *Coburn (Inspector of Taxes)* (1989) 133 S.J. 422.

Where there is more than one claim outstanding dependent on the outcome of an appeal, the consent must specify an order of priority in relation to the claims.

Section 102   SCHEDULE 16

CAPITAL ALLOWANCES: CLAIMS BY COMPANIES

Section 145A   "SCHEDULE A1

CORPORATION TAX ALLOWANCES: CLAIMS

Introductory

1.—(1) This Schedule has effect as respects claims for allowances which fall to be made under the provisions of this Act as they apply for the purposes of corporation tax.

(2) Section 42 of the Taxes Management Act 1970 (procedure for making claims) shall not apply to such claims.

Time limits

2.—(1) No claim for an accounting period of a company may be made if—
   (a) the claim affects an amount for the period which is determinable under section 41A of the Taxes Management Act 1970, and
   (b) a determination of the amount under that section has become final.

(2) Sub-paragraph (1) above shall not apply in the case of a claim made before the end of 2 years from the end of the period.

(3) Sub-paragraph (1) above shall not apply where—
   (a) the company has been assessed to corporation tax for the period, and
   (b) the assessment has not become final and conclusive.

(4) This paragraph applies to the withdrawal of a claim as it applies to the making of a claim.

3.—(1) No claim for an accounting period of a company may be made if—
   (a) the company has been assessed to corporation tax for the period, and

(b) the assessment has become final and conclusive.

(2) Sub-paragraph (1) above shall not apply in the case of a claim made before the end of 2 years from the end of the period.

(3) Sub-paragraph (1) above shall not apply where—

(a) the claim affects an amount for the period which is determinable under section 41A of the Taxes Management Act 1970, and

(b) a determination of the amount under that section has either not been made or, if made, has not become final.

(4) This paragraph applies to the withdrawal of a claim as it applies to the making of a claim.

4.—(1) No claim for an accounting period of a company may be made after the end of 6 years from the end of the period, except under paragraph 6 below.

(2) This paragraph applies to the withdrawal of a claim as it applies to the making of a claim.

5. Where under paragraph 2, 3 or 4 above a claim may not be made after a certain time, it may be made within such further time as the Board may allow.

6.—(1) A claim for an accounting period of a company may be made after the end of 6 years from the end of the period if—

(a) the company has been assessed to corporation tax for the period before the end of 6 years from the end of the period,

(b) the company has appealed against the assessment, and

(c) the assessment has not become final and conclusive.

(2) No claim for an accounting period of a company may be made under this paragraph after the end of 6 years and 3 months from the end of the period.

Method of making claim

7.—(1) A claim shall be made by being included in a return under section 11 of the Taxes Management Act 1970 (corporation tax return) for the period for which the claim is made.

(2) In sub-paragraph (1) above the reference to a claim being included in a return includes a reference to a claim being included by virtue of an amendment of the return.

(3) This paragraph applies to the withdrawal of a claim as it applies to the making of a claim.

Nature of claim

8. A claim, other than one under paragraph 6 above, shall be for an amount which is quantified at the time the claim is made.

9.—(1) A claim under paragraph 6 above shall be expressed to be conditional, as to the amount claimed, on, and only on, the outcome of one or more relevant matters specified in the claim.

(2) For the purposes of this paragraph a matter is relevant if it is relevant to the determination of the assessment of the claimant company to corporation tax for the period for which the claim is made.

Adjustments

10.—(1) All such assessments or adjustments of assessments shall be made as may be necessary to give effect to a claim or the withdrawal of a claim.

(2) An assessment under this paragraph shall not be out of time if it is made—

(a) in the case of a claim, within one year from the date mentioned in sub-paragraph (3) below, and

(b) in the case of the withdrawal of a claim, within one year from the date on which the claim is withdrawn.

(3) The date referred to above is—

(a) in a case where the claim affects an amount for the period for which the claim is made which is determinable under section 41A of the Taxes Management Act 1970, the date on which a determination of the amount under that section becomes final;

(b) in any other case, the date on which an assessment of the claimant company to corporation tax for the period for which the claim is made becomes final and conclusive.

11. Where a claim affecting an amount determinable under section 41A of the Taxes Management Act 1970 is made or withdrawn after a determination of the amount under that section has become final, the determination shall be adjusted accordingly."

Chapter II of Pt. II of the Bill proposes a number of amendments to T.M.A. 1970. This Schedule sets out a proposed new Sched. A1 to C.A.A. 1990 ("Capital Allowances: Claims by

Companies") to come into effect on an "appointed day" which will be not before March 31, 1992. T.M.A. 1970, s.42, will be excluded in dealing with claims by companies (para. 1). Para. 2 provides that a claim (or the withdrawal of a claim) for allowances may not be made if, under the proposed new s.41A of T.M.A. 1970, a determination has become final unless:

(a) it is made within two years after the end of the accounting period; or

(b) the company's corporation tax assessment has not become final and conclusive.

Corresponding provision is made in para. 3 where a company has been assessed to corporation tax and the assistance is final and conclusive.

Under paras. 4 and 6 no claim (or withdrawal) may be made more than six years after the end of an accounting period unless an assessment made within six years is under appeal and has not become final and conclusive. The limit is then extended by three months.

Para. 5 grants to the Board power to extend any two-year or six-year limit but not the extended limit under para. 6.

A claim (or withdrawal) is to be included in a return (or an amendment to a return) under T.M.A. 1970, s.11 (para. 7).

Under paras. 8 and 9, a claim must normally be quantified but a claim under para. 6 may be conditional.

Para. 10 permits the making of any necessary assessments or amendments with certain time limits and para. 11 allows the adjustment of a determination under T.M.A. 1970, s.41A, which has become final.

Section 103   SCHEDULE 17

CAPITAL ALLOWANCES: ASSIMILATION OF CLAIMS BY COMPANIES TO CLAIMS BY INDIVIDUALS

Introductory

1. The Capital Allowances Act 1990 shall be amended as follows.

Industrial buildings and structures

2. In section 1 (initial allowances: enterprise zones) in subsection (5) the words "as it applies for income tax purposes" and the words from "and" to the end shall be omitted.

Machinery and plant: general

3.—(1) Section 22 (first-year allowances: transitional relief for regional projects) shall be amended as follows.

(2) The following subsection shall be substituted for subsection (7)—

"(7) A claim for one or more first-year allowances to be made for any chargeable period may require that the amount of the allowance, or aggregate amount of the allowances, be reduced to an amount specified in that behalf in the claim."

(3) In subsection (8) the words "disclaimer or" shall be omitted.

(4) Subsection (9) shall cease to have effect.

4.—(1) Section 23 (information relating to first-year allowances) shall be amended as follows.

(2) In subsection (1) the words "by a person other than a company," the words from ", and a" to "an allowance," and, in paragraphs (b) and (c), the words "or deduction" shall be omitted.

(3) In subsection (2) the words "other than a company" and the words from ", or a" to "company," shall be omitted.

5.—(1) Section 24 (writing-down allowances and balancing adjustments) shall be amended as follows.

(2) In subsection (3) the words "in connection with a trade carried on by a person other than a company" shall be omitted.

(3) Subsection (4) shall cease to have effect.

6.—(1) Section 25 (qualifying expenditure) shall be amended as follows.

(2) In subsection (1)(a)(ii) the words from "in the case of a person" to "of a company" shall be omitted.

(3) Subsection (2) shall be omitted.

(4) In subsection (3) the words ", but not being a company," shall be omitted.

(5) In subsection (4)—

(a) in paragraph (a) the words "(whether a company or not)" shall be omitted; and

(b) in paragraph (b) the words ", in the case of a person other than a company," shall be omitted.

Machinery and plant: ships

7. In section 30 (first-year allowances) in subsection (1)(a) the words "or, in the case of a company, disclaim it" shall be omitted.

8. In section 31 (writing-down allowances) the following subsection shall be substituted for subsection (6)—

"(6) For any chargeable period of the single ship trade for which the amount of a writing-down allowance is reduced by virtue of a requirement in a claim made by virtue of section 24(3), any reference in subsections (3) to (5) above to the writing-down allowance is a reference to the reduced amount of the allowance, as specified in the claim."

Machinery and plant: leased assets and inexpensive cars

9. In section 41 (writing-down allowances) in subsection (3) the words "or is disclaimed under subsection (4) of that section," the words "or under subsection (4)" and the words "or as disclaimed" shall be omitted.

10. In section 46 (recovery of excess relief: new expenditure) in subsection (6) the words "or was disclaimed" shall be omitted.

11. In section 47 (recovery of excess relief: old expenditure) in subsection (6)(a) the words "or was disclaimed" shall be omitted.

12. In section 48 (information relating to allowances made in respect of new expenditure) in subsection (1) the words "by a person other than a company" and the words from "and a" to "allowance" shall be omitted.

13. In section 49 (information relating to allowances made in respect of old expenditure) in subsection (2) the words "other than a company" and the words from ", or a" to "company," shall be omitted.

Machinery and plant: supplementary

14. In section 79 (effect of use partly for trade etc. and partly for other purposes) in subsection (6) the words "or is disclaimed under subsection (4) of that section," the words "or (4)" and the words "or as disclaimed" shall be omitted.

15. In section 80 (effect of subsidies towards wear and tear) in subsection (6) the words "or is disclaimed under subsection (4) of that section," the words "or (4)" and the words "or as disclaimed" shall be omitted.

GENERAL NOTE

Claims by companies to capital allowances are to be brought into line with claims by individuals. These changes will relate only to the way in which claims are made and not to the way in which allowances are given. Thus, the provisions of C.A.A. 1990, ss.144 and 145 ("Corporation tax allowances and charges in taxing a trade" and "other corporation tax allowances"), remain unaffected.

The following sections of C.A.A. 1990 are, however, to be amended:

s.1(5)
s.22(7), (8) and (9)
s.23(1) and (2)
s.24(3) and (4)
s.25(1), (2), (3) and (4)
s.30(1)
s.31(6)
s.41(3)
s.46(6)
s.47(6)
s.49(2)
s.79(6)
s.80(6)

The amendments will take effect on a day appointed by the Treasury being not before March 31, 1992.

Section 127   SCHEDULE 18

DEFINITION OF "LOCAL AUTHORITY"

1. In section 74(4) of the Finance Act 1952 for "519" there shall be substituted "842A."

2. Section 52 of the Finance Act 1974 shall cease to have effect.

3. In section 149B of the Capital Gains Tax Act 1979 the following subsections shall be substituted for subsection (3)—

"(3) A local authority, a local authority association and a health service body shall be exempt from capital gains tax.

(3A) In subsection (3) above—

(a) "local authority association" has the meaning given by section 519 of the Taxes Act 1988, and

(b) "health service body" has the meaning given by section 519A of that Act.".

4. In section 272 of the Inheritance Tax Act 1984, in the definition of "local authority," for "519" there shall be substituted "842A."

5.—(1) The Taxes Act 1988 shall be amended as follows.

(2) Section 519(4) shall cease to have effect.

(3) In section 832(1), the following definition shall be substituted for the definition of "local authority" and "local authority association"—

" 'local authority association' has the meaning given by section 519;".

GENERAL NOTE

This Schedule makes amendments consequential on the replacement of domestic rates by the community charge or "poll tax" in Great Britain. See further the GENERAL NOTE to s.127.

Section 132　　　　　　　　SCHEDULE 19

REPEALS

PART I

CUSTOMS AND EXCISE

Chapter	Short title	Extent of repeal
1979 c.2.	The Customs and Excise Management Act 1979.	In section 37A(1)(b), the word "may".
1979 c.4.	The Alcoholic Liquor Duties Act 1979.	Section 12(6) to (9).
1979 c.5.	The Hydrocarbon Oil Duties Act 1979.	In section 6, in subsection (1), ", (2A)" and subsection (2A).
1981 c.63.	The Betting and Gaming Duties Act 1981.	In section 7, in subsection (1) the words "in the case of pool competitions bets to 33⅓ per cent. and in any other case" and subsection (2).
1982 c.39.	The Finance Act 1982.	Section 8(1)(a). Section 9(1) and (2). In Schedule 6, paragraph 2.
1986 c.41.	The Finance Act 1986.	In Schedule 5, paragraph 3(4) and (5).
1988 c.39.	The Finance Act 1988.	Section 6(3).
1989 c.26.	The Finance Act 1989.	Section 1(1) and (3).

The repeals in the Hydrocarbon Oil Duties Act 1979 and the Finance Act 1989 have effect in accordance with section 3(6) of this Act.

PART II

VEHICLES EXCISE DUTY

Chapter	Short title	Extent of repeal
1971 c.10.	The Vehicles (Excise) Act 1971.	In Schedule 1, in the first column of Part II, the words from "tricycles", in the second place where it occurs, to "passenger". In Schedule 4, paragraph 7.
1972 c.10 (N.I.).	The Vehicles (Excise) Act (Northern Ireland) 1972.	In Schedule 1, in column 1 of Part II, the words from "tricycles", in the second place where it occurs, to "passenger". In Schedule 4, paragraph 7.
1983 c.28.	The Finance Act 1983.	In Schedule 3, paragraph 8(4).
1985 c.54.	The Finance Act 1985.	In Schedule 2, paragraphs 3, 4 and 9.
1987 c.16.	The Finance Act 1987.	Section 2(2)(b). In Schedule 1, Part I and, in Part II, paragraph 3.
1989 c.26.	The Finance Act 1989.	Section 6(3) and (4). In Schedule 1, Part II. In Schedule 2, paragraph 3.

1. The repeals in Schedule 1 to each of the Vehicles (Excise) Act 1971 and the Vehicles (Excise) Act (Northern Ireland) 1972 are deemed to have come into force on 21st March 1990.

2. The repeals in Schedule 4 to each of the Vehicles (Excise) Act 1971 and the Vehicles (Excise) Act (Northern Ireland) 1972, the repeal in the Finance Act 1983 and the repeal of paragraph 9 of Schedule 2 to the Finance Act 1985 have effect in relation to licences taken out after 30th September 1990.

3. The remaining repeals have effect in relation to licences taken out after 20th March 1990.

PART III

VALUE ADDED TAX

Chapter	Short title	Extent of repeal
1983 c.55.	The Value Added Tax Act 1983.	Section 22. Section 33(1A). In Schedule 6, in Group 4, Note (3).
1985 c.54.	The Finance Act 1985.	In section 13(2), the word "and" at the end of paragraph (b). Section 18(4) and (5). Section 32.
1987 c.16.	The Finance Act 1987.	Section 14(4) and (5). In Schedule 2, paragraph 3.

1. The repeals of section 22 of the Value Added Tax Act 1983 and section 32 of the Finance Act 1985 have effect in relation to supplies made after the day on which this Act is passed.

2. The repeal of section 18(4) and (5) of that Act has effect in relation to assessments made on or after the day on which this Act is passed.

3. The repeals of section 33(1A) of the Value Added Tax Act 1983 and the repeals in the Finance Act 1987 have effect in relation to persons who become liable to be registered after 20th March 1990.

PART IV

INCOME TAX, CORPORATION TAX AND CAPITAL GAINS TAX

Chapter	Short title	Extent of repeal
1969 c.32.	The Finance Act 1969.	Section 52.
1970 c.10.	The Income and Corporation Taxes Act 1970.	In section 272(1)(a), the words ", subject to section 280(7) below,".
1974 c.30.	The Finance Act 1974.	Section 52.
1975 c.45.	The Finance (No. 2) Act 1975.	In section 58(10), the definition of "trading stock".
1988 c.1.	The Income and Corporation Taxes Act 1988.	Section 257C(4).
		In section 339, in subsection (2) the words "and is not a close company" and subsection (5).
		In section 349(3)(d), the words "or 479(1)".
		In section 431(2), the definitions of "policy holders' fraction" and "shareholders' fraction".
		In section 439, in subsection (7)(b), the words "(subject to subsection (8) below)" and subsection (8).
		Section 445(6).
		Section 446(4).
		Section 468(5).
		Sections 468A to 468D.
		Sections 476 and 477.
		Sections 479 and 480.
		In section 481, in subsection (1) the words "sections 479 and 480", in subsection (2) paragraphs (d) and (e), and in subsection (6) the words "479(2) to (7), 480".
		In section 482, in subsection (1) the words "479, 480 and" and in subsection (6) the words from "In relation" to the end.
		In section 483,, subsections (1) to (3) and (5).
		Section 519(4).
		Section 659.
		Section 686(5).
		In section 687(3) the words following paragraph (i).
		Section 724(2).
		In section 772(8), the words "or, in Northern Ireland, to a county court".
		In section 832(1), in the definition of "the Capital Allowances Acts", the words ", but excluding Part III of that Act".
		In Schedule 25, paragraph 2(1)(c) and the word "and" immediately following it and paragraph 4(1)(c) and the word "and" immediately following it.
1988 c.39.	The Finance Act 1988.	In Schedule 4, paragraph 13(3).
		In Schedule 8, in paragraph 1(3), the word "and" at the end of paragraph (f).
1989 c.26.	The Finance Act 1989.	Sections 78 and 79.
		In Schedule 8, paragraphs 1, 3(3) and 7.
		In Schedule 11, in paragraph 2(13)(d), the words "before 9th June 1989".
1990 c.1.	The Capital Allowances Act 1990.	Section 149(2).
		In section 161(10), the words "and of subsection (8)".

Chapter	Short title	Extent of repeal
1990 c.19.	The National Health Service and Community Care Act 1990.	Section 61(2).

1. The repeal in the Income and Corporation Taxes Act 1970 applies to disposals on or after 20th March 1990.

2. The repeals of section 52 of the Finance Act 1974 and section 519(4) of the Income and Corporation Taxes Act 1988 are deemed to have come into force on 1st April 1990.

3. The repeals in the Finance (No. 2) Act 1975 and in sections 439, 445 and 446 of the Income and Corporation Taxes Act 1988 have effect in accordance with Schedule 6 to this Act.

4. The repeal in section 339(2) of the Income and Corporation Taxes Act 1988 has effect in relation to payments made on or after 1st October 1990.

5. The repeal of section 339(5) of the Income and Corporation Taxes Act 1988 has effect in relation to accounting periods ending on or after 1st October 1990.

6. The repeal in section 431(2) of that Act and the repeal of paragraphs 1 and 3(3) of Schedule 8 to the Finance Act 1989 are deemed always to have had effect.

7. The repeal of sections 468(5) and 468A to 468D of the Income and Corporation Taxes Act 1988, and of sections 78 and 79 of the Finance Act 1989, have effect in accordance with section 52 of this Act.

8. The repeals of section 476 (apart from the repeal in subsection (4) of the words from the beginning to "affecting" and the words "and that paragraph") and sections 477, 479 and 480 of the Income and Corporation Taxes Act 1988, and the repeals in sections 349, 481, 482, 483, 686 and 687 of that Act, have effect in accordance with Schedule 5 to this Act.

9. The repeal of section 659 of the Income and Corporation Taxes Act 1988 has effect in accordance with section 81 of this Act.

10. The repeal in section 772 of that Act does not affect any proceedings instituted before 3rd April 1989.

11. The repeals in section 832 of that Act and section 149 of the Capital Allowances Act 1990 apply for chargeable periods beginning on or after 6th April 1990.

12. The repeals in Schedule 25 to the Income and Corporation Taxes Act 1988 apply to dividends paid on or after 20th March 1990.

13. The repeal in Schedule 4 to the Finance Act 1988 applies where the valuation date is on or after 20th March 1990.

14. The repeal of paragraph 7 of Schedule 8 to the Finance Act 1989 applies for accounting periods beginning on or after 1st January 1990.

15. The repeal in Schedule 11 to that Act has effect in accordance with section 58 of this Act.

16. The repeal in section 161(10) of the Capital Allowances Act 1990 applies in relation to a sale of an asset when both the time of completion and the time when possession of the asset is given are on or after 6th April 1990.

PART V

MANAGEMENT

Chapter	Short title	Extent of repeal
1970 c.9.	The Taxes Management Act 1970.	In section 11, subsection (7) and, in subsection (8), the words from "or different" to the end. In section 12(4), the words "of income of a partnership". In section 17(1), paragraph (a) of the proviso.
1971 c.68.	The Finance Act 1971.	In Schedule 6, paragraph 82.
1972 c.41.	The Finance Act 1972.	In Schedule 24, paragraph 4.
1988 c.1.	The Income and Corporation Taxes Act 1988.	In section 7(2), the words from "and accordingly" to the end. In section 11(3), the words from "and accordingly" to the end. In section 393(11), the words from the beginning to "of six years; and". Section 396(3). In Schedule 29, paragraph 4, and in the Table in paragraph 32 the entries relating to sections 8(8) and (9) and 9(4) of the Taxes Management Act 1970.
1990 c.1.	The Capital Allowances Act 1990.	In section 1(5), the words "as it applies for income tax purposes" and the words from "and" to the end. In section 22, in subsection (8) the words "disclaimer or" and subsection (9). In section 23, in subsection (1) the words "by a person other than a company", the words from ", and a" to "an allowance," and, in paragraphs (b) and (c), the words "or deduction" and in subsection (2) the words "other than a company" and the words from ", or a" to "company,". In section 24, in subsection (3) the words "in connection with a trade carried on by a person other than a company" and subsection (4). In section 25, in subsection (1)(a)(ii) the words from "in the case of a person" to "of a company", subsection (2), in subsection (3) the words ", but not being a company," and in subsection (4), in paragraph (a), the words "(whether a company or not)" and, in paragraph (b), the words ", in the case of a person other than a company,". In section 30(1)(a), the words "or, in the case of a company, disclaim it". In section 41(3), the words "or is disclaimed under subsection (4) of that section", the words "or under subsection (4)" and the words "or as disclaimed". In section 46(6), the words "or was disclaimed". In section 47(6)(a), the words "or was disclaimed". In section 48(1), the words "by a person other than a company" and the words from "and a" to "allowance".

Chapter	Short title	Extent of repeal
		In section 49(2), the words "other than a company" and the words from ", or a" to "company,".
		In section 79(6), the words "or is disclaimed under subsection (4) of that section", the words "or (4)" and the words "or as disclaimed".
		In section 80(6), the words "or is disclaimed under subsection (4) of that section", the words "or (4)" and the words "or as disclaimed".

1. The repeals in section 11 of the Taxes Management Act 1970 have effect in accordance with section 91 of this Act.

2. The repeals in section 12 of the Taxes Management Act 1970, the Finance Act 1971, the Finance Act 1972 and Schedule 29 to the Income and Corporation Taxes Act 1988 have effect in accordance with section 90 of this Act.

3. The repeal in section 17 of the Taxes Management Act 1970 has effect as regards a case where interest is paid or credited in the year 1991-92 or a subsequent year of assessment.

4. The repeals in sections 7 and 11 of the Income and Corporation Taxes Act 1988 have effect in relation to income tax falling to be set off against corporation tax for accounting periods ending after the day appointed for the purposes of section 10 of that Act.

5. The repeals in sections 393 and 396 of that Act apply in relation to accounting periods ending after that day.

6. The remaining repeals have effect in relation to allowances and charges falling to be made for chargeable periods ending after that day.

PART VI

STAMP DUTY

Chapter	Short title	Extent of repeal
1891 c.39.	The Stamp Act 1891.	In section 59(1), the words "or stock, or marketable securities,".
		Section 83.
		Section 109(1).
		In Schedule 1, the whole of the heading beginning "Bearer Instrument", and paragraph (1) of the general exemptions at the end of the Schedule.
1899 c.9.	The Finance Act 1899.	Section 5(2).
1946 c.64.	The Finance Act 1946.	Section 54(3) and (4).
		Section 56.
		Section 57(2) to (4).
1946 c.17 (N.I.).	The Finance (No. 2) Act (Northern Ireland) 1946.	Section 25(3) and (4).
		Section 27.
		Section 28(2) to (4).
1947 c.35.	The Finance Act 1947.	Section 57.
1948 c.49.	The Finance Act 1948.	Section 74.
1950 c.32 N.I.).	The Finance (No. 2) Act (Northern Ireland) 1950.	Section 3(1).
1951 c.43.	The Finance Act 1951.	Section 42.
1963 c.18.	The Stock Transfer Act 1963.	In section 2(3), in paragraph (a) the words "and section 56(4) of the Finance Act 1946", and paragraph (c) and the word "and" immediately preceding it.
1963 c.25.	The Finance Act 1963.	Section 55(1A).
		In section 59, subsections (1) to (4).
		Section 60.
		Section 61.
		In section 62, in subsection (1) the words from "and any" to the end, and subsection (4).
		Section 65(1).
		Section 67.
1963 c.22 (N.I.).	The Finance Act (Northern Ireland) 1963.	Section 4(1A).
		In section 8, subsections (1) to (4).
		Section 9.
		Section 10.
		In section 11, in subsection (1) the words from "and any" to the end, and subsection (3).
		Section 14(1).
		Section 16.
1963 c.24 (N.I.).	The Stock Transfer Act (Northern Ireland) 1963.	In section 2(3), in paragraph (a) the words "and section 27(4) of the Finance (No. 2) Act (Northern Ireland) 1946", and paragraph (c) and the word "and" immediately preceding it.
1967 c.54.	The Finance Act 1967.	Section 30.
1967 c.20 (N.I.).	The Finance Act (Northern Ireland) 1967.	Section 7.
1970 c.24.	The Finance Act 1970.	Section 33.
		In Schedule 7, paragraph 6.
1970 c.21 (N.I.).	The Finance Act (Northern Ireland) 1970.	In Schedule 2, paragraph 6.
1974 c.30.	The Finance Act 1974.	In Schedule 11, paragraphs 2 and 12.
1975 c.80.	The OECD Support Fund Act 1975.	Section 4(2).

Chapter	Short title	Extent of repeal
1976 c.40.	The Finance Act 1976.	In section 127, subsections (1) and (4) to (7).
		Section 131(3).
1980 c.48.	The Finance Act 1980.	Section 101.
1984 c.43.	The Finance Act 1984.	Section 126(3)(c) and (5).
1985 c.6.	The Companies Act 1985.	In Schedule 14, in paragraph 8 the words from "and, unless" to the end.
1985 c.54.	The Finance Act 1985.	Section 81.
1986 c.41.	The Finance Act 1986.	Section 64(1).
		Sections 65 to 72.
		Section 77.
		In section 79, subsections (2) to (8), and in subsection (12) the words "(7), (9),".
		Sections 80 to 85.
S.I. 1986/1032 (N.I.).	The Companies (Northern Ireland) Order 1986.	In Schedule 14, in paragraph 7 the words from "and unless" to the end.
1987 c.16.	The Finance Act 1987.	Sections 50 to 53.
1987 c.51.	The Finance (No. 2) Act 1987.	Section 99.
1988 c.39.	The Finance Act 1988.	Section 143.
		In Schedule 13, paragraph 19.
1989 c.26.	The Finance Act 1989.	Sections 174 and 175.

1. So far as these repeals relate to bearer instruments, they have effect in accordance with section 107 of this Act.

2. So far as these repeals relate to instruments other than bearer instruments, they have effect in accordance with section 108 of this Act.

3. So far as these repeals relate to—

(a) any provision mentioned in subsection (1), (2), (3), (4) or (5) of section 109 of this Act, or

(b) any other provision to the extent that it is ancillary to or dependent on any provision so mentioned,

the repeals have effect in accordance with the subsection concerned.

4. So far as these repeals relate to—

(a) any provision mentioned in section 109(6) of this Act, or

(b) any other provision to the extent that it is ancillary to or dependent on any provision so mentioned,

the repeals have effect in accordance with any order under section 109(7) of this Act.

5. Paragraphs 1 and 2 above have effect subject to paragraphs 3 and 4 above.

PART VII

STAMP DUTY RESERVE TAX

Chapter	Short title	Extent of repeal
1986 c.41.	The Finance Act 1986.	Part IV.
1987 c.16.	The Finance Act 1987.	Section 56.
		Schedule 7.
1987 c.51.	The Finance (No. 2) Act 1987.	Section 100.
1988 c.39.	The Finance Act 1988.	Section 144.
		In Schedule 13, paragraph 23.
1989 c.26.	The Finance Act 1989.	Sections 176 and 177.

These repeals have effect in accordance with section 110 of this Act.

PART VIII

NATIONAL SAVINGS

Chapter	Short title	Extent of repeal
1972 c.65.	The National Debt Act 1972.	Section 5(3)(b).

INDEX

References are to section numbers

29–182

GOVERNMENT TRADING ACT 1990

(1990 c. 30)

An Act to amend the Government Trading Funds Act 1973 and section 5 of the Exchequer and Audit Departments Act 1921 and to repeal the Borrowing (Control and Guarantees) Act 1946.

[26th July 1990]

PARLIAMENTARY DEBATES
Hansard, H.C. Vol. 164, col. 726; Vol. 167, col. 996; Vol. 176, col. 1209; H.L. Vol. 516, col. 1284; Vol. 520, cols. 603, 1728.
The Bill was considered in Standing Committee A on January 1, 1990 and in Committee on June 12, 1990.

INTRODUCTION

This Act affects three other pieces of legislation, namely the Government Trading Funds Act 1973 (c. 63), the Exchequer and Audit Departments Act 1921 (c. 52) and the Borrowing (Control and Guarantees) Act 1946 (c. 58), which is repealed.

The 1973 Act is affected by the following provisions made by the 1990 Act which involve the amendment of existing sections and the introduction of a new section after s.4: (1) trading funds are to be established for certain operations of a government department providing that the responsible Minister is satisfied that such operations are suitable to be financed in this way and that the interests of improved management efficiency and effectiveness are satisfied; Crown assets and liabilities may also be appropriated to a trading fund; (2) the net value of the assets appropriated to the fund, excluding public dividend capital, will be treated as a loan from the fund's authorised lender; either the National Loans Fund or the responsible Minister will be designated for this rôle by the order which establishes the fund; (3) further public dividend capital may be issued following the repayment of loans or the payment of any amount standing in the reserves into the Consolidated Fund; public dividend capital may also be replaced by loan from the authorised lender; (4) borrowing may be undertaken by the trading funds and the Treasury will determine the subsequent interest rates and terms and times of repayment; (5) the cessation in whole or in part of operations funded by a trading fund is to be regulated; procedures for the repayment of debt and public dividend capital will also be established allowing the minister responsible to pay any debt and public dividend capital remaining after the application of the aforementioned procedures out of Parliamentary money.

The introduction of a trading fund will alter the method of financing operations particularly through the removal of a direct reliance on moneys voted by Parliament to meet expenditure chargeable to revenue account. The order which establishes the fund will set a limit on the maximum borrowing to be made by any fund.

No significant increase in public service manpower is expected and all staff will remain members of the Civil Service.

New provisions in connection with government trading funds

1.—(1) For sections 1 and 2 of the Government Trading Funds Act 1973 (establishment of funds and finance) there is substituted—

C.L. STATS. (6)—22

"Establishment of trading funds

1.—(1) If it appears to any Minister of the Crown—

  (a) that any operations of a department of the government for which he is responsible are suitable to be financed by means of a fund established under this Act (referred to in this Act as a "trading fund") and, in particular, to be so managed that the revenue of the fund would consist principally of receipts in respect of goods or services provided in the course of the operations in question, and

  (b) that the financing of the operations in question by means of a trading fund would be in the interests of the improved efficiency and effectiveness of the management of those operations,

he may by order establish a trading fund for the operations in question as from a day appointed by the order.

(2) The power to make an order under this section is exercisable only with Treasury concurrence.

(3) Where a Minister of the Crown proposes to make an order in respect of any operations (not being operations then financed by means of a trading fund) and considers that—

  (a) the operations in question consist substantially in the provision of goods or services in the United Kingdom otherwise than to departments of the government, and

  (b) an opportunity to make representations to him should be given,

he shall take such steps as appear to him to be appropriate to give such an opportunity to such persons as appear to him to be appropriate.

(4) An order establishing a trading fund shall designate either—

  (a) the National Loans Fund, or

  (b) the responsible Minister,

as the source of issues to the fund by way of loan (referred to in this Act as the "authorised lender").

(5) Issues to the fund by way of loan by the responsible Minister shall be made out of money provided by Parliament, and the right to repayment of such issues ranks as an asset of the Consolidated Fund.

(6) An order establishing a trading fund for operations carried on by a person appointed in pursuance of any enactment may provide—

  (a) for the fund to be under the control and management of that person instead of the responsible Minister and, accordingly,

  (b) for this Act to have effect as if—

      (i) the reference to the responsible Minister in section 3(1) of this Act and the first reference to him in section 4(1), and

      (ii) such other references in this Act to the responsible Minister as may be specified in the order, where they are references to him in the exercise of his function of controlling or managing the fund,

were references to that person.

(7) In this Act—

  "the funded operations", in relation to a trading fund, means the operations for which the fund is established,

  "liabilities", in relation to a trading fund, does not include liabilities in respect of any amount issued to the fund under section 2B of this Act,

  "Minister of the Crown" means the holder of an office in Her Majesty's Government in the United Kingdom, and includes the Treasury,

  "order" except in section 2B(8) of this Act means an order under this section, "originating debt", in relation to a trading fund, means any amount remaining after any repayment or reduction of the amount which, by virtue of section 2(3) and (4) of this Act, is the originating debt of the fund, and

"the responsible Minister", in relation to any operations of a department of the government, means the Minister of the Crown responsible for that department.

(8) References in this Act to the provision of services include—

(a) the provision of any authority required for carrying on any activity or exercising any right, and

(b) the performance of any other functions in connection with the regulation of any activity or right.

(9) References in this Act to a Minister of the Crown include Ministers acting jointly, but an order may not designate more than one Minister as the authorised lender.

Assets and liabilities of funds

2.—(1) Where any Minister of the Crown proposes to make an order establishing a trading fund for any operations or to vary an order by extending the funded operations—

(a) he shall with Treasury concurrence determine what Crown assets and liabilities are properly attributable to the operations for which the fund is to be established or, as the case may be, the additional operations and are suitable to be appropriated to the fund, and

(b) the order shall provide for the assets and liabilities so determined to be appropriated as assets and liabilities of the fund at values or amounts determined by him in accordance with Treasury directions.

(2) The responsible Minister may from time to time, in the case of any trading fund, with Treasury concurrence determine what additional Crown assets and liabilities are properly attributable to the funded operations and suitable to be appropriated to the fund and provide by order for the assets and liabilities in question to be appropriated as assets and liabilities of the fund at values or amounts determined by him in accordance with Treasury directions.

(3) Where an order establishing a trading fund provides for any assets and liabilities to be appropriated as assets and liabilities of the fund—

(a) the amount by which the values of those assets exceed the amounts of those liabilities, less

(b) any amount treated by virtue of the order as public dividend capital,

is originating debt of the fund and is to be treated as having been issued to the fund under section 2B of this Act on the day appointed by the order.

(4) Where, in the case of a trading fund established under a previous order, an order provides for any additional assets and liabilities to be appropriated as assets and liabilities of the fund—

(a) the amount by which the values of those additional assets exceed the amounts of those additional liabilities, less

(b) any amount treated by virtue of the order as public dividend capital,

is to be added to the originating debt of the fund and is to be treated as having been issued to the fund under section 2B of this Act on the day appointed by the order.

(5) The responsible Minister may with Treasury concurrence from time to time by order provide, in the case of any trading fund, for any

assets and liabilities to cease to be assets and liabilities of the fund; but the power conferred by this subsection is not exercisable where section 4A of this Act applies.

(6) Where the responsible Minister exercises the power conferred by subsection (5) above, he may, in the case of any originating debt or public dividend capital which he may with Treasury concurrence determine to be properly attributable to the assets and liabilities in question—

    (a) out of money provided by Parliament, repay the whole or part of the debt or make a payment into the Consolidated Fund in reduction or extinguishment of the capital, and

    (b) by order made with Treasury concurrence provide for the reduction or extinguishment of any debt or capital remaining after the application of paragraph (a) above.

(7) An order providing for any assets and liabilities to be appropriated as, or to cease to be, assets and liabilities of a trading fund may describe the assets and liabilities in general terms.

Public dividend capital

2A.—(1) An order providing for any assets and liabilities to be appropriated as assets and liabilities of a trading fund may provide for any part of the amount by which the values of the assets exceed the amounts of the liabilities to be treated as public dividend capital of the fund.

(2) Where the responsible Minister—

    (a) repays out of a trading fund before the due date any amount outstanding in respect of the principal of any sums issued to the fund by the authorised lender by way of loan, or

    (b) pays any amount standing in the reserves of a trading fund into the Consolidated Fund,

he may with Treasury concurrence issue out of money provided by Parliament a corresponding amount to the fund as public dividend capital.

(3) Where any sum is issued to a trading fund under section 2B of this Act, the responsible Minister may with Treasury concurrence pay out of the fund into the Consolidated Fund a corresponding sum in reduction or extinguishment of any public dividend capital.

(4) Public dividend capital ranks as an asset of the Consolidated Fund.

(5) For any financial year in which a trading fund has public dividend capital, there shall be paid out of the fund into the Consolidated Fund such sums (if any) by way of return on that capital and its reserves as the responsible Minister may determine, with Treasury concurrence, having regard to any balance in the fund at the end of that year and the amount of the balance which appears to the responsible Minister and the Treasury to be in the nature of distributable profit.

Borrowing by funds

2B.—(1) No amount shall be paid into a trading fund by way of loan except in accordance with this section.

(2) Subject to subsection (6) below, the authorised lender may issue by way of loan to a trading fund sums required for the funded operations.

(3) Sums issued under this section shall be repaid out of the fund on such terms, and interest on them shall be paid at such variable or fixed rates and at such timcs, as the Treasury may determine.

(4) A rate of interest for any amount so issued by the responsible Minister shall be determined as if section 5 of the National Loans Act 1968 had effect in respect of it and subsections (5A) and (5B) of that section shall apply accordingly.

(5) In the case of any trading fund where the authorised lender is a Minister of the Crown, repayment of any amount outstanding in respect of the principal of any sum issued under this section (other than repayment before the due date) may, with Treasury concurrence, be made to the Minister instead of into the Consolidated Fund and applied by him as money provided by Parliament.

(6) The order establishing a trading fund shall specify the maximum amount that may be issued under this section and the aggregate of amounts issued under this section in respect of the fund (other than originating debt) shall not exceed that amount, or that amount as varied by a subsequent order.

(7) The sum of the maxima in force in respect of all trading funds at any time shall not exceed £2,000 million.

(8) The Treasury may by order made by statutory instrument increase or further increase the limit in subsection (7) above by any amount, not exceeding £1,000 million, specified in the order but not so as to make the limit exceed £4,000 million.

(9) No order under subsection (8) above shall be made unless a draft of a statutory instrument containing it has been laid before the House of Commons and approved by a resolution of that House."

(2) After section 4 of that Act (management and accounting) there is inserted—

"Operations ceasing to be funded

4A.—(1) This section applies where any operations for which a trading fund is established are to cease to be funded operations (whether the operations ceasing to be funded represent the whole or part of the funded operations or are to cease altogether or be funded operations of another fund or, while continuing to be operations of a department of the government, be financed by other means).

(2) Where the operations ceasing to be funded represent only part of the funded operations, the responsible Minister shall by order provide for such assets and liabilities of the fund as he may with Treasury concurrence determine to be properly attributable to the operations ceasing to be funded to cease to be assets and liabilities of the fund.

(3) In the following provisions of this section, "debt" means any amount outstanding in respect of the principal of or interest on sums issued under section 2B of this Act and "originating debt" includes any amount outstanding in respect of interest on such debt; and, where the operations ceasing to be funded represent only part of the funded operations—

  (a) references to assets and liabilities are to the assets and liabilities ceasing to be assets and liabilities of the fund by virtue of an order under subsection (2) above,
  (b) references to debt, originating debt or public dividend capital are to so much of any debt, originating debt or public dividend capital as the responsible Minister may with Treasury concurrence determine to be attributable to the operations ceasing to be funded.

(4) If, in a case where the operations ceasing to be funded are to cease altogether, the values of the assets of the fund exceed the amounts of the liabilities of the fund, the excess shall be applied in accordance with subsection (6) below.

(5) If in any other case—

(a) it appears to the responsible Minister that any amount standing in the reserves of the fund is surplus to any foreseeable
requirements of the funded operations, or

(b) the revenues of the fund for the last financial year exceed the
total sums properly chargeable to revenue account for that
year,

the amount or excess shall be applied in accordance with subsection (6)
below.

(6) The amount or excess in question shall be applied towards the
following objects (applying paragraph (a) before paragraph (b))—

(a) the repayment of debt, and

(b) payment into the Consolidated Fund in reduction or extinguishment of any public dividend capital,

and if, where the operations ceasing to be funded represent the whole of
the funded operations, any balance remains after the amount or excess
has been so applied, the responsible Minister shall pay the balance into
the Consolidated Fund.

(7) The responsible Minister may out of money provided by Parliament repay any debt remaining after the application of subsection (6)
above or make a payment into the Consolidated Fund in reduction or
extinguishment of any public dividend capital so remaining.

(8) Where the operations ceasing to be funded represent only part of
the funded operations, the responsible Minister may by order made
with Treasury concurrence reduce or extinguish any originating debt,
or public dividend capital, remaining after the application of the preceding subsections."

Minor and consequential amendments related to section 1

2.—(1) In section 3 of that Act (payments into and out of funds)—

(a) for subsection (1) there is substituted—

"(1) There shall be paid into a trading fund all receipts in respect of the
funded operations and there shall be paid out of the fund all expenditure
incurred by the responsible Minister in respect of those operations,
except expenditure in respect of liabilities not appropriated to the fund."

(b) in subsection (2), for "(1)(b)" there is substituted "(1)" and after
"pensions" there is inserted "(including increases of pensions)", and

(c) after subsection (3) there is inserted—

"(4) Nothing in this section affects the powers conferred in relation to
fees and charges by section 102 of the Finance (No. 2) Act 1987."

(2) In section 4 of that Act (management and accounting)—

(a) in subsection (1), "for any Crown service" is omitted and in paragraph
(a), after "fund", there is inserted—

"(i) consists principally of receipts in respect of goods or services
provided in the course of the funded operations, and
(ii)",

(b) in subsection (3), for the words from "and" to "paid" there is substituted "he may with Treasury concurrence pay that amount out of
the fund and",

(c) for subsection (4) there is substituted—

"(4) If, in the case of a trading fund not having public dividend capital,
the revenues of the fund for a financial year exceed the total sums
properly chargeable to revenue account for that year, the responsible
Minister may with Treasury concurrence—

(a) apply the excess for such purposes of the funded operations as
he may determine, or

(b) pay the whole or part of the excess into the Consolidated
Fund.",

(d) in subsection (6), in paragraph (a)—

(i) for "be in a form approved by the Treasury" there is substituted "comply with any directions given by the Treasury as to the information to be contained in the statement, the manner in which the information is to be presented or the methods and principles according to which the statement is to be prepared", and

(ii) "with respect to financial results in the previous year" is omitted,

(e) after that subsection there is inserted—

"(6A) The accounting officer shall send to the responsible Minister in respect of each financial year—

(a) the annual statement of accounts, and

(b) a report in such form and containing such information as to the performance of the funded operations as the Treasury may require,

and the responsible Minister shall publish any report received by him under this subsection, together with the annual statement of accounts (unless the Treasury otherwise directs), in such manner as the Treasury may require.

(6B) Where any enactment (other than this Act) requires, in whatever terms, a report to be prepared for any period as to the funded operations and sent to any person, or laid before Parliament, or both or so sent or laid by any time or times, an order may provide for that requirement to be treated as satisfied by preparing the report for the financial year and sending it to that person, or laying it before Parliament, or both or, as the case may be, so sending or laying it by the time or times specified in the order.", and

(f) in subsection (7), for the words from "the operations" to "this Act" there is substituted "any operations of a department of the government are funded operations of a trading fund" and for "that service" there is substituted "those operations".

(3) In section 6 (orders)—

(a) for subsection (1) there is substituted—

"(1) The power to make an order under section 1 of this Act shall be exercisable by statutory instrument and includes power to vary or revoke such an order, but no such order may alter the authorised lender in relation to any fund.",

(b) in subsection (2), for "under section 1 above" there is substituted "establishing a trading fund, or extending or restricting the funded operations,",

(c) in subsection (3), for the words from the beginning to "has" there is substituted "A statutory instrument containing an order under section 1 of this Act, if made without a draft having", and

(d) for subsection (4) there is substituted—

"(4) Where a Minister of the Crown has taken steps in pursuance of section 1(3) of this Act to give an opportunity for representations to be made about a proposed order, he shall, before laying, in accordance with subsection (2) above, a draft instrument containing the order giving effect to the proposal, lay a report before Parliament about the representations received and his conclusions."

(4) In section 7 (the Mint)—

(a) in subsection (1), for "section 2 or 4" there is substituted "sections 2, 2A, 4 or 4A", and

(b) in subsection (2), for "financed by means of a trading fund" there is substituted "funded operations".

(5) That Act, as amended by section 1 of this Act and this section, is set out in Schedule 1 to this Act.

Trading etc. accounts

3.—(1) In section 5 of the Exchequer and Audit Departments Act 1921—
(a) in subsection (1), for "shipbuilding, manufacturing, trading, or commercial services conducted by the department" there is substituted "operations of the department for which the Treasury consider it desirable that such statements should be prepared", and
(b) in subsection (3), for the words from "in " to "Parliament, and" there is substituted "he".

(2) In Schedule A to the Exchequer and Audit Departments Act 1866, for "All other shipbuilding, manufacturing, trading or commercial accounts." there is substituted "All accounts prepared by virtue of section 5 of the Exchequer and Audit Departments Act 1921.".

Repeal of Borrowing (Control and Guarantees) Act 1946

4.—(1) The Borrowing (Control and Guarantees) Act 1946 is repealed.
(2) The enactments mentioned in Part I of Schedule 2 to this Act are, in consequence, repealed to the extent specified in the third column.
(3) This section shall come into force on such day as the Treasury may by order made by statutory instrument appoint.

Short title, savings, repeals and extent

5.—(1) This Act may be cited as the Government Trading Act 1990.
(2) Subject to subsection (3) below, any order under the Government Trading Funds Act 1973 in force on the day before this Act is passed shall continue to have effect with the necessary modifications as if made under section 1 of that Act as substituted by this Act, but as if—
(a) the authorised lender were the National Loans Fund, and
(b) in the case of the HMSO Trading Fund Order 1980 the words in the Schedule after paragraph (c) were omitted.
(3) Nothing in this Act affects the operation of that Act in relation to the Crown Suppliers.
(4) The enactments mentioned in Part II of Schedule 2 to this Act are repealed to the extent specified in the third column.
(5) This Act, except section 4, extends to Northern Ireland.

SCHEDULES

Section 2   SCHEDULE 1

GOVERNMENT TRADING FUNDS ACT 1973, AS AMENDED
ARRANGEMENT OF SECTIONS

1. Establishment of trading funds.
2. Assets and liabilities of funds.
2A. Public dividend capital.
2B. Borrowing by funds.
3. Payments into, and out of, a trading fund.
4. Management and accounting.
4A. Operations ceasing to be funded.
5. Provisions as to the coinage.
6. Orders.
7. The Mint.
8. Citation.

An Act to enable certain services of the Crown to be financed by means of trading funds established in pursuance of orders made by the responsible Minister with Treasury concurrence; to make consequential provision (in the event of a trading fund being established for the Mint) as to sums received by, or due from, the Treasury in respect of the coinage; and to amend the Coinage Act 1971 in respect of the establishment and operations of the Mint.
[25th October 1973]

(Formal enacting words)

Establishment of trading funds

1.—(1) If it appears to any Minister of the Crown—

(a) that any operations of a department of the government for which he is responsible are suitable to be financed by means of a fund established under this Act (referred to in this Act as a "trading fund") and, in particular, to be so managed that the revenue of the fund would consist principally of receipts in respect of goods or services provided in the course of the operations in question, and

(b) that the financing of the operations in question by means of a trading fund would be in the interests of the improved efficiency and effectiveness of the management of those operations,

he may by order establish a trading fund for the operations in question as from a day appointed by the order.

(2) The power to make an order under this section is exercisable only with Treasury concurrence.

(3) Where a Minister of the Crown proposes to make an order in respect of any operations (not being operations then financed by means of a trading fund) and considers that—

(a) the operations in question consist substantially in the provision of goods or services in the United Kingdom otherwise than to departments of the government, and

(b) an opportunity to make representations to him should be given,

he shall take such steps as appear to him to be appropriate to give such an opportunity to such persons as appear to him to be appropriate.

(4) An order establishing a trading fund shall designate either—

(a) the National Loans Fund, or

(b) the responsible Minister,

as the source of issues to the fund by way of loan (referred to in this Act as the "authorised lender").

(5) Issues to the fund by way of loan by the responsible Minister shall be made out of money provided by Parliament, and the right to repayment of such issues ranks as an asset of the Consolidated Fund.

(6) An order establishing a trading fund for operations carried on by a person appointed in pursuance of any enactment may provide—

(a) for the fund to be under the control and management of that person instead of the responsible Minister and, accordingly,

(b) for this Act to have effect as if—

(i) the reference to the responsible Minister in section 3(1) of this Act and the first reference to him in section 4(1), and

(ii) such other references in this Act to the responsible Minister as may be specified in the order, where they are references to him in the exercise of his function of controlling or managing the fund,

were references to that person.

(7) In this Act—

"the funded operations", in relation to a trading fund, means the operations for which the fund is established,

"liabilities", in relation to a trading fund, does not include liabilities in respect of any amount issued to the fund under section 2B of this Act,

"Minister of the Crown" means the holder of an office in Her Majesty's Government in the United Kingdom, and includes the Treasury,

"order" except in section 2B(8) of this Act means an order under this section,

"originating debt", in relation to a trading fund, means any amount remaining after any repayment or reduction of the amount which, by virtue of section 2(3) and (4) of this Act, is the originating debt of the fund, and

"the responsible Minister", in relation to any operations of a department of the government, means the Minister of the Crown responsible for that department.

(8) References in this Act to the provision of services include—

(a) the provision of any authority required for carrying on any activity or exercising any right, and

(b) the performance of any other functions in connection with the regulation of any activity or right.

(9) References in this Act to a Minister of the Crown include Ministers acting jointly, but an order may not designate more than one Minister as the authorised lender.

Assets and liabilities of funds

2.—(1) Where any Minister of the Crown proposes to make an order establishing a trading fund for any operations or to vary an order by extending the funded operations—

(a) he shall with Treasury concurrence determine what Crown assets and liabilities are properly attributable to the operations for which the fund is to be established or, as the case may be, the additional operations and are suitable to be appropriated to the fund, and

(b) the order shall provide for the assets and liabilities so determined to be appropriated as assets and liabilities of the fund at values or amounts determined by him in accordance with Treasury directions.

(2) The responsible Minister may from time to time, in the case of any trading fund, with Treasury concurrence determine what additional Crown assets and liabilities are properly attributable to the funded operations and suitable to be appropriated to the fund and provide by order for the assets and liabilities in question to be appropriated as assets and liabilities of the fund at values or amounts determined by him in accordance with Treasury directions.

(3) Where an order establishing a trading fund provides for any assets and liabilities to be appropriated as assets and liabilities of the fund—

(a) the amount by which the values of those assets exceed the amounts of those liabilities, less

(b) any amount treated by virtue of the order as public dividend capital,

is originating debt of the fund and is to be treated as having been issued to the fund under section 2B of this Act on the day appointed by the order.

(4) Where, in the case of a trading fund established under a previous order, an order provides for any additional assets and liabilities to be appropriated as assets and liabilities of the fund—

(a) the amount by which the values of those additional assets exceed the amounts of those additional liabilities, less

(b) any amount treated by virtue of the order as public dividend capital,

is to be added to the originating debt of the fund and is to be treated as having been issued to the fund under section 2B of this Act on the day appointed by the order.

(5) The responsible Minister may with Treasury concurrence from time to time by order provide, in the case of any trading fund, for any assets and liabilities to cease to be assets and liabilities of the fund; but the power conferred by this subsection is not exercisable where section 4A of this Act applies.

(6) Where the responsible Minister exercises the power conferred by subsection (5) above, he may, in the case of any originating debt or public dividend capital which he may with Treasury concurrence determine to be properly attributable to the assets and liabilities in question—

(a) out of money provided by Parliament, repay the whole or part of the debt or make a payment into the Consolidated Fund in reduction or extinguishment of the capital, and

(b) by order made with Treasury concurrence provide for the reduction or extinguishment of any debt or capital remaining after the application of paragraph (a) above.

(7) An order providing for any assets and liabilities to be appropriated as, or to cease to be, assets and liabilities of a trading fund may describe the assets and liabilities in general terms.

Public dividend capital

2A.—(1) An order providing for any assets and liabilities to be appropriated as assets and liabilities of a trading fund may provide for any part of the amount by which the values of the assets exceed the amounts of the liabilities to be treated as public dividend capital of the fund.

(2) Where the responsible Minister—

(a) repays out of a trading fund before the due date any amount outstanding in respect of the principal of any sums issued to the fund by the authorised lender by way of loan, or

(b) pays any amount standing in the reserves of a trading fund into the Consolidated Fund,

he may with Treasury concurrence issue out of money provided by Parliament a corresponding amount to the fund as public dividend capital.

(3) Where any sum is issued to a trading fund under section 2B of this Act, the responsible Minister may with Treasury concurrence pay out of the fund into the Consolidated Fund a corresponding sum in reduction or extinguishment of any public dividend capital.

(4) Public dividend capital ranks as an asset of the Consolidated Fund.

(5) For any financial year in which a trading fund has public dividend capital, there shall be paid out of the fund into the Consolidated Fund such sums (if any) by way of return on that capital and its reserves as the responsible Minister may determine, with Treasury concurrence, having regard to any balance in the fund at the end of that year and the amount of the balance which appears to the responsible Minister and the Treasury to be in the nature of distributable profit.

Borrowing by funds

2B.—(1) No amount shall be paid into a trading fund by way of loan except in accordance with this section.

(2) Subject to subsection (6) below, the authorised lender may issue by way of loan to a trading fund sums required for the funded operations.

(3) Sums issued under this section shall be repaid out of the fund on such terms, and interest on them shall be paid at such variable or fixed rates and at such times, as the Treasury may determine.

(4) A rate of interest for any amount so issued by the responsible Minister shall be determined as if section 5 of the National Loans Act 1968 had effect in respect of it and subsections (5A) and (5B) of that section shall apply accordingly.

(5) In the case of any trading fund where the authorised lender is a Minister of the Crown, repayment of any amount outstanding in respect of the principal of any sum issued under this section (other than repayment before the due date) may, with Treasury concurrence, be made to the Minister instead of into the Consolidated Fund and applied by him as money provided by Parliament.

(6) The order establishing a trading fund shall specify the maximum amount that may be issued under this section and the aggregate of amounts issued under this section in respect of the fund (other than originating debt) shall not exceed that amount, or that amount as varied by a subsequent order.

(7) The sum of the maxima in force in respect of all trading funds at any time shall not exceed £2,000 million.

(8) The Treasury may by order made by statutory instrument increase or further increase the limit in subsection (7) above by any amount, not exceeding £1,000 million, specified in the order but not so as to make the limit exceed £4,000 million.

(9) No order under subsection (8) above shall be made unless a draft of a statutory instrument containing it has been laid before the House of Commons and approved by a resolution of that House.

Payments into, and out of, a trading fund

3.—(1) There shall be paid into a trading fund all receipts in respect of the funded operations and there shall be paid out of the fund all expenditure incurred by the responsible Minister in respect of those operations, except expenditure in respect of liabilities not appropriated to the fund.

(2) Without prejudice to subsection (1) above, there shall be paid out of the trading fund into the Consolidated Fund such sums as may be appropriate as representing accruing liabilities of the Treasury in respect of pensions (including increases of pensions), gratuities and other similar benefits for persons who have been employed in the funded operations and in respect of the administrative expenses attributable to those liabilities and their discharge; and—

(a) where the Treasury is the responsible Minister for the fund, it shall be for the Treasury to determine the sums payable under this subsection, the amount of any payment and the time at which it is to be made; and

(b) in other cases it shall be for the responsible Minister to determine the sums so payable in agreement with the Treasury, subject to any directions given by the Treasury as to the amount of any payment or the time at which it is to be made.

(3) The enactments relating to public receipts, expenditure and accounting shall have effect subject to the foregoing provisions of this section, except as may be directed by the Treasury from time to time; and if any question arises whether any particular sums are required by those provisions to be paid into, or out of, the trading fund, that question shall be determined by the Treasury.

(4) Nothing in this section affects the powers conferred in relation to fees and charges by section 102 of the Finance (No. 2) Act 1987.

Management and accounting

4.—(1) A trading fund established under this Act shall be under the control and management of the responsible Minister; and in the discharge of his functions in relation to the fund it shall be his duty—

(a) to manage the funded operations so that the revenue of the fund—

(i) consists principally of receipts in respect of goods or services provided in the course of the funded operations, and

(ii) is not less than sufficient, taking one year with another, to meet outgoings which are properly chargeable to revenue account; and

(b) to achieve such further financial objectives as the Treasury may from time to time, by minute laid before the House of Commons, indicate as having been determined by the responsible Minister (with Treasury concurrence) to be desirable of achievement.

(2) With Treasury concurrence, the responsible Minister may establish and maintain general, capital and other reserves in the accounts of the trading fund.

(3) If at any time it appears to the responsible Minister that any amount standing in the reserves of the trading fund is surplus to any foreseeable requirements of the funded operations, he may with Treasury concurrence pay that amount out of the fund and into the Consolidated Fund.

(4) If, in the case of a trading fund not having public dividend capital, the revenues of the fund for a financial year exceed the total sums properly chargeable to revenue account for that year, the responsible Minister may with Treasury concurrence—

(a) apply the excess for such purposes of the funded operations as he may determine, or

(b) pay the whole or part of the excess into the Consolidated Fund.

(5) Any money in the fund which appears to the responsible Minister not to be immediately required for the funded operations may be invested by him in such securities of the Government of the United Kingdom or of the Government of Northern Ireland as the Treasury may approve, including Treasury Bills and Ways and Means advances.

(6) The Treasury shall appoint an accounting officer for the fund, with responsibility for keeping its accounts and proper records in relation thereto, and preparing and signing a statement of the accounts in respect of each financial year; and—

(a) the annual statement of accounts shall comply with any directions given by the Treasury as to the information to be contained in the statement, the manner in which the information is to be presented or the methods and principles according to which the statement is to be prepared and contain such additional information as the Treasury may require to be provided for the information of Parliament; and

(b) the statement in respect of each financial year shall, on or before 30th November next following the end of that year, be transmitted to the Comptroller and Auditor General, who shall examine and certify the statement and lay copies thereof, together with his report thereon, before Parliament.

(6A) The accounting officer shall send to the responsible Minister in respect of each financial year—

(a) the annual statement of accounts, and

(b) a report in such form and containing such information as to the performance of the funded operations as the Treasury may require,

and the responsible Minister shall publish any report received by him under this subsection, together with the annual statement of accounts (unless the Treasury otherwise directs), in such manner as the Treasury may require.

(6B) Where any enactment (other than this Act) requires, in whatever terms, a report to be prepared for any period as to the funded operations and sent to any person, or laid before Parliament, or both or so sent or laid by any time or times, an order may provide for that requirement to be treated as satisfied by preparing the report for the financial year and sending it to that person, or laying it before Parliament, or both or, as the case may be, so sending or laying it by the time or times specified in the order.

(7) As respects any financial year during the whole of which any operations of a department of the government are funded operations of a trading fund, section 5 of the Exchequer and Audit Departments Act 1921 (preparation and examination of accounts of trading services conducted by government departments) shall not apply to those operations; but otherwise subsection (6) above is without prejudice to anything in that Act or the Exchequer and Audit Departments Act 1866.

Operations ceasing to be funded

4A.—(1) This section applies where any operations for which a trading fund is established are to cease to be funded operations (whether the operations ceasing to be funded represent the whole or part of the funded operations or are to cease altogether or be funded operations of another fund or, while continuing to be operations of a department of the government, be financed by other means).

(2) Where the operations ceasing to be funded represent only part of the funded operations, the responsible Minister shall by order provide for such assets and liabilities of the fund as he may with Treasury concurrence determine to be properly attributable to the operations ceasing to be funded to cease to be assets and liabilities of the fund.

(3) In the following provisions of this section, "debt" means any amount outstanding in respect of the principal of or interest on sums issued under section 2B of this Act and "originating debt" includes any amount outstanding in respect of interest on such debt; and, where the operations ceasing to be funded represent only part of the funded operations—

(a) references to assets and liabilities are to the assets and liabilities ceasing to be assets and liabilities of the fund by virtue of an order under subsection (2) above,

(b) references to debt, originating debt or public dividend capital are to so much of any debt, originating debt or public dividend capital as the responsible Minister may with Treasury concurrence determine to be attributable to the operations ceasing to be funded.

(4) If, in a case where the operations ceasing to be funded are to cease altogether, the values of the assets of the fund exceed the amounts of the liabilities of the fund, the excess shall be applied in accordance with subsection (6) below.

(5) If in any other case—

(a) it appears to the responsible Minister that any amount standing in the reserves of the fund is surplus to any foreseeable requirements of the funded operations, or

(b) the revenues of the fund for the last financial year exceed the total sums properly chargeable to revenue account for that year,

the amount or excess shall be applied in accordance with subsection (6) below.

(6) The amount or excess in question shall be applied towards the following objects (applying paragraph (a) before paragraph (b))—

(a) the repayment of debt, and

(b) payment into the Consolidated Fund in reduction or extinguishment of any public dividend capital,

and if, where the operations ceasing to be funded represent the whole of the funded operations, any balance remains after the amount or excess has been so applied, the responsible Minister shall pay the balance into the Consolidated Fund.

(7) The responsible Minister may out of money provided by Parliament repay any debt remaining after the application of subsection (6) above or make a payment into the Consolidated Fund in reduction or extinguishment of any public dividend capital so remaining.

(8) Where the operations ceasing to be funded represent only part of the funded operations, the responsible Minister may by order made with Treasury concurrence reduce or extinguish any originating debt, or public dividend capital, remaining after the application of the preceding subsections.

Provisions as to the coinage

5. If a trading fund is established under this Act for the Mint, then as from the day appointed in relation to the fund under section 1(1) of this Act—

(a) any sums received by or on behalf of the Treasury in respect of coin issued for circulation shall be paid into the Consolidated Fund; and

(b) any sums due from the Treasury as payment for coin withdrawn from circulation shall be charged on and issued out of that Fund.

Orders

6.—(1) The power to make an order under section 1 of this Act shall be exercisable by statutory instrument and includes power to vary or revoke such an order, but no such order may alter the authorised lender in relation to any fund.

(2) No order establishing a trading fund, or extending or restricting the funded operations, shall be made unless a draft of a statutory instrument containing it has been laid before the House of Commons and approved by a resolution of that House.

(3) A statutory instrument containing an order under section 1 of this Act, if made without a draft having been approved by a resolution of the House of Commons, shall be subject to annulment in pursuance of a resolution of that House.

(4) Where a Minister of the Crown has taken steps in pursuance of section 1(3) of this Act to give an opportunity for representations to be made about a proposed order, he shall, before laying, in accordance with subsection (2) above, a draft instrument containing the order giving effect to the proposal, lay a report before Parliament about the representations received and his conclusions.

The Mint

7.—(1) For purposes of this Act the Chancellor of the Exchequer is to be regarded as the Minister responsible for the administration of the Mint; and this Act, so far as it requires the concurrence of the Treasury for the making of orders, or for anything to be done under or for the purposes of sections 2, 2A, 4 or 4A, does not apply to him as responsible Minister in relation to the Mint.

(2) In section 4 of the Coinage Act 1971 (which relates to the constitution and functions of the Mint), the following shall be substituted for subsection (2)—

"(2) There shall be a deputy master of the Mint, appointed by the Treasury";

and subsections (3) and (4) are hereby repealed; and subsections (6) and (7) (expenses and receipts) shall not have effect for so long as any operations of the Mint are funded operations.

(3) Section 5 of the said Act of 1971 (coining of bullion taken by the Mint) is hereby repealed.

(4) In section 9(1) of the said Act of 1971 (prohibition of coins and tokens not issued by authority) for the words "by or with the authority of the Mint" there shall be substituted the words "with the authority of the Treasury".

Citation

8. This Act may be cited as the Government Trading Funds Act 1973.

Sections 4 and 5	SCHEDULE 2

REPEALS

PART I

REPEALS COMING INTO FORCE ON APPOINTED DAY

A. Acts

Chapter	Short title	Extent of repeal
1946 c.58.	Borrowing (Control and Guarantees) Act 1946.	The whole Act.
1968 c.64.	Civil Evidence Act 1968.	In the Schedule, the entry relating to the Borrowing (Control and Guarantees) Act 1946.
1968 c.73.	Transport Act 1968.	Section 12(6).
1974 c.47.	Solicitors Act 1974.	In Schedule 2, in paragraph 4, the words from the beginning to "in force".
1976 c.27.	Theatres Trust Act 1976.	Section 4.
1977 c.46.	Insurance Brokers (Registration) Act 1977.	In the Schedule, in paragraph 8(2)(e), the words "of section 1 of the Borrowing (Control and Guarantees) Act 1946 or".

B. Measure

Chapter	Short title	Extent of repeal
1958 No. 1.	Church Funds Investment Measure 1958.	Section 7.

PART II

REPEALS COMING INTO FORCE ON PASSING

Chapter	Short title	Extent of repeal
1973 c.63.	Government Trading Funds Act 1973.	In section 4, in subsection (1) the words "for any Crown service" and in subsection (6)(a) the words "with respect to financial results in the previous year".

INDEX

References in roman type are to sections of this Act; those in italic are to the Government Trading Funds Act 1973 (as amended).

Aviation and Maritime Security Act 1990*

(1990 c. 31)

ARRANGEMENT OF SECTIONS

---

* Annotations by Nicholas Gaskell, Senior Lecturer, Faculty of Law, University of Southampton.

SCHEDULES:
    Schedule 1—Further amendments of the Aviation Security Act 1982.
    Schedule 2—Provisions relating to compensation.
    Schedule 3—Minor and consequential amendments.
    Schedule 4—Repeals.

An Act to give effect to the Protocol for the Suppression of Unlawful Acts of Violence at Airports Servicing International Civil Aviation which supplements the Convention for the Suppression of Unlawful Acts against the Safety of Civil Aviation; to make further provision with respect to aviation security and civil aviation; to give effect to the Convention for the Suppression of Unlawful Acts against the Safety of Maritime Navigation and to the Protocol for the Suppression of Unlawful Acts against the Safety of Fixed Platforms Located on the Continental Shelf which supplements that Convention; to make other provision for the protection of ships and harbour areas against acts of violence; and for connected purposes.

[26th July 1990]

PARLIAMENTARY DEBATES
    Hansard, H.C. Vol. 164, col. 954; Vol. 168, col. 592; Vol. 174, col. 1045; Vol. 176, col. 1216; H.L. Vol. 517, col. 1586; Vol. 518, col. 856; Vol. 519, col. 452.
    The Bill was considered in Standing Committee A from February 1 to February 22, 1990 and in Committee on April 30, 1990.

GENERAL AND INTRODUCTORY NOTE
    The Act is mainly designed to deal with the threat to the safety and security of aircraft and ships caused by terrorism and similar conduct. It does so essentially by creating a number of new offences and by tightening the regulatory framework by which security is controlled in airports and harbours.
    The Act was preceded by a number of reports and responses (mainly relating to aviation security), including the following:
    Fourth Report from the Transport Committee, October 30, 1986, 1985-86 H.C. 597.
    Government Response to the Fourth Report from the Transport Committee, November 4, 1986, 1985-86 H.C. 602.
    Third Report of the Transport Committee, Airport Security, July 18, 1989, 1988-89 H.C. 509.
    Government Observations on the Third Report of the Transport Committee, December 6, 1989, 1989-90 H.C. 52.

International terrorism
    In recent years there have occurred a number of serious incidents in international aviation and maritime transport, caused by bombings or attacks, which have resulted in great loss of life. The most notable of these was the Lockerbie disaster, involving the loss of a Pan Am airliner in December 1988. There have been many other incidents involving aircraft (such as the Air India Boeing 747 that crashed south of Ireland in 1985, or the DC-10 that crashed in the African desert in September 1989), as well as airports (such as the 1985 attacks on Vienna and Rome airports) and also ships (such as the hijacking of the *Achille Lauro* in October 1985).
    Governments worldwide have been under pressure to tighten security against such terrorist attacks. In the European Community this task has been said by the British police to be more difficult because of the dismantling of customs and immigration barriers between member states. Yet it is also difficult for one state to act alone, given the ability of terrorists to board a plane or ship in any country. To achieve some form of uniformity the specialised UN agencies, such as ICAO and IMO, have produced a number of international agreements. One of the purposes of the Aviation and Maritime Security Act 1990 is to enable the U.K. to give effect to three of these: (1) the Montreal Protocol 1988; (2) the Rome Convention 1988; and (3) the Fixed Platforms Protocol 1988. These will be dealt with in Pt. I (s.1) and Pt. II (ss.9–17) respectively.

National responsibility
    The U.K. Government has faced criticism that it has not done enough to enforce security, particularly at airports. Criticisms were made by the Transport Select Committee in 1986 and 1989 and political pressure has been exerted by the Opposition, seeking to show that inadequacies resulted, in part, from Government financial cutbacks and its policy of privatisation.

Central to the debate has been the policing role of the DTp and the extent to which security services should be provided by the state, as opposed to private security organisations employed by the owners of airport and harbour facilities. During debates, the DTp was criticised for failing to circulate warnings about possible bombings of U.S. aircraft in the days before the Lockerbie disaster. In the aftermath of the Lockerbie bombing the Government was anxious to be seen as vigorously combating terrorism. Nevertheless, the Government was embarrassed in July 1990 (shortly before Royal assent) by the revelation that the father of one of the Lockerbie victims had been able to take a replica bomb from Heathrow to the U.S.A. on a British Airways plane. The purpose of the trip was to demonstrate that security had not been improved and to call for an independent inquiry into the bombing. At Second Reading in the Commons the Secretary of State for Transport, Cecil Parkinson, was keen to point out that over £7 million had already been spent on investigating that disaster. The complaint has been that it is the DTp that needs investigating.

The DTp's rôle after other disasters has also been criticised, for instance the Zeebrugge disaster in 1987 and the King's Cross Underground fire in 1988. The complaints have related both to its efforts to prevent disasters and to investigations that have been undertaken in their wake. Since Lockerbie, it has been announced that the number of aviation security inspectors will be increased from seven to 16.

Equating aviation and maritime transport

After the 1987 sinking in Zeebrugge of the *Herald of Free Enterprise* the Government established an independent Marine Accident Investigation Branch in the DTp to match the equivalent Branch for aviation which had already been operating successfully (see the note to the Merchant Shipping Act 1988, s.33 in [1988] 2 Current Law Statutes Annotated). The present Act is a further example of legislative provisions designed for one mode of transport being applied to the other (see Pts. II and III of the 1990 Act). There are logical attractions in having uniformity and it is an easy way of deflecting criticism to point to equivalent provisions in a comparable mode of transport. Nevertheless, it is not always true that such an approach is necessary or even desirable. The number and speed of movements of ships and planes differ considerably, as do the means and ability to provide security. There were criticisms from the maritime market that some of the new provisions in Pt. III were inappropriate and unduly burdensome on an already hard pressed industry. Thus, although the aviation industry may have been broadly in favour of the Act, it must be said that the same degree of enthusiasm did not exist in the maritime industry, which saw attractions in the existing voluntary arrangements about security.

Although the main Parliamentary focus was on the aviation aspects of the Bill, it is right to note that 37 out of the 54 sections are devoted to the extension of the security powers to cover the maritime industry. Moreover, Pt. I of the 1990 Act is more concerned with creating new offences than with enforcing practical improvements to aviation security. The mechanism for making such improvements was already provided by the Aviation Security Act 1982.

Civil liberties

The Act received a broad measure of cross-party support during its progress through Parliament, although there were quite a number of concerns raised relating to civil liberties. Like other legislation designed to deal with terrorism (see, for example the Prevention of Terrorism (Temporary Provisions) Act 1989) it gives very wide powers in relation to searches and information gathering and creates a host of new offences. There is the paradox of trying to protect the liberties of citizens from the activities of terrorists by giving extremely wide powers to the Government. The difficulty is to maintain a balance between the powers necessary to enable a comprehensive approach to security, allowing for an immediate and effective response to particular terrorist acts, while at the same time maintaining basic rights in a free society.

There may be the feeling that a Government is trying to reserve excessive powers to itself, avoiding Parliament, by praying in aid certain emotive words. After the Zeebrugge disaster the DTp was able to bring in sweeping new general offences on the justification of "safety". During consideration of this Act, the key words "security" and "terrorism" were emphasised in debates to counter criticism that a power might be too wide. Of particular concern, perhaps, are the powers which may be given to private security guards (see for example ss.21–24). There is still no code of practice, or uniform policy, regarding their use, especially in harbours.

Also of concern is the wide general nature of "Directions" that may be given by the Secretary of State (see for example ss.2, 3, 21–24 and *Directions*, in the General Note to Pt.I, below). The Directions need consideration, both because of the wide area in respect of which they may be made and also because of their very form. They are "flexible", *i.e.* not subject to Parliamentary scrutiny (and see generally, G. Ganz, *Quasi-Legislation* (1987)). In *R.* v. *Secretary of State for the Social Services*, ex p. *Stitt*; *R.* v. *Social Security Inspector*, ex p. *Sherwin*; *R.* v. *Same*,

ex p. *Roberts*, *The Times*, July 5, 1990, the Court of Appeal had to consider the power of the Secretary of State for Social Security to direct which categories of need qualify for payment out of the Social Fund set up by the Social Security Act 1986. The judges were astonished by such unrestricted powers given to the Executive. Purchas L.J. referred to the "wholesale unregulated and unsupervised powers" to pass subordinate legislation which had been granted to a minister. Nevertheless, the Court felt obliged to uphold the powers, given the clear and unambiguous language of the Act. The same view would probably be taken of the 1990 Act powers. A further justification for the use of Directions in ports and harbours was the fact that they were already being used in airports under the Aviation Security Act 1982. Hence, nothing "radical" was being suggested in the civil liberties context.

The difficulties of reconciling security and individual liberties were also illustrated by the debates about how much information should be made available by the Government about security and the extent to which individual passengers could demand security information from airlines (*cf.* s.7). A balance has to be struck between excessive secrecy and disclosure of security arrangements to potential terrorists. It is difficult to say yet whether the Act has achieved the right balance; there is always the danger that the Government's desire for confidentiality may facilitate avoidance of criticism for failing to take sufficient measures.

The Government was willing however to recognise certain civil liberties relating to private property (see ss.22(4), 26(6)).

SUMMARY OF THE ACT

Pt. I: Aviation security
Pt. I deals with aviation security and implements the Montreal Protocol 1988. In order to enable the DTp to obtain accurate information about the security threat, the Secretary of State is empowered to set up a (potentially) mandatory reporting system for actual or potential security incidents (s.7). New offences are created of committing acts of violence at aerodromes and of damaging aerodrome facilities or aircraft (s.1). It can also be an offence to disrupt aerodrome services (s.1).

The Aviation Security Act 1982 is amended in a number of ways which will increase the powers of the Secretary of State and create new offences in respect of persons such as passengers and visitors. Most of the powers relate to the Secretary of State being able to direct persons *other* than the DTp to take action, but with further powers of enforcement given to DTp employees.

The Secretary of State is empowered to give Directions to airlines and other businesses operating at aerodromes to conduct searches (s.2). Detailed Directions to guard against violence can now be given, not only to airlines and aerodrome managers, but also to other businesses, persons occupying aerodrome land and those who have access to aerodromes (s.3). The latter may even be directed to guard vehicles or goods kept outside the aerodrome. A new procedure allows "enforcement notices" to be served, requiring compliance with the Directions, and it is an offence to refuse or fail to comply (s.4). Where persons such as airline employees put questions to passengers and others about baggage, cargo or stores, it is an offence to answer falsely (s.5). It is also an offence to make false statements in order to obtain identity documents, for example those issued to bona fide airport employees (s.5).

Some parts of aerodromes may be designated "restricted zones" (see Sched. 1, para. 3) and it is an offence to enter one without permission (s.5). Similarly, it is an offence to board, or remain on an aircraft without permission (s.5). Anybody who deliberately obstructs authorised persons, or who impersonates them, is liable to prosecution (s.5).

S.8 and Sched. 1 make further amendments to the Aviation Security Act 1982, for instance by updating the power of the Secretary of State to request information in order to take account of the additional persons to whom Directions may now be given. Changes are made to facilitate the service of notices by the Secretary of State, for example by allowing the use of telex or fax machines. The Secretary of State is enabled by Regulation to extend the various powers to cover air cargo agents who may consign supplies to airlines (s.6).

Pt. II: Terrorism against ships or platforms
Pt. II gives effect to the Rome Convention 1988 and the Fixed Platforms Protocol 1988 and aims, in general, to penalise acts of terrorism towards ships and offshore platforms (such as oil rigs). The following offences are created: the hijacking of ships (s.9) or the seizure of platforms (s.10); damaging a ship or platform, or acting violently on board so as to endanger safety (s.11); the placing of devices such as bombs on board (s.11); destroying, damaging or interfering with the operation of marine navigational facilities, such as lighthouses (s.12); communicating false information so as to endanger the safe navigation of a ship (s.12); injuring or killing persons while trying to commit one of the above (s.14); and threatening persons in order to cause injury or damage (s.13). Although the offences do not apply generally in relation to warships, naval auxiliaries, or customs or police vessels, the various sections do provide an exception where

there is a U.K. connection, for example where the act is committed in the U.K. or by a U.K. national. The master is given power to deliver offenders to Convention countries on the giving of reasonable notice (s.15). Failure by the master to give notice, or refusal to provide evidence to officials in Convention countries, is an offence (s.15).

Pt. III: Ship and harbour security

Pt. III is the longest Part of the Act and is designed to extend to ships and ports the same sort of security provisions that apply (or are to be applied) to aerodromes and aircraft under Pt. II of the Aviation Security Act 1982.

The Secretary of State is empowered to give Directions to prevent persons or property being taken on board a ship without searches having been made (s.21). The Directions can be aimed at harbour authorities, or the owners, charterers or managers of a ship (s.21). The ship may be prevented from going to sea unless searches are made, or unless specified apparatus is installed (s.21). A harbour authority may also be directed to ensure the undertaking of searches of harbours, ships, property or persons (s.22). Corresponding powers of entry, stop and search are also granted, but only provided that there is reasonable suspicion of the presence of weapons or explosives (s.22). Obstruction of a person exercising the powers is an offence (s.22).

In addition to the specific power to give Directions about searches, there is a general power given to the Secretary of State to direct that the persons mentioned above shall take measures to guard against acts of violence (s.24). Failure to obey the various Directions without reasonable excuse is an offence (ss.21–24), as is the interference with buildings or works designed to protect against acts of violence (s.24).

In order to be able to exercise the powers to give Directions—and to check for compliance with them—the Secretary of State is allowed to require information to be provided to him by persons such as shipowners and harbour authorities (s.19). The duty to give information may be made continuous, so that, for instance, a harbour authority would be obliged to correct information that had become inaccurate (s.19). Further, extensive powers are given to the Secretary of State to order the inspection of ships or harbour areas (s.36). There are also powers to allow the Secretary of State to set up a (potentially) mandatory system for the reporting of actual or potential security incidents (s.42). It might be noted that Parliament will have only a very narrow statistical report provided to it, by the Secretary of State, on the exercise of his powers under Pt. III (s.44).

The content of the Directions themselves can be quite wide and may include, for instance, the minimum number and qualifications of those carrying out searches (s.25). The Direction can override contractual duties and a person cannot be sued for breach of contract for anything done in compliance with the Direction (s.34). This may cause complications in charterparty cases where ships are delayed because of searches being undertaken. In any event, ships may be detained on the basis that the owner, charterer or manager has failed to comply with a Direction or enforcement notice (s.35). The Directions may be framed to cover categories of persons, rather than named individuals (s.27). In an urgent case the Secretary of State is empowered to create exceptions to Directions and to notify persons who would otherwise be subject to them. It is possible to object to the Directions in certain non-urgent cases, for example where a harbour authority is ordered to carry out extensive modifications to warehouses (s.28). Enforcement notices may be served on those who fail to comply with Directions and failure to comply with a notice is an offence (ss.29–33).

The powers of harbour authorities to take security measures within harbour areas are extensive and can override existing proprietary interests (*cf.* s.26(6)) and planning laws (s.34(2)). There are limited rights of compensation granted to third parties whose property interests are affected by building or demolition works which have been required by the Secretary of State for security reasons (s.43 and Sched. 2). The compensation will not be payable by the DTp, but by the person who has been directed to perform the works.

Harbour authorities are given the power to create permanent or temporary "restricted zones" in a port, for instance around a ferry terminal (s.20). In respect of these areas, persons other than shipowners or charterers may be directed by the Secretary of State to undertake searches (s.23) or to guard against violence (s.24). These persons can include those operating in the port, such as stevedoring firms or ship's agents, and those who have access to sensitive parts of it, such as regular haulage contractors (ss.23, 24). The various Directions can even apply to land outside the harbour where the persons carry on business and the Secretary of State can order inspection of these premises (s.36).

The Directions can be given to foreign registered commercial vessels, but only in respect of activities within U.K. waters (s.26). British ships are subject to Directions even when abroad, unless this would contravene local law (s.26).

As with Pt. I, new offences are created for the giving of false statements about baggage or cargo (s.37), or in order to obtain security identity cards (s.38). Similarly, it is an offence to be in a restricted zone without permission (s.39) or to obstruct or impersonate persons authorised by the Secretary of State (s.40).

Pt. IV: Miscellaneous provisions

Pt. IV contains the usual general provisions about offences by corporations (s.50), the application of the Act to the Crown Dependencies and Dependent Territories, minor amendments (s.53, Sched. 3) and repeals (s.53 and Sched. 4). There is also a provision to amend the Civil Aviation Act 1982 to allow Air Navigation Orders to regulate the carrying of goods and in particular to lay down more specific powers to examine or seize packages (s.47).

GENERAL ABBREVIATIONS

1986 Report: Fourth Report from the Transport Committee.

1989 Report: Third Report of the Transport Committee.

1990 Act: the Aviation and Maritime Security Act 1990.

Bimco: Baltic and International Maritime Council.

BALPA: British Airline Pilots Association.

Direction: a direction issued under the Aviation Security Act 1982 or the Aviation and Maritime Security Act 1990.

DTp: Department of Transport.

GCBS: General Council of British Shipping.

Government Observations: 1989 Government Observations on the Third Report of the Transport Committee.

Government Response: 1986 Government Response to the Fourth Report from the Transport Committee.

ICAO: International Civil Aviation Organisation.

IMO: International Maritime Organisation.

JACOLA: Joint Airports Committee of Local Authorities.

TNA: Thermal Neutron Analysis.

UNCLOS: UN Convention on the Law of the Sea 1982.

CONVENTION ABBREVIATIONS

Aviation Conventions

Hague Convention 1970: Convention for the Suppression of Unlawful Seizure of Aircraft 1970.

Montreal Convention 1971: Convention for the Suppression of Unlawful Acts Against the Safety of Civil Aviation 1971 (Cmnd.4822).

Montreal Protocol 1988: Protocol for the Suppression of Unlawful Acts of Violence at Airports Serving International Civil Aviation 1988 (Cm. 378).

Tokyo Convention 1963: Convention on Offences and Certain Other Acts Committed on Board Aircraft 1963.

Maritime Conventions

Fixed Platforms Protocol 1988: Protocol for the Suppression of Unlawful Acts against the Safety of Fixed Platforms located on the Continental Shelf 1988.

Rome Convention 1988: Convention for the Suppression of Unlawful Acts against the Safety of Maritime Navigation 1988.

General Conventions on terrorism

European Communities Convention 1979: Agreement concerning the Application of the European Convention on the Suppression of Terrorism Among the Member States 1979.

European Convention 1977: European Convention on the Suppression of Terrorism 1977.

League of Nations Convention 1937: Convention for the Prevention and Punishment of Terrorism 1937.

New York Convention 1979: International Convention against the Taking of Hostages 1979.

UN Convention 1973: Convention on the Prevention and Punishment of Crimes against Internationally Protected Persons 1973.

PART I

AVIATION SECURITY

GENERAL NOTE

The International Context
   Acts of force committed against aircraft and passengers have been a threat to safety for over thirty years, although the mid-1980s saw a rash of incidents. There is no single type of perpetrator or method of violence. The aims may vary from the desire to make a profit, for example by extracting a ransom; to escape, for example from Eastern Europe; to make a political protest, for instance about the Arab-Israeli conflict; or to bargain for the release of prisoners. Aircraft may be diverted from their planned routes, or destroyed on the ground or in the air. There may be individual attacks on passengers or indiscriminate killings. Some of the activities may loosely be referred to as "aerial piracy", or "hijacking", although it is not really possible to produce a single classification for the many varieties of "terrorism" (see further E. *McWhinney, Aerial Piracy and International Terrorism: the Illegal Diversion of Aircraft and International Law*, (2nd ed. 1987)). Attacks have also been made against airports, such as those in Rome and Vienna in December 1985.
   There have been a number of Conventions which attempt to regulate safety and security on board aircraft, including the Tokyo Convention 1963, the Hague Convention 1970, the Montreal Convention 1971, and the Montreal Protocol 1988. In addition there have been a number of general international measures to control terrorism, including the League of Nations Convention 1937, the UN Convention 1973, the European Convention 1977, the European Communities Convention 1979, and the New York Convention 1979.
   A glance at the chronology will show how the legislation reflected developments over the years (see further *McWhinney, op. cit.*, A. Evans, J. Murphy (eds.), *Legal Aspects of International Terrorism* (1978) and *Shawcross & Beaumont: Air Law* (4th ed. with supps.)). The Tokyo Convention 1963 was concerned with defining the legal status of aircraft, but dealt with jurisdiction over general offences on board—including those by drunken or unruly passengers. It also contained a provision (Art. 11) on unlawful seizure. The late 1960s saw the increase in hijacking as a form of political protest and the Hague Convention 1970 was agreed to create a specific offence of seizure (hijacking) of an aircraft. Obligations were put on States to prosecute or extradite offenders. The Montreal Convention 1971 dealt with the related question of attacks against passengers and crew and acts of sabotage, such as the placing of bombs on board aircraft. It is this Convention that could be used to punish bomb attacks such as the one against Pan Am Flight 103 which crashed on Lockerbie in 1988. The Montreal Convention covers in-flight violence as well as attacks on aircraft during pre-flight preparation. The Montreal Protocol 1988 was agreed to extend protection by regulating violence at airports generally.
   Separate Conventions deal with the taking of hostages (the New York Convention 1979)—such as occurred at the Munich Olympics in 1982—and attacks against heads of state (the UN Convention 1973). There have also been efforts to make easier the extradition of terrorists (see the European Convention 1977 produced by the Council of Europe).
   Conventions are not always a successful method of controlling aerial piracy. Indeed, in May 1990 a U.S. Presidential Commission appointed to look into the Lockerbie bombing concluded that the U.S. response to terrorism should be to launch pre-emptive and retaliatory strikes (like the one on Libya in 1986). It has been noted that it took six years for the Tokyo Convention 1963 to achieve the 12 ratifications necessary to bring it into force and yet arguably it represented customary international law (*McWhinney, op. cit.*, p. 116). Moreover, not all States have implemented the various Conventions they have signed so as to provide effective mechanisms of apprehension, prosecution or extradition (*ibid.*). It has been noted that the multilateral Conventions have not been particularly successful in controlling activities such as hijacking (*ibid.*, p. 62) and a number of bilateral or regional treaties have been adopted, for instance between the U.S. and Cuba. A further problem concerns the decision of what to do with the persons who are guilty of, for example, hijacking. There is not one single category of offender: some may be considered by Western countries as terrorists or political refugees, depending on where and why the hijack occurred.

U.K. legislation and aviation security
   Apart from general legislation relating to terrorism (such as the Prevention of Terrorism (Temporary Provisions) Act 1989), U.K. legislation has been produced to give effect to the various aviation security Conventions produced from time to time. Most provisions were consolidated in the Aviation Security Act 1982 and the Civil Aviation Act 1982, but a brief table is given below to indicate the main derivations.—

31–8

Tokyo Convention 1963 (the Tokyo Convention Act 1967, and now the Civil Aviation Act 1982).

Hague Convention 1970 (the Hijacking Act 1971, now the Aviation Security Act 1982).

Montreal Convention 1971 (the Protection of Aircraft Act 1973, now the Aviation Security Act 1982).

UN Convention 1973 (the Internationally Protected Persons Act 1978).

European Convention 1977 (the Suppression of Terrorism Act 1978).

New York Convention 1979 (the Taking of Hostages Act 1982).

The Aviation and Maritime Security Act 1990 Pt. I is mainly concerned with providing amendments to the Aviation Security Act 1982 (in effect the principal Act), although s.1 of the 1990 Act stands on its own. It is the latter that gives effect to the Montreal Protocol 1988.

The Transport Select Committee

In 1985–1986 the Transport Select Committee conducted an inquiry into aviation security and, following the loss of an Air India Boeing 747 off the coast of Ireland, produced a Report in October 1986. The majority of the Committee's recommendations were accepted by the Government in its Response in November 1986. The major criticism made by the 1986 Report was that there was a need for a properly co-ordinated and soundly organised national security programme underpinned by enforceable statutory powers and controlled by a central Departmental administration. It was unhappy with a piecemeal approach that concentrated on refining security practices in response to particular incidents, rather than developing the whole structure to meet changing demands. Indeed, the Presidential Commission appointed to look into the Lockerbie bombing concluded that the U.S. Federal Aviation Administration was preoccupied with responding to incidents rather than pre-empting them.

Following the Lockerbie disaster in 1988, the Committee decided to hold a follow-up inquiry to see if the various recommendations had been implemented and that implementation, in turn, had been monitored. The 1989 Report of the Committee concluded rather generally that the "call for new powers has tended to obscure the fact that existing ones were poorly used; there was a laxity in approach to security which gives us severe doubts as to whether our recommendations were fully implemented" (see para. 3). The accusation of administrative inactivity was obviously politically sensitive, as was indicated by Patrick McLoughlin, the Minister for Aviation and Shipping, in a letter to *The Independent* on February 1, 1990 (responding to a critical article on January 27, 1990). The Government's formal response to the 1989 Report listed in two Appendices a summary of the action taken in relation to each of the 1986 recommendations and other developments in the aviation security programme (see Government Observations, p. ix).

The impression of the Committee that existing powers were not being used was criticised by the Government on the basis that it was not fully explained. The difficulty no doubt faced by the Committee is that security is often satisfied by good practices rather than legislative activity. The Aviation Security Act 1982, as amended by the Aviation and Maritime Security Act 1990, leaves many of the details of security to be implemented by the Secretary of State through the means of Directions—as opposed to formal regulation by means of statutory instrument. It is beyond the scope of this note to enter the debate as to whether particular measures (such as the use of special machines) should be adopted (by means of Direction or otherwise), save to record where legislative suggestions were made. It should be noted that a recurring issue has been the question of exactly *who* is responsible for security.

The responsibility for security

Department of Transport. The DTp is the "appropriate authority" under international law to administer the national aviation security programme. The Aviation Security Act 1982 recognised that the Secretary of State had an important function in relation to aerodrome security by allowing him to request information and give Directions. It did not specify the Directions to be given, nor did it provide that the personnel to be responsible for security at airports would be public employees, such as the police or army.

The recruitment of security staff was largely to be a matter for the airports and airlines themselves. The denationalisation of the British Airports Authority and British Airways meant that security was in the hands of private, rather than public, employees where it could more easily be argued that the profit motive would be put before safety. Security staff are generally paid less in the private sector where there are no national pay agreements. Whether a Government gives clear Directions to an employer may be less important than whether they are carried out. Responsibility for supervising those handling day-to-day security is therefore a potentially important role for the DTp. The criticisms of it relate both to whether it should be performing a primary security function (for example by employing airport police) and as to the effectiveness of its supervisory rôle.

In 1986 the Association of Chief Police Officers had wanted the police to have ultimate control over security at airports. By 1989, the Select Committee Report noted that the Association had accepted that it was not necessary for the police to assume total control and that responsibility was better shared between themselves, the airport management and airport security personnel. This reversal of positions may have been for reasons of finance (who would pay), practicality (the police would not want to control all activities, including cargo loading), or administration (which authority would cover a particular airport). Whether divided control is a good idea in an emergency is open to doubt. The Opposition proposed an amendment to require a chief constable to designate an officer, of a rank not lower than chief superintendent, to have responsibility for airport security within the relevant police area. The amendment was defeated in Committee. The legislative scheme now is such that the DTp sets the framework and the Aviation Inspectorate is supposed to ensure the requirements are met. To an outsider, it seems to be an awkward system which may be prone to misunderstanding or neglect.

Private security services. As noted, the recruitment of security staff is largely to be a matter for the airports and airlines themselves. The Minister for Aviation and Shipping (Patrick McLoughlin) disclosed at Second Reading in the Commons that since 1988 the number of security staff at major airports has increased from 2,384 to 3,599 as a result of increased requirements imposed by Government Directions under the Aviation Security Act 1982. But the Government resisted all attempts to lay down detailed statutory rules on standards of training, recruitment methods, career structure, pay or employment conditions for aviation (or maritime) security staff. The objectives were to be set out in Directions and the detail would be imposed by the persons to whom the Directions were issued. Where private security firms are used for aviation security, Directions require that they must belong to the British Security Industry Association or the International Professional Security Organisation. Their contracts must also bind them to comply with the rules of these associations.

On May 22, 1990, while the Bill was still in the Lords, the House of Commons Defence Select Committee was highly critical of the performance of private security companies engaged in guarding Ministry of Defence (MOD) facilities (see the 6th Report, "The physical safety of military installations in the U.K.", 1989–90 H.C. 171; *The Independent*, June 23, 1990). Such military bases would include the Royal Marine School of Music, bombed by the IRA in September 1989. It was said that the use of low-paid guards from cheaper security firms meant that the MOD was sometimes offered a "consistently unsatisfactory and therefore potentially dangerous guarding service". Vetting procedures on personnel were "totally inadequate" and there was a high turnover of staff. The same concerns could apply to aerodromes (and ports) where the guards would not even be under the direct control of the DTp, or the immigration service of the Home Office: *cf.* N. South, *Policing for Profit: The Private Sector* (1988), 107. Yet, for the purposes of the Prevention of Terrorism (Temporary Provisions) Act 1989, the examining officers who have powers of search and detention are only police constables, immigration officers and customs and excise officers (see s.16 and Sched. 5). One might add that there is no clear framework for complaints against private security companies, equivalent to the Police Complaints Board (*cf.* the note to s.22, below). (See also the note on *Private security services* in the General Note to Pt. III, below).

Aviation Security Inspectorate. The 1986 Report criticised the DTp for relying on three aviation security "advisers" and recommended the setting up of a formal security inspectorate with appropriate numbers and powers. The 1989 Report noted that the DTp's advisers had been increased in number (from seven to 16) and reconstituted into an Aviation Security Inspectorate. It recommended that its head be the equivalent of a Chief Constable, but the Government was only prepared to constitute the post at Grade 6 level, despite criticism during Parliamentary debates. However, it did accept the recommendation that the Aviation Security Inspectorate be given the powers equivalent to those of the Health and Safety Executive and the Factory Inspectorate (for example under the Health and Safety at Work Act 1974). The realisation of this promise is mainly to be found in s.4.

Mechanism of control. It should be noted that the DTp has exercised control over security measures undertaken by airlines and airports by means of a mixture of statutory and administrative means. Use has been made of statutory Directions under Pt. II of the Aviation Security Act 1982 as well as informal Advice Circulars. (See below for more detail on Directions). One of the criticisms made by the 1986 Report was that the Circulars were used rather too often and the Government undertook to embody all the basic features of the aviation security programme in a comprehensive series of Directions. The 1989 Observations recorded that this project had been achieved. In addition to the Aviation Security Inspectorate there is a National Aviation Security Committee, which includes industry representatives. The DTp also issues an Aviation Security Handbook, which contains standards and codes of conduct.

Directions. The general power of the Secretary of State to give security Directions derives from Pt. II of the Aviation Security Act 1982 and s.14 in particular. Directions are served specifically on airport managers, U.K. airline operators and those foreign airlines operating from the U.K. The DTp does not normally send copies to other persons and it does not admit to a public definitive list. The Secretary of State did undertake in debates that the Inspectorate would make an annual report on Directions (and enforcement notices) which would be laid before the House (see *Hansard*, H.C. Vol. 164, col. 957, the Aviation Security Act 1982, s.23 and the note to s.44). But this contains statistical information only and is an "unprinted" paper available only from the House of Lords Record Office. Presumably, the justification for the policy of secrecy is to prevent details of security coming into the hands of potential terrorists. Nevertheless, it is of some concern that a form of legislation that might lead to a prosecution is not made public. The technique of issuing Directions rather than delegated legislation also means that Parliamentary scrutiny is avoided. See also *Civil Liberties* in the INTRODUCTION, above.

A package of 'security measures relating to the control of access to airports and aircraft was contained in new and consolidated Directions issued to airports and airlines in April 1989 (see DTp Press Notice No. 158, April 6, 1989). The new Directions required passes to restricted areas to be issued only after references had been checked; staff to wear passes conspicuously (or be subject to disciplinary action); restricted areas to be patrolled; passengers' baggage to be protected from unauthorised access; aircraft to be security checked before flights; access to aircraft to be strictly controlled once checks have been done.

It seems that Directions are intended to be general in nature. If the DTp feels that a Direction is not being complied with satisfactorily, more specific "enforcement notices" could be brought into effect. These are now made possible by s.4 of the 1990 Act. There was some dissatisfaction expressed by the aviation industry with the generality of Directions: it would have preferred them to be more detailed. The Government's expressed view was that it would be inappropriate for the DTp to undertake this task as it did not have the experience of the industry. There is some inconsistency here, as the DTp inspectors must be thought to have sufficient knowledge to issue the enforcement notices. The rather laissez-faire approach also means that there will not necessarily be consistency between practices at individual airports around the country and there is the suspicion that the reluctance to be involved in the detail stems from a desire to avoid the administrative expense involved. As it is, the industry must rely on the general guidance contained in the Aviation Security Handbook.

The power of the Secretary of State to give Directions relating to matters required to be done overseas is a sensitive one, as the responsibility for security rests usually with the host government. However, it is clear that under s.14 of the Aviation Security Act 1982 it is possible to give Directions to British airlines to take security measures themselves, if the foreign government was not so doing. These powers are subject to the limitations in s.16(5) of the Aviation Security Act 1982 and the Government resisted an attempt to restrict its powers still further (see the note to Sched. 1, para. 8).

Consultation. There is no express obligation on the Secretary of State to consult aviation interests before issuing a Direction, and an amendment to the Bill to this effect (supported by the industry) was not accepted. One of the reasons was that it would oblige the DTp to consult some 50 aerodrome managers and about 250 aircraft operators (of which only about 40 are British), not counting those other bodies to whom Directions can now be given. The logical difficulty with this explanation is that the essence of the Direction system is that the expertise lies with those in the industry rather than the DTp. It seems paradoxical, therefore, to make Directions without consulting the local experts (or a cross-section of industry) as to their suitability. The answer may lie in the functions of Directions, which are designed to be general in nature, leaving the detailed implementation to the industry, subject to the control of inspectors who may issue enforcement notices under the new s.18A of the Aviation Security Act 1982 (as inserted by s.4 of the 1990 Act). There is, however, a limited duty to consult the Civil Aviation Authority before certain enforcement notices are issued (see s.18A(3) of the Aviation Security Act 1982, as inserted by s.4 of the 1990 Act).

Financing of security measures

Security costs. The increased security needed at airports costs money and concern has been expressed that the industry was reluctant to pay for expensive new machinery, for example for the detection of explosives. Although the Government increased the number of Inspectors and doubled the Aviation Security Research and Development budget, it refused to reestablish an Aviation Security Fund. Such a Fund had been established in 1978 under the Civil Aviation Act 1978 (and continued by Pt. IV of the Aviation Security Act 1982). Its purpose was to reimburse aerodrome operators, airlines and public authorities for security expenses. One advantage was said to be that it helped small airports to receive subsidies from the larger airports to finance expensive security measures. The Government abolished the Fund in 1983 (see the Aviation Security Act 1982 s.36; and S.I. Nos. 1983/81 and 1983/1644). Its reintroduction, financed by a levy on passengers, was strongly urged by the 1986 and 1989 Reports and by the Opposition during debates. The Government reiterated (in the 1989 Observations and in debates) that it considered the Fund was bureaucratic and expensive. It required levies per passenger to be set, airport charges collected, payments made to the Government, claims for reimbursement to be made and for them to be assessed and paid by the DTp. To reinstate the Fund was said to cost £50,000 a year. The Government view was that works should be financed by the airport authorities themselves. These are currently charged to airlines as part of the general ground handling charge, although the airlines have complained that they have no means of knowing the true cost of the security element.

The Government defeated an Opposition amendment at Report stage in the Commons that would have allowed the Secretary of State to reimburse directly those who incurred security expenses at airports. It was only at this stage that the Minister for Public Transport, Mr Portillo, reminded the House of the residuary provisions of s.32 of the Aviation Security Act 1982 that had remained after the repeal of the Aviation Security Fund (see generally the note to Sched. 1, para. 17). Accordingly the *power* exists to reimburse certain security expenses of the aviation industry out of general public funds. The Minister made it quite clear that the Government had no intention of exercising the powers, although updating amendments to them are made (see Sched. 1, para. 17, below).

The Government approach means that, ultimately, the costs of security will be borne by the passenger (and cargo owner) rather than the general taxpayer. This is apparently contrary to the practice of continental Europe, where security responsibilities largely fall on the police forces, although elsewhere in the Western world airlines often have to pay for security.

Costs at regional airports. The Government also resisted a more limited amendment at the Committee stage in the Lords which would have encouraged the Secretary of State to subsidise smaller airports. Many regional airports are operated by public airport companies as subsidiaries of local authorities under the Airports Act 1986. These local airports were particularly concerned about drastic increases in costs. Lord Underhill, for the Opposition, noted that the costs of security measures were not directly related to passenger throughput. He gave examples of the costs to some regional airports of implementing some of the post-Lockerbie Directions (*Hansard*, H.L. Vol. 518, col. 859). Birmingham airport has paid £86,000 in capital costs and will pay £514,000 for the running costs of additional safety requirements in the current year; East Midlands Airport has had capital expenditure of £405,000 and has current operating costs of £260,000. The equivalents for Luton Airport were £364,000 and £414,000. Lord Underhill noted that passengers at these airports might be paying disproportionately more per head than those flying from larger airports—a potential discouragement to the development of regional airports. The Government view was that a cost for security of £1–2 per head at smaller airports was not excessive. The cost of security per head at other airports is: 23.2p at Heathrow, 19.5p at Gatwick, 71p at Stansted, 21p at Glasgow and 18p at Edinburgh (*Hansard*, H.L. Vol. 518, col. 862).

JACOLA was also concerned that central Government restrictions on local government spending might affect the ability of such authorities to provide adequate security at their airports.

The cost-security balance. The question of security legislation is affected by significant uncertainties about the correct way to make travel safer in fact. The 1990 Act tightens the control which the Government can exercise, but it does not resolve the underlying technical problems, such as how to detect bombs. There is much dispute about whether to install sophisticated detection equipment, for example relying on thermal neutron analysis (TNA). The 1986 Government Response noted that the cost of installing banding machines for luggage at every check-in would be £4,500 each. Moreover, physical modifications would be required and there would be difficulties with power supplies.

However, there can be large commercial costs to the industry if it fails to take adequate security measures. The Lockerbie disaster is reported to have cost Pan Am $250 million in losses and undermined the travelling public's confidence in the airline (*The Independent*, May 11, 1990).

It must be asserted that there is no such thing as absolute security—transport would not be possible if it was required. All decisions about security standards and legislation involve difficult questions of balancing. One of the central factors in this balancing process inevitably concerns costs. It is not a matter which can be readily asserted in a debate, but safety and commercial factors are intertwined. Every delay in boarding and loading aircraft and ships will increase costs. It is possible to search every passenger and piece of luggage—but hardly practicable. The goal is therefore to find a workable system of security that will not undermine the efficiency of the transport system. The Government approach to the matter of the balance between security and cost-effectiveness has been that it "would not be right to introduce measures which would be costly to implement but which would not generally produce significant security benefits" (Government Response 1986, p. vii). In the past it has been suggested that the balance has been tipped too heavily in favour of the commercial interests. It is widely recognised that the Israeli airline El Al has the strictest security of all, but other larger airlines are less willing to incur the costs and delays in having identical systems.

A further general problem is that one country cannot act alone, as the main responsibility for security falls on the country of departure.

Particular security problems

Screening of passengers. The April 1989 Directions required that authorised persons be searched before entry into restricted areas to the same standards as passengers. Articles carried by them were also to be searched to the same standard as passenger's baggage (DTp Press Notice No. 158). Airlines such as El Al have also developed techniques of profiling passengers in order to pick up likely terrorists or "dupes" who are persuaded by the terrorists to take on board seemingly innocuous packages. Screening came too late for the victims of the Abu Nidal attack on Rome airport as the terrorists struck at the El Al and TWA check-in counters.

Screening of unaccompanied baggage. At Lockerbie a bomb was inserted in a cassette recorder carried in a suitcase thought to have been transferred from a feeder flight. In May 1990 a US Presidential Commission appointed to look into the Lockerbie bombing concluded that a major security breach was involved when Pan Am decided to allow unaccompanied luggage on its flights without searches (*The Independent*, May 16, 1990). Following Lockerbie the Secretary of State for Transport revealed that hold baggage to be carried in U.S. airlines to the U.S.A. is checked 100% and a proportion of hold baggage on other aircraft is searched at random. One of the concerns after Lockerbie was that airlines might be allowing unaccompanied baggage from feeder flights to be loaded, provided that it cleared X-ray checks (see *The Independent*, March 1, 1990).

The Opposition tried unsuccessfully to insert an amendment at Committee stage in the Commons that would have required airport managers to ensure that all transfer baggage was examined, electronically or otherwise. The Government view was that TNA machines were still being tested and that the better and more flexible mechanism was that of the Direction under the Aviation Security Act 1982. It had already accepted in its 1989 Observations that the U.K. should move to the screening of all transfer baggage (although not necessarily by the use of TNA machines). The criticism in debates was that there was no time limit stated for implementation of its undertaking. Nevertheless, it was reported in April 1990 that there was resistance amongst airlines to being forced to X-ray all luggage (*The Independent*, April 29, 1990). The Government also rejected an amendment that would have obliged airports to set aside space for carrying out security measures, for example searches.

Cargo. The 1989 Report noted (p. 8) that there was a gap in security responsibility where air cargo was concerned as the airlines relied on "known senders". This could enable the airline to abdicate responsibility. The Government agreed (Government's Observations, p. viii) to work with ICAO to develop a code of practice whereby cargo has to originate from registered suppliers with proven records of reliability. See also s.6.

Vetting of airport staff generally. Some idea of the scale of the security problem posed by checking airport staff is indicated by the fact that 80,000 employees, as well as thousands of vehicles, have access to the four largest airports in the U.K. After the Lockerbie bombing, a number of well-publicised breaches of security at airports were highlighted by journalists posing as airport employees. It is important to ensure that *all* airport staff having access to aircraft and cargo are suitable, not simply those whose function is to question passengers. The 1989 Directions tried to ensure that no one has a pass which allows them unescorted access to restricted areas of airports until their references have been checked. The 1989 Report noted that there was little incentive for employers to check the backgrounds of employees, particularly where there is a high turnover of staff. (See also the previous note on *Private security services*).

The Government accepted in 1989 that it was essential to improve the security vetting of airport staff (Government Observations, p. ix). S.3 of the Act allows the Inspectorate to require any contractor at the airport to satisfy it about the vetting of its staff and s.4 allows enforcement notices to be issued.

Vetting of security staff. The 1989 Report (para. 3) regarded the reliance on self-regulation and codes of practice as inadequate for the recruitment of staff for tasks which form part of the aviation security programme. There was again unease at the rôle of private security firms. The 1989 Report recommended that the Rehabilitation of Offenders Act 1974 be amended to force disclosure of criminal backgrounds by persons applying for security jobs. The Government seemed content to rely on its insistence that the security companies were members of appropriate trade associations (Government Observations, p. ix).

Searching of airport staff. Concern was raised in debates about the number of people exempt from searches. In debates it was suggested that some 40,000 people daily have airside passes at Heathrow. Of the security staff at Heathrow some 15,000 people are technically exempt, along with some 300 others, including Special Branch officers, vets and airport health officials, as well as 700–800 immigration officers, 700–800 customs officials and 500 police.

Issuing of passes. The difficulty of allocating responsibility between the airport authorities and the DTp is illustrated by a dispute about the issuing of passes. The 1989 Report recommended that the DTp's Aviation Security Inspectorate decide on the categories of airport worker who should receive passes. The Government's Observations indicated that the Department was not qualified to judge this matter (p. ix). All it could do was receive periodic reports. Decisions on the issuing of passes would be left to the airport operator. At Second Reading in the Commons, the Secretary of State for Transport confirmed his announcement of April 1989 that from April 1990 there would be electronic checking of all passes at 19 airports.

Detectability of explosives. The Lockerbie bombing is thought to have been caused by the Czech explosive Semtex, which is virtually impossible to detect. In 1989, the U.K. and Czechoslovakia proposed to the ICAO Council that a new legal instrument be developed requiring explosives to be marked in order to make them detectable. A sub-committee of the ICAO Legal Committee was established and, after a meeting in January 1990, it produced a draft Convention on the Marking of Explosives for the Purpose of Detection. It seems unlikely that any Convention will contain penal provisions as the manufacture of explosives is largely undertaken by State authorities. Specific amendments to the U.K. legislation will probably not be needed as the Convention will impose obligations on State Parties.

Endangering safety at aerodromes

Endangering safety at aerodromes

1.—(1) It is an offence for any person by means of any device, substance or weapon intentionally to commit at an aerodrome serving international civil aviation any act of violence which—

(a) causes or is likely to cause death or serious personal injury, and

(b) endangers or is likely to endanger the safe operation of the aerodrome or the safety of persons at the aerodrome.

(2) It is also, subject to subsection (4) below, an offence for any person by means of any device, substance or weapon unlawfully and intentionally—

(a) to destroy or seriously to damage—

(i) property used for the provision of any facilities at an aerodrome serving international civil aviation (including any apparatus or equipment so used), or

(ii) any aircraft which is at such an aerodrome but is not in service, or

(b) to disrupt the services of such an aerodrome,

in such a way as to endanger or be likely to endanger the safe operation of the aerodrome or the safety of persons at the aerodrome.

(3) Except as provided by subsection (4) below, subsections (1) and (2) above apply whether any such act as is referred to in those subsections is committed in the United Kingdom or elsewhere and whatever the nationality of the person committing the act.

(4) Subsection (2)(a)(ii) above does not apply to any act committed in relation to an aircraft used in military, customs or police service unless—

(a) the act is committed in the United Kingdom, or

(b) where the act is committed outside the United Kingdom, the person committing it is a United Kingdom national.

(5) A person who commits an offence under this section is liable on conviction on indictment to imprisonment for life.

(6) Sections 38(3)(b) (period during which aircraft in service) and 38(4) (territorial waters) of the Aviation Security Act 1982 apply for the purposes of this section as they apply for the purposes of that Act; and the references in section 38(7) of that Act (other proceedings) to Part I of that Act and to that Act include references to this section.

(7) Proceedings for an offence under this section shall not be instituted—

(a) in England and Wales, except by, or with the consent of, the Attorney General, and

(b) in Northern Ireland, except by, or with the consent of, the Attorney General for Northern Ireland.

(8) As respects Scotland, for the purpose of conferring on the sheriff jurisdiction to entertain proceedings for an offence under this section, any such offence shall, without prejudice to any jurisdiction exercisable apart from this subsection, be deemed to have been committed in any place in Scotland where the offender may for the time being be.

(9) In this section—

"act of violence" means—

(a) any act done in the United Kingdom which constitutes the offence of murder, attempted murder, manslaughter, culpable homicide or assault or an offence under section 18, 20, 21, 22, 23, 24, 28 or 29 of the Offences against the Person Act 1861 or under section 2 of the Explosive Substances Act 1883, and

(b) any act done outside the United Kingdom which, if done in the United Kingdom, would constitute such an offence as is mentioned in paragraph (a) above,

"aerodrome" has the same meaning as in the Civil Aviation Act 1982,

"military service" and "United Kingdom national" have the same meaning as in the Aviation Security Act 1982; and

"unlawfully"—

(a) in relation to the commission of an act in the United Kingdom, means so as (apart from this section) to constitute an offence under the law of the part of the United Kingdom in which the act is committed, and

(b) in relation to the commission of an act outside the United Kingdom, means so that the commission of the act would (apart from this section) have been an offence under the law of England and Wales if it had been committed in England and Wales or of Scotland if it had been committed in Scotland.

DEFINITIONS

"act of violence": subs. (9).
"aerodrome": subs. (9) and the Aviation Security Act 1982, s.38(1).
"England": Interpretation Act 1978, Sched. 1.
"military service": subs. (9) and the Aviation Security Act 1982, s.38(1).
"United Kingdom": Interpretation Act 1978, Sched. 1.
"United Kingdom national": subs. (9) and the Aviation Security Act 1982, s.38(1).
"unlawfully": subs. (9).
"Wales": Interpretation Act 1978, Sched. 1.

GENERAL NOTE

This section gives effect to the Montreal Protocol 1988 by creating offences, punishable by life imprisonment, in relation to terrorist activity at an aerodrome. (For terrorist attacks against aircraft, see the Aviation Security Act 1982, Pt. I).

Hoaxes

The Opposition tried unsuccessfully to insert a provision that would make hoax calls an offence under this section. Four types of false callers were identified in Committee: (i) the would-be terrorist (the person who might carry out an attack and threatens to); (ii) the blackmailer; (iii) the hoaxer and (iv) the would-be passenger who wants to delay an aircraft (as he himself is late). The Montreal Protocol 1988 did not deal with such situations nor, specifically, does the 1990 Act. The issue goes to the heart of legislation such as the present. It is really designed for the worst kind of international terrorist event for which life imprisonment might be an appropriate punishment. The hoaxer was excluded from s.1 mainly because there are other offences that might apply: indeed, many violent acts covered by s.1 itself would already be offences under other provisions. The ministerial justification for s.1 as a whole is significant. The section seeks to reorder offences already known in order to settle matters of jurisdiction, extradition and severity of penalty. Ultimately, a distinction is made in s.1 between threats and attacks. There is no distinction made between hoax calls about aircraft and those involving ships, or public buildings such as the Palace of Westminster. It seems unlikely that hoaxes could be considered as attempts, within the Criminal Attempts Act 1981, to commit offences under s.1, although it is possible that a would-be terrorist might be prosecuted for preparatory acts.

There are a number of existing offences that the hoaxers could commit, of which the most significant is perhaps the Criminal Law Act 1977, s.51 (bomb hoaxes). This offence had been recommended by the Law Commission in *Conspiracies to effect a public mischief and to commit a civil wrong*, W.P. No. 63 (1975), paras. 18–25 and endorsed in its *Report on conspiracy and criminal law reform*, No. 76 (1976), paras. 4.13–4.19. Other offences applying to hoaxes could include: the Criminal Law Act 1967, s.5(2) (wasting police time); the Offences against the Person Act 1861, s.47 (causing an apprehension of assault and uttering threats to assault); the Offences against the Person Act 1861 s.16 (threats to kill); the Criminal Damage Act 1971, s.2 (threats to destroy or damage property); the Theft Act 1968, s.21 (blackmail); the Telecommunications Act 1984, s.43 (improper use of public telecommunications system); the Fire Services Act 1947, s.31 (false fire alarm); the 1990 Act, s.5 (false statements relating to baggage). It has been reported that a man has been charged with an offence under s.3 of the Aviation Security Act 1982 (acts endangering the safety of aircraft) in respect of a bomb scare involving a Pan Am Boeing 747 (*The Independent*, June 7, 1990). Where there is an overlap in the possible offences that might be charged it will be a question for the relevant prosecuting authorities whether to use s.1 of the 1990 Act, or the other legislation listed above. It is not the practice to prosecute *all* jokesters. During the passage of the Bill a Government Minister was cautioned for claiming to Heathrow Security Officers that his red box contained explosives.

Where a hoax call is made to a U.K. airport from abroad, difficult questions of jurisdiction arise. There may be an offence committed in the U.K., but it would appear that there would be no extradition possible for most of the offences listed above, for example for offences under the Criminal Law Act 1967, or the Telecommunications Act 1984 (see Standing Committee A, cols. 37–38). The Government undertook to take up this matter with ICAO with a view to ensuring that prosecutions took place in the countries where the call was made. There could be extradition for an offence under s.51(4) of the Criminal Law Act 1977, as a five year prison sentence is possible for that offence. See also s.49, below.

There may also be the threat of a civil action for damages in the case of the passenger who makes a hoax call in order to delay an aircraft. British Airways is reported to be considering suing such passengers after a delay at Geneva airport resulted in a £30,000 loss.

Subs. (1)

Derivation: Montreal Protocol 1988 Art. II(1).

This subsection creates an offence of causing death or serious personal injury by specified acts of violence which endanger the safe operation of aerodromes (or the safety of persons at aerodromes). It is aimed at the terrorist who plants a bomb in an airport restaurant, or who opens fire at passengers standing at a check-in counter (as at Rome in December 1985). There must be four elements: (i) an intention to commit one of the serious personal offences listed in subs. (7); (ii) the use of some instrument; (iii) death or serious injury and (iv) danger to the airport or persons at it.

"*Intentionally*". The *mens rea* seems to relate to the act of violence and not to the consequences specified in paras. (a) or (b). This is also the effect of Art. II(1) of the Montreal Protocol. It is apparently not necessary that the defendant intends to cause death, injury or danger.

"*International civil aviation*". The international requirement derives from the Montreal Protocol, where it was included partly because of the ability to prosecute for offences committed on the territory of another state and also because of the need to have some limit over state jurisdiction. In the case of local airports, it may be difficult to decide whether they do "serve" international aviation. Does this refer to regular, scheduled flights, occasional charter services or leisure flights? A court would be entitled to look to the general purposes of the Chicago Convention 1944 and the Civil Aviation Act 1982. It is submitted that an aerodrome would fall within the definition if, at the time of the offence, international scheduled or charter passenger flights left from there, albeit infrequently. Where there is doubt as to the correct status of an airport it may be better to bring a prosecution under a pre-existing provision (such as the Criminal Damage Act 1971).

"*Device, substance or weapon*". The defendant must have used some instrument to commit the offence. This could be a grenade or gun, or some form of bomb. The expressions "device" and "substance" are so wide that they could cover items which are not apparently dangerous in themselves, such as an umbrella. It is possible, but unlikely, that an umbrella could cause serious personal injury. What is clear is that an individual does not commit an offence if he creates a disturbance by, for instance, running up and down and shouting.

It is possible to construct an argument that as a telephone is a "device", hoax calls resulting in danger to an aerodrome could be caught. However, it is difficult to see how one can use the telephone intentionally to commit the acts of violence specified in subs. (9), and it is the message given that causes the disruption rather than the physical medium by which the message is transmitted. It is submitted that the section was not intended to cover hoax calls (and see the General Note to the section, above).

"Likely to cause". The expression "likely to cause" has often been used in legislation and has been the subject of judicial decision, especially under the Road Traffic and Factories Acts (see for example the Road Traffic Act 1930, s.50 [now the Road Traffic Act 1988, s.24] and *Maguire* v. *Crouch* [1941] 1 K.B. 108). In *Bennington* v. *Peter* [1984] R.T.R. 383, Woolf J., at p. 392, accepted the following interpretation of the expression in the Heavy Goods Vehicles (Drivers' Licences) Regulations 1977:

"An event which is likely may be an event which is probable but it may also be an event which, while not probable, could well happen. But it must be more than a bare possibility."

Similarly, in *Bailey* v. *Rolls Royce (1971)* [1984] I.C.R. 688 the Court of Appeal considered s.72(1) of the Factories Act 1961. May L.J., at p. 699, considered that "likely" is the equivalent of "probable", or "more possibly than not" and certainly more than merely "possible". Slade L.J., at p. 700, and Stephenson L.J. at p. 702, rejected the idea that "likely to cause injury" means "foreseeably likely"—involving knowledge on the part of an employer of the possibility of injury. It is an objective test of likelihood which would therefore seem to require some degree of probability, rather than a mere remote possibility, that the stated event would occur. It may be that, in assessing the likelihood of injury, a court is not required to take into account some latent condition of the person injured or killed (*cf. Whitfield* v. *H & R Johnson (Tiles)*, *The Independent*, April 9, 1990—also decided on s.72(1) of the 1961 Act).

"Serious personal injury". This is not separately defined, but the emphasis on serious indicates the type of harm regulated by the offences listed in subs. (9).

"Endanger the safe operation". The word "danger" more naturally refers to people rather than functions, but its use here might seem to require something more than mere inconvenience, or hindrance. The intention seems to require some more general effect on the airport than upon the individual injured or killed. The Montreal Protocol 1988 simply refers to endangering "safety" and the references to "operation" and "persons" are Parliamentary additions.

Virtually anything could endanger the "safe operation" of an airport, but the provision is presumably designed to include attacks on airport personnel such as traffic controllers or firemen. Arguably, the definition of an act of violence (see subs. (9)) means that a minor assault on an air traffic controller would not be an offence under s.1 even if it did have the effect of endangering the safety of incoming aircraft.

The reference to "safety of persons" is presumably designed to distinguish between serious attacks on an individual (which would already be offences) from those which are likely to affect the safety of persons generally. If a terrorist machine-gunned a line of passengers and then surrendered immediately, it could be said that there was no further danger created beyond the original offences against the person. It would seem odd if he were not caught by the subsection in such circumstances, given the general objects of the legislation (and see also the preamble to the Montreal Protocol, referred to below, mentioning passenger confidence). It might be acceptable to give a wide meaning to para. (b) as such serious attacks would necessarily create a full scale security alert which itself could cause danger to others or affect the operation of the airport.

Minor offences. It should be noted that throughout Pts. I and II of the Act there are instances where it is possible to take the widest meaning of words in order to penalise conduct which might have little to do with terrorism. There will undoubtedly be duplication with existing offences and the threat of a potential life sentence is mitigated by the prosecuting discretion (see for example subs. (7)). In some cases it might be possible to persuade a judge to limit the scope of a particular offence by making reference to the general context of the Act and the Conventions which it enacts. For example, it should be possible to refer to the preamble to the Montreal Protocol 1988. This notes that the acts of violence to be penalised by s.1 "undermine the confidence of the peoples of the world in safety at such airports and disturb the safe and orderly conduct of civil aviation for all states" and "that the occurrence of such acts is a matter of grave concern to the international community and that, for the purpose of deterring such acts, there is an urgent need to provide appropriate measures for punishment of offenders". Such considerations might indicate that the person who is merely making a nuisance of himself should not be subject to prosecution under the subsection.

Subs. (2)

This subsection creates an offence for attacks on physical objects, such as the airport runway, as opposed to people. There must be more than minor acts of vandalism, such as creating graffiti. But there is no requirement that there be some sort of ulterior terrorist intent (see the discussion of "*Intentionally*", below). Nevertheless, apparently minor acts of vandalism, such as the defacing of notices, could have serious consequences (for example if a pilot followed a course to the wrong runway).

"Intentionally". Art. II(1) of the Montreal Protocol appears to relate the intention to the destruction, damage or disruption (here in paras. (a) and (b)) and not to any danger which is

consequent. It should not have to be proved that the defendant intended to endanger safety at the aerodrome. The rewording that has taken place in the U.K. Act ("intentionally ... to destroy ... in such a way as to endanger ...") might seem to link the intention to the consequence. If so, the *mens rea* is different from that in subs. (1), above—a result that would seem quite contrary to the Protocol. It is submitted that the proper interpretation of this subsection is that the prosecution do not need to show that the defendant intended, for instance, destruction *and* danger to the safety of the aerodrome.

"*Unlawfully*". The expression, defined in subs. (9), appears in the Protocol. (*Cf.* subs. (1), where it is omitted, as acts of violence are defined in subs. (7) in relation to specific U.K. offences).

"*Property used for the provision of any facilities*". The Protocol simply referred to "facilities", and it may have been thought necessary to refer to property in order to make it clear that something tangible must be destroyed, rather than something intangible, such as a sense of well-being. Property here seems to refer more to buildings, but the specific reference to apparatus and equipment means that the widest meaning can be given. Included would be communication and safety equipment, as well as leisure or recreational facilities provided for passengers. However, the damage or destruction has to endanger safety at the airport.

"*Aircraft not in service*". "In service" is defined by s.38(3) of the Aviation Security Act 1982 (derived from Art. 2(b) of the Montreal Convention). Subs. (6), below, extends that definition to this section. It includes (in addition to flying time) the period which begins with the pre-flight preparation of the aircraft for a specific flight and ends 24 hours after the aircraft lands having completed that flight. This would include aircraft on the ground in transit (with passengers aboard) and those undergoing temporary repairs at a terminal. It would exclude, for example, the time when an aircraft is stored in a hanger, before being prepared for a flight. The point about whether a plane is, or is not, "in service" under this subsection is largely academic as the Aviation Security Act 1982, s.2 creates a parallel offence in relation to aircraft which are in service.

"*Disrupt the services*". Subs. (1) requires an act of violence to be committed at an aerodrome, and subs. (2), para. (a) requires the relevant property to be destroyed or damaged at an aerodrome, but there is apparently no requirement that disruption of services is actually instigated from within the boundaries of the aerodrome itself. The services envisaged are presumably those such as the fire brigade, or the telecommunications systems. The latter could be disrupted by the cutting of wires outside the airport perimeter. The former could be diverted away from the airport by the starting of a fire outside the airport. In both cases an offence could be committed. For hoax telephone calls, see the discussion on "device" in subs. (1), above.

Subss. (3) and (4)
Consistent with the philosophy of the Montreal Convention, and the Protocol, the airport offences can be committed in any country and by any national, whether British or not. The exceptions to this wide jurisdiction are contained in subs. (4) and reflect Art. 4(1) of the Montreal Convention, which excludes aircraft used in military, customs or police services. States are free to create equivalent offences in their own law, subject to the usual jurisdictional restrictions, limited by reference to place or nationality. This course of action has already been undertaken by the U.K. in the Aviation Security Act 1982 (see s.1(2) (hijacking), s.2(4) (endangering aircraft), and s.3(5) (endangering air navigation facilities)). For the purposes of para. (a), the "United Kingdom" includes U.K. territorial waters (as defined in the Territorial Sea Act 1987): see subs. (6), extending the operation of s.38(4) of the Aviation Security Act 1982.

Subs. (5)
Art. 3 of the Montreal Convention obliges States to make the various offences punishable by "severe" penalties. The Aviation Security Act 1982 and the 1990 Act make the offences punishable by life imprisonment.

Other proceedings. S.38(7) of the Aviation Security Act 1982 provides that the relevant Part of the Act shall not be construed as (a) conferring a right of action in any civil proceedings in respect of contravention of the 1982 Act, or (b) derogating from any right of action or any other remedy (whether civil or criminal) in proceedings instituted otherwise than under the Act. The present subsection applies the same rule to s.1. Thus, an airport's rights to sue a person damaging facilities would continue to depend on the general law, for example relating to trespass and negligence, rather than on any new statutory duty that could be implied from the section.

Subs. (6)
This subsection extends the operation of various definitions in the Aviation Security Act 1982 to this section. See s.1(2)(a)(ii), above, on "in service", and subss. (3) and (4), above, on territorial waters.

Subss. (7) and (8)

In common with other recent statutes creating serious offences (see, for example, the Merchant Shipping Act 1988, s.30(8)), it is provided that the consent of a relevant law officer (in England and Wales, the Attorney-General) is required before a prosecution. The subsection prevents private prosecutions being brought, for example by the relatives of persons killed in a bomb attack. Private prosecutions are not allowed in Scotland in any event, hence the absence of a reference to the Lord Advocate. Subs. (8) has the purpose of conferring jurisdiction on the sheriff where it might not otherwise exist (for example, in relation to offences committed abroad).

Subs. (9)

"Act of violence". The use of "means" rather than "includes" restricts the expression "act of violence" only to those rather serious offences listed. These include wounding and serious bodily harm (ss.18, 20 of the Offences against the Person Act 1861), strangling (s.21), administering drugs or poison (ss.22, 23, 24) and causing explosions or throwing corrosive fluid (ss.28, 29). "Assault" is included, even though no specific reference is made to s.47 of the Offences against the Person Act 1861 (common assaults occasioning actual bodily harm). *Cf.* the Aviation Security Act 1982 s.10(2), which is slightly wider in scope.

"Aerodrome". The Protocol uses the expression "airport", but the 1990 Act refers throughout to "aerodrome", as this is the rather quaint terminology used in Pt. II of the Civil Aviation Act 1982 (and defined in s.105 of that Act: *cf.* s.88 in Pt. IV).

Powers of Secretary of State and authorised persons

Extension of power to require promotion of searches

2. After section 13 of the Aviation Security Act 1982 there is inserted—

"Power to require other persons to promote searches

13A.—(1) For purposes to which this Part of this Act applies, the Secretary of State may give a direction to any person (other than the manager of an aerodrome) who—

(a) occupies any land forming part of an aerodrome in the United Kingdom, or

(b) is permitted to have access to a restricted zone of such an aerodrome for the purposes of the activities of a business carried on by him,

requiring him to use his best endeavours to secure that such searches to which this section applies as are specified in the direction are carried out by constables or by other persons of a description specified in the direction.

(2) The searches to which this section applies are—

(a) in relation to a person falling within subsection (1)(a) above, searches—

(i) of the land which he occupies within the aerodrome, and

(ii) of persons or property which may at any time be on that land, and

(b) in relation to a person falling within subsection (1)(b) above, searches—

(i) of any land which he occupies outside the aerodrome for the purposes of his business, and

(ii) of persons or property which may at any time be on that land.

(3) Any person who, without reasonable excuse, fails to comply with a direction given to him under this section shall be guilty of an offence and liable—

(a) on summary conviction, to a fine not exceeding the statutory maximum;

(b) on conviction on indictment, to a fine or to imprisonment for a term not exceeding two years, or to both.

(4) Where a person is convicted of an offence under subsection (3) above, then, if without reasonable excuse the failure in respect of which he was convicted is continued after the conviction, he shall be guilty of a further offence and liable on summary conviction to a fine not exceeding one-tenth of level 5 on the standard scale for each day on which the failure continues."

DEFINITIONS
"aerodrome": Aviation Security Act 1982, s.38(1).
"land": Interpretation Act 1978, Sched. 1.
"person permitted": Aviation Security Act 1982, s.24A(2) (as created by Sched. 1, para. 16 of the 1990 Act).
"purposes to which this Part of this Act applies": Aviation Security Act 1982, s.10(1).
"restricted zone": Aviation Security Act 1982, s.24A (as created by Sched. 1, para. 16 of the 1990 Act).
"Secretary of State": Interpretation Act 1978, Sched. 1.
"standard scale": Criminal Justice Act 1982, s.74.
"statutory maximum": Criminal Justice Act 1982, s.74.
"United Kingdom": Interpretation Act 1978, Sched. 1.

GENERAL NOTE
Promoting searches. S.13 of the Aviation Security Act 1982 allowed the Secretary of State to give Directions requiring aerodrome managers to promote searches at aerodromes. Following various journalistic exposés of lapses in airport security at Heathrow, the Secretary of State issued new Directions under s.14 of the Aviation Security Act 1982 requiring the searching of staff and vehicles as they go airside (see the 1989 Report, p. 9). A number of exceptions were anticipated in respect of officials such as police (Government 1989 Response, p. ix).
It was obviously thought that the powers under s.13 were not wide enough. S.2 of the Aviation and Maritime Security Act 1990 extends the power to require searches by creating a new s.13A of the Aviation Security Act 1982. This allows Directions to be issued to persons other than aerodrome managers. The idea is to make sure that searches are undertaken in respect of the host of persons who have access to an airport in order to perform ancillary services.
See the General Note to Pt. I, above, on *"Directions"*. See also s.22, below, for the maritime equivalent of the new s.13A.

New s.13A(1) of the Aviation Security Act 1982
Persons on whom Directions may be served. Two distinct categories of person will now find that they may be subject to Directions. The first category comprises persons who actually occupy land at an aerodrome, such as airlines, caterers, repairers and freight forwarders. Para. (a) specifically refers to occupiers, rather than owners. The Direction would be served on a tenant, rather than a landlord. The wide definition of "land" in the Interpretation Act 1978, Sched. 1 means that occupiers of buildings on land are covered, as are, presumably, those who occupy part of a building, such as the shop-keepers within an airport terminal.
The second category consists of those persons who do not actually have premises at the airport, but who have access to the most sensitive areas of it. The phrasing of the new s.13A(1)(b) is very wide and the reference to "any person" could include even casual business visitors. Sched. 1 to the Interpretation Act 1978 would indicate that the reference to "person" would include bodies corporate. This would be particularly relevant to the discussion on the new s.13A(2)(b), below. The wording of the section (for example the reference to "manager") might indicate that it is directed towards a natural person so that it could be argued that there is a "contrary intention" (within s.5 of the 1978 Act), resulting in the exclusion of bodies corporate. It is doubtful if such an argument would be correct, particularly as the definition of "person permitted" (in s.24A(2) of the Aviation Security Act 1982, as created by Sched. 1, para. 16 of the 1990 Act) contemplates both employers and employees.
The Government refused to accept an Opposition amendment that would have required the DTp to copy to an airport manager all Directions issued to third parties, although it stated that it "will ensure that he is generally informed about Directions given" under the new section (*Hansard*, H.L. Vol. 518, col. 858, and see *Hansard*, H.L. Vol. 519, col. 453).
Obligations that may be imposed. The Direction requires the person to whom it is directed to "secure" that searches are carried out. The person is not required to perform the searches himself, but will presumably be expected to pay for others to undertake the task, such as private security companies. The actual powers of search are contained in s.13(3) of the Aviation Security Act 1982 (*cf.* s.22(3) of the 1990 Act, below). The reference to "best endeavours" is

designed to take into account the fact that the person receiving the Direction will not undertake the search personally. Presumably it is possible to take account of the financial and other resources of the person concerned. See also s.13A(3) of the Aviation Security Act 1982, below.

Persons who will carry out the searches. At the time of the Protection of Aircraft Act 1978 (consolidated in the Aviation Security Act 1982) the British Airports Authority (BAA) and some other airport authorities had their own police forces. The BAA no longer has its own force nor, with one or two exceptions, do other airport authorities. The controversy as to who will provide security services has been mentioned already (see *The responsibility for security*, in the General Note to Pt. I). The new subsection allows the Secretary of State to describe in the Direction the persons who may provide the services. As noted, it is likely that private security firms would have to belong to one of the appropriate trade organisations.

The Bill, as originally drafted, excluded "constables", as reference to them was thought unnecessary. As members of local police forces might possibly carry out searches, the appropriate person could now call for their assistance. This would be discretionary and subject to payment (*cf. Harris* v. *Sheffield United Football Club* [1988] Q.B. 77).

"Purposes to which this Part of this Act applies". The Directions can only be for the purposes defined by the Aviation Security Act 1982, s.10. Broadly they are the protection against acts of violence: (a) of aircraft (and persons and property on board); (b) of aerodromes (and persons and property thereat) and (c) of air navigation installations.

"In writing". Although the Direction must be in writing, there are powers to issue urgent Directions (otherwise than in writing) under s.17 of the Aviation Security Act 1982 (as amended by Sched. 1, para. 9, below).

"Restricted zone". See s.11A of the Aviation Security Act 1982, as inserted by Sched. 1, para. 3 of the 1990 Act, which allows the Secretary of State to create restricted zones for the whole or any part of an aerodrome, or for air navigation installations (such as navigational beacons or radar equipment) situated outside the aerodrome.

New s.13A(2) of the Aviation Security Act 1982

Searches that may be ordered. The type of searches that may be ordered include those on the land that is occupied, or of persons or property *at any time* on that land. Thus, a casual visitor to any airport premises may find that he is liable to search by a private security guard. (For the powers of search see s.13(3) of the Aviation Security Act 1982 and *cf.* s.22(3) of the 1990 Act, below). There was concern during debates that the powers to order searches were excessive in that they allowed searches of premises that may not be in the vicinity of the airport. Thus, a catering company which delivers food to Heathrow may be ordered (on the basis of para. 2(b)) to conduct a search at its factory in the Midlands of *any* person who may visit the premises—even though the airport is a hundred miles away.

In debates, the Minister (Standing Committee A, col. 51) emphasised that para. 2(b)(i) required the land outside the aerodrome to be occupied "for the purposes of his business". This was clearly designed to exclude domestic premises (except perhaps where a person operated from home). The question was raised of whether the definition would include, for example, an airline's offices in the Strand. The Minister seemed to suggest that such premises could not be searched because they had nothing to do with airport operation but this is not exactly what the provision says; it simply requires the premises to be occupied for the "business", not for airport related activities. The business is the running of an airline, and ticket or information facilities would be included. However, reference must be made back to s.13A(1)(b) which concentrates on a person who has access for the purposes of the business. If the Direction is addressed to an individual it is easier to see the suggested connection, but not if the Direction is sent to a body corporate, such as an airline which runs many offices. (See also the discussion on *Persons on whom Directions may be served*, above; for similar problems in relation to ports see s.23, below).

New s.13A(3) of the Aviation Security Act 1982

Offence. An offence is committed by a person who fails to comply with a Direction, subject to a reasonable excuse defence. Note that a person will not be held to have failed to comply with a Direction where an enforcement notice has been issued which specifies the basis of non-compliance (see the new s.18E(4), s.4 below). This does not apply to matters which are not specified in the notice, or to enforcement proceedings already started under s.13A(3).

Some concern was expressed at the extent of the Government powers in relation to small airports which might not have the resources to cope with the Directions. S.16 of the Aviation Security Act 1982 allows wide powers concerned with construction, etc. of buildings. The reasonable excuse defence has also to be read with the limited "best endeavours" requirement in 13A(1). *Cf.* the formulation in s.14(1A) of the Aviation Security Act 1982 (s.3 of the 1990 Act, below).

Where the offence is tried summarily under the new subs. (3)(a) the fine is not to exceed the statutory maximum, Level 5 on the standard scale laid down by the Criminal Justice Act 1982, s.74 (currently £2,000).

New s.13A(4) of the Aviation Security Act 1982
A small fine might not deter some persons faced by large costs in instituting search procedures. Accordingly, where the person continues in the failure to obey the Direction, subs. (4) allows for a further conviction to be punished by a fine calculated on a day-by-day basis. For each day on which the failure continues a fine of about £200 a day will clock up.

At the Committee stage in the Lords, the Government added a "reasonable excuse" defence for failing to comply with a Direction or enforcement notice after an initial conviction or failure to comply. It was thought to be necessary because although a person might not have a reasonable excuse (under subs. (3)) at the time of the original failure to comply he may have one at the later stage. An example was given by the Minister for Aviation and Shipping, Mr McCloughlin, (on consideration by the Commons of the Lords' amendments: *Hansard*, H.C. Vol. 174, col. 1045) of an airport manager convicted of not operating an automatic pass reading system. When charged subsequently with continued failure to comply, he could possibly cite as a reasonable excuse the inability of the manufacturer to produce equipment without which he could not comply with the Direction.

Extension of Secretary of State's powers under section 14 of Aviation Security Act 1982

3.—(1) In section 14 of the Aviation Security Act 1982, for subsections (1) and (2) there is substituted—
   "(1) Subsection (1A) below applies to any person who—
   (a) is the operator of one or more aircraft registered or operating in the United Kingdom,
   (b) is the manager of an aerodrome in the United Kingdom,
   (c) occupies any land forming part of an aerodrome in the United Kingdom, or
   (d) is permitted to have access to a restricted zone of such an aerodrome for the purposes of the activities of a business carried on by him.
   (1A) Subject to the following provisions of this section, the Secretary of State may give a direction in writing to any person to whom this subsection applies requiring him to take such measures for purposes to which this Part of this Act applies as are specified in the direction—
   (a) in the case of a direction given to a person as the operator of any aircraft, in respect of all the aircraft registered or operating in the United Kingdom of which (at the time when the direction is given or at any subsequent time) he is the operator, or in respect of any such aircraft, or any class of such aircraft, specified in the direction;
   (b) in the case of a direction given to a person as the manager of an aerodrome, in respect of that aerodrome;
   (c) in the case of a direction given to a person as a person occupying any land forming part of an aerodrome, in respect of any such land as is specified in the direction; and
   (d) in the case of a direction given to a person as a person who is permitted to have access to a restricted zone as mentioned in subsection (1)(d) above, in respect of such activities carried on by that person in that zone as are specified in the direction.
   (2) Without prejudice to the generality of subsection (1A) above, the measures to be specified in a direction given under this section to any person to whom that subsection applies may

include the provision by that person of persons charged with the duty (at such times as may be specified in the direction)—

(a) where the direction is given to a person as the operator of aircraft, of guarding the aircraft against acts of violence;

(b) where the direction is given to a person as the manager of an aerodrome, of guarding the aerodrome, or persons or property (including aircraft) in any part of the aerodrome, against acts of violence ;

(c) where the direction is given to a person as falling within subsection (1)(c) above, of guarding against acts of violence any aircraft in the aerodrome which is for the time being under his control; or

(d) where the direction is given to a person as falling within subsection (1)(d) above, of guarding—

   (i) any land outside the aerodrome occupied by him for the purposes of his business, any vehicles or equipment used for those purposes and any goods which are in his possession for those purposes, and

   (ii) any aircraft which is for the time being under his control,

   for purposes to which this Part of this Act applies."

(2) Subsection (4) of that section is omitted.

(3) In subsection (6) of that section—

(a) for the words from "such an operator," in the first place where those words occur, to "subsection (1) above," there is substituted "a person to whom subsection (1A) above applies," and

(b) for the words "an operator or manager," in the second place where they occur, there is substituted "a person."

DEFINITIONS

"aerodrome": Aviation Security Act 1982, s.38(1).

"land": Interpretation Act 1978, Sched. 1.

"purposes to which this Part of this Act applies": Aviation Security Act 1982, s.10(1).

"person": Interpretation Act 1978, Sched. 1.

"restricted zone": Aviation Security Act 1982, s.24A (as created by Sched. 1, para. 16 of the 1990 Act).

"Secretary of State": Interpretation Act 1978, Sched. 1.

"United Kingdom": Interpretation Act 1978, Sched. 1.

GENERAL NOTE

Directions. The general power of the Secretary of State to give security Directions derives from s.14 of the Aviation Security Act 1982. Current Directions cover aspects of security such as searching passengers and their property, the control of access to restricted areas, and searching and checking of aircraft (private communication from DTp and Press Notices 1989 Nos. 158 and 185). Directions are intended to be general in nature. If the DTp feels that a Direction is not being complied with satisfactorily more specific "enforcement notices" could be brought into effect under s.18A of the Aviation Security Act 1982 (as inserted by s.4 of the 1990 Act, below).

See further the General Note to Part I, "*Directions*". As noted there, Directions are served specifically on airport managers and airline operators (both U.K. and those foreign airlines operating from the U.K.). The purpose of s.3 is to enable the Secretary of State to give general Directions to businesses other than airport and aircraft operators. These will include catering suppliers, cleaning firms, aircraft maintenance and servicing firms and suppliers of aircraft stores. *Cf.* s.2 above.

Subs. (1)

New s.14(1) of the Aviation Security Act 1982

Paras. (a) and (b) are the same as in the original s.14; (c) and (d) are completely new. Their inclusion is to widen the categories of persons to whom Directions may be given. See also the note to s.2, above, for examples.

New s.14(1A) of the Aviation Security Act 1982

This subsection is really an expansion of the existing s.14(1) to take account of the extensions in the new s.14(1), above. The extent of the obligation to take measures to comply with a Direction varies, in paras. (a) to (c), according to the control exercised by a person. For instance, a Direction given to an aircraft maintenance company, under para. (c), to take certain security measures will only apply to the hangars and workshops actually occupied by it. In the case of a person who does not occupy land at an airport, but who does business in a restricted zone (see the Aviation Security Act 1982, s.24A, as created by Sched. 1, para. 16 of the 1990 Act), the Direction must relate to the activities carried on in that zone, and not to other activities outside. Note that the existing s.14(5) of the Aviation Security Act 1982 provides that a Direction cannot require any search of persons or property (*cf.* s.13 of the Aviation Security Act 1982), or modifications to aircraft.

Absolute requirement. There is no "best endeavours" requirement in s.14(1A) as in s.13A, above. Where the Secretary of State gives a Direction under s.14(1A) the recipient is required to take measures within his own control, for example by having an employee guard an aircraft. This is intended to be an absolute requirement. Under s.13A the person to whom the Direction is addressed is required to ensure that someone else, such as a police officer, carries out a search. The best endeavours formula is not applied throughout Pt. II, but note that there is a "reasonable excuse" defence in s.14(7) of the Aviation Security Act 1982.

New s.14(2) of the Aviation Security Act 1982

This subsection gives specific examples of the type of measure to which the previous paragraph refers in general. In particular, persons may be required to guard aircraft or premises. Para. 2(d) certainly goes beyond the general ambit of para. 1A(d). The latter only refers to measures within the restricted zone: the former, in subpara. (i), extends to measures on land occupied by the person *outside* the aerodrome. This subparagraph is exceptionally wide, from a civil liberties point of view. A catering company supplying food to Heathrow from a factory in Southampton may be required to provide guards at that factory and at its vehicle pound. A tarmac supplier could be required to guard piles of gravel stored at its yard.

Control. The concept of control in paras. (c) and (d) is deliberately narrower than "possession". Control is meant to be a "visible test for determining who is best able, by being on the spot, to ensure the safeguarding of an aircraft from interference." (Mr Portillo, Standing Committee A, col. 60).

Difficulties of interpretation could arise where third party engineering work is carried out, for example where the registered owner of an aircraft arranges for servicing to be undertaken by another airline in its own hangar. It is debatable whether the first airline retains possession, but it would seem that the second airline had control of the aircraft in its own hangar. It would probably be relevant to consider any agreement between the two airlines concerning control. However, there may be a distinction between legal control (often described in terms of responsibility) and actual control (which may or may not be justified on the basis of the servicing contract). It is submitted that the Act is more concerned with actual control. It is doubtful if the second airline would be in "control" if the aircraft were still in the hands of the first airline's employees, albeit that technically the contract imposed responsibility on the second airline from a particular time.

There may be similar problems when a contract cleaning firm or an outside firm of structural engineers are employed to provide services to an aircraft. It may be difficult to decide whether the firms had exclusive control of an aircraft or not.

Subs. (2)

Subs. (4) allowed a Direction to an aircraft operator to cover all its registered aircraft. The matter is now covered by the new s.14(1A)(a) and 14(2)(a).

Subs. (3)

Subs. (6) allows the Secretary of State to give a Direction to persons about to become operators or managers. The amendments simply extend the categories of such persons to include those in the new s.14(1A)—*i.e.* to include the persons listed in s.14(1)(c) and (d).

Enforcement notices in respect of directions under Part II of Aviation Security Act 1982

4. In the Aviation Security Act 1982 after section 18 there is inserted—

> **"Enforcement notices**
>   18A.—(1) Where an authorised person is of the opinion that any person has failed to comply with any general requirement of a direc-

tion given to him under section 12, 13, 13A or 14 of this Act, the authorised person may serve on that person a notice (in this Part of this Act referred to as an "enforcement notice")—

  (a) specifying those general requirements of the direction with which he has, in the opinion of the authorised person, failed to comply, and

  (b) specifying, subject to section 18B of this Act, the measures that ought to be taken in order to comply with those requirements.

(2) For the purposes of this section a requirement of a direction given by the Secretary of State under section 12, 13, 13A or 14 of this Act is a "general requirement" if the provision imposing the requirement—

  (a) has been included in two or more directions given to different persons (whether or not at the same time), and

  (b) is framed in general terms applicable to all the persons to whom those directions are given.

(3) Before serving any enforcement notice which relates to a direction given under section 12(2) of this Act, the authorised person shall inform the Civil Aviation Authority of the measures proposed to be specified in the notice, and shall take account of any advice given to him by that Authority with respect to those proposals.

Contents of enforcement notice

18B.—(1) An enforcement notice may specify in greater detail measures which are described in general terms in those provisions of the direction to which it relates which impose general requirements, but may not impose any requirement which could not have been imposed by a direction given by the Secretary of State under the provision under which the direction was given.

(2) An enforcement notice may be framed so as to afford the person on whom it is served a choice between different ways of complying with the specified general requirements of the direction.

(3) Subject to subsection (4) below, an enforcement notice which relates to a direction given under section 12 of this Act must require the person to whom the direction was given not to cause or permit things to be done as mentioned in subsection (1)(a) or (b) or (2) of that section, as the case requires, until the specified measures have been taken.

(4) In serving an enforcement notice which relates to a direction under section 12(2) of this Act, the authorised person shall allow, and shall specify in the notice, such period as appears to him to be reasonably required for taking the measures specified in the notice; and the notice shall not take effect before the end of the period so specified.

(5) An enforcement notice which relates to a direction given under section 13, 13A or 14 of this Act must either—

  (a) require the person to whom the direction was given to take the specified measures within a specified period which—

      (i) where the measures consist of or include the construction, execution, alteration, demolition or removal of a building or other works, must not be less than thirty days beginning with the date of service of the notice, and

      (ii) in any other case, must not be less than seven days beginning with that date; or

  (b) require him not to do specified things, or cause or permit specified things to be done, until the specified measures have been taken.

(6) Subject to section 18E(2) of this Act, an enforcement notice requiring a person not to cause or permit anything to be done shall be construed as requiring him to take all such steps as in any particular circumstances are practicable and necessary to prevent that thing from being done.

Offences relating to enforcement notices

18C.—(1) Any person who, without reasonable excuse, fails to comply with an enforcement notice served on him shall be guilty of an offence and liable—

(a) on summary conviction, to a fine not exceeding the statutory maximum;

(b) on conviction on indictment, to a fine.

(2) Where a person is convicted of an offence under subsection (1) above, then, if without reasonable excuse the failure in respect of which he was convicted is continued after the conviction, he shall be guilty of a further offence and liable on summary conviction to a fine not exceeding one-tenth of level 5 on the standard scale for each day on which the failure continues.

(3) Any person who intentionally interferes with any building constructed or works executed on any land in compliance with an enforcement notice or with anything installed on, under, over or across any land in compliance with such a notice shall be guilty of an offence and liable—

(a) on summary conviction, to a fine not exceeding the statutory maximum;

(b) on conviction on indictment, to a fine.

Objections to enforcement notices

18D.—(1) The person on whom an enforcement notice is served may serve on the Secretary of State a notice in writing of his objection to the enforcement notice, specifying the grounds of the objection.

(2) Any notice of objection under subsection (1) above must be served—

(a) where the enforcement notice specifies measures falling within section 18B(5)(a)(i) of this Act, before the end of the period of thirty days beginning with the date on which the enforcement notice was served, or

(b) in any other case, before the end of the period of seven days beginning with that date.

(3) The grounds of objection to an enforcement notice are—

(a) that the general requirements of the direction which are specified in the notice for the purposes of section 18A(1)(a) of this Act have been complied with,

(b) that the notice purports to impose a requirement which could not have been imposed by a direction given under the provision under which the direction to which the notice relates was given, or

(c) that any requirement of the notice—

(i) is unnecessary for complying with the general requirements specified as mentioned in paragraph (a) above and should be dispensed with, or

(ii) having regard to the terms of those general requirements, is excessively onerous or inconvenient and should be modified in a manner specified in the notice of objection under subsection (1) above.

(4) Where the person on whom an enforcement notice is served serves a notice under subsection (1) above objecting to the enforce-

ment notice, the Secretary of State shall consider the grounds of the objection and, if so required by the objector, shall afford to him an opportunity of appearing before and being heard by a person appointed by the Secretary of State for the purpose, and shall then serve on the objector a notice in writing either—

(a) confirming the enforcement notice as originally served, or

(b) confirming it subject to one or more modifications specified in the notice under this subsection, or

(c) cancelling the enforcement notice.

(5) An enforcement notice to which an objection has been made under subsection (1) above—

(a) if it contains such a requirement as is mentioned in section 18B(3) or (5)(b) of this Act, shall continue to have effect as originally served until it has been cancelled, or it has been confirmed subject to modification by a notice under subsection (4) above, and

(b) in any other case, shall not take effect until it has been confirmed (with or without modification) by a notice under subsection (4) above.

Enforcement notices: supplementary

18E.—(1) An enforcement notice served on any person—

(a) may be revoked by a notice served on him by an authorised person, and

(b) may be varied by a further enforcement notice.

(2) Sections 15 and 16 of this Act apply to an enforcement notice as they apply to the direction to which the notice relates.

(3) The ownership of any property shall not be affected by reason only that it is placed on or under or affixed to, any land in compliance with an enforcement notice.

(4) Where an authorised person has served an enforcement notice specifying the general requirements of a direction with which the person on whom it is served has, in the opinion of the authorised person, failed to comply, the person on whom the notice is served shall not be taken, for the purposes of section 12(9), 13(4), 13A(3) or 14(7) of this Act, to have failed to comply with the direction by reason of the matters specified in the notice.

(5) Subsection (4) above does not apply in relation to any proceedings commenced before the service of the enforcement notice.

(6) Where an enforcement notice has been served in relation to a direction, the fact that the notice specifies certain general requirements of the direction as those with which the person on whom the notice is served has, in the opinion of the authorised person, failed to comply shall not in any proceedings be evidence that any other requirement of the direction has been complied with.

(7) In this section "direction" means a direction under section 12, 13, 13A or 14 of this Act."

DEFINITIONS

"authorised person": Aviation Security Act 1982, s.24A (as created by Sched. 1, para. 16 of the 1990 Act).

"direction": s.18E(7) of the Aviation Security Act 1982 (as created by s.4 of the 1990 Act).

"general requirement": s.18A(2) of the Aviation Security Act 1982 (as created by s.4 of the 1990 Act).

"measures": Aviation Security Act 1982, s.38(1).

"Secretary of State": Interpretation Act 1978, Sched. 1.

GENERAL NOTE

New s.18A of the Aviation Security Act 1982

Enforcement notices. During the Second Reading debate in the Commons the Secretary of State for Transport stated that further powers were needed to give the aviation security inspectors more flexible and effective means to enforce Directions so that "deficiencies in security can be remedied on the spot" (*Hansard*, H.C. Vol. 164, col. 956). It is not quite clear which deficiencies he had in mind. S.17 of the Aviation Security Act 1982 already allows for urgent Directions to be given. The new s.18A introduces the concept of the enforcement notice (*cf.* ss.21, 22 of the Health and Safety at Work Act 1974). It gives powers to authorised persons (expected to be the DTp's aviation security inspectors) to issue enforcement notices when there is a failure to comply with a Direction under ss.12-14 of the Aviation Security Act 1982. The serving of an enforcement notice is not a penalty as such. A person served with an enforcement notice may be required to carry out remedial action. It seems that the relationship between the Direction and the enforcement notice is that the former will lay down general obligations (see the new s.18A(2)), such as to search an aircraft, while the latter can be used to specify exactly how the search is to be carried out.

The new s.18A(3) requires the Civil Aviation Authority (CAA) to be consulted about the measures specified in the notice. Failure to do so, or to take account of any advice given, could result in an application for judicial review, or a collateral challenge. This requirement to consult could presumably operate as a brake on the taking of urgent enforcement action (but see s.17 of the Aviation Security Act 1982).

General nature of the enforcement notice. The new s.18A(1) requires the enforcement notice to specify two matters: (a) the general requirements of a Direction with which a person, to whom it is addressed, has failed to comply, and (b) the detailed measures which that person has to take in order to effect compliance. Those details are subject to the new s.18B, below.

"General requirement". S.18A(2) defines a general requirement for the purposes of s.18A. The intention, apparently, is to enable the enforcement notice to be triggered by a failure to comply with a commonly framed provision contained within a Direction. If parts of a Direction that have been issued to an airport are not being complied with, the inspector can bring them to the notice of the individual.

New s.18B of the Aviation Security Act 1982

Contents of the enforcement notice. As indicated by s.18A(1), an enforcement notice must specify what a person has to do in order to comply with a Direction that has been given. Under s.18B(1) an enforcement notice may apparently impose conditions that are more onerous than those that appear in the original Direction, although they must be of a kind that the Secretary of State was originally empowered to make. *Cf.* the objection procedure under s.18D(3)(b) and (c). Note also ss.15 and 16 of the Aviation Security Act 1982 which contain, respectively, matters which may be included in Directions and limitations on their scope. The new s.18E(2), below, applies these sections, *mutatis mutandis*, to enforcement notices.

S.18B(2) allows the notice to give the recipient a choice between different methods of compliance, for instance by employing extra staff, or engaging sub-contractors. When deciding exactly how an enforcement notice should be complied with (for example whether to offer such a choice) an inspector would have to take into account the practical difficulties faced by the person concerned. He would also have to anticipate possible objections under s.18D on the basis that the notice was unnecessary, or excessively onerous or inconvenient.

Time for compliance: restrictions in relation to aircraft. S.12 of the Aviation Security Act 1982 allows Directions to be given in relation to an aircraft, for instance forbidding the aircraft to fly unless it has been searched, or certain equipment has been installed on it. The new s.18B(3) requires an enforcement notice for s.12 to contain an interim ban on activities such as those mentioned above (for example flying) until the measures specified in the notice have been taken. Where modifications or alterations of the aircraft are required the inspector is obliged by s.18B(4) to allow a reasonable period for them to be done. The enforcement notice will not take effect until the end of that period. An aircraft would not therefore be grounded if the necessary equipment was not immediately available from a supplier.

Time for compliance: ss.13–14. S.18B(5) deals with the question of when compliance with an enforcement notice is required. S.18B(5)(a) generally requires that a period of seven or 30 days be given, depending on whether building work is necessary. S.18B(5)(b) and s.18B(6) relate to interim measures that may be necessary before more extensive works are completed. The enforcement notice could result in certain operations having to cease until the specified action is taken.

When deciding exactly how an enforcement notice should be complied with (for example whether to allow more than the minimum time for compliance under s.18B(5)(a), or whether to impose an immediate prohibition under s.18B(5)(b)) an inspector would have to take into account the practical difficulties faced by the person concerned. He would also have to anticipate possible objections under s.18D on the basis that the notice was unnecessary, or excessively onerous or inconvenient.

Annual reports. The Secretary of State did undertake that the inspectorate make an annual report on enforcement notices (and Directions) which would be laid before the House (*Han-*

sard, H.C. Vol. 164, col. 957). See now the Aviation Security Act 1982, as amended by Sched. 1, para.14, below.

New s.18C of the Aviation Security Act 1982
   Enforcement notice offences. Two new offences are created. It is an offence to fail to comply with an enforcement notice, subject to a reasonable excuse test. The penalties could include an unlimited fine on indictment. As with the new s.13A(4) (see s.2 of the 1990 Act, above) continued failure to comply could result in a cumulative daily penalty.
   It is also an offence intentionally to interfere with buildings, works or installations which are on land in compliance with an enforcement notice. There is no requirement that the interferer *knows*, for example, that the building was constructed as part of a security scheme in respect of which there are statutory notices. Moreover, interference does not necessarily include damage (*cf.* the Criminal Damage Act 1971).

New s.18D of the Aviation Security Act 1982
   Objections to enforcement notices. Despite the fact that there must be consultation with the CAA under s.18A(3), a recipient of an enforcement notice may serve a formal objection (under the new s.18D) within the appropriate time limit, if any.
   Grounds of objection. There are four basic grounds of objection under the new s.18D(3): (a) that the general grounds of the Direction itself had already been met; (b) that the enforcement notice imposed requirements that went beyond those allowed for the appropriate Direction; (c)(i) that the enforcement notice is unnecessary and should be cancelled; (c)(ii) that the enforcement notice should be modified because it is excessively onerous or inconvenient.
   Objection (a) is self explanatory and will largely be a question of fact. Objection (b) requires consideration of the appropriate provision under which the Direction was issued. For example, an enforcement notice relating to a s.14 Direction could not require searches to be carried out, as s.14(5) of the Aviation Security Act 1982 does not permit this. Objections (c)(i) and (c)(ii) will again involve questions of fact. It will not be an objection that the person will find it difficult to carry out the order: it must be *excessively* onerous or inconvenient. The disjunctive was deliberately inserted to replace a conjunctive in the original Bill. Hence an objector need only show that the requirements are either excessively onerous, *or* inconvenient, but not both. The present wording leaves it unclear whether "excessively" also applies to "inconvenient", so that the alternative objection is that the order will be *excessively* inconvenient, rather than 'merely' inconvenient. It is submitted that the content shows that the objector must show excessive inconvenience.
   An enforcement notice takes precedence over existing laws (see s.19 of the Aviation Security Act 1982, as amended by Sched. 1, para. 10, below), but no doubt potential overlaps will be borne in mind. The Government resisted an attempt to add as an additional ground for objection that the enforcement notice *conflicted* with the requirements of other statutory or regulatory bodies.
   Suspension of effect of notice. In general, notices shall not take effect if an objection has been made—at least until they have been confirmed or modified (see s.18D(5)). The exceptions concern those notices enforcing s.12 of the Aviation Security Act 1982 which s.18B(3) of the Act requires to continue in effect and those enforcing ss.13–14 where an inspector has decided (under s.18B(5)(b)) that certain acts are not to take place until specified measures are taken.
   Procedure after objection. Under s.18D(4) the objector has the right to a hearing, if desired. After consideration of the objection, the Secretary of State can cancel, confirm or modify the enforcement notice.

New s.18E of the Aviation Security Act 1982
   This section contains various supplementary provisions relating to enforcement notices. It allows for revocation or variation of notices (subs. (1)) and applies provisions of the 1982 Act which expand upon, or limit, their scope (subs. (2)).
   S.18E(3) is a saving provision to preserve existing rights for movable property; s.18E(4) and (5) remove the possibility of overlapping offences; and s.18E(6) means that an enforcement notice is not to be taken as an admission that there *has* been compliance with general requirements other than those mentioned in it.

Offences relating to security at aerodromes etc.

Offences relating to security at aerodromes etc.

   5. After section 21 of the Aviation Security Act 1982 there is inserted—

"Offences relating to security at aerodromes etc.

False statements relating to baggage, cargo etc.

21A.—(1) Subject to subsection (3) below, a person commits an offence if, in answer to a question which—

(a) relates to any baggage, cargo or stores (whether belonging to him or to another) that is or are intended for carriage by a civil aircraft registered or operating in the United Kingdom, and

(b) is put to him for purposes to which this Part of this Act applies—

(i) by any of the persons mentioned in subsection (2) below,

(ii) by any employee or agent of such a person in his capacity as employee or agent, or

(iii) by a constable,

he makes a statement which he knows to be false in a material particular, or recklessly makes a statement which is false in a material particular.

(2) The persons referred to in subsection (1)(b) above are—

(a) the manager of an aerodrome in the United Kingdom,

(b) the operator of one or more aircraft registered or operating in the United Kingdom, and

(c) any person who—

(i) is permitted to have access to a restricted zone of an aerodrome for the purposes of the activities of a business carried on by him, and

(ii) has control in that restricted zone over the baggage, cargo or stores to which the question relates.

(3) Subsection (1) above does not apply in relation to any statement made by an authorised person in the exercise of the power conferred by section 20(2)(aa) of this Act.

(4) A person guilty of an offence under subsection (1) above shall be liable on summary conviction to a fine not exceeding level 5 on the standard scale.

(5) In this section—

"cargo" includes mail;

"civil aircraft" has the same meaning as in section 3 of this Act; and

"stores" means any goods intended for sale or use on an aircraft, including spare parts and other articles of equipment, whether or not for immediate fitting.

False statements in connection with identity documents

21B.—(1) Subject to subsection (4) below, a person commits an offence if—

(a) for the purpose of, or in connection with, an application made by him or another for the issue of an identity document to which this subsection applies, or

(b) in connection with the continued holding by him or another of any such document which has already been issued,

he makes to any of the persons specified in subsection (3) below, to any employee or agent of such a person or to a constable, a statement which he knows to be false in a material particular, or recklessly makes to any of those persons, or to any such employee or agent or to a constable, a statement which is false in a material particular.

(2) Subsection (1) above applies to any identity document which is to be or has been issued by any of the persons specified in subsection (3) below in accordance with arrangements the maintenance of which is required by a direction given by the Secretary of State under section 14 of this Act.

(3) The persons referred to in subsection (1) above are—
(a) the manager of an aerodrome in the United Kingdom,
(b) the authority responsible for an air navigation installation in the United Kingdom,
(c) the operator of one or more aircraft registered or operating in the United Kingdom, and
(d) any person who is permitted to have access to a restricted zone of an aerodrome or air navigation installation for the purposes of the activities of a business carried on by him.

(4) Subsection (1) above does not apply in relation to any statement made by an authorised person in the exercise of the power conferred by section 20(2)(aa) of this Act.

(5) A person guilty of an offence under subsection (1) above shall be liable on summary conviction to a fine not exceeding level 5 on the standard scale.

Unauthorised presence in restricted zone
21C.—(1) A person shall not—
(a) go, with or without a vehicle, onto any part of a restricted zone of—
      (i) an aerodrome, or
      (ii) an air navigation installation which does not form part of an aerodrome,
except with the permission of the manager of the aerodrome, the authority responsible for the air navigation installation or a person acting on behalf of that manager or authority, and in accordance with any conditions subject to which that permission is for the time being granted, or
(b) remain on any part of such a restricted zone after being requested to leave by the manager of the aerodrome, the authority responsible for the air navigation installation or a person acting on behalf of that manager or authority.

(2) Subsection (1)(a) above does not apply unless it is proved that, at the material time, notices stating that the area concerned was a restricted zone were posted so as to be readily seen and read by persons entering the restricted zone.

(3) A person who contravenes subsection (1) above without lawful authority or reasonable excuse shall be guilty of an offence and liable on summary conviction to a fine not exceeding level 5 on the standard scale.

Unauthorised presence on board aircraft
21D.—(1) A person shall not—
(a) get into or onto an aircraft at an aerodrome in the United Kingdom except with the permission of the operator of the aircraft or a person acting on his behalf, or
(b) remain on an aircraft at such an aerodrome after being requested to leave by the operator of the aircraft or a person acting on his behalf.

(2) A person who contravenes subsection (1) above without lawful authority or reasonable excuse shall be guilty of an offence and liable on summary conviction to a fine not exceeding level 5 on the standard scale.

Offences relating to authorised persons
21E.—(1) A person who—
(a) intentionally obstructs an authorised person acting in the exercise of a power conferred on him by or under this Part of this Act, or

(b) falsely pretends to be an authorised person,
commits an offence.

(2) A person guilty of an offence under subsection (1)(a) above
shall be liable—

(a) on summary conviction, to a fine not exceeding the statutory
maximum;

(b) on conviction on indictment, to a fine or to imprisonment for a
term not exceeding two years or to both.

(3) A person guilty of an offence under subsection (1)(b) above
shall be liable on summary conviction to a fine not exceeding level 5
on the standard scale."

DEFINITIONS

"air navigation installation": Aviation Security Act 1982, s.38(1).
"authorised person": Sched. 1, para.16.
"cargo": s.21A(5).
"civil aircraft": s.21A(5) and s.3 of the Aviation Security Act 1982.
"employee": Sched. 1, para.16.
"person": Interpretation Act 1978, Sched. 1.
"restricted zone": Sched. 1, para.16.
"Secretary of State": Interpretation Act 1978, Sched. 1.
"stores": s.21A(5).
"United Kingdom": Interpretation Act 1978, Sched. 1.

GENERAL NOTE

New s.21A of the Aviation Security Act 1982
    False statements relating to baggage. The 1989 Report recommended that the giving of false
answers to questions about baggage and its contents should be a criminal offence (para. 49) and
the 1989 Government Observations accepted the proposal (p. viii). The Transport Committee
had in mind couriers who are used to carrying baggage in circumstances where it is cheaper than
sending it unaccompanied. The couriers might be tempted to avoid delays by giving false
answers to questions such as "did you pack these bags yourself?". General safety might also be
increased if passengers were more aware of the need to disclose the carriage of potentially
dangerous goods, such as fireworks and camping gas containers. (See generally the Civil
Aviation Authority's new booklet, *The Air Traveller's Code*, issued in 1990).
    The new s.21A does indeed create a new offence of making false statements in relation to
baggage, but it is not limited to couriers. The offence could be committed by passengers or, for
instance, by airline or airport employees. There is no offence of *refusing* to answer a question.
Presumably, in such a case it would be presumed that the baggage contained something
unsatisfactory and it would be searched under existing powers.
    The false statement has to be made in answer to a question relating to the matters listed in
s.21A(1)(a). It appears that there is no offence if a false statement is volunteered and in such a
case it seems difficult to argue that there is an attempt. It may be possible in certain circumstances to imply that one of the persons listed in s.21A(1)(b) has asked a question, for example
if it appears on a notice at the check-out, but the provision must not be stretched too far.
    The section states that it is the *question*, as opposed to the false statement, that has to relate to
baggage, cargo or stores. It might be argued that any false statement in answer to such a
question, for example relating to travel intentions, would be an offence. However, the better
opinion is that the reference to "material particular" reinforces the view that the false answer
must also relate to baggage, cargo or stores.
    The exact extent of "material particular" will vary according to the facts, but its inclusion in
the section is clearly designed to avoid there being an offence in respect of minor, or irrelevant,
statements. But the maker of a false statement will do so at his peril, as what may be irrelevant
to him may be important to the security authorities. For instance, a passenger may state that a
radio had been bought in the U.K. in order to conceal the fact that it had been purchased abroad
and that no duty had been paid on it. But it may be that there was a security alert about radios
from that country and the authorities may wish to inspect them more closely. The *mens rea*
element of the offence is also satisfied by proof of recklessness. Passengers are often asked
whether luggage has been out of their sight at any time since it was packed. It would be ludicrous
to expect a passenger to refer to the period when he was sitting in the front seat of a car while the
luggage was in the boot, yet moments of inattention at airports could give the determined
terrorist the time to insert a bomb in a suitcase. See also *Testing the system*, below, for corporate
liability. It is no defence to assert that the false statement was a joke. The Government Minister

who, in exasperation at delays, stated that his red box contained a bomb would presumably be guilty.

The baggage, cargo or stores have to be intended for carriage in an aircraft. It would not apply, for example, to questions about food brought into an airport and intended for consumption in one of the passenger lounges.

Persons who may put questions. The question has to have been put by (a) the manager of a U.K. aerodrome, or (b) the operator of an aircraft registered or operating in the U.K., or (c) persons such as officials who have control over baggage, cargo or stores in a restricted zone, or (d) employees or agents of the persons above, or (e) police constables. It is clear that this is a very wide list and it may place a passenger in some difficulty in knowing exactly who is demanding the information. The questions do not have to be answered at a specific place, such as a check-in desk. An employee of a baggage handling agency might stop a passenger in a lounge and demand to know what is in the passenger's hand luggage. The passenger might believe that he had no obligation to give a correct (or any) answer to a person who did not appear to be a security officer. Nevertheless, an offence might be committed.

In the case of a large airline or airport authority, it is possible that some minor employee might make a misstatement and there was some concern lest this give rise to corporate liability (see also s.50, below). The response was that it was appropriate for there to be corporate liability, for example where short staffing is deliberate. The Minister for Public Transport, Mr Portillo, said at Committee Stage in the Commons that "we do not envisage corporate liability when the statement is made by employees when knowledge does not lie in the minds of those responsible for the direction of the company" (Standing Committee A, col.78).

"Statement". A statement for the purposes of s.21A(1) might be made orally, in answer to an oral question, or in writing. The Government resisted an amendment to include written statements on the basis that it was unnecessary as the wording in the Act covered both oral and written questions and answers. This is probably more important in the shipping than the aviation context. See below, s.37.

Testing the system. S.21A(3) allows an authorised person, such as an inspector, to deliberately make a false statement, for instance to check airport security arrangements. This would not include, for example, false statements by investigative journalists, as they would not be "authorised persons" as defined by Sched. 1, para. 16, *i.e.* those to whom written authority had been given by the Secretary of State. The Minister indicated that there would be a limited number of persons authorised (Standing Committee A, col. 77). They would mainly be inspectors and not aerodrome managers or airline employees.

Tests might involve delays at airports which could give rise to the possibility of an airline or airport attempting to sue the DTp. One of the purposes of s.21A(3) is apparently to provide a defence to any such suit. The inspector must, however, be purporting to exercise the power in the new s.20(2)(aa) of the Aviation Security Act 1982 (as inserted by Sched. 1, para. 11, below).

New s.21B of the Aviation Security Act 1982

False statements and identity documents. The new s.21B creates an offence where a person makes a false statement in order to obtain or renew a document such as an identity card. The Secretary of State denied that the offences in s.5 of the 1990 Act were aimed at members of the press who, for example, had gained access to airports by subterfuge in order to point out security lapses. Nevertheless, it was made clear that members of the press were not excluded and that they could be prosecuted for lying to obtain a security pass.

Unlike the new s.21A, above, it is not necessary that a specific question be addressed to the maker of the statement, although in most cases the offence is likely to be relevant when a false application is submitted on a form which itself asks questions.

The persons to whom the statement must be made are broadly the same as those for s.21A, above, but with the addition of the new s.21B(3)(b)—the authority responsible for an air navigation installation (for example an air traffic control centre).

The type of identity document to which the section applies are those issued by the persons above in accordance with general arrangements set up by the Secretary of State in a Direction under s.14 of the Aviation Security Act 1982.

For authorised security tests (under the new s.21B(4) of the Aviation Security Act 1982) see the note to the new s.21A(3), above.

New s.21C of the Aviation Security Act 1982

"Restricted zone". The new s.11A of the Aviation Security Act 1982 (see Sched. 1, para. 3 of the 1990 Act) allows for the creation of restricted zones within an aerodrome or, indeed, at an air navigation installation elsewhere (for example an air traffic control centre). The new s.21C gives the zone some substance by providing an offence for going onto a restricted zone without

permission. The permission itself may be given subject to conditions, for example to keep away from aircraft, and it would be an offence to disobey the conditions.

A person making deliveries to an airport would expect to be checked on entry, but it may be that a restricted zone is not physically separated from the rest of the aerodrome and the visitor may not be aware that there is a restriction. This might apply even more to an air traffic control centre where only the nerve centre of the building is designated. Accordingly, s.21C(2) provides that there is no offence unless there are notices which can be "readily seen". At night such notices would presumably have to be illuminated.

It may be that a person enters a restricted zone with permission, or in circumstances where he had no means of knowing that the zone existed (for example where there were inadequate notices). In such a case, the airport manager would be entitled to ask him to leave and it would be an offence to fail to do so, under s.21C(b) and s.21C(3).

Note that s.1(1) of the Official Secrets Act 1911 (left untouched by the Official Secrets Act 1989) creates an offence for persons entering "prohibited places", as defined by s.3. In general these are places such as *military* aerodromes, or nuclear establishments (see S.I. 1975 No. 182 and the well-known Committee of 100 case, *Chandler* v. *D.P.P.* [1964] A.C. 763, where anti-nuclear demonstrators were convicted of blocking the runway of an R.A.F. base in Essex).

New s.21D of the Aviation Security Act 1982

S.21D appears to be the only example in the 1990 Act where the aviation provision has been created to mirror the maritime one, and not vice versa: for the maritime equivalent see the Merchant Shipping Act 1970, s.78. It is now an offence to enter, or climb on to, an aircraft, or to remain on it, without permission. The aircraft must be at an aerodrome in the U.K. The aerodrome does not have to be one serving international civil aviation (as in s.1 of the 1990 Act), but the section does not appear to extend to seaplanes.

New s.21E of the Aviation Security Act 1982

S.21E creates an offence of obstructing or impersonating an authorised person. It is not quite clear who exactly will be covered by the expression "authorised person". It is defined in the new s.24A to mean a person authorised in writing by the Secretary of State and all the indications are that the authorisations will be limited to the DTp's aviation security inspectors—although there is nothing to stop the Secretary of State authorising a wider category of persons, such as aerodrome managers, private security guards and airline employees. On the basis that only inspectors will be authorised, there may be gaps in relation to the new offences created by s.21A–D, for example. What is the sanction if a person refuses to leave a restricted zone, after being told to do so by an aerodrome manager, or refuses to leave an aircraft when so requested by the pilot? These persons will certainly commit offences under ss.21C and 21D, but what of the "friend" who interferes with the officials trying to eject the trespasser? It is these sort of problems that are multiplied by the absence of an official police force at aerodromes, whose officers can be summoned to exercise their statutory powers.

Note that the punishment for obstructing an authorised person, *i.e.* an aviation security inspector, may in some circumstances be greater than that for one of the principal offences (for example under s.21D).

Air cargo agents

Air cargo agents

6. After section 21E of the Aviation Security Act 1982 there is inserted—

"Air cargo agents

Air cargo agents

21F.—(1) The Secretary of State may by regulations made by statutory instrument make provision, for purposes to which this Part of this Act applies, in relation to persons (in this section referred to as "air cargo agents") who carry on a business of handling cargo which is to be delivered (whether by them or any other person) to the operator of any aircraft for carriage from any aerodrome in the United Kingdom by a civil aircraft.

(2) Regulations under this section may, in particular—

(a) enable the Secretary of State to maintain a list of air cargo agents who are approved by him for purposes related to aviation security, to include the name of an air cargo agent on that list, on application being made to the Secretary of State in accordance with the regulations, if he is satisfied as to such matters as are specified in the regulations, and to remove the name of any person from that list in such circumstances as are so specified,

(b) provide that any provision of this Part of this Act which applies in relation to persons who are permitted to have access to a restricted zone of an aerodrome for the purposes of the activities of a business (including any such provision which creates a criminal offence) shall also apply, with such modifications as are specified in the regulations, in relation to air cargo agents included on any such list,

(c) amend sections 21A(2), 21B(3) and 32(2) of this Act by including references to air cargo agents included on any such list,

(d) make provision (including any such provision as is mentioned in paragraphs (a) to (c) above) relating to a class of air cargo agents specified in the regulations and not to other air cargo agents,

(e) make different provision for different cases, and

(f) make such incidental, supplementary or transitional provision as the Secretary of State considers necessary or expedient in consequence of any provision made by the regulations.

(3) Before making any regulations under this section the Secretary of State shall consult organisations appearing to him to represent persons affected by the proposed regulations.

(4) Any statutory instrument containing regulations under this section shall be subject to annulment in pursuance of a resolution of either House of Parliament.

(5) Without prejudice to the generality of sections 12 and 14 of this Act, the exemptions that may be included in any direction given to an operator of aircraft under section 12 or 14 which requires the carrying out of searches of cargo, or the taking of any other measures in relation of cargo, include exemptions from such requirements in relation to cargo received from any air cargo agent included on any list maintained by the Secretary of State under regulations under this section or from any air cargo agent falling within a class of such air cargo agents specified in the direction.

(6) In this section—

"cargo" includes stores and mail; and

"stores" means any goods intended for sale or use on an aircraft, including spare parts and other articles of equipment, whether or not for immediate fitting."

DEFINITIONS

"aerodrome": Aviation Security Act 1982, s.38(1).
"air cargo agents": new s.21F(1) of the Aviation Security Act 1982.
"cargo": new s.21F(6) of the Aviation Security Act 1982.
"operator": Aviation Security Act 1982, s.38(1).
"person": Interpretation Act 1978, Sched. 1.
"restricted zone": Sched. 1, para.16.
"Secretary of State": Interpretation Act 1978, Sched. 1.
"stores": s.21F(6).
"United Kingdom": Interpretation Act 1978, Sched. 1.

GENERAL NOTE

This section was added at Committee stage in the Commons to cover the position of agents supplying consignments of cargo, mail or stores that might be delivered to airlines without the agents themselves going to the airport. Technically, they might not fall within the categories of persons who have "access" to restricted areas (for example within s.14 of the Aviation Security

Act 1982, as amended). Yet they would be responsible for sending materials into those areas. The section goes towards meeting the recommendations in the 1989 Report which suggested a code of practice whereby all cargo has to originate from registered shippers.

The section is a regulation-making power that may not necessarily be used. The Secretary of State is empowered to maintain a list of approved agents. It is expected that agents would apply for inclusion on the list and would be interviewed by an aviation security inspector at the agents' premises so that checks may be made on the facilities available for implementing security procedures. An agent with a poor record in complying with Directions may be removed from the list by the Secretary of State, following written notification of the proposed course of action and the reasons for it. There would not be a formal objection procedure, despite the great commercial impact that removal from the list might have.

Once on the list, security Directions could be issued, for example requiring persons or property at the agents' premises to be searched or for cargo to be guarded. There is a general power to extend to air cargo agents, by regulation, the relevant Parts of the Aviation Security Act 1982, for example relating to those persons having access to restricted zones (see s.13A(b), s.14(1)(d)). Similarly, the Secretary of State could extend to air cargo agents the new offences in ss.21A and 21B relating to false statements.

There would be a duty to consult before making regulations.

Air cargo agents. The expression is defined very widely in the new s.21F(1) to be persons (i) who carry on a business of handling cargo, (ii) which is delivered by them or others, (iii) to an operator of any aircraft, (iv) for the purpose of carriage, (v) from any U.K. aerodrome, (vi) by a civil aircraft. The reference to delivery by "any other person" was added at Report stage in the Lords to cover the situation where cargo agents use third parties, such as haulage contractors, to make the delivery. The agents could not escape from the effect of security Directions by employing a sub-contractor. Note that the definitions of cargo and stores in subs. (6) have the effect of including agents who supply spare parts, or items such as fuel which may be used in transit, or duty free goods for sale to passengers.

Cf. s.41, below, for the maritime equivalent of s.21F.

Reporting of certain occurrences

Duty to report certain occurrences

7. After section 21F of the Aviation Security Act 1982 there is inserted—

"Reporting of certain occurrences relating to aviation security

Duty to report certain occurrences

21G.—(1) For purposes to which this Part of this Act applies, the Secretary of State may by regulations made by statutory instrument require such persons as are specified in the regulations to make a report to him, in such manner and within such period as are so specified, of any occurrence of a description so specified.

(2) Before making any regulations under this section, the Secretary of State shall consult organisations appearing to him to represent persons affected by the proposed regulations.

(3) Regulations under this section may—

(a) provide that any person who, in making a report required by the regulations, makes a statement which he knows to be false in a material particular, or recklessly makes a statement which is false in a material particular, is to be guilty of an offence and liable—

(i) on summary conviction, to a fine not exceeding the statutory maximum;

(ii) on conviction on indictment, to a fine or to imprisonment for a term not exceeding two years or to both, and

(b) provide for persons to be guilty of an offence in such other circumstances as may be specified in the regulations and to be liable on summary conviction to a fine not exceeding level 5 on the standard scale.

(4) Regulations under this section may require the reporting of occurrences taking place outside the United Kingdom only if those occurrences relate to aircraft registered in the United Kingdom.

(5) Any statutory instrument containing regulations under this section shall be subject to annulment in pursuance of a resolution of either House of Parliament."

DEFINITIONS

"person": Interpretation Act 1978, Sched. 1.

"Secretary of State": Interpretation Act 1978, Sched. 1.

"United Kingdom": Interpretation Act 1978, Sched. 1.

GENERAL NOTE

Reporting security incidents. This section was added at Committee stage in the Commons, following a proposal of the British Airline Pilots Association (BALPA) and the recommendations of the 1989 Report (para. 18). The latter recommended the establishment of a mandatory security incident reporting system. This must not be confused with the voluntary, and anonymous, reporting system in respect of near-miss incidents or operational failures on aircraft.

S.7 is a regulation making power enabling the Secretary of State to set up a system for the reporting of actual or potential security incidents. This would replace the present voluntary system that has no statutory backing. The existing system does not provide enough reports or sufficient detail to enable the DTp effectively to monitor the national aviation security programme.

In general the type of incidents that will be reportable will be those that reveal weaknesses in aviation security and breaches of Directions. Subs. (3)(a) makes it an offence to make a false report and subs. (3)(b) allows for offences in other undefined circumstances. One example given was the possibility of making it an offence *not* to report a reportable incident. If the latter position is adopted the system will indeed be mandatory. The persons who would be required to make the report would be those persons who have been served with Directions under the Aviation Security Act 1982 as amended (see for example the list of persons in s.14(1), as inserted by s.3 of the 1990 Act, above). Incidents outside the U.K. will only be reportable in so far as they relate to U.K. registered aircraft.

As the section is enabling, detailed discussion on matters such as which incidents should be reportable must await further reflection and the promulgation of regulations. Subs. (2) requires consultation, for example with BALPA. The section does not say what will happen to the information and whether it will be published, or issued in a neutralised form not indicating the parties alleged to have been in breach of a Direction or to have caused a "near-miss". (*Cf.* the Merchant Shipping Act 1988, s.33). The incidence of reporting may vary, depending on whether the persons reporting are guaranteed anonymity. A holder of an airport shop franchise might be reluctant to "inform" on the security lapses of the airport authority if it thought this might jeopardise the renewal of a lease. It appears that the information will appear in the form of a summary in the annual report of the chief aviation security inspector (see s.23 of the Aviation Security Act 1982 , as amended by Sched. 1, para. 14, below, and the General Note to Pt. I, above).

Public information. The Opposition proposed, unsuccessfully, an amendment that would have obliged airlines to answer requests from members of the public about security precautions on their aircraft. There was some concern after Lockerbie that U.S. Government personnel were informed about bomb threats and were able to cancel flights, but that this information was not made known to ordinary members of the public. It is difficult to see how such a legal obligation could work practically, given the number of passengers, and the number of bomb hoaxes (467 in 1989). There is also the danger of inadvertently providing information to terrorists.

Other amendments

Other amendments of Aviation Security Act 1982

8.—(1) The further amendments of the Aviation Security Act 1982 specified in Schedule 1 to this Act have effect.

(2) Paragraphs 4(3), 5(3) and 6(3) of that Schedule do not have effect in any case where the relevant conviction of an offence under section 12(9), 13(4)(a) or 14(7)(a) of the Aviation Security Act 1982 occurred before the commencement of those paragraphs.

GENERAL NOTE

Subs. (1)

Schedule 1 of the 1990 Act contains many amendments to the Aviation Security Act 1982. These will be considered in the note to that Schedule, but the main changes relate to: the provision of information (under s.11 of the Aviation Security Act 1982); the designation of restricted zones (s.11A); Directions by the Secretary of State (ss.12–17); compensation for compliance with Directions (s.22); the annual report of the Secretary of State (s.23); the service of documents (s.24); interpretation (s.25); and reimbursement of expenses (s.32). Most noteworthy, perhaps, are the provisions for revised information-gathering powers and for daily penalties to be imposed for failure to comply with a Direction after being convicted of an offence.

Subs. (2)

This subsection makes it clear that the daily fine provisions of Sched. 1 of the 1990 Act do not apply where convictions for failing to comply with Directions (under the Aviation Security Act 1982) took place before the coming into force of the 1990 provisions.

PART II

OFFENCES AGAINST THE SAFETY OF SHIPS AND FIXED PLATFORMS

GENERAL NOTE

Pt. II of the Act gives effect to the Rome Convention 1988 and the Fixed Platforms Protocol 1988, described in more detail below. The Act does go slightly further than the Convention in respect of certain public vessels such as U.K. customs craft, to which the Convention would not apply. The Rome Convention 1988 is very similar in content to the air Conventions mentioned in the GENERAL NOTE to Pt. I, above, such as the Hague and Montreal Conventions. There are, however, a number of differences between the sea and air Conventions.

Pt. II and the Rome Convention 1988 are only relevant to determine whether an offence has been committed. Of more general significance, perhaps, are the type of preventive security measures which are dealt with under Pt. III, below.

Terrorism and piracy generally

Terrorist activity against ships has been far less frequent than against aircraft, but commercial piracy has always been a problem. The 1980s have seen increases in both types of activity. Politically inspired attacks on ships and their passengers and crews have been exemplified by the hijacking of the *Achille Lauro* in October 1985 and the attack on the *City of Poros* in July 1988. Commercial pirates have been making attacks against ships, particularly in areas such as the Straits of Malacca and off West Africa, often using fast vessels and modern weaponry.

Governments seem to react more readily to the threat of terrorism, although the incidence of commercial piracy is certainly higher. The reason for this is partly because of the higher media profile of terrorism, but also because much commercial piracy involves no injury or death. Traditional pirates and terrorists both depend on the threat of violence to achieve their aims: it may be that the terrorists are more prepared to put those threats into effect. The maritime world understands piracy and the measures to counter it are not new. If terrorism is a modern phenomenon, it must still be asked whether it poses problems of a fundamentally different nature requiring different legal solutions.

The most recent study of piracy by the International Maritime Bureau recorded some 733 pirate attacks on commercial vessels in the period 1981–87: see E. Ellen (ed.), *Piracy at Sea*, (1989), pp. 5–8 and Appendix 1 (p. 241). In that same period 27 incidents were recorded in which people were killed and 50 incidents in which injuries occurred (*Piracy at Sea, op. cit.*, pp. 278–9). It is not possible to say exactly how many individuals were killed or injured as the statistics are admittedly incomplete because of recording variations (*Piracy at Sea, op. cit.*, p. 5). It can be said, however, that the overwhelming number of attacks are commercial rather than political and that, so far, there has not been the sort of catastrophic attack resulting in large loss of life, as at Lockerbie in 1988 and with the Air India Boeing 747 in 1985. But a recent workshop concluded that the 1990s would see a doubling of maritime terrorist incidents (see E. Ellen (ed.), *Violence at sea* (2nd ed. 1987), p. 9 and J.D. Simon, "The implications of the *Achille Lauro* hijacking for the maritime community", *ibid.*, pp. 19–22).

Although aircraft bombings are nearly always likely to result in large loss of life, it should not be thought that the potential for similar maritime catastrophes is less. Ships are not so fragile as aircraft, but a strategically placed bomb on a cross-Channel ferry or a cruise liner could be disastrous. Most of these ferries can carry over 1000–1500 passengers; the *Queen Elizabeth 2* can carry 1740. The sinking of the *Herald of Free Enterprise* shows that even modern ships are susceptible to rapid submersion.

Political hijacking is not novel to this century, but it has been said that the modern history of political piracy started with the *Santa Maria* incident in 1961 (see P. Birnie, "Piracy Past, Present and Future", in *Piracy at Sea*, *op. cit.*, p. 143 *et seq.*). The most serious maritime terrorist incidents in recent years have been those to the *Achille Lauro* and the *City of Poros*. The *Achille Lauro* was an Italian cruise liner on a voyage to Egypt and Israel in October 1985 with 750 passengers and 331 crew. After leaving Alexandria on October 3, the ship was taken over outside Egyptian waters by four Palestinian terrorists apparently protesting against an Israeli attack on the PLO in Tunisia. The ship was ordered to Syria, where it was denied entry. An elderly wheelchair-bound U.S. citizen was killed and thrown overboard—an action that has continued to horrify more than some other incidents involving greater loss of life. The ship was refused entry to Cyprus and returned to Egypt where safe passage was negotiated in exchange for the release of the hostages and the ship. The Palestinians were not detained, tried or extradited by Egypt, although the U.S. forced the aircraft carrying them to land in Italy. The Italians commenced proceedings against them, refusing a U.S. extradition request.

The *City of Poros* was a Greek passenger ferry with 471 passengers and 22 crew which was on a one day cruise around the Saronic Gulf in July 1988. Three terrorists amongst the passengers made a random machine gun and grenade attack on passengers, as a result of which 11 people died and 60 were injured. It is suspected that the attack was part of a hijack attempt in retaliation for the shooting down by the U.S. of an Iranian airliner shortly before. The hijack went wrong when there was an explosion in a car containing accomplices at the Piraeus dockside. (See various reports in Lloyd's List and *The Times* from July 13, 1988). The IMO guidelines on ship and port security did not apply to one day cruises (see (1988) 6 Commercial Crime International 1) and there are doubts about how far it is possible to protect such ships which may have 500 or more passengers boarding in short periods of time (see Fairplay, July 21, 1988, 2).

It is not only large cruise ships or ferries that have been vulnerable to political attacks. In November 1987 Abu Nidal terrorists hijacked the 17 ton French pleasure craft *Silco*, which was cruising off the Gaza coast, and took eight hostages (*The Times*, November 9–11, 1987). A further category of cases might be those that involve seizures of vessels by governments as part of disputes with other countries. See, for example, the incidents involving the *Pueblo* and the *Mayaguez* (Birnie, *op. cit.*, pp. 145–6).

From these few examples it can be seen that the range of vessels at risk is large and that each may prevent different problems of security.

Piracy: the legal background

Piracy has long been considered illegal under international law and relevant provisions may be found in the Geneva Convention on the High Seas 1958 (especially Articles 14–23) and UNCLOS 1982 (especially Articles 100–107 and 110–111). States have an international obligation to repress piracy (Articles 14 and 100, respectively), seize pirate vessels (Articles 19 and 105, respectively), or pursue them from territorial waters to the high seas (Articles 23 and 110, respectively). The U.K. recognises the international law of piracy as defined in the 1958 Geneva Convention on the High Seas (see the Tokyo Convention Act 1967, s.4).

There are also two definitional problems in the Conventions. First, they outlaw "illegal acts of violence or detention, or any act of depredation *committed for private ends* by the crew or passengers of a private ship . . ." (Articles 15 and 101, respectively, emphasis added). There has been much debate about whether some of the political incidents described above are really piracy as they are not committed for "private ends" (see Birnie, *op. cit.*, p. 137, *cf.* S. Menefee, "The *Achille Lauro* and similar incidents as piracy: two arguments", in *Piracy at Sea*, *op. cit.*, pp. 179–180). It may be very difficult to describe the demands of the hijackers of the *Achille Lauro* for the release of 50 Palestinian prisoners as private and the gunmen on the *City of Poros* did not have robbery as a motive. Note that an unsuccessful attempt at robbery is still the crime of piracy *jure gentium* (see *Re Piracy Jure Gentium* [1934] A.C. 586).

The second problem of definition in the 1958 and 1982 Conventions is that they assume that the illegal acts are committed "against another ship" (Articles 15 and 101, respectively) and this may not fit easily into scenarios where hijackers only seize the ship on which they are passengers. (*Cf.* Menefee, *op. cit.*, for the somewhat strained view that the acts may be committed against the carrying ship on the high seas). Internationally, these definitional problems cause uncertainty about state rights in respect of terrorist hijackings—is there a right of seizure or hot pursuit? The jurist is then driven back to the familiar refuge of arguing that the Conventions are not exclusive and that there is customary international law to apply (*cf.* Menefee, *op. cit.*, p. 180). Even more unsatisfactory is the reliance by a state on its own municipal law (*cf.* Birnie, *op. cit.*, p. 147).

It should be noted that in Scottish law, piracy can apparently involve acts by a crew against its *own* ship, as they are regarded as a form of aggravated theft. See for example *Cameron* v. *Advocate (H.M.)* 1971 S.C. 50, where the crew of a trawler threatened and robbed a master, putting him ashore and taking possession of the ship.

Finally, in public international law, piracy can probably only occur on the high seas: similar conduct in national waters will be a matter for the laws of the coastal state. It seems that there is no equivalent common law offence of piracy (see *Existing U.K. legislation on maritime security*, below). However, this narrow definition would not necessarily apply in the private law fields, such as in a policy of marine insurance (*Athens Maritime Enterprises Corp.* v. *The Hellenic Mutual War Risks Association (Bermuda)*; *Andreas Lemos, The* [1983] Q.B. 647, 654 *et seq.*): see also J. Ignarski, "Terrorism in a maritime context: Law insurance and the legal implications of armed merchant ships", in *Violence at sea, op. cit.*, pp. 181–190.

Terrorism: legal and practical developments

Until the *Achille Lauro* hijacking, there does not appear to have been much legal discussion about maritime terrorism as a separate topic, as opposed to piracy or state attacks on neutral shipping (and see S. Menefee, "Terrorism at sea: the historical development of an international response", in *Violence at sea, op. cit.*, pp. 191–220). At the international level, the IMO Assembly adopted in 1979 a Resolution calling for measures to prevent and control "barratry and other unlawful seizure of ships and their cargoes". After consultations with industry bodies such as the ICS (International Chamber of Shipping), the 12th Session of the IMO Assembly adopted the "Recommendations on the Prevention and Suppression of Unlawful seizures of ships and their cargoes and other forms of maritime fraud" (Res. A.504 (XII) November 1981). The emphasis here was obviously on commercial depredations. The piracy problem was recognised by the production by IMO of a resolution, A.545(XIII), on November 17, 1983, on "measures to prevent acts of piracy and armed robbery against ships". For other bodies who have produced practical guidance, such as Bimco and the IMB (International Maritime Bureau), see *Piracy at Sea, op. cit.*, pp. 318–324 and *Violence at sea, op. cit.*, generally.

The *Achille Lauro* hijacking prompted a further IMO resolution, A.584(14), on November 20, 1985, on "measures to prevent unlawful acts which threaten the safety of ships and the security of their passengers and crews". This was directed towards producing technical ways of ensuring security and the Maritime Safety Committee of IMO prepared and adopted measures which were circulated to Governments and others. This lead was endorsed when IMO was requested by the General Assembly of the UN to make recommendations about terrorism aboard or against ships (see Resolution 40/61, December 9, 1985).

The question of further legislation was raised at the 57th Session of the IMO Council in November 1986. Austria, Egypt and Italy (the latter two most directly affected by the *Achille Lauro* incident) introduced a draft Convention and it was agreed to give the matter urgent consideration. An ad hoc preparatory Committee met in March and May 1987. It decided that "fixed platforms" should not be included in the scope of the draft Convention but agreed to consider an optional Protocol (for an account of the sessions see generally the documents PCUA 1/4 and PCUA 2/5). The Committee produced drafts of a Convention and Protocol (see LEG/Es.1/3, July 3, 1983).

The work of the ad hoc Committee was then referred to an extra-ordinary session of the IMO Legal Committee on October 19 and 20, 1987. Its attention was particularly drawn to four matters raised by the drafts, namely: (a) the position of demise charterers; (b) the obligation of States to accept offenders detained by the master; (c) the relationship of crew disciplinary questions to the Convention and (d) the harmonisation of terminology with UNCLOS. Following its Report (LEG/Es.1/5, October 27, 1987), the 58th Session of the IMO Council in June 1987 agreed to convene a diplomatic conference in Rome from March 1–10, 1988. The conference, which was attended by 69 States, adopted two treaty instruments, the Rome Convention 1988 and the Fixed Platforms Protocol 1988.

The Rome Convention 1988 and the Fixed Platforms Protocol 1988

The speed with which the international community moved from production of drafts to diplomatic conference indicated the priority that was attached to the terrorist problem. Birnie (*op. cit.*, p. 153) noted the small number of hijacking and terrorist offences that occur at sea and the lack of universality of the aircraft Convention and wondered about the likely success of the maritime equivalent. By June 1990, six states had become contracting parties to the Convention and Protocol.

For analysis of the Rome Convention, see D. Freestone, "The 1988 International Convention for the Suppression of Unlawful Acts against the Safety of Maritime Navigation" (1988) 3 IJECL 305, M. Halberstam, "Terrorism on the High Seas: The *Achille Lauro*, Piracy, and the IMO Convention on Maritime Safety" (1988) 82 A.J.I.L. 269-310.

In addition to the four matters specifically raised before the Legal Committee in 1987, noted above, a number of other questions arose for consideration during drafting.

Geographical extent. There was some dispute as to the geographical extent of the Convention. Under Art. 4 it applies, *inter alia*, if the ship is navigating or is scheduled to navigate into or through or from waters beyond the outer limit of the territorial sea of a state and also where an offender is found in the territorial sea of another State Party. The uncertainty was as to whether the Convention was to apply in straits used for international navigation, for example between two parts of the high seas. Para. 23 of the Final Act recorded the interpretation difficulty and stated that the Convention will apply in straits used for international navigation, without prejudice to the legal status of the waters forming such straits in accordance with relevant Conventions and other rules of law. In theory the Convention was not meant to apply to ships engaged on wholly domestic voyages such as the coasting trade (SUA/Conf/6, December 21, 1987) (*cf.* SUA/Conf/CW/Wp 23). This was to be a matter for national law. In the 1990 Act the Convention provisions have been given the widest possible application so as to apply to a ship whether the ship is in the U.K. or elsewhere (see for example s.9). There is a geographical limit to U.K. waters in s.9(2)(b); this is because the subsection goes beyond the Convention anyway as Art. 2 of the Convention excludes certain public ships. Note that the territorial waters of the U.K. are treated as part of the U.K. (see s.17(2) and LEG/ES.1/5, October 27, 1987, para. 55).

Nationality. Art. 6(1) of the Convention requires a State Party to establish jurisdiction in a minimum number of circumstances. These are where (a) the offence is committed in relation to a ship flying the State's flag, or (b) in the territory of a State, or (c) by a national of the State. Art. 6(2) allowed the state also to establish jurisdiction in three other specific circumstances. These were when (a) the offence was committed by a stateless person habitually resident in the State, or (b) during the commission of the offence a national of the State was seized, threatened, injured or killed, or (c) if the offence was committed in order to force the State to do or abstain from doing an act.

However, Pt. II of the 1990 Act does not impose any general restrictions based on the nationality of the defendant, see ss.9(1), 10(1), 11(4), 12(5), 13(3). The only exception relates to the public ship provisions derived from Art. 2 (see ss.9(2), 11(5), 12(6), and 13(4)). An offence under the Act will be committed by any person on the high seas in relation to any nationality of vessel even if none of the victims or attackers is a national of a State Party. The justification for the extension of jurisdiction under the Act is not quite clear, given the feeling that it might not be a good idea to have a proliferation of competing jurisdictions (*cf.* Leg/Es.1/5, October 27, 1987, p. 4). Art. 6(5) did state that the Convention was not to exclude any criminal jurisdiction exercised in accordance with national law, but this would seem to refer more to pre-existing provisions.

Demise charterers. Art. 6(2)(d) of the draft Convention produced by the ad hoc Committee would have allowed a State to establish jurisdiction when a demise charterer of a ship had its principal place of business in a State. Some countries considered that the demise provision was contrary to UNCLOS Arts. 91 and 92 which only recognised the exclusive jurisdiction of the flag state: it was wrong to extend on the basis of private control (SUA/Conf/6, December 21, 1987). Although there was disagreement about the effect of UNCLOS, Art. 6(2)(d) was dropped. Again, the 1990 Act would seem to have been extended to cover situations covered by this provision.

Interpretation. It should be noted that many provisions of the Convention and Protocol are derived from the Montreal Convention and Protocol. In general, the air instruments may assist in the interpretation of ambiguities in their maritime counterparts (*cf.* Steyn J. in *The European Enterprise* [1989] 2 Lloyd's Rep. 185, 192), but care should be taken to notice that there are differences in the texts. Moreover, the effects of damage on an aircraft may be much more drastic than for a ship.

Criminal extent. There is no doubt that the main mischief against which the Convention is aimed is that of terrorism. This is referred to explicitly in the third paragraph of the preamble to the Convention. However, the next paragraph, and the long title of the Convention, refer more widely to "unlawful acts against the safety of maritime navigation". The question arises of how far the Convention was intended to apply to what might be called "ordinary criminal violence", not relevant to the type of terrorist acts referred to in the UN and IMO Resolutions preceding the Convention. The Federal Republic of Germany voiced its concern, at the drafting stage, that the Convention ought not to cover minor offences, such as those in relation to on-board discipline (see SUA/Conf/CW/WP 11, March 2, 1988). It noted that the combination of the draft Arts. 1 and 3 would apply the Convention to ordinary criminal violence against small pleasure boats. Those provisions were not materially altered in the Convention or the equivalent provisions of the 1990 Act. There seems no reason why there could not be terrorism to a small pleasure craft—and there is every reason to apply it to the sort of hijacking of the pleasure craft *Silco* (see *Terrorism and piracy generally*, above, and the discussion on "ship", s.17, below).

The question of whether the Convention needed to, and did, extend to non-terrorist acts (if they can be defined) is more problematical. France considered that Art. 3(1)(e) and (f) were not really necessary in the maritime, as opposed to the air context, for damage to facilities or false communication could have very serious consequences for aircraft where the smallest harm could cause disaster. The only restriction in the maritime Convention is as to the "endangering safety" requirement (SUA/Conf/6, December 21, 1987). Similarly, it was said that a threat to commit one of the Convention offences, in Art. 3(2)(c), is not really a form of terrorism, but this is surely wrong.

Crew discipline. At one stage it was suggested that a provision be added to the Rome Convention 1988 stating that nothing in it was to create any new offence in relation to the normal maintenance of crew discipline. The Legal Committee noted that most delegations thought that there was no need for such a provision (see LEG/Es.1/5) The reasons varied, but the general feeling seemed to be that the ordinary powers of the master were adequate to control routine disciplinary matters. Nevertheless, it was recognised that there may be occasions where acts of the crew crossed the border of matters for internal discipline. This problem was resolved by the inclusion of a paragraph in the preamble to the Convention noting "that acts of the crew which are subject to normal shipboard discipline are outside the purview of this Convention". Accordingly, it is clear that members of the crew are not in any way excluded from the potential list of offences, but that some weight should be given to the intention of the Convention when interpreting provisions such as Art. 3(1)(c) (see s.11(1)(b)). So far as U.K. law is concerned there are adequate powers available under the Merchant Shipping Acts to discourage crew indiscipline and other general offences would be available in relation to personal attacks and property damage (see *Existing U.K. legislation on maritime security*, below).

Particular concern was expressed in the Commons about the position of the 25,000 workers on offshore platforms and the implications of offences such as ss.9(1) and 10(1) for those workers taking industrial action. This might include the occupation of a rig as part of a pay or safety dispute. Two disputes were mentioned (*Hansard*, H.C. Vol. 164, col. 982–3) where union officials had boarded a ship to inspect it for safety and where the crew of an emergency response vessel objected to the change of employer forced by an oil major. In both cases there were threats of criminal prosecutions and the question was raised about how far the new Act would add to such potential threats. At Second Reading in the Commons the Minister of Aviation and Shipping, Mr Patrick McLoughlin, agreed that the powers were widely drawn and could only point to the safeguard offered by the executive discretion provisions in s.16.

Political offences. Neither the Convention nor the Act allows for any defence of political necessity. Indeed the rationale of the Convention was to overcome the restrictions in UNCLOS Art. 101 restricting piracy to commercial depredations (see *The legal background to piracy*, above). The Libyan delegation unsuccessfully pressed for non-application of the Convention where there was "armed conflict for the struggle of peoples against colonial domination, foreign occupation and systems of racist regimes in exercise of its right of self-determination" (see Wp15/ rev.1/, March 4, 1988).

Public international law provisions. There are a number of provisions of a public international law nature which are not reproduced in the Act, for example Art. 12 (co-operation).

Existing U.K. legislation on maritime security

Special legislative provisions relating to maritime security matters are not unusual because of the inherent dangers posed by the sea. Thus, it is an offence under the Merchant Shipping Act 1970 s.30 for seamen to strike while a ship is at sea and the Mineral Workings (Offshore Installations) Act 1971, s.5, gives powers to the manager of a platform in order to avoid dangerous incidents. Special references are common in general security legislation. Thus, the Prevention of Terrorism (Temporary Provisions) Act 1989, s.16, provides specific powers to examine persons arriving at or leaving from designated ports in Great Britain or Northern Ireland. There are powers to allow examination, search and detention and to require production of documents (see Sched. 5 of the 1989 Act). Theoretically, a hijacker could commit the offence of taking a conveyance without authority under s.12 of the Theft Act 1968 as, under subs. (7), "conveyance" includes water transport. But the maximum penalty is only six months' imprisonment—clearly inadequate for a major hijacking.

As already indicated (see *Piracy: the legal background*, above), the Tokyo Convention Act 1967, s.4, confirms piracy on the high seas as an offence *jure gentium*. But, as noted by Law Commission in *The territorial and extra territorial extent of the criminal law* (Law Commission No. 91 (H.C. 75) 1978, para. 102), it is doubtful if piracy existed independently at common law in England and Wales. It is unlikely, therefore, that there is a separate offence of piracy in U.K. territorial waters. Moreover, acts by the crew and passengers against their own ship would probably not fall within the international definition of "piracy" (see *Piracy: the legal background*, above).

In so far as piracy is essentially a form of "aggravated theft" (*Piracy at Sea, op. cit.*, p. 6) it is already covered by the ordinary law, for example relating to robbery (see the Theft Act 1968, s.8). The penalty for robbery can already be life imprisonment. Similar punishments are possible for terrorist acts of violence, such as homicide. Indeed, the Government admitted during debates that there were parallels or duplications in Pt. II with existing criminal provisions.

It must therefore be asked whether the creation of a new species of terrorist offence really serves any purpose other than to demonstrate Governmental or international determination to confront the problem. In this sense, all that Pt. II of the Aviation and Maritime Security Act 1990 does is to apply a maximum penalty of life imprisonment expressly to terrorist offences against ships. Whether this threat is sufficient to deter the type of politically motivated terrorists of modern times may be open to doubt—particularly as they face death or injury at the hands of the security forces. Perhaps the matter should be seen in an international context where some countries have been less than willing to take rigorous action against terrorists, or to provide lasting punishments. Part of the reason is the differing international perceptions of what is terrorism. It is noticeable that after the *Achille Lauro* hijacking, three hijackers were sentenced by an Italian court to 30, 24 and 15 years imprisonment and three others (including the alleged ring-leader) were sentenced to life imprisonment *in absentia* (McWhinney, *op. cit.*, pp. 180–181). Although Pt. II may not make a significant difference to U.K. law and practice, it has to be viewed as a contribution to an international compact to renounce terrorism. It may also be relevant to the problem of piracy.

Hijacking of ships

9.—(1) A person who unlawfully, by the use of force or by threats of any kind, seizes a ship or exercises control of it, commits the offence of hijacking a ship, whatever his nationality and whether the ship is in the United Kingdom or elsewhere, but subject to subsection (2) below.

(2) Subsection (1) above does not apply in relation to a warship or any other ship used as a naval auxiliary or in customs or police service unless—

   (a) the person seizing or exercising control of the ship is a United Kingdom national, or

   (b) his act is committed in the United Kingdom, or

   (c) the ship is used in the naval or customs service of the United Kingdom or in the service of any police force in the United Kingdom.

(3) A person guilty of the offence of hijacking a ship is liable on conviction on indictment to imprisonment for life.

DEFINITIONS
   "naval service": s.17(1).
   "person": s.50, and the Interpretation Act 1978, Sched. 1.
   "ship": s.17(1).
   "United Kingdom": s.17(2), and the Interpretation Act 1978, Sched. 1.
   "United Kingdom national": s.17(1).

GENERAL NOTE

Subs. (1)
   Derivation: Rome Convention 1988 Art. 3(1)(a). *Cf.* the Hague Convention 1970, Art. 1 and the Aviation Security Act 1982, s.1.
   "Hijacking". This subsection creates a new offence of hijacking a ship, although the facts may justify an alternative charge (see the General Note to Pt. II, above). There may be a few cases of hijacking where robbery is not a motive and the threats are insufficient to justify charges of serious violence. The Law Commission had suggested in December 1978 that hijacking of ships be an offence (see *The territorial and extra-territorial extent of the criminal law*, Law Commission No. 91 (H.C. 75) 1978, p. 46).
   The subsection does not reproduce the Convention verbatim, as Art. 3(1)(a) required that a person act "unlawfully and intentionally". Presumably, it is difficult to accomplish a seizure inadvertently. The essence of the offence is taking control of a ship by force, or threats "of any kind". Such threats presumably need not be physical threats amounting to assault. They could include threats to damage property, or to encourage some accomplices elsewhere to take certain action. It is not clear if the threatened conduct has to be unlawful itself, as opposed to the seizure. A threat might be made to leak politically or personally embarrassing material.
   The definition of ship in s.17(1) excludes laid up vessels, but it does not necessarily have to be read in the light of the definition in the Merchant Shipping Act 1894, s.742. Ships could include

quite small vessels, such as a yacht or, indeed, a small rowing boat. It might seem rather absurd to apply notions of hijacking to acts of delinquency involving punts on a river, but see the discretion to prosecute filter provided by s.16, below.

There is no limit placed upon the offences by reason of geography or nationality, except in relation to the warship exception in subs. (2), below.

Seize or exercise control. It would be possible to seize or control part of a vessel, for example the bridge, or engine room, or ballroom. This scenario is quite possible in the context of hostage taking. Where a single terrorist, or a small gang, is involved it may sometimes be difficult to assert that there could be a takeover of the whole ship: there may be an uneasy situation where the crew and hijackers are each in control of part. The words "seize a ship" seem to suggest that the *actus reus* is committed only if there is a complete seizure. "Control" can be exercised over part of a ship, but the "control of it" would again seem to indicate a complete and total command. It is submitted that a better interpretation would be to consider the exercise of control in as broad a way as possible so as to bring within the offence those who may physically be able to control only a part, but who intend that their influence should extend over the whole ship. Attempted hijacking would be an offence under the Criminal Attempts Act 1981. This could be used, as an alternative, for the failed hijack which resulted in only partial control being achieved, but it may be difficult to do so where there was only an intention to seize part of the ship in the first place. In any event, it is very likely that another offence will have been committed, under the general law, or for example under s.11.

"Unlawfully". This is not separately defined (*cf.* s.11(7)). The requirement is meant to exclude persons such as police or customs officers who might try to detain a ship, or the Admiralty Marshal who might try to enforce an order of arrest from the Admiralty Court (see PCUA 1/4).

"Person". (*Cf.* s.50 for bodies corporate). During negotiations for the Convention, Cuba and Nicaragua tried to add "or a government " to the list of persons who could commit an offence (see WP33, March 7, 1988). The concept of "state terrorism", where a country uses terrorism as part of its foreign policy, had been advanced in 1984 (see McWhinney, *op. cit.*, p. 153), but the amendment was presumably aimed at the U.S.A., which had mined harbours in Nicaragua and "diverted" to an Italian NATO base an Egyptian plane carrying the suspected hijackers of the *Achille Lauro* (as well as bombing Libya in 1986).

Hoaxes. See the note to s.1, above, which indicates the existing offences that could be created by hoax terrorist threats.

Subs. (2)
Derivation: Rome Convention 1988, Art. 2. The latter excluded from the scope of the Convention warships and state-owned ships used as naval auxiliaries or for customs or police purposes. The Government exercised its powers to increase the scope of the Convention where the hijacking is committed by a U.K. national, by any person within the U.K. or where U.K. naval, customs or police vessels are concerned (anywhere in the world).

Subs. (3)
Derivation: Rome Convention 1988, Art. 5, Fixed Platforms Protocol 1988, Art. 1.

Seizing or exercising control of fixed platforms

10.—(1) A person who unlawfully, by the use of force or by threats of any kind, seizes a fixed platform or exercises control of it, commits an offence, whatever his nationality and whether the fixed platform is in the United Kingdom or elsewhere.

(2) A person guilty of an offence under this section is liable on conviction on indictment to imprisonment for life.

DEFINITIONS
"fixed platform": s.17(1).
"United Kingdom": s.17(2), and the Interpretation Act 1978, Sched. 1.
"unlawfully": *cf.* s.11(7).

GENERAL NOTE
Derivation: Fixed Platforms Protocol 1988 Art. 2(1)(c). *Cf.* s.9, above, the Hague Convention 1970, Art. 1 and the Aviation Security Act 1982, s.1.

"Hijacking" a platform. In effect, this section is the equivalent of the hijacking provision in s.9, above, although a platform to which this section applies cannot be taken anywhere. The

definition in s.17(1) makes it clear that only fixed platforms are covered. However, a semi-submersible or jack-up oil rig would fall within the definition of *ship* in s.17(1) (and thus be covered by s.9), so there is no chance of a type of platform falling between the two definitions.

Industrial disputes. Concern was expressed at the extent to which a provision inspired by terrorism might, in turn, be used to "terrorise" workers in an industrial dispute (see the discussion on *Crew discipline*, in the General Note to Pt. II, above, and s.11, below). The opposition proposed an amendment which would have provided a defence if an act was committed incidentally in the course of an industrial dispute. The Government rejected this partly because it wished to give precise effect to the Convention provision, but also because of the prosecution discretion given by s.16.

Destroying ships or fixed platforms or endangering their safety

11.—(1) Subject to subsection (5) below, a person commits an offence if he unlawfully and intentionally—
  (a) destroys a ship or a fixed platform,
  (b) damages a ship, its cargo or a fixed platform so as to endanger, or to be likely to endanger, the safe navigation of the ship, or as the case may be, the safety of the platform, or
  (c) commits on board a ship or on a fixed platform an act of violence which is likely to endanger the safe navigation of the ship, or as the case may be, the safety of the platform.
  (2) Subject to subsection (5) below, a person commits an offence if he unlawfully and intentionally places, or causes to be placed, on a ship or fixed platform any device or substance which—
  (a) in the case of a ship, is likely to destroy the ship or is likely so to damage it or its cargo as to endanger its safe navigation, or
  (b) in the case of a fixed platform, is likely to destroy the fixed platform or so to damage it as to endanger its safety.
  (3) Nothing in subsection (2) above is to be construed as limiting the circumstances in which the commission of any act—
  (a) may constitute an offence under subsection (1) above, or
  (b) may constitute attempting or conspiring to commit, or aiding, abetting, counselling, procuring or inciting, or being art and part in, the commission of such an offence.
  (4) Except as provided by subsection (5) below, subsections (1) and (2) above apply whether any such act as is mentioned in those subsections is committed in the United Kingdom or elsewhere and whatever the nationality of the person committing the act.
  (5) Subsections (1) and (2) above do not apply in relation to any act committed in relation to a warship or any other ship used as a naval auxiliary or in customs or police service unless—
  (a) the person committing the act is a United Kingdom national, or
  (b) his act is committed in the United Kingdom, or
  (c) the ship is used in the naval or customs service of the United Kingdom or in the service of any police force in the United Kingdom.
  (6) A person guilty of an offence under this section is liable on conviction on indictment to imprisonment for life.
  (7) In this section—
    "act of violence" means—
    (a) any act done in the United Kingdom which constitutes the offence of murder, attempted murder, manslaughter, culpable homicide or assault or an offence under section 18, 20, 21, 22, 23, 24, 28 or 29 of the Offences against the Person Act 1861 or under section 2 of the Explosive Substances Act 1883, and
    (b) any act done outside the United Kingdom which, if done in the United Kingdom, would constitute such an offence as is mentioned in paragraph (a) above, and
    "unlawfully"—

(a) in relation to the commission of an act in the United Kingdom, means so as (apart from this Act) to constitute an offence under the law of the part of the United Kingdom in which the act is committed, and

(b) in relation to the commission of an act outside the United Kingdom, means so that the commission of the act would (apart from this Act) have been an offence under the law of England and Wales if it had been committed in England and Wales or of Scotland if it had been committed in Scotland.

DEFINITIONS
"act of violence": subs. (7).
"England": Interpretation Act 1978, Sched. 1.
"fixed platform": s.17(1).
"naval service": s.17(1).
"person": s.50, and the Interpretation Act 1978, Sched. 1.
"ship": s.17(1).
"United Kingdom": s.17(2), and the Interpretation Act 1978, Sched. 1.
"United Kingdom national": s.17(1).
"unlawfully": subs. (7).
"Wales": Interpretation Act 1978, Sched. 1.

GENERAL NOTE
Destroying or endangering ships or platforms. The section creates a number of offences in respect of persons who deliberately endanger ships and platforms: by destroying or damaging them, or by committing acts of violence on board, or by placing on them devices such as bombs.

"Intentionally". The drafting of the international and domestic legislation makes it rather unclear whether the prosecution must prove that the defendant intended merely to do the relevant act (such as destroying, or damaging a ship), or whether it must also be shown that he intended the consequence (for example the endangering of the ship or platform). It is submitted that the better view is that, despite the gravity of the offence, there are grounds for requiring only the lower degree of proof of *mens rea*. The wording of Art. 3 of the Rome Convention 1988 seems to lend some support to this. For example, Art. 3(1)(b) (the equivalent of s.11(1)(c)) seems to emphasise the need to look at whether the *act* of violence is likely to endanger the vessel, as opposed to whether the defendant *intended* this. (See also the discussion on s.1(1)(b), above).

"Likely to" endanger or destroy. These expressions (in subss. (1) and (2)) gave rise to much discussion during the drafting of the Convention. They are based on Art. 1 of the Montreal Convention 1971 (see the Aviation Security Act 1982, ss.2 and 3). In the air context any damage is "likely" to cause destruction: at sea, this will not necessarily be the case. The expression "might foreseeably" was proposed at one stage of the negotiations (see PCUA 1/4), but the present text was the result of a compromise at the ad hoc Committee. Australia (SUA/Conf/10, January 20, 1988) considered that "likely" was too narrow, as terrorism might include violence not harming the ship and suggested that "could" would be better. This proposal was also rejected.

Accordingly, there may be cases of violence or damage (or the placement of "devices or substances") which do *not* endanger safe navigation. Wanton destruction of a valuable cargo, for example computers in a container, might not affect the operation of the ship as a vessel (as opposed to a floating warehouse). In the case of a platform, similar considerations should apply, for example to destruction of non-flammable stores. The use of the words "likely to endanger" show that there must be more than a mere possibility of danger (see also the note to s.1(1), above).

Industrial disputes. (See the discussion in s.10, above, and on *Crew discipline* in the General Note to Pt. II, above). There may be occasions when a member of the crew deliberately damages a ship, perhaps after a dispute with the master. In such a case it is questionable whether it was intended that an offence could be committed under an Act mainly designed to deal with terrorism, as quite a small amount of damage could cause danger. Some protection against the possibility of a life sentence for an act of ill discipline is afforded by the "likely to endanger" requirement (see above), but it is submitted that on an ordinary meaning of the words an offence could be committed by a crew member. If such is the literal interpretation of the provision, there is a very strong case for the Attorney-General to refuse to give consent to proceedings, under s.16, where the actions have not crossed the borderline between ill-discipline and terrorism.

It seems that it was not the intention of the Government that the section be used in relation to operational negligence.

Hoaxes. See the notes to ss.1, 10, 12(3). In October 1989 a suspected bomb was found aboard a gas platform in Morecambe Bay at the time of the Conservative Party Conference in Blackpool. 300 men were kept on board for about 10 hours until the package was discovered to be a hoax. It would appear that the 1990 Act would not create any new offences in relation to such an incident and a prosecution would have to be brought under existing legislation such as the Criminal Law Act 1977, s.51, as mentioned in the note to s.1, above. By virtue of the Continental Shelf Act 1989 U.K. law applies on platforms. *N.B.* the 1977 Act would not apply to the platforms in the Scottish sector: see s.65(10) of that Act.

Subs. (1)
  Para. (a)
  Derivation: Rome Convention 1988, Art. 3(1)(c), Fixed Platforms Protocol 1988, Art. 2(1) (c). *Cf.* the Montreal Convention 1971, Art. 1(1)(b); the Aviation Security Act 1982, s.2.
  Destroying a ship or platform. There is no definition of "destruction" and it is presumed that the paragraph requires the actual (or constructive) total loss of the ship or platform.

  Para. (b)
  Derivation: Rome Convention 1988, Art. 3(1)(c), Fixed Platforms Protocol 1988, Art. 2(1) (c). *Cf.* the Montreal Convention 1971, Art. 1(1)(b); the Aviation Security Act 1982, s.2.
  Damaging a ship, cargo or platform. An offence under this paragraph is committed where there is (i) damage, which (ii) endangers (or is likely to endanger) the safe navigation of (iii) the ship, its cargo or a platform. Examples would include cases of the person who severed electrical cabling to the bridge, or smashed a radar set, or set fire to cargo (causing evacuation of the engine room).

  Para. (c)
  Derivation: Rome Convention 1988, Art. 3(1)(b); Fixed Platforms Protocol 1988, Art. 2(1) (b). *Cf.* the Montreal Convention 1971, Art. 1(1)(a); the Aviation Security Act 1982, s.2.
  Acts of violence endangering safety. The offence here is of endangering safety by committing an act of violence on board a ship or platform, for example by assaulting the officer of the watch. The sub-paragraph differs from the Convention and Protocol which require an act of violence to be performed "against a person" which itself endangers the safe navigation of the ship. As it is possible to commit an act of violence against a thing the Act might appear to include as an offence an act of vandalism which could affect safe navigation. However, subs. (7) makes it clear that the Convention formula is to be followed. Accordingly, the subsection does not overlap with the Criminal Damage Act 1971, for which the punishment is 10 years, as opposed to life imprisonment under the 1990 Act (see subs. (6), below).

Subs. (2)
  Derivation: Rome Convention 1988, Art. 3(1)(d); Fixed Platforms Protocol 1988, Art. 2(1) (d). *Cf.* the Montreal Convention 1971, Art. 1(1)(c); the Aviation Security Act 1982, s.2(2).
  Placing bombs, etc. The subsection creates an offence of endangering the safety of ships or platforms by placing items such as bombs or explosives on board. The placing must also result in likely destruction or the endangerment of safety (see note to subs. (1), above).
  "Places". The subsection does not say how the device or substance has to be placed on board. The Convention and Protocol make it clear that the placing can be by "any means whatsoever". This would include the using of a "dupe" to take a bomb aboard. In the U.K. this would presumably be covered by the offence of procuring, preserved by subs. (3).
  "Device or substance". Although the provision is aimed mainly at explosives, it is not limited to them. Poisonous chemicals could cause the evacuation of the bridge. Comparatively innocuous compounds could be introduced into machinery in order to cause it to seize up.

Subs. (3)
  The subsection preserves the normal preparatory offences, such as aiding and abetting (and see subs. (2), above). Note also the offence under s.13 of threatening to commit an offence under s.11(1).

Subs. (4)
  There is no limit placed upon the offences by reason of geography or nationality—except in relation to the warship exception in subs. (5), below.

Subs. (5)
  Derivation: Rome Convention 1988, Art. 2. See the note to s.9(2), above.

Subs. (7)
   Cf. the note to s.1(9), above.
   "Unlawfully".
   Derivation: Rome Convention 1988, Art. 3(1). The Convention did not define "unlawfully".
Cf. the note to s.9(1), above.

Other acts endangering or likely to endanger safe navigation

12.—(1) Subject to subsection (6) below, it is an offence for any person unlawfully and intentionally—

   (a) to destroy or damage any property to which this subsection applies, or

   (b) seriously to interfere with the operation of any such property,

where the destruction, damage or interference is likely to endanger the safe navigation of any ship.

(2) Subsection (1) above applies to any property used for the provision of maritime navigation facilities, including any land, building or ship so used, and including any apparatus or equipment so used, whether it is on board a ship or elsewhere.

(3) Subject to subsection (6) below, it is also an offence for any person intentionally to communicate any information which he knows to be false in a material particular, where the communication of the information endangers the safe navigation of any ship.

(4) It is a defence for a person charged with an offence under subsection (3) above to prove that, when he communicated the information, he was lawfully employed to perform duties which consisted of or included the communication of information and that he communicated the information in good faith in performance of those duties.

(5) Except as provided by subsection (6) below, subsections (1) and (3) above apply whether any such act as is mentioned in those subsections is committed in the United Kingdom or elsewhere and whatever the nationality of the person committing the act.

(6) For the purposes of subsections (1) and (3) above any danger, or likelihood of danger, to the safe navigation of a warship or any other ship used as a naval auxiliary or in customs or police service is to be disregarded unless—

   (a) the person committing the act is a United Kingdom national, or

   (b) his act is committed in the United Kingdom, or

   (c) the ship is used in the naval or customs service of the United Kingdom or in the service of any police force in the United Kingdom.

(7) A person guilty of an offence under this section is liable on conviction on indictment to imprisonment for life.

(8) In this section "unlawfully" has the same meaning as in section 11 of this Act.

DEFINITIONS
   "maritime navigational facilities": subs. (2).
   "naval service": s.17(1).
   "person": s.50, and the Interpretation Act 1978, Sched. 1.
   "ship": s.17(1).
   "United Kingdom": s.17(2), and the Interpretation Act 1978, Sched. 1.
   "United Kingdom national": s.17(1).
   "unlawfully": subs. (8); s.11(7).

GENERAL NOTE
   The section creates two sets of offences of endangering safe navigation: (i) destroying, damaging or interfering with navigational facilities and (ii) communicating false information. Note that these offences are committed only in relation to ships and not platforms.

Subss. (1) and (2)
   Derivation: Rome Convention 1988, Art. 3(1)(e). *Cf*. the Montreal Convention 1971, Art. 1 (1)(d) and the Aviation Security Act 1982, s.3.

Interfering with navigational facilities. Subs. (1) creates offences where persons damage, destroy or seriously interfere with navigational facilities. The activities must endanger the safe navigation of the ship (*cf.* s.11, above).

"Intentionally". See the note to s.11, above.

"Marine navigational facilities". The Convention provides no definition of the facilities, but the Act effectively repeats the Aviation Security Act 1982, s.3(2), which is the equivalent provision for aircraft. The facilities could include radar or satellite navigation equipment on board ship, or on land. They could also include floating buoys or beacons and lighthouses on land. An act of vandalism could damage the building housing the equipment, but the damage would need to endanger navigation for there to be an offence.

Subs. (3)

Derivation: Rome Convention 1988, Art. 3(1)(f). *Cf.* the Montreal Convention 1971, Art. 1 (1)(e); the Aviation Security Act 1982, s.3(3).

Communicating false information. This provision was introduced by the New Zealand delegation who justified it by giving the example of somebody deliberately misleading shipping in a crowded or difficult waterway (see WP/1, March 1, 1988). There were criticisms of the provision for being overly vague (see the FRG in WP/11, March 2, 1988).

The words "in a material particular" in the subsection do not appear in the Convention and it is not clear what they achieve. On the Convention wording it might be possible for someone to commit an offence by giving some false information that is quite trivial, but without realising the consequences (note that under the Convention the communication also has to be unlawful, see below). It is difficult to give a precise example, but perhaps someone gives the wrong time to a vessel for a prank and the master decides to leave early, expecting to be able to navigate safely over a rock normally covered at high tide. It may be that the reference to "material" particular in the Act is meant to signify that the defendant is to be aware of the causative potential of the false communication. But the Convention simply requires the defendant to know of the falsity of the information, not that it is likely to cause danger to safe navigation. There are indications that this was deliberate (see the note to s.11, *Intentionally*, above and *cf.* Art. 3(1)(c) and (d)) and so the Act may have created an offence narrower than that in the Convention.

The Convention provision required that the communication be unlawful, although the Act appears—in part at least—to have omitted this element of the offence (see subs. (4), below).

It is possible that a bomb hoaxer could be convicted under this subsection. A charge was brought in relation to a bomb scare under the equivalent aviation provision, s.3 of the Aviation Security Act 1982 (see the note to s.1, above).

Subs. (4)

Defence. The subsection creates a limited defence to a subs. (3) charge where a person can show that false information was given as part of his job. The type of person could include a coast guard officer who is instructed to test the alertness of those in charge of a ship. In debates the example was given of a person instructed by the security service to transmit false information to a ship which had been hijacked. Although such information could endanger the ship it would be intended to direct it to a position from where a recovery attempt might be made. (*Cf.* the Aviation Security Act 1982, s.3(4)).

The defence is very restricted as the defendant must show that his job involved communicating information generally and that he acted in good faith. As the subs. (3) offence requires the navigation of the ship to be endangered, it will be difficult for the defendant in good faith to say that this was justified by the holding of an exercise. Good faith would probably be established by showing an intent to revoke an incorrect communication at the earliest opportunity.

"Lawfully". Under Art. 3(1)(f) of the Rome Convention 1988 a person has to communicate the false information "unlawfully and intentionally". The intentional requirement is dealt with in subs. (3), above, while the unlawfulness point appears only partly in subs. (4), in an inverted manner. The defence refers only to lawful employment, although arguably lawfulness (under the Convention) could be construed more widely. Moreover, the onus is on the defence to establish the lawfulness, while under the Convention it would appear that unlawfulness is an ingredient of the *actus reus* that would have to be proved by the prosecution. It is not quite clear by reference to whose law the matter is to be judged. Presumably the reference to "lawfully" in subs. (4) does not allow reference to s.11(7), which defines "unlawfully". Where the communication takes place outside the United Kingdom it would presumably be a defence to prove that the act was done as part of the person's lawful employment in that place.

Subs. (5)

There is no limit placed upon the offences by reason of geography or nationality, except in relation to the warship exception in subs. (5), below.

Subs. (6)
   Derivation: Rome Convention 1988, Art. 2. See the note to s.9(2), above.

Offences involving threats

   13.—(1) A person commits an offence if—
   (a) in order to compel any other person to do or abstain from doing any act, he threatens that he or some other person will do in relation to any ship or fixed platform an act which is an offence by virtue of section 11(1) of this Act, and
   (b) the making of that threat is likely to endanger the safe navigation of the ship or, as the case may be, the safety of the fixed platform.
   (2) Subject to subsection (4) below, a person commits an offence if—
   (a) in order to compel any other person to do or abstain from doing any act, he threatens that he or some other person will do an act which is an offence by virtue of section 12(1) of this Act, and
   (b) the making of that threat is likely to endanger the safe navigation of any ship.
   (3) Except as provided by subsection (4) below, subsections (1) and (2) above apply whether any such act as is mentioned in those subsections is committed in the United Kingdom or elsewhere and whatever the nationality of the person committing the act.
   (4) Section 12(6) of this Act applies for the purposes of subsection (2)(b) above as it applies for the purposes of section 12(1) and (3) of this Act.
   (5) A person guilty of an offence under this section is liable on conviction on indictment to imprisonment for life.

DEFINITIONS
   "fixed platform": s.17(1).
   "person": s.50, and the Interpretation Act 1978, Sched. 1.
   "ship": s.17(1).
   "United Kingdom": s.17(2), and the Interpretation Act 1978, Sched. 1.

GENERAL NOTE

Subs. (1)
   Derivation: Rome Convention 1988, Art. 3(2)(c); Fixed Platforms Protocol 1988, Art. 2(2)(c).
   Threats to ships or platforms. The subsection creates an offence of endangering safety by threatening to commit a s.11(1) offence (for example by destroying or damaging a ship or platform). The threat has to be aimed at compelling another person, such as the ship's master, to do or abstain from doing something. An example would be where a terrorist forced a master to anchor by the threat of opening fire on the ship.

Subs. (2)
   Derivation: Rome Convention 1988, Art. 3(2)(c); Fixed Platforms Protocol 1988, Art. 2(2)(c).
   Threats to maritime navigation facilities. The subsection creates an offence similar to that in subs. (1), above, but in relation to threats to commit a s.12(1) offence (for example to damage navigational facilities ashore in a way that would endanger shipping).

Subss. (3) and (4)
   There is no limit placed upon the offences by reason of geography or nationality, except in relation to the warship exception in subs. (4). For the purposes of subs. (2)(b) only, reference can be made to s.12(6).

Ancillary offences

   14.—(1) Where a person (of whatever nationality) does outside the United Kingdom any act which, if done in the United Kingdom, would constitute an offence falling within subsection (2) below, his act shall constitute that offence if it is done in connection with an offence under section 9, 10, 11 or 12 of this Act committed or attempted by him.

(2) The offences falling within this subsection are murder, attempted murder, manslaughter, culpable homicide and assault and offences under sections 18, 20, 21, 22, 23, 28 and 29 of the Offences against the Person Act 1861 and section 2 of the Explosive Substances Act 1883.

(3) Subsection (1) above has effect without prejudice to section 686 or 687 of the Merchant Shipping Act 1894 (offences committed on board British ships or by British seamen) or section 22 of the Oil and Gas (Enterprise) Act 1982 (application of criminal law to offshore installations).

(4) It is an offence for any person in the United Kingdom to induce or assist the commission outside the United Kingdom of any act which—

(a) would, but for subsection (2) of section 9 of this Act, be an offence under that section, or

(b) would, but for subsection (5) of section 11 of this Act, be an offence under that section, or

(c) would, but for subsection (6) of section 12 of this Act, be an offence under that section, or

(d) would, but for subsection (4) of section 13 of this Act, be an offence under that section.

(5) A person who commits an offence under subsection (4) above is liable on conviction on indictment to imprisonment for life.

(6) Subsection (4) above has effect without prejudice to the operation, in relation to any offence under section 9, 11, 12 or 13 of this Act—

(a) in England and Wales, or in Northern Ireland, of section 8 of the Accessories and Abettors Act 1861, or

(b) in Scotland, of any rule of law relating to art and part guilt.

DEFINITIONS
"person": s.50, and the Interpretation Act 1978, Sched. 1.
"United Kingdom": s.17(2), and the Interpretation Act 1978, Sched. 1.

GENERAL NOTE
Derivation: Rome Convention 1988, Art. 3(1)(g).
This section implements the provision of the Rome Convention that makes it an offence to injure or kill in the course of one of the other Art. 3 offences (ss.9–12 of the Act). There is a large measure of overlap with existing offences (*cf.* the note to s.1(1), above).
There was some suggestion during the drafting of the Convention that injuring or killing in the course of committing one of the other offences should merely be an aggravating provision, rather than a separate offence. The view which prevailed was that it was important to address these attacks specifically, not least because the citizens of particular states may be singled out (as happened on board the *Achille Lauro*). (See PCUA 1/4, March 16, 1987).
The section leaves unaffected the general jurisdictional rules of maritime (and offshore exploration) law, for example that the U.K. courts have jurisdiction over offences committed aboard U.K. registered ships (see subs. (3)).
Attempts. Derivation: Rome Convention 1988, Art. 3(2)(a); Fixed Platforms Protocol 1988, Art. 2(2).
See generally the Criminal Attempts Act 1981.

Master's power of delivery

15.—(1) The provisions of this section shall have effect for the purposes of any proceedings before any court in the United Kingdom.

(2) If the master of a ship, wherever that ship may be, and whatever the State (if any) in which it may be registered, has reasonable grounds to believe that any person on board the ship has—

(a) committed any offence under section 9, 11, 12 or 13 of this Act,

(b) attempted to commit such an offence, or

(c) aided, abetted, counselled, procured or incited, or been art and part in, the commission of such an offence, in relation to any ship other than a warship or other ship used as a naval auxiliary or in customs or police service, he may deliver that person to an appropriate officer in the United Kingdom or any other Convention country.

(3) Where the master of a ship intends to deliver any person in the United Kingdom or any other Convention country in accordance with subsection (2) above he shall give notification to an appropriate officer in that country—

(a) of his intention to deliver that person to an appropriate officer in that country; and

(b) of his reasons for intending to do so.

(4) Any notification under subsection (3) above must be given—

(a) before the ship in question has entered the territorial sea of the country concerned; or

(b) if in the circumstances it is not reasonably practicable to comply with paragraph (a) above, as soon as reasonably practicable after the ship has entered that territorial sea.

(5) Where the master of a ship delivers any person to an appropriate officer in any country under subsection (2) above he shall—

(a) make to an appropriate officer in that country such oral or written statements relating to the alleged offence as that officer may reasonably require; and

(b) deliver to an appropriate officer in that country such other evidence relating to the alleged offence as is in the master's possession.

(6) The master of a ship who without reasonable excuse fails to comply with subsection (3) or (5) above is guilty of an offence and liable on summary conviction to a fine not exceeding level 3 on the standard scale.

(7) It is a defence for a master of a ship charged with an offence under subsection (6) above of failing to comply with subsection (3) above to show that he believed on reasonable grounds that the giving of the notification required by subsection (3) above would endanger the safety of the ship and, except where the country concerned is the United Kingdom, that either—

(a) he notified some other competent authority in the country concerned within the time required by subsection (4) above, or

(b) he believed on reasonable grounds that the giving of notification to any competent authority in that country would endanger the safety of the ship.

(8) In this section—

"appropriate officer" means—

(a) in relation to the United Kingdom, a constable or immigration officer, and

(b) in relation to any other Convention country, an officer having functions corresponding to the functions in the United Kingdom either of a constable or of an immigration officer,

"Convention country" means a country in which the Convention for the Suppression of Unlawful Acts against the Safety of Maritime Navigation, which was signed at Rome on March 10, 1988, is for the time being in force; and Her Majesty may by Order in Council certify that any country specified in the Order is for the time being a Convention country and any such Order in Council for the time being in force shall be conclusive evidence that the country in question is for the time being a Convention country, and

"master" has the same meaning as in the Merchant Shipping Act 1894.

DEFINITIONS
"appropriate officer": subs. (8).

"Convention country": subs. (8).
"master": subs. (8) and the Merchant Shipping Act, s.742.
"ship": s.17(1).
"United Kingdom": s.17(2), and the Interpretation Act 1978, Sched. 1.

GENERAL NOTE
Derivation: Rome Convention 1988, Art. 8.
Delivery of offenders. The purpose of the section is to allow the master of a ship flagged in a State Party to deliver up offenders to the authorities of another State Party. This provision was added to the Rome Convention to give some protection to the master who has detained an offender on board his ship, but who faces a certain reluctance from States to relieve him of his burden. States might, for political reasons, refuse to accept terrorists so as to avoid becoming the focus of future attacks designed to free them.
There was discussion as to whether it would be right to allow an individual to create obligations for States (see Leg/Es.1/5, October 27, 1987). It was also suggested that the discretion should be restricted to those circumstances where there was no other reasonable alternative (*ibid.*). In the end there were no restrictions imposed on the discretion, although there were requirements as to reasonable suspicion of an offence and notification to the receiving State: see Arts. 8(1) and 8(2) (s.15(2) and (3)). However, Art. 8(3) imposed a duty on the receiving State to accept delivery, except where it has grounds to consider that the Convention is not applicable, and then it must give a statement of reasons. If it does accept, it can, under Art. 8(5), request the flag State to accept delivery. It does not appear that the flag State has any obligation to do so, although it must consider the request and give reasons. The 1990 Act contains no provisions regulating the duties of the U.K. authorities in this regard.
"On board". The master has power to deliver an offender even if the master does not believe an offence has been committed while the offender is on board his ship. It may be that the master believes the person has committed an offence in relation to another ship, or has made threats while not on board any ship. The original Bill was narrower than the Convention in requiring the offence to be committed on board the carrying ship.

Subs. (1)
This subsection gives effect to the delivery provisions as they would arise before a U.K. court.

Subs. (2)
Derivation: Rome Convention 1988, Art. 8(1).
The master's choice. The master is given the option of delivering the offender: he is not obliged to give him up by this section. The option does not have to be exercised by a ship in U.K. waters. Delivery may be made to any State Party and the U.K. would be obliged to take delivery from the master of a ship belonging to another flag state. However, it would be possible to dispute that the master had reasonable grounds on which to base his suspicion. Under Art. 8 of the Convention, a State Party which refuses to accept delivery is obliged to accompany it with a statement of reasons. Where delivery is accepted, the receiving State can request the flag State to take delivery, although there is no obligation on it to do so.
"Other than a warship". This exception follows the Convention (see the note to s.9(2)), but it puts the master who has on board a person whom he suspects of having committed an offence against a warship in a rather difficult position. He may well have the right to detain under his general powers as master, but the specific power of delivery given by the Convention would not be available.

Subss. (3) and (4)
Derivation: Rome Convention 1988, Art. 8(2) and see, in turn, the Tokyo Convention 1963, Art. 9(2).
Notification. There may be some initial reluctance, at a port, for the authorities to receive a person whom the master describes as a terrorist. Art. 8(2) of the Rome Convention 1988 puts a qualified obligation on the master to notify the receiving State of his intention to deliver an offender. Subss. (3) and (4) give effect to this obligation. The notification has to be made to a police or immigration officer in the U.K., and their equivalents overseas. The notification must state the intention to deliver *and* the reasons for it. Presumably, it will be sufficient for a master to provide, in outline only, the basis for his belief that the person concerned has committed an offence.
Time of notification. States were concerned that the master should make his intentions known at the earliest opportunity. If possible, this should be before the ship enters the territorial sea of the receiving country. In many cases a master may be ignorant of the precise territorial sea claimed by a State. If he has doubts about this, or if he is already in territorial

waters when the offence took place, he should give notice as soon as "reasonably practicable" thereafter. Art. 8(2) of the Rome Convention 1988 uses the expression "whenever practicable", but it is not thought that there is any material difference. During negotiations an amendment requiring notification "at the earliest possible time" was rejected (see SUA/Conf/ CW/Wp 39).

Subs. (5)
Derivation: Rome Convention 1988, Art. 8(4).
Reporting. The flag State has an obligation to furnish the receiving State with evidence in the master's possession: see now, para. (b) of this subsection. Para. (a) of the subsection seems to go slightly further than the Convention in obliging the master to provide written or oral statements to appropriate officers. Arguably, this is merely an expansion of the obligation to give reasons in subs. 3(b), although subs. (3) is really directed to the position before, rather than after, delivery.

Subss. (6) and (7)
Offence. The Convention puts an obligation on the flag State to enforce the master's obligations of notification and reporting. This subsection gives effect to that obligation by making it an offence for the master to fail to comply with the requirements, for example by failing to notify in time of his intention to deliver.
Defences. There is a defence of reasonable excuse in subs. (6), as well as the inbuilt qualification in subs. (4) relating to reasonable practicality. Subs. (7) provides a separate defence for the type of circumstance where a master does not want to provide notification of his intentions as this might assist terrorists in making a further attack on his vessel. The defence does not appear in the Convention and is really a more specific example of the practicality defence, above.

Prosecution of offences and proceedings

16.—(1) Proceedings for an offence under any provision of this Part of this Act shall not be instituted—
   (a) in England and Wales, except by, or with the consent of, the Attorney General, and
   (b) in Northern Ireland, except by, or with the consent of, the Attorney General for Northern Ireland.
   (2) As respects Scotland, for the purpose of conferring on the sheriff jurisdiction to entertain proceedings for an offence under or by virtue of this Part of this Act, any such offence shall, without prejudice to any jurisdiction exercisable apart from this subsection, be deemed to have been committed in any place in Scotland where the offender may for the time being be.

DEFINITIONS
"England": Interpretation Act 1978, Sched. 1.
"Wales": Interpretation Act 1978, Sched. 1.

GENERAL NOTE
See the note to s.1(7), above on the discretion to prosecute.
In Scotland, procurators fiscal have a wide discretion about when to prosecute, but are subject to Directions from the Lord Advocate. When a new Act is passed, the Lord Advocate circulates information and sets out the policy on prosecutions. During debates, the Minister undertook to ask him to take into account the point that Pt. II is not intended to be used in industrial disputes cases (Standing Committee A, col. 104). See also *Crew Discipline*, in the General Note to Pt. II, above.

Interpretation of Part II

17.—(1) In this Part of this Act—
   "fixed platform" means—
      (a) any offshore installation, within the meaning of the Mineral Workings (Offshore Installations) Act 1971, which is not a ship, and
      (b) any other artificial island, installation or structure which—
         (i) permanently rests on, or is permanently attached to, the seabed,

(ii) is maintained for the purposes of the exploration or exploitation of resources or for other economic purposes, and

(iii) is not connected with dry land by a permanent structure providing access at all times and for all purposes;

"naval service" includes military and air force service;

"ship" means any vessel (including hovercraft, submersible craft and other floating craft) other than one which—

(a) permanently rests on, or is permanently attached to, the seabed, or

(b) has been withdrawn from navigation or laid up; and

"United Kingdom national" means an individual who is—

(a) a British citizen, a British Dependent Territories citizen, a British National (Overseas) or a British Overseas citizen,

(b) a person who under the British Nationality Act 1981 is a British subject, or

(c) a British protected person (within the meaning of that Act).

(2) For the purposes of this Part of this Act the territorial waters adjacent to any part of the United Kingdom shall be treated as included in that part of the United Kingdom.

GENERAL NOTE
S.17 is the definition section for Pt. II, only.

Subs. (1)
"Fixed platform". (Derivation: Fixed Platforms Protocol 1988, Art. 1(3)). Essentially, the definition would cover the type of fixed production and exploration platforms found in the North Sea and elsewhere. It would include accommodation platforms, such as that involved in the Piper Alpha tragedy. The main type of rig that would be excluded would be the mobile semi-submersible or jack-up rigs used in exploration. These would be "other floating craft" within the definition of "ship", below.

"Ship". (Derivation: Rome Convention 1988, Art. 1). *Cf.* the definition in the Merchant Shipping Act 1894, s.742. The Convention definition is deliberately wide, as the intention of the Diplomatic Conference was that there should be no gaps between the definitions of ships and fixed platforms and that they should be complementary (see SUA/Conf/CW/RD, April 20, 1988). It is clear that it applies to any vessel whatsoever (whether propelled by oars or not). The ship does not have to be seagoing (the expression was dropped by the ad hoc Preparatory Committee at the drafting stage of the Convention (see PCUA 1/4). In addition to "other floating craft", the Convention mentions "dynamically supported craft". This was intended to cover hydrofoils and hovercraft, although only the latter are mentioned in the section. It is assumed that the former are also intended to be covered, as are surface effect ships. The Convention definition in Art. 2 excluded warships and the like, but see s.9(2).

"Other floating craft". This does not cover fixed platforms, which are defined separately. But it would cover unpowered craft such as barges and structures such as floating cranes, or (probably) floating dry docks.

"Permanently attached". The Convention was meant to apply to any drilling units when "permanently" attached to the sea-bed. It is quite possible for semi-submersible exploration rigs to be towed to a site before being ballasted down in order to enable exploratory drilling to take place. Likewise, jack-up oil rigs could have their legs lowered while drilling was to take place. Such craft would fall within the definition of "ship" rather than "fixed platform", as they lack the necessary degree of permanence.

"Withdrawn from navigation or laid up". This phrase was used in the Rome Convention 1988, Art. 2 in place of "ship in service" which gave rise to problems of application (see PCUA 1/4). Withdrawal from navigation was a replacement for "out of commission" which was thought inappropriate, *inter alia*, for commercial craft (*ibid.*). On the basis that the vessel was not in service there would be less likelihood of danger to persons, although a laid-up ship could certainly cause danger if it were cast adrift, or scuttled in a waterway. There may be a difficult question of transition between a state of service and laying up. A ship is not laid up simply because it is waiting for work. Factors relevant to lay-up would include: withdrawal of navigating crew and installation of watchkeeping personnel; altered insurance arrangements; notifications given to harbour authority; and whether the vessel had been maintained in class.

"United Kingdom National". See generally the British Nationality Act 1981.

"British citizen": British Nationality Act 1981, Pt. I.
"British Dependent Territories Citizen": British Nationality Act 1981, Pt. II, s.50 and Sched. 6.
"British National (Overseas)": British Nationality Act 1981, Pt. II, s.50 and the Hong Kong (British Nationality) Order 1986 (S.I. No. 948).
"British Overseas citizen": British Nationality Act 1981, Pt. III, s.50 and the Hong Kong (British Nationality) Order 1986 (S.I. No. 948).
"British subject": British Nationality Act 1981, Pt. IV.
"British protected person": British Nationality Act 1981, s.50.

Subs. (2)
Territorial waters. See the Territorial Waters Act 1987. The Diplomatic Conference rejected an attempt to enlarge the scope of application of the Rome Convention and Protocol to the Exclusive Economic Zone.

PART III

PROTECTION OF SHIPS AND HARBOUR AREAS AGAINST ACTS OF VIOLENCE

GENERAL NOTE

General purpose of Pt. III.
Pt. III extends to maritime activities the same sort of powers that are available to the Secretary of State under the Aviation Security Act 1982, Pt. II (as amended by Pt. I of the 1990 Act). Indeed, on a number of occasions, it was said that the intention was to create a mirror image of the security arrangements applying to aviation. In order to avoid undue repetition, references will be made to equivalent provisions in Pt. I, where appropriate. See the *Summary of the Act*, at the beginning of this Annotation, for an overview of Pt. III.

The necessity for control
During debates a number of complaints were made to the effect that undertakings had been given to the shipping industry that legislation on security would go no further than the Rome Convention 1988. The thrust of the complaints was that there was no real comparison between the security situation applying to airports and aircraft and that applying to ports and ships. There would certainly appear to be a difference in scale. The Secretary of State gave some examples of the respective positions at Second Reading in the Commons. In the peak period in 1989 Heathrow handled 1,000 aircraft movements per day; 142,000 passengers, with 160,000 items of baggage, passed per day through the terminals; Dover handled 100,000 passengers and 10,000 vehicles per day. Fewer passengers pass through ports, but the amount of cargo is immeasurably greater. Individual vessel movements in ports are probably less extensively regulated than aircraft at airports. Traditionally, a wider class of persons has had access to ports for leisure purposes, for example in order to fish or to see off passengers. Unlike in aviation, there is often no clear division between the equivalent of the airside and the terminal parts of airports. Although a quayside is a natural division, this is not an equivalent to that between the airside and the airport terminal, as many functions relating to the preparation of a ship take place on the quay. Moreover, there has traditionally been freedom of navigation in and around ports, and that would certainly not be the case with runways.

The Government view was that there was no legal framework for ensuring that adequate security precautions are taken to counter terrorism against ships and ports. The same might be said about road and rail transport. The aim was to "achieve a level of security appropriate to the threat to shipping" (*Hansard*, H.C. Vol. 164, col. 959). It is clear from the general reserved nature of the provisions that wide Draconian restrictions are not anticipated. Nevertheless, there were fears expressed that there would be enormous costs associated with providing security in ports catering for Irish traffic, such as Fishguard. It was said in debates that the cost of Special Branch policing in Pembroke Dock is about £1 million out of a total police budget in Dyfed-Powys of £30 million (Standing Committee A, col. 127). Similarly, a port like Southampton is an extensive complex of berths, jetties, factories and modern marina and housing developments. It could be extremely expensive to provide for a significant security infrastructure.

British merchant fleet. Concern has been expressed many times about the difficult trading position of the British fleet (see the General Note to the Merchant Shipping Act 1988 in [1988] 2 Current Law Statutes Annotated) and the Government was sensitive to suggestions that its position should not be further weakened by including security provisions in the Act that discriminated against British, as opposed to foreign flagged, ships. Accordingly, it is possible to trace a number of provisions that were produced or amended so as to apply equally to British and foreign ships. See for example ss.19(1)(a), 21(1), 21(2), 35(1), 36(1).

It has already been noted that the *power* exists to reimburse certain security expenses of the aviation industry out of general public funds (see s.32 of the Aviation Security Act 1982 and the General Note to Pt. I, *Financing of security measures*). No equivalent powers exist for the maritime industry, nor have any been created under the "parallel" principle that has otherwise been applied to Pts. II and III of the 1990 Act.

Enforcement responsibility
See the General Note to Part I on aviation security.
Private security services. The powers given to the Secretary of State are certainly far-reaching in peace-time and some concern was expressed in debates because of the disbandment of the British Transport Police and the use of private security firms (see also the note on *Private security services* in the General Note to Pt. I, above). Constables may be sworn by two justices of the peace under the Harbours, Docks and Piers Clauses Act 1847, s.79, which, in practice, is incorporated into the local legislation of most harbours. In 1989, 25 newly-appointed private security guards were employed by Sealink at Harwich as replacements for more expensive British Transport Police. The Government has under review the rôle, if any, of ports police authorities.

The competence, experience, regulation and accountability of private security forces is obviously a matter for concern (and see N. South, *Policing for Profit—The Private Security Sector*, 1988). Doubts have been expressed about their training standards, the fact that they have a very high turnover of staff and often employ persons with criminal records. One alternative would be to set up a compulsory system of licensing, involving registration of private security forces generally, but the view of the Home Office has been to prefer self-regulation, for example by the British Security Industry Association. When the Bill was introduced the Government had not yet decided whether it would apply the same practice as it does in aviation Directions. The latter specify that where private security companies are used their contracts must bind them to comply with the rules of the British Security Industry Association or the International Security Organisation. At the Committee stage in the Lords, the Minister of State, Foreign and Commonwealth Office, Lord Brabazon of Tara, confirmed that the same rules would be applied (*Hansard*, H.L. Vol. 518, col. 876). There is, nevertheless, no body equivalent to the Police Complaints Authority (and *cf.* the Government concession in s.22(4), below).

It might be argued that there is a great deal of difference between the routine security work of private guards employed to protect property at a factory and the sort of security work at ports that would involve the safety of members of the public. The Government view seemed to be that the rôle was not essentially different from that performed by guards who protect public buildings. The Minister did try to allay some fears by indicating that the Home Office and DTp were reviewing the future rôles of ports police forces and the extent to which a private security company can be converted into a ports police force under the 1847 Act, as at Harwich. It is open to the Chief Constable to object to those appointed as constables under the Harbours, Docks and Piers Clauses Act 1847 when the justices are considering the application. This is not exactly the same as a full vetting process, but it seems that the issue will have to await the inter-Departmental review.

It was noted in debates that the powers given enabled the Secretary of State to lay down a complete code for the policing and security arrangements at any harbour in the country. The use of such codes, for example under the Health and Safety at Work Act 1974 and the Police and Criminal Evidence Act 1984, has been criticised because it carries with it a lack of Parliamentary scrutiny. It would seem that the Secretary of State could give Directions under s.25 requiring a harbour to be policed by constables under the Police Act 1964, or by a private firm (as a person receiving a Direction was entitled to employ someone else to do the work). In the latter case detailed rules could then be made concerning training and experience. It may be that Directions would adopt the aviation practice of checking the last 20 years of an individual's records before employing him.

Civil liberties aspects
The concern over the civil liberties aspects of the powers of search are accented in modern ports which have marinas and associated housing developments in which ordinary members of the public can be expected (and see the note to the Act, above). Nevertheless, the Government was not prepared to exclude private dwellings as it was said that they could be a "soft target" for terrorists (but see s.22(4), below). One Government response to the concerns about the wide powers to be exercised in ports and harbours was simply to say that it was reproducing provisions that had already been applied to aviation.

At Second Reading in the Commons, the parliamentary adviser to the Police Federation expressed the concern of the police about some of the powers to be conferred by Pt. III. For example, under s.25(4) of the 1990 Act there is a reference to the carrying of firearms by constables, for which they would need firearms certificates under the Firearms Act 1968. It would be incongruous if private security services carried weapons while the metropolitan and county forces did not. However, it appears that under the Firearms Act 1968 the only persons who are exempted from firearms control are constables of regular police forces. The exemption would not apply to private security guards, even if they were created constables under the Harbours, Docks and Piers Clauses Act 1847. (See the note to ss.25(4), below).

One amendment suggested in Committee was the introduction of a set of standards and codes for the carrying out of searches by private security firms. Whether such a proposal will be considered remains to be seen.

Platforms

Note that Pt. III, unlike Pt. II, does not extend to offshore platforms (despite the rather ambiguous comments of the Minister during debates (Standing Committee A, col. 162). The Government resisted an opposition attempt to extend the general powers to make Directions (for example under s.24, below) to the operators, owners or managers of fixed platforms. The main reason for this was said to be that Pt. II already dealt with securing platforms against terrorist attack. A separate point concerning procedures involving evacuation in the event of a bomb, fire or other emergency was stated to fall within the general remit of the Department of Energy. The latter was said to have issued regulations necessary for the purpose. Presumably these are the Offshore Installations (Emergency Procedures) Regulations 1976 (S.I. No. 1542), requiring there to be an emergency procedure manual and creating offences for non-compliance. These Regulations are really designed for general safety rather than to increase security. Note also that under the Petroleum Act 1987, ss.21-23, there are safety zones around platforms.

The justification for not including specific provisions in the 1990 Act is not particularly convincing, except in terms of inter-departmental rivalry. A fixed platform has as much need of security as a harbour—arguably more so, bearing in mind the potential for large loss of life (as in the *Piper Alpha* explosion). Moreover, the DTp is responsible for some aspects of offshore safety, for example fire fighting, life-saving and evacuation equipment and for stand-by vessels and supply boats.

Masters

Pt. III creates a number of new offences that may be committed by masters, see for example s.19(1) (provision of information) and s.21(2) (going to sea without modifications to ship). There is no power to serve Directions on a master under s.24 (the main Direction-making power), although enforcement notices could be served in some circumstances (see s.29(3), below). The latter was considered by the officers' organisation, NUMAST (National Union of Aviation, Marine and Shipping Transport Officers), to be the most objectionable provision in the Act.

The opposition was concerned at the increasing number of offences that could be committed by employees, such as masters, and proposed amendments that would have removed them from the list of possible offenders, *e.g.* one amendment would have excluded masters from the list of people from whom the Secretary of State can require information under s.19 (and see also in respect of s.21, below). The worry was that masters were likely to be made scapegoats. The Minister for Aviation and Shipping, Patrick McCloughlin, did undertake to make the master the last line of contact and not the first (Standing Committee A, col. 120). It was also noted that the DTp did not intend to operate enforcement notices against masters involving matters outside their responsibilities where it can pursue the ship's operator (*Hansard*, H.L. Vol. 518, col. 869). However, the Act does not say that the master can only be served when it is impossible to locate the operator and the Government rejected an amendment to this effect at Report stage in the Lords. At Report stage in the Commons, the Government had already resisted an Opposition attempt to force the Secretary of State to give a Direction to a master only after using his "best endeavours" to secure compliance with the Direction by the owner charterer, or manager. It was said that this could cause problems in urgent cases, particularly where foreign owners were concerned. The difficulty with foreign ships is often that it is often only practicable to deal with the master. By the time owners are contacted the ship may have sailed.

For powers of detention, see s.35, below (and also the difficulties in relation to s.19, below). Note that in relation to offences such as that under s.19(6) there is a reasonable excuse defence.

General purposes

Purposes to which Part III applies

18.—(1) The purposes to which this Part of this Act applies are the protection against acts of violence—

(a) of ships, and of persons or property on board ships, and

(b) of harbour areas, of such persons as are at any time present in any part of a harbour area and of such property as forms part of a harbour area or is at any time (whether permanently or temporarily) in any part of a harbour area.

(2) In this Part of this Act "act of violence" means any act (whether actual or potential, and whether done or to be done in the United Kingdom or elsewhere) which either—

(a) being an act done in Great Britain, constitutes, or

(b) if done in Great Britain would constitute,

the offence of murder, attempted murder, manslaughter, culpable homicide or assault, or an offence under section 18, 20, 21, 22, 23, 24, 28 or 29 of the Offences against the Person Act 1861, under section 2 of the Explosive Substances Act 1883 or under section 1 of the Criminal Damage Act 1971 or, in Scotland, the offence of malicious mischief.

(3) In this Part of this Act "harbour area" means—

(a) the aggregate of—

(i) any harbour in the United Kingdom in respect of which a harbour authority (within the meaning of the Harbours Act 1964 or, in Northern Ireland, the Harbours Act (Northern Ireland) 1970) has statutory powers or duties of improvement, maintenance or management, and

(ii) any land which is adjacent to such a harbour and which is either land occupied by the harbour authority or land in respect of which the harbour authority has statutory powers or duties of improvement, maintenance or management, or

(b) any hoverport in Great Britain which does not form part of any area mentioned in paragraph (a)(i) or (ii) above.

DEFINITIONS

"act of violence": s.46(1).

"British ship": s.46(1).

"harbour": s.46(1).

"harbour area": ss.18(3); 46(1).

"harbour authority": s.46(1).

"hoverport": s.46(1).

"person": Interpretation Act 1978, Sched. 1.

"property": s.46(1).

"purposes to which this part of this Act applies": s.18(1).

"ship": s.46(1).

"United Kingdom": Interpretation Act 1978, Sched. 1.

GENERAL NOTE

Derivation: the Aviation Security Act 1982, s.10.

This section defines the purposes to which Pt. III of the 1990 Act applies. In general, those purposes are the protection of ships, harbours and the people who use them from acts of violence. The reason for stating the purpose is that, in following sections, the Secretary of State is given a variety of powers which can only be exercised to further the purposes set out generally in s.18. See, for example, ss.20(1), 21(1), 22(1), 23(1), 24(2), 41(1) and 42(1). In effect, therefore, s.18 is a limitation on executive power.

Subs. (2)

"Act of violence". Cf. s.1(9).

Subs. (3)

Harbour authorities commonly exercise their statutory powers (for example to regulate the movement of ships or vehicles) over a wide area. This would include land not owned by the authority, but would normally be strictly defined by the statutory provision which established it. Some authorities may have acquired, by inheritance or purchase, land outside the strict limits of the harbour. It may be sensible for such land to be included in any overall security planning. If such land, over which a harbour authority has statutory powers, is to be included in a "harbour area" it must be adjacent to that harbour. Some harbour authorities may own land which is nearby, for example in a city centre. It is assumed that "adjacent" means immediately next to the harbour and not separated from it by any other land.

Under the Hovercraft Act 1968, s.4, a hoverport means any area, whether on land or elsewhere, which is designed, equipped, set apart or commonly used for affording facilities for the arrival and departure of hovercraft.

Powers of Secretary of State

Power of Secretary of State to require information

19.—(1) The Secretary of State may, by notice in writing served on any of the following persons—
  (a) the owner, charterer, manager or master of—
       (i) a British ship, or
       (ii) any other ship which is in, or appears to the Secretary of State to be likely to enter, a harbour area,
  (b) a harbour authority,
  (c) any person who carries on harbour operations in a harbour area, and
  (d) any person who is permitted to have access to a restricted zone of a harbour area for the purposes of the activities of a business carried on by him,
require that person to provide the Secretary of State with such information specified in the notice as the Secretary of State may require in connection with the exercise by the Secretary of State of his functions under this Part of this Act.

(2) A notice under subsection (1) above shall specify a date (not being earlier than seven days from the date on which the notice is served) before which the information required by the notice in accordance with subsection (1) above is to be furnished to the Secretary of State.

(3) Any such notice may also require the person on whom it is served, after he has furnished to the Secretary of State the information required by the notice in accordance with subsection (1) above, to inform the Secretary of State if at any time the information previously furnished to the Secretary of State (including any information furnished in pursuance of a requirement imposed by virtue of this subsection) is rendered inaccurate by any change of circumstances (including the taking of any further measures for purposes to which this Part of this Act applies or the alteration or discontinuance of any measures already being taken).

(4) In so far as such a notice requires further information to be furnished to the Secretary of State in accordance with subsection (3) above, it shall require that information to be furnished to him before the end of such period (not being less than seven days from the date on which the change of circumstances occurs) as is specified in the notice for the purposes of this subsection.

(5) Any person who—
  (a) without reasonable excuse, fails to comply with a requirement imposed on him by a notice under this section, or
  (b) in furnishing any information so required, makes a statement which he knows to be false in a material particular, or recklessly makes a statement which is false in a material particular,
commits an offence.

(6) A person guilty of an offence under subsection (5) above is liable—

(a) on summary conviction, to a fine not exceeding the statutory maximum;

(b) on conviction on indictment, to a fine or to imprisonment for a term not exceeding two years or to both.

(7) A notice served on a person under subsection (1) above may at any time —

(a) be revoked by a notice in writing served on him by the Secretary of State, or

(b) be varied by a further notice under subsection (1) above.

DEFINITIONS
"British ship": s.46(1).
"functions to which this part of this Act applies": *cf.* s.18(1).
"harbour": s.46(1).
"harbour area": ss.18(3); 46(1).
"harbour authority": s.46(1).
"harbour operations": s.46(1).
"manager": s.46(1).
"master": s.46(1).
"owner": s.46(1).
"permitted to have access": s.46(3).
"person": Interpretation Act 1978, Sched. 1.
"restricted zone": s.46(1).
"Secretary of State": Interpretation Act 1978, Sched. 1.
"ship": s.46(1).
"statutory maximum": Criminal Justice Act 1982, s.74.

GENERAL NOTE
Derivation: the Aviation Security Act 1982, s.11 (and see Sched. 1, para. 2 of the 1990 Act).
Directions. See the General Note to Pt. I, above.
Directions about information. The section allows the Secretary of State to serve a notice on ship and harbour users requiring them to provide information relevant to security matters and, where appropriate, to update that information when circumstances change. At Report stage in the Lords, Lord Brabazon gave an indication of the type of information required in the aviation context. It was designed to enable the compilation of a comprehensive list of persons to whom Directions could be given. The sort of information that might be required could also include details of existing security measures and details about employees. In Pt. III, harbour authorities might be asked to provide details of all persons occupying land forming part of the harbour and all persons carrying on harbour operations or having access to restricted zones (created under s.20, below). The harbour authority could also be under a duty to keep the list up to date.
It should be noted that the very wide ambit of s.19(1)(d) could include many individuals or businesses with very little connection to the shipping business. In addition to transport companies, it could include regular suppliers of food or building materials to businesses within the harbour, even if the supplier's place of business is hundreds of miles away (*cf.* the note to s.2, above). Not all visitors to harbours can be served with notices, only those that have access to the restricted zones created under s.20, below. There is to be a minimum period of seven days in which to provide the information. Failure to do so without reasonable excuse is an offence, as is the deliberate or reckless provision of false information. However, the information has to be false in a "material particular". Under subs. (7) there are powers to revoke or vary the notice. For offences by bodies corporate, see s.50, below.
The Opposition failed in an attempt to exclude masters from criminal liability for failing to comply with the section (and see *Masters*, in the General Note to Pt. III, above). The seven day period under subs. (2) could be said to defeat the Government's purpose of demanding information from the master whose foreign owners cannot be contacted. The Minister for Public Transport, Mr Portillo, appeared to suggest that there were powers of detention if a Direction is not complied with (*Hansard*, H.C. Vol. 168, col. 599), but it would appear from s.35, below, that it does not refer to Directions under s.19. If this is right, a foreign master would be able to sail away during the seven day period.
For service of notices, see s.45, below.

Designation of restricted zones of harbour areas

20.—(1) A harbour authority may, and shall if so requested in writing by the Secretary of State, apply to the Secretary of State for the designation of the whole or any part of the harbour area as a restricted zone for the purposes of this Part of this Act.

(2) An application under subsection (1) above shall be in such form, and accompanied by such plans, as the Secretary of State may require.

(3) If the Secretary of State approves an application under subsection (1) above with or without modifications, he shall designate the restricted zone accordingly.

(4) Before approving an application with modifications, the Secretary of State shall consult the harbour authority.

(5) If a harbour authority is requested in writing by the Secretary of State to make an application under subsection (1) above within a specified period but fails to do so within that period, the Secretary of State may designate the whole or any part of the harbour area as a restricted zone.

(6) The whole or any part of a harbour area may be designated as a restricted zone, or part of a restricted zone, for specified days or times of day only.

(7) The Secretary of State shall give notice to the harbour authority of any designation under this section and the designation of the restricted zone shall take effect on the giving of the notice.

(8) Where the whole or any part of a harbour area has been designated under this section as a restricted zone—

  (a) subsections (1) to (7) above also have effect in relation to any variation of the designation, and

  (b) the designation may at any time be revoked by the Secretary of State.

DEFINITIONS
"harbour area": ss.18(3); 46(1).
"harbour authority": s.46(1).
"purposes of this Part of this Act": s.18(1).
"permitted to have access": s.46(3).
"restricted zone": s.46(1).
"Secretary of State": Interpretation Act 1978, Sched. 1.

GENERAL NOTE
  Cf. Aviation Security Act 1982, s.11A (as inserted by Sched. 1, para. 3, below).
  Restricted zones. Power is given to create restricted zones within harbours. Harbour authorities may apply to create such a zone, or may be ordered to do so by the Secretary of State. The restricted zone might be created for part of a harbour, for example the dockside, or cargo storage sheds. Zones may be created for particular times (for example at night, or while ships are at a berth).
  The zones are relevant to the provisions in the Act which allow notices and Directions (for example under ss.19 and 24) to be served on persons having access to them, or allow inspection of the property of such persons (see, for example, s.36). The Act also creates offences that can be committed in relation to the zones, for example unauthorised presence within them (see, for example, s.39).
  Presumably, the designation of part of a harbour area as a restricted zone might have financial consequences for an authority, as it might reduce commercial activities. The Government refused to accept an amendment that would have entitled the ports to claim compensation from public funds for the dislocation. Here, as in aviation, the view of the Government was that security costs should be borne by the industry itself and recouped from users. *Cf.* s.22 of the Aviation Security Act 1982 and s.43 of the 1990 Act (introduced at Report stage in the Commons) which deal with third party compensation.
  For prohibited zones in ports see the Official Secrets Act 1911, ss.1 and 3, and the note to s.5, above.
  For service of notices, see s.45, below.

Power to impose restrictions in relation to ships

  21.—(1) For purposes to which this Part of this Act applies, the Secretary of State may give a direction in writing to a harbour authority or to the owner, charterer, manager or master of a British ship, or of any other ship which is in a harbour area, requiring that person—

(a) not to cause or permit persons or property to go or be taken on board any ship to which the direction relates, or to come or be brought into proximity to any such ship, unless such searches of those persons or that property as are specified in the direction have been carried out by constables or by other persons of a description specified in the direction, or

(b) not to cause or permit any such ship to go to sea unless such searches of the ship as are specified in the direction have been carried out by constables or by other persons of a description so specified.

(2) For purposes to which this Part of this Act applies, the Secretary of State may give a direction in writing to the owner, charterer, manager or master of—

(a) a British ship, or

(b) any other ship which is in a harbour area,

requiring him not to cause or permit the ship to go to sea unless such modifications or alterations of the ship, or of apparatus or equipment installed in or carried on board the ship, as are specified in the direction have first been carried out, or such additional apparatus or equipment as is so specified is first installed in or carried on board the ship.

(3) In giving any direction under subsection (2) above, the Secretary of State shall allow, and shall specify in the direction, such period as appears to him to be reasonably required for carrying out the modifications or alterations or installing or obtaining the additional apparatus or equipment in question; and the direction shall not take effect before the end of the period so specified.

(4) Subject to the following provisions of this Part of this Act, a direction given to an owner, charterer or manager of a ship under subsection (1) or (2) above may be given so as to relate either to all the ships falling within that subsection of which at the time when the direction is given or at any subsequent time he is the owner, charterer or manager or only to one or more such ships specified in the direction; and a direction given to a harbour authority under subsection (1) above may be given so as to relate either to all ships which at the time when the direction is given or at any subsequent time are in any part of the harbour area, or to a class of such ships specified in the direction.

(5) Subject to the following provisions of this Part of this Act, a direction under subsection (1) above may be given so as to relate—

(a) either to all persons or only to one or more persons, or persons of one or more descriptions, specified in the direction, and

(b) either to property of every description or only to particular property, or property of one or more descriptions, so specified.

(6) Subject to the following provisions of this Part of this Act, any direction given under this section to any person not to cause or permit anything to be done shall be construed as requiring him to take all such steps as in any particular circumstances are practicable and necessary to prevent that thing from being done.

(7) A direction may be given under this section to a person appearing to the Secretary of State to be about to become such a person as is mentioned in subsection (1) or (2) above, but a direction given to a person by virtue of this subsection shall not take effect until he becomes a person so mentioned and, in relation to a direction so given, the preceding provisions of this section shall apply with the necessary modifications.

(8) Any person who, without reasonable excuse, fails to comply with a direction given to him under this section is guilty of an offence and liable—

(a) on summary conviction, to a fine not exceeding the statutory maximum;

(b) on conviction on indictment, to a fine or to imprisonment for a term not exceeding two years or to both.

(9) Where a person is convicted of an offence under subsection (8) above, then, if without reasonable excuse the failure in respect of which he was convicted is continued after the conviction, he is guilty of a further offence and liable on summary conviction to a fine not exceeding one-tenth of level 5 on the standard scale for each day on which the failure continues.

DEFINITIONS
  "British ship": s.46(1).
  "harbour": s.46(1).
  "harbour area": ss.18(3); 46(1).
  "harbour authority": s.46(1).
  "manager": s.46(1).
  "master": s.46(1).
  "owner": s.46(1).
  "person": Interpretation Act 1978, Sched. 1.
  "property": s.46(1).
  "purposes to which this Part of this Act applies": s.18(1).
  "Secretary of State": Interpretation Act 1978, Sched. 1.
  "ship": s.46(1).
  "standard scale": Criminal Justice Act 1982, s.74.
  "statutory maximum": Criminal Justice Act 1982, s.74.

GENERAL NOTE
  Derivation: the Aviation Security Act 1982, s.12.
  Directions. See the General Note to Pt. I, above. Note the scope of Directions permitted under ss.25–27 and the power to revoke or vary a Direction given by s.46(2). For the service of documents, see s.45, below.
  Restrictions in relation to ships. The section gives the Secretary of State the power to make Directions in order to impose three types of restriction: (i) people or property may be prevented from going or being taken aboard (or near) a ship unless there has been a search; (ii) ships may not go to sea unless they have been searched; and (iii) ships may be prevented from going to sea unless specified modifications or alterations have been carried out. Note that the qualifications of those carrying out modifications may also be specified (see s.25(2), below). The obligation to make modifications and alterations could be particularly expensive, especially where delay is involved.
  At the Committee stage in the Lords, Lord Brabazon stated that s.21 is likely to be used only in unusual and extreme circumstances. "It will need to be used only where co-operation has not been forthcoming after consultation or in emergencies where a quick, direct responsive course of action is needed" (*Hansard*, H.L. Vol. 518, col. 871). Although speaking in the context of Directions served on masters, it seems that the statement was meant to apply generally. Accordingly, the main way in which improvements to security will be made is by the issuing of Directions under s.24, below.
  The Bill only covered British ships, but it is now clear from subs. (2)(b) that the powers apply not only to British ships anywhere in the world, but also to foreign ships visiting British ports. The GCBS had objected that otherwise the provision would discriminate against British ships.
  Directions can relate to all ships owned, chartered or managed by a person. Thus, a British shipowner can face restrictions on a fleet of ships, even if they are operating in different parts of the world. The master was added to the list of persons to whom Directions could be given at the suggestion of the GCBS on the basis that it would be sensible to include him as he will be present to see whether the searches have been carried out. In the case of a foreign flag ship, he may be the only person that can be identified and contacted. (*Cf.* s.19 and s.24). The Government resisted an Opposition attempt to force the Secretary of State to give a Direction to a master only after using his best endeavours to secure compliance with the Direction by the owner charterer, or manager. It was said that this could cause problems in urgent cases, particularly where foreign owners were concerned. It was in the scope of responsibility of a master to prohibit persons coming near the ship, or to prevent it sailing (and see the note on *Masters*, in the General Note to Pt. III, above).
  Searches may be carried out by policemen or other specified persons (including, presumably, private security guards). The Direction may exclude persons from the searching requirement, for example specified harbour authority officials.
  Offences. It is an offence to fail to comply with a Direction. No offence is committed under subs. (2) if the works are not carried out and the ship remains in port. The offence only occurs when the ship goes to sea without the works having been completed. There is a defence of reasonable excuse and note the qualification in subs. (7) on the duty to comply. Note also the

penalties in subs. (9) for continued refusal to comply after an initial conviction (and see the note to s.2, above, inserting a new s.13A(4) in the Aviation Security Act 1982). For offences by bodies corporate, see s.50, below.

Power to require harbour authorities to promote searches in harbour areas

22.—(1) For purposes to which this Part of this Act applies, the Secretary of State may give a direction in writing to a harbour authority requiring it to use its best endeavours to secure that such searches to which this section applies as are specified in the direction are carried out by constables or by other persons of a description specified in the direction.

(2) The searches to which this section applies, in relation to a harbour area, are searches—

(a) of the harbour area or any part of it,

(b) of any ship which at the time when the direction is given or at any subsequent time is in the harbour area, and

(c) of persons and property (other than ships) which may at any time be in the harbour area.

(3) Where a direction under this section to a harbour authority is for the time being in force, then, subject to subsections (4) and (5) below, if a constable or any other person specified in the direction in accordance with this section has reasonable cause to suspect that an article to which this subsection applies is in, or may be brought into, any part of the harbour area, he may, by virtue of this subsection and without a warrant, search any part of the harbour area or any ship, vehicle, goods or other moveable property of any description which, or any person who, is for the time being in any part of the harbour area, and for that purpose—

(a) may enter any building or works in the harbour area, or enter upon any land in the harbour area, if need be by force,

(b) may go on board any such ship and inspect the ship,

(c) may stop any such ship and, for so long as may be necessary for that purpose, prevent it from being moved, and

(d) may stop any such vehicle, goods, property or person and detain it or him for so long as may be necessary for that purpose.

(4) In the case of premises used only as a private dwelling any power to search or enter conferred by subsection (3) above may not be exercised except—

(a) under the authority of a warrant issued by a justice of the peace; and

(b) by a constable who is a member of a body of constables maintained—

(i) in England, Scotland or Wales by a police authority or an authority which has entered into an agreement with the Police Complaints Authority under section 96(1) of the Police and Criminal Evidence Act 1984; or

(ii) in Northern Ireland, by the Police Authority for Northern Ireland or an authority which has entered into an agreement with the Independent Commission for Police Complaints for Northern Ireland under Article 16 of the Police (Northern Ireland) Order 1987.

(5) If, on an application made by a constable, a justice of the peace is satisfied that there are reasonable grounds for suspecting that an article to which subsection (3) above applies is in any premises used only as a private dwelling, he may issue a warrant authorising a constable to enter and search the premises.

(6) Subsection (3) above applies to the following articles—

(a) any firearm, or any article having the appearance of being a firearm, whether capable of being discharged or not,

(b) any explosive, any article manufactured or adapted (whether in the form of a bomb, grenade or otherwise) so as to have the appearance of being an explosive, whether it is capable of producing a practical

31–65

effect by explosion or not, or any article marked or labelled so as to indicate that it is or contains an explosive, and

(c) any article (not falling within either of the preceding paragraphs) made or adapted for use for causing injury to or incapacitating a person or for destroying or damaging property, or intended by the person having it with him for such use, whether by him or by any other person.

(7) Any person who—

(a) without reasonable excuse, fails to comply with a direction given to him under this section, or

(b) intentionally obstructs a person acting in the exercise of a power conferred on him by subsection (3) above,

commits an offence.

(8) A person guilty of an offence under subsection (7) above is liable—

(a) on summary conviction, to a fine not exceeding the statutory maximum;

(b) on conviction on indictment, to a fine or to imprisonment for a term not exceeding two years or to both.

(9) Where a person is convicted of an offence under subsection (7)(a) above, then, if without reasonable excuse the failure in respect of which he was convicted is continued after the conviction, he is guilty of a further offence and liable on summary conviction to a fine not exceeding one-tenth of level 5 on the standard scale for each day on which the failure continues.

(10) Subsection (3) above has effect without prejudice to the operation, in relation to any offence under this Act—

(a) in England and Wales, of sections 17, 24 and 25 of the Police and Criminal Evidence Act 1984 (which confer power to arrest without warrant and to enter premises for the purpose of making an arrest) or of section 3 of the Criminal Law Act 1967 (use of force in making arrest etc.), or

(b) in Scotland, of any rule of law relating to the power to arrest without warrant, or

(c) in Northern Ireland, of Articles 19, 26 and 27 of the Police and Criminal Evidence (Northern Ireland) Order 1989 or of section 3 of the Criminal Law Act (Northern Ireland) 1967.

DEFINITIONS

"article": s.46(1).
"constable": s.46(1).
"England": Interpretation Act 1978, Sched. 1.
"explosive": s.46(1).
"firearm": s.46(1).
"harbour": s.46(1).
"harbour authority": s.46(1).
"land": Interpretation Act 1978, Sched. 1.
"person": Interpretation Act 1978, Sched. 1.
"property": s.46(1).
"purposes to which this Part of this Act applies": s.18(1).
"Secretary of State": Interpretation Act 1978, Sched. 1.
"ship": s.46(1).
"standard scale": Criminal Justice Act 1982, s.74.
"statutory maximum": Criminal Justice Act 1982, s.74.
"Wales": Interpretation Act 1978, Sched. 1.

GENERAL NOTE

Derivation: the Aviation Security Act 1982, s.13 (*cf.* s.2 of the 1990 Act).

Directions. See the General Notes to Pt. I and the notes to s.2, above. Note the scope of Directions permitted under ss.25–27 and the power to revoke or vary a Direction given by s.46(2). For service of Directions, see s.45, below.

Promoting searches: harbour authorities. The section gives the Secretary of State power to direct harbour authorities to ensure that searches are undertaken. The obligation can extend to any part of a harbour, to any ship that may enter it and to any persons or property that may be there.

Searches. Police officers or other specified persons (including, potentially, private security guards) are given the power to search persons or property, without warrant. There must be reasonable cause for suspicion that firearms, explosives or the like are to be brought into the harbour area. The search may take place anywhere in the harbour and may include vehicles. The searcher may (i) board, inspect or detain ships; (ii) stop and detain persons, vehicles and property; and (iii) use force to enter land or buildings in the harbour. The specific reference to force in para. (3)(a) only might seem to suggest that there will be no power to use force in relation to persons or ships. But it may be that it is inherent in any power to stop and detain that force may be necessary. Note the restriction in relation to private dwellings imposed by subs. (4) and (5) (see *Civil liberties*, below).

Offences. Offences are committed by (i) a harbour authority for failing to comply with a Direction and (ii) persons who intentionally obstruct those exercising the search powers. For offences by bodies corporate, see s.50, below. For continuing offences see subs. (9) and the note to s.13A(4) of the Aviation Security Act 1982 (as inserted by s.2, above).

Civil liberties. Great concern was expressed about the civil liberties aspects of the wide ranging powers, including the right of detention, given under subs. (3), which does not contain any time limits as under the Prevention of Terrorism (Temporary Provisions) Act 1989, s.14. There were worries about who would undertake searches in airports, and harbours, and about the level of their qualifications (and see the General Note to Pt. I). Those concerned, particularly about the civil liberties aspects of having searches undertaken by private security guards, included not just MPs but also bodies such as the Police Federation and the British Ports Federation. The Government emphasised that the detention could only be for the specific purpose mentioned in the subsection (and see s.18, above). It does not seem a good answer to say that there is a natural time limit imposed by the specified purpose as that is far too broad, especially considering that the powers may be exercised by private security guards. Nor is it an answer to say that judicial review can be made of the Directions. That would be relevant to a harbour authority initially receiving a Direction, but not to an individual detained later. Also, individuals may assume that private security guards do not have wide powers given by the section. Proof of identification may well be a source of dispute. See also the note on *Private security services* in the General Note to Pt. I, above.

In many harbours, such as Southampton, there are marina developments containing private housing. The Government agreed to meet concerns about the powers in relation to such housing by introducing at the Third Reading in the Lords what are now subss. (4) and (5). Subs. (4) restricts the power of search of, and entry to, private dwellings to police officers with warrants (which can now be issued pursuant to subs. (5)). Thus, private security guards cannot exercise the powers. It should also be noted that the type of constable who can enter and search is more restricted than that defined in s.46. The latter would include all types of ports police. Subs. (4) includes constables in a body maintained (i) by a police authority under the Police Act 1964, or in Scotland, the Police (Scotland) Act 1976, and (ii) by other constabularies which have entered agreements with the Police Complaints Authority. It is believed that there are only two private police forces falling within the latter category, namely the British Transport Police and the Port of London Police. The agreements are made under the Police and Criminal Evidence Act 1984, s.96, and in effect draw the forces into the codes of practice of that Act. Note that neither s.22 nor any other provision in the Act allows for searches of private dwellings *outside* the harbour (and see the note to s.23, below).

The definition of private dwelling in subs. (4) would only apply to premises used solely as such. There may be buildings, such as shops, which have residential accommodation over the business accommodation. It is assumed that "premises" will be interpreted so as to apply the search and entry restriction to that part of the building used as accommodation, rather than to the building as a whole. If the whole building were to be considered as the "premises" then they would not be "used only" as a private dwelling. This approach would defeat the purpose of subs. (4). The position would be more difficult in relation to a flat that was used partly as an office: it would probably not fall within the subsection.

Power to require other persons to promote searches

23.—(1) For purposes to which this Part of this Act applies, the Secretary of State may give a direction to any person (other than a harbour authority) who—

(a) carries on harbour operations in a harbour area, or
(b) is permitted to have access to a restricted zone of a harbour area for the purposes of the activities of a business carried on by him,

C.L. STATS. (0)—25(2)

requiring him to use his best endeavours to secure that such searches to
which this section applies as are specified in the direction are carried out by
constables or by other persons of a description specified in the direction.
 (2) The searches to which this section applies are—
 (a) in relation to a person falling within subsection (1)(a) above,
    searches—
      (i) of any land which he occupies within the harbour area, and
      (ii) of persons or property which may at any time be on that land;
    and
 (b) in relation to a person falling within subsection (1)(b) above,
    searches—
      (i) of any land which he occupies outside the harbour area for the
    purposes of his business, and
      (ii) of persons or property which may at any time be on that land.
 (3) Any person who, without reasonable excuse, fails to comply with a
direction given to him under this section is guilty of an offence and liable—
 (a) on summary conviction, to a fine not exceeding the statutory
    maximum;
 (b) on conviction on indictment, to a fine or to imprisonment for a term
    not exceeding two years or to both.
 (4) Where a person is convicted of an offence under subsection (3) above,
then, if without reasonable excuse the failure in respect of which he was
convicted is continued after the conviction, he is guilty of a further offence
and liable on summary conviction to a fine not exceeding one-tenth of level 5
on the standard scale for each day on which the failure continues.

DEFINITIONS
 "constable": s.46(1).
 "harbour": s.46(1).
 "harbour area": ss.18(3); 46(1).
 "harbour authority": s.46(1).
 "harbour operations": s.46(1).
 "land": Interpretation Act 1978, Sched. 1.
 "manager": s.46(1).
 "permitted to have access": s.46(3).
 "person": Interpretation Act 1978, Sched. 1.
 "property": s.46(1).
 "purposes to which this Part of this Act applies": s.18(1).
 "restricted zone": s.46(1).
 "Secretary of State": Interpretation Act 1978, Sched. 1.
 "standard scale": Criminal Justice Act 1982, s.74.
 "statutory maximum": Criminal Justice Act 1982, s.74.

GENERAL NOTE
 See the note, above, on s.2 (inserting a new s.13A in the Aviation Security Act 1982).
 Direction. See the General Note to Pt. I, above. Note the scope of Directions permitted
under ss.25-27 and the power to revoke or vary a Direction given by s.46(2). For service of
Directions, see s.45, below.
 Promoting searches: persons other than harbour authorities. S.22 allows the Secretary of State
to compel harbour authorities to use best endeavours to promote security searches. S.23 gives
the Secretary of State similar powers in relation to two other categories of person who may
operate in harbours: those (i) who carry on harbour operations or (ii) who have access to
restricted zones (set up under s.20). Harbour operations (as defined by s.57 of the Harbours
Act 1964) mean activities such as the berthing of ships (for example by towing companies) and
the handling and warehousing of goods (for example by stevedoring companies). This definition would appear to be narrower than the aviation equivalent, which refers to persons
"occupying land" despite the reference to land in subs. (2). However, subs. (1)(b) is sufficiently wide to cover most persons who operate within harbours.
 Indeed, concern was expressed at the Committee stage in the Commons that the reference to
"any person" brings too many people into the section. Like the aviation equivalent, the
Direction can relate to land occupied *outside* the harbour area (see subs. (2)). A freight
forwarder having access to restricted zones in the port of Southampton could occupy land in

Glasgow in connection with its business. (See also s.41, below, for sea cargo agents.) The Government response was that the powers would be used sparingly, but it was not quite clear who would be performing the searches away from the designated areas. The recipient of the Direction would have to ensure that the searches were undertaken by the police "or other persons" described in the Direction - such as private security companies (see the note to s.22, above). Subs. (2)(b)(i) does not allow for the searching of private dwellings outside the harbour, but only land occupied for the purposes of business. Private residences could only be searched under existing general powers.

Offences. Failure, without reasonable excuse, to comply with a Direction is an offence. For offences by bodies corporate, see s.50, below. For continuing offences see subs. (4) and the note to s.13A(4) of the Aviation Security Act 1982 (as inserted by s.2, above).

General power to direct measures to be taken for purposes to which Part III applies

24.—(1) Subsection (2) below applies to—
  (a) any person who is the owner, charterer or manager of one or more ships which—
      (i) are British ships, or
      (ii) are in a harbour area,
  (b) any harbour authority,
  (c) any person other than a harbour authority who carries on harbour operations in a harbour area, and
  (d) any person who is permitted to have access to a restricted zone of a harbour area for the purposes of the activities of a business carried on by him.

(2) Subject to the following provisions of this section, the Secretary of State may give a direction in writing to any person to whom this subsection applies requiring him to take such measures for purposes to which this Part of this Act applies as are specified in the direction—
  (a) in the case of a direction given to a person as the owner, charterer or manager of a ship, in respect of all the ships falling within subsection (1)(a) above of which (at the time when the direction is given or at any subsequent time) he is the owner, charterer or manager, or in respect of any such ships specified in the direction,
  (b) in the case of a direction given to a harbour authority, in respect of the harbour area,
  (c) in the case of a direction given to a person as a person falling within subsection (1)(c) above, in respect of the harbour operations carried on by him, and
  (d) in the case of a direction given to a person as a person who is permitted to have access to a restricted zone as mentioned in subsection (1)(d) above, in respect of such activities carried on by that person in that zone as are specified in the direction.

(3) Without prejudice to the generality of subsection (2) above, the measures to be specified in a direction given under this section to any person to whom that subsection applies may include the provision by that person of persons charged with the duty (at such times as may be specified in the direction)—
  (a) where the direction is given to a person as the owner, charterer or manager of ships, of guarding the ships against acts of violence,
  (b) where the direction is given to a harbour authority, of guarding the harbour area, or persons or property (including ships) in any part of the harbour area, against acts of violence,
  (c) where the direction is given to a person as falling within subsection (1)(c) above, of guarding against acts of violence any ship in the harbour area which is for the time being under his control, or
  (d) where the direction is given to a person as falling within subsection (1)(d) above, of guarding—
      (i) any land outside the harbour area occupied by him for the

purposes of his business, any vehicles or equipment used for those purposes and any goods which are in his possession for those purposes, and

(ii) any ship which is for the time being under his control,

for purposes to which this Part of this Act applies.

(4) A direction given under this section may be either of a general or of a specific character, and may require any measures specified in the direction to be taken at such time or within such period as may be so specified.

(5) A direction under this section—

(a) shall not require any search (whether of persons or of property), and

(b) shall not require the modification or alteration of any ship, or of any of its apparatus or equipment, or the installation or carriage of additional apparatus or equipment, or prohibit any ship from being caused or permitted to go to sea without some modification or alteration of the ship or its apparatus or equipment or the installation or carriage of additional apparatus or equipment.

(6) A direction may be given under this section to a person appearing to the Secretary of State to be about to become a person to whom subsection (2) above applies, but a direction given to a person by virtue of this subsection shall not take effect until he becomes a person to whom subsection (2) above applies and, in relation to a direction so given, the preceding provisions of this section shall apply with the necessary modifications.

(7) Any person who—

(a) without reasonable excuse, fails to comply with a direction given to him under this section, or

(b) intentionally interferes with any building constructed or works executed on any land in compliance with a direction under this section or with anything installed on, under, over or across any land in compliance with such a direction,

commits an offence.

(8) A person guilty of an offence under subsection (7) above is liable—

(a) on summary conviction, to a fine not exceeding the statutory maximum;

(b) on conviction on indictment, to a fine or to imprisonment for a term not exceeding two years or to both.

(9) Where a person is convicted of an offence under subsection (7)(a) above, then, if without reasonable excuse the failure in respect of which he was convicted is continued after the conviction, he is guilty of a further offence and liable on summary conviction to a fine not exceeding one-tenth of level 5 on the standard scale for each day on which the failure continues.

(10) The ownership of any property shall not be affected by reason only that it is placed on or under, or affixed to, any land in compliance with a direction under this section.

DEFINITIONS

"act of violence": s.46(1).

"harbour": s.46(1).

"harbour area": ss.18(3); 46(1).

"harbour authority": s.46(1).

"harbour operations": s.46(1).

"land": Interpretation Act 1978, Sched. 1.

"manager": s.46(1).

"master": s.46(1).

"measures": s.46(1).

"owner": s.46(1).

"permitted to have access": s.46(3).

"person": Interpretation Act 1978, Sched. 1.

"property": s.46(1).

"purposes to which this Part of this Act applies": s.18(1).

"restricted zone": s.46(1).

"Secretary of State": Interpretation Act 1978, Sched. 1.
"ship": s.46(1).
"standard scale": Criminal Justice Act 1982, s.74.
"statutory maximum": Criminal Justice Act 1982, s.74.

GENERAL NOTE

Derivation: the Aviation Security Act 1982, s.14 (as amended by this Act).

Directions. See the General Note to Pt. I, above. S.24 can be described as the main Direction-making power of Pt. III. Under it the Secretary of State is given the power to impose a security regime on those using or having access to harbours. The powers can be used to force operators to create contingency plans (for example covering evacuation), to exercise those plans and to train their staff appropriately. The general aim of the Act is to draw a distinction between imposing a direct requirement on individuals to perform actions that are within their control, but to ask them to take "reasonable steps" when it is necessary for them to persuade a person, or use the agency of someone else, to achieve what the Act requires of them.

Persons to whom Direction may be issued. The categories of person to whom Directions can be made are broadly comparable to those in relation to aviation (see the note to s.3, above) and, with one exception, to those in s.19(1), above. In addition to (i) harbour authorities, (ii) those carrying out harbour operations (under the Harbours Act 1964, s.57) and (iii) those having access to restricted zones (created under s.20), the Directions can be issued to (iv) ship operators and (v) those who are about to fall within one of the above categories. In the case of such prospective owners, operators, etc., subs. (6) makes it clear that the Direction only takes effect when, for example, they *actually* become owners.

Note that the Direction cannot be served on a master (*cf.* s.19(1)), for example to require him to incur capital expenditure, but only on an owner, charterer or manager. The owner, as defined by s.46, means a registered owner where the ship is registered. Under the new system established under the Merchant Shipping Act 1988, there is no compulsion to register, although most commercial owners will do so. In the case of unregistered ships, Directions could certainly be served on the legal owner and, possibly, the beneficial owner. All types of charterer could be served, whether demise, voyage or time. In practice, it may be difficult for time and voyage charterers to effect actual security measures themselves on board a ship which, by definition, they do not possess. There may be difficult contractual questions over the responsibility for paying for the costs of security measures, or the losses (for example caused by delay) which might result from their implementation. It may be that the costs could be quite significant for certain categories of vessel, such as passenger ships. In some cases it may be appropriate to seek contractual indemnities. A "manager" would normally refer to a professional firm undertaking ship management on behalf of an owner (for example a bank).

Measures to be taken. Subs. (2) gives a wide general power to direct the appropriate persons to take action relevant to their interest. For example, shipowners can receive Directions in respect of ships: persons having access to restricted zones can be directed in respect of activities within that zone. Subs. (3) details specific Directions that can be given under s.24, for example by requiring shipowners to guard their ships against acts of violence. Note in particular that under subs. (3)(d) a person having access to restricted zones may be obliged to guard vehicles and equipment kept *outside* the harbour. Subs. (5) imposes two limits on the extent of the Direction. First, it cannot require searches (*cf.* ss.22, 23, above). Secondly, the Direction cannot oblige a ship operator to incur expenditure on making modifications or alterations to the ship or its equipment; nor could a ship be delayed for that purpose. Such Directions would be allowed under s.21(2). The type of Direction under s.24 that can be envisaged for ship operators would be those which relate to the deployment of personnel. The presence of subs. (5)(b), dealing with ships, also serves to emphasise that capital expenditure *can* be required of persons such as harbour authorities, for example in the construction of perimeter fencing.

Note the power under subs. (4) to impose time limits and, under s.46(2), to revoke or vary a Direction. See also the scope of Directions permitted under ss.25–28. For the ability to make formal objections to certain Directions, see s.28, below. For service of Directions, see s.45, below.

Guarding. A question was raised in debates as to exactly how an individual, as opposed to a company, would guard against acts of violence. The Ministerial reply took guarding to mean "ensuring the establishment of reasonable protection so that no unauthorised person enters a particular area or goes aboard a vessel or aircraft." (Standing Committee A, col. 148). This might involve routine precautions, such as maintaining a normal state of vigilance over movements of people. Where there is a special, or heightened, risk the provisions relating to the arming of constables would come into play. There was no intention of requiring defenceless civilians to be put in the front line, so long as there was someone present to challenge intruders (employing force if the intrusion continues). What is quite clear is that guarding does not

require an individual to carry firearms (and see also ss.25(4) and 26(1)). The Government
rejected an amendment that would have allowed a harbour authority to show that it had taken
"reasonable steps" to guard. This might have allowed it to say that a telephone call had been
made, or letter sent. That was considered to be too loose as the authority would have its own
personnel and should have the absolute duty to ensure the Direction was complied with. Note
the existence of subss. (7) and (9) for those who have a reasonable excuse.

Property rights. Subs. (10) preserves rights in property, for example where a harbour
authority is required to install surveillance equipment on land belonging to a shipping line. The
subsection seems to be drafted with movable property in mind as it talks of property being
placed or fixed in relation to land. S.46, however, includes land within the definition of
property. It can hardly have been intended that s.24 can be used to alter the ownership of real
property (see also s.26, below).

Offence. Failure to comply with a Direction is an offence. For continued refusal to comply
after an initial conviction see the note to s.2, above (inserting a new s.13A(4) in the Aviation
Security Act 1982). For offences by bodies corporate, see s.50, below.

Supplemental provisions with respect to directions

Matters which may be included in directions under sections 21 to 24

25.—(1) A direction under subsection (1) of section 21 or under section 22
or 23 of this Act may specify the minimum number of persons by whom any
search to which the direction relates is to be carried out, the qualifications
which persons carrying out any such search are to have, the manner in which
any such search is to be carried out, and any apparatus, equipment or other
aids to be used for the purpose of carrying out any such search.

(2) A direction under subsection (2) of section 21 of this Act may specify
the qualifications required to be had by persons carrying out any modifications or alterations, or the installation of any additional apparatus or
equipment, to which the direction relates.

(3) A direction under section 24 of this Act may specify—

(a) the minimum number of persons to be employed for the purposes of
any measures required by the direction to be taken by the person to
whom it is given, and the qualifications which persons employed for
those purposes are to have, and

(b) any apparatus, equipment or other aids to be used for those purposes.

(4) Where a direction under any of the preceding provisions of this Part of
this Act requires searches to be carried out, or other measures to be taken,
by constables, the direction may require the person to whom it is given to
inform the chief officer of police for the police area in which the searches are
to be carried out or the other measures taken that the Secretary of State
considers it appropriate that constables should be duly authorised to carry,
and should carry, firearms when carrying out the searches or taking the
measures in question.

(5) Nothing in subsections (1) to (4) above shall be construed as limiting
the generality of any of the preceding provisions of this Part of this Act.

(6) In this section "qualifications" includes training and experience.

(7) In the application of this section to Northern Ireland for the words in
subsection (4) above from "chief officer" to "measures taken" there are
substituted the words "chief constable of the Royal Ulster Constabulary".

DEFINITIONS
"constable": s.46(1).
"firearm": s.46(1).
"person": Interpretation Act 1978, Sched. 1.
"qualifications": subs. (6).
"Secretary of State": Interpretation Act 1978, Sched. 1.

GENERAL NOTE
Derivation: the Aviation Security Act 1982, s.15.
Content of Directions. This section expands upon the matters which may be included in
Directions. In particular, in relation to searches under ss.21–23, the Direction may specify: (i)

the minimum number of persons to be involved in a search; (ii) their qualifications, training and experience; (iii) the manner of the search; (iv) the equipment to be used in a search; and (v) the qualifications of persons performing security modifications or alterations to ships. In respect of the more general s.24 Directions, specifications may include: (i) the minimum number of persons to be employed to accomplish the necessary objective; (ii) their qualifications; and (iii) the equipment to be used by them.

Subs. (4)

Use of armed police. The version of this clause in the original Bill referred to the recipient of a Direction being required to use best endeavours to ensure that constables would be armed. This was ambiguous, as it suggested that a harbour authority might have to obtain arms. The present subs. (4) encapsulates the Government's view that the mechanism for securing searches by armed constables would operate when a person receiving a Direction gets in touch with the Chief Constable of the local police force, who would then ensure that arms were carried by his men. Note the effect of s.26(1), below.

Lord Brabazon stated in Committee in the Lords that the Government envisaged Directions requiring the arming of the police to be issued very infrequently and that none had ever been issued under the Aviation Security Act 1982 (*Hansard*, H.L. Vol. 518, col. 866). It was thought necessary to have the provision in case of an increased threat of terrorist attack and in order to avoid breakdowns in communication, for example with the Home Office, especially after office hours and at weekends.

Limitations on scope of directions under sections 21 to 24

26.—(1) Without prejudice to section 25(4) of this Act, a direction shall not require or authorise any person to carry a firearm.

(2) A direction shall not have effect in relation to any ship used in naval, customs or police service.

(3) A direction shall not have effect in relation to any ship which is registered outside the United Kingdom and of which the owner is the Government of a country outside the United Kingdom, or is a department or agency of such a Government, except at a time when any such ship is being used for commercial purposes or is for the time being allocated by that Government, department or agency for such use.

(4) A direction (except in so far as it requires any building or other works to be constructed, executed, altered, demolished or removed) shall not be construed as requiring or authorising the person to whom the direction was given, or any person acting as his employee or agent, to do anything which, apart from the direction, would constitute an act of violence; but nothing in this subsection shall restrict the use of such force as is reasonable in the circumstances (whether at the instance of the person to whom the direction was given or otherwise) by a constable, or its use by any other person in the exercise of a power conferred by section 22(3) of this Act.

(5) In so far as a direction requires anything to be done or not done at a place outside the United Kingdom—

(a) it shall not have effect except in relation to British ships, and

(b) it shall not have effect so as to require anything to be done or not done in contravention of any provision of the law (whether civil or criminal) in force at that place, other than any such provision relating to breach of contract.

(6) In so far as a direction given to a harbour authority or to any person mentioned in section 24(1)(c) or (d) of this Act requires a building or other works to be constructed, executed, altered, demolished or removed on land outside the harbour area, or requires any other measures to be taken on such land, the direction shall not confer on the person to whom it is given any rights as against a person having—

(a) an interest in that land, or

(b) a right to occupy that land, or

(c) a right restrictive of its use;

and accordingly, the direction shall not be construed as requiring the person to whom it is given to do anything which would be actionable at the suit or instance of a person having such interest or right in his capacity as a person having that interest or right.

(7) Nothing in this section shall be construed as derogating from any exemption or immunity of the Crown in relation to the provisions of this Part of this Act.

(8) In this section "direction" means a direction under section 21, 22, 23 or 24 of this Act.

DEFINITIONS
"act of violence": s.46(1).
"British ship": s.46(1).
"direction": subs. (8).
"employee": s.46(1).
"firearm": s.46(1).
"harbour": s.46(1).
"harbour area": ss.18(3); 46(1).
"harbour authority": s.46(1).
"land": Interpretation Act 1978, Sched. 1.
"naval service": s.46(1).
"person": Interpretation Act 1978, Sched. 1.
"ship": s.46(1).
"United Kingdom": Interpretation Act 1978, Sched. 1.

GENERAL NOTE
Derivation: the Aviation Security Act 1982, s.16.
The section contains a number of limitations on the scope of Directions permitted under ss.21–24, although the phrasing of the restrictions also serves to indicate, in a number of cases, the range of Directions possible.

Subs. (1)
The Secretary of State is not entitled to permit persons such as private security guards to carry firearms, including airguns and air pistols. It is only the ordinary police forces which are exempt from the requirements of the Firearms Act 1968. Ports police are not exempt. They require firearms certificates like ordinary members of the public and thus would fall under the control of the appropriate Chief Constable.

Subss. (2) and (3)
In common with other provisions of the Act (see for example s.9(2)), public service vessels cannot be the subject of Directions. The exception is for foreign public vessels used for commercial purposes (*cf.* the State Immunity Act 1978, implementing the Convention for the Unification of Certain Rules Concerning the Immunity of State-owned Ships 1926).

Subs. (4)
Use of force. In general, Directions cannot sanction the use of force constituting an "act of violence" within s.18(2)—including assault. Force can be used: (i) where building works are required; (ii) where it is reasonable in the circumstances and is exercised by a constable; and (iii) where a constable or other authorised person undertakes a search sanctioned by s.22.

Subs. (5)
Geographic limits. It is clear that Directions can be given in respect of activities outside U.K. territorial limits, but these can only be effective in relation to British ships (for example cruising in the Caribbean). Even the recipient of the Direction cannot be made to contravene local law, although the Direction can override contractual provisions relating to breach. This would appear to be intended to prevent a shipowner, for instance, refusing to obey a Direction to make modifications under s.21(2) on the basis that it would be in breach of a charterparty requiring him to obey the charterer's orders immediately. The wording of para. (b) is a little unfortunate because it seems more appropriate for legislative, rather than contractual, provisions. It would be contrary to the intention of Pt. III if potential breaches of contract justified non-compliance with Directions.

Subs. (6)
Property rights. The general power to require building works arises under s.24. What is not entirely clear is the effect that Directions (or enforcement notices under s.29, below) in respect

of such works will have on existing property rights, especially of persons on whose land work is to take place. The effect of s.24(1), above, on the owner of equipment installed on somebody else's land has already been noted. What of the owner of the land on which it is installed? At the least, landowners affected by building works might be able to take advantage of the compensation provisions in s.43. The distinction appears to be between land inside and land outside the harbour area. (See also s.34, below).

Land outside the harbour area. Subs. (6) only deals with building works *outside* the harbour area. It provides that the Direction does not confer any rights as against those with proprietary interests. Accordingly, there is no power, for example, to direct a harbour authority to commit trespass on land outside the harbour in order to install security equipment. It is clear that subs. (6) preserves the rights of a private property owner *outside* the harbour area (within s.18(3)) to refuse permission for work to be carried out on his land, and those rights are not pre-empted. Accordingly, neither the harbour authority nor the DTp would have any implied compulsory purchase powers in respect of such land. To this extent, security prevails over all except private property. Of course, there is nothing to prevent landowners consenting to work on their land.

Land within the harbour area. At Report stage in the Commons the Minister for Public Transport, Mr Portillo, explained that most works would need to take place in harbour areas (*Hansard*, H.C. Vol. 164, col. 594). S.34(2) makes it clear that the Act takes precedence over other Acts and to this extent, the Directions can presumably override planning laws. He gave the example of a harbour authority given a Direction to construct a wall which may impinge on the property of a shipping line within the harbour. The Direction was said to take precedence, with the harbour authority paying compensation (under s.43). On this point, concerning the rights of third parties with property in the harbour, the Minister was forced to retract assurances made in Committee about the effect of the Act on private rights.

The Ministerial explanation does not spell out how far, if at all, the recipient of the Direction has compulsory purchase powers within a harbour. If a harbour authority is directed to construct a building on land belonging to another, what happens to the ownership of the land? The logic of subs. (6) indicates that rights can be created against the private owner. In the case of a perimeter fence, there would be no need for compulsory purchase, but a landowner might refuse to allow access for a fence to be constructed. However, it follows from subs. (6) that the operation of Pt. III could not be frustrated by third parties with property within the harbour, such as an electricity board (with cables) or a gas company (with pipelines). S.26(4) would seem to confirm that force could be used to compel construction work.

The position on boundary rules was said in debates, somewhat vaguely, to rely on "planning law" (and see the note to s.43, below). It is possible to imagine planning blight in respect of some areas within a port owned by a person not falling within the s.19(1) list as a person performing harbour operations (for example the owner of a marina-type private dwelling).

General or urgent directions under sections 21 to 24

27.—(1) A direction given to any person under section 21, 22, 23 or 24 of this Act need not be addressed to that particular person, but may be framed in general terms applicable to all persons to whom such a direction may be given or to any class of such persons to which that particular person belongs.

(2) If it appears to the Secretary of State that an exception from any direction given under any of those sections is required as a matter of urgency in any particular case he may, by a notification given (otherwise than in writing) to the person for the time being subject to the direction, authorise that person to disregard the requirements of the direction—

    (a) in relation to such ships or class of ships, in relation to such harbour area or part of a harbour area, in relation to such land outside a harbour area, in relation to such activities or in relation to such persons or property or such description of persons or property, and

    (b) on such occasion or series of occasions, or for such period,

as he may specify; and the direction shall have effect in that case subject to any exceptions so specified.

(3) Any notification given to any person under subsection (2) above with respect to any direction shall cease to have effect (if it has not already done so)—

    (a) if a direction in writing is subsequently given to that person varying or revoking the original direction, or

(b) if no such direction in writing is given within the period of thirty days beginning with the date on which the notification was given, at the end of that period.

(4) Any notification given under subsection (2) above shall be regarded as given to the person to whom it is directed if it is given—

(a) to any person authorised by that person to receive any such direction or notification,

(b) where that person is a body corporate, to the secretary, clerk or similar officer of the body corporate, and

(c) in any other case, to anyone holding a comparable office or position in that person's employment.

DEFINITIONS
"harbour": s.46(1).
"harbour area": ss.18(3); 46(1).
"harbour authority": s.46(1).
"person": Interpretation Act 1978, Sched. 1.
"property": s.46(1).
"ship": s.46(1).

GENERAL NOTE
Derivation: the Aviation Security Act 1982, s.17.

Subs. (1)
Nature of a Direction. Directions under ss.21–24 do not have to be addressed to a particular individual, but may be framed generally, for example to shipowners in Southampton. Nevertheless, for an offence to be committed it would seem that the Direction in writing must have been "given" to the individual (see for example s.24(2)).
Note the power to revoke or vary a Direction given by s.46(2).

Subss. (2) and (3)
Exceptions. This subsection allows the giving of exemptions to Directions in urgent cases, for example where higher standards were necessary after an alert indicated security deficiencies.
Under ss.21–24 Directions have to be given in writing and s.46(2) includes a power to vary or revoke the Direction. This would normally be done in writing, but the present subsection allows the urgent exemptions to be given by telephone or in person. The exception will last until a written revocation of the Direction is received, or for 30 days.
For service of notifications, see s.45, below.

Subs. (4)
The "secretary" and "clerk" referred to would be senior officers, such as a company secretary, rather than clerical officers. The GCBS suggested that paras. (b) and (c) be omitted because, in the case of a foreign flag ship, it may not be possible to identify a secretary, clerk or similar officer. However, the DTp said that it preferred to have the option of dealing with companies if it was not possible to contact a master.

Objections to certain directions under section 24

28.—(1) This section applies to any direction given under section 24 of this Act which—

(a) requires a person to take measures consisting of or including the construction, execution, alteration, demolition or removal of a building or other works, and

(b) does not contain a statement that the measures are urgently required and that accordingly the direction is to take effect immediately.

(2) At any time before the end of the period of thirty days beginning with the date on which a direction to which this section applies is given, the person to whom the direction is given may serve on the Secretary of State a notice in writing objecting to the direction, on the grounds that the measures specified in the direction, in so far as they relate to the construction, execution, alteration, demolition or removal of a building or other works—

(a) are unnecessary and should be dispensed with, or
(b) are excessively onerous or inconvenient and should be modified in a
    manner specified in the notice.

(3) Where the person to whom such a direction is given serves a notice
under subsection (2) above objecting to the direction, the Secretary of State
shall consider the grounds of the objection and, if so required by the
objector, shall afford to him an opportunity of appearing before and being
heard by a person appointed by the Secretary of State for the purpose, and
shall then serve on the objector a notice in writing either—
(a) confirming the direction as originally given, or
(b) confirming it subject to one or more modifications specified in the
    notice under this subsection, or
(c) withdrawing the direction;
and the direction shall not take effect until it has been confirmed (with or
without modification) by a notice served under this subsection.

DEFINITIONS
  "measures": s.46(1).
  "person": Interpretation Act 1978, Sched. 1.
  "Secretary of State": Interpretation Act 1978, Sched. 1.

GENERAL NOTE
  Derivation: the Aviation Security Act 1982, s.18.
  Objection. Apart from the possibility of judicial review, there are no provisions allowing
formal appeals to the courts. The section provides a right to object to, rather than appeal
against, certain Directions. In effect it allows the Direction to be suspended until the objection
procedure is completed, whereupon the Secretary of State can confirm the Direction. The type
of Direction to which objection may be made is the most drastic sort that involves some building
work, for instance an order to demolish a building. If the Direction states that its measures are
urgently required, and that they are to take effect immediately, there is no power of objection
under the section. Otherwise, the objection must be made within 30 days.
  Note the power to revoke or vary a Direction given by s.46(2). For service of notices, see s.45,
below.

Subs. (1)
  "Under s.24". The right to object to a Direction only arises if it is one of the non-urgent
building Directions permitted under s.24 and not one relating, for example, to the searching of
ships (under s.21), the searching of harbours (s.22), the searching of land (s.23), or if it is a
general Direction relating to port areas (under s.24). The British Ports Federation pressed for
wider powers of appeal to include these Directions, particularly because of the cost implications; heavy costs could arise, not simply in relation to buildings, but also in the number of
persons employed in searches. The Government objection was that, as extensive consultation
would take place with the industry, there was no need for an appeal. Although there would be
no formal right to object under the section, there would be nothing to stop an aggrieved person
approaching the Secretary of State informally and asking for the exercise of the powers of
variation given by s.46(2). However, the person would then not be able to rely on the
suspensory effect of subs. (3).

Subs. (2)
  Grounds for objection. The grounds on which objection may be made are that the measures
specified are (i) unnecessary, or (ii) excessively onerous or inconvenient. Under s.28(2) it may
be an objection to a Direction that the recipient will have to pay excessively onerous compensation of a third party. The minimum objection period of 30 days could be extended by the
Secretary of State while the compensation issue is resolved, for example, by referring the
matter to the Lands tribunal.

Enforcement notices

29.—(1) Where an authorised person is of the opinion that any person has
failed to comply with any general requirement of a direction given to him
under section 21, 22, 23 or 24 of this Act, the authorised person may serve on
that person a notice (in this Part of this Act referred to as an "enforcement
notice")—

(a) specifying those general requirements of the direction with which he has, in the opinion of the authorised person, failed to comply, and

(b) specifying, subject to section 30 of this Act, the measures that ought to be taken in order to comply with those requirements.

(2) For the purposes of this section a requirement of a direction given by the Secretary of State under section 21, 22, 23 or 24 of this Act is a "general requirement" if the provision imposing the requirement—

(a) has been included in two or more directions given to different persons (whether or not at the same time), and

(b) is framed in general terms applicable to all the persons to whom those directions are given.

(3) If an enforcement notice is served under this section on the owner, charterer or manager of a ship, then (whether or not that service is effected by virtue of section 45(8) of this Act) an authorised person may serve on the master of the ship—

(a) a copy of the enforcement notice and of the direction to which it relates, and

(b) a notice stating that the master is required to comply with the enforcement notice,

and, if he does so, sections 31, 32 and 33 of this Act shall have effect as if the enforcement notice had been served on him as well as on the owner, charterer or manager of the ship.

DEFINITIONS
"authorised person": s.46(1).
"enforcement notice": s.46(1).
"manager": s.46(1).
"master": s.46(1).
"owner": s.46(1).
"person": Interpretation Act 1978, Sched. 1.
"ship": s.46(1).

GENERAL NOTE
Derivation: *cf.* the Aviation Security Act 1982, s.18A (as inserted by s.4 of the 1990 Act).

Enforcement notices. See generally the note to s.4, above. At first sight, it is difficult to see why an enforcement notice should be necessary, as it might be supposed that it can only repeat a requirement set out in a Direction. The answer appears to lie in the intended content of the two documents. In essence the enforcement notice enables an inspector to set out in detail exactly how an individual should comply with the general requirements of a Direction, for example under s.22. The general Direction might specify that searches are to take place in certain places; the enforcement notice might set out exactly the manner in which the search is to be undertaken. Nevertheless, the relationship between the Direction and the enforcement notice still seems awkward.

For service of notices, see s.45, below. For revocation or variation of notices, see s.33, below. For objections to notices, see s.31, below.

The concept of enforcement notices is not entirely new: *cf.* the Health and Safety at Work Act 1974, s.21, and the Merchant Shipping Act 1984, Pt. I, where official inspectors have powers to issue "improvement notices" to persons in breach of statutory duties.

Subs. (3)
This subsection does not have an equivalent in the aviation context. It allows an inspector to serve a copy of an enforcement notice (and relevant Direction) on a ship's master so as to make it effective and binding on him. Note that the original may be served on the master under s.45(8) *as agent* of owner, charterer or manager. That service, as such, does not bind the master personally and lay him open to the penalties under s.31. For the enforcement notice to bind him the requirements of subs. (3)(a) and (b) must be met. For the likely practice of the DTp see *Masters* in the General Note to Pt. III, above. At Committee stage in the Lords, Lord Brabazon noted that the power to place requirements on masters would be taken "sensibly and sensitively" (*Hansard*, H.L. Vol. 518, col. 881). The Government would not expect a master to carry out works required initially as part of a Direction under s.24 if that would involve him in personal expenditure. It might be different if the master had delegated to him by the ship's operator the financial power to spend company money.

Contents of enforcement notice

30.—(1) An enforcement notice may specify in greater detail measures which are described in general terms in those provisions of the direction to which it relates which impose general requirements, but may not impose any requirement which could not have been imposed by a direction given by the Secretary of State under the provision under which the direction was given.

(2) An enforcement notice may be framed so as to afford the person on whom it is served a choice between different ways of complying with the specified requirements of the direction.

(3) Subject to subsection (4) below, an enforcement notice which relates to a direction given under section 21 of this Act must require the person to whom the direction was given not to cause or permit things to be done as mentioned in subsection (1)(a) or (b) or (2) of that section, as the case requires, until the specified measures have been taken.

(4) In serving an enforcement notice which relates to a direction under section 21(2) of this Act, the authorised person shall allow, and shall specify in the notice, such period as appears to him to be reasonably required for taking the measures specified in the notice; and the notice shall not take effect before the end of the period so specified.

(5) An enforcement notice which relates to a direction given under section 22, 23 or 24 of this Act must either—

(a) require the person to whom the direction was given to take the specified measures within a specified period which—

(i) where the measures consist of or include the construction, execution, alteration, demolition or removal of a building or other works, must not be less than thirty days beginning with the date of service of the notice, and

(ii) in any other case, must not be less than seven days beginning with that date; or

(b) require him not to do specified things, or cause or permit specified things to be done, until the specified measures have been taken.

(6) Subject to section 33(2) of this Act, an enforcement notice requiring a person not to cause or permit anything to be done shall be construed as requiring him to take all such steps as in any particular circumstances are practicable and necessary to prevent that thing from being done.

DEFINITIONS
  "authorised person": s.46(1).
  "enforcement notice": s.46(1).
  "measures": s.46(1).
  "person": Interpretation Act 1978, Sched. 1.

GENERAL NOTE
  Derivation: *cf.* the Aviation Security Act 1982, s.18B (as inserted by s.4 of the 1990 Act).
  Contents of the enforcement notice. See also the note to s.4, above. The enforcement notice must state how the recipient of the Direction has failed to comply with it and which measures are required in order to achieve compliance (see s.29(1), above). It must not exceed the requirements that could have been imposed in the first place by the Secretary of State. The section lays down time limits for compliance with the enforcement notice, depending on the nature of the measures required.

Offences relating to enforcement notices

31.—(1) Any person who, without reasonable excuse, fails to comply with an enforcement notice served on him is guilty of an offence and liable—

(a) on summary conviction, to a fine not exceeding the statutory maximum;

(b) on conviction on indictment, to a fine.

(2) Where a person is convicted of an offence under subsection (1) above, then, if without reasonable excuse the failure in respect of which he was

convicted is continued after the conviction, he is guilty of a further offence and liable on summary conviction to a fine not exceeding one-tenth of level 5 on the standard scale for each day on which the failure continues.

(3) Any person who intentionally interferes with any building constructed or works executed on any land in compliance with an enforcement notice or with anything installed on, under, over or across any land in compliance with such a notice is guilty of an offence and liable—

(a) on summary conviction, to a fine not exceeding the statutory maximum;

(b) on conviction on indictment, to a fine.

DEFINITIONS
"enforcement notice": s.46(1).
"land": Interpretation Act 1978, Sched. 1.
"person": Interpretation Act 1978, Sched. 1.
"standard scale": Criminal Justice Act 1982, s.74.
"statutory maximum": Criminal Justice Act 1982, s.74.

GENERAL NOTE
Derivation: *cf.* the Aviation Security Act 1982, s.18C (as inserted by s.4 of the 1990 Act).
Offences. Failure to comply with an enforcement notice is an offence: continued failure could result in a day-by-day fine (see the note to s.2, above, inserting a new s.13A(4) in the Aviation Security Act 1982). There are two possible defences, (i) reasonable excuse and (ii) that there was not a failure to comply as the defendant had taken all steps that were practicable and necessary (within s.29(6), above).
It is also an offence intentionally to interfere with buildings or installations on land for the purpose of complying with an enforcement notice.

Objections to enforcement notices

32.—(1) The person on whom an enforcement notice is served may serve on the Secretary of State a notice in writing of his objection to the enforcement notice, specifying the grounds of the objection.

(2) Any notice of objection under subsection (1) above must be served—

(a) where the enforcement notice specifies measures falling within section 30(5)(a)(i) of this Act, before the end of the period of thirty days beginning with the date on which the enforcement notice was served, or

(b) in any other case, before the end of the period of seven days beginning with that date.

(3) The grounds of objection to an enforcement notice are—

(a) that the general requirements of the direction which are specified in the notice for the purposes of section 29(1)(a) of this Act have been complied with,

(b) that the notice purports to impose a requirement which could not have been imposed by a direction given under the provision under which the direction to which the notice relates was given, or

(c) that any requirement of the notice—

(i) is unnecessary for complying with the general requirements specified as mentioned in paragraph (a) above and should be dispensed with, or

(ii) having regard to the terms of those general requirements, is excessively onerous or inconvenient and should be modified in a manner specified in the notice of objection under subsection (1) above.

(4) Where the person on whom an enforcement notice is served serves a notice under subsection (1) above objecting to the enforcement notice, the Secretary of State shall consider the grounds of the objection and, if so required by the objector, shall afford to him an opportunity of appearing before and being heard by a person appointed by the Secretary of State for the purpose, and shall then serve on the objector a notice in writing either—

(a) confirming the enforcement notice as originally served, or
(b) confirming it subject to one or more modifications specified in the notice under this subsection, or
(c) cancelling the enforcement notice.

(5) An enforcement notice to which an objection has been made under subsection (1) above—
(a) if it contains such a requirement as is mentioned in section 30(3) or (5)(b) of this Act, shall continue to have effect as originally served until it has been cancelled, or it has been confirmed subject to modification by a notice under subsection (4) above, and
(b) in any other case, shall not take effect until it has been confirmed (with or without modification) by a notice under subsection (4) above.

DEFINITIONS
   "enforcement notice": s.46(1).
   "person": Interpretation Act 1978, Sched. 1.
   "Secretary of State": Interpretation Act 1978, Sched. 1.

GENERAL NOTE
   Derivation: *cf.* the Aviation Security Act 1982, s.18D (as inserted by s.4 of the 1990 Act).
   Objections to enforcement notices. As with Directions themselves (see s.28), it is possible to object to enforcement notices within certain time limits, although there is no restriction on the type of measure in respect of which an appeal may be made. The grounds of objection are the same as for aviation (see the note to s.4, above). An objector can argue (i) that he has complied with the Direction, (ii) that the enforcement notice exceeds its powers, (iii) that the requirements are unnecessary, or (iv) that the requirements are excessively onerous or inconvenient.

Enforcement notices: supplementary

33.—(1) An enforcement notice served on any person—
(a) may be revoked by a notice served on him by an authorised person, and
(b) may be varied by a further enforcement notice.

(2) Sections 25 and 26 of this Act apply to an enforcement notice as they apply to the direction to which the notice relates.

(3) The ownership of any property shall not be affected by reason only that it is placed on or under or affixed to, any land in compliance with an enforcement notice.

(4) Where an authorised person has served an enforcement notice specifying the general requirements of a direction with which the person on whom it is served has, in the opinion of the authorised person, failed to comply, the person on whom the notice is served shall not be taken, for the purposes of section 21(8), 22(7), 23(3) or 24(7) of this Act, to have failed to comply with the direction by reason of the matters specified in the notice.

(5) Subsection (4) above does not apply in relation to any proceedings commenced before the service of the enforcement notice.

(6) Where an enforcement notice has been served in relation to a direction, the fact that the notice specifies certain general requirements of the direction as those with which the person on whom the notice is served has, in the opinion of the authorised person, failed to comply shall not in any proceedings be evidence that any other requirement of the direction has been complied with.

(7) In this section "direction" means a direction under section 21, 22, 23 or 24 of this Act.

DEFINITIONS
   "authorised person": s.46(1).
   "direction": subs. (7).
   "enforcement notice": s.46(1).

"land": Interpretation Act 1978, Sched. 1.
"person": Interpretation Act 1978, Sched. 1.
"property": s.46(1).

GENERAL NOTE
    Derivation: *cf.* the Aviation Security Act 1982, s.18E (as inserted by s.4 of the 1990 Act).
    The section aligns the position under enforcement notices with that under Directions. Thus, subs. (2) applies to enforcement notices the sections of the Act dealing with the scope of, and restrictions affecting, Directions. Subs. (3) is the equivalent of s.24(10). Subss. (4) and (5) prevent the possibility of overlapping offences.

Operation of directions under Part III in relation to rights and duties under other laws

34.—(1) In subsections (2) to (4) below references to a direction are references to a direction under section 21, 22, 23 or 24 of this Act as the direction has effect subject to any limitation imposed on its operation—
    (a) by section 26 of this Act, or
    (b) by any exemption or immunity of the Crown;
and any reference in those subsections to compliance with a direction is a reference to compliance with it subject to any limitation so imposed.
    (2) In so far as a direction requires anything to be done or not done in the United Kingdom, the direction shall have effect notwithstanding anything contained in any contract (whether a United Kingdom contract or not) or contained in, or having effect by virtue of, any other Act or any rule of law; and accordingly no proceedings (whether civil or criminal) shall lie against any person in any United Kingdom court by reason of anything done or not done by him or on his behalf in compliance with a direction.
    (3) In so far as a direction requires anything to be done or not done at a place outside the United Kingdom, the direction shall have effect notwithstanding anything contained in any contract (whether a United Kingdom contract or not); and accordingly, where a direction is inconsistent with anything in such a contract, it shall (without prejudice to any proceedings in a court other than a United Kingdom court) be construed as requiring compliance with the direction notwithstanding that compliance would be in breach of that contract.
    (4) No proceedings for breach of contract shall lie against any person in a United Kingdom court by reason of anything done or not done by him or on his behalf at a place outside the United Kingdom in compliance with a direction, if the contract in question is a United Kingdom contract.
    (5) Subsections (1) to (4) above have effect in relation to an enforcement notice as they have effect in relation to a direction under section 21, 22, 23 or 24 of this Act.
    (6) In this section "United Kingdom court" means a court exercising jurisdiction in any part of the United Kingdom under the law of the United Kingdom or of part of the United Kingdom, and "United Kingdom contract" means a contract which is either expressed to have effect in accordance with the law of the United Kingdom or of part of the United Kingdom or (not being so expressed) is a contract the law applicable to which is the law of the United Kingdom or of part of the United Kingdom.

DEFINITIONS
    "person": Interpretation Act 1978, Sched. 1.
    "United Kingdom": Interpretation Act 1978, Sched. 1.
    "United Kingdom contract": subs. (6).
    "United Kingdom court": subs. (6).

GENERAL NOTE
    Derivation: the Aviation Security Act 1982, s.19.
    This section describes the relationship between Directions and enforcement notices under Pt. III and existing law (see also the note to s.26, above).

Within the U.K. The Direction will override (i) any contract, whether U.K. law is the proper law or not, (ii) any Act, or (iii) any common law rule, or (iv) any equitable rule. The section operates as a complete bar to any proceedings in the U.K. resulting from compliance.

Outside the U.K. Under s.26(5), Directions and (by s.33(2)) enforcement notices which relate to measures to be taken outside of the U.K. can only be effective in relation to British ships. Subs. (3) means that a Direction or enforcement notice in relation to a British ship again overrides any contract, whatever the proper law. Compliance will be required even if this is a breach. For example, a demise charterer may be required to modify the ship in breach of the charterparty. If the contract is a U.K. contract, the charterer could not be sued for breach in a U.K. court. However, if the contract is governed by some other system of law, a U.K. court would be obliged to consider the effect of that law in deciding whether there was a breach.

Detention of ships

35.—(1) Where an authorised person is satisfied that the owner, charterer, manager or master of a ship has failed to comply with—

(a) a direction given to him under section 21 or 24 of this Act in respect of that ship, or

(b) an enforcement notice which has been served on him in respect of that ship and which relates to such a direction,

and the authorised person certifies in writing to that effect, stating particulars of the non-compliance, the ship may be detained until the authorised person otherwise directs.

(2) Where the authorised person does not himself detain the ship, he shall deliver the certificate to the officer detaining the ship.

(3) On detaining the ship, the authorised person or other officer shall deliver to the master of the ship a copy of the certificate.

(4) Section 692 of the Merchant Shipping Act 1894 (enforcement of detention of ships) applies in the case of detention under this section as if it were authorised or ordered under that Act.

DEFINITIONS
"authorised person": s.46(1).
"enforcement notice": s.46(1).
"manager": s.46(1).
"master": s.46(1).
"ship": s.46(1).

GENERAL NOTE
This provision does not have an exact equivalent in the Aviation Security Act 1982. In common with most maritime regulatory provisions, a power of detention is given to prevent ships sailing away in order to avoid the effects of a Direction or enforcement notice. An inspector must certify in writing that there has been non-compliance before that person, or an official such as a customs officer, actually detains the vessel. S.692 of the Merchant Shipping Act 1894 deals with matters such as the expenses of detention and offences for wrongful sailing.

It would appear from subs. (1)(a) that there would be no power of detention if the master failed to obey a Direction under s.19 and sailed away within the seven day period allowed by s.19(2) for the provision of information (and see s.19, above).

Inspection of ships and harbour areas

36.—(1) For the purpose of enabling the Secretary of State to determine whether to give a direction to any person under any of sections 21 to 24 of this Act, or of ascertaining whether any such direction or any enforcement notice is being or has been complied with, an authorised person shall have power, on production (if required) of his credentials, to inspect—

(a) any British ship,

(b) any other ship while in a harbour area,

(c) any part of any harbour area, or

(d) any land outside a harbour area which is occupied for the purposes of a business by a person who—

(i) carries on (or appears to the authorised person to be about to carry on) harbour operations in a harbour area for the purposes of that business, or

(ii) is permitted (or appears to the authorised person to be about to be permitted) to have access to a restricted zone of a harbour area for the purposes of the activities of that business.

(2) An authorised person inspecting a ship or any part of a harbour area or any land outside a harbour area under subsection (1) above shall have power—

(a) to subject any property found by him on the ship (but not the ship itself or any apparatus or equipment installed in it) or, as the case may be, to subject that part of the harbour area or any property found by him there or on that land, to such tests,

(b) to take such steps—

(i) to ascertain what practices or procedures are being followed in relation to security, or

(ii) to test the effectiveness of any practice or procedure relating to security, or

(c) to require the owner, charterer, manager or master of the ship, the harbour authority or the occupier of the land to furnish to him such information,

as the authorised person may consider necessary for the purpose for which the inspection is carried out.

(3) Subject to subsection (4) below, an authorised person, for the purpose of exercising any power conferred on him by subsection (1) or (2) above in relation to a ship, in relation to a harbour area or in relation to any land outside a harbour area, shall have power—

(a) for the purpose of inspecting a ship, to go on board it and to take all such steps as are necessary to ensure that it is not moved, or

(b) for the purpose of inspecting any part of a harbour area, to enter any building or works in the harbour area or enter upon any land in the harbour area, or

(c) for the purpose of inspecting any land outside a harbour area, to enter upon the land and to enter any building or works on the land.

(4) The powers conferred by subsection (3) above shall not include power for an authorised person to use force for the purpose of going on board any ship, entering any building or works or entering upon any land.

(5) Any person who—

(a) without reasonable excuse, fails to comply with a requirement imposed on him under subsection (2)(c) above, or

(b) in furnishing any information so required, makes a statement which he knows to be false in a material particular, or recklessly makes a statement which is false in a material particular,

commits an offence.

(6) A person guilty of an offence under subsection (5) above is liable—

(a) on summary conviction, to a fine not exceeding the statutory maximum;

(b) on conviction on indictment, to a fine or to imprisonment for a term not exceeding two years or to both.

DEFINITIONS

"authorised person": s.46(1).

"British ship": s.46(1).

"enforcement notice": s.46(1).

"harbour": s.46(1).

"harbour area": ss.18(3); 46(1).

"harbour operations": s.46(1).

"land": Interpretation Act 1978, Sched. 1.

"manager": s.46(1).

"master": s.46(1).
"owner": s.46(1).
"permitted to have access": s.46(3).
"person": Interpretation Act 1978, Sched. 1.
"property": s.46(1).
"restricted zone": s.46(1).
"Secretary of State": Interpretation Act 1978, Sched. 1.
"ship": s.46(1).
"statutory maximum": Criminal Justice Act 1982, s.74.

GENERAL NOTE

Derivation: *cf*. the Aviation Security Act 1982, s.20 (as inserted by Sched. 1, para. 11, below).

Inspection powers. It will be necessary for the DTp to create a maritime inspectorate to be "authorised persons" under s.46(1). The wording is wide enough to include any category of persons and yet very wide powers of entry are granted. Lord Brabazon did confirm that such persons would only be "trained DTp staff" (*Hansard*, H.L. Vol. 518, col. 884). It seems probable that the aviation position will be copied, with an inspectorate, under a chief inspecting officer, in the Marine Policy Division of the DTp. This section would give such inspectors wide powers to inspect ships and harbours. The power extends to land outside harbours occupied by persons who operate in the harbour, or have access to its restricted areas (created under s.20).

The powers would allow the inspector (i) to undertake tests on suspect substances found on board, (ii) to investigate security procedures and conduct security exercises, and (iii) to require the ship's operators or master to provide him with information. Failure to provide information, or giving false information, is an offence.

Despite the wide powers of entry, it is clear from subs. (4) that force may not be used.

Cf. the Health and Safety at Work Act 1974, s.20, and the Merchant Shipping Act 1979, s.27.

Offences relating to security of ships and harbour areas

False statements relating to baggage, cargo etc.

37.—(1) Subject to subsection (3) below, a person commits an offence if, in answer to a question which—

(a) relates to any baggage, cargo or stores (whether belonging to him or to another) that is or are intended for carriage by sea—

(i) by a British ship, or

(ii) by any other ship to or from the United Kingdom, and

(b) is put to him for purposes to which this Part of this Act applies—

(i) by any of the persons mentioned in subsection (2) below, or

(ii) by any employee or agent of such a person in his capacity as employee or agent,

(iii) by a constable,

he makes a statement which he knows to be false in a material particular, or recklessly makes a statement which is false in a material particular.

(2) The persons referred to in subsection (1)(b) above are—

(a) a harbour authority,

(b) the owner, charterer or manager of any ship, and

(c) any person who—

(i) is permitted to have access to a restricted zone of a harbour area for the purposes of the activities of a business carried on by him, and

(ii) has control in that restricted zone over the baggage, cargo or stores to which the question relates.

(3) Subsection (1) above does not apply in relation to any statement made by an authorised person in the exercise of the power conferred by section 36(2)(b) of this Act.

(4) A person guilty of an offence under subsection (1) above is liable on summary conviction to a fine not exceeding level 5 on the standard scale.

(5) In this section—

"cargo" includes mail;

"ship" does not include a ship used in naval, customs or police
service; and
"stores" means any goods intended for sale or use in a ship, including
fuel and spare parts and other articles of equipment, whether or
not for immediate fitting.

DEFINITIONS
"authorised person": s.46(1).
"cargo": subs. (5).
"employee": s.46(1).
"harbour": s.46(1).
"harbour area": ss.18(3); 46(1).
"harbour authority": s.46(1).
"manager": s.46(1).
"owner": s.46(1).
"permitted to have access": s.46(3).
"person": Interpretation Act 1978, Sched. 1.
"purposes to which this Part of this Act applies": s.18(1).
"restricted zone": s.46(1).
"ship": s.46(1) and subs. (5).
"standard scale": Criminal Justice Act 1982, s.74.
"stores": subs. (5).
"United Kingdom": Interpretation Act 1978, Sched. 1.

GENERAL NOTE
Derivation: *cf.* the Aviation Security Act 1982, s.21A, (as inserted by the 1990 Act, s.5).
False statements relating to baggage. The section is almost identical to the aviation equivalent
(see the note to s.5, above) and creates an offence for the giving of false information relating to
baggage, cargo or stores. It is aimed mainly at the passenger who gives a false answer to
questions about the contents of his luggage. The wording does not seem particularly apt to deal
with the passenger asked about his car, which would probably have to be fitted in as "cargo" for
the section to apply. The contents of the car would clearly be baggage. However, it should be
noted that the section could also apply to shippers who, for example misdescribe their dangerous cargo, perhaps in order to achieve a lower rate of freight.
The section requires there to have been a positive question: mere non-disclosure is not
enough. However, there is nothing that says that the question cannot be contained in a standard
form. The Government did not accept an Opposition amendment that would have made it an
offence if the false statement was in any "documentation", not just in answer to a question; it
was stated in response that the section was not designed to deal with all types of documentation.
S.41 was available to produce regulations for sea cargo agencies.
It should also be noted that the question does not have to be put by a policeman or DTp
official. It could be posed by the employee of a shipping line or a firm of stevedores.
There is a defence under subs. (3) for the inspector who decides to test security by giving
incorrect answers (see the note to the new s.21A(3) of the Aviation Security Act 1982 as
inserted by s.5, above).

False statements in connection with identity documents

38.—(1) Subject to subsection (4) below, a person commits an offence if—
(a) for the purpose of, or in connection with, an application made by him
or another for the issue of an identity document to which this subsection applies, or
(b) in connection with the continued holding by him or another of any
such document which has already been issued,
he makes to any of the persons specified in subsection (3) below, to any
employee or agent of such a person or to a constable, a statement which he
knows to be false in a material particular, or recklessly makes to any of those
persons, to any such employee or agent or to a constable, a statement which
is false in a material particular.
(2) Subsection (1) above applies to any identity document which is to be or
has been issued by any of the persons specified in subsection (3) below in
accordance with arrangements the maintenance of which is required by a
direction given by the Secretary of State under section 24 of this Act.

(3) The persons referred to in subsection (1) above are—
(a) a harbour authority,
(b) the owner, charterer or manager of any ship, and
(c) any person who is permitted to have access to a restricted zone of a harbour area for the purposes of the activities of a business carried on by him.

(4) Subsection (1) above does not apply in relation to any statement made by an authorised person in the exercise of the power conferred by section 36(2)(b) of this Act.

(5) A person guilty of an offence under subsection (1) above is liable on summary conviction to a fine not exceeding level 5 on the standard scale.

DEFINITIONS
"employee": s.46(1).
"harbour": s.46(1).
"harbour area": ss.18(3); 46(1).
"harbour authority": s.46(1).
"manager": s.46(1).
"owner": s.46(1).
"permitted to have access": s.46(3).
"person": Interpretation Act 1978, Sched. 1.
"restricted zone": s.46(1).
"Secretary of State": Interpretation Act 1978, Sched. 1.
"ship": s.46(1).
"standard scale": Criminal Justice Act 1982, s.74.

GENERAL NOTE
Derivation: *cf.* the Aviation Security Act 1982, s.21B, (as inserted by the 1990 Act, s.5).
False statements and identity documents. See the note to s.5, above, for the aviation equivalent. The section creates an offence for making false statements in order to obtain the sort of security identity cards that would enable the wearer to gain access to sensitive areas. As with s.37, above, there is no offence committed by an inspector who asks a false question as part of a security exercise (see the note to the new s.21A(3) of the Aviation Security Act 1982 as inserted by s.5, above).

Unauthorised presence in restricted zone

39.—(1) A person shall not—
(a) go, with or without a vehicle or vessel, onto or into any part of a restricted zone of a harbour area except with the permission of the harbour authority or a person acting on behalf of the harbour authority and in accordance with any conditions subject to which that permission is for the time being granted, or
(b) remain in any part of such a restricted zone after being requested to leave by the harbour authority or a person acting on behalf of the harbour authority.

(2) Subsection (1)(a) above does not apply unless it is proved that, at the material time, notices stating that the area concerned was a restricted zone were posted so as to be readily seen and read by persons entering the restricted zone.

(3) A person who contravenes subsection (1) above without lawful authority or reasonable excuse is guilty of an offence and liable on summary conviction to a fine not exceeding level 5 on the standard scale.

DEFINITIONS
"harbour": s.46(1).
"harbour area": ss.18(3); 46(1).
"harbour authority": s.46(1).
"person": Interpretation Act 1978, Sched. 1.
"restricted zone": s.46(1).
"standard scale": Criminal Justice Act 1982, s.74.

    Derivation: *cf.* the Aviation Security Act 1982, s.21C, (as inserted by the 1990 Act, s.5).
    Like its aviation equivalent, this section creates offences for persons who (i) enter a restricted zone (created by s.20) without permission, or (ii) fail to act in accordance with conditions laid down for entry, or (iii) remain after being requested to leave. The permission can be granted by the harbour authority, for example through the harbour master. It should be noted that a restricted zone could cover water as well as land. It could thus be an offence to take a vessel into the zone. This sort of zone might be created near quays where explosives are loaded. In theory it could also be used around naval vessels, for example in Portsmouth Harbour, but note also the existence of the prohibited places under the Official Secrets Act 1911, ss.1, 3.
    There is a general defence of lawful authority or reasonable excuse. It is a defence to the entry charge that the status of the zone was not indicated by notices that could easily be seen by persons generally. It does not seem to matter that the defendant had actually seen a relevant notice if it did not meet the objective standard.

Offences relating to authorised persons

    40.—(1) A person who—
    (a) intentionally obstructs an authorised person acting in the exercise of a power conferred on him by or under this Part of this Act, or
    (b) falsely pretends to be an authorised person,
commits an offence.
    (2) A person guilty of an offence under subsection (1)(a) above is liable—
    (a) on summary conviction, to a fine not exceeding the statutory maximum;
    (b) on conviction on indictment, to a fine or to imprisonment for a term not exceeding two years or to both.
    (3) A person guilty of an offence under subsection (1)(b) above is liable on summary conviction to a fine not exceeding level 5 on the standard scale.

DEFINITIONS
    "person": Interpretation Act 1978, Sched. 1.
    "standard scale": Criminal Justice Act 1982, s.74.
    "statutory maximum": Criminal Justice Act 1982, s.74.

GENERAL NOTE
    Derivation: *cf.* the Aviation Security Act 1982, s.21E, (as inserted by the 1990 Act, s.5).
    Obstruction or impersonation of authorised officers, such as security inspectors, is an offence.

Sea cargo agents

Sea cargo agents

    41.—(1) The Secretary of State may by regulations made by statutory instrument make provision, for purposes to which this Part of this Act applies, in relation to persons (in this section referred to as "sea cargo agents") who carry on a business of handling cargo which is to be delivered (whether by them or any other person) to the owner, charterer or manager of any ship for carriage by sea from any harbour area.
    (2) Regulations under this section may, in particular—
    (a) enable the Secretary of State to maintain a list of sea cargo agents who are approved by him for purposes related to maritime security, to include the name of a sea cargo agent on that list, on application being made to the Secretary of State in accordance with the regulations, if he is satisfied as to such matters as are specified in the regulations, and to remove the name of any person from that list in such circumstances as are so specified,
    (b) provide that any provision of this Part of this Act which applies in relation to persons who are permitted to have access to a restricted zone of a harbour area for the purposes of the activities of a business

(including any such provision which creates a criminal offence) shall also apply, with such modifications as are specified in the regulations, in relation to sea cargo agents included on any such list,

(c) amend sections 37(2) and 38(3) of this Act by including references to sea cargo agents included on any such list,

(d) make provision (including any such provision as is mentioned in paragraphs (a) to (c) above) relating to a class of sea cargo agents specified in the regulations and not to other sea cargo agents,

(e) make different provision for different cases, and

(f) make such incidental, supplementary or transitional provision as the Secretary of State considers necessary or expedient in consequence of any provision made by the regulations.

(3) Before making any regulations under this section the Secretary of State shall consult organisations appearing to him to represent persons affected by the proposed regulations.

(4) Any statutory instrument containing regulations under this section shall be subject to annulment in pursuance of a resolution of either House of Parliament.

(5) Without prejudice to the generality of sections 21 and 24 of this Act, the exemptions that may be included in any direction given to an owner, charterer, manager or master of a ship under section 21 or 24 which requires the carrying out of searches of cargo, or the taking of any other measures in relation to cargo, include exemptions from such requirements in relation to cargo received from any sea cargo agent included on any list maintained by the Secretary of State under regulations under this section or from any sea cargo agent falling within a class of such sea cargo agents specified in the direction.

(6) In this section—

"cargo" includes stores and mail;

"carriage by sea" does not include carriage by any ship used in naval, customs or police service; and

"stores" means any goods intended for sale or use in a ship, including fuel and spare parts and other articles of equipment, whether or not for immediate fitting.

DEFINITIONS
"cargo": subs. (6).
"carriage by sea": subs. (6).
"harbour": s.46(1).
"harbour area": ss.18(3); 46(1).
"owner": s.46(1).
"manager": s.46(1).
"master": s.46(1).
"permitted to have access": s.46(3).
"purposes to which this Part of this Act applies": s.18(1).
"restricted zone": s.46(1).
"Secretary of State": Interpretation Act 1978, Sched. 1.
"ship": s.46(1).
"stores": subs. (6).

GENERAL NOTE
Cf. s.6, above, for the aviation equivalent.
This section was added at Committee stage in the Commons to cover the position of agents supplying consignments of cargo, mail or stores to ship operators. The supplies might be delivered to ships without the agents themselves going to the port. Technically, they might not fall within the categories of persons who have "access" to restricted areas (for example within s.19 of the 1990 Act), yet they would be responsible for sending materials into those areas. Note that the section applies even if the agent uses a sub-contractor, such as a haulier, to make the actual delivery.
The section is a regulation-making power that may not necessarily be used. The Secretary of State is empowered to maintain a list of approved sea cargo agents. It is expected that agents

would apply for inclusion on the list and would be interviewed by an maritime security inspector at the agents' premises so that checks might be made on the facilities available for implementing security procedures. An agent with a poor record in complying with Directions may be removed from the list by the Secretary of State, following written notification of the proposed course of action and the reasons for it. There would not be a formal objection procedure, despite the great commercial impact that removal from the list might have. Once on the list, security Directions could be issued, for example requiring persons or property at the agents' premises to be searched or for cargo to be guarded.

Reporting of certain occurrences

Duty to report certain occurrences

42.—(1) For purposes to which this Part of this Act applies, the Secretary of State may by regulations made by statutory instrument require such persons as are specified in the regulations to make a report to him, in such manner and within such period as are so specified, of any occurrence of a description so specified.

(2) Before making any regulations under this section, the Secretary of State shall consult organisations appearing to him to represent persons affected by the proposed regulations.

(3) Regulations under this section may—

(a) provide that any person who, in making a report required by the regulations, makes a statement which he knows to be false in a material particular, or recklessly makes a statement which is false in a material particular, is to be guilty of an offence and liable—

(i) on summary conviction, to a fine not exceeding the statutory maximum;

(ii) on conviction on indictment, to a fine or to imprisonment for a term not exceeding two years or to both; and

(b) provide for persons to be guilty of an offence in such other circumstances as may be specified in the regulations and to be liable on summary conviction to a fine not exceeding level 5 on the standard scale.

(4) Regulations under this section may require the reporting of occurrences taking place outside the United Kingdom only if those occurrences relate to British ships.

(5) Any statutory instrument containing regulations under this section shall be subject to annulment in pursuance of a resolution of either House of Parliament.

DEFINITIONS

"British ship": s.46(1).
"person": Interpretation Act 1978, Sched. 1.
"purposes to which this Part of this Act applies": s.18(1).
"Secretary of State": Interpretation Act 1978, Sched. 1.
"ship": s.46(1).
"standard scale": Criminal Justice Act 1982, s.74.
"United Kingdom": Interpretation Act 1978, Sched. 1.

GENERAL NOTE

Cf. the Aviation Security Act 1982, s.21G (inserted by s.7 of the 1990 Act).

Reporting security incidents. The section allows the Secretary of State to set up a system whereby security incidents can be reported to him. The advantage of such a system would be that it would provide the DTp with feedback about the effectiveness of the national security programme. The provision parallels that for aviation (see the note to s.7, above), although there are apparently no plans at present to make such regulations.

General supplemental provisions

Compensation in respect of certain measures taken under Part III

43.—(1) The provisions of this section have effect where, in compliance with a direction under Section 24 of this Act or in compliance with an enforcement notice, the person to whom the direction was given or on whom the notice was served takes any measures consisting of the construction, execution, alteration, demolition or removal of a building or other works on land either within or outside a harbour area.

(2) If the value of any interest in that land to which a person is entitled is depreciated in consequence of the taking of those measures, or the person having such an interest suffers loss in consequence of them by being disturbed in his enjoyment of any of that land, he is entitled to compensation equal to the amount of the depreciation or loss.

(3) If any land other than the land on which the measures are taken is injuriously affected by the taking of those measures, any person having an interest in that other land who suffers loss in consequence of its being injuriously affected is entitled to compensation equal to the amount of the loss.

(4) Any compensation to which a person is entitled under this section shall be payable to him by the person by whom the measures in question were taken.

(5) The provisions of Schedule 2 to this Act have effect for the purposes of this section; and subsections (1) to (4) above have effect subject to the provisions of that Schedule.

DEFINITIONS
   "enforcement notice": s.46(1).
   "harbour": s.46(1).
   "harbour area": ss.18(3); 46(1).
   "land": Interpretation Act 1978, Sched. 1.
   "person": Interpretation Act 1978, Sched. 1.

GENERAL NOTE
   Derivation: the Aviation Security Act 1982, s.22.
   Compensation. This section was added at Report Stage in the Commons and is designed to mirror the aviation provisions. The idea is to provide compensation to third parties who are affected by building works being carried out by harbour authorities in compliance with a Direction under s.24 (or enforcement notice under s.29). An example would be a landowner whose property was affected by the siting of posts for a perimeter fence, or gates for access. The compensation will be paid by the harbour authority (not the DTp) and is designed to cover the cost of loss or depreciation in the value of the land owned by the third party. Apparently, the aviation provision is rarely used. The example given in debates was of a Direction given to a harbour authority to take security measures, as a result of which a local newsagent was displaced. The newsagent would be entitled to compensation, but a company such as P & O Ferries, directed to install electronic screening equipment, would not.
   The compensation was apparently designed to be payable only to those who cannot be served Directions (Standing Committee A, col. 124). However, a close reading of the section indicates that this is not strictly correct. It is not a question of whether a Direction "cannot" be served, but whether one *has* been served on the person seeking compensation. It would seem possible for a general Direction to be served on a harbour authority requiring a certain type of security screen to be constructed. The authority might decide to alter or demolish buildings in which a shipping line has some sort of interest. In such a case it would seem that the line could claim compensation from the authority, although it would not have been entitled to any if the Direction had been addressed to it.
   Note that there are no compulsory purchase powers, although it appears that a distinction is made between land within and land without the harbour area (see the note to s.26(6)). This means that a landowner outside the harbour would be in a strong position to negotiate terms if he was not prepared to allow the work to be undertaken first and submit later to the s.43/Sched. 2 compensation procedure. The Government recognised that this was part of the price for recognising the rights of third parties outside a harbour area.

The section must be read together with Sched. 2, below.

Amount of compensation. Disputes as to levels of compensation will be resolved by the mechanisms indicated in Sched. 2. Land values will be calculated in accordance with the Land Compensation Act 1961. Note also ss.26(6) and 28(2).

Planning law. It is not immediately clear what the relationship is between the powers of the Secretary of State to give Directions as to buildings and the ordinary rules of planning law (for example about the height and style of buildings and the compulsory purchase rules). S.34(2) effectively allows the Secretary of State to override existing legislation, so an authority may be able to avoid seeking planning permission. No doubt such a Direction will be used sparingly but, although it is understandable that there is a desire to avoid delays in obtaining planning permission, there is scope for potential conflict. The Direction may specify that a security wall or fence is created, but what about its size or composition? If the Direction does not specify details, is the authority entirely free to chose its own materials without consultation with the planning authority? In the case of the perimeter fence, given above, there would be no need for compulsory purchase and the question of how far the third party can be compelled to assist has been noted (see s.26 above).

It should be noted that for many ports there are already wide and special powers relating to development, created either by Private Acts, or by harbour revision and empowerment orders (under the Harbours Act 1964). Moreover, under the General Development Order 1988 (S.I. No. 1813), development by statutory undertakers is permitted on operational land. In respect of many developments, harbour authorities are effectively their own planning authority, but it should be noted that there are areas where planning permission is needed, especially where a port has diversified, for example where a hotel or private housing is constructed in a marina.

Annual report by Secretary of State as to notices and directions under Part III

44.—(1) The Secretary of State shall, on or before 31st January in each year, lay before each House of Parliament a report stating the number of notices served by him under section 19 of this Act, the number of directions given by him under sections 21, 22, 23 and 24 of this Act and the number of enforcement notices served by authorised persons during the period of twelve months which expired with the preceding December.

(2) Each such report shall deal separately with notices served under section 19 of this Act, directions given under section 21 of this Act, directions given under section 22 of this Act, directions given under section 23 of this Act, directions given under section 24 of this Act and enforcement notices, and, in relation to each of those matters, shall show separately—

  (a) the number of notices or directions which, during the period to which the report relates, were served on or given to persons as being, or as appearing to the Secretary of State to be about to become, owners, charterers, managers or masters of ships,

  (b) the number of notices or directions which during that period were served on or given to persons as being, or as appearing to the Secretary of State to be about to become, harbour authorities,

  (c) the number of notices or directions which during that period were served on or given to persons as being, or as appearing to the Secretary of State to be about to become, persons carrying on harbour operations in a harbour area, and

  (d) the number of notices or directions which during that period were served on or given to persons as being, or as appearing to the Secretary of State to be about to become, persons permitted to have access to a restricted zone of a harbour area for the purposes of the activities of a business.

(3) Each such report shall also show separately the number of copies of enforcement notices which during that period were served on masters of ships under section 29(3) of this Act.

DEFINITIONS

  "enforcement notice": s.46(1).
  "harbour": s.46(1).
  "harbour area": ss.18(3); 46(1).

"harbour authority": s.46(1).
"harbour operations": s.46(1).
"manager": s.46(1).
"master": s.46(1).
"owner": s.46(1).
"permitted to have access": s.46(3).
"person": Interpretation Act 1978, Sched. 1.
"restricted zone": s.46(1).
"Secretary of State": Interpretation Act 1978, Sched. 1.
"ship": s.46(1).

GENERAL NOTE
   Derivation: the Aviation Security Act 1982, s.23.
   Under the Aviation Security Act 1982, s.23, the Secretary of State has to make an annual
report to Parliament detailing the statistics of aviation Directions issued (and note Sched. 1,
para. 14). There was no maritime equivalent, and at one stage the Government did not propose
one. S.44 of the Aviation and Maritime Security Act 1990 was eventually added at Committee
stage. Accordingly, the Secretary of State now has an obligation to provide Parliament with
basic details of the number of notices, Directions and enforcement notices issued in respect of
maritime security matters.
   However, the report is very limited in its coverage, relating only to statistical matters. It will
not enable Parliament to scrutinise the DTp in order to ensure quality, consistency and
uniformity of Directions. This report is apparently in addition to the annual report to be made
by the chief inspector of security to be established. It is envisaged that the annual reports of the
aviation inspectorate (and a maritime equivalent if and when established) will include comments on the development and implementation of the national security programme.

Service of documents

   45.—(1) This section has effect in relation to any notice, any document
containing a direction and any other document authorised or required by
any provision of this Part of this Act to be served on or given to any person.
   (2) Any such document may be given to or served on any person—
   (a) by delivering it to him, or
   (b) by leaving it at his proper address, or
   (c) by sending it by post to him at that address, or
   (d) by sending it to him at that address by telex or other similar means
        which produce a document containing the text of the communication.
   (3) Any such document may, in the case of a body corporate, be given to
or served on the secretary, clerk or similar officer of that body.
   (4) For the purposes of this section and section 7 of the Interpretation Act
1978 (service of documents by post) in its application to this section, the
proper address of any person to whom or on whom any document is to be
given or served is his usual or last known address or place of business
(whether in the United Kingdom or elsewhere), except that in the case of a
body corporate or its secretary, clerk or similar officer it shall be the address
of the registered or principal office of that body in the United Kingdom (or,
if it has no office in the United Kingdom, of its principal office, wherever it
may be).
   (5) In the case of a person registered under any of the United Kingdom
registration provisions as the owner of any ship so registered, the address for
the time being recorded in relation to him in the register in which the ship is
registered shall also be treated for the purposes of this section and section 7
of the Interpretation Act 1978 as his proper address.
   (6) If the person to or on whom any document mentioned in subsection (1)
above is to be given or served has notified the Secretary of State of an
address within the United Kingdom, other than an address determined
under subsection (4) or (5) above, as the one at which he or someone else on
his behalf will accept documents of the same description as that document,
that address shall also be treated for the purposes of this section and section
7 of the Interpretation Act 1978 as his proper address.

(7) Any document mentioned in subsection (1) above shall, where there are two or more owners registered under any of the United Kingdom registration provisions, be treated as duly served on each of those owners—

  (a) in the case of a ship in relation to which a managing owner is for the time being registered under section 59(1) of the Merchant Shipping Act 1894, if served on that managing owner, and

  (b) in the case of any other ship, if served on any one of the registered owners.

(8) Where an enforcement notice is to be served under section 29 of this Act on the owner, charterer or manager of a ship, it shall be treated as duly served on him if it is served on the master of the ship in question, but (except as provided by section 29(3) of this Act) the master shall not be obliged by virtue of this subsection to comply with the notice.

(9) Where any document mentioned in subsection (1) above is to be served (for the purposes of subsection (8) above or otherwise) on the master of a ship, it shall be treated as duly served if it is left on board that ship with the person being or appearing to be in command or charge of the ship.

(10) In this section "the United Kingdom registration provisions" means—

  (a) Part I of the Merchant Shipping Act 1894,

  (b) section 5 of the Merchant Shipping Act 1983,

  (c) Part II of the Merchant Shipping Act 1988, and

  (d) any Order in Council under section 1 of the Hovercraft Act 1968.

DEFINITIONS
"enforcement notice": s.46(1).
"manager": s.46(1).
"master": s.46(1).
"owner": s.46(1).
"proper address": subs. (4).
"person": Interpretation Act 1978, Sched. 1.
"Secretary of State": Interpretation Act 1978, Sched. 1.
"ship": s.46(1).
"United Kingdom": Interpretation Act 1978, Sched. 1.
"United Kingdom registration provisions": subs. (10).

GENERAL NOTE
  The section sets out the procedure for the service of the various documents authorised under Pt. III.

Interpretation of Part III

46.—(1) In this Part of this Act, except in so far as the context otherwise requires—

  "act of violence" shall be construed in accordance with section 18(2) of this Act,

  "article" includes any substance, whether in solid or liquid form or in the form of a gas or vapour,

  "authorised person" means a person authorised in writing by the Secretary of State for the purposes of this Part of this Act,

  "British ship" means a ship which—

  (a) is registered in the United Kingdom under Part I of the Merchant Shipping Act 1894, section 5 of the Merchant Shipping Act 1983, Part II of the Merchant Shipping Act 1988 or any Order in Council under section 1 of the Hovercraft Act 1968, or

  (b) is not registered under the law of any country and is entitled to be registered in the United Kingdom under Part I of the Merchant Shipping Act 1894,

  "constable" includes any person having the powers and privileges of a constable, "employee," in relation to a body corporate, includes officer,

"enforcement notice" has the meaning given by section 29(1) of this Act,

"explosive" means any article manufactured for the purpose of producing a practical effect by explosion, or intended for that purpose by a person having the article with him,

"firearm" includes an airgun or air pistol,

"harbour"—
  (a) in relation to Great Britain, means a harbour within the meaning of the Harbours Act 1964, and
  (b) in relation to Northern Ireland, has the same meaning as in the Harbours Act (Northern Ireland) 1970,

"harbour area" has the meaning given by section 18(3) of this Act,

"harbour authority"—
  (a) in Great Britain, means—
        (i) a harbour authority within the meaning of the Harbours Act 1964, or
        (ii) the manager of any hoverport which does not form part of an area mentioned in section 18(3)(a)(i) or (ii) of this Act, and
  (b) in Northern Ireland, has the same meaning as in the Harbours Act (Northern Ireland) 1970,

"harbour operations" has the same meaning as in the Harbours Act 1964,

"hoverport" has the same meaning as in the Hovercraft Act 1968,

"manager," in relation to a hoverport, means the person by whom the hoverport is managed,

"master" has the same meaning as in the Merchant Shipping Act 1894,

"measures" (without prejudice to the generality of that expression) includes the construction, execution, alteration, demolition or removal of any building or other works (whether on dry land or on the seabed or other land covered by water), and also includes the institution or modification, and the supervision and enforcement, of any practice or procedure,

"naval service" includes military and air force service,

"owner," in relation to a ship registered in the United Kingdom or in any other country, means registered owner,

"property" includes any land, buildings or works, any ship or vehicle and any baggage, cargo or other article of any description,

"restricted zone," in relation to a harbour area, means any part of the harbour area designated under section 20 of this Act or, where the whole of the harbour area is so designated, that area, and

"ship" includes hovercraft and every other description of vessel used in navigation.

(2) Any power to give a direction under any provision of this Part of this Act includes power to revoke or vary any such direction by a further direction.

(3) For the purposes of this Part of this Act a person is permitted to have access to a restricted zone of a harbour area if he is permitted to enter that zone or if arrangements exist for permitting any of his employees or agents to enter that zone.

GENERAL NOTE

This is the general definitions section for Pt. III only.

PART IV

MISCELLANEOUS AND GENERAL

Miscellaneous

Carriage of goods by air

47. In section 60 of the Civil Aviation Act 1982 (power to give effect to Chicago Convention and to regulate air navigation etc.), in subsection (3)—
  (a) in paragraph (f) the words "and goods" and the words from "and for" to the end are omitted, and
  (b) after that paragraph there is inserted—
    "(ff) as to the conditions under which goods may be carried by air, for prohibiting the carriage by air of goods of such classes as may be specified in the Order, and for conferring, on such persons as may be so specified, powers relating to the enforcement of any such condition or prohibition (including powers to examine, take samples of, seize and detain any goods, powers to open any baggage or packages containing goods or to require them to be opened and powers to require the production of any documents);".

DEFINITIONS
  "Chicago Convention": Civil Aviation Act 1982, s.105.

GENERAL NOTE
  This section amends a provision of the Civil Aviation Act 1982 which gives effect to the Chicago Convention 1944 regulating air navigation. The amendment enables the Civil Aviation Authority to inspect any document relating to suspected or declared dangerous goods. It will also be able to examine and send for analysis the contents of any package or baggage which it believes contains dangerous goods.

Powers in relation to certain aircraft

48.—(1) Except as provided by subsection (2) below, this section applies to any aircraft which—
  (a) is registered in, or owned by, any State which appears to the Secretary of State to be contravening any international agreement relating to civil aviation to which that State and the United Kingdom are parties—
    (i) by prohibiting any one or more aircraft registered in the United Kingdom from flying over its territory, or
    (ii) by prohibiting any one or more such aircraft from landing in its territory, or
  (b) is being operated under the direction of nationals of such a State.
  (2) This section does not apply to any aircraft by reason only of any prohibition which affects only aircraft belonging to or exclusively employed in the service of the Crown.
  (3) For the purposes of this section a State which has taken steps to prevent certain aircraft from flying over or landing in its territory is to be taken to prohibit them from doing so.
  (4) Subsection (5) below applies where an aircraft to which this section applies—
  (a) has landed in the United Kingdom and is situated at an aerodrome,
  (b) has landed on any land in the United Kingdom outside an aerodrome, with the consent of the occupier of that land, and is situated on that land, or
  (c) has landed in the United Kingdom and is situated on land outside an aerodrome to which it has been moved with the consent of the occupier of that land,

but that subsection does not apply where the aircraft has landed in the United Kingdom in accordance with permission granted by the Secretary of State under any enactment.

(5) Where this subsection applies, the Secretary of State may give a direction, in a case falling within subsection (4)(a) above to the manager of the aerodrome or in a case falling within subsection (4)(b) or (c) above to the occupier of the land, requiring him to take all such steps as may be reasonably practicable to prevent any person, other than a constable, from gaining access to the aircraft unless—

(a) it is necessary for that person to do so for the purpose of preparing the aircraft for a flight out of the United Kingdom (either directly or following an intermediate stop elsewhere in the United Kingdom for non-traffic purposes),

(b) that person is acting—
  (i) with the permission of a constable, or
  (ii) in the exercise of powers conferred by subsection (7) below or by or under any other enactment, or

(c) that person is a person specified in the direction acting in circumstances so specified.

(6) A direction under subsection (5) above may also prohibit the person to whom it is given from gaining access to the aircraft except in such circumstances as may be specified in the direction.

(7) Where a direction has been given under subsection (5) above, a constable or any other person specified for the purposes of this subsection in the direction—

(a) may, for the purpose of ascertaining whether the direction is being complied with or, if the direction so provides, for the purpose of moving the aircraft as mentioned in paragraph (b) below or causing it to be so moved—
  (i) enter any part of the aerodrome or other land concerned (including any building or works in that aerodrome or on that land), and
  (ii) go into or onto the aircraft, if need be by force,

(b) may, if the direction so provides, move the aircraft or cause it to be moved—
  (i) in a case falling within subsection (4)(a) above, to such other part of the aerodrome concerned as is specified in the direction, for the purpose of preventing any interference with the functioning of the aerodrome, or
  (ii) in a case falling within subsection (4)(b) or (c) above, to any aerodrome specified in the direction, for the purpose of facilitating the preparation of the aircraft for a flight out of the United Kingdom,

(c) may require—
  (i) the commander of the aircraft, or
  (ii) in the absence of the commander, any other person who the person making the requirement has reason to believe has in his possession documents relating to the aircraft,
  to produce any such documents, and

(d) may remove and detain any such documents.

(8) Subject to subsection (9) below, a direction under subsection (5) above shall have effect notwithstanding anything contained in any contract (whether a United Kingdom contract or not) or contained in, or having effect by virtue of, any other enactment or rule of law; and accordingly no proceedings (whether civil or criminal) shall lie against any person in any United Kingdom court by reason of anything done or not done by him or on his behalf in compliance with a direction.

(9) The giving of a direction under subsection (5) above does not affect—

(a) any liability to pay airport charges incurred in respect of the aircraft to which the direction relates, or

(b) the exercise of any power arising under section 88 of the Civil Aviation Act 1982 (detention and sale of aircraft for unpaid airport charges).

(10) If a person who has removed and detained any documents under subsection (7)(d) above is satisfied that the aircraft is being prepared for a flight out of the United Kingdom (either directly or following an intermediate stop elsewhere in the United Kingdom for non-traffic purposes), he shall return them to the commander of the aircraft.

(11) A person commits an offence if—

(a) without reasonable excuse, he fails to comply with a direction given to him under subsection (5) above,

(b) he intentionally obstructs a person acting in the exercise of a power conferred by subsection (7) above, or

(c) knowing that a direction under subsection (5) above has effect in relation to an aircraft, he gains access to the aircraft without lawful authority or reasonable excuse and otherwise than in accordance with the direction.

(12) A person guilty of an offence under subsection (11) above is liable—

(a) on summary conviction, to a fine not exceeding the statutory maximum;

(b) on conviction on indictment, to a fine or to imprisonment for a term not exceeding two years or to both.

(13) In this section—

"aerodrome" has the same meaning as in the Civil Aviation Act 1982,

"airport charges" has the same meaning as in section 88 of the Civil Aviation Act 1982,

"commander", in relation to an aircraft, has the same meaning as in section 94 of the Civil Aviation Act 1982,

"manager", in relation to an aerodrome, has the same meaning as in the Aviation Security Act 1982,

"reward" has the same meaning as in the Civil Aviation Act 1982,

"stop for non-traffic purposes" means a landing for any purpose other than the taking on board or discharging of passengers carried for reward or of cargo so carried, and

"United Kingdom court" and "United Kingdom contract" have the same meaning as in section 19 of the Aviation Security Act 1982;

and for the purposes of this section a person gains access to an aircraft if, and only if, he goes into or onto the aircraft, carries out any work on the aircraft or delivers anything to the aircraft or to persons on board the aircraft.

DEFINITIONS

"aerodrome": subs. (13).
"airport charges": subs. (13).
"commander": subs. (13).
"gains access": subs. (13).
"land": Interpretation Act 1978, Sched. 1.
"manager": subs. (13).
"reward": subs. (13).
"Secretary of State": Interpretation Act 1978, Sched. 1.
"statutory maximum": Criminal Justice Act 1982, s.74.
"stop for non-traffic purposes": subs. (13).
"United Kingdom": Interpretation Act 1978, Sched. 1.
"United Kingdom contract": subs. (13).
"United Kingdom court": subs. (13).

GENERAL NOTE

This section was added at Committee stage in the Commons and was summarised by the Minister for Public Transport, Mr Portillo, as "big clause, small loophole" (Standing Committee A, col. 171). It provides the Secretary of State with the power to act against foreign-registered aircraft that land in the U.K. from a state that has banned U.K. registered civil aircraft from its airspace in breach of an international agreement between that state and the U.K. In effect, it is a trade protectionist measure, which can presumably be used as a bargaining counter with foreign Governments (*cf.* the Merchant Shipping Act 1974, Pt. II; the Merchant Shipping Act 1988, s.38).

Offences are created of failing to comply with a Direction, intentionally obstructing anyone acting under a Direction and entering an aircraft without lawful authority or reasonable excuse for some purpose other than as provided for in the Direction.

International agreement. The Government was confident that the section did not breach the Chicago Convention 1944. The section is clearly comprehensive in that all flights into or out of the U.K. are either subject to bilateral or multilateral agreements or have the permission of the Secretary of State.

Subs. (4)

Permission. Although aircraft from countries that have banned U.K. civil aircraft would not be generally welcome, the Secretary of State might make exceptions for official visits, air shows, or for humanitarian reasons.

Subs. (5)

In effect, an aircraft that does land, despite a ban (for example as a result of an emergency), will be cocooned. It would not be possible for it to be serviced, except to enable it to leave the U.K. Thus, the aircraft could not be re-equipped or converted from one purpose to another. Apparently, this possibility is not as fanciful as might be supposed.

General

Extradition by virtue of Orders in Council under section 2 of Extradition Act 1870

49. The offences to which an Order in Council under section 2 of the Extradition Act 1870 can apply shall include—
  (a) offences under sections 1, 9, 10, 11, 12 and 13 of this Act, and
  (b) attempts to commit such offences.

GENERAL NOTE

Extradition. The various international Conventions dealing with terrorism and the like contain detailed provisions on extradition (see for example the Montreal Convention 1971, Art. 8; the Rome Convention 1988, Art. 11; and the Fixed Platforms Protocol 1988, Art. 1(1)). The ability to extradite offenders was considered a vital issue in the aviation and maritime conventions. During negotiations for the Rome Convention one delegation suggested that an article be included which stated that none of the offences created by the Convention should be considered as political offences and thus not subject to extradition (see LEG/ES.1/5). There is a restricted equivalent of this in the European Convention 1977 Art. 2 (*cf.* M. Zander, "Extradition of terrorists from Ireland: a major judicial setback" (1990) 140 New L.J. 474). The final version of Art. 11 of the Rome Convention simply refers extradition to existing treaties or the law of the State from which extradition was requested. However, it should be noted that Art. 10 obliges a State Party which does not extradite an offender, to prosecute him itself.

The 1990 Act simply adds the offences listed in subs. (a) to the existing general extradition legislation (see the Extradition Acts 1870–1935, as consolidated now in the Extradition Act 1989). Under the Extradition Act 1989 (see s.53 (1) and Sched. 3, para. 9; and s.54(2) and Sched. 4) an offence is extraditable if it attracts a minimum sentence on indictment of 12 months' imprisonment in both countries. That definition applies now to all Commonwealth countries and will apply later in 1990 to extraditions involving countries that have ratified the European Convention on extradition. As for other foreign countries, extradition will continue to depend on the terms of bilateral treaties drawn up under the 1870 Act (as preserved by s.1 and Sched. 1 of the Extradition Act 1989), until they have been renegotiated. Those treaties (in effect by virtue of Orders in force under s.2 of the Extradition Act 1870) rely on a *list* system for their definition of extradition crimes (as opposed to one based on length of *sentence*). (See the statement by the Minister for Public Transport, Standing Committee A, cols. 37-38 and C. Warbrick [1989] 3 Current Law Statutes Annotated, c.33).

See s.1, above for discussion of hoax calls and extradition.

Note also the changes to the Extradition Act 1989 made by the Criminal Justice (International Co-operation) Act 1990.

Offences by bodies corporate

50.—(1) Where an offence under this Act (including any provision of Part III as applied by regulations made under section 41 of this Act) or under regulations made under section 42 of this Act has been committed by a body corporate and is proved to have been committed with the consent or connivance of, or to be attributable to any neglect on the part of, any director, manager, secretary or other similar officer of the body corporate, or any person who was purporting to act in any such capacity, he as well as the body corporate shall be guilty of that offence and shall be liable to be proceeded against and punished accordingly.

(2) Where the affairs of a body corporate are managed by its members, subsection (1) above shall apply in relation to the acts and defaults of a member in connection with his functions of management as if he were a director of the body corporate.

GENERAL NOTE
Cf. the Merchant Shipping Act 1988, s.51.
The purpose of this section is to provide an incentive to managers of companies to comply with the Act. It enables prosecutions to be brought against individual managers where they consented to or connived at the offence committed by their company, or where it is attributable to their neglect. Thus, a senior manager can be guilty where he knows that a Direction dealing with searching is not being complied with because to do so would require the hiring of more staff.

The section catches senior executives, such as directors or company secretaries (not typists). However, the expression "manager" is sufficiently wide to cover fairly junior managers. Members of a company may also be prosecuted where they are engaged in management.

Extension of Act outside the United Kingdom

51.—(1) Her Majesty may by Order in Council make provision for extending any of the provisions of section 1, Parts II and III and section 50 of this Act with such exceptions, adaptations or modifications as may be specified in the Order, to any of the Channel Islands, the Isle of Man or any colony.

(2) Section 15 of the Visiting Forces Act 1952, section 94 of the Merchant Shipping Act 1970, section 7 of the Suppression of Terrorism Act 1978, section 39(3) of the Aviation Security Act 1982 and section 108 of the Civil Aviation Act 1982 (extension to Channel Islands, Isle of Man and other countries) apply respectively to the provisions of this Act amending each of those Acts.

DEFINITIONS
"colony": Interpretation Act 1978, Sched. 1.

GENERAL NOTE
Subs. (1) allows for the main provisions of the Act to be extended to the Crown Dependencies and Dependent Territories.

As the various Acts listed in subs. (2) are amended by the 1990 Act, the provisions of those Acts relating to their extension outside the U.K. must apply to the sections of the 1990 Act that amend them.

Expenses

52. There shall be paid out of money provided by Parliament any expenses of the Secretary of State under this Act and any increase attributable to this Act in the sums so payable under any other Act.

Minor and consequential amendments and repeals

53.—(1) The enactments mentioned in Schedule 3 to this Act have effect subject to the minor and consequential amendments specified in that Schedule.

(2) The enactments mentioned in Schedule 4 to this Act (which include spent provisions) are hereby repealed to the extent specified in the third column of that Schedule.

GENERAL NOTE
    See the notes to Sched. 3, below.

Short title, commencement and extent

54.—(1) This Act may be cited as the Aviation and Maritime Security Act 1990.

(2) The following provisions of this Act shall not come into force until the end of the period of two months beginning with the day on which this Act is passed—
    section 1,
    section 5,
    Part II,
    paragraphs 1, 2(6), 4, 5, 6 and 11(5) of Schedule 1,
    Schedule 3, and
    in Schedule 4, the repeals in the Criminal Jurisdiction Act 1975, in
        sections 11(5)(a), 14(7)(a) and 20(5) of the Aviation Security
        Act 1982 and in the Extradition Act 1989.

(3) This Act extends to Northern Ireland.

GENERAL NOTE
    Commencement. Royal Assent was on July 26, 1990 and the Act, therefore, is now fully in force. There was a delay before the coming into force of a number of provisions listed in subs. (2). This was to take account of the fact that new offences are created, and so the public and practitioners needed time to become aware of them.

SCHEDULES

Section 8   SCHEDULE 1

FURTHER AMENDMENTS OF THE AVIATION SECURITY ACT 1982

Obstruction

1. In section 7 (powers exercisable on suspicion of intended offence under Part I) in subsection (2) for "wilfully obstructs or impedes" there is substituted "intentionally obstructs."

Provision of information

2.—(1) Section 11 (power of Secretary of State to require information) is amended as follows.
(2) For subsection (1) there is substituted—
    "(1) The Secretary of State may, by notice in writing served on any person who—
        (a) is the operator of one or more aircraft registered or operating in the United Kingdom,
        (b) is the manager of an aerodrome in the United Kingdom,
        (c) occupies any land forming part of an aerodrome in the United Kingdom, or
        (d) is permitted to have access to a restricted zone of an aerodrome for the purposes of the activities of a business carried on by him,
    require that person to provide the Secretary of State with such information specified in the notice as the Secretary of State may require in connection with the exercise by the Secretary of State of his functions under this Part of this Act."
(3) In subsection (2) for "four weeks" there is substituted "seven days."
(4) In subsection (3)—
    (a) for "shall" there is substituted "may," and
    (b) for paragraphs (a) and (b) there is substituted "the information previously furnished to the Secretary of State (including any information furnished in pursuance of a requirement imposed by virtue of this subsection) is rendered inaccurate by any change of

circumstances (including the taking of any further measures for purposes to which this Part of this Act applies or the alteration or discontinuance of any measures already being taken)."

(5) In subsection (4) for the words from "the further" to "be" there is substituted "the change of circumstances occurs."

(6) In subsection 5(a) the words "refuses or" are omitted.

(7) In subsection (6) for the words from "time" onwards there is substituted "time—

(a) be revoked by a notice in writing served on him by the Secretary of State, or

(b) be varied by a further notice under subsection (1) above."

Designation of restricted zones of aerodromes

3. After section 11 there is inserted—

"Designation of restricted zones

11A.—(1) The manager of an aerodrome in the United Kingdom may, and shall if so requested in writing by the Secretary of State, apply to the Secretary of State for the designation of the whole or any part of the aerodrome as a restricted zone for the purposes of this Part of this Act.

(2) Where the aerodrome includes an air navigation installation, the manager—

(a) shall, before making any application under subsection (1) above, consult the authority responsible for the air navigation installation, and

(b) shall send a copy of the application to that authority.

(3) An application under subsection (1) above shall be in such form, and accompanied by such plans, as the Secretary of State may require.

(4) If the Secretary of State approves an application under subsection (1) above with or without modifications, he shall designate the restricted zone accordingly.

(5) Before approving an application with modifications, the Secretary of State shall consult—

(a) the manager of the aerodrome, and

(b) the authority responsible for any air navigation installation which forms part of the aerodrome.

(6) If the manager of an aerodrome is requested in writing by the Secretary of State to make an application under subsection (1) above within a specified period but fails to do so within that period, the Secretary of State may designate the whole or any part of the aerodrome as a restricted zone.

(7) The whole or any part of an aerodrome may be designated as a restricted zone, or part of a restricted zone, for specified days or times of day only.

(8) The Secretary of State shall give notice of any designation under this section to—

(a) the manager of the aerodrome, and

(b) the authority responsible for any air navigation installation which forms part of the aerodrome,

and the designation of the restricted zone shall take effect on the giving of the notice.

(9) In relation to an air navigation installation in the United Kingdom which does not form part of an aerodrome, this section has effect as if any reference to an aerodrome were a reference to such an air navigation installation and any reference to the manager of an aerodrome were a reference to the authority responsible for such an air navigation installation.

(10) Where the whole or any part of an aerodrome has been designated under this section as a restricted zone—

(a) subsections (1) to (9) above also have effect in relation to any variation of the designation, and

(b) the designation may at any time be revoked by the Secretary of State."

Directions by Secretary of State

4.—(1) Section 12 (power to impose restrictions in relation to aircraft) is amended as follows.

(2) In subsection (9) for "refuses or" there is substituted ", without reasonable excuse,".

(3) After subsection (9) there is inserted—

"(10) Where a person is convicted of an offence under subsection (9) above, then, if without reasonable excuse the failure in respect of which he was convicted is continued after the conviction, he shall be guilty of a further offence and liable on summary conviction to a fine not exceeding one-tenth of level 5 on the standard scale for each day on which the failure continues."

5.—(1) Section 13 (power to require aerodrome managers to promote searches at aerodromes) is amended as follows.

(2) In subsection (4)—
(a) in paragraph (a) for "refuses or" there is substituted "without reasonable excuse,", and
(b) in paragraph (b) for "wilfully obstructs or impedes" there is substituted "intentionally obstructs."
(3) After subsection (4) there is inserted—
"(4A) Where a person is convicted of an offence under subsection (4)(a) above, then, if without reasonable excuse the failure in respect of which he was convicted is continued after the conviction, he shall be guilty of a further offence and liable on summary conviction to a fine not exceeding one-tenth of level 5 on the standard scale for each day on which the failure continues."
(4) In subsection (5)—
(a) in paragraph (a) for the words from "section 2" to "that Act" there is substituted "sections 17, 24 and 25 of the Police and Criminal Evidence Act 1984 (which confer power to arrest without warrant and to enter premises for the purpose of making an arrest) or of section 3 of the Criminal Law Act 1967", and
(b) in paragraph (c) for "section 2 or" there is substituted "Articles 19, 26 and 27 of the Police and Criminal Evidence (Northern Ireland) Order 1989 or of section".
6.—(1) Section 14 (general power to direct measures to be taken for purposes to which Part II applies) is amended as follows.
(2) In subsection (7)—
(a) in paragraph (a) the words "refuses or" are omitted, and
(b) in paragraph (b) for "wilfully" there is substituted "intentionally."
(3) After subsection (7) there is inserted—
"(7A) Where a person is convicted of an offence under subsection (7)(a) above, then, if without reasonable excuse the failure in respect of which he was convicted is continued after the conviction, he shall be guilty of a further offence and liable on summary conviction to a fine not exceeding one-tenth of level 5 on the standard scale for each day on which the failure continues."

Supplemental provisions with respect to directions

7.—(1) Section 15 (matters which may be included in directions under sections 12 to 14) is amended as follows.
(2) In subsection (1) after "13" there is inserted "or 13A."
(3) For subsection (2) there is substituted—
"(2) A direction under subsection (2) of section 12 of this Act must require all the persons carrying out any modifications or alterations, or the installation of any additional apparatus or equipment, to be persons approved by the Civil Aviation Authority."
(4) Subsection (3) is omitted.
(5) In subsection (4)(a) for the words from "an operator" to "aerodrome" there is substituted "the person to whom it is given."
(6) For subsection (5) there is substituted—
"(5) Where a direction under any of the preceding provisions of this Part of this Act requires searches to be carried out, or other measures to be taken, by constables, the direction may require the person to whom it is given to inform the chief officer of police for the police area in which the searches are to be carried out or the other measures taken that the Secretary of State considers it appropriate that constables should be duly authorised to carry, and should carry, firearms when carrying out the searches or taking the measures in question."
(7) After subsection (7) there is inserted—
"(8) In the application of this section to Northern Ireland for the words in subsection (5) above from "chief officer" to "measures taken" there are substituted the words "chief constable of the Royal Ulster Constabulary"."
8.—(1) Section 16 (limitations on scope of directions under sections 12 to 14) is amended as follows.
(2) In subsection (4)—
(a) for the words from "the operator" to "or agent of such an operator or manager" there is substituted "the person to whom the direction was given, or any person acting as his employee or agent," and
(b) for "(whether at the instance of such an operator or manager or otherwise)" there is substituted "(whether at the instance of the person to whom the direction was given or otherwise)."
(3) For subsection (6) there is substituted—
"(6) In so far as a direction given to the manager of an aerodrome or to any person mentioned in section 14(1)(c) or (d) of this Act requires a building or other works to be

constructed, executed, altered, demolished or removed on land outside the aerodrome, or requires any other measures to be taken on such land, the direction shall not confer on the person to whom it is given any rights as against a person having—

  (a) an interest in that land, or
  (b) a right to occupy that land, or
  (c) a right restrictive of its use;

and accordingly, the direction shall not be construed as requiring the person to whom it is given to do anything which would be actionable at the suit or instance of a person having such interest or right in his capacity as a person having that interest or right."

(4) In subsection (8) after "13" there is inserted ", 13A."

9.—(1) Section 17 of that Act (general or urgent directions under sections 12 and 14) is amended as follows.

(2) In subsection (1) for "or 14" there is substituted ", 13, 13A or 14."

(3) In subsection (2)—

  (a) for "either" there is substituted "any," and
  (b) in paragraph (a) after "class of aircraft," there is inserted "in relation to such aerodrome or part of an aerodrome, in relation to such land outside an aerodrome, in relation to such activities."

10. In section 19 (operation of directions under Part II in relation to rights and duties under other laws) after subsection (4) there is inserted—

"(4A) Any reference in this section to a direction under any of the preceding provisions of this Part of this Act includes a reference to an enforcement notice."

11.—(1) Section 20 (inspection of aircraft and aerodromes) is amended as follows.

(2) In subsection (1)—

  (a) after "any such direction" there is inserted "or any enforcement notice," and
  (b) for the words from "any person authorised" to " "authorised person")" there is substituted "an authorised person", and
  (c) at the end there is inserted "or
      (c) any land outside an aerodrome which is occupied for the purposes of a business by a person who—
            (i) also occupies (or appears to the authorised person to be about to occupy) land within an aerodrome for the purposes of that business, or
            (ii) is permitted (or appears to the authorised person to be about to be permitted) to have access to a restricted zone of a aerodrome for the purposes of the activities of that business."

(3) In subsection (2)—

  (a) for "or any part of an aerodrome" there is substituted ", any part of an aerodrome or any land outside an aerodrome,"
  (b) in paragraph (a) after "there" there is inserted "or on that land,"
  (c) after paragraph (a) there is inserted the following paragraph—
      "(aa) to take such steps—
        (i) to ascertain what practices or procedures are being followed in relation to security, or
        (ii) to test the effectiveness of any practice or procedure relating to security,", and
  (d) in paragraph (b) for "or the manager of the aerodrome" there is substituted "the manager of the aerodrome or the occuper of the land".

(4) In subsection (3)—

  (a) for "or in relation to an aerodrome" there is substituted ", in relation to an aerodrome or in relation to any land outside an aerodrome", and
  (b) at the end there is inserted "or
      (c) for the purpose of inspecting any land outside an aerodrome, to enter upon the land and to enter any building or works on the land."

(5) In subsection (5), paragraph (a) and, in paragraph (b), the words "refuses or" are omitted.

Air navigation installations

12.—(1) Section 21 (air navigation installations) is amended as follows.

(2) In subsection (1) after "13," there is inserted "13A,".

(3) In subsection (7) after "18(1)" there is inserted ", 18A, 18B, 18E."

Compensation

13.—(1) Section 22 (compensation in respect of certain measures taken under Part II) is amended as follows.

(2) In subsection (1)—

(a) for the words from "the manager" to "an air navigation installation" there is substituted "or in compliance with an enforcement notice, the person to whom the direction was given or on whom the notice was served," and

(b) for "the aerodrome or that" there is substituted "an aerodrome or."

(3) In subsection (4) the words from "(whether" to "installation)" are omitted.

Annual report by Secretary of State

14.—(1) Section 23 (annual report by Secretary of State as to notices and directions under Part II) is amended as follows.

(2) In subsection (1) for the words from "and the number" to "14 of this Act" there is substituted ", the number of directions given by him under sections 12, 13, 13A and 14 of this Act and the number of enforcement notices served by authorised persons."

(3) In subsection (2)—

(a) for "and directions given under section 14 of this Act" there is substituted ", directions given under section 13A and directions given under section 14 of this Act and enforcement notices," and

(b) after paragraph (b) there is inserted—

"(bb) the number of notices or directions which during that period were served on or given to persons as being, or as appearing to the Secretary of State to be about to become, persons occupying land forming part of an aerodrome or air navigation installation;

(bc) the number of notices or directions which during that period were served on or given to persons as being, or as appearing to the Secretary of State to be about to become, persons permitted to have access to a restricted zone of an aerodrome or air navigation installation for the purposes of the activities of a business;".

(4) In subsection (3) after "13" there is inserted ", 13A".

Service of documents

15. For section 24 there is substituted—

"Service of documents

24.—(1) This section has effect in relation to any notice, any document containing a direction and any other document authorised or required by any provision of this Part of this Act to be served on or given to any person.

(2) Any such document may be given to or served on any person—

(a) by delivering it to him, or

(b) by leaving it at his proper address, or

(c) by sending it by post to him at that address, or

(d) by sending it to him at that address by telex or other similar means which produce a document containing the text of the communication.

(3) Any such document may, in the case of a body corporate, be given to or served on the secretary, clerk or similar officer of that body.

(4) For the purposes of this section and section 7 of the Interpretation Act 1978 (service of documents by post) in its application to this section, the proper address of any person to whom or on whom any document is to be given or served is his usual or last known address or place of business (whether in the United Kingdom or elsewhere), except that in the case of a body corporate or its secretary, clerk or similar officer, it shall be the address of the registered or principal office of that body in the United Kingdom (or, if it has no office in the United Kingdom, of its principal office, wherever it may be).

(5) If the person to or on whom any document mentioned in subsection (1) above is to be given or served has notified the Secretary of State of an address within the United Kingdom, other than his proper address within the meaning of subsection (4) above, as the one at which he or someone else on his behalf will accept documents of the same description as that document, that address shall also be treated for the purposes of this section and section 7 of the Interpretation Act 1978 as his proper address.

(6) Where an authorised person—

(a) intends to serve an enforcement notice on any person ("the intended recipient"), and

(b) is of the opinion that all the requirements of the notice could be complied with by an employee or agent of the intended recipient,

the authorised person may, after consulting that employee or agent, serve the notice on the intended recipient by delivering it to that employee or agent or by sending it to that employee or agent at the proper address of the employee or agent by such means as are mentioned in subsection (2)(d) above.

(7) An authorised person who serves an enforcement notice under subsection (6) above on an employee or agent of the intended recipient shall serve a copy of the notice on the intended recipient.

(8) Nothing in subsection (6) above shall be taken to impose on the employee or agent to whom the enforcement notice is delivered or sent any obligation to comply with it."

Interpretation

16. After section 24 there is inserted—

"Interpretation of Part II

24A.—(1) In this Part of this Act, except in so far as the context otherwise requires—

"act of violence" has the meaning given by section 10(2) of this Act,

"authorised person" means a person authorised in writing by the Secretary of State for the purposes of this Part of this Act,

"employee," in relation to a body corporate, includes officer,

"enforcement notice" has the meaning given by section 18A(1) of this Act, and

"restricted zone", in relation to an aerodrome or air navigation installation, means any part of the aerodrome or installation designated under section 11A of this Act or, where the whole of the aerodrome or installation is so designated, that aerodrome or installation.

(2) For the purposes of this Part of this Act a person is permitted to have access to a restricted zone of an aerodrome or air navigation installation if he is permitted to enter that zone or if arrangements exist for permitting any of his employees or agents to enter that zone."

Reimbursement of expenses

17. In section 32(2) of that Act (which enables the Secretary of State, out of money provided by Parliament, to reimburse certain expenses incurred in relation to aviation security)—
(a) after paragraph (c) there is inserted "or
  (d) a person to whom a direction has been or could be given by the Secretary of State under section 14 of this Act by virtue of subsection (1)(c) or (d) of that section," and
(b) for the words from "have at any time" to "installation" there is substituted "have, in the case of a person mentioned in paragraph (a), (b) or (c) above, been at any time on or after June 1, 1972 or, in the case of a person mentioned in paragraph (d) above, been at any time after the passing of the Aviation and Maritime Security Act 1990, incurred or may, in any case, be incurred by any such person in relation to those aircraft, to that aerodrome or air navigation installation or to the land or activities concerned,".

Offences by bodies corporate

18. In section 37 of that Act (offences by bodies corporate) for "or under regulations made under section 33" there is substituted "(including any provision of Part II as applied by regulations made under section 21F of this Act) or under regulations made under section 21G."

Revocation and variation of directions

19. In section 38(6) of that Act (revocation and variation of directions) the words "given under that provision" are omitted.

Provisions relating to compensation

20.—(1) Schedule 1 is amended as follows.
(2) In paragraph 2 for the words "manager of the aerodrome" there is substituted "person."
(3) In paragraph 3—
(a) for the words from "the manager" to "the aerodrome" there is substituted "any person on land outside an aerodrome or air navigation installation," and
(b) after "direction" (in both places) there is inserted "or enforcement notice."
(4) Paragraph 8 is omitted.

GENERAL NOTE
See generally the notes to Pt. I, above. This Schedule contains amendments to the Aviation

Security Act 1982 which update it and align it more fully with the new maritime provisions in Pt. III.

Para. 2
   Subpara. (2): provision of information. The power to require information is widely drawn so as to enable the Secretary of State to obtain general information about aviation and maritime security. As originally drafted the Bill would have limited the power to seek information to that required for deciding whether to make a Direction and if it had been complied with. Judicial review would presumably be available if the DTp tried to obtain information that was not strictly necessary. Some concern was expressed in Parliament about the civil liberties aspects of the powers, especially where records were kept about individuals. The Minister stated that it was not the intention that information should relate to persons in particular. It would concern matters such as the airlines involved, the numbers of flights and passengers and which firms had access to restricted zones and the arrangements for controlling access or patrolling the zones. (*Cf.* s.19.)
   Subpara. (3): seven days. The information required by the Secretary of State might take some time to compile. Under the Aviation Security Act 1982, s.11, the person concerned had four weeks in which to make any reply and concern was expressed that the new time limit was too short. The Minister, Mr Portillo, admitted that this might be so, but was only prepared to give a commitment to the Standing Committee that the DTp would apply the provision sensitively on a case-by-case basis, taking account of circumstances (Standing Committee A, col. 89).

Para. 3
   Restricted zones. See the note to s.5, above (inserting a new s.21C in the Aviation Security Act 1982) and *cf.* s.20, for the maritime equivalent.

Para. 4
   Subpara. (3) adds a new day-by-day penalty for continuing offences (see the note to s.2, above, inserting a new s.13A(4) in the Aviation Security Act 1982).

Para. 5
   Subpara. (3) adds a new day-by-day penalty for continuing offences (see the note to s.2, above, inserting a new s.13A(4) in the Aviation Security Act 1982).
   Subpara. (4). These amendments take account of the repeal of s.2 of the Criminal Law Act 1967 and its Northern Irish equivalent.

Para. 6
   Subpara. (3) adds a new day-by-day penalty for continuing offences (see the note to s.2, above, inserting a new s.13A(4) in the Aviation Security Act 1982).

Para. 7
   Cf. s.25(4) and (7) for notes on the maritime equivalents.

Para. 8
   S.16 imposes general limitations on the scope of Directions that the Secretary of State can give. The industry sought an amendment to subs. (5), which deals with Directions about matters needing to be undertaken abroad, for example at foreign airports. There had been complaints about the operation of the Immigration (Carrier's Liability) Act 1987 as airlines have found it impossible to comply with the provisions of the Act without the co-operation of handling agents and others in the host country. The Government resisted an amendment designed to limit the power to give Directions in such circumstances by stating that there were already limits within subs. (5) based on legality and a "reasonable excuse" defence was available to meet any prosecution.

Para. 10
   S.19 is the aviation equivalent of s.34 of the 1990 Act. It provides that a Direction can override laws, statutory or otherwise. The amendment makes it clear that this overriding effect applies equally to enforcement notices. JACOLA had been concerned at the overlap with security requirements imposed by other bodies such as the Health and Safety Executive and the Customs and Excise Commissioners.

Para. 11
   Cf. s.36 for the maritime equivalent.

Inspection of aircraft. S.20 allows for the inspection of aircraft. The amendments to subs. (1) extend the geographical area of possible inspection in line with the general extension of the coverage of the Act (see the note to s.3, above). The amendments relating to "authorised person" take account of the new definition in s.24A of the Aviation Security Act 1982, as inserted by para. 16, below. The amendment to subs. (2) allows for security tests or exercises by authorised persons (see the note to the new s.21A(3) of the Aviation Security Act 1982, as inserted by s.5 of the 1990 Act, above.

Para. 14

S.23 of the Aviation Security Act 1982, is amended to include reports on the number of enforcement notices issued. The new s.13A is also brought within the annual reporting provisions, so that information must be provided about, *inter alia*, the number of Directions served on occupiers of land at aerodromes. *Cf.* s.44 for the maritime equivalent.

Para. 15

Cf. s.45 for the maritime equivalent.

Para. 16

This paragraph provides a new definitions section for Pt. II of the Aviation Security Act 1982. *Cf.* s.46 of the 1990 Act for the maritime equivalent.

Para. 17

S.32 (1) of the Aviation Security Act 1982 continued the Aviation Security Fund, set up in 1978. In 1983, the Fund was wound up (see the Aviation Security Act 1982, s.36, (S.I. Nos. 1983/81; 1983/1644)). However, the effect of s.36(2) of the Aviation Security Act 1982 is that s.32(2) and (4) continue to have effect as if all payments under those subsections fell to be defrayed out of Parliament, instead of under the Fund—subject to the consent of the Treasury. In fact, both those subsections allow the Secretary of State to reimburse certain expenses of airlines and airports. Para. 17 of Sched. 1 of the 1990 Act adds to the list of persons to whom such payments can be made those persons now listed in s.14(c) and (d) of the Aviation Security Act 1982 (as inserted by s.3 of the 1990 Act). These are the occupiers of land and persons having access to restricted areas. See generally *The responsibility for security* in the General Note to Pt. I.

Para. 18

This paragraph adds offences relating to air cargo agents to the list of those which can be committed by company officers. *Cf.* s.50.

Section 43   SCHEDULE 2

PROVISIONS RELATING TO COMPENSATION

1. This Schedule applies to compensation under section 43 of this Act (in this Schedule referred to as "the principal section").
2. No compensation to which this Schedule applies shall be payable unless the person to whom it is payable in accordance with the principal section (or in accordance with regulations made under paragraph 5 below) serves on the person by whom the measures in question were taken a notice in writing claiming compensation under that section, and that notice is served before the end of the period of two years from the completion of the measures.
3. In relation to any measures taken by any person on land outside a harbour area, any reference in the principal section to a direction or enforcement notice, or to compliance with a direction or enforcement notice, is to be construed as if subsection (6) of section 26 of this Act were omitted.
4. In calculating value for any of the purposes of the principal section—
(a) rules (2) to (4) of the rules set out in section 5 of the Land Compensation Act 1961 apply with the necessary modifications, and
(b) if the interest to be valued is subject to a mortgage, it is to be treated as if it were not subject to the mortgage.
5. Regulations made by the Secretary of State by statutory instrument may make provision—
(a) requiring compensation to which this Schedule applies, in such cases as may be specified in the regulations, to be paid to a person other than the person entitled to it in accordance with the principal section,
(b) as to the application of any compensation to which this Schedule applies, or any part of it, in cases where the right to claim compensation is exercisable by reference to an interest in

land which is subject to a mortgage, or to a rentcharge, or to the trusts of a settlement, or, in Scotland, to a feuduty or ground annual or to the purposes of a trust, or which was so subject at a time specified in the regulations, or

(c) as to any assumptions to be made, or matters to be taken into or left out of account, for the purpose of assessing any compensation to which this Schedule applies.

6. A statutory instrument containing regulations made under paragraph 5 above shall be subject to annulment in pursuance of a resolution of either House of Parliament.

7. Any dispute arising under the principal section or under this Schedule, whether as to the right to any compensation or as to the amount of any compensation or otherwise, shall be referred to and determined by the Lands Tribunal.

8. In the application of this Schedule to Scotland—

(a) the reference in paragraph 4(a) to section 5 of the Land Compensation Act 1961 is to be construed as a reference to section 12 of the Land Compensation (Scotland) Act 1963, and

(b) the reference in paragraph 7 to the Lands Tribunal is to be construed as a reference to the Lands Tribunal for Scotland.

9. In the application of this Schedule to Northern Ireland—

(a) the reference in paragraph 4(a) to section 5 of the Land Compensation Act 1961 is to be construed, notwithstanding paragraph 4 of Schedule 1 to the Land Compensation (Northern Ireland) Order 1982 (which confines the operation of that Order to matters within the legislative competence of the Parliament of Northern Ireland), as a reference to Article 6(1) of that Order, and

(b) the reference in paragraph 7 to the Lands Tribunal is to be construed as a reference to the Lands Tribunal for Northern Ireland.

10. In this Schedule "mortgage" includes any charge or lien on any property for securing money or money's worth, and any heritable security within the meaning of section 9(8) of the Conveyancing and Feudal Reform (Scotland) Act 1970.

GENERAL NOTE

Derivation: the Aviation Security Act 1982, Sched. 1.

The Schedule lays down details of the compensation payable to persons whose interests are affected by building work necessary for maritime security purposes. See the note to s.43, above.

Section 53(1)   SCHEDULE 3

MINOR AND CONSEQUENTIAL AMENDMENTS

The Visiting Forces Act 1952 (c. 67)

1.—(1) Section 3 of the Visiting Forces Act 1952 (restriction, as respects certain offences, of trial by United Kingdom courts of offenders connected with visiting force) is amended as follows.

(2) In subsection (1) after paragraph (e) there is inserted "or

(f) the alleged offence is an offence under section 1(2)(a)(ii) of the Aviation and Maritime Security Act 1990, where one or more such aircraft was or were the only aircraft alleged to have been thereby destroyed or seriously damaged; or

(g) the alleged offence is the offence of hijacking a warship in the service of that force or any other ship used as a naval auxiliary in that service or consists of inducing or assisting, in relation to any such warship or other ship, the commission of any such act as is mentioned in section 14(4)(a) of the Aviation and Maritime Security Act 1990; or

(h) the alleged offence is an offence under section 11, 12, or 13 of that Act in relation to a ship, or consists of inducing or assisting the commission of any such act as is mentioned in section 14(4)(b), (c) or (d) of that Act in relation to a ship, where (in either case) one or more warships in the service of that force or other ships used as naval auxiliaries in that service were the only ships alleged to have been, or to have been likely to be, thereby destroyed or damaged or whose safe navigation is alleged to have been, or to have been likely to be, thereby endangered".

(3) In subsection (4) for "paragraphs (b) and (c)" in the first place where those words occur there is substituted "paragraphs (b), (c) and (f)", and for "paragraphs (d) and (e)" there is substituted "paragraphs (d), (e), (g) and (h)".

The Merchant Shipping Act 1970 (c. 36)

2.—(1) In section 78 of the Merchant Shipping Act 1970 (unauthorised presence on board ship) for "level 2 on the standard scale" (which was substituted by virtue of section 46 of the Criminal Justice Act 1982) there is substituted "level 5 on the standard scale".

(2) Sub-paragraph (1) above does not affect the punishment for any offence committed before the commencement of this paragraph.

The Criminal Jurisdiction Act 1975 (c. 59)

3. In section 2 of the Criminal Jurisdiction Act 1975 (hijacking of vehicles or ships in Northern Ireland or the Republic of Ireland) in subsection (1)(a) the words "or any ship or hovercraft" are omitted.

4. In Schedule 1 to the Criminal Jurisdiction Act 1975 (offences in Republic of Ireland triable in Northern Ireland) in Part I after paragraph 11 there is inserted—

"Endangering safety at aerodromes

11A. An offence under section 1 of the Aviation and Maritime Security Act 1990 (endangering safety at aerodromes).

Offences relating to ships and fixed platforms

11B. An offence under section 9 of the Aviation and Maritime Security Act 1990 (hijacking of ships) or under section 10 of that Act (seizing or exercising control of fixed platforms)."

The Northern Ireland (Emergency Provisions) Act 1978 (c. 5)

5. In Schedule 4 to the Northern Ireland (Emergency Provisions) Act 1978 (the scheduled offences) in Part I after paragraph 19D there is inserted—

"Aviation and Maritime Security Act 1990

19E. Offences under the following provisions of the Aviation and Maritime Security Act 1990—
(a) section 1 (endangering safety at aerodromes);
(b) section 9 (hijacking of ships);
(c) section 10 (seizing or exercising control of fixed platforms)."

The Suppression of Terrorism Act 1978 (c. 26)

6. In Schedule 1 to the Suppression of Terrorism Act 1978 (list of offences for purposes of section 1 of that Act) after paragraph 18 there is inserted—
"18A. An offence under section 1 of the Aviation and Maritime Security Act 1990.

Offences relating to ships and fixed platforms

18B. An offence under Part II of the Aviation and Maritime Security Act 1990 (other than an offence under section 15 of that Act)."

The Criminal Justice Act 1982 (c. 48)

7. At the end of Part II of Schedule 1 to the Criminal Justice Act 1982 (statutory offences excluded from provisions for early release of prisoners) there is inserted—

"AVIATION AND MARITIME SECURITY ACT 1990 (c. 31)

Section 1 (endangering safety at aerodromes).
Section 9 (hijacking of ships).
Section 10 (seizing or exercising control of fixed platforms).
Sections 11, 12, 13 and 14 (other offences relating to ships and fixed platforms)."

The Police and Criminal Evidence Act 1984 (c. 60)

8. At the end of Part II of Schedule 5 to the Police and Criminal Evidence Act 1984 (serious arrestable offences) there is added—

"Aviation and Maritime Security Act 1990 (c. 31)

11. Section 1 (endangering safety at aerodromes).
12. Section 9 (hijacking of ships).
13. Section 10 (seizing or exercising control of fixed platforms)."

The Extradition Act 1989 (c. 33)

9.—(1) Section 22 of the Extradition Act 1989 (extension of purposes of extradition for offences under Acts giving effect to international Conventions) is amended as follows.

(2) At the end of subsection (2) there is inserted—

"(i) the Protocol for the Suppression of Unlawful Acts of Violence at Airports Serving International Civil Aviation, supplementary to the Montreal Convention, which was signed at Montreal on February 24, 1988 ("the Montreal Protocol");

(j) the Convention for the Suppression of Unlawful Acts against the Safety of Maritime Navigation, which was signed at Rome on March 10, 1988 ("the Rome Convention");

(k) the Protocol for the Suppression of Unlawful Acts against the Safety of Fixed Platforms Located on the Continental Shelf, which was also signed at Rome on March 10, 1988 ("the Rome Protocol")."

(3) At the end of subsection (4) there is inserted—

"(i) in relation to the Montreal Protocol, an offence under section 1 of the Aviation and Maritime Security Act 1990;

(j) in relation to the Rome Convention, an offence under section 9 or 12 of that Act or an offence under section 11 or 13 of that Act committed in relation to a ship (within the meaning of Part II of that Act); and

(k) in relation to the Rome Protocol, an offence under section 10 of that Act or an offence under section 11 or 13 of that Act committed in relation to a fixed platform (within the meaning of Part II of that Act)."

10. In Schedule 1 to the Extradition Act 1989 (provisions deriving from Extradition Act 1870 and associated enactments) in paragraph 15 (deemed extension of jurisdiction of foreign states) after paragraph (k) there is inserted—

"or

(l) an offence under section 1, 9, 10, 11, 12 or 13 of the Aviation and Maritime Security Act 1990 or an attempt to commit such an offence,".

The Police and Criminal Evidence (Northern Ireland) Order 1989
(S.I. 1989/1341 (N.I.12))

11. At the end of Part II of Schedule 5 to the Police and Criminal Evidence (Northern Ireland) Order 1989 (serious arrestable offences) there is added—

"Aviation and Maritime Security Act 1990 (c. 31)

10. Section 1 (endangering safety at aerodromes).
11. Section 9 (hijacking of ships).
12. Section 10 (seizing or exercising control of fixed platforms)."

GENERAL NOTE
The Schedule contains a number of comparatively small, but significant amendments.

Para. 1
Visiting Forces Act 1952. A number of the more serious terrorist-type offences under the 1990 Act are added to the list of offences in respect of which there are restrictions on U.K. courts trying visiting servicemen.

Para. 2
Merchant Shipping Act 1970. The penalty for unauthorised presence on board a ship is increased in respect of offences committed after the coming into force of the 1990 Act.

Para. 3
Criminal Jurisdiction Act 1975. The unlawful seizure or control of ships or hovercraft in Northern Ireland is removed from s.2 of the 1975 Act, as s.9 of the 1990 Act covers the hijacking of ships whether in the U.K. or elsewhere. See also the repeal in Sched. 4.

Para. 4
  Criminal Jurisdiction Act 1975. The offences of endangering safety at aerodromes and those relating to ships and platforms are added to the list of offences which are triable in Northern Ireland even if committed in the Republic of Ireland.

Para. 5
  Northern Ireland (Emergency Provisions) Act 1978. The offences under ss.1, 9 and 10 are added to the list of scheduled offences in the 1978 Act so that various provisions in that Act will apply.

Para. 7
  Criminal Justice Act 1982. The paragraph excludes from the provisions of the 1982 Act dealing with the early release of prisoners those offences covered by the Montreal Protocol 1988 and the Rome Convention 1988. This gives effect to international obligations.

Para. 8
  Police and Criminal Evidence Act 1984. The offences under ss.1, 9 and 10 are added to the list of serious arrestable offences.

Para. 9
  Extradition Act 1989. See also the note to s.49.

Para. 11
  Police and Criminal Evidence (Northern Ireland) Order 1989. The offences under ss.1, 9 and 10 are added to the list of serious arrestable offences.

Section 53(2)   SCHEDULE 4

REPEALS

Chapter	Short title	Extent of repeal
1975 c. 59.	The Criminal Jurisdiction Act 1975.	In section 2(1)(a), the words "or any ship or hovercraft".
1982 c. 16.	The Civil Aviation Act 1982.	In section 60(3)(f), the words "and goods" and the words from "and for" onwards. In section 105(1), in the definition of "relevant overseas territory", the words from "and any" onwards.
1982 c. 36.	The Aviation Security Act 1982.	In section 11(5)(a), the words "refuses or". In section 14, subsection (4) and, in subsection (7)(a), the words "refuses or". Section 15(3). In section 20, in subsection (5) paragraph (a), the word "or" immediately following it and, in paragraph (b), the words "refuses or". In section 22(4), the words from "(whether" to "installation)". Sections 34 and 35. In section 38, in subsection (1) the definition of "act of violence" and in subsection (6) the words "given under that provision". In section 39(3), the words from "other than a colony" onwards. In Schedule 1, paragraph 8.
1989 c. 33.	The Extradition Act 1989.	In section 22(4), the word "and" immediately following paragraph (g). In Schedule 1, in paragraph 15, the word "or" immediately following paragraph (j).

INDEX

References in roman type are to sections of the Act: references in italic are to sections of the Aviation Security Act 1982 (as amended).